TM 9-230-289-20P
CUCV
Commercial Utility Cargo Vehicle
Unit Maintenance
Repair Parts and Special Tools List
May 1992

The CUCV or Commercial Utility Cargo Vehicle is a US Military vehicle based on readily available commercial trucks. Originally intended to augment the purpose-built, but expensive GAMA Goat 6x6 and older Jeeps. The first generation was based on Dodge / Chrysler trucks.

This book is focused on the M1008 series second generation CUCV which was General Motor's first major light-truck military vehicle production since World War II. They began production in 1984 and ended production in 1996 with most units being produced as 1984 model year units. Later production was focused on replacements for existing CUCV's. The majority of units were built from existing heavy duty light truck commercial parts. The M1009 was an upgraded/up-rated Chevy K5 Blazer with a 3/4 ton capacity. The M1008 series trucks were a 1-1/4 ton or 5/4 ton rated truck. In all 70,000 units were produced with three power trains.

This manual is the Unit Maintenance Repair Parts and Special Tools List for these vehicles. Including the 6.5 liter and other models. It is published as a convenience to enthusiasts who may wish to have a quality professionally printed copy of the manual.

This publisher has also printed other manuals for this series of vehicles. Should you have suggestions or feedback on ways to improve this book please send email to Books@OcotilloPress.com

---

Edited 2021 Ocotillo Press
ISBN 978-1-954285-83-5

Ocotillo Press
Houston, TX 77017
Books@OcotilloPress.com

Disclaimer: The user of this book is responsible for following safe and lawful practices at all times. The publisher assumes no responsibility for the use of the content of this book. The publisher has made an effort to ensure that the text is complete and properly typeset, however omissions, errors, and other issues may exist that the publisher is unaware of.

TECHNICAL MANUAL

UNIT MAINTENANCE REPAIR PARTS AND SPECIAL TOOLS LISTS (INCLUDING DEPOT MAINTENANCE REPAIR PARTS AND SPECIAL TOOLS LISTS) FOR

**TRUCK, CARGO, TACTICAL, 1-1/4 TON, 4X4, M1008
(2320-01-123-6827)
TRUCK, CARGO, TACTICAL, 1-1/4 TON, 4X4, M1008A1
(2320-01-123-2671)
TRUCK, UTILITY, TACTICAL, 3/4 TON, 4X4, M1009
(2320-01-123-2665)
TRUCK, AMBULANCE, TACTICAL, 1-1/4 TON, 4X4, M1010
(231 0-01-1 23-2666)
TRUCK, SHELTER CARRIER, TACTICAL, 1-1/4 TON, 4X4, M1028
(2320-01-127-5077)
TRUCK, SHELTER CARRIER W/PTO, TACTICAL, 1 -1/4 TON, 4X4, M1028A1
(2320-01-158-0820)
TRUCK, SHELTER CARRIER W/PTO, TACTICAL, 1-1/4 TON, 4X4, M1028A2
(2320-01-295-0822)
TRUCK, SHELTER CARRIER, TACTICAL, 1-1/4 TON, 4X4, M1028A3
(2320-01-325-1937)
TRUCK, CHASSIS, TACTICAL, 1-1/4 TON, 4X4, M1031
(2320-01-133-5368)**

This manual supersedes TM 9-2320-289-20P, 16 September 1988 and all changes.

**DEPARTMENTS OF THE ARMY, THE AIR FORCE,
AND HEADQUARTERS, MARINE CORPS
1 MAY 1992**

DEPARTMENTS OF THE ARMY, THE AIR FORCE,
AND HEADQUARTERS, MARINE CORPS
Washington, D.C., 1 May 1992

UNIT MAINTENANCE REPAIR PARTS AND SPECIAL TOOLS LISTS
(INCLUDING DEPOT MAINTENANCE REPAIR PARTS AND SPECIAL TOOLS LISTS)
FOR

TRUCK, CARGO, TACTICAL, 1 -1/4 TON, 4X4, M1008
(2320-01-123-6827)
TRUCK, CARGO, TACTICAL, 1-1/4 TON, 4X4, M1008A1
(2320-01-123-2671)
TRUCK, UTILITY, TACTICAL, 3/4 TON, 4X4, M1009
(2320-01-123-2665)
TRUCK, AMBULANCE, TACTICAL, 1-1/4 TON, 4X4, M1010
(2310-01-123-2666)
TRUCK, SHELTER CARRIER, TACTICAL, 1-1/4 TON, 4X4, M1028
(2320-01-127-5077)
TRUCK, SHELTER CARRIER W/PTO, TACTICAL, 1-1/4 TON, 4X4, M1028A1
(2320-01-158-0820)
TRUCK, SHELTER CARRIER W/PTO, TACTICAL, 1-1/4 TON, 4X4, M1028A2
(2320-01-295-0822)
TRUCK, SHELTER CARRIER, TACTICAL, 1-1/4 TON, 4X4, M1028A3
(2320-01-325-1937)
TRUCK, CHASSIS, TACTICAL, 1-1/4 TON, 4X4, M1031
(2320-01-133-5368)

Current as of 7 February 1992

REPORTING ERRORS AND RECOMMENDING IMPROVEMENTS

You can help improve this manual. If you find any mistakes or if you know of a way to improve the procedures, please let us know. Mail your letter, DA Form 2028 (Recommended Changes to Publications and Blank forms), or DA Form 2028-2, located in the back of this manual, direct to: Commander, U.S. Army Tank-Automotive Command, ATTN: AMSTA-MB, Warren, MI 48397-5000. A reply will be furnished to you.

---

* **This manual supersedes TM 9-2320-289-20P, dated 16 September 1988, and all changes.**

TABLE OF CONTENTS

TABLE OF CONTENTS (Con't)

TABLE OF CONTENTS (Con't)

TABLE OF CONTENTS (Con't)

TABLE OF CONTENTS (Con't)

TABLE OF CONTENTS (Con't)

TABLE OF CONTENTS (Con't)

TABLE OF CONTENTS (Con't)

UNIT MAINTENANCE REPAIR PARTS AND SPECIAL TOOLS LIST S
(INCLUDING DEPOT MAINTENANC E
REPAIR PARTS AND SPECIA L
TOOLS LISTS)

SECTION I. INTRODUCTIO N

1. Scope.

This RPSTL lists and authorizes spares and repair parts; Special tools; special test, measurement, and diagnostic equipment (TMDE); and other special support equipment required for performance of Unit Maintenance of the CUCV Series Truck. It authorizes the requisitioning, issue, and disposition of spares, repair parts and special tools as indicated by the source, maintenance and recoverability (SMR) codes.

2. General.

In addition to Section 1. Introduction, this Repair Paris and Special Tools List is divided into the following sections:

a. *Section II. Repair Parts List.* A list of spares and repair parts authorized by this RPSTL for use in the performance of maintenance. The list also Includes parts which must be removed for replacement of the authorized parts. Parts lists are composed of functional groups in ascending alphanumeric sequence, with the parts in each group listed in ascending figure and item number sequence. Bulk materials are listed in item name sequence. Repair kits are listed separately in their own functional group within Section II. Repair parts for reparable special tools are also listed in the section. Items listed are shown on the associated illustration(s) /figure(s).

b. *Section ///. Special Tools List.* A list of special tools, special TMDE, and other special support equipment authorized by this RPSTL (as indicated by Basis of Issue (BOI) information in DESCRIPTION AND USABLE ON CODE column) for the performance of maintenance.

c. *Section IV. Cross-reference Indexes.* A list, in National Item Identification Number (NIIN) sequence, of all National stock numbered items appearing in the listing, followed by a list in alphanumeric sequence of all part numbers appearing in the listings. National stock numbers and part numbers are cross-referenced to each illustration/figure and item number appearance. The figure and item number index lists figure and item numbers in alphanumeric sequence and cross-references NSN, CAGE, and part numbers.

3. Explanation of Columns (Sections II and III).

a. ITEM NO. *(Column (1)).* Indicates the number used to identify items called out in the illustration.

b. *SMR CODE (Column (2)). The* Source, Maintenance, and Recoverability (SMR) code is a 5-position code containing supply/requisitioning information, maintenance category authorization criteria, and disposition instructions, as shown in the following breakout:

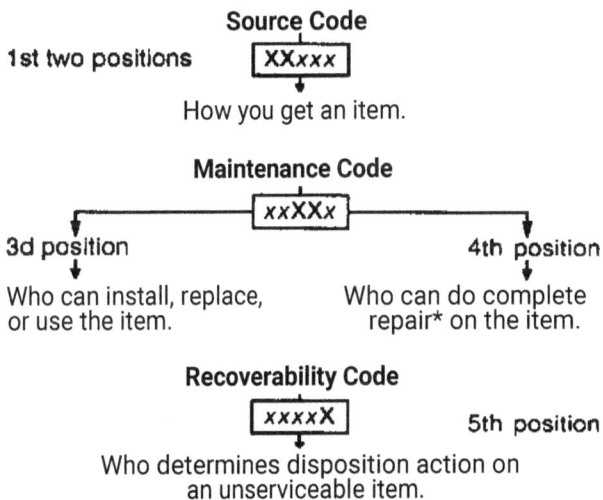

Source Code

1st two positions | XXxxx |

How you get an item.

Maintenance Code

| xxXXx |

3d position — Who can install, replace, or use the item.

4th position — Who can do complete repair* on the item.

Recoverability Code

| xxxxX | 5th position

Who determines disposition action on an unserviceable item.

Complete Repair: Maintenance capacity, capability, and authority to perform all corrective maintenance tasks of the "Repair" function in a use/user environment in order to restore serviceability to a failed item.

(1) *Source Code. The* source code tells you how to get an item needed for maintenance, repair, or overhaul of an end item/equipment. Explanations of source codes follows:

Code	Application/Explanation
PA PB PC** PD PE PF PG	Stocked items; use the applicable NSN to request/requisition items with these source codes. They are authorized to the category indicated by the code entered in the 3d position of the SMR code. ** Items coded PC are subject to deterioration.

KD KF KB	Items with these codes are not to be requested/requisitioned individually. They are part of a kit which is authorized to the maintenance category indicated in the 3d position of the SMR code. The complete kit must be requisitioned and applied.

MO - (Made at UM/ AVUM Level) MF - (Made at DS/ AVUM Level) MH - (Made at GS Level) ML- (Made at Specialized Repair Activity (SRA)) MD - (Made at Depot)	Items with these codes are not to be requested/requisitioned individually. They must be made from bulk material which is identified by the part number in the DESCRIPTION AND USABLE ON CODE (UOC) column and listed in the Bulk Material group of the repair parts list in this RPSTL. If the item is authorized to you by the 3d position code of the SMR code, but the source code indicates it is made at a higher level, order the item from the higher level of maintenance.

AO - (Assembled by UM/ AVUM Level) AF - (Assembled by DS/AVIM Level) AH - (Assembled by GS Category) AL- (Assembled by SRA) AD - (Assembled by Depot)	Items with these codes are not to be requested/requisitioned individually. The parts that make up the assembled item must be requisitioned or fabricated and assembled at the level of maintenance indicted by the source code. If the 3d position code of the SMR code authorizes you to replace the item, but the source code indicates the item is assembled at a higher level, order the item from the higher level of maintenance.

XA -	Do not requisition an "XA"-coded item. Order its next higher assembly. (Also refer to the NOTE following.)
XB -	If an "XB" item Is not available from salvage, order it using the CAGE and part number given.
XC -	Installation drawing, diagram, instruction sheet, field service drawing, that is identified by the manufacturer's part number.
XD -	Item is not stocked. Order an "XD"-coded item through normal supply channels using the CAGE and part number given, if no NSN is available.

NOTE: Cannibalization or controlled exchange, when authorized, may be used as a source of supply for items with the above source codes, except for those source coded "XA" or those aircraft support items restricted by requirements of AR 700-42.

(2) *Maintenance Code.* Maintenance codes tell you the level(s) of maintenance authorized to USE and REPAIR support items. The maintenance codes are entered in the third and fourth positions of the SMR code as follows:

(a) The maintenance code entered in the third position tells you the lowest maintenance level authorized to remove, replace, and use an item. The maintenance code entered in the third position will indicate authorization to one of the following levels of maintenance.

Code	Application/Explanation
C -	Crew or operator maintenance done within unit maintenance or aviation unit maintenance.
O -	Unit maintenance or aviation unit category can remove, replace, and use the item.
F -	Direct support or aviation intermediate level can remove, replace, and use the item.
H -	General support level can remove, replace, and use the item.
L -	Specialized repair activity can remove, replace, and use the item.
D -	Depot level can remove, replace, and use the item.

(b) The maintenance code entered in the fourth position tells whether or not the item is to be repaired and identifies the lowest maintenance level with the capability to do complete repair (i.e., perform all authorized repair functions), (NOTE: Some limited repair may be done on the item at a lower level of maintenance, if authorized by the Maintenance Allocation Chart (MAC) and SMR codes.) This position will contain one of the following maintenance codes:

Code	Application/Explanation
O -	Unit maintenance or aviation unit is the lowest level that can do complete repair of the item.
F -	Direct support or aviation intermediate is the lowest level than can do complete repair of the item.

H - General support is the lowest level that can do complete repair of the item.

L - Specialized repair activity is the lowest level that can do complete repair of the item.

D - Depot is the lowest level that can do complete repair of the item.

Z - Nonreparable. No repair is authorized.

B - No repair is authorized. (No parts or special tools are authorized for the maintenance of a "B"-coded item.) However, the item maybe reconditioned by adjusting, lubricating, etc., at the user level.

(3) *Recoverability Code.* Recoverability codes are assigned to items to indicate the disposition action on unserviceable items. The recoverability code is entered in the fifth position of the SMR code as follows:

Code   Application/Explanation

Z - Nonreparable item. When unserviceable, condemn and dispose of the item at the level of maintenance shown in the 3d position of the SMR code.

O - Reparable item. When uneconomically reparable, condemn and dispose of the item at unit maintenance or aviation unit level.

F - Reparable item. When uneconomically reparable, condemn and dispose of the item at the direct support or aviation intermediate level.

H - Reparable item. When uneconomically reparable, condemn and dispose of the item at the general support level.

D - Reparable item. When beyond lower level repair capability, return to depot, Condemnation and disposal of item not authorized below depot level.

L - Reparable item. Condemnation and disposal of item not authorized below specialized repair activity (SRA).

A - Item requires special handling or condemnation procedures because of specific reasons (e.g., precious metal content, high dollar value, critical material, or hazardous material). Refer to appropriate manuals/directives for specific instructions.

c. CAGEC (Column (3)), me Commercial and Government Entity (CAGE) Code (C) is a 5-digit alphanumeric code which is used to Identify the manufacturer, distributor, or Government agency, etc., that supplies the item.

d. *PART NUMBER (Column (4)).* Indicates the primary number used by the manufacturer (individual, company, firm, corporation, or Government activity), which controls the design and characteristics of the item by means of its engineering drawings, specifications standards, and inspection requirements to identify an item or range of items.

NOTE: When you use an NSN to requisition an item, the item you receive may have a different part number from the part ordered.

e. *DESCRIPTION AND USABLE ON CODE (UOC) (Column (5)). This* column includes the following information:

(1) The Federal item name and, when required, a minimum description to Identify the Item.

(2) Physical security classification. Not Applicable.

(3) Items that are included in kits and sets are listed below the name of the kit or set on Figure KIT,

(4) Spare/repair parts that make up an assembled item are listed immediately following the assembled item line entry.

(5) Part numbers for bulk materials are referenced in this column in the line item entry for the item to be manufactured/fabricated.

(6) When the item is not used with ail serial numbers of the same model, the effective serial numbers are shown on the last line(s) of the description (before UOC).

(7) The usable on code, when applicable (see paragraph 5, Special Information).

(8) In the Special Tools List section, the basis of issue (BOI) appears as the last line(s) in the entry for each special tool, special TMDE, and other special support equipment. When density of equipments supported exceeds density spread indicated in the basis of issue, the total authorization is increased proportionately.

(9) The statement "END OF FIGURE" appears just below the last item description in Column 5 for a given figure in both Section II and Section III.

f. QTY *(Column (6)). The QTY* (quantity per figure column) indicates the quantity of the item used in the breakout shown on the illustration/figure, which is prepared for a functional group, subfunctional group, or an assembly. A "V" appearing in this column in lieu of a quantity indicates that the quantity is variable and the quantity may vary from application to application.

4. Explanation of Columns (Section IV).

a. *NATIONAL STOCK NUMBER (NSN) INDEX.*

(1) *STOCK NUMBER column.* This column lists the NSN by National Item Identification Number (NIIN)

sequence. The NIIN consists of the last nine
NSN

digits of the NSN (i.e., 5305-01-674-1467). When

NIIN

using this column to locate an item, ignore the first 4 digits of the NSN. However, the complete NSN should be used when ordering items by stock number.

(2) FIG. column. This column lists the number of the figure where the item is identified/located. The figures are in numerical order in Section II and Section III.

(3) ITEM column. The item number identifies the item associated with the figure listed in the adjacent FIG. column. This item is also identified by the NSN listed on the same line.

b. PART NUMBER INDEX. Part numbers in this index are listed by part number in ascending alphanumeric sequence (i.e., vertical arrangement of letter and number combination which places the first letter or digit of each group in order A through Z, followed by the numbers 0 through 9 and each following letter or digit in like order).

(1) CAGEC column. The Commercial and Government Entity (CAGE) Code (C) is a 5-digit alphanumeric code used to identify the manufacturer, distributor, or Government agency, etc., that supplies the item.

(2) PART NUMBER column. Indicates the primary number used by the manufacturer (individual, firm, corporation, or Government activity), which controls the design and characteristics of the item by means of its engineering drawings, specifications standards, and inspection requirements to identify an item or range of items.

(3) STOCK NUMBER column. This column lists the NSN for the associated part number and manufacturer identified in the PART NUMBER and CAGE columns to the left.

(4) FIG. column. This column lists the number of the figure where the item is identified/located in Sections II and III.

(5) ITEM column. The item number is that number assigned to the item as it appears in the figure referenced in the adjacent figure number column.

c. FIGURE AND ITEM NUMBER INDEX.

(1) FIG. column. This column lists the number of the figure where the item is identified/located in Sections II and III.

(2) ITEM column. The item number is that number assigned to the item as it appears in the figure referenced in the adjacent figure number column.

(3) STOCK NUMBER column. This column lists the NSN for the item.

(4) CAGEC column. The Commercial and Government Entity (CAGE) Code (C) is a 5-digit alphanumeric code used to identify the manufacturer, distributor, or Government agency, etc., that supplies the item.

(5) PART NUMBER column. Indicates the primary number used by the manufacturer (individual, firm, corporation, or Government activity), which controls the design and characteristics of the item by means of its engineering drawings, specifications standards and inspection requirements to identify an item or range of items.

5. Special Information.

a. USABLE ON CODE. The usable on code appears in the lower left corner of the Description column heading. Usable on codes are shown as "UOC:......" in the Description column (justified left) on the first line following applicable item description/nomenclature. Uncoded items are applicable to all models. Identification of the usable on codes used in the RPSTL are:

Code	Used On
194	M1008, Type "B" Cargo, Shelter
208	M1008A1, Type "B" Cargo, Troop Seat
209	M1009, Type "A" Utility
210	M1010, Type "C" Ambulance
230	MI 028, Type "E" Shelter Carrier
252	M1028A1, Type"F" Shelter Carrier w/PTO
254	M1028A2, Type "F" Shelter Carrier w/PTO
256	M1028A3, Type "E Shelter Carrier
231	M1031, Type "D" Chassis

b. FABRICATION INSTRUCTIONS. Bulk materials required to manufacture items are listed in the Bulk Material Functional Group of this RPSTL. Part numbers for bulk materials are also referenced in the Description column of the line item entry for the item to be manufactured/fabricated. Detailed fabrication instructions for items source coded to be manufactured or fabricated are found in TM 9-2320-28920 or TM 9-2320-289-34.

c. ASSEMBLY INSTRUCTIONS. Detailed assembly instructions for items source coded to be assembled from component spare/repair parts are found in *TM 9 2320-289-20* or *TM 9-2320-289-34*. Items that makeup the assembly are listed immediately following the assembly item entry or reference is made to an applicable figure.

d. *KITS.* Line item entries for repair parts kits appear in group 9401 in Section II.

e. *INDEX NUMBERS.* Items which have the word BULK in the figure column will have an index number shown in the item number column. This index number is a cross-reference between the National Stock Number/Part Number Index and the bulk material list in Section II.

f. *ASSOCIATED PUBLICATIONS. The* publications listed below pertain to the CUCV Series Truck and its components:

Publication	Short Title
LO 9-2320-289-12	CUCV Series Truck
TM 9-2320-289-10	CUCV Series Truck
TM 9-2320-289-20	CUCV Series Truck
TM 9-2320-289-20P	CUCV Series Truck
TM 9-2320-289-34	CUCV Series Truck

g. The illustrations In this manual are identical to those published in *TM 9-2320-289-34P*. Only those parts coded "C" or "O" in the third position of the SMR code are listed in the tabular listing; therefore, there maybe a break in the item number sequence. Only illustrations containing organizational/unit level authorized items appear in this manual.

6. How to Locate Repair Parts.

a. *When National Stock Number or Part Number is Not Known:*

(1) First. Using the table of contents, determine the assembly group or subassembly group to which the item belongs. This is necessary since figures are prepared for assembly groups and subassembly groups, and listings are divided into the same groups.

(2) Second. Find the figure covering the assembly group or subassembly group to which the item belongs.

(3) Third. Identify the item on the figure and use the Figure and Item Number Index to find the NSN.

b. *When National Stock Number or Part Number is Known:*

(1) First. Using the National Stock Number or Part Number Index, find the pertinent National Stock Number or Part Number. The NSN index is in National Item Identification Number (NIIN) sequence (see paragraph 4.a.(1)). The part numbers in the Part Number index are listed in ascending alphanumeric sequence (see paragraph 4. b). Both indexes cross-reference you to the illustration/figure and item number of the item you are looking for.

(2) Second. Turn to the figure and item number, verify that the item is the one you're looking for, then locate the item number in the repair parts list for the figure.

7. Abbreviations.

For standard abbreviations see MIL-STD-12D, *Military Standard Abbreviations for Use on Drawings, Specifications, Standards, and in Technical Documents.*

Abbreviations	Explanation
NIIN	National Item Identification Number (consists of the last 9 digits of the NSN)
RPSTL	Repair Parts and Special Tools List

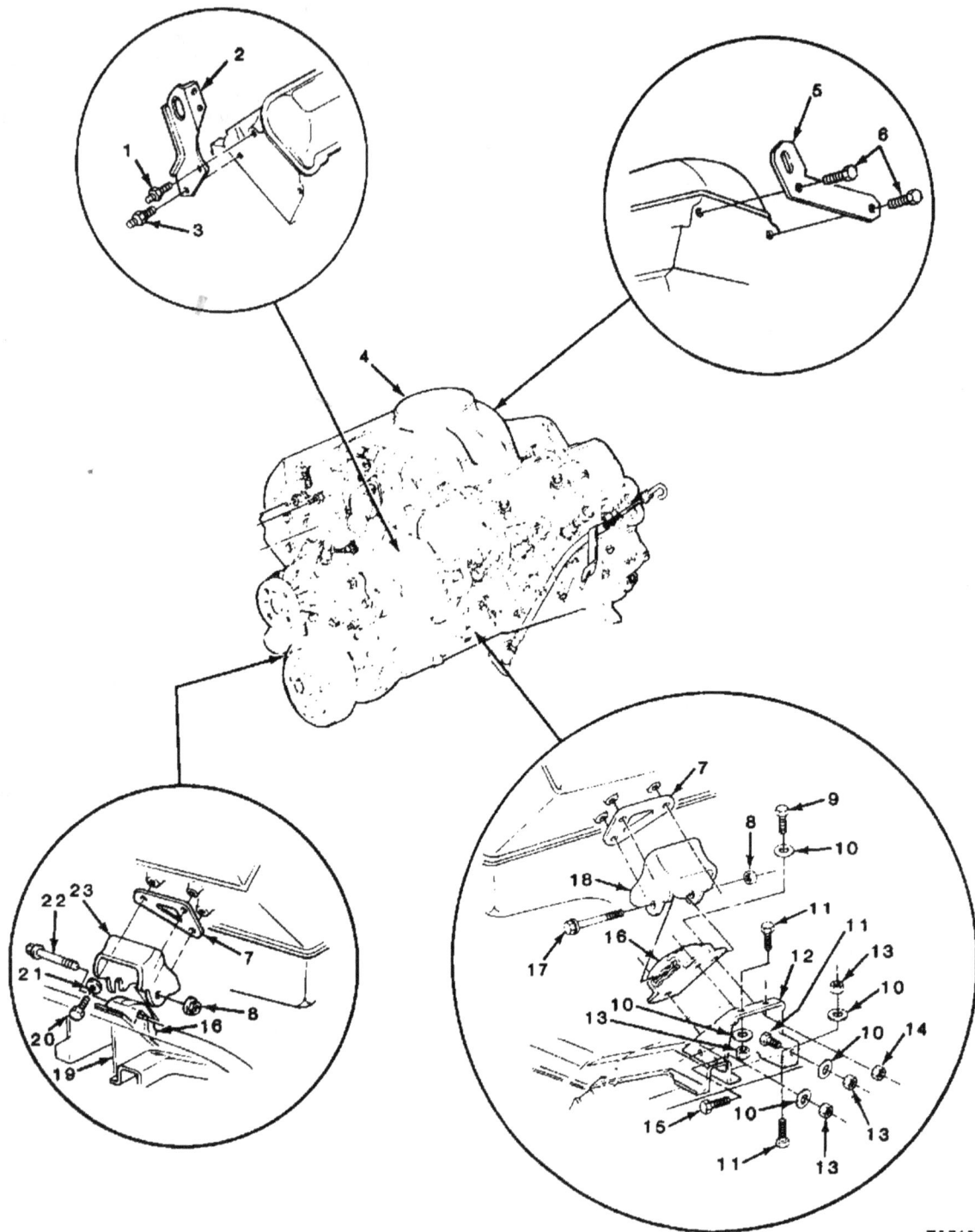

TA510808

FIGURE 1. ENGINE ASSEMBLY MOUNTS, LIFTING BRACKETS,
AND MOUNTING HARDWARE.

(1)	(2)	(3)	(4)	(5)	(6)
ITEM NO	SMR CODE	CAGEC	PART NUMBER	DESCRIPTION AND USABLE ON CODES (UOC)	QTY

GROUP 01 ENGINE

GROUP 0100 ENGINE ASSEMBLY

FIG. 1 ENGINE ASSEMBLY, MOUNTS, LIFTING BRACKETS, AND MOUNTING HARDWARE

1	PAOZZ	11862	1403394-6	STUD,CONTINUOUS THR	1
2	PAOZZ	11862	14033945	BRACKET,ENGINE LIFT FRONT	1
3	PAOZZ	11862	22535073	STUD,CONTINUOUS THR	1
5	PAOZZ	11862	14033947	BRACKET,ANGLE REAR	1
6	PAOZZ	11862	11504595	SCREW,CAP,HEXAGON H	2

END OF FIGURE

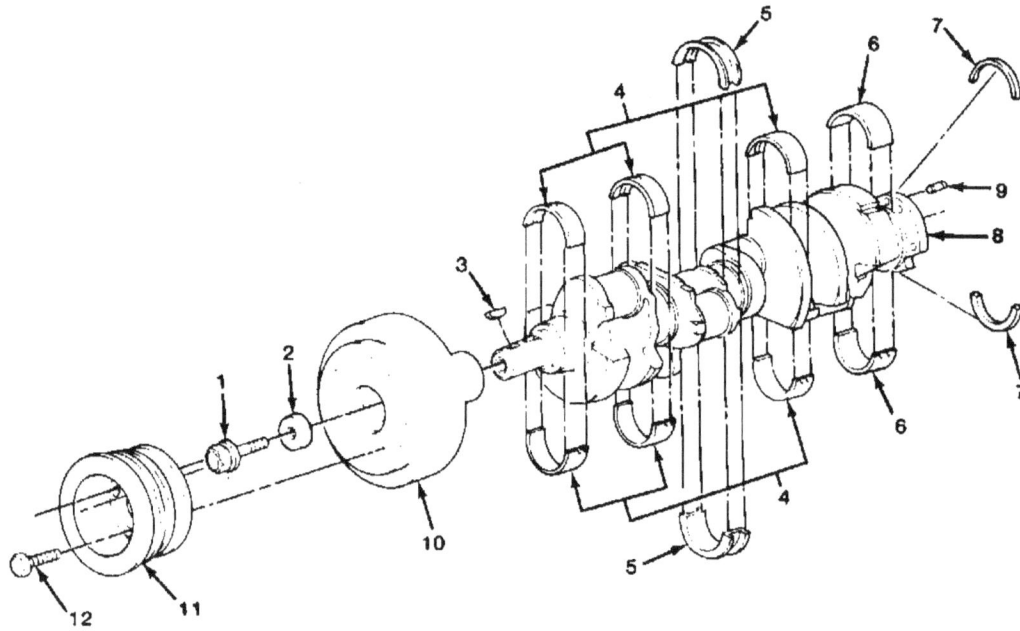

FIGURE 2. ENGINE CRANKSHAFT AND RELATED PARTS.

TA510810

(1) ITEM NO	(2) SMR CODE	(3) CAGEC	(4) PART NUMBER	(5) DESCRIPTION AND USABLE ON CODES (UOC)	(6) QTY
				GROUP 0102 CRANKSHAFT	
				FIG. 2 ENGINE CRANKSHAFT AND RELATED PARTS	
11	PAOZZ	11862	14067703	PULLEY,CONE UOC:194,208,209,230,231,252,254,256	1
11	PAOZZ	11862	14067702	PULLEY,CONE UOC:210,230	1
12	PAOZZ	11862	11504595	SCREW,CAP,HEXAGON H	4
				END OF FIGURE	

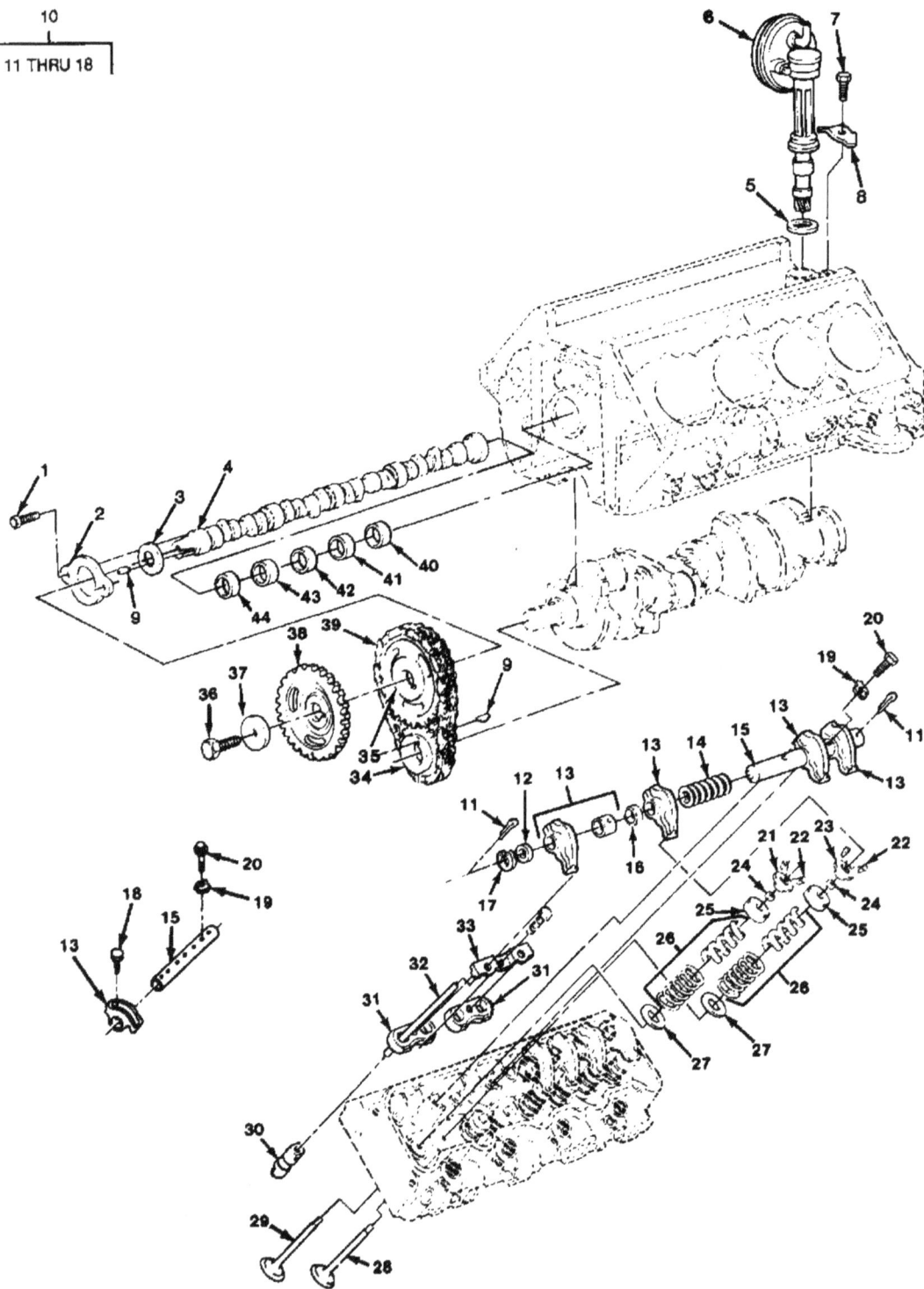

FIGURE 3. CAMSHAFT, VALVES, ROCKER ARMS, AND RELATED PARTS.

TA510814

(1) ITEM NO	(2) SMR CODE	(3) CAGEC	(4) PART NUMBER	(5) DESCRIPTION AND USABLE ON CODES (UOC)	(6) QTY
				GROUP 0105 VALVES, CAMSHAFTS, AND TIMING SYSTEM	
				FIG. 3 CAMSHAFT, VALVES, ROCKER ARMS, AND RELATED PARTS	
5	PAOZZ	11862	14022649	GASKET PART OF KIT P/N 15633467	1
6	PAOZZ	11862	7849302	PUMP,AIR,EMISSION C	1
7	PAOZZ	11862	1635490	BOLT,SELF-LOCKING	1
8	PAOZZ	11862	14022650	CLAMP	1

END OF FIGURE

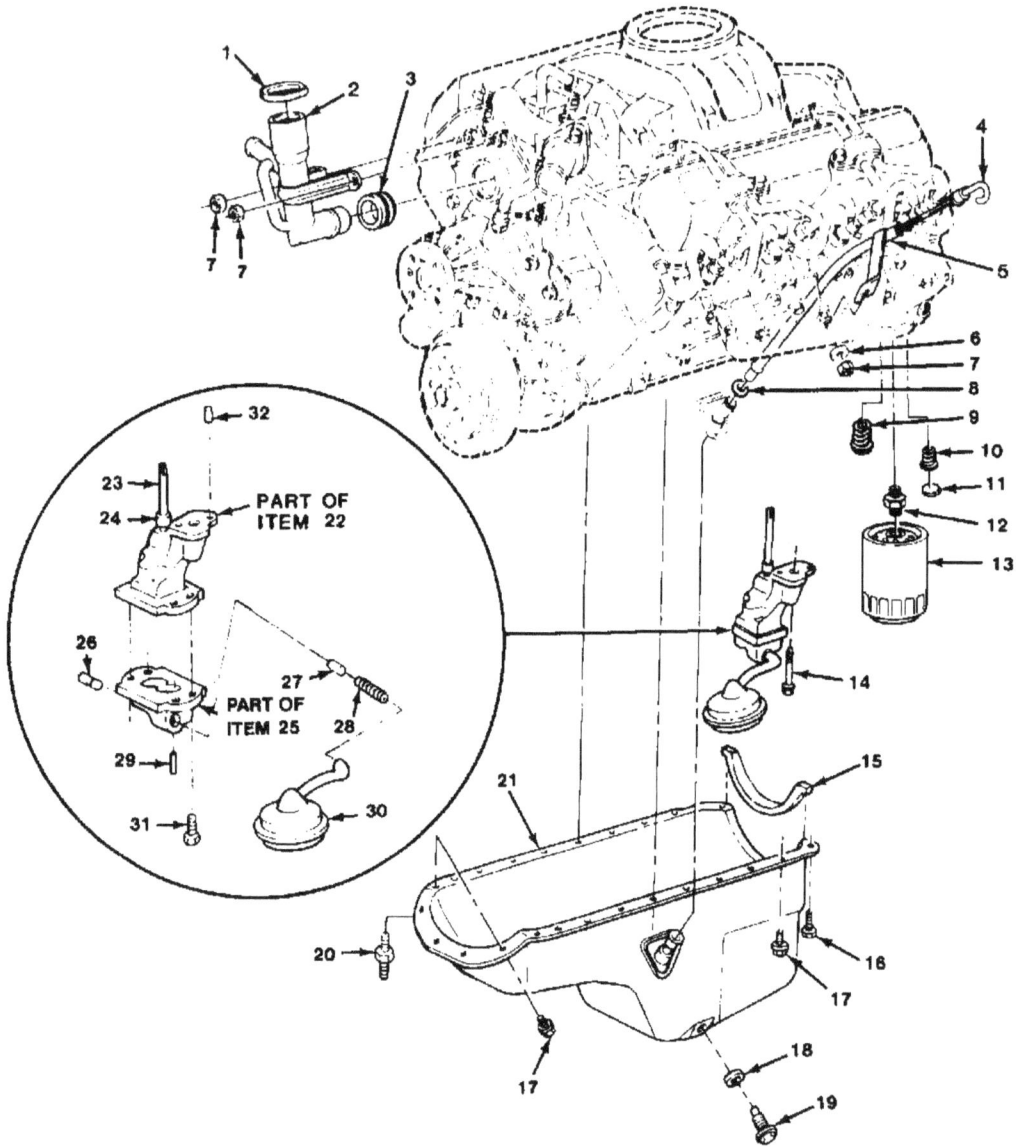

FIGURE 4. ENGINE OIL PUMP ASSEMBLY FILTER, PAN, AND RELATED PARTS.

TA510815

(1) ITEM NO	(2) SMR CODE	(3) CAGEC	(4) PART NUMBER	(5) DESCRIPTION AND USABLE ON CODES (UOC)	(6) QTY
				GROUP 0106 ENGINE LUBRICATION SYSTEM	
				FIG. 4 ENGINE OIL PUMP ASSEMBLY, FILTER, PAN, AND RELATED PARTS	
1	PAOZZ	70040	FC106	CAP,FILLER OPENING	1
2	PAOZZ	11862	14071059	FILLER NECK	1
3	PAOZZ	11862	14028942	GROMMET,NONMETALLIC	1
4	PAOZZ	11862	14050523	GAGE ROD-CAP,LIQUID	1
5	PAOZZ	11862	14045268	TUBE,BENT,METALLIC	1
6	PAOZZ	11862	14036369	WASHER,FLAT	1
7	PAOZZ	11862	22521550	NUT,PLAIN,HEXAGON	3
8	PAOZZ	24617	274244	PACKING,PREFORMED	1
9	PAOZZ	11862	25011208	VALVE,REGULATING,OI	1
10	PAOZZ	11862	25011206	VALVE,SAFETY RELIEF	1
11	PAOZZ	11862	14066310	PLUG,PISTON PIN	1
12	PAOZZ	11862	14022700	REDUCER,BOSS	1
13	PAOZZ	70040	PF-35	FILTER,FLUID	1
15	PAOZZ	11862	14022683	SEAL,NONMETALLIC SP	1
16	PAOZZ	11862	11508534	BOLT,MACHINE	2
17	PAOZZ	24617	11507029	SCREW,CAP,HEXAGON H	21
18	PAOZZ	11862	14079550	GASKET	1
19	PAOZZ	11862	337185	PLUG,MACHINE THREAD	1
20	PAOZZ	11862	14066307	STUD,SHOULDERED	1
21	PAOZZ	11862	14061649	OIL PAN	1

END OF FIGURE

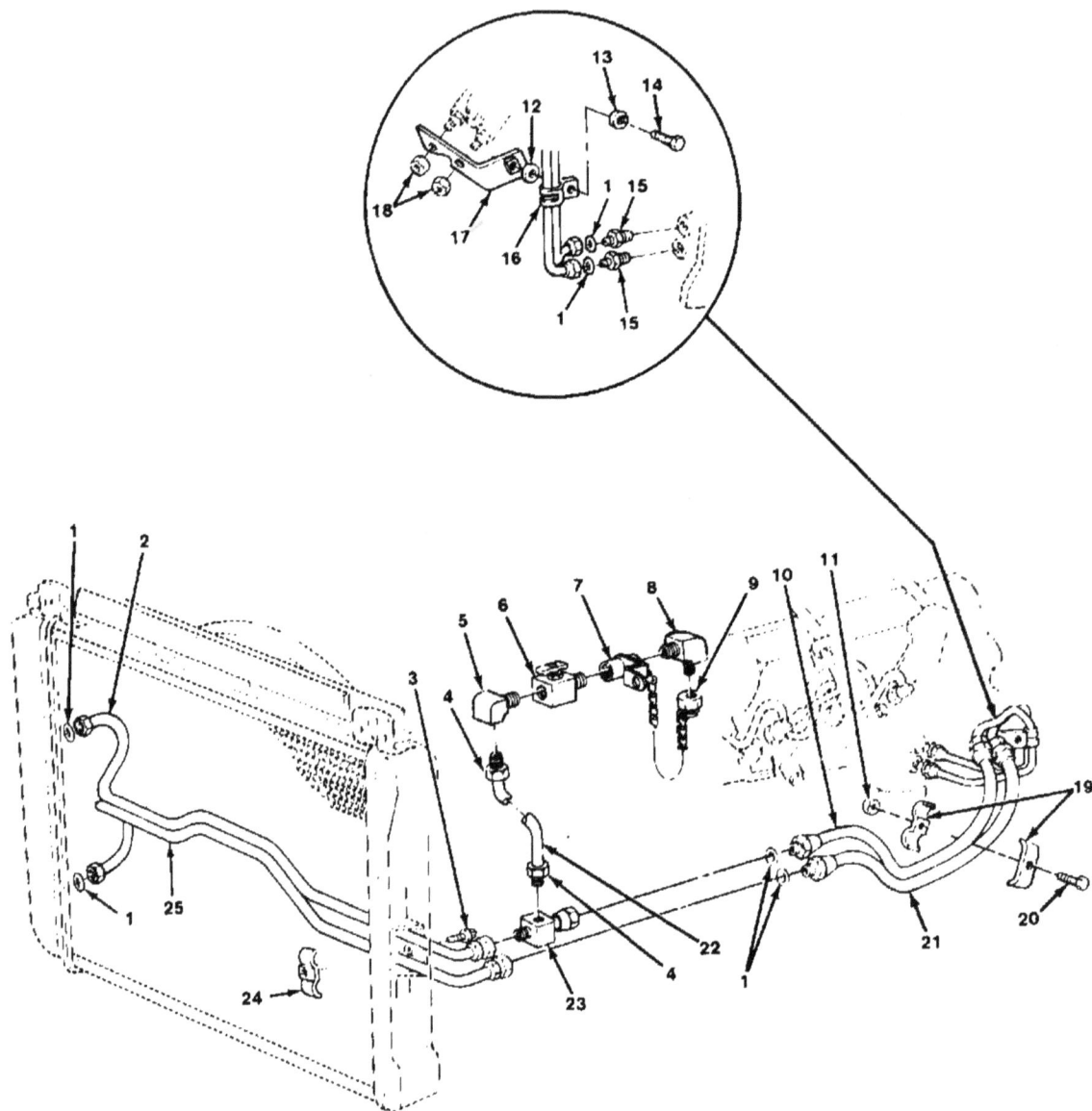

TA510816

FIGURE 5. OIL COOLER LINES, SAMPLING VALVE, AND RELATED PARTS.

(1) ITEM NO	(2) SMR CODE	(3) CAGEC	(4) PART NUMBER	(5) DESCRIPTION AND USABLE ON CODES (UOC)	(6) QTY
				GROUP 0106 ENGINE LUBRICATION SYSTEM	
				FIG. 5 OIL COOLER LINES, SAMPLING VALVE, AND RELATED PARTS	
1	PAOZZ	11862	14055585	SEAL RING,METAL	6
2	PAOZZ	11862	14061344	TUBE ASSEMBLY,METAL	1
3	PAOZZ	96906	MS90728-8	SCREW,CAP,HEXAGON H	1
4	PAOZZ	11862	137396	INVERTED NUT,TUBE C	2
5	PAOZZ	72582	224425	ELBOW,PIPE TO TUBE	1
6	PAOZZ	79470	6820	COCK,SHUTOFF,SCREW	1
7	PAOZZ	11862	15599988	BRACKET,DOUBLE ANGL	1
8	PAOZZ	72582	118754	ELBOW,PIPE TO TUBE	1
9	PAOZZ	70411	SP2489-FM	CAP,FILLER OPENING	1
10	PAOZZ	11862	15548901	HOSE ASSEMBLY,NONME UOC:194,208,209,230,231,252,254,256	1
10	PAOZZ	11862	14063336	HOSE ASSEMBLY,NONME UOC:210,230	1
11	PAOZZ	96906	MS35691-406	NUT,PLAIN,HEXAGON	1
12	PAOZZ	11862	14061350	DISK,OIL COOLER	1
13	PAOZZ	96906	MS35338-44	WASHER,LOCK	1
14	PAOZZ	96906	MS90728-6	SCREW,CAP,HEXAGON H	1
15	PAOZZ	11862	14055586	ADAPTER,STRAIGHT,PI	2
16	PAOZZ	11862	14047899	CLAMP,LOOP	1
17	PAOZZ	11862	14061348	BRACKET,ANGLE	1
18	PAOZZ	11862	22521550	NUT,PLAIN,HEXAGON	2
19	PAOZZ	11862	14061352	STRAP,RETAINING	2
20	PAOZZ	96906	MS90728-10	SCREW,CAP,HEXAGON H	1
21	PAOZZ	11862	15548902	HOSE ASSEMBLY,NONME UOC:194,208,209,230,231,252,254,256	1
21	PAOZZ	11862	14063337	HOSE ASSEMBLY,NONME UOC:210,230	1
22	MFOZZ	11862	15599986	PIPE ASM (9-68"LG) MAKE FROM PIPE, P/N 3696822	1
23	PAOZZ	11862	15599987	TEE,TUBE	1
24	PAOZZ	11862	14036784	STRAP,RETAINING	1
25	PAOZZ	11862	14061345	TUBE ASSEMBLY,METAL	1

END OF FIGURE

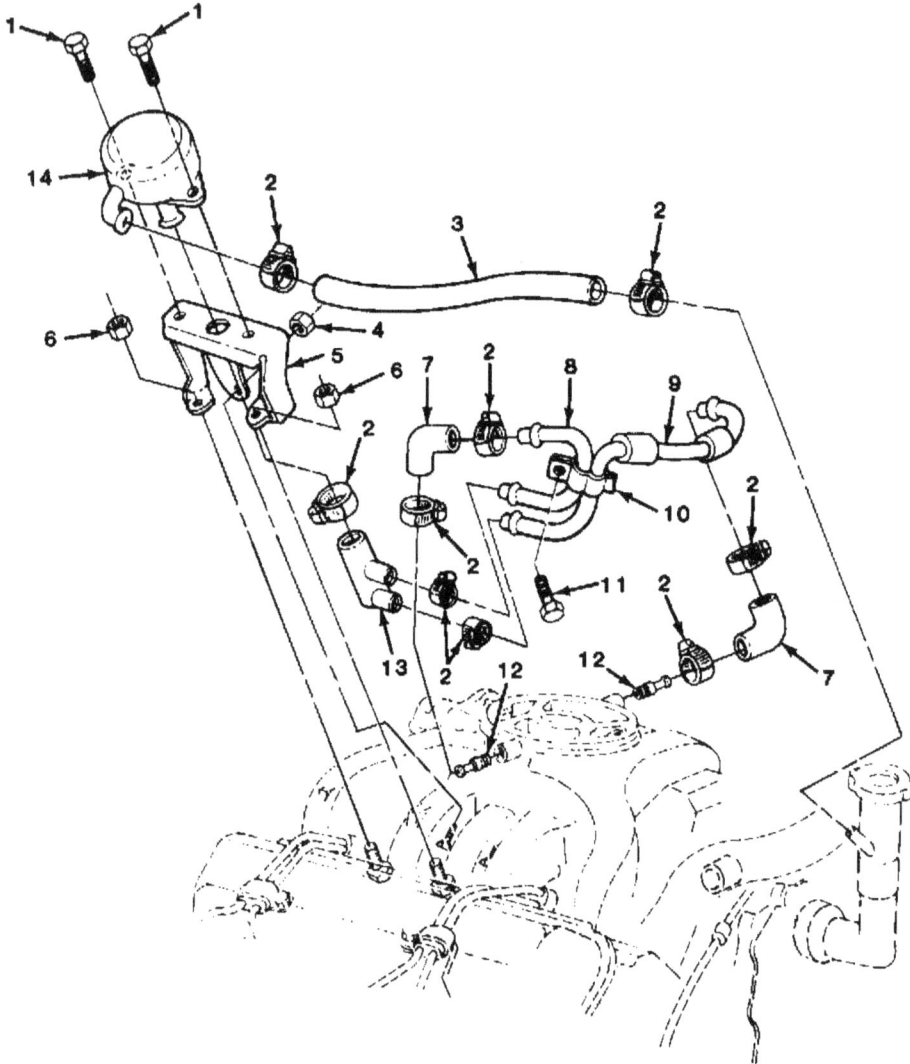

TA510817

FIGURE 6. CRANKCASE DEPRESSION VALVE AND RELATED PARTS.

(1) ITEM NO	(2) SMR CODE	(3) CAGEC	(4) PART NUMBER	(5) DESCRIPTION AND USABLE ON CODES (UOC)	(6) QTY

GROUP 0106 ENGINE LUBRICATION SYSTEM

FIG. 6 CRANKCASE DEPRESSION VALVE
AND RELATED PARTS

1	PAOZZ	11862	11508353	BOLT,MACHINE	2
2	PAOZZ	96906	MS35842-11	CLAMP,HOSE	9
3	PAOZZ	11862	14067732	HOSE,PREFORMED	1
4	PAOZZ	24617	11502488	NUT,PLAIN,HEXAGON	1
5	PAOZZ	11862	14067733	BRACKET ASSEMBLY,CR	1
6	PAOZZ	11862	22521550	NUT,PLAIN,HEXAGON	2
7	PAOZZ	11862	14050445	HOSE,PREFORMED	2
8	PAOZZ	11862	14050442	TUBE,BENT,METALLIC	1
9	PAOZZ	11862	14050443	TUBE,BENT,METALLIC	1
10	PAOZZ	11862	14050441	CLAMP,LOOP	1
11	PAOZZ	11862	11509135	SCREW,ASSEMBLED WAS	1
12	PAOZZ	11862	14050444	ADAPTER,STRAIGHT,TU	2
13	PAOZZ	11862	14050446	CONNECTOR,CRANKCASE	1
14	PAOZZ	11862	25042462	SENSOR,AIR CHARGED	1

END OF FIGURE

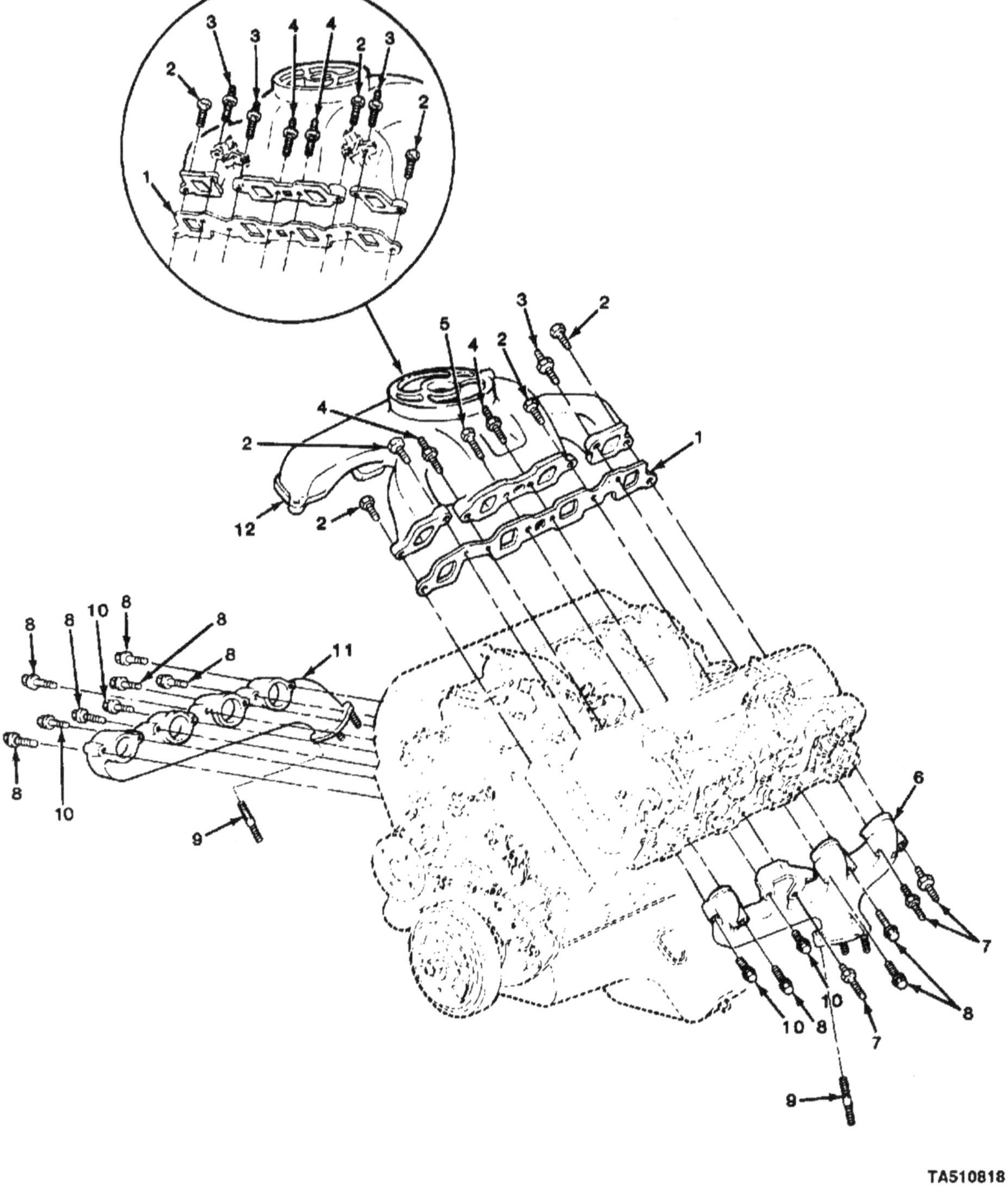

FIGURE 7. INTAKE AND EXHAUST MANIFOLDS.

TA510818

(1) ITEM NO	(2) SMR CODE	(3) CAGEC	(4) PART NUMBER	(5) DESCRIPTION AND USABLE ON CODES (UOC)	(6) QTY
				GROUP 0108 MANIFOLDS	
				FIG. 7 INTAKE AND EXHAUST MANIFOLDS	
6	PAOZZ	11862	14022657	MANIFOLD,EXHAUST LEFT	1
7	PAOZZ	11862	14028924	STUD,SHOULDERED AND	3
8	PAOZZ	11862	14028922	BOLT,MACHINE	9
9	PAOZZ	11862	14022654	STUD,PLAIN	6
10	PAOZZ	11862	14028923	SCREW,CAP,HEXAGON H	4
11	PAOZZ	11862	14025568	MANIFOLD,EXHAUST RIGHT	1
				END OF FIGURE	

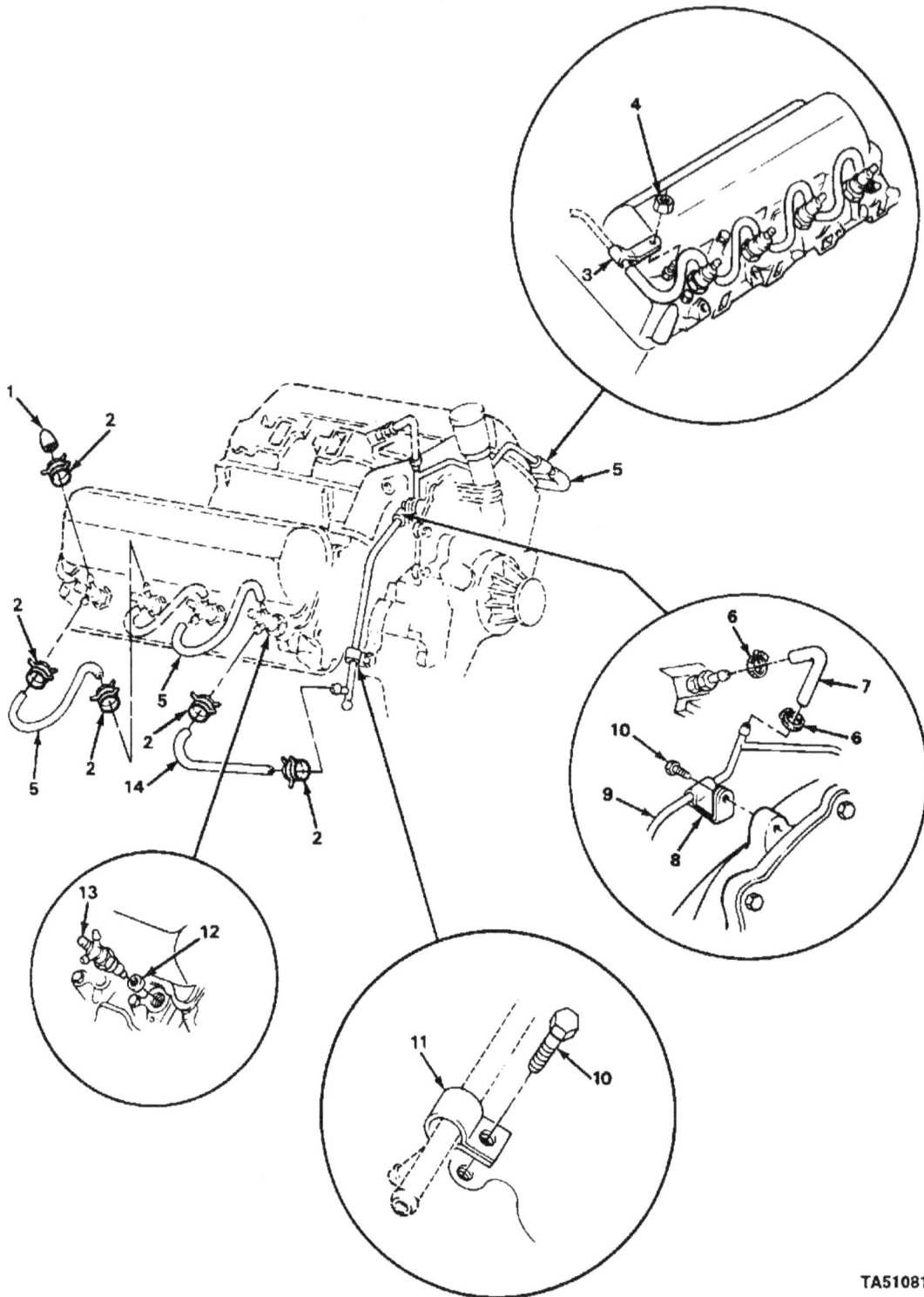

TA510819

FIGURE 8. FUEL INJECTOR AND RELATED PARTS.

(1) ITEM NO	(2) SMR CODE	(3) CAGEC	(4) PART NUMBER	(5) DESCRIPTION AND USABLE ON CODES (UOC)	(6) QTY
				GROUP 03 FUEL SYSTEM	
				GROUP 0301 CARBURETOR, FUEL INJECTOR	
				FIG. 8 FUEL INJECTOR AND RELATED PARTS	
1	PAOZZ	11862	14066301	CAP	2
2	PAOZZ	11862	11663000	CLAMP	18
3	PAOZZ	11862	14033893	CLAMP,LOOP	1
4	PAOZZ	11862	22521550	NUT,PLAIN,HEXAGON	1
5	MOOZZ	11862	14066306	HOSE,NONMETALLIC (7" LG) MAKE FROM P/N 14066305	7
6	PAOZZ	11862	25518880	CLAMP,HOSE	2
7	MOOZZ	11862	9439363	HOSE, NON MET (3" LG) MAKE FROM HOSE,P/N 9439402	1
8	PAOZZ	11862	14033895	CLAMP,LOOP	1
9	PAOZZ	11862	14061569	TUBE,BENT,METALLIC	1
10	PAOZZ	11862	11504512	BOLT,MACHINE	2
11	PAOZZ	96906	MS21333-45	CLAMP,LOOP	1
14	PAOZZ	11862	14066305	TUBING,NONMETALLIC (7.01" LG) CUT TO SIZE	1

END OF FIGURE

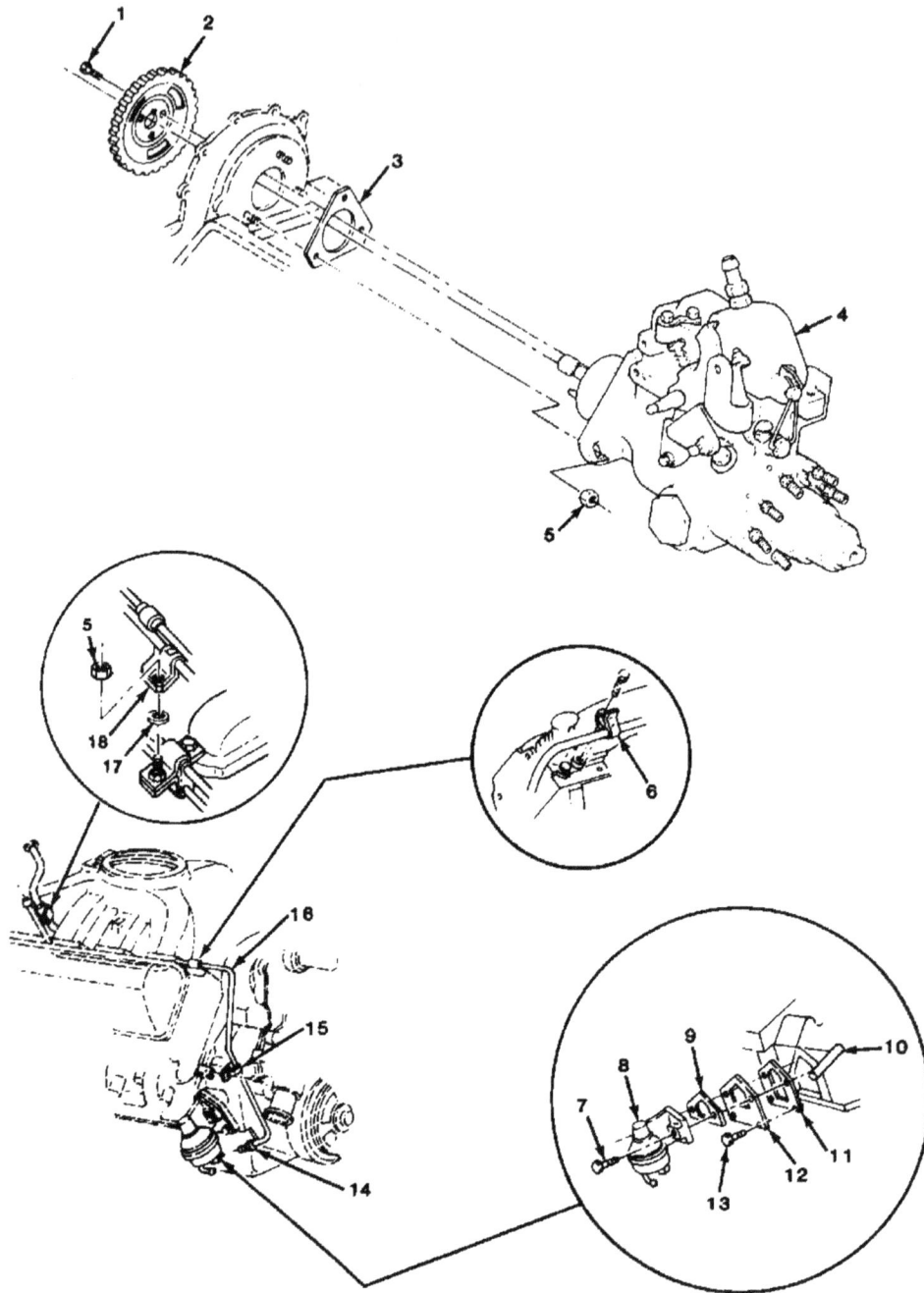

TA510820

FIGURE 9. SUPPLY PUMP, INJECTOR PUMP, AND RELATED PARTS.

(1) ITEM NO	(2) SMR CODE	(3) CAGEC	(4) PART NUMBER	(5) DESCRIPTION AND USABLE ON CODES (UOC)	(6) QTY
				GROUP 0302 FUEL PUMPS	
				FIG. 9 SUPPLY PUMP, INJECTOR PUMP, AND RELATED PARTS	
7	PAOZZ	96906	MS90728-64	SCREW,CAP,HEXAGON H	2
8	PAOZZ	11862	6471831	PUMP,FUEL,CAM ACTUA	1
9	PAOZZ	11862	9776705	GASKET PART OF KIT P/N 15633467	1
10	PAOZZ	11862	14050425	PIN,STRAIGHT,HEADLE	1
11	PAOZZ	11862	3705044	GASKET PART OF KIT P/N 15633467	1
12	PAOZZ	11862	3719599	PLATE,FUEL PUMP	1
13	PAOZZ	11862	11509669	BOLT,ASSEMBLED WASH	2

END OF FIGURE

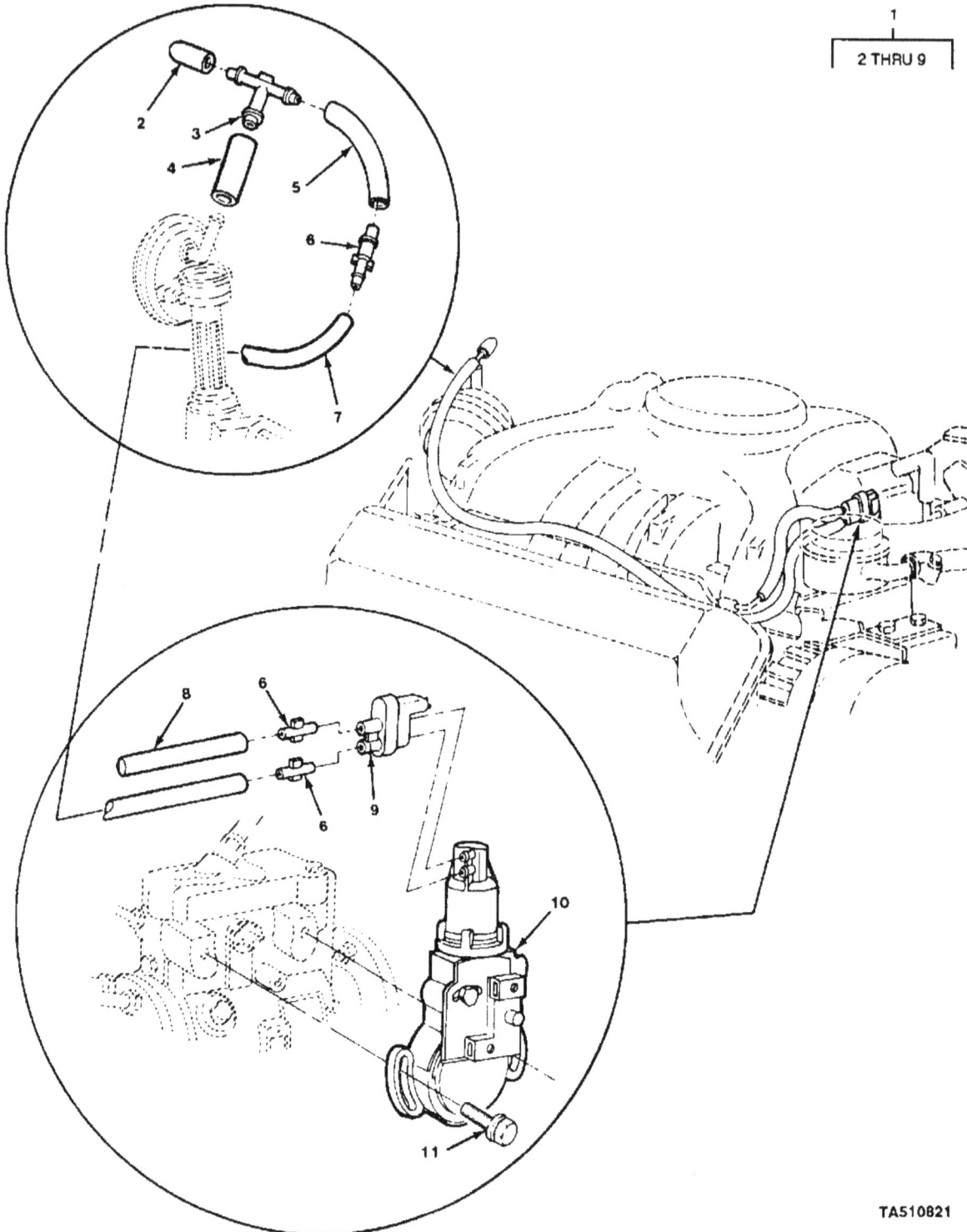

FIGURE 10. VACUUM VALVE AND HOSES.

TA510821

(1) ITEM NO	(2) SMR CODE	(3) CAGEC	(4) PART NUMBER	(5) DESCRIPTION AND USABLE ON CODES (UOC)	(6) QTY
				GROUP 0302 FUEL PUMPS	
				FIG. 10 VACUUM VALVE AND HOSES	
1	XDOOO	11862	14045233	DUPLEX HOSE,RUBBER	1
2	PAOZZ	11862	343350	.CAP,PROTECTIVE,DUST	1
3	PAOZZ	11862	3970076	.TEE	1
4	MOOZZ	11862	M51	.HOSE,RUBBER (2" LG) MAKE FROM HOSE,P/N 9438124	1
5	MOOZZ	11862	M140	.HOSE,RUBBER (5.51" LG) MAKE FROM HOSE,P/N 3987364	1
6	PAOZZ	11862	560625	.CONNECTOR,HOSE	3
7	MOOZZ	11862	M495	.HOSE,RUBBER (19.49" LG) MAKE FROM HOSE,P/N 9738381	1
8	MOOZZ	11862	M127	.HOSE,RUBBER (5" LG) MAKE FROM HOSE,P/N 9438381	1
9	PAOZZ	11862	22506637	.ADAPTER	1
10	PAOZZ	11862	14057219	VALVE,VACUUM REGULA	1
11	PAOZZ	96906	MS51869-28	SCREW,TAPPING	2

END OF FIGURE

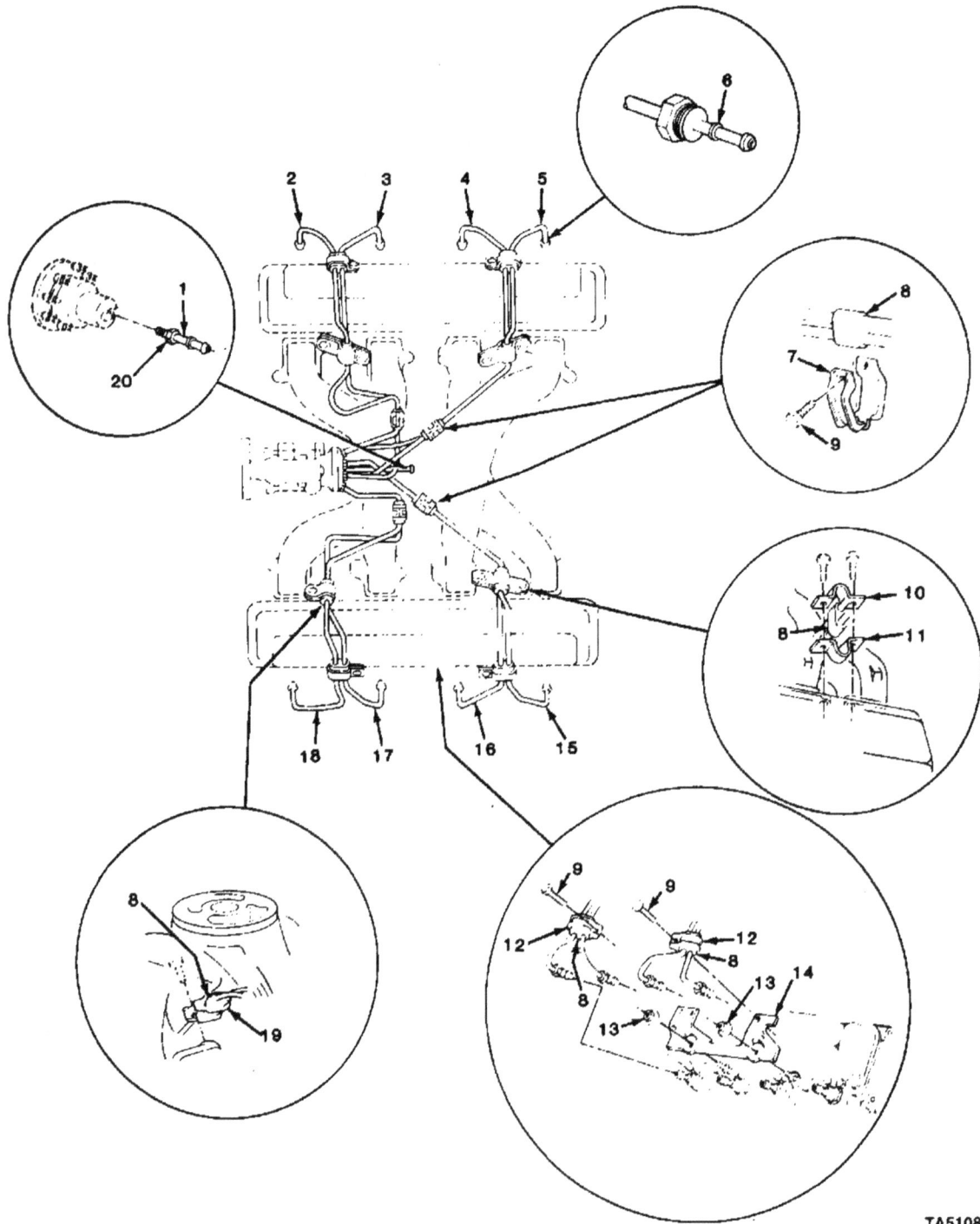

FIGURE 11. INJECTOR LINES AND RELATED PARTS.

TA510823

(1) ITEM NO	(2) SMR CODE	(3) CAGEC	(4) PART NUMBER	(5) DESCRIPTION AND USABLE ON CODES (UOC)	(6) QTY
				GROUP 0302 FUEL PUMPS	
				FIG. 11 INJECTOR LINES AND RELATED PARTS	
7	PAOZZ	11862	14033955	CLAMP,LOOP	4
8	PAOZZ	11862	560614	GROMMET,NONMETALLIC	12
9	PAOZZ	11862	11503617	SCREW,TAPPING	8
10	PAOZZ	11862	14033921	STRAP,RETAINING	3
11	PAOZZ	11862	14033922	STRAP,RETAINING	3
12	PAOZZ	11862	560613	CLAMP,LOOP	4
13	PAOZZ	11862	22521550	NUT,PLAIN,HEXAGON	4
19	PAOZZ	11862	14033953	CLAMP,LOOP	1

END OF FIGURE

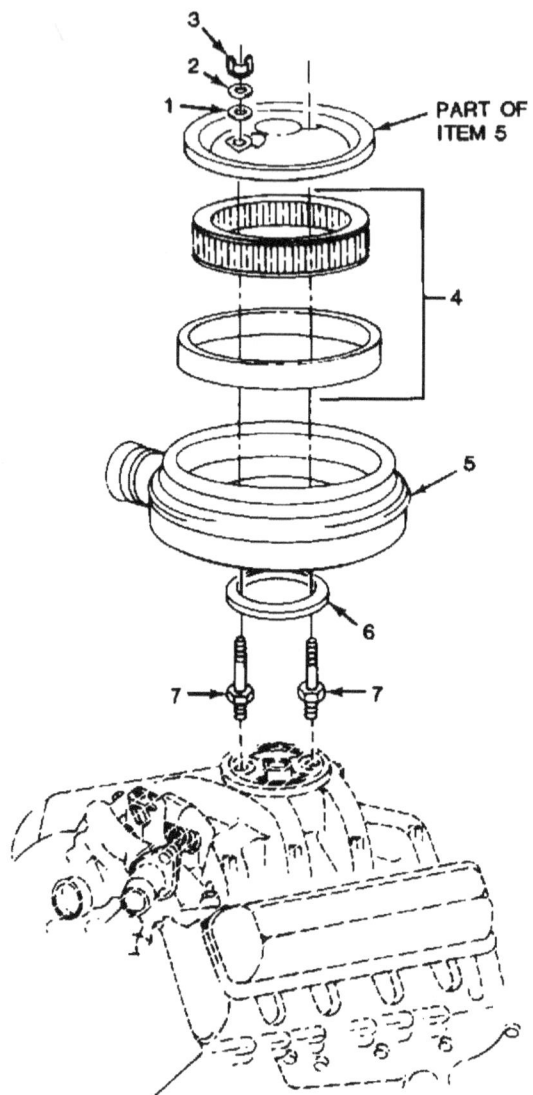

PART OF
ITEM 5

TA510824

FIGURE 12. AIR CLEANER.

(1) ITEM NO	(2) SMR CODE	(3) CAGEC	(4) PART NUMBER	(5) DESCRIPTION AND USABLE ON CODES (UOC)	(6) QTY
				GROUP 0304 AIR CLEANER	
				FIG. 12 AIR CLEANER	
1	PAOZZ	11862	3827499	WASHER,FLAT	2
2	PAOZZ	11862	3790768	WASHER,FLAT	2
3	PAOZZ	11862	14001197	NUT,PLAIN,WING	2
4	PAOZZ	70040	A644C	FILTER ELEMENT,INTA	1
5	PAOZZ	11862	25041910	AIR CLEANER,INTAKE INCLUDES ITEM #4	1
6	PAOZZ	11862	15530620	GROMMET,NONMETALLIC	1
7	PAOZZ	11862	14033948	STUD,SHOULDERED AND	2

END OF FIGURE

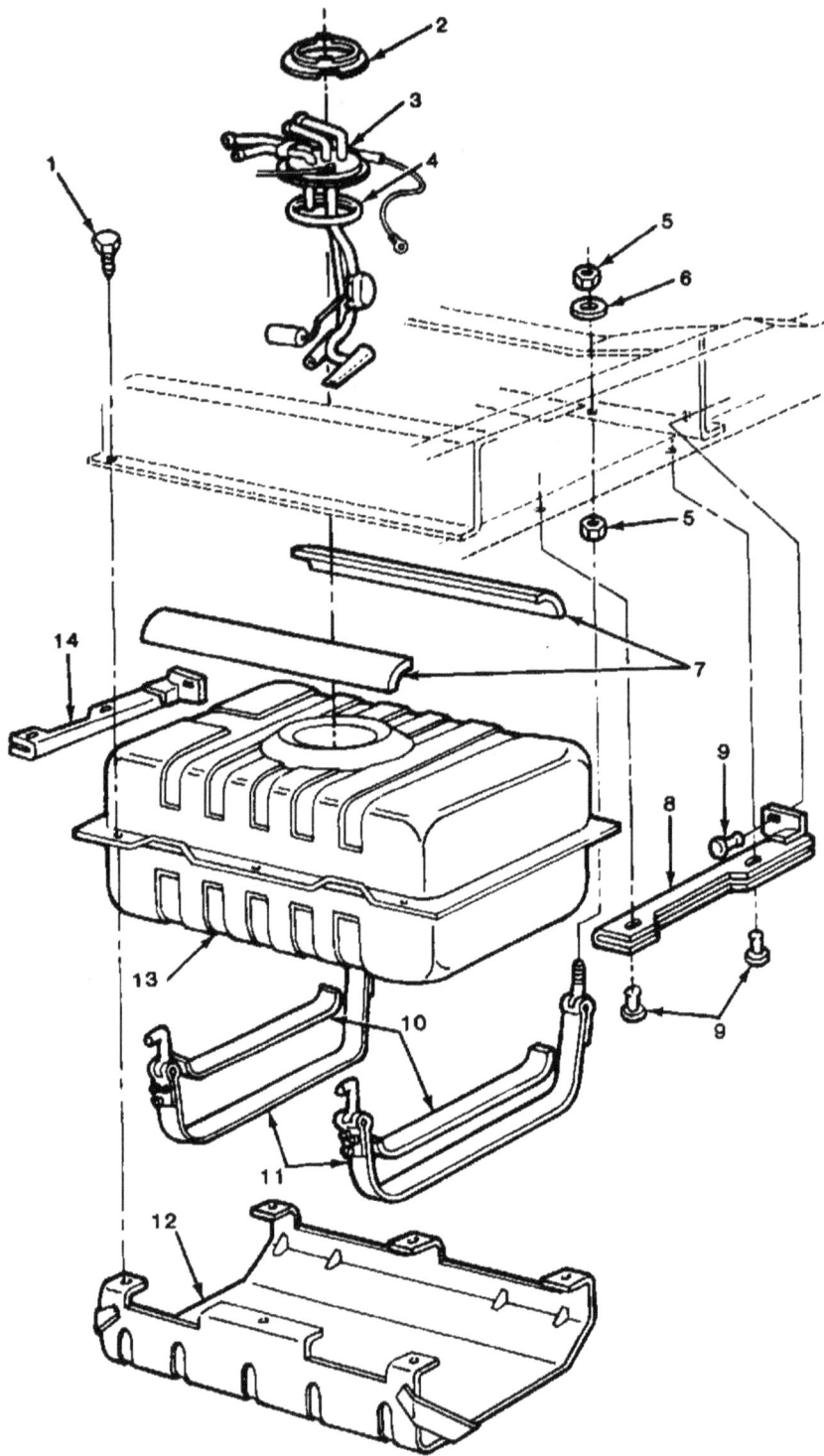

TA510825

FIGURE 13. FUEL TANK AND RELATED PARTS (M1009).

(1) ITEM NO	(2) SMR CODE	(3) CAGEC	(4) PART NUMBER	(5) DESCRIPTION AND USABLE ON CODES (UOC)	(6) QTY
				GROUP 0306 TANKS, LINES, FITTINGS, HEADERS	
				FIG. 13 FUEL TANK AND RELATED PARTS (M1009)	
1	PAOZZ	96906	MS90728-59	SCREW,CAP,HEXAGON H UOC:209	6
2	PAOZZ	11862	22516548	CAP,FUEL SENDER UOC:209	1
3	PAOZZ	11862	25004140	GAGE,GAS FLOW INCLUDES ITEM #4 UOC:209	1
4	PAOZZ	11862	22515965	GASKET UOC:209	1
5	PAOZZ	96906	MS51967-12	NUT,PLAIN,HEXAGON UOC:209	4
6	PAOZZ	96906	MS27183-15	WASHER,FLAT UOC:209	2
7	PAOZZ	11862	6263877	FELT,MECHANICAL,PRE UOC:209	2
8	PAOZZ	11862	14020491	GUARD ASSEMBLY,FUEL LEFT UOC:209	1
9	PAOZZ	11862	480534	RETAINER,PANEL HOLE UOC:209	6
10	PAOZZ	11862	6260631	ANTISQUEAK,FUEL TAN UOC:209	2
11	PAOZZ	11862	334675	STRAP,RETAINING UOC:209	2
12	PAOZZ	11862	368752	SHIELD ASSEMBLY,FUE UOC:209	1
13	PAOZZ	11862	14050685	TANK,FUEL,ENGINE UOC:209	1
14	PAOZZ	11862	14020492	BRACKET,ENGINE ACCE RIGHT UOC:209	1

END OF FIGURE

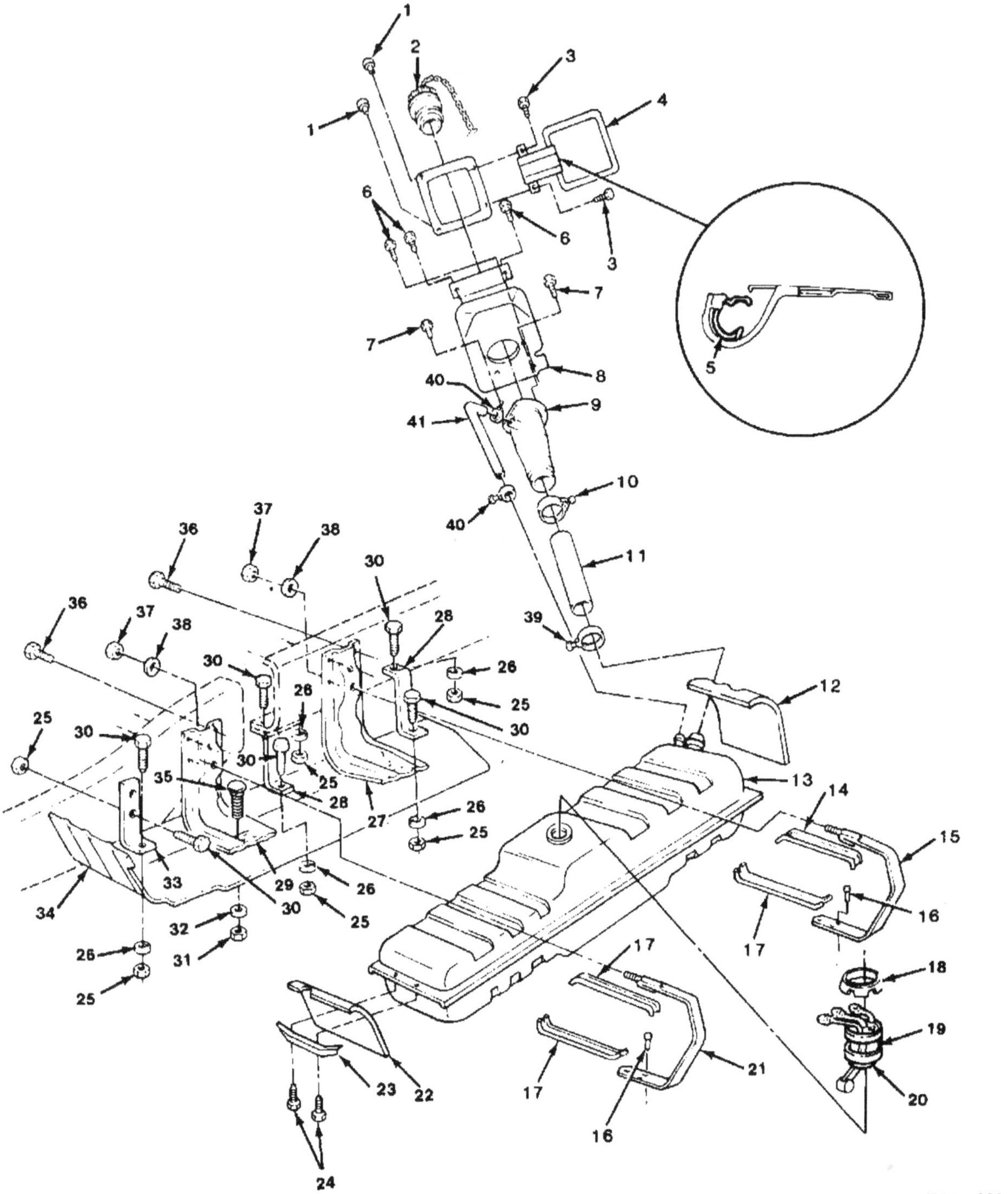

FIGURE 14. FUEL TANK AND RELATED PARTS (ALL EXCEPT M1009).

TA510826

(1) ITEM NO	(2) SMR CODE	(3) CAGEC	(4) PART NUMBER	(5) DESCRIPTION AND USABLE ON CODES (UOC)	(6) QTY
				GROUP 0306 TANKS, LINES, FITTINGS, HEADERS	
				FIG. 14 FUEL TNAK AND RELATED PARTS (ALL EXCEPT M1009)	
1	PAOZZ	11862	14010707	BUMPER,NONMETALLIC UOC:194,208,230,252,254,256	2
2	PAOZZ	11862	14063326	CAP,FILLER OPENING UOC:194,208,210,230,231,252,254,256	1
3	PAOZZ	96906	MS51869-24	SCREW,CAP,SOCKET HE UOC:194,208,230,252	2
4	PAOZZ	11862	14052026	DOOR,ACCESS UOC:194,208,230,252,254,256	1
5	PAOZZ	11862	4813235	SPRING,FLAT UOC:194,208,230,252	1
6	PAOZZ	96906	MS51869-24	SCREW,CAP,SOCKET HE UOC:194,208,230,252,254,256	3
7	PAOZZ	11862	14026247	SCREW,ASSEMBLED WAS UOC:194,208,230,252,254,256	3
8	PAOZZ	11862	14063363	HOUSING,FILLER NECK UOC:194,208,230,252,254,256	1
9	PAOZZ	11862	14063333	FILLER NECK UOC:210,231	1
9	PAOZZ	11862	14063327	FILLER NECK UOC:194,208,230,252,254,256	1
10	PAOZZ	96906	MS35842-14	CLAMP,HOSE UOC:194,208,210,230,231,252,254,256	1
11	PAOZZ	11862	14063334	HOSE,PREFORMED UOC:210,231	1
11	PAOZZ	11862	14063328	HOSE,PREFORMED UOC:194,208,230,252,254,256	1
12	PAOZZ	11862	334523	PAD,CUSHIONING UOC:194,208,210,230,231,252,254,256	1
13	PAOZZ	11862	14071984	TANK,FUEL,ENGINE UOC:194,208,210,230,231,252,254,256	1
14	MOOZZ	11862	6263870	INSULATOR F/TNK ST (3.00"X19.25") MAKE FROM FELT, P/N 6263877 UOC:194,208,210,230,231,252,254,256	1
15	PAOZZ	11862	6262755	STRAP ASSEMBLY,FUEL UOC:194,208,210,230,231,252,254,256	1
16	XDOZZ	24617	9414411	RIVET,SOLID UOC:194,208,210,230,231,252,254,256	6
17	MOOZZ	11862	6263871	INSULATOR F/TNK ST (3.00"X15.75") MAKE FROM FELT, P/N 6263877 UOC:194,208,210,230,231,252,254,256	3
18	PAOZZ	11862	22516548	CAM,FUEL SENDER UOC:194,208,210,230,231,252,254,256	1
19	PAOZZ	11862	22515965	GASKET UOC:194,208,210,230,231,252,254,256	1
20	PAOZZ	11862	25004137	TRANSMITTER,LIQUID INCLUDES ITEM #33	1

(1) ITEM NO	(2) SMR CODE	(3) CAGEC	(4) PART NUMBER	(5) DESCRIPTION AND USABLE ON CODES (UOC)	(6) QTY
				UOC:194,208,210,230,231,252,254,256	
21	PAOZZ	11862	359847	BAND,RETAINING	1
				UOC:194,208,210,230,231,252,254,256	
22	PAOZZ	11862	334521	SHIELD,FUEL TANK,FR	1
				UOC:194,208,210,230,231,252,254,256	
23	PAOZZ	11862	334522	BRACKET,ANGLE	1
				UOC:194,208,210,230,231,252,254,256	
24	PAOZZ	96906	MS51850-86	SCREW,TAPPING	2
				UOC:194,208,210,230,231,252,254,256	
25	PAOZZ	96906	MS51967-6	NUT,PLAIN,HEXAGON	7
				UOC:194,208,210,230,231,252,254,256	
26	PAOZZ	96906	MS35338-45	WASHER,LOCK	5
				UOC:194,208,210,230,231,252,254,256	
27	PAOZZ	11862	341287	SUPPORT ASSEMBLY,FU	1
				UOC:194,208,210,230,231,252,254,256	
28	PAOZZ	11862	344714	BRACKET,DOUBLE ANGL	2
				UOC:194,208,210,230,231,252,254,256	
29	PAOZZ	11862	467525	SUPPORT ASSEMBLY,FU	1
				UOC:194,208,210,230,231,252,254,256	
30	PAOZZ	96906	MS90728-33	BOLT,MACHINE	7
				UOC:194,208,210,230,231,252,254,256	
31	PAOZZ	24617	9422295	NUT,SELF-LOCKING,CO	2
				UOC:194,208,210,230,231,252,254,256	
32	PAOZZ	96906	MS27183-12	WASHER,FLAT	2
				UOC:194,208,210,230,231,252,254,256	
33	PAOZZ	11862	15599221	BRACKET,ANGLE	1
				UOC:194,208,210,230,231,252,254,256	
34	PAOZZ	11862	474955	SHIELD,FUEL TANK	1
				UOC:194,208,210,230,231,252,254,256	
35	PAOZZ	11862	14072666	BOLT,RIBBED NECK	2
				UOC:194,208,210,230,231,252,254,256	
36	PAOZZ	96906	MS90728-59	SCREW,CAP,HEXAGON H	8
				UOC:194,208,210,230,231,252,254,256	
37	PAOZZ	96906	MS51967-12	NUT,PLAIN,HEXAGON	2
				UOC:194,208,210,230,231,252,254,256	
38	PAOZZ	96906	MS27183-15	WASHER,FLAT	2
				UOC:194,208,210,230,231,252,254,256	
39	PAOZZ	96906	MS35842-13	CLAMP,HOSE	1
				UOC:194,208,210,230,231,252,254,256	
40	PAOZZ	96906	MS35842-11	CLAMP,HOSE	2
				UOC:194,208,210,230,231,252,254,256	
41	PAOZZ	11862	14063335	HOSE,PREFORMED	1
				UOC:210,231	
41	PAOZZ	11862	14036751	HOSE,PREFORMED	1
				UOC:194,208,230,252,254,256	

END OF FIGURE

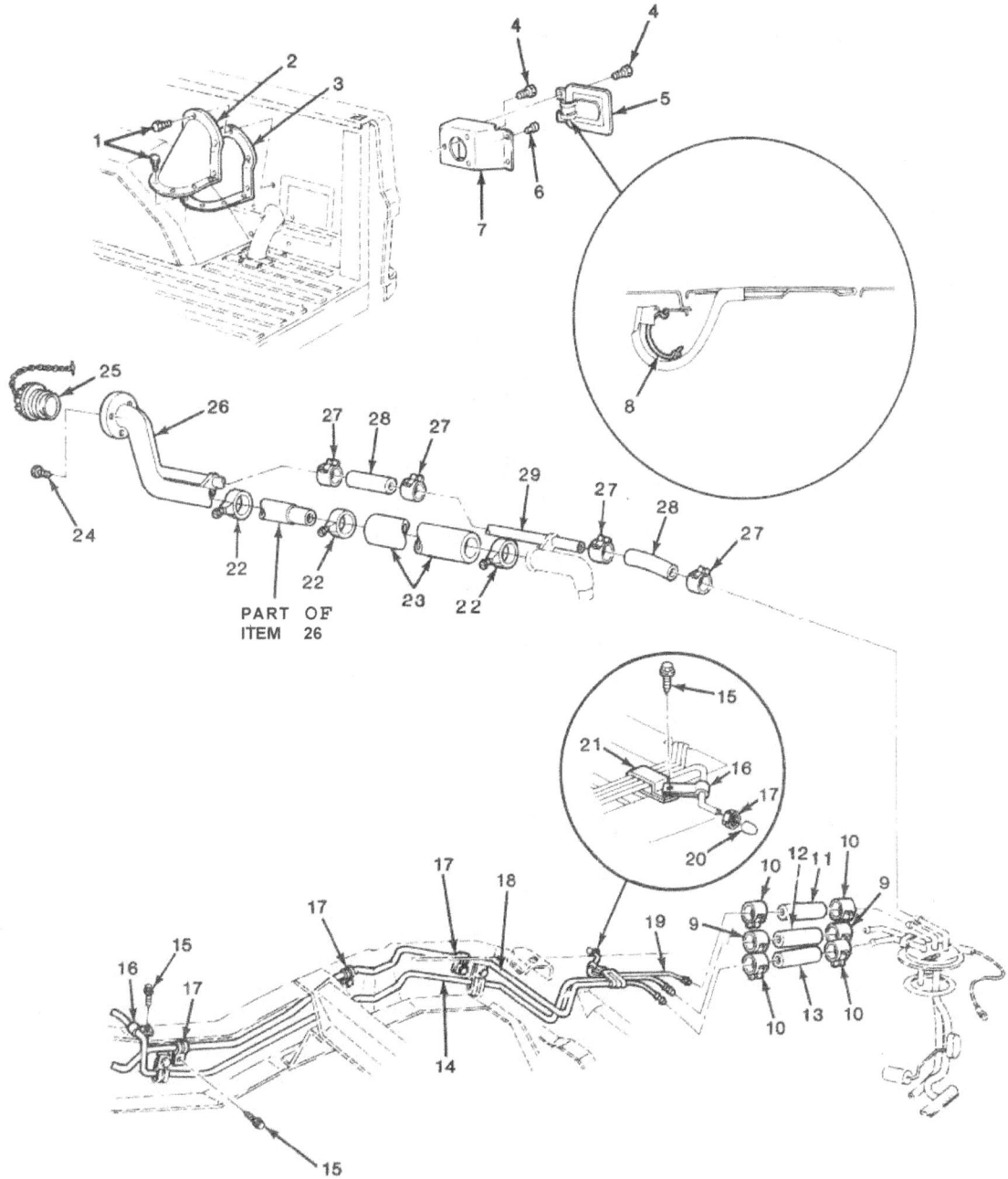

TA510827

(1) ITEM NO	(2) SMR CODE	(3) CAGEC	(4) PART NUMBER	(5) DESCRIPTION AND USABLE ON CODES (UOC)	(6) QTY
				GROUP 0306 TANKS, LINES, FITTINGS, HEADERS	
				FIG. 15 REAR FUEL LINES AND RELATED PARTS (M1009)	
1	PAOZZ	24617	9419327	SCREW UOC:209	11
2	PAOZZ	11862	476916	COVER,FILLER NECK UOC:209	1
3	PAOZZ	11862	476927	GASKET UOC:209	1
4	PAOZZ	96906	MS51869-24	SCREW,CAP,SOCKET HE UOC:209	5
5	PAOZZ	11862	14052026	DOOR,ACCESS UOC:209	1
6	PAOZZ	11862	14010707	BUMPER,NONMETALLIC UOC:209	2
7	PAOZZ	11862	14063329	HOUSING,FILLER PIPE UOC:209	1
8	PAOZZ	11862	4813235	SPRING,FLAT UOC:209	1
9	PAOZZ	19207	11608950-4	CLAMP,HOSE UOC:209	3
10	PAOZZ	11862	25518880	CLAMP,HOSE UOC:209	4
11	MOOZZ	11862	9439068	HOSE FUEL TANK DRAI (7.48"LG) MAKE FROM HOSE,P/N 9439104 UOC:209	1
12	MOOZZ	11862	9439128	HOSE FU FEED REAR (8.27"LG) MAKE FROM HOSE,P/N 9439162 UOC:209	1
13	MOOZZ	11862	9439010	HOSE,FUEL RET RR (7.48"LG) MAKE FROM HOSE,P/N 9439046 UOC:209	1
14	MOOZZ	11862	14018658	PIPE ASM-FUEL FEED (78.69"LG) MAKE FROM TUBE, P/N 3750950 UOC:209	1
15	PAOZZ	11862	11504447	SCREW,TAPPING UOC:209	5
16	PAOZZ	11862	1638274	CLAMP,LOOP UOC:209	2
17	PAOZZ	96906	MS21333-98	CLAMP,LOOP UOC:209	3
18	MFOZZ	11862	14018647	PIPE FUEL RTN REAR (73.44"LG) MAKE FROM TUBE, P/N 603827 UOC:209	1
19	MFOZZ	11862	14063317	PIPE ASM F/T DRAIN (17.05"LG) MAKE FROM TUBE, P/N 1324714 UOC:209	1
20	PAOZZ	11862	14063319	CAP,FUEL TANK DRAIN UOC:209	1

(1) ITEM NO	(2) SMR CODE	(3) CAGEC	(4) PART NUMBER	(5) DESCRIPTION AND USABLE ON CODES (UOC)	(6) QTY
21	PAOZZ	11862	14018630	CLAMP,LOOP UOC:209	1
22	PAOZZ	96906	MS35842-13	CLAMP,HOSE UOC:209	3
23	PAOZZ	11862	14049494	HOSE,NONMETALLIC (14.06"LG) UOC:209	1
24	PAOZZ	11862	14026247	SCREW,ASSEMBLED WAS UOC:209	3
25	PAOZZ	11862	14063326	CAP,FILLER OPENING UOC:209	1
26	PAOZZ	11862	14063325	FILLER NECK UOC:209	1
27	PAOZZ	96906	MS35842-11	CLAMP,HOSE UOC:209	4
28	MOOZZ	11862	14041258	HOSE F/T FILL VENT (6.50"LG) MAKE FROM HOSE,P/N 9438383 UOC:209	2
29	PAOZZ	11862	468484	TUBE,METALLIC UOC:209	1

END OF FIGURE

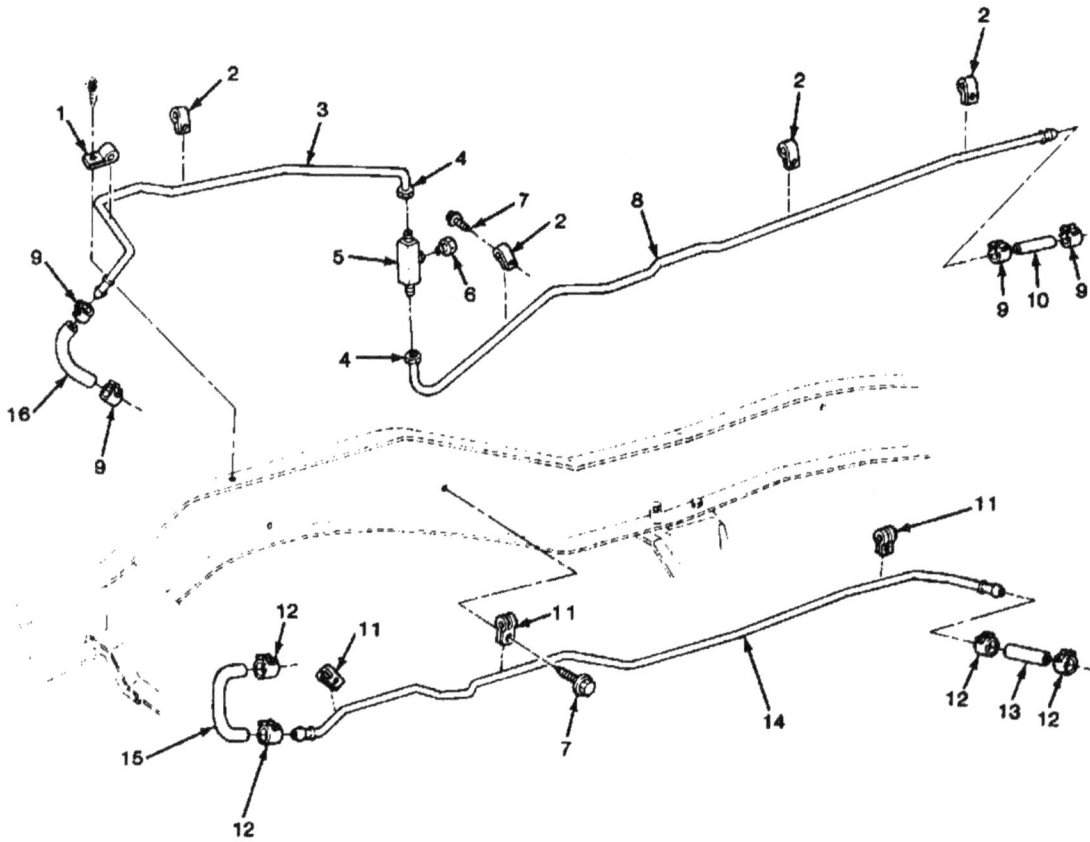

TA510828

FIGURE 16. FRONT FUEL LINES AND RELATED PARTS (M1009).

(1) ITEM NO	(2) SMR CODE	(3) CAGEC	(4) PART NUMBER	(5) DESCRIPTION AND USABLE ON CODES (UOC)	(6) QTY
				GROUP 0306 TANKS, LINES, FITTINGS, HEADERS	
				FIG. 16 FRONT FUEL LINES AND RELATED PARTS (M1009)	
1	PAOZZ	11862	1638274	CLAMP, LOOP UOC:209	1
2	PAOZZ	96906	MS21333-111	CLAMP, LOOP UOC:209	4
3	MOOZZ	11862	15599209	PIPE F/FEED FRONT (30.67"LG) MAKE FROM TUBE, P/N 3750950 UOC:209	1
4	PAOZZ	24617	142433	INVERTED NUT, TUBE C UOC:209	2
5	PAOZZ	72582	178917	TEE, PIPE TO TUBE UOC:209	1
6	PAOZZ	6N299	0917425	PLUG, PIPE UOC:209	1
7	PAOZZ	11862	11504447	SCREW, TAPPING UOC:209	7
8	MOOZZ	11862	14063315	PIPE-FUEL FEED INTE (51.86"LG) MAKE FROM TUBE, P/N 3750950 UOC:209	1
9	PAOZZ	11862	477402	CLAMP, HOSE UOC:209	4
10	MOOZZ	11862	9439117	HOSE, NONMETALLIC (3.94"LG) MAKE FROM HOSE, P/N 9439162 UOC:209	1
11	PAOZZ	96906	MS21333-98	CLAMP, LOOP UOC:209	3
12	PAOZZ	11862	25518880	CLAMP, HOSE UOC:209	4
13	MOOZZ	11862	9439001	HOSE, FU, RET, INT (3.94"LG) MAKE FROM HOSE, P/N 9439046 UOC:209	1
14	MOOZZ	11862	474957	TUBE, BENT, METALLIC (71.45"LG) MAKE FROM TUBE, P/N 603827 UOC:209	1
15	MOOZZ	11862	9438227	HOSE FUEL RTURN FRN (9.84"LG) MAKE FROM HOSE, P/N 9438257 UOC:209	1
16	PAOZZ	11862	14063391	HOSE, PREFORMED UOC:209	1

END OF FIGURE

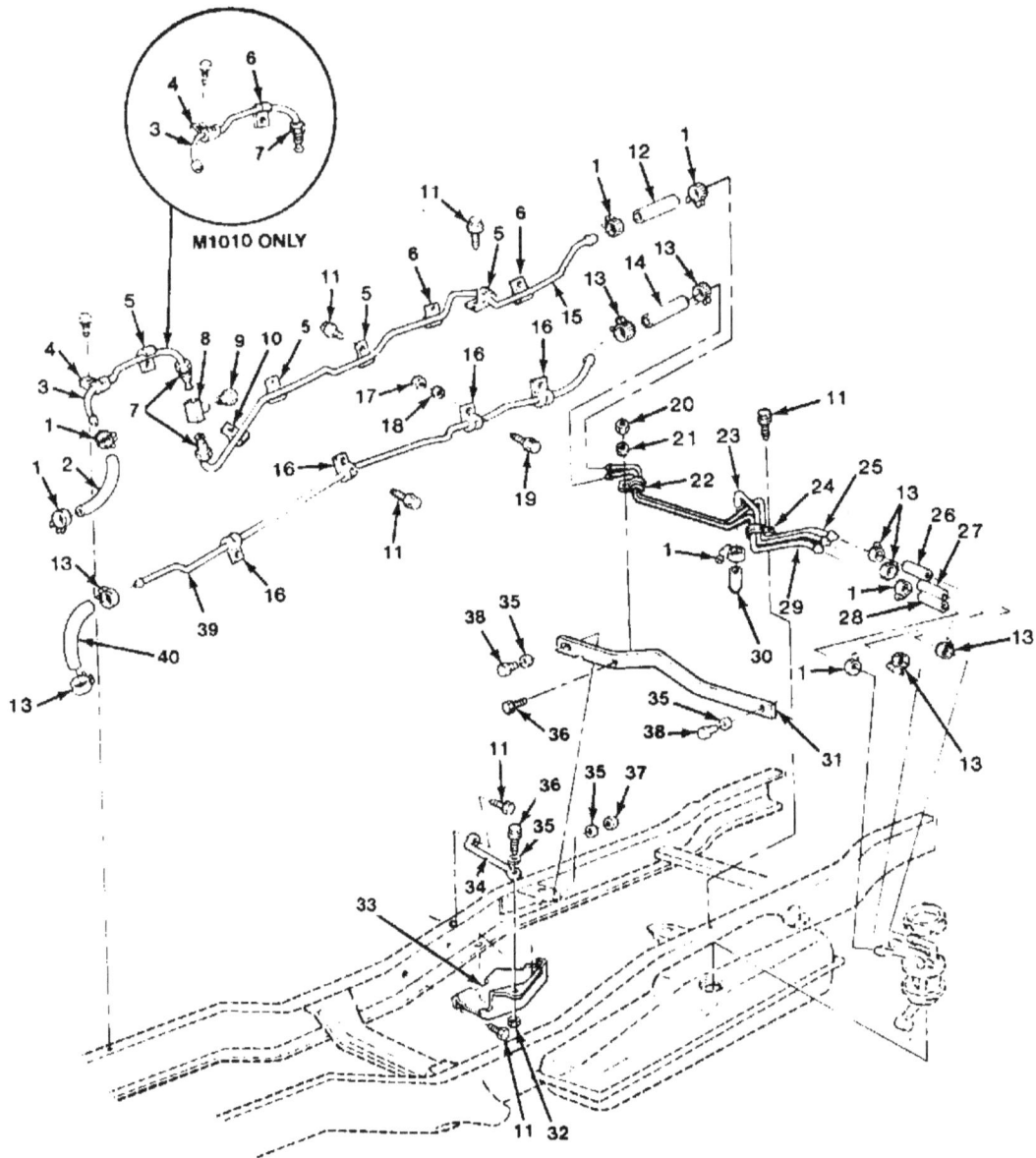

TA510829

FIGURE 17. FUEL LINES AND RELATED PARTS (ALL EXCEPT M1009).

GROUP 0306 TANKS, LINES, FITTINGS,
AND HEADERS

FIG. 17 FUEL LINES AND RELATED PARTS
(ALL EXCEPT M1009)

1	PAOZZ	11862	477402	CLAMP,HOSE UOC:194,208,210,230,231,252,254,256	7
2	PAOZZ	11862	14063391	HOSE,PREFORMED UOC:194,208,210,230,231,252,254,256	1
3	MOOZZ	11862	15599209	PIPE F/FEED FRONT (30.67"LG) MAKE FROM TUBE, P/N 3750950 UOC:194,208,210,230,231,252,254,256	1
4	PAOZZ	11862	1638274	CLAMP,LOOP UOC:194,208,210,230,231,252,254,256	1
5	PAOZZ	96906	MS21333-111	CLAMP,LOOP UOC:194,208,230,231,252,254,256	4
6	PAOZZ	96906	MS21333-111	CLAMP,LOOP UOC:210	3
7	PAOZZ	24617	142433	INVERTED NUT,TUBE C UOC:194,208,210,230,231,252,254,256	2
8	PAOZZ	72582	178917	TEE,PIPE TO TUBE UOC:194,208,210,230,231,252,254,256	1
9	PAOZZ	24617	444620	PLUG,PIPE UOC:194,208,230,231,252,254,256	1
10	PAOZZ	11862	25527423	CLAMP,LOOP UOC:210,230	1
11	PAOZZ	11862	11504447	SCREW,TAPPING UOC:194,208,210,230,231,252,254,256	12
12	MOOZZ	11862	9439117	HOSE,NONMETALLIC (3.94"LG) MAKE FROM HOSE, P/N 9439162 UOC:194,208,210,230,231,252,254,256	1
13	PAOZZ	11862	25518880	CLAMP,HOSE UOC:194,208,210,230,231,252,254,256	8
14	MOOZZ	11862	9439010	HOSE,FUEL RET RR (7.48"LG) MAKE FROM HOSE, P/N 9439046 UOC:194,208,210,230,231,252,254,256	1
15	MOOZZ	11862	14063314	PIPE-FUEL FEED INT (57.14"LG) MAKE FROM TUBE, P/N 3750950 UOC:194,208,210,230,231,252,254,256	1
16	PAOZZ	96906	MS21333-45	CLAMP,LOOP UOC:194,208,210,230,231,252,254,256	4
17	PAOZZ	96906	MS35691-406	NUT,PLAIN,HEXAGON UOC:194,208,210,230,231,252,254,256	1
18	PAOZZ	96906	MS35338-44	WASHER,LOCK UOC:194,208,210,230,231,252,254,256	1
19	PAOZZ	96906	MS90725-5	SCREW,CAP,HEXAGON H UOC:194,208,210,230,231,252,254,256	1
20	PAOZZ	96906	MS51967-6	NUT,PLAIN,HEXAGON UOC:194,208,210,230,231,252,254,256	1
21	PAOZZ	96906	MS35338-45	WASHER,LOCK UOC:194,208,210,230,231,252,254,256	1

(1) ITEM NO	(2) SMR CODE	(3) CAGEC	(4) PART NUMBER	(5) DESCRIPTION AND USABLE ON CODES (UOC)	(6) QTY
22	PAOZZ	11862	467524	CLAMP,LOOP UOC:194,208,210,230,231,252,254,256	1
23	MOOZZ	11862	14045605	PIPE ASM F/T DRAIN (12.25"LG) MAKE FROM TUBE, P/N 1324714 UOC:194,208,210,230,231,252,254,256	1
24	PAOZZ	11862	14034543	CLAMP,LOOP UOC:194,208,210,230,231,252,254,256	1
25	MFOZZ	11862	14061227	PIPE F/RTN HOSE RR (37.96"LG) MAKE FROM TUBE, P/N 603827 UOC:194,208,210,230,231,252,254,256	1
26	MOOZZ	11862	9439004	HOSE F/RETURN RR (5.12"LG) MAKE FROM HOSE,P/N 9439046 UOC:194,208,210,230,231,252,254,256	1
27	MOOZZ	11862	9439059	HOSE FUEL TANK DRAI (3.94"LG) MAKE FROM HOSE,P/N 9439104 UOC:194,208,210,230,231,252,254,256	1
28	MOOZZ	11862	9439120	HOSE F/FEED RR (5.12" LG) MAKE FROM HOSE,P/N 9439162 UOC:194,208,210,230,231,252,254,256	1
29	MOOZZ	11862	14061223	PIPE ASM-FUEL FEED (37.86"LG) MAKE FROM TUBE, P/N 3750950 UOC:194,208,210,230,231,252,254,256	1
30	PAOZZ	11862	14063319	CAP,FUEL TANK DRAIN UOC:194,208,210,230,231,252,254,256	1
31	PAOZZ	11862	467509	BRACKET,ANGLE UOC:194,208,210,230,231,252,254,256	1
32	PAOZZ	96906	MS17829-5C	NUT,SELF-LOCKING,HE UOC:194,208,210,230,231,252,254,256	1
33	POAZZ	11862	15522392	SHIELD,FUEL HOSE UOC:194,208,210,230,231,252,254,256	1
34	PAOZZ	11862	14034546	BRACE,FUEL HOSE SHI UOC:194,208,210,230,231,252,254,256	1
35	PAOZZ	96906	MS27183-12	WASHER,FLAT UOC:194,208,210,230,231,252,254,256	5
36	PAOZZ	96906	MS90728-32	BOLT,MACHINE UOC:194,208,210,230,231,252,254,256	3
37	PAOZZ	24617	9422295	NUT,SELF-LOCKING,CO UOC:194,208,210,230,231,252,254,256	2
38	PAOZZ	96906	MS90728-33	BOLT,MACHINE UOC:194,208,210,230,231,252,254,256	2
39	MFOZZ	11862	15599999	PIPE FUEL RETRN FRT (74.60"LG) MAKE FROM TUBE, P/N 603827 UOC:194,208,210,230,231,252,254,256	1
40	MOOZZ	11862	9438227	HOSE FUEL RTURN FRN (9.84"LG)MAKE FROM HOSE,P/N 9438257 UOC:194,208,210,230,231,252,254,256	1

END OF FIGURE

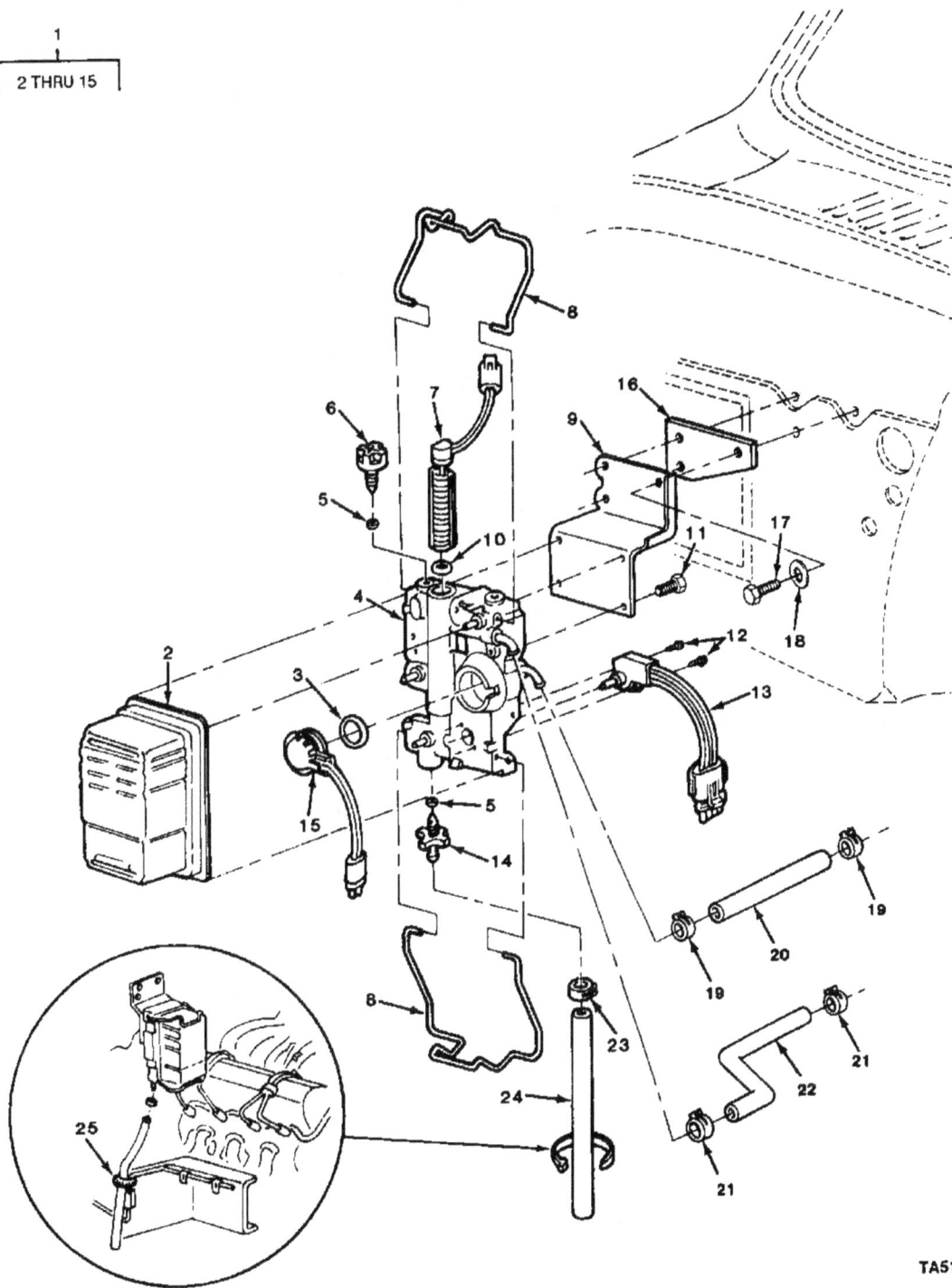

FIGURE 18. FUEL FILTER AND RELATED PARTS.

TA510830

(1) ITEM NO	(2) SMR CODE	(3) CAGEC	(4) PART NUMBER	(5) DESCRIPTION AND USABLE ON CODES (UOC)	(6) QTY
				GROUP 0309 FUEL FILTERS	
				FIG. 18 FUEL FILTER AND RELATED PARTS	
1	PAOOO	84760	27290	FILTER,FLUID	1
2	PAOZZ	11862	14075347	.FILTER,FLUID	1
3	PAOZZ	87460	22591	.PACKING,PREFORMED	1
4	PAOFF	87460	24285	.HOUSING,FUEL FILTER	1
5	PAOZZ	87460	27820	.PACKING,PREFORMED	2
6	PAOZZ	87460	24267	.PLUG,VENT	1
7	PAOZZ	87460	29090	.HEATER ASSEMBLY,FUE	1
8	PAOZZ	87460	24265	.CLAMP,LOOP	2
9	PFOZZ	87460	24281	.BRACKET,ANGLE	1
10	PAOZZ	87460	15349	.PACKING,PREFORMED	1
11	PAOZZ	87460	24437	.SCREW,TAPPING,THREA	4
12	PAOZZ	87460	24322	.SCREW,TAPPING,THREA	2
13	PAOZZ	87460	27284	.SENSOR,FUEL FILTER	1
14	PAOZZ	87460	23796	.COCK,POPPET DRAIN	1
15	PAOZZ	61928	15596614	.SWITCH,PRESSURE	1
16	PFOZZ	11862	14043724	COVER,ACCESS	1
17	PAOZZ	96906	MS18154-58	SCREW,CAP,HEXAGON H	3
18	PAOZZ	96906	MS35338-46	WASHER,LOCK	3
19	PAOZZ	11862	25518880	CLAMP,HOSE	2
20	PAOZZ	11862	14063302	HOSE,PREFORMED	1
21	PAOZZ	19207	11608950-4	CLAMP,HOSE	2
22	PAOZZ	11862	14063301	HOSE,PREFORMED	1
23	PAOZZ	96906	MS35842-10	CLAMP,HOSE	1
24	MOOZZ	11862	9439092	HOSE,NONMETALLIC (25.59"LG) MAKE FROM HOSE,P/N 9439104	1
25	PAOZZ	11862	9785074	CLIP,SPRING TENSION	1

END OF FIGURE

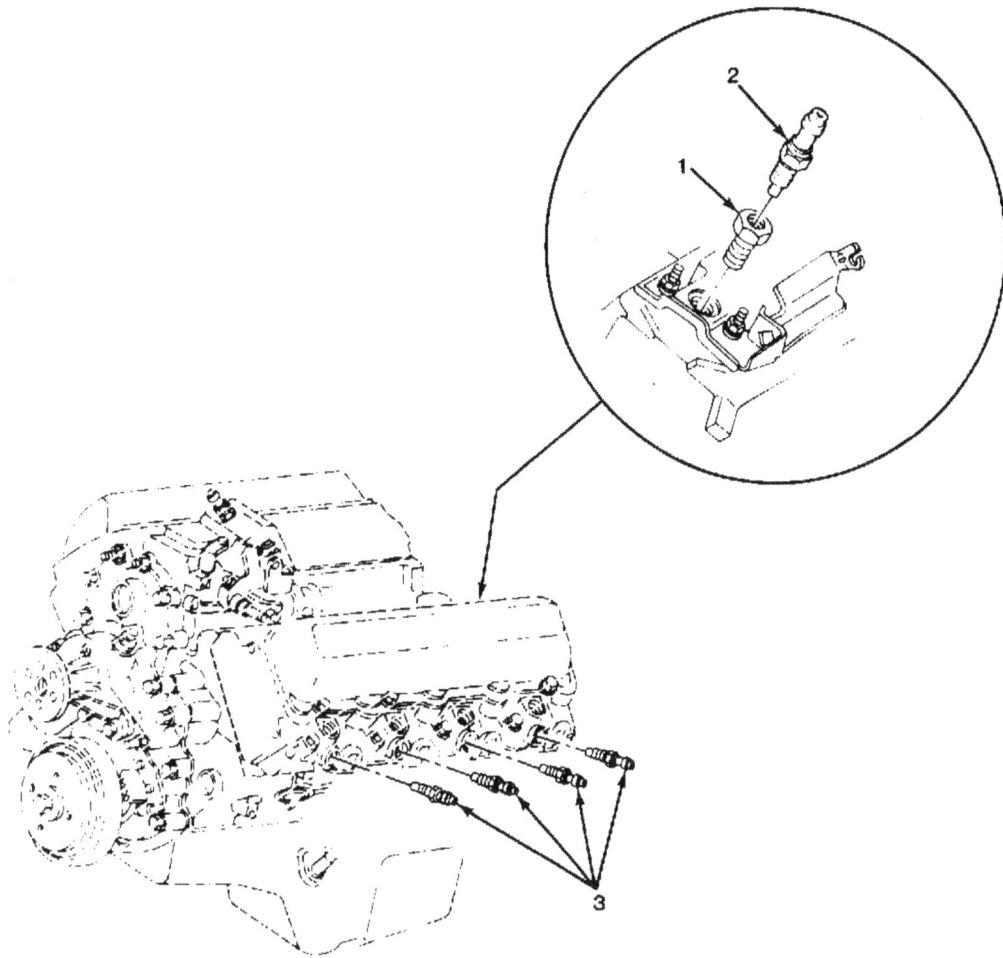

TA510831

FIGURE 19. GLOW PLUGS AND TEMPERATURE SENSOR.

(1) ITEM NO	(2) SMR CODE	(3) CAGEC	(4) PART NUMBER	(5) DESCRIPTION AND USABLE ON CODES (UOC)	(6) QTY
				GROUP 0311 ENGINE STARTING AIDS	
				FIG. 19 GLOW PLUGS AND TEMPERATURE SENSOR	
1	PAOZZ	24617	444034	BUSHING,PIPE UOC:208,209,210,230,231,252,254,256	1
2	PAOZZ	70040	10045847	SENSOR,TEMPERATURE INCLUDES ADAPTER FOR TWO TERMINAL SWITCH TO CONNECT TO ONE TERMINAL WIRING HARNESS	1
3	PAOZZ	11862	5613939	GLOW PLUG	8
				END OF FIGURE	

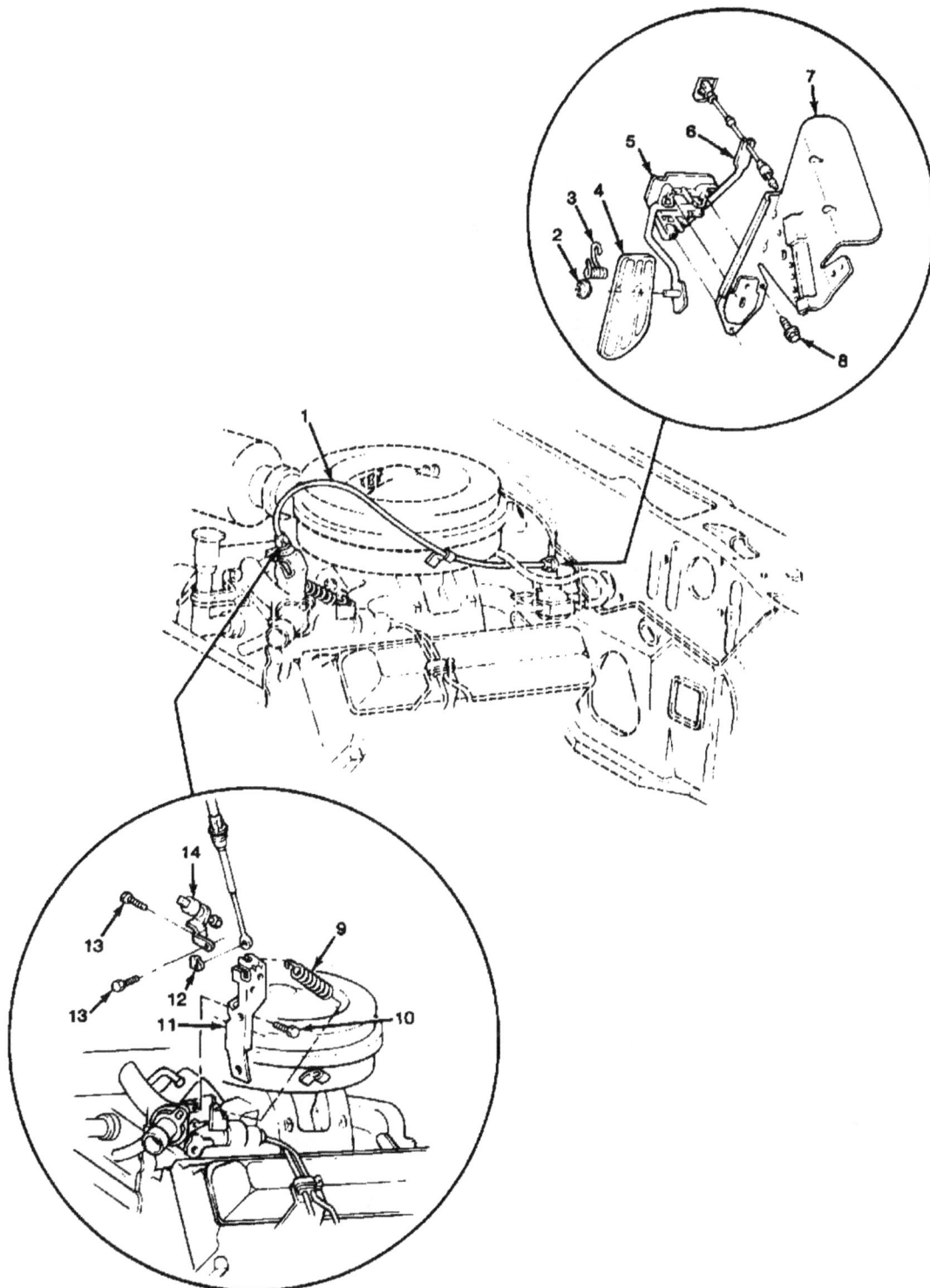

TA510832

FIGURE 20. ACCELERATOR LINKAGE AND RELATED PARTS.

(1) ITEM NO	(2) SMR CODE	(3) CAGEC	(4) PART NUMBER	(5) DESCRIPTION AND USABLE ON CODES (UOC)	(6) QTY
				GROUP 0312 ACCELERATOR, THROTTLE, OR CHOKE CONTROLS	
				FIG. 20 ACCELERATOR LINKAGE AND RELATED PARTS	
1	PAOZZ	11862	14038644	CONTROL ASSEMBLY,PU	1
2	PAOZZ	73342	3909063	PUSH ON NUT	1
3	PAOZZ	11862	336989	SPRING,HELICAL,TORS	1
4	PAOZZ	11862	468234	PEDAL,CONTROL	1
5	PAOZZ	11862	3993087	SUPPORT,ACCELERATOR	1
6	PAOZZ	11862	15590123	LEVER,REMOTE CONTRO	1
7	PAOZZ	11862	342405	REINFORCEMENT,ACCEL	1
8	PAOZZ	24617	9422956	SCREW,TAPPING	3
9	PAOZZ	11862	14024997	SPRING,HELICAL,EXTE	1
10	PAOZZ	24617	11504986	BOLT,MACHINE	2
11	PAOZZ	11862	14038647	SUPPORT,ACCELERATOR	1
12	PAOZZ	11862	15567924	CLIP,RETAINING	1
13	PAOZZ	11862	11501095	BOLT,MACHINE	2
14	PAOZZ	11862	14066255	RELAY,ELECTROMAGNET	1

END OF FIGURE

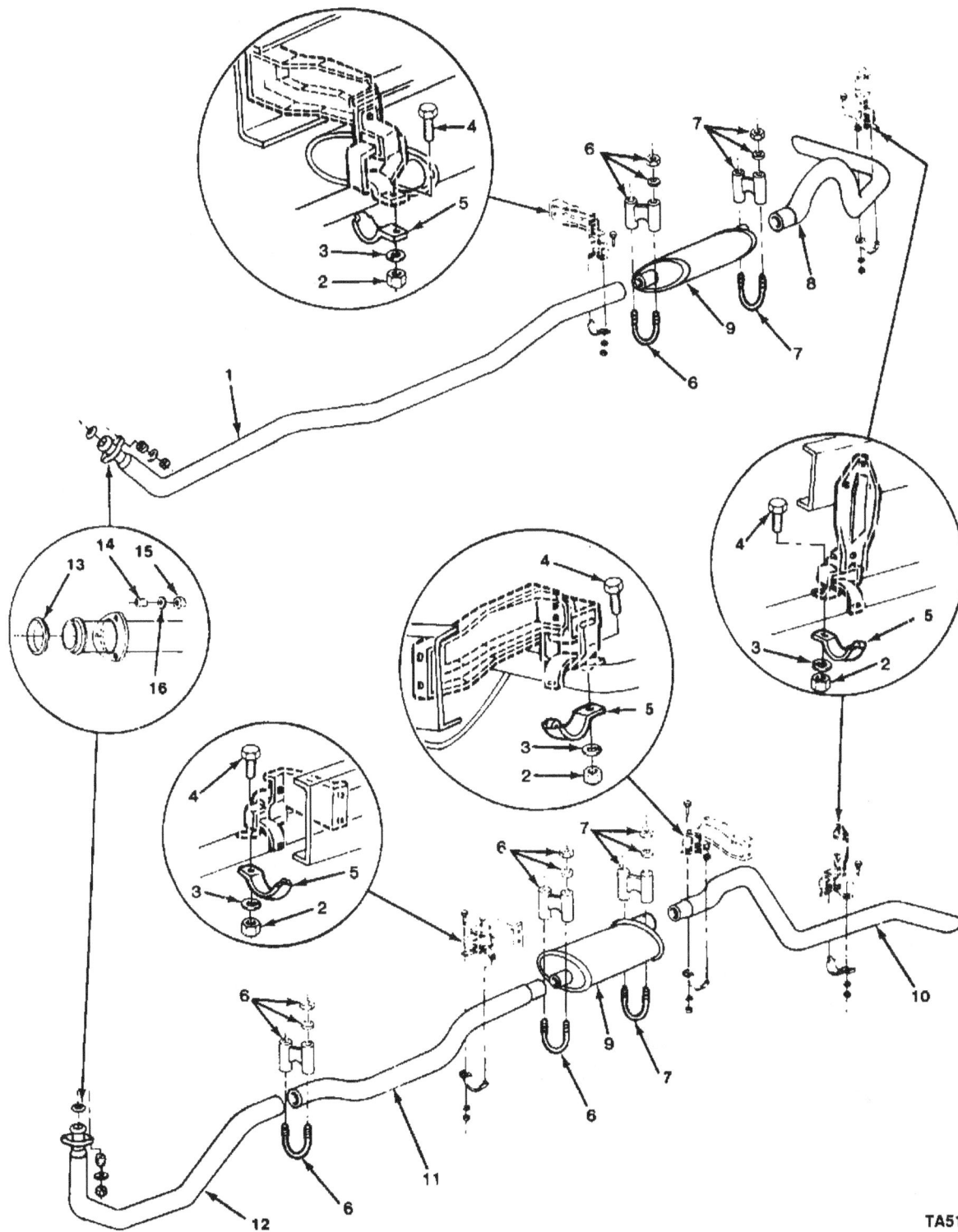

FIGURE 21. EXHAUST MUFFLERS AND PIPES (ALL EXCEPT M1009).

TA510833

(1) ITEM NO	(2) SMR CODE	(3) CAGEC	(4) PART NUMBER	(5) DESCRIPTION AND USABLE ON CODES (UOC)	(6) QTY
				GROUP 04 EXHAUST SYSTEM	
				GROUP 0401 MUFFLERS AND PIPES	
				FIG. 21 EXHAUST MUFFLERS AND PIPES (ALL EXCEPT M1009)	
1	PAOZZ	11862	14037856	PIPE,EXHAUST UOC:194,208,210,230,231,252,254,256	1
1	PAOZZ	11862	15595224	PIPE,EXHAUST UOC:194,208,210,230,231,252,254,256	1
2	PAOZZ	96906	MS51967-6	NUT,PLAIN,HEXAGON UOC:194,208,210,230,231,252,254	5
3	PAOZZ	96906	MS35338-45	WASHER,LOCK UOC:194,208,210,230,231,252,254,256	5
4	PAOZZ	96906	MS90728-37	BOLT,MACHINE UOC:194,208,210,230,231,252,254	5
5	PAOZZ	11862	341160	STRAP,RETAINING UOC:194,208,210,230,231,252,254,256	5
6	PAOZZ	96906	MS52150-31HE	CLAMP,LOOP UOC:194,208,210,230,231,252,254,256	3
7	PAOZZ	96906	MS52150-30HE	CLAMP,LOOP UOC:194,208,210,230,231,252,254,256	2
8	PAOZZ	79260	45823	PIPE,EXHAUST RIGHT REAR UOC:194,208,210,230,231,252,254,256	1
9	PAOZZ	11862	14063795	MUFFLER,EXHAUST UOC:194,208,210,230,231,252,254,256	2
9	PAOZZ	11862	14089132	MUFFLER,EXHAUST APPLIES TO VEHICLES STARTING WITH VIN FF3000 UOC:194,208,210,230,231,252,254,256	2
10	PAOZZ	11862	14029956	PIPE,EXHAUST LEFT REAR UOC:194,208,210,230,231,252,254,256	1
11	PAOZZ	11862	14045525	PIPE,EXHAUST LEFT CENTER UOC:194,208,210,230,231,252,254,256	1
11	PAOZZ	11862	15595271	PIPE,EXHAUST APPLIES TO VEHICLES STARTING WITH VIN FF3000 UOC:194,208,210,230,231,252,254,256	1
12	PAOZZ	11862	14045521	PIPE,EXHAUST LEFT FRONT UOC:194,208,210,230,231,252,254,256	1
13	PAOZZ	11862	14072686	SEAL,EXHAUST PIPE UOC:194,208,210,230,231,252,254,256	2
14	PAOZZ	11862	587575	SPRING,HELICAL,COMP UOC:194,208,210,230,231,252,254,256	6
15	PAOZZ	80205	NAS1408A6	NUT,SELF-LOCKING,HE UOC:194,208,210,230,231,252,254,256	6
16	PAOZZ	96906	MS27183-16	WASHER,FLAT UOC:194,208,210,230,231,252,254,256	6

END OF FIGURE

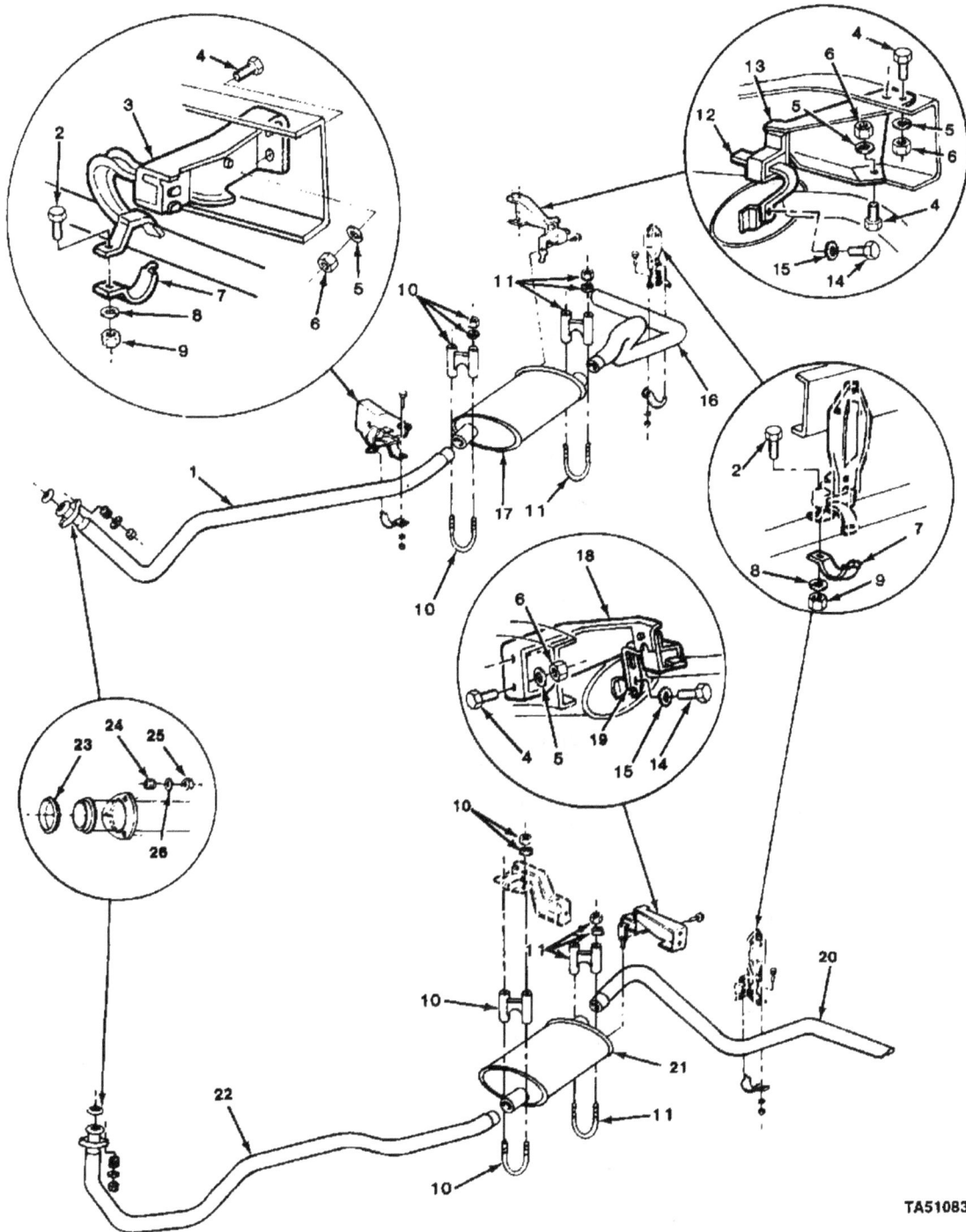

FIGURE 22. EXHAUST MUFFLERS AND PIPES (MI 009).

TA510834

(1) ITEM NO	(2) SMR CODE	(3) CAGEC	(4) PART NUMBER	(5) DESCRIPTION AND USABLE ON CODES (UOC)	(6) QTY
				GROUP 0401 MUFFLERS AND PIPES	
				FIG. 22 EXHAUST MUFFLERS AND PIPES (M1009)	
1	PAOZZ	11862	15595216	PIPE,EXHAUST (RIGHT) APPLIES TO VEHICLES BEFORE VIN FF136169 UOC:209	1
1	XDOZZ	11862	15599216	PIPE,EXHAUST (RIGHT) APPLIES TO VEHICLES STARTING WITH VIN FF136169 UOC:209	1
2	PAOZZ	96906	MS90728-37	BOLT,MACHINE UOC:209	3
3	PAOZZ	11862	14037808	BRACKET,PIPE UOC:209	1
4	PAOZZ	96906	MS18154-58	SCREW,CAP,HEXAGON H UOC:209	7
5	PAOZZ	96906	MS35338-46	WASHER,LOCK UOC:209	7
6	PAOZZ	96906	MS51967-8	NUT,PLAIN,HEXAGON UOC:209	7
7	PAOZZ	11862	341160	STRAP,RETAINING UOC:209	3
8	PAOZZ	96906	MS35338-45	WASHER,LOCK UOC:209	3
9	PAOZZ	96906	MS51967-6	NUT,PLAIN,HEXAGON UOC:209	3
10	PAOZZ	96906	MS52150-31HE	CLAMP,LOOP UOC:209	2
11	PAOZZ	96906	MS52150-30HE	CLAMP,LOOP UOC:209	2
12	PAOZZ	11862	14037836	HANGER,ENGINE EXHAU UOC:209	1
13	PAOZZ	11862	14037812	SUPPORT ASSEMBLY,MU UOC:209	1
14	PAOZZ	96906	MS90728-34	BOLT,MACHINE UOC:209	2
15	PAOZZ	96906	MS35335-34	WASHER,LOCK UOC:209	2
16	PAOZZ	11862	14044996	PIPE,EXHAUST RIGHT REAR UOC:209	1
17	PAOZZ	11862	14067430	MUFFLER AND INLET P RIGHT UOC:209	1
18	PAOZZ	11862	14034547	BRACKET,TAIL PIPE UOC:209	1
19	PAOZZ	11862	14024561	BRACKET,DOUBLE ANGL UOC:209	1
20	PAOZZ	11862	14044995	PIPE,EXHAUST LEFT REAR UOC:209	1
21	PAOZZ	11862	14067429	MUFFLER AND INLET P UOC:209	1
22	PAOZZ	11862	14067759	PIPE,EXHAUST (LEFT) APPLIES TO	1

(1) ITEM NO	(2) SMR CODE	(3) CAGEC	(4) PART NUMBER	(5) DESCRIPTION AND USABLE ON CODES (UOC)	(6) QTY
				VEHICLES BEFORE VIN FF136169 UOC:209	
22	PAOZZ	11862	15599269	PIPE,EXHAUST (LEFT) APPLIES TO VEHICLES STARTING WITH VIN FF136169 UOC:209	1
23	PAOZZ	11862	14072686	SEAL,EXHAUST PIPE PART OF KIT P/N 15633467 UOC:209	2
24	PAOZZ	11862	587575	SPRING,HELICAL,COMP UOC:209	6
25	PAOZZ	80205	NAS1408A6	NUT,SELF-LOCKING,HE UOC:209	6
26	PAOZZ	96906	MS27183-16	WASHER,FLAT UOC:209	6

END OF FIGURE

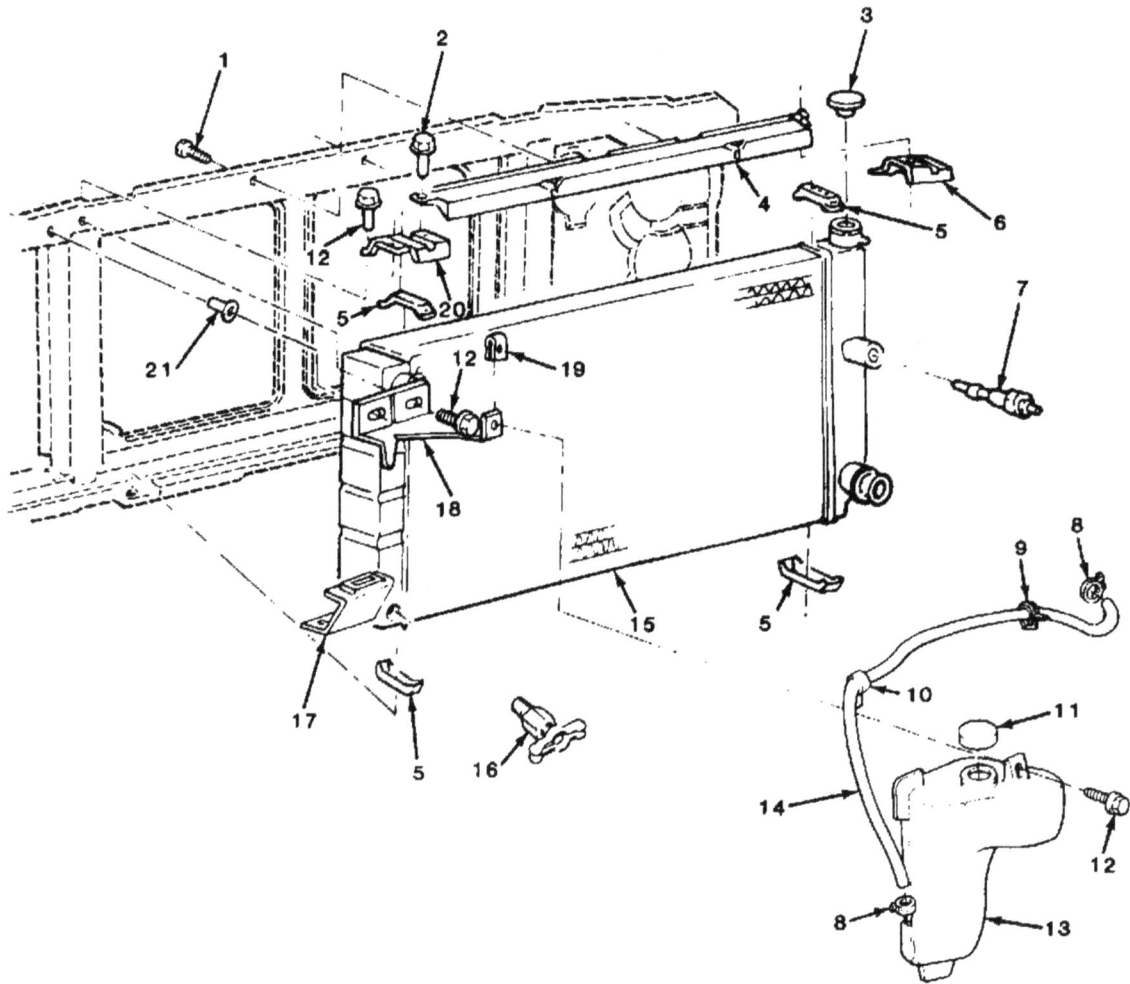

TA510835

FIGURE 23. RADIATOR, COOLANT RECOVERY RESERVOIR, AND RELATED PARTS.

(1) ITEM NO	(2) SMR CODE	(3) CAGEC	(4) PART NUMBER	(5) DESCRIPTION AND USABLE ON CODES (UOC)	(6) QTY
				GROUP 05 COOLING SYSTEM	
				GROUP 0501 RADIATOR, EVAPORATIVE COOLER, OR HEAT EXCHANGER	
				FIG. 23 RADIATOR, COOLANT RECOVERY RESERVOIR, AND RELATED PARTS	
1	PAOZZ	11862	11508566	SCREW,TAPPING	2
2	PAOZZ	11862	11504115	SCREW,TAPPING	2
3	PAOZZ	11862	6410785	CAP,FILLER OPENING	1
4	PFOZZ	11862	14039948	PANEL,RADIATOR	1
5	PAOZZ	11862	6264100	PAD,RADIATOR RETAIN	4
6	PFOZZ	11862	14039950	BRACKET,MOUNTING RA	1
7	PAOZZ	11862	358375	PROBE ASSEMBLY,TRAN	1
8	PAOZZ	96906	MS35842-10	CLAMP,HOSE	2
9	PAOZZ	11862	3816659	STRAP,LINE SUPPORTI	1
10	PAOZZ	96906	MS21333-114	CLAMP,LOOP	1
11	PAOZZ	11862	14011345	CAP ASSY	1
12	PAOZZ	11862	2014469	BOLT,ASSEMBLED WASH	7
13	PFOZZ	11862	14052221	TANK,RADIATOR,OVERF	1
14	MOOZZ	11862	14072430	HOSE COLLANT RES (59.00"LG) MAKE FROM HOSE, P/N 9438373	1
15	PAOFF	61928	3058966	RADIATOR,ENGINE COO	1
16	PAOZZ	11862	9437207	COCK,DRAIN	1
17	PFOZZ	11862	14072427	BRACKET,RESERVOIR,C	1
18	PFOZZ	11862	14072426	BRACKET,RESERVOIR,C	1
19	PAOZZ	24617	1494253	NUT,CLIP-ON	1
20	PFOZZ	11862	14039949	BRACKET,MOUNTING	1
21	PAOZZ	11862	3792287	NUT,PLAIN,BLIND RIV	1

END OF FIGURE

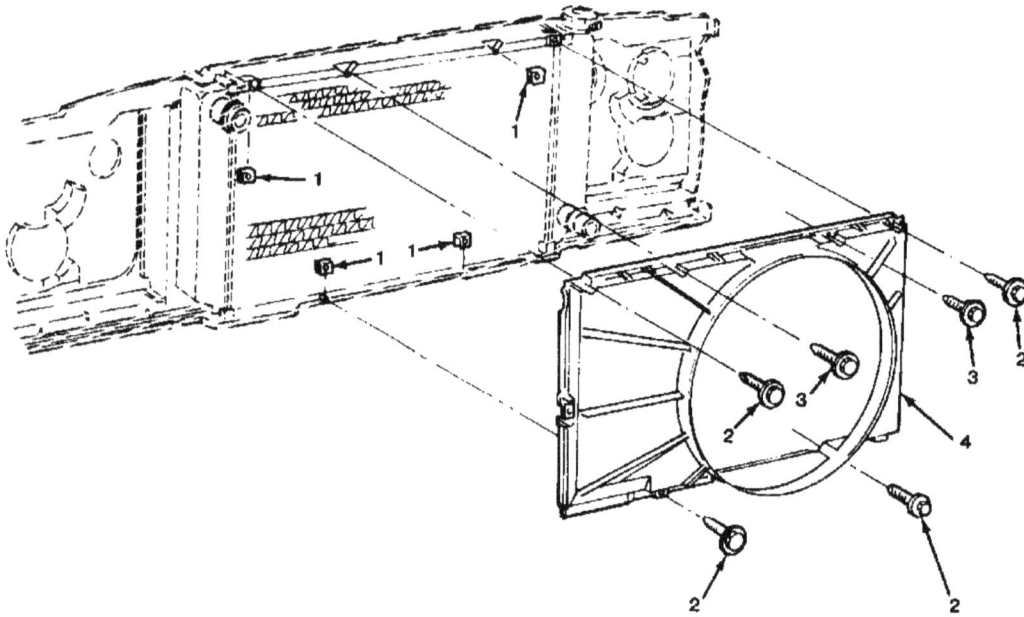

TA510836

FIGURE 24. RADIATOR SHROUD.

(1) ITEM NO	(2) SMR CODE	(3) CAGEC	(4) PART NUMBER	(5) DESCRIPTION AND USABLE ON CODES (UOC)	(6) QTY
				GROUP 0502 COWLING, DEFELCTORS, AIR DUCTS, SHROUDS, ETC.	
				FIG. 24 RADIATOR SHROUD	
1	PAOZZ	11862	3982098	NUT,PLAIN,HEXAGON	4
2	PAOZZ	11862	9440334	BOLT,ASSEMBLED WASH	4
3	PAOZZ	11862	11508566	SCREW,TAPPING	2
4	PFOZZ	11862	15522697	SHROUD,FAN,RADIATOR APPLIES TO VEHICLES STARTING WITH VIN FF136169 AND VIN FF300021	1

END OF FIGURE

(1) ITEM NO	(2) SMR CODE	(3) CAGEC	(4) PART NUMBER	(5) DESCRIPTION AND USABLE ON CODES (UOC)	(6) QTY

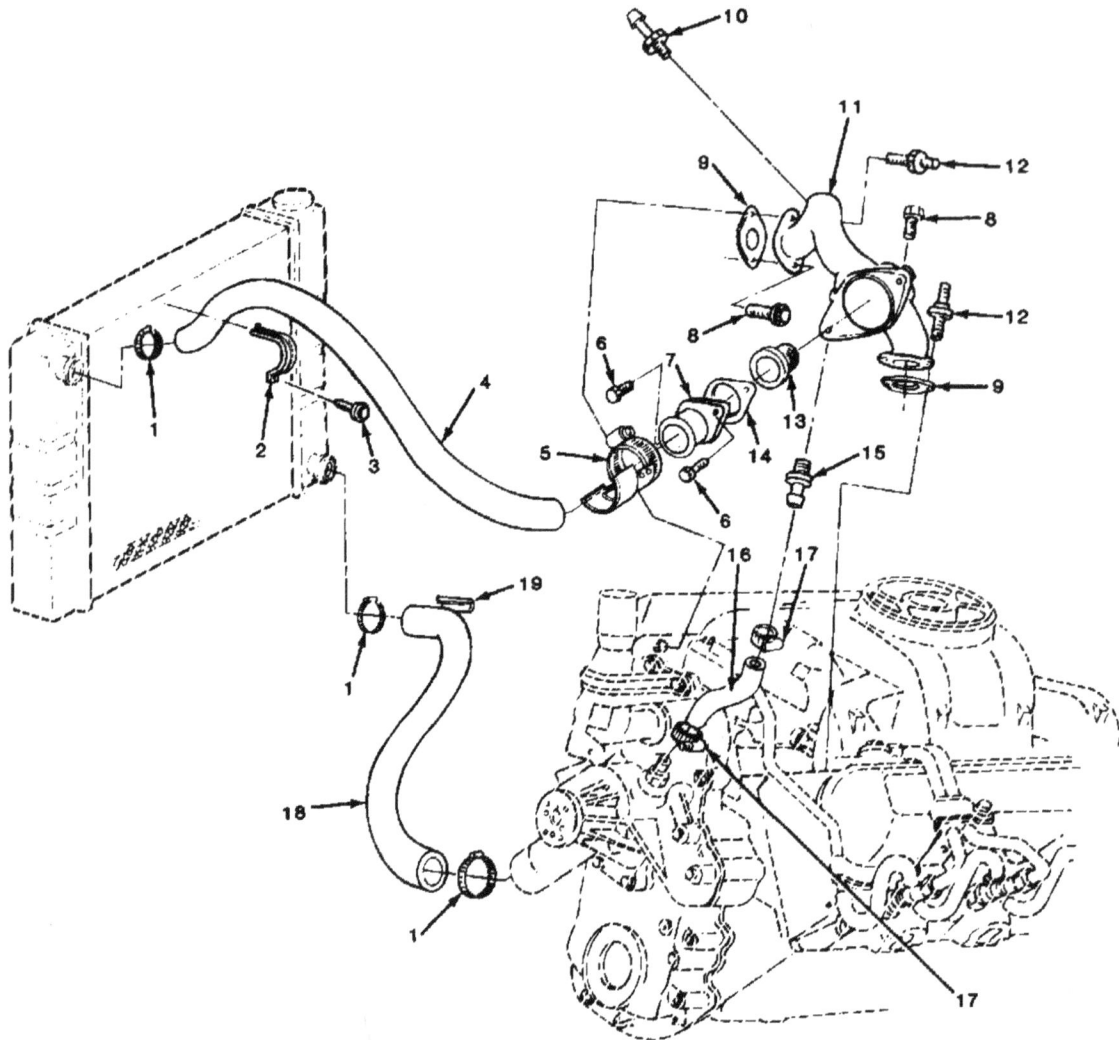

TA510837

FIGURE 25. ENGINE THERMOSTAT AND HOSES.

SECTION II					
(1)	(2)	(3)	(4)	(5)	(6)
ITEM NO	SMR CODE	CAGEC	PART NUMBER	DESCRIPTION AND USABLE ON CODES (UOC)	QTY

GROUP 0503 WATER MANIFOLD, HEADERS, THERMOSTATS, AND HOUSING GASKET

FIG. 25 ENGINE THERMOSTAT AND HOSES

1	PAOZZ	96906	MS35842-13	CLAMP,HOSE UOC:194,208,209,210,230,231,252,254	3
2	PAOZZ	11862	14036779	STRAP,RETAINING	1
3	PAOZZ	11862	11508566	SCREW,TAPPING	1
4	PAOZZ	11862	14036744	HOSE,PREFORMED	1
5	PAOZZ	11862	14071983	CLAMP,HOSE	1
6	PAOZZ	11862	11513606	BOLT,MACHINE	2
7	PAOZZ	11862	14028918	FLANGE,WATER OUTLET	1
8	PAOZZ	11862	1635490	BOLT,SELF-LOCKING	2
9	PAOZZ	11862	23500846	GASKET PART OF KIT P/N 12516166	2
10	PAOZZ	11862	14067737	ELBOW,PIPE TO HOSE UOC:194,208,209,230,231,252,254,256	1
10	PAOZZ	11862	14067727	ELBOW,PIPE TO HOSE UOC:210,230	1
11	PAOZZ	11862	14028917	WATER OUTLET,ENGINE	1
12	PAOZZ	11862	22535073	STUD,CONTINOUS THR UOC:194,208,209,210,230,231,252,254	2
13	PAOZZ	11862	14077122	THERMOSTAT,FLOW CON	1
14	PAOZZ	11862	14028916	GASKET PART OF KIT P/N 12516166	1
15	PAOZZ	11862	354501	ADAPTER,STRAIGHT,PI	1
16	MOOZZ	11862	14033823	HOSE,NONMETALLIC (4.25" LG) MAKE FROM HOSE, P/N MS521304B203R	1
17	PAOZZ	96906	MS35842-11	CLAMP,HOSE	2
18	PAOZZ	11862	14067763	HOSE,PREFORMED	1
19	PAOZZ	11862	14000217	GUARD,RADIATOR HOSE	1

END OF FIGURE

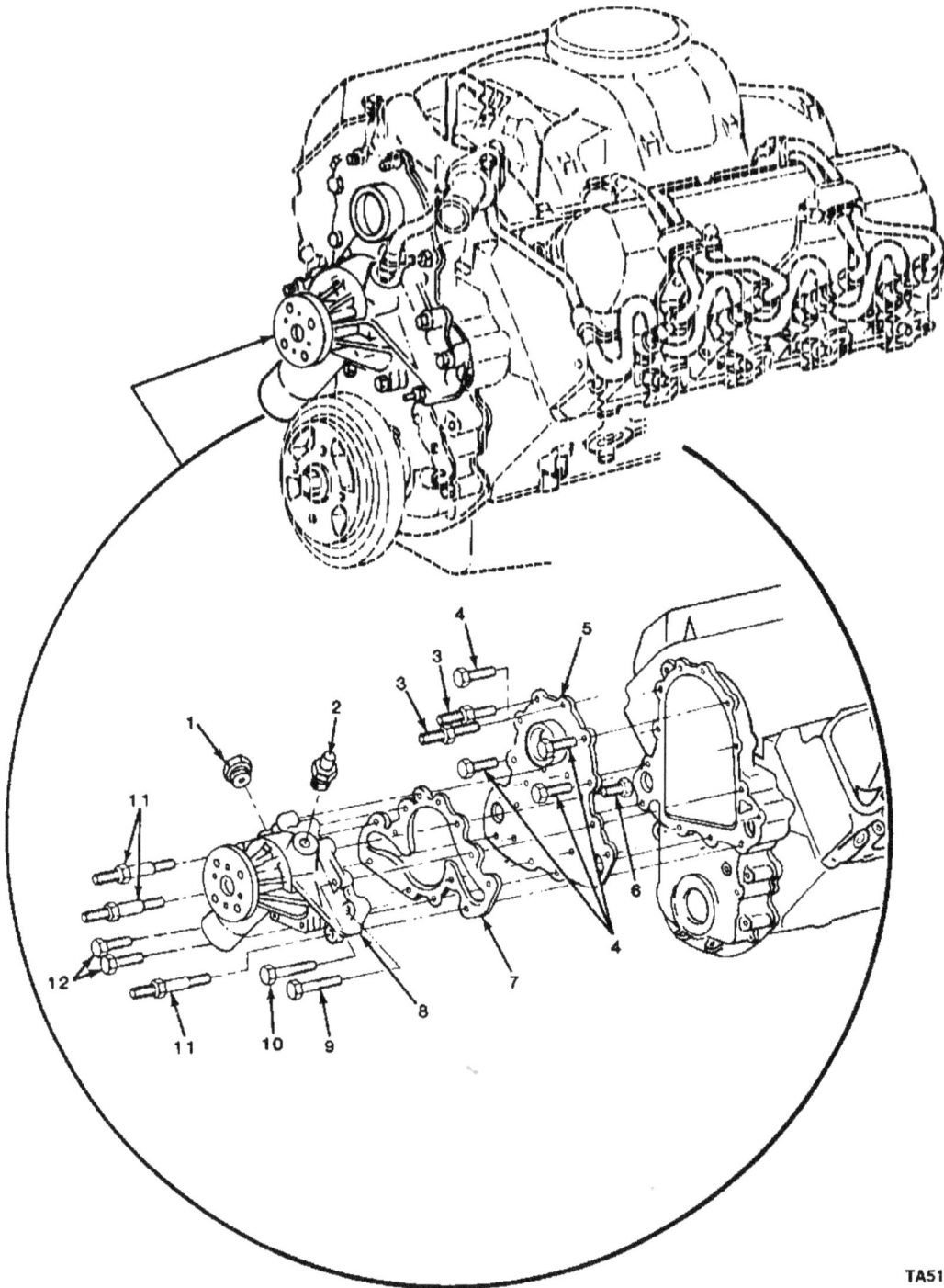

TA510838

FIGURE 26. WATER PUMP.

(1)	(2)	(3)	(4)	(5)	(6)
ITEM NO	SMR CODE	CAGEC	PART NUMBER	DESCRIPTION AND USABLE ON CODES (UOC)	QTY

GROUP 0504 WATER PUMP

FIG. 26 WATER PUMP

| 1 | PAOZZ | 30379 | 444789 | PLUG,PIPE | 1 |
| 2 | PAOZZ | 11862 | 354501 | ADAPTER,STRAIGHT,PI | 1 |

END OF FIGURE

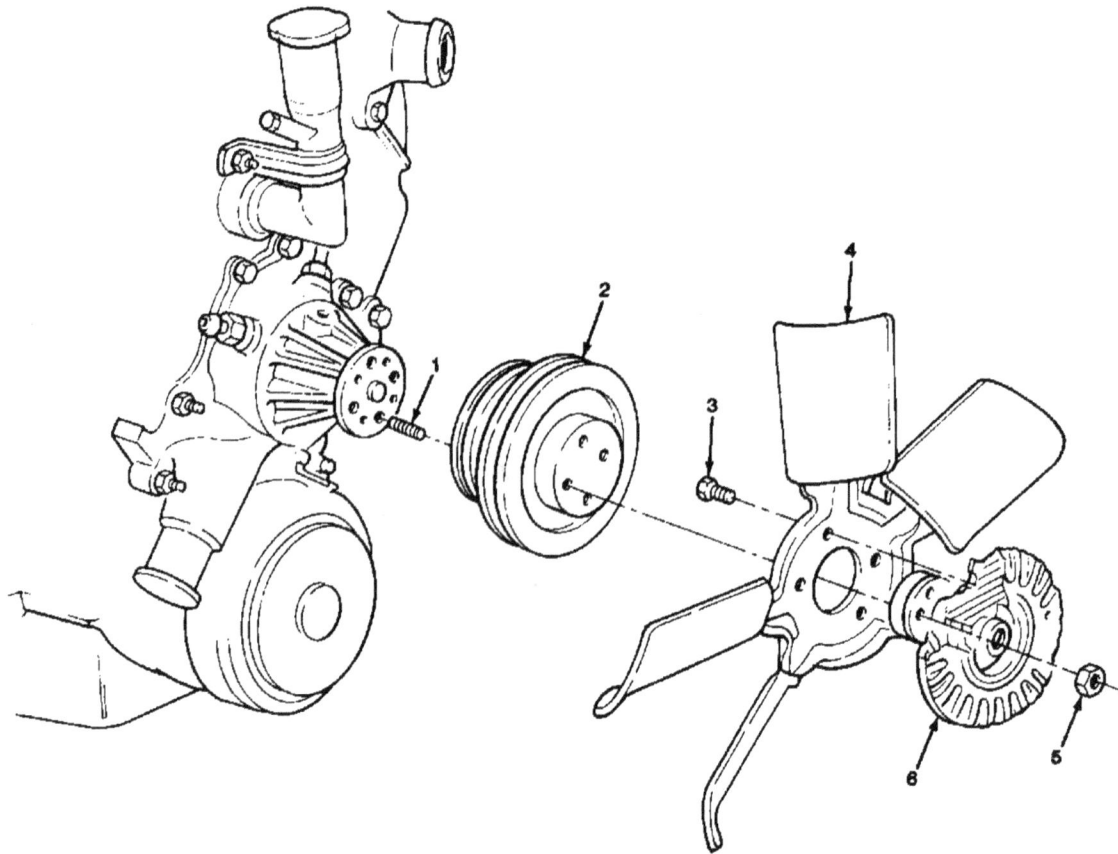

TA510839

FIGURE 27. ENGINE FAN ASSEMBLY

SECTION II (1) ITEM NO	(2) SMR CODE	(3) CAGEC	(4) PART NUMBER	(5) DESCRIPTION AND USABLE ON CODES (UOC)	(6) QTY
				GROUP 0505 FAN ASSEMBLY	
				FIG. 27 ENGINE FAN ASSEMBLY	
1	PAOZZ	11862	14061661	STUD,SHOULDERED	4
2	PAOZZ	11862	14067704	PULLEY,CONE	1
				UOC:194,208,209,230,231,252,254	
2	PAOZZ	11862	14067705	PULLEY,CONE	1
				UOC:210,230	
3	PAOZZ	11862	14020698	BOLT,ASSEMBLED WASH	4
4	PAOZZ	11862	14077928	IMPELLER,FAN,AXIAL	1
5	PAOZZ	96906	MS51967-6	NUT,PLAIN,HEXAGON	4
6	PAOZZ	11862	14032395	HUB,FAN CLUTCH	1

END OF FIGURE

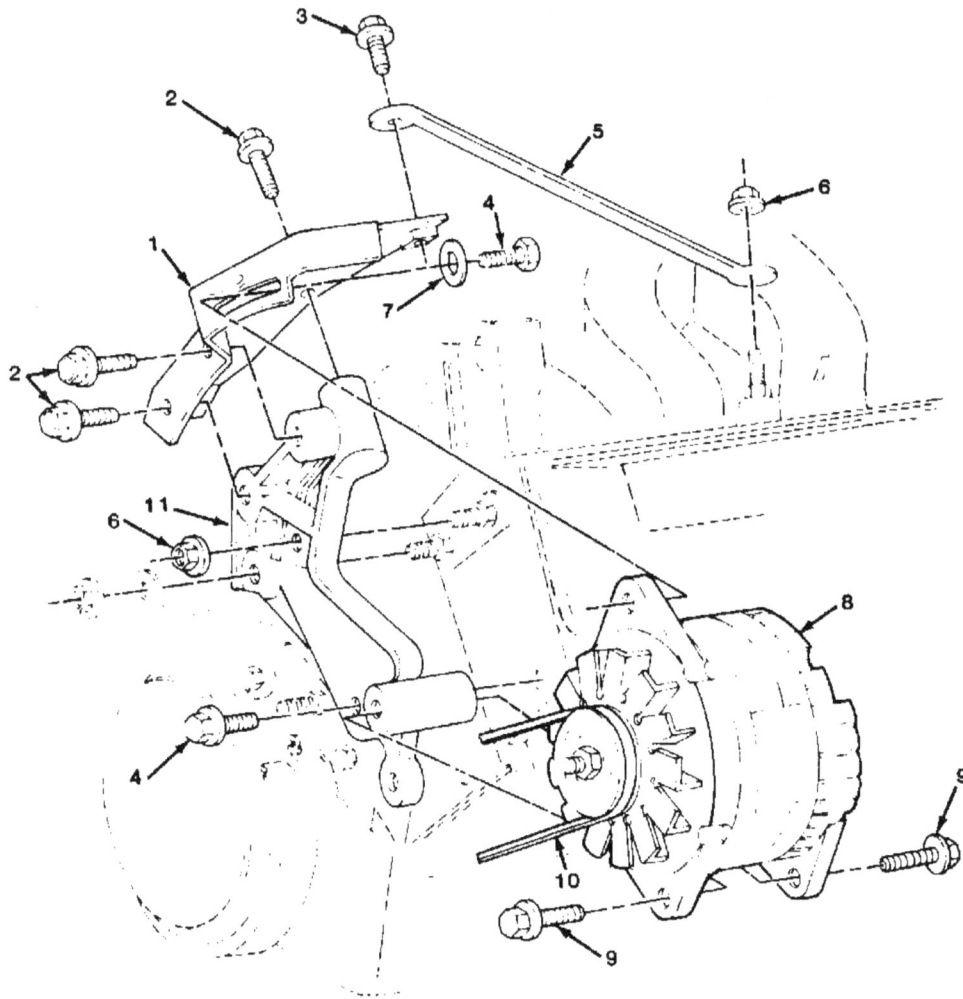

TA510840

FIGURE 28. ALTERNATOR AND MOUNTING HARDWARE, LEFT SIDE (ALL EXCEPT M1010).

(1) ITEM NO	(2) SMR CODE	(3) CAGEC	(4) PART NUMBER	(5) DESCRIPTION AND USABLE ON CODES (UOC)	(6) QTY
				GROUP 06 ELECTRICAL SYSTEM	
				GROUP 0601 GENERATOR, ALTERNATOR	
				FIG. 28 ALTERNATOR AND MOUNTING HARDWARE, LEFT SIDE (ALL EXCEPT M1010)	
1	PAOZZ	11862	14077149	BRACKET,ENGINE ACCE UOC:194,208,209,230,231,252,254,256	1
2	PAOZZ	11862	1635490	BOLT,SELF-LOCKING UOC:194,208,209,230,231,252,254,256	3
3	PAOZZ	11862	11504595	SCREW,CAP,HEXAGON H UOC:194,208,209,230,231,252,254,256	1
4	PAOZZ	11862	1635490	BOLT,SELF-LOCKING UOC:194,208,209,230,231,252,254,256	2
5	PAOZZ	11862	14077151	BRACKET,DOUBLE ANGL UOC:194,208,209,230,231,252,254,256	1
6	PAOZZ	11862	11503643	NUT UOC:194,208,209,230,231,252,254,256	2
7	PAOZZ	96906	MS27183-16	WASHER,FLAT UOC:194,208,209,230,231,252,254,256	1
8	PAOFF	11862	1105500	GENERATOR,ENGINE AC UOC:194,208,209,230,231,252,254,256	2
9	PAOZZ	11862	1610819	BOLT,MACHINE UOC:194,208,209,230,231,252,254,256	2
10	PAOZZ	20796	43-3226	BELT,V UOC:194,208,209,230,231,252,254,256	1
11	PAOZZ	11862	14077147	BRACKET,ENGINE ACCE UOC:194,208,209,230,231,252,254,256	1

END OF FIGURE

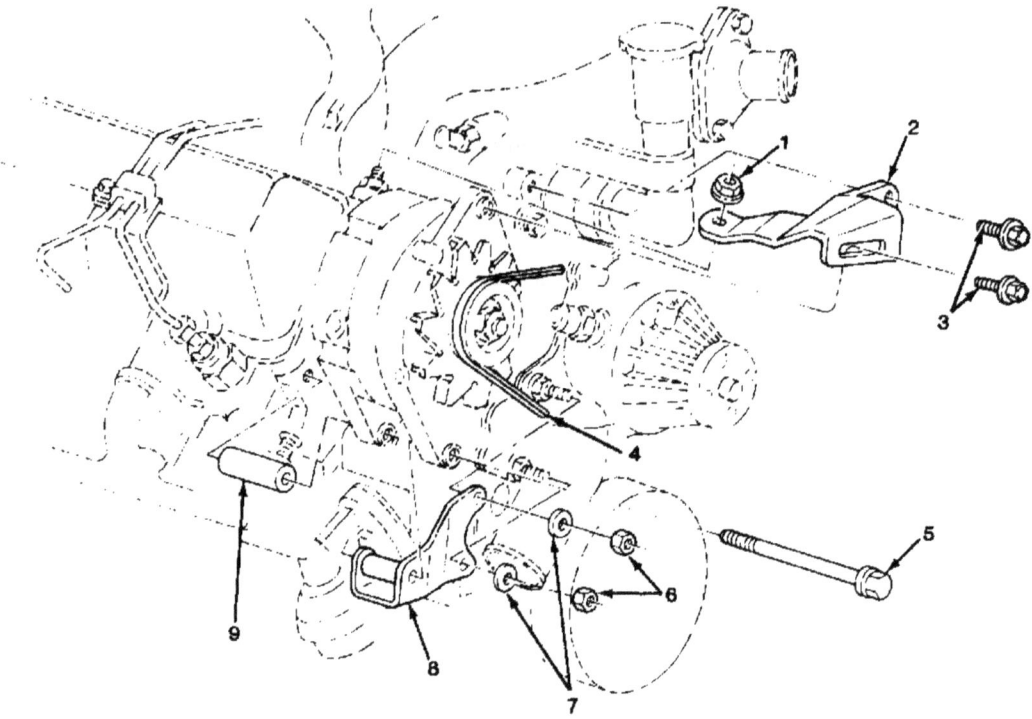

FIGURE 29. ALTERNATOR AND MOUNTING HARDWARE, RIGHT SIDE (ALL EXCEPT M1010).

(1) ITEM NO	(2) SMR CODE	(3) CAGEC	(4) PART NUMBER	(5) DESCRIPTION AND USABLE ON CODES (UOC)	(6) QTY
				GROUP 0601 GENERATOR, ALTERNATOR	
				FIG. 29 ALTERNATOR AND MOUNTING HARDWARE, RIGHT SIDE (ALL EXCEPT M1010)	
1	PAOZZ	11862	14005953	SHIELD,EXPANSION UOC:194,208,209,230,231,252,254,256	1
2	PAOZZ	11862	14067724	BRACKET,ENGINE ACCE UOC:194,208,209,230,231,252,254,256	1
3	PAOZZ	11862	1635490	BOLT, SELF-LOCKING UOC:194,208,209,230,231,252,254,256	2
4	PAOZZ	20796	42-6923	BELT,V UOC:194,208,209,230,231,252,254,256	1
5	PAOZZ	11862	14067717	BOLT,MACHINE UOC:194,208,209,230,231,252,254,256	1
6	PAOZZ	11862	11506101	NUT UOC:194,208,209,230,231,252,254,256	2
7	PAOZZ	96906	MS27183-16	WASHER,FLAT UOC:194,208,209,230,231,252,254,256	2
8	PAOZZ	11862	14067714	BRACKET,ENGINE ACCE UOC:194,208,209,230,231,252,254,256	1
9	PAOZZ	11862	14067725	SPACER,SLEEVE UOC:194,208,209,230,231,252,254,256	1

END OF FIGURE

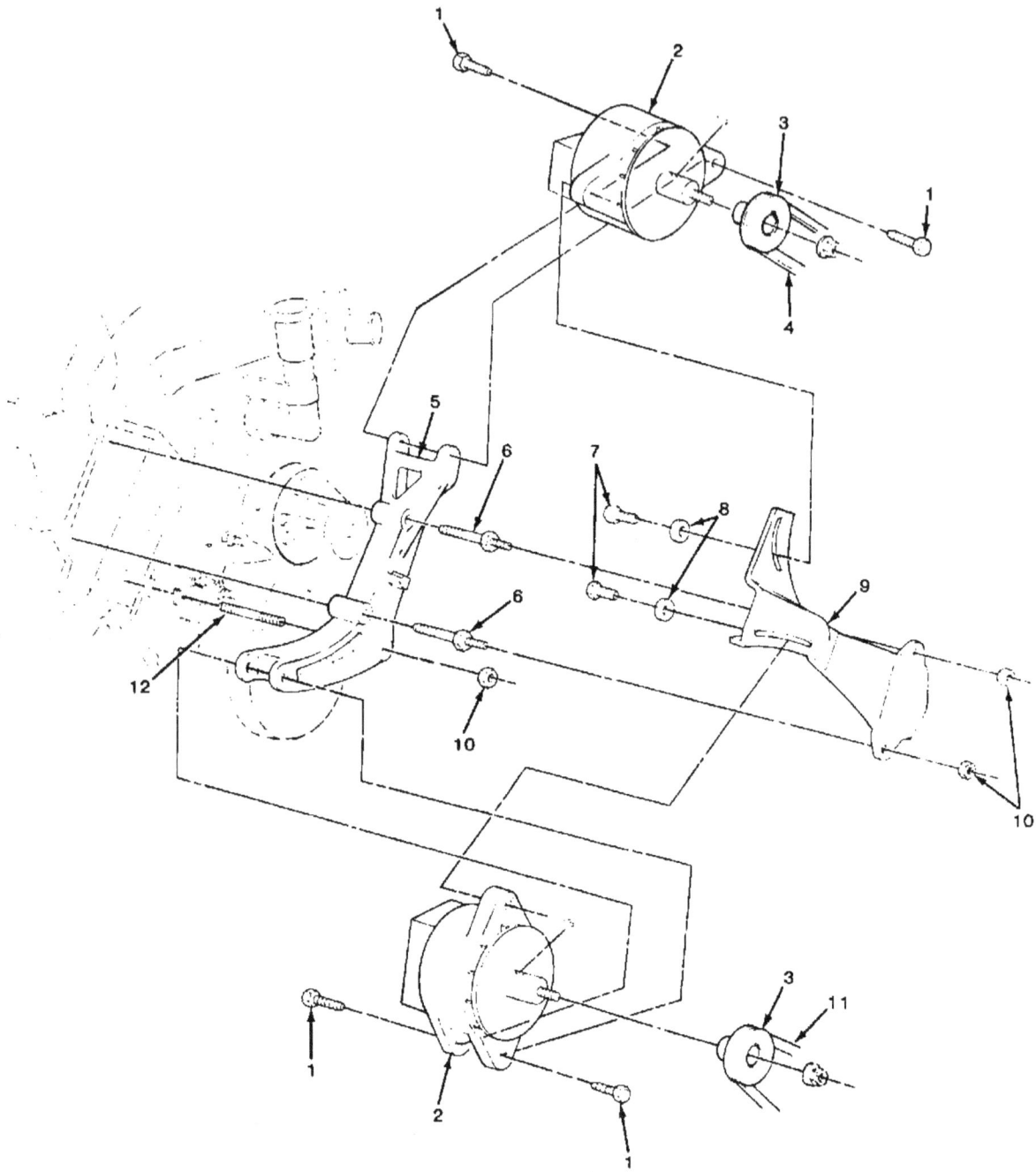

TA510842

FIGURE 30. ALTERNATOR AND MOUNTING HARDWARE (M1010).

(1) ITEM NO	(2) SMR CODE	(3) CAGEC	(4) PART NUMBER	(5) DESCRIPTION AND USABLE ON CODES (UOC)	(6) QTY
				GROUP 0601 GENERATOR, ALTERNATOR	
				FIG. 30 ALTERNATOR AND MOUNTING HARDWARE (M1010)	
1	PAOZZ	11862	9440280	SCREW,CAP,HEXAGON H UOC:210,230	4
2	PAOFF	35510	4629JA	GENERATOR,ENGINE AC FOR COMPONENT PARTS SEE FIG. 31 UOC:210,230	2
3	PAOZZ	11862	15599204	PULLEY,GROOVE UOC:210,230	2
4	PAOZZ	20796	42-6919	BELT,V UOC:210,230	1
5	PAOZZ	11862	14067715	BRACKET,ENGINE ACCE UOC:210,230	1
6	PAOZZ	11862	14067718	STUD,RECESSED UOC:210,230	2
7	PAOZZ	96906	MS90728-109	SCREW,CAP,HEXAGON H UOC:210,230	2
8	PAOZZ	11862	3954735	WASHER,FLAT UOC:210,230	2
9	PAOZZ	11862	14067721	BRACKET,ENGINE ACCE UOC:210,230	1
10	PAOZZ	11862	11506101	NUT UOC:210,230	3
11	PAOZZ	20796	42-6921	BELT,V UOC:210,230	1
12	PAOZZ	11862	1623159	STUD,PLAIN UOC:210,230	1

END OF FIGURE

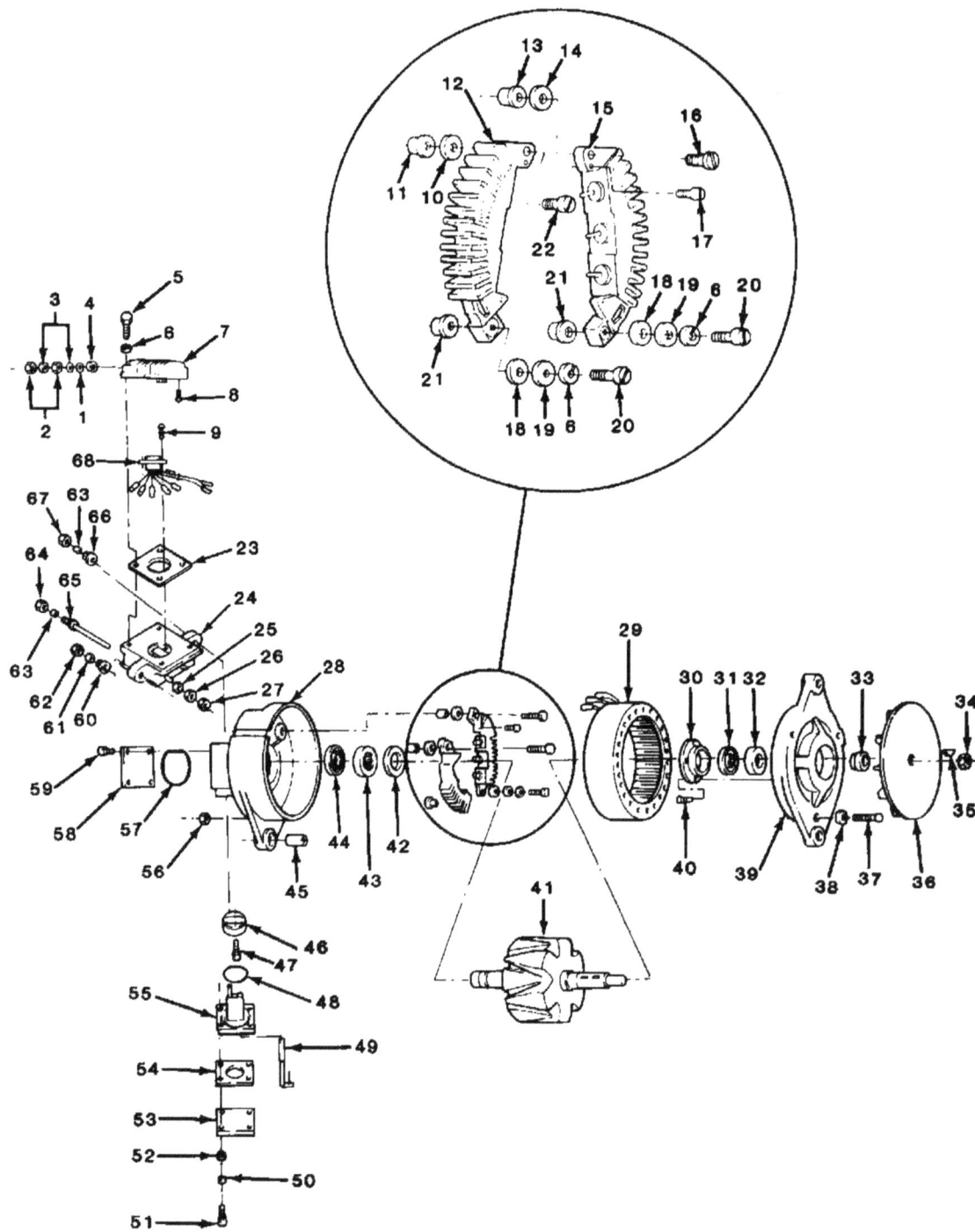

FIGURE 31. ALTERNATOR COMPONENT PARTS (M1010).

TA510844

SECTION II					
(1)	(2)	(3)	(4)	(5)	(6)
ITEM NO	SMR CODE	CAGEC	PART NUMBER	DESCRIPTION AND USABLE ON CODES (UOC)	QTY

GROUP 0601 GENERATOR, ALTERNATOR

FIG. 31 ALTERNATOR COMPONENT PARTS (M1010)

1	PAOZZ	35510	5413	WASHER,FLAT UOC:210	1
2	PAOZZ	35510	4340	NUT,PLAIN,HEXAGON UOC:210	2
3	PAOZZ	35510	31256	WASHER,LOCK UOC:210	2
4	PAOZZ	35510	7983	INSULATOR,WASHER UOC:210	1
5	PAOZZ	35510	99525	SCREW,MACHINE UOC:210	4
6	PAOZZ	35510	2434	WASHER,LOCK UOC:210	6
7	PAOZZ	35510	95300	REGULATOR,ENGINE GE UOC:210	1
8	PAOZZ	35510	99459	SCREW,ASSEMBLED WAS UOC:210	1

END OF FIGURE

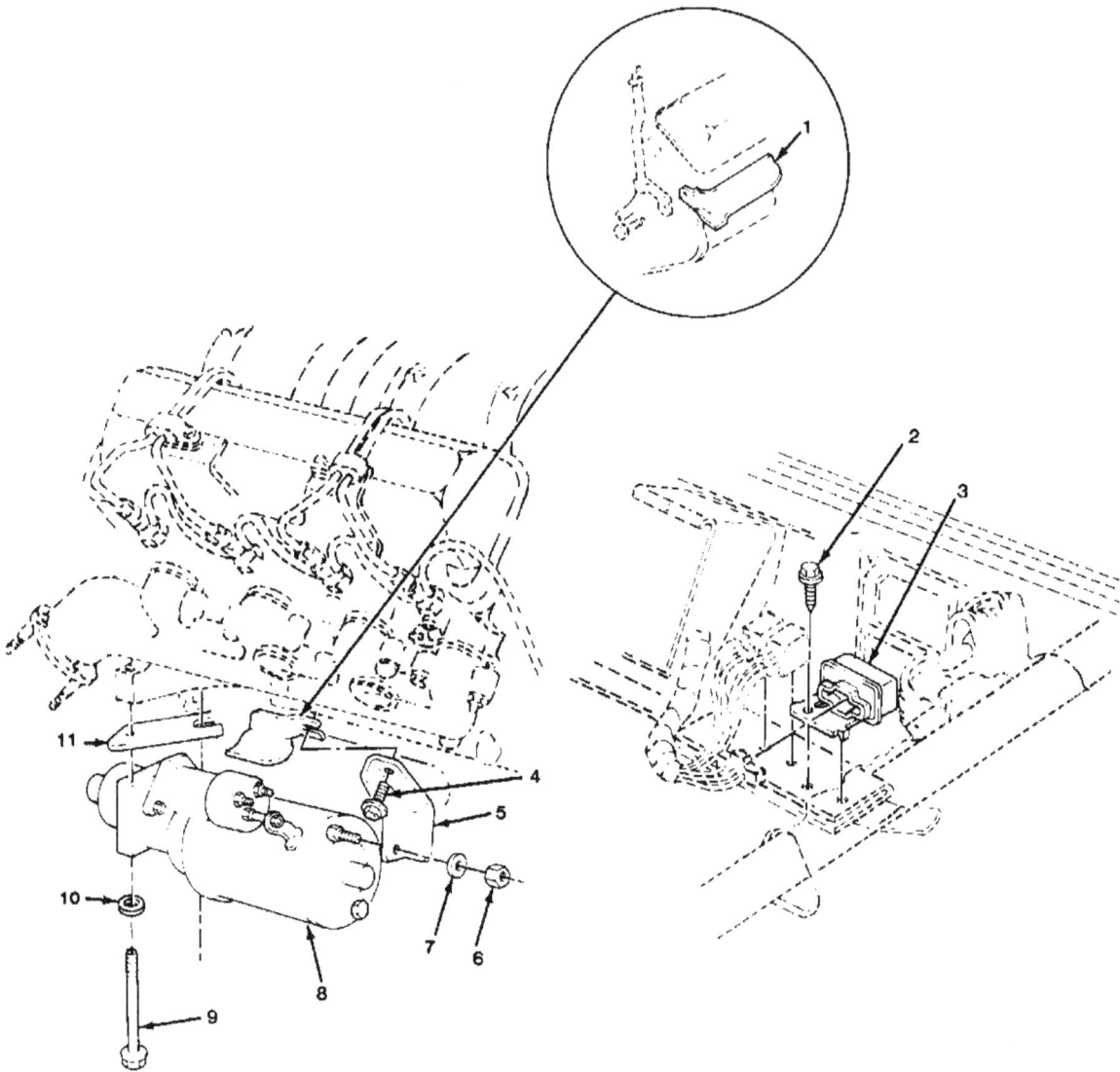

TA510846

FIGURE 32. STARTER MOTOR AND RELAY.

(1) ITEM NO	(2) SMR CODE	(3) CAGEC	(4) PART NUMBER	(5) DESCRIPTION AND USABLE ON CODES (UOC)	(6) QTY
				GROUP 0603 STARTING MOTOR	
				FIG. 32 STARTER MOTOR AND RELAY	
1	PAOZZ	11862	14066657	SHIELD,STARTER MOTO	1
2	PAOZZ	24617	9419663	SCREW,TAPPING	1
3	PAOZZ	11862	15591718	RELAY,ELECTROMAGNET	1
4	PAOZZ	11862	14060613	BOLT,MACHINE	1
5	PAOZZ	11862	14028931	BRACKET,ANGLE	1
6	PAOZZ	21450	131245	NUT,SELF-LOCKING,HE	1
7	PAOZZ	96906	MS27183-10	WASHER,FLAT	1
8	PAOFF	16764	1113591	STARTER,ENGINE,ELEC	1
9	PAOZZ	11862	15544950	BOLT,CLOSE TOLERANC	2
10	PAOZZ	11862	22521054	WASHER,FLAT	2
11	PAOZZ	11862	23500396	SPACER,PLATE (1.0 MM AS REQUIRED)	1

END OF FIGURE

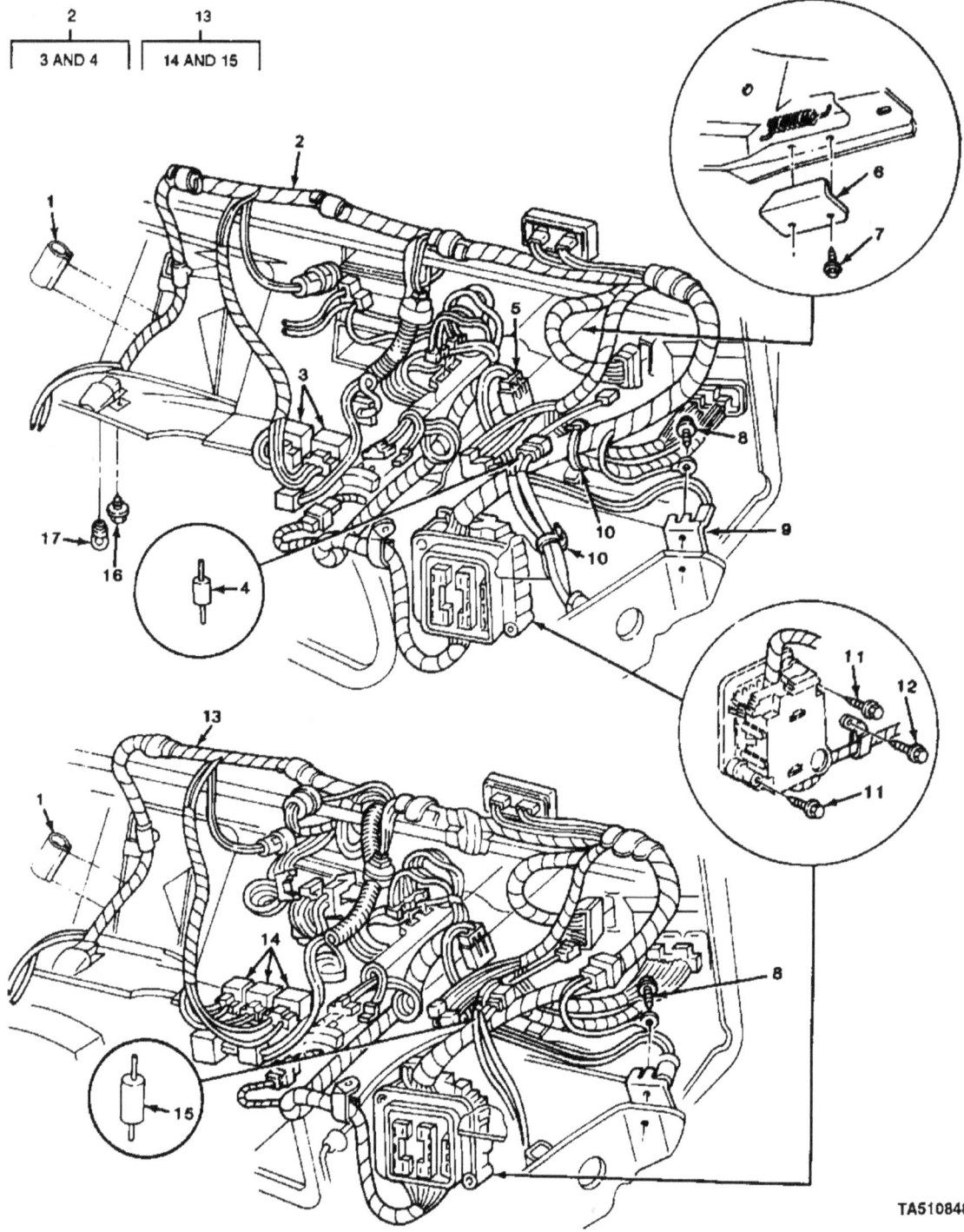

FIGURE 33. INSTRUMENT PANEL WIRING HARNESS.

TA510848

(1) ITEM NO	(2) SMR CODE	(3) CAGEC	(4) PART NUMBER	(5) DESCRIPTION AND USABLE ON CODES (UOC)	(6) QTY
				GROUP 0607 INSTRUMENT OR ENGINE CONTROL PANEL	
				FIG. 33 INSTRUMENT PANEL WIRING HARNESS	
1	PAOZZ	11862	3999572	ADHESIVE,DRY MOUNTI	1
4	PAOZZ	11862	12006377	.RECTIFIER,CONNECTOR UOC:194,208,209,230,231,252,254,256	1
5	PAOZZ	11862	15591138	MODULE,INDICATOR,CO	1
17	PAOZZ	08806	1003	LAMP,INCANDESCENT	1

END OF FIGURE

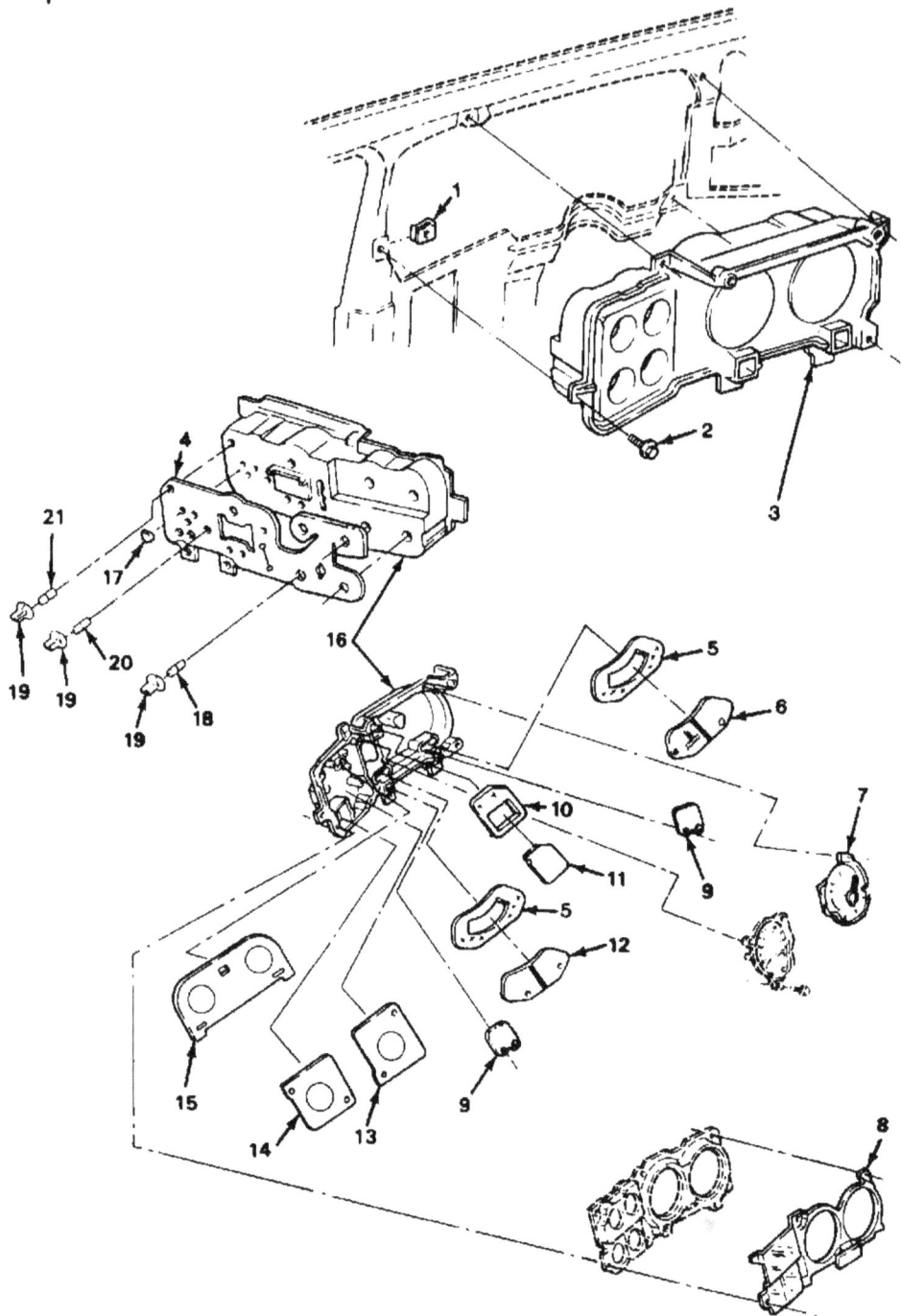

FIGURE 34. INSTRUMENT CLUSTER ASSEMBLY

TA510849

(1) ITEM NO	(2) SMR CODE	(3) CAGEC	(4) PART NUMBER	(5) DESCRIPTION AND USABLE ON CODES (UOC)	(6) QTY
				GROUP 0607 INSTRUMENT OR ENGINE CONTROL PANEL	
				FIG. 34 INSTRUMENT CLUSTER ASSEMBLY	
1	PAOZZ	96906	MS90724-34	NUT,SHEET SPRING	4
2	PAOZZ	11862	11513932	SCREW,ASSEMBLED WAS	4
3	PAOOO	11862	25052807	PANEL,INSTRUMENT	1
4	PAOZZ	11862	25053623	.PRINTED WIRING BOAR	1
5	PAOZZ	11862	25015099	.GASKET	2
6	PAOZZ	11862	25022883	.LENS,LIGHT	1
7	PAOZZ	70040	6433429	.INDICATOR,LIQUID QU	1
8	PAOZZ	11862	25017376	.BEZEL,INSTRUMENT MO	1
9	PAOZZ	11862	6497476	.LENS,LIGHT	2
10	PAOZZ	11862	6497483	.GASKET	1
11	PAOZZ	11862	6497475	.FILTER,INDICATOR LI	1
12	PAOZZ	11862	25022884	.FILTER,INDICATOR LI UOC:194,208,209,210,230,231,252,254	1
13	PAOZZ	11862	25053501	.FILTER,INDICATOR LI	1
14	PAOZZ	11862	25053500	.FILTER,SIGNAL LIGHT	1
15	PAOZZ	11862	25076586	.FILTER,INDICATOR LI	1
16	PAOZZ	11862	25053622	.CASE,INSTRUMENT CLU	1
17	PAOZZ	11862	8986000	.CLIP,ELECTRICAL	3
18	PAOZZ	08806	194	LAMP,INCANDESCENT	1
19	PAOZZ	77060	2973932	LAMPHOLDER	14
20	PAOZZ	08806	194	LAMP,INCANDESCENT LEFT	1
21	PAOZZ	08806	168	LAMP,INCANDESCENT	12

END OF FIGURE

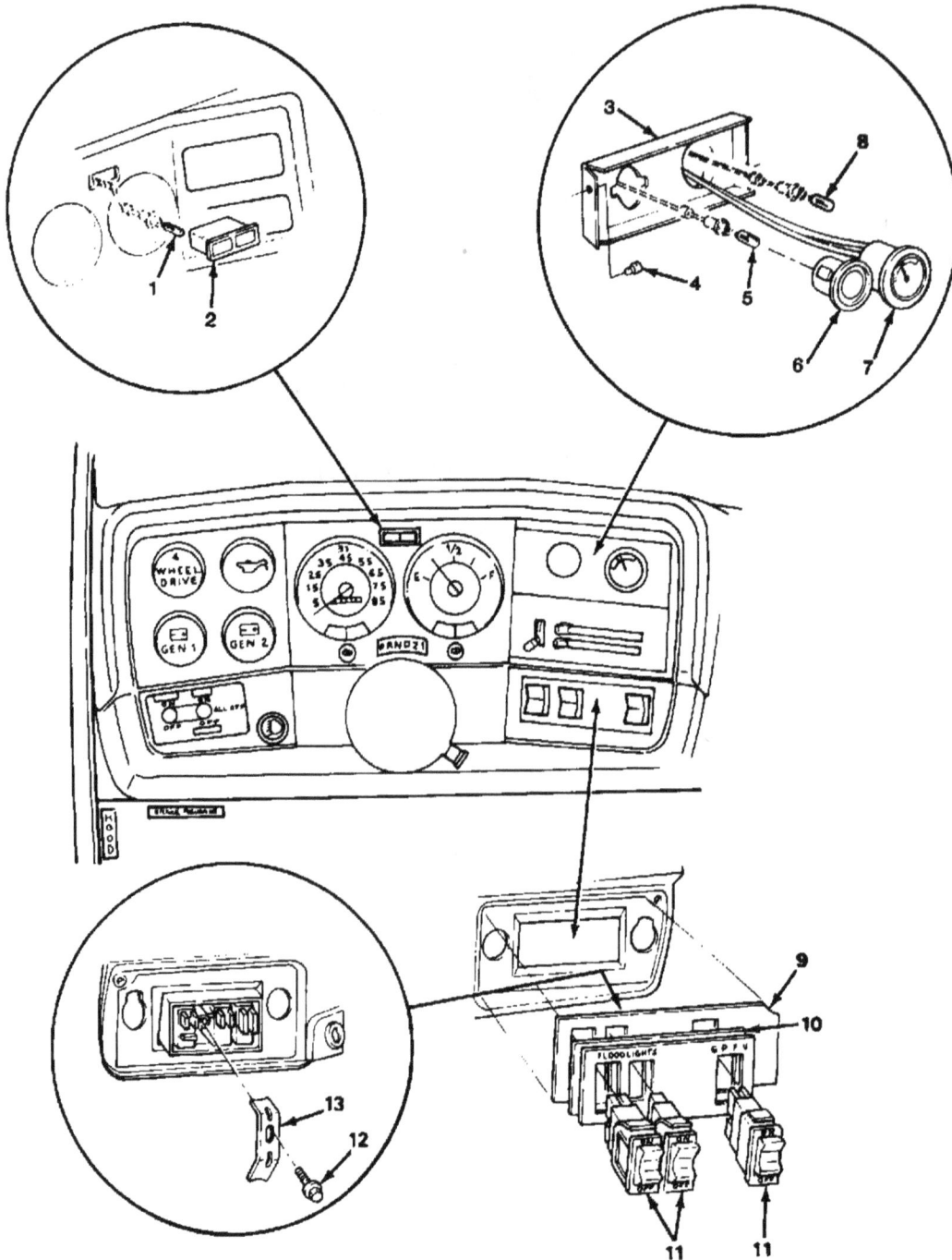

FIGURE 35. DOOR AJAR AND GLOW PLUG INDICATOR, VOLTMETER, GAS-PARTICULATE
FILTER UNIT, AND FLOODLIGHT SWITCH.

TA510850

(1)	(2)	(3)	(4)	(5)	(6)
ITEM NO	SMR CODE	CAGEC	PART NUMBER	DESCRIPTION AND USABLE ON CODES (UOC)	QTY

GROUP 0607 INSTRUMENT OR ENGINE
CONTROL PANEL

FIG. 35 DOOR AJAR AND GLOW PLUG
INDICATOR, VOLTMETER,
GAS-PARTICULATE FILTER UNIT, AND
FLOODLIGHT SWITCH

(1)	(2)	(3)	(4)	(5)	(6)
1	PAOZZ	08806	168	LAMP,INCANDESCENT	2
2	PAOZZ	11862	14066662	LENS,LIGHT UOC:194,208,209,210,230,231,252,254	1
3	PAOZZ	11862	14072406	BRACKET,MOUNTING UOC:194,208,209,230,231,252,254,256	1
3	PAOZZ	11862	14072409	BRACKET,MOUNTING UOC:210	1
4	PAOZZ	11862	9441669	RIVET,BLIND	2
5	PAOZZ	08806	168	LAMP,INCANDESCENT UOC:210	1
6	PAOZZ	11862	14075858	HOUSING,INDICATOR UOC:210	1
7	PAOZZ	70040	6474942A	METER,SPECIAL SCALE	1
8	PAOZZ	08806	1445	.LAMP,INCANDESCENT VOLTMETER	1
9	PAOZZ	11862	14072410	COVER,ACCESSORY,SWI UOC:210	1
10	PAOZZ	11862	14072448	COVER,ELECTRICAL SW UOC:210	1
11	PAOZZ	11862	14072338	SWITCH,PUSH UOC:210	3
12	PAOZZ	24617	9415163	SCREW,ASSEMBLED WAS UOC:210	1
13	PAOZZ	11862	14072412	RETAINER,ELECTRICAL UOC:210	1

END OF FIGURE

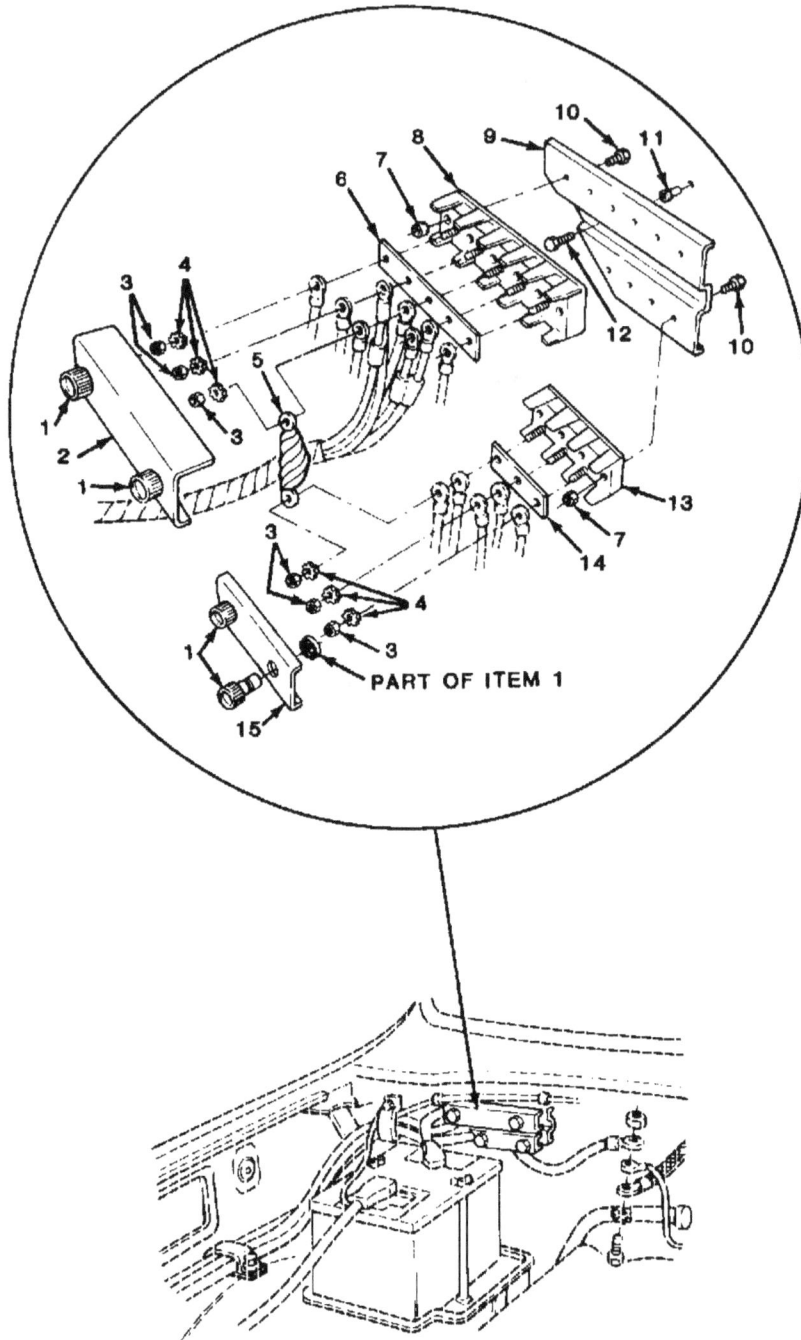

TA510851

FIGURE 36. ACCESSORY WIRING TERMINAL BOARD AND COMPONENTS.

(1) ITEM NO	(2) SMR CODE	(3) CAGEC	(4) PART NUMBER	(5) DESCRIPTION AND USABLE ON CODES (UOC)	(6) QTY
				GROUP 0608 MISCELLANEOUS ITEMS	
				FIG. 36 ACCESSORY WIRING TERMINAL BOARD AND COMPONENTS	
1	PAOZZ	96906	MS18029-24	NUT ASSEMBLY	4
2	MOOZZ	96906	MS18029-13L-5	BOARD,VEH ACC WRG MAKE FROM COVER, P/N MS18029-4S-8	1
3	PAOZZ	96906	MS35650-3314	NUT,PLAIN,HEXAGON	8
4	PAOZZ	96906	MS35335-34	WASHER,LOCK	8
5	PAOZZ	11862	15599225	CAPACITOR ASSEMBLY	1
6	PAOZZ	11862	14072336	BUS,CONDUCTOR	1
7	PAOZZ	96906	MS35649-262	NUT,PLAIN,HEXAGON	10
8	MOOZZ	96906	MS27212-4-5	TERMINAL BOARD MAKE FROM BOARD,P/N MS27212-4-8	1
9	PAOZZ	11862	14075900	TERMINAL BOARD BRAC	1
10	PAOZZ	96906	MS51849-33	SCREW,MACHINE	10
11	PAOZZ	11862	14005953	SHIELD,EXPANSION	2
12	PAOZZ	11862	9437702	BOLT,MACHINE	2
13	MOOZZ	96906	MS27212-4-3	BOARD,VEH ACC WRG MAKE FROM BOARD, P/N MS27212-4-8 UOC:194,208,209,210,230,231,252	1
14	MOOZZ	11862	14072337	CONNECTOR LINK (3.625" LG) MAKE FROM ITEM 6 (P/N 14072336)	1
15	MOOZZ	96906	MS18029-13S-3	COVER MAKE FROM COVER,P/N MS18029-13S-8	1

END OF FIGURE

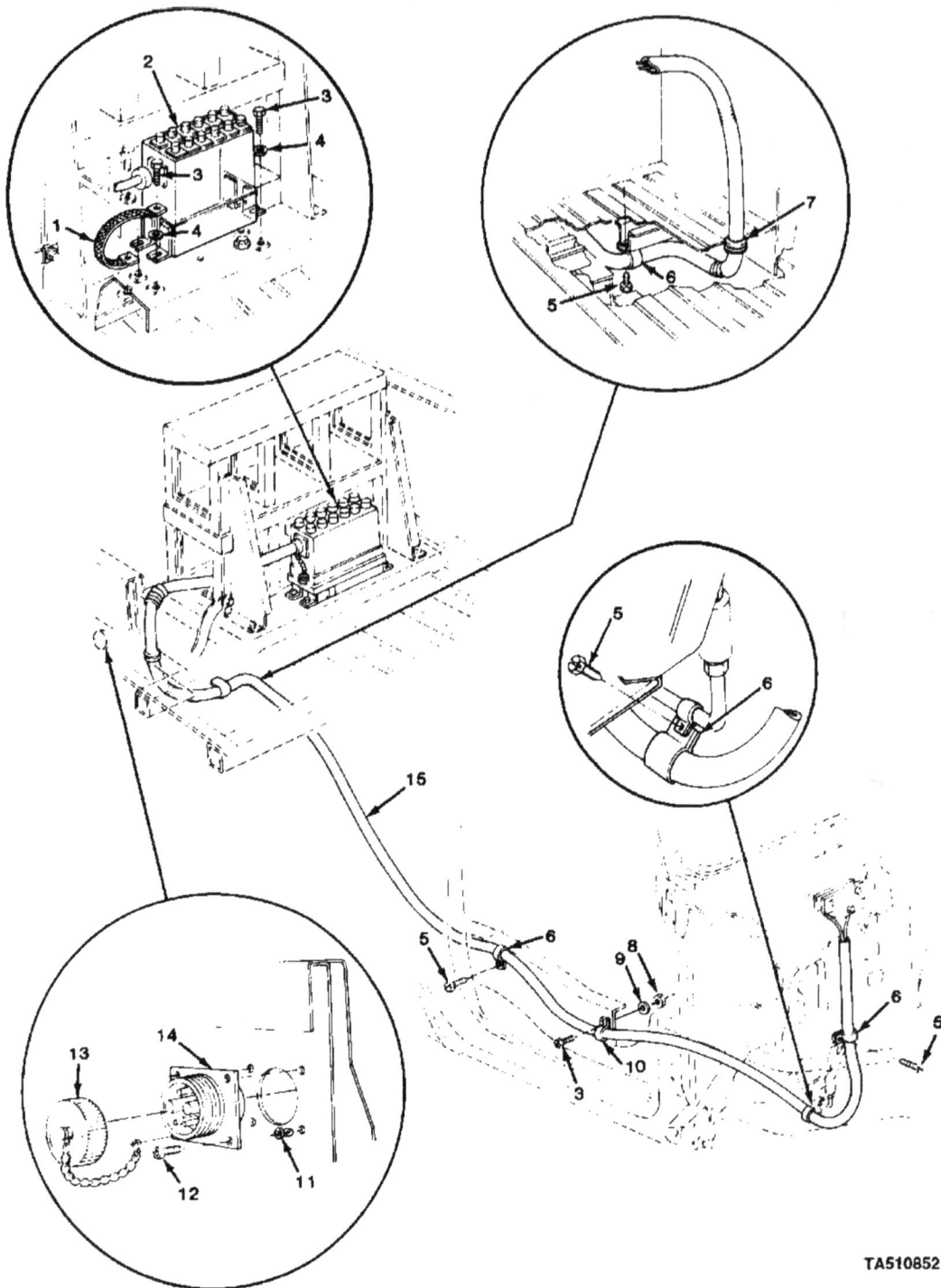

FIGURE 37. POWER JUNCTION BOX AND CABLE.

TA510852

(1) ITEM NO	(2) SMR CODE	(3) CAGEC	(4) PART NUMBER	(5) DESCRIPTION AND USABLE ON CODES (UOC)	(6) QTY
				GROUP 0608 MISCELLANEOUS ITEMS	
				FIG. 37 POWER JUNCTION BOX AND CABLE	
1	XDOZZ	80063	SC-B-75180-IV	LEAD, ELECTRICAL UOC:208,230	1 1
2	PAOFF	80063	SC-D-691391	INTERCONNECTING BOX FOR COMPONENT PARTS SEE TM11-5820 862-13&P UOC:194,208	1
3	PAOZZ	96906	MS90728-6	SCREW, CAP, HEXAGON H UOC:208,230	5
4	PAOZZ	96906	MS35335-33	WASHER, LOCK UOC:208,230	4
5	PAOZZ	11862	11504447	SCREW, TAPPING UOC:194,208,230,252,254,256	4
6	PAOZZ	11862	2043151	CLAMP, LOOP UOC:194,208,230,252,254,256	4
7	PAOZZ	11862	343124	GROMMET, NONMETALLIC UOC:208,230	1
8	PAOZZ	96906	MS51967-2	NUT, PLAIN, HEXAGON UOC:194,208	1
9	PAOZZ	96906	MS35338-44	WASHER, LOCK UOC:208,230	1
10	PAOZZ	96906	MS21333-116	CLAMP, LOOP UOC:208,230	1
11	PAOZZ	00613	C-5139-2	RECEPTACLE, TURNLOCK UOC:208,209	4
12	PAOZZ	96906	MS35206-267	SCREW, MACHINE UOC:208,230	4
13	PAOZZ	96906	MS25043-32DA	COVER, ELECTRICAL CO UOC:208,230	1
14	PAOZZ	19207	8701347	SHELL, ELECTRICAL CO UOC:208,230	1
15	PAOZZ	11862	12039254	CABLE ASSEMBLY, POWE UOC:208,230,252,254,256	1

END OF FIGURE

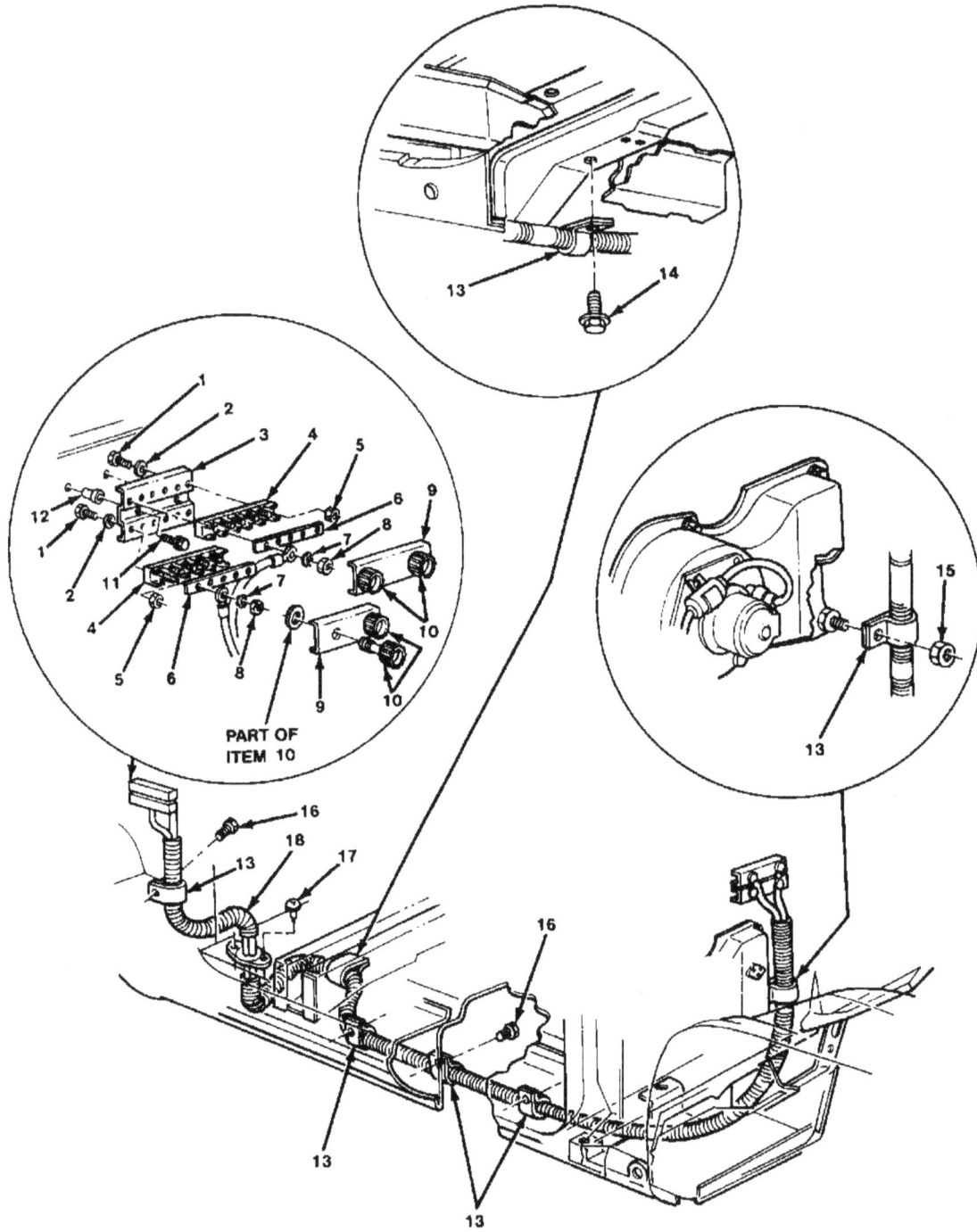

TA510853

FIGURE 38. RADIO FEED HARNESS (M1009).

(1) ITEM NO	(2) SMR CODE	(3) CAGEC	(4) PART NUMBER	(5) DESCRIPTION AND USABLE ON CODES (UOC)	(6) QTY
				GROUP 0608 MISCELLANEOUS ITEMS	
				FIG. 38 RADIO FEED HARNESS (M1009)	
1	PAOZZ	96906	MS51849-33	SCREW, MACHINE UOC:209	12
2	PAOZZ	96906	MS27183-6	WASHER, FLAT UOC:209	12
3	PAOZZ	11862	15599989	TERMINAL BOARD BRAC UOC:209	1
4	MOOZZ	96906	MS27212-4-5	TERMINAL BOARD MAKE FROM BOARD, P/N MS27212-4-8 UOC:209	2
5	PAOZZ	96906	MS35649-262	NUT, PLAIN, HEXAGON UOC:209	12
6	PAOZZ	11862	14072336	BUS, CONDUCTOR UOC:209	2
7	PAOZZ	96906	MS35335-34	WASHER, LOCK UOC:209	10
8	PAOZZ	96906	MS35650-3314	NUT, PLAIN, HEXAGON UOC:209	10
9	MOOZZ	96906	MS18029-13L-5	BOARD, VEH ACC WRG MAKE FROM COVER, P/N MS18029-4S-8 UOC:209	2
10	PAOZZ	96906	MS18029-24	NUT ASSEMBLY UOC:209	4
11	PAOZZ	11862	9437702	BOLT, MACHINE UOC:209	2
12	PAOZZ	11862	14005953	SHIELD, EXPANSION UOC:209	2
13	PAOZZ	11862	2043151	CLAMP, LOOP UOC:209	5
14	PAOZZ	11862	11508534	BOLT, MACHINE UOC:209	1
15	PAOZZ	24617	11506003	NUT, PLAIN, ASSEMBLED UOC:209	1
16	PAOZZ	11862	9436175	RIVET, BLIND UOC:209	4
17	PAOZZ	79846	ABA64LBA	RIVET, BLIND UOC:209	2
18	PAOZZ	11862	12044586	LEAD AND CONDUIT AS UOC:209	1

END OF FIGURE

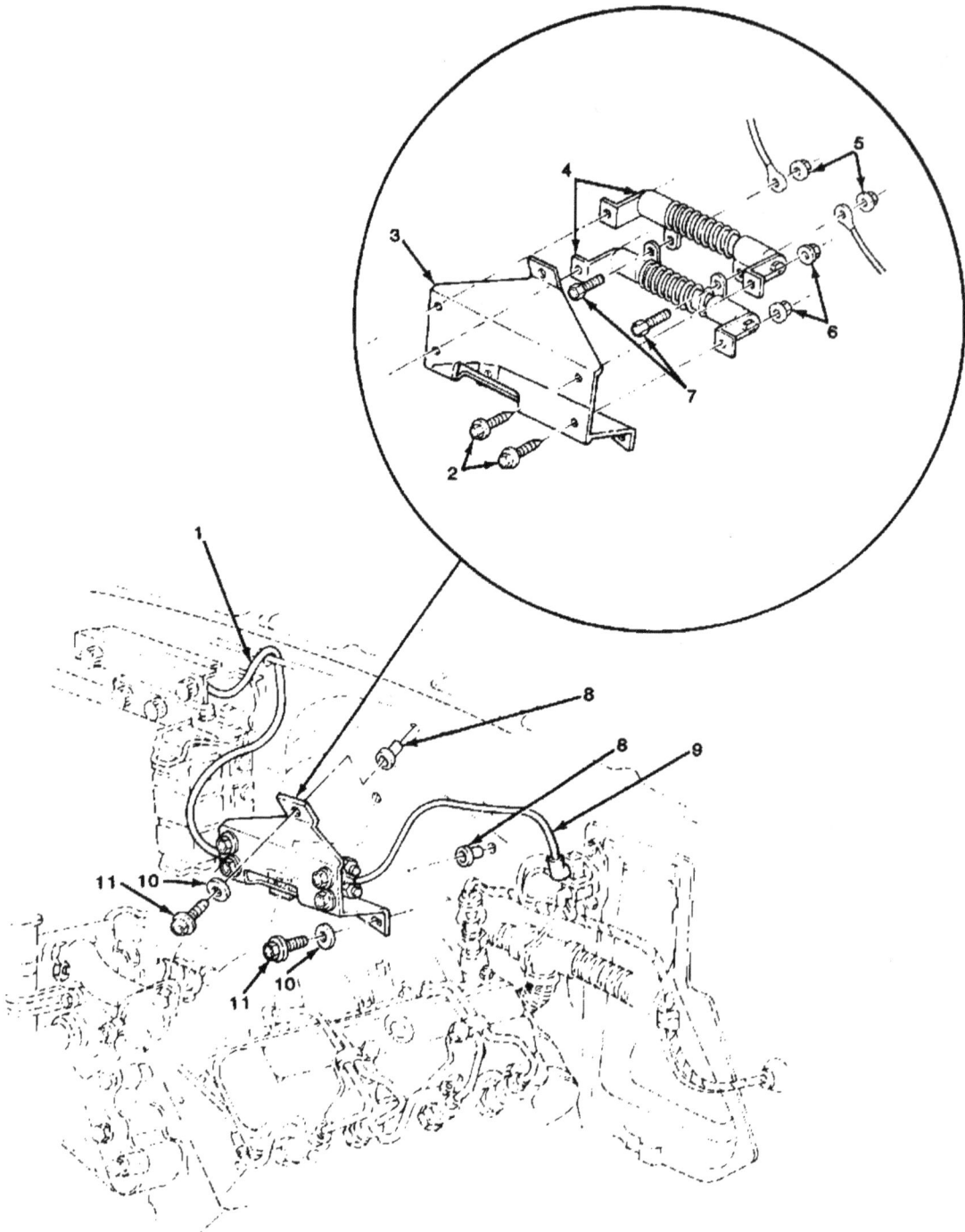

TA510854

FIGURE 39. BATTERY BOOSTER RESISTOR.

(1) ITEM NO	(2) SMR CODE	(3) CAGEC	(4) PART NUMBER	(5) DESCRIPTION AND USABLE ON CODES (UOC)	(6) QTY
				GROUP 0608 MISCELLANEOUS ITEMS	
				FIG. 39 BATTERY BOOSTER RESISTOR	
1	PAOZZ	77060	12039297	LEAD,IGNITION,ENGIN	1
2	PAOZZ	11862	9439770	BOLT,ASSEMBLED WASH	4
3	PAOZZ	11862	14076848	BRACKET,RESISTOR	1
4	PAOZZ	11862	14076847	RESISTOR,FIXED,WIRE	2
5	PAOZZ	72582	271163	NUT,PLAIN,ASSEMBLED	2
6	PAOZZ	24617	271172	NUT,SELF-LOCKING,AS	4
7	PAOZZ	96906	MS51849-55	SCREW,MACHINE	2
8	PAOZZ	11862	14005953	SHIELD,EXPANSION	3
9	PAOZZ	77060	12039298	LEAD,IGNITION,ENGIN	1
10	PAOZZ	96906	MS35335-33	WASHER,LOCK	3
11	PAOZZ	11862	9437702	BOLT,MACHINE	3

END OF FIGURE

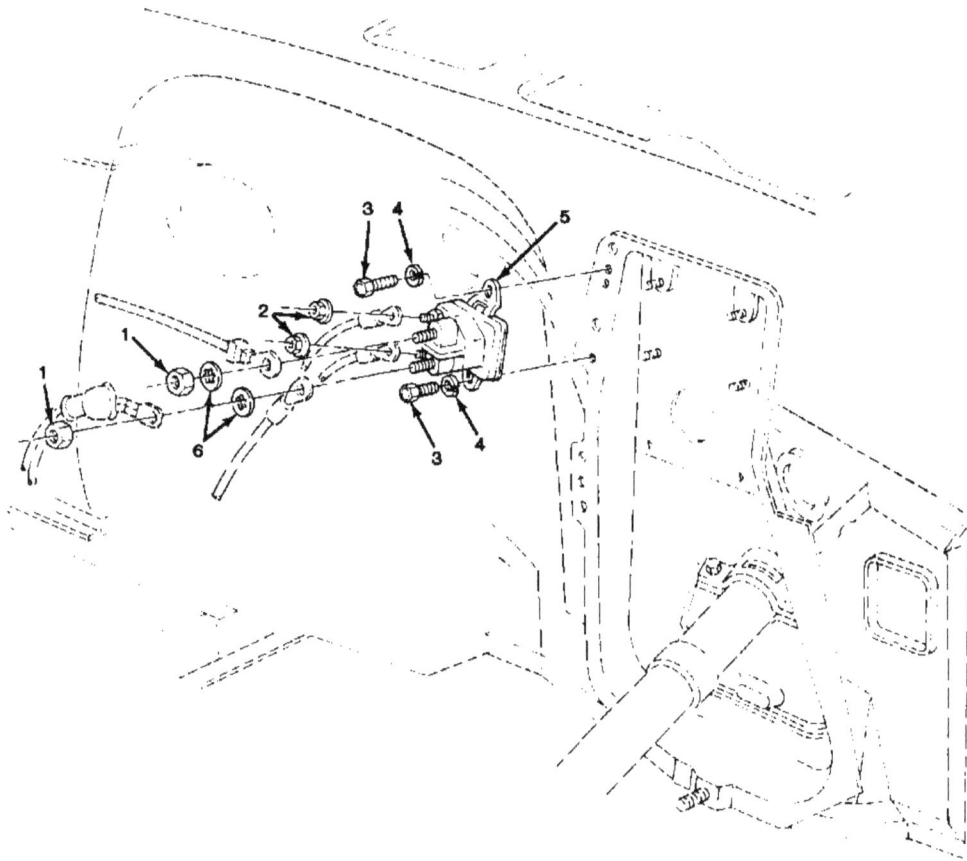

TA510855

FIGURE 40. GLOW PLUG RELAY

(1) ITEM NO	(2) SMR CODE	(3) CAGEC	(4) PART NUMBER	(5) DESCRIPTION AND USABLE ON CODES (UOC)	(6) QTY
				GROUP 0608 MISCELLANEOUS ITEMS	
				FIG. 40 GLOW PLUG RELAY	
1	PAOZZ	96906	MS51968-5	NUT, PLALIN, HEXAGON	2
2	PAOZZ	96906	MS35649-205	NUT, PLAIN, HEXAGON	2
3	PAOZZ	11862	9440166	SCREW, TAPPING	2
4	PAOZZ	96906	MS35338-44	WASHER, LOCK	2
5	PAOZZ	72055	98226	RELAY, ELECTROMAGNET	1
6	PAOZZ	96906	MS35333-41	WASHER, LOCK	2

END OF FIGURE

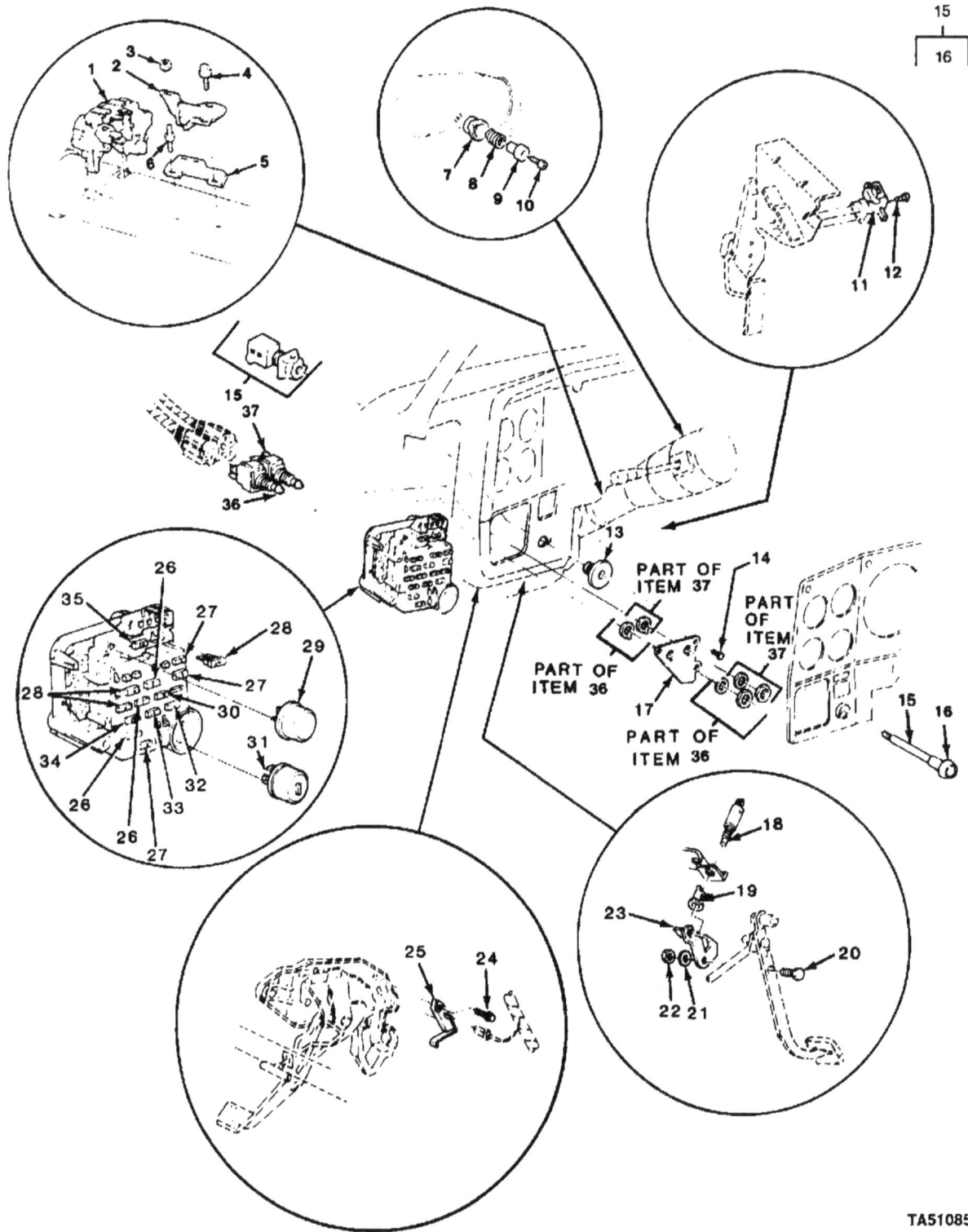

FIGURE 41. HEADLAMP, BLACKOUT LAMP AND TAILLAMP SWITCHES AND FUSES.

TA510856

(1) ITEM NO	(2) SMR CODE	(3) CAGEC	(4) PART NUMBER	(5) DESCRIPTION AND USABLE ON CODES (UOC)	(6) QTY
				GROUP 0608 MISCELLANEOUS ITEMS	
				FIG. 41 HEADLAMP, BLACKOUT LAMP, AND TAILLAMP SWITCHES AND FUSES	
1	PAOZZ	11862	22514861	SWITCH,SAFETY,NEUTR	1
7	PAOZZ	11862	22507977	KNOB	1
8	PAOZZ	11862	556743	SPRING,HELICAL,COMP	1
9	PAOZZ	11862	556742	PUSH BUTTON	1
10	PAOZZ	11862	1640902	SCREW,TAPPING	1
11	PAOZZ	11862	1242101	SWITCH,DOWN SHIFT TRNS D/SHIFT	1
13	PAOZZ	11862	6258213	NUT,BEZEL	1
14	PAOZZ	11862	2477054	RIVET,BLIND	3
15	PAOOO	11862	1995217	SWITCH ASSEMBLY	1
16	PAOZZ	11862	469302	.KNOB	1
17	PAOZZ	11862	14072413	BRACKET,ELECTRICAL	1
18	PAOZZ	11862	1261219	SWITCH,PUSH	1
19	PAOZZ	11862	1361699	CLIP,RETAINING	1
20	PAOZZ	96906	MS90728-60	SCREW,CAP,HEXAGON H	1
21	PAOZZ	96906	MS35338-46	WASHER,LOCK	1
22	PAOZZ	96906	MS51967-8	NUT,PLAIN,HEXAGON	1
23	PAOZZ	11862	14040525	ACTUATOR,STOP LIGHT UOC:209	1
23	PAOZZ	11862	14000395	STRIKER,BRAKE PEDAL UOC:194,208,210,230,231,252,254,256	1
24	PAOZZ	11862	9418944	SCREW,TAPPING	1
25	PAOZZ	11862	477361	SWITCH,SENSITIVE	1
26	PAOZZ	11862	12004005	FUSE,INCLOSED LINK	3
27	PAOZZ	11862	12004007	FUSE,INCLOSED LINK	3
28	PAOZZ	11862	12004009	FUSE,INCLOSED LINK	3
29	PAOZZ	94988	552-12V	FLASHER,THERMAL	1
30	PAOZZ	11862	12004010	FUSE,INCLOSED LINK	1
31	PAOZZ	94988	224-12V	FLASHER,THERMAL	1
32	PAOZZ	11862	12004011	FUSE,INCLOSED LINK	1
33	PAOZZ	11862	12004008	FUSE,INCLOSED LINK	1
34	PAOZZ	11862	12004011	FUSE,INCLOSED LINK UOC:210	1
35	PAOZZ	11862	12004009	FUSE,INCLOSED LINK UOC:210	1
36	PAOZZ	11862	14072358	SWITCH,TOGGLE	1
37	PAOZZ	11862	14072339	SWITCH,TOGGLE	1

END OF FIGURE

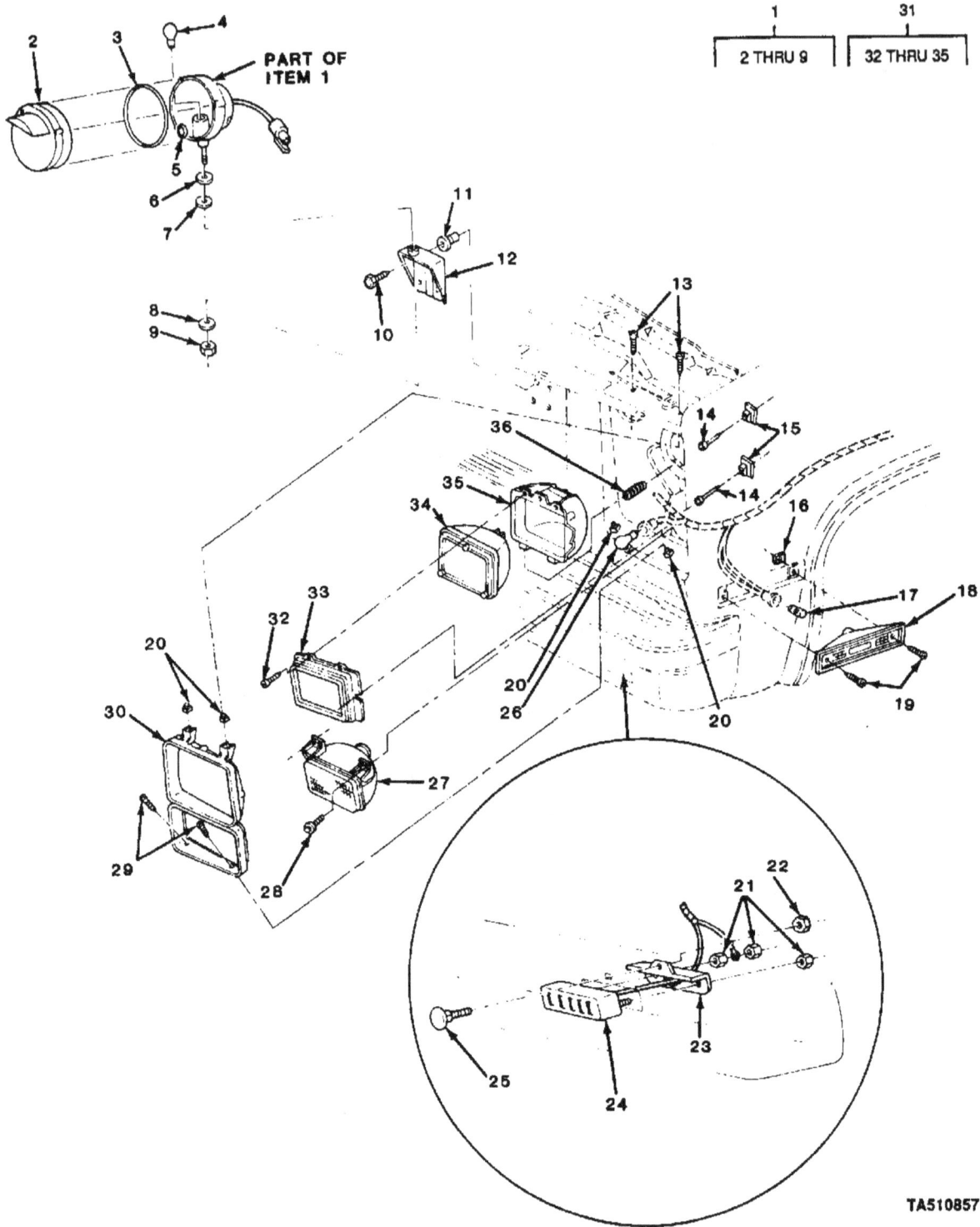

FIGURE 42. BLACKOUT HEADLAMP AND HEADLAMP ILLUMINATING COMPONENTS.

(1) ITEM NO	(2) SMR CODE	(3) CAGEC	(4) PART NUMBER	(5) DESCRIPTION AND USABLE ON CODES (UOC)	(6) QTY
				GROUP 0609 LIGHTS	
				FIG. 42 BLACKOUT HEADLAMP AND HEADLAMP ILLUMINATING COMPONENTS	
1	PAOZZ	11862	14072333	BLACKOUT LIGHT	1
2	PAOZZ	5A910	DC8218	.RETAINER,LENS	1
3	PAOZZ	34904	DC8226	.GASKET	1
4	PAOZZ	96906	MS35478-1073	.LAMP,INCANDESCENT	1
5	PAOZZ	5A910	DC8211	.GASKET	1
6	PAOZZ	5A910	DC8228	.WASHER,SADDLE	1
7	PAOZZ	19207	5294507	.WASHER,FINISHING	1
8	PAOZZ	96906	MS35338-46	.WASHER,LOCK	1
9	PAOZZ	96906	MS51967-8	.NUT,PLAIN,HEXAGON	1
10	PAOZZ	11862	9440334	BOLT,ASSEMBLED WASH	4
11	PAOZZ	11862	14005953	SHIELD,EXPANSION	4
12	PAOZZ	11862	14072431	BRACKET	1
13	PAOZZ	96906	MS51862-26	SCREW,TAPPING	4
14	PAOZZ	11862	9438150	SETSCREW	4
15	PAOZZ	11862	362379	NUT,HEADLIGHT MOUNT	4
16	PAOZZ	96906	MS90724-34	NUT,SHEET SPRING	4
17	PAOZZ	08806	194	LAMP,INCANDESCENT	2
18	PAOZZ	11862	915449	LENS,LIGHT LEFT	1
18	PAOZZ	11862	915450	LENS,LIGHT RIGHT	1
19	PAOZZ	11862	15605040	SCREW,TAPPING	4
20	PAOZZ	11862	347347	GROMMET,NONMETALLIC	8
21	PAOZZ	72582	271163	NUT,PLAIN,ASSEMBLED	6
22	PAOZZ	24617	11506003	NUT,PLAIN,ASSEMBLED	2
23	PAOZZ	11862	14072421	BRACKET,DOUBLE ANGL	2
24	PAOZZ	11862	15559316	LIGHT,MARKER,CLEARA	2
25	PAOZZ	24617	11503778	BOLT,SQUARE NECK	2
26	PAOZZ	08806	2057NA	LAMP,INCANDESCENT	2
27	PAOZZ	11862	915908	LENS,LIGHT	2
28	PAOZZ	96906	MS51871-4	SCREW,TAPPING	6
29	PAOZZ	11862	11504656	SCREW,TAPPING	4
30	PAOZZ	11862	14043873	RETAINER,LENS LEFT	1
30	PAOZZ	11862	14043874	RETAINER,LENS RIGHT	1
31	PAOOO	11862	16500591	HEADLIGHT	2
32	PAOZZ	11862	5966249	.SCREW	4
33	PAOZZ	11862	16501759	.RING ASSEMBLY,RETAI UOC:194,208,209,210,230,231,252,254	1
34	PAOZZ	08806	H6054	.LAMP,INCANDESCENT	1
35	PAOZZ	11862	5968095	.HOUSING,LIGHT	1
36	PAOZZ	11862	459461	SPRING,HELICAL,EXTE	2

END OF FIGURE

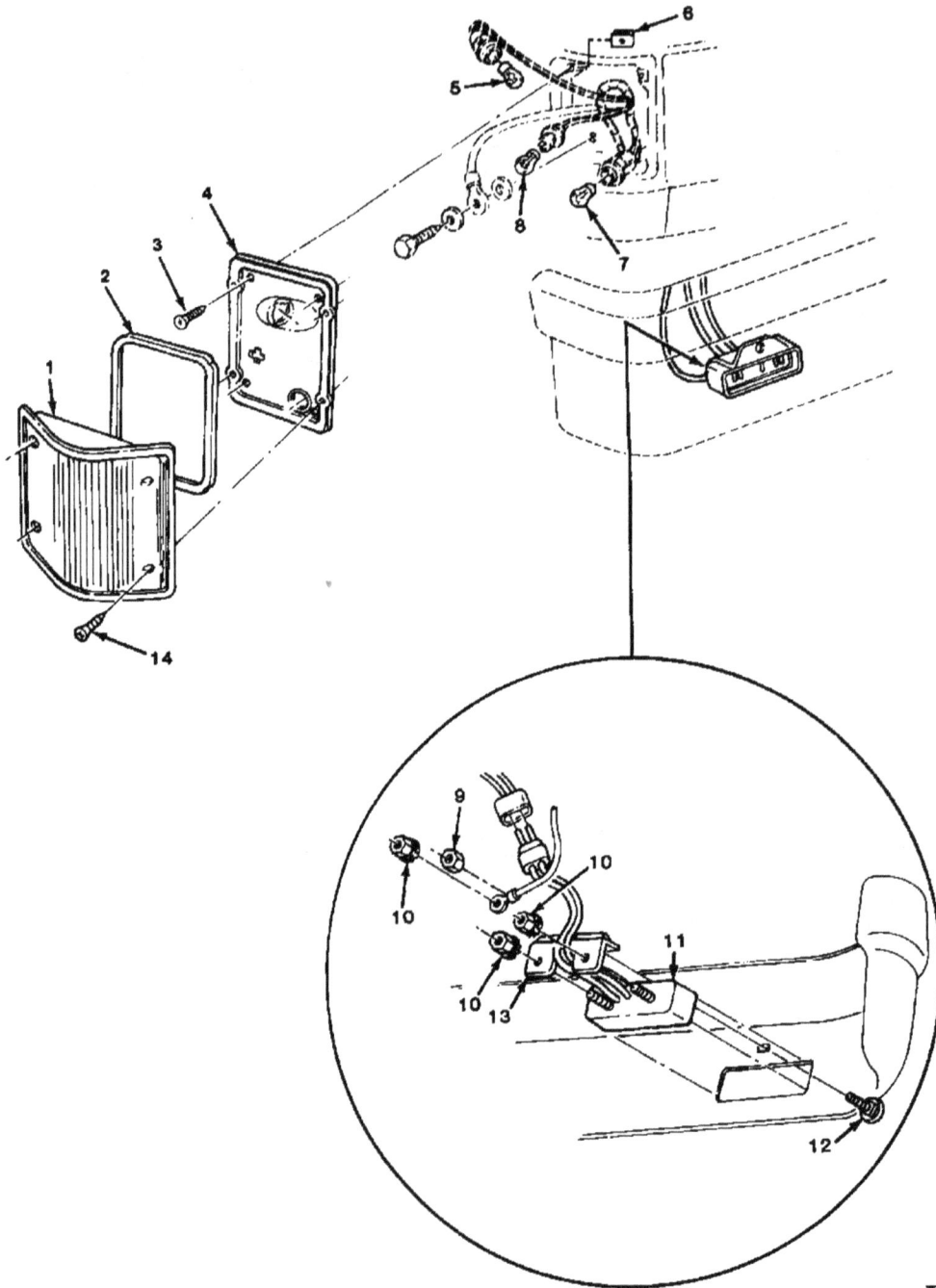

FIGURE 43. REAR BLACKOUT LAMPS AND TAILLAMPS ILLUMINATING COMPONENTS
(ALL EXCEPT M1010 AND M1031).

TA510858

(1) ITEM NO	(2) SMR CODE	(3) CAGEC	(4) PART NUMBER	(5) DESCRIPTION AND USABLE ON CODES (UOC)	(6) QTY
				GROUP 0609 LIGHTS	
				FIG. 43 REAR BLACKOUT LAMPS AND TAILLAMPS ILLUMINATING COMPONENTS (ALL EXCEPT M1010 AND M1031)	
1	PAOZZ	11862	5965775	LENS,LIGHT LEFT UOC:194,208,209,230,252,254,256	1
1	PAOZZ	11862	5965776	LENS,LIGHT RIGHT UOC:194,208,209,230,252,254,256	1
2	PAOZZ	11862	5965748	GASKET UOC:194,208,209,230,252,254,256	2
3	PAOZZ	96906	MS51861-38	SCREW,TAPPING UOC:194,208,209,230,252,254,256	8
4	PAOZZ	11862	5965771	HOUSING,LIGHT LEFT UOC:194,208,209,230,252,254,256	1
4	PAOZZ	11862	5965772	HOUSING,TAIL LAMP RIGHT UOC:194,208,209,230,252,254,256	1
5	PAOZZ	08806	2057	LAMP,INCANDESCENT UOC:194,208,209,230,252,254,256	2
6	PAOZZ	96906	MS90724-34	NUT,SHEET SPRING UOC:194,208,209,230,252,254,256	8
7	PAOZZ	08806	1156	LAMP,INCANDESCENT UOC:194,208,209,230,252,254,256	2
8	PAOZZ	08806	168	LAMP,INCANDESCENT UOC:194,208,209,230,252,254,256	2
9	PAOZZ	24617	11506003	NUT,PLAIN,ASSEMBLED UOC:194,208,209,230,252,254,256	2
10	PAOZZ	72582	271163	NUT,PLAIN,ASSEMBLED UOC:194,208,209,230,252,254,256	6
11	PAOZZ	11862	15559312	LIGHT,MARKER,CLEARA UOC:194,208,209,230,252,254,256	2
12	PAOZZ	24617	11503778	BOLT,SQUARE NECK UOC:194,208,209,230,252	2
13	PAOZZ	11862	14072433	BRACKET,DOUBLE ANGL UOC:209	2
13	PAOZZ	11862	14072434	BRACKETR,DOUBLE ANGL UOC:194,208,230,252,254,256	2
14	PAOZZ	11862	11504655	SCREW,TAPPING UOC:194,208,209,230,252,254,256	8

END OF FIGURE

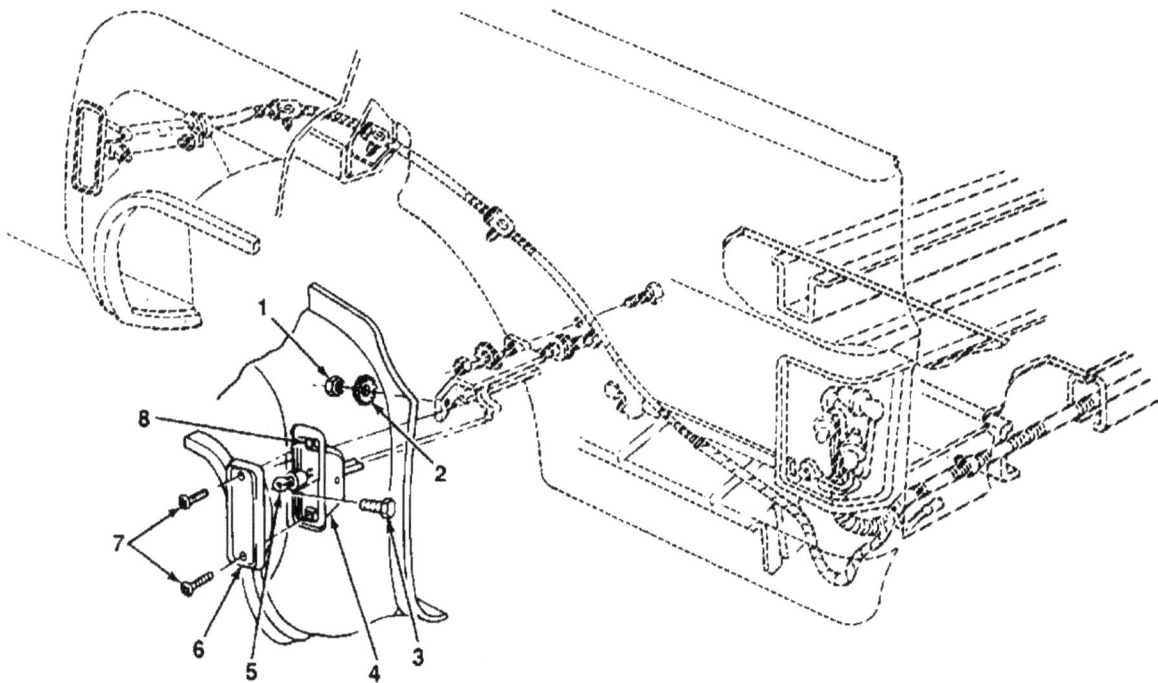

TA510859

FIGURE 44. REAR FENDER SIDE MARKERS (M1028A2 AND M1082A3).

(1) ITEM NO	(2) SMR CODE	(3) CAGEC	(4) PART NUMBER	(5) DESCRIPTION AND USABLE ON CODES (UOC)	(6) QTY
				GROUP 0609 LIGHTS	
				FIG. 44 REAR FENDER SIDE MARKERS (M1028A2 AND M1028A3)	
1	PAOZZ	96906	MS51967-2	NUT,PLAIN,HEXAGON UOC:254,256	2
2	PAOZZ	96906	MS35335-33	WASHER,LOCK UOC:254,256	2
3	PAOZZ	11862	9440033	BOLT,MACHINE UOC:254,256	2
4	PAOZZ	11862	330492	HOUSING,LIGHT UOC:254,256	4
5	PAOZZ	08806	168	LAMP,INCANDESCENT UOC:254,256	1
6	PAOZZ	11862	339885	LIGHT,MARKER,CLEARA UOC:254,256	2
6	PAOZZ	11862	339887	LENS,LIGHT UOC:254,256	2
7	PAOZZ	11862	11504655	SCREW,TAPPING UOC:254,256	2
8	PAOZZ	96906	MS90724-34	NUT,SHEET SPRING UOC:254,256	2

END OF FIGURE

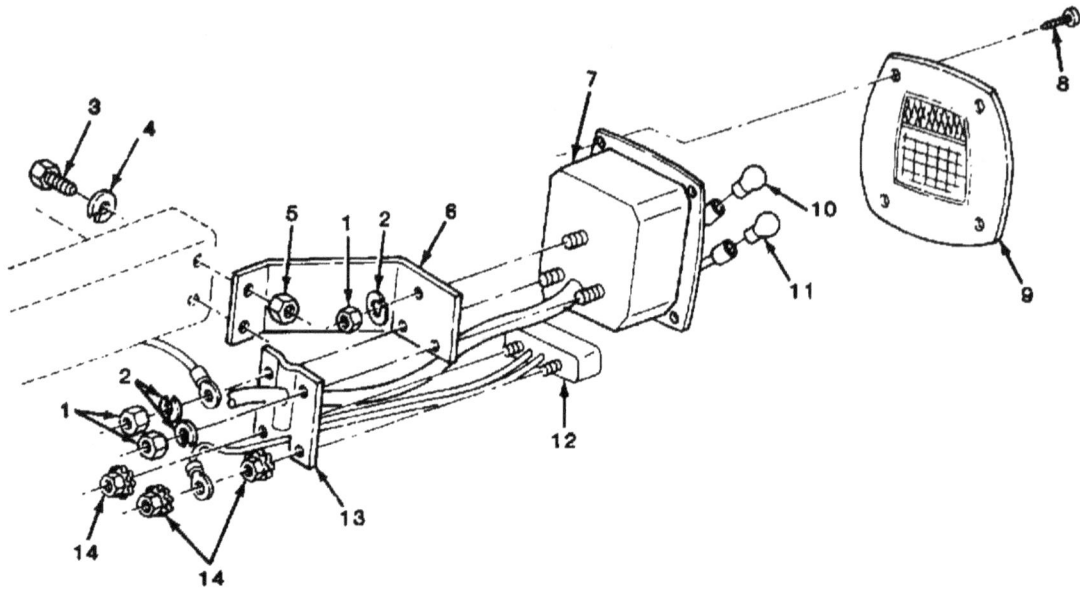

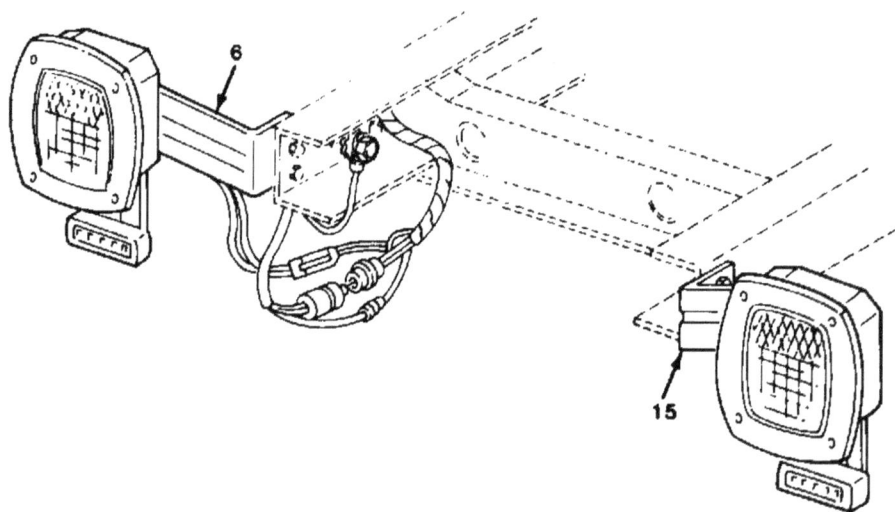

FIGURE 45. REAR BLACKOUT LAMPS AND TAILAMP ILLUMINATING COMPONENTS
(M1010 AND M1031).

TA510860

(1) ITEM NO	(2) SMR CODE	(3) CAGEC	(4) PART NUMBER	(5) DESCRIPTION AND USABLE ON CODES (UOC)	(6) QTY
				GROUP 0609 LIGHTS	
				FIG. 45 REAR BLACKOUT LAMPS AND TAILLAMP ILLUMINATING COMPONENTS (M1010 AND M1031)	
1	PAOZZ	96906	MS51967-2	NUT,PLAIN,HEXAGON UOC:210,231	6
2	PAOZZ	96906	MS35335-33	WASHER,LOCK UOC:210,231	6
3	PAOZZ	96906	MS90728-60	SCREW,CAP,HEXAGON H UOC:210,231	4
4	PAOZZ	96906	MS35340-46	WASHER,LOCK UOC:210,231	4
5	PAOZZ	96906	MS51967-8	NUT,PLAIN,HEXAGON UOC:210,231	4
6	PAOZZ	11862	370873	BRACKET,ANGLE UOC:210,231	1
7	PAOOO	11862	370867	STOP LIGHT-TAILLIGH LEFT UOC:210,231	1
7	PAOOO	11862	370868	STOP LIGHT-TAILLIGH RIGHT UOC:210,231	1
8	PAOZZ	11862	11504736	.SCREW,TAPPING UOC:210,231	4
9	PAOZZ	11862	475922	.LENS,LIGHT UOC:210,231	1
10	PAOZZ	08806	1156	.LAMP,INCANDESCENT UOC:210,231	1
11	PAOZZ	08806	1157	.LAMP,INCANDESCENT UOC:210,231	1
12	PAOZZ	11862	15559312	LIGHT,MARKER,CLEARA UOC:210,231	2
13	PAOZZ	11862	14072481	STRAP,RETAINING UOC:210,231	2
14	PAOZZ	72582	271163	NUT,PLAIN,ASSEMBLED UOC:210,231	6
15	PAOZZ	11862	370874	BRACE,LAMPHOLDER UOC:210,231	1

END OF FIGURE

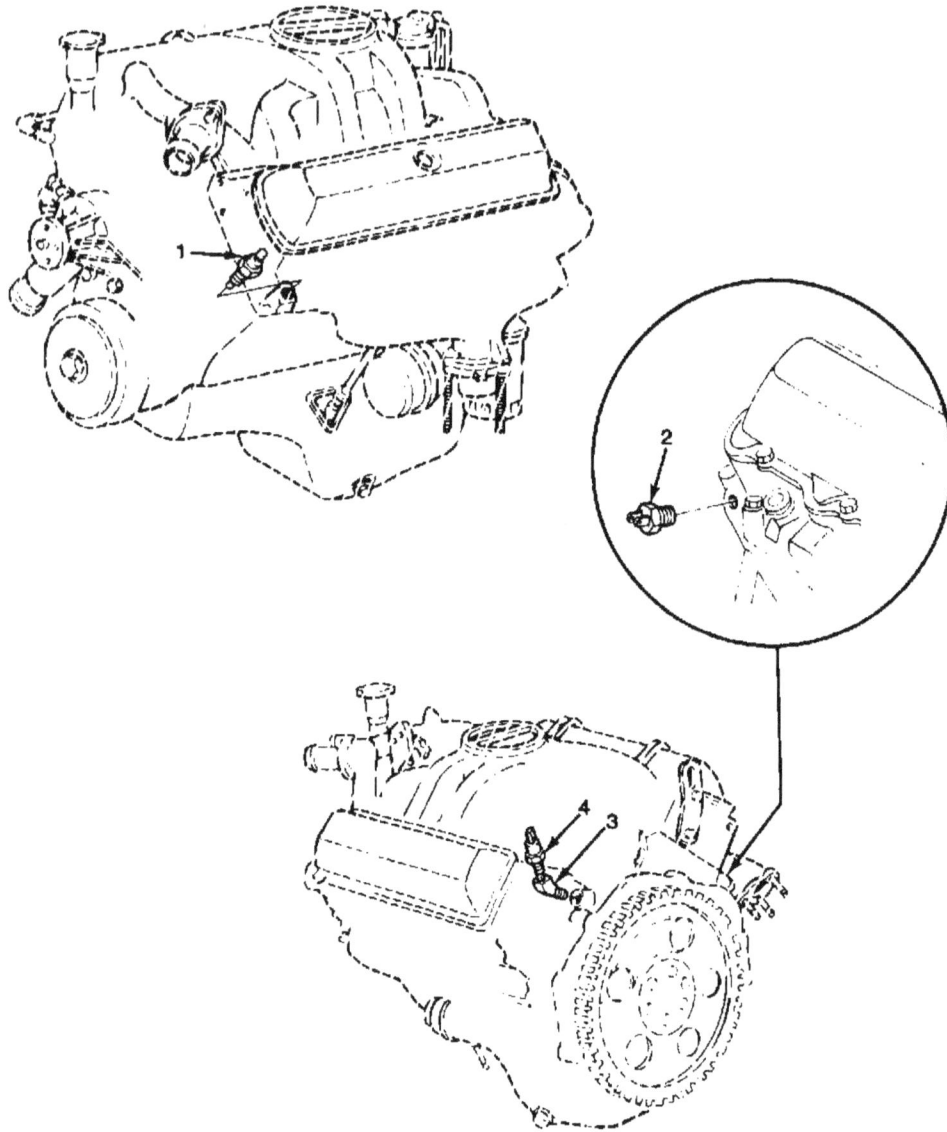

TA510861

FIGURE 46. ENGINE OIL PRESSURE AND WATER TEMPERATURE SENDING UNITS.

(1) ITEM NO	(2) SMR CODE	(3) CAGEC	(4) PART NUMBER	(5) DESCRIPTION AND USABLE ON CODES (UOC)	(6) QTY
				GROUP 0610 SENDING UNITS AND WARNING SWITCHES	
				FIG. 46 ENGINE OIL PRESSURE AND WATER TEMPERATURE SENDING UNITS	
1	PAOZZ	11862	25037177	TRANSMITTER,TEMPERA	1
2	PAOZZ	11862	14071047	SWITCH,COLD AVANCE	1
3	PAOZZ	11862	14040817	ELBOW,PIPE	1
4	PAOZZ	11862	3815936	SWITCH,PRESSURE	1
				END OF FIGURE	

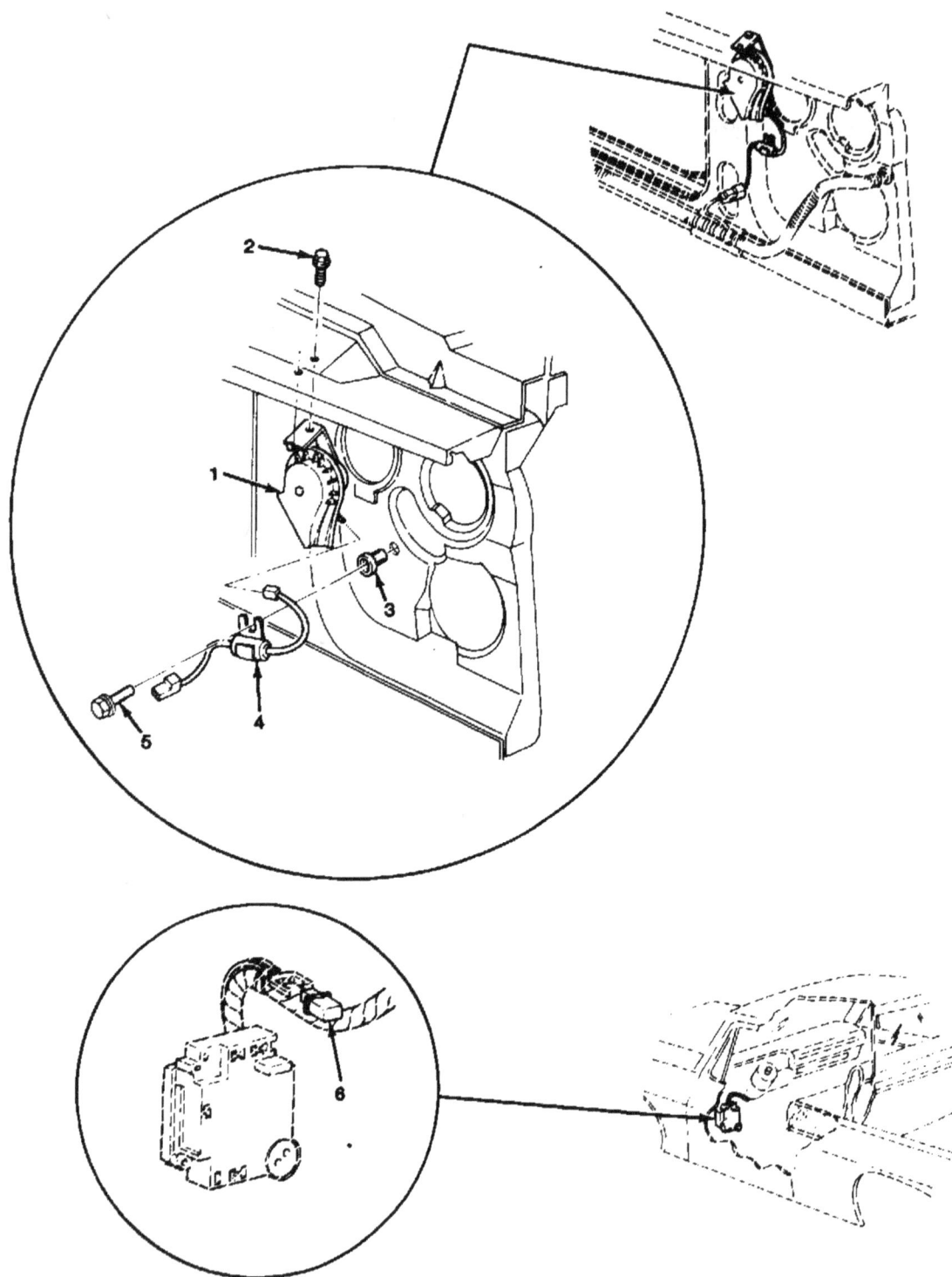

TA510862

FIGURE 47. TRUCK HORN AND RELATED PARTS.

(1) ITEM NO	(2) SMR CODE	(3) CAGEC	(4) PART NUMBER	(5) DESCRIPTION AND USABLE ON CODES (UOC)	(6) QTY
				GROUP 0611 HORN, SIREN	
				FIG. 47 TRUCK HORN AND RELAED PARTS	
1	PAOZZ	11862	1892163	HORN,ELECTRICAL	1
2	PAOZZ	11862	11501812	SCREW,TAPPING	1
3	PAOZZ	00613	C-5139-2	RECEPTACLE,TURNLOCK	1
4	PAOZZ	11862	15599224	CAPACITOR,FIXED,PAP	1
5	PAOZZ	11862	9437702	BOLT,MACHINE	1
6	PAOZZ	11862	25523703	RELAY,ELECTROMAGNET	1

END OF FIGURE

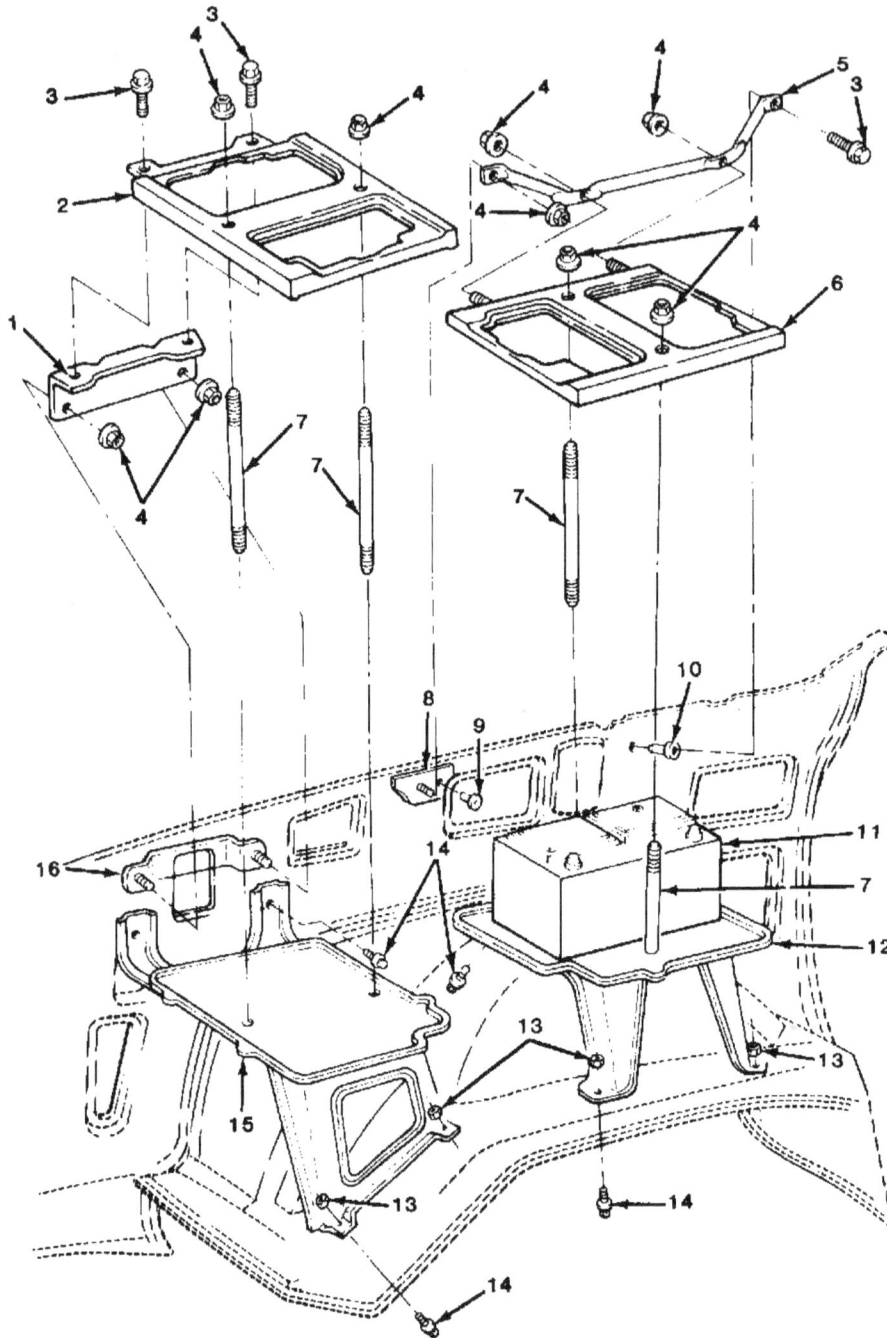

TA510863

FIGURE 48. BATTERIES, BATTERY TRAYS, AND RELATED PARTS.

(1) ITEM NO	(2) SMR CODE	(3) CAGEC	(4) PART NUMBER	(5) DESCRIPTION AND USABLE ON CODES (UOC)	(6) QTY
				GROUP 0612 BATTERIES, STORAGE	
				FIG. 48 BATTERIES, BATTERY TRAYS, AND RELATED PARTS	
1	PAOZZ	11862	15599900	BRACKET,ENGINE ACCE	1
2	PAOZZ	11862	14076856	RETAINER,BATTERY	1
3	PAOZZ	11862	9440334	BOLT,ASSEMBLED WASH	3
4	PAOZZ	24617	11506003	NUT,PALIN,ASSEMBLED	9
5	PAOZZ	11862	14075896	RETAINER,BATTERY	1
6	PAOZZ	11862	14076857	RETAINER,BATTERY	1
7	PAOZZ	11862	14075894	STUD,PLAIN	4
8	PAOZZ	11862	15599902	RETAINER,BATTERY	1
9	PAOZZ	96906	MS20613-4P4	RIVET,SOLID	1
10	PAOZZ	11862	14005953	SHIELD,EXPANSION	1
11	PAOFA	81343	31-620	BATTERY,STORGAE (OPTIONAL WITH P/N MS52149-11	2
11	PAOFA	96906	MS52149-1	BATTERY,STORAGE (OPTIONAL WITH P/N 31-620 AND NOT APPLICABLE W/ WINTERIZED BATTERY BOX)	2
12	PAOZZ	11862	14075389	TRAY,BATTERY	1
13	PAOZZ	11862	1359887	NUT,PLAIN,HEXAGON	4
14	PAOZZ	11862	2014469	BOLT,ASSEMBLED WASH	8
15	PAOZZ	11862	14075388	TRAY,BATTERY	1
16	PAOZZ	11862	15599901	RETAINER,BATTERY	1

END OF FIGURE

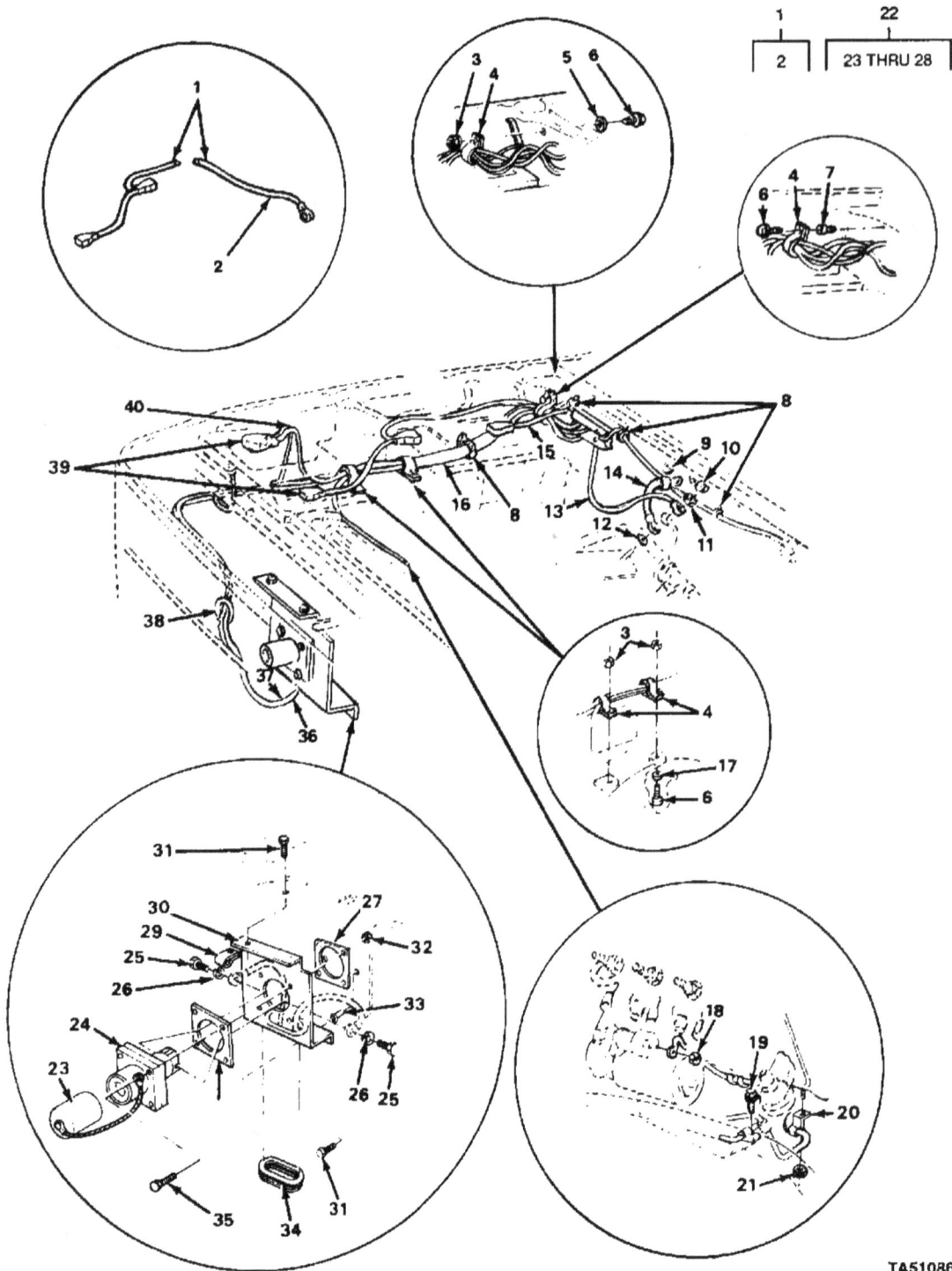

FIGURE 49. CABLES AND SLAVE CONNECTOR.

TA510864

(1) ITEM NO	(2) SMR CODE	(3) CAGEC	(4) PART NUMBER	(5) DESCRIPTION AND USABLE ON CODES (UOC)	(6) QTY
				GROUP 0612 BATTERIES, STORAGE	
				FIG. 49 CABLES AND SLAVE CONNECTOR	
1	PAOOO	11862	12039293	LEAD, STORAGE BATTER	1
2	MOOZZ	11862	FLW-12	.WIRE, FUSELINK (10 IN LG) MAKE FROM WIRE, P/N 6293923	1
3	PAOZZ	24617	271172	NUT,SELFL-LOCKING,AS	3
4	PAOZZ	11862	2043151	CLAMP,LOOP UOC:208	3
5	PAOZZ	96906	MS27183-9	WASHER,FLAT	1
6	PAOZZ	96906	MS90728-6	SCREW,CAP,HEXAGON H UOC:194,208,209,210,230,231,252,254	3
7	PAOZZ	11862	14005953	SHIELD,EXPANSION	1
8	PAOZZ	11862	3816659	STRAP,LINE SUPPORTI	4
9	PAOZZ	96906	MS35335-34	WASHER,LOCK	1
10	PAOZZ	11862	11509371	SCREW,ASSEMBLED WAS	1
11	PAOZZ	11862	14005953	SHIELD,EXPANSION	1
12	PAOZZ	96906	MS35335-36	WASHER,LOCK	1
13	PAOZZ	11862	12039271	LEAD,ELECTRICAL	1
14	PAOZZ	11862	6287160	LEAD,STORAGE BATTER	1
15	PAOZZ	58499	6258	LEAD,STORAGE BATTER	1
16	PAOZZ	11862	12039272	LEAD,ELECTRICAL	1
17	PAOZZ	96906	MS27183-10	WASHER,FLAT	2
18	PAOZZ	11862	11504108	NUT,PLAIN,HEXAGON	1
19	PAOZZ	11862	11504447	SCREW,TAPPING UOC:208	1
20	PAOZZ	11862	14040813	CLIP,SPRING TENSION RIGHT	1
21	PAOZZ	11862	11503739	NUT, PLAIN,HEXAGON	1
22	PAOOO	19207	11674728	CONNECTOR,RECEPTACL	1
23	PAOZZ	19207	11675004	.CAP,PROTECTIVE,DUST	1
24	PAOZZ	19207	11682345	.CONNECTOR,RECEPTACL	1
25	PAOZZ	96906	MS90727-57	.SCREW,CAP,HEXAGON H	2
26	PAOZZ	96906	MS35338-46	.WASHER,LOCK	2
27	PAOZZ	19207	11674730	.INSULATOR,PLATE	1
28	PAOZZ	19207	11674729	.GASKET	1
29	PAOZZ	11862	3982098	NUT,PLAIN,HEXAGON	2
30	PAOZZ	11862	14072432	BRACKET,DOUBLE ANGL	1
31	PAOZZ	11862	9440334	NUT,PLAIN,EXTENDED	4
32	PAOZZ	11862	11508446	NUT,PLAIN,EXTENDED	4
33	PAOZZ	11862	14005953	SHIELD,EXPANSION	2
34	PAOZZ	11862	3979756	GROMMET,NONMETALLIC	1
35	PAOZZ	11862	11508858	SCREW,ASSEMBLED WASH	4
36	PAOZZ	11862	12039257	LEAD,ELECTRICAL	1
37	PAOZZ	11862	12039267	LEAD,ELECTRICAL	1
38	MOOZZ	11862	8919163	CONDT BAT BST CBL (6.OO"LG)) MAKE FROM CONDUIT,P/N 8919355	1
39	PAOZZ	96906	MS75004-2	TERMINAL,LUG	1
39	PAOZZ	96906	MS75004-1	TERMINAL,LUG	1
40	PAOZZ	58499	6262	LEAD,STORAGE BATTER	1

END OF FIGURE

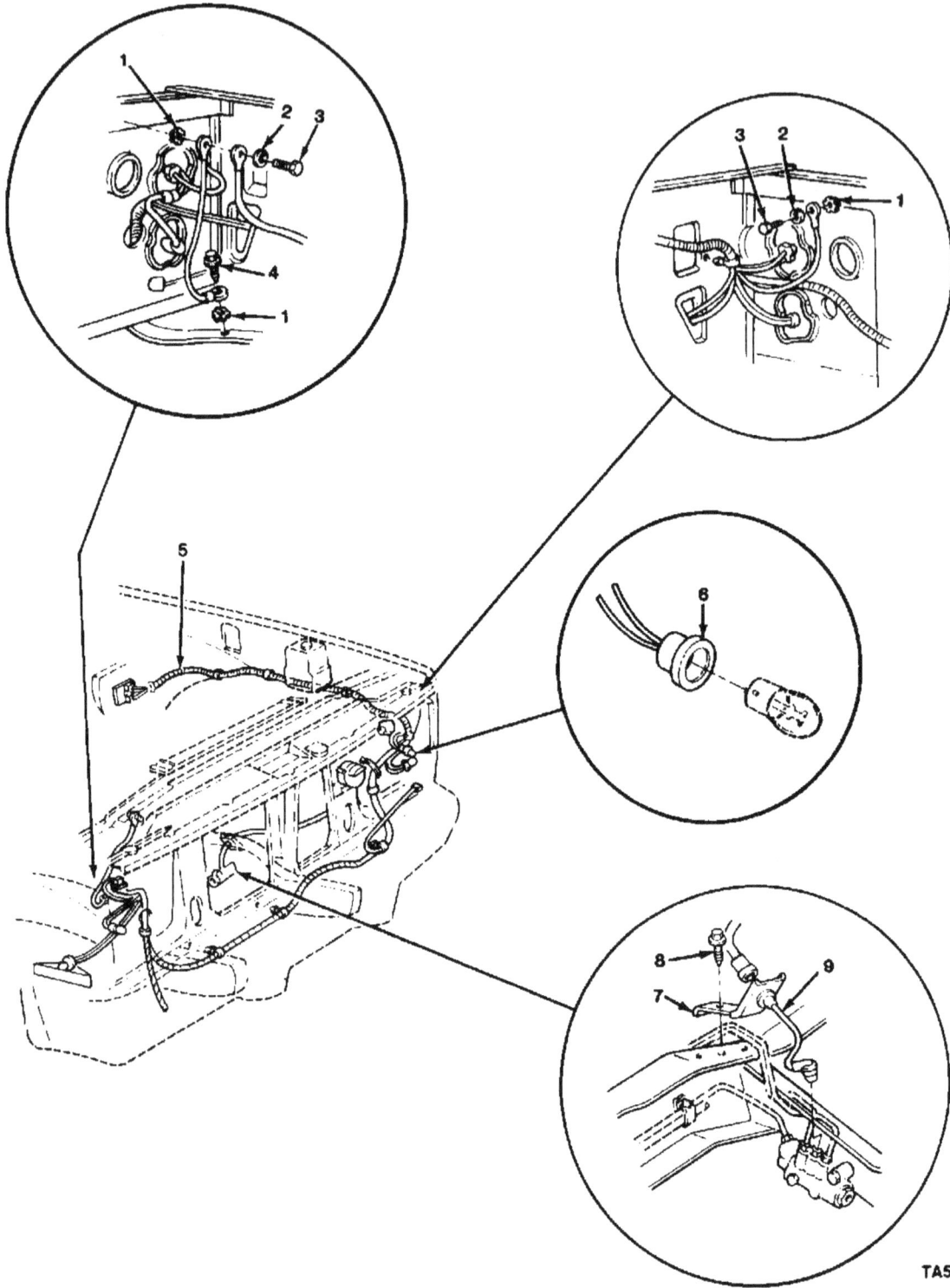

FIGURE 50. FRONT WIRING HARNESS.

TA510865

(1) ITEM NO	(2) SMR CODE	(3) CAGEC	(4) PART NUMBER	(5) DESCRIPTION AND USABLE ON CODES (UOC)	(6) QTY
				GROUP 0613 HULL OR CHASSIS WIRING HARNESS	
				FIG. 50 FRONT WIRING HARNESS	
6	PAOZZ	11862	12013813	LAMPHOLDER	2
7	PAOZZ	11862	469339	BRACKET,DOUBLE ANGL	1
8	PAOZZ	24617	9416187	SCREW,TAPPING	1
9	PAOZZ	11862	12001184	CABLE ASSEMBLY,SPEC	1
				END OF FIGURE	

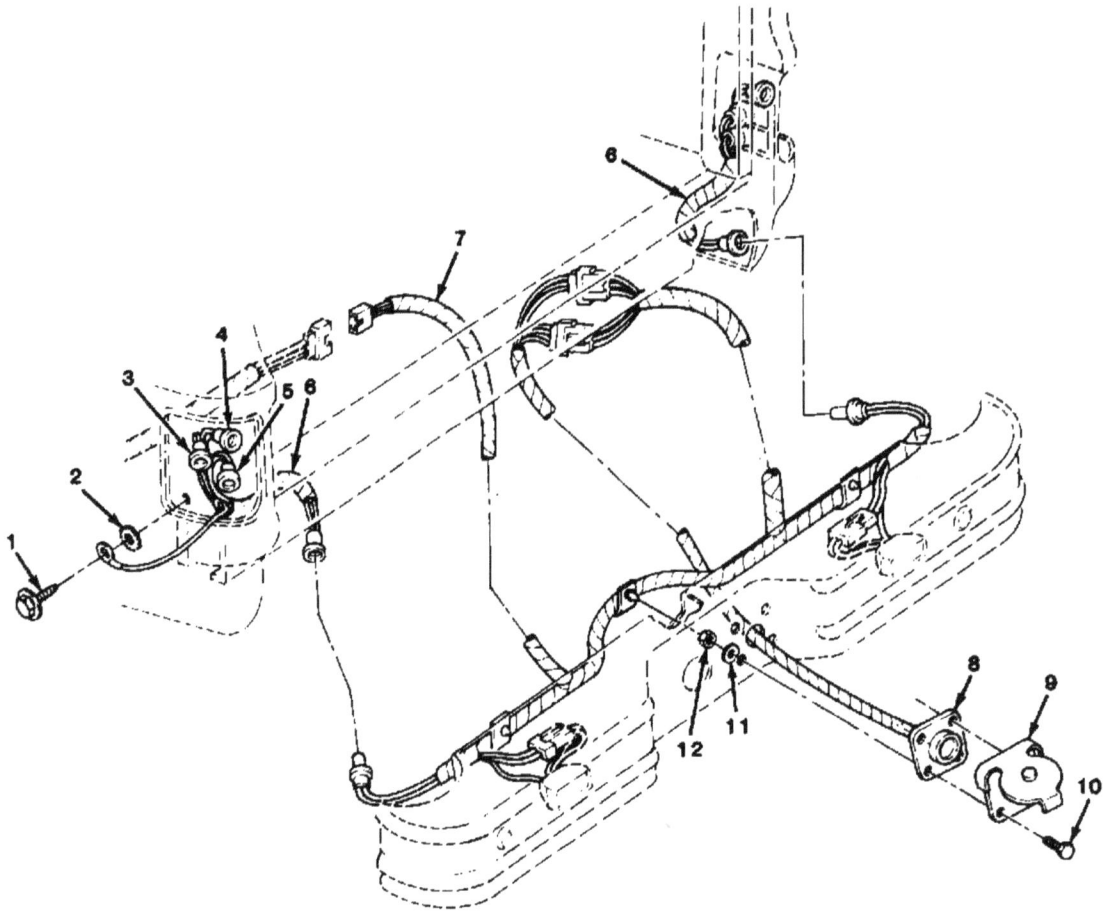

TA510868

FIGURE 51. BLACKOUT AND TAILAMP WIRING HARNESS (ALL EXCEPT M1010
AND M1031) AND TRAILER WIRING HARNESS (ALL EXCEPT MI 010).

(1) ITEM NO	(2) SMR CODE	(3) CAGEC	(4) PART NUMBER	(5) DESCRIPTION AND USABLE ON CODES (UOC)	(6) QTY
				GROUP 0613 HULL OR CHASSIS WIRING HARNESS	
				FIG. 51 BLACKOUT AND TAILLAMP WIRING HARNESS (ALL EXCEPT M1010 AND M1031) AND TRAILER WIRING HARNESS (ALL EXCEPT M1010)	
1	PAOZZ	96906	MS51850-86	SCREW,TAPPING UOC:194,208,209,230,252,254,256	2
2	PAOZZ	96906	MS35335-33	WASHER,LOCK UOC:194,208,230,252,254,256	1
3	PAOZZ	11862	6298886	LAMPHOLDER UOC:194,208,209,230,252,254,256	2
4	XDOZZ	11862	8914822	SOCKET,TAIL LAMP UOC:194,208,209,230,252,254,256	2
5	PAOZZ	11862	8909518	LAMPHOLDER UOC:194,208,209,230,252,254,256	2
6	PAOZZ	11862	8906150	WIRING HARNESS,BRAN UOC:194,208,209,230,252,254,256	2
7	PAOZZ	11862	12039205	WIRING HARNESS,BRAN UOC:194,208,230,252,254,256	1
8	PAOZZ	11862	12039208	WIRING HARNESS,BRAN UOC:194,208,209,230,252,254,256	1
9	PAOZZ	19207	7731428	COVER,ELECTRICAL CO UOC:194,208,209,230,252,254,256	1
10	PAOZZ	96906	MS90728-6	SCREW,CAP,HEXAGON H UOC:194,208,209,230,252,254,256	4
11	PAOZZ	96906	MS27183-10	WASHER,FLAT UOC:194,209,230,252,254,256	4
12	PAOZZ	96906	MS35691-406	NUT,PLAIN,HEXAGON UOC:194,208,209,230,252,254,256	4

END OF FIGURE

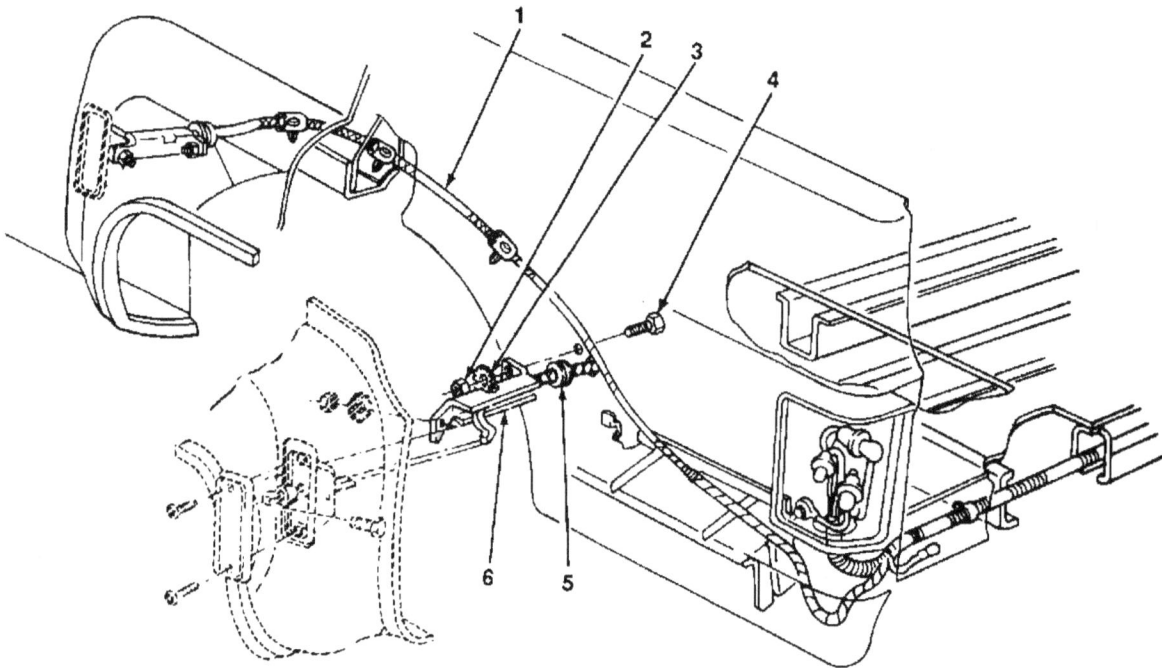

TA510869

FIGURE 52. REAR FENDER WIRING HARNESS (M1028A2 AND M1028A3).

(1) ITEM NO	(2) SMR CODE	(3) CAGEC	(4) PART NUMBER	(5) DESCRIPTION AND USABLE ON CODES (UOC)	(6) QTY
				GROUP 0613 HULL OR CHASSIS WIRING HARNESS	
				FIG.52 REAR FENDER WIRING HARNESS (M1028112 AND M1028A3)	
2	PAOZZ	96906	MS51967-2	NUT,PLAIN,HEXAGON UOC:254,256	2
3	PAOZZ	96906	MS35335-33	WASHER,LOCK UOC:254,256	2
4	PAOZZ	11862	9440033	BOLT,MACHINE UOC:254,256	2
5	PAOZZ	11862	15591130	GROMMET,NONMETALLIC UOC:254,256	8

END OF FIGURE

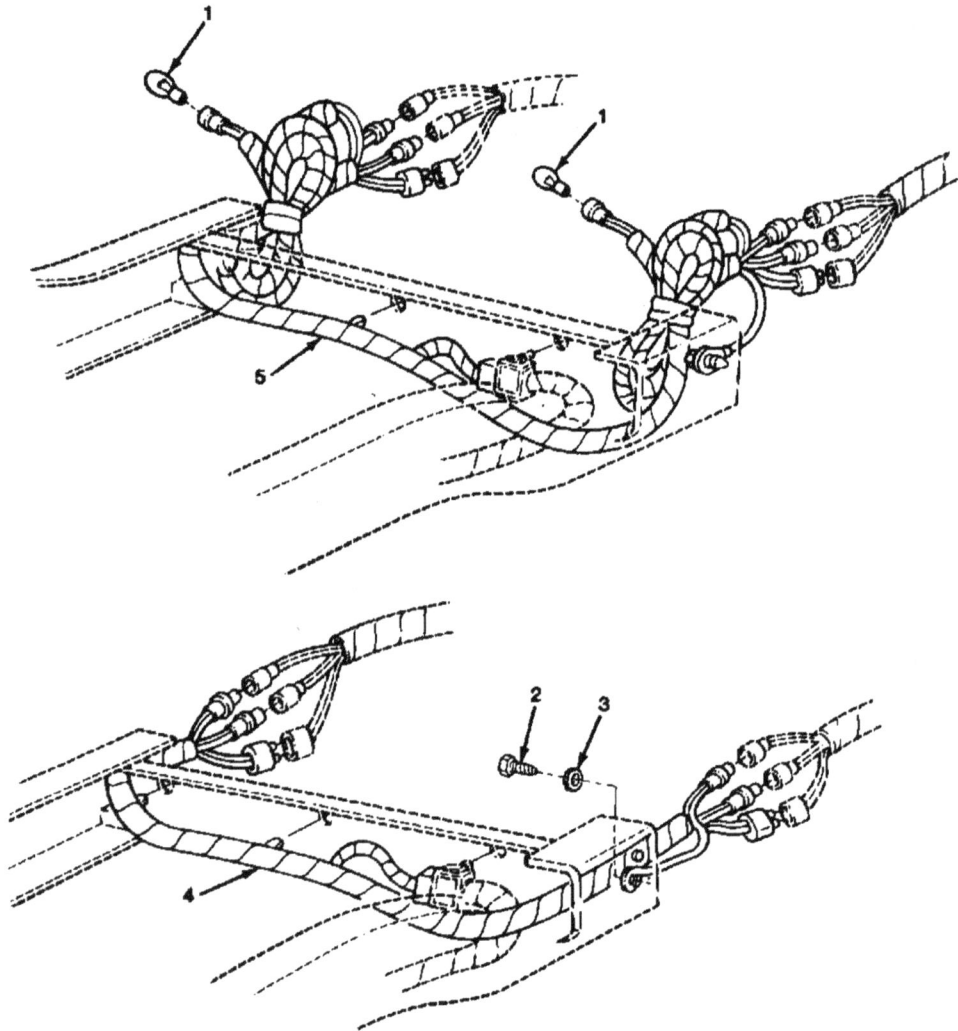

TA510870

FIGURE 53. BLACKOUT AND TAILLAMP WIRING HARNESSES (M1010 AND M1031).

(1) ITEM NO	(2) SMR CODE	(3) CAGEC	(4) PART NUMBER	(5) DESCRIPTION AND USABLE ON CODES (UOC)	(6) QTY
				GROUP 0613 HULL OR CHASSIS WIRING HARNESS	
				FIG. 53 BLACKOUT AND TAILLAMP WIRING HARNESS (M1010 AND M1031)	
1	PAOZZ	08806	194	LAMP, INCANDESCENT UOC:210,231	2
2	PAOZZ	11862	11504447	SCREW, TAPPING UOC:210,231	1
3	PAOZZ	96906	MS35335-34	WASHER, LOCK UOC:210,231	1
				END OF FIGURE	

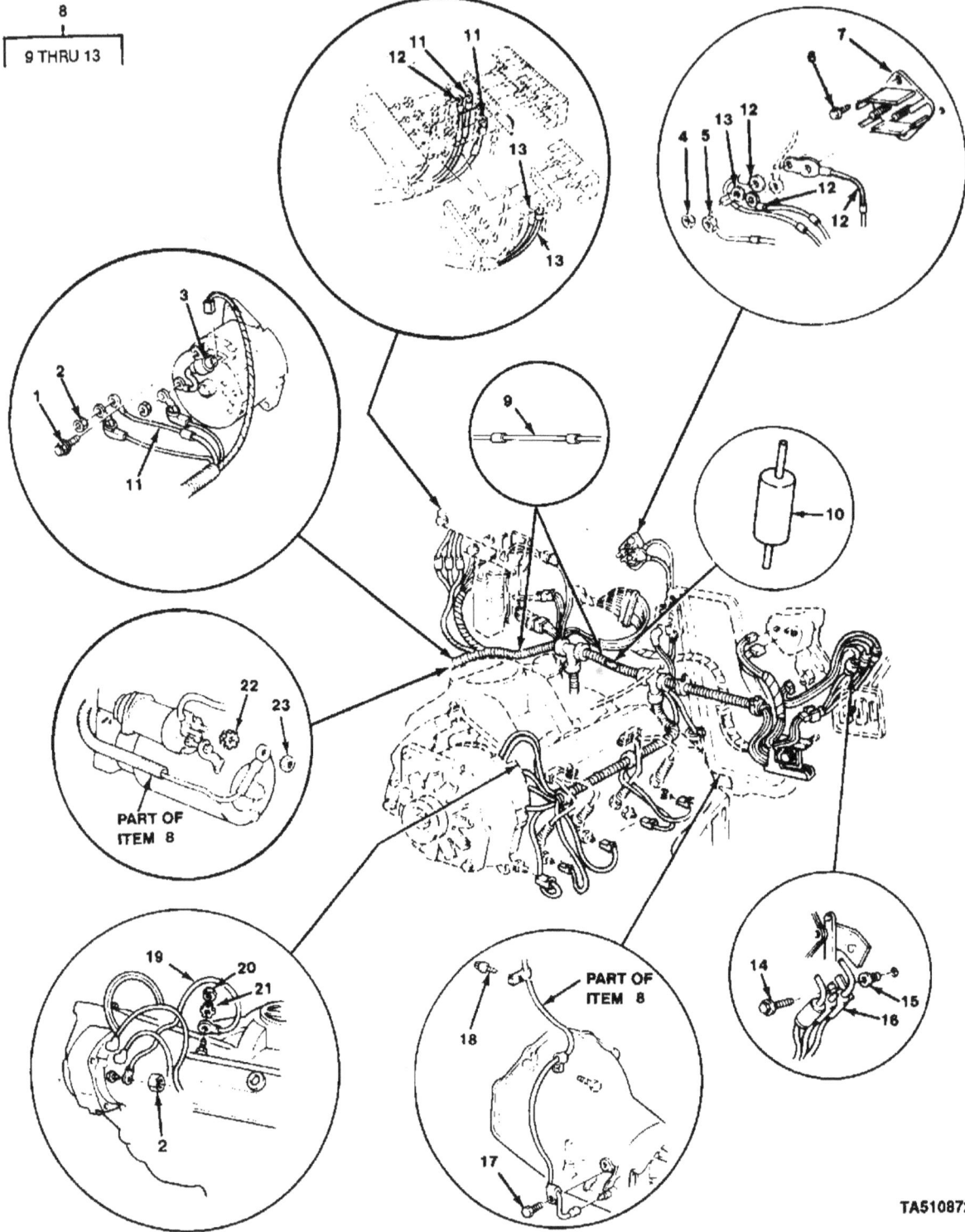

FIGURE 54. ENGINE WIRING HARNESS (ALL EXCEPT M1010).

TA510872

(1) ITEM NO	(2) SMR CODE	(3) CAGEC	(4) PART NUMBER	(5) DESCRIPTION AND USABLE ON CODES (UOC)	(6) QTY
				GROUP 0613 HULL OR CHASSIS WIRING HARNESS	
				FIG. 54 ENGINE WIRING HARNESS (ALL EXCEPT M1010)	
1	PAOZZ	24617	11508687	BOLT,MACHINE UOC:194,208,209,230,231,252,254,256	1
2	PAOZZ	24617	11506003	NUT,PLAIN,ASSEMBLED UOC:194,208,209,230,231,252,254,256	2
3	PAOZZ	11862	1988380	CAPACITOR.,FIXED,PAP UOC:194,208,209,230,231,252,254,256	1
4	PAOZZ	24617	271166	NUT,PLAIN,ASSEMBLED	1
5	PAOZZ	24617	271172	NUT,SELF-LOCKING,AS	1
6	PAOZZ	24617	1640810	SCREW,TAPPING	2
7	PAOZZ	11862	3996270	TERMINAL BOARD	1
10	PAOZZ	11862	12006377	.RECTIFIER,CONNECTOR UOC:194,208,209,230,231,252,254,256	1
14	PAOZZ	11862	9437702	BOLT,MACHINE	1
15	PAOZZ	11862	14005953	SHIELD,EXPANSION	1
16	PAOZZ	11862	15599222	CAPACITOR ASSEMBLY	1
19	PAOZZ	11862	12039253	LEAD,ELECTRICAL UOC:194,208,209,230,231,252,254,256	1
20	PAOZZ	11862	14005953	SHIELD,EXPANSION UOC:194,208,209,210,230,231,252,254	1
21	PAOZZ	96906	MS35335-36	WASHER,LOCK	1
22	PAOZZ	96906	MS35335-33	WASHER,LOCK	1

END OF FIGURE

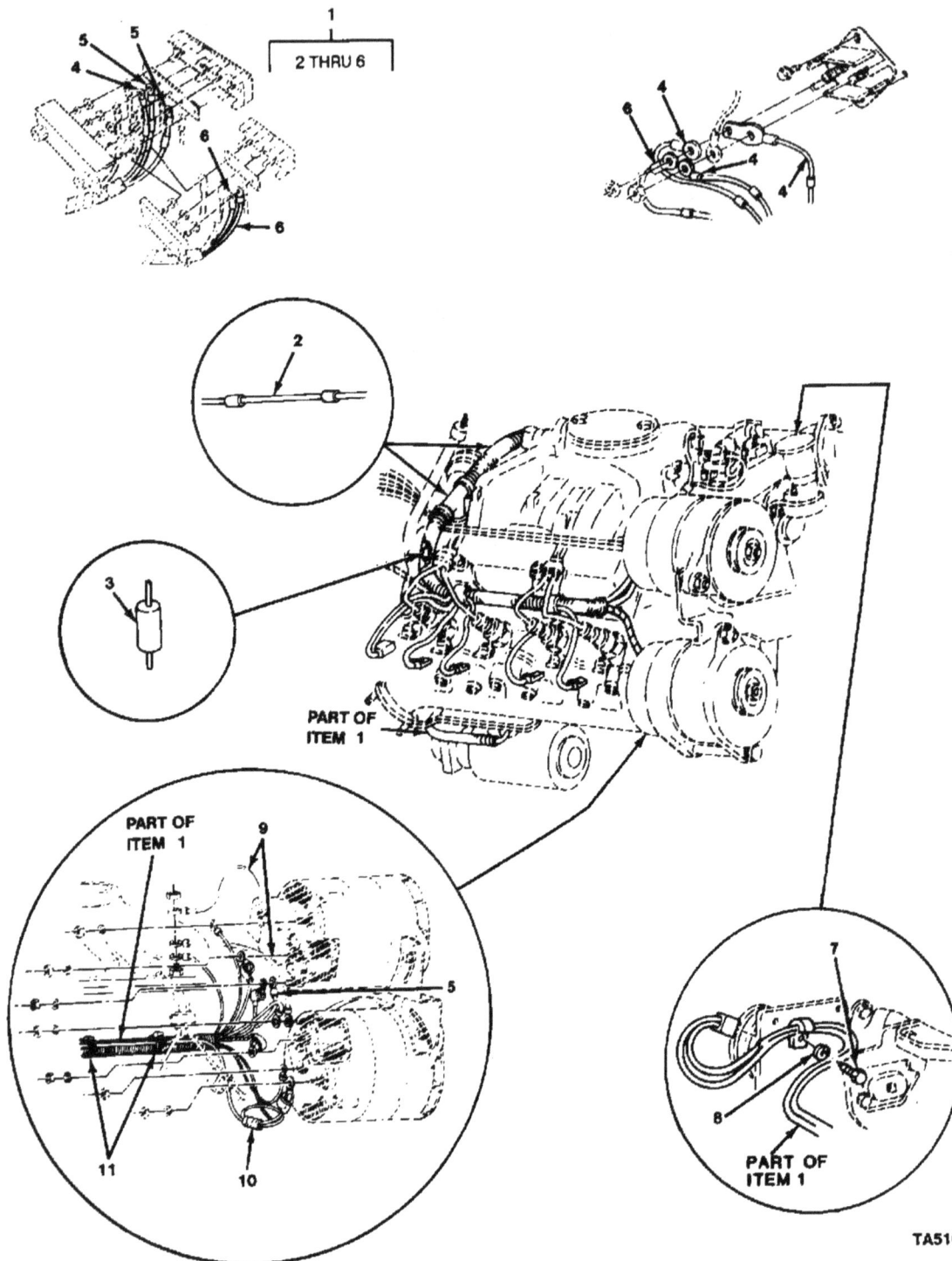

FIGURE 55. ENGINE WIRING HARNESS (M1010).

TA510873

(1)	(2)	(3)	(4)	(5)	(6)
ITEM	SMR		PART		
NO	CODE	CAGEC	NUMBER	DESCRIPTION AND USABLE ON CODES (UOC)	QTY

GROUP 0613 HULL OR CHASSIS WIRING
HARNESS

FIG. 55 ENGINE WIRING HARNESS
(M1010)

3	PAOZZ	11862	12006377	.RECTIFIER,CONNECTOR UOC:210	3
7	PAOZZ	11862	11502656	BOLT,MACHINE UOC:210,230	1
8	PAOZZ	96906	MS35338-45	WASHER,LOCK UOC:210,230	1
9	PAOZZ	11862	12039253	LEAD,ELECTRICAL UOC:210	2

END OF FIGURE

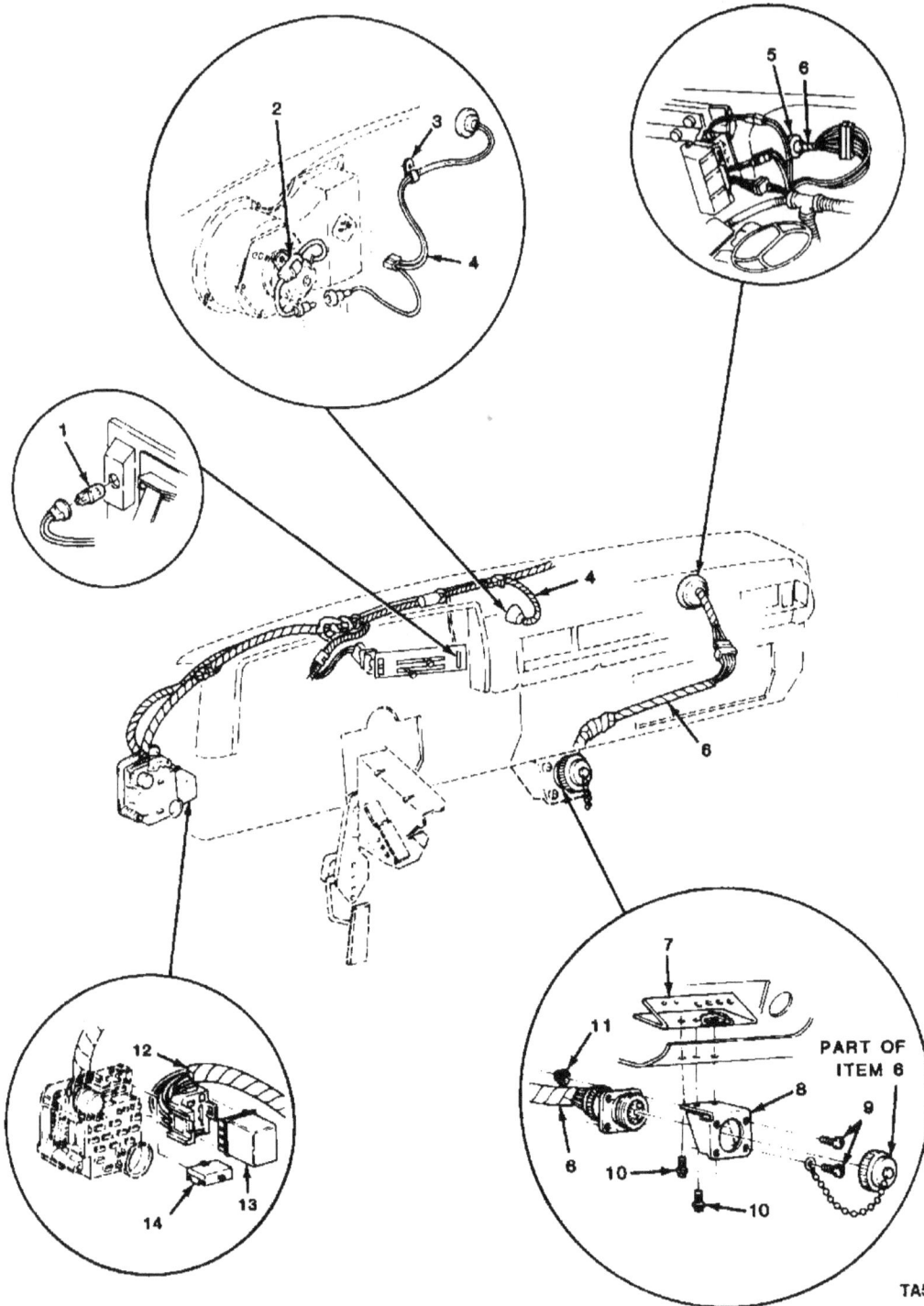

TA510875

FIGURE 56. HEATER CONTROL, DIAGNOSTIC, AND DOOR ALARM WIRING HARNESSES.

(1) ITEM NO	(2) SMR CODE	(3) CAGEC	(4) PART NUMBER	(5) DESCRIPTION AND USABLE ON CODES (UOC)	(6) QTY
				GROUP 0613 HULL OR CHASSIS WIRING HARNESS	
				FIG. 56 HEATER CONTROL, DIAGNOSTIC, AND DOOR ALARM WIRING HARNESSES	
1	PAOZZ	08806	194	LAMP, INCANDESCENT UOC:194,208,209,210,230,231,252	1
2	PAOZZ	11862	15599223	CAPACITOR, FIXED, PAP	1
7	PAOZZ	11862	14072340	BRACKET, ANGLE	1
8	PAOZZ	11862	14074480	BRACKET, ANGLE	1
9	PAOZZ	96906	MS35206-245	SCREW, MACHINE	4
10	PAOZZ	11862	1244067	BOLT, ASSEMBLED WASH	3
11	PAOZZ	72582	271163	NUT, PLAIN, ASSEMBLED	4
13	PAOZZ	11862	22529441	ALARM, DOOR ASSEMBLY UOC:210	1
14	PAOZZ	11862	1253637	BUZZER	1

END OF FIGURE

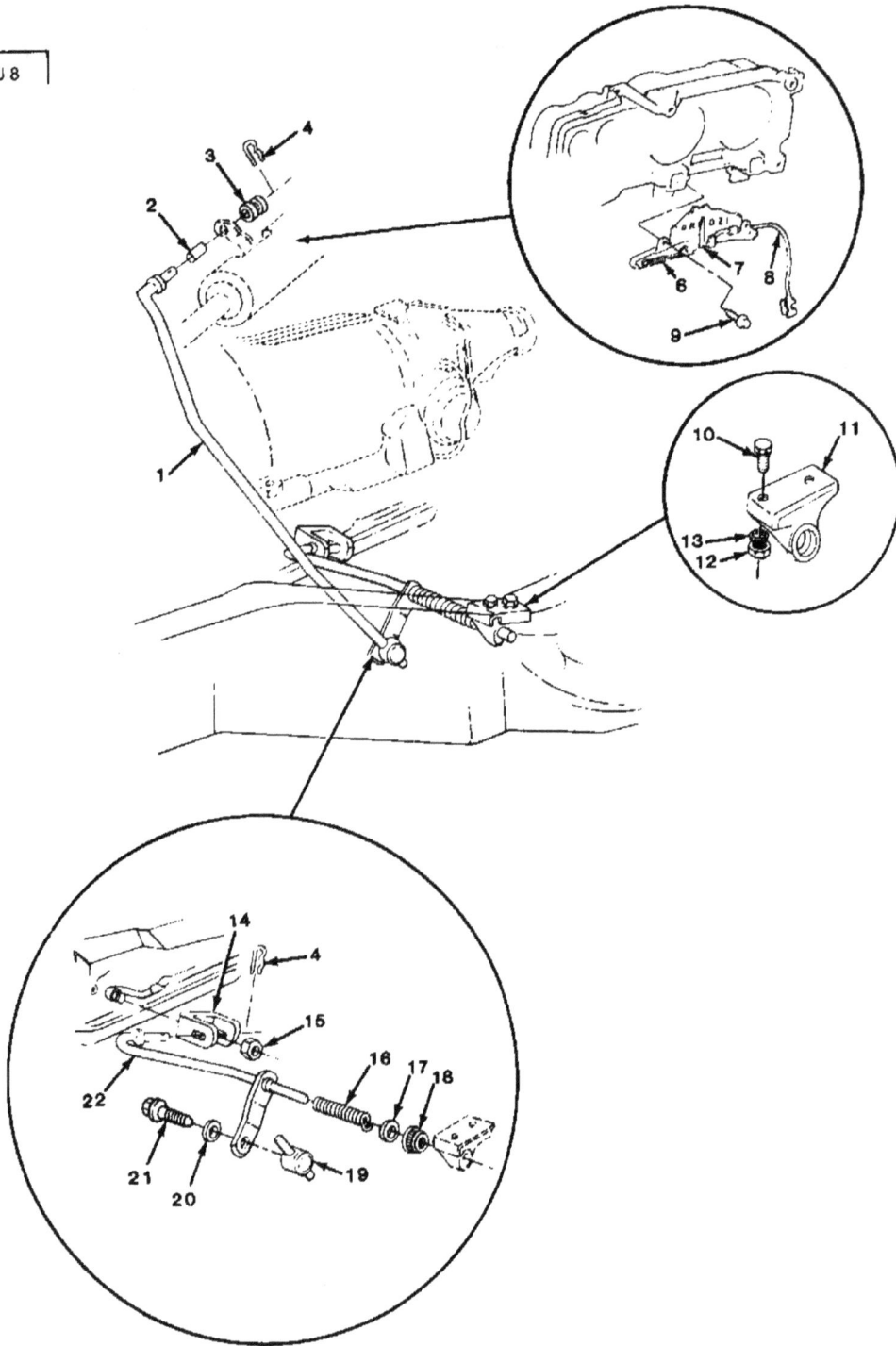

FIGURE 57. SHIFTING

TA510876

(1) ITEM NO	(2) SMR CODE	(3) CAGEC	(4) PART NUMBER	(5) DESCRIPTION AND USABLE ON CODES (UOC)	(6) QTY
				GROUP 07 TRANSMISSION	
				GROUP 0705 TRANSMISSION SHIFTING COMPONENTS	
				FIG. 57 SHIFTING LINKAGE	
5	PAOOO	11862	25078571	SHIFT INDICATOR,HYD	1
6	PAOZZ	11862	8985418	.SPRING,HELICAL,EXTE	1
7	PAOZZ	70040	25023641	.POINTER,SHIFT INDIC	1
8	PAOZZ	11862	25078578	.CABLE,SHIFT INDICAT	1
9	PAOZZ	96906	MS51850-86	SCREW,TAPPING	2
				END OF FIGURE	

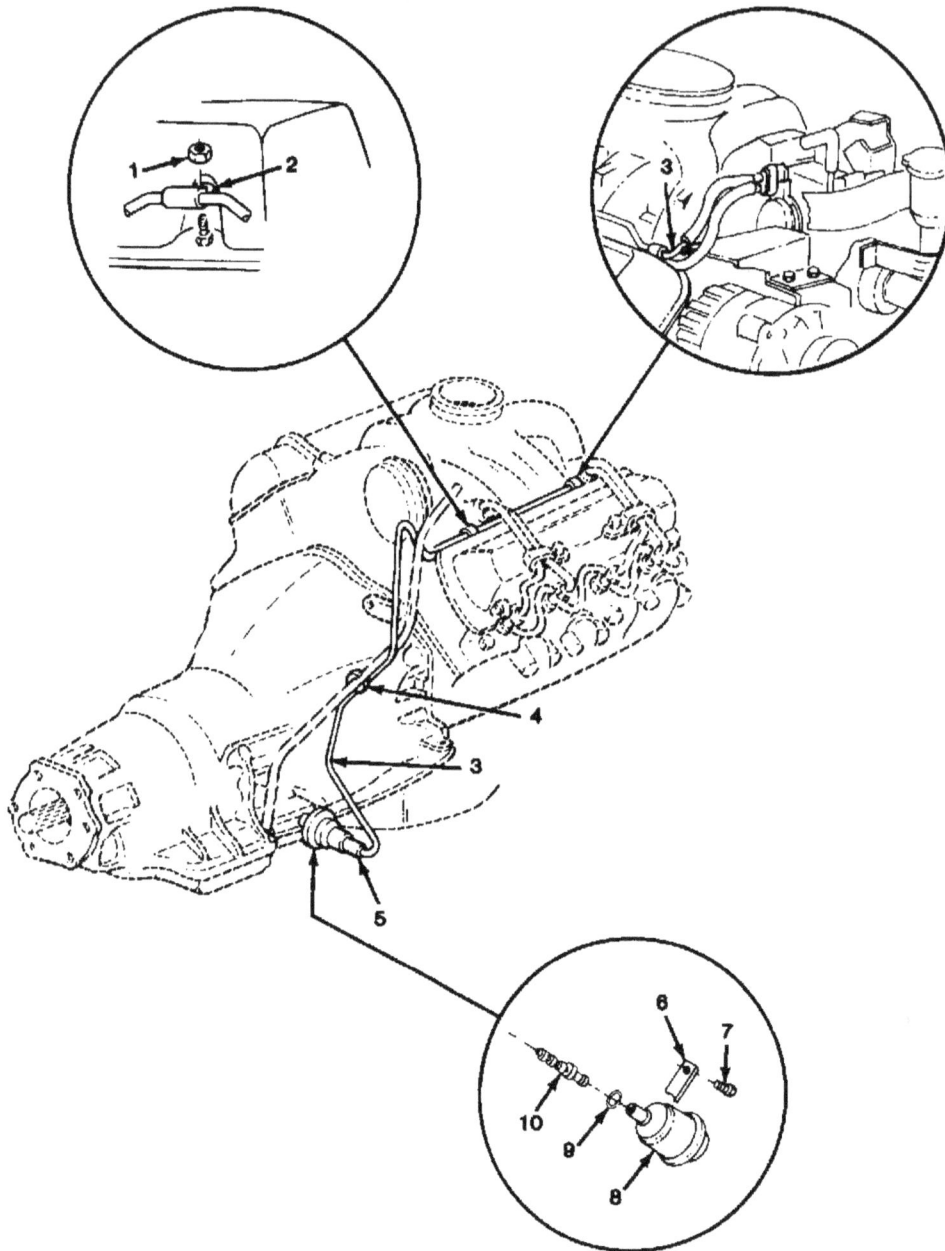

TA510877

FIGURE 58. VACUUM MODULATOR VALVE.

(1)	(2)	(3)	(4)	(5)	(6)
ITEM NO	SMR CODE	CAGEC	PART NUMBER	DESCRIPTION AND USABLE ON CODES (UOC)	QTY

GROUP 0705 TRANSMISSION SHIFTING COMPONENTS

FIG. 58 VACUUM MODULATOR VALVE

1	PAOZZ	11862	22521550	NUT,PLAIN,HEXAGON	2
2	PAOZZ	11862	2044779	CLAMP	2
3	MFOZZ	11862	15599235	PIPE-TRNS VAC MOD (49.11"LG) MAKE FROM TUBE, P/N 603827	1
4	PAOZZ	11862	2043150	CLAMP,LOOP	1
5	MFOZZ	11862	326560	HOSE-TRNS VAL MOD P (1.30"LG) MAKE FROM HOSE,P/N 9439274	1

END OF FIGURE

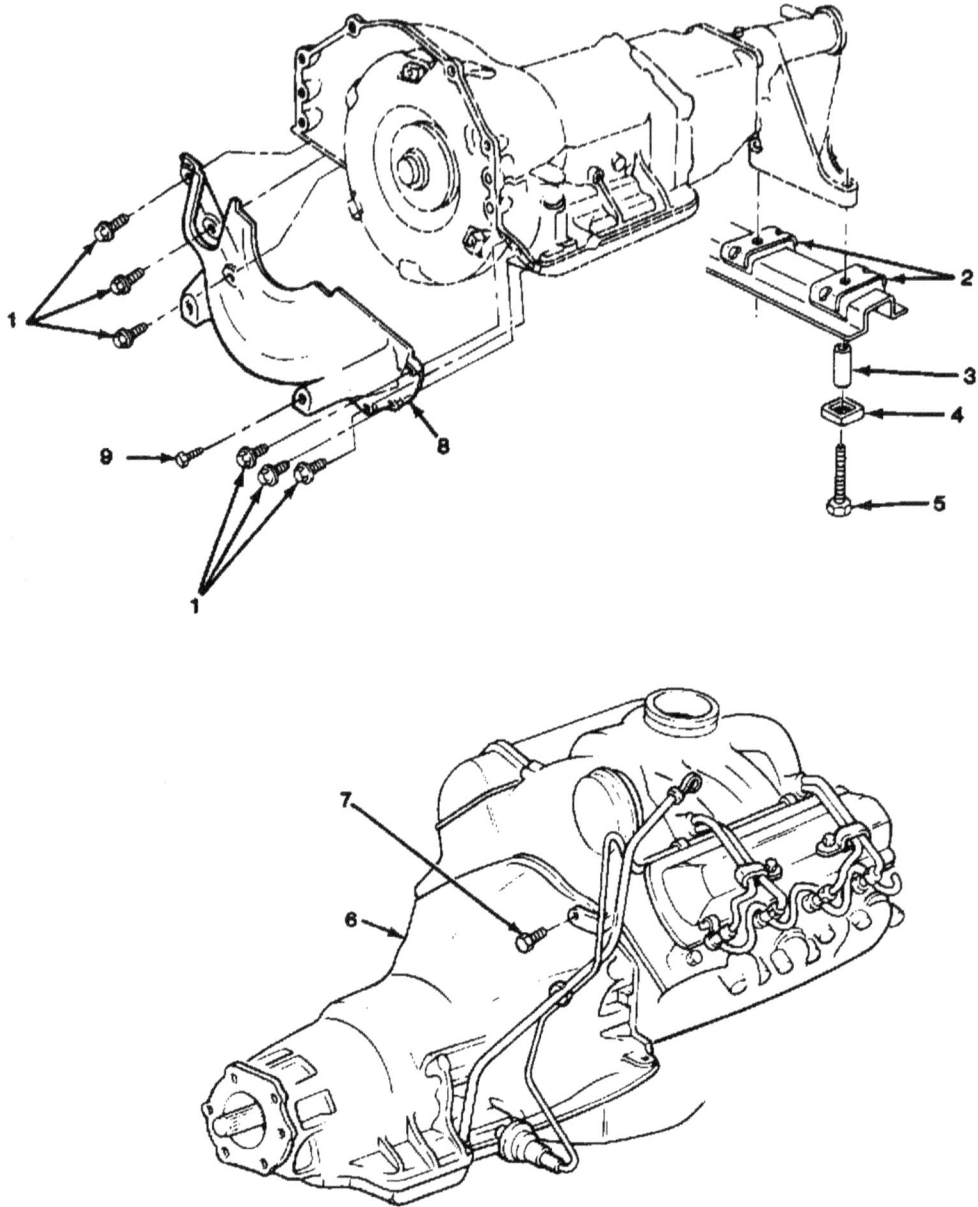

TA510878

FIGURE 59. TRANSMISSION ASSEMBLY AND MOUNTS.

(1) ITEM NO	(2) SMR CODE	(3) CAGEC	(4) PART NUMBER	(5) DESCRIPTION AND USABLE ON CODES (UOC)	(6) QTY
				GROUP 0710 TRANSMISSION ASSEMBLY AND ASSOCIATED PARTS	
				FIG. 59 TRANSMISSION ASSEMBLY AND MOUNTS	
1	PAOZZ	11862	1635490	BOLT,SELF-LOCKING	6
8	PAOZZ	11862	15522022	COVER,ACCESS	1
9	PAOZZ	96906	MS90728-83	SCREW,CAP,HEXAGON H UOC:194,208,209,210,230,231,252,254	2

END OF FIGURE

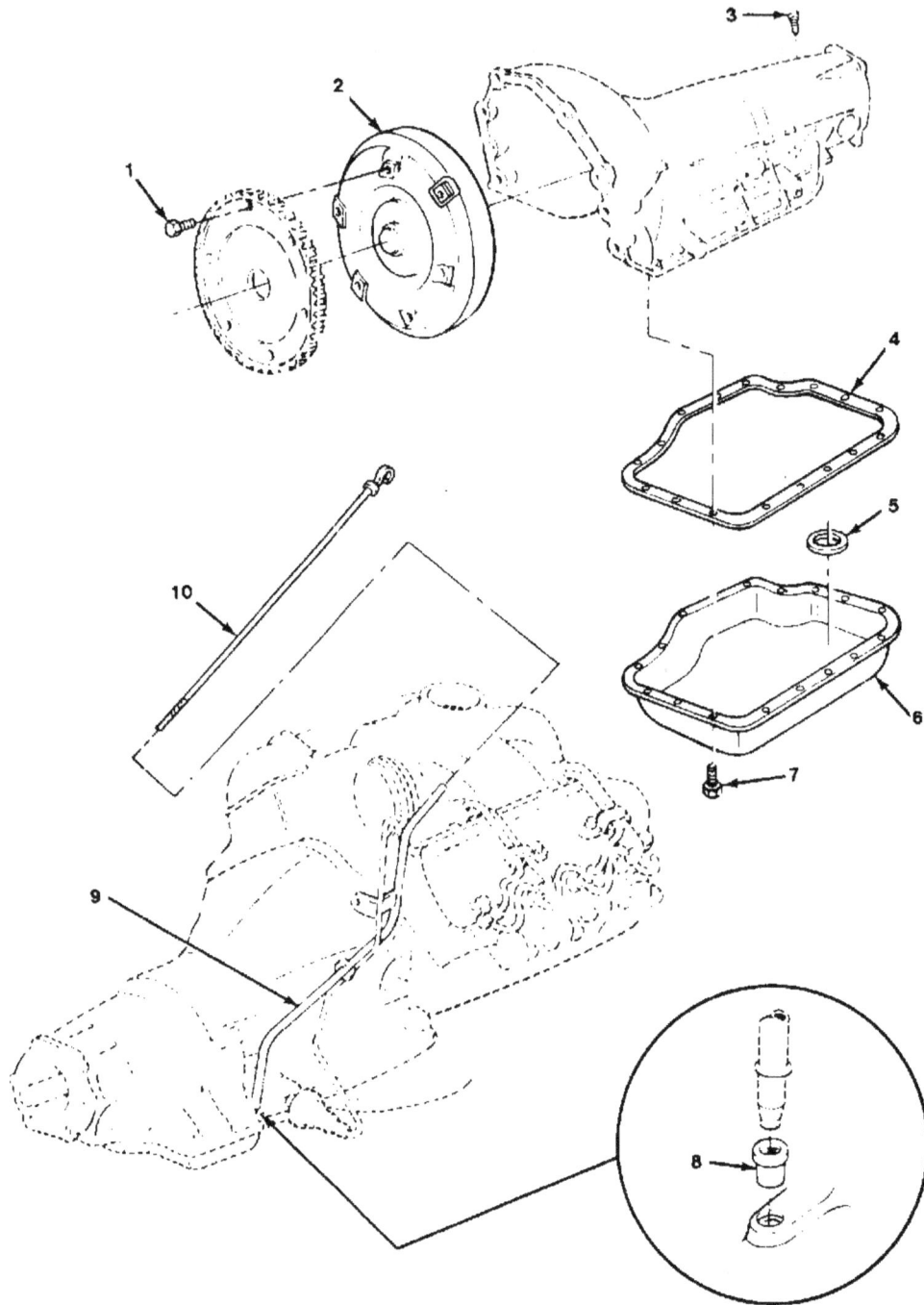

TA510879

FIGURE 60. TORQUE CONVERTER, OIL PAN, AND FILLER TUBE.

(1) ITEM NO	(2) SMR CODE	(3) CAGEC	(4) PART NUMBER	(5) DESCRIPTION AND USABLE ON CODES (UOC)	(6) QTY
				GROUP 0710 TRANSMISSION ASSEMBLY AND ASSOCIATED PARTS	
				FIG. 60 TORQUE CONVERTER, OIL PAN, AND FILLER TUBE	
4	PAOZZ	11862	8655625	GASKET USE WITH P/N 8633203	1
5	PBOZZ	11862	3787240	MAGNET,CHIP COLLECT	1
6	PAOZZ	11862	8633203	OIL PAN	1
6	PAOZZ	11862	8655020	OIL PAN	1
7	PAOZZ	11862	9440224	BOLT,MACHINE	13
8	PAOZZ	11862	1259475	SEAL,OIL FILLER PIP	1
9	PAOZZ	11862	14045642	TUBE,BENT,METALLIC UOC:194,208,209,210,230,231,252,254	1
10	PAOZZ	11862	334532	GAGE ROD-CAP,LIQUID	1

END OF FIGURE

13

14 THRU 29

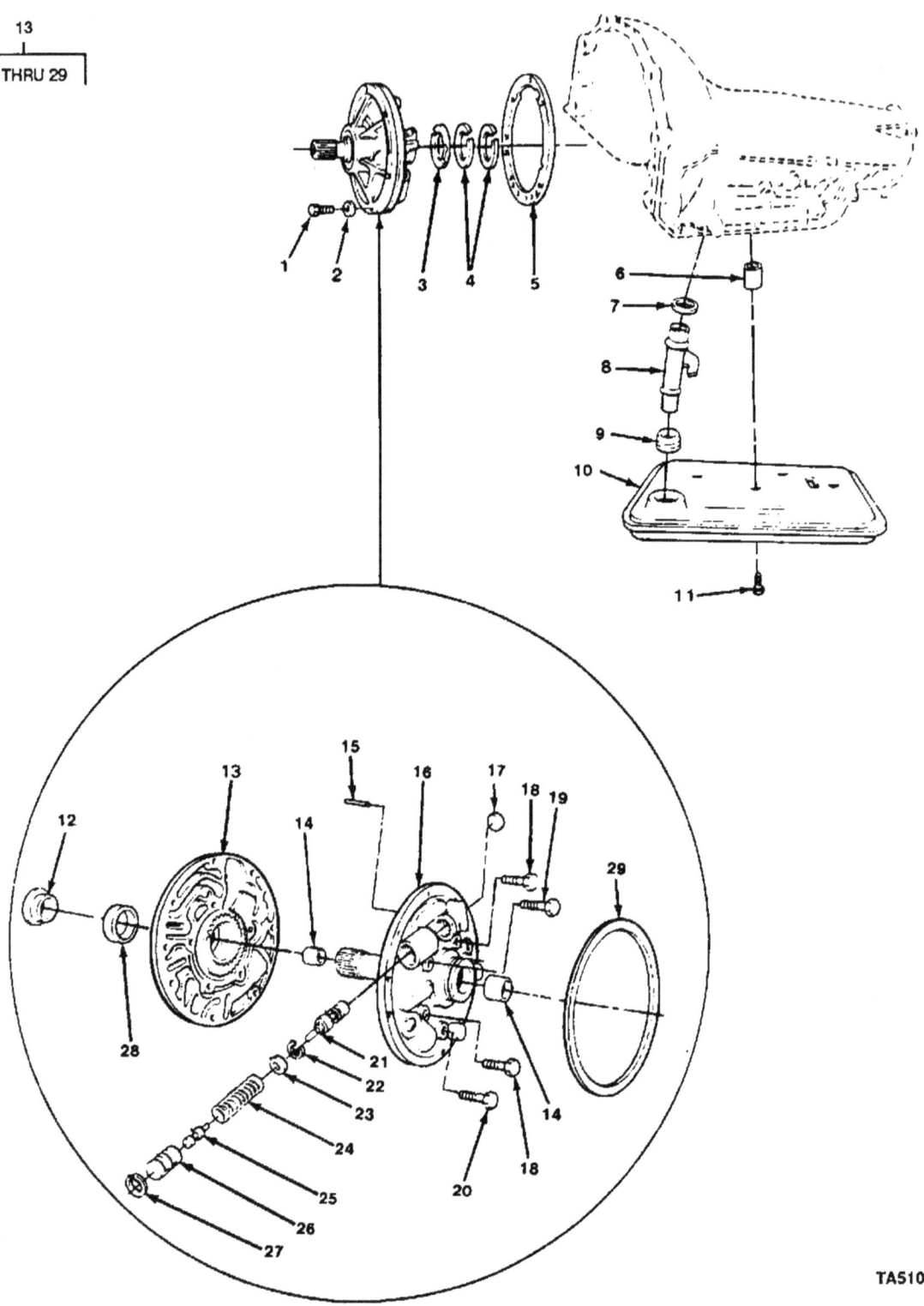

TA510886

FIGURE 61. OIL PUMP ASSEMBLY AND TRANSMISSION FILTER.

(1) ITEM NO	(2) SMR CODE	(3) CAGEC	(4) PART NUMBER	(5) DESCRIPTION AND USABLE ON CODES (UOC)	(6) QTY
				GROUP 0721 COOLERS, PUMPS, MOTORS	
				FIG. 61 OIL PUMP ASSEMBLY AND TRANSMISSION FILTER	
7	PAOZZ	73342	6771005	SEAL,NONMETALLIC RO PART OF KIT P/N 8625905	1
8	PAOZZ	11862	8629526	TUBE,BENT,METALLIC	1
9	PAOZZ	11862	6437746	GROMMET,TRANSMISSION	1
10	PAOZZ	11862	6259423	PARTS KIT,FLUID PRE	1
11	PAOZZ	11862	8633208	BOLT,SHOULDER	1

END OF FIGURE

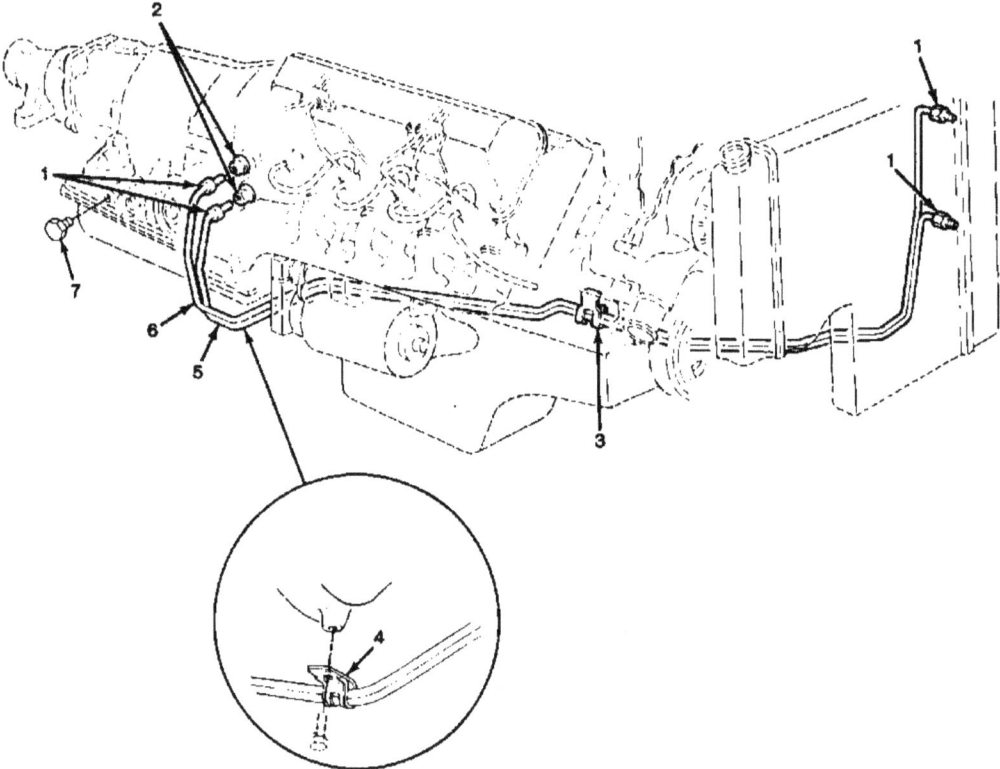

TA510887

FIGURE 62. TRANSMISSION OIL COOLER LINES.

(1) ITEM NO	(2) SMR CODE	(3) CAGEC	(4) PART NUMBER	(5) DESCRIPTION AND USABLE ON CODES (UOC)	(6) QTY
				GROUP 0721 COOLERS, PUMPS, MOTORS	
				FIG. 62 TRANSMISSION OIL COOLER LINERS	
1	PAOZZ	72582	137398	INVERTED NUT,TUBE C	4
2	PAOZZ	11862	8637742	ADAPTER,STRAIGHT,PI (5" FLARED)	2
3	PAOZZ	11862	3997718	CLIP,SPRING TENSION	1
4	PAOZZ	11862	15517986	CLAMP,LOOP	1
5	MOOZZ	11862	14045626	TUBE,METALLIC (73.95"LG) MAKE FROM TUBE, P/N 1324714	1
6	MOOZZ	11862	14045628	PIPE ASM-TRNS OIL C (80.64"LG) MAKE FROM TUBE, P/N 1324714	1
7	PAOZZ	14569	1007-2	PLUG,PIPE (1/8 PIPE)	1

END OF FIGURE

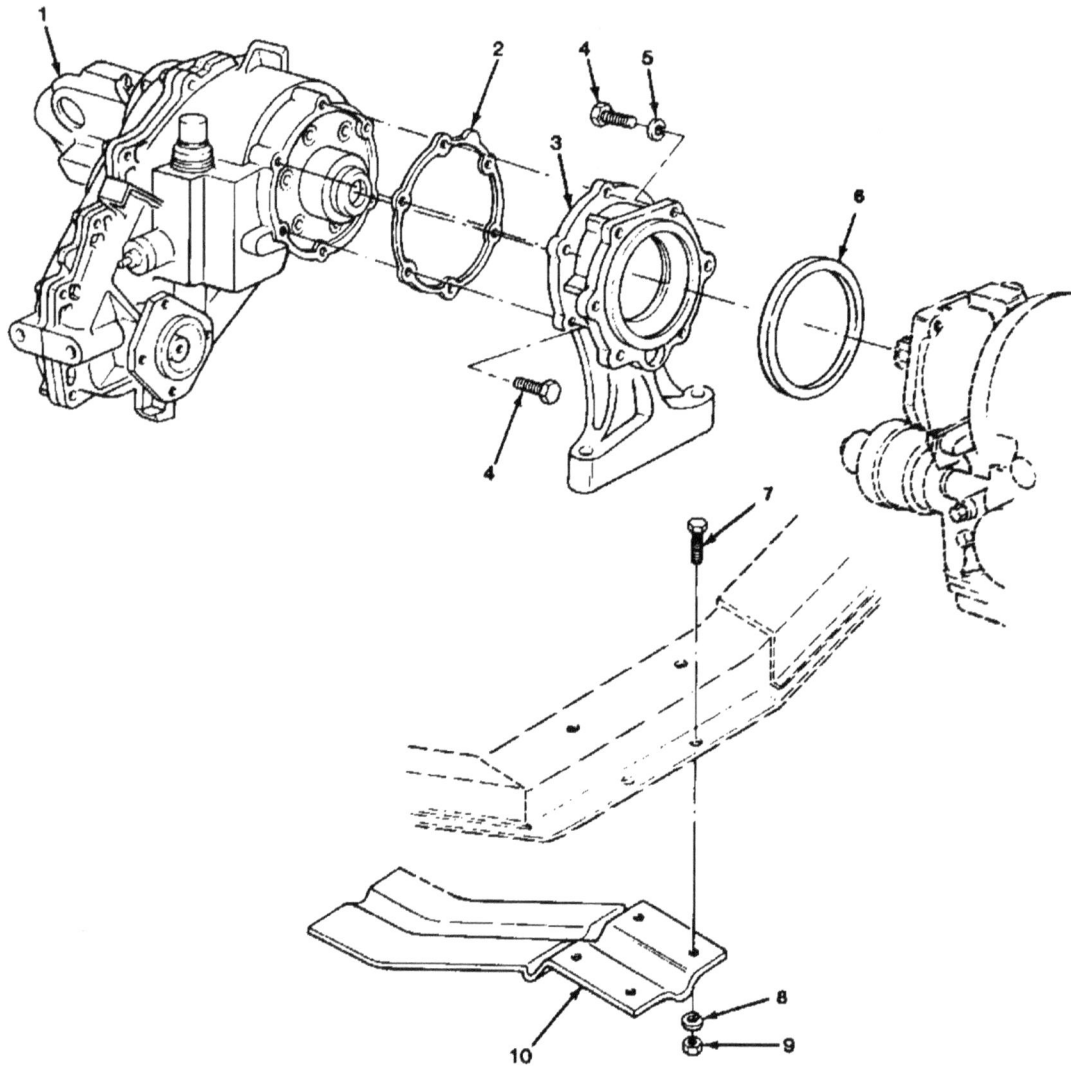

TA510888

FIGURE 63. TRANSFER CASE ASSEMBLY AND ADAPTER (MODEL 208).

(1) ITEM NO	(2) SMR CODE	(3) CAGEC	(4) PART NUMBER	(5) DESCRIPTION AND USABLE ON CODES (UOC)	(6) QTY
				GROUP 08 TRANSFER, FINAL DRIVE. PLANETARY, AND DROP GEARBOX ASSEMBLIES	
				GROUP 0801 POWER TRANSFER, FINAL DRIVE, PLANETARY, OR DROP GEARBOX ASSEMBLIES FIG. 63 TRANSFER CASE ASSEMBLY AND ADAPTER (MODEL 208)	
7	PAOZZ	96906	MS90728-62	SCREW,CAP,HEXAGON H UOC:194,208,209,210,230	4
8	PAOZZ	96906	MS27183-14	WASHER,FLAT UOC:194,208,209,210,230	4
9	PAOZZ	80205	NAS1408A6	NUT,SLEF-LOCKING,HE UOC:194,208,209,210,230	4
10	PAOZZ	11862	14067764	COVER,ACCESS UOC:194,208,209,210,230,252,254,256	1

END OF FIGURE

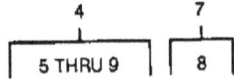

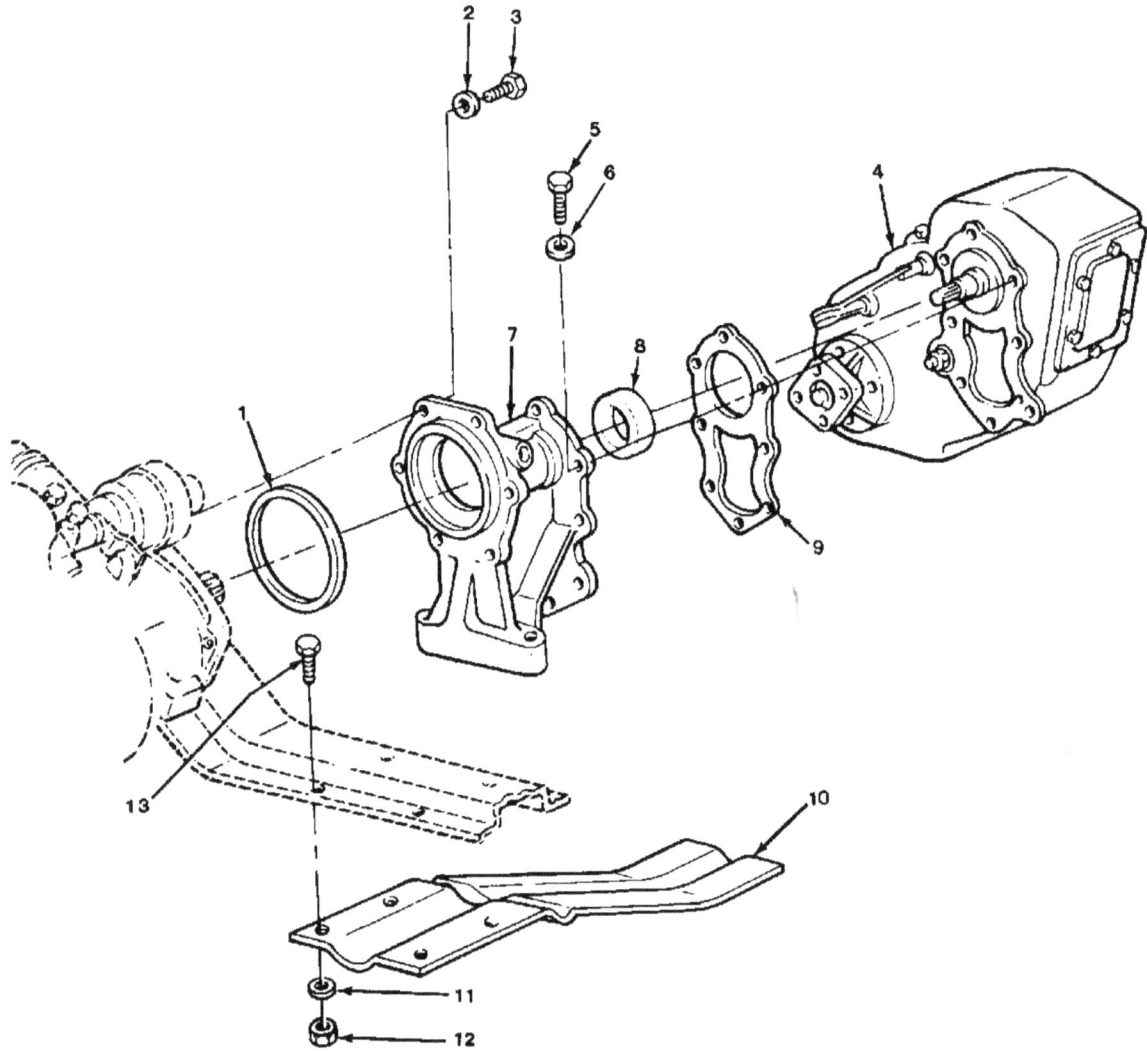

TA510889

FIGURE 64. TRANSFER CASE ASSEMBLY AND ADAPTER (MODEL 205).

(1) ITEM NO	(2) SMR CODE	(3) CAGEC	(4) PART NUMBER	(5) DESCRIPTION AND USABLE ON CODES (UOC)	(6) QTY
				GROUP 0801 POWER TRANSFER,FINAL DRIVER, PLANETARY, OR DROP GEARBOX ASSEMBLIES	
				FIG. 64 TRANSFER CASE ASSEMBLY AND ADAPTER (MODEL 205)	
10	PAOZZ	11862	14029158	PLATE,TRANSFER CASE UOC:231,252,254,256	1
11	PAOZZ	96906	MS27183-14	WASHER,FLAT UOC:231,252,254,256	4
12	PAOZZ	80205	NAS1408A6	NUT,SELF-LOCKING,HE UOC:231,252,254,256	4
13	PAOZZ	96906	MS90728-62	SCREW,CAP,HEXAGON H UOC:231,252,254,256	4
				END OF FIGURE	

1	7	10	26	33
2 THRU 4	8	11	27 THRU 30	34 THRU 36

40	53	64	69
41 THRU 43	54 THRU 58	65	70 THRU 72

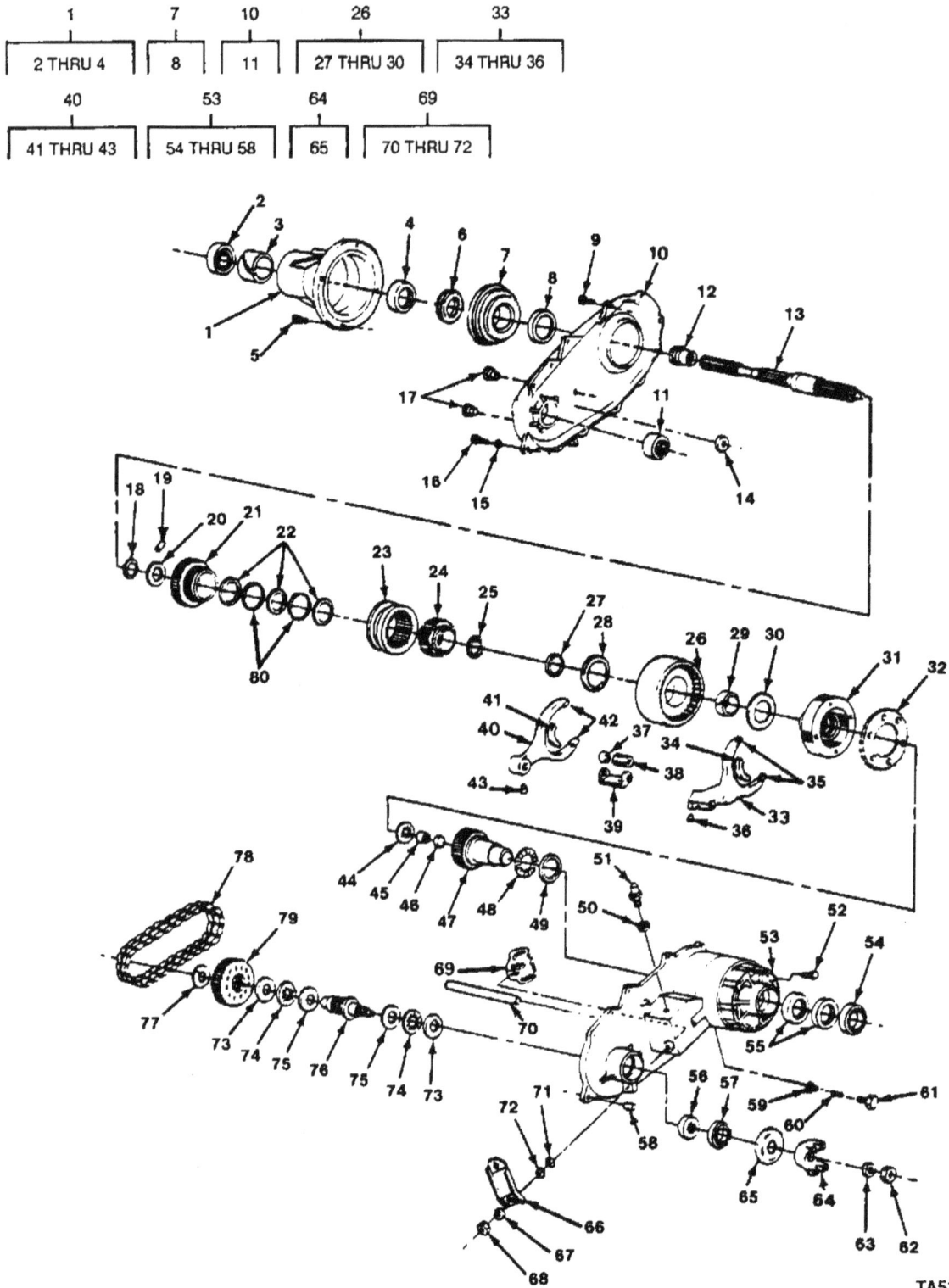

TA510890

FIGURE 65. TRANSFER CASE COMPONENT PARTS (MODEL 208).

(1) ITEM NO	(2) SMR CODE	(3) CAGEC	(4) PART NUMBER	(5) DESCRIPTION AND USABLE ON CODES (UOC)	(6) QTY
				GROUP 0801 POWER TRANSFER, FINAL DRIVE, PLANETARY, OR DROP GEARBOX ASSEMBLIES	
				FIG. 65 TRANSFER CASE COMPONENT PARTS (MODEL 208)	
17	PAOZZ	11862	14037987	PLUG,MACHINE THREAD UOC:194,208,209,210,230	2
50	PAOZZ	76760	99780	GASKET UOC:194,208,209,210,230	1
51	PAOZZ	11862	14037986	SWITCH,PUSH UOC:194,208,209,210,230	1

END OF FIGURE

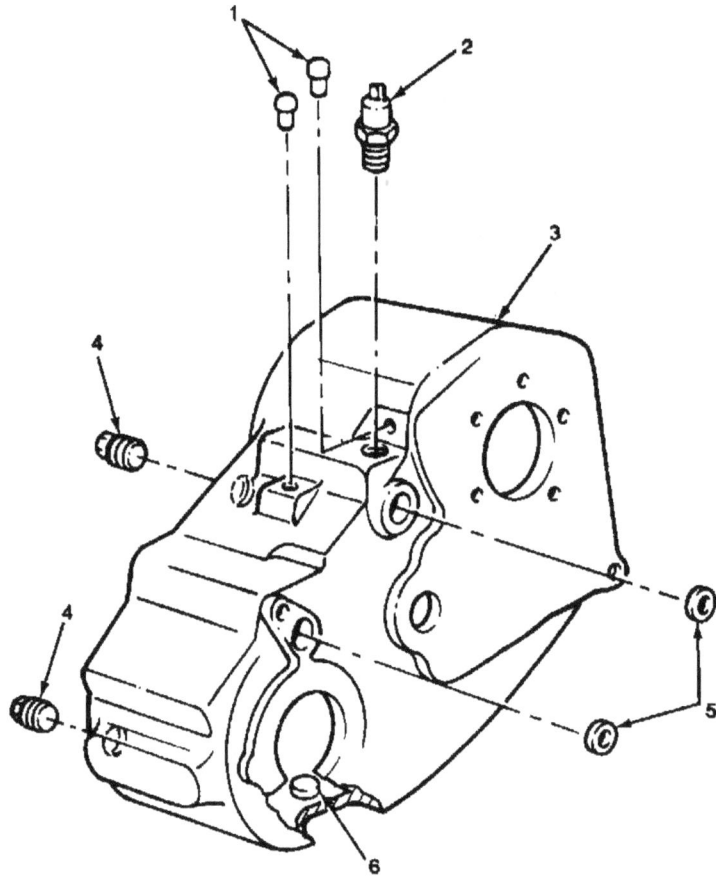

FIGURE 66. TRANSFER CASE HOUSING (MODEL 205).

TA510892

(1) ITEM NO	(2) SMR CODE	(3) CAGEC	(4) PART NUMBER	(5) DESCRIPTION AND USABLE ON CODES (UOC)	(6) QTY
				GROUP 0801 POWER TRANSFER, FINAL DRIVE, PLANETARY, OR DROP GEARBOX ASSEMBLIES	
				FIG. 66 TRANSFER CASE HOUSING (MODEL 205)	
2	PAOZZ	11862	15594176	SWITCH,PUSH UOC:231,252,254,256	1
4	PAOZZ	89346	103868	.PLUG,PIPE UOC:231,252,254,256	2
				END OF FIGURE	

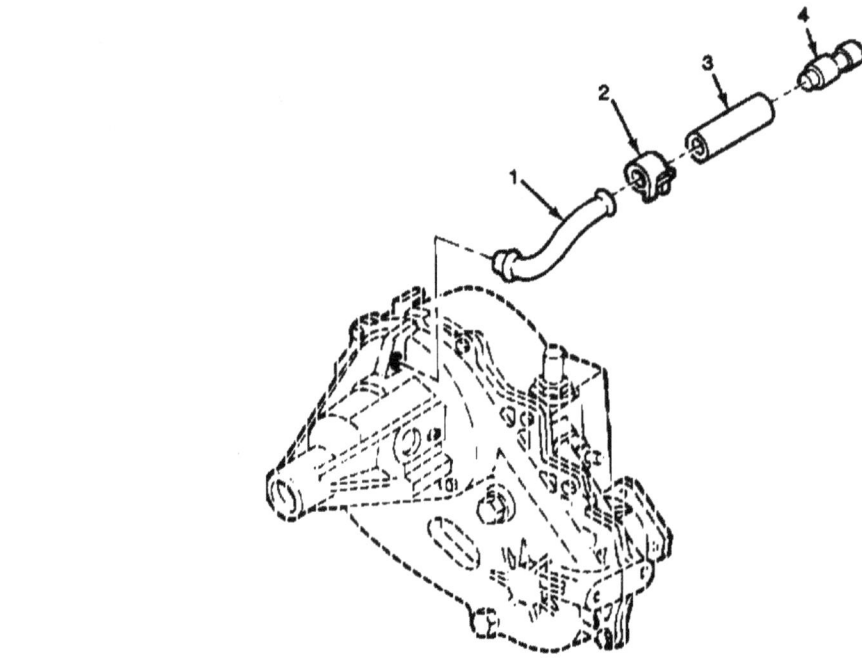

MODEL 208

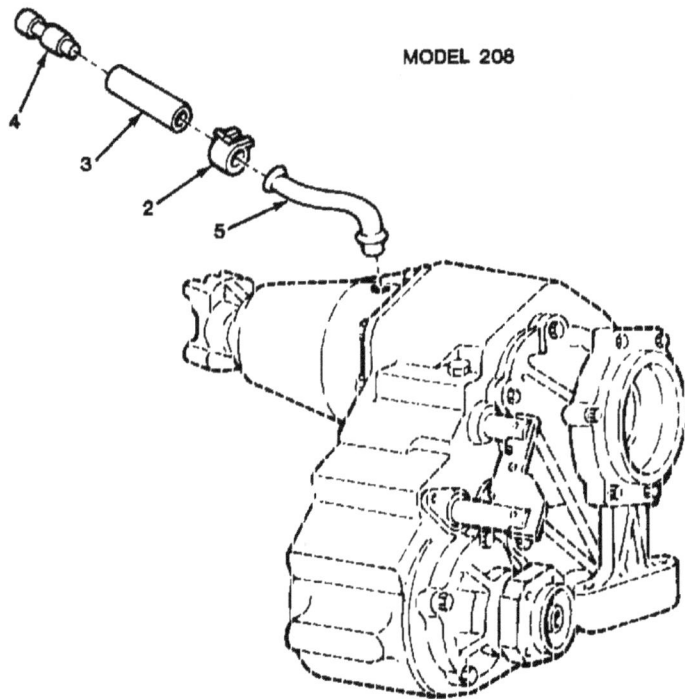

TA510893

MODEL 205

FIGURE 67. CASE VENT COMPONENT PARTS.

(1) ITEM NO	(2) SMR CODE	(3) CAGEC	(4) PART NUMBER	(5) DESCRIPTION AND USABLE ON CODES (UOC)	(6) QTY
				GROUP 0801 POWER TRANSFER, FINAL DRIVE, PLANETARY, OR DROP GEARBOX ASSEMBLIES	
				FIG. 67 CASE VENT COMPONENT PARTS	
1	PAOZZ	11862	14032995	TUBE ASSEMBLY,METAL (MODEL 208) UOC:194,208,209,210,230	1
2	PAOZZ	96906	MS35842-10	CLAMP,HOSE	1
3	MOOZZ	11862	9439048	HOSE,NONMETALLIC (1.77"LG) MAKE FROM HOSE,P/N 9439104	1
4	PAOZZ	11862	8640496	SHAFT,SHOULDERED	1
5	PAOZZ	11862	14032996	TUBE,BENT,METALLIC UOC:231,252,254,256	1

END OF FIGURE

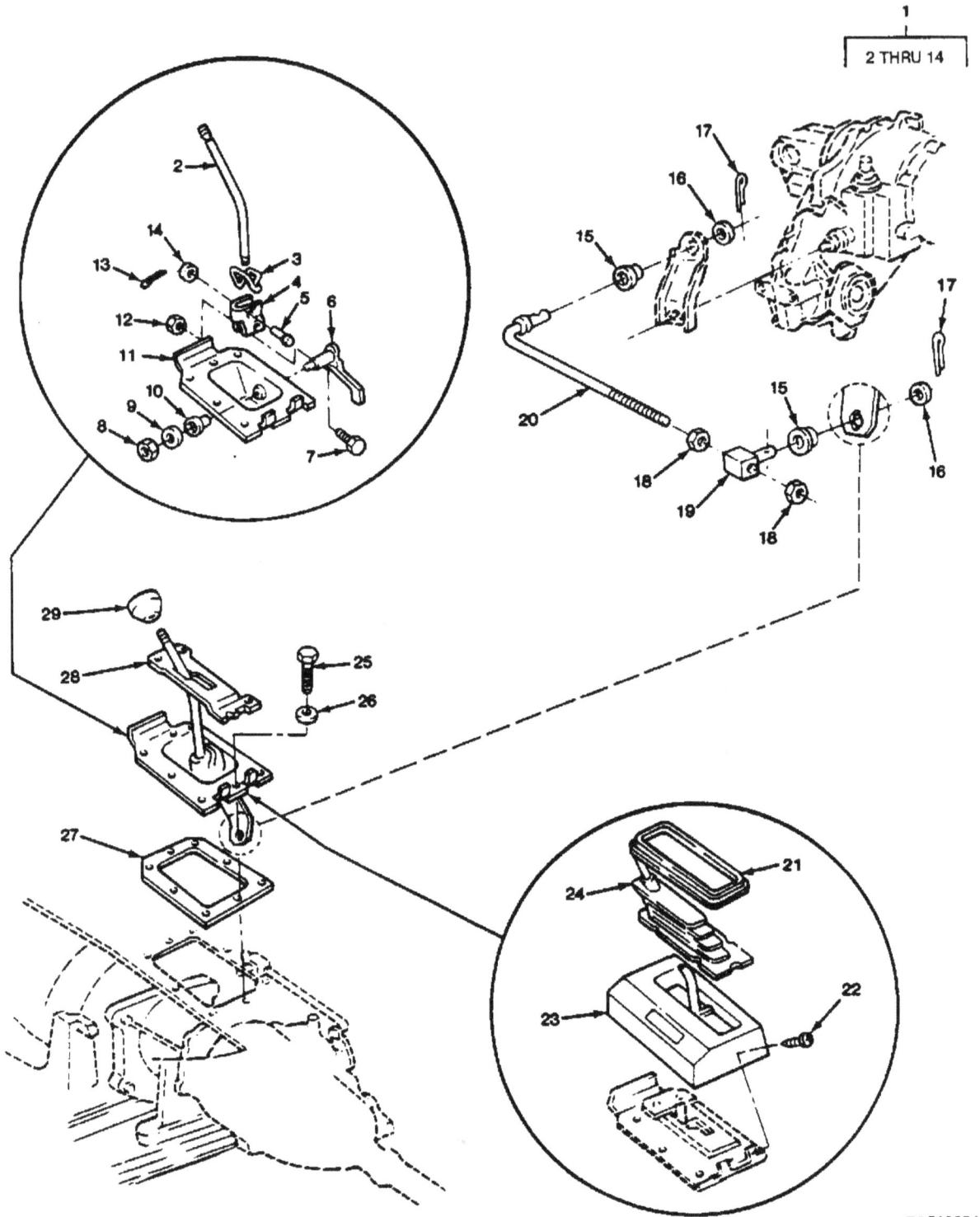

FIGURE 68. GEARSHIFT LEVER AND LINKAGE (MODEL 208).

TA510894

(1) ITEM NO	(2) SMR CODE	(3) CAGEC	(4) PART NUMBER	(5) DESCRIPTION AND USABLE ON CODES (UOC)	(6) QTY
				GROUP 0803 GEARSHIFT, VACUUM BOOSTER, AND CONTROLS	
				FIG. 68 GEARSHIFT LEVER AND LINKAGE (MODEL 208)	
1	AOOOO	11862	14063331	LVR ASM T/CASE CTL UOC:210	1
1	AOOOO	11862	14071950	LVR ASM T/CASE CTL UOC:194,208,209,230	1
2	PAOZZ	11862	14045658	.LEVER,MANUAL CONTRO UOC:194,208,209,230	1
2	PAOZZ	11862	14063332	.ROD,SHIFT LINKAGE UOC:210	1
3	PAOZZ	11862	14029108	.SPRING,HELICAL,TORS UOC:194,208,209,210,230	1
4	PAOZZ	11862	14029107	.SHIFTER FORK UOC:194,208,209,210,230	1
5	PAOZZ	11862	14029111	.PIN,STRAIGHT,HEADED UOC:194,208,209,210,230	1
6	PAOZZ	11862	14037889	.LEVER,MANUAL CONTO UOC:194,208,209,210,230	1
7	PAOZZ	11862	14045504	.SCREW,CAP,HEXAGON H UOC:194,208,209,210,230	2
8	PAOZZ	24617	9422295	.NUT,SELF-LOCKING,CC UOC:194,208,209,210,230	1
9	PAOZZ	11862	466578	.WASHER,FLAT UOC:194,208,209,210,230	1
10	PAOZZ	11862	3992925	.BUSHING,SLEEVE UOC:194,208,209,210,230,	2
11	PAOZZ	11862	14071952	.HOUSING,MECHANICAL UOC:194,208,209,210,230	1
12	PAOZZ	21450	131245	.NUT,SELF-LOCKING,HE UOC:194,208,209,210,230	2
13	PAOZZ	96906	MS24665-283	.PIN,COTTER UOC:194,208,209,210,230	1
14	PAOZZ	96906	MS27183-12	.WASHER,FLAT UOC:194,208,209,210,230	1
15	PAOZZ	11862	1234418	GROMMET,NONMETALLIC UOC:194,208,209,210,230	2
16	PAOZZ	11862	382105	WASHER,FLAT UOC:194,208,209,210,230	2
17	PAOZZ	89749	IF316	PIN,COTTER UOC:194,208,209,210,230	2
18	PAOZZ	96906	MS35691-29	NUT,PLAIN,HEXAGON UOC:194,208,209,210,230	2
19	PAOZZ	11862	718368	SWIVEL,TRANSFER CAS UOC:194,208,209,210,230	1
20	PAOZZ	11862	14029122	PIN,STRAIGHT,HEADED UOC:194,208,209,210,230	1
21	PAOZZ	11862	14029117	PLATE,TRANSFER CASE UOC:194,208,209,210,230	1

(1) ITEM NO	(2) SMR CODE	(3) CAGEC	(4) PART NUMBER	(5) DESCRIPTION AND USABLE ON CODES (UOC)	(6) QTY
22	PAOZZ	11862	20365263	SCREW, TAPPING UOC:194,208,209,210,230	4
23	PAOZZ	11862	14037893	LEVER, REMOTE CONTRO UOC:194,208,209,210,230	1
24	PAOZZ	11862	14029116	BOOT, DUST AND MOIST UOC:194,208,209,210,230	1
25	PAOZZ	96906	MS90728-6	SCREW, CAP, HEXAGON H UOC:194,208,209,210,230	8
26	PAOZZ	96906	MS9549-10	WASHER, FLAT UOC:194,208,209,210,230	8
27	PAOZZ	11862	14071954	GASKET UOC:194,208,209,210,230	1
28	PAOZZ	11862	14045697	GUIDE, TRANSFER CASE UOC:194,208,209,210,230	1
29	PAOZZ	11862	15588503	KNOB UOC:194,208,209,210,230	1

END OF FIGURE

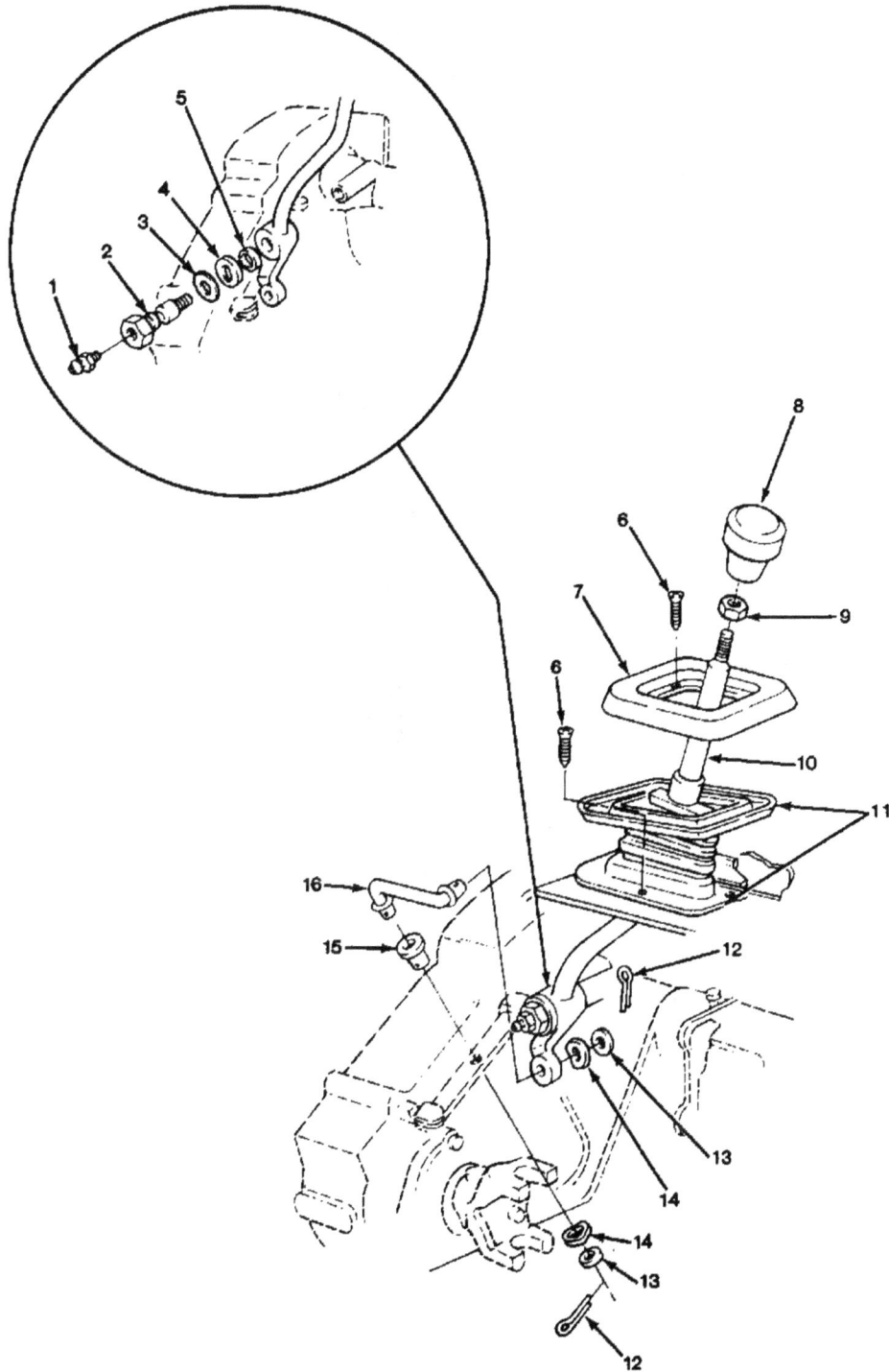

FIGURE 69. GEARSHIFT LEVER AND LINKAGE (MODEL 205).

TA510895

(1) ITEM NO	(2) SMR CODE	(3) CAGEC	(4) PART NUMBER	(5) DESCRIPTION AND USABLE ON CODES (UOC)	(6) QTY
				GROUP 0803 GEARSHIFT, VACUUM BOOSTER, AND CONTROLS	
				FIG. 69 GEARSHIFT LEVER AND LINKAGE (MODEL 205)	
1	PAOZZ	11862	9417901	FITTING,LUBRICATION UOC:231,252,254,256	1
2	PAOZZ	11862	14009313	BOLT,FLUID PASSAGE UOC:231,252,254,256	1
3	PAOZZ	11862	4497001	WASHER,SPRING TENSI UOC:231,252,254,256	1
4	PAOZZ	11862	3838153	WASHER,FLAT UOC:231,252,254,256	1
5	PAOZZ	11862	2423517	WASHER,FLAT UOC:231,252,254,256	1
6	PAOZZ	24617	9431995	SCREW,TAPPING UOC:231,252	8
7	PAOZZ	11862	14032789	PLATE,RETAINING,SHA UOC:231,252,254,256	1
8	PAOZZ	11862	15588504	KNOB UOC:231,252,254,256	1
9	PAOZZ	96906	MS35691-29	NUT,PLAIN,HEXAGON UOC:231,252,254,256	1
10	PAOZZ	11862	14055531	LEVER,MANUAL CONTRO UOC:231,252,254,256	1
11	PAOZZ	11862	14071955	BOOT,DUST AND MOIST UOC:231,252,254,256	1
12	PAOZZ	89749	IF316	PIN,COTTER UOC:231,252,254,256	2
13	PAOZZ	96906	MS27183-14	WASHER,FLAT UOC:231,252,254,256	2
14	PAOZZ	11862	3953987	WASHER,SPRING TENSI UOC:231,252,254,256	2
15	PAOZZ	11862	14049556	GROMMET,NONMETALLIC UOC:231,252,254,256	1
16	PAOZZ	11862	14054220	ROD,TRANSFER CASE UOC:231,252,254,256	1

END OF FIGURE

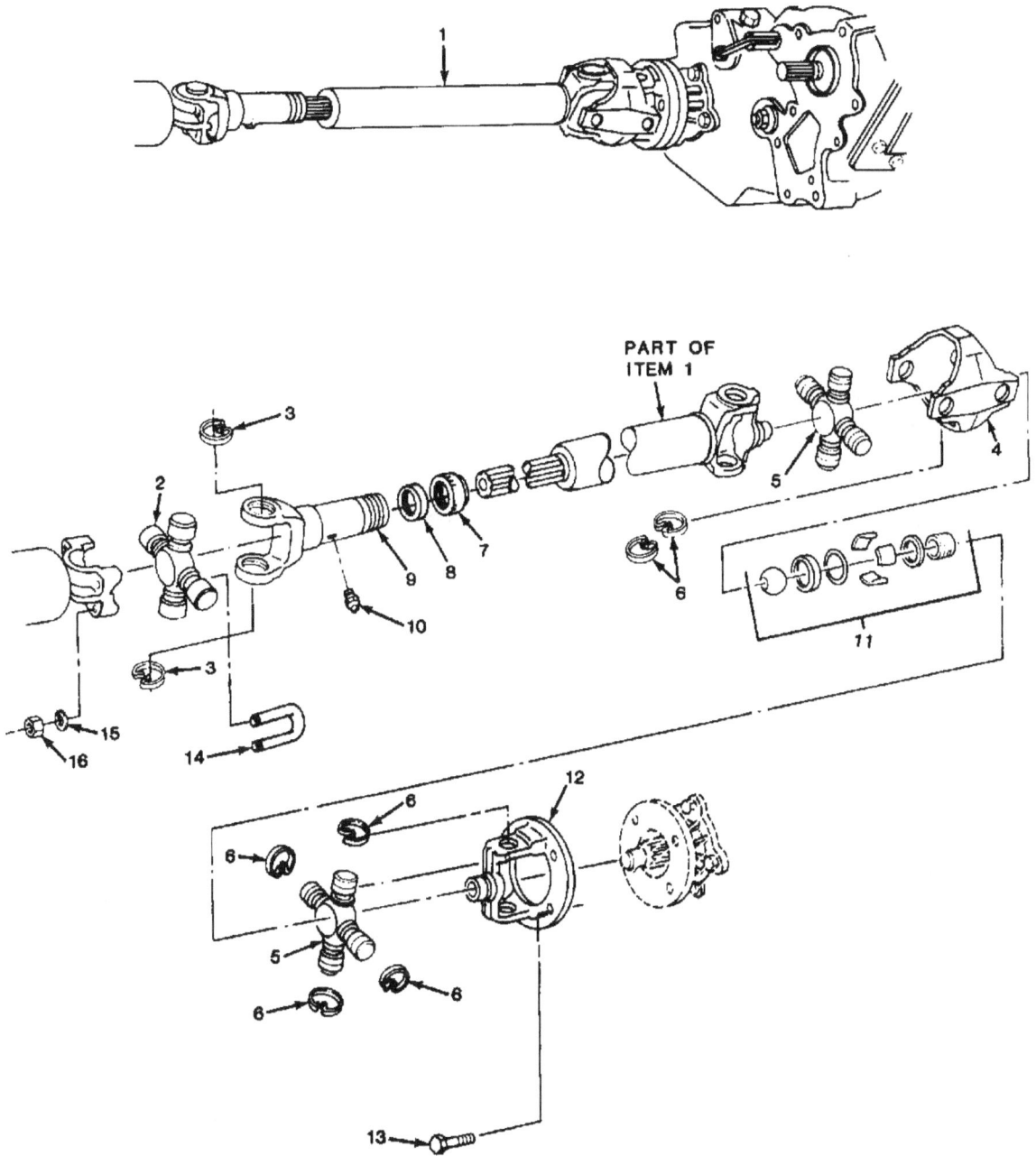

FIGURE 70, FRONT PROPELLER SHAFT ASSEMBLY (ALL EXCEPT M1009, FIRST DESIGN).

TA510896

(1) ITEM NO	(2) SMR CODE	(3) CAGEC	(4) PART NUMBER	(5) DESCRIPTION AND USABLE ON CODES (UOC)	(6) QTY
				GROUP 09 PROPELLER, PROPELLER SHAFTS, UNIVERSAL JOINTS, COUPLER, AND CLAMP ASSEMBLY	
				GROUP 0900 PROPELLER SHAFTS	
				FIG. 70 FRONT PROPELLER SHAFT ASSEMBLY (ALL EXCEPT M1009, FIRST DESIGN)	
1	PAOFF	11862	7845102	PROPERLLER SHAFT (FIRST DESIGN APPLIES TO VEHICLES BEFORE VIN ENDING WITH 354457) UOC:194,208,210,230,231,252,254,256	1
2	PAOZZ	11862	386451	.PARTS KIT,UNIVERSAL INCLUDES ITEM #3 UOC:194,208,210,230,231,252,254,256	1
3	PAOZZ	11862	3721887	.RING,RETAINING UOC:194,208,210,230,231,252,254,256	2
5	PAOZZ	11862	7806140	.PARTS KIT,UNIVERSAL INCLUDES ITEM #6 UOC:194,208,210,230,231,252,254,256	2
6	PAOZZ	11862	1456507	.RING,RETAINING UOC:194,208,210,230,231,252,254,256	8
7	PAOZZ	11862	458418	.CAP,DUST,PROPELLER UOC:194,208,210,230,231,252,254,256	1
8	PAOZZ	11862	7827942	.PACKING,PREFORMED UOC:194,208,210,230,231,252,254,256	1
9	PAOZZ	11862	15596686	.YOKE,UNIVERSAL JOIN INCLUDES ITEM #10 UOC:194,208,210,230,231,252,254,256	1
10	PAOZZ	11862	9417901	.FITTING,LUBRICATION UOC:194,208,210,230,231,252,254,256	1
13	PAOZZ	96906	MS90728-86	SCREW,CAP,HEXAGON H UOC:194,208,210,230,231,252,254,256	4
14	PAOZZ	72712	1358938	BOLT,U UOC:194,208,210,230,231,252,254,256	2
15	PAOZZ	96906	MS35338-45	WASHER,LOCK UOC:194,208,210,230,231,252,254,256	4
16	PAOZZ	96906	MS51967-6	NUT,PLAIN,HEXAGON UOC:194,208,210,230,231,252,254,256	4

END OF FIGURE

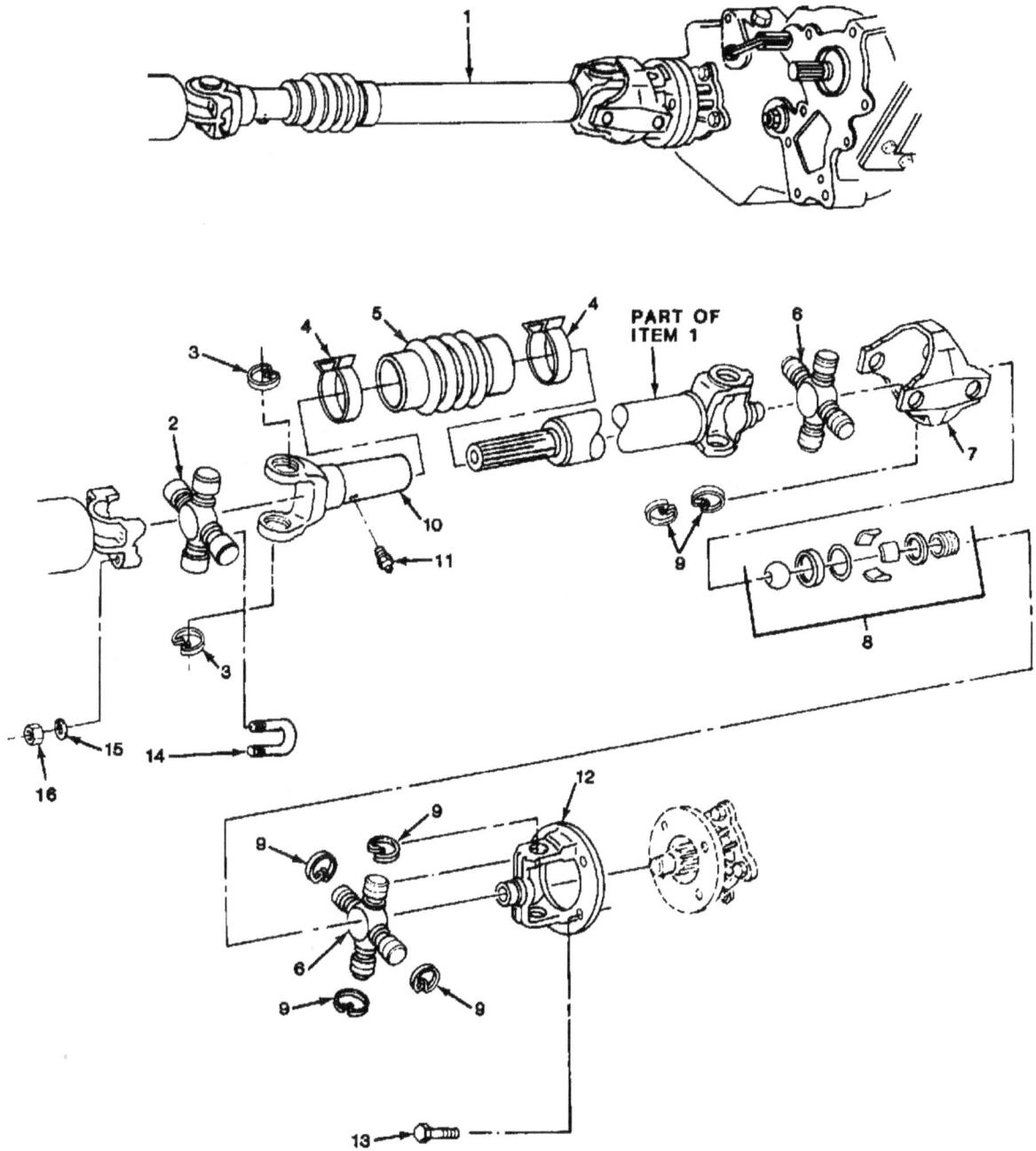

TA510897

FIGURE 71. FRONT PROPELLER SHAFT ASSEMBLY (ALL EXCEPT M1009, SECOND DESIGN).

(1) ITEM NO	(2) SMR CODE	(3) CAGEC	(4) PART NUMBER	(5) DESCRIPTION AND USABLE ON CODES (UOC)	(6) QTY
				GROUP 0900 PROPELLER SHAFTS	
				FIG. 71 FRONT PROPELLER SHAFT ASSEMBLY (ALL EXCEPT M1009, SECOND DESIGN)	
1	PAOFF	11862	26013913	PROPELLER SHAFT WIT (SECOND DESIGN WITH 205 TRANSFER CASE APPLIES TO VEHICLES AFTER VIN ENDING WITH 354457) UOC:231,252,254,256	1
1	PAOFF	11862	7845102	PROPERLLER SHAFT (SECOND DESIGN WITH 208 TRANSFER CASE APPLIES TO VEHICLES AFTER VIN ENDING WITH 354457) UOC:194,208,210,230	1
2	PAOZZ	11862	386451	.PARTS KIT,UNIVERSAL INCLUDES ITEM #3 UOC:194,208,210,230,231,252,254,256	1
3	PAOZZ	11862	3721887	.RING,RETAINING UOC:194,208,210,230,231,252,254,256	2
4	PAOZZ	11862	7840235	.CLIP,RETAINING UOC:194,208,210,230,231,252,254,256	2
5	PAOZZ	11862	7845127	.BOOT,DUST AND MOIST UOC:194,208,210,230,231,252,254,256	1
6	PAOZZ	11862	7806140	.PARTS KIT,UNIVERSAL INCLUDES ITEM #9 UOC:194,208,210,230,231,252,254,256	2
9	PAOZZ	11862	1456507	.RING,RETAINING UOC:194,208,210,230,231,252,254,256	8
10	PAOZZ	11862	7845119	.PROPELLER SHAFT INCLUDES ITEM #11 UOC:194,208,210,230,231,252,254,256	1
11	PAOZZ	11862	9417901	.FITTING,LUBRICATION UOC:194,208,210,230,231,252,254,256	1
13	PAOZZ	96906	MS90728-86	SCREW,CAP,HEXAGON H UOC:194,208,210,230,231,252,254,256	4
14	PAOZZ	11862	1358938	BOLT,U UOC:194,208,210,230,231,252,254,256	2
15	PAOZZ	96906	MS35338-45	WASHER,LOCK UOC:194,208,210,230,231,252,254,256	4
16	PAOZZ	96906	MS51967-6	NUT,PLAIN,HEXAGON UOC:194,208,210,230,231,252,254,256	4

END OF FIGURE

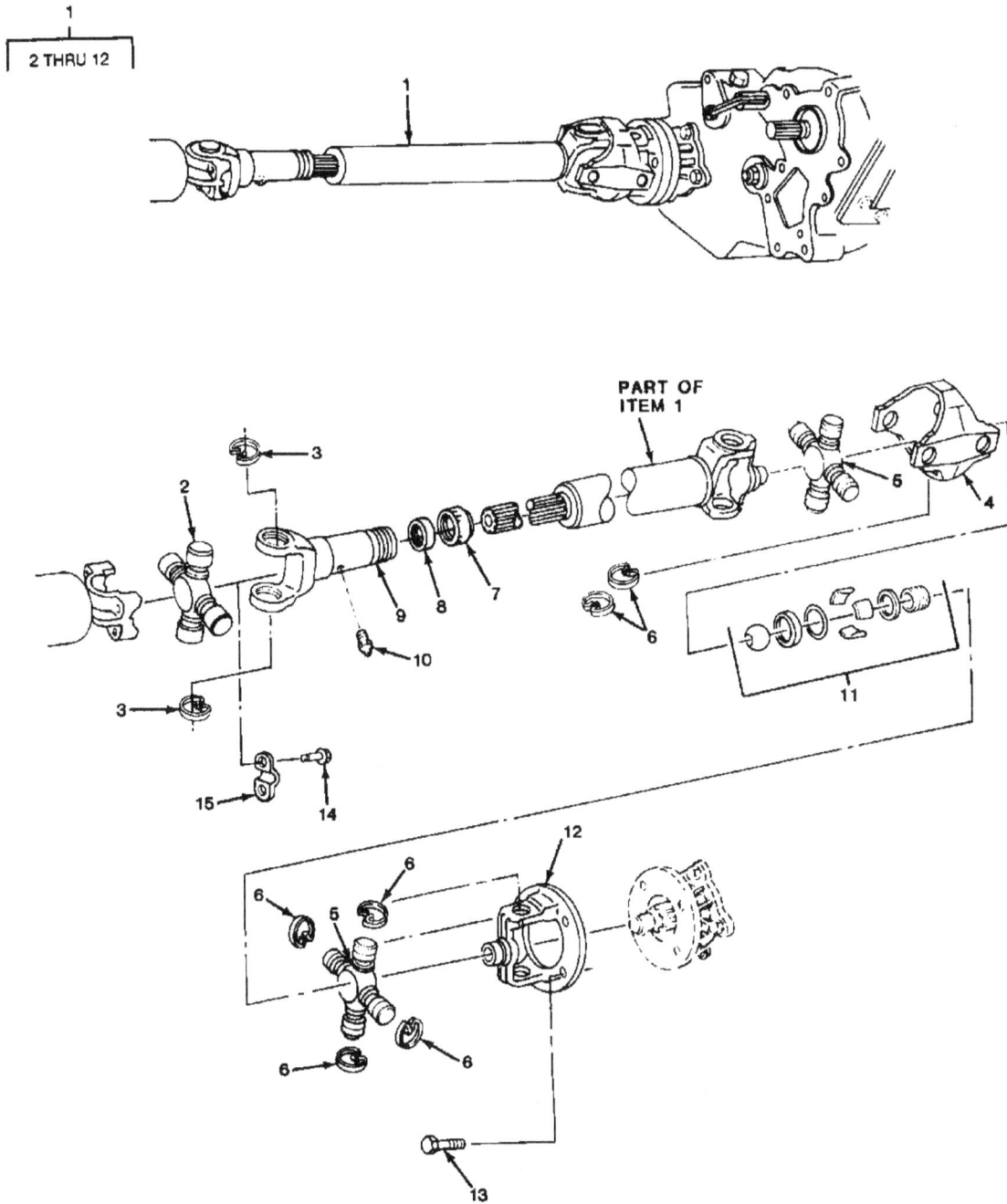

TA510898

FIGURE 72. FRONT PROPELLER SHAFT ASSEMBLY (M1009, FIRST DESIGN).

(1) ITEM NO	(2) SMR CODE	(3) CAGEC	(4) PART NUMBER	(5) DESCRIPTION AND USABLE ON CODES (UOC)	(6) QTY
				GROUP 0900 PROPELLER SHAFTS	
				FIG. 72 FRONT PROPELLER SHAFT ASSEMBLY (M1009, FIRST DESIGN)	
1	PAOFF	11862	7830927	PROPELLER SHAFT (FIRST DESIGN APPLIES TO VEHICLES BEFORE VIN ENDING WITH 168593 AND IS INTERCHANGEABLE WITH P/N 7845043) UOC:209	1
2	PAOZZ	11862	386451	.PARTS KIT,UNIVERSAL INCLUDES ITEM #3 UOC:209	1
3	PAOZZ	11862	3721887	.RING,RETAINING UOC:209	2
5	PAOZZ	11862	7806140	.PARTS KIT,UNIVERSAL INCLUDES ITEM #6 UOC:209	2
6	PAOZZ	11862	1456507	.RING,RETAINING UOC:209	8
7	PAOZZ	11862	458418	.CAP,DUST,PROPELLER UOC:209	1
8	PAOZZ	11862	7827942	.PACKING,PREFORMED UOC:209	1
9	PAOZZ	11862	15596686	.YOKE,UNIVERSAL JOIN INCLUDES ITEM #10 UOC:209	1
10	PAOZZ	11862	9417901	.FITTING,LUBRICATION UOC:209	1
12	PAOZZ	11862	7815849	.YOKE,UNIVERSAL JOIN UOC:209	1
13	PAOZZ	96906	MS90728-86	SCREW,CAP,HEXAGON H UOC:209	4
14	PAOZZ	11862	14018700	SCREW,CAP,HEXAGON H UOC:209	4
15	PAOZZ	11862	3882979	CLAMP,HUB UOC:209	2

END OF FIGURE

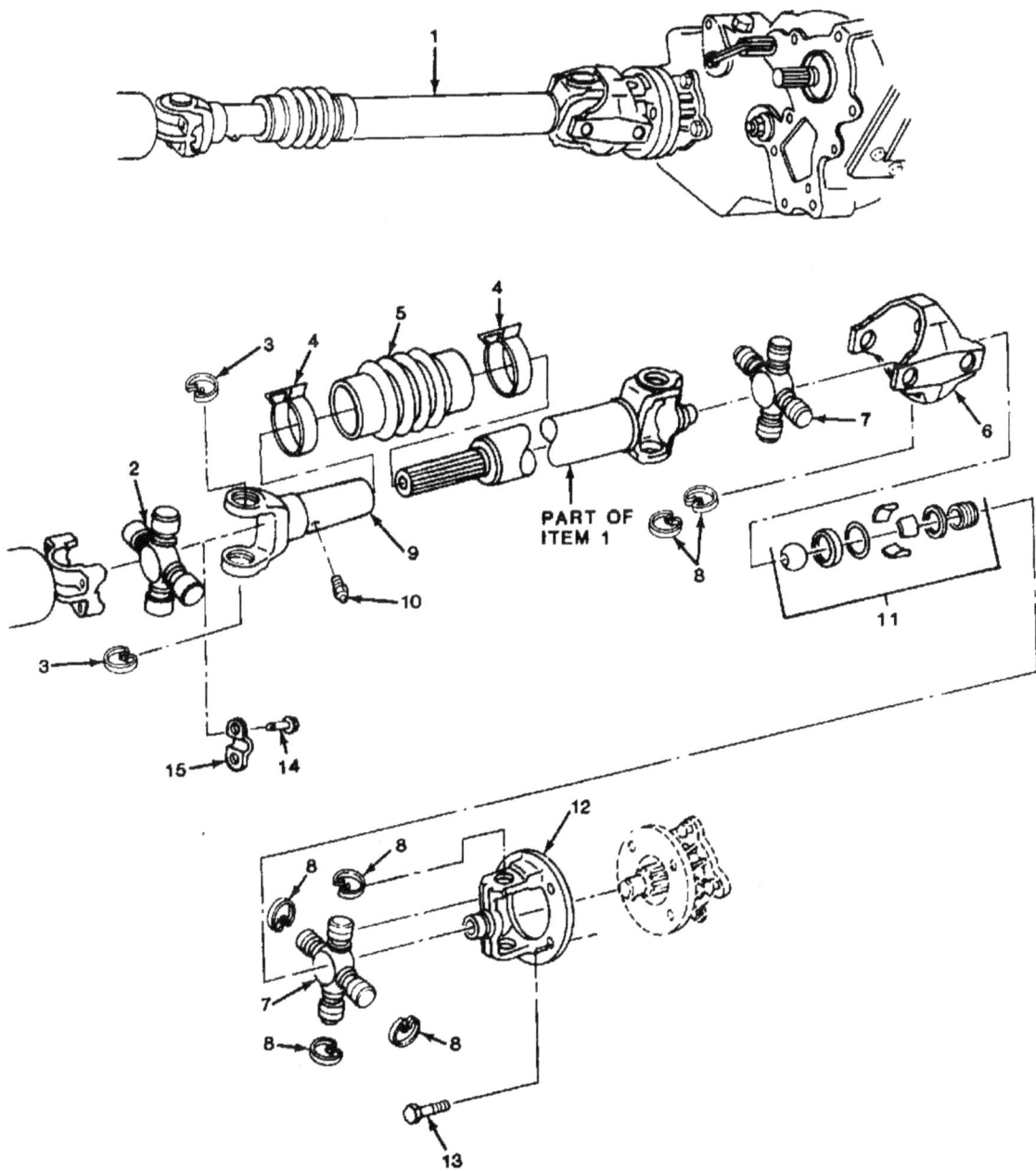

TA510899

FIGURE 73. FRONT PROPELLER SHAFT ASSEMBLY (M1009, SECOND DESIGN).

(1) ITEM NO	(2) SMR CODE	(3) CAGEC	(4) PART NUMBER	(5) DESCRIPTION AND USABLE ON CODES (UOC)	(6) QTY
				GROUP 0900 PROPELLER SHAFTS	
				FIG. 73 FRONT PROPELLER SHAFT ASSEMBLY (M1009, SECOND ASSEMBLY)	
1	PAOFF	11862	26013911	PROPELLER SHAFT WIT (SECOND DESIGN APPLIES TO VEHICLES AFTER VIN ENDING WITH 168593 AND REPLACES P/N 7830927) UOC:209	1
2	PAOZZ	11862	386451	.PARTS KIT,UNIVERSAL INCLUDES ITEM #3 UOC:209	1
3	PAOZZ	11862	3721887	.RING,RETAINING UOC:209	2
4	PAOZZ	11862	7840235	.CLIP,RETAINING UOC:209	2
5	PAOZZ	11862	7845127	.BOOT,DUST AND MOIST UOC:209	1
7	PAOZZ	11862	7806140	.PARTS KIT,UNIVERSAL INCLUDES ITEM #8 UOC:209	2
8	PAOZZ	11862	1456507	.RING,RETAINING UOC:209	8
9	PAOZZ	11862	7845119	.PROPELLER SHAFT INCLUDES ITEM #10 UOC:209	1
10	PAOZZ	11862	9417901	.FITTING,LUBRICATION UOC:209	1
12	PAOZZ	11862	7815849	.YOKE,UNIVERSAL JOIN UOC:209	1
13	PAOZZ	96906	MS90728-86	SCREW,CAP,HEXAGON H UOC:209	4
14	PAOZZ	11862	14018700	SCREW,CAP,HEXAGON H UOC:209	4
15	PAOZZ	11862	3882979	CLAMP,HUB UOC:209	2

END OF FIGURE

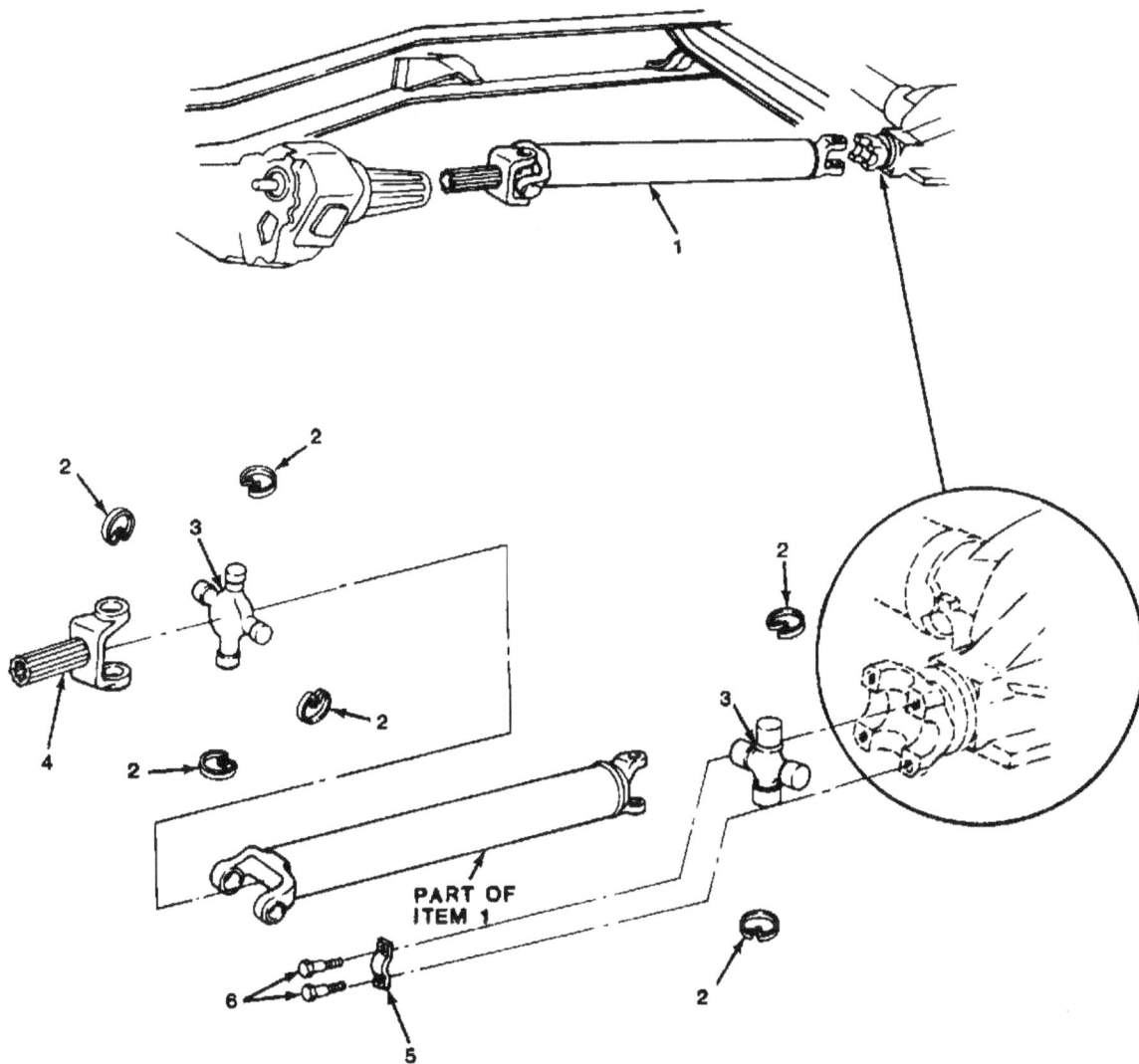

FIGURE 74. REAR PROPELLER SHAFT ASSEMBLY

TA510900

(1) ITEM NO	(2) SMR CODE	(3) CAGEC	(4) PART NUMBER	(5) DESCRIPTION AND USABLE ON CODES (UOC)	(6) QTY
				GROUP 0900 PROPELLER SHAFTS	
				FIG. 74 REAR PROPELLERS SHAFT ASSEMBLY	
1	PAOOO	11862	14067762	PROPELLER SHAFT WITH 208 TRANSFER CASE UOC:194,208,210,230	1
1	PAOOO	11862	7844074	PROPELLER SHAFT WIT UOC:209	1
1	PAOOO	11862	14020403	PROPELLER SHAFT WITH 205 TRANSFER CASE UOC:231,252	1
1	PAOZZ	97271	911105-5130	PROPELLER SHAFT WIT UOC:254,256	1
1	PFOOO	11862	14071980	PROPELLER SHAFT WIT UOC:254,256	1
2	PAOZZ	11862	1456507	.RING,RETAINING UOC:194,208,209,210,230,231,252	6
3	PAOZZ	11862	7806140	.PARTS KIT,UNIVERSAL INCLUDES ITEM #2 UOC:194,208,210,230,231,252	2
3	PAOZZ	11862	7806140	.PARTS KIT,UNIVERSAL INCLUDES ITEM #2 UOC:209	2
4	PAOZZ	11862	14029852	.SLIP YOKE ASSEMBLY UOC:194,208,210,230,231,252	1
4	PAOZZ	11862	7838665	.YOKE,UNIVERSAL JOIN UOC:209	1
5	PAOZZ	11862	3920486	STRAP,RETAINING UOC:194,208,210,230,231,252	2
5	PAOZZ	11862	7846740	STRAP,RETAINING UOC:209	2
5	PAOZZ	11862	14046907	BRACKET,VEHICULAR C UOC:254,256	2
6	PAOZZ	11862	14018700	SCREW,CAP,HEXAGON H UOC:194,208,209,210,230,231,252	4
6	PAOZZ	11862	458300	BOLT,SELF-LOCKING UOC:254,256	4

END OF FIGURE

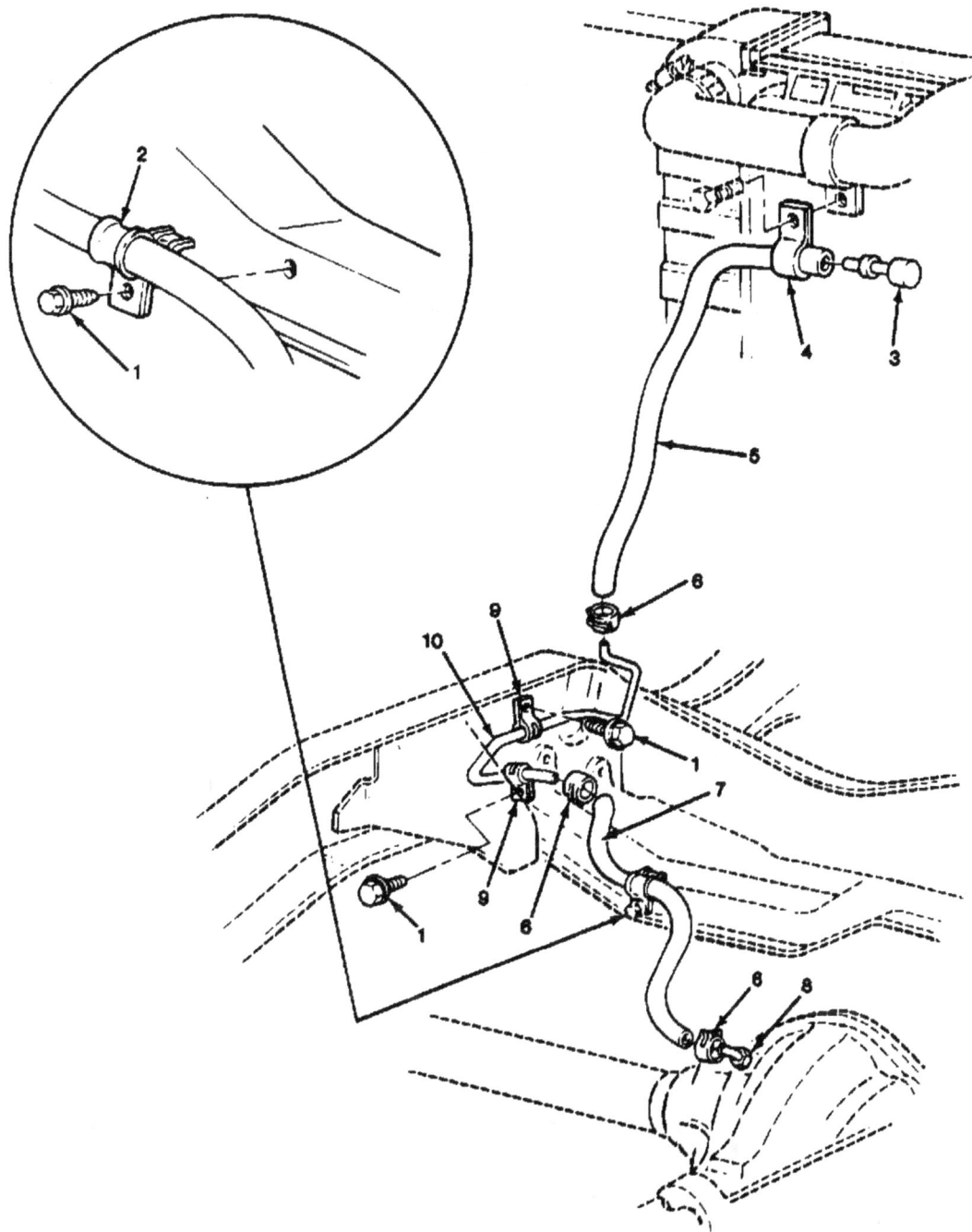

TA510902

FIGURE 75. FRONT AXLE BREATHER.

(1) ITEM NO	(2) SMR CODE	(3) CAGEC	(4) PART NUMBER	(5) DESCRIPTION AND USABLE ON CODES (UOC)	(6) QTY
				GROUP 10 FRONT AXLE	
				GROUP 1000 FRONT AXLE ASSEMBLY	
				FIG. 75 FRONT AXLE BREATHER	
1	PAOZZ	11862	11504447	SCREW,TAPPING	3
2	PAOZZ	96906	MS21333-112	CLAMP,LOOP	1
3	PAOZZ	11862	8640496	SHAFT,SHOULDERED	1
4	PAOZZ	96906	MS21333-48	CLAMP,LOOP	1
5	MOOZZ	11862	9439088	HOSE-FRT AX VENT (20.67"LG)MAKE FROM HOSE,P/N 9439104	1
6	PAOZZ	96906	MS35842-10	CLAMP,HOSE	3
7	MOOZZ	11862	9439091	HOSE-FRT AX VENT (23.62"LG)MAKE FROM HOSE,P/N 9439104	1
8	PAOZZ	11862	14056299	ELBOW,HOSE UOC:194,208,210,230,231,252,254,256	1
9	PAOZZ	96906	MS21333-110	CLAMP,LOOP	2
10	MFOZZ	11862	14029235	PIPE-FRT AX VNT (23.82"LG) MAKE FROM TUBE, P/N 465246	1

END OF FIGURE

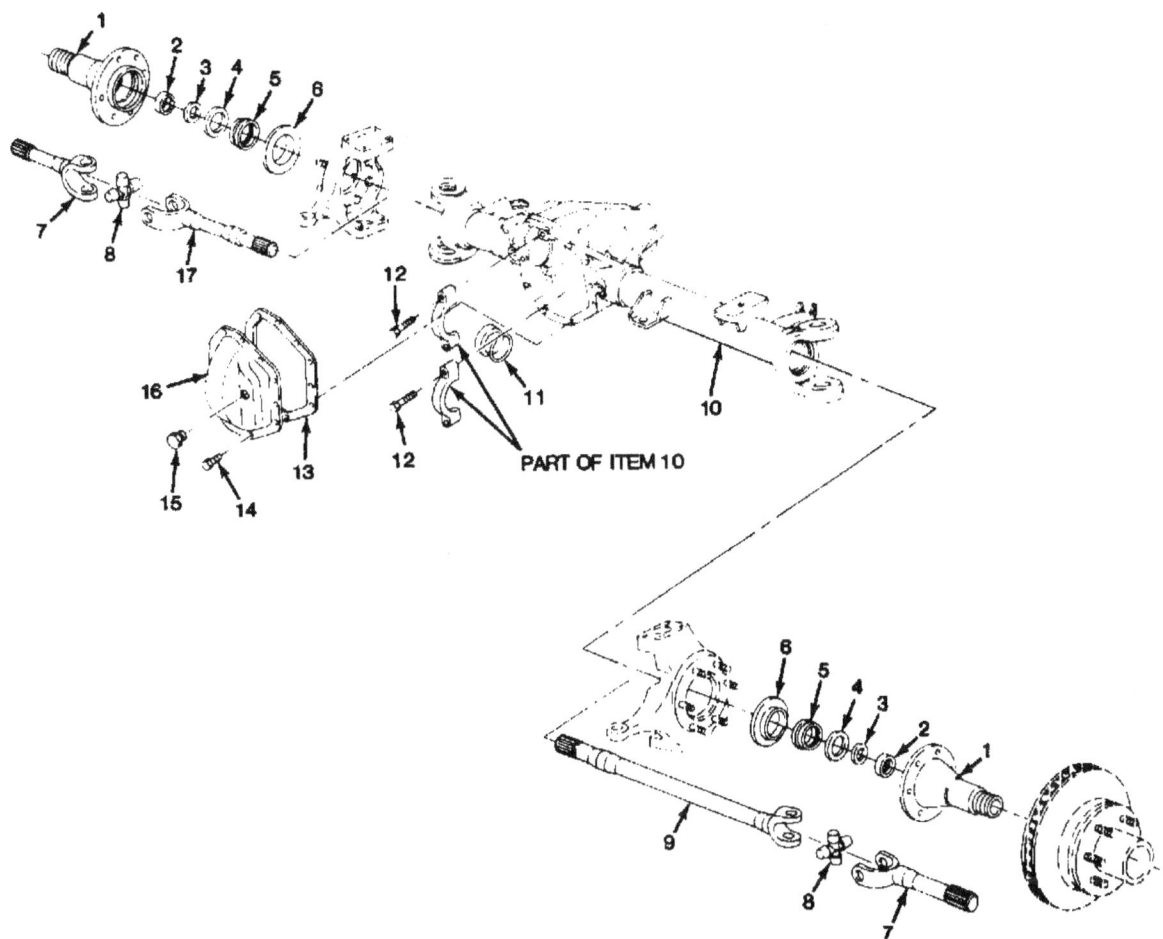

TA510903

FIGURE 76. FRONT AXLE COMPONENT PARTS AND SPINDLE ASSEMBLIES
(ALL EXCEPT M1009).

(1) ITEM NO	(2) SMR CODE	(3) CAGEC	(4) PART NUMBER	(5) DESCRIPTION AND USABLE ON CODES (UOC)	(6) QTY
				GROUP 1000 FRONT AXLE ASSEMBLY	
				FIG. 76 FRONT AXLE COMPONENTS PARTS AND SPINDLE ASSEMBLIES (ALL EXCEPT M1009)	
1	PAOZZ	97271	700013L	PARTS KIT,VEHICULAR INCLUDES ITEMS 4,5 UOC:194,208,210,230,231,252,254,256	2
2	PAOZZ	11862	14009626	PARTS KIT,STEERING INCLUDES ITEMS 3,4,5 UOC:194,208,210,230,231,252,254,256	2
3	PAOZZ	97271	620062-B	SEAL,PLAIN ENCASED UOC:194,208,210,230,231,252,254,256	2
4	PAOZZ	97271	37312	SPACER,RING UOC:194,208,210,230,231,252,254,256	2
5	PAOZZ	11862	462811	SEAL,PLAIN ENCASED UOC:194,208,210,230,231,252,254,256	2
15	PAOZZ	72447	36472	PLUG,PIPE UOC:194,208,210,230,231,252,254,256	1

END OF FIGURE

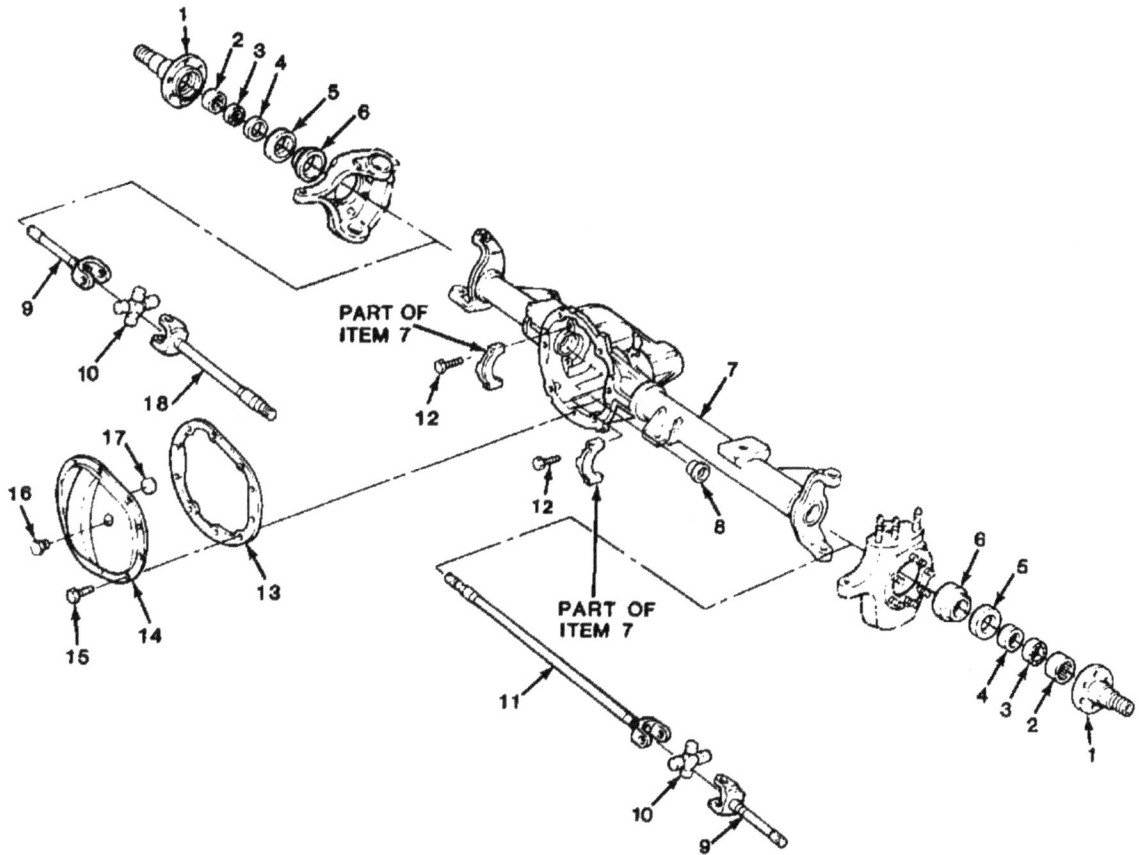

TA510904

FIGURE 77. FRONT AXLE COMPONENT PARTS AND SPINDLE ASSEMBLIES (M1009).

GROUP 1000 FRONT AXLE ASSEMBLY

FIG. 77 FRONT AXLE COMPONENT PARTS
AND SPINDLE ASSEMBLIES (M1009)

ITEM NO	SMR CODE	CAGEC	PART NUMBER	DESCRIPTION AND USABLE ON CODES (UOC)	QTY
1	PAOZZ	11862	14072919	SPINDLE,WHEEL,NONDR INCLUDES ITEM 2,3 APPLIES TO 1984 MODELS ONLY UOC:209	2
1	PAOZZ	97271	29907X	SPINDLE,WHEEL,NONDR INCLUDES ITEMS 2,3,4 AND APPLIES TO VEHICLES STARTING WITH VIN ENDING WITH F136169 UOC:209	2
1	PAOZZ	11862	464039	SPINDLE,WHELL,DRIVI INCLUDES ITEM 2,3,4 UOC:209	2
2	PAOZZ	11862	3965121	PARTS KIT,BEARING R UOC:209	2
3	PAOZZ	11862	376855	SEAL,PLAIN ENCASED UOC:209	2
4	PAOZZ	11862	376852	WASHER,RECESSED UOC:209	2
5	PAOZZ	11862	376851	SEAL,PLAIN ENCASED UOC:209	2
16	PAOZZ	96906	MS51884-9	PLUG,PIPE UOC:209	1

END OF FIGURE

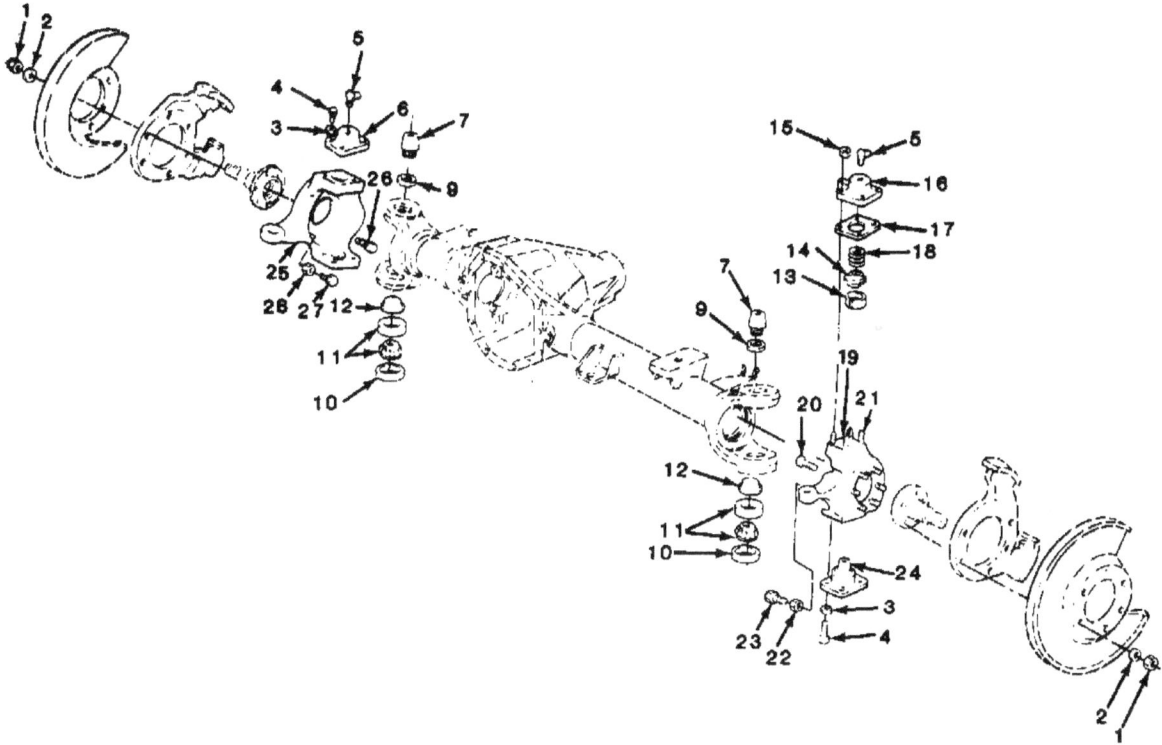

FIGURE 78. STEERING KNUCKLE ASSEMBLY (ALL EXCEPT M1009).

TA510908

(1) ITEM NO	(2) SMR CODE	(3) CAGEC	(4) PART NUMBER	(5) DESCRIPTION AND USABLE ON CODES (UOC)	(6) QTY
				GROUP 1004 STEERING AND LEANING WHEEL MECHANISM	
				FIG. 78 STEERING KNUCKLE ASSEMBLY (ALL EXCEPT M1009)	
1	PAOZZ	97271	36880	NUT,PLAIN UOC:194,208,210,230,231,252,254,256	12
2	PAOZZ	97271	38081-1	WASHER,LOCK UOC:194,208,210,230,231,252,254,256	12
5	PAOZZ	24617	9411031	FITTING,LUBRICATION UOC:194,208,210,230,231,252,254,256	4

END OF FIGURE

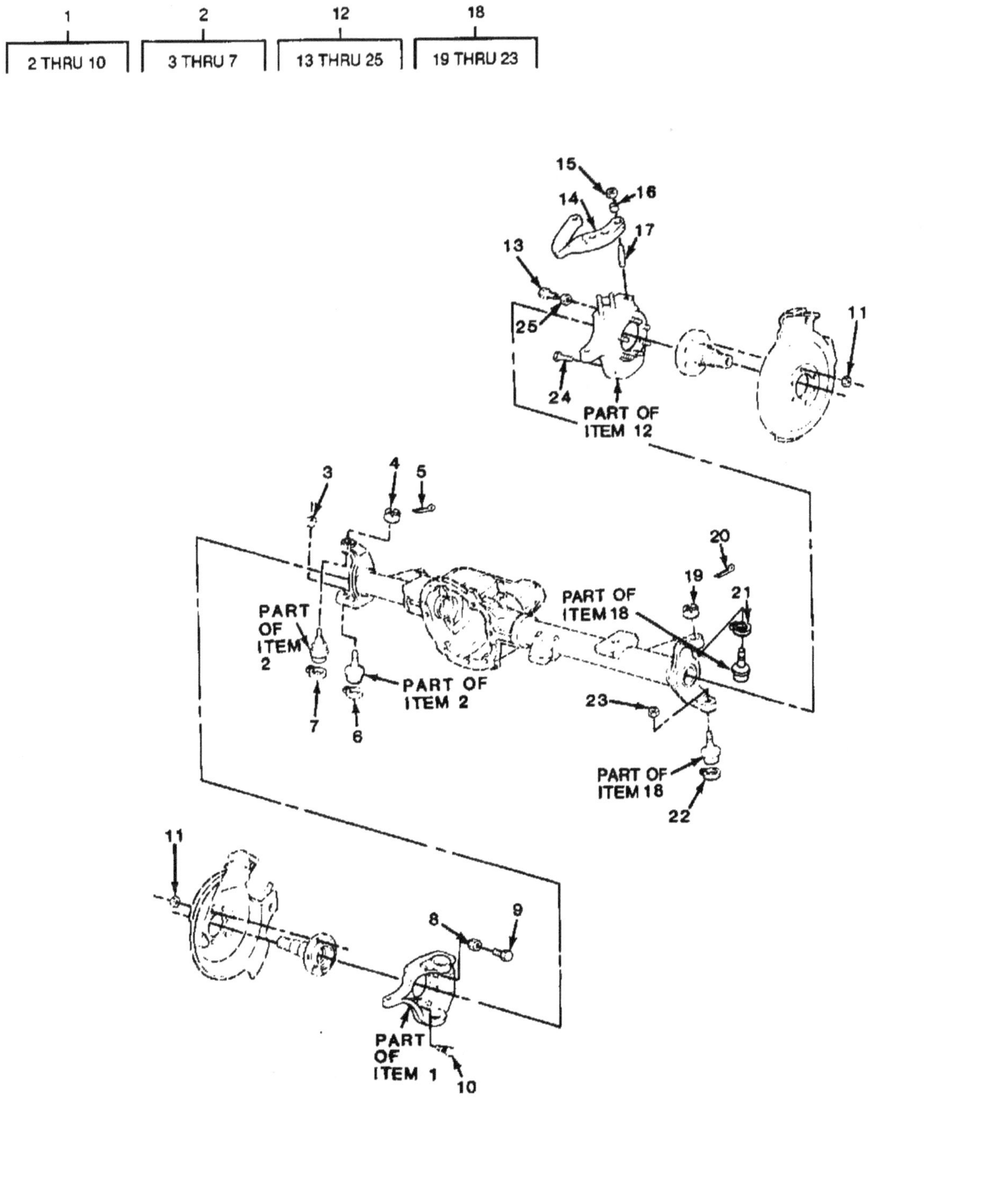

FIGURE 79. STEERING KNUCKLE ASSEMBLY (M1009).

TA510909

(1) ITEM NO	(2) SMR CODE	(3) CAGEC	(4) PART NUMBER	(5) DESCRIPTION AND USABLE ON CODES (UOC)	(6) QTY
				GROUP 1004 STEERING AND LEANING WHEEL MECHANISM	
				FIG. 79 STEERING KNUCKLE ASSEMBLY (M1009)	
8	PAOZZ	96906	MS35691-21	.NUT,PLAIN,HEXAGON UOC:209	1
9	PAOZZ	11862	3711876	.SCREW,CAP,HEXAGON H UOC:209	1
11	PAOZZ	11862	14056133	.NUT,SELF-LOCKING,HE UOC:209	12
13	PAOZZ	11862	3711876	.SCRW,CAP,HEXAGON H UOC:209	1
25	PAOZZ	96906	MS35691-21	.NUT,PLAIN,HEXAGON UOC:209	1

END OF FIGURE

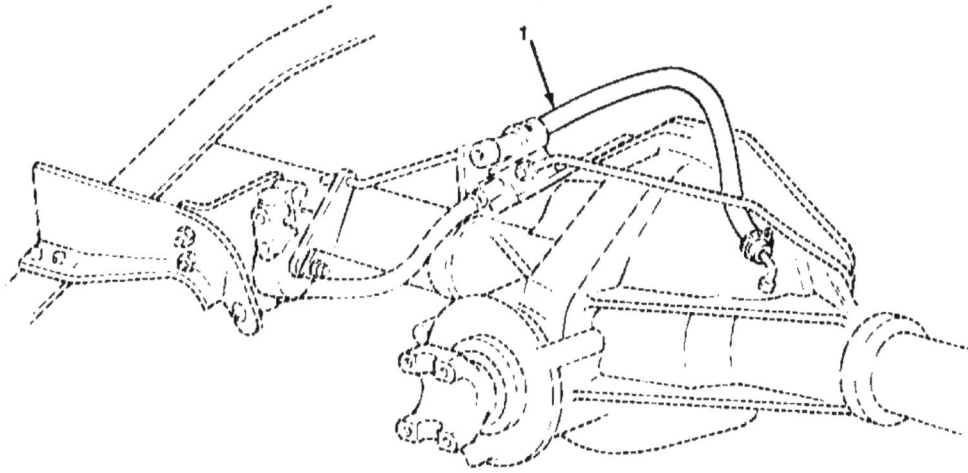

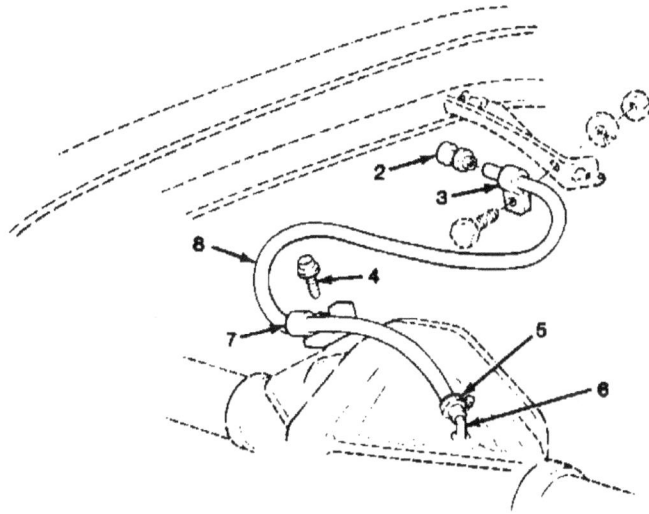

TA510911

FIGURE 80. REAR AXLE BREATHER (ALL EXCEPT MI 009).

(1) ITEM NO	(2) SMR CODE	(3) CAGEC	(4) PART NUMBER	(5) DESCRIPTION AND USABLE ON CODES (UOC)	(6) QTY
				GROUP 11 REAR AXLE	
				GROUP 1100 REAR AXLE ASSEMBLY	
				FIG. 80 REAR AXLE BREATHER (ALL EXCEPT M1009)	
1	MOOZZ	11862	14040775	HOSE NON METALLIC (14.38" LG) MAKE FROM HOSE,P/N 9438315 UOC:210,231	1
2	PAOZZ	11862	8640496	SHAFT,SHOULDERED UOC:194,208,210,230,231,252	1
3	PAOZZ	11862	3866187	HANGER,PIPE UOC:210	1
4	PAOZZ	11862	11504447	SCREW,TAPPING UOC:194,208,210,230,231,252	1
5	PAOZZ	96906	MS35842-10	CLAMP,HOSE UOC:194,208,210,230,231,252	1
6	PAOZZ	11862	14056297	ELBOW,HOSE UOC:194,208,210,230,231,252	1
7	PAOZZ	96906	MS21333-112	CLAMP,LOOP UOC:194,208,210,230,231,252	1
8	MOOZZ	11862	474935	HOSE RR AX VENT (24.00"LG.) MAKE FROM HOSE,P/N 9438315 UOC:194,208,230,252	1

END OF FIGURE

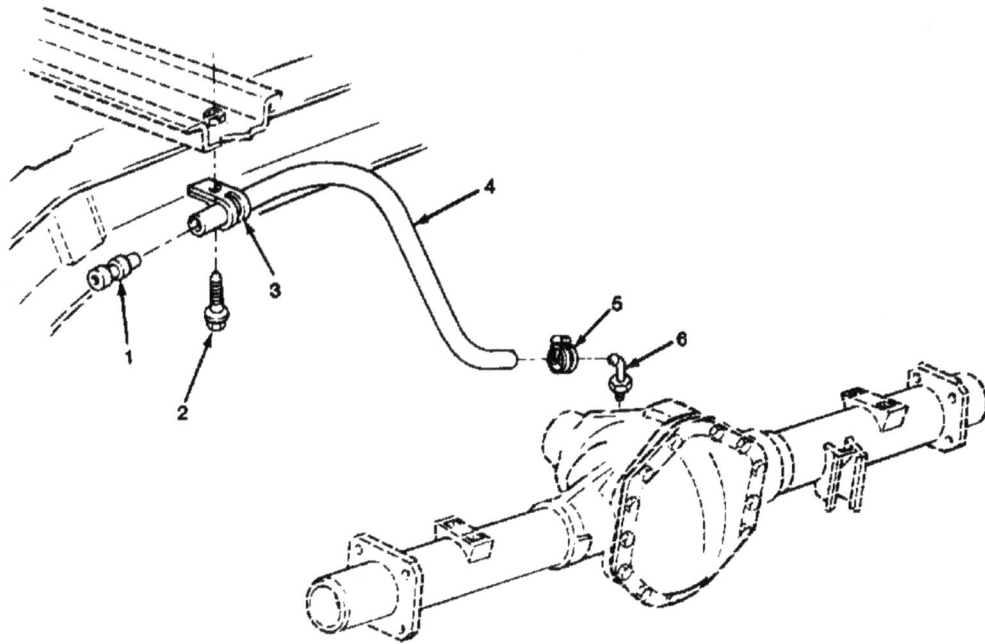

TA510912

FIGURE 81. REAR AXLE BREATHER (M1009).

(1) ITEM NO	(2) SMR CODE	(3) CAGEC	(4) PART NUMBER	(5) DESCRIPTION AND USABLE ON CODES (UOC)	(6) QTY
				GROUP 1100 REAR AXLE ASSEMBLY	
				FIG. 81 REAR AXLE BREATHER (M1009)	
1	PAOZZ	11862	8640496	SHAFT,SHOULDERED UOC:209	1
2	PAOZZ	11862	11504447	SCREW,TAPPING UOC:209	1
3	PAOZZ	96906	MS21333-112	CLAMP,LOOP UOC:209	1
4	MOOZZ	11862	474935	HOSE RR AX VENT (24.00"LG) MAKE FROM HOSE,P/N 9738315 UOC:209	1
5	PAOZZ	96906	MS35842-10	CLAMP,HOSE UOC:209	1
6	PAOZZ	11862	14072930	ELBOW,FLANGE TO HOS UOC:209	1

END OF FIGURE

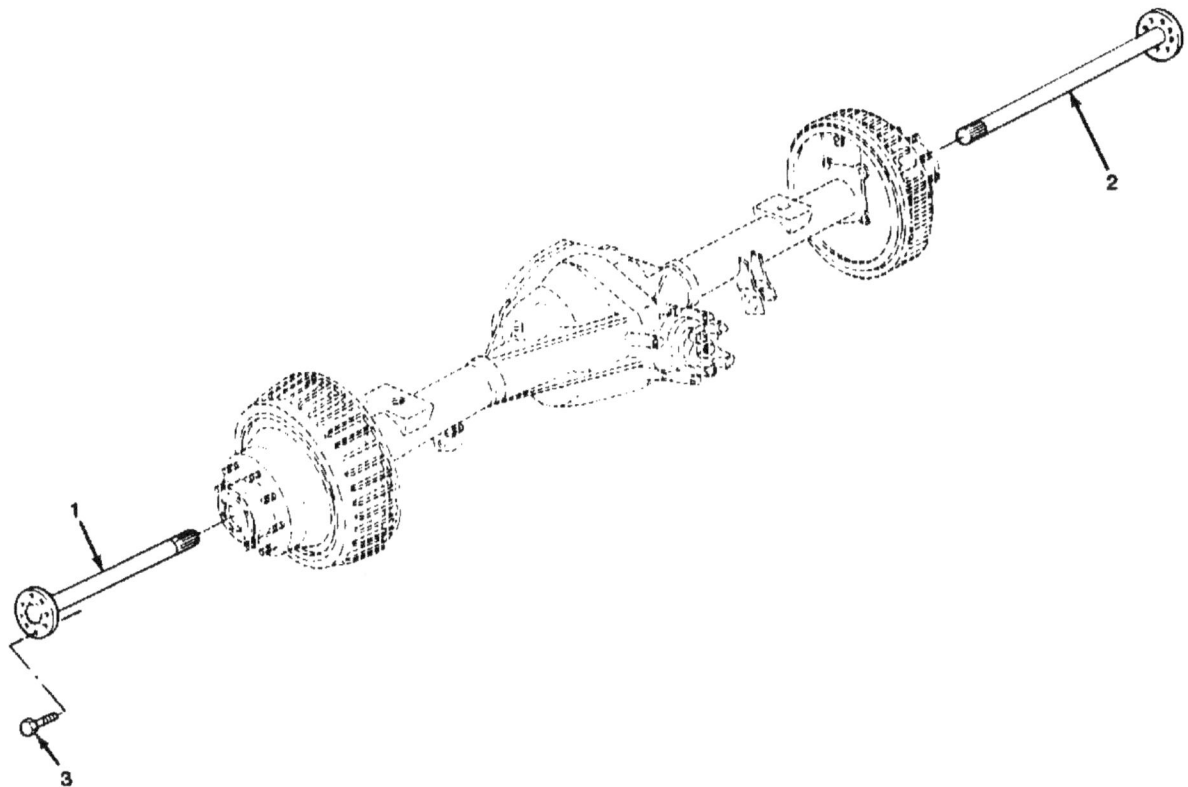

TA510913

FIGURE 82. AXLE SHAFTS (ALL EXCEPT MI 009).

(1) ITEM NO	(2) SMR CODE	(3) CAGEC	(4) PART NUMBER	(5) DESCRIPTION AND USABLE ON CODES (UOC)	(6) QTY
				GROUP 1100 REAR AXLE SHAFTS	
				FIG. 82 AXLE SHAFTS (ALL EXCEPT M1009)	
1	PAOZZ	11862	3977384	SHAFT,AXLE,AUTOMOTI RIGHT UOC:194,208,210,230,231,252	1
1	PAOZZ	11862	15599687	SHAFT,AXLE,AUTOMOTI UOC:254,256	1
2	PAOZZ	11862	3977383	SHAFT,AXLE,AUTOMOTI UOC:194,208,210,230,231,252	1
3	PAOZZ	11862	376869	BOLT,SELF-LOCKING UOC:194,208,210,230,231,252,254,256	16

END OF FIGURE

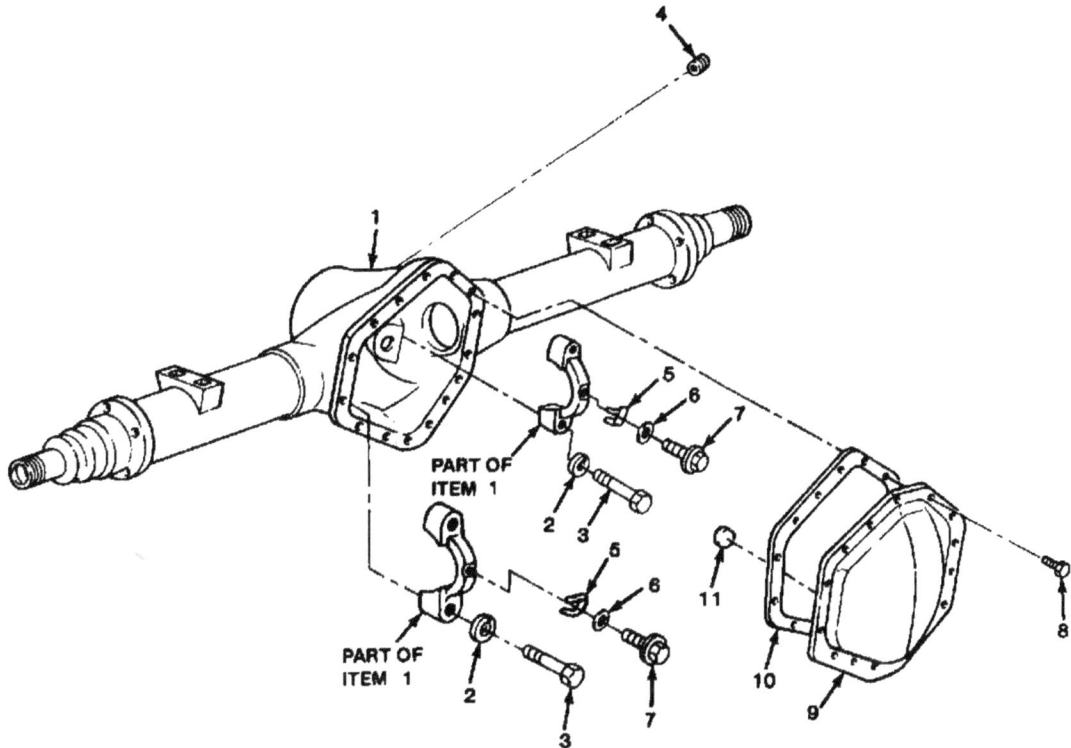

FIGURE 83. REAR AXLE HOUSING (ALL EXCEPT M1009).

TA510915

(1) ITEM NO	(2) SMR CODE	(3) CAGEC	(4) PART NUMBER	(5) DESCRIPTION AND USABLE ON CODES (UOC)	(6) QTY
				GROUP 1101 HOUSING, BEAM, HOUSING COVERS, PLUGS, SEALS, ETC.	
				FIG. 83 REAR AXLE HOUSING (ALL EXCEPT M1009)	
4	PAOZZ	30379	444789	PLUG,PIPE UOC:194,208,210,230,231,252	1
8	PAOZZ	11862	15521977	BOLT,SELF-LOCKING UOC:194,208,210,230,231,252	14
9	PAOZZ	11862	3977386	COVER,ACCESS UOC:194,208,210,230,231,252	1
9	PAOZZ	11862	14071884	COVER,TRANSMISSION UOC:254,256	1
10	PAOZZ	11862	3977387	GASKET UOC:194,208,210,230,231,252	1
11	PAOZZ	11862	3787240	MAGNET,CHIP COLLECT UOC:194,208,210,230,231,252	1

END OF FIGURE

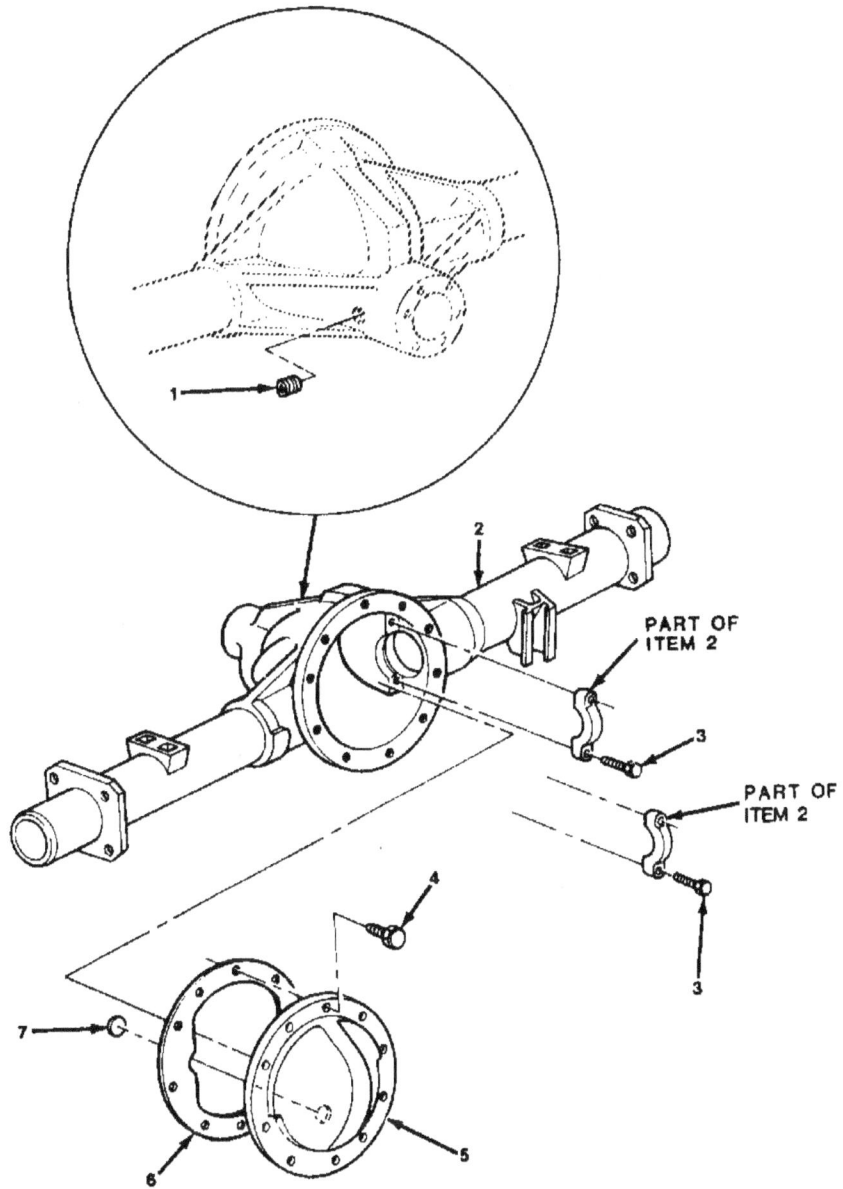

FIGURE 84. REAR AXLE HOUSING (MI 009).

TA510916

(1) ITEM NO	(2) SMR CODE	(3) CAGEC	(4) PART NUMBER	(5) DESCRIPTION AND USABLE ON CODES (UOC)	(6) QTY
				GROUP 1101 HOUSING, BEAM, HOUSING COVERS, PLUGS, SEALS, ETC.	
				FIG. 84 REAR AXLE HOUSING (M1009)	
1	PAOZZ	30379	444789	PLUG,PIPE UOC:209	1
4	PAOZZ	11862	10008936	BOLT,SELF-LOCKING UOC:209	10
5	PAOZZ	11862	1252415	COVER,GEAR CARRIER UOC:209	1
6	PAOZZ	11862	26016662	GASKET UOC:209	1
7	PBOZZ	11862	3787240	MAGNET,CHIP COLLECT UOC:209	1
				END OF FIGURE	

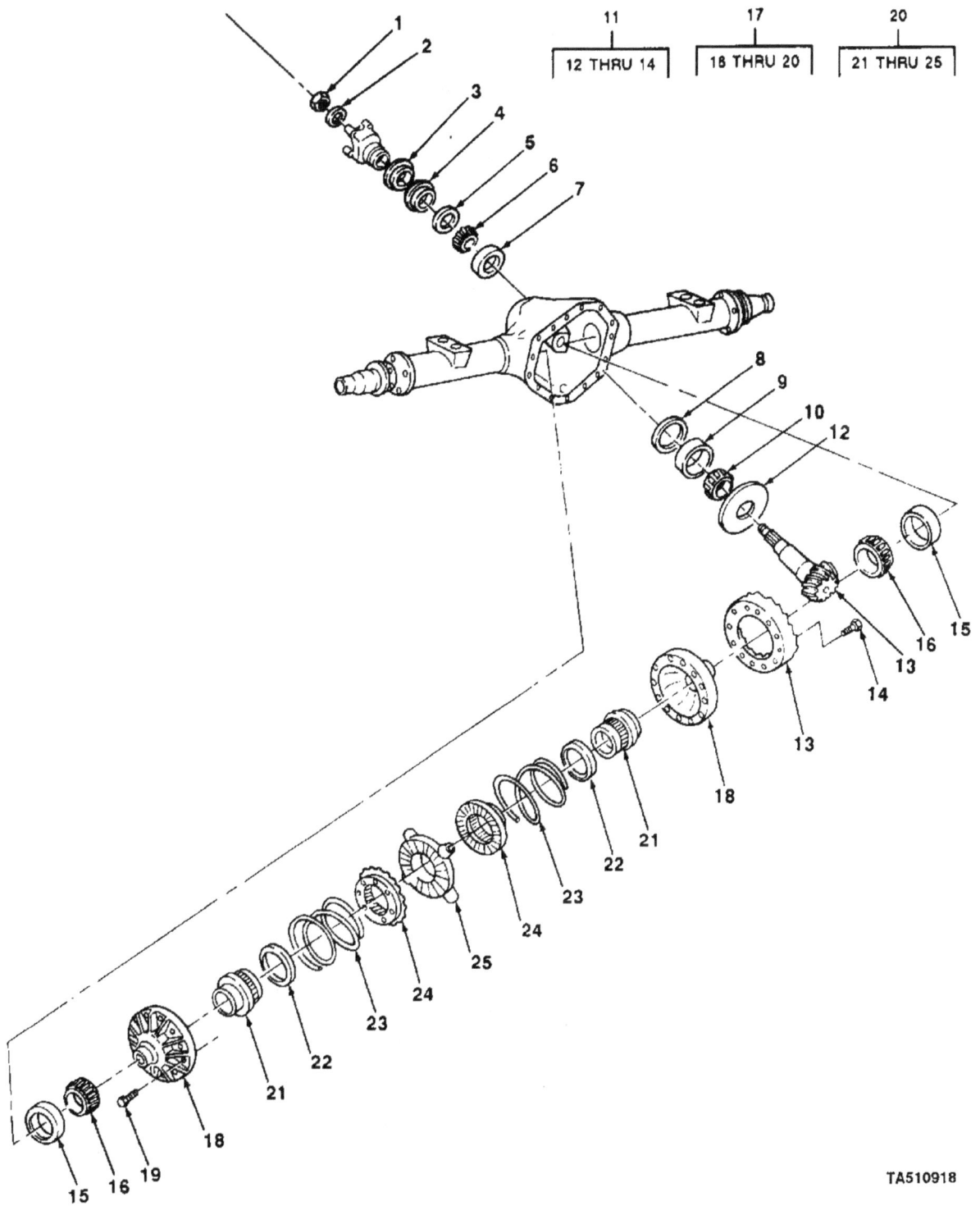

FIGURE 85. DIFFERENTIAL LOCK ASSEMBLY, RING, PINION, AND RELATED
PARTS (M1028A2 AND M1028A3).

TA510918

(1) ITEM NO	(2) SMR CODE	(3) CAGEC	(4) PART NUMBER	(5) DESCRIPTION AND USABLE ON CODES (UOC)	(6) QTY
				GROUP 1102 DIFFERENTIAL	
				FIG. 85 DIFFERENTIAL LOCK ASSEMBLY, RING, PINION, AND RELATED PARTS (M1028A2 AND M1028A3)	
6	PAOZZ	60038	HM88542	CONE AND ROLLERS,TA UOC:254,256	1
7	PAOZZ	60038	88510	CUP,TAPERED ROLLER UOC:254,256	1
9	PAOZZ	60038	HM807010	CUP,TAPERED ROLLER UOC:254,256	1
10	PAOZZ	60038	HM807040	CONE AND ROLLERS,TA UOC:254,256	1
15	PAOZZ	60038	453X	CUP,TAPERED ROLLER UOC:254,256	1
16	PAOZZ	60038	469	CONE AND ROLLERS,TA UOC:254,256	1

END OF FIGURE

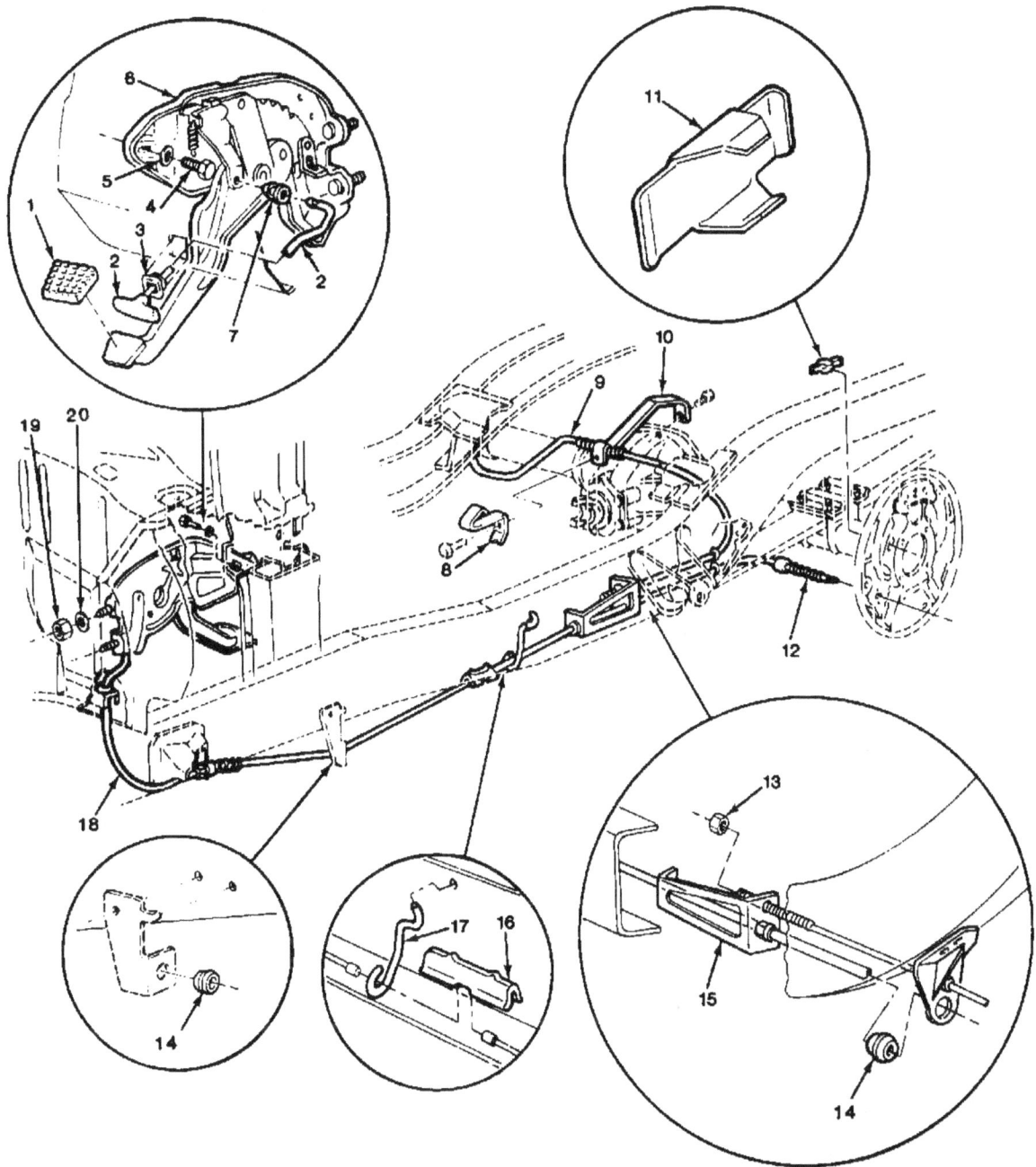

TA510921

FIGURE 86. PARKING BRAKE PEDAL AND RELEASE MECHANISM.

(1) ITEM NO	(2) SMR CODE	(3) CAGEC	(4) PART NUMBER	(5) DESCRIPTION AND USABLE ON CODES (UOC)	(6) QTY
				GROUP 12 BRAKES	
				GROUP 1201 HANDBRAKES	
				FIG. 86 PARKING BRAKE PEDAL AND RELEASE MECHANISM	
1	PAOZZ	11862	3893181	PAD, PEDAL	1
2	PAOZZ	11862	334540	LEVER, MANUAL CONTRO	1
3	PAOZZ	11862	341990	GROMMET, NONMETALLIC	1
4	PAOZZ	96906	MS90728-33	BOLT, MACHINE	1
5	PAOZZ	96906	MS35340-45	WASHER, LOCK	1
6	PAOZZ	11862	14053591	LEVER, MANUAL CONTRO	1
7	PAOZZ	11862	334541	GROMMET, NONMETALLIC	1
8	PAOZZ	11862	14054122	CLIP, SPRING TENSION UOC:194,208,210,230,231,252,254,256	1
8	PAOZZ	11862	15557723	CLIP, SPRING TENSION UOC:254,256	1
9	PAOZZ	11862	14054174	CONTROL ASSEMBLY, PU UOC:209	1
9	PAOZZ	11862	14064664	CONTROL ASSEMBLY, PU UOC:194,208,210,230,231,252,254,256	1
10	PAOZZ	11862	14072697	CLIP, SPRING TENSION UOC:209	1
10	PAOZZ	11862	14054120	CLIP, SPRING TENSION UOC:254,256	1
11	PAOZZ	19207	7001423	PLUG, PROTECTIVE, DUS UOC:194,208,210,230,231,252,254,256	6
12	PAOZZ	11862	14054173	CONTROL ASSEMBLY, PU UOC:209	1
12	PAOZZ	11862	14064663	CONTROL ASSEMBLY, PU UOC:194,208,210,230,231,252,254,256	1
13	PAOZZ	96906	MS17829-5C	NUT, SELF-LOCKING, HE	1
14	PAOZZ	11862	15530620	GROMMET, NONMETALLIC	2
15	PAOZZ	11862	14072692	EQUALIZER, PARKING B	1
16	PAOZZ	11862	25516531	CLIP, RETAINING	1
17	PAOZZ	11862	368786	GUIDE, CABLE, PARKING UOC:209	1
18	PAOZZ	11862	14055591	CABLE ASSEMBLY, PARK UOC:209	1
18	PAOZZ	11862	14053593	CONTROL ASSEMBLY, PU UOC:194,208,210,230,231,252,254,256	1
19	PAOZZ	96906	MS51967-6	NUT, PLAIN, HEXAGON	2
20	PAOZZ	96906	MS27183-11	WASHER, FLAT	2

END OF FIGURE

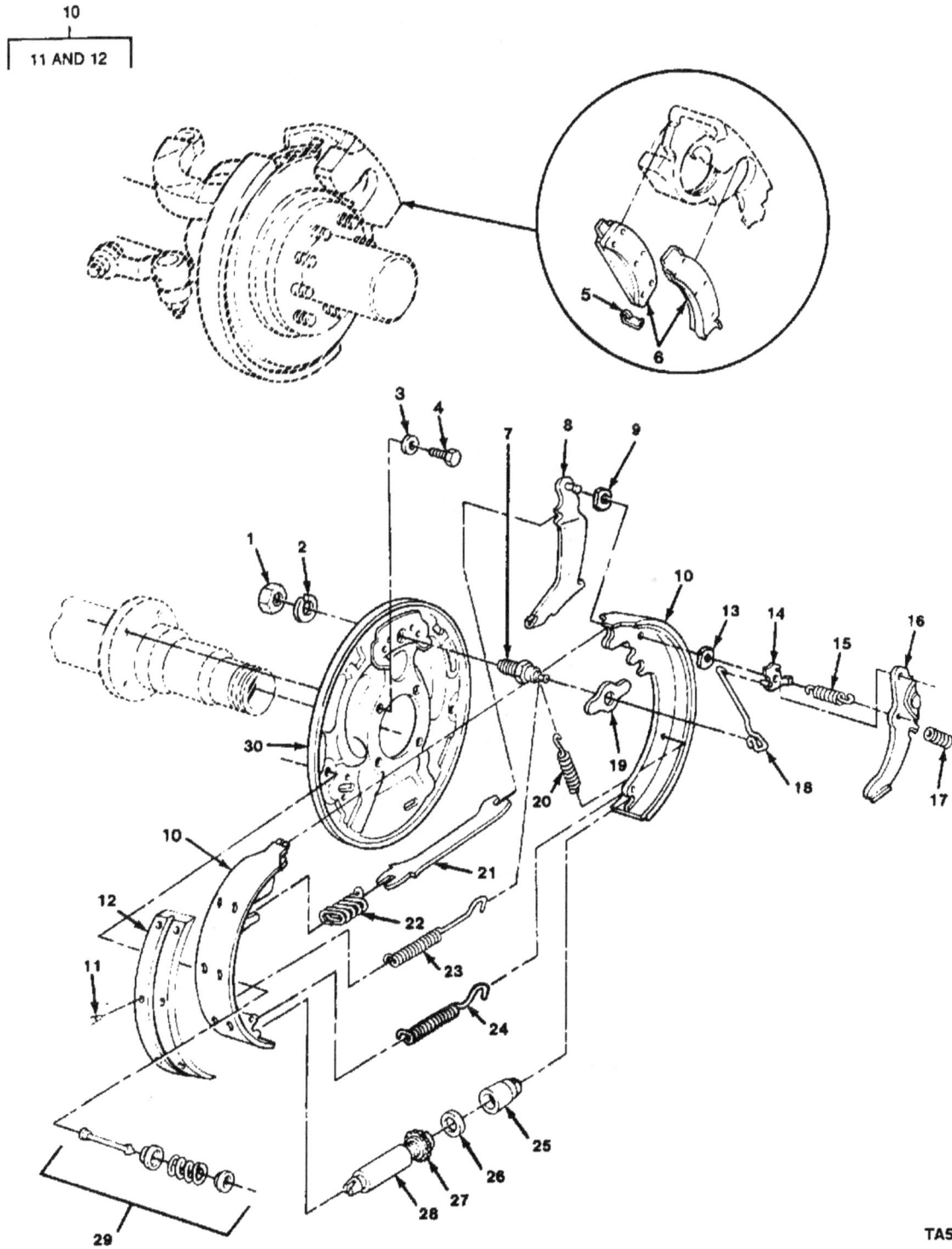

FIGURE 87. REAR BRAKESHOE ASSEMBLY COMPONENTS, FRONT BRAKE PADS,
AND RELATED PARTS (ALL EXCEPT M1009).

GROUP 1202 SERVICE BRAKES

FIG. 87 REAR BRAKESHOE ASSEMBLY
COMPONENTS, FRONT BRAKE PADS, AND
RELATED PARTS (ALL EXCEPT M1009)

ITEM NO	SMR CODE	CAGEC	PART NUMBER	DESCRIPTION AND USABLE ON CODES (UOC)	QTY
1	PAOZZ	96906	MS51968-24	NUT,PLAIN,HEXAGON UOC:194,208,210,230,231,252	2
2	PAOZZ	96906	MS35340-51	WASHER,LOCK UOC:194,208,210,230,231,252	2
3	PAOZZ	96906	MS35340-48	WASHER,LOCK UOC:194,208,210,230,231,252	8
4	PAOZZ	96906	MS90727-109	SCREW,CAP,HEXAGON H UOC:194,208,210,230,231,252	8
5	PAOZZ	14892	4150515	CLIP,BRAKE SHOE UOC:194,208,210,230,231,252,254,256	2
6	PAOZZ	14892	3368689	DISK BRAKE SHOE SET UOC:194,208,210,230,231,252,254,256	1
7	PAOZZ	11862	3856834	PIN,BRAKE SHOE ANCH UOC:194,208,210,230,231,252,254,256	2
8	PAOZZ	11862	334307	LEVER,MANUAL CONTRO LEFT SIDE UOC:194,208,210,230,231,252,254,256	1
8	PAOZZ	11862	334308	LEVER,MANUAL CONTRO RIGHT SIDE UOC:194,208,210,230,231,252,254,256	1
9	PAOZZ	11862	5454797	WASHER,SPRING TENSI UOC:194,208,210,230,231,252,254,256	2
10	PAOFF	11862	372379	BRAKE SHOE SET,INTE UOC:194,208,210,230,231,252,254,256	1
13	PAOZZ	96906	MS16633-1031	RING,RETAINING UOC:194,208,210,230,231,252	2
14	PAOZZ	11862	3856855	PIVOT,BRAKE SHOE AD LEFT UOC:194,208,210,231,252,254,256	1
14	PAOZZ	11862	3856856	PIVOT,BRAKE SHOE RIGHT UOC:194,208,210,230,231,252,254,256	1
15	PAOZZ	11862	5461145	SPRING,HELICAL,EXTE LEFT UOC:194,208,210,230,231,252,254,256	2
16	PAOZZ	11862	357845	LEVER ASSEMBLY,BRAK LEFT UOC:194,208,210,230,231,252,254,256	1
16	PAOZZ	11862	357846	LEVER,LOC-RELEASE RIGHT UOC:194,208,210,230,231,252,254,256	1
17	PAOZZ	11862	5461984	SPRING,BRAKE SHOE UOC:194,208,210,230,231,252,254,256	2
18	PAOZZ	11862	3856857	CONNECTING LINK,RIG LEFT UOC:194,208,210,230,231,252,254,256	1
18	PAOZZ	11862	3856858	LINK,ANCHOR,BRAKE S RIGHT UOC:194,208,210,230,231,252,254,256	1
19	PAOZZ	11862	18002428	NUT SPACER,PLATE UOC:194,208,210,230,231,252,254,256	2
20	PAOZZ	11862	3856843	SPRING,HELICAL,EXTE UOC:194,208,210,230,231,252,254,256	2
21	PAOZZ	11862	3898059	STRUT,PARKING BRAKE UOC:194,208,210,230,231,252,254,256	2

(1) ITEM NO	(2) SMR CODE	(3) CAGEC	(4) PART NUMBER	(5) DESCRIPTION AND USABLE ON CODES (UOC)	(6) QTY
22	PAOZZ	11862	1312281	SPRING KIT UOC:194,208,210,230,231,252,254,256	2
23	PAOZZ	11862	3767138	SPRING,HELICAL,EXTE UOC:194,208,210,230,231,252,254,256	2
24	PAOZZ	11862	3856850	SPRING,HELICAL,EXTE UOC:194,208,210,230,231,252,254,256	2
25	PAOZZ	11862	15522081	SOCKET,BRAKE SHOE UOC:194,208,210,230,231,252,254,256	2
26	PAOZZ	11862	3856849	SHIM UOC:194,208,10,230,231,252,254,256	2
27	PAOZZ	11862	15522077	ADJUSTER,SLACK,BRAK LEFT UOC:194,208,210,230,231,252,254,256	1
27	PAOZZ	11862	15522078	ADJUSTING SCREW ASS RIGHT UOC:194,208,210,230,231,252,254,256	1
28	PAOZZ	11862	15522079	NUT,BRAKE SHOE ADJU LEFT UOC:194,208,210,230,231,252,254,256	1
28	PAOZZ	11862	15522080	ADJUSTING SCREW ASS RIGHT UOC:194,208,210,230,231,252,254,256	1
29	PAOZZ	11862	372249	PARTS KIT,BRAKE SHO UOC:194,208,210,230,231,252,254,256	2
30	PAOZZ	11862	14068905	PLATE,BACKING,BRAKE LEFT UOC:194,208,210,230,231,252,254,256	1
30	PAOZZ	11862	14068906	PLATE,BACKING,BRAKE RIGHT UOC:194,208,210,230,231,252,254,256	1

END OF FIGURE

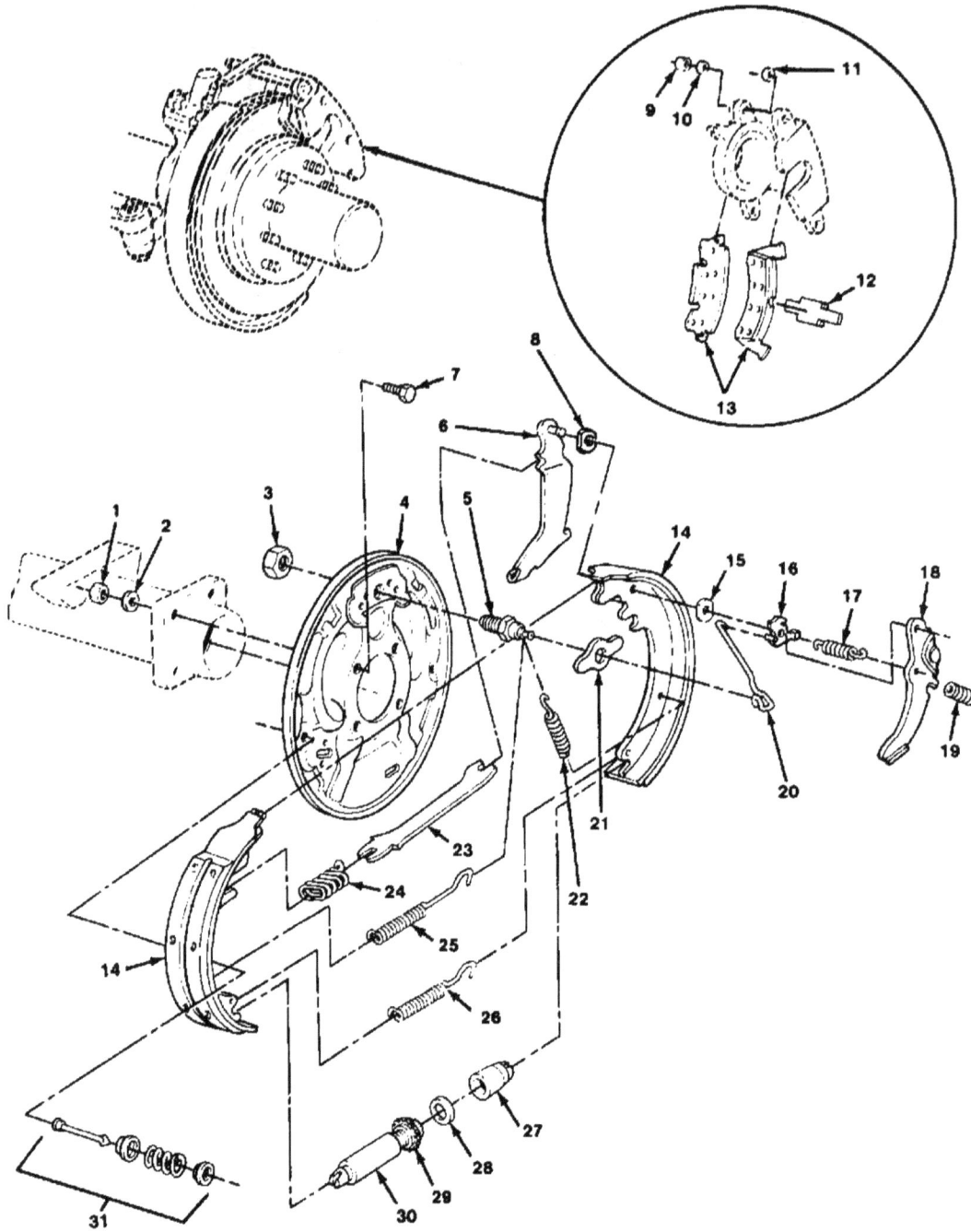

TA510923

FIGURE 88. REAR BRAKESHOE ASSEMBLY COMPONENTS, FRONT BRAKE
PADS, AND RELATED PARTS (MI 009).

(1) ITEM NO	(2) SMR CODE	(3) CAGEC	(4) PART NUMBER	(5) DESCRIPTION AND USABLE ON CODES (UOC)	(6) QTY
				GROUP 1202 SERVICE BRAKES	
				FIG. 88 REAR BRAKESHOE ASSEMBLY COMPONENTS, FRONT BRAKE PADS, AND RELATED PARTS (M1009)	
3	PAOZZ	11862	3760300	NUT,PLAIN,ROUND UOC:209	2
5	PAOZZ	11862	14009982	LINK,ANCHOR,BRAKE S UOC:209	2
6	PAOZZ	11862	15594177	PARTS KIT,PARKING B LEFT UOC:209	1
6	PAOZZ	11862	15594178	PARTS KIT,PARKING B RIGHT UOC:209	1
8	PAOZZ	11862	5454797	WASHER,SPRING TENSI UOC:209	2
9	PAOZZ	11862	18004057	SPACER,SLEEVE UOC:209	4
10	PAOZZ	76462	18001032	BUSHING,NONMETALLIC UOC:209	4
11	PAOZZ	11862	5470497	PACKING,PREFORMED UOC:209	4
12	PAOZZ	11862	5469497	CLIP,SPRING TENSION UOC:209	2
13	PAOZZ	11862	12321435	DISK BRAKE SHOE SET UOC:209	1
14	PAOZZ	11862	1155445	BRAKE SHOE SET UOC:209	1
15	PAOZZ	96906	MS16633-1031	RING,RETAINING UOC:209	2
16	PAOZZ	11862	3856855	PIVOT,BRAKE SHOE AD LEFT UOC:209	1
16	PAOZZ	11862	3856856	PIVOT,BRAKE SHOE RIGHT UOC:209	1
17	PAOZZ	11862	5461145	SPRING,HELICAL,EXTE UOC:209	2
18	PAOZZ	11862	357890	LEVER,MANUAL CONTRO RIGHT UOC:209	1
18	PAOZZ	11862	357889	LEVER,MANUAL CONTRO LEFT UOC:209	1
19	PAOZZ	11862	5461984	SPRING,BRAKE SHOE UOC:209	2
20	PAOZZ	11862	5461156	LINK,ANCHOR,BRAKE S RIGHT UOC:209	1
20	PAOZZ	11862	14055315	LINK,ADJUSTING BRAK LEFT UOC:209	1
21	PAOZZ	11862	18002428	NUT SPACER,PLATE UOC:209	2
22	PAOZZ	11862	3820163	SPRING,HELICAL,EXTE UOC:209	2
23	PAOZZ	11862	468661	STRUT,PARKING BRAKE UOC:209	2

(1) ITEM NO	(2) SMR CODE	(3) CAGEC	(4) PART NUMBER	(5) DESCRIPTION AND USABLE ON CODES (UOC)	(6) QTY
24	PAOZZ	11862	1312281	SPRING KIT UOC:209	2
25	PAOZZ	11862	3694822	SPRING,HELICAL,EXTE UOC:209	2
26	PAOZZ	11862	3887347	SPRING,HELICAL,EXTE UOC:209	2
27	PAOZZ	11862	468675	SCREW UOC:209	2
28	PAOZZ	11862	5462496	SHIM UOC:209	2
29	PAOZZ	11862	345943	ADJUSTING SCREW ASS LEFT UOC:209	1
29	PAOZZ	11862	345944	ADJUSTING SCREW ASS RIGHT UOC:209	1
30	PAOZZ	11862	468673	NUT,ADJUSTER BRAKE LEFT UOC:209	1
30	PAOZZ	11862	468674	NUT,ADJUSTER BRAKE RIGHT UOC:209	1
31	PAOZZ	11862	372249	PARTS KIT,BRAKE SHO UOC:209	2

END OF FIGURE

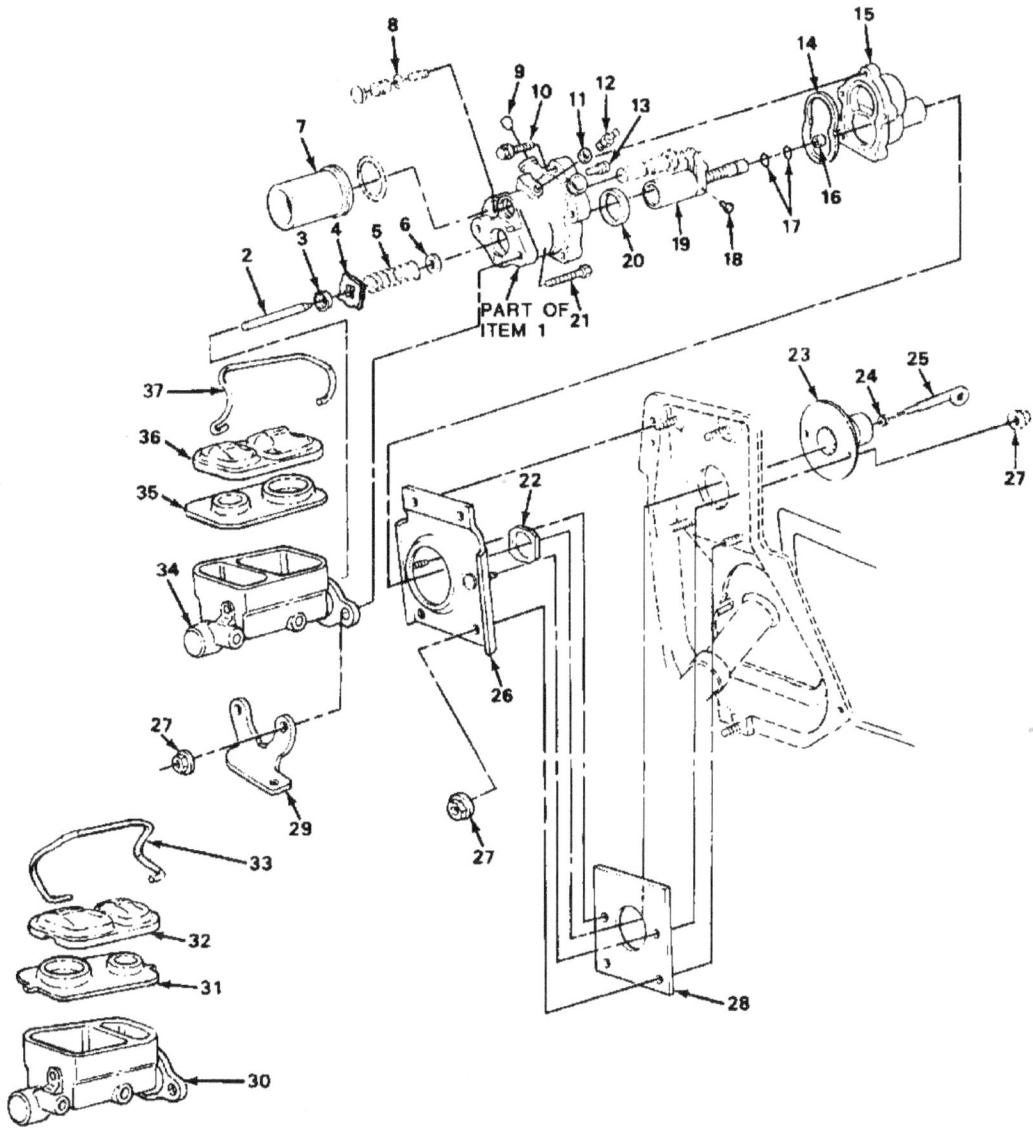

FIGURE 89. POWER BOOSTER AND MASTER CYLINDER ASSEMBLIES.

TA510924

(1) ITEM NO	(2) SMR CODE	(3) CAGEC	(4) PART NUMBER	(5) DESCRIPTION AND USABLE ON CODES (UOC)	(6) QTY
				GROUP 1204 HYDRAULIC BRAKE SYSTEM	
				FIG. 89 POWER BOOSTER AND MASTER CYLINDER ASSEMBLIES	
1	PAOZZ	14892	2770317	BRAKE BOOSTER ASSEM UOC:209	1
1	PAOZZ	14892	2770209	BOOSTER,HYDRAULIC B UOC:194,208,210,230,231,252,254,256	1
11	XDOZZ	14892	2770614	.PACKING,PREFORMED UOC:209	2
12	XAOZZ	14892	129494	.FITTING,BRAKE BOOST	1
25	PAOZZ	11862	345683	.ROD,PEDAL CONTROL UOC:194,208,210,230,231,252,254,256	1
27	PAOZZ	11862	11502812	NUT,SELF-LOCKING,EX	8
28	PAOZZ	11862	14004810	GASKET	1
29	PAOZZ	11862	14045698	BRACKET,ANGLE	1
30	PAOOO	14892	2232073	CYLINDER ASSEMBLY,H UOC:194,208,210,230,231,252,254,256	1
31	PAOZZ	14892	2229044	.GASKET UOC:194,208,210,230,231,252,254,256	1
32	PBOZZ	14892	2232076	.COVER,MASTER CYLIND UOC:194,208,210,230,231,252,254,256	1
33	PBOZZ	14892	2229046	.HANDLE,BAIL UOC:194,208,210,230,231,252,254,256	2
34	PAOOO	14892	2232072	CYLINDER,HYDRAULIC UOC:209	1
35	PAOZZ	14892	2227168	.GASKET UOC:209	1
36	PBOZZ	14892	2232077	.COVER,RESERVOIR UOC:209	1
37	PBOZZ	14892	2229448	.CLIP,SPRING TENSION UOC:209	1

END OF FIGURE

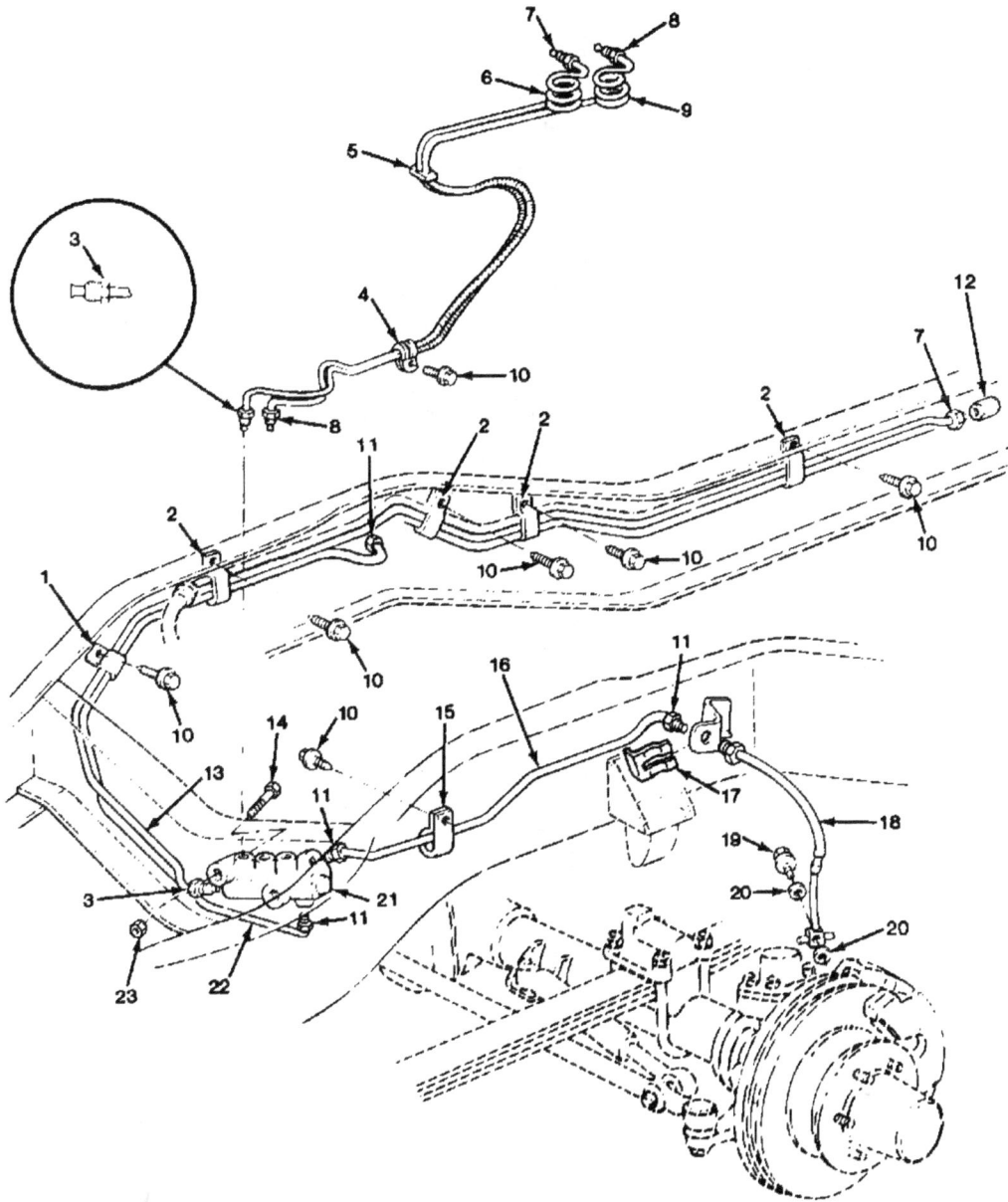

TA510925

FIGURE 90. FRONT BRAKE LINES AND RELATED PARTS.

GROUP 1204 HYDRAULIC BRAKE SYSTEM

FIG. 90 FRONT BRAKE LINES AND
RELATED PARTS

ITEM NO	SMR CODE	CAGEC	PART NUMBER	DESCRIPTION AND USABLE ON CODES (UOC)	QTY
1	PAOZZ	11862	343438	CLAMP,LOOP	1
2	PAOZZ	11862	15599973	CLAMP,LOOP	4
3	PAOZZ	11862	9424955	INVERTED NUT,TUBE C	2
4	PAOZZ	11862	25527423	CLAMP,LOOP	1
5	PAOZZ	11862	3816659	STRAP,LINE SUPPORTI	1
6	MFOZZ	11862	15599260	PIPE ASM RR BRK CB (78.49" LG) MAKE FROM TUBE, P/N 603827 UOC:209	1
6	MFOZZ	11862	15599262	PIPE ASM RR BRK (75.25"LG) MAKE FROM TUBE, P/N 603827 UOC:194,208,210,230,231,252,254,256	1
7	PAOZZ	24617	137397	INVERTED NUT,TUBE C	2
8	PAOZZ	11862	15607227	NUT	2
9	MFOZZ	11862	15599259	PIPE ASM FRT BRK (72.68" LG) MAKE FROM PIPE, P/N 3696822 UOC:209	1
9	MFOZZ	11862	15599261	PIPE ASM FRT BRK CB (76.63"LG) MAKE FROM PIPE, P/N 3696822 UOC:194,208,210,230,231,252,254,256	1
10	PAOZZ	11862	11504447	SCREW,TAPPING	7
11	PAOZZ	24617	9432075	INVERTED NUT,TUBE C	4
12	PAOZZ	96906	MS51877-4	COUPLING,TUBE	1
13	MFOZZ	11862	14034586	PIPE ASM RR BRK (91.51" LG) MAKE FROM TUBE, P/N 603827 UOC:209	1
13	MFOZZ	11862	15522444	PIPE ASSY (89.68"LG) MAKE FROM TUBE, P/N 603827 UOC:194,208,210,230,231,252,254,256	1
14	PAOZZ	96906	MS90728-40	BOLT,MACHINE	2
15	PAOZZ	11862	342677	CLAMP,LOOP	1
16	MFOZZ	11862	14034571	PIPE ASM FRT BRK (29.43" LG) MAKE FROM PIPE, P/N 3696822 UOC:209	1
16	MFOZZ	11862	14054257	PIPE ASM FRT BRK LH (30.44"LG) MAKE FROM PIPE, P/N 3696822 UOC:194,208,210,230,231,252,254,256	1
17	PAOZZ	11862	22527167	SPRING,SPECIAL YOKE	2
18	PAOZZ	11862	14036723	HOSE ASSEMBLY,NONME LEFT UOC:209	1
18	PAOZZ	11862	14036736	HOSE ASSEMBLY,NONME RIGHT UOC:209	1
18	PAOZZ	11862	14054269	HOSE ASSEMBLY,NONME LEFT UOC:194,208,210,230,231,252,254,256	1
18	PAOZZ	11862	14054270	HOSE ASSEMBLY,NONME RIGHT UOC:194,208,210,230,231,252,254,256	1
19	PAOZZ	11862	14094948	BOLT,FLUID PASSAGE	2
20	PAOZZ	11862	14000172	WASHER,FLAT	4

(1) ITEM NO	(2) SMR CODE	(3) CAGEC	(4) PART NUMBER	(5) DESCRIPTION AND USABLE ON CODES (UOC)	(6) QTY
21	PAOZZ	11862	25515635	VALVE,SAFETY RELIEF UOC:209	1
21	PAOZZ	11862	1257203	VALVE,BRAKE UOC:194,208,210,230,231,252,254,256	1
21	PAOZZ	11862	1257087	VALVE ASSEMBLY UOC:254,256	1
22	MFOZZ	11862	14034572	PIPE ASM FRT BRK (42.13"LG) MAKE FROM PIPE, P/N 3696822	1
23	PAOZZ	24617	9422295	NUT,SELF-LOCKING,CO	2

END OF FIGURE

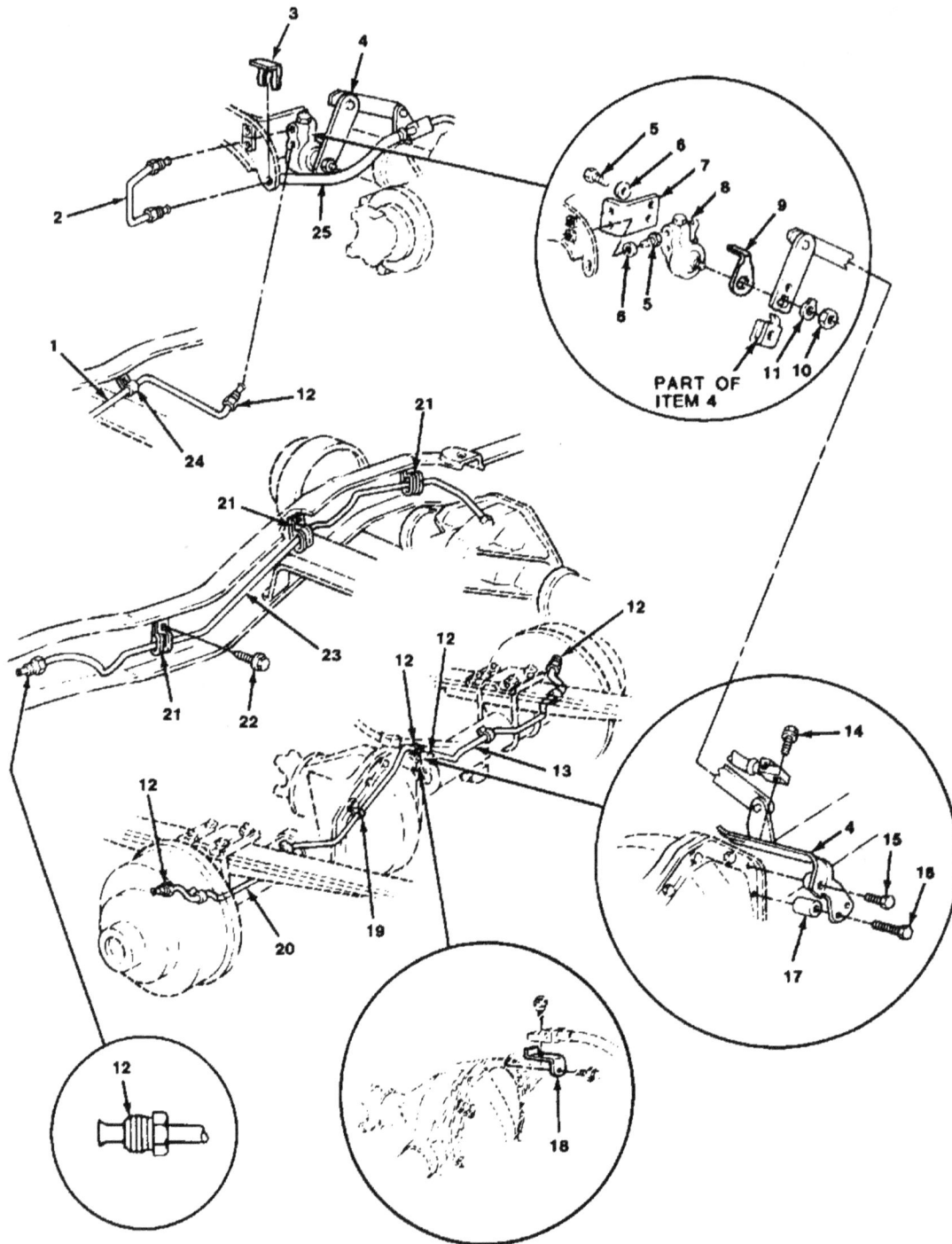

FIGURE 91. REAR BRAKE LINES, WEIGHT PROPORTIONAL VALVE, AND RELATED PARTS.

TA510926

(1) ITEM NO	(2) SMR CODE	(3) CAGEC	(4) PART NUMBER	(5) DESCRIPTION AND USABLE ON CODES (UOC)	(6) QTY
				GROUP 1204 HYDRAULIC BRAKE SYSTEM	
				FIG. 91 REAR BRAKE LINES, WEIGHT PROPORTIONAL VALVE, AND RELATED PARTS	
1	MFOZZ	11862	14036797	PIPE ASM RR BRK RR (78.68"LG) MAKE FROM TUBE, P/N 603827 UOC:194,208,210,230,231,252,254,256	1
2	PAOZZ	11862	14036792	TUBE ASSEMBLY,METAL UOC:194,208,210,230,231,252,254,256	1
3	PAOZZ	11862	22527167	SPRING,SPECIAL YOKE	1
4	PAOZZ	11862	15549248	LEVER ASSEMBLY UOC:194,208,210,230,231,252,254,256	1
5	PAOZZ	96906	MS90728-31	BOLT,MACHINE UOC:194,208,210,230,231,252,254,256	4
6	PAOZZ	96906	MS35340-45	WASHER,LOCK UOC:194,208,210,230,231,252,254,256	4
7	PAOZZ	11862	14036773	BRACKET,ANGLE UOC:194,208,210,230,231,252,254,256	1
8	PAOZZ	11862	15538215	VALVE,BRAKE,PROPORT UOC:194,208,210,230,231,252,254,256	1
9	PAOZZ	11862	14061396	GAGE,SETTING UOC:194,208,210,230,231,252,254,256	1
10	PAOZZ	96906	MS51967-6	NUT,PLAIN,HEXAGON UOC:194,208,210,230,231,252,254,256	1
11	PAOZZ	11862	14036775	BUSHING,PIPE UOC:194,208,210,230,231,252,254,256	1
12	PAOZZ	24617	9432075	INVERTED NUT,TUBE C	6
13	MFOZZ	11862	14036706	PIPE ASM RR BRK (31.29"LG) MAKE FROM PIPE, P/N 3696822 UOC:209	1
13	MFOZZ	11862	14036712	PIPE ASM RR BRK (35.35"LG) MAKE FROM PIPE, P/N 3696822 UOC:194,208,210,230,231,252,254,256	1
14	PAOZZ	11862	1239146	BOLT,SHOULDER	1
15	PAOZZ	96906	MS90728-63	SCREW,CAP,HEXAGON H UOC:194,208,210,230,231,252,254,256	1
16	PAOZZ	11862	9439637	SCREW,CAP,HEXAGON H UOC:194,208,210,230,231,252,254	1
17	PAOZZ	11862	14055556	SPACER,SLEEVE UOC:194,208,210,230,231,252,254,256	1
18	PAOZZ	11862	359816	BRACKET,DOUBLE ANGL UOC:209	1
19	PAOZZ	11862	331416	CLIP,SPRING TENSION	1
19	PAOZZ	11862	6259071	CLIP,SPRING TENSION UOC:254,256	1
20	MFOZZ	11862	14036705	PIPE ASM RR BRK C/O (38.59" LG) MAKE FROM PIPE, P/N 3696822 UOC:209	1
20	MFOZZ	11862	14036711	PIPE ASM RR BRK (41.54"LG) MAKE FROM PIPE, P/N 3696822	1

				UOC:194,208,210,230,231,252,254,256	
21	PAOZZ	96906	MS21333-45	CLAMP,LOOP	3
				UOC:194,208,210,230,231,252,254,256	
21	PAOZZ	96906	MS21333-98	CLAMP,LOOP	3
				UOC:209	
22	PAOZZ	11862	11504447	SCREW,TAPPING	3
23	MFOZZ	11862	14034599	PIPE ASM RR BRK (73.51" LG) MAKE FROM TUBE, P/N 603827	1
				UOC:209	
24	PAOZZ	11862	15599973	CLAMP,LOOP	1
				UOC:194,208,210,230,231,252,254,256	
25	PAOZZ	11862	17981073	HOSE ASSEMBLY,NONME	1

END OF FIGURE

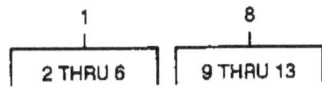

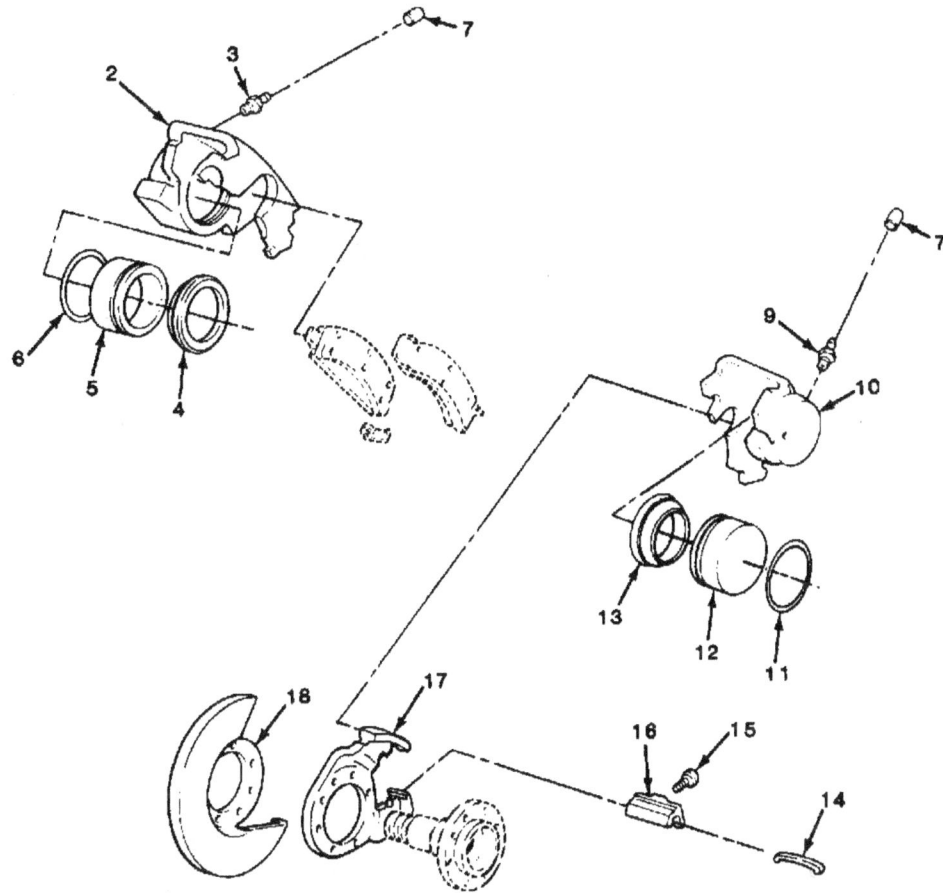

FIGURE 92. FRONT BRAKE CALIPER ASSEMBLIES (ALL EXCEPT M1009).

TA510927

SECTION II (1) ITEM NO	(2) SMR CODE	(3) CAGEC	(4) PART NUMBER	(5) DESCRIPTION AND USABLE ON CODES (UOC)	(6) QTY
				GROUP 1204 HYDRAULIC BRAKE SYSTEM	
				FIG. 92 FRONT CALIPER ASSEMBLIES (ALL EXCEPT M1009)	
1	AFOFF	14892	2238739	CALIPER ASSEMBLY,DI LEFT UOC:194,208,210,230,231,252,254,256	1
2	PAOFF	11862	14002543	.CALIPER ASSEMBLY,DI UOC:194,208,210,230,231,252,254,256	1
7	PAOZZ	11862	5469581	CAP,PROTECTIVE,DUST UOC:194,208,210,230,231,252,254,256	2
8	AFOFF	14892	2238740	CALIPER ASSEMBLY,DI RIGHT UOC:194,208,210,230,231,252,254,256	1
10	PAOFF	14892	2238742	.CALIPER ASSEMBLY,DI UOC:194,208,210,230,231,252,254,256	1
14	PAOZZ	14892	4150514	CLIP,SPRING TENSION UOC:194,208,210,230,231,252,254,256	2
15	PAOZZ	11862	331478	SCREW,SHOULDER UOC:194,208,210,230,231,252,254,256	2
16	PAOZZ	11862	14023439	KEY,CALIPER SUPPORT UOC:194,208,210,230,231,252,254,256	2
17	PAOZZ	14892	3203466	CALIPER,DISC BRAKE RIGHT UOC:194,208,210,230,231,252,254,256	1
17	PAOZZ	14894	3203465	BRACKET,BRAKE SHOE LEFT UOC:194,208,210,230,231,252,254,256	1
18	PAOZZ	97271	38001	SHIELD,BRAKE DISK LEFT UOC:194,208,210,230,231,252,254,256	1
18	PAOZZ	97271	38000	SHIELD,BRAKE DISK RIGHT UOC:194,208,210,230,231,252,254,256	1

END OF FIGURE

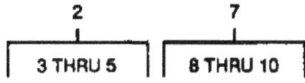

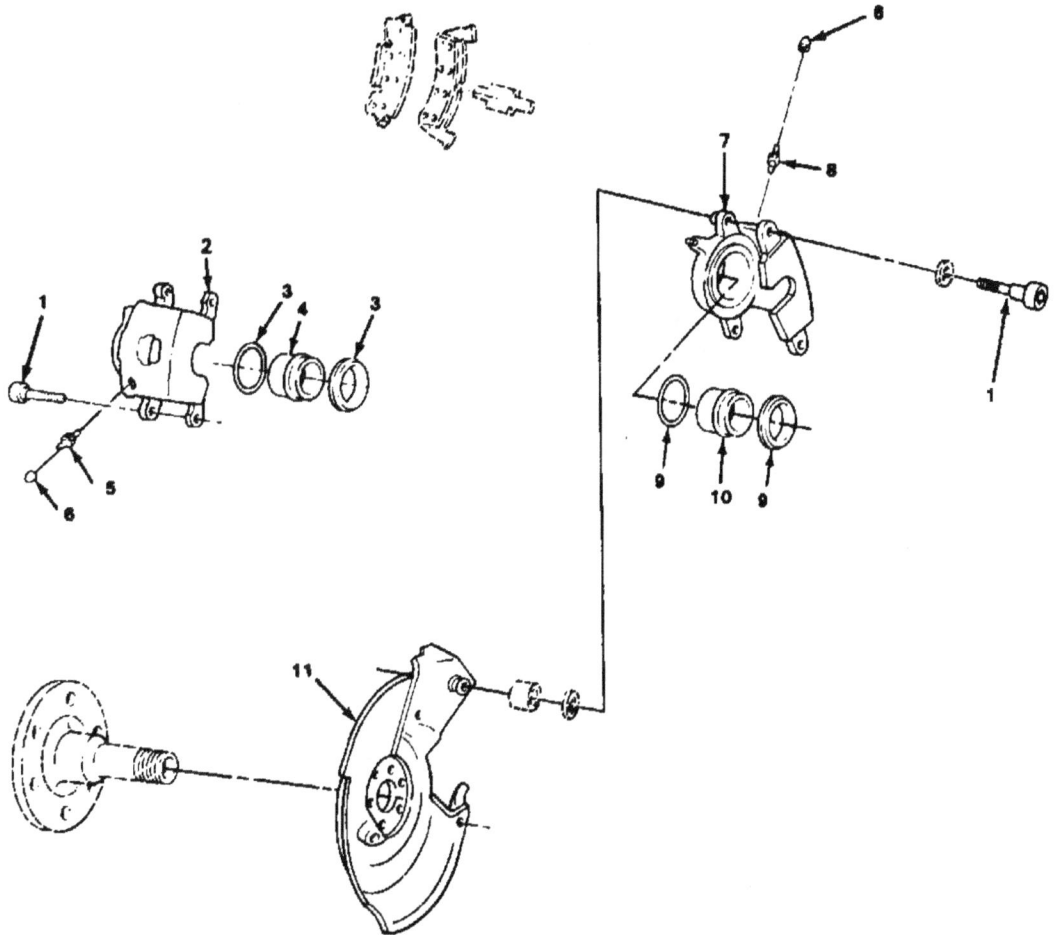

FIGURE 93. FRONT BRAKE CALIPER ASSEMBLIES (M1009).

TA510928

(1) ITEM NO	(2) SMR CODE	(3) CAGEC	(4) PART NUMBER	(5) DESCRIPTION AND USABLE ON CODES (UOC)	(6) QTY
				GROUP 1204 HYDRAULIC BRAKE SYSEM	
				FIG. 93 FRONT BRAKE CALIPER ASSEMBLIES (M1009)	
1	PAOZZ	11862	5468226	BOLT UOC:209	4
2	PAOFF	11862	18015381	CALIPER,DISC BRAKE LEFT HAND UOC:209	1
5	PAOZZ	11862	18013395	.VALVE,SAFETY RELIEF UOC:209	1
6	PAOZZ	11862	5469581	CAP,PROTECTIVE,DUST UOC:209	2
7	PAOFF	11862	18007952	CALIPER,DISC BRAKE RIGHT HAND UOC:209	1
8	PAOZZ	11862	18013395	.VALVE,SAFETY RELIEF UOC:209	1
11	PAOZZ	11862	14023429	PLATE,BACKING,BRAKE LEFT UOC:209	1
11	PAOZZ	11862	14023430	PLATE,BACKING,BRAKE RIGHT UOC:209	1

END OF FIGURE

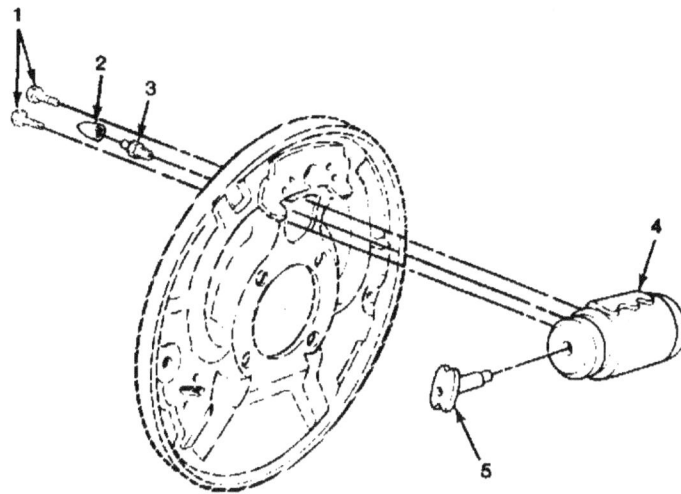

TA510929

FIGURE 94. REAR BRAKE WHEEL CYLINDER.

(1)	(2)	(3)	(4)	(5)	(6)
ITEM NO	SMR CODE	CAGEC	PART NUMBER	DESCRIPTION AND USABLE ON CODES (UOC)	QTY

GROUP 1204 HYDRAULIC BRAKE SYSTEM

FIG. 94 REAR WHEEL BRAKE CYLINDER

1	PAOZZ	24617	456697	BOLT,MACHINE	4
2	PAOZZ	11862	5469581	CAP,PROTECTIVE,DUST	2
3	PAOZZ	11862	18003151	BLEEDER VALVE,HYDRA	2
4	PAOZZ	11862	18004890	CYLINDER ASSEMBLY,H UOC:209	2
4	PAOZZ	11862	18004794	CYLINDER,HYDRAULIC UOC:194,208,210,230,231,252,254,256	2
5	PAOZZ	11862	2622667	LINK,WHEEL CYLINDER	4

END OF FIGURE

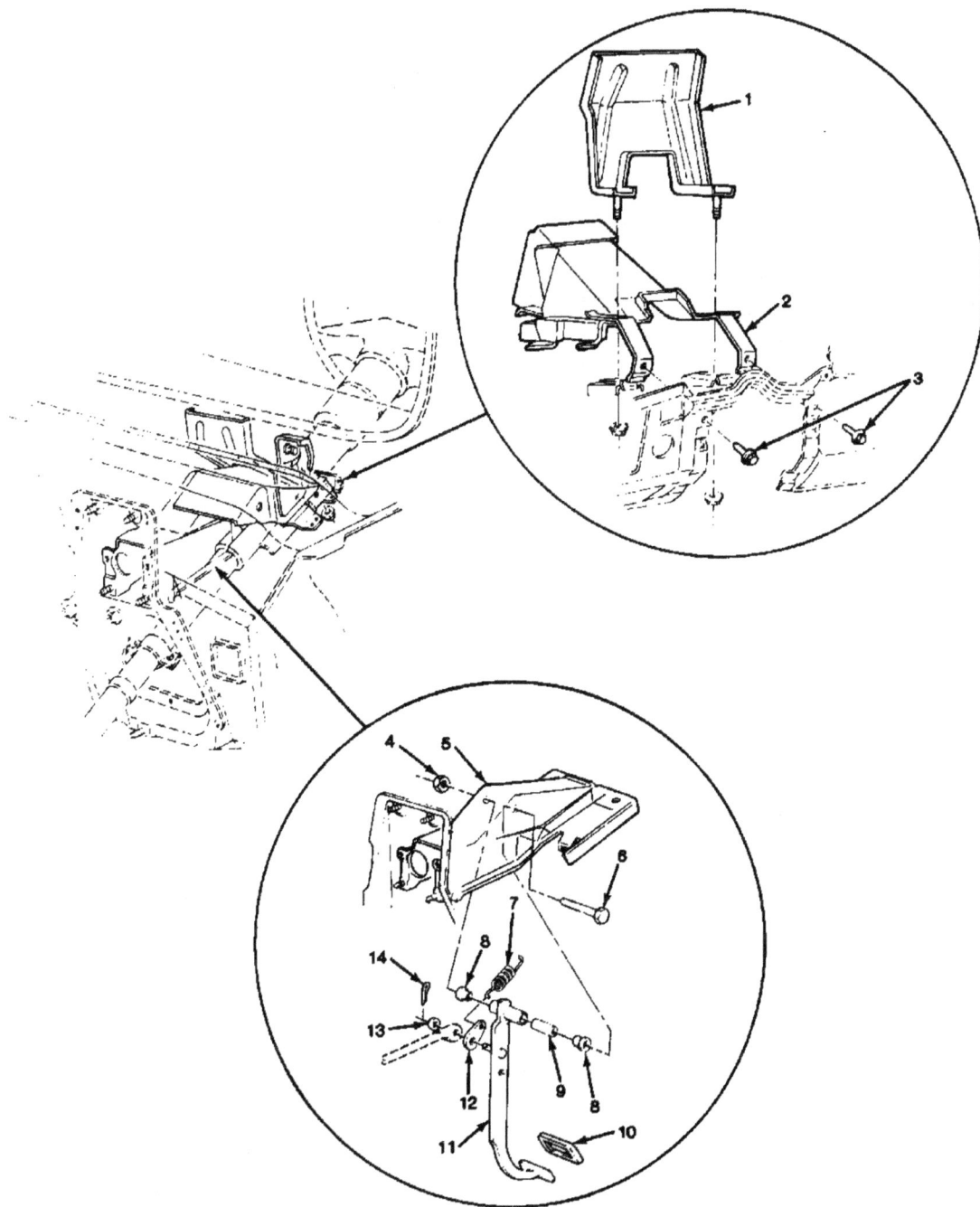

TA510930

FIGURE 95. BRAKE PEDAL, MOUNTING BRACKETS, AND RELATED PARTS.

GROUP 1206 MECHANICAL BRAKE SYSTEM

FIG. 95 BRAKE PEDAL, MOUNTING
BRACKETS, AND RELATED PARTS

ITEM NO	SMR CODE	CAGEC	PART NUMBER	DESCRIPTION AND USABLE ON CODES (UOC)	QTY
4	PAOZZ	11862	9422299	NUT,SELF-LOCKING,HE	1
5	PBOZZ	11862	15593849	BRACKET,BRAKE PEDAL	1
6	PAOZZ	96906	MS18154-96	SCREW,CAP,HEXAGON H	1
7	PAOZZ	11862	3850084	SPRING,HELICAL,EXTE	1
8	PAOZZ	11862	346381	BUSHING,SLEEVE	2
9	PAOZZ	11862	6264951	SPACER,SLEEVE	1
10	PAOZZ	11862	15522095	COVER,BRAKE PEDAL P	1
11	PAOZZ	11862	355561	PEDAL ASSEMBLY,BRAK	1
12	PAOZZ	11862	336926	CONNECTING LINK,RIG	1
13	PAOZZ	11862	3702807	WASHER,FLAT	1
14	PAOZZ	11862	1244707	PIN,LOCK	1

END OF FIGURE

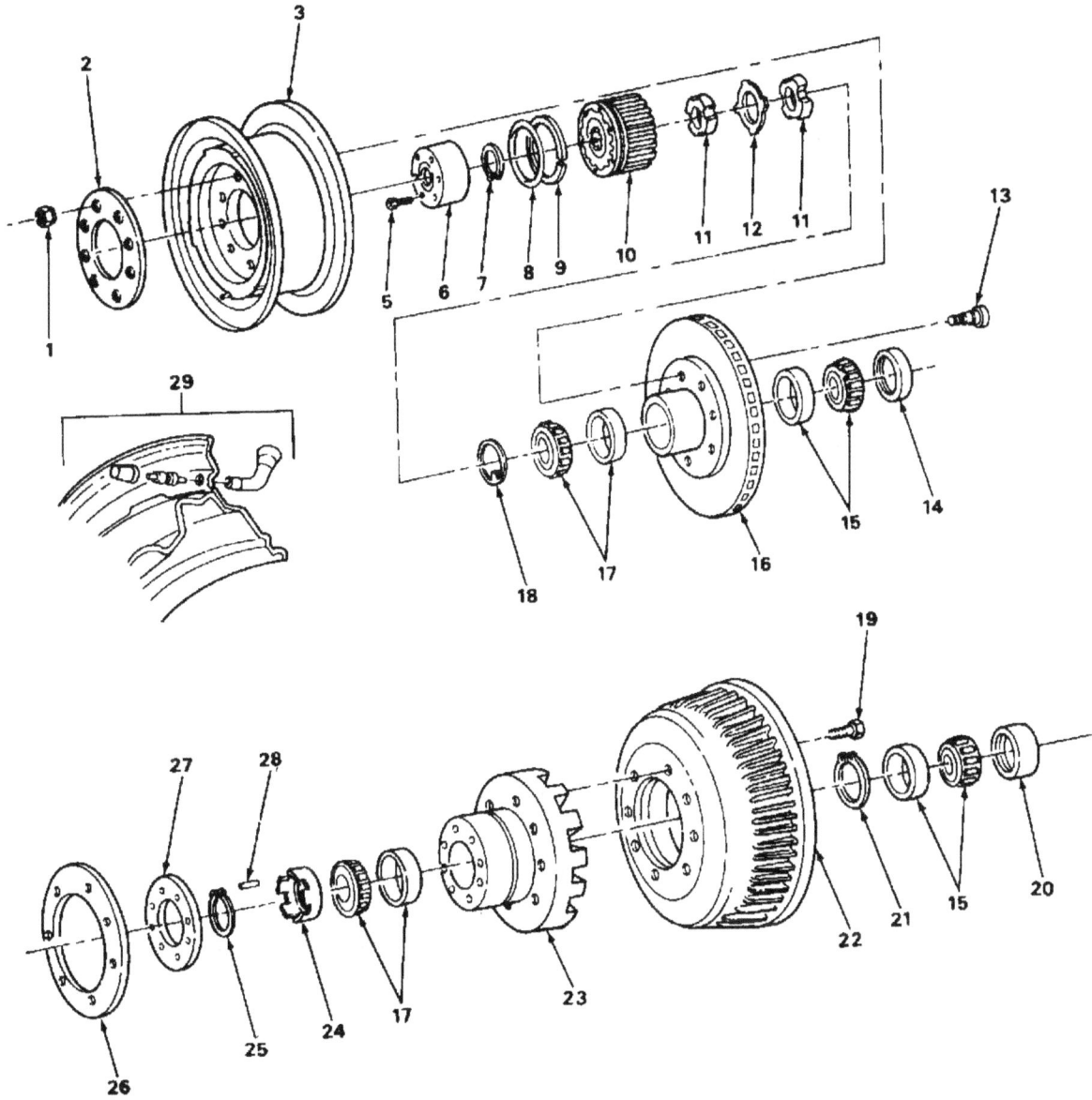

FIGURE 96. FRONT HUB, ROTOR, REAR HUB, BRAKEDRUM, AND
RELATED PARTS (ALL EXCEPT M1009).

TA510931

(1) ITEM NO	(2) SMR CODE	(3) CAGEC	(4) PART NUMBER	(5) DESCRIPTION AND USABLE ON CODES (UOC)	(6) QTY
				GROUP 13 WHEELS AND TRACKS	
				GROUP 1311 WHEEL ASSEMBLY	
				FIG. 96 FRONT HUB, ROTOR, REAR HUB, BRAKEDRUM, AND RELATED PARTS (ALL EXCEPT M1009)	
1	PAOZZ	11862	3978901	NUT,PLAIN,CONE SEAT UOC:194,208,210,230,231,252,254,256	32
1	PAOZZ	23862	334387	NUT UOC:254,256	32
2	PAOZZ	11862	472536	RING,WHEEL CLAMPING UOC:254,256	4
3	PAOZZ	11862	14035374	WHEEL,PNEUMATIC TIR	5
3	PAOZZ	11862	15668598	WHEEL,PNEUMATIC TIR UOC:254,256	1
4	PAOOO	27647	25113	LOCK HUB,FRONT UOC:194,208,210,230,231,252,254,256	2
5	PAOZZ	27647	9477	.SCREW PART OF KIT P/N 15528 UOC:194,208,210,230,231,252,254,256	6
6	PAOZZ	27647	15149	.HUB CAP,WHEEL UOC:194,208,210,230,231,252,254,256	1
7	PAOZZ	96906	MS16624-1131	.RING,RETAINING PART OF KIT P/N 15528 UOC:194,208,210,230,231,252,254,256	1
8	KFOZZ	27647	9952	.SEAL "O" RING PART OF KIT P/N 15528 UOC:194,208,210,230,231,252,254,256	1
9	PAOZZ	11862	14070396	.RING,RETAINING PART OF KIT P/N 15528 UOC:194,208,210,230,231,252,254,256	1
10	PAOZZ	27647	13109	.HUB BODY ASSEMBLY,F UOC:194,208,210,230,231,252,254,256	1
11	PAOZZ	11862	14050679	DISC,OUTER LOCKNUT UOC:194,208,210,230,231,252,254,256	4
11	PAOZZ	11862	15582233	DISC,INNER LOCKOUT UOC:194,208,210,230,231,252,254,256	4
12	PAOZZ	11862	14038051	DISC,LOCK RING UOC:194,208,210,230,231,252,254,256	2
13	PAOZZ	09386	102007	BOLT UOC:194,208,210,230,231,252,254,256	16
13	XDOZZ	11862	15634658	BOLT UOC:254,256	8
14	PAOZZ	80201	27467	SEAL,PLAIN UOC:194,208,210,230,231,252,254,256	2
14	PAOZZ	80201	27467	SEAL,PLAIN UOC:254,256	1
15	PAOZZ	60038	387AS-382A	BEARING,ROLLER,TAPE UOC:194,208,210,230,231,252,254,256	4
16	PAOFF	09386	SR104396	HUB,WHEEL,VEHICULAR INCLUDES ITEM 13 UOC:194,208,210,230,231,252,254,256	2

(1) ITEM NO	(2) SMR CODE	(3) CAGEC	(4) PART NUMBER	(5) DESCRIPTION AND USABLE ON CODES (UOC)	(6) QTY
16	PAOZZ	09386	104192	ROTOR AND HUB UOC:254,256	2
17	PAOZZ	43334	LM104949LM104911	BEARING,ROLLER,TAPE UOC:194,208,210,230,231,252,254,256	4
18	PAOZZ	97271	33734	WASHER UOC:194,208,210,230,231,252,254,256	2
19	PAOZZ	11862	3988538	SCREW,CAP,HEXAGON H UOC:194,208,210,230,231,252	16
20	PAOZZ	11862	469694	SEAL ASSY UOC:194,208,210,230,231,252,254,256	2
21	PAOZZ	11862	474309	RING,RETAINING UOC:194,208,210,230,231,252	2
22	PAOZZ	11862	6260830	BRAKE DRUM UOC:194,208,210,230,231,252	2
23	PAOZZ	11862	3977397	HUB,WHEEL,VEHICULAR UOC:194,208,210,230,231,252	2
23	PAOFF	11862	15634663	HUB,WHEEL,VEHICULAR INCLUDES DRUM UOC:254,256	2
24	PAOZZ	11862	341509	NUT,PLAIN,ROUND UOC:194,208,210,230,231,252	2
25	PAOZZ	11862	341511	REAR WHEEL HUB RETA UOC:194,208,210,230,231,252	2
26	PAOZZ	11862	15634661	SPACER,PLATE UOC:254,256	2
27	PAOZZ	24617	327739	GASKET UOC:194,208,210,230,231,252	2
28	PAOZZ	11862	341510	KEY,MACHINE UOC:194,208,210,230,231,252	2
29	PAOZZ	11862	273487	VALVE,PNEUMATIC TIR UOC:194,208,210,230,231,252,254,256	5
29	PAOZZ	11862	9591270	VALVE,PNEUMATIC TIR UOC:254,256	5
29	PAOZZ	6V625	30-600	VALVE,PNEUMATIC TIR USED ON WHEELS WITH PIN 9591597 UOC:194,208,210,230,231,252,254,256	5

END OF FIGURE

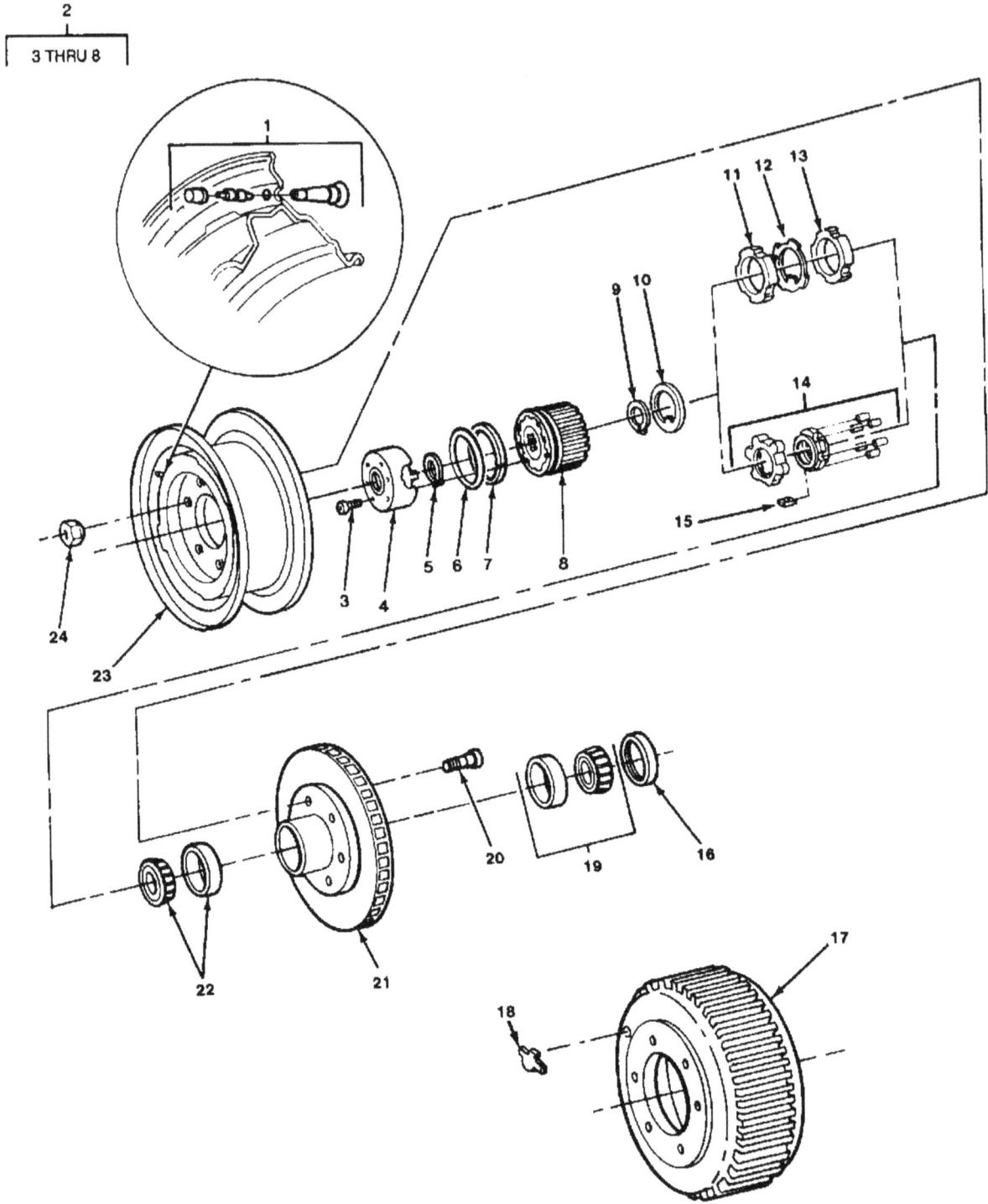

FIGURE 97. FRONT HUB, ROTOR, BRAKEDRUM, AND RELATED PARTS (M1009).

TA510932

(1) ITEM NO	(2) SMR CODE	(3) CAGEC	(4) PART NUMBER	(5) DESCRIPTION AND USABLE ON CODES (UOC)	(6) QTY
				GROUP 1311 WHEEL ASSEMBLY	
				FIG. 97 FRONT HUB, ROTOR, BRAKEDRUM, AND RELATED PARTS (M1009)	
1	PAOZZ	17875	T14R	VALVE,PNEUMATIC TIR UOC:209	5
2	PAOOO	27647	M257	LOCK,DRIVE SHAFT,DI UOC:209	2
3	PAOZZ	27647	9477	.SCREW PART OF KIT P/N 11967 UOC:209	6
4	PAOZZ	27647	15147	.HUB CAP ASSEMBLY UOC:209	1
5	PAOZZ	96906	MS16624-1125	.RING,RETAINING PART OF KIT P/N 11967 UOC:209	2
6	PAOZZ	27647	13446	.PACKING,PREFORMED UOC:209	1
7	PAOZZ	11862	14070348	.RING,RETAINING PART OF KIT P/N 11967 UOC:209	1
8	PAOZZ	27647	13113	.HUB,BODY UOC:209	1
9	PAOZZ	96906	MS16624-1125	RING,RETAINING UOC:209	2
10	PAOZZ	11862	14072921	SPACER,RING UOC:209	2
11	PAOZZ	11862	14034413	NUT,PLAIN,ROUND APPLIES TO VEHICLES STARING WITH VIN ENDING WITH F136169 UOC:209	2
12	PAOZZ	79410	17-01-014-001	WASHER,KEY APPLIES TO VEHICLES STARTING WITH VIN ENDING WITH F136169 UOC:209	2
13	PAOZZ	11862	14034410	NUT,PLAIN,ROUND APPLIES TO VEHICLES STARTING WITH VIN ENDING WITH F136169 UOC:209	2
14	PAOZZ	76445	40424	NUT,PLAIN,ROUND APPLIES TO 84 MODEL UOC:209	2
15	XDOZZ	11862	14072927	KEY,MACHINE APPLIES TO 84 MODEL UOC:209	2
16	PAOZZ	11862	6273948	SEAL,PLAIN ENCASED UOC:209	2
17	PAOFF	11862	14070352	BRAKE DRUM UOC:209	2
18	PAOZZ	19207	6262328	PLUG,PROTECTIVE,DUS UOC:209	2
19	PAOZZ	11862	7455617	BEARING,ROLLER,TAPE UOC:209	2
20	PAOZZ	09386	96735	BOLT,RIBBED SHOULDE	12

(1) ITEM NO	(2) SMR CODE	(3) CAGEC	(4) PART NUMBER	(5) DESCRIPTION AND USABLE ON CODES (UOC)	(6) QTY
				UOC:209	
21	PAOFF	11862	14026765	ROTOR ASSEMBLY,DISC INCLUDES ITEM 20	2
				UOC:209	
22	PAOZZ	43334	LM501349-LM501310	BEARING,ROLLER,TAPE	2
				UOC:209	
23	PAOZZ	11862	14063307	RIM,WHEEL,PNEUMATIC	5
				UOC:209	
24	PAOZZ	11862	358501	NUT,PLAIN,CONE SEAT	24
				UOC:209	

END OF FIGURE

FIGURE 98. TIRES.

(1) ITEM NO	(2) SMR CODE	(3) CAGEC	(4) PART NUMBER	(5) DESCRIPTION AND USABLE ON CODES (UOC)	(6) QTY
				GROUP 1313 TIRES,TUBES, TIRE CHAINS	
				FIG. 98 TIRES	
1	PAOOO	22337	212-776	TIRE,PNEUMATIC UOC:209	5
1	PAOOO	81348	GP2A/LT235/85R16 /E/LTAW	TIRE,PNEUMATIC UOC:194,208,210,230,231,252,254,256	5
				END OF FIGURE	

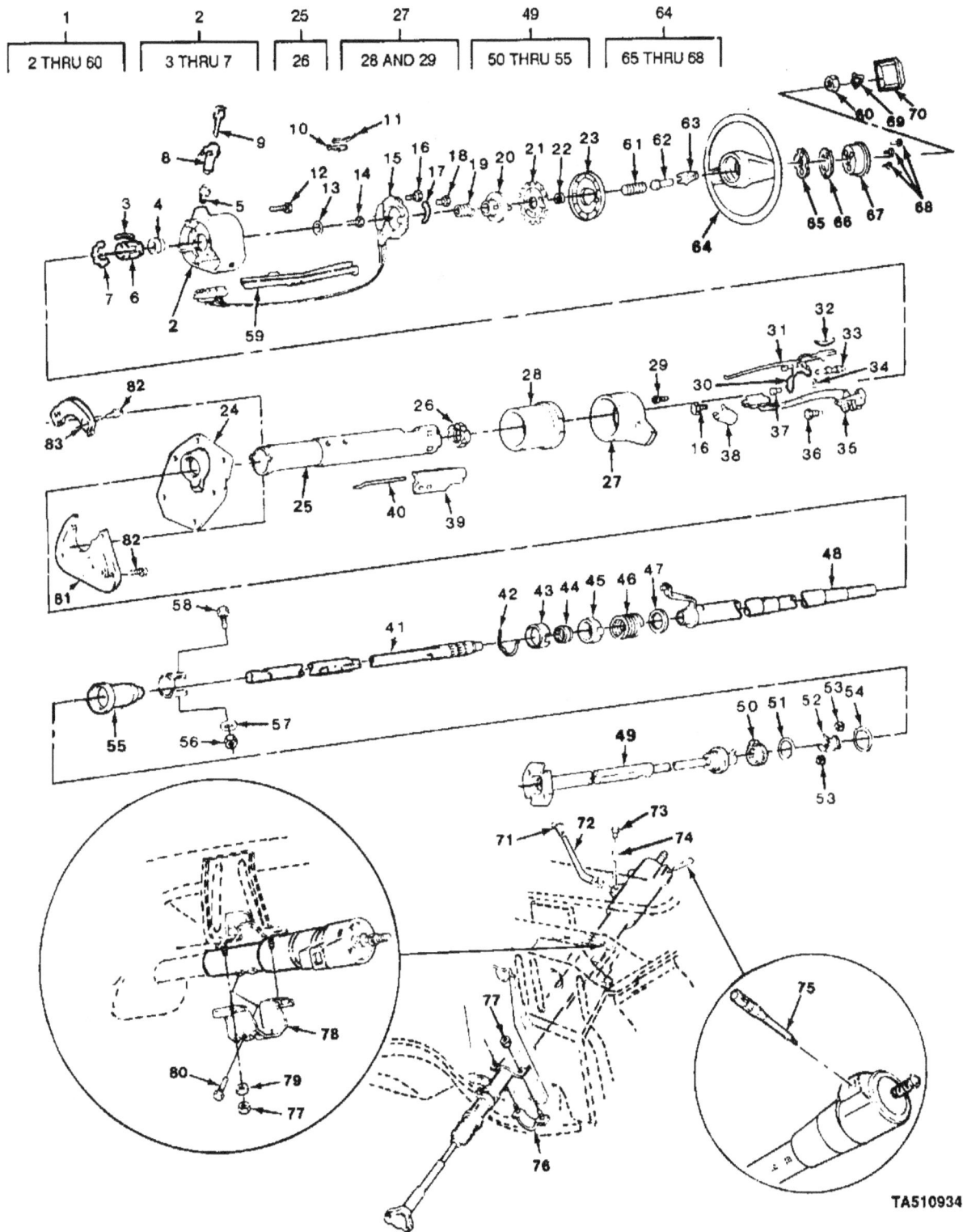

FIGURE 99. STEERING WHEEL AND COLUMN.

TA510934

(1) ITEM NO	(2) SMR CODE	(3) CAGEC	(4) PART NUMBER	(5) DESCRIPTION AND USABLE ON CODES (UOC)	(6) QTY
				GROUP STEERING	
				GROUP 1401 MECHANICAL STEERING GEAR ASSEMBLY	
				FIG. 99 STEERING WHEEL AND COLUMN	
60	PAOZZ	11862	7846970	.NUT,PLAIN,HEXAGON	1
61	PAOZZ	11862	404234	SPRING,HELICAL,COMP	1
62	PAOZZ	11862	474102	PARTS KIT,HORN BUTT INCLUDES ITEMS 61 & 63	1
63	PAOZZ	11862	409190	INSULATOR,HORN CONT	1
64	PAOOO	11862	9762199	STEERING WHEEL	1
65	PAOZZ	24617	9749363	.SPRING	1
66	PAOZZ	11862	9754764	.SPACER,RING	1
67	PAOZZ	11862	17983936	.HORN BUTTON,VEHICLE	1
68	PAOZZ	11862	9767270	.SCREW,CAP,SOCKET HE	3
69	PAOZZ	11862	419454	RING,RETAINING	1
70	PAOZZ	11862	17987489	HORN BUTTON,VEHICLE	1
71	PAOZZ	11862	14049351	KNOB	1
71	PAOZZ	11862	470205	KNOB APPLIES TO VEHICLES STARTING WITH VIN FF136163 AND VIN FF300021	1
72	PAOZZ	11862	14034728	LEVER,MANUAL CONTRO	1
72	PAOZZ	11862	14081915	LEVER,MANUAL CONTRO APPLIES TO VEHICLES STARTING WITH VIN FF136169 AND VIN FF300021	1
73	PAOZZ	11862	3793014	PIN,STRAIGHT,HEADED	1
74	PAOZZ	11862	1604854	BUSHING,SLEEVE APPLIED TO VEHICLES STARTING WITH VIN FF136169 AND VIN FF 300021	1
75	PAOZZ	11862	22510143	LEVER,MANUAL CONTRO	1

END OF FIGURE

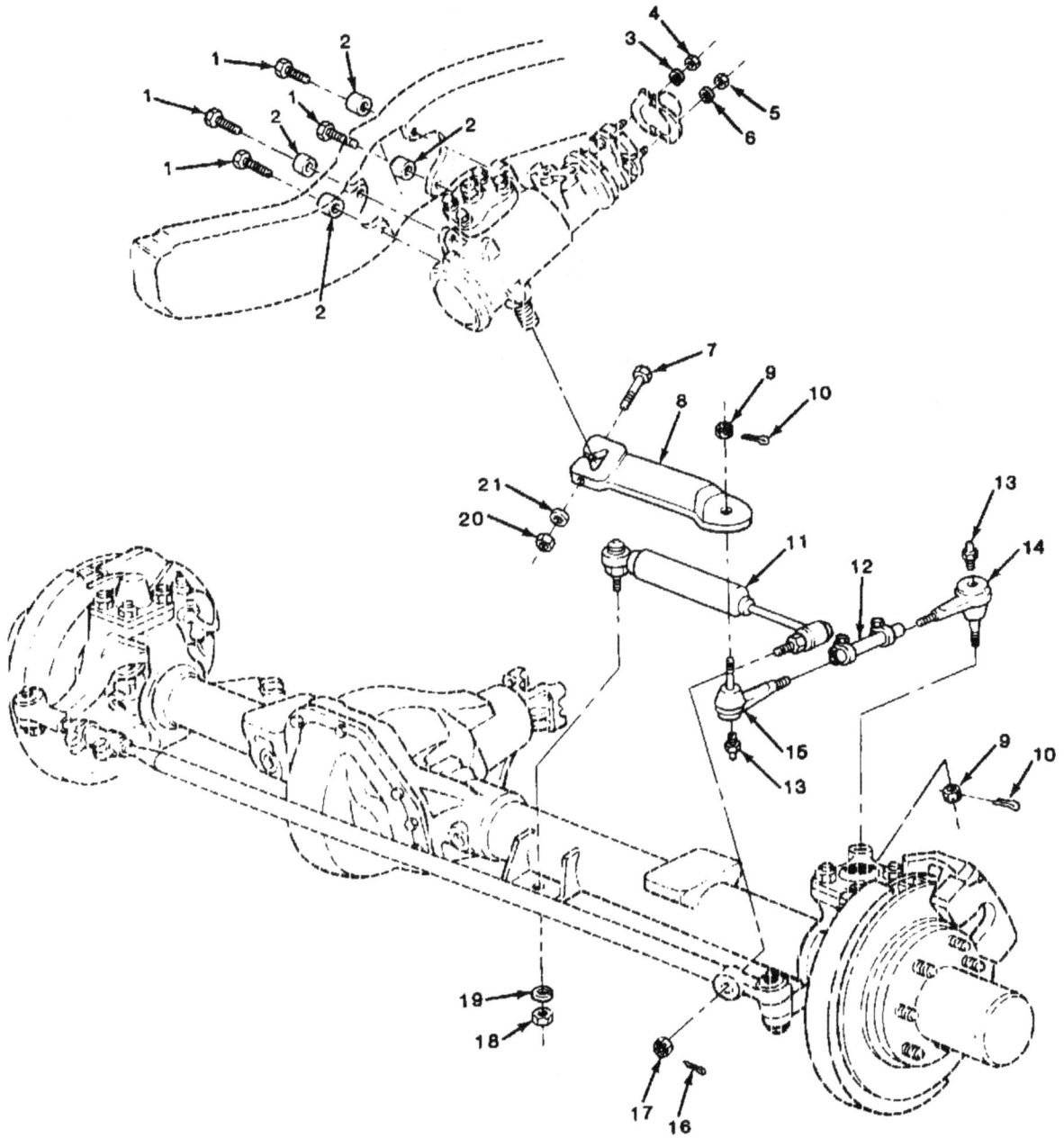

TA510935

FIGURE 100. PITMAN ARM, ABSORBER, AND RELATED PARTS.

GROUP 1401 MECHANICAL STEERING GEAR
ASSEMBLY

FIG. 100 PITMAN ARM, ABSORBER, AND
RELATED PARTS

ITEM NO	SMR CODE	CAGEC	PART NUMBER	DESCRIPTION AND USABLE ON CODES (UOC)		QTY
1	PAOZZ	11862	343178	SCREW,CAP,HEXAGON H		4
2	PAOZZ	11862	343179	SPACER,SLEEVE		4
3	PAOZZ	96906	MS35338-45	WASHER,LOCK		1
4	PAOZZ	96906	MS51968-6	NUT,PLAIN,HEXAGON		1
5	PAOZZ	96906	MS51968-9	NUT,PLAIN,HEXAGON		1
6	PAOZZ	96906	MS35338-46	WASHER,LOCK		1
7	PAOZZ	96906	MS90727-145	SCREW,CAP,HEXAGON H		1
8	PAOZZ	11862	14064660	ARM,STEERING GEAR		1
9	PAOZZ	96906	MS35692-53	NUT,PLAIN,SLOTTED,H		2
10	PAOZZ	96906	MS24665-357	PIN,COTTER		2
11	PAOZZ	11862	4993563	CYLINDER ASSEMBLY,A		1
12	PAOZZ	11862	14007644	SLEEVE ASSEMBLY,CON		1
13	PAOZZ	11862	9417901	FITTING,LUBRICATION		2
14	PAOZZ	11862	362297	TIE ROD END,STEERIN	SHORT	1
15	PAOZZ	11862	362298	TIE ROD END,STEERIN	LONG	1
16	PAOZZ	89749	IF316	PIN,COTTER		1
17	PAOZZ	96906	MS35692-37	NUT,PLAIN,SLOTTED,H		1
18	PAOZZ	96906	MS35690-824	NUT,PLAIN,HEXAGON		1
19	PAOZZ	96906	MS35338-48	WASHER,LOCK		1
20	PAOZZ	11862	9422303	NUT SELF-LOCKINNG,HE		1
21	PAOZZ	96906	MS27183-20	WASHER,FLAT		1

END OF FIGURE

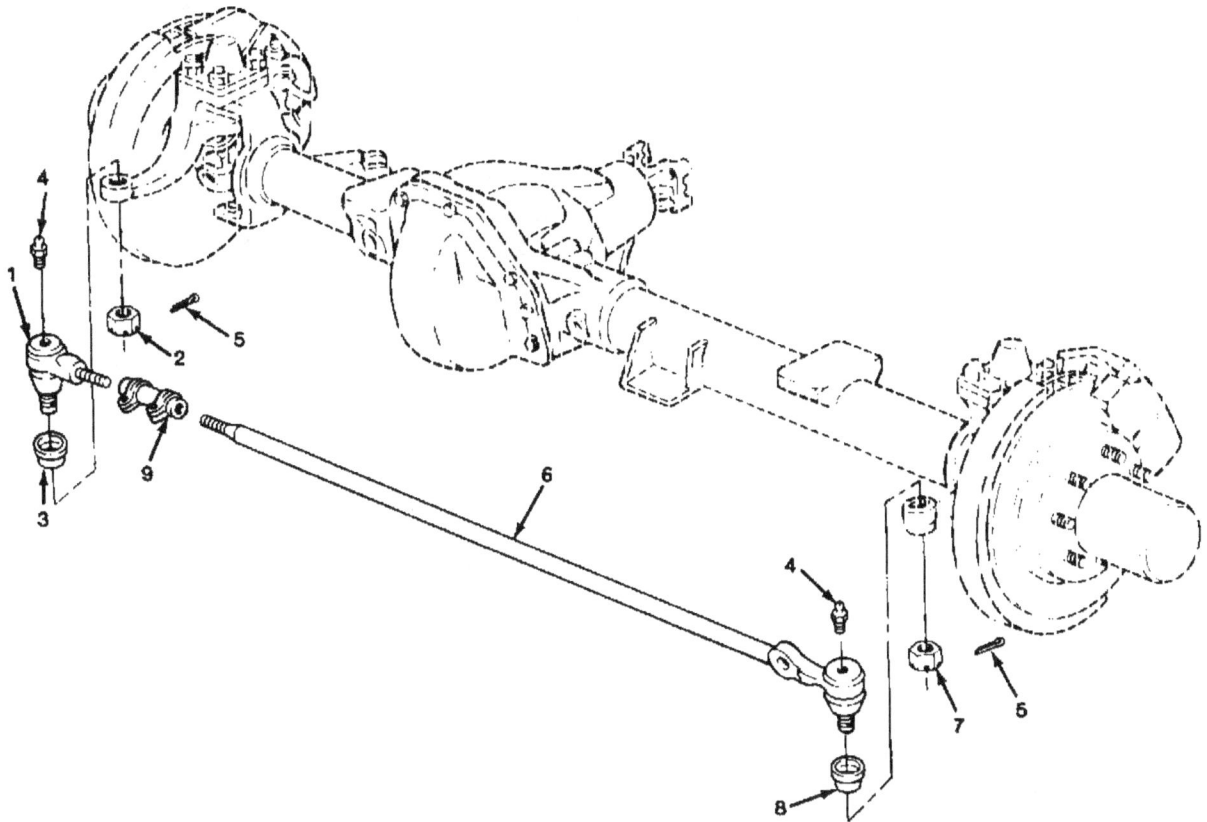

TA510936

FIGURE 101. TIE-ROD ASSEMBLY (ALL EXCEPT M1009).

(1) ITEM NO	(2) SMR CODE	(3) CAGEC	(4) PART NUMBER	(5) DESCRIPTION AND USABLE ON CODES (UOC)	(6) QTY
				GROUP 1401 MECHANICAL STEERING GEAR ASSEMBLY	
				FIG. 101 TIE-ROD ASSEMBLY (ALL EXCEPT M1009)	
1	PAOOO	72210	D23980-J	TIE ROD END,STEERIN RIGHT UOC:194,208,210,230,231,252,254,256	1
2	PAOZZ	24617	125384	.NUT,PLAIN,SLOTTED,H UOC:194,208,210,230,231,252,254,256	1
3	PAOZZ	11862	6259074	.PACKING,PREFORMED UOC:194,208,210,230,231,252,254,256	1
4	PAOZZ	11862	9417901	FITTING,LUBRICATION UOC:194,208,210,230,231,252,254,256	2
5	PAOZZ	96906	MS24665-425	PIN,COTTER UOC:194,208,210,230,231,252,254,256	2
6	PAOOO	72210	24004-J	TIE ROD END,STEERIN LEFT UOC:194,208,210,230,231,252,254,256	1
7	PAOZZ	24617	125384	.NUT,PLAIN,SLOTTED,H UOC:194,208,210,230,231,252,254,256	1
8	PAOZZ	97271	S19587-T	.PACKING,PREFORMED UOC:194,208,210,230,231,252,254,256	1
9	PAOZZ	72210	S23981-H	ADJUSTING SLEEVE,TI UOC:194,208,210,230,231,252,254,256	1

END OF FIGURE

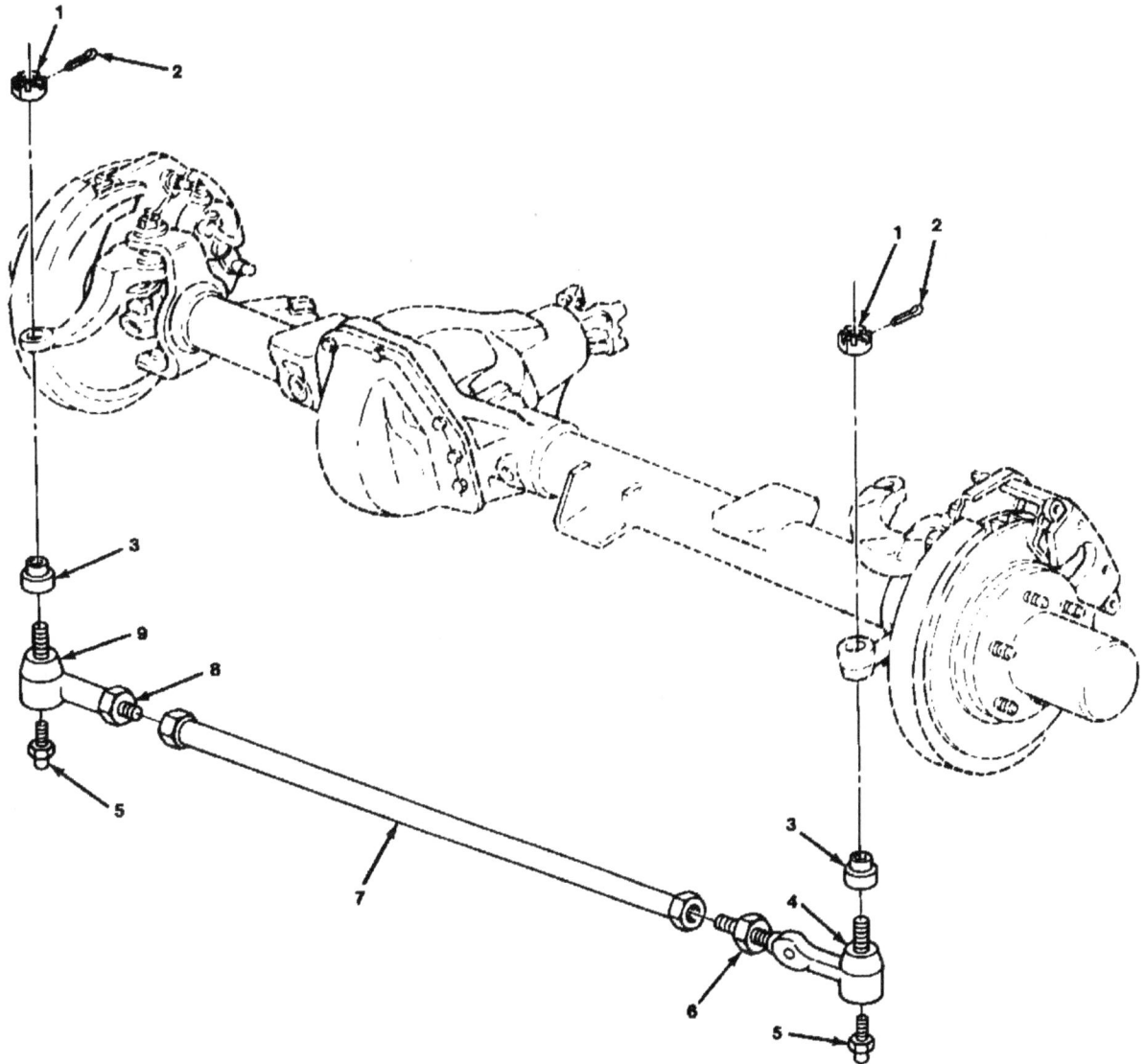

TA510937

FIGURE 102. TIE-ROD ASSEMBLY (M1009).

(1) ITEM NO	(2) SMR CODE	(3) CAGEC	(4) PART NUMBER	(5) DESCRIPTION AND USABLE ON CODES (UOC)	(6) QTY
				GROUP 1401 MECHANICAL STEERING GEAR ASSEMBLY	
				FIG. 102 TIE-ROD ASSEMBLY (M1009)	
1	PAOZZ	11862	467117	NUT,PLAIN,SLOTTED,H UOC:209	2
2	PAOZZ	11862	11514337	PIN,COTTER UOC:209	2
3	PAOZZ	11862	6259074	PACKING,PREFORMED UOC:209	2
4	PAOZZ	11862	14026803	TIE ROD END,STEERIN LEFT UOC:209	1
5	PAOZZ	11862	9417901	FITTING,LUBRICATION UOC:209	2
6	PAOZZ	11862	14026805	NUT,PLAIN,HEXAGON UOC:209	1
7	PAOZZ	11862	14026804	TIE ROD,STEERING UOC:209	1
8	PAOZZ	30076	160635	NUT,PLAIN,HEXAGON UOC:209	1
9	PAOZZ	11862	14026802	TIE ROD END,STEERIN RIGHT UOC:209	1

END OF FIGURE

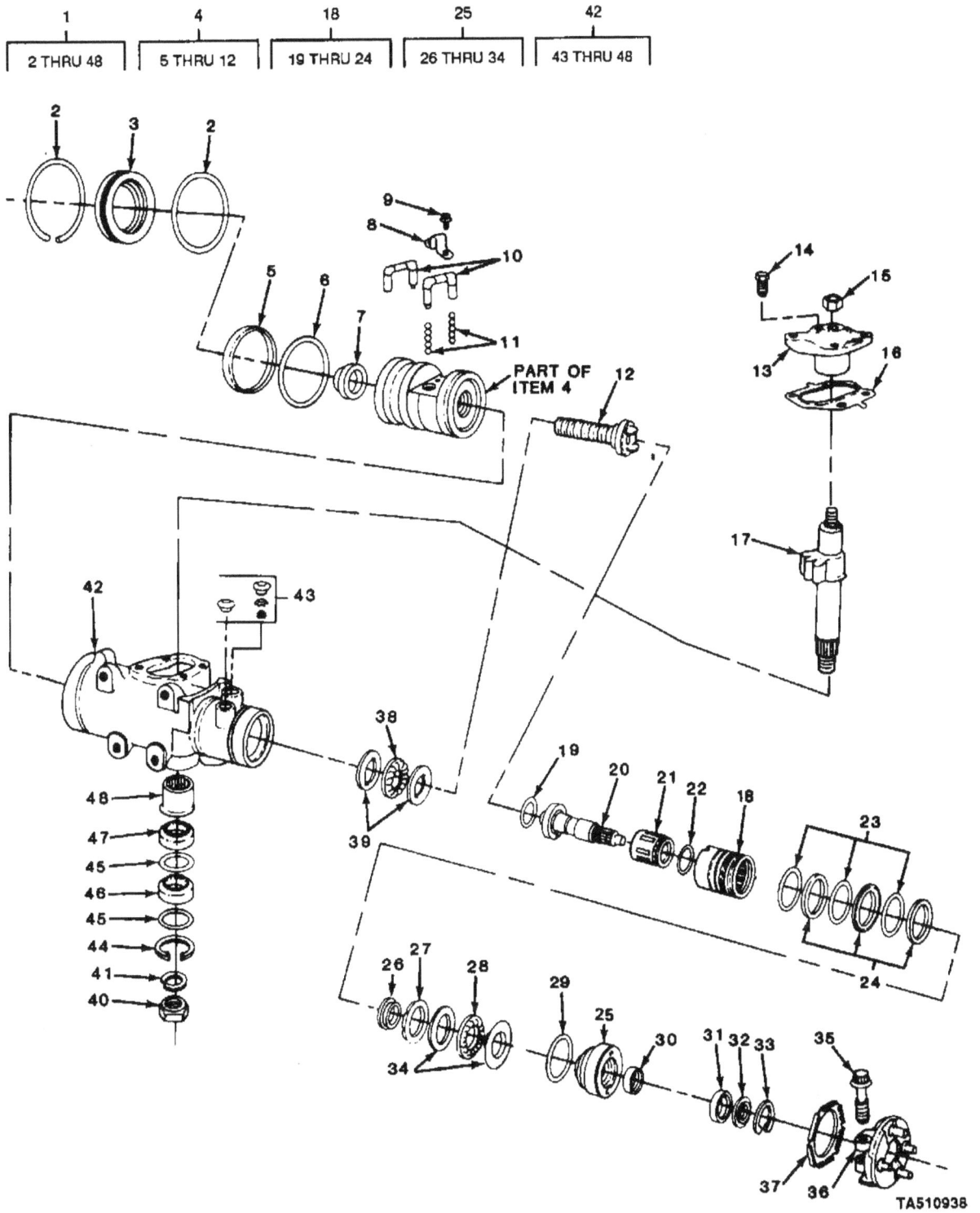

FIGURE 103. POWER STEERING GEAR AND

(1) ITEM NO	(2) SMR CODE	(3) CAGEC	(4) PART NUMBER	(5) DESCRIPTION AND USABLE ON CODES (UOC)	(6) QTY
				GROUP 1407 POWER STEERING GEAR ASSEMBLY	
				FIG. 103 POWER STEERING GEAR AND COMPONENT PARTS	
1	PAOHH	11862	7846959	STEERING GEAR	1
				END OF FIGURE	

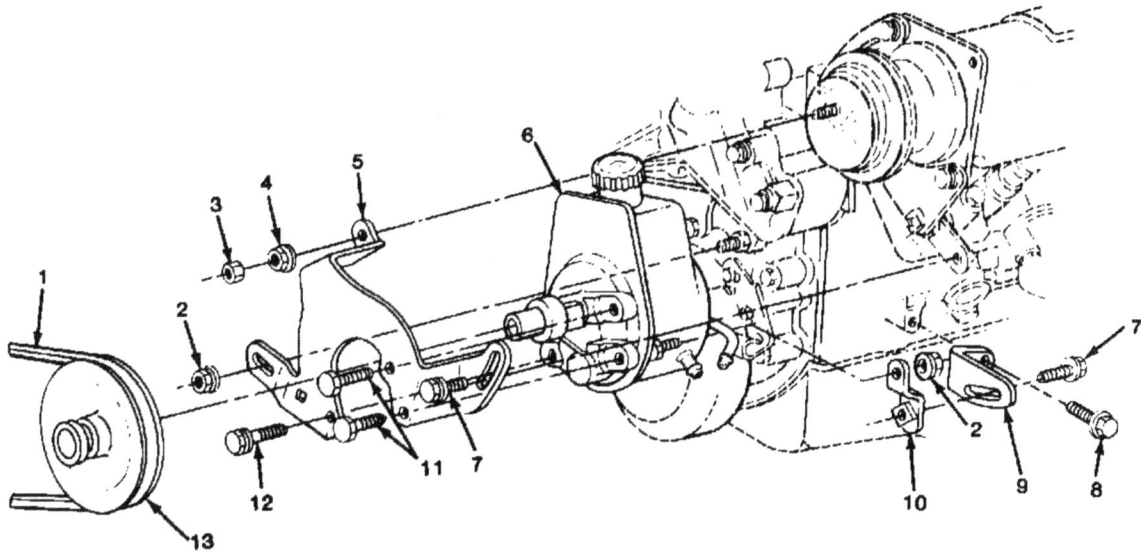

TA510939

FIGURE 104. HYDRAULIC PUMP.

(1) ITEM NO	(2) SMR CODE	(3) CAGEC	(4) PART NUMBER	(5) DESCRIPTION AND USABLE ON CODES (UOC)	(6) QTY
				GROUP 1410 HYDRAULIC PUMP OR FLUID MOTOR ASSEMBLY	
				FIG. 104 HYDRAULIC PUMP	
1	PAOZZ	20796	42-5023	BELT,V	1
2	PAOZZ	11862	11506101	NUT	2
3	PAOZZ	11862	11503643	NUT UOC:194,208,209,230,231,252,254,256	1
4	PAOZZ	73342	11501033	NUT UOC:210	1
5	PAOZZ	11862	14033879	BRACKET,POWER STEER	1
6	PAOFH	52788	7838936	PUMP ASSEMBLY,POWER	1
7	PAOZZ	11862	1635490	BOLT,SELF-LOCKING	2
8	PAOZZ	11862	11504595	SCREW,CAP,HEXAGON H	1
9	PAOZZ	11862	14033880	BRACKET,ANGLE	1
10	PAOZZ	11862	14033881	BRACKET,DOUBLE ANGL	1
11	PAOZZ	11862	11504512	BOLT,MACHINE	2
12	PAOZZ	11862	11505299	BOLT,MACHINE	1
13	PAOZZ	11862	14023174	PULLEY,GROOVE UOC:210,230	1
13	PAOZZ	11862	14067701	PULLEY,CONE UOC:194,208,209,230,231,252,254,256	1

END OF FIGURE

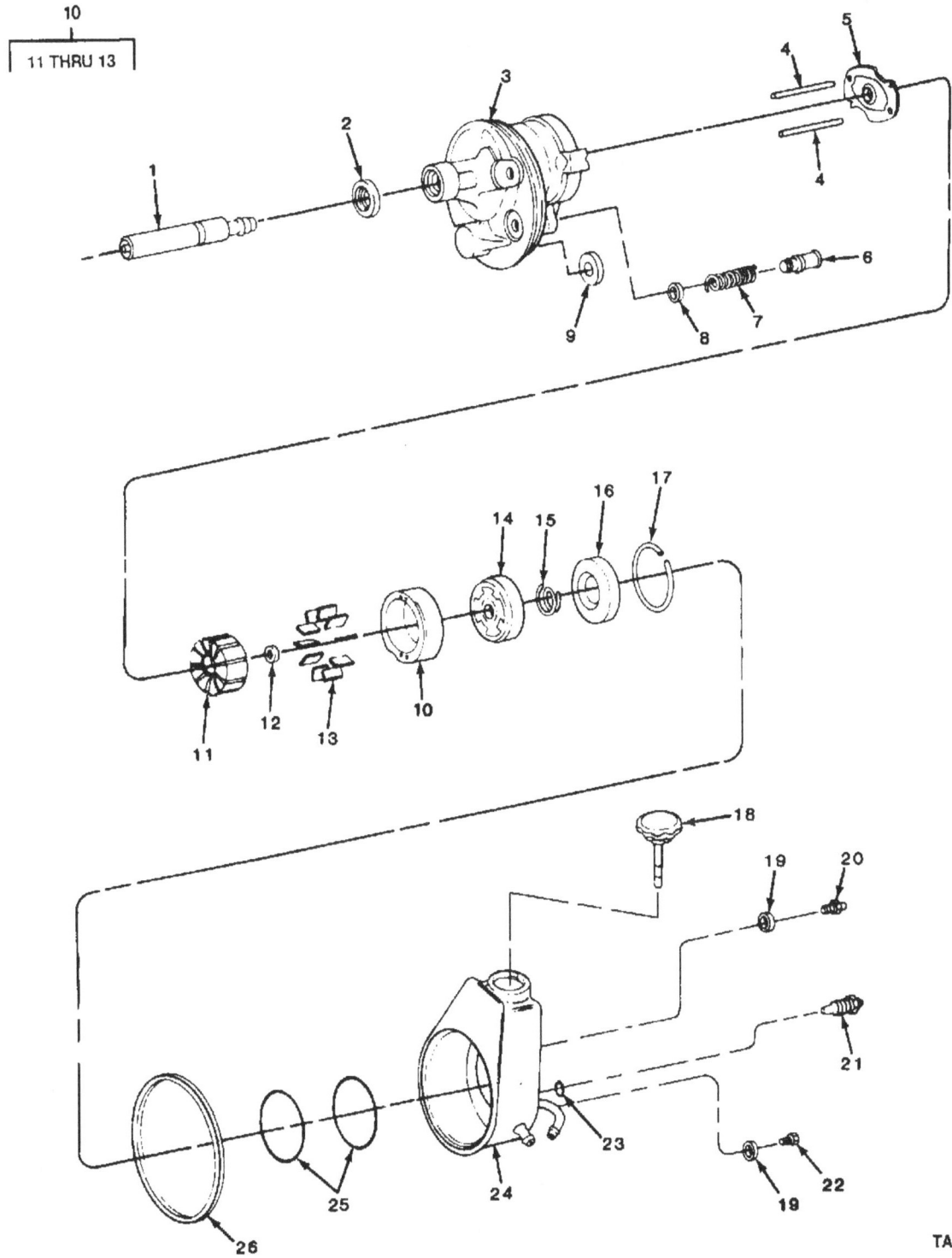

FIGURE 105. HYDRAULIC PUMP COMPONENT PARTS.

TA510940

(1) ITEM NO	(2) SMR CODE	(3) CAGEC	(4) PART NUMBER	(5) DESCRIPTION AND USABLE ON CODES (UOC)	(6) QTY
				GROUP 1410 HYDRAULIC PUMP OR FLUID MOTOR ASSEMBLY	
				FIG. 105 HYDRAULIC PUMP COMPONENT PARTS	
18	PAOZZ	11862	7834183	.GAGE ROD-CAP,LIQUID	1
				END OF FIGURE	

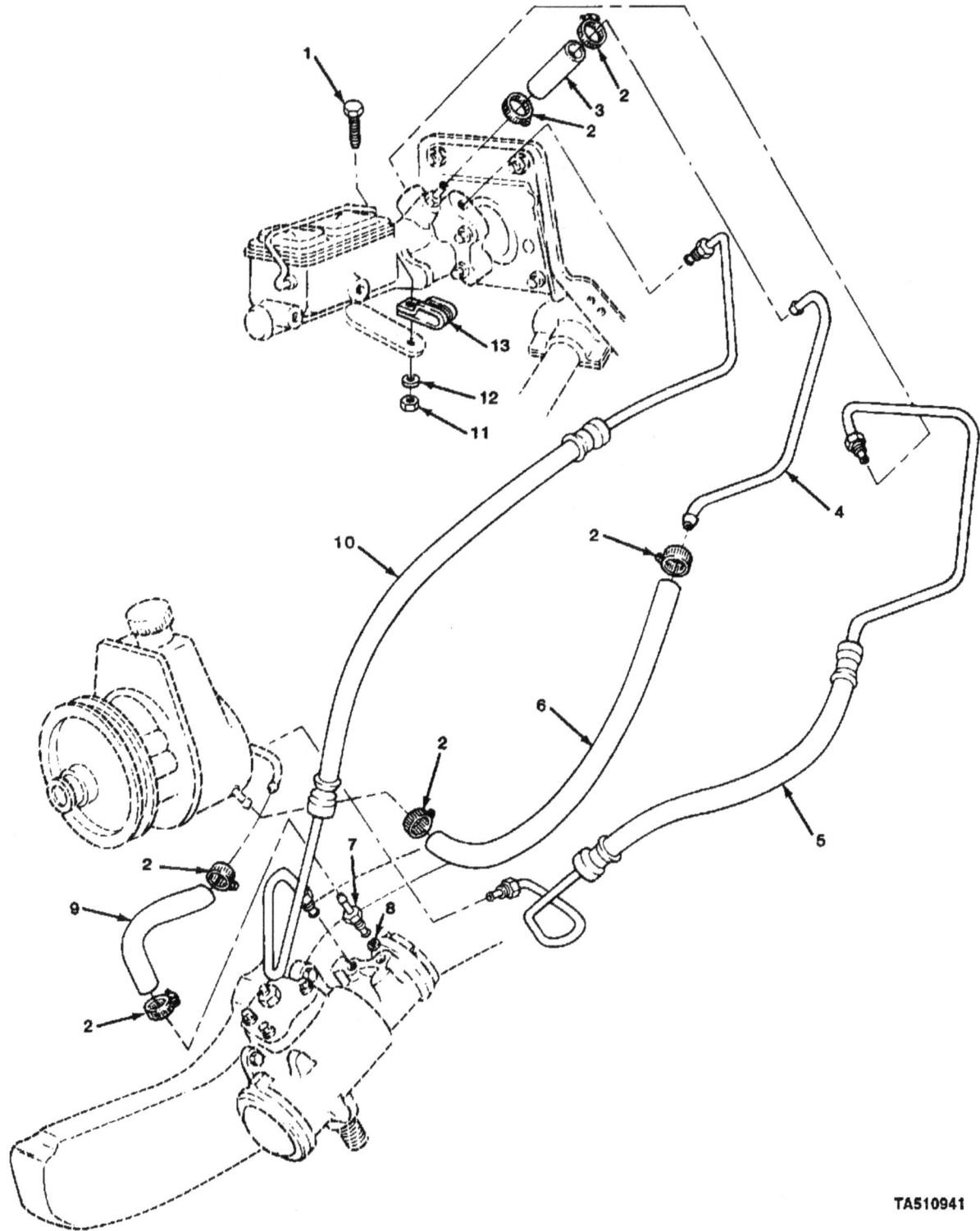

FIGURE 106. HYDRAULIC STEERING LINES

TA510941

GROUP 1411 HOSES, LINES, FITTINGS

FIG. 106 HYDRAULIC STEERING LINES

ITEM NO	SMR CODE	CAGEC	PART NUMBER	DESCRIPTION AND USABLE ON CODES (UOC)	QTY
1	PAOZZ	96906	MS90728-32	BOLT,MACHINE	1
2	PAOZZ	11862	25518880	CLAMP,HOSE	6
3	MOOZZ	11862	350371	HOSE P/S BSTR RTN (1.75"LG) MAKE FROM HOSE,P/N 7828506	1
4	MFOZZ	11862	14040735	PIPE P/S BSTR RTN (15.90"LG) MAKE FROM TUBE, P/N 603827	1
5	PAOZZ	11862	7838941	HOSE ASSEMBLY,NONME	1
6	MOOZZ	11862	1488565	HOSE P/S BSTR RTN (20.50"LG) MAKE FROM HOSE,P/N 7828506	1
7	PAOZZ	11862	22514738	TUBE AND ADAPTER AS	1
8	PAOZZ	11862	7829923	PACKING,PREFORMED	1
9	MOOZZ	11862	3773687	HOSE P/S FR OTLT (13.00"LG) MAKE FROM HOSE,P/N 7828506	1
10	PAOZZ	11862	7838942	HOSE ASSEMBLY,NONME	1
11	PAOZZ	96906	MS51967-6	NUT,PLAIN,HEXAGON	1
12	PAOZZ	96906	MS35340-45	WASHER,LOCK	1
13	PAOZZ	11862	338696	CLAMP,LOOP	1

END OF FIGURE

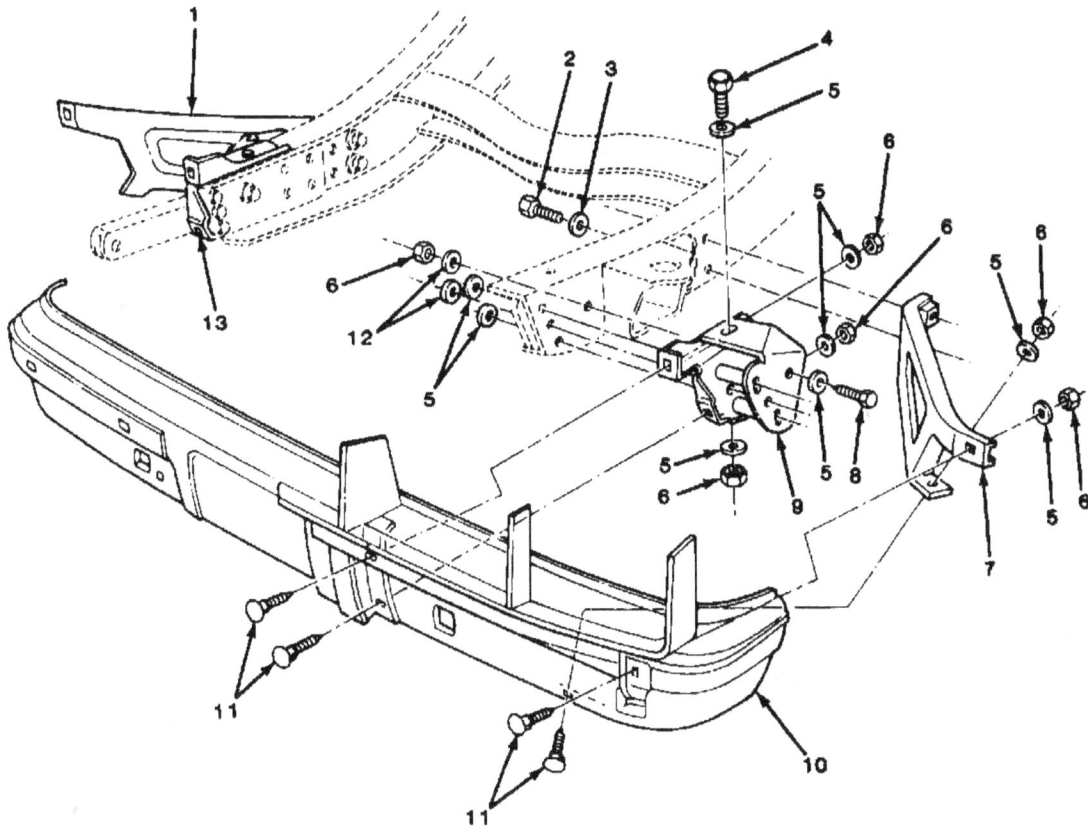

TA510942

FIGURE 107. FRONT BUMPER AND RELATED PARTS.

(1) ITEM NO	(2) SMR CODE	(3) CAGEC	(4) PART NUMBER	(5) DESCRIPTION AND USABLE ON CODES (UOC)	(6) QTY
				GROUP 15 FRAME, TOWING ATTACHMENTS, DRAWBARS, AND ARTICULATION SYSTEMS	
				GROUP 1501 FRAME ASSEMBLY	
				FIG. 107 FRONT BUMPER AND RELATED PARTS	
1	PAOZZ	11862	14045516	BRACE,FENDER	1
2	PAOZZ	96906	MS90728-87	SCREW,CAP,HEXAGON H	4
3	PAOZZ	11862	3790768	WASHER,FLAT	4
4	PAOZZ	96906	MS90728-111	SCREW,CAP,HEXAGON H	2
5	PAOZZ	96906	MS27183-18	WASHER,FLAT	24
6	PAOZZ	96906	MS51967-14	NUT,PLAIN,HEXAGON	18
7	PAOZZ	11862	14045515	BRACE,FENDER	1
8	PAOZZ	96906	MS90728-119	SCREW,CAP,HEXAGON H	8
9	PAOZZ	11862	14067791	BRACE,FENDER LEFT	1
10	PFOZZ	11862	14072422	BUMPER,VEHICULAR	1
11	PAOZZ	11862	14072425	BOLT,SQUARE NECK	8
12	PAOZZ	96906	MS27183-19	WASHER,FLAT	4
13	PAOZZ	11862	14067792	BRACKET ASSEMBLY,BU RIGHT	1

END OF FIGURE

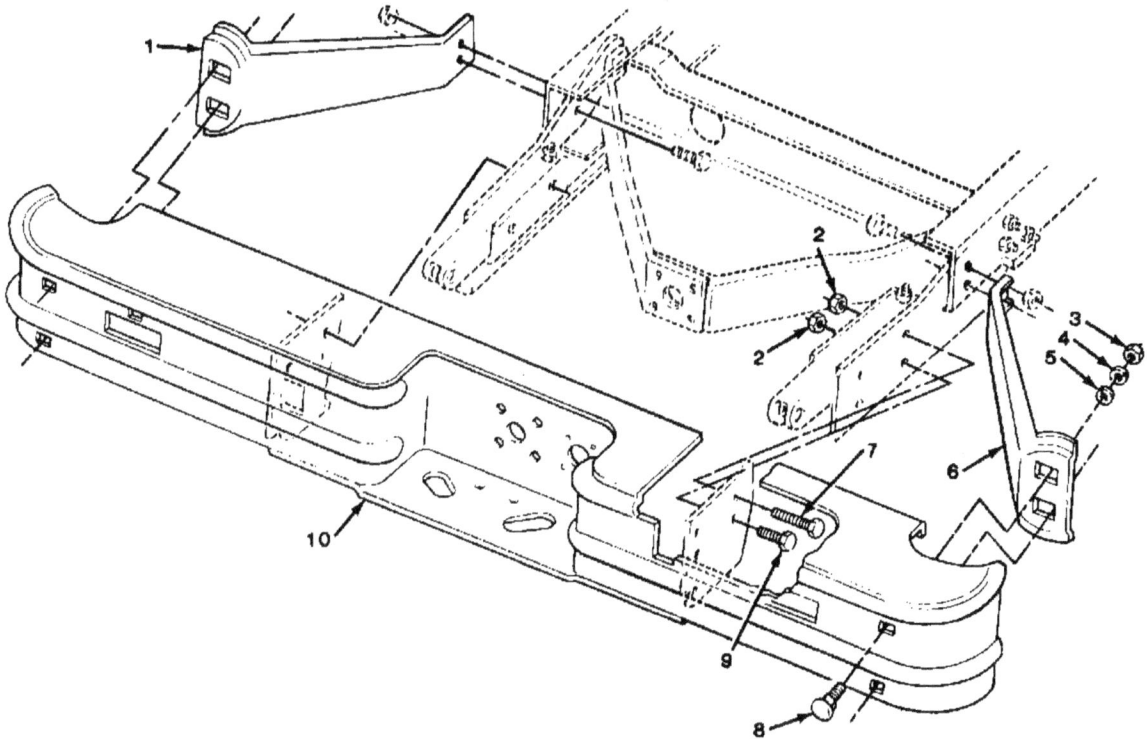

TA510943

FIGURE 108. REAR BUMPER AND MOUNTING PARTS (ALL EXCEPT M1009 AND M1010).

(1) ITEM NO	(2) SMR CODE	(3) CAGEC	(4) PART NUMBER	(5) DESCRIPTION AND USABLE ON CODES (UOC)	(6) QTY
				GROUP 1501 FRAME ASSEMBLY	
				FIG. 108 REAR BUMPER AND MOUNTING PARTS (ALL EXCEPT M1009 AND M1010)	
1	PAOZZ	11862	14014799	BRACE,FENDER UOC:194,208,230,231,252,254,256	1
2	PAOZZ	24617	9422301	NUT,SELF-LOCKING,HE UOC:194,208,230,231,252,254,256	8
3	PAOZZ	96906	MS51967-14	NUT,PLAIN,HEXAGON UOC:194,208,230,231,252,254,256	4
4	PAOZZ	96906	MS35340-48	WASHER,LOCK UOC:194,208,230,231,252,254,256	4
5	PAOZZ	96906	MS27183-18	WASHER,FLAT UOC:194,208,230,231,252,254,256	4
6	PAOZZ	11862	14014800	BRACE,FENDER UOC:194,208,230,231,252,254,256	1
7	PAOZZ	96906	MS90728-119	SCREW,CAP,HEXAGON H UOC:194,208,230,231,252,254,256	4
8	PAOZZ	11862	14072425	BOLT,SQUARE NECK UOC:194,208,230,231,252,254,256	4
9	PAOZZ	96906	MS90728-111	SCREW,CAP,HEXAGON H UOC:194,208,230,231,252,254,256	4
10	PFOZZ	11862	14072435	BUMPER,VEHICULAR UOC:194,208,230,231,252,254,256	1

END OF FIGURE

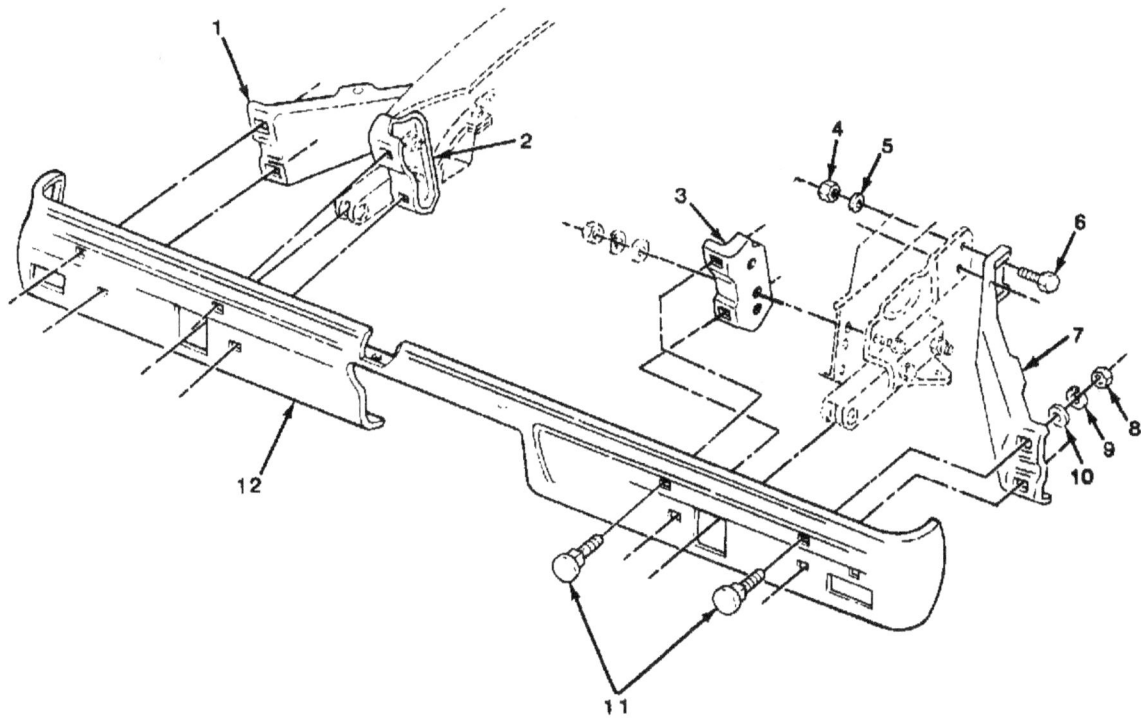

TA510944

FIGURE 109. REAR BUMPER AND MOUNTING PARTS (M1009).

(1) ITEM NO	(2) SMR CODE	(3) CAGEC	(4) PART NUMBER	(5) DESCRIPTION AND USABLE ON CODES (UOC)	(6) QTY
				GROUP 1501 FRAME ASSEMBLY	
				FIG. 109 REAR BUMPER AND MOUNTING PARTS (M1009)	
1	PAOZZ	11862	14067783	BRACE,FENDER UOC:209	1
2	PAOZZ	11862	14021357	BRACE,FENDER UOC:209	1
3	PAOZZ	11862	14021358	BRACE,FENDER UOC:209	1
4	PAOZZ	96906	MS51967-12	NUT,PLAIN,HEXAGON UOC:209	4
5	PAOZZ	96906	MS35340-47	WASHER,LOCK UOC:209	4
6	PAOZZ	96906	MS90728-87	SCREW,CAP,HEXAGON H UOC:209	4
7	PAOZZ	11862	14067784	BRACE,FENDER UOC:209	1
8	PAOZZ	96906	MS51967-14	NUT,PLAIN,HEXAGON UOC:209	8
9	PAOZZ	96906	MS35340-48	WASHER,LOCK UOC:209	8
10	PAOZZ	96906	MS27183-18	WASHER,FLAT UOC:209	8
11	PAOZZ	11862	14072425	BOLT,SQUARE NECK UOC:209	8
12	PFOZZ	11862	14072436	BUMPER,VEHICULAR UOC:209	1

END OF FIGURE

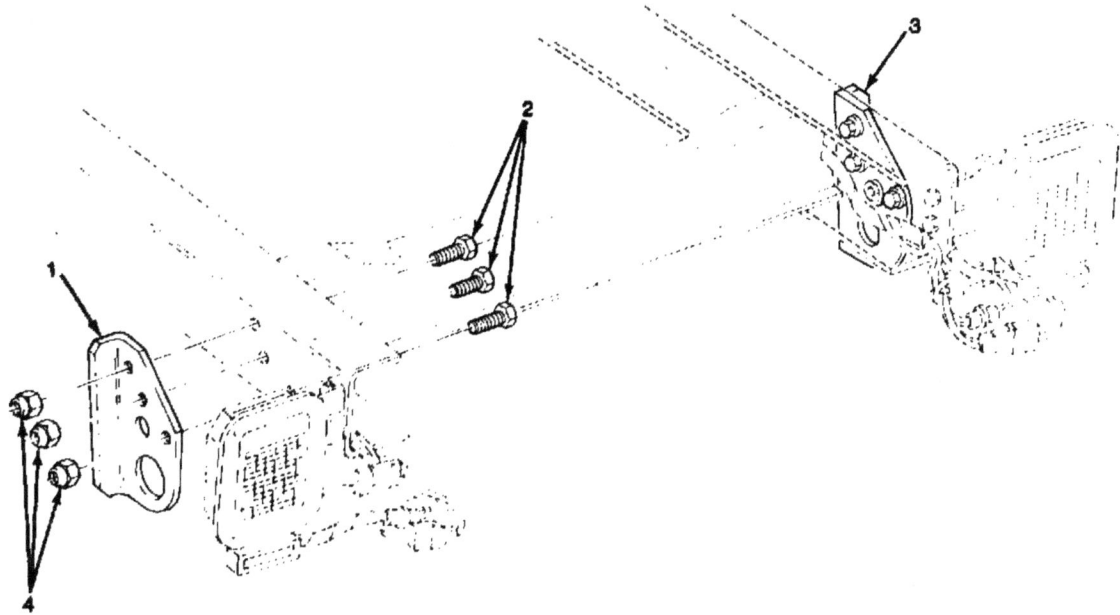

TA510945

FIGURE 110. REAR TIE-DOWNS (M1031).

(1) ITEM NO	(2) SMR CODE	(3) CAGEC	(4) PART NUMBER	(5) DESCRIPTION AND USABLE ON CODES (UOC)	(6) QTY
				GROUP 1501 FRAME ASSEMBLY	
				FIG. 110 REAR TIE-DOWNS (M1031)	
1	PAOZZ	11862	15599219	BRACKET,ANGLE LEFT UOC:231	1
2	PAOZZ	96906	MS90728-111	SCREW,CAP,HEXAGON H UOC:231	6
3	PAOZZ	11862	15599220	BRACKET,ANGLE UOC:231	1
4	PAOZZ	24617	9422301	NUT,SELF-LOCKING,HE UOC:231	6
				END OF FIGURE	

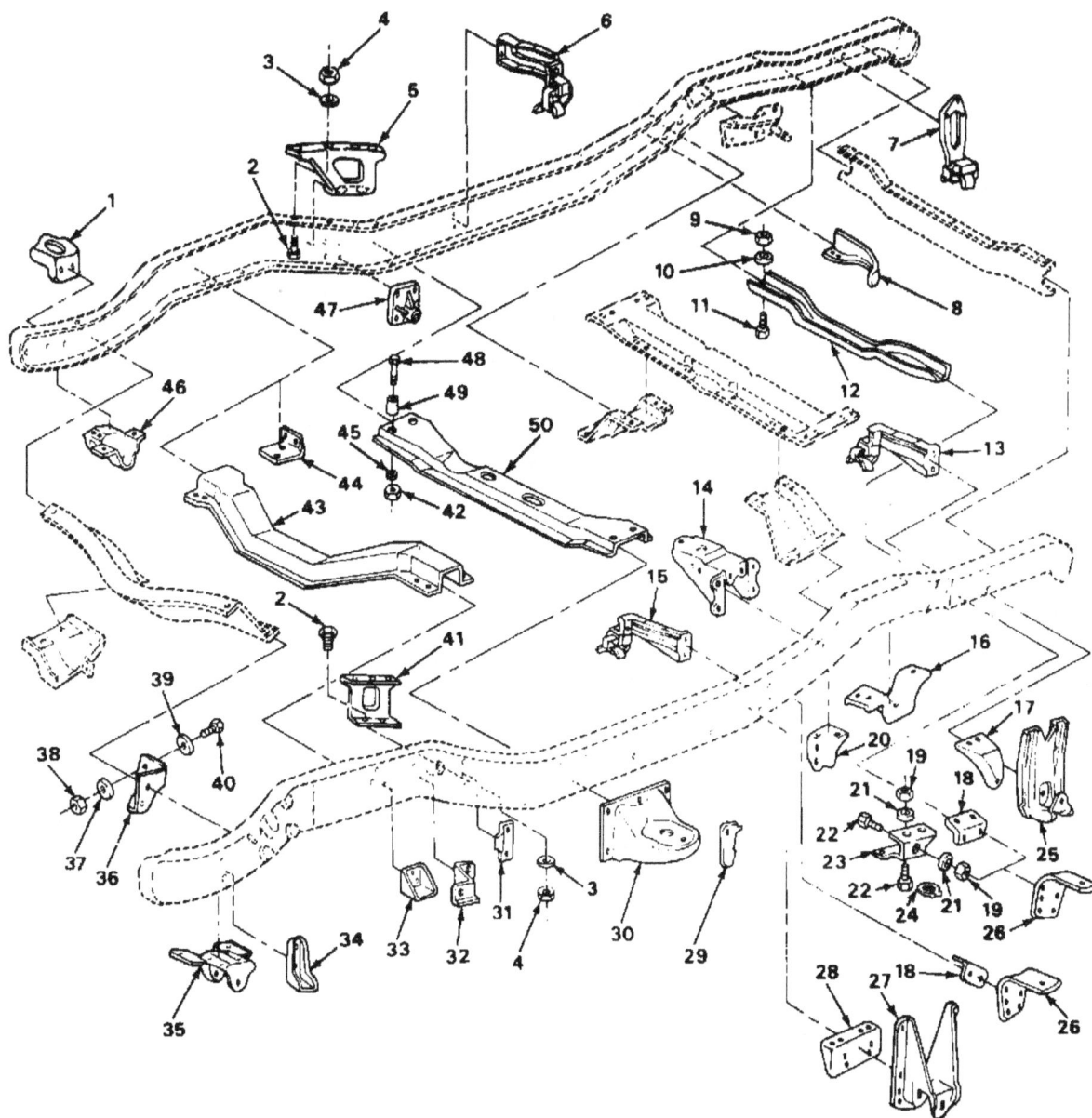

TA510947

FIGURE 111. FRAME ASSEMBLY RELATED PARTS (ALL EXCEPT M1009).

(1) ITEM NO	(2) SMR CODE	(3) CAGEC	(4) PART NUMBER	(5) DESCRIPTION AND USABLE ON CODES (UOC)	(6) QTY
				GROUP 1501 FRAME ASSEMBLY	
				FIG. 111 FRAME ASSEMBLY RELATED PARTS (ALL EXCEPT M1009)	
2	PAOZZ	11862	9424320	SCREW,CAP,HEXAGON H UOC:194,208,210,230,231,252,254,256	10
3	PAOZZ	96906	MS27183-16	WASHER,FLAT UOC:194,208,210,230,231,252,254,256	10
4	PAOZZ	80205	NAS1408A6	NUT,SELF-LOCKING,HE UOC:194,208,210,230,231,252,254,256	10
5	PAOZZ	11862	15599998	BRACKET,SIDE MEMBER RIGHT UOC:194,208,210,230,231,252,254,256	1
6	PAOZZ	11862	14022538	BRACKET,PIPE UOC:194,208,210,230,231,252,254,256	1
7	PAOZZ	11862	14034504	BRACKET,PIPE RIGHT UOC:194,208,210,230,231,252,254,256	1
7	PAOZZ	11862	14034503	HANGER,PIPE LEFT UOC:194,208,210,230,231,252,254,256	1
9	PAOZZ	80205	NAS1408A6	NUT,SELF-LOCKING,HE UOC:194,208,210,230,231,252,254,256	1
10	PAOZZ	11862	3914674	WASHER,FLAT UOC:194,208,210,230,231,252,254,256	1
11	PAOZZ	96906	MS90728-59	SCREW,CAP,HEXAGON H UOC:194,208,210,230,231,252,254,256	1
12	PAOZZ	11862	15595211	BAR,SPARE WHEEL UOC:194,208,210,230,231,252,254,256	1
13	PAOZZ	11862	14034501	BRACKET,PIPE UOC:194,208,210,230,231,252,254,256	1
15	PAOZZ	11862	14022537	BRACKET,PIPE UOC:194,208,210,230,231,252,254,256	1
19	PAOZZ	96906	MS51967-8	NUT,PLAIN,HEXAGON UOC:254,256	2
21	PAOZZ	96906	MS35338-46	WASHER,LOCK UOC:254,256	2
22	PAOZZ	96906	MS90728-60	SCREW,CAP,HEXAGON H UOC:254,256	3
23	PAOZZ	11862	14001067	BRACKET,DOUBLE ANGL UOC:254,256	2
23	PAOZZ	11862	14001068	BRACKET,DOUBLE ANGL UOC:254,256	2
24	PAOZZ	11862	337957	RETAINER,PACKING UOC:254,256	2
41	PAOZZ	11862	15599997	BRAKCET,SIDE MEMBER LEFT UOC:194,208,210,230,231,252,254,256	1

END OF FIGURE

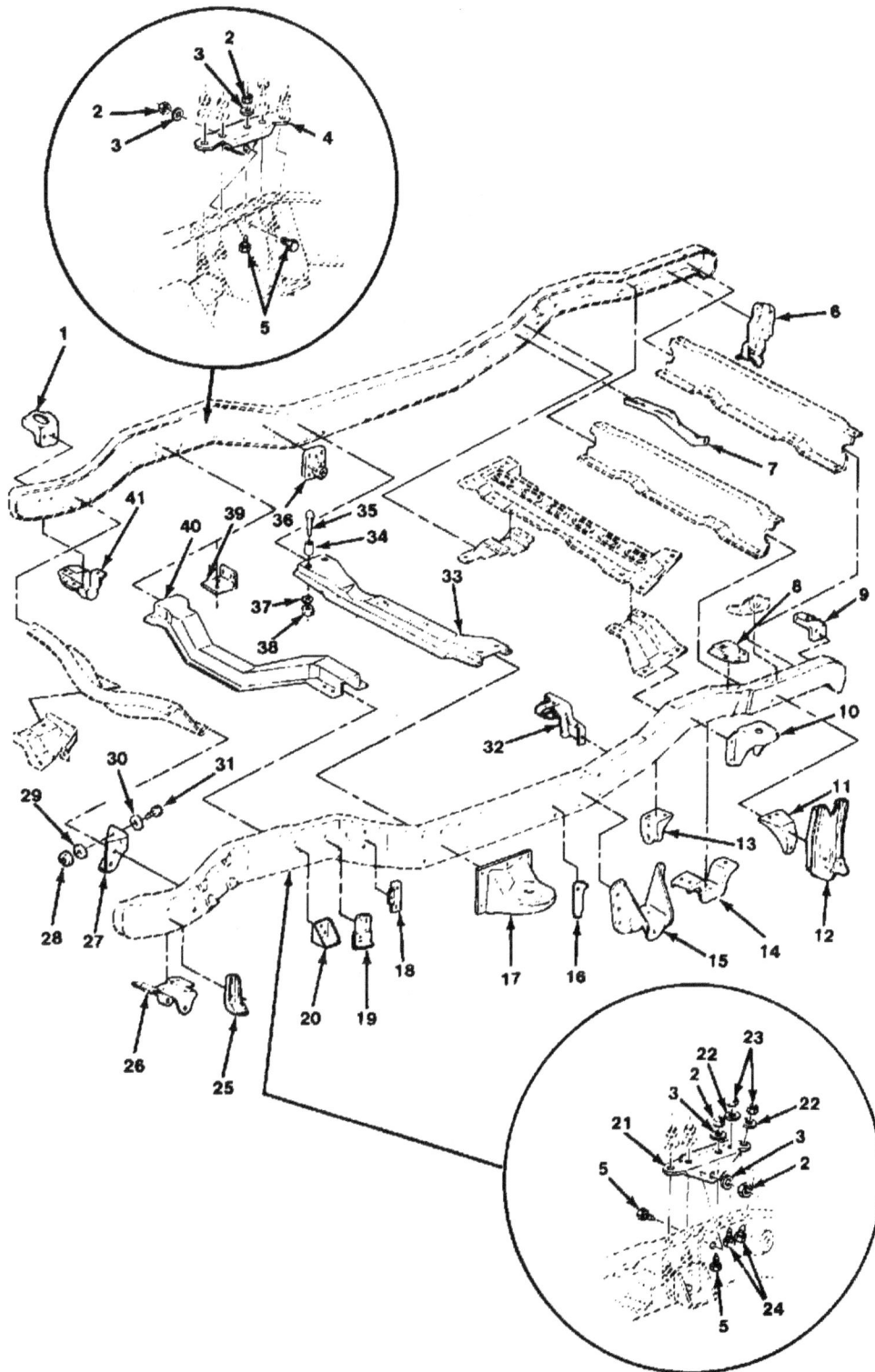

TA510949

FIGURE 112. FRAME ASSEMBLY RELATED PARTS (M1009).

(1) ITEM NO	(2) SMR CODE	(3) CAGEC	(4) PART NUMBER	(5) DESCRIPTION AND USABLE ON CODES (UOC)	(6) QTY
				GROUP 1501 FRAME ASSEMBLY	
				FIG. 112 FRAME ASSEMBLY RELATED PARTS (M1009)	
2	PAOZZ	11862	9422299	NUT,SELF-LOCKING UOC:209	8
3	PAOZZ	24617	3990160	WASHER,FLAT UOC:209	8
4	XBOZZ	11862	TX001488	BRACKET,RH UOC:209	1
5	PAOZZ	11862	9440344	BOLT,MACHINE UOC:209	8
6	PAOZZ	11862	14020478	SUPPORT ASSEMBLY,MU RIGHT UOC:209	1
6	PAOZZ	11862	14034513	SUPPORT,MUFFLER AND LEFT UOC:209	1
21	XBOZZ	11862	TX001487	BRACKET,LH UOC:209	1
22	PAOZZ	96906	MS35340-46	WASHER,LOCK UOC:209	4
23	PAOZZ	11862	9418931	NUT,PLAIN,HEXAGON UOC:209	3
24	PAOZZ	96906	MS90728-63	SCREW,CAP,HEXAGON H UOC:209	2
32	PAOZZ	11862	14007142	HANGER,ENGINE EXHAU UOC:209	1

END OF FIGURE

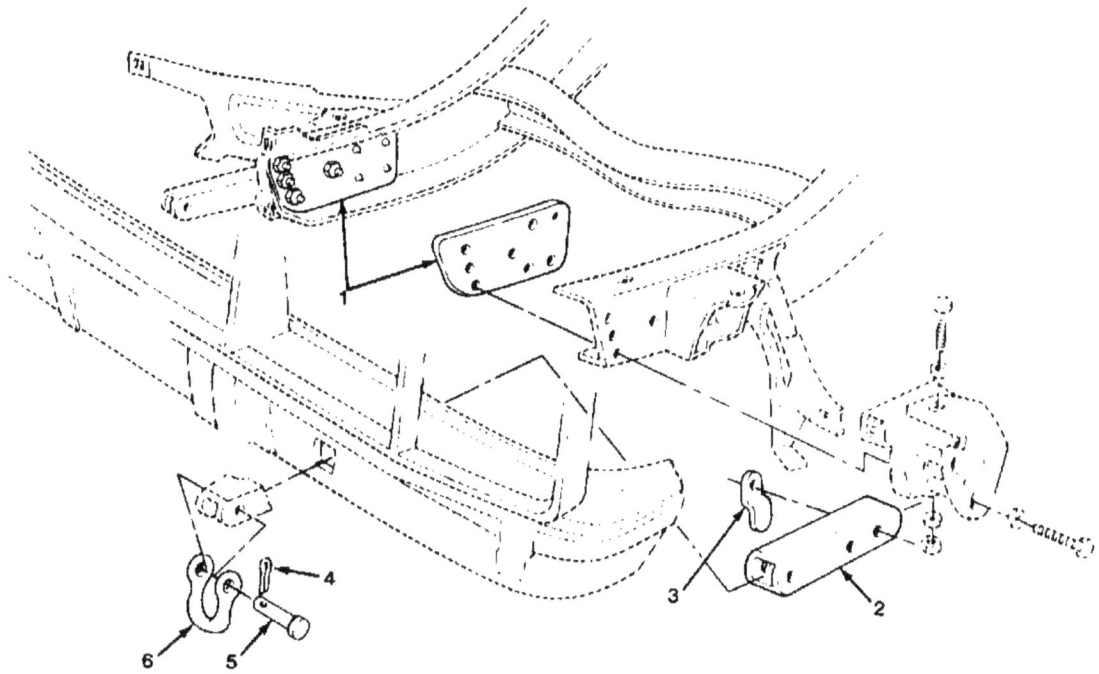

TA510950

FIGURE 113. CLEVISES AND SUPPORTS.

(1) ITEM NO	(2) SMR CODE	(3) CAGEC	(4) PART NUMBER	(5) DESCRIPTION AND USABLE ON CODES (UOC)	(6) QTY
				GROUP 1503 PINTLES AND TOWING ATTACHEMENTS	
				FIG. 113 CLEVISES AND SUPPORTS	
1	PAOZZ	11862	14067790	PLATE,TIE-DOWN	2
2	PAOZZ	11862	14067795	EXTENSION,TIE DOWN	2
3	PAOZZ	11862	14067796	BRACKET,DOUBLE ANGL	2
4	PAOZZ	96906	MS24665-497	PIN,COTTER	2
5	PAOZZ	11862	14067794	PIN,STRAIGHT,HEADED	2
6	PAOZZ	19207	7358030	SHACKLE	2

END OF FIGURE

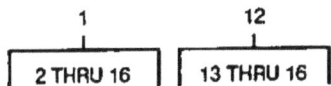

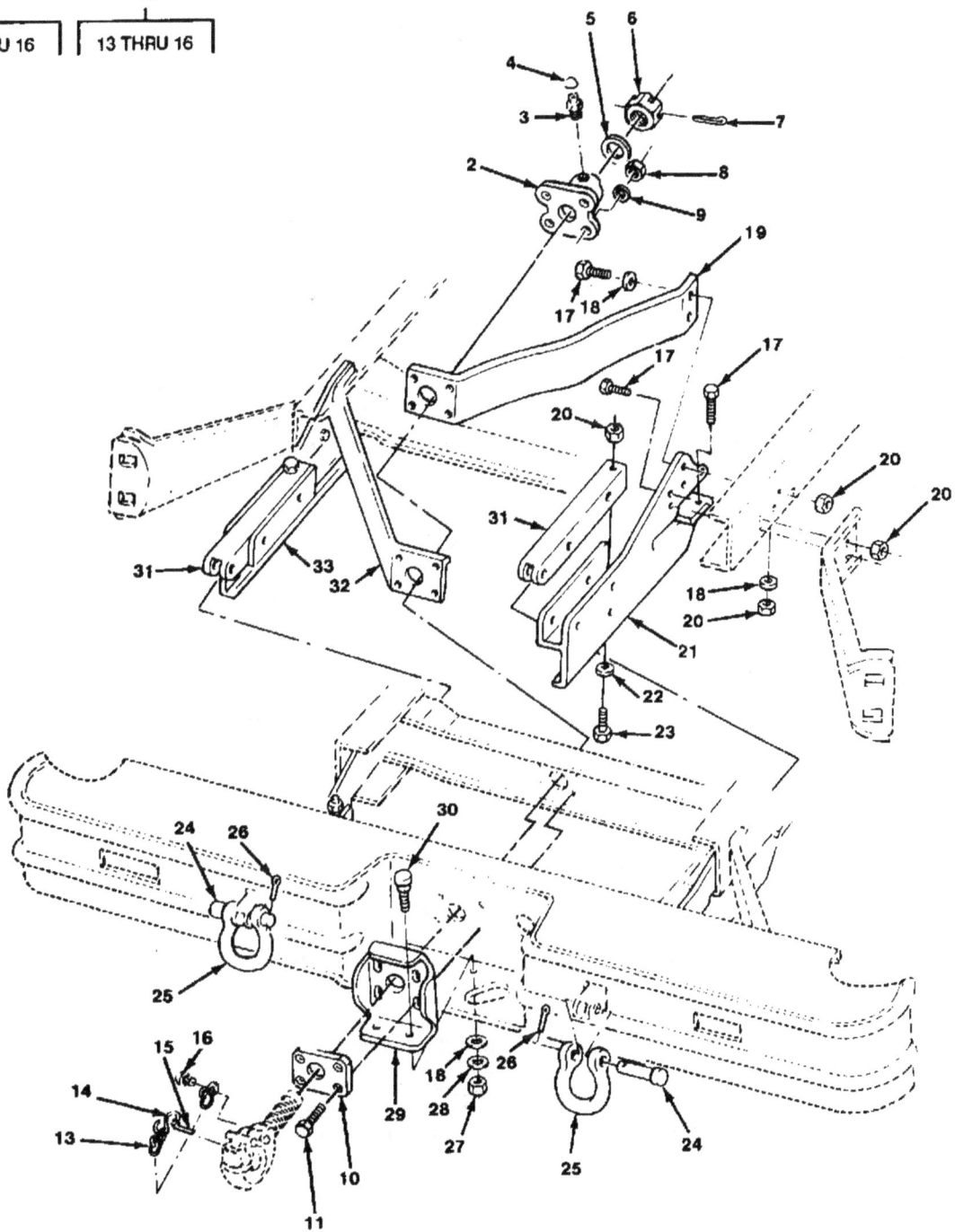

TA510951

FIGURE 114. PINTLE ASSEMBLY AND CLEVIS (M1008, M1028, AND M1028A1).

SECTION II (1) ITEM NO	(2) SMR CODE	(3) CAGEC	(4) PART NUMBER	(5) DESCRIPTION AND USABLE ON CODES (UOC)	(6) QTY
				GROUP 1503 PINTLES AND TOWING ATTACHMENTS	
				FIG. 114 PINTLE ASSEMBLY AND CLEVIS (M1008, M1028, AND M1028A1)	
1	PAOOO	96906	MS51335-1	PINTLE ASSEMBLY,TOW UOC:194,208,230,252	1
2	PAOZZ	74410	XA-T-61-SR	.COLLAR,SHAFT UOC:194,208,230,252,254,256	1
3	PAOZZ	96906	MS15001-1	.FITTING,LUBRICATION UOC:194,208,230,252,254,256	1
4	PAOZZ	74410	XB-767-10	.CAP,PROTECTIVE,DUST UOC:194,208,230,252,254,256	1
5	PAOZZ	74410	XA-T-88	.WASHER,FLAT UOC:194,208,230,252,254,256	1
6	PAOZZ	96906	MS35692-94	.NUT,PLAIN,SLOTTED,H UOC:194,208,230,252,254,256	1
7	PAOZZ	96906	MS24665-628	.PIN,COTTER UOC:194,208,230,252,254,256	1
8	XDOZZ	74410	XB-766	.NUT,PLAIN,HEXAGON UOC:194,208,230,252,254,256	4
9	PAOZZ	74410	XB-T-45-1	.WASHER,LOCK UOC:194,208,230,252,254,256	4
10	PAOZZ	74410	XA-T-61-SF	.BRACKET,PINTLE HOOK UOC:194,208,230,252,254,256	1
11	PAOZZ	96906	MS90727-117	.SCREW,CAP,HEXAGON H UOC:194,208,230,252,254,256	4
12	PAOOO	96906	MS51335-1	.PINTLE ASSEMBLY,TOW UOC:194,208,230,252,254,256	1
13	MOOZZ	74410	XX123	..CHAIN (5" LG) MAKE FROM CHAIN, P/N RRC271BTY2CLDIA072 UOC:194,208,230,252,254,256	1
14	PAOZZ	96906	MS87006-53	..HOOK,CHAIN,S UOC:194,208,230,252,254,256	1
15	PAOZZ	80020	36344N24	..PIN,COTTER UOC:194,208,230,252,254,256	1
16	PAOZZ	96906	MS21318-47	..SCREW,DRIVE UOC:194,208,230,252,254,256	1
17	PAOZZ	96906	MS90728-113	SCREW,CAP,HEXAGON H UOC:194,208,230,252	12
18	PAOZZ	96906	MS27183-18	WASHER,FLAT UOC:194,208,230,252	8
19	PAOZZ	11862	14067786	BAR,REINFORCEMENT,P UOC:194,208,230,252,254,256	1
20	PAOZZ	24617	9422301	NUT,SELF-LOCKING,HE UOC:194,208,230,252	14
21	PAOZZ	11862	14067780	BRACKET,SPECIAL UOC:194,208,230,252,254,256	1
22	PAOZZ	96906	MS27183-19	WASHER,FLAT UOC:194,208,230,252	2
23	PAOZZ	96906	MS90728-119	SCREW,CAP,HEXAGON H	2

(1) ITEM NO	(2) SMR CODE	(3) CAGEC	(4) PART NUMBER	(5) DESCRIPTION AND USABLE ON CODES (UOC)	(6) QTY
				UOC:194,208,230,252	
24	PAOZZ	11862	14067794	PIN,STRAIGHT,HEADED	2
				UOC:194,208,230,252	
25	PAOZZ	11862	14067793	SHACKLE	2
				UOC:194,208,230,252	
26	PAOZZ	96906	MS24665-497	PIN,COTTER	2
				UOC:194,208,230,252	
27	PAOZZ	96906	MS51967-14	NUT,PLAIN,HEXAGON	2
				UOC:194,208,230,252,254,256	
28	PAOZZ	96906	MS35340-48	WASHER,LOCK	2
				UOC:194,208,230,252,254,256	
29	PAOZZ	11862	14078806	REINFORCEMENT,BUMPE	1
				UOC:194,208,230,252,254,256	
30	PAOZZ	11862	14072425	BOLT,SQUARE NECK	2
				UOC:194,208,230,252,254,256	
31	PAOZZ	11862	14067787	EXTENSION,TIE DOWN	2
				UOC:194,208,230,252,254,256	
32	PAOZZ	11862	14067785	BRACKET,TOW HOOK	1
				UOC:194,208,230,252,254,256	
33	PAOZZ	11862	14067779	BRACKET,SPECIAL	1
				UOC:194,208,230,5252,254,256	

END OF FIGURE

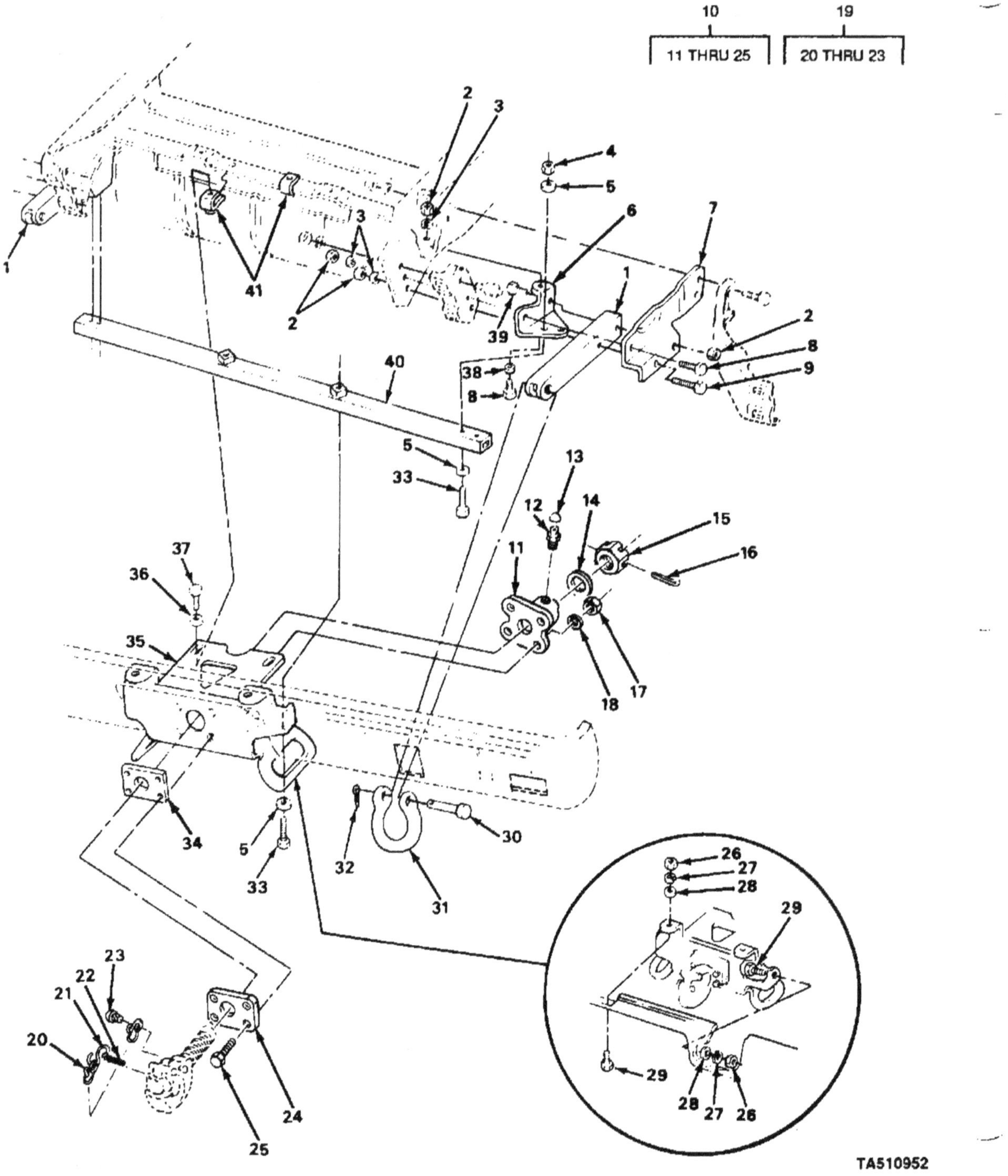

FIGURE 115. PINTLE ASSEMBLY AND CLEVIS (M1009)

TA510952

GROUP 1503 PINTLES AND TOWING
ATTACHMENTS

FIG. 115 PINTLE ASSEMBLY AND CLEVIS
(M1009)

ITEM NO	SMR CODE	CAGEC	PART NUMBER	DESCRIPTION AND USABLE ON CODES (UOC)	QTY
1	PAOZZ	11862	14067770	EXTENSION,TIE DOWN UOC:209	2
2	PAOZZ	96906	MS51967-14	NUT,PLAIN,HEXAGON UOC:209	10
3	PAOZZ	96906	MS35340-48	WASHER,LOCK UOC:209	6
4	PAOZZ	96906	MS51967-12	NUT,PLAIN,HEXAGON UOC:209	4
5	PAOZZ	11862	3790768	WASHER,FLAT UOC:209	10
6	PAOZZ	11862	14067773	BRACKET,REINFORCEME LEFT UOC:209	1
6	PAOZZ	11862	14067774	BRACKET,TOW HOOK RIGHT UOC:209	1
7	PAOZZ	11862	14067771	BRACKET,DOUBLE ANGL LEFT UOC:209	1
7	PAOZZ	11862	14067772	BRACKET,DOUBLE ANGL RIGHT UOC:209	1
8	PAOZZ	96906	MS90728-111	SCREW,CAP,HEXAGON H UOC:209	4
9	PAOZZ	96906	MS90728-119	SCREW,CAP,HEXAGON H UOC:209	2
10	PAOOO	96906	MS51335-1	PINTLE ASSEMBLY,TOW UOC:209	1
11	PAOZZ	74410	XA-T-61-SR	.COLLAR,SHAFT UOC:209	1
12	PAOZZ	96906	MS15001-1	.FITTING,LUBRICATION UOC:209	1
13	PAOZZ	74410	XB-767-10	.CAP,PROTECTIVE,DUST UOC:209	1
14	PAOZZ	74410	XA-T-88	.WASHER,FLAT UOC:209	1
15	PAOZZ	96906	MS35692-94	.NUT,PLAIN,SLOTTED,H UOC:209	1
16	PAOZZ	96906	MS24665-628	.PIN,COTTER UOC:209	1
17	XDOZZ	74410	XB-766	.NUT,PLAIN,HEXAGON UOC:209	4
18	PAOZZ	74410	XB-T-45-1	.WASHER,LOCK UOC:209	4
19	PAOOO	96906	MS51335-1	.PINTLE ASSEMBLY,TOW UOC:209	1
20	MOOZZ	74410	XX123	..CHAIN (5" LG) MAKE FROM CHAIN, P/ N RRC271BTY2CLDIA072 UOC:209	1
21	PAOZZ	96906	MS87006-53	..HOOK,CHAIN,S	1

(1) ITEM NO	(2) SMR CODE	(3) CAGEC	(4) PART NUMBER	(5) DESCRIPTION AND USABLE ON CODES (UOC)	(6) QTY
				UOC:209	
22	PAOZZ	80020	36344N24	.PIN,COTTER.	1
				UOC:209	
23	PAOZZ	96906	MS21318-47	..SCREW,DRIVE	1
				UOC:209	
24	PAOZZ	74410	XA-T-61-SF	.BRACKET,PINTLE HOOK	1
				UOC:209	
25	PAOZZ	96906	MS90727-117	SCREW,CAP,HEXAGON H	4
				UOC:209	
26	PAOZZ	96906	MS51967-8	NUT,PLAIN,HEXAGON	4
				UOC:209	
27	PAOZZ	96906	MS35338-46	WASHER,LOCK	4
				UOC:209	
28	PAOZZ	96906	MS27183-14	WASHER,FLAT	4
				UOC:209	
29	PAOZZ	96906	MS90728-60	SCREW,CAP,HEXAGON H	4
				UOC:209	
30	PAOZZ	11862	14067794	PIN,STRAIGHT,HEADED	2
				UOC:209	
31	PAOZZ	11862	14067793	SHACKLE	2
				UOC:209	
32	PAOZZ	96906	MS24665-497	PIN,COTTER	2
				UOC:209	
33	PAOZZ	96906	MS90728-92	SCREW,CAP,HEXAGON H	6
				UOC:209	
34	PAOZZ	11862	14067789	SPACER,PLATE	2
				UOC:209	
35	PAOZZ	11862	14067776	BRACKET,TOW HOOK	1
				UOC:209	
36	PAOZZ	96906	MS27183-15	WASHER,FLAT	2
				UOC:209	
37	PAOZZ	96906	MS90728-87	SCREW,CAP,HEXAGON H	2
				UOC:209	
38	PAOZZ	96906	MS27183-18	WASHER,FLAT	2
				UOC:209	
39	PAOZZ	96906	MS90728-117	SCREW,CAP,HEXAGON H	2
				UOC:209	
40	PAOZZ	11862	14067775	BRACKET,TOW HOOK	1
				UOC:209	
41	PAOZZ	11862	480567	NUT,CLIP-ON	2
				UOC:209	

END OF FIGURE

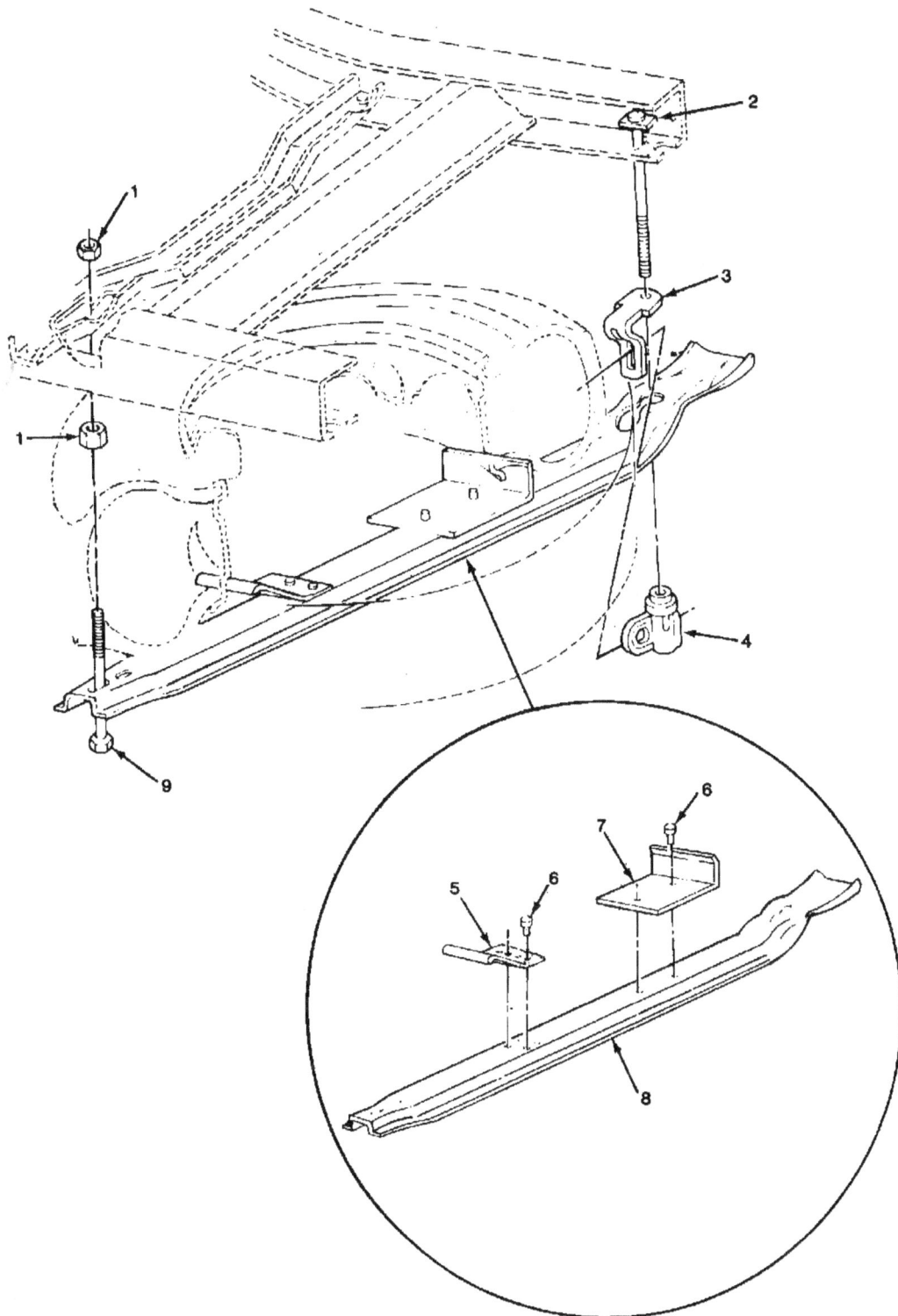

TA510953

FIGURE 116. SPARE WHEEL CARRIER (ALL EXCEPT M1009).

(1) ITEM NO	(2) SMR CODE	(3) CAGEC	(4) PART NUMBER	(5) DESCRIPTION AND USABLE ON CODES (UOC)	(6) QTY
				GROUP 1504 SPARE WHEEL CARRIER AND TIRE LOCK	
				FIG. 116 SPARE WHEEL CARRIER (ALL EXCEPT M1009)	
1	PAOZZ	96906	MS51967-14	NUT,PLAIN,HEXAGON UOC:194,208,210,230,231,252,254,256	2
2	PAOZZ	11862	3991022	BOLT,MACHINE UOC:194,208,210,230,231,252,254,256	1
3	PAOZZ	11862	15599915	HOLD DOWN,SPARE TIR UOC:194,208,210,230,231,252,254,256	1
4	PAOZZ	11862	6274031	NUT,PLAIN,HEXAGON UOC:194,208,210,230,231,252,254,256	1
5	PAOZZ	11862	350037	PILOT,WHEEL CARRIER UOC:194,208,210,230,231,252,254,256	1
6	PAOZZ	24617	189448	RIVET,SOLID UOC:194,208,210,230,231,252,254,256	4
7	PAOZZ	11862	6274036	PILOT,WHEEL CARRIER UOC:194,208,210,230,231,252,254,256	1
8	PAOZZ	11862	350036	STRAP,SPARE WHEEL UOC:194,208,210,230,231,252,54,256	1
9	PAOZZ	11862	371603	SCREW,CAP,HEXAGON H UOC:194,208,210,230,231,252,254,256	1

END OF FIGURE

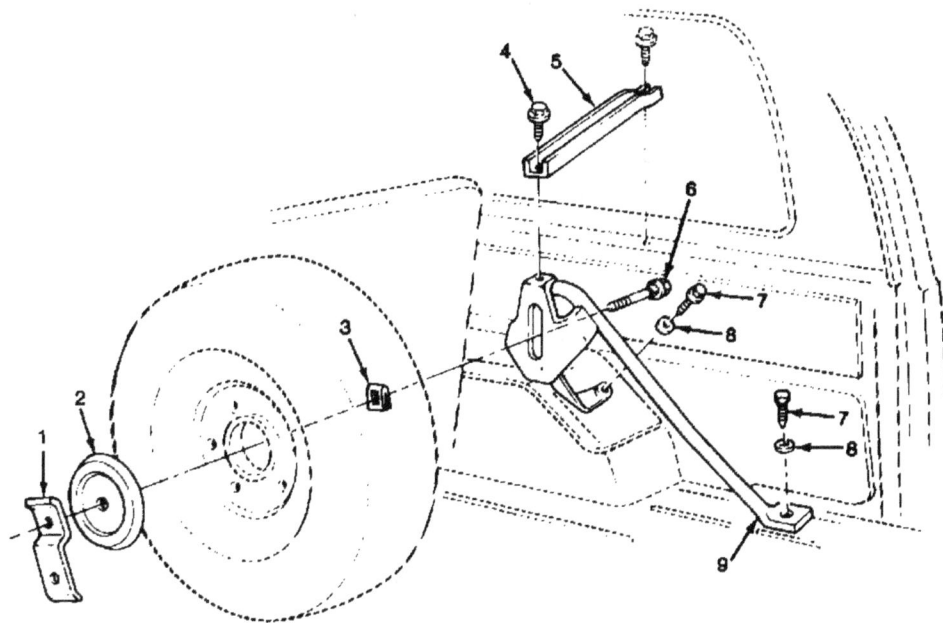

TA510954

FIGURE 117. SPARE WHEEL CARRIER (M1009).

(1) ITEM NO	(2) SMR CODE	(3) CAGEC	(4) PART NUMBER	(5) DESCRIPTION AND USABLE ON CODES (UOC)	(6) QTY
				GROUP 1504 SPARE WHEEL CARRIER AND TIRE LOCK	
				FIG. 117 SPARE WHEEL CARRIER (M1009)	
1	PAOZZ	11862	330046	RETAINER,SPARE TIRE UOC:209	1
2	PAOZZ	11862	14027926	PLATE,RESILIENT MOU UOC:209	1
3	PAOZZ	11862	3725668	PUSH ON NUT UOC:209	1
4	PAOZZ	24617	443945	SCREW UOC:209	2
5	PAOZZ	11862	14007545	BRACE,SPARE WHEEL S UOC:209	1
6	PAOZZ	11862	15599432	BOLT,SQUARE NECK UOC:209	1
7	PAOZZ	11862	3954730	SETSCREW UOC:209	2
8	PAOZZ	96906	MS27183-18	WASHER,FLAT UOC:209	2
9	PAOZZ	11862	343951	SUPPORT ASSEMBLY,WH UOC:209	1

END OF FIGURE

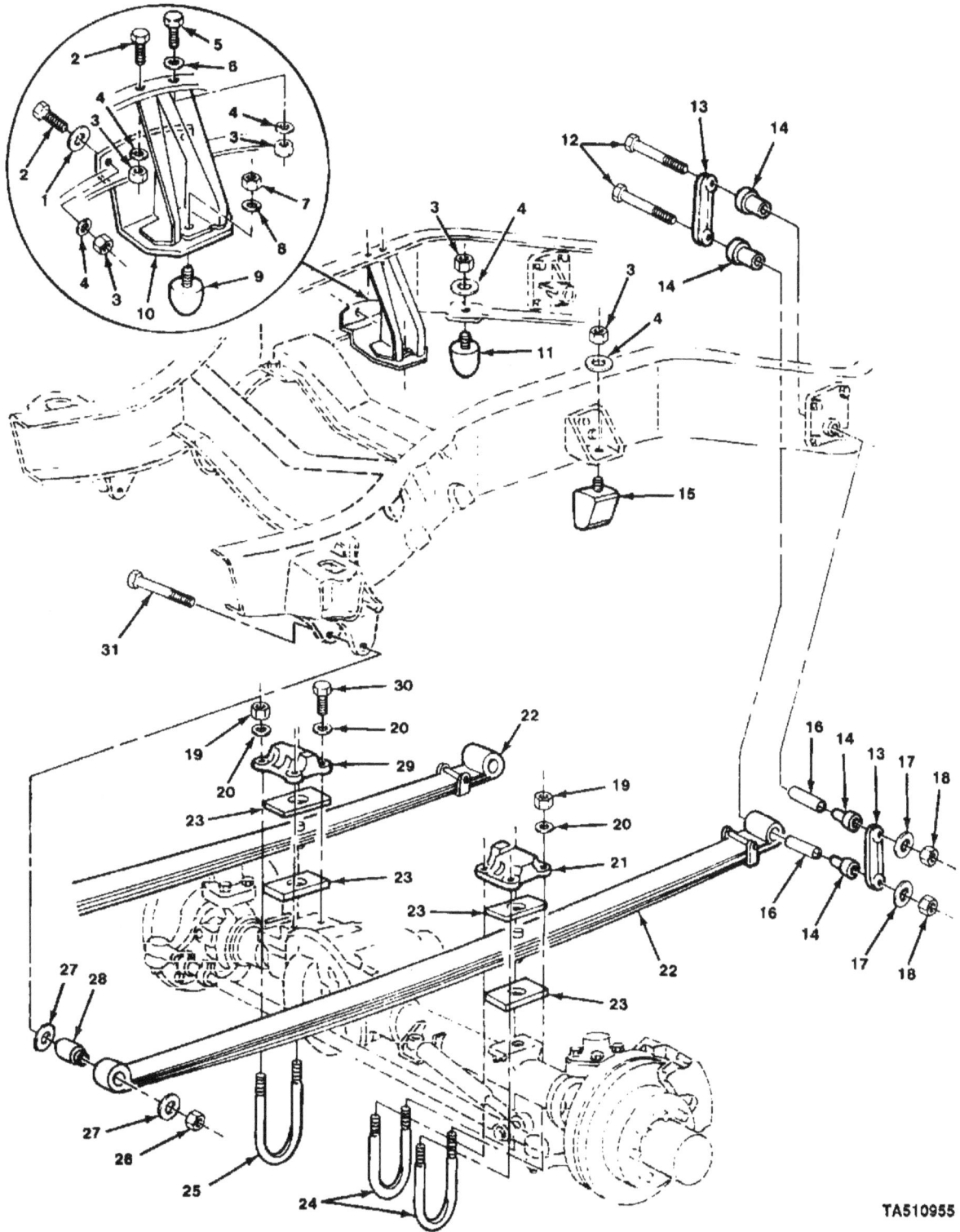

TA510955

FIGURE 118. FRONT SPRINGS AND RELATED PARTS (ALL EXCEPT M1009).

(1) ITEM NO	(2) SMR CODE	(3) CAGEC	(4) PART NUMBER	(5) DESCRIPTION AND USABLE ON CODES (UOC)	(6) QTY
				GROUP 16 SPRINGS AND SHOCK ABSORBERS	
				GROUP 1601 SPRINGS	
				FIG. 118 FRONT SPRINGS AND RELATED PARTS (ALL EXCEPT M1009)	
1	PAOZZ	96906	MS27183-14	WASHER,FLAT UOC:194,208,210,230,231,252,254	2
2	PAOZZ	96906	MS90728-60	SCREW,CAP,HEXAGON H UOC:194,208,210,230,231,252,254,256	4
3	PAOZZ	96906	MS51967-8	NUT,PLAIN,HEXAGON UOC:194,208,210,230,231,252,254,256	8
4	PAOZZ	96906	MS35338-46	WASHER,LOCK UOC:194,208,210,230,231,252,254,256	10
5	PAOZZ	96906	MS90728-62	SCREW,CAP,HEXAGON H UOC:194,208,210,230,231,252,254,256	1
6	PAOZZ	96906	MS27183-16	WASHER,FLAT UOC:194,208,210,230,231,252,254,256	1
7	PAOZZ	96906	MS51967-14	NUT,PLAIN,HEXAGON UOC:194,208,210,230,231,252,254	1
8	PAOZZ	96906	MS35340-48	WASHER,LOCK UOC:194,208,210,230,231,252,254,256	1
9	PAOZZ	11862	14029200	BUMPER,NONMETALLIC UOC:194,208,210,231,252,254,256	1
10	PAOZZ	11862	14045654	BRACKET ASSEMBLY,FR UOC:194,208,210,230,231,252,254,256	1
11	PAOZZ	11862	359878	BUMPER ASSEMBLY,FRO UOC:194,208,210,230,231,252	2
15	PAOZZ	11862	359877	BUMPER ASSEMBLY,FRO UOC:194,208,210,230,231,252,254,256	2

END OF FIGURE

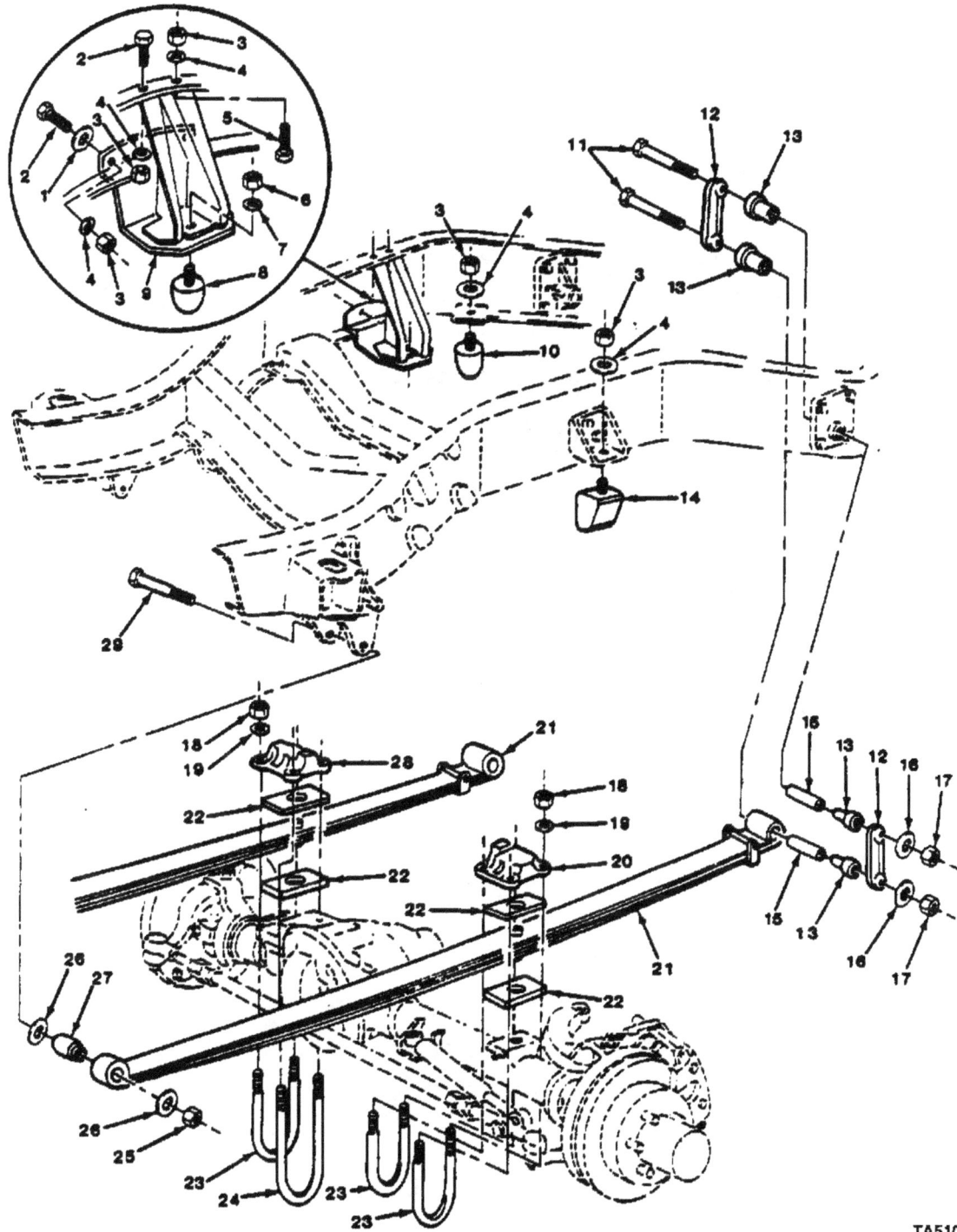

TA510956

FIGURE 119. FRONT SPRINGS AND RELATED PARTS (M1009).

(1) ITEM NO	(2) SMR CODE	(3) CAGEC	(4) PART NUMBER	(5) DESCRIPTION AND USABLE ON CODES (UOC)	(6) QTY
				GROUP 1601 SPRINGS	
				FIG. 119 FRONT SPRINGS AND RELATED PARTS (M1009)	
1	PAOZZ	96906	MS27183-14	WASHER,FLAT UOC:209	2
2	PAOZZ	96906	MS90728-60	SCREW,CAP,HEXAGON H UOC:209	3
3	PAOZZ	96906	MS51967-8	NUT,PLAIN,HEXAGON UOC:209	8
4	PAOZZ	96906	MS35338-46	WASHER,LOCK UOC:209	8
5	PAOZZ	96906	MS90728-63	SCREW,CAP,HEXAGON H UOC:209	1
6	PAOZZ	96906	MS51967-14	NUT,PLAIN,HEXAGON UOC:209	1
7	PAOZZ	96906	MS35340-48	WASHER,LOCK UOC:209	1
8	PAOZZ	11862	14029200	BUMPER,NONMETALLIC UOC:209	1
9	PAOZZ	11862	15522381	BRACKET,BUMPER UOC:209	1
10	PAOZZ	11862	359878	BUMPER ASSEMBLY,FRO UOC:209	2
14	PAOZZ	11862	359877	BUMPER ASSEMBLY,FRO UOC:209	2

END OF FIGURE

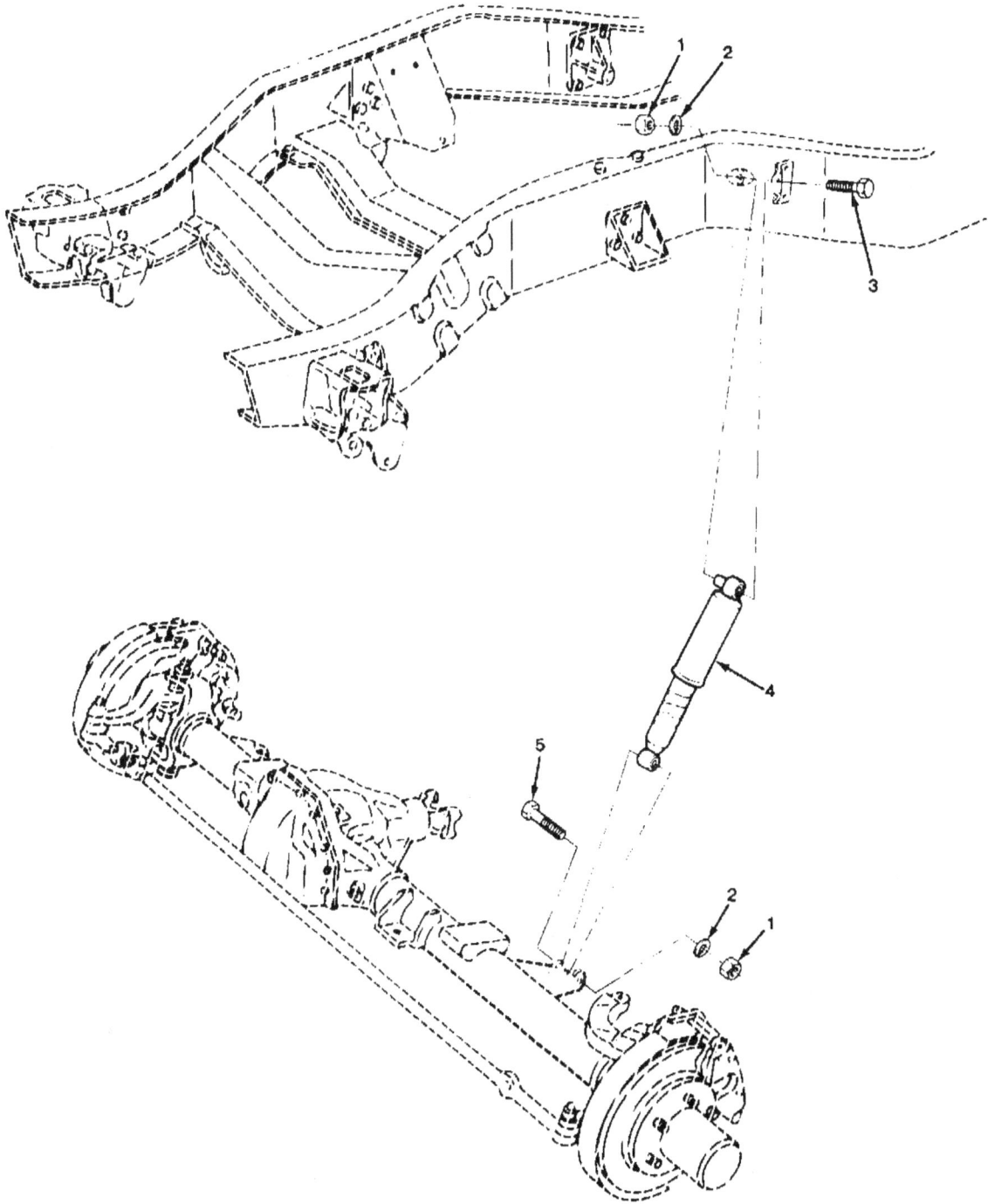

TA510960

FIGURE 120. FRONT SHOCK ABSORBERS.

(1) ITEM NO	(2) SMR CODE	(3) CAGEC	(4) PART NUMBER	(5) DESCRIPTION AND USABLE ON CODES (UOC)	(6) QTY
				GROUP 1604 SHOCK ABSORBER EQUIPMENT	
				FIG. 120 FRONT SHOCK ABSORBERS	
1	PAOZZ	96906	MS51967-14	NUT,PLAIN,HEXAGON	4
2	PAOZZ	96906	MS35340-48	WASHER,LOCK	4
3	PAOZZ	96906	MS90728-121	SCREW,CAP,HEXAGON H	2
4	PAOZZ	11862	3187843	SHOCK ABSORBER,DIRE UOC:209	2
4	PAOZZ	11862	3187846	SHOCK ABSORBER,DIRE UOC:194,208,210,230,231,252,254,256	2
5	PAOZZ	96906	MS90728-119	SCREW,CAP,HEXAGON H	2

END OF FIGURE

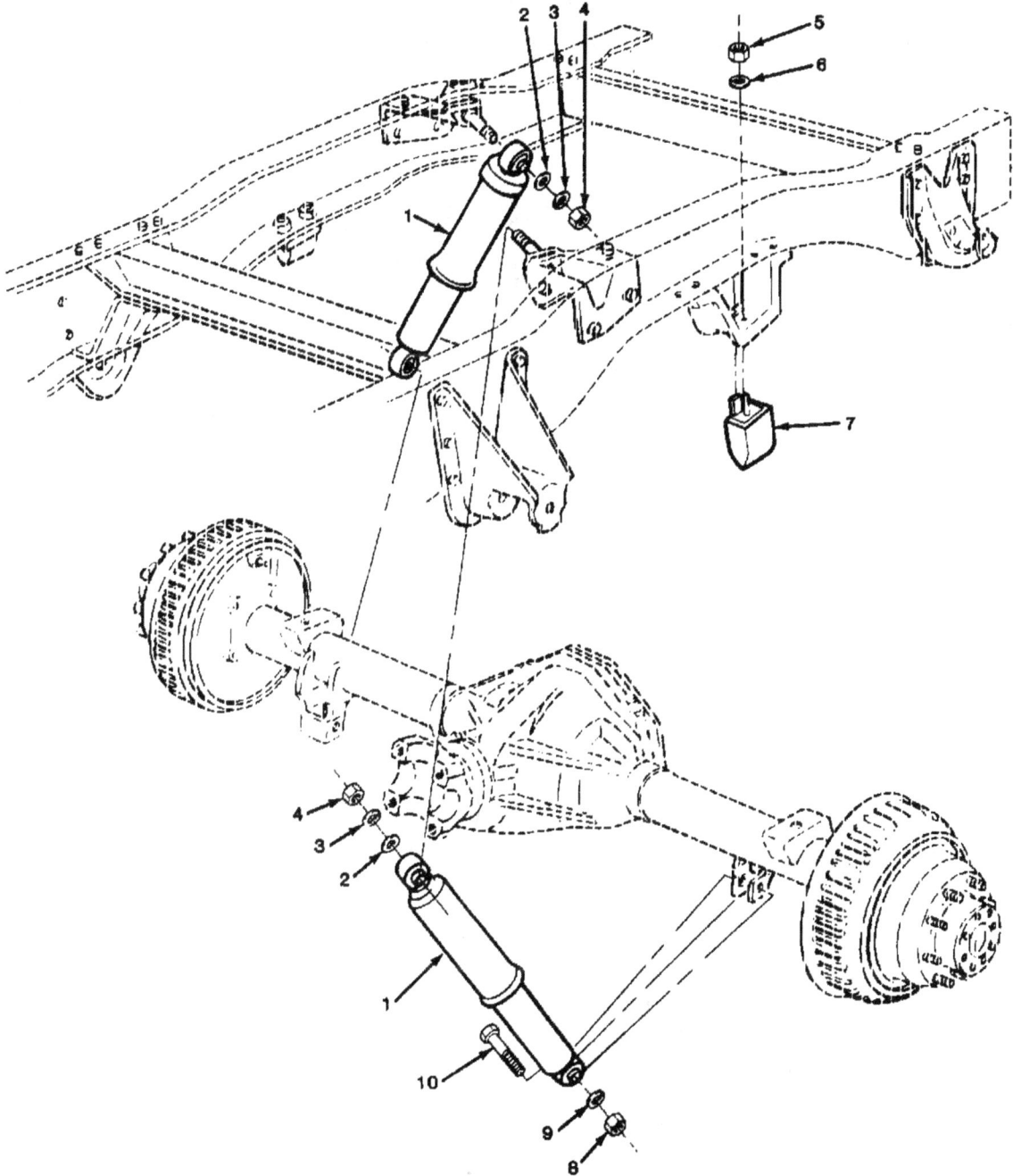

TA510961

FIGURE 121. REAR SHOCK ABSORBERS (ALL EXCEPT M1009).

GROUP 1604 SHOCK ABSORBER EQUIPMENT

FIG. 121 REAR SHOCK ABSORBERS (ALL
EXCEPT M1009)

ITEM NO	SMR CODE	CAGEC	PART NUMBER	DESCRIPTION AND USABLE ON CODES (UOC)	QTY
1	PAOZZ	11862	3187845	SHCOK ABSORBER,DIRE UOC:194,208,210,230,231,252,254,256	2
2	PAOZZ	96906	MS27183-18	WASHER,FLAT UOC:194,208,210,230,231,252,254,256	2
3	PAOZZ	96906	MS35340-49	WASHER,LOCK UOC:194,208,210,230,231,252,254,256	2
4	PAOZZ	96906	MS51967-14	NUT,PLAIN,HEXAGON UOC:194,208,210,230,252,254,256	2
5	PAOZZ	96906	MS51967-8	NUT,PLAIN,HEXAGON UOC:194,208,210,230,231,252,254,256	2
6	PAOZZ	96906	MS35338-46	WASHER,LOCK UOC:194,208,210,230,231,252,254,256	2
7	PAOZZ	11862	3764438	BUMPER,RUBBER ASSEM UOC:194,208,210,230,231,252,254,256	2
8	PAOZZ	96906	MS51967-17	NUT,PLAIN,HEXAGON UOC:194,208,210,230,231,252,254,256	2
9	PAOZZ	96906	MS35338-49	WASHER,LOCK UOC:194,208,210,230,231,252,254,256	2
10	PAOZZ	11862	9419138	SCREW,CAP,HEXAGON H UOC:194,208,210,230,231,252,254,256	2

END OF FIGURE

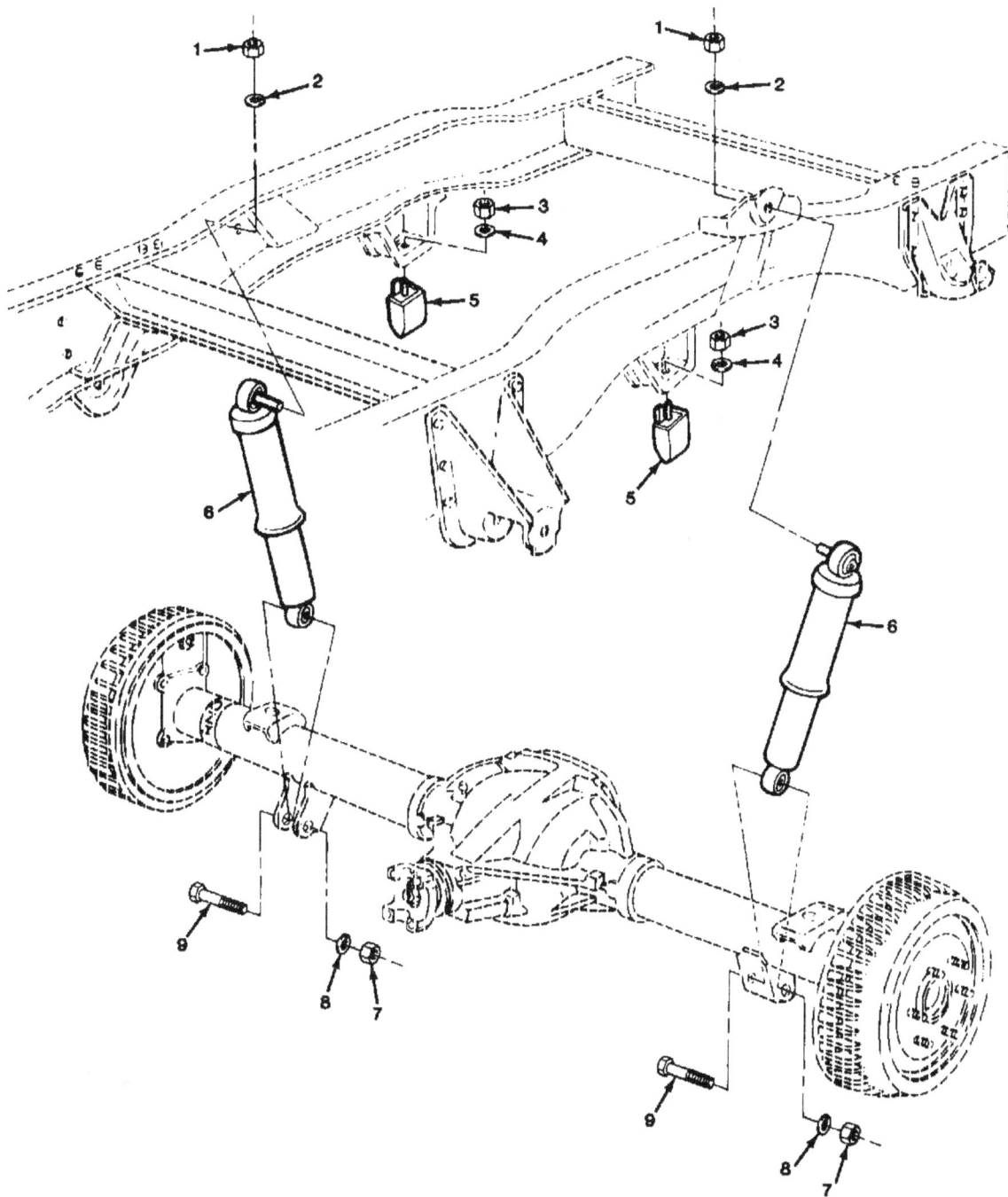

TA510962

FIGURE 122. REAR SHOCK ABSORBERS (M1009).

(1) ITEM NO	(2) SMR CODE	(3) CAGEC	(4) PART NUMBER	(5) DESCRIPTION AND USABLE ON CODES (UOC)	(6) QTY
				GROUP 1604 SHOCK ABSORBER EQUIPMENT	
				FIG. 122 REAR SHOCK ABSORBERS (M1009)	
1	PAOZZ	96906	MS51968-20	NUT,PLAIN,HEXAGON UOC:209	2
2	PAOZZ	96906	MS35340-50	WASHER,LOCK UOC:209	2
3	PAOZZ	96906	MS51967-8	NUT,PLAIN,HEXAGON UOC:209	2
4	PAOZZ	96906	MS35338-46	WASHER,LOCK UOC:209	2
5	PAOZZ	11862	3764438	BUMPER,RUBBER ASSEM UOC:209	2
6	PAOZZ	11862	3187844	SHOCK ABSORBER,LEVE UOC:209	2
7	PAOZZ	96906	MS51967-17	NUT,PLAIN,HEXAGON UOC:209	2
8	PAOZZ	96906	MS35338-49	WASHER,LOCK UOC:209	2
9	PAOZZ	11862	9419138	SCREW,CAP,HEXAGON H UOC:209	2

END OF FIGURE

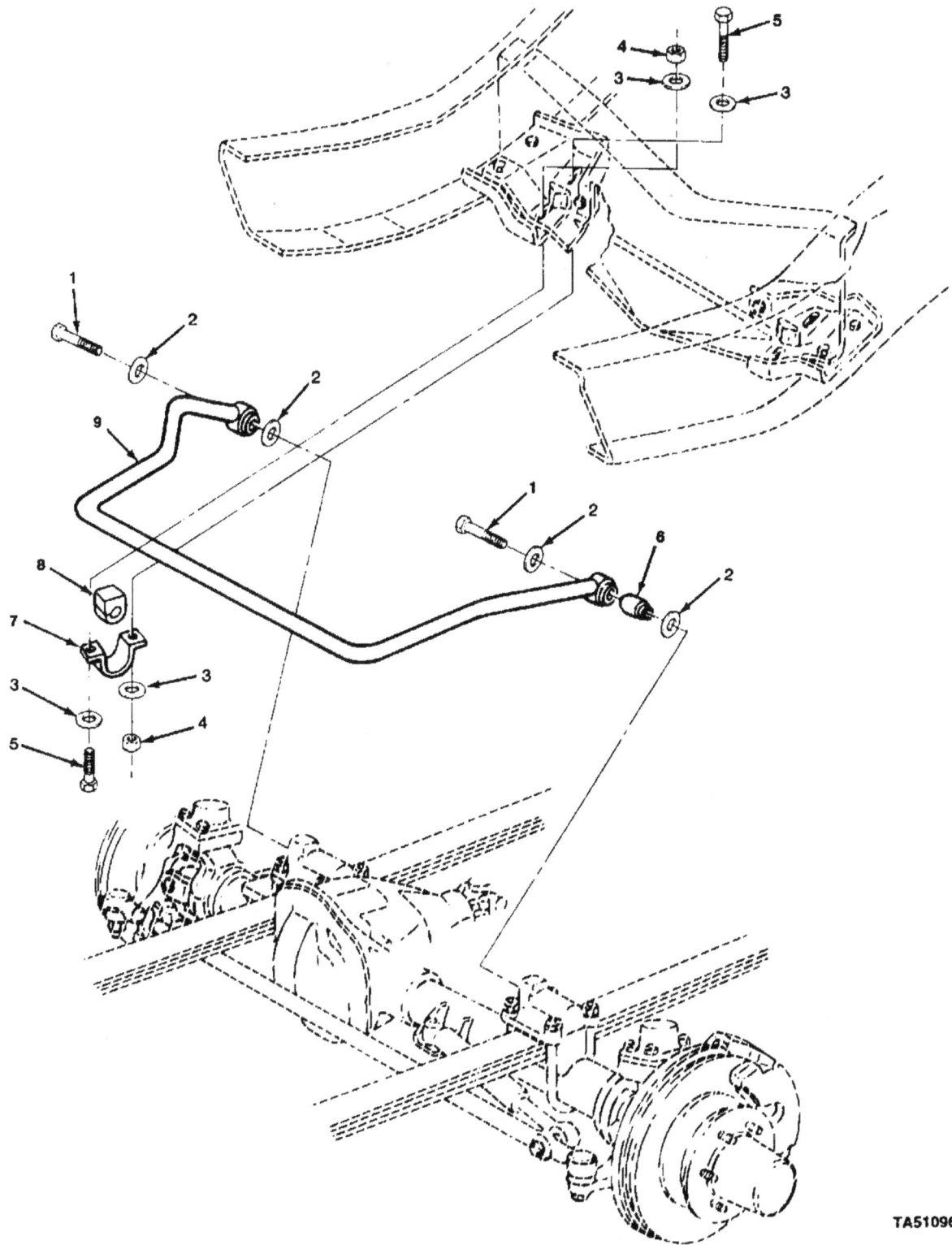

FIGURE 123. FRONT STABILIZER BAR

TA510963

(1) ITEM NO	(2) SMR CODE	(3) CAGEC	(4) PART NUMBER	(5) DESCRIPTION AND USABLE ON CODES (UOC)	(6) QTY
				GROUP 1605 TORQUE, RADIUS, AND STABILIZER RODS	
				FIG. 123 FRONT STABILIZER BAR	
1	PAOZZ	11862	328130	BOLT,SELF-LOCKING	2
2	PAOZZ	11862	328131	WASHER,FLAT	4
3	PAOZZ	24617	3990160	WASHER,FLAT	8
4	PAOZZ	11862	9422299	NUT,SELF-LOCKING,HE	4
5	PAOZZ	96906	MS90728-89	SCREW,CAP,HEXAGON H	4
6	PAOZZ	11862	328128	BUSHING,SLEEVE	2
7	PAOZZ	11862	14015726	STRAP,RETAINING	2
8	PAOZZ	11862	14015724	BUSHING,NONMETALLIC	2
9	PAOFF	11862	328132	SHAFT ASSEMBLY,FRON	1

END OF FIGURE

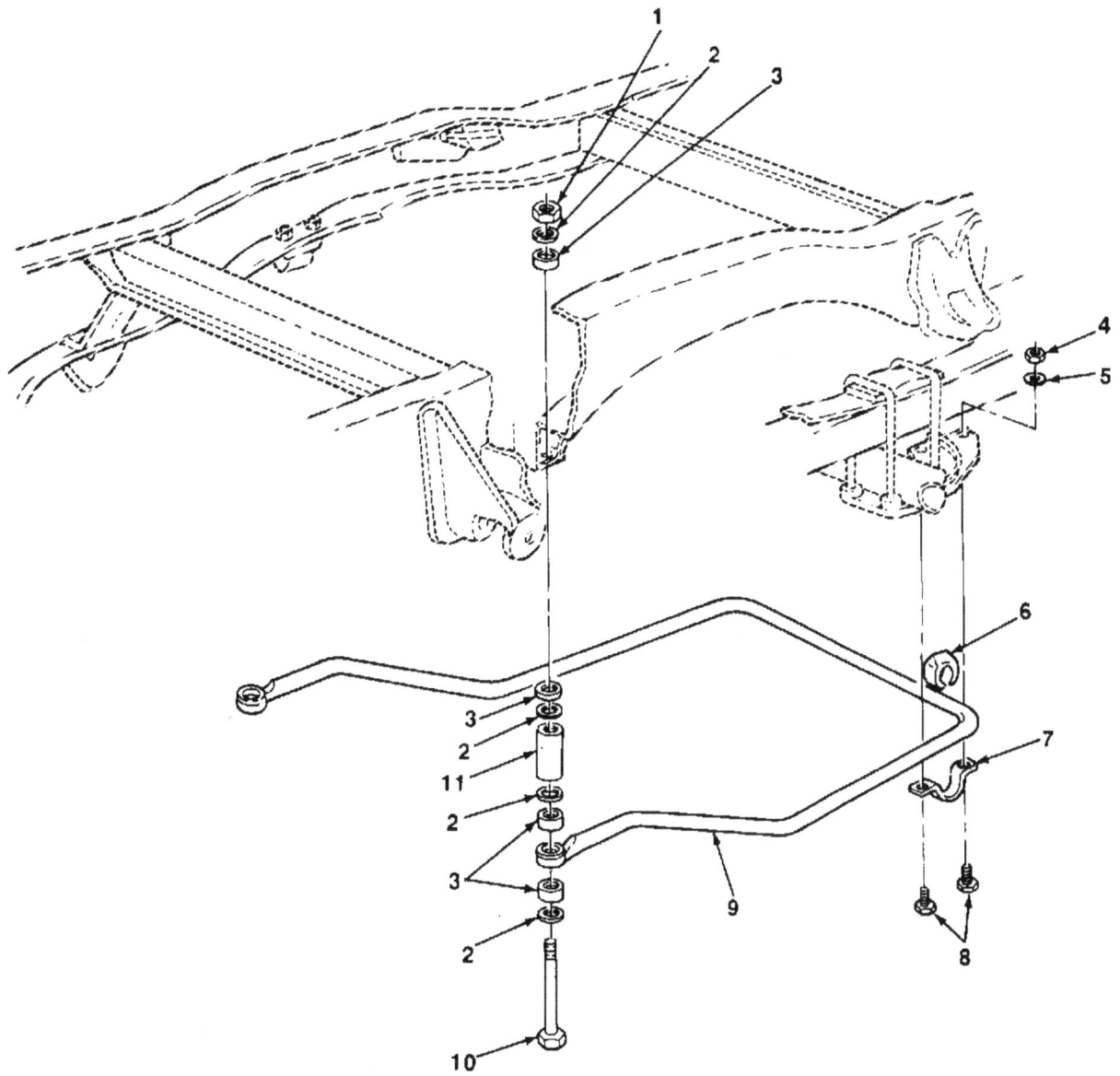

TA510964

FIGURE 124. REAR STABILIZER BAR (M1028A2 AND M1028A3).

GROUP 1605 TORQUE, RADIUS, AND
STABILIZER RODS

FIG. 124 REAR STABILIZER BAR
(M1028A2 AND M1028A3)

1	KFOZZ	11862	1365065	NUT,SPECIAL PART OF KIT P/N 6258545 UOC:254,256	2
2	KFOZZ	11862	3993729	RETAINER,WASHER SPE PART OF KIT P/N 6258545 UOC:254,256	4
3	PAOZZ	11862	6270704	GROMMET STABIL LINK PART OF KIT P/N 6258545 UOC:254,256	4
4	PAOZZ	96906	MS51967-8	NUT,PLAIN,HEXAGON UOC:254,256	4
5	PAOZZ	96906	MS35338-46	WASHER,LOCK UOC:254,256	2
6	PAOZZ	11862	404062	BUSHING,SLEEVE UOC:254,256	2
7	PAOZZ	11862	406887	BRACKET,VEHICULAR C UOC:254,256	2
8	PAOZZ	96906	MS90728-65	SCREW,CAP,HEXAGON H UOC:254,256	2
9	PAOZZ	11862	328107	BAR,STABILIZER UOC:254,256	1
10	KFOZZ	11862	328111	BOLT,STAB,LINK PART OF KIT P/N 6258545 UOC:254,256	2
11	KFOZZ	11862	328108	SPACER,STAB,LINK PART OF KIT P/N 6258545 UOC:254,256	2

END OF FIGURE

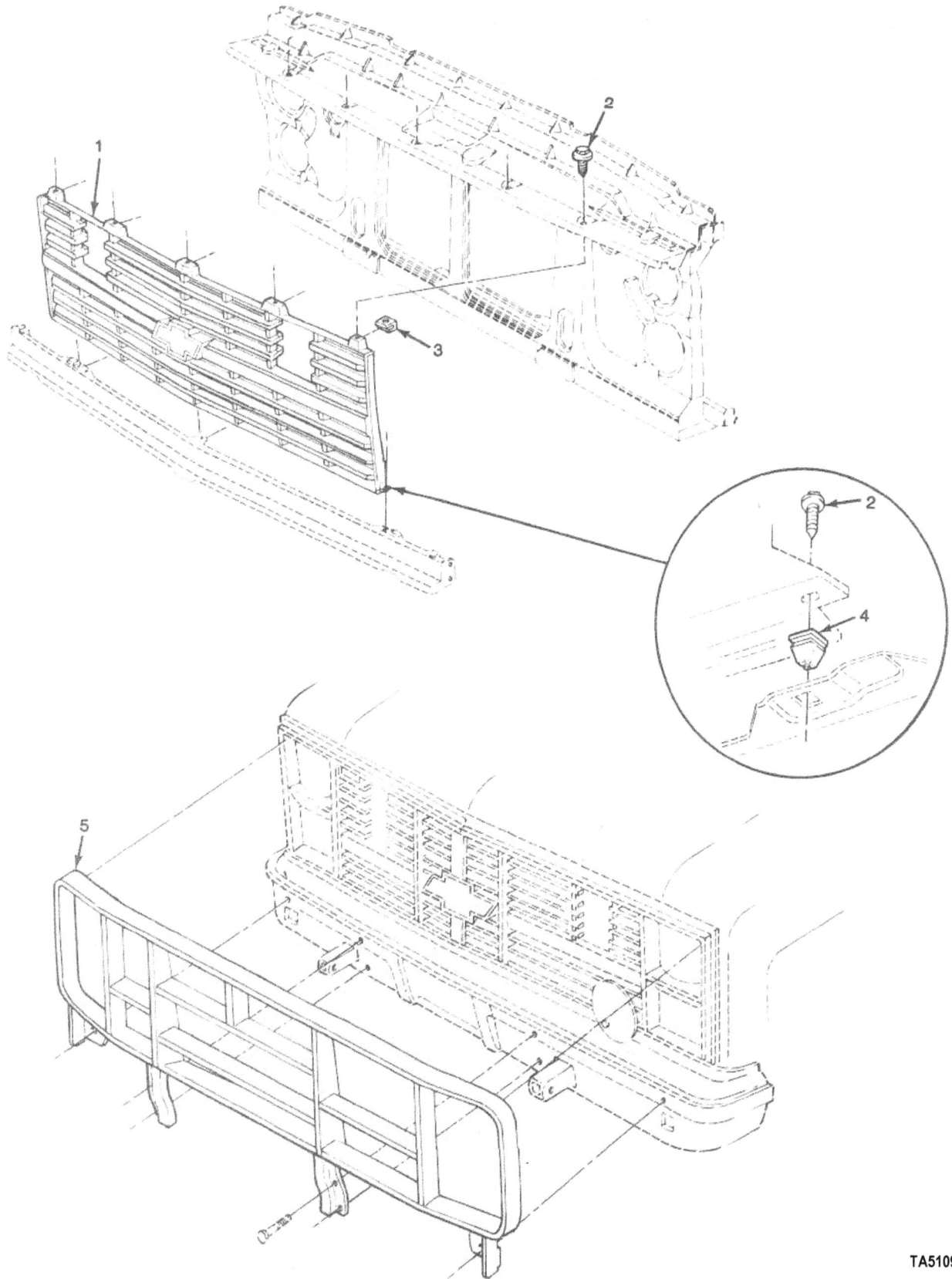

TA510965

(1) ITEM NO	(2) SMR CODE	(3) CAGEC	(4) PART NUMBER	(5) DESCRIPTION AND USABLE ON CODES (UOC)	(6) QTY
				GROUP 18 BODY, CAB, FOOD, AND HULL	
				GROUP 1801 BODY, CAB, HOOD, AND HULL ASSEMBLIES	
				FIG. 125 BRUSH GUARD AND GRILLE	
1	PFOZZ	11862	15554915	GRILLE,RADIATOR,VEH	1
2	PAOZZ	24617	11503395	SCREW,ASSEMBLED WAS	8
3	PAOZZ	96906	MS90724-34	NUT,SHEET SPRING	5
4	PAOZZ	11862	347347	GROMMET,NONMETALLIC	3
5	PFOZZ	11862	14072488	GUARD,GRILLE,RADIAT	1
				END OF FIGURE	

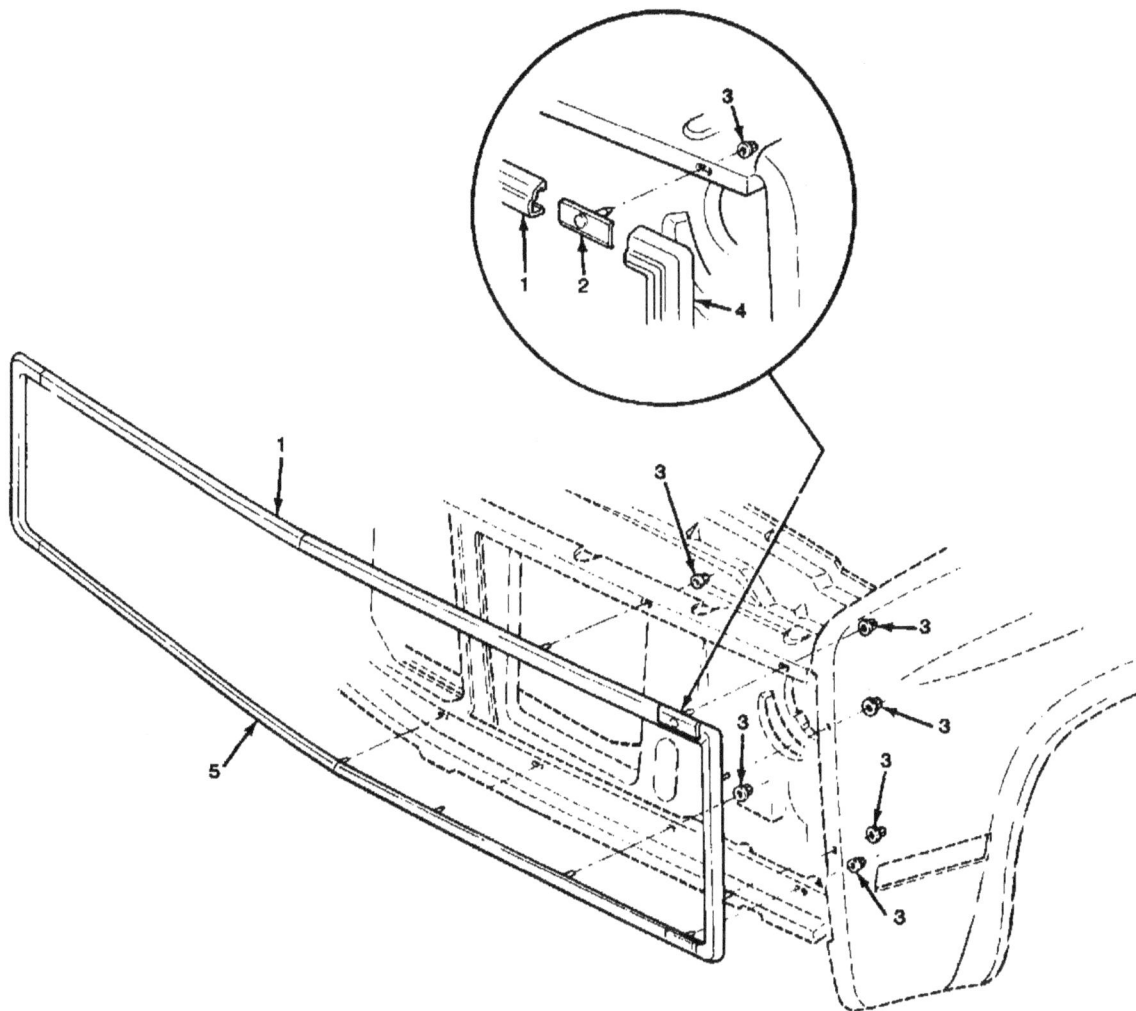

TA510966

FIGURE 126. FRONT MOLDINGS.

(1) ITEM NO	(2) SMR CODE	(3) CAGEC	(4) PART NUMBER	(5) DESCRIPTION AND USABLE ON CODES (UOC)	(6) QTY
				GROUP 1801 BODY, CAB, HOOD, AND HULL ASSEMBLIES	
				FIG. 126 FRONT MOLDINGS	
1	PAOZZ	11862	15599285	MOLDING ASSEMBLY,FR	1
2	PAOZZ	11862	14072850	RETAINER,MOLDING	4
3	PAOZZ	24617	9420621	PUSH ON NUT	18
4	PAOZZ	11862	15599283	MOLDING,METAL LEFT	1
4	PAOZZ	11862	15599284	MOLDING,METAL RIGHT	1
5	PAOZZ	11862	15599286	MOLDING,METAL	1

END OF FIGURE

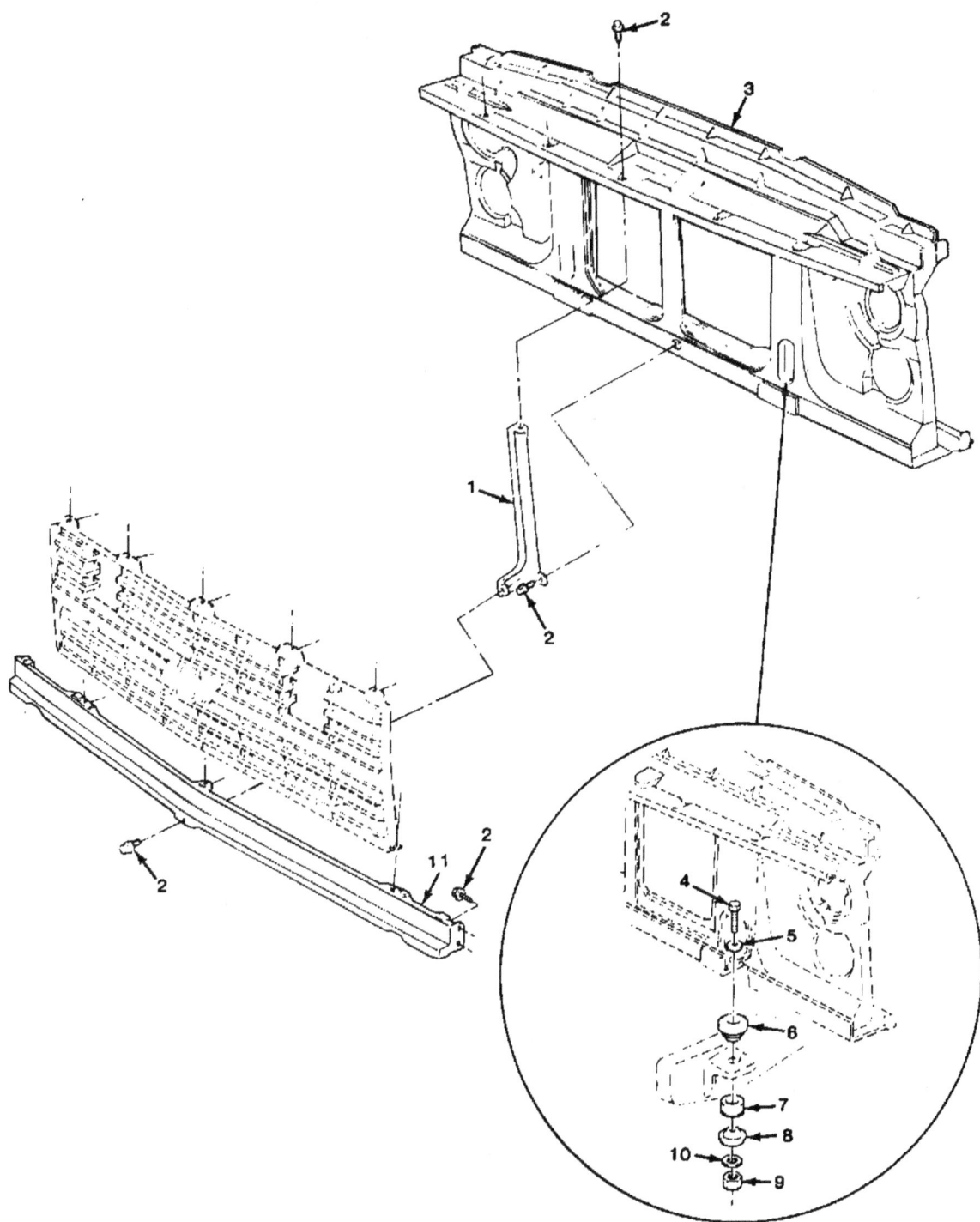

FIGURE 127. FRONT SUPPORT PANELS.

TA510967

(1) ITEM NO	(2) SMR CODE	(3) CAGEC	(4) PART NUMBER	(5) DESCRIPTION AND USABLE ON CODES (UOC)	(6) QTY
				GROUP 1801 BODY, CAB, HOOD, AND HULL ASSEMBLIES	
				FIG. 127 FRONT SUPPORT PANELS	
1	PAOZZ	11862	14021243	SUPPORT ASSEMBLY,HO	1
2	PAOZZ	11862	2014469	BOLT,ASSEMBLED WASH	7
11	PAOZZ	11862	14043880	PANEL,FRONT END	1
				END OF FIGURE	

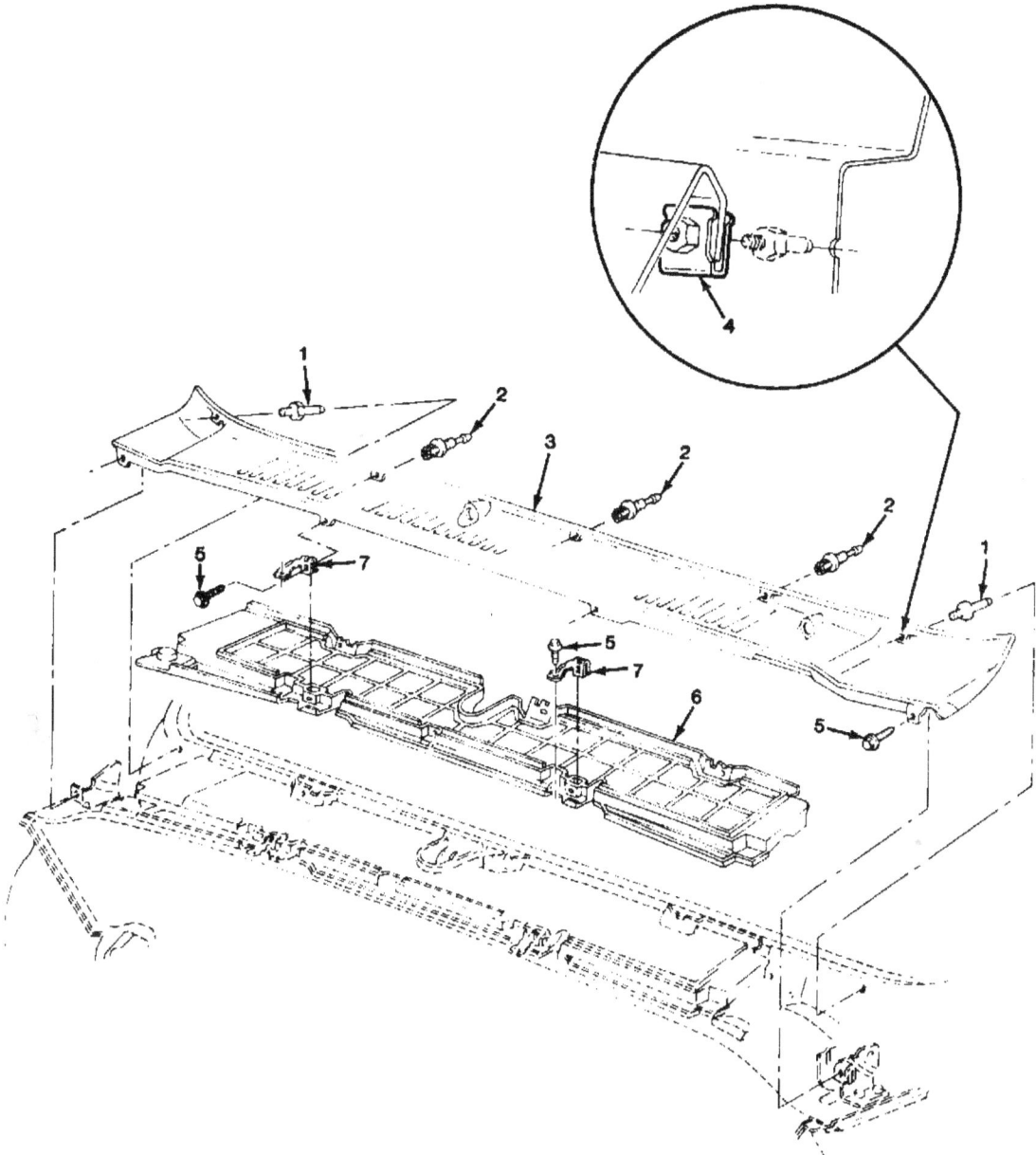

TA510968

FIGURE 128. COWL TOP VENTILATOR PANEL.

SECTION II					
(1)	(2)	(3)	(4)	(5)	(6)
ITEM NO	SMR CODE	CAGEC	PART NUMBER	DESCRIPTION AND USABLE ON CODES (UOC)	QTY

GROUP 1801 BODY, CAB, HOOD, AND HULL ASSEMBLIES

FIG. 128 COWL TOP VENTILATOR PANEL

1	PAOZZ	11862	15598770	RETAINER,COWL,TOP V	2
2	PAOZZ	11862	15598769	RETAINER,AIR VENT,T	3
3	PAOZZ	11862	15598708	PANEL,AIR INLET GRI	1
4	PAOZZ	11862	3982098	NUT,PLAIN,HEXAGON	2
5	PAOZZ	11862	14026247	SCREW,ASSEMBLED WAS	6
6	PAOZZ	11862	15598709	PLENUM,AIR	1
7	PAOZZ	11862	14027555	BRACKET	2

END OF FIGURE

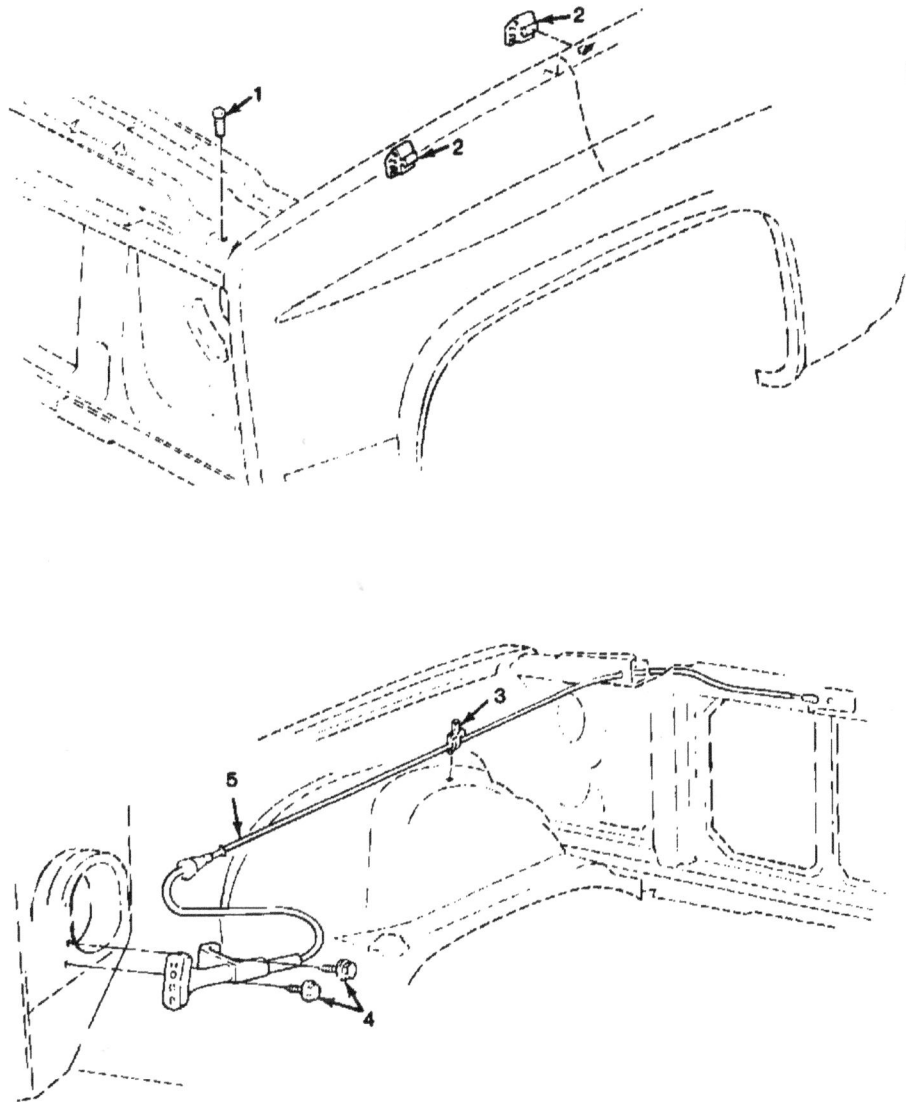

TA510969

FIGURE 129. FRONT HOOD LATCH RELEASE CABLE.

(1) ITEM NO	(2) SMR CODE	(3) CAGEC	(4) PART NUMBER	(5) DESCRIPTION AND USABLE ON CODES (UOC)	(6) QTY
				GROUP 1801 BODY, CAB, HOOD AND HULL ASSEMBLIES	
				FIG. 129 FRONT HOOD LATCH RELEASE CABLE	
1	PAOZZ	11862	472450	BUMPER,NONMETALLIC	2
2	PAOZZ	11862	6262054	BUMPER,NONMETALLIC	4
3	PAOZZ	11862	3816659	STRAP,LINE SUPPORTI	1
4	PAOZZ	24617	11503396	SCREW,ASSEMBLED WAS	2
5	PAOZZ	11862	14039963	CONTROL ASSEMBLY,PU	1

END OF FIGURE

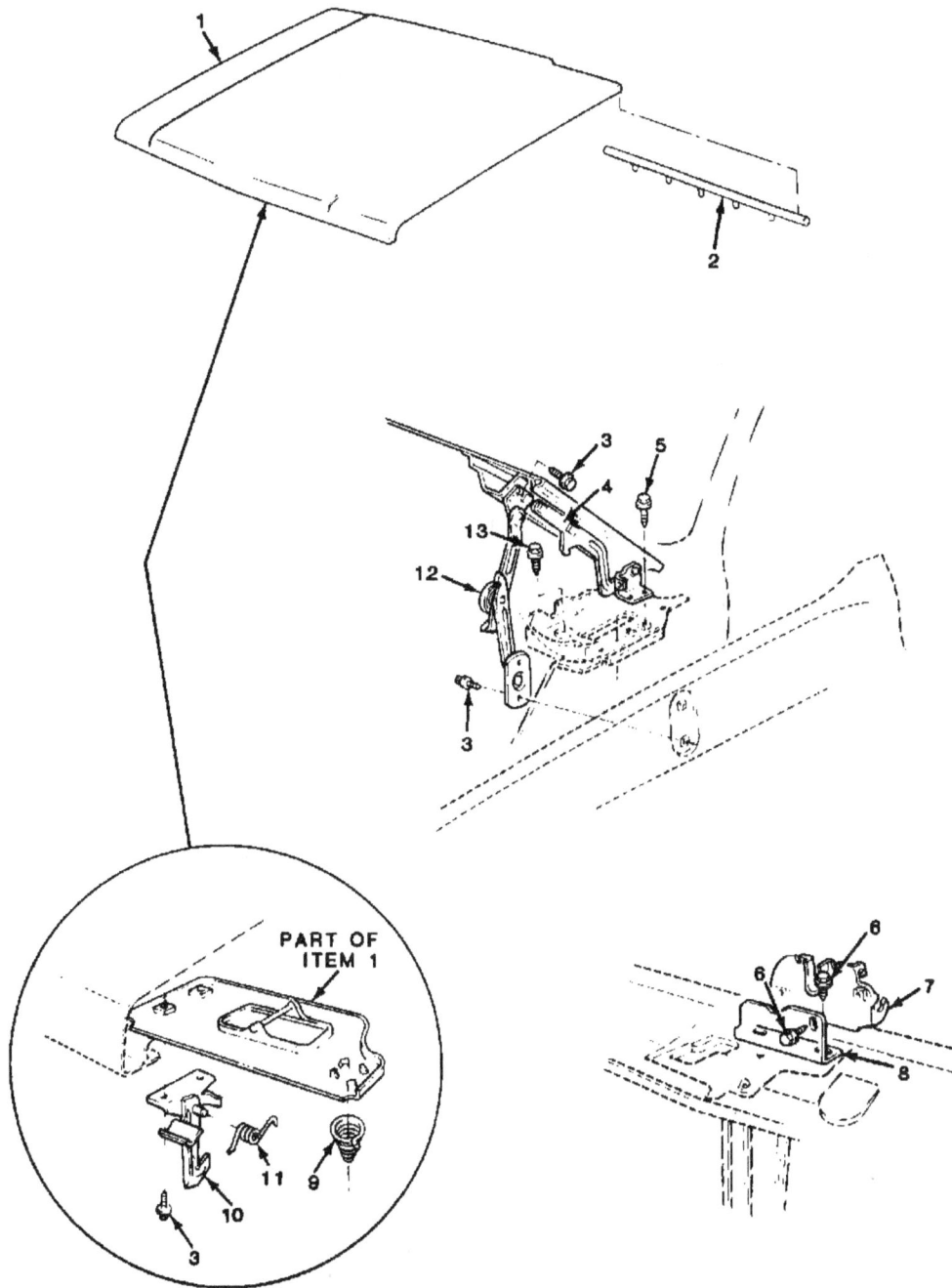

PART OF
ITEM 1

TA510970

FIGURE 130. FRONT HOOD, LATCH, AND HINGES.

(1) ITEM NO	(2) SMR CODE	(3) CAGEC	(4) PART NUMBER	(5) DESCRIPTION AND USABLE ON CODES (UOC)		(6) QTY
				GROUP 1801 BODY, CAB, HOOD, AND HULL ASSEMBLIES		
				HINGES		
1	PAOZZ	11862	15629509	HOOD,ENGINE COMPART		1
2	PAOZZ	11862	14018523	SEAL,NONMETALLIC SP		1
3	PAOZZ	11862	2014469	BOLT,ASSEMBLED WASH		14
4	PAOZZ	11862	14043823	HINGE,HOOD,VEHICULA	LEFT	1
4	PAOZZ	11862	14043824	HINGE,HOOD,VEHICULA	RIGHT	1
5	PAOZZ	96906	MS90728-59	SCREW,CAP,HEXAGON H		4
6	PAOZZ	11862	11508164	SCREW,ASSEMBLED WAS		4
7	PAOZZ	11862	14070703	LATCH HOOD VEHICULA		1
8	PAOZZ	11862	14018531	BRACKET,ANGLE		1
9	PAOZZ	11862	14018532	SPRING,HELICAL,COMP		1
10	PAOOO	11862	14018526	LATCH SET,MORTISE		1
11	PAOZZ	11862	14018529	.SPRING		1
12	PAOZZ	11862	14021253	HINGE,HOOD,VEHICULA	LEFT	1
12	PAOZZ	11862	14021254	HINGE,HOOD,VEHICULA	RIGHT	1
13	PAOZZ	11862	11508566	SCREW,TAPPING		4

END OF FIGURE

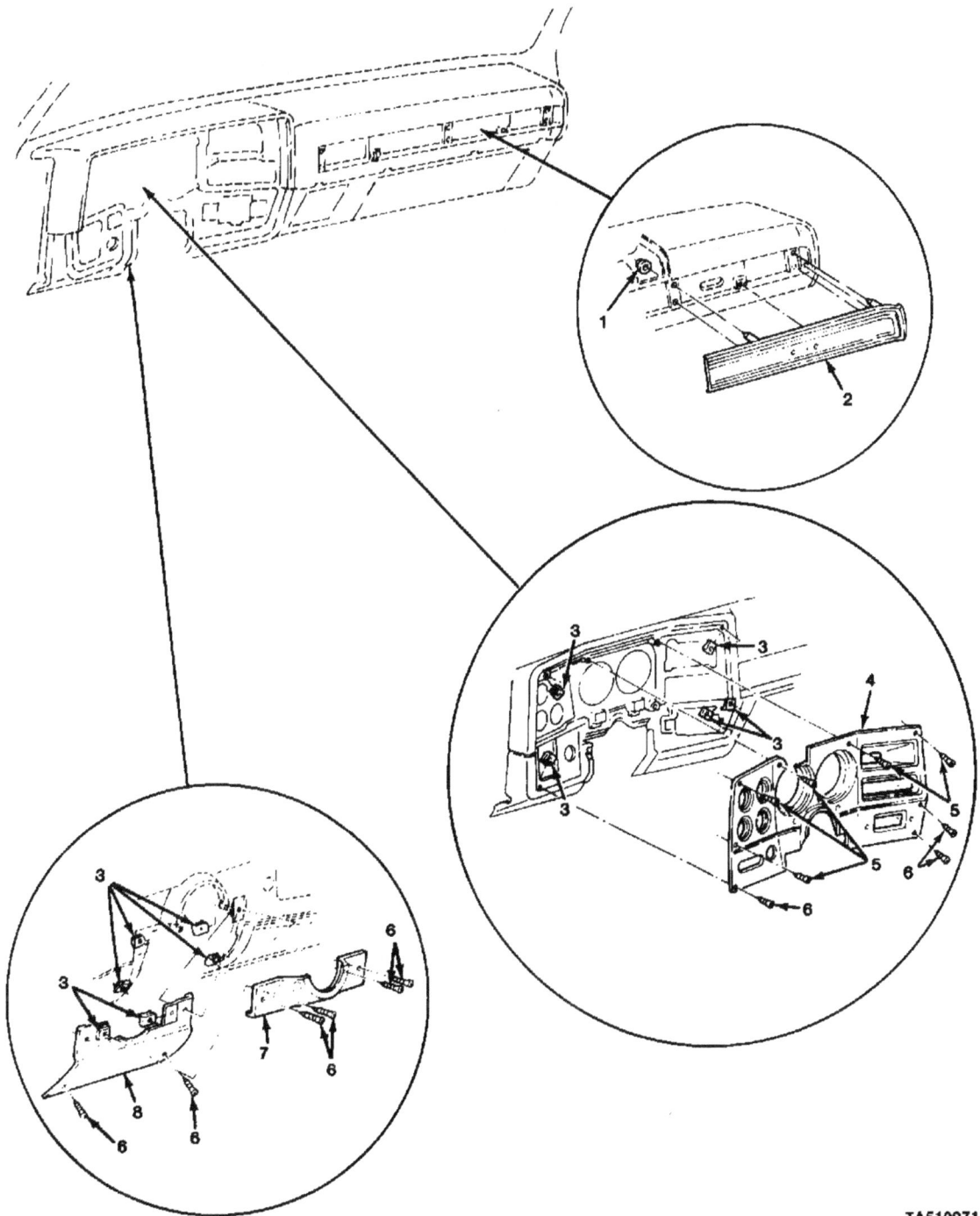

TA510971

FIGURE 131. INSTRUMENT PANEL TRIM

(1) ITEM NO	(2) SMR CODE	(3) CAGEC	(4) PART NUMBER	(5) DESCRIPTION AND USABLE ON CODES (UOC)	(6) QTY
				GROUP 1801 BODY, CAB, HOOD, AND HULL ASSEMBLIES	
				FIG. 131 INSTRUMENT PANEL TRIM	
1	PAOZZ	11862	11501047	NUT	5
2	PFOZZ	11862	14023039	PANEL,INSTRUMENT,PA	1
3	PAOZZ	96906	MS90724-34	NUT,SHEET SPRING	11
4	PAOZZ	11862	14072405	PLATE,INSTRUMENT PA	1
5	PAOZZ	24617	11501153	SCREW,ASSEMBLED WAS	5
6	PAOZZ	24617	11501151	SCREW,TAPPING	9
7	PAOZZ	11862	14023008	SUPPORT,STEERING CO	1
8	PAOZZ	11862	6274970	COVER,PANEL	1
				END OF FIGURE	

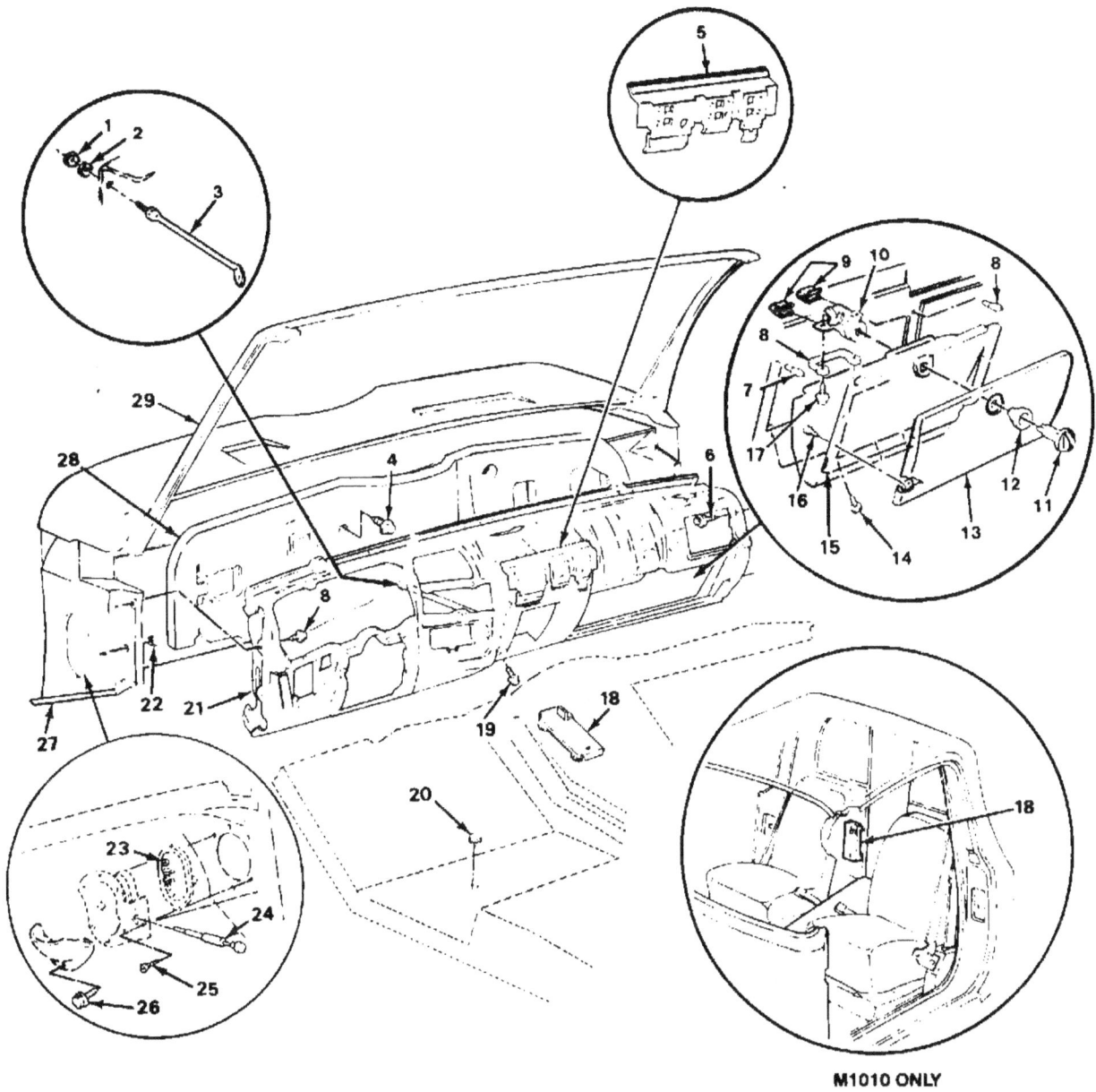

M1010 ONLY

TA510972

FIGURE 132. INSTRUMENT PANEL COMPONENTS.

(1) ITEM NO	(2) SMR CODE	(3) CAGEC	(4) PART NUMBER	(5) DESCRIPTION AND USABLE ON CODES (UOC)	(6) QTY
				GROUP 1801 BODY, CAB, HOOD, AND HULL ASSEMBLIES	
				FIG. 132 INSTRUMENT PANEL COMPONENTS	
7	PAOZZ	11862	3765243	BUMPER,NONMETALLIC	2
8	PAOZZ	11862	6274550	STRIKE,CATCH UOC:194,208,209,210,230,231,252	1
9	PAOZZ	96906	MS90724-34	NUT,SHEET SPRING	2
10	PAOZZ	11862	14044471	CYLINDER,LOCK,VEHIC	1
11	PAOZZ	11862	6260421	CYLINDER,LOCK,VEHIC	1
12	PAOZZ	11862	3957093	MOLDING,METAL	1
13	PAOZZ	11862	6264131	DOOR,ACCESS	1
14	PAOZZ	11862	11509135	SCREW,ASSEMBLED WAS	4
15	PAOZZ	11862	343915	GLOVE BOX	1
16	PAOZZ	24617	9420408	SCREW,TAPPING	4
17	PAOZZ	24617	9415163	SCREW,ASSEMBLED WAS	2
29	PAOZZ	11862	15598706	FRAME,WINDOW,VEHICU	1

END OF FIGURE

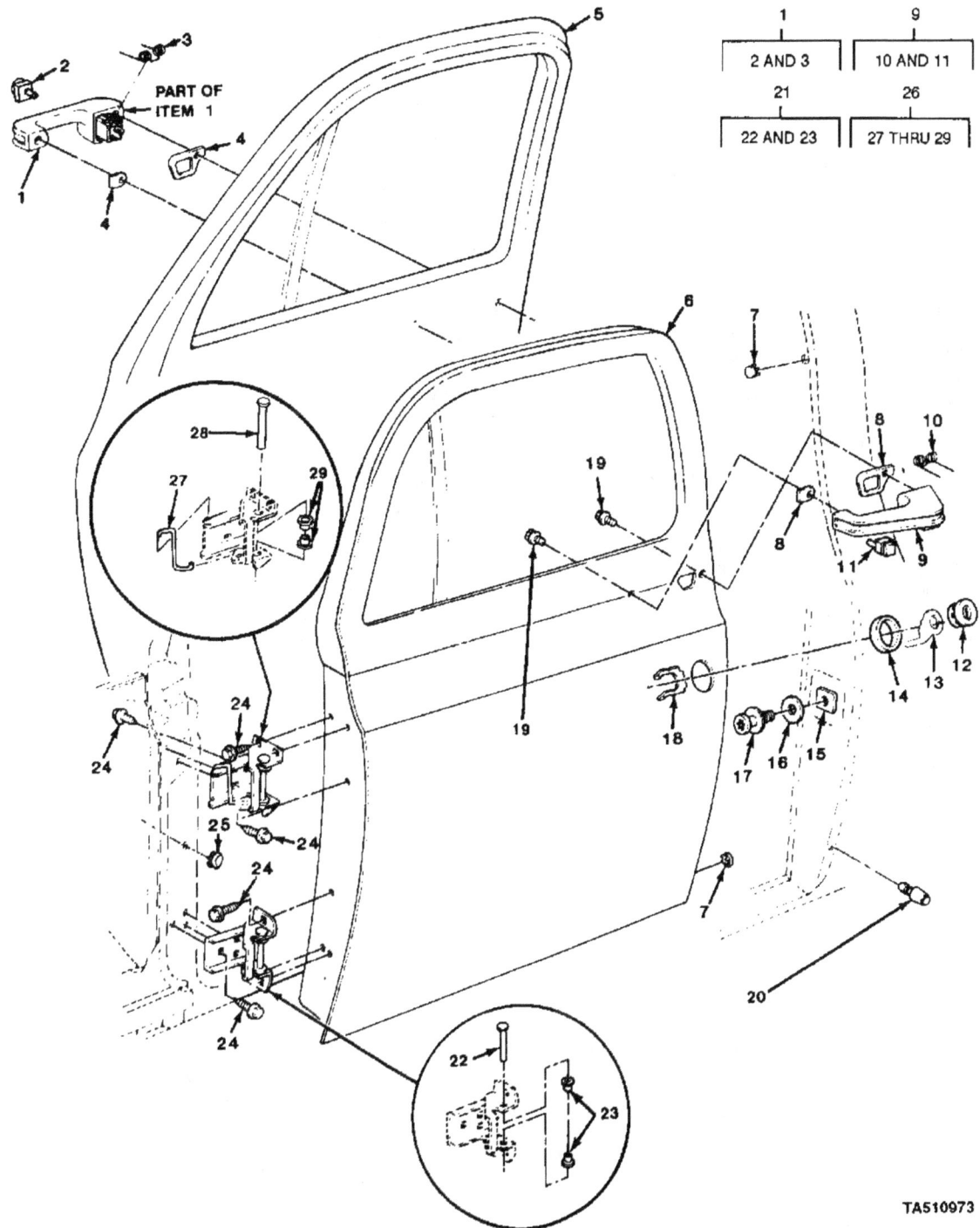

FIGURE 133. SIDE DOORS AND COMPONENTS.

TA510973

(1) ITEM NO	(2) SMR CODE	(3) CAGEC	(4) PART NUMBER	(5) DESCRIPTION AND USABLE ON CODES (UOC)	(6) QTY
				GROUP 1801 BODY, CAB, HOOD, AND HULL ASSEMBLIES	
				FIG. 133 SIDE DOORS AND COMPONENTS	
1	PAOOO	11862	14072494	HANDLE,DOOR	1
2	PAOZZ	11862	327062	.BUTTON,DOOR HANDLE	1
3	PAOZZ	11862	327065	.SPRING,HELICAL,TORS	1
4	PAOZZ	11862	6258562	GASKET SET	2
5	PAOZZ	11862	15593230	DOOR ASSEMBLY,CAB RIGHT	1
6	PAOZZ	11862	15571643	DOOR,VEHICULAR LEFT	1
7	PAOZZ	11862	4410574	PLUG,PROTECTIVE,DOS	4
8	PAOZZ	11862	6258561	GASKET SET	2
9	PAOOO	11862	14072493	HANDLE,DOOR	1
10	PAOZZ	11862	327065	.SPRING,HELICAL,TORS	1
11	PAOZZ	11862	327062	.BUTTON,DOOR HANDLE	1
12	PAOZZ	11862	15599677	CYLINDER,LOCK,VEHIC	2
13	PAOZZ	11862	7040173	PAWL LEFT	1
13	PAOZZ	11862	7040174	PAWL RIGHT	1
14	PAOZZ	11862	4587931	GASKET	2
15	XDOZZ	11862	6272627	STRIKE,CATCH	2
16	AOZZ	11862	1260895	WASHER,FLAT	2
17	PAOZZ	11862	9601750	BOLT,SHOULDER	2
18	PAOZZ	11862	9728247	RETAINER	2
19	PAOZZ	11862	9439771	BOLT,ASSEMBLED WASH	4
20	PAOZZ	11862	3900684	BUMPER,NONMETALLIC	4
21	PAOOO	11862	14000091	HINGE,ACCESS DOOR LEFT	1
21	PAOOO	11862	14000092	HINGE,DOOR VEHICULA RIGHT	1
22	PAOZZ	11862	6271989	.PIN,STRAIGHT,HEADED	1
23	PAOZZ	11862	9721917	.BEARING,SLEEVE	2
24	PAOZZ	11862	9438916	SCREW,TAPPING	24
25	PAOZZ	11862	3944769	CAP-PLUG,PROTECTIVE	2
26	PAOOO	11862	14000093	HINGE,ACCESS DOOR LEFT	1
26	PAOOO	11862	14000094	HINGE RIGHT	1
27	PAOZZ	11862	327960	.ROD,HINGE TORQUE RH	1
27	PAOZZ	11862	327959	.ROD,HINGE TORQUE LH LEFT	1
28	PAOZZ	11862	6271989	.PIN,STRAIGHT,HEADED	1
29	PAOZZ	11862	9721917	.BEARING,SLEEVE	2

END OF FIGURE

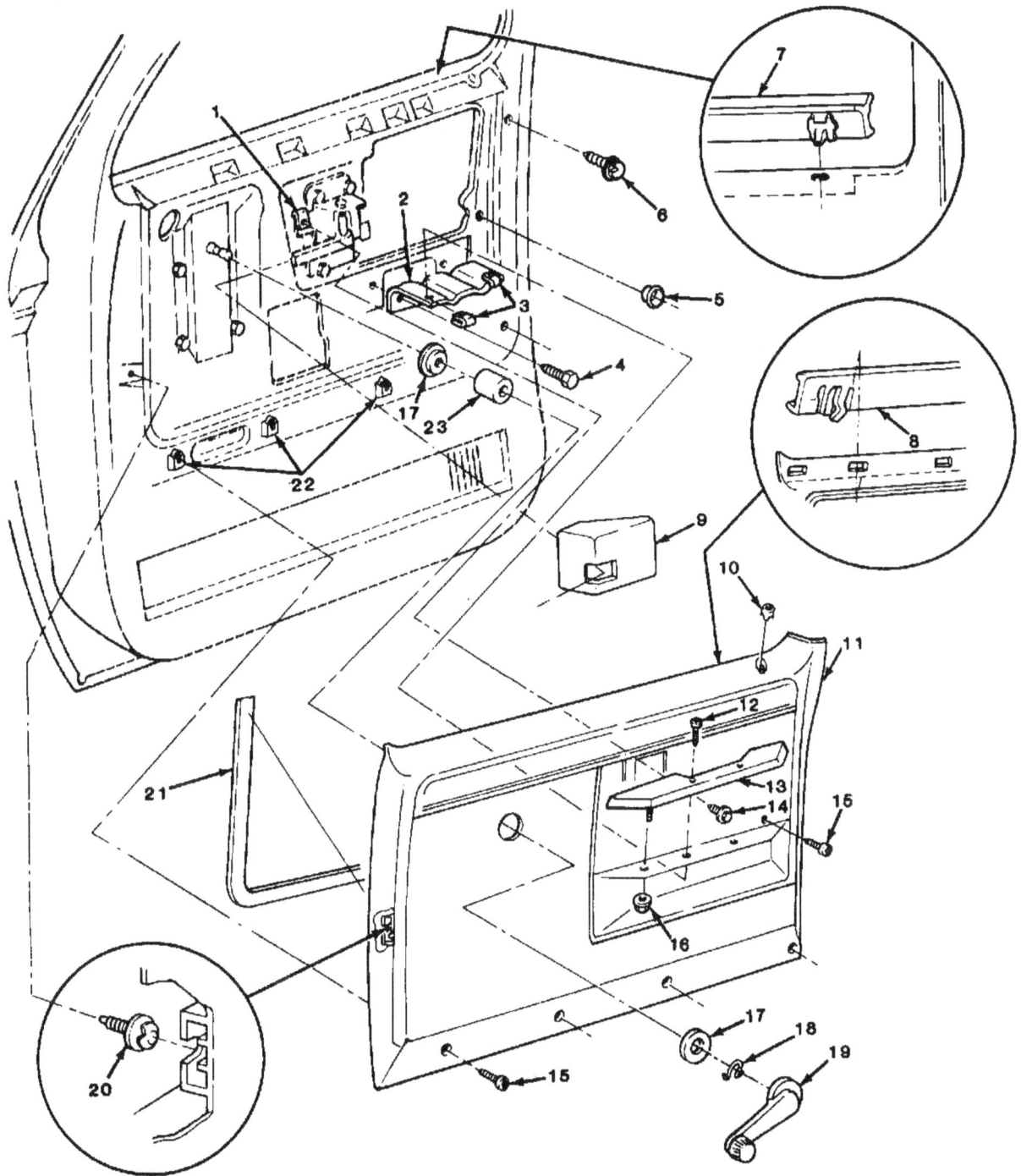

TA510974

FIGURE 134. INSIDE DOOR TRIM PANEL AND RELATED PARTS.

GROUP 1801 BODY, CAB, HOOD, AND HULL
ASSEMBLIES

FIG. 134 INSIDES DOOR TRIM PANEL AND
RELATED PARTS

ITEM NO	SMR CODE	CAGEC	PART NUMBER	DESCRIPTION AND USABLE ON CODES (UOC)	QTY
1	PAOZZ	96906	MS90724-34	NUT, SHEET SPRING	2
2	PAOZZ	11862	362433	BRACKET, ANGLE LEFT	1
2	PAOZZ	11862	362434	BRACKET, ANGLE RIGHT	1
3	PAOZZ	96906	MS90724-40	NUT, SHEET SPRING	4
4	PAOZZ	11862	9439770	BOLT, ASSEMBLED WASH	4
5	PAOZZ	11862	1355003	NUT	4
6	PAOZZ	11862	20696927	FASTENER, SPRING TEN	2
7	PAOZZ	11862	14027775	SEAL, RUBBER SPECIAL LEFT	1
7	PAOZZ	11862	14027776	SEAL, RUBBER SPECIAL OUTER RIGHT	1
8	PAOZZ	11862	15569071	SEAL	1
8	PAOZZ	11862	15569072	SEAL, NONMETALLIC SP INNER RIGHT	1
9	PAOZZ	11862	14026383	SEAL, NONMETALLIC SP LEFT	1
9	PAOZZ	11862	14026384	SEAL, NONMETALLIC SP RIGHT	1
10	PAOZZ	11862	330485	GROMMET	2
11	PAOZZ	11862	15597667	PANEL, BODY, VEHICULA LEFT	1
11	PAOZZ	11862	15597668	PANEL, BODY, VEHICULA RIGHT	1
12	PAOZZ	24617	9414724	SCREW, TAPPING	4
13	PAOZZ	11862	14026409	PAD, CUSHIONING LEFT	1
13	PAOZZ	11862	14026410	PAD, CUSHIONING RIGHT	1
14	PAOZZ	11862	11503537	SCREW, ASSEMBLED WAS	2
15	PAOZZ	24617	1640810	SCREW, TAPPING	10
16	PAOZZ	24617	9420621	PUSH ON NUT	2
17	PAOZZ	11862	14010954	ESCUTCHEON PLATE	4
18	PAOZZ	11862	4168122	RETAINER, SPECIAL	2
19	PAOZZ	11862	14030586	HANDLE, WINDOW REGUL	2
20	PAOZZ	11862	363137	FASTENER, SPRING TEN	2
21	MOOZZ	11862	15590415	SEAL, FRONT DOOR (46.5" X 0.36" X 0.50") MAKE FROM SEAL, P/N 363139	2
22	PAOZZ	11862	15590422	RETAINER, DOOR TRIM	6
23	PAOZZ	11862	364372	BUSHING, NONMETALLIC	2

END OF FIGURE

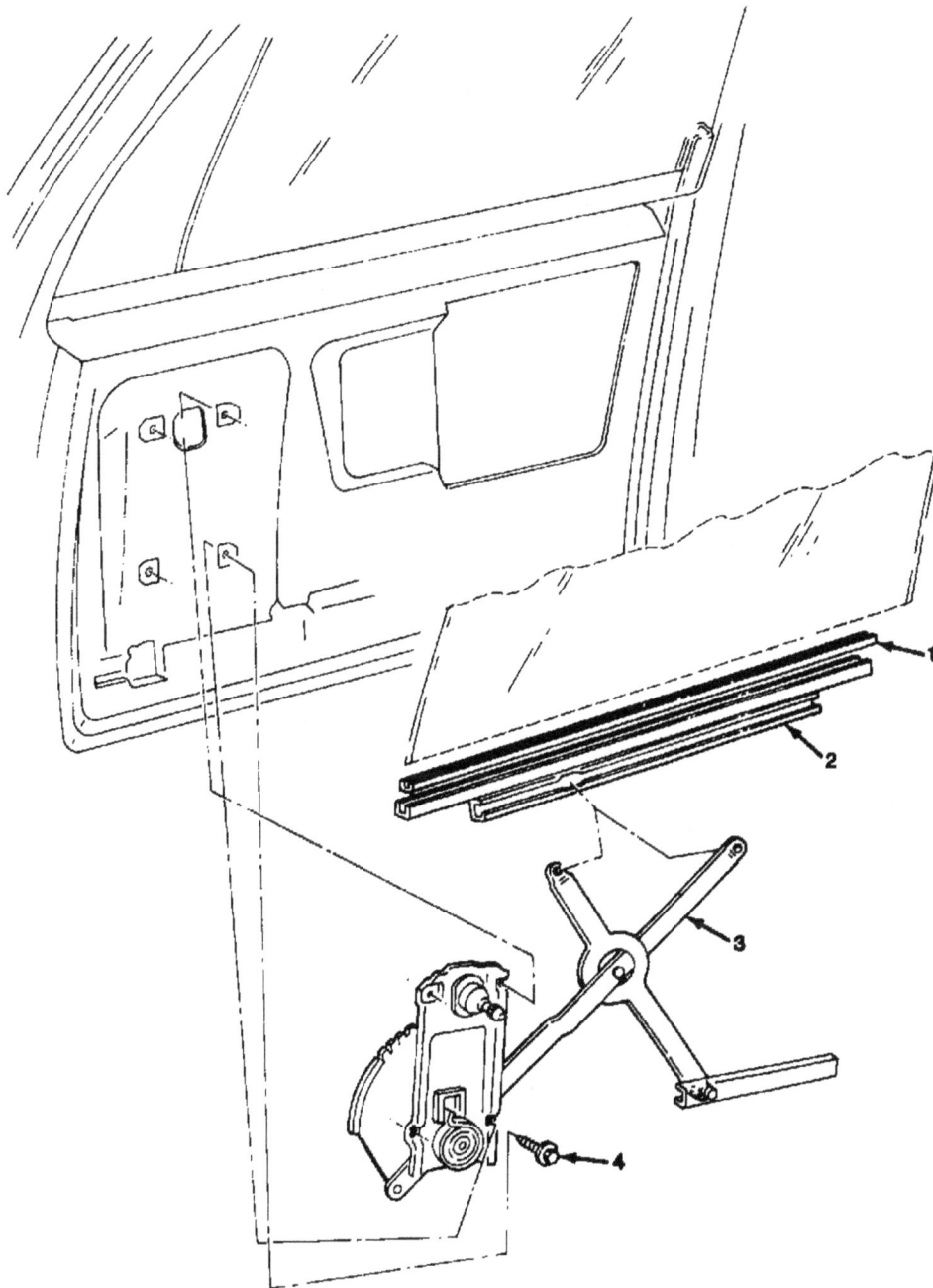

TA510975

FIGURE 135. SIDE DOOR WINDOW REGULATOR.

(1) ITEM NO	(2) SMR CODE	(3) CAGEC	(4) PART NUMBER	(5) DESCRIPTION AND USABLE ON CODES (UOC)	(6) QTY
				GROUP 1801 BODY, CAB, HOOD, AND HULL ASSEMBLIES	
				FIG. 135 SIDE DOOR WINDOW REGULATOR	
1	MOOZZ	11862	365953	FILLER,GLASS CHANNE (25.62" LG.) MAKE FROM FILLER,P/N 370389	1
2	PAOZZ	11862	15590401	CHANNEL,LIFT,VEHICL LEFT	1
2	PAOZZ	11862	15590402	CHANNEL,LIFT,VEHICL RIGHT	1
3	PAOZZ	11862	14027431	REGULATOR,VEHICLE W LH	1
3	PAOZZ	11862	14027432	REGULATOR,VEHICLE W RH	1
4	PAOZZ	11862	9439770	BOLT,ASSEMBLED WASH	8

END OF FIGURE

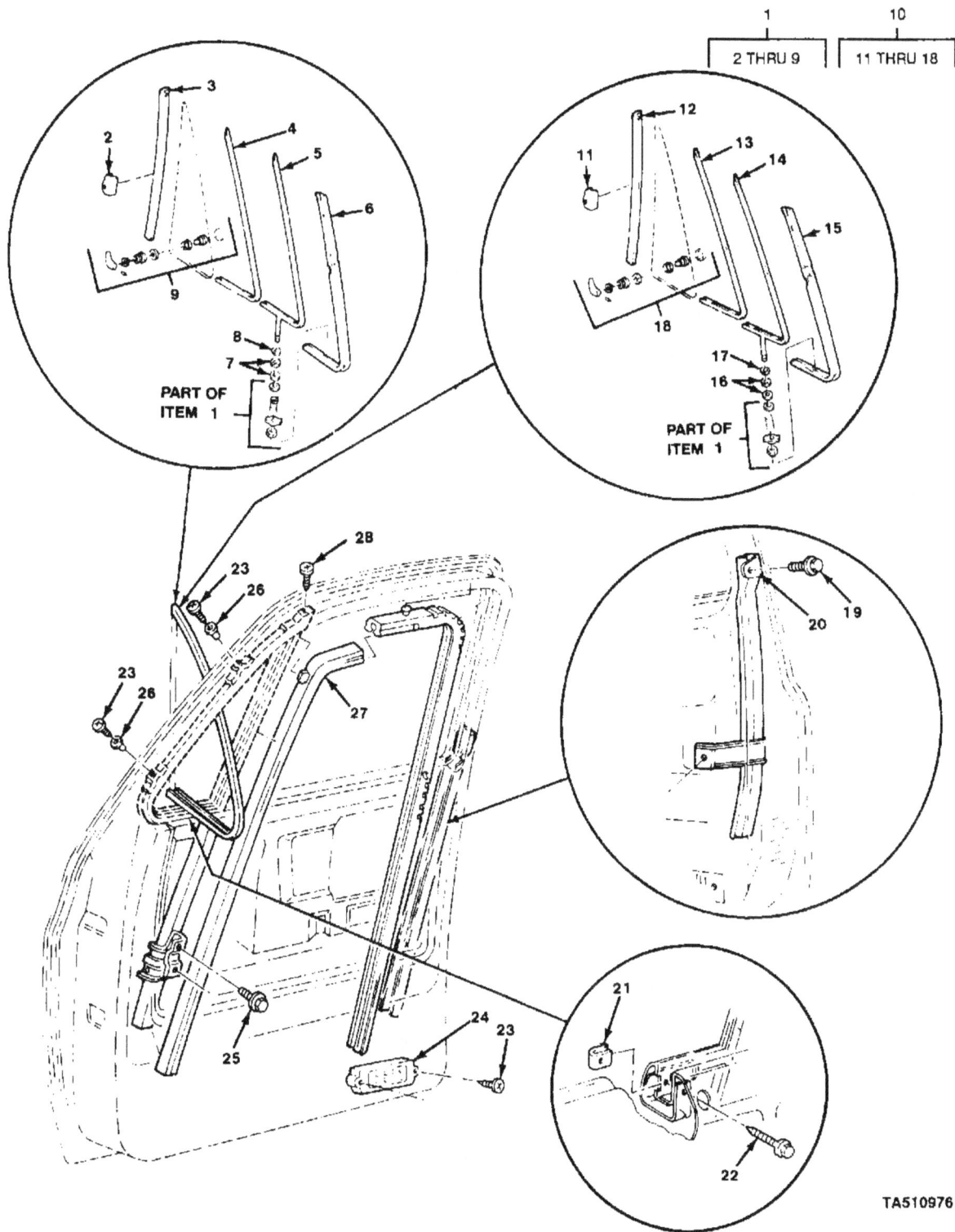

FIGURE 136. SIDE DOOR COMPONENTS.

TA510976

(1) ITEM NO	(2) SMR CODE	(3) CAGEC	(4) PART NUMBER	(5) DESCRIPTION AND USABLE ON CODES (UOC)	(6) QTY
				GROUP 1801 BODY, CAB, HOOD, AND HULL ASSEMBLIES	
				FIG. 136 SIDE DOOR COMPONENTS	
1	PAOOO	11862	15635685	VENT WING ASSEMBLY, RIGHT	1
2	PAOZZ	11862	20264729	.STRIKE,CATCH	1
3	PAOZZ	11862	20264731	.SEAL,NONMETALLIC SP	1
4	MOOZZ	11862	365953-1	.FILLER,GLASS CHANNE (25.10" LG.) MAKE FROM RUBBER, P/N 370390	1
5	PAOZZ	11862	20264737	.CHANNEL,LIFT,VEHICL	1
6	PAOZZ	11862	20354946	.WEATHER STRIP	1
7	PAOZZ	11862	365443	.WASHER,FLAT	2
8	PAOZZ	11862	3762400	.STOP,DOOR VENTILATO	1
9	PAOZZ	11862	15617126	.PARTS KIT,VEHICULAR	1
10	PAOOO	11862	15635684	VENTILATOR,AIR CIRC LEFT	1
11	PAOZZ	11862	20264728	.STRIKE,CATCH	1
12	PAOZZ	11862	20264730	.SEAL,RUBBER SPECIAL	1
13	MOOZZ	11862	365953-1	.FILLER,GLASS CHANNE (25.10" LG.) MAKE FROM RUBBER, P/N 370390	1
14	PAOZZ	11862	20264736	.VENTILLATOR,AIR CIRC	1
15	PAOZZ	11862	20354945	.WEATHER STRIP	1
16	PAOZZ	11862	365443	.WASHER,FLAT	2
17	PAOZZ	11862	3762400	.STOP,DOOR VENTILATO	1
18	PAOZZ	11862	12300197	.PARTS KIT,VEHICULAR	1
19	PAOZZ	11862	9439770	BOLT,ASSEMBLED WASH	4
20	PAOZZ	11862	337715	CHANNEL,LIFT,VEHICL LEFT	1
20	PAOZZ	11862	337716	CHANNEL,LIFT,VEHICL RIGHT	1
21	PAOZZ	96906	MS90724-34	NUT,SHEET SPRING	2
22	PAOZZ	11862	15531547	SCREW,TAPPING	2
23	PAOZZ	11862	11501149	SCREW,TAPPING	8
24	PAOZZ	11862	461610	VALVE ASSEMBLY,DOOR	2
25	PAOZZ	11862	9439770	BOLT,ASSEMBLED WASH	4
26	PAOZZ	11862	14013789	SPACER,SLEEVE	4
27	PAOZZ	11862	14027777	NONMETALLIC SPECIAL LEFT	1
27	PAOZZ	11862	14027778	NONMETALLIC SPECIAL RIGHT	1
28	PAOZZ	11862	15590443	SCREW,ASSEMBLED WAS	2

END OF FIGURE

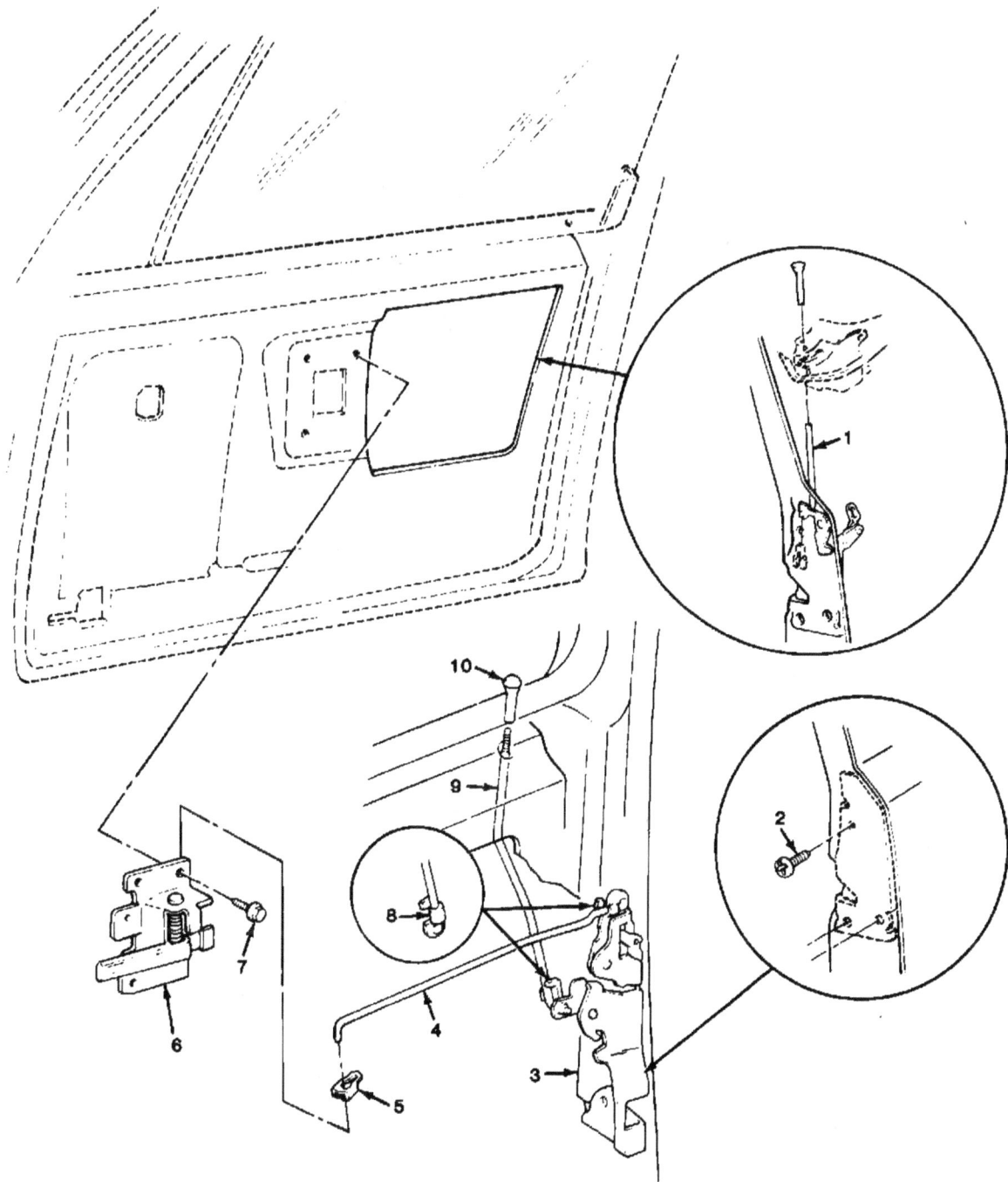

TA510977

FIGURE 137. SIDE DOOR LOCK ASSEMBLY

GROUP 1801 BODY, CAB, HOOD, AND HULL
ASSEMBLIES

FIG. 137 SIDE DOOR LOCK ASSEMBLY

1	PAOZZ	11862	327067	CONNECTING LINK,RIG			2
2	PAOZZ	11862	9439772	SCREW,SELF-LOCKING			6
3	PAOZZ	11862	14039763	LOCK ASSEMBLY,VEHIC	LEFT		1
3	PAOZZ	11862	14039764	LOCK ASSEMBLY,VEHIC	RIGHT		1
4	PAOZZ	11862	14039765	CONNECTING LINK,RIG	LEFT		1
4	PAOZZ	11862	14039766	CONNECTING LINK,RIG	RIGHT		1
5	PAOZZ	11862	375180	CLIP,SPRING TENSION			2
6	PAOZZ	11862	15597653	CONTROL ASSEMBLY,RE	LEFT		1
6	PAOZZ	11862	15597654	CONTROL ASSEMBLY,LC	RIGHT		1
7	PAOZZ	11862	9439770	BOLT,ASSEMBLED WASH			6
8	PAOZZ	11862	15545178	CLIP,RETAINING			4
9	PAOZZ	11862	14039767	CONNECTING LINK,RIG	LEFT		1
9	PAOZZ	11862	14039768	CONNECTING LINK,RIG	RIGHT		1
10	PAOZZ	11862	7591126	KNOB			2

END OF FIGURE

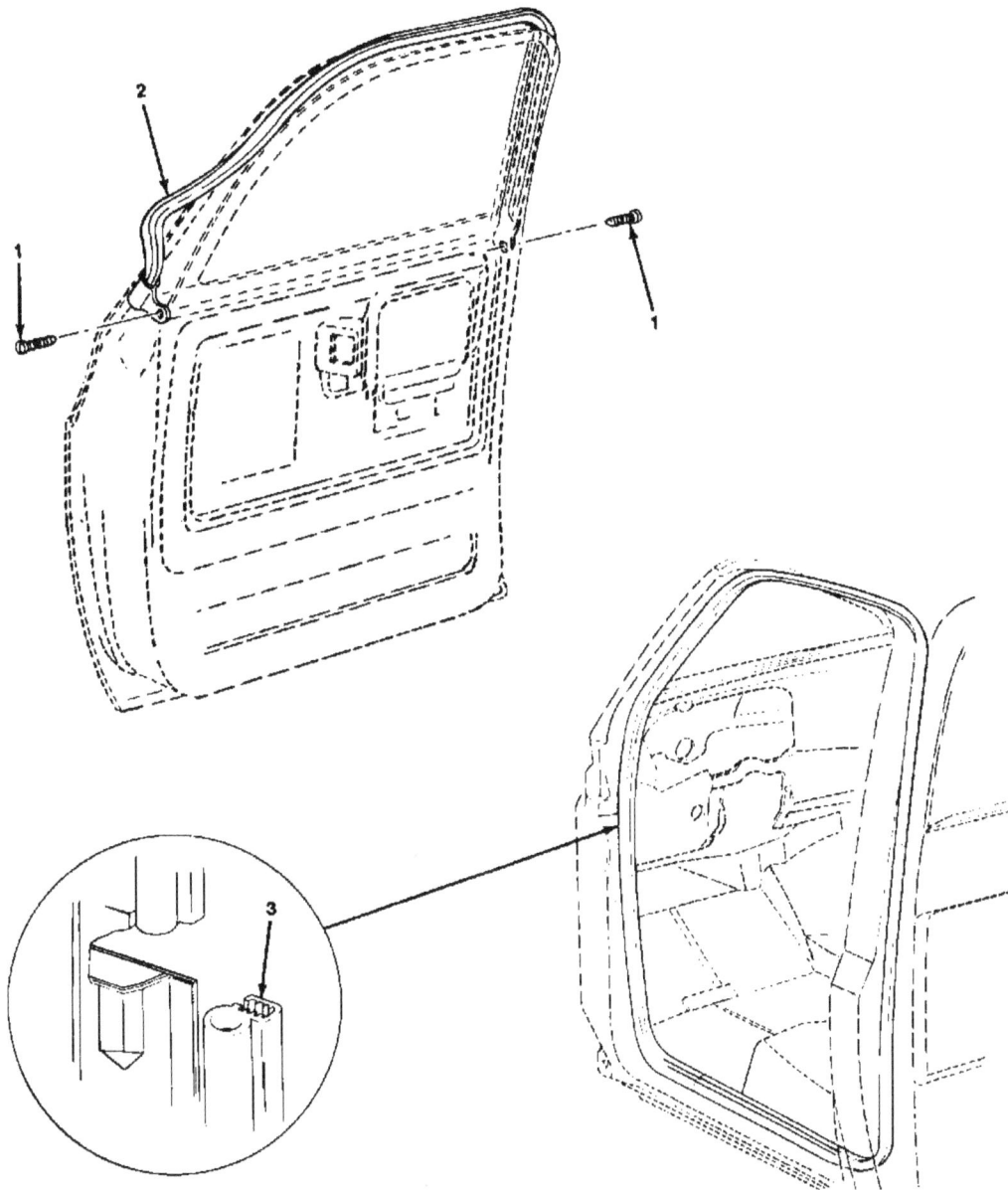

TA510978

FIGURE 138. SIDE DOOR WEATHERSTRIPS.

(1) ITEM NO	(2) SMR CODE	(3) CAGEC	(4) PART NUMBER	(5) DESCRIPTION AND USABLE ON CODES (UOC)	(6) QTY
				GROUP 1801 BODY, CAB, HOOD, AND HULL ASSEMBLIES	
				FIG. 138 SIDE DOOR WEATHERSTRIPS	
1	PAOZZ	11862	14022885	SCREW,TAPPING UOC:209	4
2	PAOZZ	11862	14016511	MOLDING,FRAME LEFT UOC:209	1
2	PAOZZ	11862	14016512	MOLDING,FRAME RIGHT UOC:209	1
3	PAOZZ	11862	15522764	WEATHER STRIP	2
				END OF FIGURE	

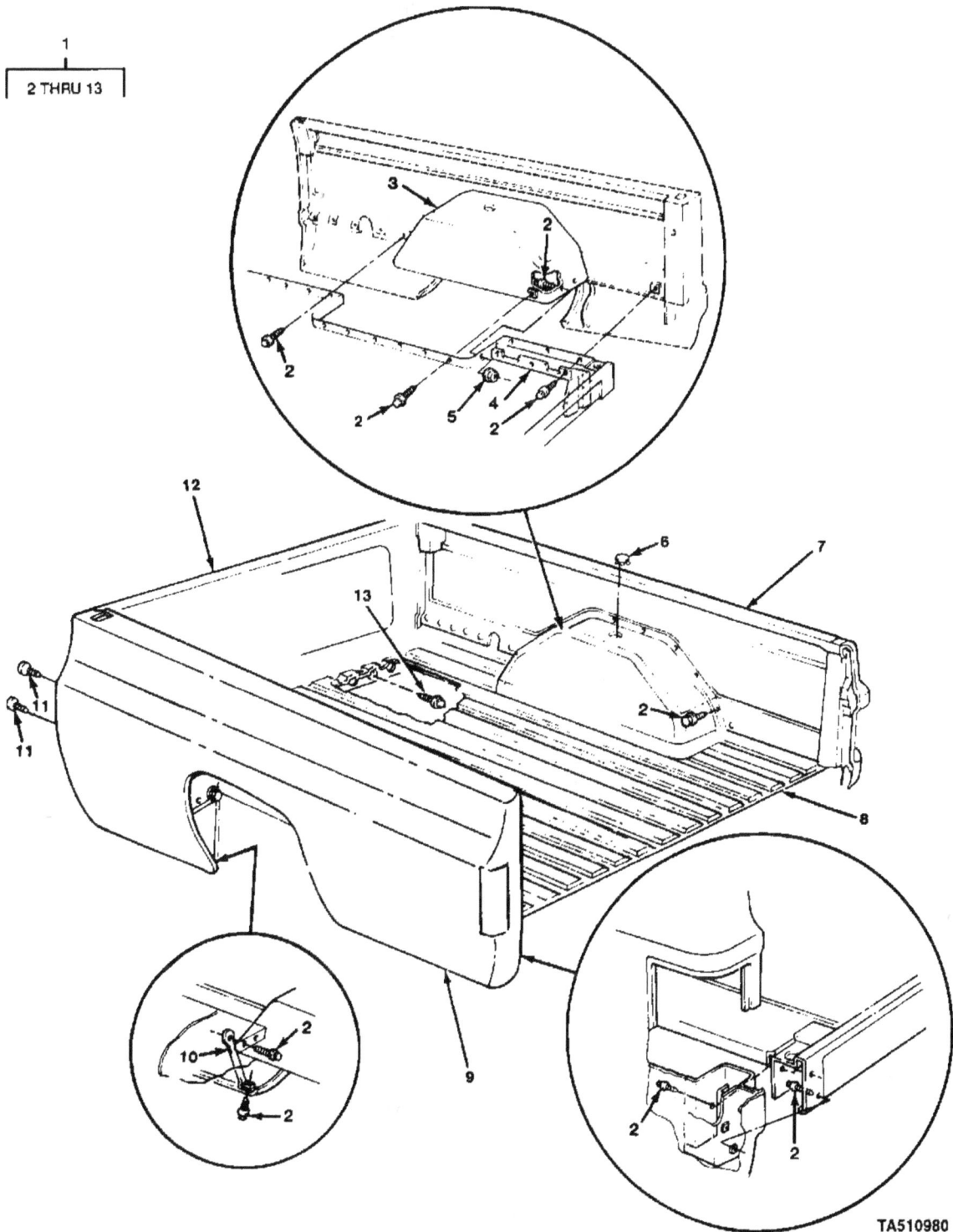

FIGURE 139. CARGO BOX AND COMPONENTS (M1008, M1008A1 , M1028,
M1028A1 , M1028A2, AND M1028A3).

TA510980

GROUP 1801 BODY, CAB, HOOD, AND HULL
ASSEMBLIES

FIG. 139 CARGO BOX AND COMPONENTS
(M1008, M1008A1, M1028, M1028A1,
M1028A2, AND M1028A31)

6   PAOZZ   11862   14049810   .PLUG,PROTECTIVE,DUS   2
                                             UOC:194,208,230,252,254,256

                                             END OF FIGURE

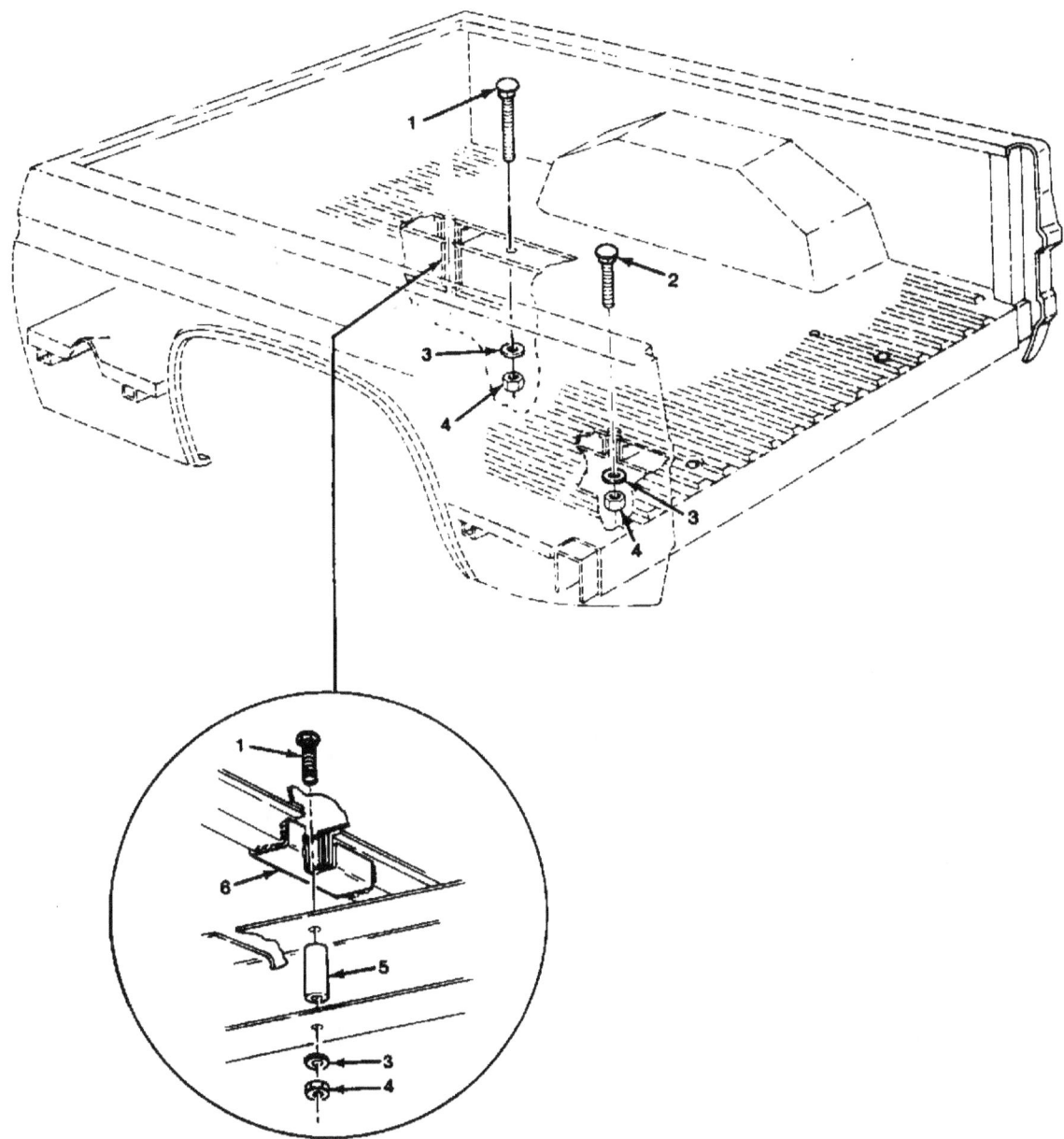

TA510981

FIGURE 140. CARGO BOX MOUNTING (M1008, M1008A1, M1028, M1028A1, M1028A2, AND M1028A3).

(1) ITEM NO	(2) SMR CODE	(3) CAGEC	(4) PART NUMBER	(5) DESCRIPTION AND USABLE ON CODES (UOC)	(6) QTY
				GROUP 1801 BODY, CAB, HOOD, AND HULL ASSEMBLIES	
				FIG. 140 CARGO BOX MOUNTING (M1008, M1008A1, M1028, M1028A1, M1028A2, AND M1028A3)	
1	PAOZZ	11862	14039924	BOLT,SQUARE NECK UOC:194,208,230,231,252,254,256	4
2	PAOZZ	11862	15599971	BOLT,SQUARE NECK UOC:194,208,230,231,252,254,256	4
3	PAOZZ	96906	MS27183-18	WASHER,FLAT UOC:194,208,230,231,252,254,256	8
4	PAOZZ	96906	MS51967-14	NUT,PLAIN,HEXAGON UOC:194,208,230,231,252,254,256	8
5	PAOZZ	11862	14076894	SPACER,PLATE USE WITH BOLT P/N 15599971 UOC:194,208,220,231,252,254,256	4
5	PAOZZ	11862	15599250	SPACER,SLEEVE USE WITH BOLT P/N 14039924 UOC;194,208,230,231,252,254,256	4
6	PAOZZ	11862	14076887	STRAP,RETAINING UOC:194,208,230,231,252,254,256	6

END OF FIGURE

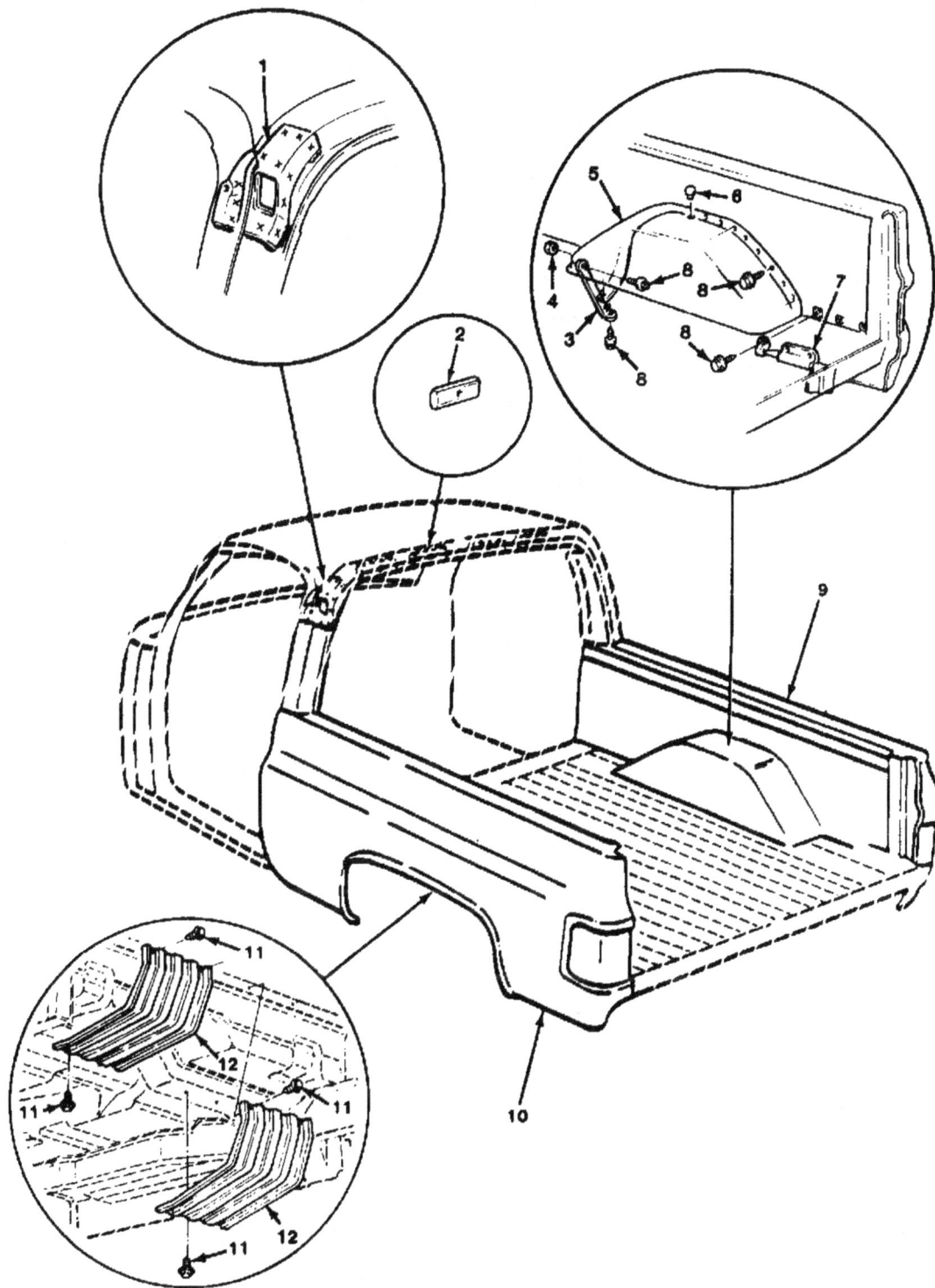

TA510982

FIGURE 141. BODY CARGO AND COMPONENTS (M1009).

(1) ITEM NO	(2) SMR CODE	(3) CAGEC	(4) PART NUMBER	(5) DESCRIPTION AND USABLE ON CODES (UOC)	(6) QTY
				GROUP 1801 BODY, CAB, HOOD, AND HULL ASSEMBLIES	
				FIG. 141 BODY CARGO AND COMPONENTS (M1009)	
3	PAOZZ	11862	330438	BRACE ASSEMBLY,PANE UOC:209	2
4	PAOZZ	96906	MS51967-6	NUT,PLAIN,HEXAGON UOC:209	2
5	PAOZZ	11862	14027451	PANEL,WHEEL HOUSE LEFT UOC:209	1
5	PAOZZ	11862	14027454	LINER SECTION,VEHIC RIGHT UOC:209	1
6	PAOZZ	11862	14049810	PLUG,PROTECTIVE,DUS UOC:209	2
7	PAOZZ	11862	467911	SHIELD,PANEL STONE LEFT UOC:209	1
7	PAOZZ	11862	467912	SHIELD,PANEL STONE RIGHT UOC:209	1
8	PAOZZ	11862	2014469	BOLT,ASSEMBLED WASH UOC:209	36
11	PAOZZ	11862	11504447	SCREW,TAPPING UOC:209	8
12	PAOZZ	11862	471089	GUARD,MUFFLER-EXHAU UOC:209	2

END OF FIGURE

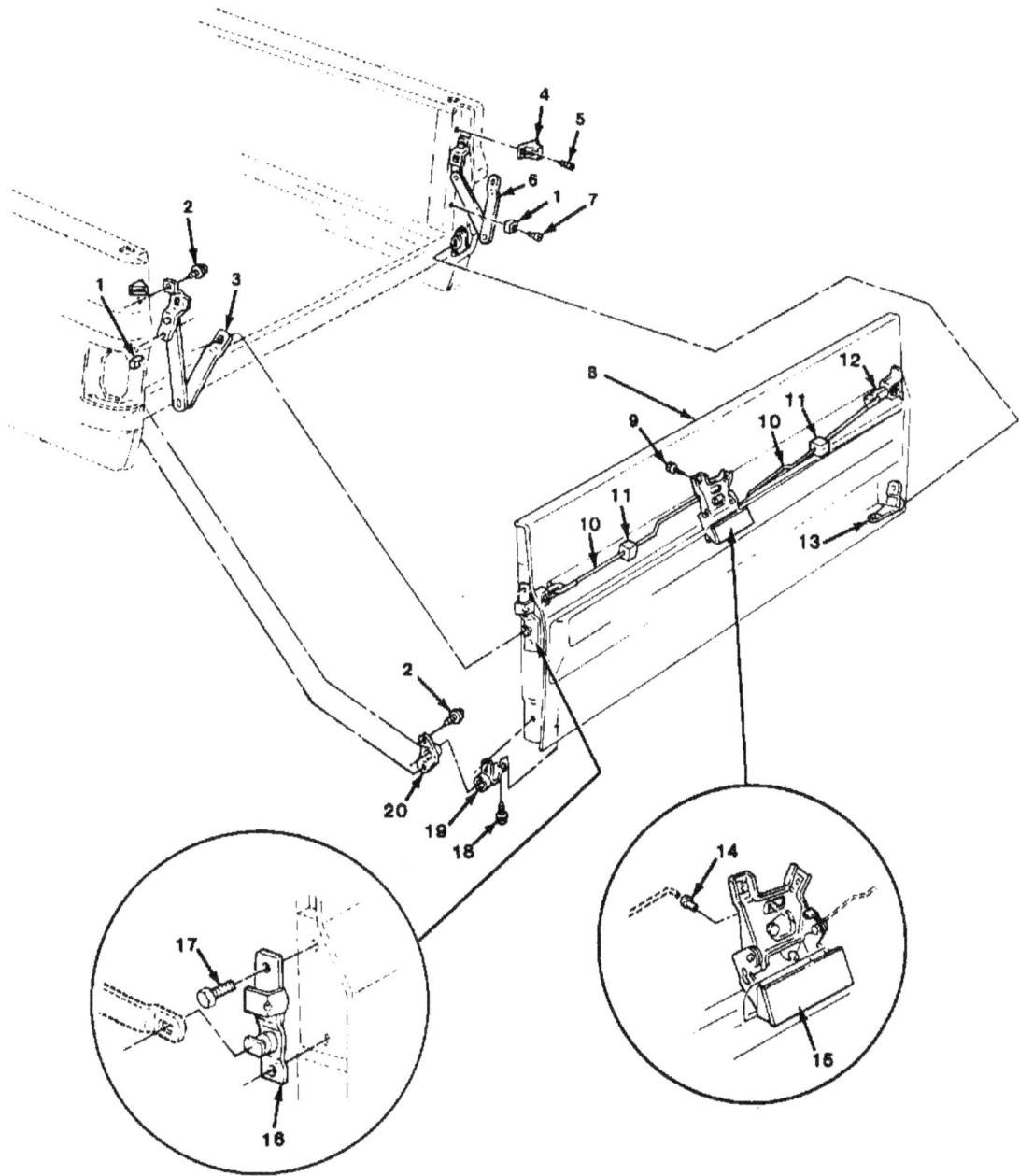

TA510983

FIGURE 142. CARGO END GATE AND COMPONENTS (M1008, M1008A1,
M1028, M1028A1 , M1028A2, AND M1028A3).

(1) ITEM NO	(2) SMR CODE	(3) CAGEC	(4) PART NUMBER	(5) DESCRIPTION AND USABLE ON CODES (UOC)	(6) QTY
				GROUP 1801 BODY, CAB, HOOD, AND HULL ASSEMBLIES	
				FIG. 142 CARGO ENDGATE AND COMPONENTS (M1008, M1008A1, M1028, M1028A1, M1028A2, AND M1028A3)	
1	PAOZZ	11862	6262029	BUMPER,END GATE LIN UOC:194,208,230,252,254,256	2
2	PAOZZ	96906	MS90728-59	SCREW,CAP,HEXAGON H UOC:194,208,230,252,254,256	8
3	PAOZZ	11862	458025	STRIKER PLATE AND L UOC:194,208,230,252,254,256	1
4	PAOZZ	11862	14032787	BUMPER,NONMETALLIC UOC:194,208,230,252,254,256	2
5	PAOZZ	96906	MS51869-24	SCREW,CAP,SOCKET HE UOC:194,208,230,252,254,256	2
6	PAOZZ	11862	458026	STRIKER PLATE ASSEM UOC:194,208,230,252,254,256	1
7	PAOZZ	96906	MS51861-45	SCREW,TAPPING UOC:194,208,230,252,254,256	2
8	PAOZZ	11862	15628608	TAILGATE,VEHICLE BO UOC:194,208,230,252,254,256	1
9	PAOZZ	11862	9431663	SCREW,ASSEMBLED WAS UOC;194,208,230,252,254,256	3
10	PAOZZ	11862	14021389	ROD,TAILGATE LATCH UOC:194,208,230,252,254,256	2
11	PAOZZ	11862	14007449	BUMPER,NONMETALLIC UOC:194,208,230,252,254,256	2
12	PAOZZ	11862	15594644	LATCH,END GATE UOC:194,208,230,252,254,256	1
13	PAOZZ	11862	15596976	TRUNION ASSEMBLY RIGHT UOC:194,208,230,252,254,256	1
14	PAOZZ	11862	3889864	CLIP,SPLIT TUBULAR UOC:194,208,230,252,254,256	2
15	PAOZZ	11862	14021275	HANDLE,DOOR UOC:194,208,230,252,254,256	1
16	PAOZZ	11862	15594643	LATCH,DOOR,VEHICULA UOC:194,208,230,252,254,256	1
17	PAOZZ	24617	9414712	SCREW,TAPPING,THREA UOC:194,208,230,252,254,256	4
18	PAOZZ	11862	2014469	BOLT,ASSEMBLED WASH UOC:194,208,230,252,254,256	8
19	PAOZZ	11862	15596975	BUSHING ASSEMBLY,EN LEFT UOC:194,208,230,252,254,256	1
20	PAOZZ	11862	14021385	TRUNNION ASSEMBLY LEFT UOC:194,208,230,252,254,256	1
20	PAOZZ	11862	14021386	TRUNNION ASSEMBLY,E RIGHT UOC:194,208,230,252,254,256	1

END OF FIGURE

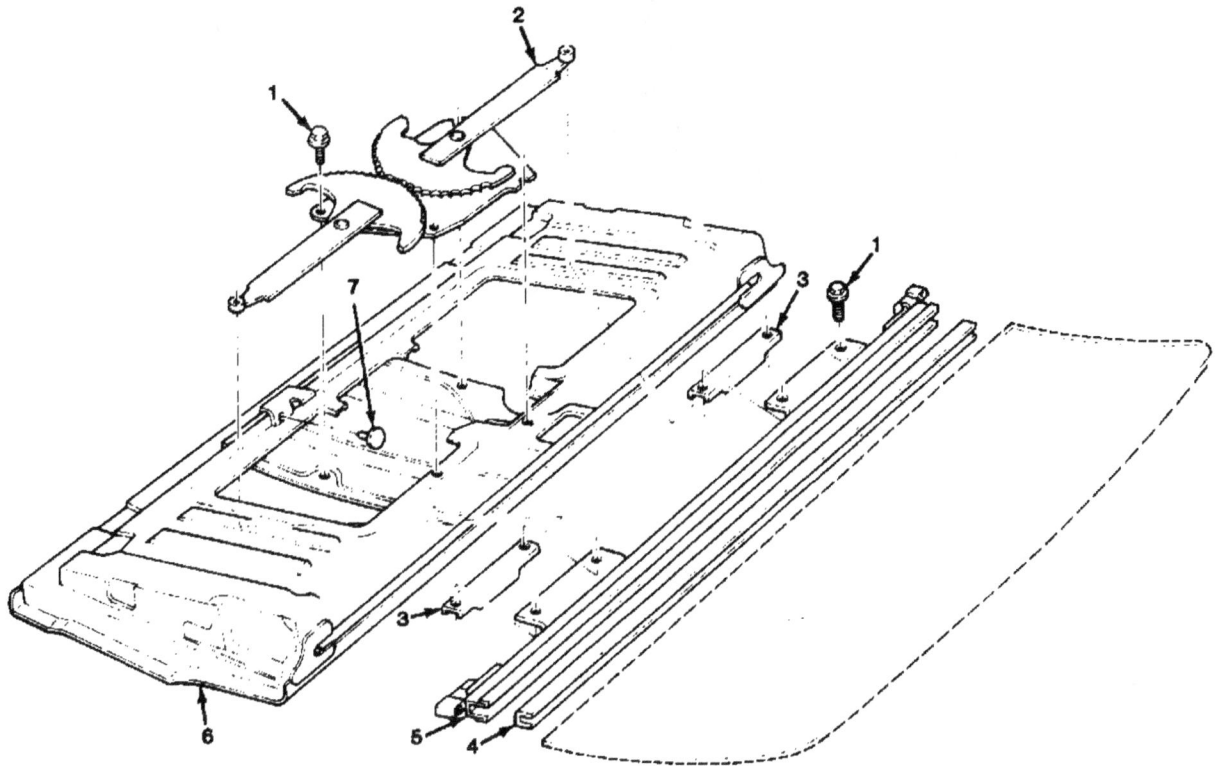

TA510984

FIGURE 143. ENDGATE AND COMPONENTS (M1009).

(1) ITEM NO	(2) SMR CODE	(3) CAGEC	(4) PART NUMBER	(5) DESCRIPTION AND USABLE ON CODES (UOC)	(6) QTY
				GROUP 1801 BODY, CAB, HOOD, AND HULL ASSEMBLIES	
				FIG. 143 ENDGATE AND COMPONENTS (M1009)	
1	PAOZZ	11862	1244067	BOLT,ASSEMBLED WASH UOC:209	8
2	PAOOO	11862	15641780	REGULATOR,WINDOW,VE UOC:209	1
2	PAOZZ	11862	4158246	ROLLER,LINEAR-ROTAR UOC:209	1
3	PAOZZ	11862	20171141	CHANNEL,LIFT,VEHICL UOC:209	2
4	MOOZZ	11862	14027542	FILLER E/GATE SASH (60.00"LG) MAKE FROM RUBBER, P/N 370390 UOC:209	1
5	PAOZZ	11862	340053	CHANNEL,LIFT,VEHICL UOC:209	1
6	PAOZZ	11862	15614462	TAILGATE,VEHICLE BO UOC:209	1
7	PAOZZ	11862	8785295	BUMPER,NONMETALLIC UOC:209	1

END OF FIGURE

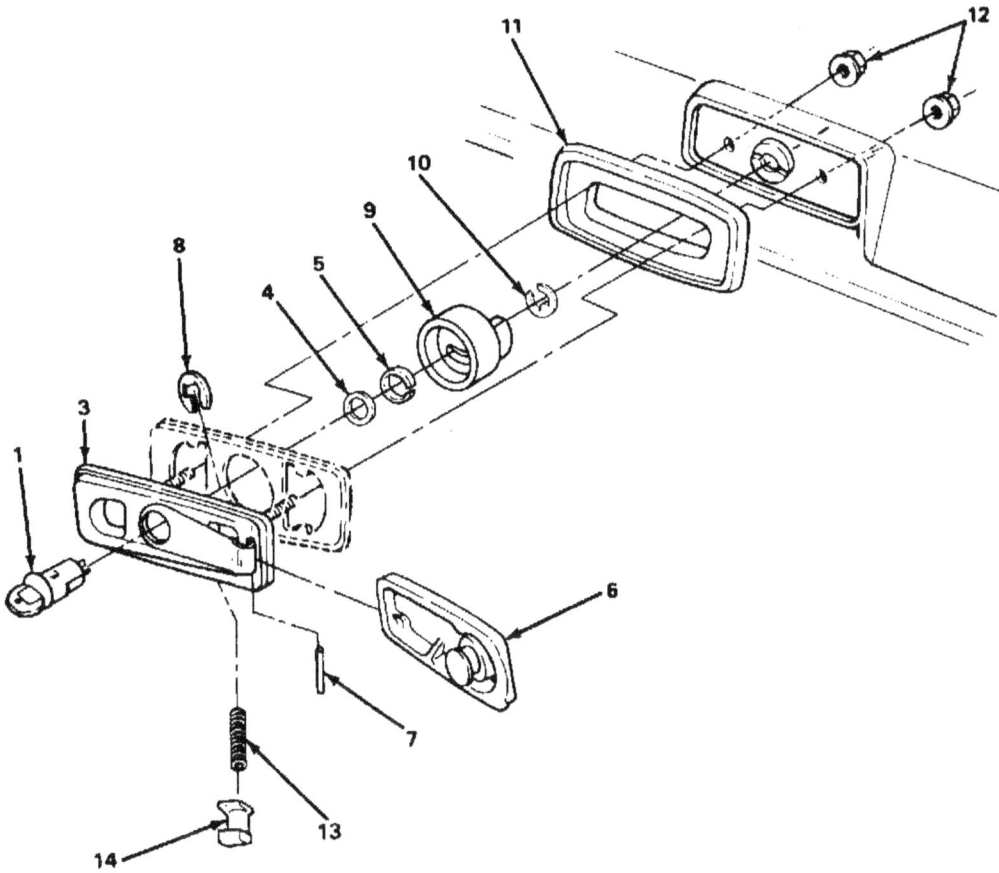

TA510985

FIGURE 144. ENDGATE WINDOW HANDLE ASSEMBLY (M1009).

(1) ITEM NO	(2) SMR CODE	(3) CAGEC	(4) PART NUMBER	(5) DESCRIPTION AND USABLE ON CODES (UOC)	(6) QTY
				GROUP 1801 BODY, CAB, HOOD, AND HULL ASSEMBLIES	
				FIG. 144 ENDGATE WINDOW HANDLE ASSEMBLY (M1009)	
1	PAOZZ	11862	15599678	CYLINDER,LOCK,VEHIC UOC:209	1
2	PAOZZ	11862	14072497	HANDLE ASSEMBLY,WIN UOC:209	1
3	PAOZZ	11862	14072499	.LATCH,DOOR,VEHICULA UOC:209	1
4	PAOZZ	11862	5713274	.WASHER,SPRING TENSI UOC:209	1
5	PAOZZ	11862	5713276	.RING,RETAINING UOC:209	1
6	PAOZZ	11862	9703344	.HANDLE,DOOR UOC:209	1
7	PAOZZ	11862	5717887	.PIN,STRAIGHT,HEADLE UOC:209	1
8	PAOZZ	96906	MS16633-1021	RING,RETAINING UOC:209	1
9	PAOZZ	11862	9702916	CLUTCH,WINDOW REGUL UOC:209	1
10	PAOZZ	96906	MS16624-1024	RING,RETAINING UOC:209	1
11	PAOZZ	11862	327015	GASKET UOC:209	1
12	PAOZZ	24617	271172	NUT,SELF-LOCKING,AS UOC:209	2
13	PAOZZ	11862	4303911	SPRING,HELICAL,COMP UOC:209	1
14	PAOZZ	11862	5713268	PAWL UOC:209	1

END OF FIGURE

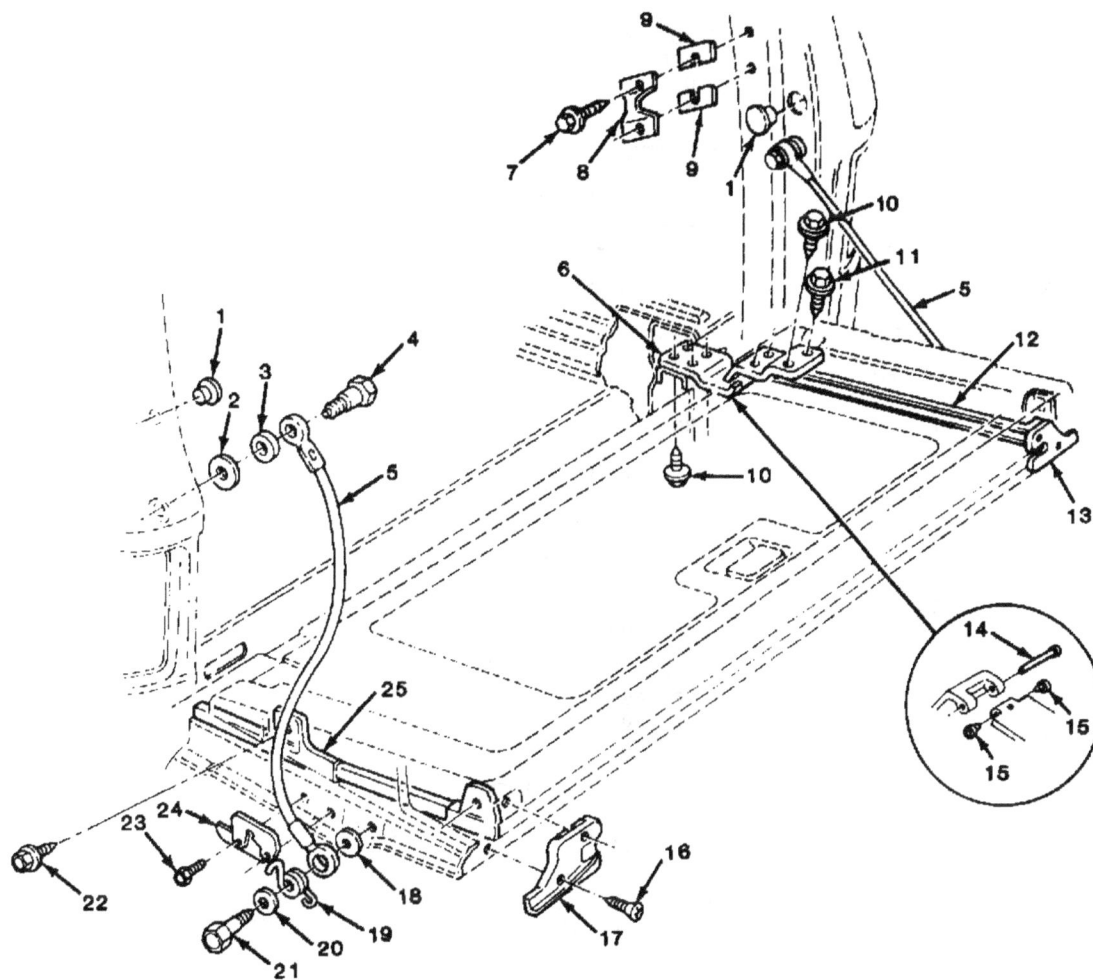

TA510988

FIGURE 145. ENDGATE HINGES AND RELATED PARTS (M1009).

GROUP 1801 BODY, CAB, HOOD, AND HULL
ASSEMBLIES

FIG. 145 ENDGATE HINGES AND RELATED
PARTS (M1009)

ITEM NO	SMR CODE	CAGEC	PART NUMBER	DESCRIPTION AND USABLE ON CODES (UOC)	QTY
1	PAOZZ	11862	14050440	PLUG,PROTECTIVE,DUS UOC:209	2
2	PAOZZ	11862	1260895	WASHER,FLAT UOC:209	2
3	PAOZZ	11862	14021292	SPACER,SLEEVE UOC:209	2
4	PAOZZ	11862	7740374	BOLT,SHOULDER UOC:209	2
5	PAOZZ	11862	6274850	WIRE ROPE ASSEMBLY, UOC:209	2
6	PAOZZ	11862	337788	HINGE,BUTT UOC:209	2
7	PAOZZ	11862	2014469	BOLT,ASSEMBLED WASH UOC:209	4
8	PAOZZ	11862	6274847	STRIKE,CATCH LEFT UOC:209	1
8	PAOZZ	11862	6274848	STRIKER,END GATE RIGHT UOC:209	1
9	PAOZZ	11862	6274849	SPACER,PLATE UOC:209	1
10	XDOZZ	11862	9438039	BOLT,ASSEMBLED WASH UOC:209	14
11	PAOZZ	11862	9437242	BOLT,MACHINE UOC:209	2
12	PAOZZ	11862	6274836	GUIDE,WINDOW,VEHICU RIGHT UOC:209	1
13	PAOZZ	11862	15522708	CAP ASSEMBLY,TAILGA RIGHT UOC:209	1
14	PAOZZ	11862	6271989	PIN,STRAIGHT,HEADED UOC:209	2
15	PAOZZ	11862	335524	BUSHING,SLEEVE UOC:209	4
16	PAOZZ	96906	MS51862-35	SCREW,TAPPING UOC:209	4
17	PAOZZ	11862	15522707	CAP ASSEMBLY,TAILGA LEFT UOC:209	1
18	PAOZZ	96906	MS27183-16	WASHER,FLAT UOC:209	2
19	PAOZZ	11862	14021315	SPRING,HELICAL,TORS LEFT UOC:209	1
19	PAOZZ	11862	14021316	SPRING,HELICAL,TORS RIGHT UOC:209	1
20	PAOZZ	96906	MS27183-19	WASHER,FLAT UOC:209	2
21	PAOZZ	11862	14021317	BOLT,SHOULDER UOC:209	2

(1) ITEM NO	(2) SMR CODE	(3) CAGEC	(4) PART NUMBER	(5) DESCRIPTION AND USABLE ON CODES (UOC)	(6) QTY
22	PAOZZ	11862	9439771	BOLT,ASSEMBLED WASH UOC:209	4
23	PAOZZ	24617	9414712	SCREW,TAPPING UOC:209	2
24	PAOZZ	11862	334132	GUIDE,END GATE SUPP UOC:209	2
25	PAOZZ	11862	470949	GUIDE,WINDOW,VEHICU UOC:209	1

END OF FIGURE

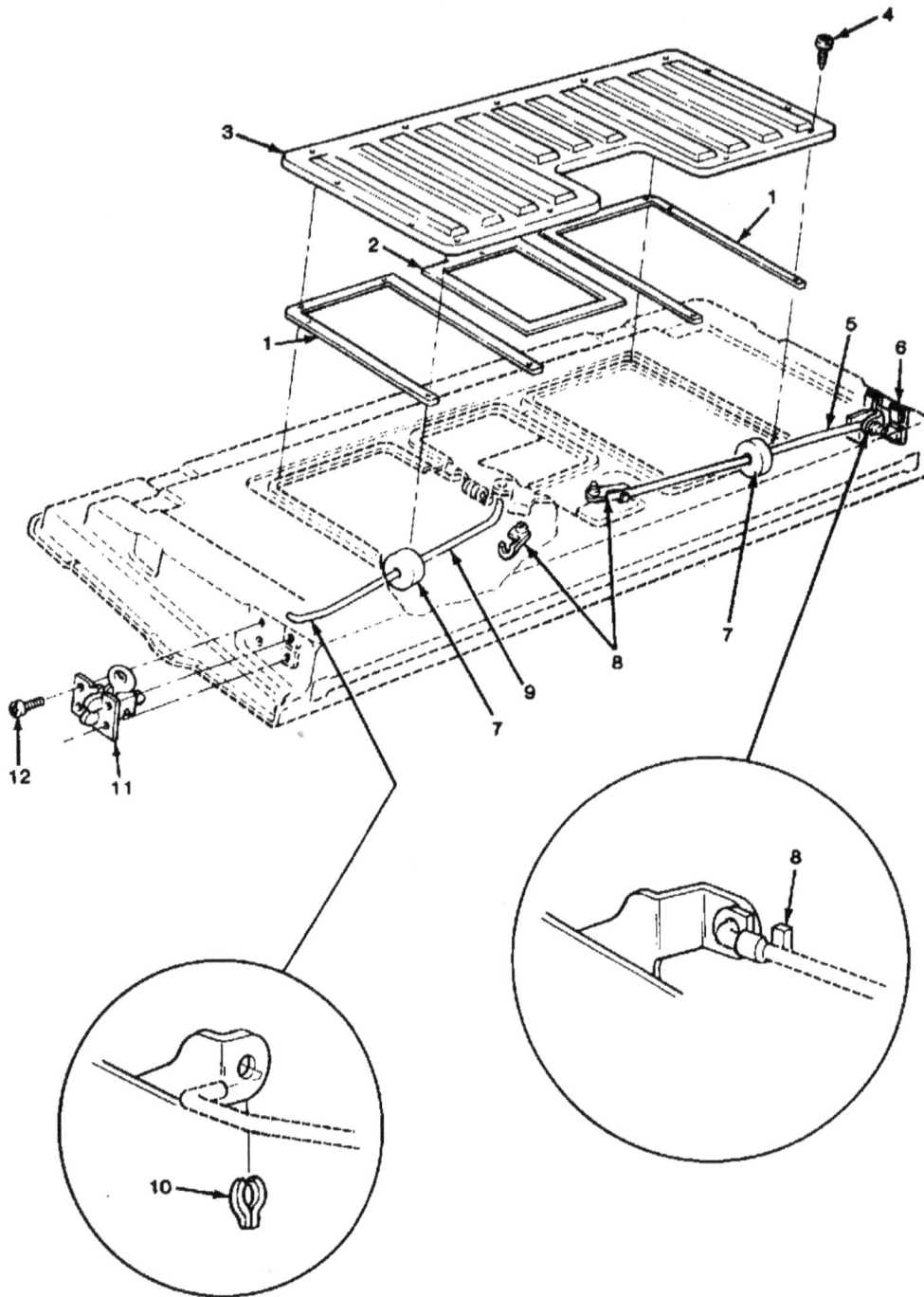

FIGURE 146. ENDGATE LATCHES AND RELATED PARTS (M1009).

TA510987

(1) ITEM NO	(2) SMR CODE	(3) CAGEC	(4) PART NUMBER	(5) DESCRIPTION AND USABLE ON CODES (UOC)	(6) QTY
				GROUP 1801 BODY, CAB, HOOD, AND HULL ASSEMBLIES	
				FIG. 146 ENDGATE LATCHES AND RELATED PARTS (M1009)	
1	PAOZZ	11862	15593570	SEAL UOC:209	2
2	PAOZZ	11862	15593571	GASKET UOC:209	1
3	PAOZZ	11862	6274890	COVER,ACCESS UOC:209	1
4	PAOZZ	24617	9419327	SCREW UOC:209	16
5	PAOZZ	11862	14039716	CONNECTING LINK,RIG RIGHT UOC:209	1
6	PAOZZ	11862	14039710	LATCH ASSEMBLY,END RIGHT UOC:209	1
7	PAOZZ	11862	14007449	BUMPER,NONMETALLIC UOC:209	2
8	PAOZZ	11862	15545178	CLIP,RETAINING UOC:209	3
9	PAOZZ	11862	473917	ROD,LATCH,END GATE, LEFT UOC:209	1
10	PAOZZ	11862	3905674	CLIP,SPRING TENSION UOC:209	1
11	PAOZZ	11862	473995	LATCH ASSEMBLY,END LEFT UOC:209	1
12	PAOZZ	11862	9439772	SCREW,SELF-LOCKING UOC:209	8

END OF FIGURE

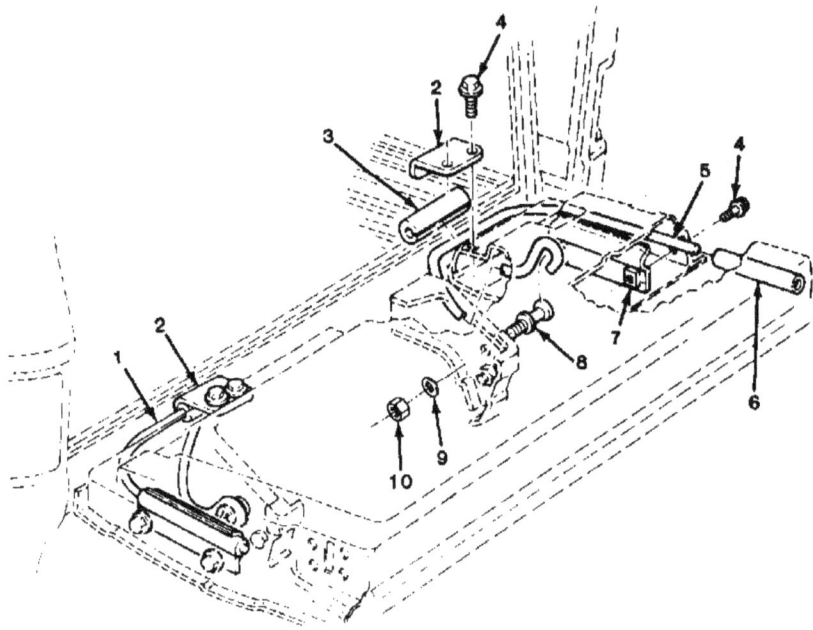

TA510988

FIGURE 147. ENDGATE TORQUE RODS (M1009).

(1) ITEM NO	(2) SMR CODE	(3) CAGEC	(4) PART NUMBER	(5) DESCRIPTION AND USABLE ON CODES (UOC)	(6) QTY
				GROUP 1801 BODY, CAB, HOOD, AND HULL ASSEMBLIES	
				FIG. 147 ENDGATE TORQUE RCDS (M10009)	
1	PAOZZ	11862	334101	ROD,TAILGATE,VEHICU LEFT UOC:209	1
2	PAOZZ	11862	6274854	BRACKET,ANGLE UOC:209	2
3	PAOZZ	22593	30103	GASKET LEFT UOC:209	1
3	PAOZZ	11862	334104	SEAL,NONMETALLIC SP RIGHT UOC:209	1
4	PAOZZ	11862	9439771	BOLT,ASSEMBLED WASH UOC:209	4
5	PAOZZ	11862	334102	ROD,END GATE,VEHICU RIGHT UOC:209	1
6	PAOZZ	11862	6274853	RUBBER ROUND SECTION UOC:209	2
7	PAOZZ	11862	337899	BRACKET,DOUBLE ANGL UOC:209	2
8	PAOZZ	11862	473894	STUD ASSEMBLY,ROD,T UOC:209	2
9	PAOZZ	96906	MS35340-48	WASHER,LOCK UOC:209	2
10	PAOZZ	96906	MS51967-14	NUT,PLAIN,HEXAGON UOC:209	2

END OF FIGURE

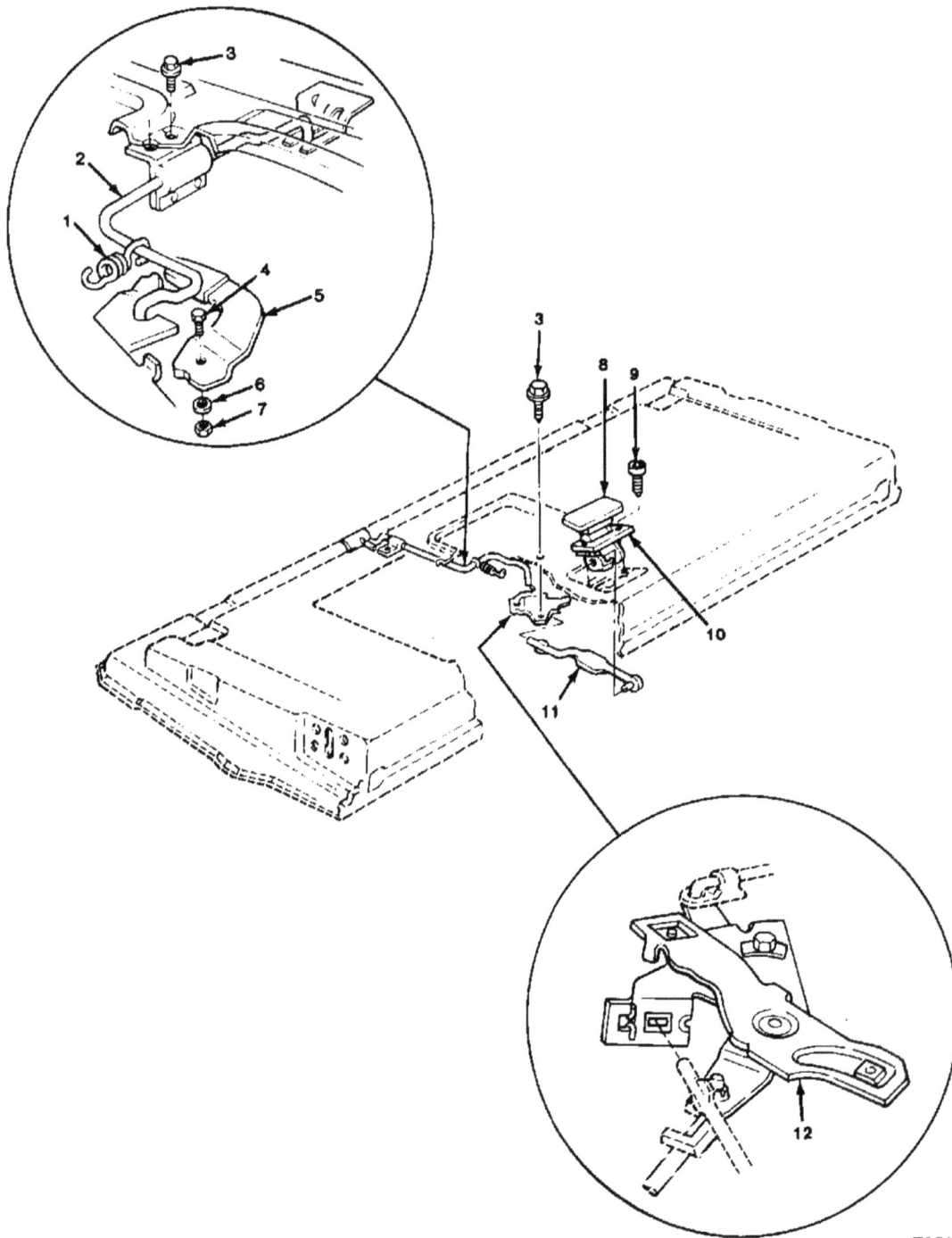

FIGURE 148. ENDGATE LATCH HANDLE (M1009).

TA510989

(1) ITEM NO	(2) SMR CODE	(3) CAGEC	(4) PART NUMBER	(5) DESCRIPTION AND USABLE ON CODES (UOC)	(6) QTY
				GROUP 1801 BODY, CAB, HOOD, AND HULL ASSEMBLIES	
				FIG. 148 ENDGATE LATCH HANDLE (M1009)	
1	PAOZZ	11862	15593866	SPRING,HELICAL,EXTE UOC:209	1
2	PAOZZ	11862	331638	ROD ASSEMBLY,LATCH, UOC:209	1
3	PAOZZ	11862	1244067	BOLT,ASSEMBLED WASH UOC:209	5
4	PAOZZ	96906	MS90728-6	SCREW,CAP,HEXAGON H UOC:209	1
5	PAOZZ	11862	335452	LEVER,MANUAL CONTRO UOC:209	1
6	PAOZZ	96906	MS35338-44	WASHER,LOCK UOC:209	1
7	PAOZZ	96906	MS35691-406	NUT,PALIN,HEXAGON UOC:209	1
8	PAOZZ	11862	4495180	HANDLE ASSEMBLY,TAI UOC:209	1
9	PAOZZZ	11862	8782501	SCREW,TAPPING UOC:209	2
10	PAOZZ	11862	470993	GASKET UOC:209	1
11	PAOZZ	11862	8742340	CONNECTING LINK,RIG UOC:209	1
12	PAOZZ	11862	14039712	LEVER,REMOTE CONTRO UOC:209	1

END OF FIGURE

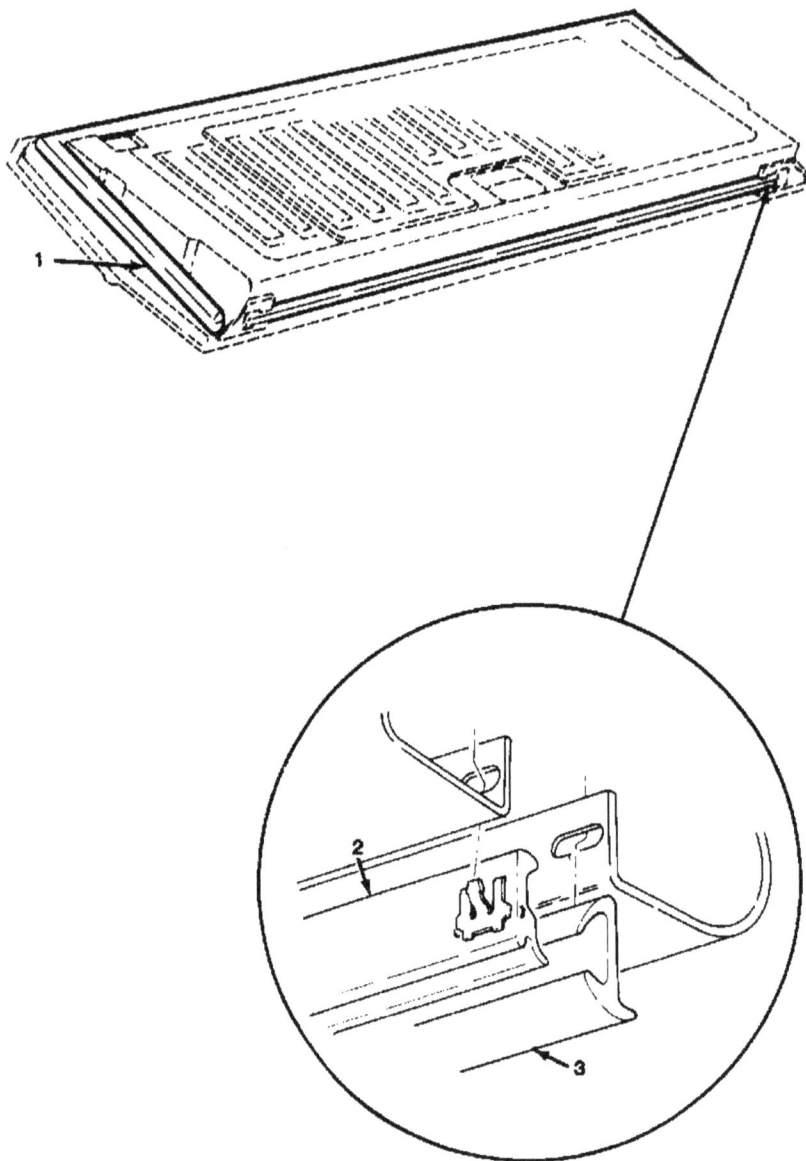

TA510990

FIGURE 149. ENDGATE WEATHERSTRIPS (M1009).

(1) ITEM NO	(2) SMR CODE	(3) CAGEC	(4) PART NUMBER	(5) DESCRIPTION AND USABLE ON CODES (UOC)	(6) QTY
				GROUP 1801 BODY, CAB, HOOD, AND HULL ASSEMBLIES	
				FIG. 149 ENDGATE WEATHERSTRIPS (M1009)	
1	PAOZZ	11862	326934	SEAL,NONMETALLIC SP UOC:209	1
2	PAOZZ	11862	327006	SEAL,NONMETALLIC SP UOC:209	1
3	PAOZZ	11862	327005	SEAL,NONMETALLIC SP UOC:209	1

END OF FIGURE

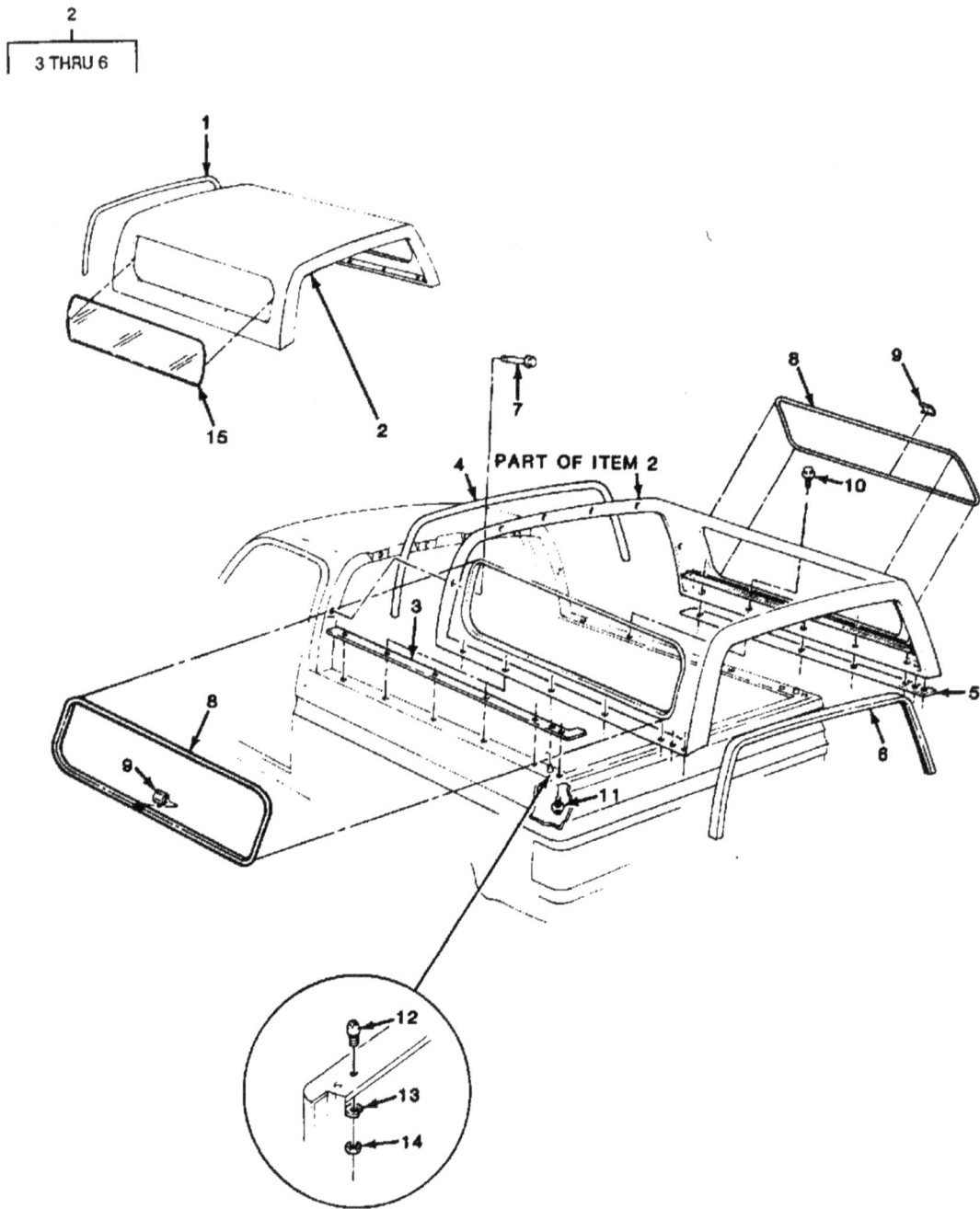

TA510991

FIGURE 150. TOP ASSEMBLY AND COMPONENTS (M1009).

(1)	(2)	(3)	(4)	(5)	(6)
ITEM NO	SMR CODE	CAGEC	PART NUMBER	DESCRIPTION AND USABLE ON CODES (UOC)	QTY

GROUP 1801 BODY, CAB, HOOD, AND HULL ASSEMBLIES

FIG. 150 TOP ASSEMBLY AND COMPONENTS (M1009)

| 10 | PAOZZ | 11862 | 458985 | SCREW,TAPPING
UOC:209 | 10 |

END OF FIGURE

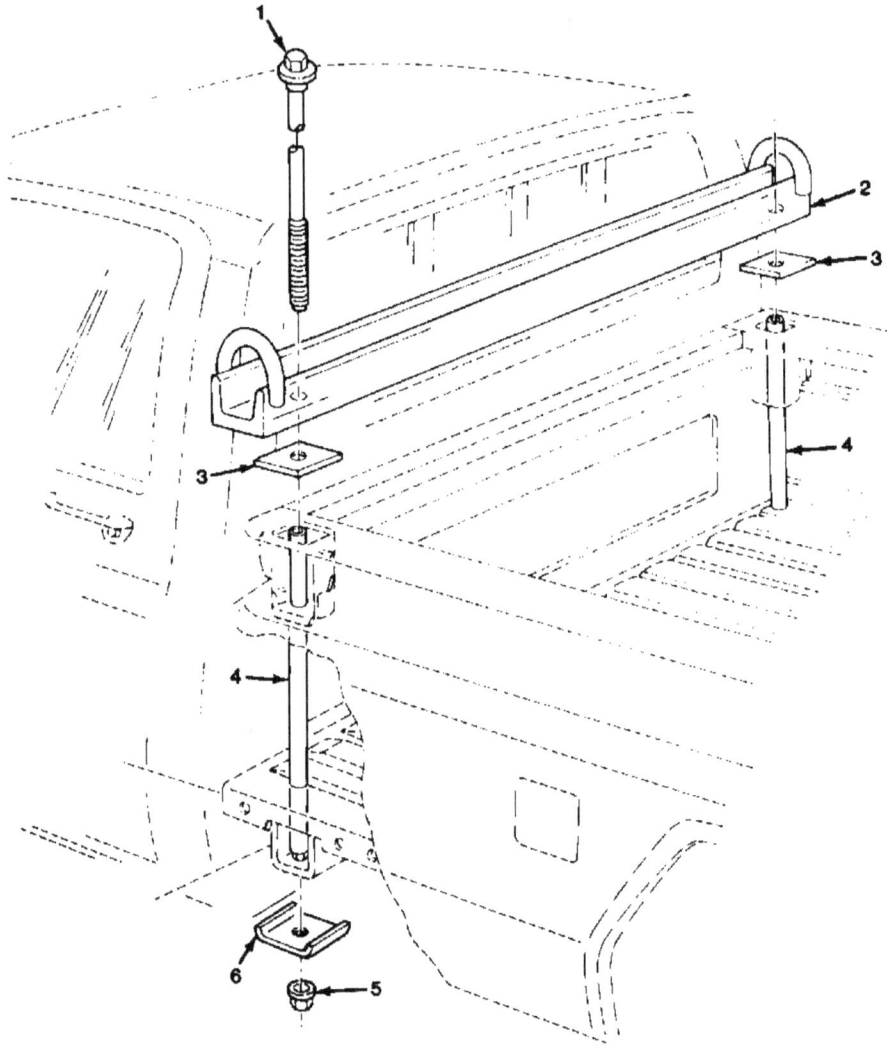

TA510992

FIGURE 151. FRONT TIE-DOWN BRACKETS (M1028, M1028A1, M1028A2, AND M1028A3).

(1) ITEM NO	(2) SMR CODE	(3) CAGEC	(4) PART NUMBER	(5) DESCRIPTION AND USABLE ON CODES (UOC)	(6) QTY
				GROUP 1801 BODY, CAB, HOOD, AND HULL ASSEMBLIES	
				FIG. 151 FRONT TIE-DOWN BRACKETS (M1028, M1028A1, M1028A2, ANC M1028A3)	
1	PAOZZ	11862	15599929	BOLT, EXTERNALLY REL UOC:230,252,254,256	2
2	PAOZZ	11862	14072452	CLAMP, LOOP UOC:230,252,254,256	1
3	PAOZZ	11862	14072460	PAD, BRACKET SUPPORT UOC:230,252,254,256	2
4	PAOZZ	11862	14072454	SPACER, SLEEVE UOC:230,252,254,256	2
5	PAOZZ	11862	9439757	NUT, PLAIN, EXTENDED UOC:230,252,254,256	2
6	PAOZZ	11862	14072459	PLATE, REINFORCEMENT UOC:230,252,254,256	2

END OF FIGURE

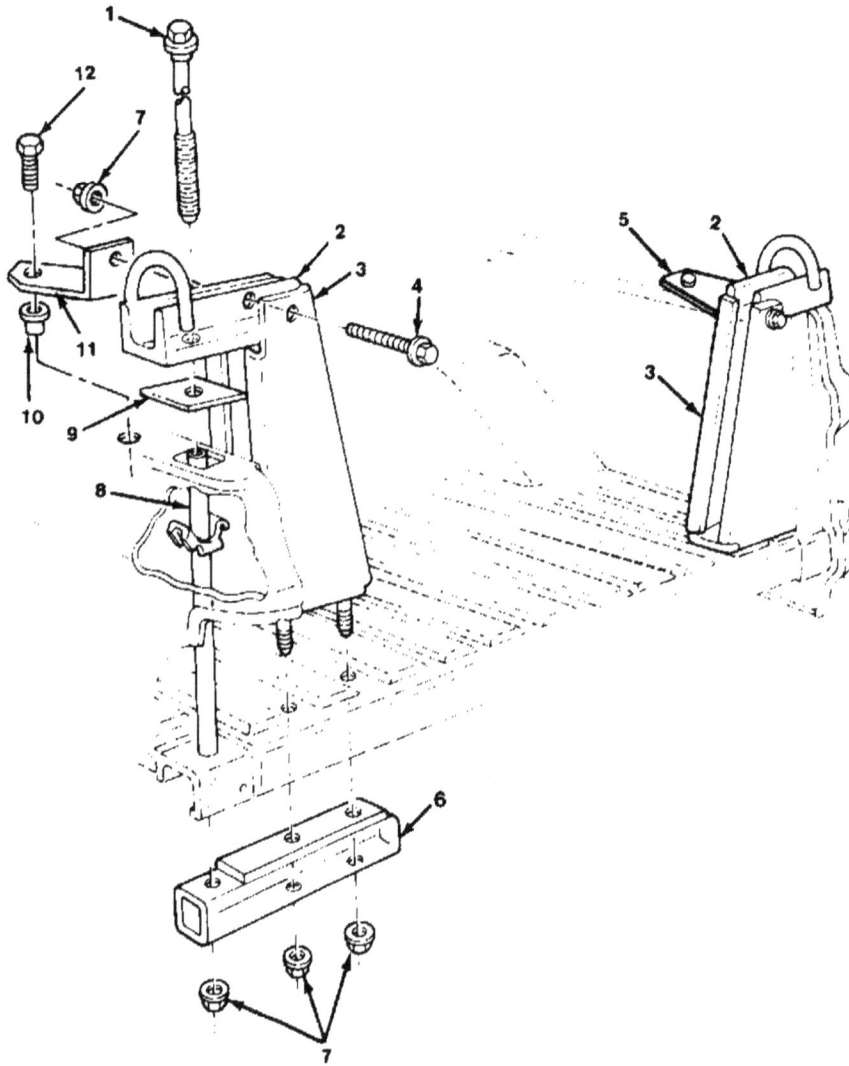

TA510993

FIGURE 152. REAR TIE-DOWN BRACKETS (M1028, M1028A1, M1028A2, AND M1028A3).

GROUP 1801 BODY, CAB, HOOD, AND HULL
ASSEMBLIES

FIG. 152 REAR TIE-DOWN BRACKETS
(M1028,M1028A1, M1028A2,AND
M102A31)

ITEM NO	SMR CODE	CAGEC	PART NUMBER	DESCRIPTION AND USABLE ON CODES (UOC)	QTY
1	PAOZZ	11862	15599929	BOLT,EXTERNALLY REL UOC:230,252,254,256	2
2	PAOZZ	11862	15591705	BRACKET,TIE DOWN UOC:230,252,254,256	2
3	PAOZZ	23862	15591706	BRACKET,TOW HOOK RIGHT UOC:230,252,254,256	1
3	PAOZZ	11862	15591709	BRACKET,TIE DOWN LEFT UOC:230,252,254,256	1
4	PAOZZ	11862	14072458	SETSCREW UOC:230,252,254,256	2
5	PAOZZ	1T998	15591710	BRACKET,ANGLE RIGHT UOC:230,252,254,256	1
6	PAOZZ	11862	14072455	REINFORCEMENT,REAR UOC:230,252,254,256	2
7	PAOZZ	96906	MS51967-14	NUT,PLAIN,HEXAGON UOC:230,252,254,256	8
8	PAOZZ	11862	14072454	SPACER,SLEEVE UOC:230,252,254,256	2
9	PAOZZ	11862	14072460	PAD,BRACKET SUPPORT UOC:230,252,254,256	2
10	PAOZZ	11862	3792287	NUT,PLAIN,BLIND RIV UOC:230,252,254,256	2
11	PAOZZ	11862	15591707	BRACKET,ANGLE LEFT UOC:230,252,254	1
12	PAOZZ	11862	9440300	SCREW,CAP,HEXAGON H UOC:230,252,254,256	2

END OF FIGURE

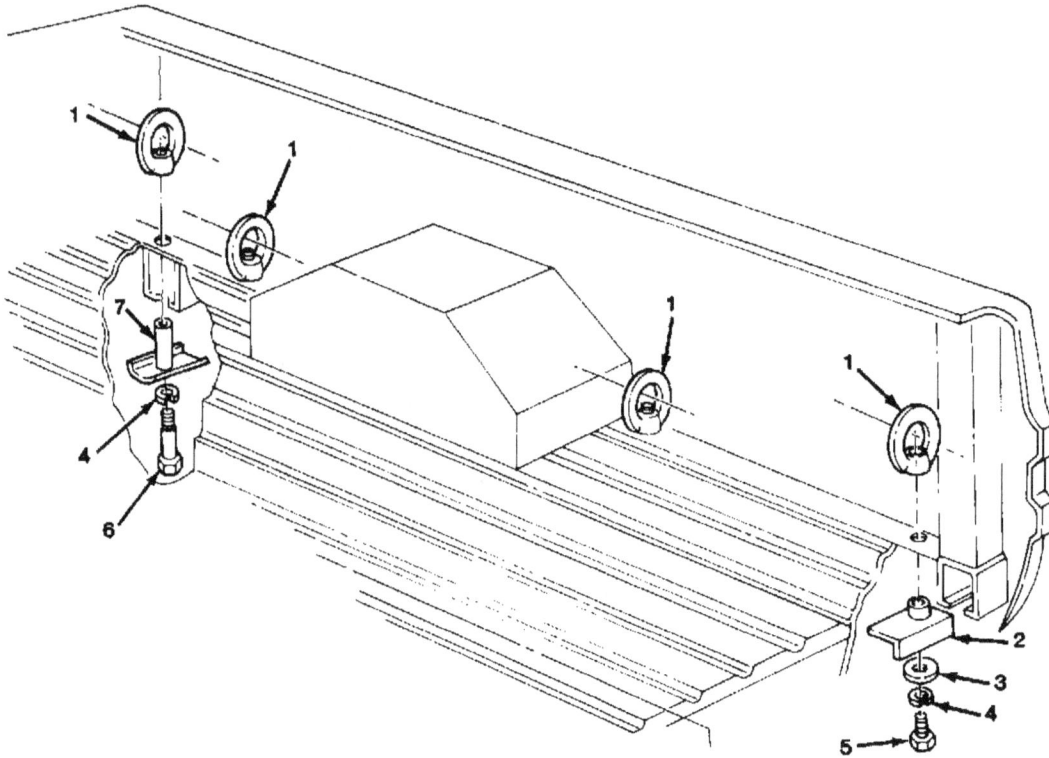

TA510994

FIGURE 153. CARGO TIE-DOWNS (M1008 AND M1008A1).

(1) ITEM NO	(2) SMR CODE	(3) CAGEC	(4) PART NUMBER	(5) DESCRIPTION AND USABLE ON CODES (UOC)	(6) QTY
				GROUP 1801 BODY, CAB, HOOD, AND HULL ASSEMBLIES	
				FIG. 153 CARGO TIE-DOWNS (M1008 AND M1008A1)	
1	PAOZZ	11862	14072307	NUT,EYE UOC:194,208	8
2	PAOZZ	11862	14072305	STRAP,RETAINING UOC:194,208	2
3	PAOZZ	11862	94009398	WASHER,FLAT UOC:194,208	2
4	PAOZZ	96906	MS35340-48	WASHER,LOCK UOC:194,208	8
5	PAOZZ	96906	MS90728-114	SCREW,CAP,HEXAGON H UOC:194,208	2
6	PAOZZ	96906	MS90728-125	SCREW,CAP,HEXAGON H UOC:194,208	6
7	PAOZZ	11862	14072306	REINFORCEMENT,CARGO UOC:194,208	6

END OF FIGURE

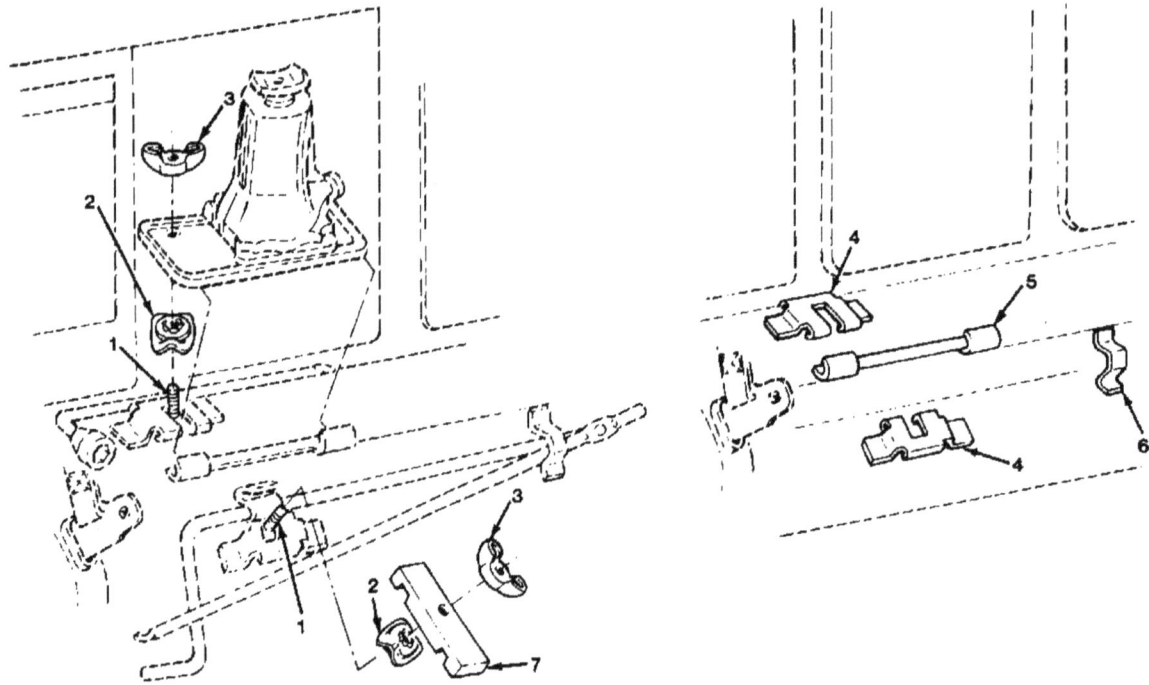

ALL EXCEPT M1009 AND M1010

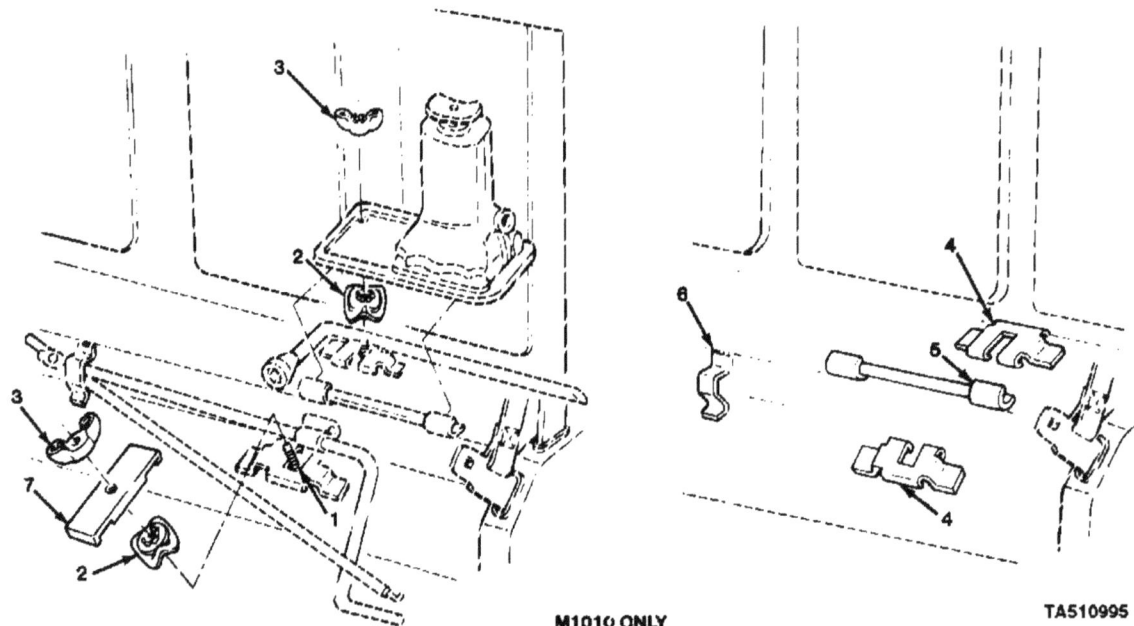

M1010 ONLY

TA510995

FIGURE 154. JACK STOWAGE COMPONENTS (ALL EXCEPT M1009).

(1) ITEM NO	(2) SMR CODE	(3) CAGEC	(4) PART NUMBER	(5) DESCRIPTION AND USABLE ON CODES (UOC)	(6) QTY
				GROUP 1801 BODY, CAB, HOOD, AND HULL ASSEMBLIES	
				FIG. 154 JACK STOWAGE COMPONENTS (ALL EXCEPT M1009)	
1	PAOZZ	11862	14032814	BOLT,SQUARE NECK UOC:194,208,210,230,231,252,254,256	2
2	PAOZZ	24617	9409613	PUSH ON NUT UOC:194,208,210,230,231,252,254,256	2
3	PAOZZ	96906	MS35425-72	NUT,PLAIN,WING UOC:194,208,210,230,231,252,254,256	2
7	PAOZZ	11862	467299	STRAP,RETAINING UOC:194,208,210,230,231,252,254,256	1

END OF FIGURE

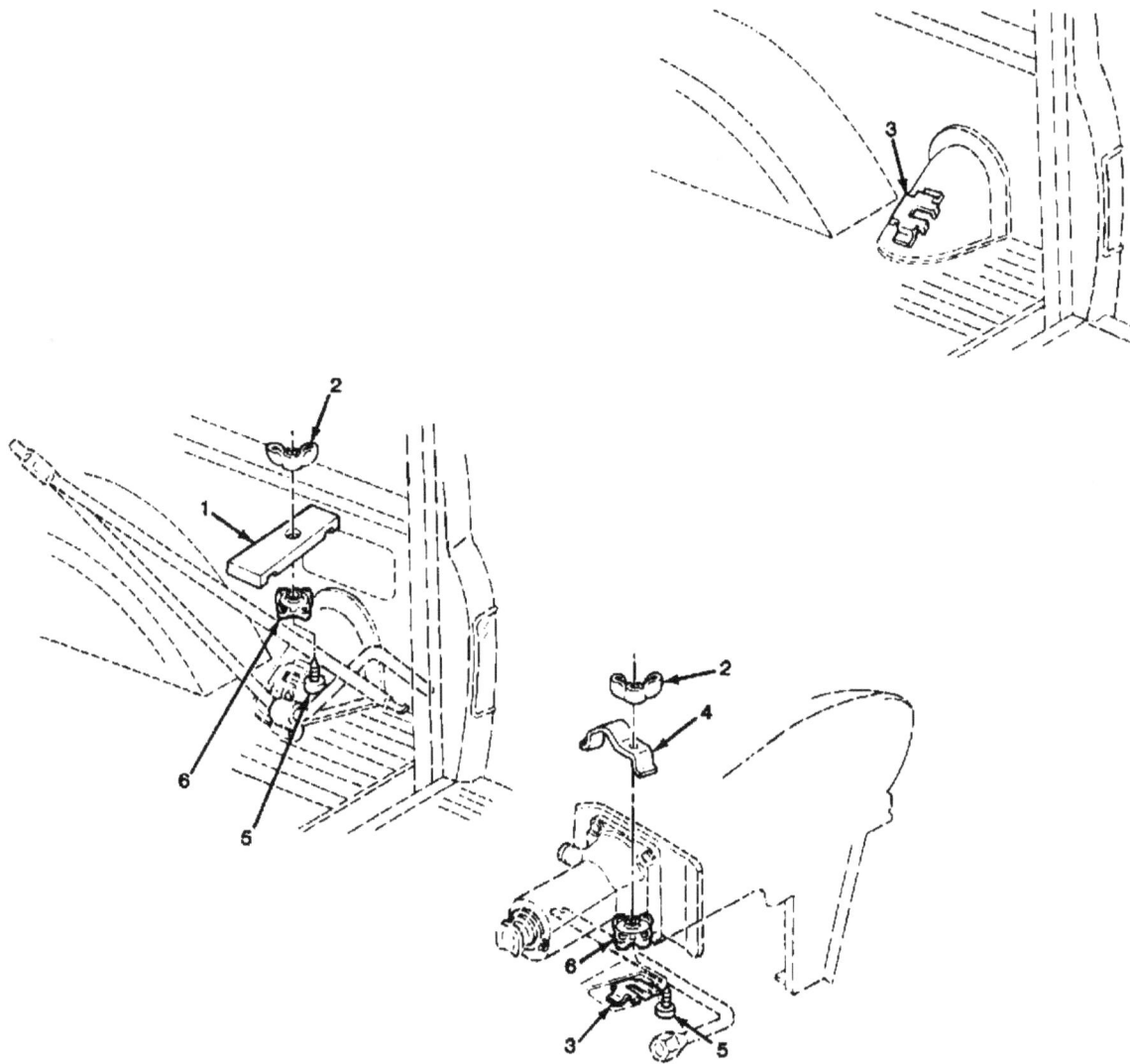

TA510996

FIGURE 155. JACK STOWAGE COMPONENTS (M1009).

(1) ITEM NO	(2) SMR CODE	(3) CAGEC	(4) PART NUMBER	(5) DESCRIPTION AND USABLE ON CODES (UOC)	(6) QTY
				GROUP 1801 BODY, CAB, HOOD, AND HULL ASSEMBLIES	
				FIG. 155 JACK STOWAGE COMPONENTS (M1009)	
1	PAOZZ	11862	467299	STRAP,RETAINING UOC:209	1
2	PAOZZ	96906	MS35425-72	NUT,PLAIN,WING UOC:209	2
4	PAOZZ	11862	14032812	RETAINER,JACK UOC:209	1
5	PAOZZ	11862	14032814	BOLT,SQUARE NECK UOC:209	2
6	PAOZZ	24617	9409613	PUSH ON NUT UOC:209	2

END OF FIGURE

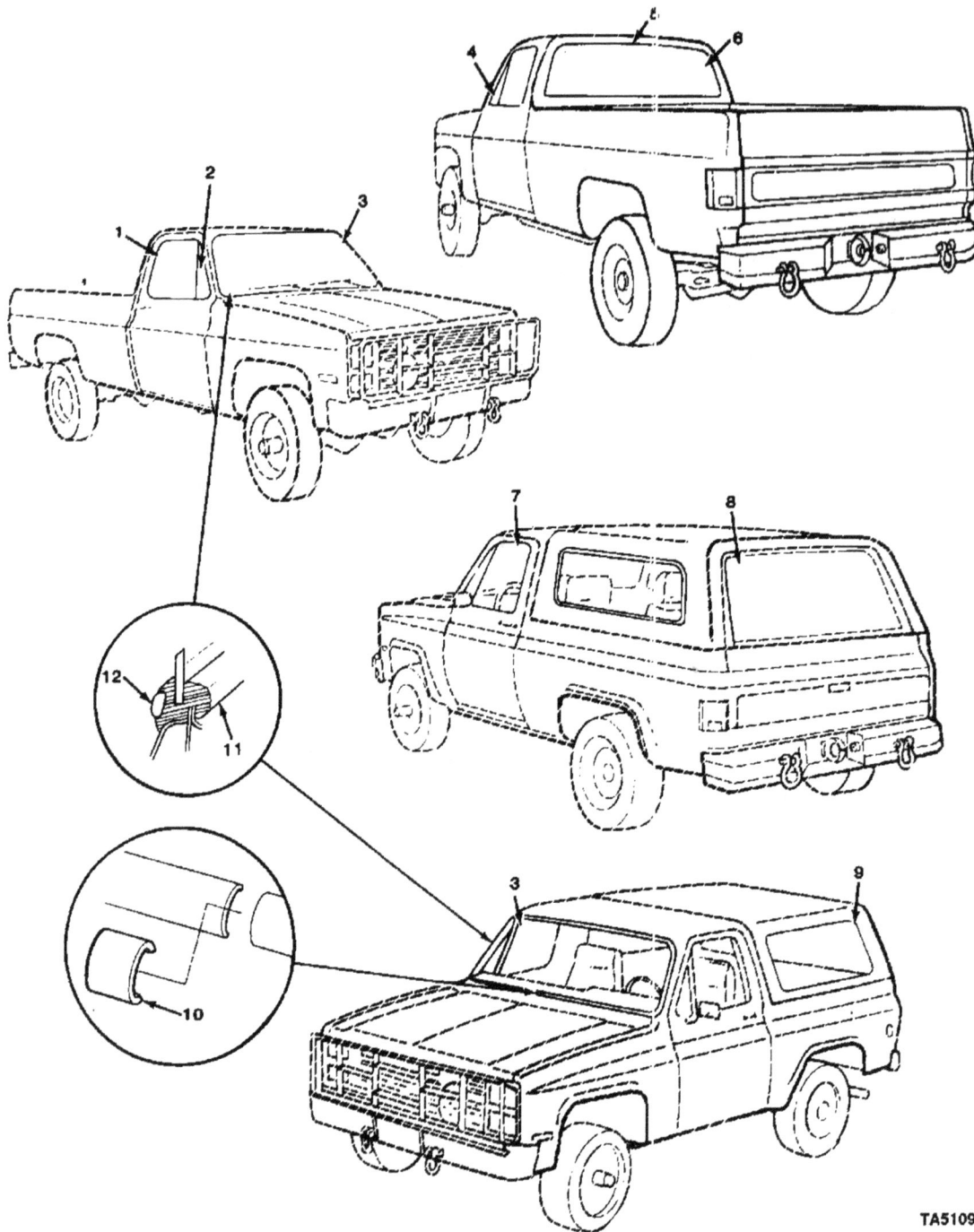

TA510997

FIGURE 156. WINDSHIELD AND WINDOW GLASS.

(1) ITEM NO	(2) SMR CODE	(3) CAGEC	(4) PART NUMBER	(5) DESCRIPTION AND USABLE ON CODES (UOC)	(6) QTY
				GROUP 1802 FENDERS, RUNNING BOARDS WITH MOUNTING AND ATTACHING PARTS, OUTRIGGERS, WINDSHIELD, GLASS, ETC.	
				FIG. 156 WINDSHIELD AND WINDOW GLASS	
1	PAOZZ	75829	14022842	WINDOW,VEHICULAR RIGHT	1
2	PAOZZ	11862	20264744	WINDOW,VEHICULAR RIGHT	1
4	PAOZZ	11862	20264743	WINDOW,VEHICULAR LEFT	1
7	PAOZZ	75829	14022841	WINDOW,VEHICULAR LEFT	1
8	PAOZZ	75829	14076899	WINDOW,VEHICULAR UOC:209	1

END OF FIGURE

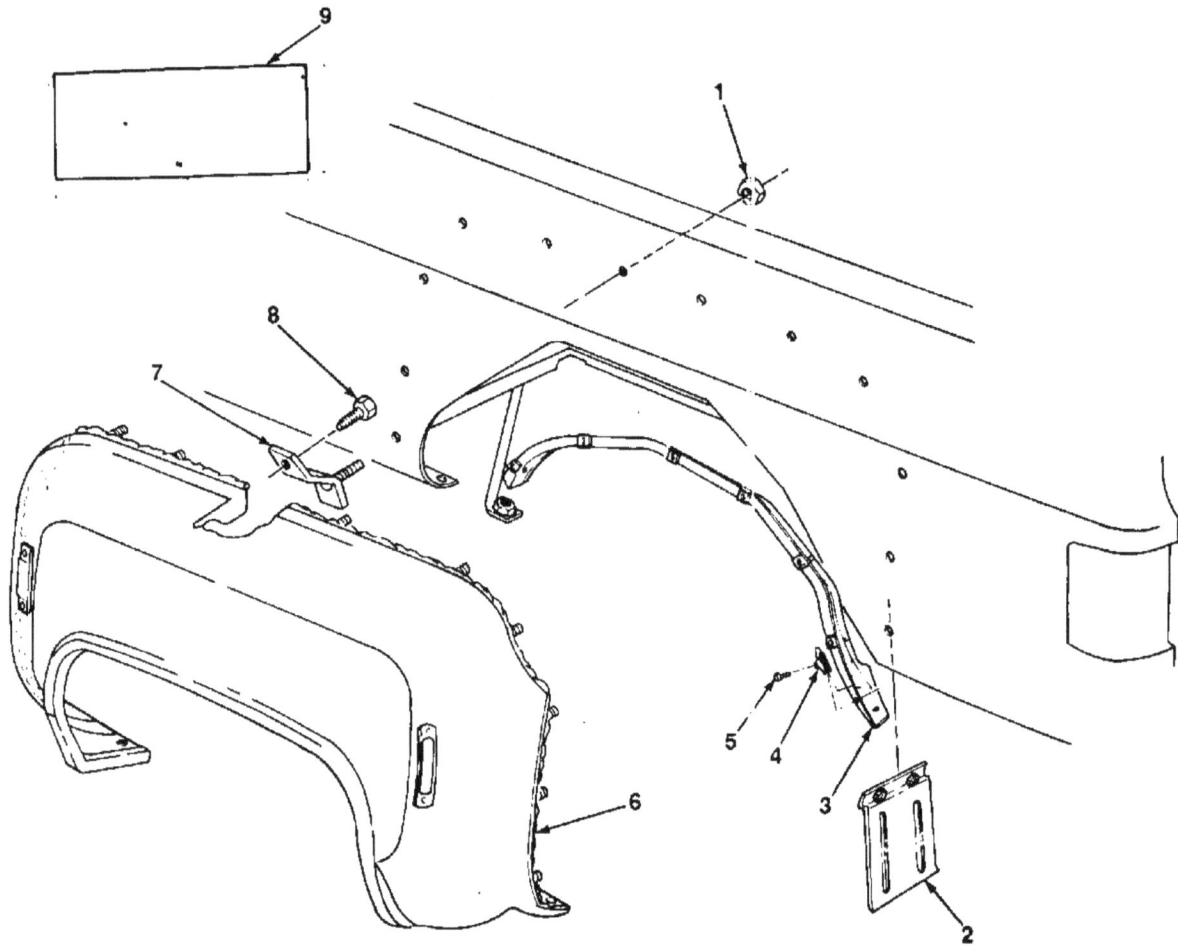

TA510999

FIGURE 157, REAR FENDER AND RELATED PARTS (M1028A2 AND M1028A3).

(1) ITEM NO	(2) SMR CODE	(3) CAGEC	(4) PART NUMBER	(5) DESCRIPTION AND USABLE ON CODES (UOC)	(6) QTY
				GROUP 1802 FENDERS, RUNNING BOARDS WITH MOUNTING AND ATTACHING PARTS, OUTRIGGERS, WINDSHIELD, GLASS, ETC.	
				FIG. 157 REAR FENDER AND RELATED PARTS (M1028A2 AND M1028A3)	
1	PAOZZ	11862	1359887	NUT,PLAIN,HEXAGON UOC:254,256	2
4	PAOZZ	24617	1494253	NUT,CLIP-ON UOC:254,256	2
5	PAOZZ	96906	MS51869-24	SCREW,CAP,SOCKET HE UOC:254,256	2

END OF FIGURE

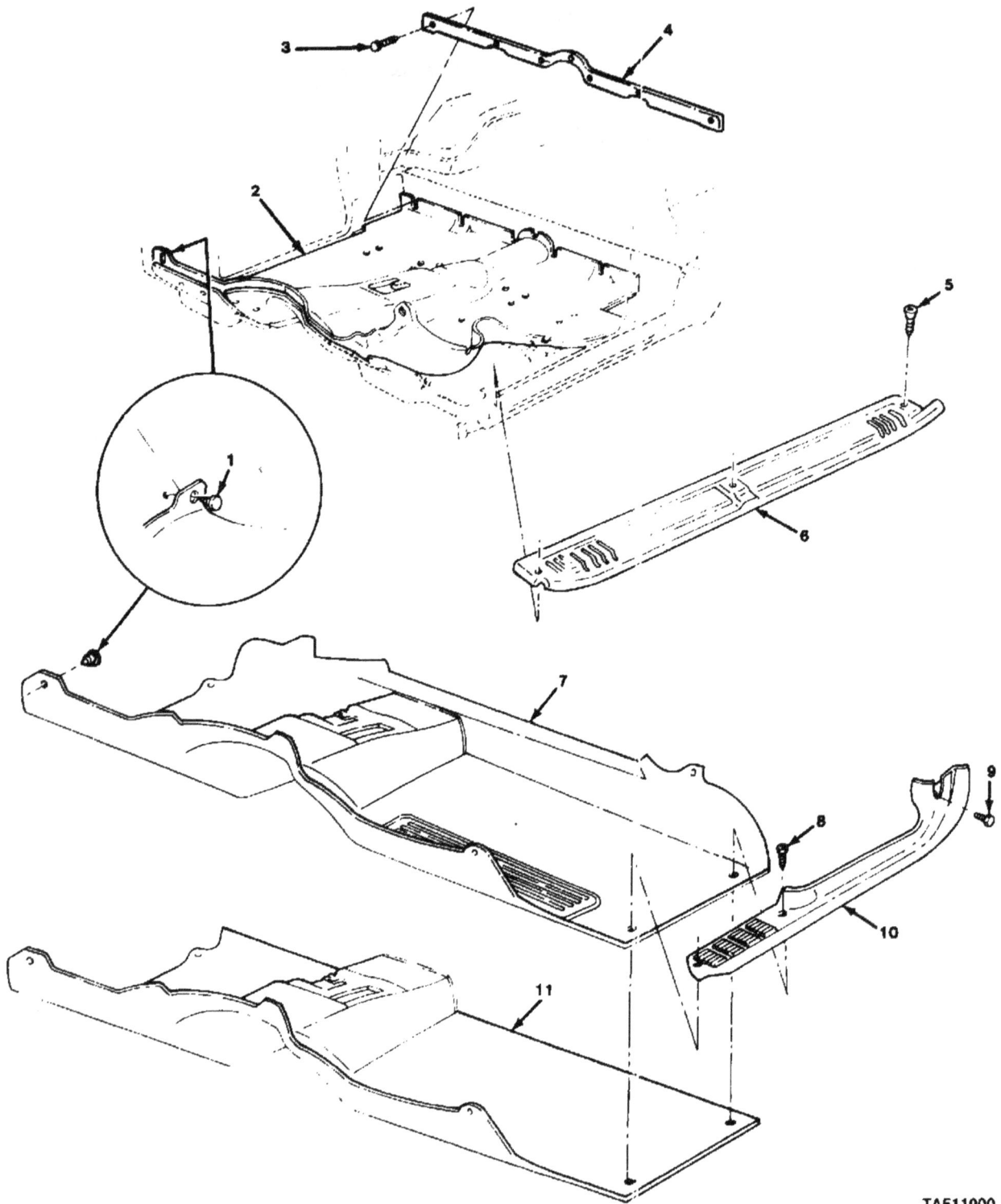

FIGURE 158. FLOORMATS, INSULATORS, AND RELATED PARTS.

TA511000

(1) ITEM NO	(2) SMR CODE	(3) CAGEC	(4) PART NUMBER	(5) DESCRIPTION AND USABLE ON CODES (UOC)	(6) QTY
				GROUP 1805 FLOORS, SUBFLOORS, AND RELATED PARTS	
				FIG. 158 FLOORMATS, INSULATORS, AND RELATED PARTS	
1	PAOZZ	11862	20030401	FASTENER,SPRING TEN	2
2	PFOZZ	11862	15591702	MAT,FLOOR UOC:209	1
3	PAOZZ	11862	11500668	SCREW,ASSEMBLED WAS UOC:209	7
4	PBOZZ	11862	474022	FRAME SECTION,STRUC UOC:209	1
5	PAOZZ	96906	MS51862-26	SCREW,TAPPING UOC:209	6
6	PAOZZ	11862	467247	PLATE,DOOR,LEFT UOC:209	1
6	PAOZZ	11862	467248	TREAD,METALLIC,NONS RIGHT UOC:209	1
7	PAOZZ	11862	15594983	MAT,FLOOR UOC:194,208,210,230,231,252,254,256	1
8	PAOZZ	11862	11502634	SCREW,TAPPING UOC:194,208,210,230,231,252,254,256	4
9	PAOZZ	24617	11503606	SCREW,TAPPING UOC:194,208,210,230,231,252,254,256	2
10	PAOZZ	11862	15594895	PLATE,DOOR,KICK LEFT UOC:194,208,210,230,231,252,254,256	1
10	PAOZZ	11862	15594896	MOLDING,METAL RIGHT UOC:194,208,210,230,231,252,254,256	1
11	PAOZZ	11862	462233	INSULATOR,FLOOR,VEH	1

END OF FIGURE

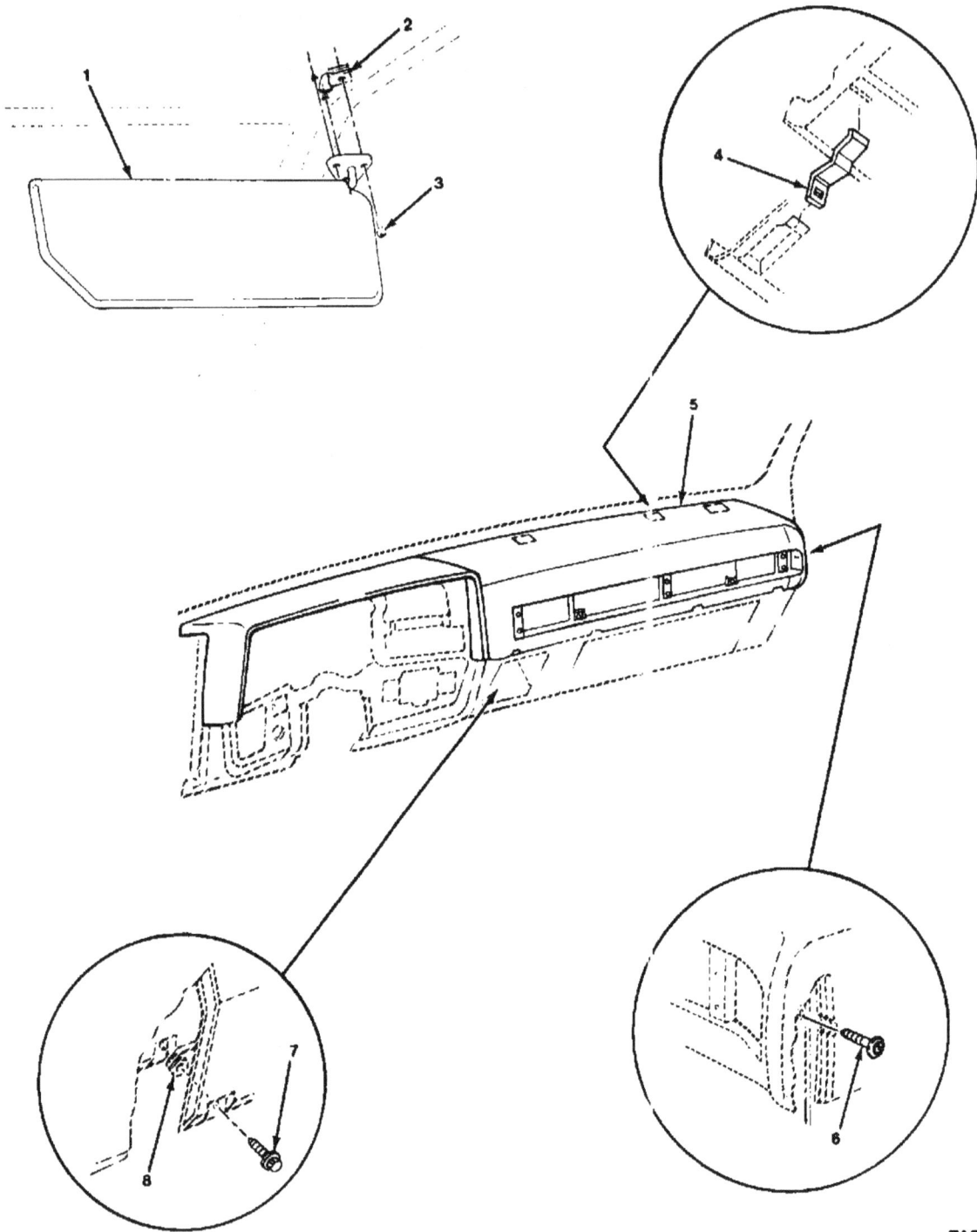

TA511001

FIGURE 159. SUNVISOR AND INSTRUMENT PANEL PAD.

(1) ITEM NO	(2) SMR CODE	(3) CAGEC	(4) PART NUMBER	(5) DESCRIPTION AND USABLE ON CODES (UOC)	(6) QTY
				GROUP 1806 UPHOLSTERY, SEATS, AND CARPETS	
				FIG. 159 SUNVISOR AND INSTRUMENT PANEL PAD	
1	PAOZZ	11862	14013753	VISOR,SUN,VEHICLE LEFT	1
1	PAOZZ	11862	14013754	VISOR,SUN,VEHICLE RIGHT	1
2	PAOZZ	96906	MS90724-34	NUT,SHEET SPRING	6
3	PAOZZ	11862	11501149	SCREW,TAPPING	6
4	PFOZZ	11862	14031893	CLIP,SPRING TENSION	6
5	PAOZZ	11862	15646949	PAD ASSEMBLY INSTRU	1
6	PAOZZ	11862	14044340	SCREW,ASSEMBLED WAS	1
7	PAOZZ	24617	11503395	SCREW,ASSEMBLED WAS	4
8	PAOZZ	11862	347347	GROMMET,NONMETALLIC	4

END OF FIGURE

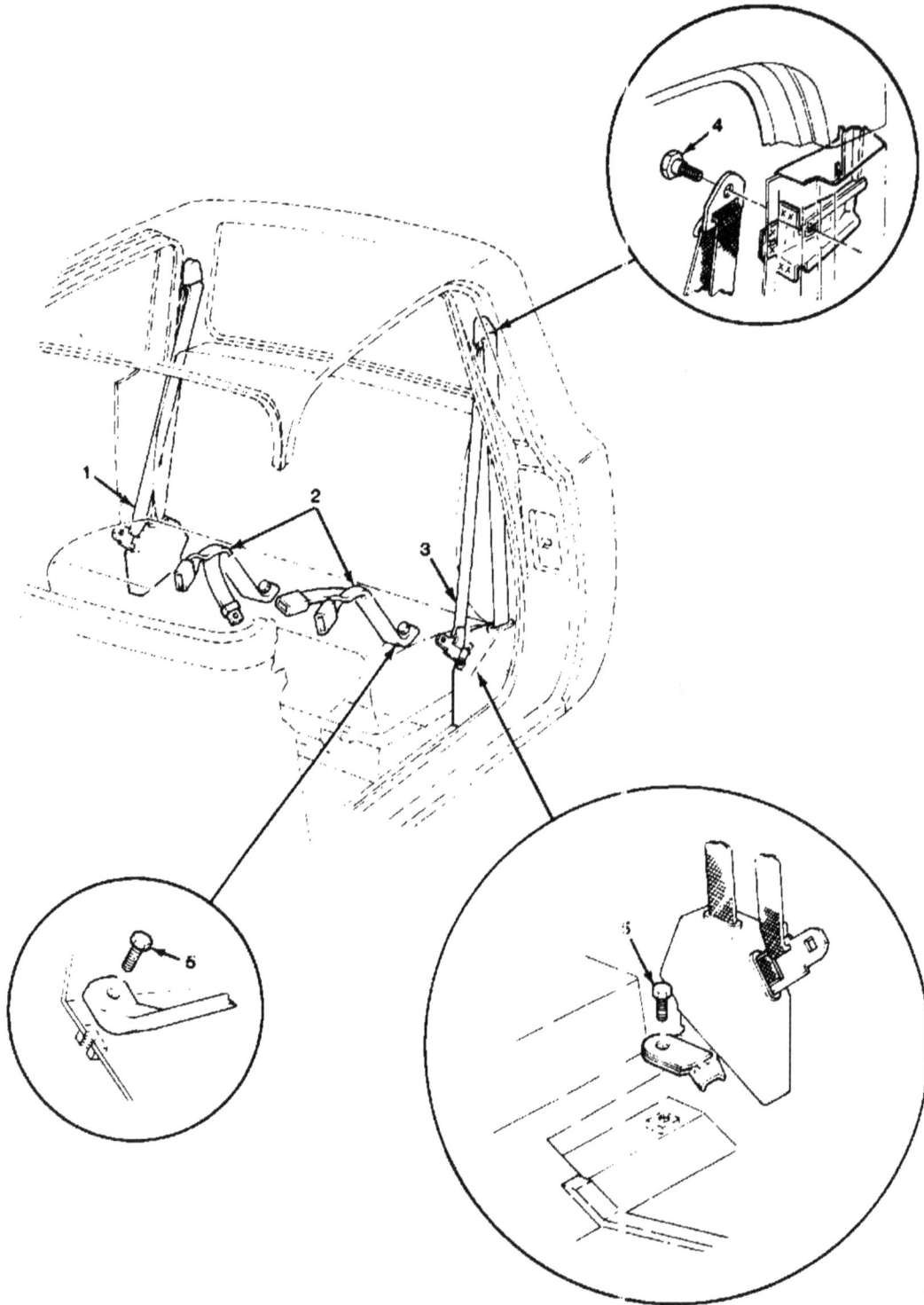

FIGURE 160. SEATBELTS AND MOUNTING PARTS (ALL E XCEPT M1009 AND M1010).

TA511002

(1) ITEM NO	(2) SMR CODE	(3) CAGEC	(4) PART NUMBER	(5) DESCRIPTION AND USABLE ON CODES (UOC)	(6) QTY
				GROUP 1806 UPHOLSTERY, SEATS,AND CARPETS	
				FIG. 160 SEATBELTS AND MOUNTING PARTS (ALL EXCEPT M1009 AND M1010)	
1	PAOZZ	11862	14079058	BELT,VEHICULAR SAFE RIGHT UOC:194,208,230,231,252	1
2	PAOZZ	11862	14079056	BELT,VEHICULAR SAFE UOC:194,208,230,231,252,254,256	1
3	PAOZZ	11862	14079057	BELT,VEHICULAR SAFE LEFT UOC:194,208,230,231,252,254,256	1
4	PAOZZ	11862	342221	BOLT,SHOULDER UOC:194,208,230,231,252,254,256	2
5	PAOZZ	11862	471083	BOLT,MACHINE UOC:194,208,230,231,252,254,256	4

END OF FIGURE

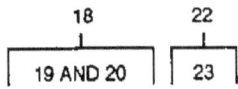

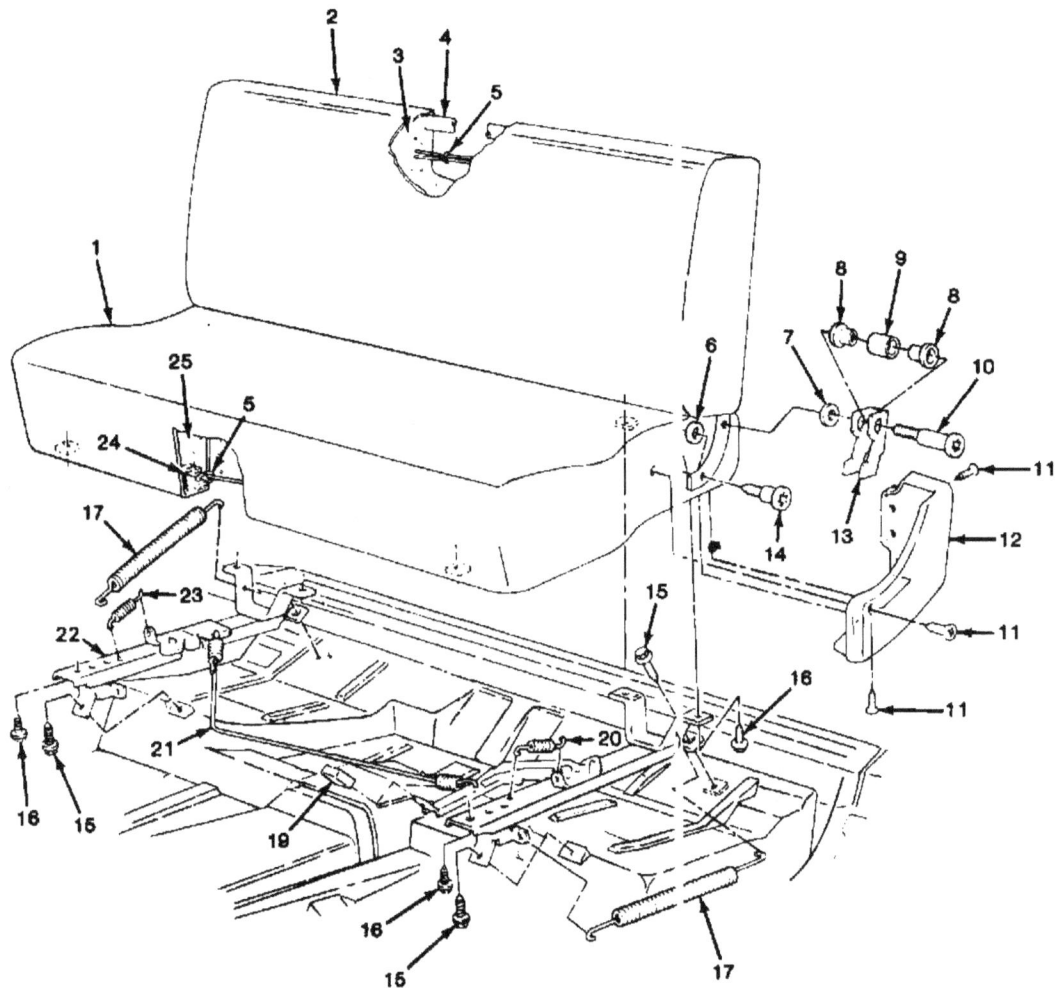

FIGURE 161. BENCH SEAT AND COMPONENTS (ALL EXCEPT M1009 AND M1010).

TA511003

GROUP 1806 UPHOLSTERY, SEATS, AND
CARPETS

FIG. 161 BENCH SEAT AND COMPONENTS
(ALL EXCEPT M1009 AND M1010)

ITEM NO	SMR CODE	CAGEC	PART NUMBER	DESCRIPTION AND USABLE ON CODES (UOC)	QTY
6	PAOZZ	11862	343978	SHIM UOC:194,208,230,231,252,254,256	2
7	PAOZZ	11862	3914674	WASHER,FLAT UOC:194,208,230,231,252,254,256	2
8	PAOZZ	11862	14066195	BUSHING,SLEEVE UOC:194,208,230,231,252,254,256	4
9	PAOZZ	11862	14066196	BUSHING,NONMETALLIC UOC:194,208,230,231,252,254,256	2
10	PAOZZ	11862	14021211	SCREW,SHOULDER UOC:194,208,230,231,252,254,256	2
11	PAOZZ	24617	9417325	SCREW,TAPPING UOC:194,208,230,231,252,254,256	10
12	PAOZZ	11862	14037059	COVER,TRIM SEAT LEFT UOC:194,208,230,231,252,254,256	1
12	PAOZZ	11862	14037060	COVER,TRIM SEAT RIGHT UOC:194,208,230,231,252,254,256	1
13	PAOZZ	11862	14021209	CATCH,SEAT FRAME LEFT UOC:194,208,230,231,252,254,256	1
13	PAOZZ	11862	14021210	CATCH,SEAT FRAME RIGHT UOC:194,208,230,231,252,254,256	1
14	PAOZZ	11862	14021213	SCREW,SHOULDER UOC:194,208,230,231,252,254,256	2
15	PAOZZ	11862	9438916	SCREW,TAPPING UOC:194,208,230,231,252,254,256	4
16	PAOZZ	11862	2014469	BOLT,ASSEMBLED WASH UOC:194,208,230,231,252,254,256	6
17	PAOZZ	11862	20056525	SPRING,HELICAL,EXTE UOC:194,208,230,231,252,254,256	2
18	PAOOO	11862	14022777	LEVER,MANUAL CONTRO LEFT UOC:194,208,230,231,252,254,256	1
19	PAOZZ	11862	465536	.KNOB UOC:194,208,230,231,252,254,256	1
20	PAOZZ	11862	329457	.SPRING,HELICAL,EXTE UOC:194,208,230,231,252,254,256	1
21	PAOZZ	11862	14022786	CLIP ASSEMBLY UOC:194,208,230,231,252,254,256	1
22	PAOOO	11862	14022778	LEVER,MANUAL CONTRO RIGHT UOC:194,208,230,231,252,254,256	1
23	PAOZZ	11862	329457	.SPRING,HELICAL,EXTE UOC:194,208,230,231,252,254,256	1

END OF FIGURE

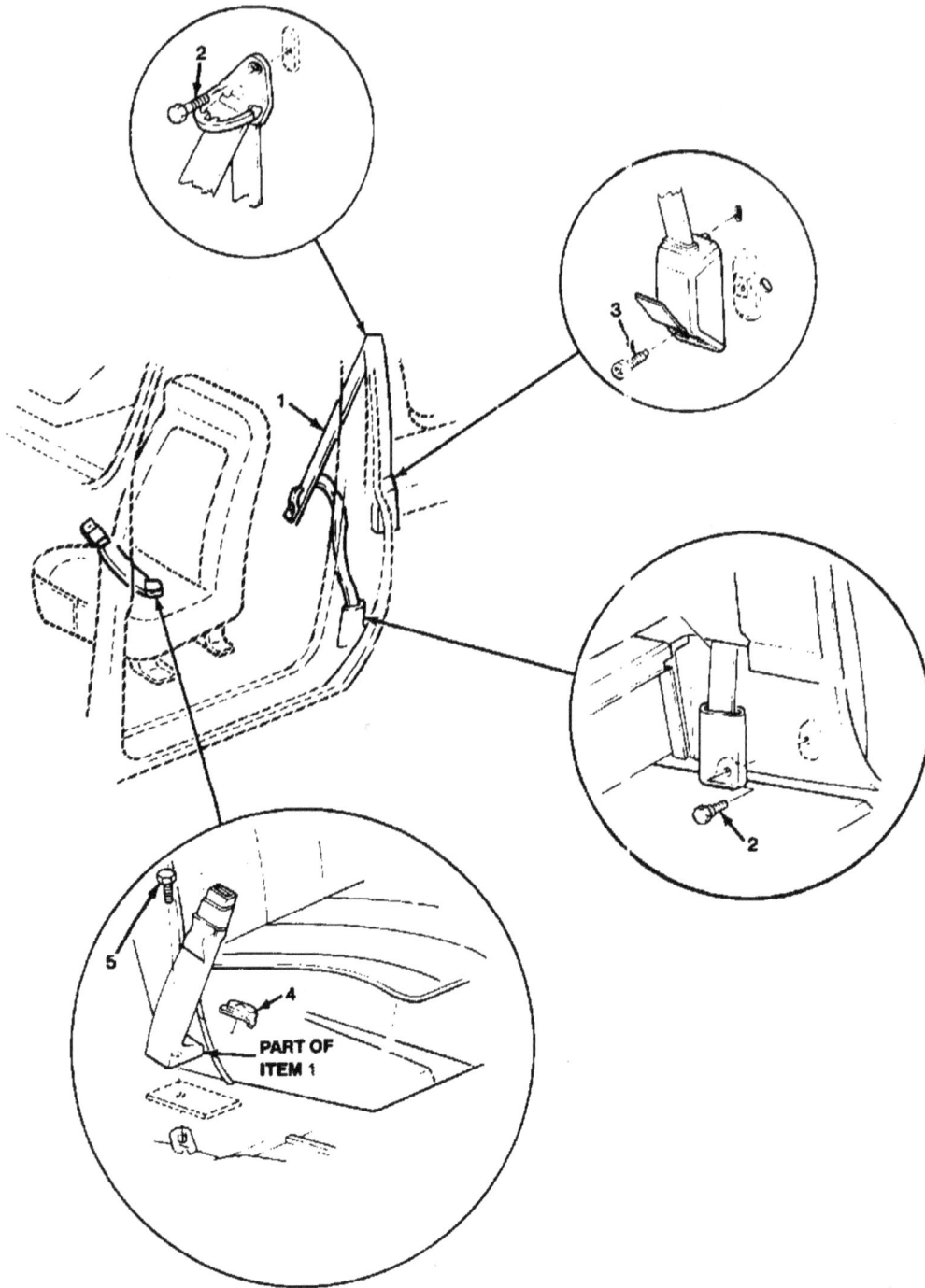

TA511004

FIGURE 162. DRIVER'S SEATBELT AND MOUNTING PARTS (M1009).

(1) ITEM NO	(2) SMR CODE	(3) CAGEC	(4) PART NUMBER	(5) DESCRIPTION AND USABLE ON CODES (UOC)	(6) QTY
				GROUP 1806 UPHOLSTERY, SEATS, AND CARPETS	
				FIG. 162 DRIVER'S SEATBELT AND MOUNTING PARTS (M1009)	
1	PAOZZ	11862	15591247	BELT,VEHICULAR SAFE UOC:209	1
2	PAOZZ	11862	342221	BOLT,SHOULDER UOC:209	2
3	PAOZZ	11862	3954730	SETSCREW UOC:209	1
4	PAOZZ	11862	1731168	PLUG,PROTECTIVE,DUS UOC:209	1
5	PAOZZ	11862	471083	BOLT,MACHINE UOC:209	1

END OF FIGURE

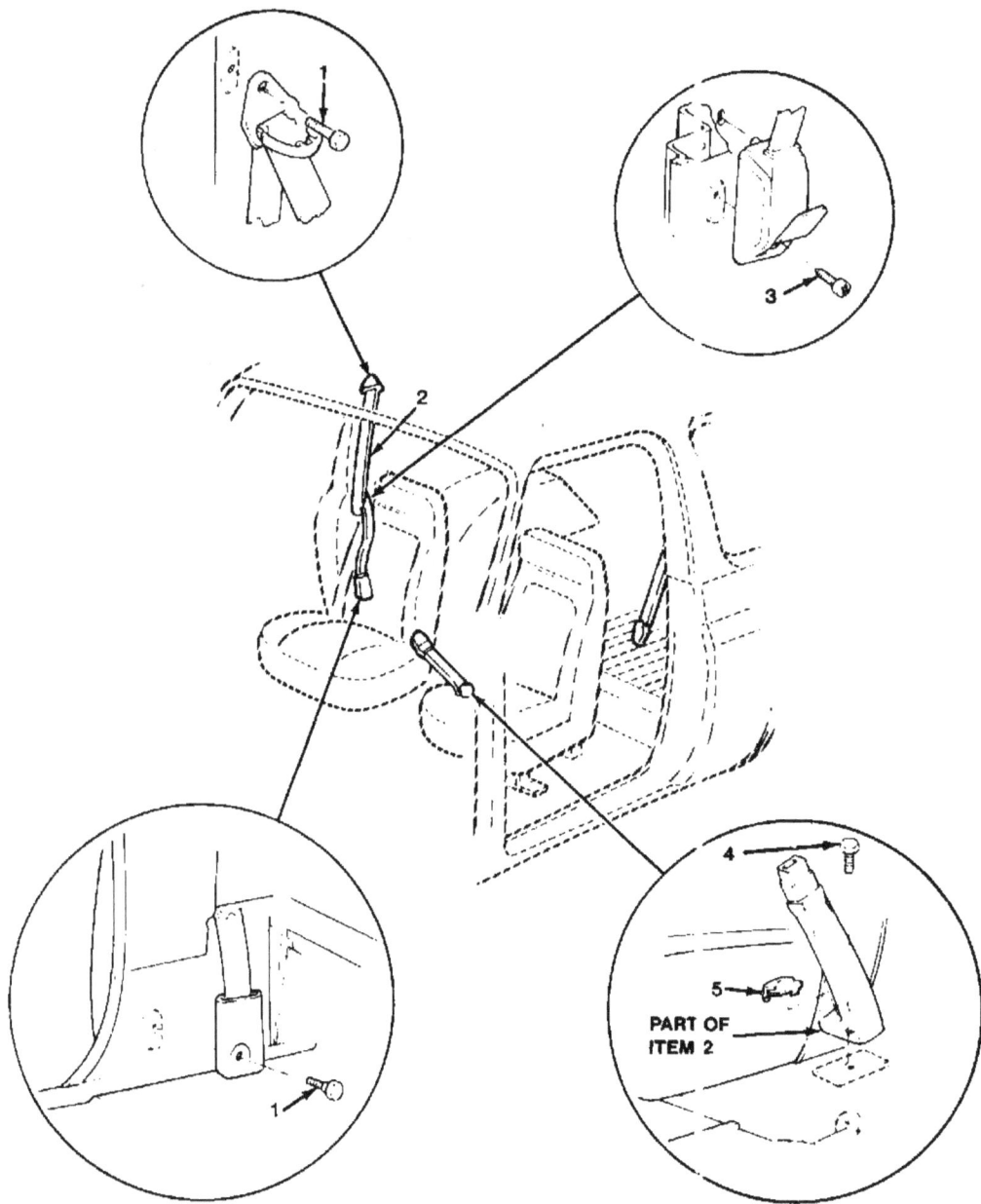

TA511005

FIGURE 163. PASSENGER'S SEATBELT AND MOUNTING PARTS (M1009).

(1)	(2)	(3)	(4)	(5)	(6)
ITEM NO	SMR CODE	CAGEC	PART NUMBER	DESCRIPTION AND USABLE ON CODES (UOC)	QTY

GROUP 1806 UPHOLSTERY, SEATS, AND CARPETS

FIG. 163 PASSENGER'S SEATBELT AND MOUNTING PARTS (M1009)

(1)	(2)	(3)	(4)	(5)	(6)
1	PAOZZ	11862	342221	BOLT,SHOULDER UOC:209	2
2	PAOZZ	11862	15591248	BELT,VEHICULAR SAFE UOC:209	1
3	PAOZZ	11862	3954730	SETSCREW UOC:209	1
4	PAOZZ	11862	471083	BOLT,MACHINE UOC:209	1
5	PAOZZ	11862	1731168	PLUG,PROTECTIVE,DUS UOC:209	1

END OF FIGURE

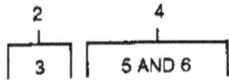

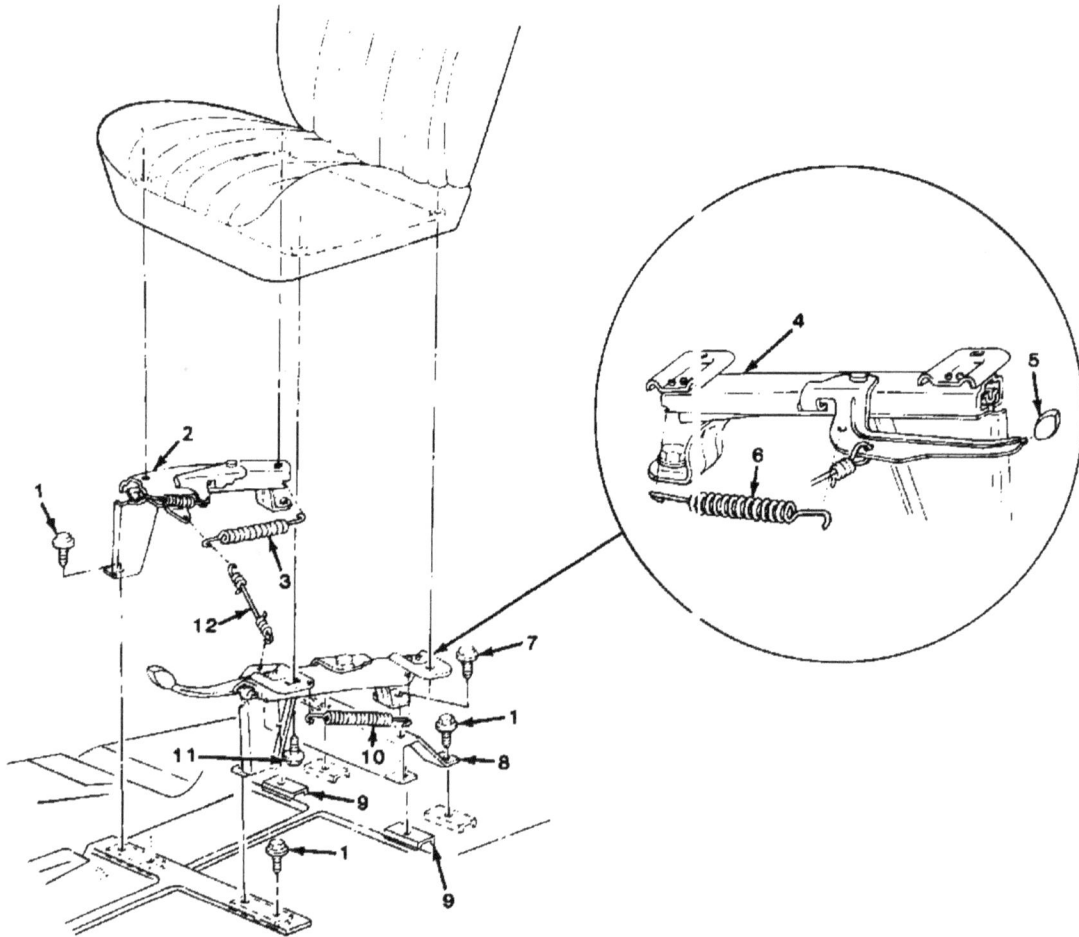

TA511006

FIGURE 164. DRIVER'S SEAT ADJUSTER ASSEMBLY (M1009).

(1) ITEM NO	(2) SMR CODE	(3) CAGEC	(4) PART NUMBER	(5) DESCRIPTION AND USABLE ON CODES (UOC)	(6) QTY
				GROUP 1806 UPHOLSTERY, SEATS, AND CARPETS	
				FIG. 164 DRIVER'S SEAT ADJUSTER ASSEMBLY (M1009)	
1	PAOZZ	11862	9438916	SCREW,TAPPING UOC:209	8
2	PAOOO	11862	14075823	ADJUSTER ASSEMBLY,S UOC:209	1
3	PAOZZ	11862	9711038	.SPRING,HELICAL,EXTE UOC:209	1
4	PAOOO	11862	14075824	ADJUSTER ASSEMBLY,S UOC:209	1
5	PAOZZ	11862	9834636	.HANDLE,MANUAL CONTR UOC:209	1
6	PAOZZ	11862	20351007	.SPRING,HELICAL,EXTE UOC:209	1
7	PAOZZ	11862	334195	BOLT,ASSEMBLED WASH UOC:209	2
8	PAOZZ	11862	14075821	BRACKET,SEAT ADJUST UOC:209	1
10	PAOZZ	11862	20056525	SPRING,HELICAL,EXTE UOC:209	1
11	PAOZZ	11862	14060613	BOLT,MACHINE UOC:209	4
12	PAOZZ	11862	20243999	WIRE,SEAT ADJUSTMEN UOC:209	1

END OF FIGURE

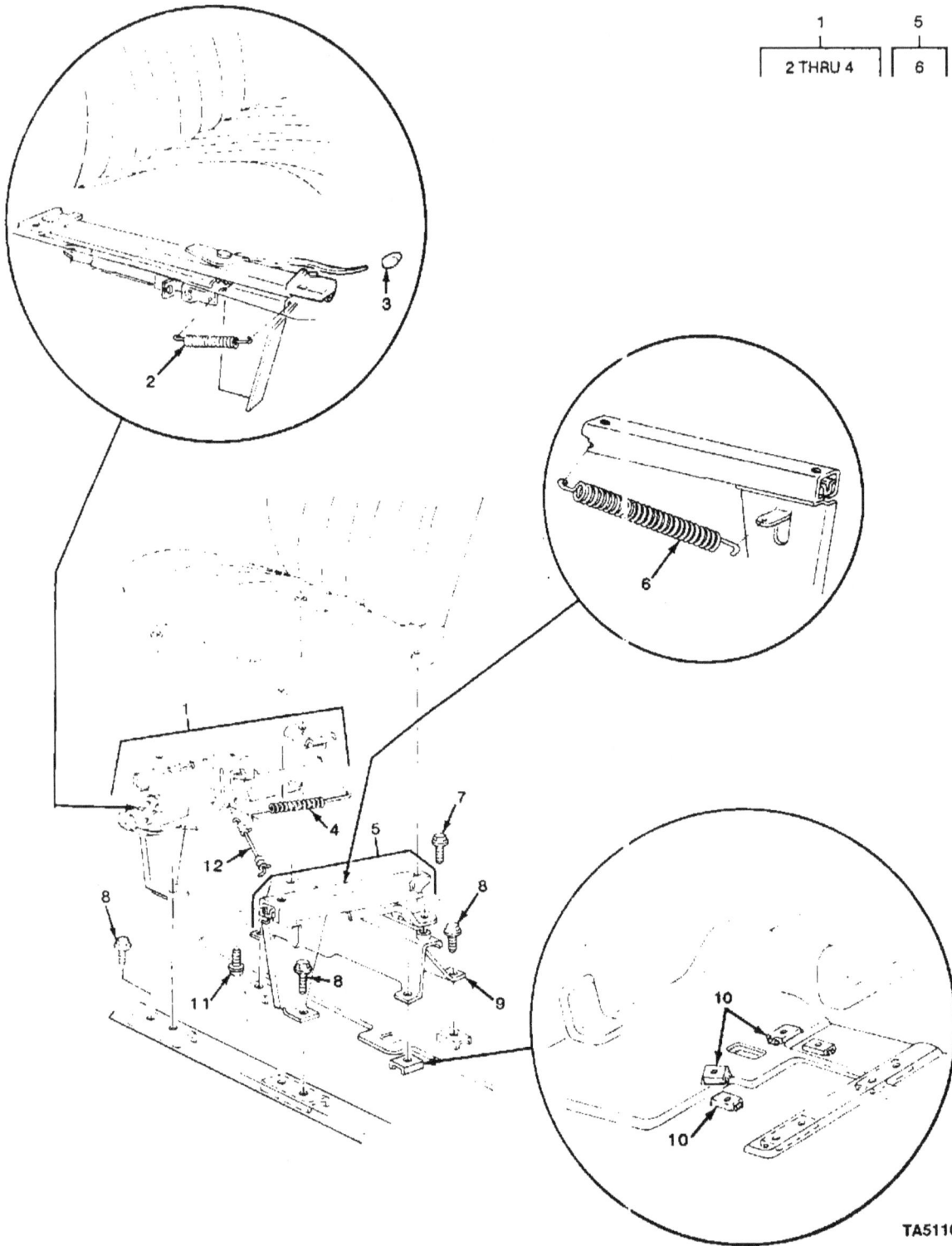

FIGURE 165. PASSENGER'S SEAT ADJUSTER ASSEMBLY (M1009).

TA511007

(1) ITEM NO	(2) SMR CODE	(3) CAGEC	(4) PART NUMBER	(5) DESCRIPTION AND USABLE ON CODES (UOC)	(6) QTY
				GROUP 1806 UPHOLSTERY, SEATS, AND CARPETS	
				FIG. 165 PASSENGER'S SEAT ADJUSTER ASSEMBLY (M1009)	
1	PAOOO	11862	15599975	ADJUSTER ASSEMBLY,S UOC:209	1
2	PAOZZ	11862	9645073	.SPRING,HELICAL,EXTE UOC:209	1
3	PAOZZ	11862	9834636	.HANDLE,MANUAL CONTR UOC:209	1
4	PAOZZ	11862	9826897	.SPRING,HELICAL,EXTE UOC:209	1
5	PAOOO	11862	15599976	.SUPPORT,SEAT ADJUST UOC:209	1
6	PAOZZ	11862	20056525	.SPRING,HELICAL,EXTE UOC:209	1
7	PAOZZ	11862	334195	BOLT,ASSEMBLED WASH UOC:209	2
8	PAOZZ	11862	9438916	SCREW,TAPPING UOC:209	8
9	PAOZZ	11862	14075822	BRACKET,ADJUSTMENT UOC:209	1
11	PAOZZ	11862	14060613	BOLT,MACHINE UOC:209	4
12	PAOZZ	11862	20243999	WIRE,SEAT ADJUSTMEN UOC:209	1

END OF FIGURE

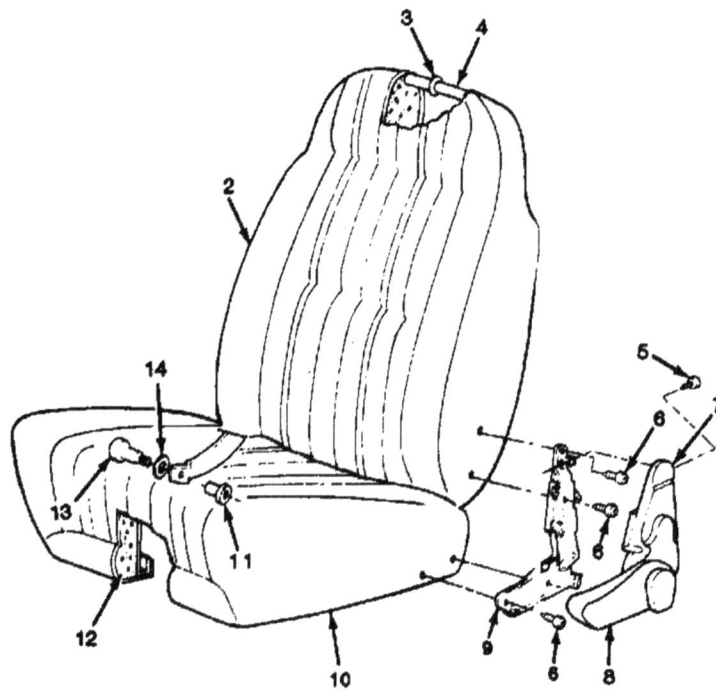

FIGURE 166. DRIVER'S SEAT ASSEMBLY AND COMPONENTS (M1009).

TA511008

(1) ITEM NO	(2) SMR CODE	(3) CAGEC	(4) PART NUMBER	(5) DESCRIPTION AND USABLE ON CODES (UOC)	(6) QTY
				GROUP 1806 UPHOLSTERY, SEATS, AND CARPETS	
				FIG. 166 DRIVER'S SEAT ASSEMBLY AND COMPONENTS (M1009)	
1	PAOFF	11862	14075820	SEAT,VEHICULAR UOC:209	1
5	PAOZZ	11862	11503537	.SCREW,ASSEMBLED WAS UOC:209	4
6	PAOZZ	11862	20025648	.SCREW,TAPPING UOC:209	4
7	PAOZZ	11862	20293843	.COVER,RECLINING HIN UOC:209	1
8	PAOZZ	11862	20289493	.COVER,SEAT LOCK UOC:209	1
9	PAOZZ	11862	16604537	.LOCK,SEAT,HINGE UOC:209	1
10	PAOZZ	11862	14075818	.COVER,SEAT,VEHICULA UOC:209	1
11	PAOZZ	11862	14059238	.BUSHING,SLEEVE UOC:209	2
13	PAOZZ	11862	14056723	.SCREW,SHOULDER UOC:209	2
14	PAOZZ	11862	1727059	.WASHER,FLAT UOC:209	2

END OF FIGURE

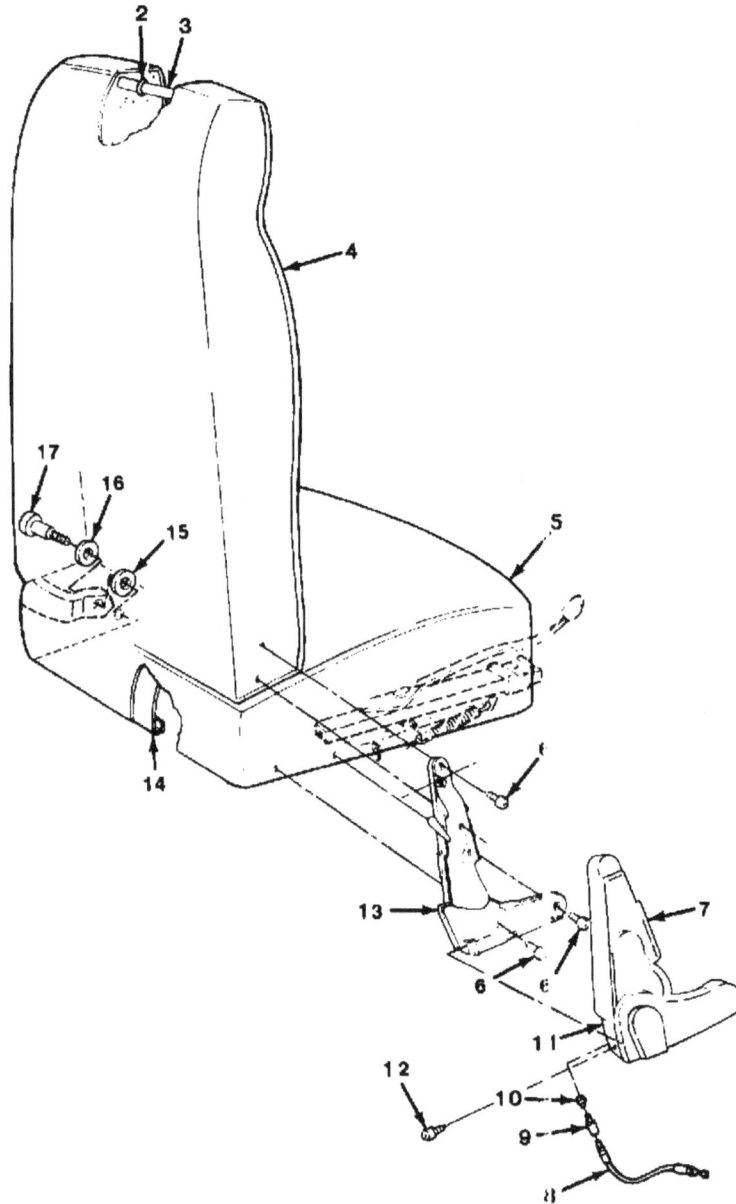

TA511009

FIGURE 167. PASSENGER'S SEAT ASSEMBLY AND COMPONENTS (M1009),

(1) ITEM NO	(2) SMR CODE	(3) CAGEC	(4) PART NUMBER	(5) DESCRIPTION AND USABLE ON CODES (UOC)	(6) QTY
				GROUP 1806 UPHOLSTERY, SEATS, AND CARPETS	
				FIG. 167 PASSENGER'S SEAT ASSEMBLY AND COMPONENTS (M1009)	
1	PAOFF	11862	14075819	SEAT,VEHICULAR UOC:209	1
6	PAOZZ	11862	20025648	.SCREW,TAPPING UOC:209	4
7	PAOZZ	11862	20293842	.COVER,SEAT BACK HIN UOC:209	1
8	PAOZZ	11862	20369919	.CABLE,PASSENGER SEA UOC:209	1
9	PAOZZ	11862	20369920	.LOCK,BELT RELEASE,V UOC:209	1
10	PAOZZ	11862	20573776	.GROMMET,NONMETALLIC UOC:209	1
11	PAOZZ	11862	15627452	.COVER,SEAT,LOCK UOC:209	1
12	PAOZZ	11862	11503537	.SCREW,ASSEMBLED WAS UOC:209	4
13	PAOZZ	11862	20410901	.LOCK,SEAT,BACK UOC:209	1
15	PAOZZ	11862	14059238	.BUSHING,SLEEVE UOC:209	2
16	PAOZZ	11862	1727059	.WASHER,FLAT UOC:209	2
17	PAOZZ	11862	14056723	.SCREW,SHOULDER UOC:209	2

END OF FIGURE

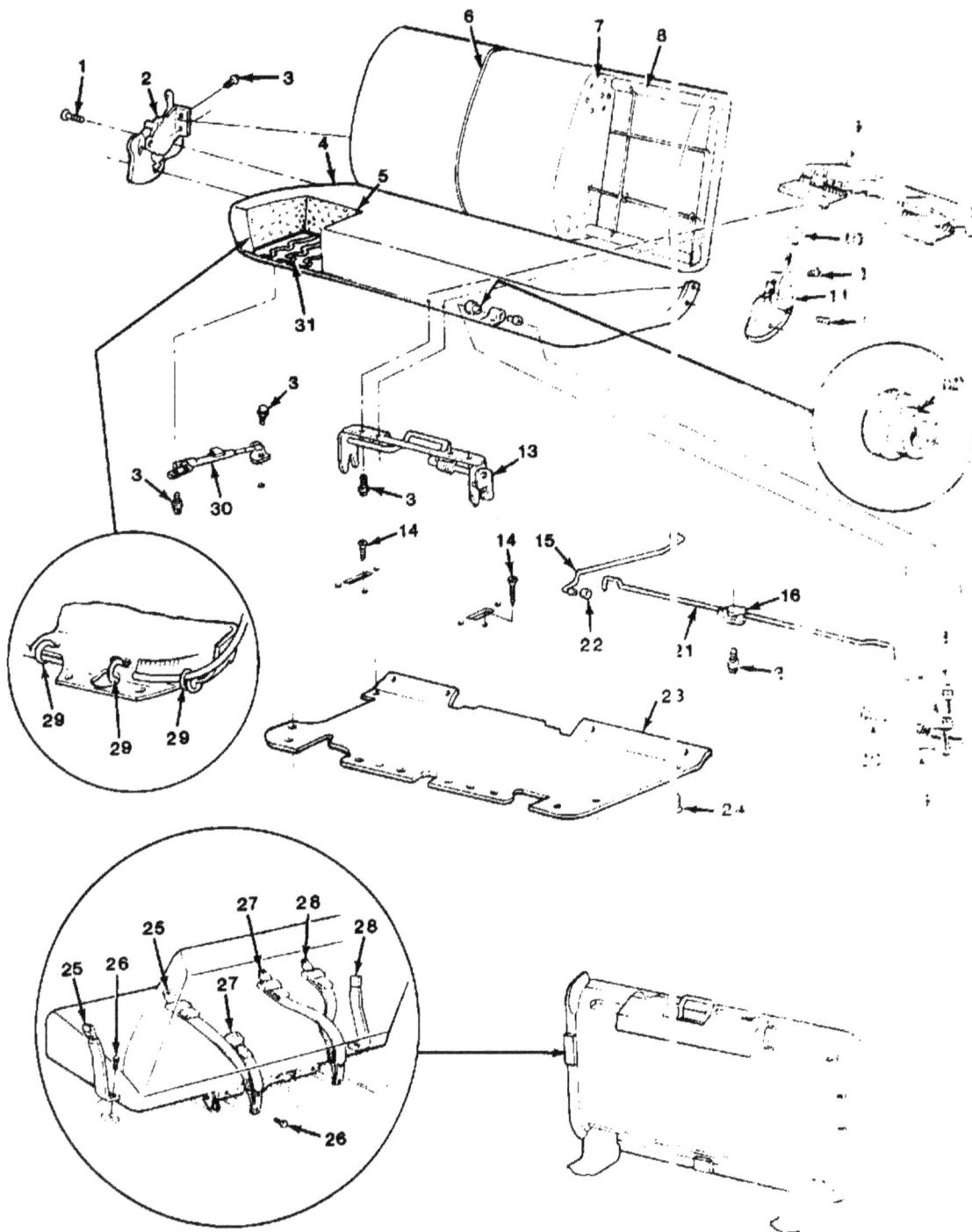

FIGURE 168. REAR BENCH SEAT ASSEMBLY AND COMPONENTS (M1009)

GROUP 1806 UPHOLSTERY, SEATS, AND
CARPETS

FIG. 168 REAR BENCH SEAT ASSEMBLY
AND COMPONENTS (M1009)

ITEM NO	SMR CODE	CAGEC	PART NUMBER	DESCRIPTION AND USABLE ON CODES (UOC)	QTY
1	PAOZZ	11862	14013724	SCREW,TAPPING UOC:209	4
2	PAOZZ	11862	15569010	HINGE AND LATCH,SEA RIGHT UOC:209	1
3	PAOZZ	11862	2014469	BOLT,ASSEMBLED WASH UOC:209	10
9	PAOZZ	11862	14014293	COVER,LATCH SEAT UOC:209	1
10	PAOZZ	11862	473187	KNOB UOC:209	1
11	PAOZZ	11862	15569009	HINGE,SEAT,VEHICULA LEFT UOC:209	1
12	PAOZZ	11862	335524	BUSHING,SLEEVE UOC:209	4
13	PAOZZ	11862	470984	LATCH AND GUIDE ASS UOC:209	1
14	PAOZZ	24617	9419327	SCREW UOC:209	2
15	PAOZZ	11862	473197	ROD ASSEMBLY,SEAT L UOC:209	1
16	PAOZZ	11862	14027799	CLAMP,RIM CLENCHING UOC:209	1
17	PAOZZ	96906	MS35340-48	WASHER,LOCK UOC:209	2
18	PAOZZ	24617	9432194	SCREW,CAP,HEXAGON H UOC:209	2
19	PAOZZ	11862	471018	HINGE,LOWER FRONT,R UOC:209	2
20	PAOZZ	11862	470974	PIN,STRAIGHT,HEADED UOC:209	2
21	PAOZZ	11862	471010	LEVER,MANUAL CONTRO UOC:209	1
22	PAOZZ	96906	MS16633-1015	RING,RETAINING UOC:209	2
23	PAOZZ	11862	14074479	PANEL,SEAT CUSHION UOC:209	1
24	PAOZZ	11862	14069636	SCREW,ASSEMBLED WAS UOC:209	16
25	PAOZZ	11862	14075375	BELT,VEHICULAR SAFE LEFT UOC:209	1
26	PAOZZ	11862	3954730	SETSCREW UOC:209	4
27	PAOZZ	11862	14075374	BELT,VEHICULAR SAFE CENTER UOC:209	1
28	PAOZZ	11862	14075376	BELT,VEHICULAR SAFE RIGHT UOC:209	1

ITEM NO	SMR CODE	CAGEC	PART NUMBER	DESCRIPTION AND USABLE ON CODES (UOC)	QTY
30	PAOZZ	11862	471079	STRUT,STOWACE,REAR UOC:209	1

END OF FIGURE

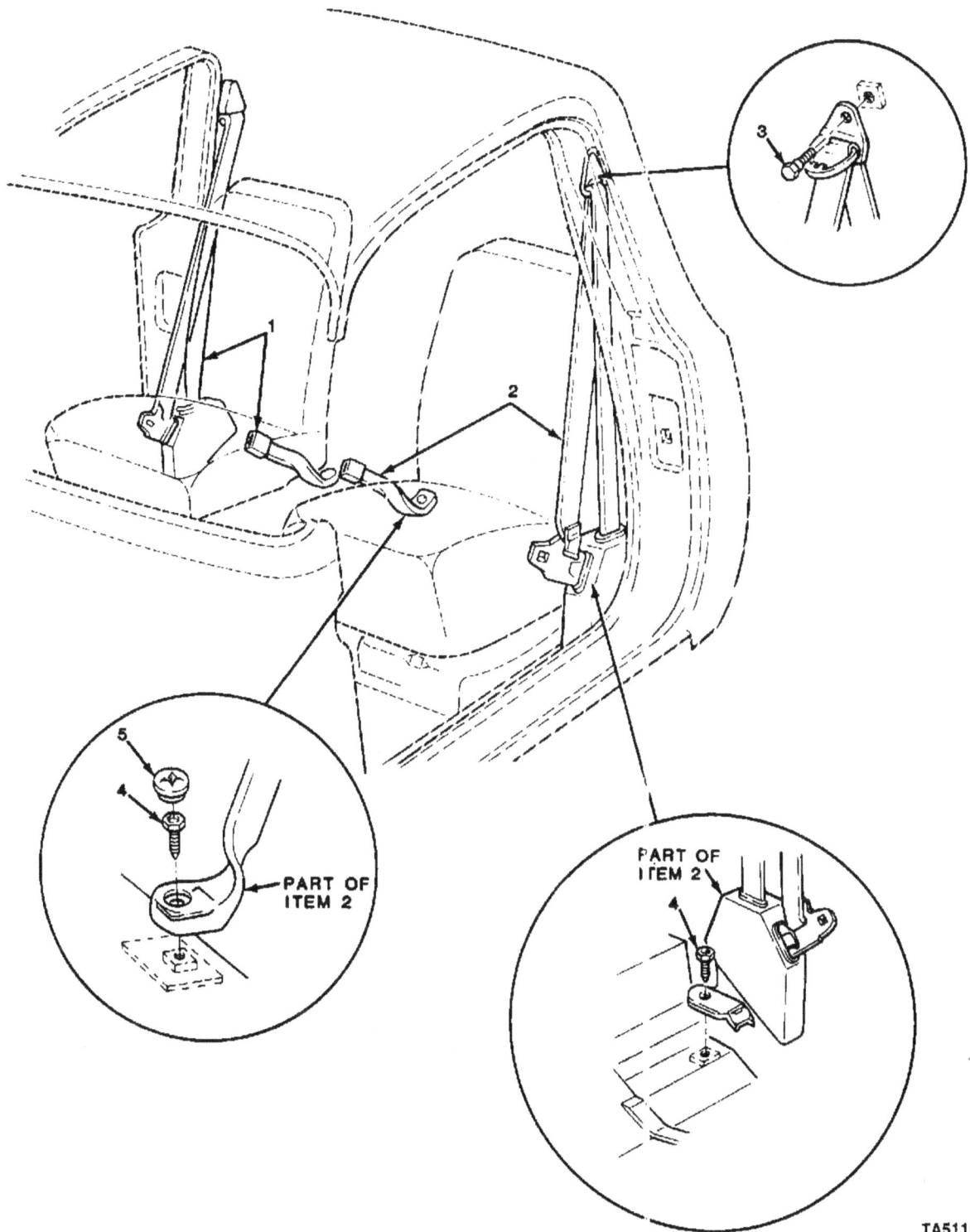

TA511011

FIGURE 169. SEATBELTS AND MOUNTING PARTS (M1010).

(1) ITEM NO	(2) SMR CODE	(3) CAGEC	(4) PART NUMBER	(5) DESCRIPTION AND USABLE ON CODES (UOC)	(6) QTY
				GROUP 1806 UPHOLSTERY, SEATS, AND CARPETS	
				FIG. 169 SEATBELTS AND MOUNTING PARTS (M1010)	
1	PAOZZ	11862	15577694	BELT,VEHICULAR SAFE RIGHT UOC:210	1
2	PAOZZ	11862	14075379	BELT,VEHICULAR SAFE LEFT UOC:210	1
3	PAOZZ	11862	342221	BOLT,SHOULDER UOC:210	2
4	PAOZZ	11862	471083	BOLT,MACHINE UOC:210	4
5	PAOZZ	11862	1731168	PLUG,PROTECTIVE,DUS UOC:210	2

END OF FIGURE

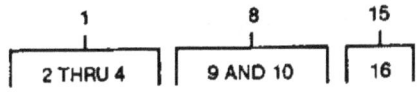

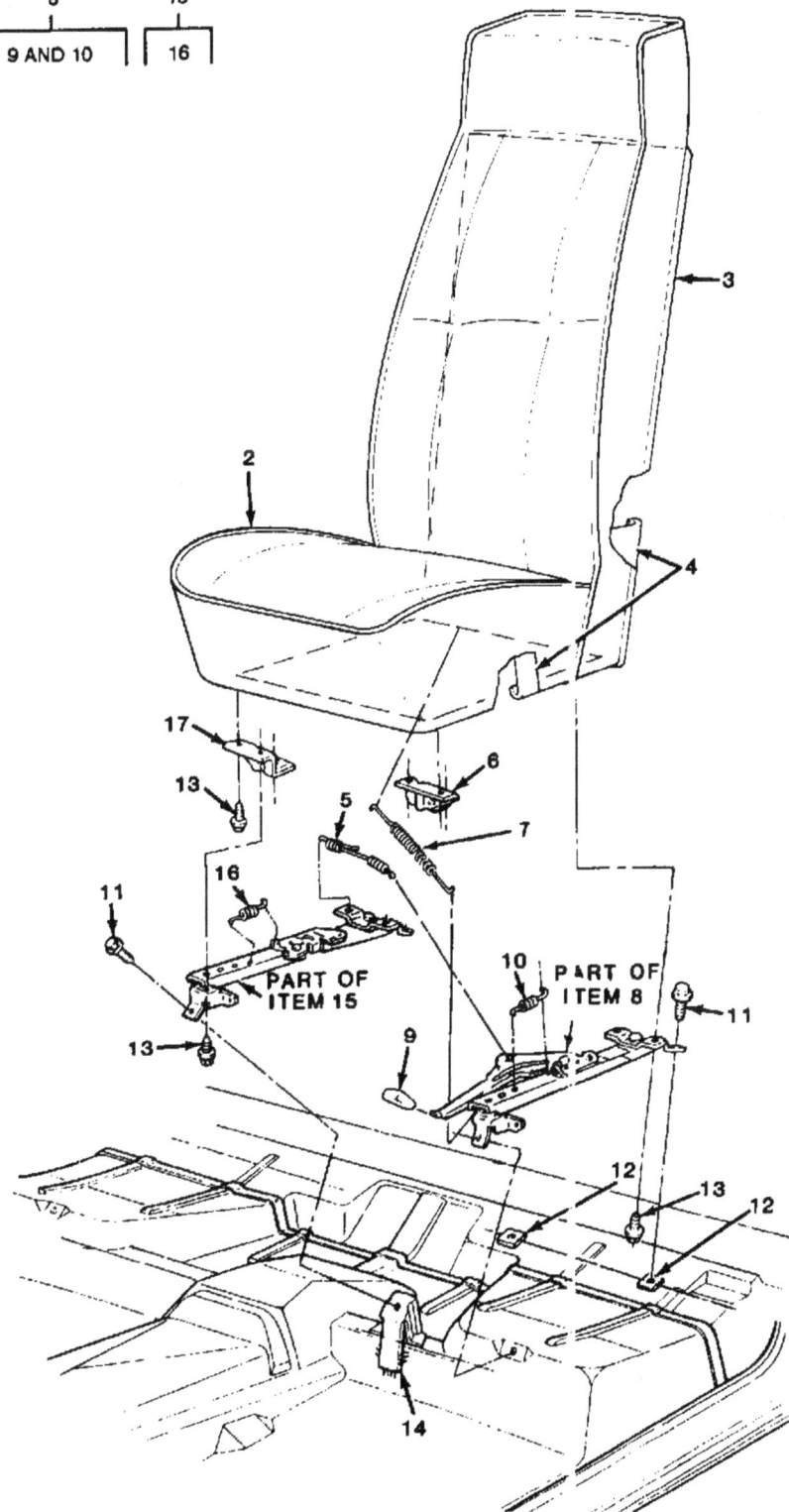

FIGURE 170. SEAT ASSEMBLY DRIVER'S SEAT, ADJUSTER ASSEMBLY,
AND RELATED PARTS (M1010).

TA511012

(1) ITEM NO	(2) SMR CODE	(3) CAGEC	(4) PART NUMBER	(5) DESCRIPTION AND USABLE ON CODES (UOC)	(6) QTY
				GROUP 1806 UPHOLSTERY, SEATS, AND CARPETS	
				FIG. 170 SEAT ASSEMBLY, DRIVER'S SEAT, ADJUSTER ASSEMBLY, AND RELATED PARTS (M1010)	
1	PAOFF	11862	14075815	CUSHION,SEAT,VEHICU UOC:210	2
5	PAOZZ	11862	14025679	WIRE ASSEMBLY,LOCK UOC:210	1
6	PAOZZ	11862	14025673	BRACKET,DOUBLE ANGL UOC:210	1
7	PAOZZ	11862	20056525	SPRING,HELICAL,EXTE UOC:210	1
8	PAOOO	11862	14023889	LEVER,MANUAL CONTRO LEFT UOC:210	1
9	PAOZZ	11862	465536	.KNOB UOC:210	1
10	PAOZZ	11862	329457	.SPRING,HELICAL,EXTE UOC:210	1
11	PAOZZ	11862	9438916	SCREW,TAPPING UOC:210	4
13	PAOZZ	11862	2014469	BOLT,ASSEMBLED WASH UOC:210	10
15	PAOOO	11862	14023890	LEVER,MANUAL CONTRO RIGHT UOC:210	1
16	PAOZZ	11862	329457	.SPRING,HELICAL,EXTE UOC:210	1
17	PAOZZ	11862	14025674	BRACKET,DOUBLE ANGL UOC:210	1

END OF FIGURE

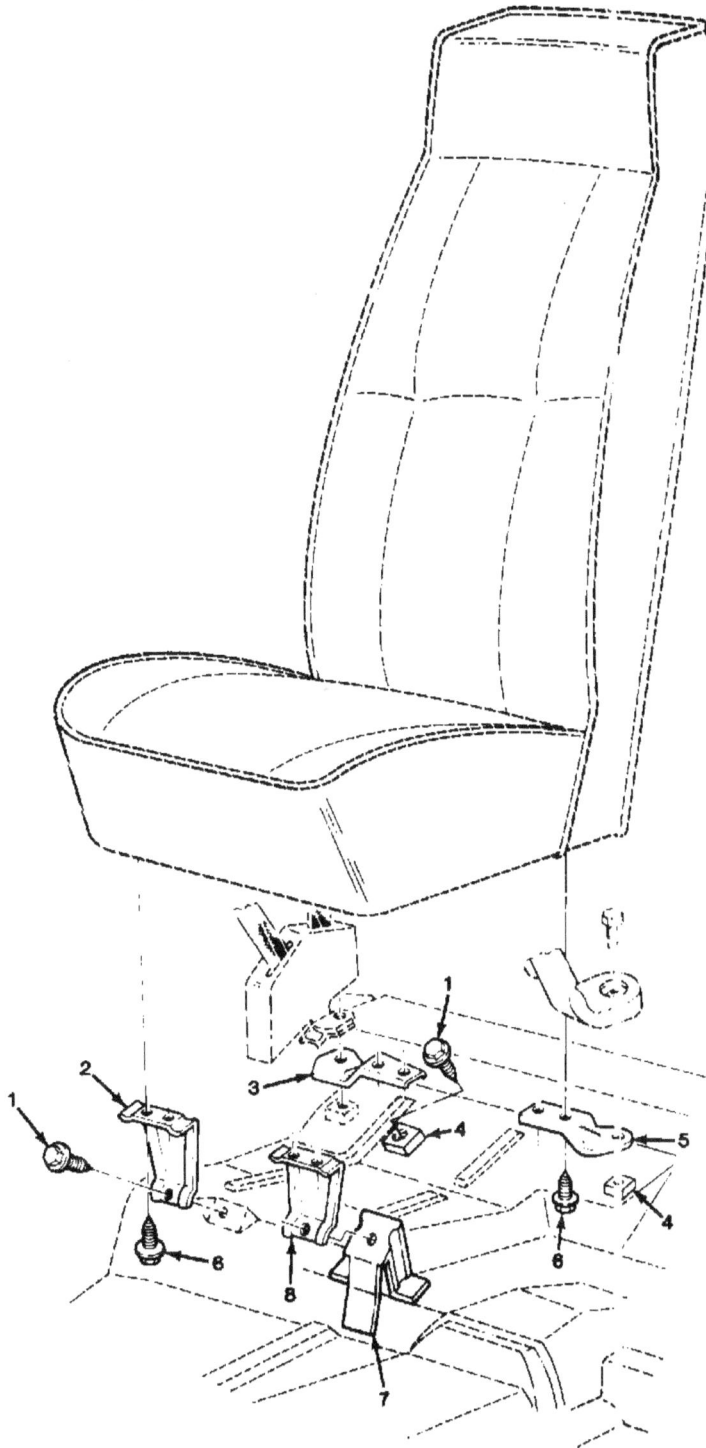

TA511013

FIGURE 171. SEAT MOUNTING PARTS (M1010).

(1) ITEM NO	(2) SMR CODE	(3) CAGEC	(4) PART NUMBER	(5) DESCRIPTION AND USABLE ON CODES (UOC)	(6) QTY
				GROUP 1806 UPHOLSTERY, SEATS, AND CARPETS	
				FIG. 171 SEAT MOUNTING PARTS (M1010)	
1	PAOZZ	11862	9438916	SCREW,TAPPING UOC:210	3
2	PAOZZ	11862	14027346	SUPPORT,SEAT FRAME RIGHT UOC:210	1
3	PAOZZ	11862	14027348	SUPPORT,SEAT,VEHICU RIGHT UOC:210	1
5	PAOZZ	11862	14027347	SUPPORT,SEAT,VEHICU LEFT UOC:210	1
6	PAOZZ	11862	2014469	BOLT,ASSEMBLED WASH UOC:210	8
8	PAOZZ	11862	14027345	SUPPORT,SEAT,VEHICU LEFT UOC:210	1

END OF FIGURE

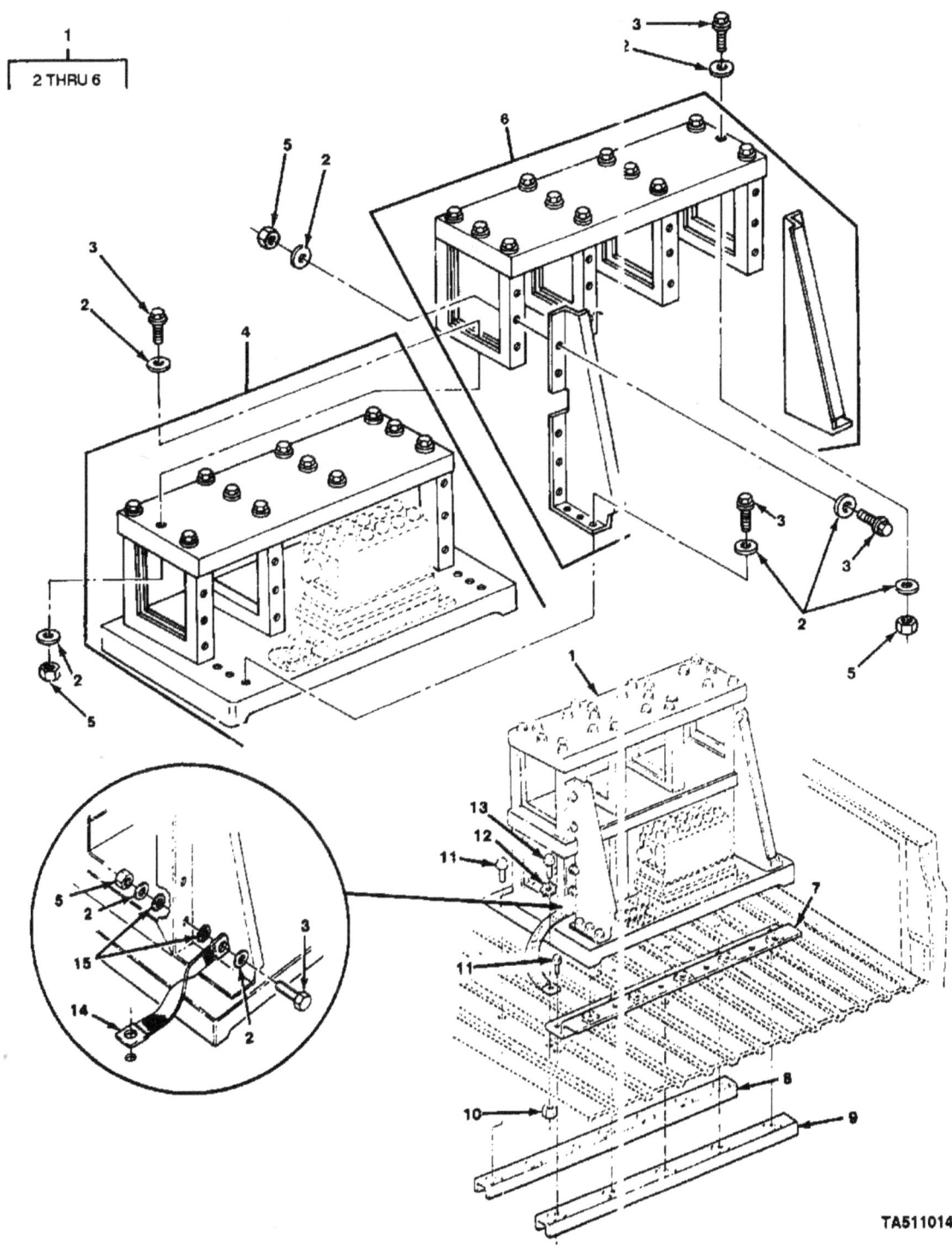

FIGURE 172. COMMUNICATIONS RACK ASSEMBLY AND RELATED PARTS (M1028A1).

TA511014

(1) ITEM NO	(2) SMR CODE	(3) CAGEC	(4) PART NUMBER	(5) DESCRIPTION AND USABLE ON CODES (UOC)	(6) QTY
				GROUP 1808 STOWAGE RACKS, BOXES, STRAPS, CARRYING CASES, CABLE REELS, HOSE REELS, ETC.	
				FIG. 172 COMMUNICATIONS RACK ASSEMBLY AND RELATED PARTS (M1028A1)	
1	PAOOO	80063	SC-D-866091	RACK,ELECTRICAL EQU UOC:208	1
2	PAOZZ	96906	MS35338-139	.WASHER,LOCK UOC:208	110
3	PAOZZ	96906	MS90725-6	.SCREW,CAP,HEXAGON H UOC:208	61
4	PAOZZ	80063	DL-SC-B-691368	.RACK ASSEMBLY UOC:194,208	1
5	PAOZZ	96906	MS51971-1	.NUT,PLAIN,HEXAGON UOC:208	49
6	PAOZZ	80063	SC-D-691375	.RACK,ELECTRICAL EQU UOC:194,208	1
7	PAOZZ	80063	SC-C-691545	BRACKET,DOUBLE ANGL UOC:208	1
8	PAOZZ	11862	15599959	STRAP,RETAINING UOC:208	1
9	PAOZZ	11862	15599958	STRAP,RETAINING UOC:208	1
10	PAOZZ	24617	271172	NUT,SELF-LOCKING,AS UOC:208	1
11	PAOZZ	11862	9440334	BOLT,ASSEMBLED WASH UOC:208	12
12	PAOZZ	96906	MS35335-33	WASHER,LOCK UOC:208	1
13	PAOZZ	96906	MS90728-6	SCREW,CAP,HEXAGON H UOC:208	1
14	XDOZZ	80063	SC-B-75180-IV	LEAD,ELECTRICAL UOC:208	1
15	PAOZZ	96906	MS45904-68	WASHER,LOCK UOC:208	2

END OF FIGURE

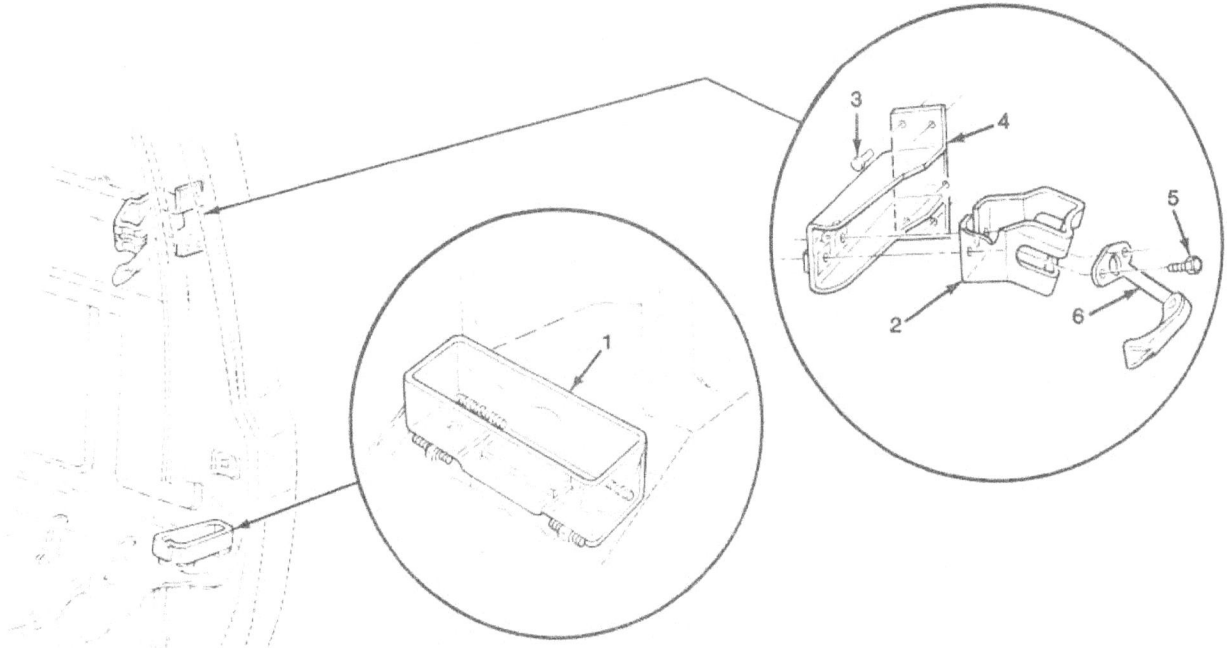

ALL EXCEPT MI010 AND MI009

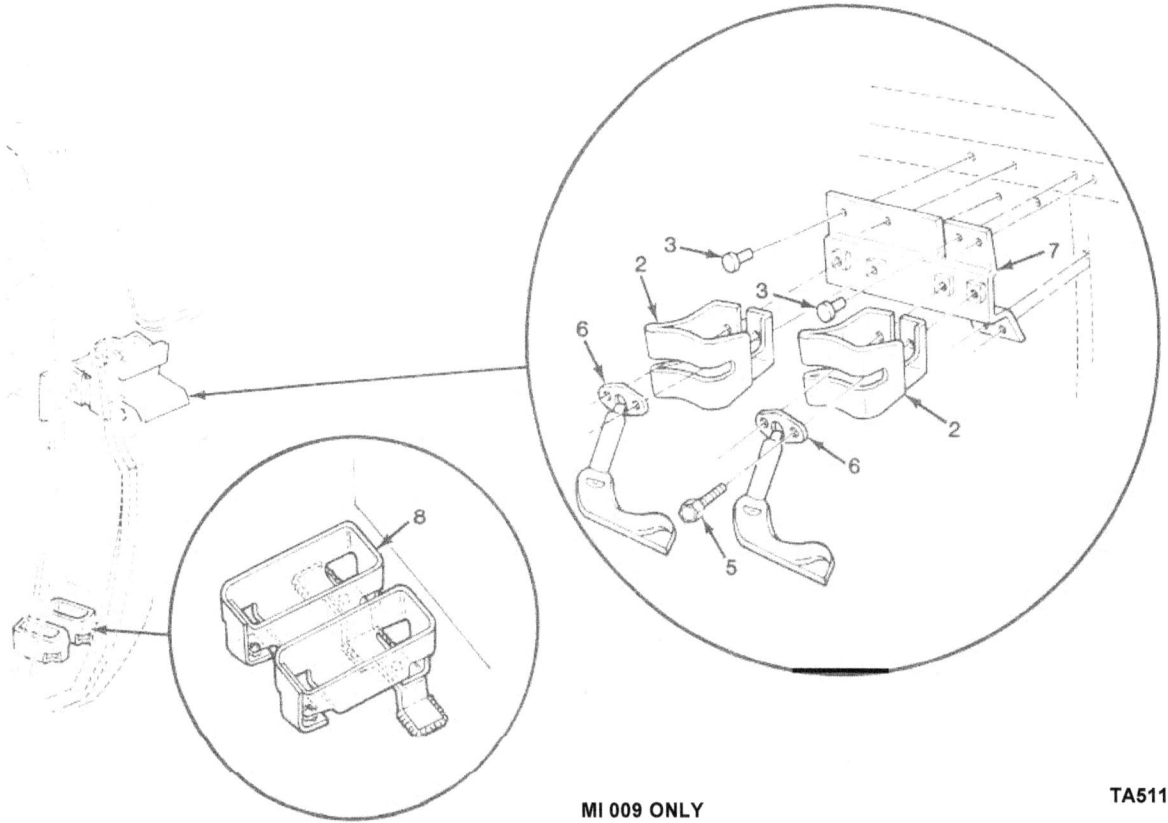

MI 009 ONLY

TA511015

(1) ITEM NO	(2) SMR CODE	(3) CAGEC	(4) PART NUMBER	(5) DESCRIPTION AND USABLE ON CODES (UOC)	(6) QTY
				GROUP 1808 STOWAGE RACKS, BOXES, STRAPS, CARRYING CASES, CABLE REELS, HOSE REELS, ETC.	
				FIG. 173 WEAPONS MOUNT (ALL EXCEPT M1010)	
1	PAOZZ	11862	14074435	SUPPORT,WEAPON MOUN UOC:194,208,230,231,252,254,256	2
2	PAOZZ	11862	14074437	BRACKET,MOUNTING,CA UOC:194,208,209,230,231,252,254,256	2
3	PAOZZ	11862	2477054	RIVET,BLIND UOC:194,208,209,230,231,252,254,256	8
4	PAOZZ	11862	14074441	BRACKET,WEAPON MOUN LEFT UOC:194,208,230,231,252,254,256	1
4	PAOZZ	11862	14074442	BRACKET,WEAPON MOUN RIGHT UOC:194,208,230,231,252,254,256	1
5	PAOZZ	11862	9440033	BOLT,MACHINE UOC:194,208,209,230,231,252,254,256	4
6	PAOZZ	11862	14074438	LATCH ASSEMBLY,WEAP UOC:194,208,209,230,231,252,254,256	2
7	PAOZZ	11862	15599965	BRACKET,MOUNTING LEFT UOC:209	1
8	PAOZZ	11862	15599271	SUPPORT,WEAPON UOC:209	1

END OF FIGURE

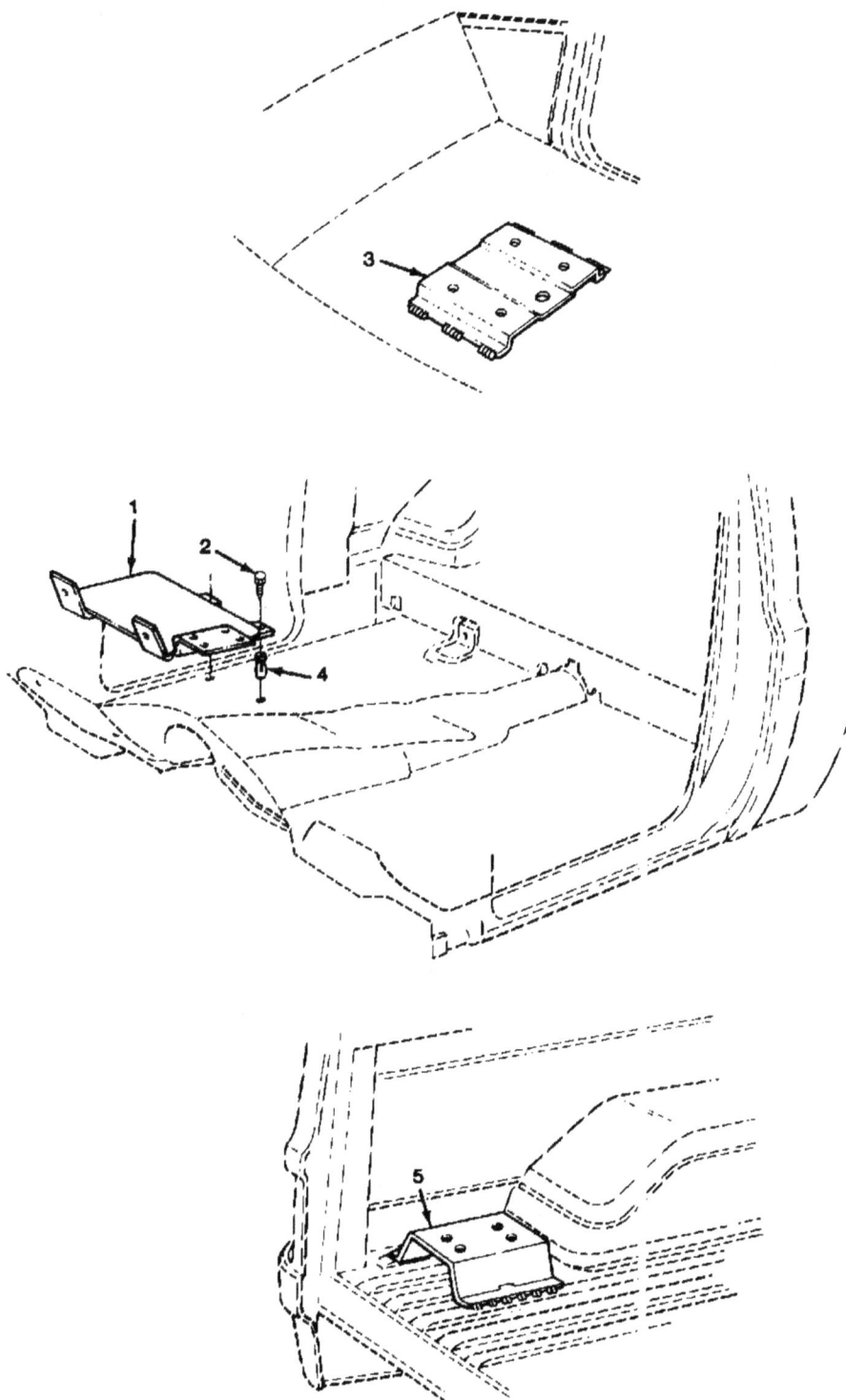

TA511016

FIGURE 174. BRACKETS AND MOUNTING PARTS.

(1) ITEM NO	(2) SMR CODE	(3) CAGEC	(4) PART NUMBER	(5) DESCRIPTION AND USABLE ON CODES (UOC)	(6) QTY
				GROUP 1808 STOWAGE RACKS, BOXES, STRAPS, CARRYING CASES, CABLE REELS, HOSE REELS, ETC.	
				FIG. 174 BRACKETS AND MOUNTING PARTS	
1	PAOZZ	11862	14074439	BRACKET ASSEMBLY,CH	1
2	PAOZZ	24617	9421432	SCREW,MACHINE	4
4	PAOZZ	11862	14005953	SHIELD,EXPANSION	4

END OF FIGURE

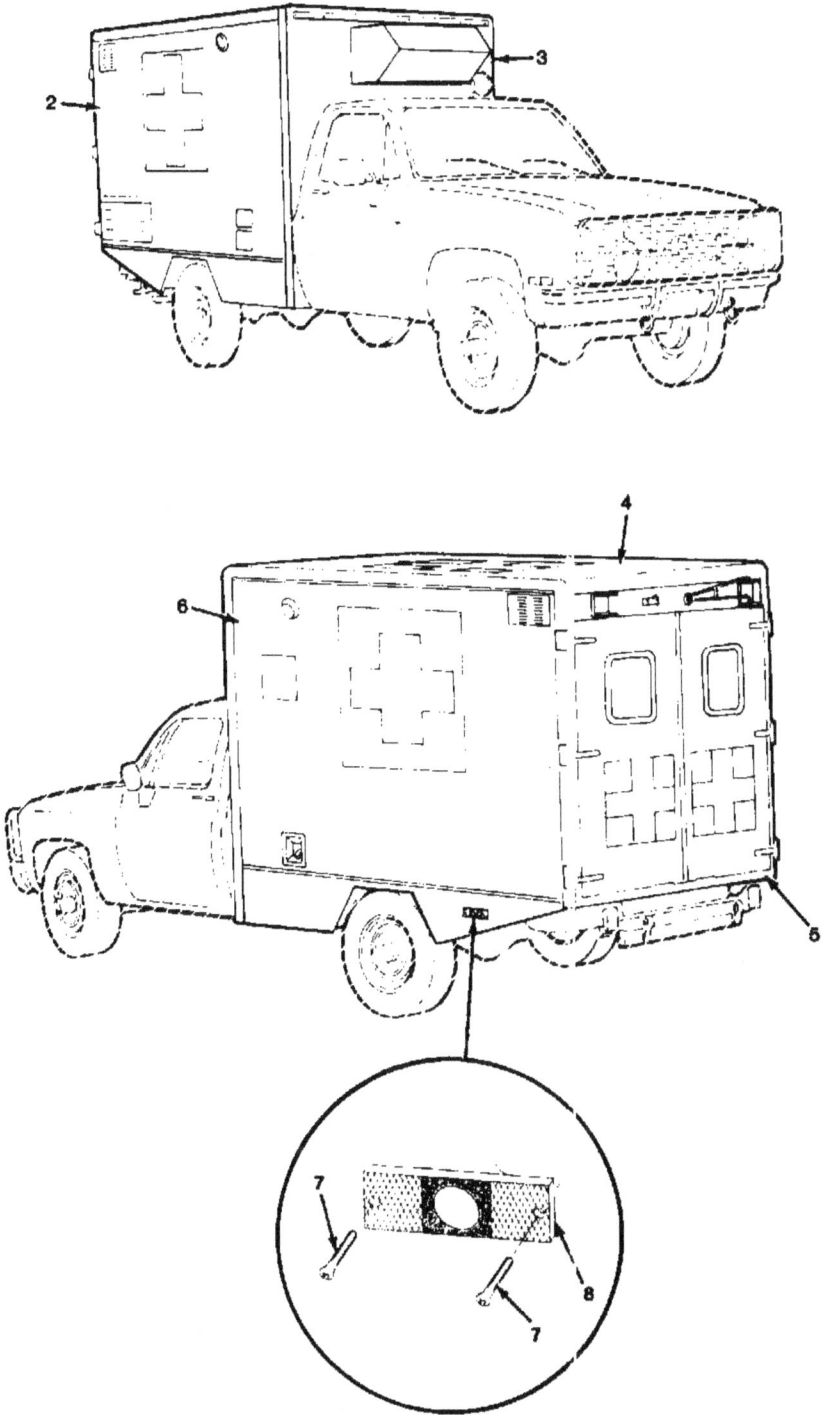

FIGURE 175. BODY ASSEMBLY (M1010).

TA511017

(1) ITEM NO	(2) SMR CODE	(3) CAGEC	(4) PART NUMBER	(5) DESCRIPTION AND USABLE ON CODES (UOC)	(6) QTY
				GROUP 1812 SPECIAL PURPOSE BODIES	
				FIG. 175 BODY ASSEMBLY (M1010)	
7	PAOZZ	25022	07-1016	.SCREW,TAPPING THRD UOC:210	4
8	PAOZZ	13548	99012R	.LENS,LIGHT UOC:210	2
				END OF FIGURE	

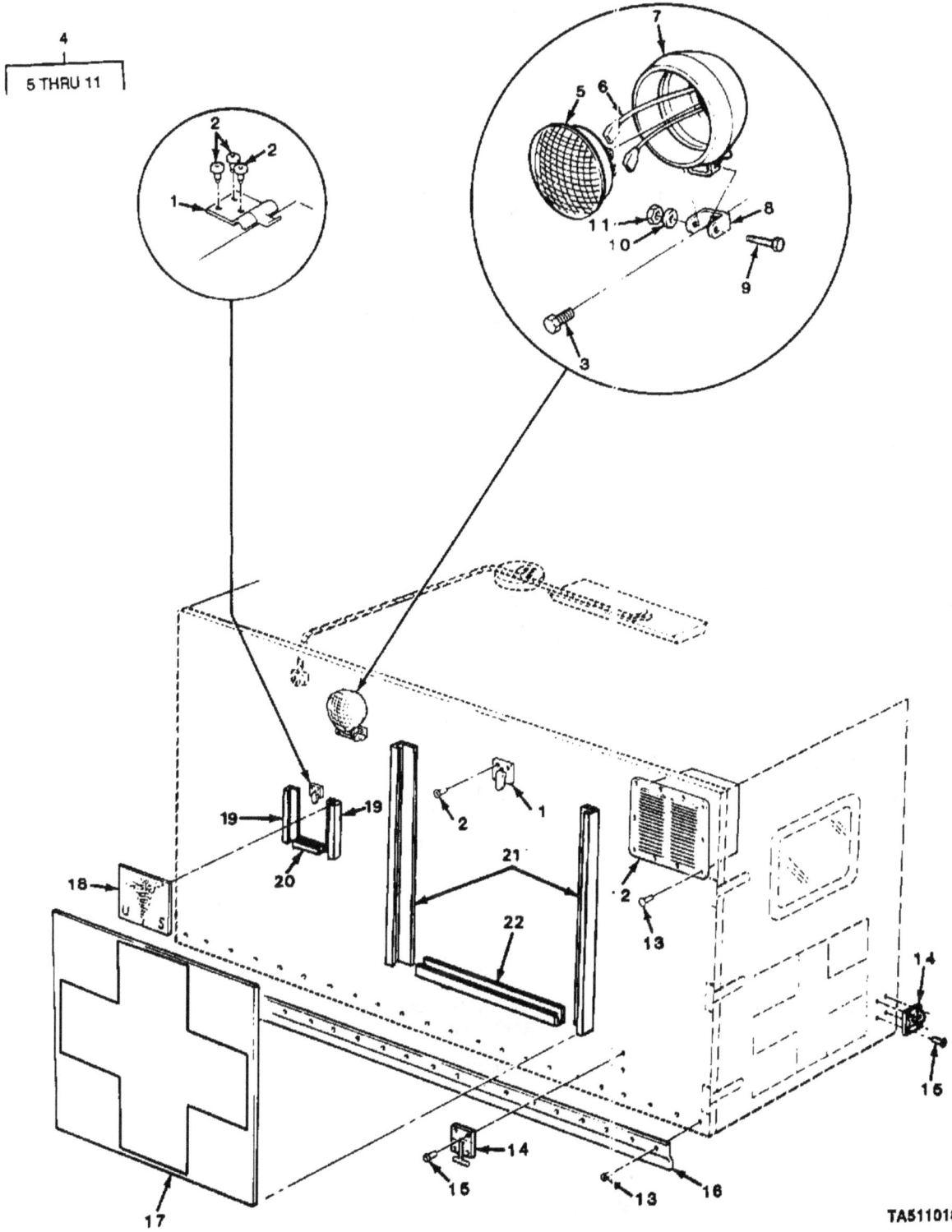

FIGURE 176. LEFT SIDE OUTER PANEL COMPONENT PARTS (M1010).

TA511018

(1) ITEM NO	(2) SMR CODE	(3) CAGEC	(4) PART NUMBER	(5) DESCRIPTION AND USABLE ON CODES (UOC)	(6) QTY
				GROUP 1812 SPECIAL PURPOSE BODIES	
				FIG. 176 LEFT OUTER PANEL COMPONENT PARTS (M1010)	
1	PAOZZ	25022	09-0954	CLIP,SPRING TENSION UOC:210	2
2	PAOZZ	96906	MS20600-B4W3	RIVET,BLIND UOC:210	6
3	PAOZZ	96906	MS90728-60	SCREW,CAP,HEXAGON H UOC:210	1
4	PAOOO	25022	19-0817	FLOODLIGHT,ELECTRIC UOC:210	1
5	PAOZZ	08806	4411	.LAMP,INCANDESCENT UOC:210	1
6	PAOZZ	25022	19-0884	.CABLE ASSEMBLY,SPEC UOC:210	2
7	PAOZZ	25022	19-0882	.HOUSING,FLOODLIGHT UOC:210	1
8	PAOZZ	25022	19-0885	.BRACKET,FLOODLIGHT UOC:210	1
9	PAOZZ	96906	MS90728-40	.BOLT,MACHINE UOC:210	1
10	PAOZZ	96906	MS35338-45	.WASHER,LOCK UOC:210	1
11	PAOZZ	96906	MS51967-5	.NUT,PLAIN,HEXAGON UOC:210	1
12	PAOZZ	25022	31-0030	VENTILATOR,AIR CIRC UOC:210	1
13	PAOZZ	96906	MS20600B6W4	RIVET,BLIND UOC:210	V
14	PAOZZ	25022	09-0093	LATCH SET,RIM UOC:210	1
15	PAOZZ	96906	MS21141-U0604	RIVET,BLIND UOC:210	8
16	PAOZZ	25022	99-4308-1	MOLDING,METAL UOC:210	1
17	PAOZZ	25022	23-0196	PLATE,DESIGNATION UOC:210	1
18	PAOZZ	25022	23-0193	PLATE,DESIGNATION UOC:210	1
19	PAOZZ	25022	99-4582-1	BRACKET,MOUNTING UOC:210	2
20	PAOZZ	25022	99-4581-1	BRACKET,MOUNTING UOC:210	1
21	PAOZZ	25022	99-4580-1	BRACKET,MOUNTING UOC:210	2
22	PAOZZ	25022	99-4579-1	BRACKET,MOUNTING UOC:210	1

END OF FIGURE

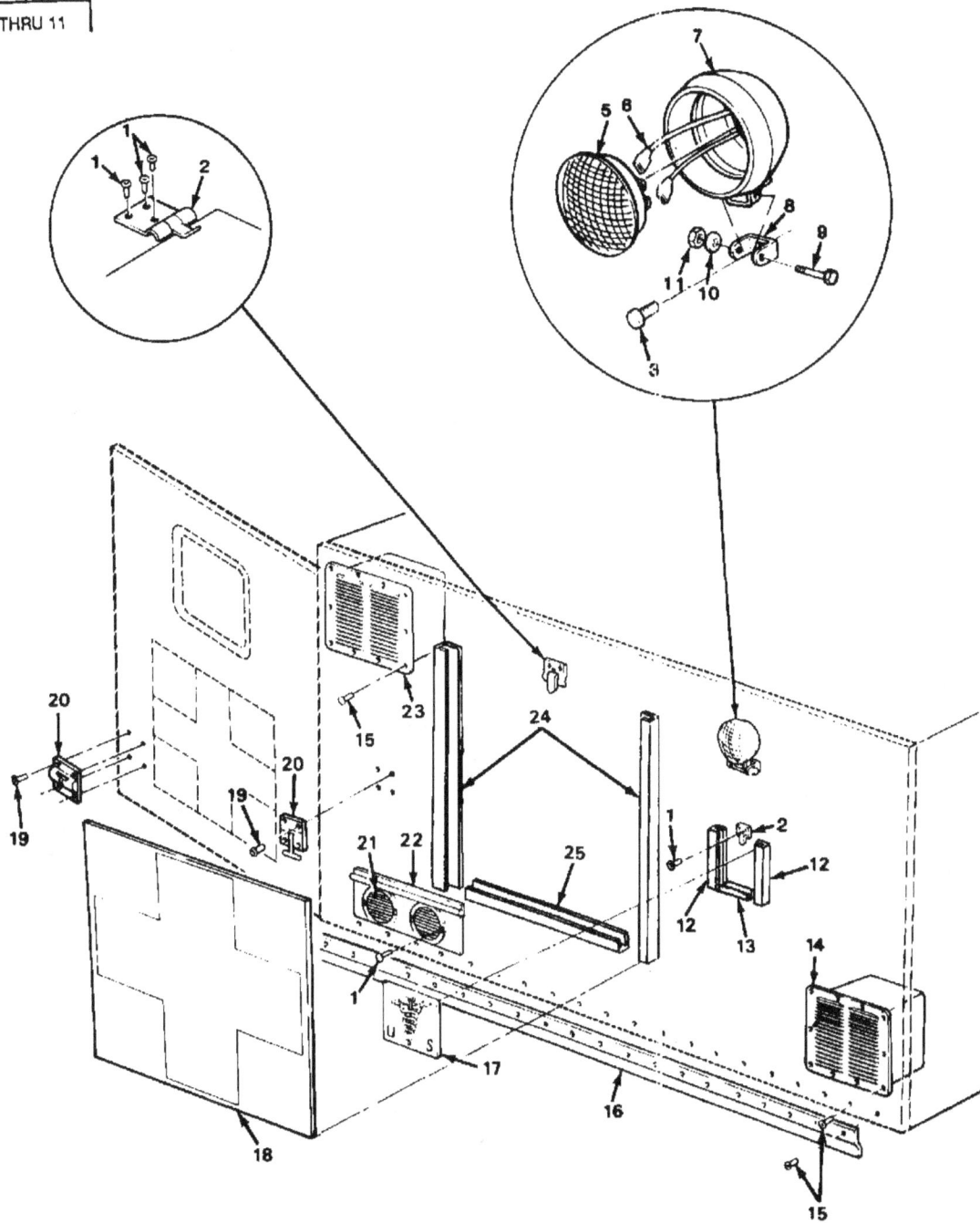

FIGURE 177. RIGHT SIDE OUTER PANEL COMPONENT PARTS (M1010).

TA511019

(1) ITEM NO	(2) SMR CODE	(3) CAGEC	(4) PART NUMBER	(5) DESCRIPTION AND USABLE ON CODES (UOC)	(6) QTY
				GROUP 1812 SPECIAL PURPOSE BODIES	
				FIG. 177 RIGHT SIDE OUTER PANEL COMPONENT PARTS (M1010)	
1	PAOZZ	96906	MS20600-B4W3	RIVET,BLIND UOC:210	10
2	PAOZZ	25022	09-0954	CLIP,SPRING TENSION UOC:210	2
3	PAOZZ	96906	MS90728-60	SCREW,CAP,HEXAGON H UOC:210	1
4	PAOOO	25022	19-0817	FLOODLIGHT,ELECTRIC UOC:210	1
5	PAOZZ	08806	4411	.LAMP,INCANDESCENT UOC:210	1
6	PAOZZ	25022	19-0884	.CABLE ASSEMBLY,SPEC UOC:210	2
7	PAOZZ	25022	19-0882	.HOUSING,FLOODLIGHT UOC:210	1
8	PAOZZ	25022	19-0885	.BRACKET,FLOODLIGHT UOC:210	1
9	PAOZZ	96906	MS90728-40	.BOLT,MACHINE UOC:210	1
10	PAOZZ	96906	MS35338-45	.WASHER,LOCK UOC:210	1
11	PAOZZ	96906	MS51967-5	.NUT,PLAIN,HEXAGON UOC:210	1
12	PAOZZ	25022	99-4582-1	BRACKET,MOUNTING UOC:210	2
13	PAOZZ	25022	99-4581-1	BRACKET,MOUNTING UOC:210	1
14	PAOZZ	99688	78404	VENTILATOR,AIR CIRC UOC:210	1
15	PAOZZ	96906	MS20600B6W4	RIVET,BLIND UOC:210	V
16	PAOZZ	25022	99-4308-1	MOLDING,METAL UOC:210	1
17	PAOZZ	25022	23-0193	PLATE,DESIGNATION UOC:210	1
18	PAOZZ	25022	23-0196	PLATE,DESIGNATION UOC:210	1
19	PAOZZ	96906	MS21141-U0604	RIVET,BLIND UOC:210	8
20	PAOZZ	25022	09-0093	LATCH SET,RIM UOC:210	1
21	PAOZZ	25022	22-0881	PLUG UOC:210	1
22	PAOZZ	25022	99-4888-0	COVER,ACCESS UOC:210	1
23	PAOZZ	25022	31-0030	VENTILATOR,AIR CIRC UOC:210	1
24	PAOZZ	25022	99-4580-1	BRACKET,MOUNTING	2

(1)	(2)	(3)	(4)	(5)	(6)
ITEM NO	SMR CODE	CAGEC	PART NUMBER	DESCRIPTION AND USABLE ON CODES (UOC)	QTY
				UOC:210	
25	PAOZZ	25022	99-4579-1	BRACKET,MOUNTING	1
				UOC:210	
				END OF FIGURE	

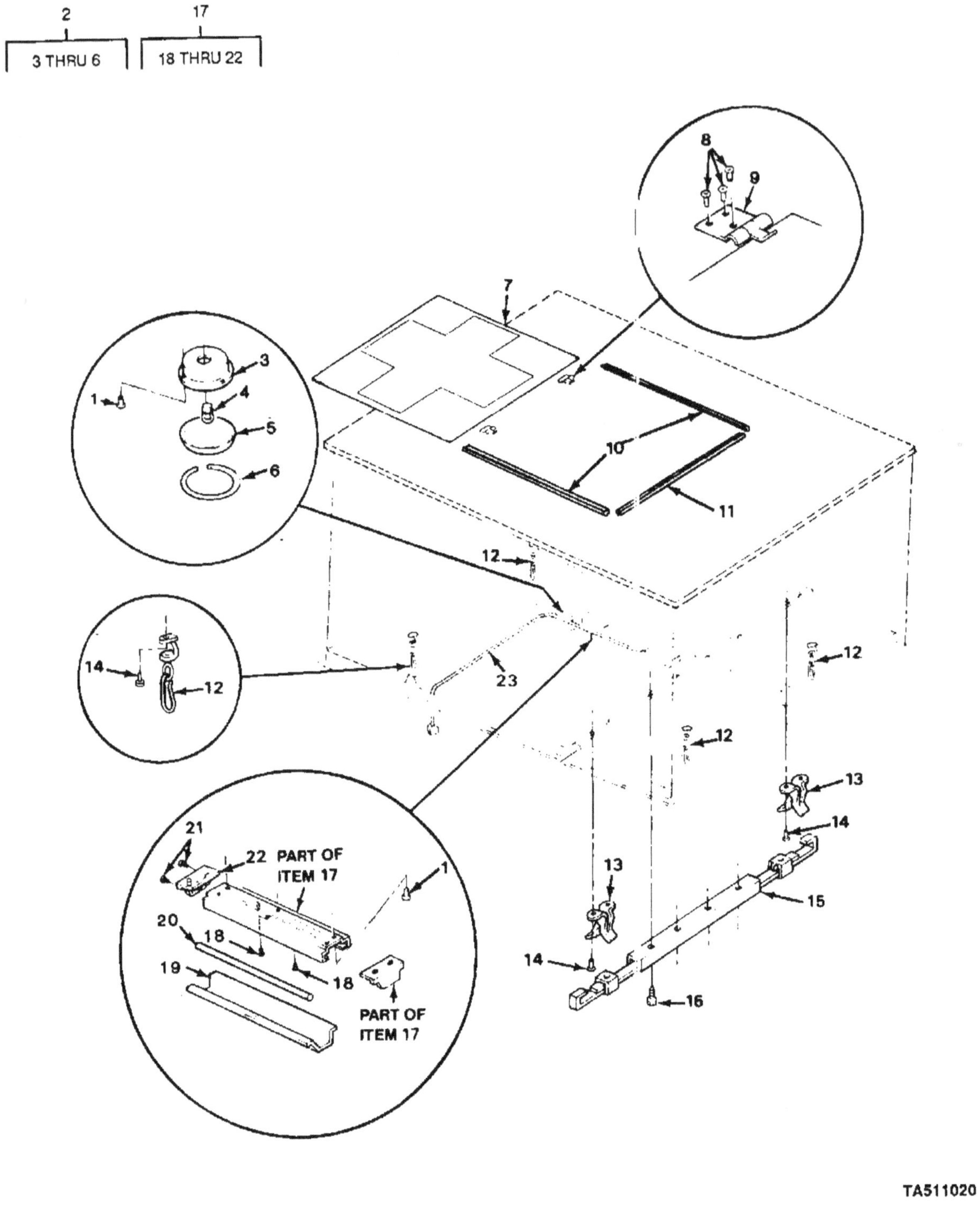

FIGURE 178. ROOF PANEL COMPONENT PARTS (M1010).

TA511020

(1) ITEM NO	(2) SMR CODE	(3) CAGEC	(4) PART NUMBER	(5) DESCRIPTION AND USABLE ON CODES (UOC)	(6) QTY
				GROUP 1812 SPECIAL PURPOSE BODIES	
				FIG. 178 ROOF PANEL COMPONENT PARTS (M1010)	
1	PAOZZ	96906	MS20600B6W4	RIVET,BLIND UOC:210	9
2	AOOOO	25022	19-0445	LIGHT,DOME UOC:210	1
3	PAOZZ	25022	19-0893	.LIGHT,DOME UOC:210	1
4	PAOZZ	08806	1157	.LAMP,INCANDESCENT UOC:210	1
5	PAOZZ	25022	19-0861	.LENS,LIGHT UOC:210	1
6	PAOZZ	25022	19-0969	.RING,RETAINING UOC:210	1
7	PAOZZ	25022	23-0198	PLATE,DESIGNATION UOC:210	1
8	PAOZZ	96906	MS20600-B4W3	RIVET,BLIND UOC:210	6
9	PAOZZ	25022	09-0954	CLIP,SPRING TENSION UOC:210	2
10	PAOZZ	25022	99-4577-1	BRACKET,MOUNTING UOC:210	2
11	PAOZZ	25022	99-4578-1	BRACKET,MOUNTING UOC:210	1
12	PAOZZ	25022	99-1088-0	SWIVEL,LINK AND LIN UOC:210	4
13	PAOZZ	25022	09-0959	CLIP,SPRING TENSION UOC:210	2
14	PAOZZ	96906	MS20600-B4W4	RIVET,BLIND UOC:210	8
15	PAOZZ	25022	22-0875	HANGER,UPPER LITTER UOC:210	1
16	PAOZZ	96906	MS90728-29	BOLT,MACHINE UOC:210	4
17	PAOOO	25022	19-0818	LIGHT,DOME UOC:210	1
18	PAOZZ	96906	MS35206-243	.SCREW,MACHINE UOC:210	2
19	PAOZZ	25022	51-1942	.LENS,LIGHT UOC:210	1
20	PAOZZ	08805	F48T12/CW/WM	.LAMP,FLUORESCENT UOC:210	1
21	PAOZZ	24617	9414238	.SCREW UOC:210	2
22	PAOZZ	25022	51-1991	.INVERTER,POWER,STAT UOC:210	1
23	PAOZZ	25022	19-0820	WIRING HARNESS,BRAN UOC:210	1

END OF FIGURE

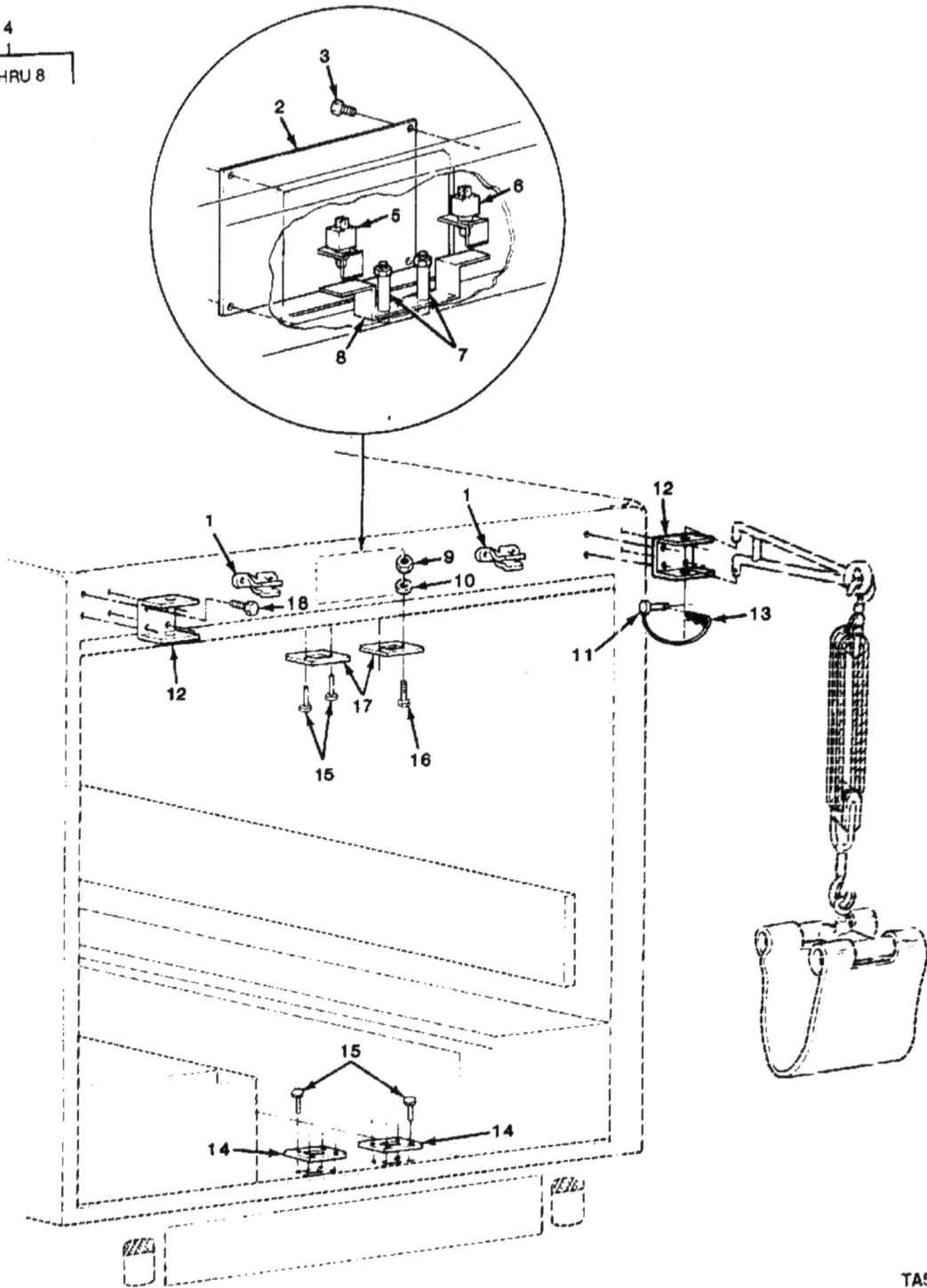

FIGURE 179. REAR FRAME COMPONENT PARTS (M1010).

TA511021

(1) ITEM NO	(2) SMR CODE	(3) CAGEC	(4) PART NUMBER	(5) DESCRIPTION AND USABLE ON CODES (UOC)	(6) QTY
				GROUP 1812 SPECIAL PURPOSE BODIES	
				FIG. 179 REAR FRAME COMPONENT PARTS (M1010)	
1	PAOZZ	25022	09-0959	CLIP,SPRING TENSION UOC:210	2
2	PAOZZ	25022	99-4356-1	PLATE,MENDING UOC:210	1
3	PAOZZ	24617	9414714	SCREW,MACHINE UOC:210	4
4	PAOOO	25022	99-4256-0	SWITCH,TOGGLE UOC:210	1
5	PAOZZ	25022	51-1902	.SWITCH,PUSH UOC:210	1
6	PAOZZ	25022	51-1901	.SWITCH,PUSH UOC:210	1
7	PAOZZ	25022	06-0075	.TUBE,METALLIC UOC:210	2
8	PAOZZ	25022	99-4256-2	.BRACKET,HEATER UOC:210	1
9	PAOZZ	96906	MS35649-202	NUT,PLAIN,HEXAGON UOC:210	2
10	PAOZZ	96906	MS35338-43	WASHER,LOCK UOC:210	2
11	PAOZZ	11862	3929059	PIN,LOCK UOC:210	1
12	PAOZZ	25022	99-4315-1	BRACKET UOC:210	2
13	PAOZZ	25022	09-0963	LANYARD,VEHICULAR UOC:210	1
14	PAOZZ	25022	51-1305	FRAME SECTION,STRUC UOC:210	2
15	PAOZZ	96906	MS21141-U0604	RIVET,BLIND UOC:210	10
16	PAOZZ	96906	MS51957-71	SCREW,MACHINE UOC:210	2
17	PAOZZ	25022	51-1304	STRIKE,CATCH UOC:210	2
18	PAOZZ	96906	MS90728-36	BOLT,MACHINE UOC:210	8

END OF FIGURE

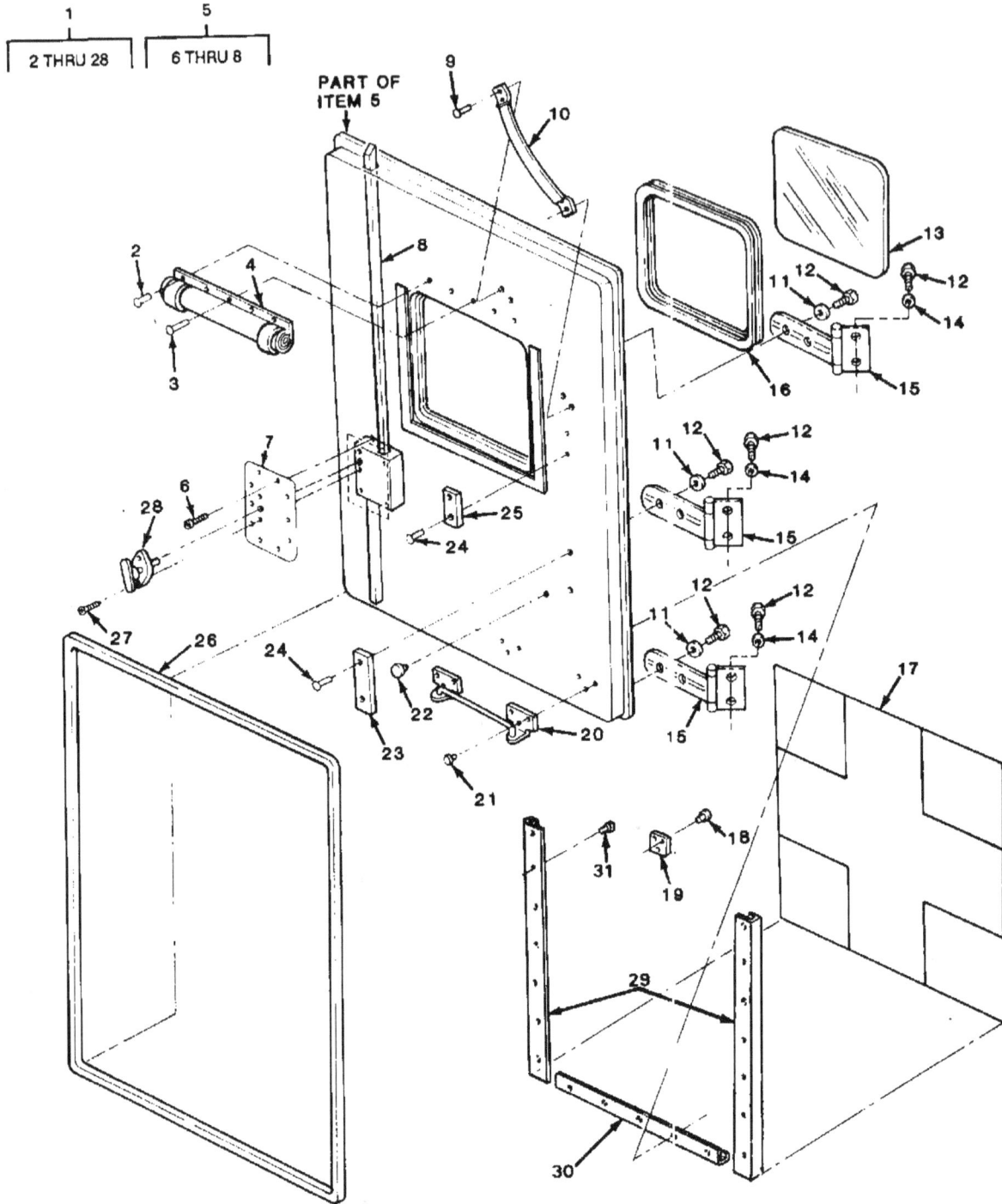

FIGURE 180. LEFT REAR DOOR ASSEMBLY (M1010).

TA511022

(1) ITEM NO	(2) SMR CODE	(3) CAGEC	(4) PART NUMBER	(5) DESCRIPTION AND USABLE ON CODES (UOC)	(6) QTY
				GROUP 1812 SPECIAL PURPOSE BODIES	
				FIG. 180 LEFT REAR DOOR ASSEMBLY (M1010)	
1	XDOFF	25022	99-1265-01	DOOR,METAL,SWINGING UOC:210	1
2	PAOZZ	96906	MS20600-B6W5	.RIVET,BLIND UOC:210	4
3	PAOZZ	96906	MS20600-B4W4	.RIVET,BLIND UOC:210	1
4	PAOZZ	25022	51-2294	.CURTAIN,BLACKOUT UOC:210	1
5	PAOOO	25022	13-1105	.DOOR,METAL,SWINGING INCLUDES ITEMS 11, 12, 15 UOC:210	1
6	PAOZZ	24617	447143	..SCREW,TAPPING UOC:210	10
7	PAOZZ	25022	51-2204	..PANEL,ACCESS DOOR UOC:210	1
8	PAOZZ	25022	51-0999	..BAR,LOCK,DOOR,VEHIC UOC:210	1
9	PAOZZ	96906	MS20600MP6W10	.RIVET,BLIND UOC:210	4
10	PAOZZ	25022	99-4675-1	.STRAP UOC:210	1
11	PAOZZ	96906	MS27183-13	.WASHER,FLAT UOC:210	6
12	PAOZZ	96906	MS90728-60	.SCREW,CAP,HEXAGON H UOC:210	12
13	PAOZZ	25022	51-1603	.WINDOW,OBSERVATION UOC:210	1
14	PAOZZ	96906	MS35338-46	.WASHER,LOCK UOC:210	6
15	PAOZZ	25022	51-0998	.HINGE,TEE UOC:210	3
16	PAOZZ	25022	51-1721	.FRAME,WINDOW DOOR,V UOC:210	1
17	PAOZZ	25022	23-0200	.PLATE,DESIGNATION UOC:210	1
18	PAOZZ	96906	MS20600-B4W3	.RIVET,BLIND UOC:210	3
19	PAOZZ	25022	09-0954	.CLIP,SPRING TENSION UOC:210	1
20	PAOZZ	25022	52-0914	.HOLDER,BACK,DOOR,VE UOC:210	1
21	PAOZZ	96906	MS21141-U0604	.RIVET,BLIND UOC:210	6
22	PAOZZ	25022	17-0209	.BUMPER,VEHICULAR UOC:210	1
23	PAOZZ	25022	17-0178	.BUMPER UOC:210	1

SECTION II					
(1)	(2)	(3)	(4)	(5)	(6)
ITEM NO	SMR CODE	CAGEC	PART NUMBER	DESCRIPTION AND USABLE ON CODES (UOC)	QTY
24	PAOZZ	96906	MS24662-153	.RIVET,BLIND UOC:210	4
25	PAOZZ	25022	17-0177	.BUMPER UOC:210	1
26	PAOZZ	25022	17-0202	.WEATHER STRIP UOC:210	1
27	PAOZZ	24617	165079	.SCREW,MACHINE UOC:210	2
28	PAOZZ	25022	51-0988	.HANDLE,DOOR UOC:210	1
29	PAOZZ	25022	99-4583-1	BRACKET,MOUNTING UOC:210	2
30	PAOZZ	25022	99-4584-1	BRACKET,MOUNTING UOC:210	1
31	PAOZZ	96906	MS20600B6W4	RIVET,BLIND UOC:210	V

END OF FIGURE

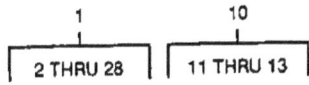

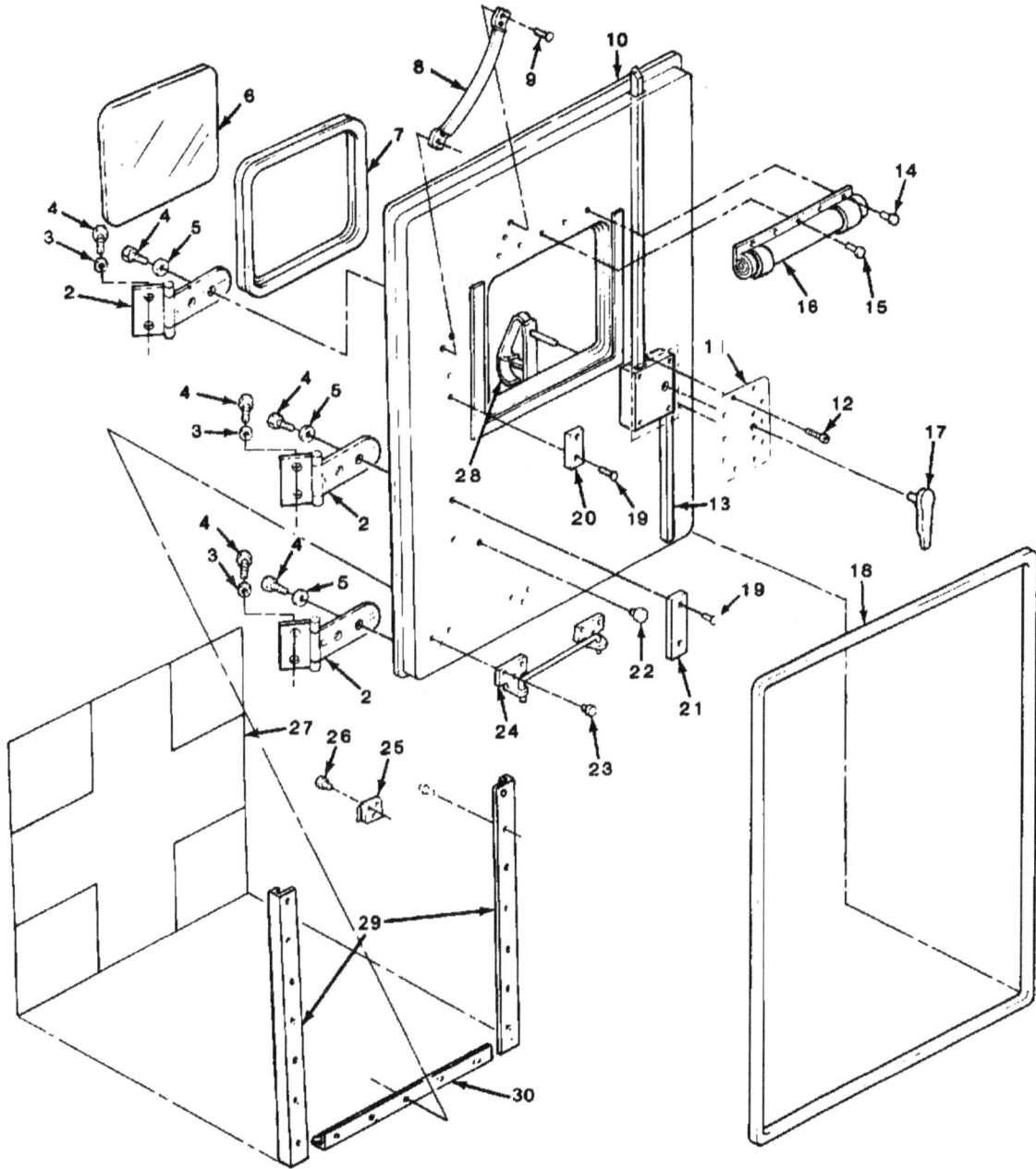

FIGURE 181. RIGHT REAR DOOR ASSEMBLY (111010).

TA511023

GROUP 1812 SPECIAL PURPOSE BODIES

FIG. 181 RIGHT REAR DOOR ASSEMBLY
(M1010)

1	XDOFF	25022	99-1265-02	DOOR,METAL,SWINGING UOC:210	1
2	PAOZZ	25022	51-0998	.HINGE,TEE UOC:210	3
3	PAOZZ	96906	MS35338-46	.WASHER,LOCK UOC:210	6
4	PAOZZ	96906	MS90728-60	.SCREW,CAP,HEXAGON H UOC:210	12
5	PAOZZ	96906	MS27183-13	.WASHER,FLAT UOC:210	6
6	PAOZZ	25022	51-1603	.WINDOW,OBSERVATION UOC:210	1
7	PAOZZ	25022	51-1721	.FRAME,WINDOW DOOR,V UOC:210	1
8	PAOZZ	25022	99-4675-1	.STRAP UOC:210	1
9	PAOZZ	96906	MS20600MP6W10	.RIVET,BLIND UOC:210	4
10	PAOOO	25022	13-1104	.DOOR,METAL,SWINGING INDLUDES ITEMS 2,4,5 UOC:210	1
11	PAOZZ	25022	51-2204	..PANEL,ACCESS DOOR UOC:210	1
12	PAOZZ	24617	447143	..SCREW,TAPPING UOC:210	10
13	PAOZZ	25022	51-0999	..BAR,LOCK,DOOR,VEHIC UOC:210	1
14	PAOZZ	96906	MS20600-B6W5	.RIVET,BLIND UOC:210	4
15	PAOZZ	96906	MS20600-B4W4	.RIVET,BLIND UOC:210	1
16	PAOZZ	25022	51-2294	.CURTAIN,BLACKOUT UOC:210	1
17	PAOZZ	25022	51-0989	.HANDLE,DOOR UOC:210	1
18	PAOZZ	25022	17-0201	.WEATHER STRIP UOC:210	1
19	PAOZZ	96906	MS24662-153	.RIVET,BLIND UOC:210	4
20	PAOZZ	25022	17-0177	.BUMPER UOC:210	1
21	PAOZZ	25022	17-0178	.BUMPER UOC:210	1
22	PAOZZ	25022	17-0209	.BUMPER,VEHICULAR UOC:210	1
23	PAOZZ	96906	MS21141-U0604	.RIVET,BLIND UOC:210	6

(1) ITEM NO	(2) SMR CODE	(3) CAGEC	(4) PART NUMBER	(5) DESCRIPTION AND USABLE ON CODES (UOC)	(6) QTY
24	PAOZZ	25022	52-0914	.HOLDER,BACK,DOOR,VE UOC:210	1
25	PAOZZ	25022	09-0954	.CLIP,SPRING TENSION UOC:210	1
26	PAOZZ	96906	MS20600-B4W3	.RIVET,BLIND UOC:210	3
27	PAOZZ	25022	23-0200	.PLATE,DESIGNATION UOC:210	1
28	PAOZZ	25022	99-4680-1	.HANDLE,BAIL UOC:210	1
29	PAOZZ	25022	99-4583-1	BRACKET,MOUNTING UOC:210	2
30	PAOZZ	25022	99-4584-1	BRACKET,MOUNTING UOC:210	1
31	PAOZZ	96906	MS20600B6W4	RIVET,BLIND UOC:210	V

END OF FIGURE

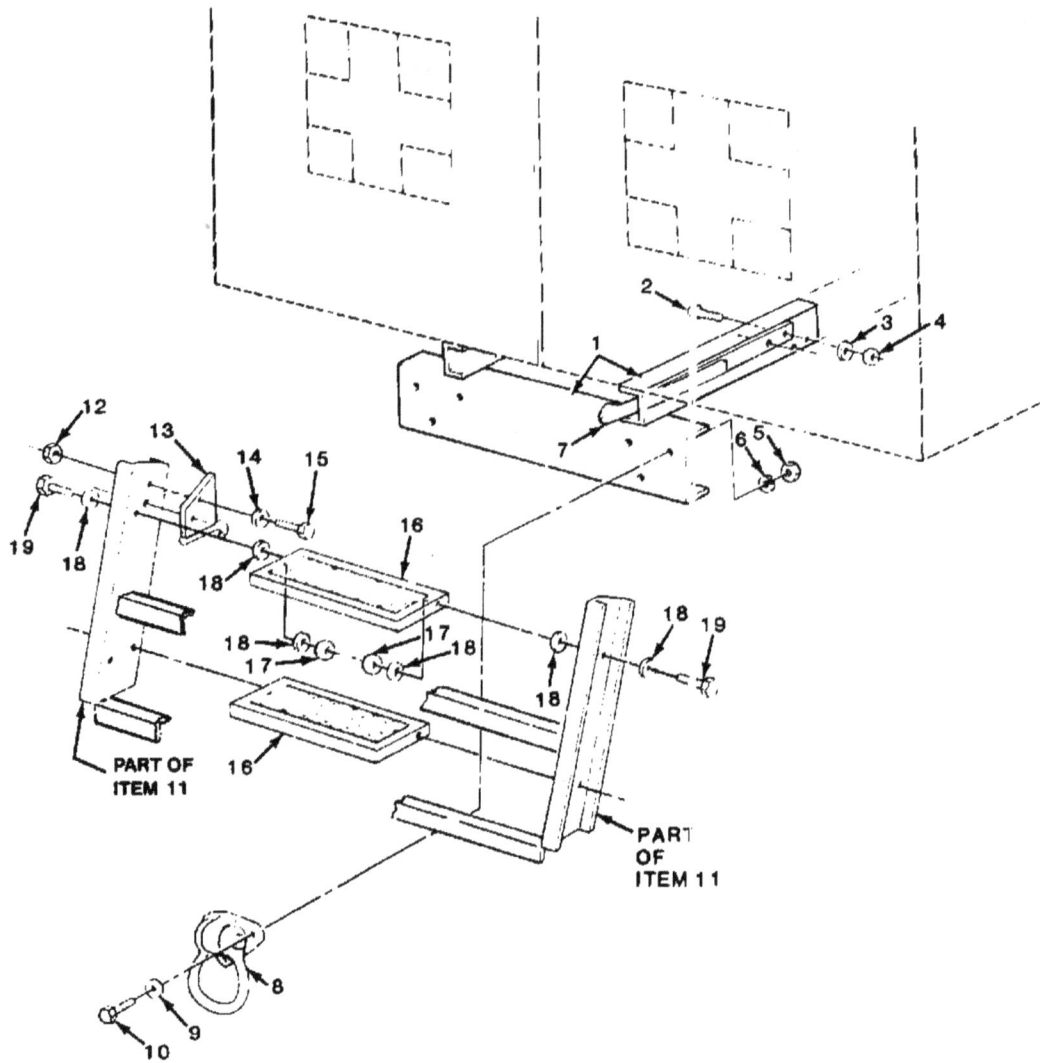

11

12 THRU 19

PART OF
ITEM 11

PART OF
ITEM 11

PART
OF
ITEM 11

TA511024

FIGURE 182. REAR BUMPER AND STEP ASSEMBLY (M1010)

(1) ITEM NO	(2) SMR CODE	(3) CAGEC	(4) PART NUMBER	(5) DESCRIPTION AND USABLE ON CODES (UOC)	(6) QTY
				GROUP 1812 SPECIAL PURPOSE BODIES	
				FIG. 182 REAR BUMPER AND STEP ASSEMBLY (M1010)	
2	PAOZZ	96906	MS90728-8	SCREW,CAP,HEXAGON H UOC:210	2
3	PAOZZ	96906	MS27183-9	WASHER,FLAT UOC:210	4
4	PAOZZ	96906	MS35691-1	NUT,PLAIN,HEXAGON UOC:210	2
5	PAOZZ	96906	MS51967-14	NUT,PLAIN,HEXAGON UOC:210	6
6	PAOZZ	96906	MS35340-48	WASHER,LOCK UOC:210	6
7	PAOZZ	25022	09-0955	RETAINER,SPRING UOC:210	1
8	PAOZZ	74410	TH-0681	RING,HITCH UOC:210	2
9	PAOZZ	96906	MS27183-17	WASHER,FLAT UOC:210	6
10	PAOZZ	96906	MS90728-114	SCREW,CAP,HEXAGON H UOC:210	6
11	PAOOO	25022	99-4340-0	LADDER,VEHICLE BOAR UOC:210	1
12	PAOZZ	96906	MS35691-1	.NUT,PLAIN,HEXAGON UOC:210	2
13	PAOZZ	25022	99-4469-0	.HOOK,LADDER,VEHICLE UOC:210	1
14	PAOZZ	96906	MS27183-9	.WASHER,FLAT UOC:210	2
15	PAOZZ	96906	MS90728-8	.SCREW,CAP,HEXAGON H UOC:210	2
16	PAOZZ	25022	99-4456-0	.STEP,VEHICULAR UOC:210	2
17	PAOZZ	96906	MS35691-9	.NUT,PLAIN,HEXAGON UOC:210	4
18	PAOZZ	96906	MS27183-11	.WASHER,FLAT UOC:210	12
19	PAOZZ	96906	MS90728-34	.BOLT,MACHINE UOC:210	4

END OF FIGURE

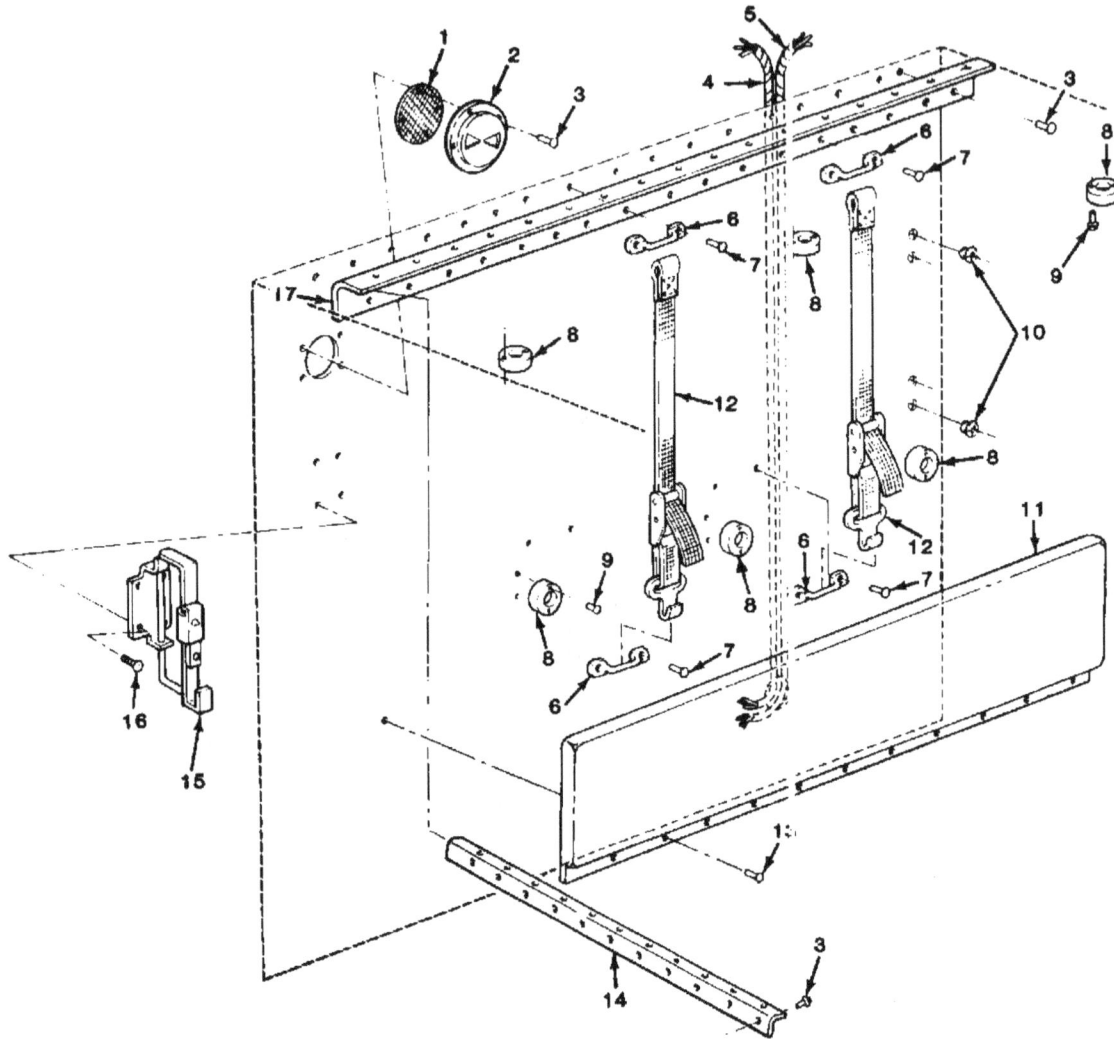

TA511025

FIGURE 183. LEFT SIDE INNER PANEL RELATED PARTS (M1010).

(1) ITEM NO	(2) SMR CODE	(3) CAGEC	(4) PART NUMBER	(5) DESCRIPTION AND USABLE ON CODES (UOC)	(6) QTY
				GROUP 1812 SPECIAL PURPOSE BODIES	
				FIG. 183 LEFT SIDE INNER PANEL RELATED PARTS (M1010)	
1	PAOZZ	25022	22-0832	STRAINER ELEMENT,SE UOC:210	1
2	PAOZZ	25022	22-0884	VENTILATOR,AIR CIRC INCLUDES ITEM 1 UOC:210	1
3	PAOZZ	96906	MS20600B6W4	RIVET,BLIND UOC:210	51
6	PAOZZ	25022	51-0979	STRAP,RETAINING UOC:210	4
7	PAOZZ	96906	MS21141-U0604	RIVET,BLIND UOC:210	8
8	PAOZZ	25022	19-0942	BASE,LAMPHOLDER UOC:210	6
9	PAOZZ	96906	MS20600-B6W10	RIVET,BLIND UOC:210	12
10	PAOZZ	25022	19-0849	STRAIN RELIEF UOC:210	4
11	PAOZZ	25022	22-0861	PAD,CUSHIONING UOC:210	1
12	PAOZZ	25022	22-0877	STRAP,RETAINING UOC:210	2
13	PAOZZ	96906	MS24662-155	RIVET,BLIND UOC:210	14
14	PAOZZ	25022	99-4420-2	MOLDING,FRONT UOC:210	1
15	PAOZZ	25022	09-0965	BRACKET,PIVOT UOC:210	1
16	PAOZZ	24617	171108	SCREW,TAPPING UOC:210	4
17	PAOZZ	25022	99-4420-1	MOLDING,METAL UOC:210	1

END OF FIGURE

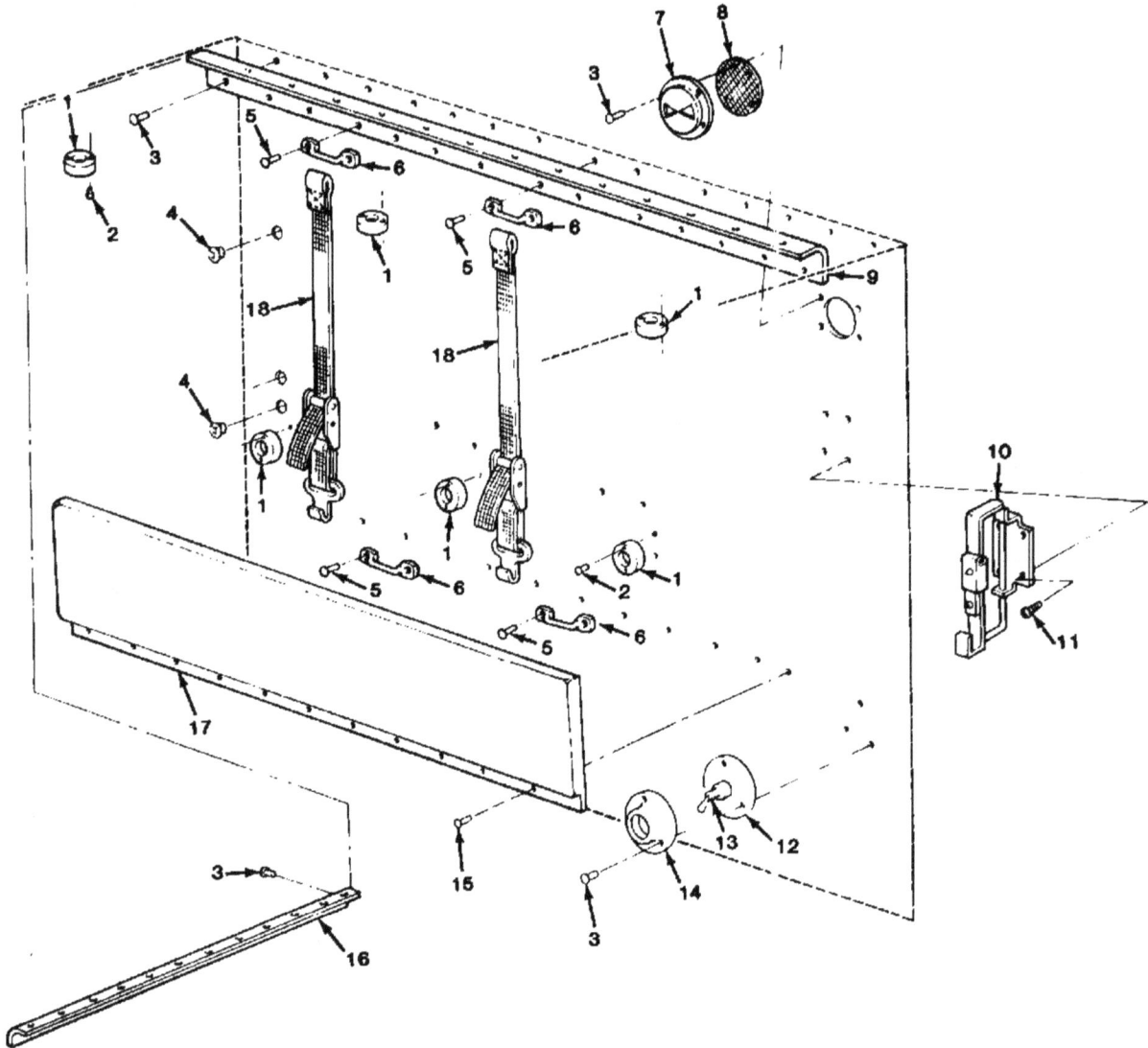

TA511026

FIGURE 184. RIGHT SIDE INNER PANEL RELATED PARTS (M1010).

(1) ITEM NO	(2) SMR CODE	(3) CAGEC	(4) PART NUMBER	(5) DESCRIPTION AND USABLE ON CODES (UOC)	(6) QTY
				GROUP 1812 SPECIAL PURPOSE BODIES	
				FIG. 184 RIGHT SIDE INNER PANEL RELATED PARTS (M1010)	
1	PAOZZ	25022	19-0942	BASE,LAMPHOLDER UOC:210	6
2	PAOZZ	96906	MS20600-B6W10	RIVET,BLIND UOC:210	12
3	PAOZZ	96906	MS20600B6W4	RIVET,BLIND UOC:210	54
4	PAOZZ	25022	19-0849	STRAIN RELIEF UOC:210	3
5	PAOZZ	96906	MS21141-U0604	RIVET,BLIND UOC:210	8
6	PAOZZ	25022	51-0979	STRAP,RETAINING UOC:210	4
7	PAOZZ	25022	22-0884	VENTILATOR,AIR CIRC INCLUDES ITEM #8 UOC:210	1
8	PAOZZ	25022	22-0832	STRAINER ELEMENT,SE UOC:210	1
9	PAOZZ	25022	99-4420-1	MOLDING,METAL UOC:210	1
10	PAOZZ	25022	09-0965	BRACKET,PIVOT UOC:210	1
11	PAOZZ	24617	171108	SCREW,TAPPING UOC:210	4
12	PAOZZ	25022	37-0020	PLATE,SWITCH UOC:210	1
13	PAOZZ	25022	51-1959	SWITCH,TOGGLE UOC:210	1
14	PAOZZ	25022	37-0019	COVER,ELECTRICAL SW UOC:210	1
15	PAOZZ	96906	MS24662-155	RIVET,BLIND UOC:210	14
16	PAOZZ	25022	99-4420-2	MOLDING,FRONT UOC:210	1
17	PAOZZ	25022	22-0861	PAD,CUSHIONING UOC:210	1
18	PAOZZ	25022	22-0877	STRAP,RETAINING UOC:210,230	2

END OF FIGURE

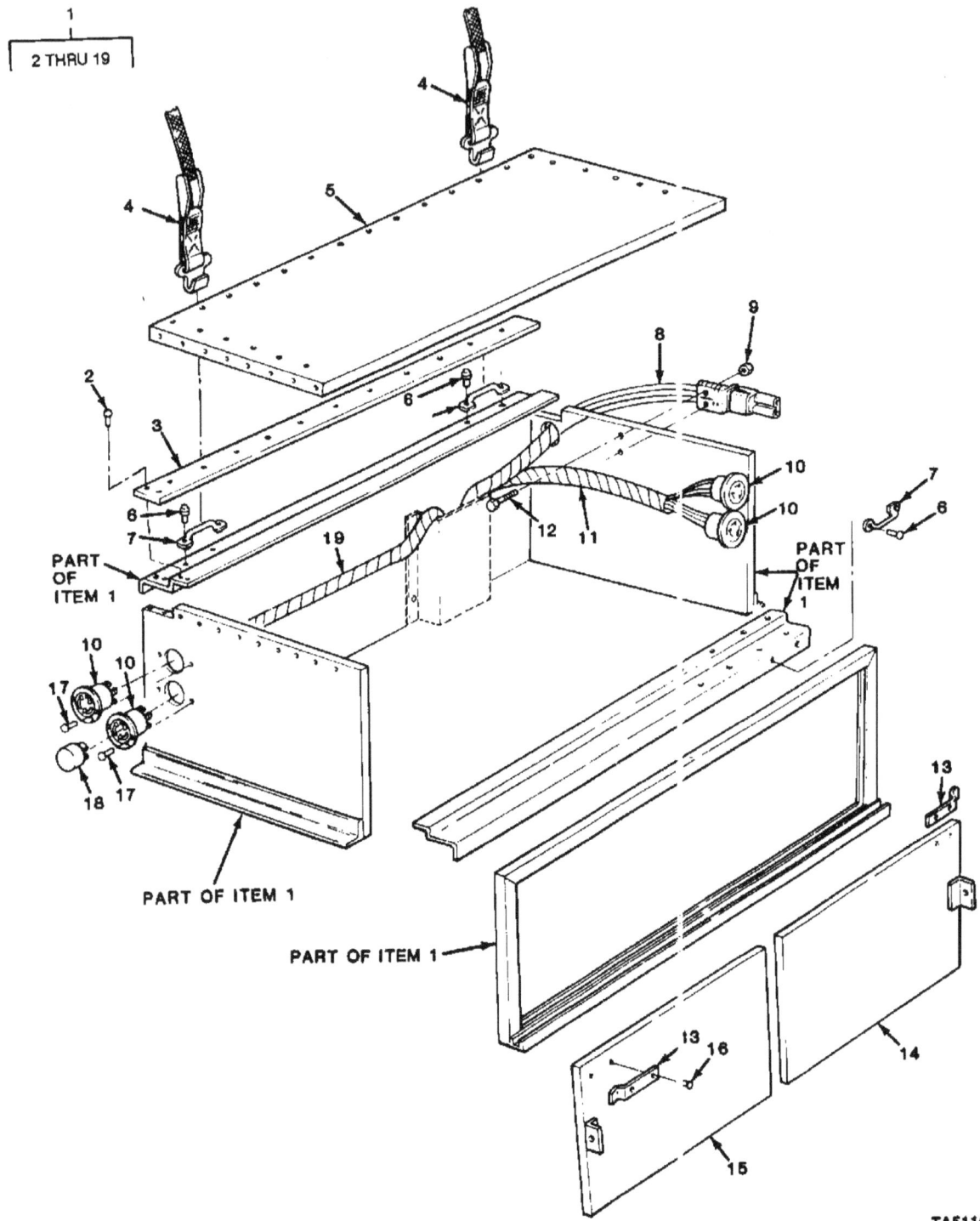

FIGURE 185. LEFT SIDE STOWAGE BOX ASSEMBLY AND COMPONENT PARTS M1010).

TA511027

(1) ITEM NO	(2) SMR CODE	(3) CAGEC	(4) PART NUMBER	(5) DESCRIPTION AND USABLE ON CODES (UOC)	(6) QTY
				GROUP 1812 SPECIAL PUPOSE BODIES	
				FIG. 185 LEFT SIDE STOWAGE BOX ASSEMBLY AND COMPONENT PARTS (M1010)	
1	XAOFF	25022	99-4447-0	BOX,VEHICULAR ACCES UOC:210	1
2	PAOZZ	96906	MS20601-B6W6	.RIVET,BLIND UOC:210	30
3	PAOZZ	25022	51-2297	.PLASTIC STRIP UOC:210	2
4	PAOZZ	25022	22-0880	.STRAP,WEBBING,LITTLE UOC:210	4
5	XAOZZ	25022	22-0867	.LITTLE,VEHICULAR MO UOC:210	1
6	PAOZZ	96906	MS21141-U0604	.RIVET,BLIND UOC:210	8
7	PAOZZ	25022	51-0979	.STRAP,RETAINING UOC:210	4
9	PAOZZ	96906	MS35691-1	.NUT,PLAIN,HEXAGON UOC:210	2
12	PAOZZ	96906	MS90728-10	.SCREW,CAP,HEXAGON H UOC:210	2
13	PAOZZ	25022	51-0991	.CLIP,SPRING TENSION UOC:210	2
14	PAOZZ	25022	99-4894-02	.DOOR,HATCH,VEHICLE UOC:210	1
15	PAOZZ	25022	99-4894-01	.DOOR,HATCH,VEHICLE UOC:210	1
16	PAOZZ	96906	MS20600B6W4	.RIVET,BLIND UOC:210	4
17	PAOZZ	96906	MS20600-B4W4	.RIVET,BLIND UOC:210	8
18	PAOZZ	81348	WC596/9-1	.CONNECTOR,PLUG,ELEC UOC:210	4

END OF FIGURE

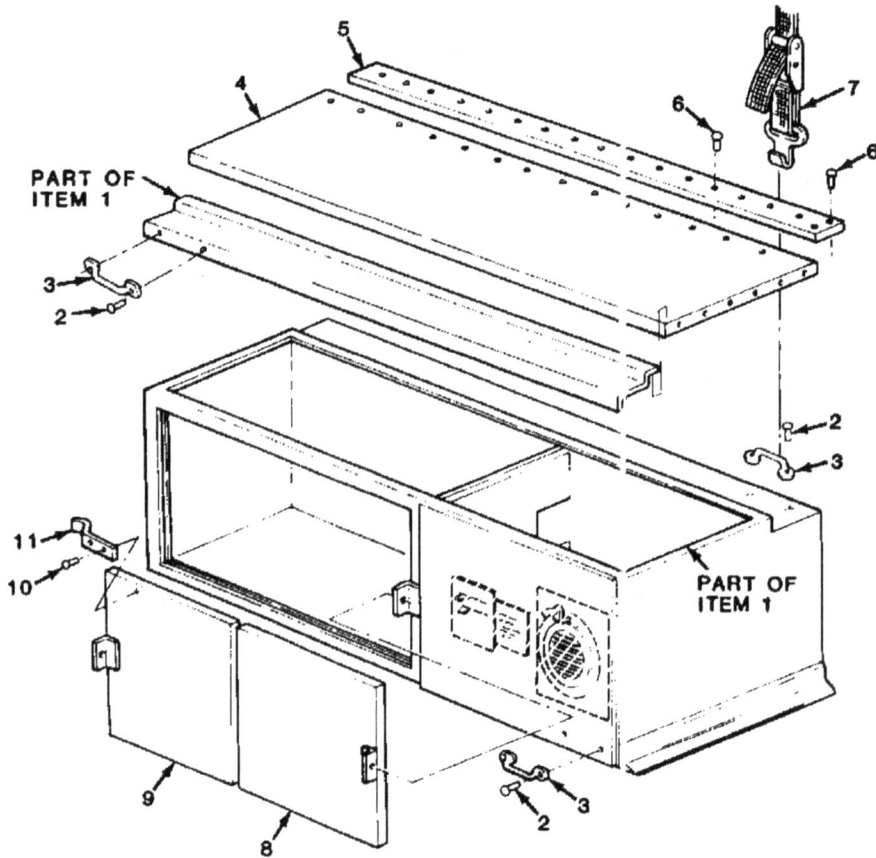

TA511028

FIGURE 186. RIGHT SIDE STOWAGE BOX ASSEMBLY AND COMPONENT PARTS (M1010).

(1) ITEM NO	(2) SMR CODE	(3) CAGEC	(4) PART NUMBER	(5) DESCRIPTION AND USABLE ON CODES (UOC)	(6) QTY
				GROUP 1812 SPECIAL PURPOSE BODIES	
				FIG. 186 RIGHT SIDE STOWAGE BOX ASSEMBLY AND COMPONENT PARTS (M1010)	
2	PAOZZ	96906	MS21141-U0604	.RIVET,BLIND UOC:210	12
3	PAOZZ	25022	51-0979	.STRAP,RETAINING UOC:210	6
5	PAOZZ	25022	51-2297	.PLASTIC STRIP UOC:210	2
6	PAOZZ	96906	MS20601-B6W6	.RIVET,BLIND UOC:210	30
7	PAOZZ	25022	22-0880	.STRAP,WEBBING,LITTLE UOC:210	4
8	PAOZZ	25022	99-4893-01	.DOOR,HATCH,VEHICLE UOC:210	1
9	PAOZZ	25022	99-4893-02	.DOOR,HATCH,VEHICLE UOC:210	1
10	PAOZZ	96906	MS20600B6W4	.RIVET,BLIND UOC:210	4
11	PAOZZ	25022	51-0991	.CLIP,SPRING TENSION UOC:210	2

END OF FIGURE

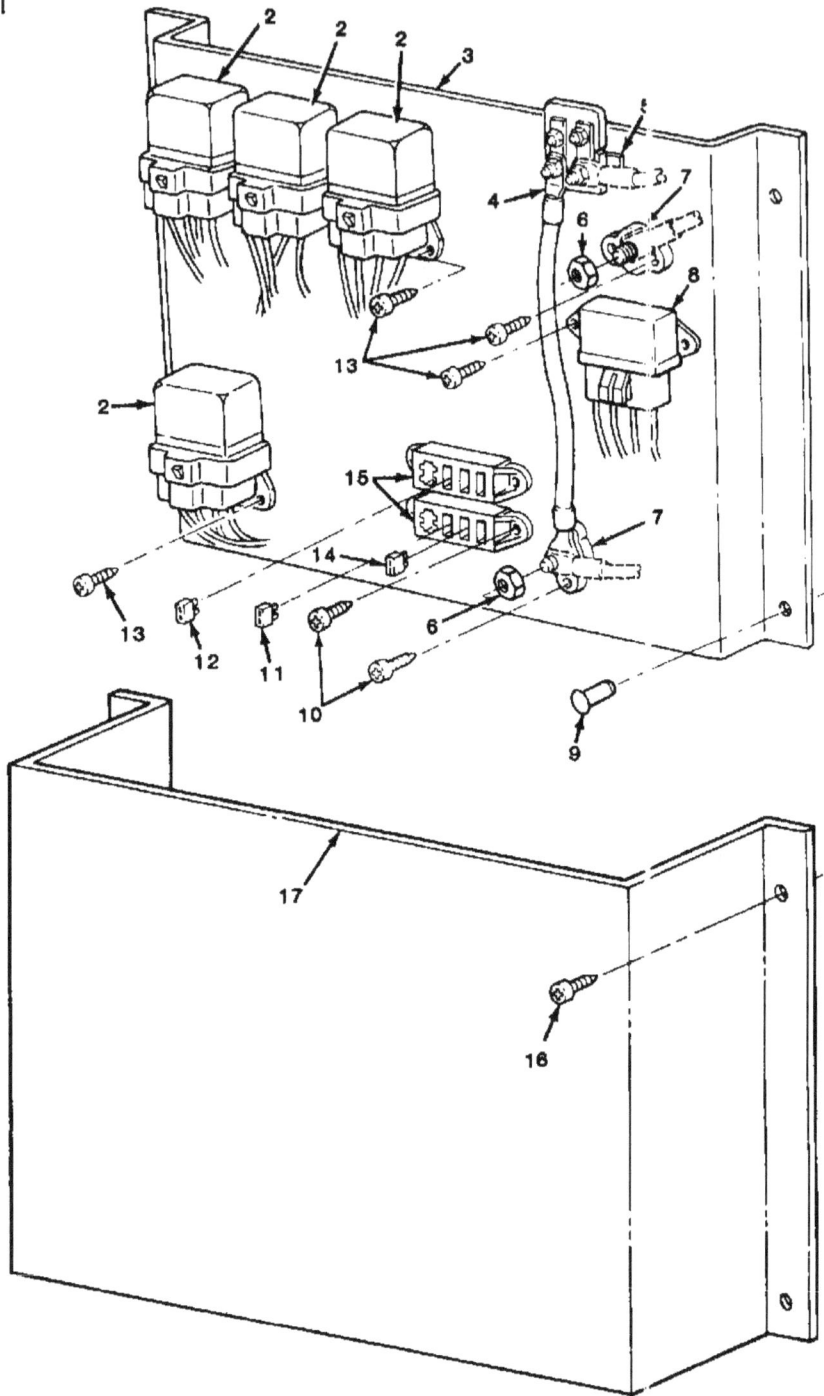

FIGURE 187. RELAY PANEL ASSEMBLY COMPONENTS AND F ELATED PARTS (M1010).

TA511029

(1) ITEM NO	(2) SMR CODE	(3) CAGEC	(4) PART NUMBER	(5) DESCRIPTION AND USABLE ON CODES (UOC)	(6) QTY
				GROUP 1812 SPECIAL PURPOSE BODIES	
				FIG. 187 RELAY PANEL ASSEMBLY COCMPONENTS AND RELATED PARTS	
2	PAOZZ	25022	19-0875	.RELAY,ELECTROMAGNET UOC:210	4
4	PAOZZ	25022	19-0910	.CABLE ASSEMBLY,SPEC UOC:210	1
5	PAOZZ	25022	19-0909	.CIRCUIT BREAKER UOC:210	1
6	PAOZZ	25022	07-01-01	.NUT,PALIN,HEXAGON UOC:210	2
7	PAOZZ	25022	19-0877	.TERMINAL,LUG UOC:210	2
8	PAOZZ	25022	19-0876	.RELAY SUBASSEMBLY UOC:210	1
10	PAOZZ	24617	9426623	.SCREW,TAPPING UOC:210	8
11	PAOZZ	11862	12004011	.FUSE,INCLOSED LINK UOC:210	2
12	PAOZZ	11862	12004008	.FUSE,INCLOSED LINK UOC:210	4
13	PAOZZ	24617	9418719	.SCREW UOC:210	12
14	PAOZZ	11862	12004010	.FUSE,INCLOSED LINK UOC:210	1
16	PAOZZ	24617	9414714	SCREW,MACHINE UOC:210	4
17	PAOZZ	25022	99-4360-1	COVER,PANEL UOC:210	1

END OF FIGURE

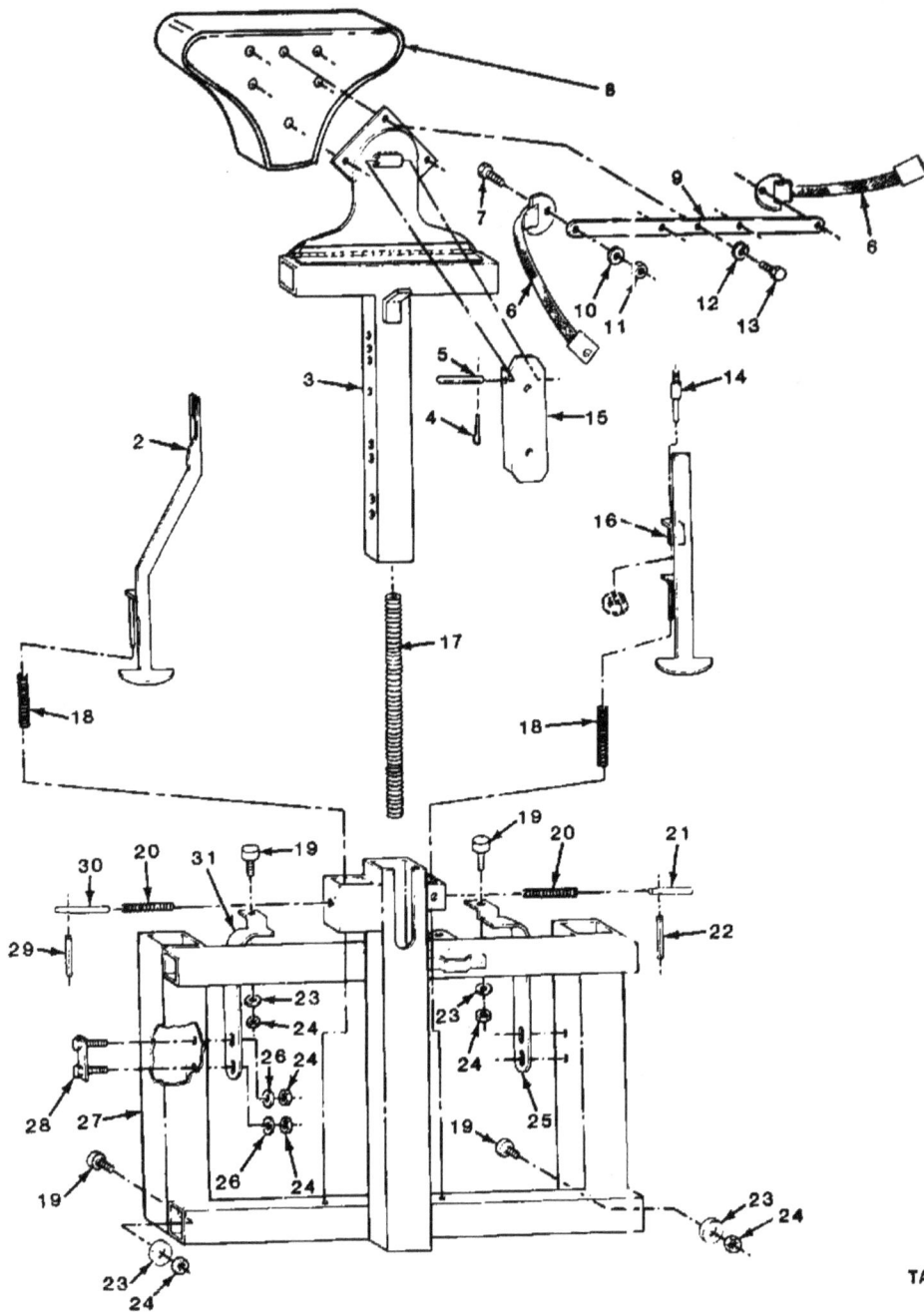

FIGURE 188. ATTENDANT'S SEAT ASSEMBLY AND COMPONENT PARTS (M1010).

TA511030

(1) ITEM NO	(2) SMR CODE	(3) CAGEC	(4) PART NUMBER	(5) DESCRIPTION AND USABLE ON CODES (UOC)	(6) QTY
				GROUP 1812 SPECIAL PURPOSE BODIES	
				FIG. 188 ATTENDANT'S SEAT ASSEMBLY AND COMPONENT PARTS (M1010)	
1	PAOOO	25022	36-0039	SEAT,VEHICULAR UOC:210	1
2	PAOZZ	25022	36-0045	.ARM,ADJUSTING,VEHIC UOC:210	1
3	PFOZZ	25022	36-0044	.STEM,STEAT VEHICULAR UOC:210	1
4	PAOZZ	96906	MS24665-134	.PIN,COTTER UOC:210	1
5	PAOZZ	25022	36-0056	.PIN UOC:210	1
6	PAOZZ	25022	36-0055	.BELT,VEHICULAR SAFE UOC:210	1
7	PAOZZ	96906	MS90727-85	.SCREW,CAP,HEXAGON H UOC:210	2
8	PAOZZ	25022	36-0054	.SEAT,VEHICLAR UOC:210	1
9	PAOZZ	25022	36-0070	.BRACKET,SEAT BELT UOC:210	1
10	PAOZZ	96906	MS27183-15	.WASHER,FLAT UOC:210	2
11	PAOZZ	96906	MS35691-29	.NUT,PLAIN,HEXAGON UOC:210	2
12	PAOZZ	96906	MS35338-47	.WASHER,LOCK UOC:210	6
13	PAOZZ	96906	MS90728-3	.SCREW,CAP,HEXAGON H UOC:210	6
14	PAOZZ	25022	36-0071	.PIN,SHOULDER,HEADLE UOC:210	1
15	PAOZZ	25022	36-0047	.BRACKET,SEAT SUPPOR UOC:210	1
16	PAOZZ	25022	36-0046	.ARM,ADJUSTING,VEHIC UOC:210	1
17	PAOZZ	25022	36-0048	.SPRING,HELICAL,COMP UOC:210	1
18	PAOZZ	25022	36-0049	.SPRING,HELICAL,COMP UOC:210	2
19	PAOZZ	25022	09-0056	.ROLLER,SEAT UOC:210	4
20	PAOZZ	25022	36-0050	.SPRING,HELAICAL,COMP UOC:210	2
21	PAOZZ	25022	36-0075	.PIN UOC:210	1
22	PAOZZ	96906	MS16562-147	.PIN,SPRING UOC:210	1
23	PAOZZ	96906	MS35338-46	.WASHER,LOCK UOC:210	8
24	PAOZZ	96906	MS51968-8	.NUT,PLAIN,HEXAGON	8

(1) ITEM NO	(2) SMR CODE	(3) CAGEC	(4) PART NUMBER	(5) DESCRIPTION AND USABLE ON CODES (UOC)	(6) QTY
				UOC:210	
25	PAOZZ	25022	36-0074	.BRACKET,ANGLE RIGHT	1
				UOC:210	
26	PAOZZ	96906	MS27183-13	.WASHER,FLAT	4
				UOC:210	
27	PFOZZ	25022	36-0043	.BASE,SEAT VEHICULAR	1
				UOC:210	
28	PAOZZ	25022	36-0073	.PIN,SUPPORT	2
				UOC:210	
29	PAOZZ	96906	MS16562-50	.PIN,SPRING	1
				UOC:210	
30	PAOZZ	25022	36-0051	.PIN	1
				UOC:210	
31	PAOZZ	25022	36-0072	.BRACKET,ANGLE LEFT	1
				UOC:210	

END OF FIGURE

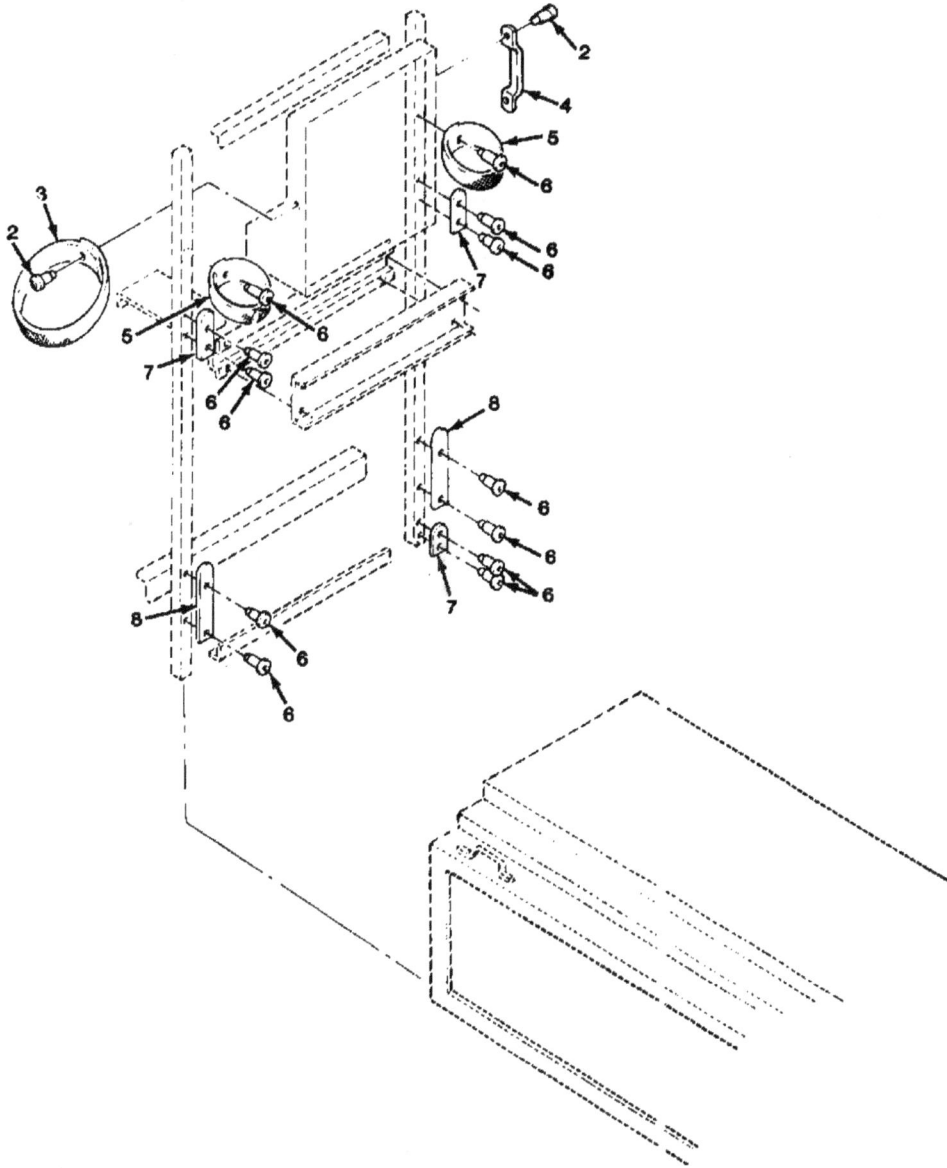

TA511032

FIGURE 190. FRONT HALF-PARTITION ASSEMBLY (M1010)

(1) ITEM NO	(2) SMR CODE	(3) CAGEC	(4) PART NUMBER	(5) DESCRIPTION AND USABLE ON CODES (UOC)	(6) QTY
				GROUP 1812 SPECIAL PURPOSE BODIES	
				FIG. 190 FRONT HALF-PARTITION ASSEMBLY (M1010)	
2	PAOZZ	96906	MS21141-U0604	.RIVET,BLIND UOC:210	3
3	PAOZZ	25022	22-0876	.STRAP,WEBBING UOC:210	1
4	PAOZZ	25022	51-0979	.STRAP,RETAINING UOC:210	1
5	PAOZZ	25022	22-0878	.STRAP,WEBBING UOC:210	2
6	PAOZZ	96906	MS24662-153	.RIVET,BLIND UOC:210	12
7	PAOZZ	25022	17-0177	.BUMPER UOC:210	3
8	PAOZZ	25022	17-0178	.BUMPR UOC:210	2

END OF FIGURE

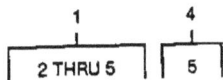

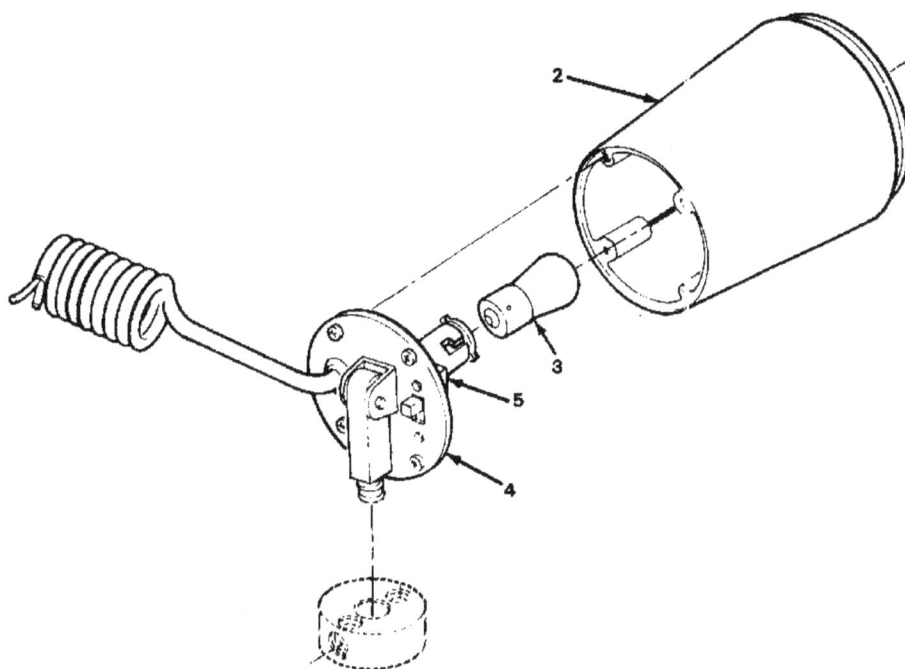

```
  1           4
┌───────┐   ┌───┐
│2 THRU 5│   │ 5 │
└───────┘   └───┘
```

TA511033

FIGURE 191. INTERIOR FOCUS LIGHT (M1010).

(1) ITEM NO	(2) SMR CODE	(3) CAGEC	(4) PART NUMBER	(5) DESCRIPTION AND USABLE ON CODES (UOC)	(6) QTY
				GROUP 1812 SPECIAL PURPOSE BODIES	
				FIG. 191 INTERIOR FOCUS LIGHT (M1010)	
1	PAOOO	25022	19-0816	FIXTURE,LIGHTING UOC:210	4
2	PAOZZ	25022	19-0940	.LENS,LIGHT UOC:210	1
3	PAOZZ	08806	1003	.LAMP,INCANDESCENT UOC:210	1
4	PAOOO	25022	19-0941	.LIGHT,EXTENSION UOC:210	1
5	XDOZZ	25022	19-0941-1	..SWITCH,TOGGLE UOC:210	1

END OF FIGURE

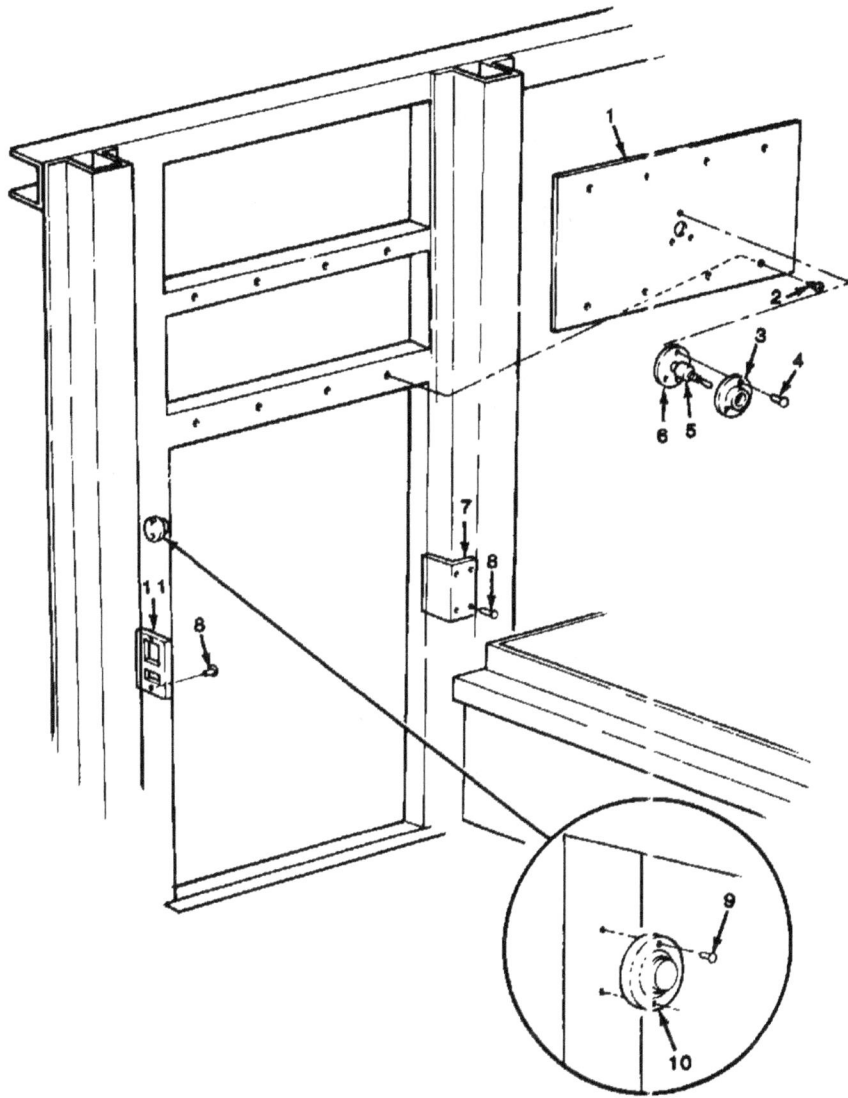

TA511034

FIGURE 192. FRONT FRAME ASSEMBLY COMPONENTS (M1010).

(1)	(2)	(3)	(4)	(5)	(6)
ITEM	SMR		PART		
NO	CODE	CAGEC	NUMBER	DESCRIPTION AND USABLE ON CODES (UOC)	QTY

GROUP 1812 SPECIAL PURPOSE BODIES

FIG. 192 FRONT FRAME ASSEMBLY
COMPONENTS (M1010)

1	PAOZZ	25022	99-4282-1	PANEL,SWITCH MOUNTI UOC:210	1
2	PAOZZ	24617	9414714	SCREW,MACHINE UOC:210	8
3	PAOZZ	25022	37-0019	COVER,ELECTRICAL SW UOC:210	1
4	PAOZZ	96906	MS20600B6W4	RIVET,BLIND UOC:210	3
5	PAOZZ	25022	51-1959	SWITCH,TOGGLE UOC:210	1
6	PAOZZ	25022	37-0020	PLATE,SWITCH UOC:210	1
7	PAOZZ	25022	99-4408-1	STRIKER,STOP UOC:210	1
8	PAOZZ	96906	MS21141-U0604	RIVET,BLIND UOC:210	6
9	PAOZZ	96906	MS20600-B4W4	RIVET,BLIND UOC:210	2
10	PAOZZ	25022	51-1926	SWITCH,SENSITIVE UOC:210	1
11	PAOZZ	25022	51-1304	STRIKE,CATCH UOC:210	1

END OF FIGURE

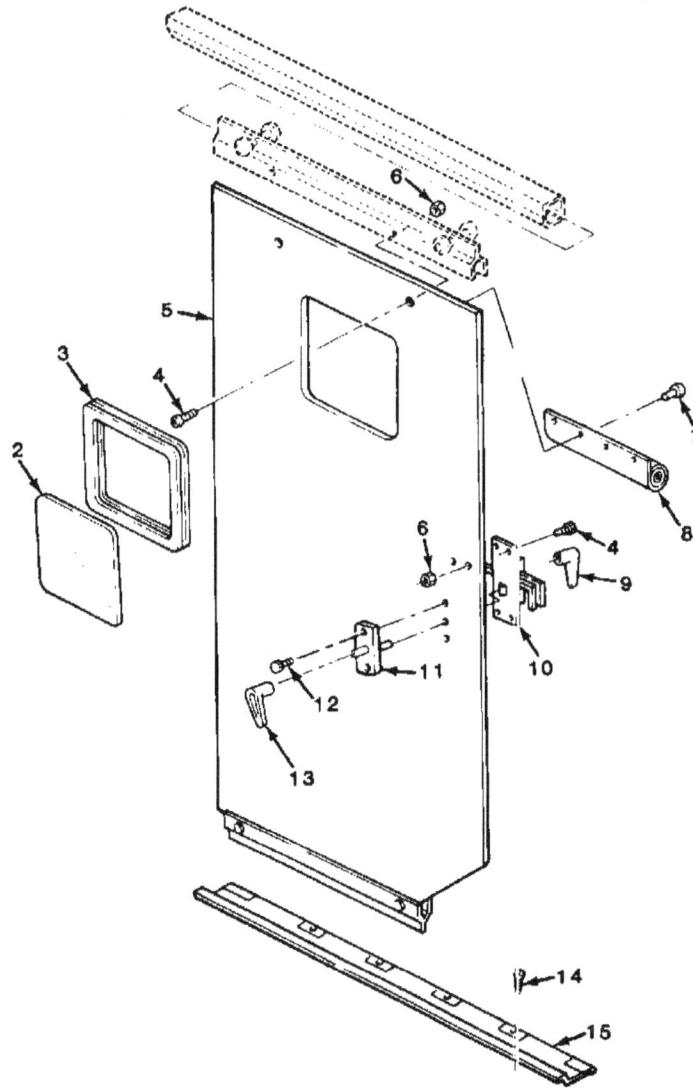

FIGURE 193. INTERIOR SLIDING DOOR ASSEMBLY AND COMPONENT PARTS (M1010).

TA511035

GROUP 1812 SPECIAL PURPOSE BODIES

FIG. 193 INTERIOR SLIDING DOOR
ASSEMBLY AND COMPONENT PARTS (M1010)

ITEM NO	SMR CODE	CAGEC	PART NUMBER	DESCRIPTION AND USABLE ON CODES (UOC)	QTY
1	PAOOO	25022	99-4324-0	DOOR,VEHICULAR UOC:210	1
2	PAOZZ	25022	51-1604	.WINDOW,OBSERVATION UOC:210	1
3	PAOZZ	25022	51-1724	.SEAL,RUBBER SPECIAL UOC:210	1
4	PAOZZ	21450	126281	.BOLT,SQUARE NECK UOC:210	6
5	PAOOO	25022	22-0864	.DOOR,VEHICULAR UOC:210	1
6	PAOZZ	88044	AN365-1024A	.NUT,SELF-LOCKING,HE UOC:210	6
7	PAOZZ	96906	MS24662-153	.RIVET,BLIND UOC:210	4
8	PAOZZ	25022	22-0873	.CURTAIN,BLACKOUT UOC:210	1
9	PAOZZ	25022	09-0951	.HANDLE,DOOR UOC:210	1
10	PAOZZ	25022	09-0952	.LOCK,DOOR,VEHICULAR UOC:210	1
11	PAOZZ	25022	99-4683-1	.PIN UOC:210	1
12	PAOZZ	96906	MS21207-10-10	.SCREW,TAPPING UOC:210	2
13	PAOZZ	25022	08-0475	.HANDLE,DOOR UOC:210	1
14	PAOZZ	24617	163881	RIVET UOC:210	4
15	PFOZZ	25022	99-4257-1	TRACK,SLIDING DOOR UOC:210	1

END OF FIGURE

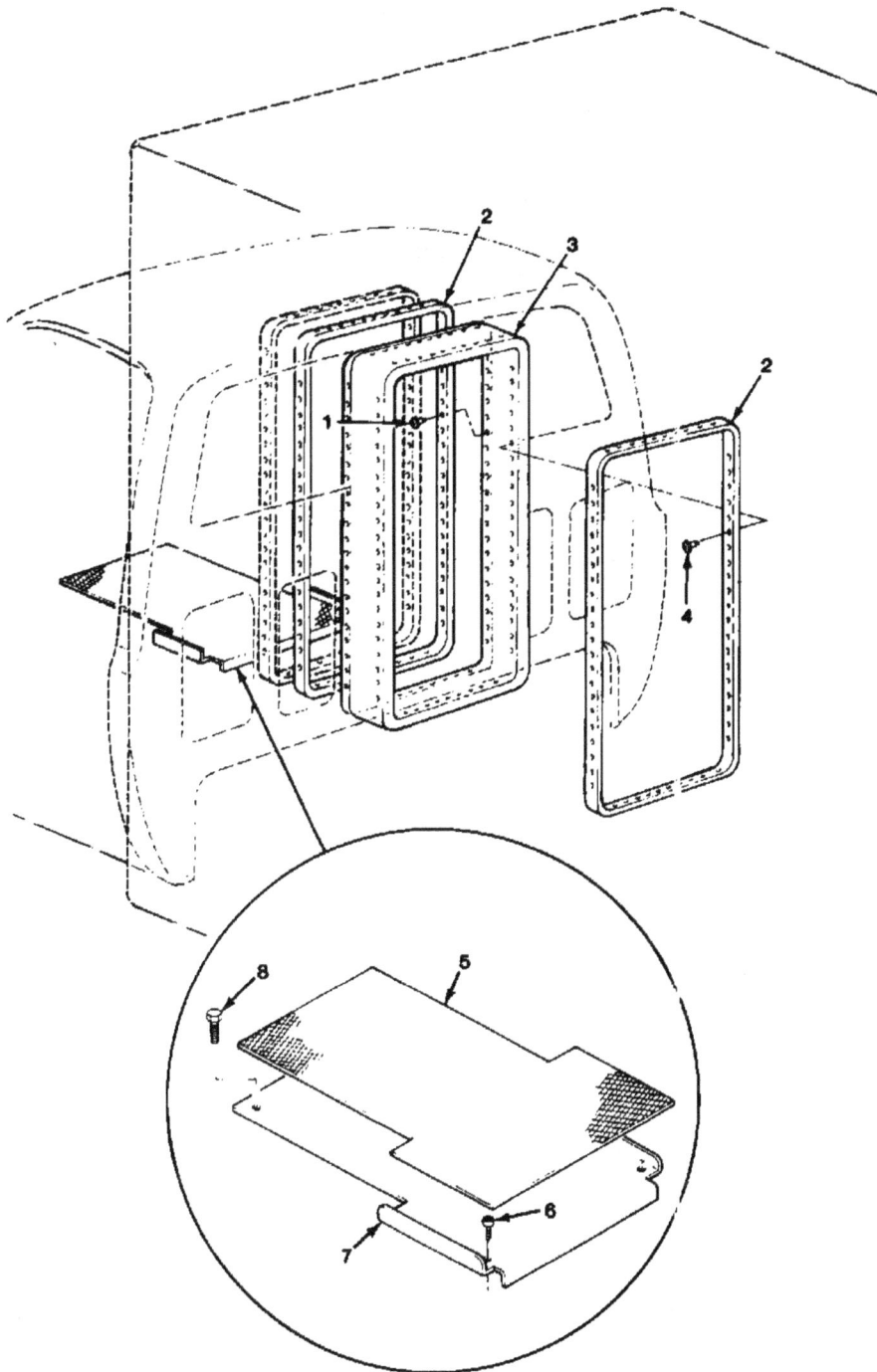

TA511036

FIGURE 194. PULLMAN COLLAR AND RELATED PARTS (M1010).

(1) ITEM NO	(2) SMR CODE	(3) CAGEC	(4) PART NUMBER	(5) DESCRIPTION AND USABLE ON CODES (UOC)	(6) QTY
				GROUP 1812 SPECIAL PURPOSE BODIES	
				FIG. 194 PULLMAN COLLAR AND RELATED PARTS (M1010)	
5	PAOZZ	25022	17-0195	MAT,FLOOR UOC:210	1
6	PAOZZ	96906	MS24627-67	SCREW,TAPPING UOC:210	2
7	PAOZZ	25022	99-4892-0	RAMP,CAB UOC:210	1
8	PAOZZ	96906	MS90728-8	SCREW,CAP,HEXAGON H UOC:210	2

END OF FIGURE

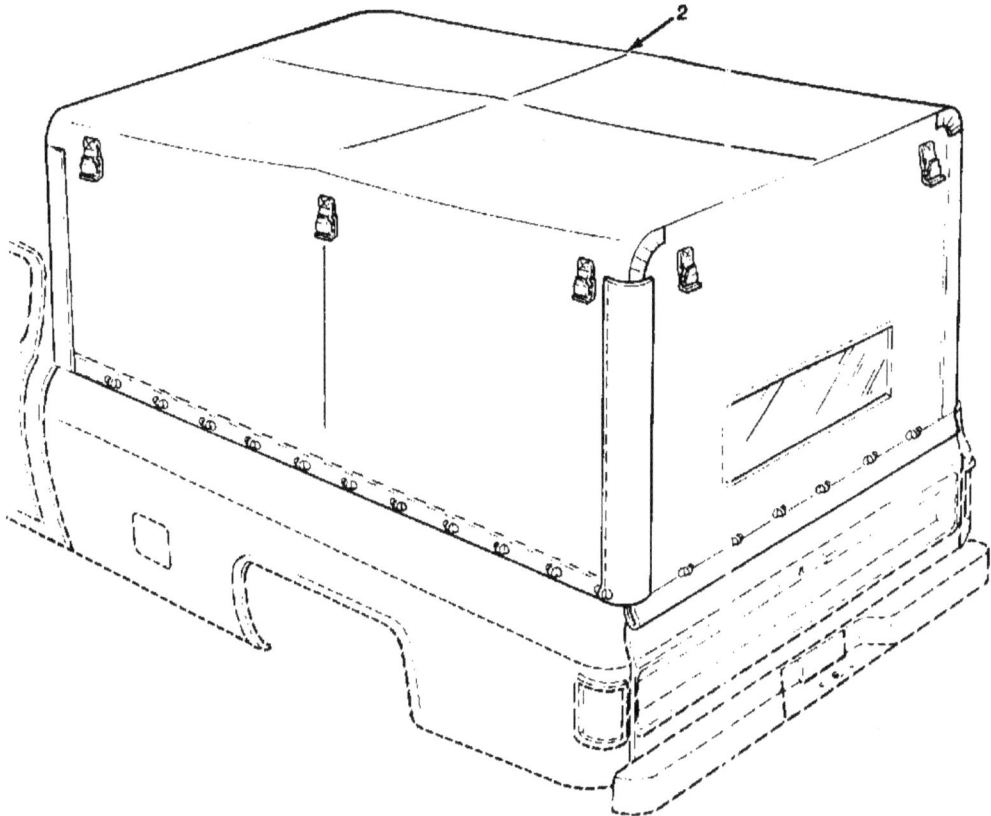

TA511037

FIGURE 195. CARGO COVER ASSEMBLY (M1008 AND M1008A1).

(1) ITEM NO	(2) SMR CODE	(3) CAGEC	(4) PART NUMBER	(5) DESCRIPTION AND USABLE ON CODES (UOC)	(6) QTY
				GROUP 22 BODY, CHASSIS, AND HULL ACCESSORY ITEMS	
				GROUP 2201 CANVAS, RUBBER, OR PLASTIC ITEMS	
				FIG. 195 CARGO COVER ASSEMBLY (M1008 AND M1008A1)	
1	PDOFF	11862	14072479	PARTS KIT,CARGO COV FOR COMPONENT PARTS SEE FIG'S 196,197 UOC:194,208	1
2	PAOFF	11862	14072475	.TOP ASSEMBLY,TRUCK UOC:194,208	1
				END OF FIGURE	

SECTION II   TM9-2320-289-20P
(1)   (2)   (3)   (4)   (5)   (6)
ITEM   SMR
NO   CODE   CAGEC PART
              NUMBER   DESCRIPTION AND USABLE ON CODES (UOC)   QTY

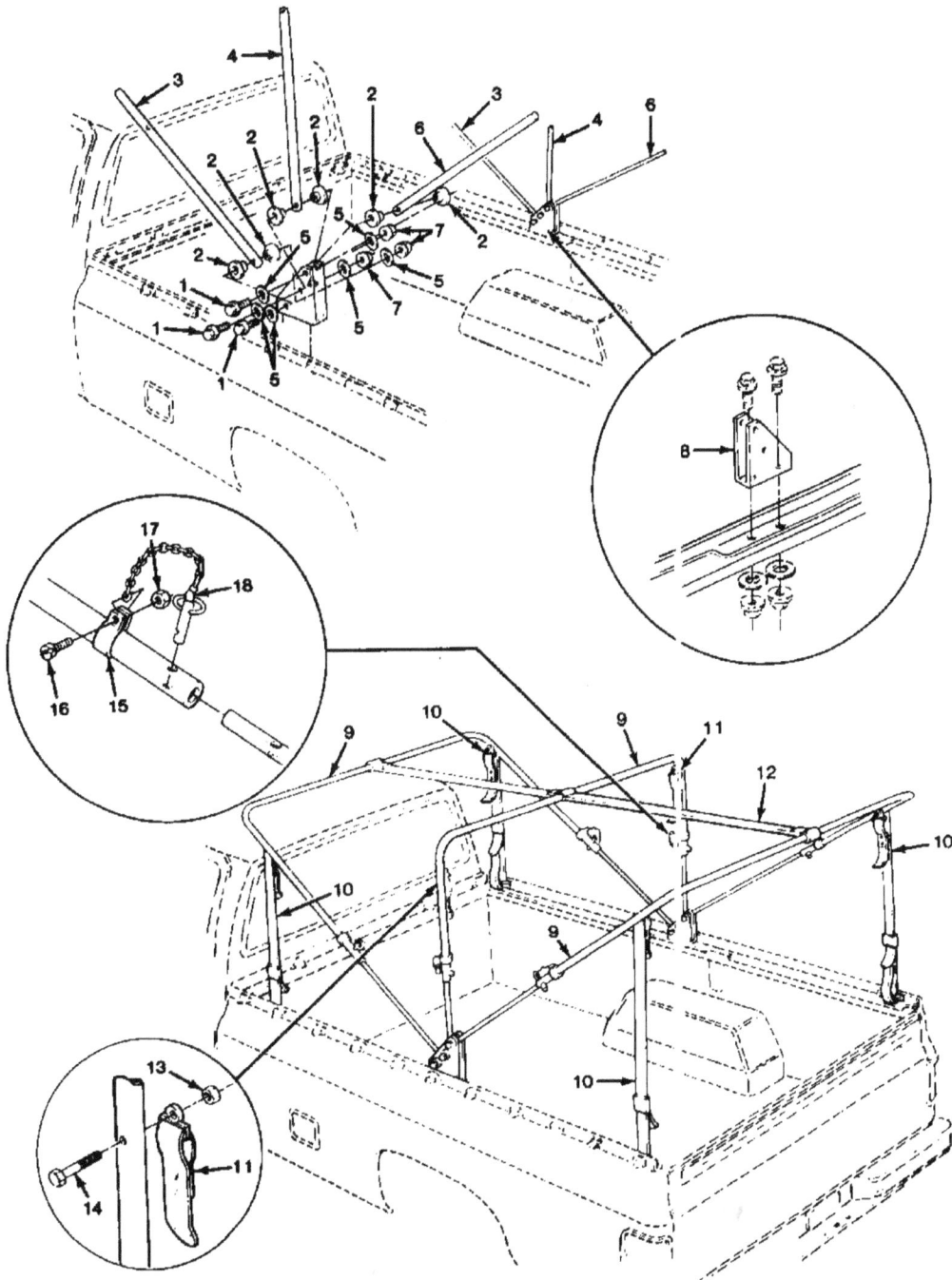

TA511038

FIGURE 196. COVER FRAME COMPONENTS (M1008 AND M1008A1).

(1) ITEM NO	(2) SMR CODE	(3) CAGEC	(4) PART NUMBER	(5) DESCRIPTION AND USABLE ON CODES (UOC)	(6) QTY
				GROUP 2201 CANVAS, RUBBER, OR PLASTIC ITEMS	
				FIG. 196 COVER FRAME COMPONENTS (M1008 AND M1008A1)	
1	PAOZZ	96906	MS90728-39	BOLT,MACHINE UOC:194,208	6
2	PAOZZ	11862	15599919	BUSHING,SLEEVE UOC:194,208	12
3	MOOZZ	11862	14072471	STRUT-C/CVR (33.75" LG) MAKE FROM STRUT,P/N 15599621 UOC:194,208	2
4	MOOZZ	11862	14072472	STRUT-C/CVR RF BOW (22.50" LG) MAKE FROM STRUT, P/N 15599621 UOC:194,208	2
5	PAOZZ	96906	MS27183-12	WASHER,FLAT UOC:194,208	12
6	MOOZZ	11862	14072473	STRUT-C/CVR RF BOW (32.34" LG) MAKE FROM STRUT, P/N 15599621 UOC:194,208	2
7	PAOZZ	96906	MS51943-33	NUT,SELF-LOCKING,HE UOC:194,208	6
8	PAOZZ	11862	14072468	BRACKET,BOW HINGE,V UOC:194,208	2
9	PAOZZ	11862	14072470	BOW,VEHICULAR TOP UOC:194,208	3
10	PAOZZ	19207	12255559	STRAP,WEBBING UOC:194,208	4
11	PAOZZ	19207	12255567	STRAP,WEBBING UOC:194,208	2
12	PAOZZ	11862	14072469	STRAP,VEHICULAR TOP UOC:194,208	1
13	PAOZZ	72582	9419454	NUT,SELF-LOCKING,HE UOC:194,208	6
14	PAOZZ	24617	157456	SCREW,MACHINE UOC:194,208	6
15	PAOZZ	19207	12255561	CLAMP,LOOP UOC:194,208	6
16	PAOZZ	96906	MS51957-30	SCREW,MACHINE UOC:194,208	6
17	PAOZZ	24617	9423530	NUT,PLAIN,ASSEMBLED UOC:194,208	6
18	PAOZZ	19207	11669126-1	PIN,QUICK RELEASE UOC:194,208	6

END OF FIGURE

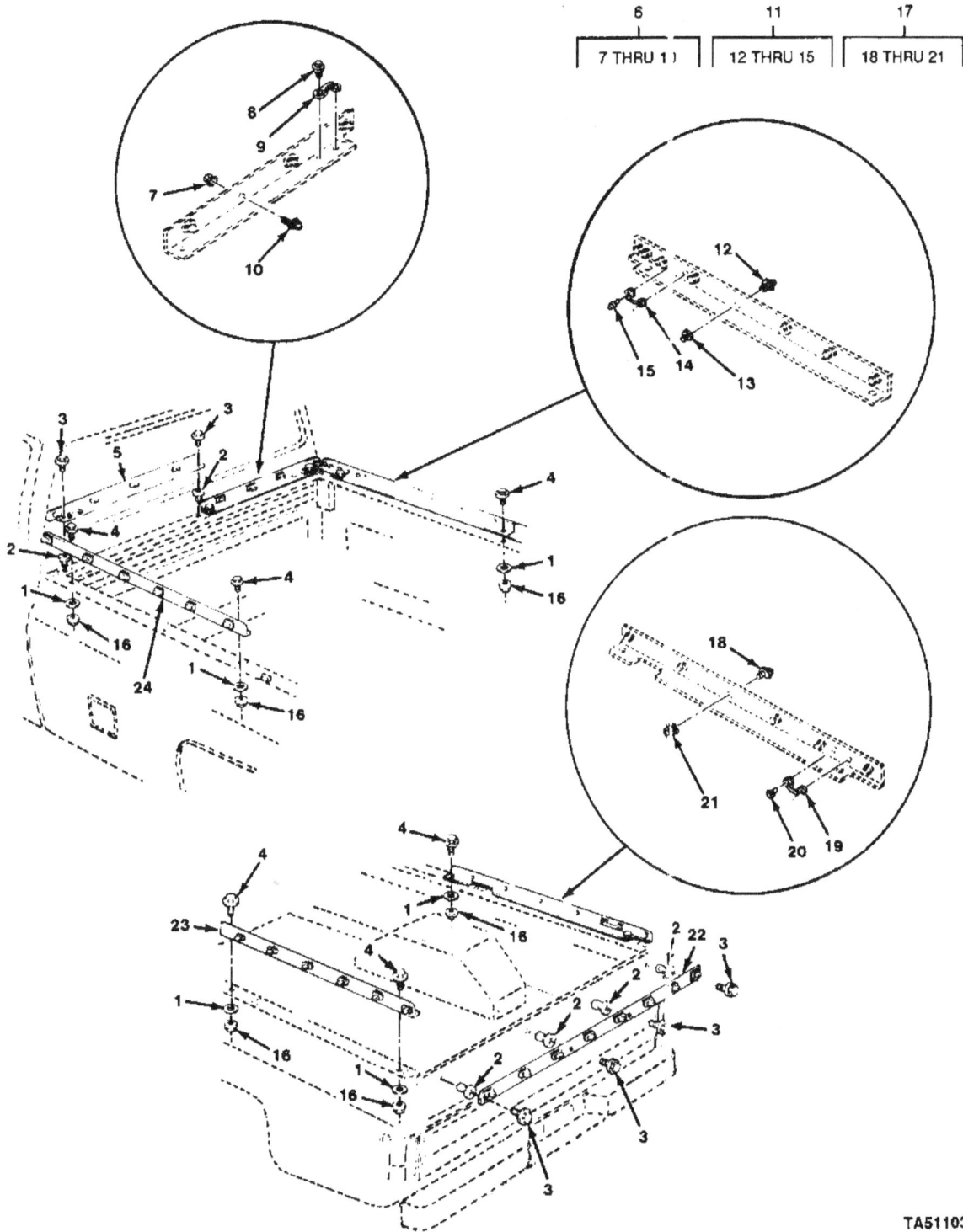

FIGURE 197. CARGO COVER MOUNTING PARTS (M1008 AND M1008A1).

TA511039

(1) ITEM NO	(2) SMR CODE	(3) CAGEC	(4) PART NUMBER	(5) DESCRIPTION AND USABLE ON CODES (UOC)	(6) QTY
				GROUP 2201 CANVAS, RUBBER, OR PLASTIC ITEMS	
				FIG. 197 CARGO COVER MOUNTING PARTS (M1008 AND M1008A1)	
1	PAOZZ	96906	MS27183-14	WASHER,FLAT UOC:194,208	8
2	PAOZZ	11862	14005953	SHIELD,EXPANSION UOC:194,208	8
3	PAOZZ	96906	MS90728-8	SCREW,CAP,HEXAGON H UOC:194,208	8
4	PAOZZ	24617	9415153	SCREW,ASSEMBLED WAS UOC:194,208	8
5	PAOZZ	11862	14072461	RAIL,BOW RECEPTACLE LEFT UOC:194,208	1
6	PAOZZ	11862	14072462	RAIL,CARGO COVER RIGHT UOC:194,208	1
7	PAOZZ	24617	271172	.NUT,SELF-LOCKING,AS UOC:194,208	4
8	PAOZZ	96906	MS21141-U0604	.RIVET,BLIND UOC:194,208	2
9	PAOZZ	96906	MS51939-2	.LOOP,STRAP FASTENER UOC:194,208	1
10	PAOZZ	19207	12255564-2	.STUD,TURNBUTTON FAS UOC:194,208	4
11	PAOOO	11862	14072464	RAIL,CARGO COVER RIGHT UOC:194,208	1
12	PAOZZ	19207	12255564-2	STUD,TURNBUTTION FAS UOC:194,208	6
13	PAOZZ	24617	271172	.NUT,SELF-LOCKING,AS UOC:194,208	6
14	PAOZZ	96906	MS51939-2	.LOOP,STRAP FASTENER UOC:194,208	2
15	PAOZZ	96906	MS21141-U0604	.RIVET,BLIND UOC:194,208	4
16	PAOZZ	24617	456004	NUT,SELF-LOCKING,HE UOC:194,208	8
17	PAOOO	11862	14072466	RAIL,CARGO COVER RIGHT UOC:194,208	1
18	PAOZZ	19207	12255564-2	.STUD,TURNBUTTON FAS UOC:194,208	6
19	PAOZZ	96906	MS51939-2	.LOOP,STRAP FASTENER UOC:194,208	1
20	PAOZZ	96906	MS21141-U0604	.RIVET,BLIND UOC:194,208	2
21	PAOZZ	24617	271172	.NUT,SELF-LOCKING,AS UOC:194,208	6
22	PAOZZ	11862	14072467	RAIL,CARGO COVER REAR UOC:194,208	1
23	PAOOO	11862	14072465	RAIL,CARGO COVER UOC:194,208	1

(1) ITEM NO	(2) SMR CODE	(3) CAGEC	(4) PART NUMBER	(5) DESCRIPTION AND USABLE ON CODES (UOC)	(6) QTY
24	PAOOO	11862	14072463	RAIL,CARGO COVER UOC:194,208	1
				END OF FIGURE	

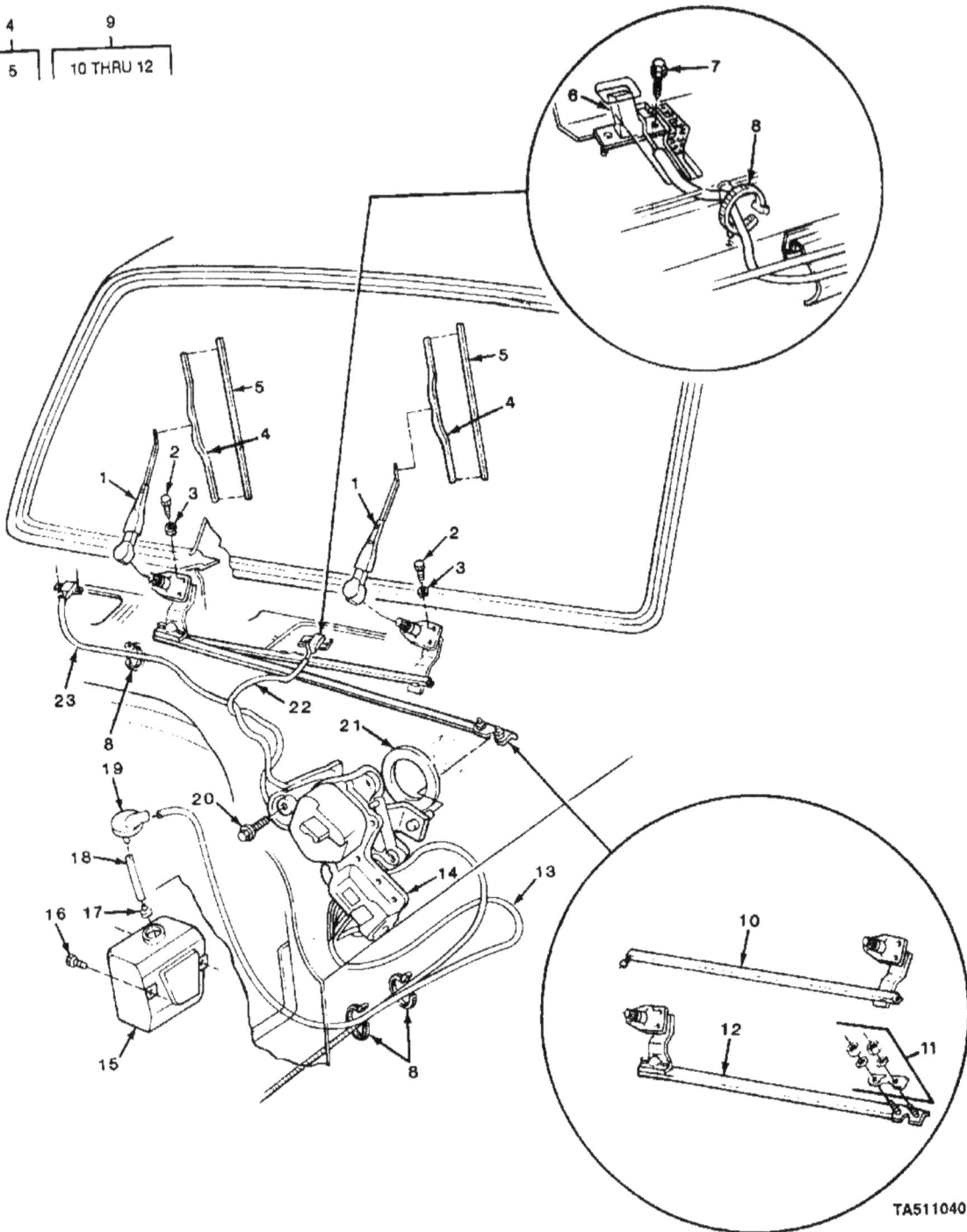

FIGURE 198. WINDSHIELD WIPER MOTOR AND PUMP ASSMBLY, WIPER ARM
LINK ASSEMBLY, WIPER BLADE ASSEMBLY, AND RELATED PARTS.

TA511040

GROUP 2202 ACCESSORY ITEMS

FIG. 198 WINDSHIELD WIPER MOTOR AND
PUMP ASSEMBLY, WIPER ARM LINK
ASSEMBLY, WIPER BLADE ASSEMBLY, AND
RELATED PARTS

ITEM NO	SMR CODE	CAGEC	PART NUMBER	DESCRIPTION AND USABLE ON CODES (UOC)	QTY
1	PAOZZ	11862	15591703	ARM,WINDSHIELD WIPE	2
2	PAOZZ	24617	9421985	SCREW,TAPPING	6
3	PAOZZ	96906	MS35335-34	WASHER,LOCK	6
4	PAOOO	11862	15591704	BLADE,WINDSHIELD WI	2
5	XAOZZ	11862	14044931	.REFILL BLADE,WIPER	2
6	PAOZZ	11862	14076838	NOZZLE ASSEMBLY,WIN	2
7	PAOZZ	24617	9419163	SCREW,CAP,HEXAGON H	2
8	PAOZZ	11862	3816659	STRAP,LINE SUPPORTI	6
9	AOOOO	11862	22021655	TRANS & LINK ASM W/	1
10	PAOZZ	11862	22029629	.LINK,WIPER,WINDSHIE LEFT	1
11	PAOZZ	11862	4918562	.PARTS KIT, WINDSHIEL	1
12	PAOZZ	11862	22029630	.WIPER ASSEMBLY,WIND RIGHT	1
13	MOOZZ	11862	3782730	HOSE ASM PMP (46.00"LG) MAKE FROM HOSE, P/N 3987364	1
14	PAOFF	72560	22048352	MOTOR,WINDSHIELD WI FORM COMPONENT PARTS SEE FIG 199	1
15	PAOZZ	11862	3990892	JAR ASSEMBLY,WINDSH	1
16	PAOZZ	96906	MS51871-4	SCREW,TAPPING	2
17	PAOZZ	11862	3986821	STRAINER,SUCTION	1
18	MOOZZ	11862	329198	HOSE (CUT TO 7.0") MAKE FROM HOSE, P/N 3987364	1
19	PAOZZ	11862	3798372	CAP,FILLER OPENING	1
20	PAOZZ	11862	3824124	BOLT,ASSEMBLED WASH	3
21	PAOZZ	11862	20489125	GASKET	1
22	MOOZZ	11862	337714	HOSE ASM NOZZLE L/H (16.00" LG) MAKE FROM HOSE, P/N 1359744	1
23	MOOZZ	11862	3782732	HOSE ASM NOZZLE R/H (36.00" LG) MAKE FROM HOSE, P/N 1359744	1

END OF FIGURE

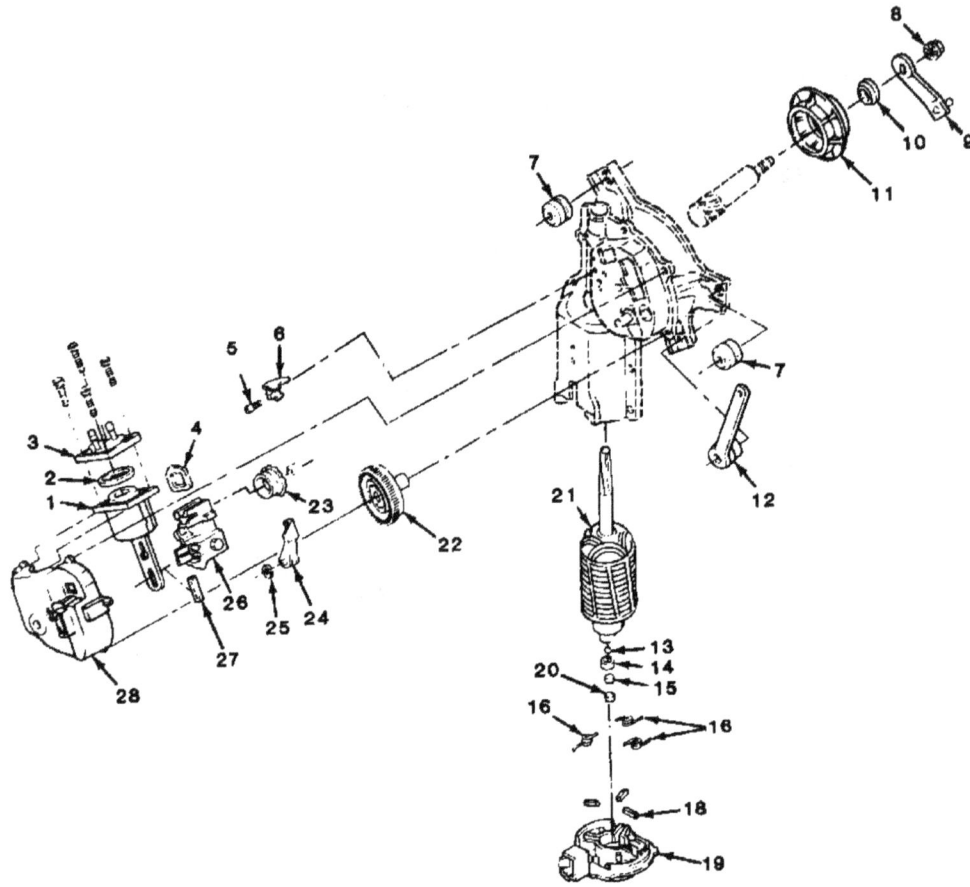

TA511041

FIGURE 199. WIPER MOTOR COMPONENT PARTS.

(1) ITEM NO	(2) SMR CODE	(3) CAGEC	(4) PART NUMBER	(5) DESCRIPTION AND USABLE ON CODES (UOC)	(6) QTY
				GROUP 2202 ACCESSORY ITEMS	
				FIG. 199 WIPER MOTOR COMPONENT PARTS	
7	PAOZZ	11862	22049531	SPACER AND GROMMET	3
8	PAOZZ	11862	22054153	NUT,SELF-LOCKING,EX	1
9	PAOZZ	11862	22038927	LEVER,REMOTE CONTRO	1
10	PAOZZ	11862	22054156	GASKET	1
12	PAOZZ	11862	22021679	GROMMET	1
28	PAOZZ	11862	22038928	COVER,WASHER,WINDSH	1

END OF FIGURE

3
┌─────────┐
│ 4 THRU 9 │
└─────────┘

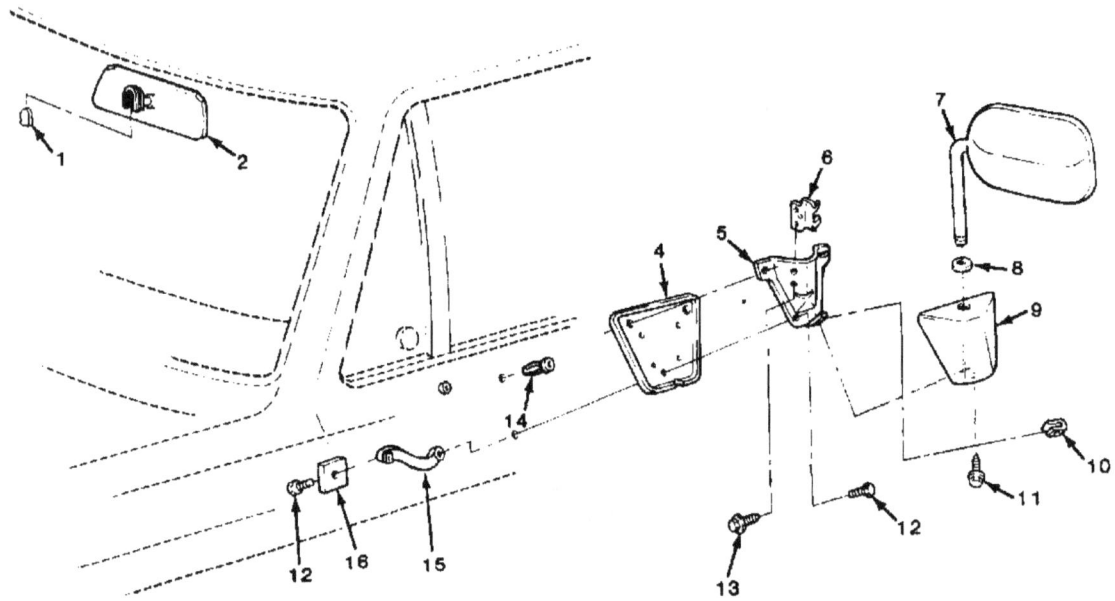

TA511042

FIGURE 200. REARVIEW MIRRORS.

(1) ITEM NO	(2) SMR CODE	(3) CAGEC	(4) PART NUMBER	(5) DESCRIPTION AND USABLE ON CODES (UOC)	(6) QTY
				GROUP 2202 ACCESSORY ITEMS	
				FIG. 200 REARVIEW MIRRORS	
1	PAOZZ	11862	9831062	SUPPORT,REARVIEW MI INCLUDES GLUE UOC:194,208,209,231	1
2	PAOZZ	11862	918656	MIRROR ASSEMBLY,REA UOC:194,208,209,231	1
3	ACOOO	11862	14072485	MIRROR ASSEMBLY,REA LEFT UOC:194,208,209,210,230,231,252	1
3	ACOOO	11862	14072486	MIRROR ASSEMBLY,REA RIGHT UOC:194,208,209,210,230,231,252	1
4	PAOZZ	11862	14008191	.GASKET UOC:194,208,209,210,230,231,252	1
5	PAOZZ	11862	14007429	.BRACKET,MIRROR UOC:194,208,209,210,230,231,252	1
6	PAOZZ	11862	14007430	.CLAMP,REAR VIEW MIR UOC:194,208,209,210,230,231,252	1
7	PAOZZ	11862	14072487	.MIRROR ASSEMBLY, REA UOC:194,208,209,210,230,231,252	1
7	PAOZZ	11862	15634659	.MIRROR,ASSEMBLY,REA UOC:254,256	1
7	PAOZZ	11862	15634660	.MIRROR ASSEMBLY,REA UOC:254,256	1
8	PAOZZ	11862	14007435	.GROMMET,NONMETALLIC UOC:194,208,209,210,230,231,252	1
9	PAOZZ	11862	14072489	.COVER,MIRROR,REAR V LEFT UOC:194,208,209,210,230,231,252	1
10	PAOZZ	11862	52351724	NUT,SHEET SPRING	2
11	PAOZZ	11862	15554576	SCREW,ASSEMBLED WAS	2
12	PAOZZ	11862	14007511	BOLT,ASSEMBLED WASH	8
13	PAOZZ	24617	9426277	BOLT	4
14	PAOZZ	11862	14005953	SHIELD,EXPANSION UOC:194,208,209,210,230,231,252	4
15	PAOZZ	11862	14007541	ARM,REARVIEW MIRROR LEFT UOC:194,208,209,210,230,231,252	1
15	PAOZZ	11862	14007542	ARM,REARVIEW MIRROR RIGHT UOC:194,208,209,210,230,231,252	1
16	PAOZZ	11862	14007539	WASHER,FLAT	2

END OF FIGURE

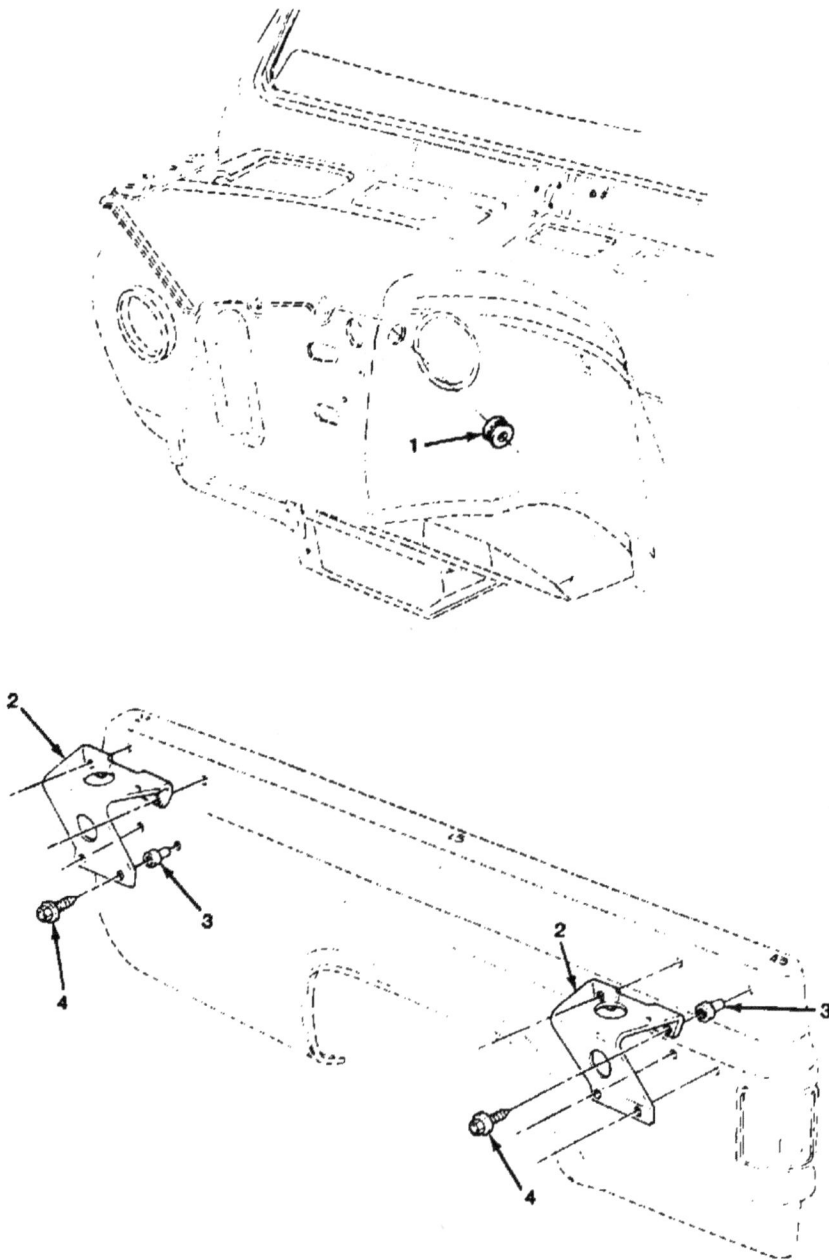

TA511043

FIGURE 201. ANTENNA MOUNTING (ALL EXCEPT M1009 AND M1010).

(1) ITEM NO	(2) SMR CODE	(3) CAGEC	(4) PART NUMBER	(5) DESCRIPTION AND USABLE ON CODES (UOC)	(6) QTY
				GROUP 2202 ACCESSORY ITEMS	
				FIG. 201 ANTENNA MOUNTING (ALL EXCEPT M1009 AND M1010)	
1	PAOZZ	11862	14076298	GROMMET,NOMETALLIC UOC:194,208,230,252,254,256	1
2	PAOZZ	11862	14072445	BRACKET,ANGLE UOC:194,208,230,252,254,256	4
3	PAOZZ	11862	15599994	NUT,PLAIN,BLIND RIV UOC:194,208,230,231,252,254,256	16
4	PAOZZ	11862	9440300	SCREW,CAP,HEXAGON H UOC:194,208,230,252,254,256	16

END OF FIGURE

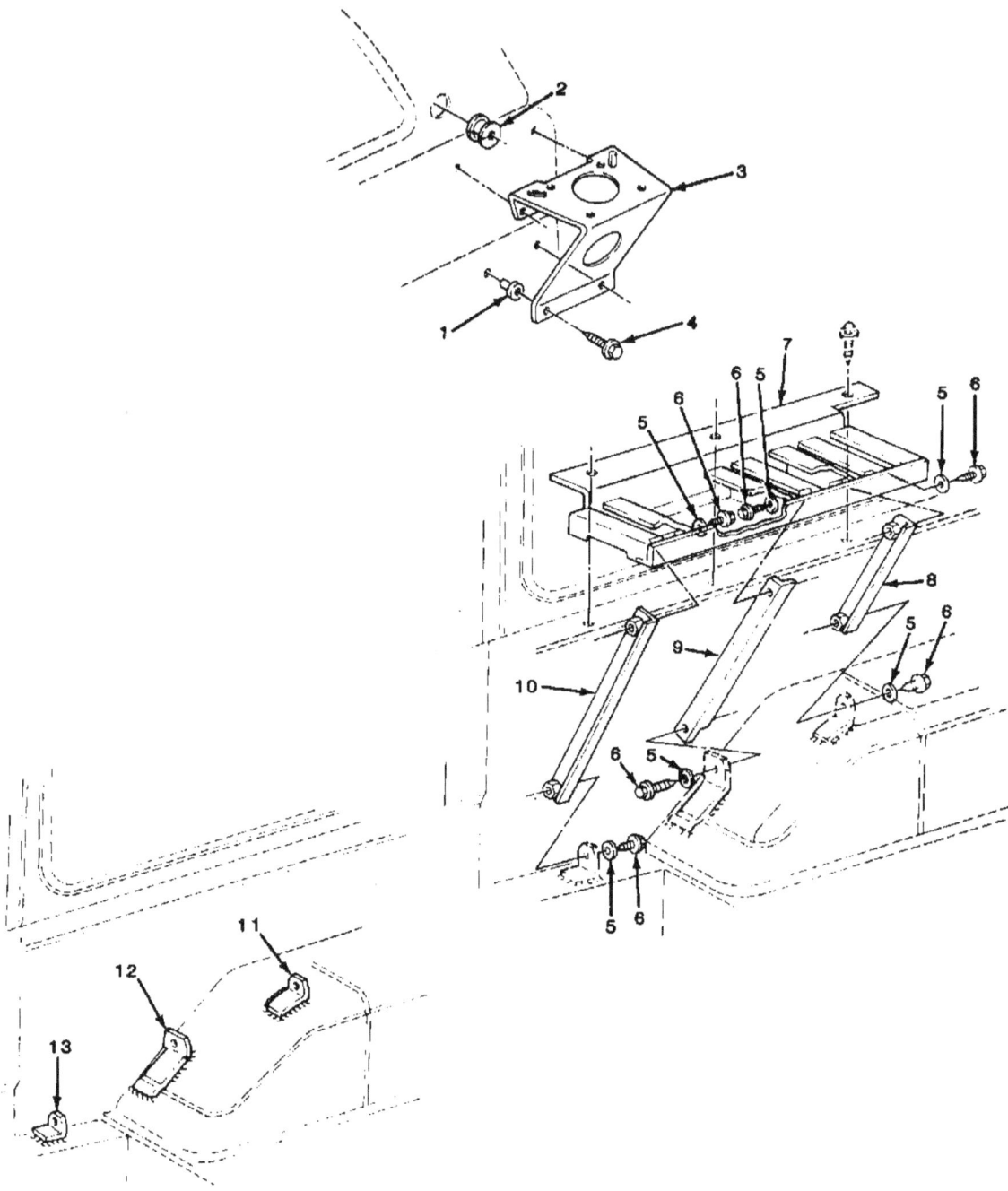

TA511044

FIGURE 202. RADIO AND ANTENNA BRACKETS (M1009).

(1) ITEM NO	(2) SMR CODE	(3) CAGEC	(4) PART NUMBER	(5) DESCRIPTION AND USABLE ON CODES (UOC)	(6) QTY
				GROUP 2202 ACCESSORY ITEMS	
				FIG. 202 RADIO AND ANTENNA BRACKETS (M1009)	
1	PAOZZ	11862	15599994	NUT,PLAIN,BLIND RIV UOC:209	8
2	PAOZZ	11862	15599990	GROMMET,NONMETALLIC UOC:209	2
3	PAOZZ	11862	14072445	BRACKET,ANGLE UOC:209	2
4	PAOZZ	11862	9440300	SCREW,CAP,HEXAGON H UOC:209	8
5	PAOZZ	96906	MS35340-45	WASHER,LOCK UOC:209	6
6	PAOZZ	96906	MS90728-34	BOLT,MACHINE UOC:209	6
7	PAOZZ	11862	15599962	BRACKET UOC:209	1
8	PAOZZ	11862	14072441	BRACKET,ANGLE UOC:209	1
9	PAOZZ	11862	14072440	BRACKET,ANGLE UOC:209	1
10	PAOZZ	11862	14072439	BRACKET,ANGLE UOC:209	1
11	PAOZZ	11862	15599964	BRACKET,ANGLE UOC:209	1
12	PAOZZ	11862	15599963	BRACKET,DOUBLE ANGL UOC:209	1
13	PAOZZ	11862	14072442	BRACKET,ANGLE UOC:209	1

END OF FIGURE

TA511045

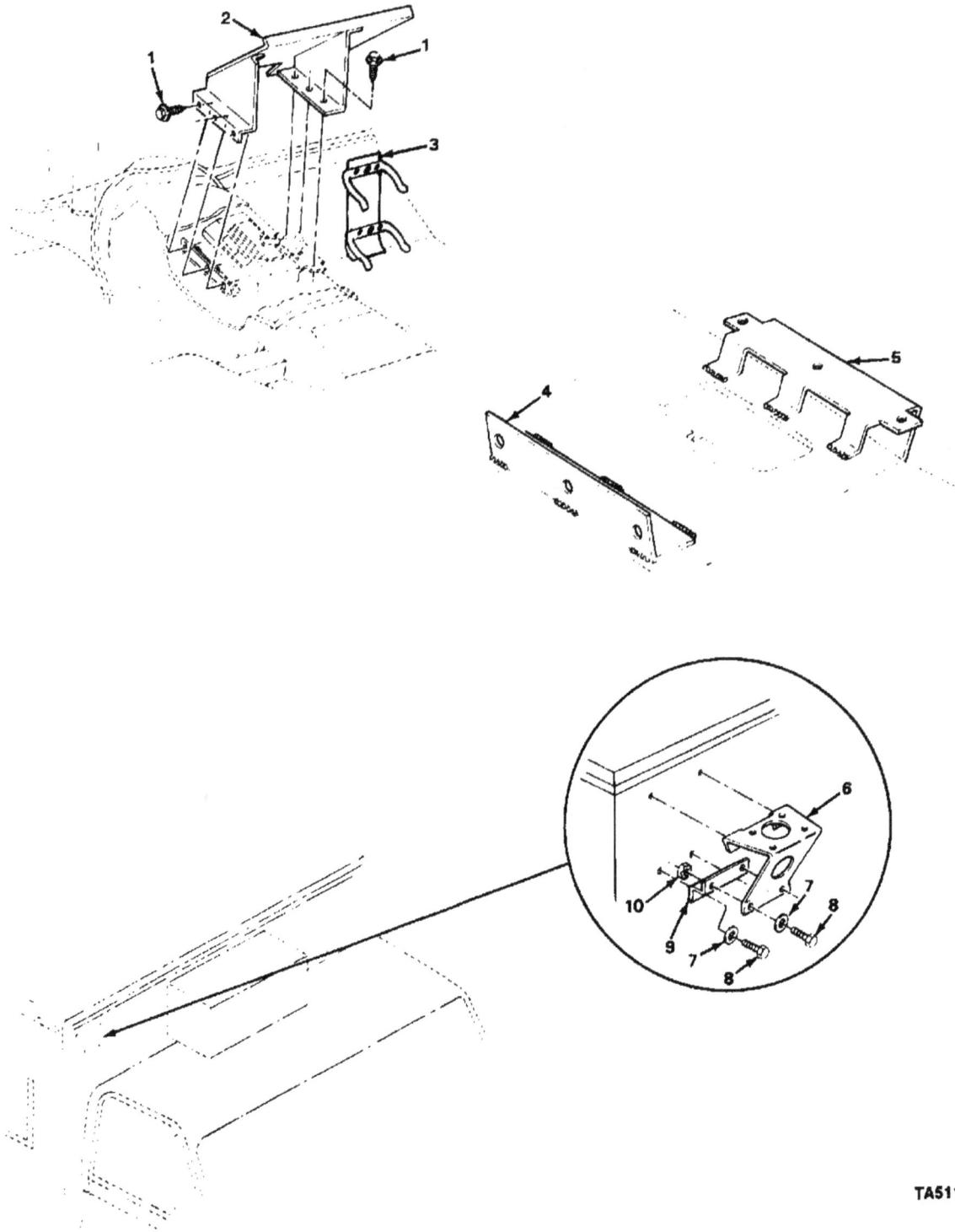

FIGURE 203. RADIO, FIRE EXTINGUISHER, AND ANTENNA BRACKETS (M1010).

(1) ITEM NO	(2) SMR CODE	(3) CAGEC	(4) PART NUMBER	(5) DESCRIPTION AND USABLE ON CODES (UOC)	(6) QTY
				GROUP 2202 ACCESSORY ITEMS	
				FIG. 203 RADIO, FIRE EXTINGUISHER, AND ANTENNA BRACKETS (M1010)	
1	PAOZZ	24617	9425117	BOLT,MACHINE UOC:210	6
2	PAOZZ	11862	14075846	BRACKET,DOUBLE ANGL UOC:210	1
3	PAOZZ	19207	7357009	BRACKET,FIRE EXTING UOC:210	1
6	PAOZZ	25022	99-4602-1	BRACKET,ANGLE UOC:210	1
7	PAOZZ	96906	MS35338-45	WASHER,LOCK UOC:210	6
8	PAOZZ	96906	MS90728-34	BOLT,MACHINE UOC:210	6
9	PAOZZ	25022	99-4341-1	BRACKET,DOUBLE ANGL UOC:210	1
10	PAOZZ	96906	MS35691-9	NUT,PLAIN,HEXAGON UOC:210	2

END OF FIGURE

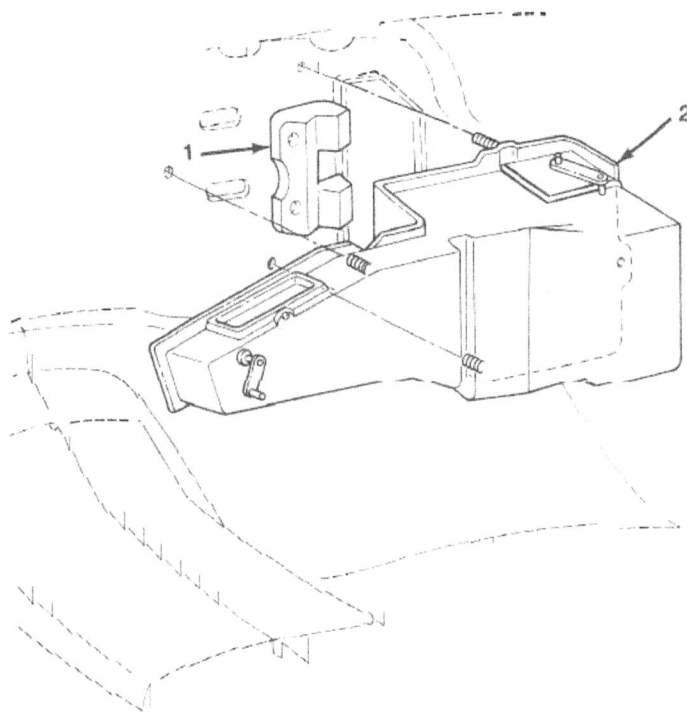

TA511046

(1)	(2)	(3)	(4)	(5)	(6)
ITEM NO	SMR CODE	CAGEC	PART NUMBER	DESCRIPTION AND USABLE ON CODES (UOC)	QTY

GROUP 2207 WINTERIZATION EQUIPMENT

FIG. 204 HEATER ASSEMBLY

| 1 | PAOZZ | 11862 | 6273325 | SEAL,RUBBER SPECIAL | 1 |
| 2 | AC000 | 11862 | 3054308 | HEATER,ASM FOR COMPONENT PARTS SEE FIG 205 | 1 |

END OF FIGURE

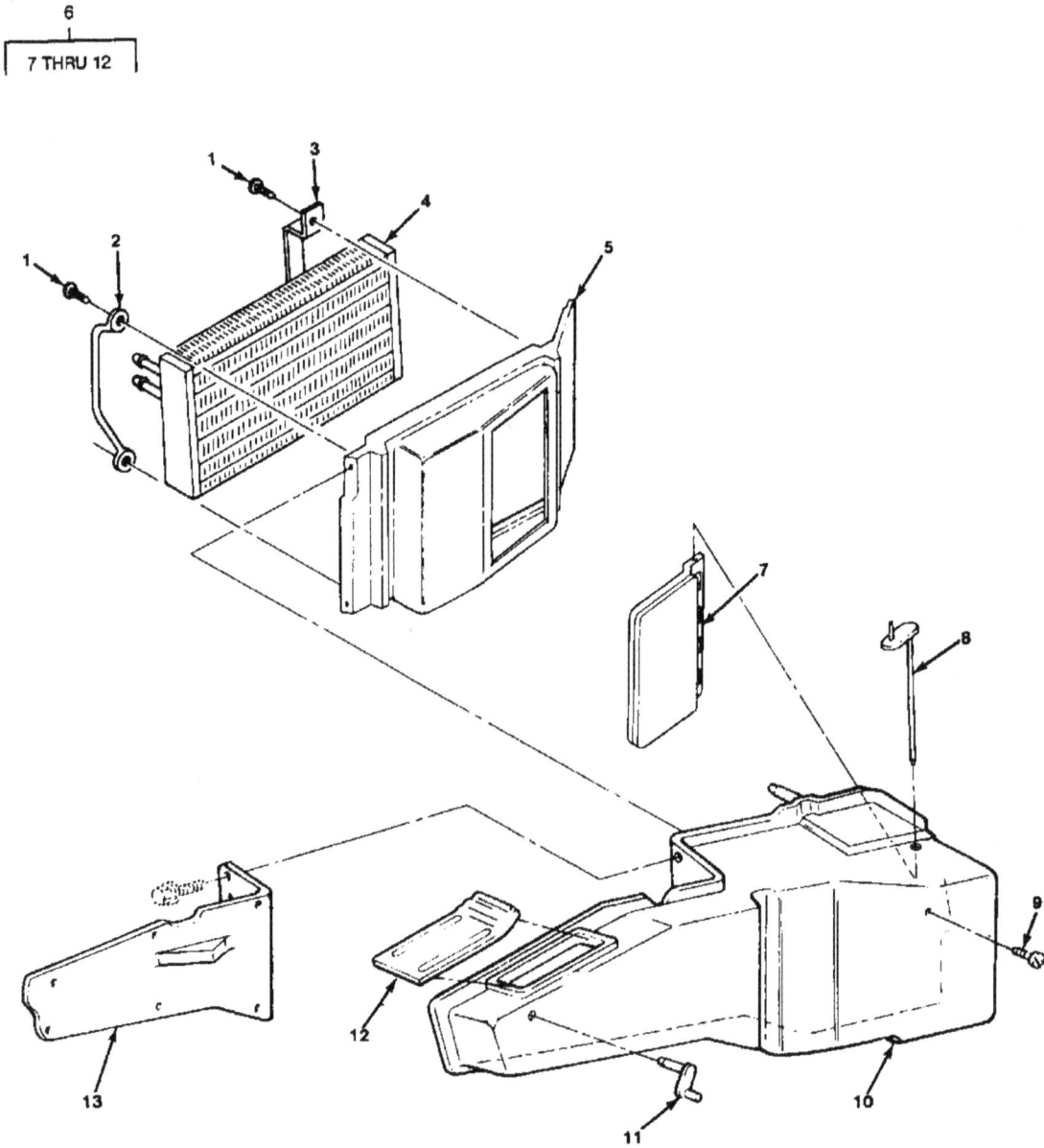

TA511047

FIGURE 205. HEATER ASSEMBLY COMPONENTS.

(1) ITEM NO	(2) SMR CODE	(3) CAGEC	(4) PART NUMBER	(5) DESCRIPTION AND USABLE ON CODES (UOC)	(6) QTY
				GROUP 2207 WINTERIZATION EQUIPMENT	
				FIG. 205 HEATER ASSEMBLY COMPONENTS	
1	PAOZZ	24617	9419699	BOLT,MACHINE UOC:194,208,209,210,230,231,252,254	4
2	PAOZZ	11862	3025501	STRAP,RETAINING	1
3	PAOZZ	11862	3024673	STRAP,RETAINING	1
4	PAOZZ	11862	3027247	CORE,HEATER ASSEMBL	1
5	PAOZZ	11862	3048083	SHROUD,VALVE SEAT	1
6	PAOZZ	11862	3054315	HOUSING,HEATER COMP	1
7	PAOZZ	11862	3024867	.VALVE,HEATER CONTRC	1
8	PAOZZ	11862	3030075	.SHAFT AND LEVER ASS	1
9	PAOZZ	24617	11500999	.SCREW,ASSEMBLED WAS	1
10	PAOZZ	27462	3054316	.HOUSING ASSEMBLY, HE	1
11	PAOZZ	11862	3030072	.SHAFT AND LEVER ASS	1
12	PAOZZ	11862	3027308	.VALVE,DEFROSTER	1
13	PAOZZ	11862	3048067	PLATE AND BOLT ASSE	1

END OF FIGURE

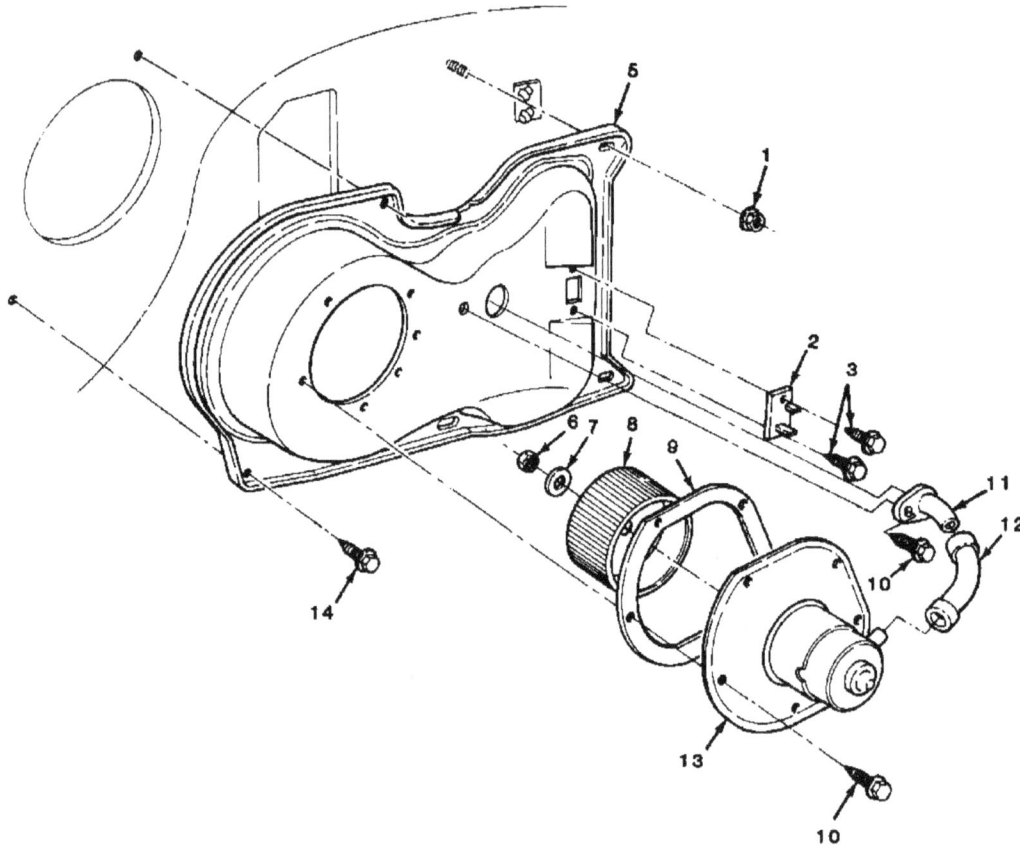

TA511048

FIGURE 206. HEATER BLOWER MOTOR ASSEMBLY AND COMPONENT PARTS.

(1) ITEM NO	(2) SMR CODE	(3) CAGEC	(4) PART NUMBER	(5) DESCRIPTION AND USABLE ON CODES (UOC)	(6) QTY
				GROUP 2207 WINTERIZATION EQUIPMENT	
				FIG. 206 HEATER BLOWER MOTOR ASSEMBLY AND COMPONENT PARTS	
1	PAOZZ	24617	11506003	NUT,PLAIN,ASSEMBLED	3
2	PAOZZ	11862	500890	RESISTORK,FIXED,WIRE	1
3	PAOZZ	11862	11513932	SCREW,ASSEMBLED WAS	2
4	AOOOO	11862	3058097	BLOWER ASM	1
5	PAOZZ	11862	3029730	.CASE ASSEMBLY,BLOWE	1
6	PAOZZ	11862	3042351	.NUT,SHEET SPRING	1
7	PAOZZ	11862	3015545	.WWASHER,FAN SUPPORT	1
8	PAOZZ	11862	3037550	.IMPELLER,FAN,CENTRI	1
9	PAOZZ	11862	3039873	.GASKET	1
10	PAOZZ	11862	11500742	.SCREW,TAPPING	6
11	PAOZZ	11862	3013475	.ELBOW,TUBE	1
12	PAOZZ	11862	3036927	.ELBOW,TUBE	1
13	PAOZZ	11862	22020945	.MOTOR,DIRECT CURREN	1
14	PAOZZ	24617	11500997	SCREW,ASSEMBLED WAS	2

END OF FIGURE

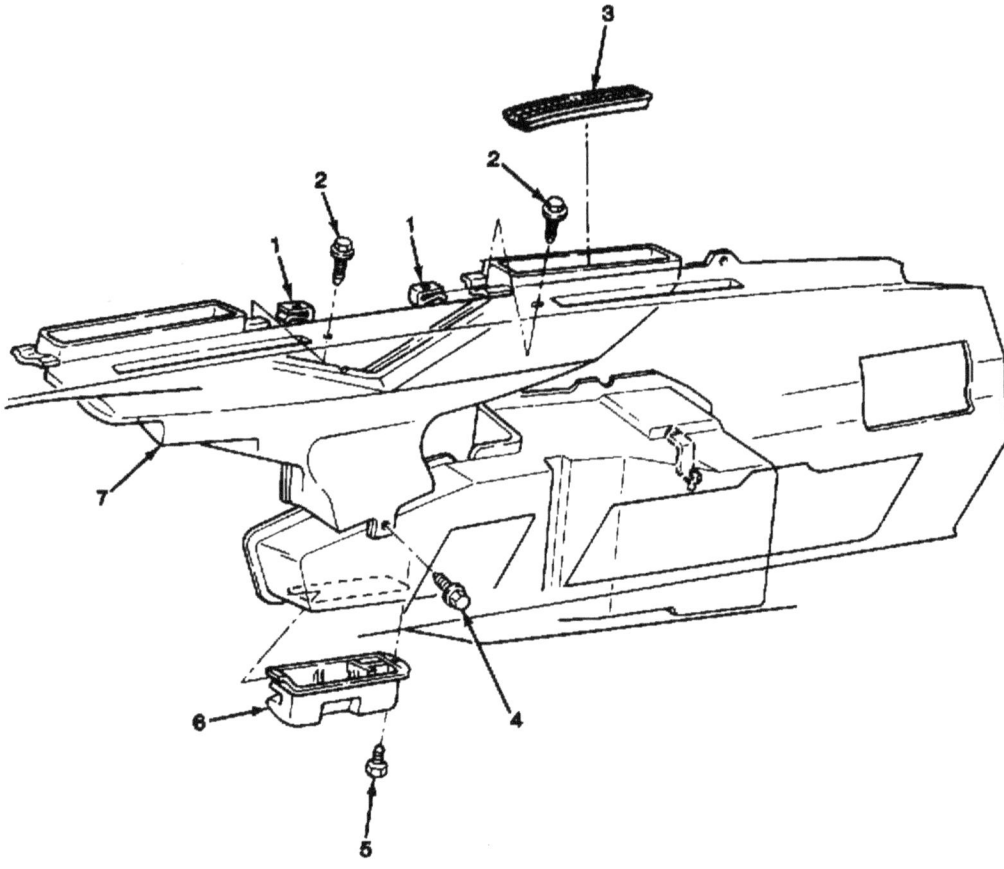

TA511049

FIGURE 207. HEATER ASSEMBLY AIR DUCTS.

(1) ITEM NO	(2) SMR CODE	(3) CAGEC	(4) PART NUMBER	(5) DESCRIPTION AND USABLE ON CODES (UOC)	(6) QTY
				GROUP 2207 WINTERIZATION EQUIPMENT	
				FIG. 207 HEATER ASSEMBLY AIR DUCTS	
4	PAOZZ	24617	9440025	SCREW,TAPPING	1
5	PAOZZ	24617	11503396	SCREW,ASSEMBLED WAS	1
6	PAOZZ	11862	14013122	DUCT ASSEMBLY,HEATI RIGHT	1
				END OF FIGURE	

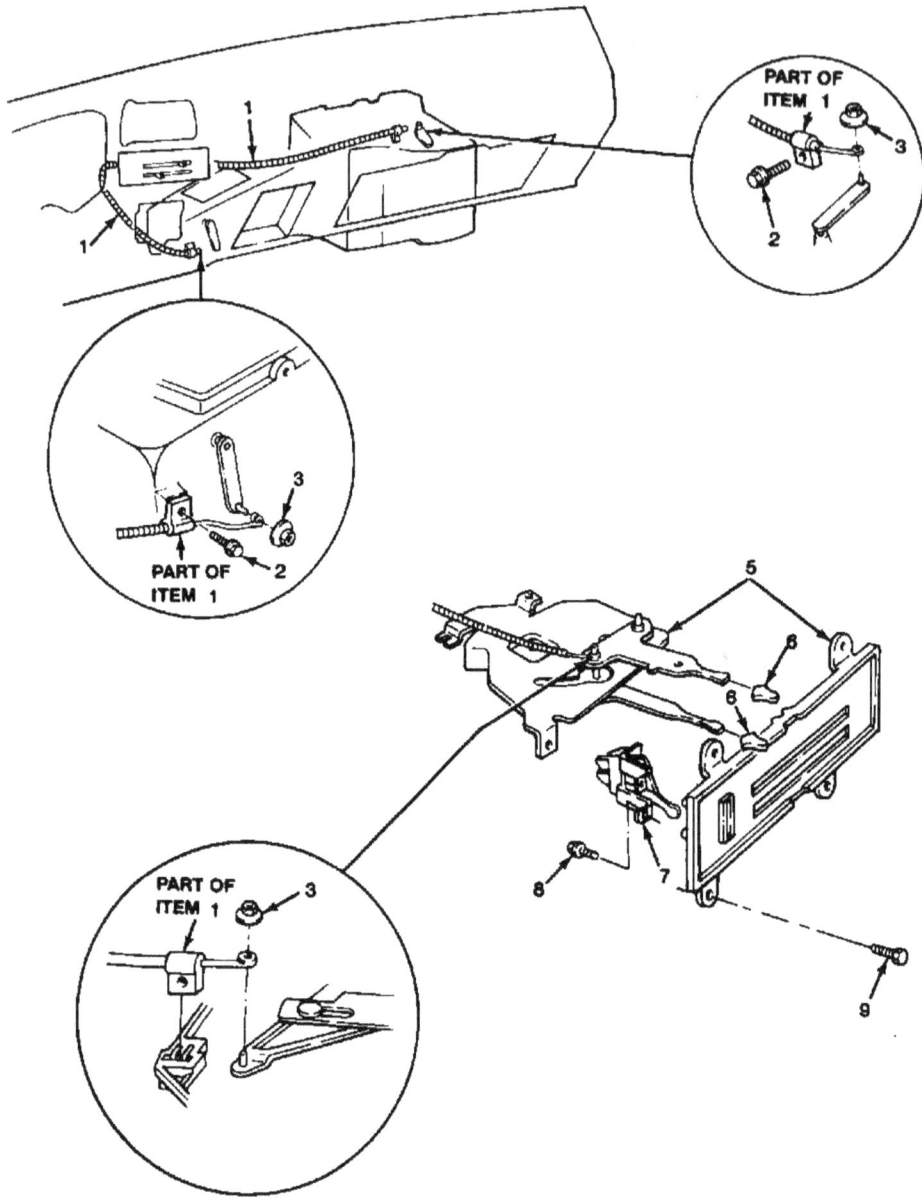

TA511050

FIGURE 208. HEATER CABLE AND CONTROL ASSEMBLY

(1) ITEM NO	(2) SMR CODE	(3) CAGEC	(4) PART NUMBER	(5) DESCRIPTION AND USABLE ON CODES (UOC)	(6) QTY
				GROUP 2207 WINTERIZATION EQUIPMENT	
				FIG. 208 HEATER CABLE AND CONTROL ASSEMBLY	
1	PAOZZ	11862	6258364	CONTRO ASSEMBLY,PU	2
2	PAOZZ	96906	MS51850-86	SCREW,TAPPING	2
3	PAOZZ	11862	11501937	NUT	4
4	PAOOO	11862	16034561	CONTROL,HEATER	1
5	PAOZZ	11862	1226174	.PARTS KIT,HEATER CO	1
6	PAOZZ	11862	336406	.KNOB	2
7	PAOZZ	16758	16015256	.SWITCH,LEVER	1
8	PAOZZ	24617	9419663	.SCREW,TAPPING	2
9	PAOZZ	24617	9415163	SCREW,ASSEMBLED WAS	4

END OF FIGURE

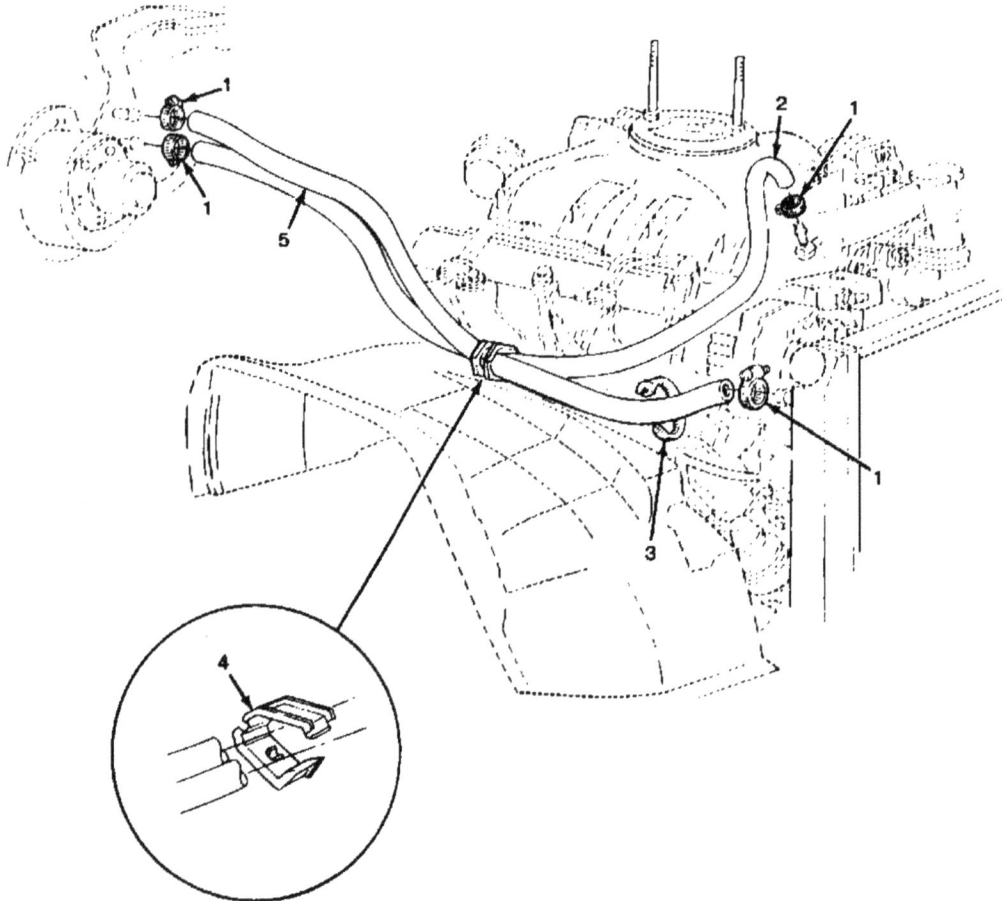

TA511051

FIGURE 209. HEATER HOSES.

(1) ITEM NO	(2) SMR CODE	(3) CAGEC	(4) PART NUMBER	(5) DESCRIPTION AND USABLE ON CODES (UOC)	(6) QTY
				GROUP 2207 WINTERIZATION EQUIPMENT	
				FIG. 209 HEATER HOSES	
1	PAOZZ	96906	MS35842-11	CLAMP,HOSE	4
2	MOOZZ	11862	487425	HOSE HEATER INLET (48.00" LG) MAKE FROM HOSE,P/N 482420 UOC:210	1
2	MOOZZ	11862	482995	HOSE,NONMETALLIC (42.00" LG) MAKE FROM HOSE,P/N 495692 UOC:194,208,209,230,252,254,256	1
3	PAOZZ	11862	12337820	STRAP,LINE SUPPORTI UOC:210,230	1
4	PAOZZ	11862	3825416	CLAMP,LOOP	1
5	MOOZZ	11862	10012288-45	HOSE,PREFORMED (44.75" LG) MAKE FROM HOSE,P/N 482420	1

END OF FIGURE

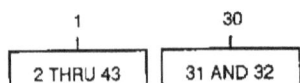

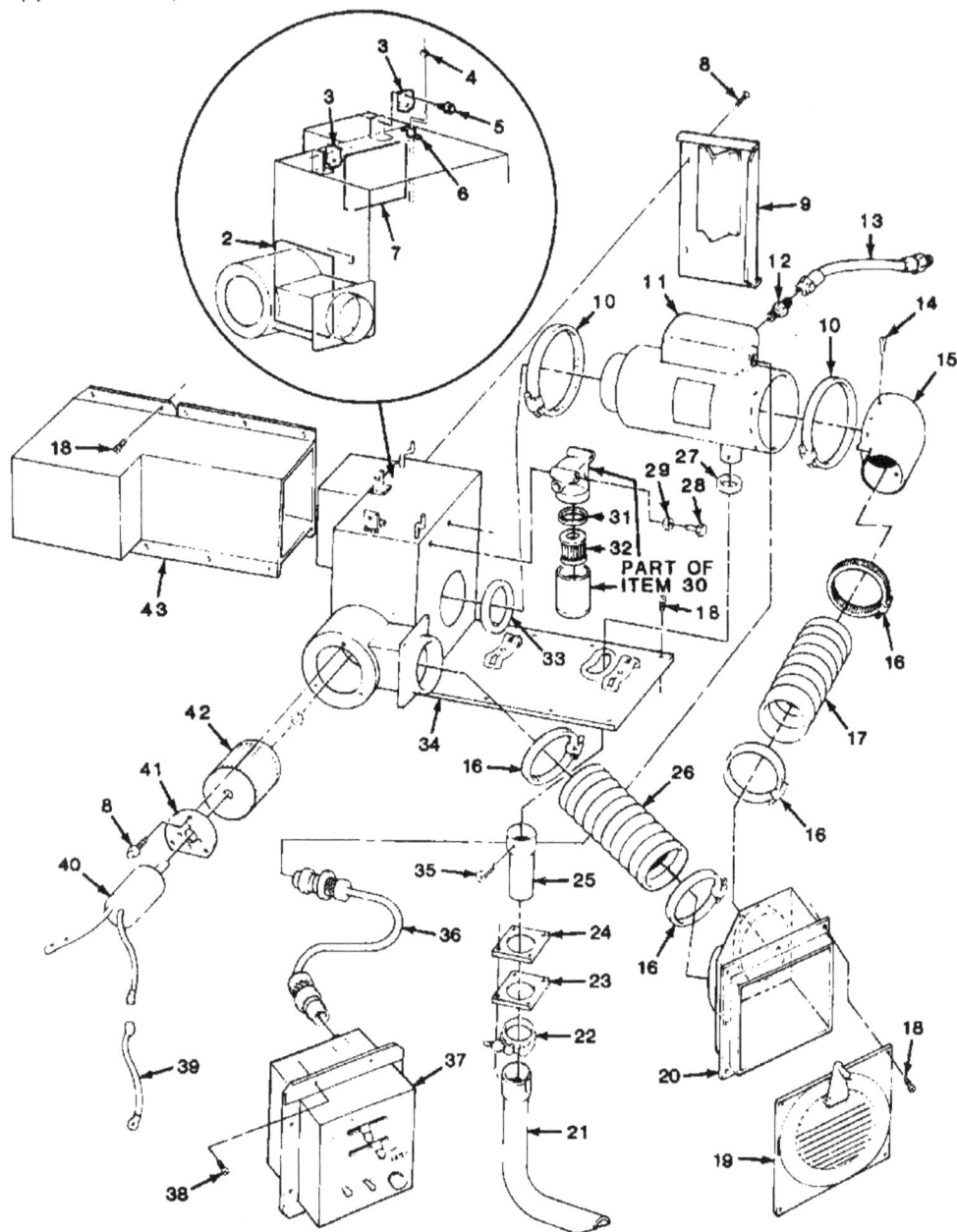

FIGURE 210. PERSONNEL HEATER ASSEMBLY (M1010).

TA511052

(1) ITEM NO	(2) SMR CODE	(3) CAGEC	(4) PART NUMBER	(5) DESCRIPTION AND USABLE ON CODES (UOC)	(6) QTY
				GROUP 2207 WINTERIZATION EQUIPMENT	
				FIG. 210 PERSONNEL HEATER ASSEMBLY (M1010)	
1	AOOOO	25022	22-0871	PARTS KIT,MANIFOLD UOC:210	1
2	PAOZZ	99688	58636	.GASKET UOC:210	1
3	PAOZZ	99688	58659	.CLIP,SPRING TENSION UOC:210	2
4	PAOZZ	99688	62229	.PUSH ON NUT UOC:210	2
5	PAOZZ	96906	MS51861-24	.SCREW,TAPPING UOC:210	2
6	PAOZZ	99688	58627	.SPRING,HELICAL,TORS UOC:210	1
7	PAOZZ	99688	58637	.GASKET UOC:210	1
8	PAOZZ	24617	9421073	.SCREW,TAPPING UOC:210	7
9	PAOZZ	99688	85941	.COVER,DOOR UOC:210	1
10	PAOZZ	96906	MS35842-16	.CLAMP,HOSE UOC:210	2
11	PAOFF	78385	10530B	.HEATER,VEHICULAR,CC UOC:210	1
12	PAOZZ	72983	248X4	.ADAPTER,STRAIGHT,PI UOC:210	1
13	PAOZZ	99688	58625	.HOSE ASSEMBLY,NONME UOC:210	1
14	PAOZZ	96906	MS35206-247	.SCREW,MACHINE UOC:210	4
15	PAOZZ	99688	58623	.ADAPTER,AIR CONDITI UOC:210	1
16	PAOZZ	96906	MS35842-15	.CLAMP,HOSE UOC:210	4
17	MOOZZ	99688	58628	.HOSE,AIR DUCT (CUT TO 16.0" LG)MAKE FROM HOSE,P/N 319029 UOC:210	1
18	PAOZZ	96906	MS21141-U0604	.RIVET,BLIND UOC:210	8
19	PFOZZ	99688	784030	.VENTILATOR,AIR CIRC UOC:210	1
20	XOOZZ	99688	78405	.VENT,HEATER UOC:210	1
21	PAOZZ	99688	58649	.PIPE,EXHAUST UOC:210	1
22	PAOZZ	99688	58620	.CLAMP,HOSE UOC:210	1
23	PAOZZ	99688	46090	.COLLAR,AIR CONDITIO UOC:210	1

(1) ITEM NO	(2) SMR CODE	(3) CAGEC	(4) PART NUMBER	(5) DESCRIPTION AND USABLE ON CODES (UOC)	(6) QTY
24	PAOZZ	99688	58635	.GASKET UOC:210	1
25	PAOZZ	99688	58651	.CONNECTOR,EXHAUST P UOC:210	1
26	MOOZZ	99688	58629	.HOSE,AIR DUCT (CUT TO 23.0"LG) MAKE FROM HOSE,P/N 319029 UOC:210	1
27	PAOZZ	99688	58632	.GASKET UOC:210	1
28	PAOZZ	96906	MS51849-70	.SCREW,MACHINE UOC:210	2
29	PAOZZ	6906	MS27183-42	.WASHER,FLAT UOC:210	2
30	PAOOO	96906	MS51085-1	.FILTER,FLUID UOC:210	1
31	PAOZZ	96906	MS29513-125	.PACKING,PREFORMED UOC:210	1
32	PAOZZ	90005	26422-B	.FILTER ELEMENT,FLUI UOC:210	1
33	POOZZ	99688	58624	.GASKET UOC:210	1
34	PFOZZ	99688	85942	.BASE,HEATER UOC:210	1
35	PAOZZ	96906	MS24665-446	.PIN,COTTER UOC:210	1
36	PAOZZ	99688	65148	.WIRING HARNESS,BRAN UOC:210	1
37	PAOFF	99688	859430	.PANEL,HEATER CONTRO UOC:210	1
38	PAOZZ	96906	MS20600B6W4	.RIVET,BLIND UOC:210	28
39	PAOZZ	99688	65149	.LEAD,ELECTRICAL UOC:210	1
40	PAOZZ	0A7R8	PV23135R	.MOTOR,DIRECT CURREN 24 VOLT D.C. UOC:210	1
41	PAOZZ	99688	46023	.PLATE,MOUNTING,GROM UOC:210	1
42	PAOZZ	99688	58634	.IMPELLER,FAN,CENTRI UOC:210	1
43	PFOZZ	99688	78406	.DUCT,FRESH AIR UOC:210	1

END OF FIGURE

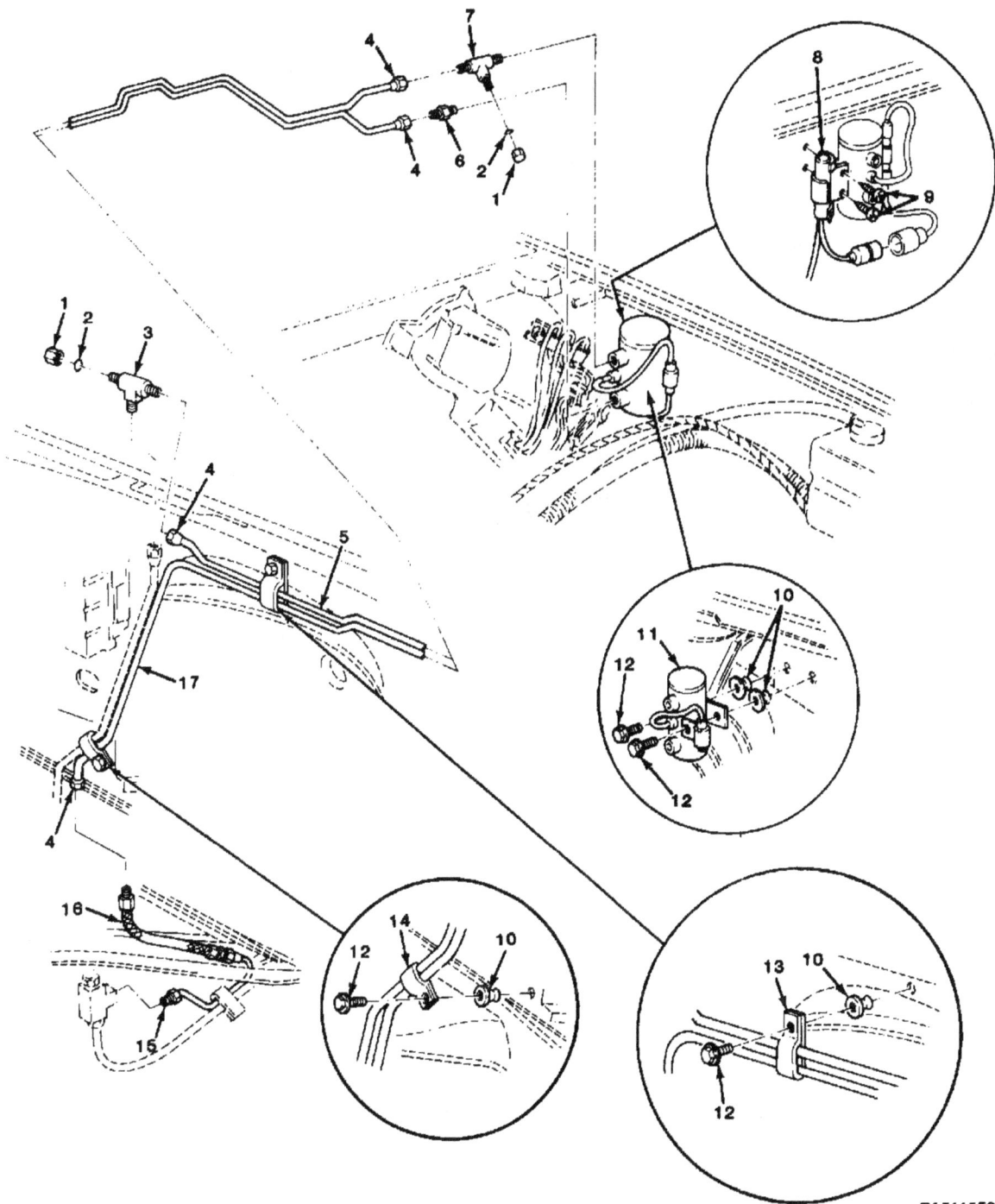

TA511058

FIGURE 211. PERSONNEL HEATER FUEL PUMP, LINES, AND RELATED PARTS (M1010).

GROUP 2207 WINTERIZATION EQUIPMENT

FIG. 211 PERSONNEL HEATER FUEL PUMP,
LINES, AND RELATED PARTS

ITEM NO	SMR CODE	CAGEC	PART NUMBER	DESCRIPTION AND USABLE ON CODES (UOC)	QTY
1	PAOZZ	24617	9409761	NUT,PLAIN,CAP UOC:210,230	2
2	PAOZZ	11862	9409754	WASHER,FINISHING UOC:210,230	2
3	PAOZZ	93061	144F-5	TEE,TUBE UOC:210,230	1
5	MFOZZ	11862	14072371	PIPE ASM-AUX HTR (44.45"LG) MAKE UOC:210,230	1
6	PAOZZ	81343	SAEJ513	ADAPTER,STRAIGHT,PI UOC:210,230	1
8	PAOZZ	11862	14072347	SWITCH,HEATER FUEL UOC:210,230	1
9	PAOZZ	24617	9415163	SCREW,ASEMBLED WAS UOC:210,230	2
10	PAOZZ	11862	14005953	SHIELD,EXPANSION UOC:210,230	4
11	PAOZZ	96906	MS51321-1	PUMP,FUEL,ELECTRICA UOC:210,230	1
12	PAOZZ	11862	14007511	BOLT,ASSEMBLED WASH UOC:210,230	4
13	PAOZZ	11862	343444	CLAMP,LOOP UOC:210,230	1
14	PAOZZ	11862	14004512	CLAMP,LOOP UOC:210,230	1
15	PAOZZ	16764	110200	ADAPTER,STRAIGHT,PI UOC:210,230	1
16	PAOZZ	11862	14072368	HOSE ASSEMBLY,NONME UOC:210,230	1
17	MFOZZ	11862	14072369	PIPE ASM-AUX HTR (65.22"LG) MAKE FROM TUBE, P/N 1324714 UOC:210,230	1

END OF FIGURE

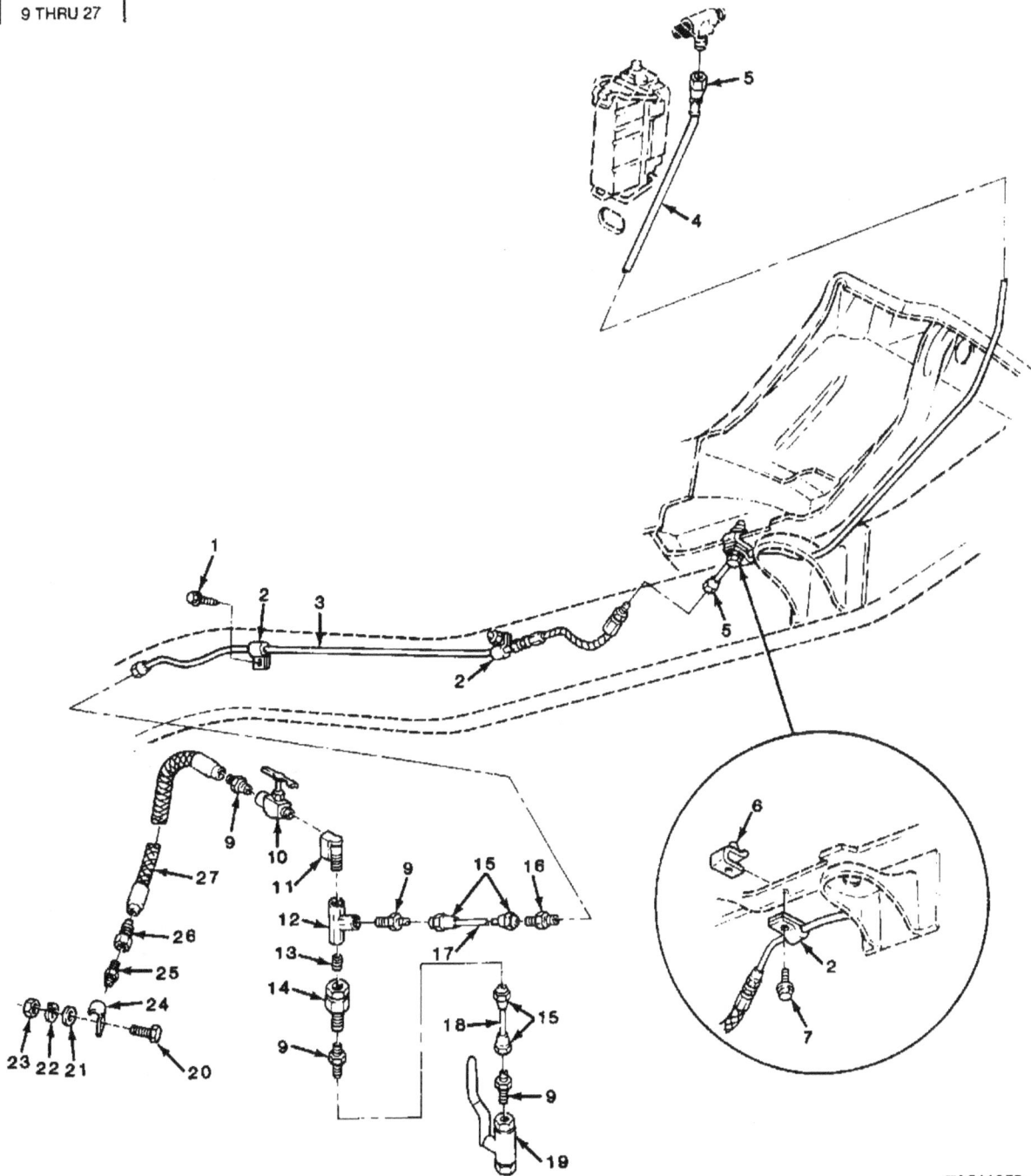

8

9 THRU 27

TA511059

FIGURE 212. PERSONNEL HEATER FUEL LINES AND RELATED PARTS (M1010).

(1) ITEM NO	(2) SMR CODE	(3) CAGEC	(4) PART NUMBER	(5) DESCRIPTION AND USABLE ON CODES (UOC)	(6) QTY
				GROUP 2207 WINTERIZATION EQUIPMENT L	
				FIG. 212 PERSONNEL HEATER FUEL LINES AND RELATED PARTS (M1010)	
1	PAOZZ	11862	11504447	SCREW,TAPPING UOC:210,230	1
2	PAOZZ	96906	MS21333-110	CLAMP,LOOP UOC:210,230	3
3	PAOZZ	11862	14063324	HOSE, ASSEMBLY,NONME UOC:210,230	1
6	PAOZZ	24617	1494253	NUT,CLIP-ON UOC:210,230	1
7	PAOZZ	96906	MS90728-31	BOLT,MACHINE UOC:210,230	1

END OF FIGURE

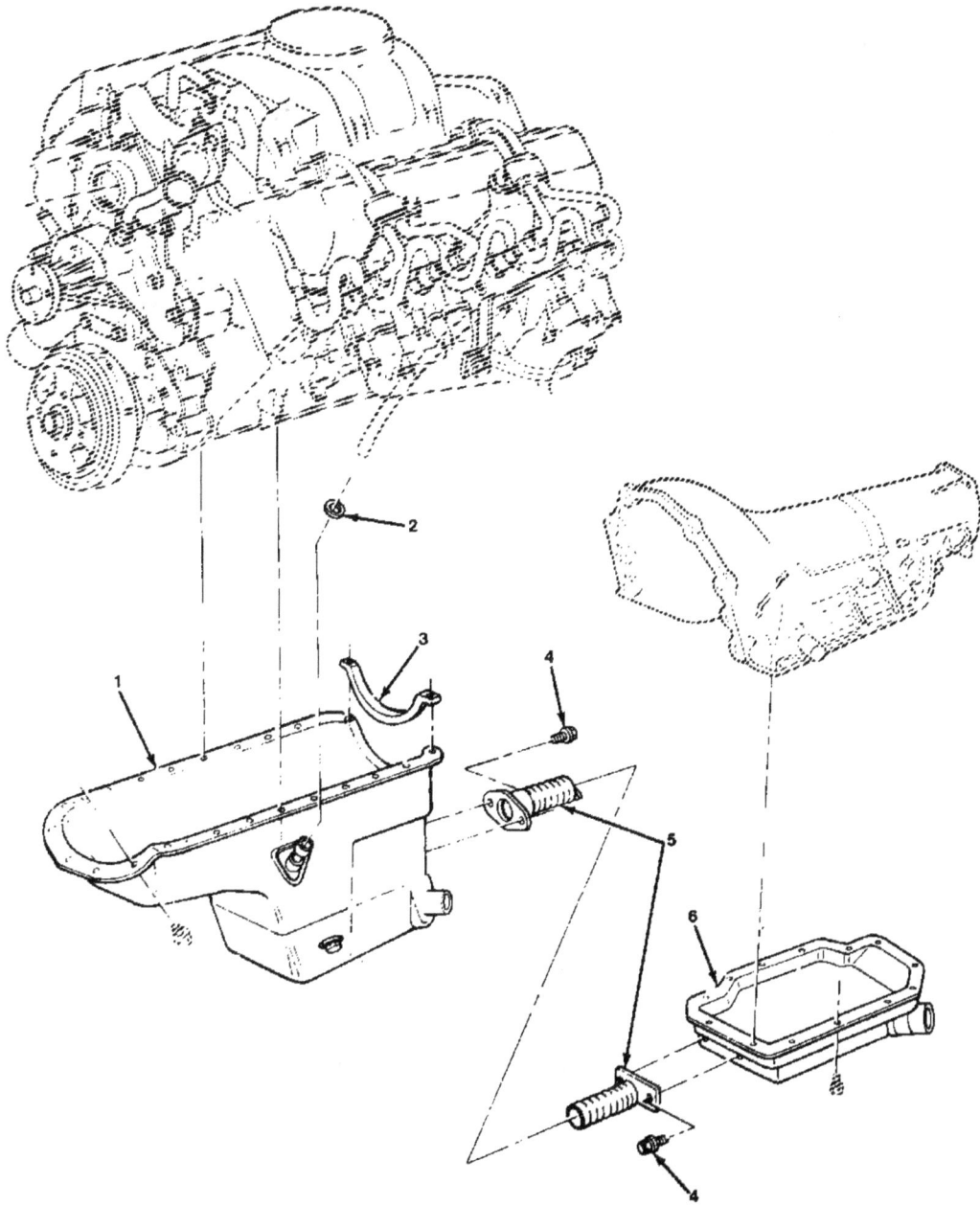

TA511061

FIGURE 213. TRANSMISSION AND OIL PAN.

(1) ITEM NO	(2) SMR CODE	(3) CAGEC	(4) PART NUMBER	(5) DESCRIPTION AND USABLE ON CODES (UOC)	(6) QTY
				GROUP 33 SPECIAL PURPOSE KITS	
				GROUP 3303 WINTERIZATION KITS	
				FIG. 213 TRANSMISSION AND OIL PAN	
2	PAOZZ	24617	274244	PACKING, PREFORMED	1
3	PAOZZ	11862	14022683	SEAL, NONMETALLIC SP	1
4	PAOZZ	11862	9439930	SCREW, CAP, HEXAGON H	4
5	PAOZZ	11862	15599200	PIPE, EXHAUST	1
6	PAOZZ	11862	15599201	OIL, PAN AND HEAT EX	1
7	PAOZZ	11862	337185	PLUG, MACHINE THREAD	1
8	PAOZZ	11862	14079550	GASKET	1

END OF FIGURE

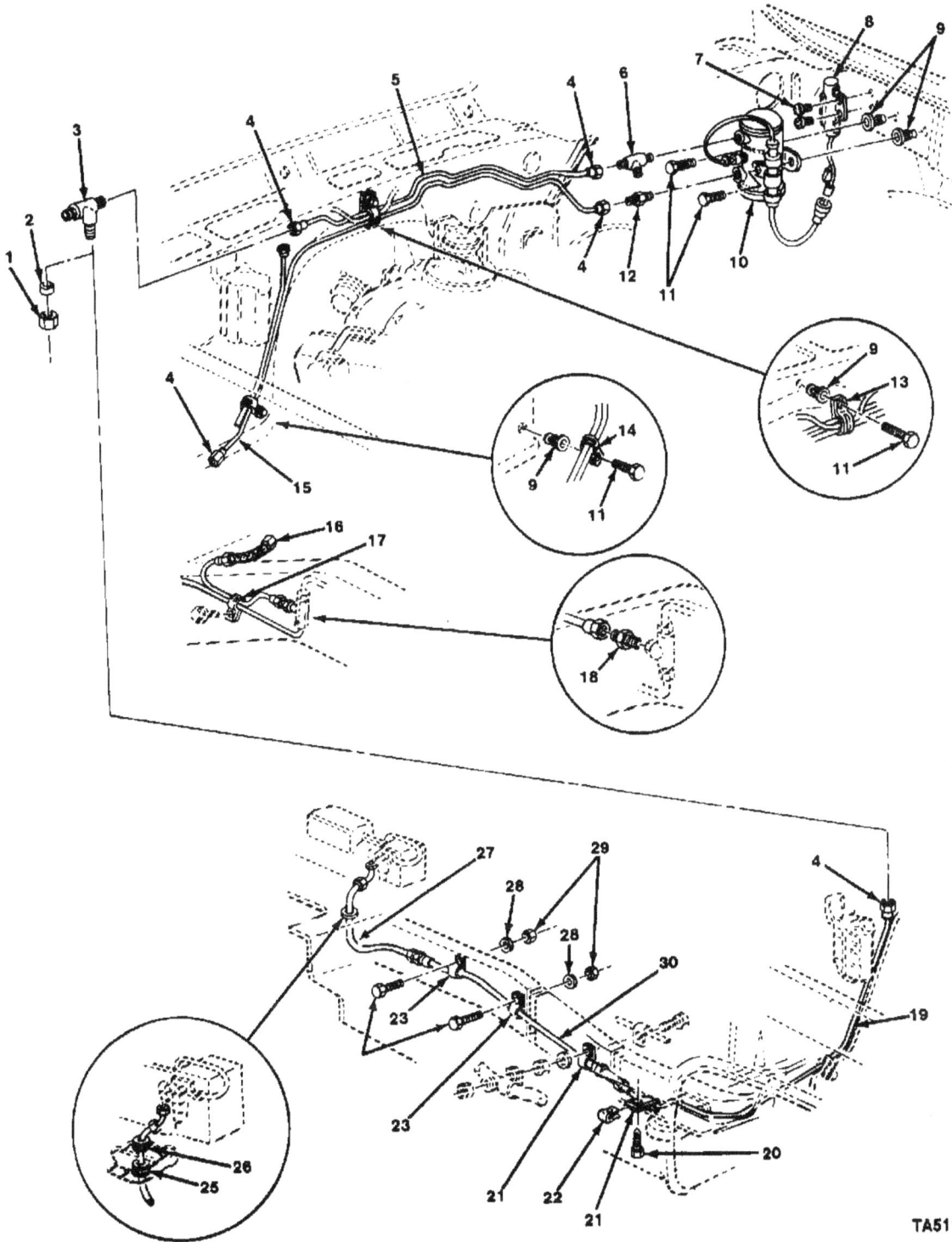

FIGURE 214. AUXILIARY HEATER FUEL PUMP, LINES, AND RELATED PARTS (M1008).

TA511062

GROUP 3303 SPECIAL PURPOSE KITS

FIG. 214 AUXILIARY HEATER FUEL PUMP,
LINES, AND RELATED PARTS (M1008)

ITEM NO	SMR CODE	CAGEC	PART NUMBER	DESCRIPTION AND USABLE ON CODES (UOC)	QTY
1	PAOZZ	24617	9409761	NUT,PLAIN,CAP UOC:209,230,231	1
2	PAOZZ	11862	9409754	WASHER,FINISHING UOC:209,230,231	1
3	PAOZZ	93061	144F-5	TEE,TUBE UOC:194,208,230,231,252,254,256	1
4	PAOZZ	81343	5 010111B	NUT,TUBE COUPLING UOC:194,208,209,230,231,252,254,256	6
5	MFOZZ	11862	14072371	PIPE ASM-AUX HTR (44.45" LG) MAKE FROM TUBE, P/N 1324714 UOC:194,208,209,230,231,252,254,256	1
6	PAOZZ	24617	140642	TEE,PIPE TO TUBE UOC:194,208,230,231,252,254,256	1
7	PAOZZ	24617	9414713	SCREW,TAPPING UOC:194,208,230,231,252,254,256	2
8	PAOZZ	11862	14072347	SWITCH,HEATER FUEL UOC:194,208,209,230,231,252,254,256	1
9	PAOZZ	11862	14005953	SHIELD,EXPANSION UOC:194,208,209,230,231,252,254,256	4
10	PAOZZ	96906	MS51321-1	PUMP,FUEL,ELECTRICA UOC:194,208,209,230,231,252,254,256	1
11	PAOZZ	11862	14007511	BOLT,ASSEMBLED WASH UOC:194,208,209,230,231,252,254,256	2
12	PAOZZ	81240	CM118749	ADAPTER,STRAIGHT,PI UOC:194,208,230,231,252,254,256	1
13	PAOZZ	11862	343444	CLAMP,LOOP UOC:194,208,230,231,252,254,256	1
14	PAOZZ	11862	14004512	CLAMP,LOOP UOC:194,208,230,231,252,254,256	1
15	MFOZZ	11862	14072369	PIPE ASM-AUX HTR (65.22" LG) MAKE FROM TUBE, P/N1324714 UOC:194,208,230,231,252,254,256	1
16	PAOZZ	11862	14072368	HOSE ASSEMBLY,NONME UOC:194,208,230,231,252,254,256	1
17	PAOZZ	11862	25527423	CLAMP,LOOP UOC:194,208,230,231,252,254,256	1
18	PAOZZ	16764	110200	ADAPTER,STRAIGHT,PI UOC:194,208,230,231,252,254,256	1
19	PAOZZ	11862	14063323	TUBE ASSEMBLY,METAL UOC:194,208	1
20	PAOZZ	96906	MS90728-31	BOLT,MACHINE UOC:194,208	1
	PAOZZ	96906	MS21333-110	CLAMP,LOOP UOC:194,208,230,231,252,254,256	2
22	PAOZZ	24617	1494253	NUT,CLIP-ON UOC:194,208	1
	PAOZZ	96906	MS21333-46	CLAMP,LOOP	2

(1) ITEM NO	(2) SMR CODE	(3) CAGEC	(4) PART NUMBER	(5) DESCRIPTION AND USABLE ON CODES (UOC)	(6) QTY
				UOC:194,208	
24	PAOZ	96906	MS90728-59	SCREW,CAP,HEXAGON H	2
				UOC:194,208	
25	PAOZZ	11862	3886908	GROMMET,NONMETALLIC	1
				UOC:194,208	
26	PAOZZ	96906	MS35489-103	GROMMET,NONMETALLIC	1
				UOC:194,208	
27	PAOZZ	11862	14076390	HOSE ASSEMBLY, NONME	1
				UOC:194,208	
28	PAOZZ	11862	11500046	WASHER,LOCK	2
				UOC:194,208	
29	PAOZZ	96906	MS51967-8	NUT,PLAIN,HEXAGON	2
				UOC:194,208	
30	PAOZZ	11862	14063324	HOSE ASSEMBLY,NONME	1
				UOC:194,208	

END OF FIGURE

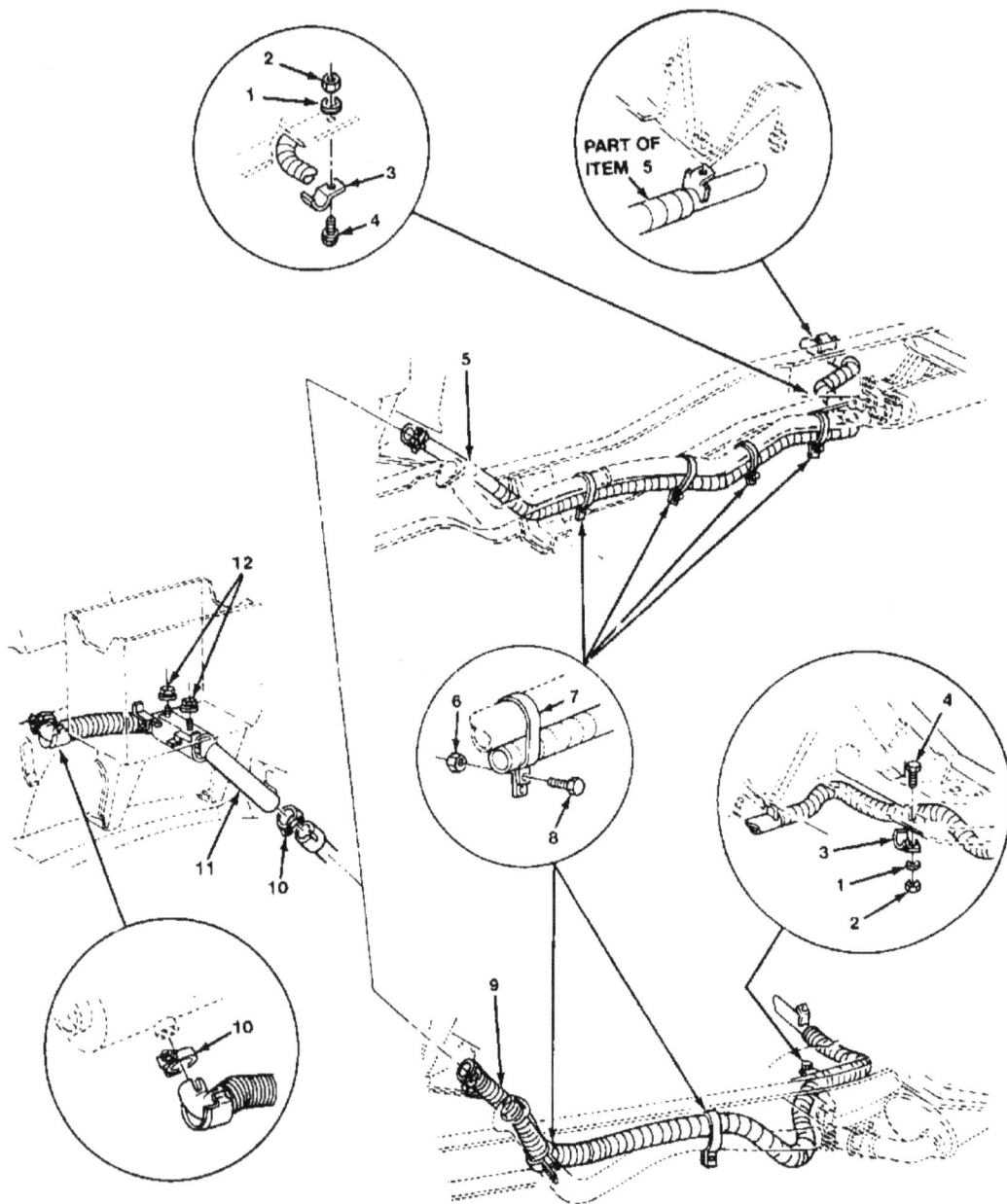

PART OF
ITEM 5

TA511063

FIGURE 215. WARM AIR HEATER EXHAUST (ALL EXCEPT M1010).

(1) ITEM NO	(2) SMR CODE	(3) CAGEC	(4) PART NUMBER	(5) DESCRIPTION AND USABLE ON CODES (UOC)	(6) QTY
				GROUP 3303 WINTERIZATION KITS	
				FIG. 215 WARM AIR HEATER EXHAUST (ALL EXCEPT M1010)	
1	PAOZZ	96906	MS27183-12	WASHER, FLAT UOC:194,208,209,230,231,252,254,256	1
2	PAOZZ	96906	MS51943-33	NUT, SELF-LOCKING, HE UOC:194,208,209,230,231,252,254,256	1
3	PAOZZ	11862	120877	STRAP, RETAINING UOC:194,208,209,230,231,252,254,256	1
4	PAOZZ	24617	9417350	BOLT, ASSEMBLED WASH UOC:194,208,209,230,231,252,254,256	1
5	PAOZZ	11862	14075801	PIPE, EXHAUST UOC:194,208,230,231,252,254,256	1
6	PAOZZ	21450	131245	NUT, SELF-LOCKING, HE UOC:194,208,230,231,252,254,256	4
6	PAOZZ	21450	131245	NUT, SELF-LOCKING, HE UOC:209	2
7	PAOZZ	96906	MS35842-15	CLAMP, HOSE UOC:194,208,230,231,252,254,256	4
7	PAOZZ	96906	MS35842-15	CLAMP, HOSE UOC:209	2
8	PAOZZ	96906	MS90728-8	SCREW, CAP, HEXAGON H UOC:194,208,230,231,252,254,256	4
8	PAOZZ	96906	MS90728-8	SCREW, CAP, HEXAGON H UOC:209	2
9	PAOZZ	11862	15599211	PIPE ASSEMBLY, EXHAU UOC:209	1
10	PAOZZ	63208	650-24	CLAMP, HOSE	2
11	XDOZZ	11862	15599287	PIPE	1
12	PAOZZ	24617	9416918	NUT, PLAIN, EXTENDED	2

END OF FIGURE

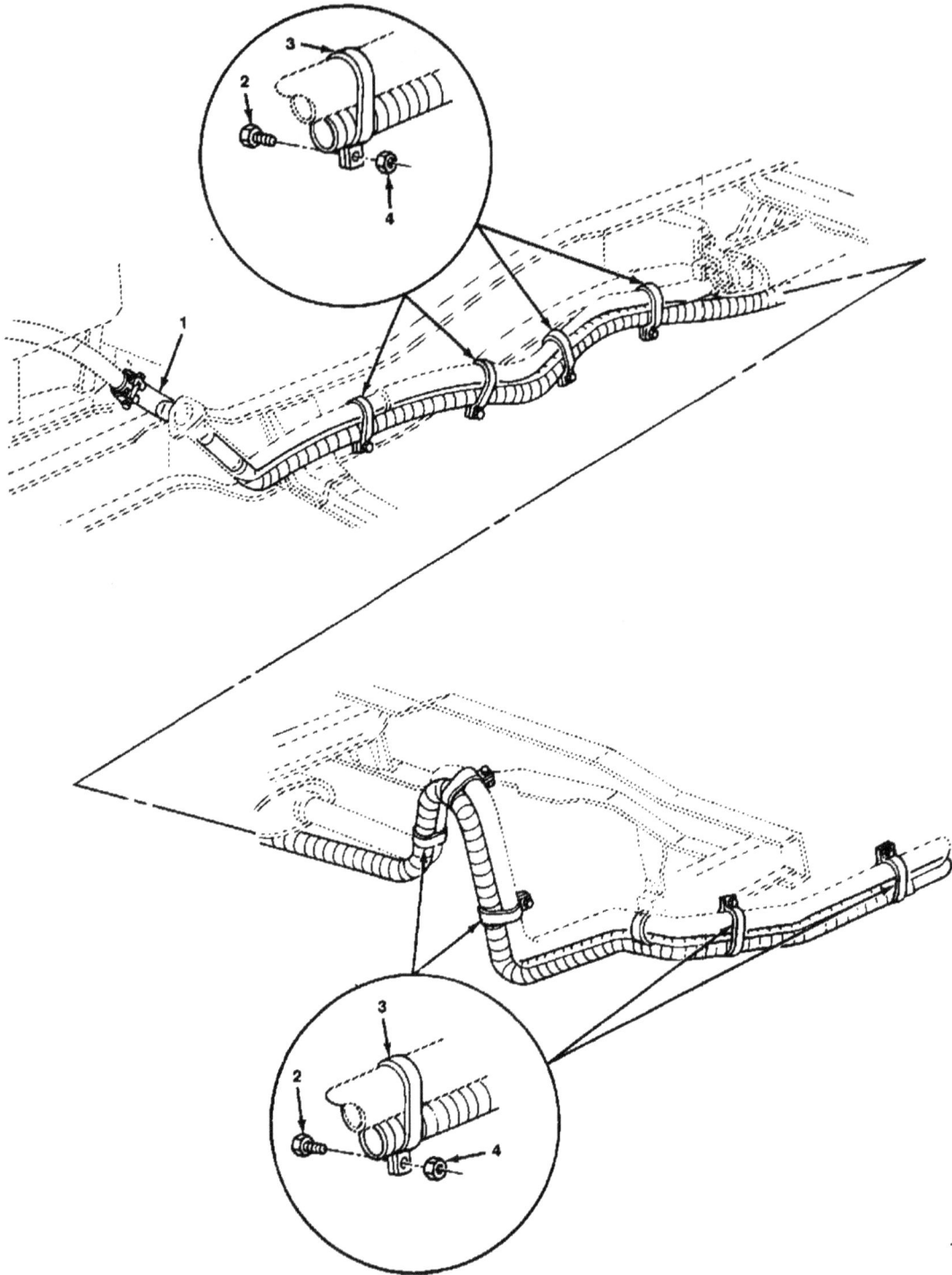

FIGURE 216. WARM AIR HEATER EXHAUST (M1010).

TA511064

(1) ITEM NO	(2) SMR CODE	(3) CAGEC	(4) PART NUMBER	(5) DESCRIPTION AND USABLE ON CODES (UOC)	(6) QTY
				GROUP 3303 WINTERIZATION KITS	
				FIG. 216 WARM AIR HEATER EXHAUST (M1010)	
1	PAOZZ	11862	15599290	PIPE ASSEMBLY,EXHAU UOC:210	1
2	PAOZZ	96906	MS90728-8	SCREW,CAP,HEXAGON H UOC:210	11
3	PAOZZ	96906	MS35842-15	CLAMP,HOSE UOC:210	11
4	PAOZZ	21450	131245	NUT,SELF-LOCKING,HE UOC:210	11

END OF FIGURE

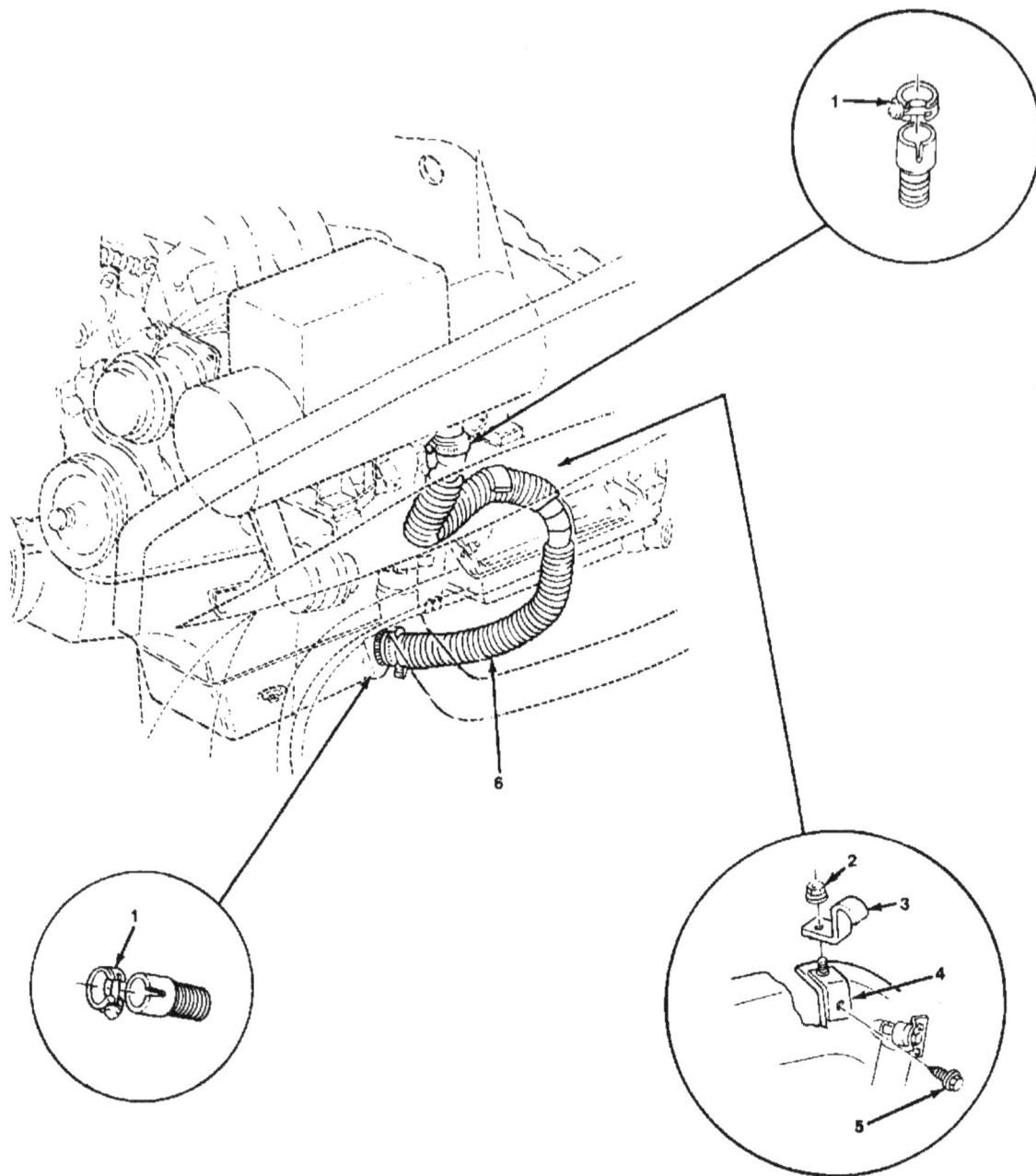

TA511065

FIGURE 217. COOLANT HEATER EXHAUST.

SECTION II					
(1) ITEM NO	(2) SMR CODE	(3) CAGEC	(4) PART NUMBER	(5) DESCRIPTION AND USABLE ON CODES (UOC)	(6) QTY

GROUP 3303 WINTERIZATION KITS

FIG. 217 COOLANT HEATER EXHAUST

1	PAOZZ	63208	650-24	CLAMP,HOSE	2
2	PAOZZ	24617	9416918	NUT,PLAIN,EXTENDED	1
3	PAOZZ	11862	120877	STRAP,RETAINING	1
				UOC:194,208,230,231,252,254,256	
4	PAOZZ	11862	15599245	BRACKET,ANGLE	1
5	PAOZZ	24617	9416187	SCREW,TAPPING	1
6	PAOZZ	11862	15599243	PIPE,EXHAUST	1

END OF FIGURE

ALL EXCEPT
M1009

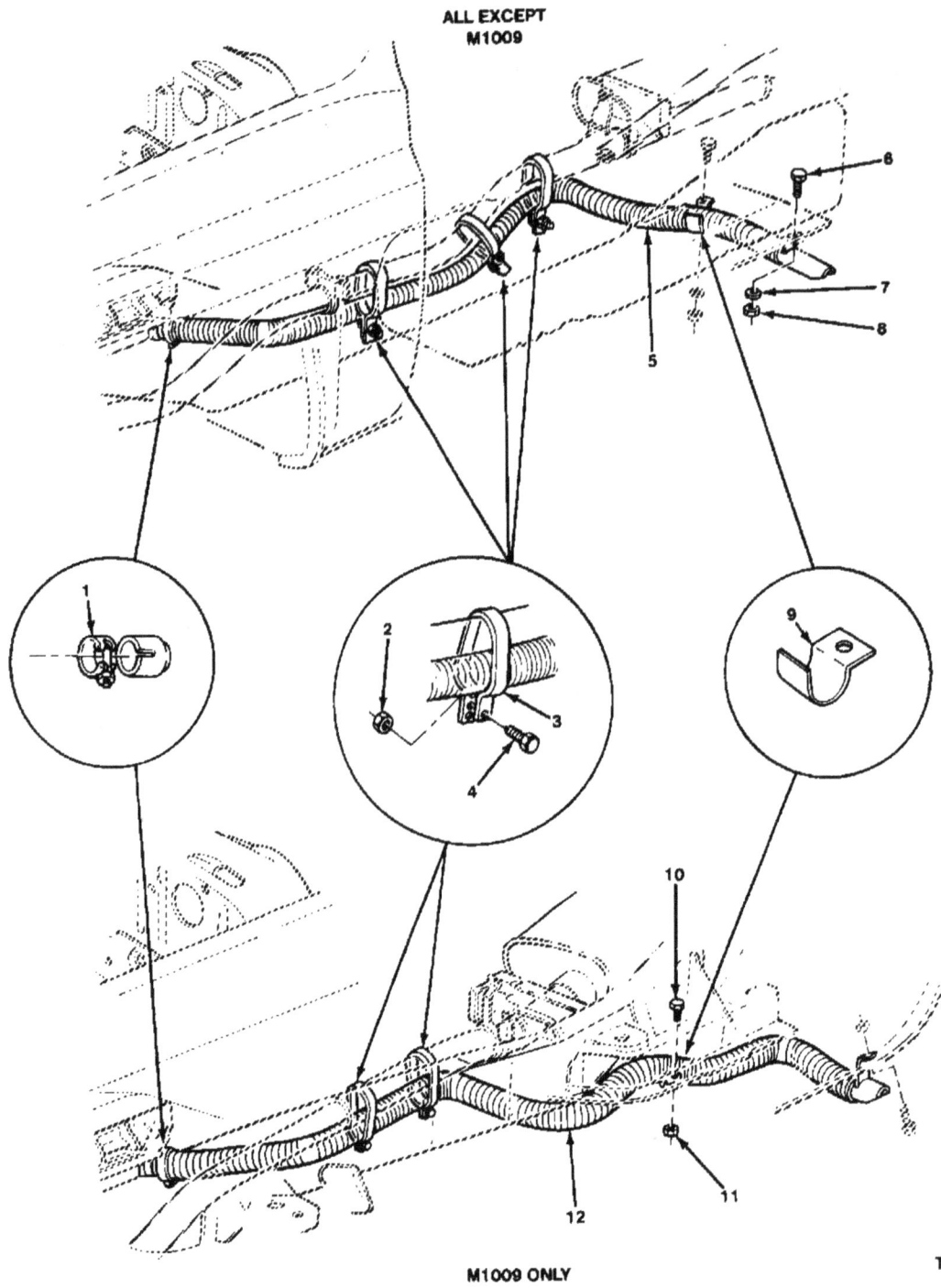

M1009 ONLY

TA511056

FIGURE 218. COOLANT HEATER REAR EXHAUST.

(1) ITEM NO	(2) SMR CODE	(3) CAGEC	(4) PART NUMBER	(5) DESCRIPTION AND USABLE ON CODES (UOC)	(6) QTY
				GROUP 3303 WINTERIZATION KITS	
				FIG. 218 COOLANT HEATER REAR EXHAUST	
1	PAOZZ	63208	650-24	CLAMP,HOSE UOC:194,208,209,210,230,231,252,254	1
2	PAOZZ	21450	131245	NUT,SELF-LOCKING,HE UOC:194,208,210,230,231,252,254,256	3
2	PAOZZ	21450	131245	NUT,SELF-LOCKING,HE UOC:209	2
3	PAOZZ	96906	MS35842-15	CLAMP,HOSE UOC:194,208,210,230,231,252,254,256	3
3	PAOZZ	96906	MS35842-15	CLAMP,HOSE UOC:209	2
4	PAOZZ	96906	MS90728-8	SCREW,CAP,HEXAGON H UOC:194,208,210,230,231,252,254,256	3
4	PAOZZ	96906	MS90728-8	SCREW,CAP,HEXAGON H UOC:209	2
5	PAOZZ	11862	15599215	PIPE,EXHAUST UOC:194,208,230,231,252,254,256	1
5	PAOZZ	11862	14074499	PIPE ASEMBLY,EXHAU UOC:210	1
6	PAOZZ	24617	9417350	BOLT,ASSEMBLED WASH UOC:194,208,210,230,231,252,254,256	1
7	PAOZZ	96906	MS27183-12	WASHER,FLAT UOC:194,208,230,231,252,254,256	1
7	PAOZZ	96906	MS27183-12	WASHER,FLAT UOC:209	2
8	PAOZZ	96906	MS51943-33	NUT,SELF-LOCKING,HE UOC:194,208,210,230,231,252,254,256	1
9	PAOZZ	11862	120877	STRAP,RETAINING UOC:194,208,210,230,231,252,254,256	1
10	PAOZZ	24617	9417350	BOLT,ASSEMBLED WASH UOC:209	1
11	PAOZZ	96906	MS51943-33	NUT,SELF-LOCKING,HE UOC:209	1
12	PAOZZ	11862	15599212	PIPE,EXHAUST UOC:209	1

END OF FIGURE

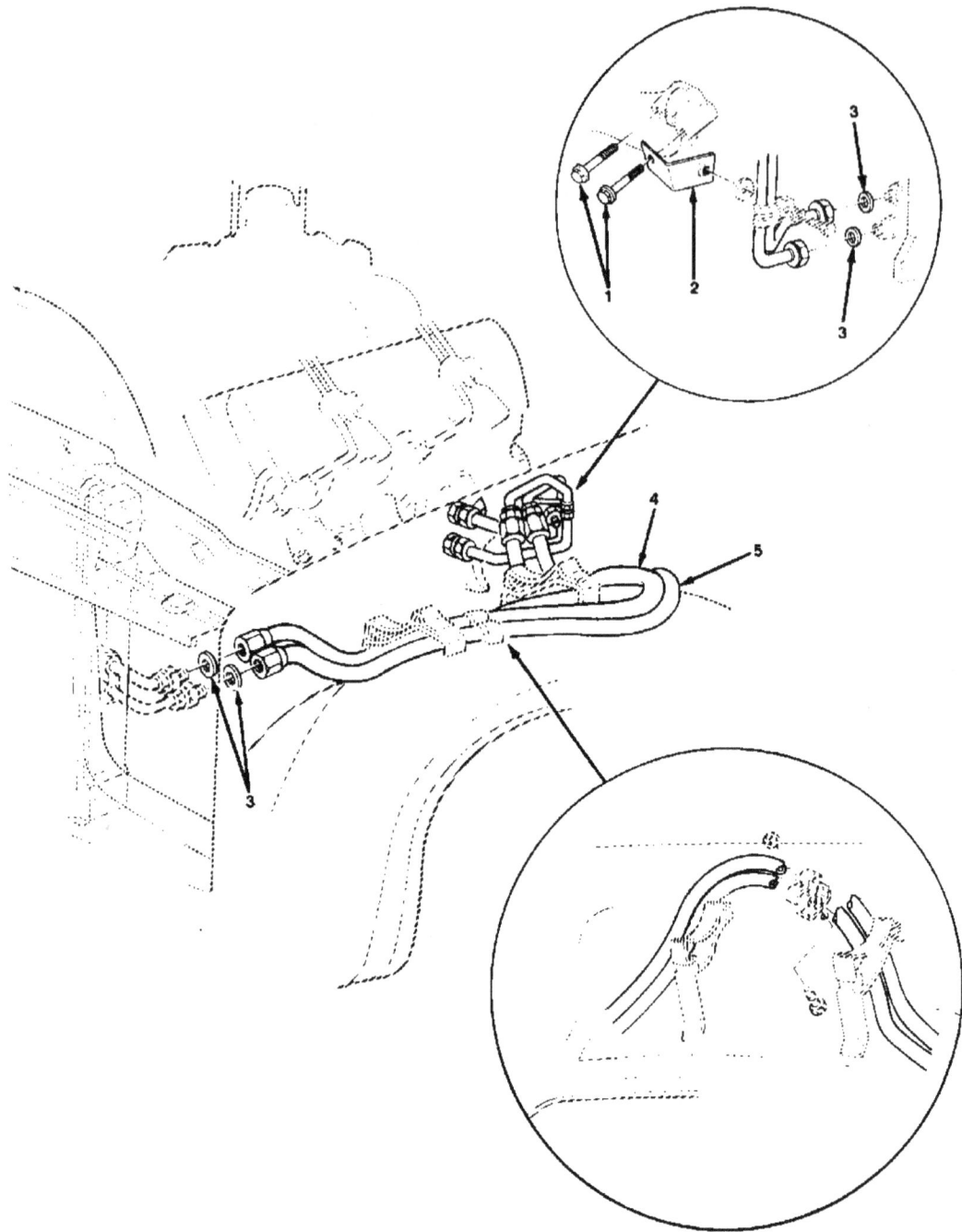

TA511067

FIGURE 219. ENGINE OIL COOLER LINES.

(1) ITEM NO	(2) SMR CODE	(3) CAGEC	(4) PART NUMBER	(5) DESCRIPTION AND USABLE ON CODES (UOC)	(6) QTY
				GROUP 3303 WINTERIZATION KITS	
				FIG. 219 ENGINE OIL COOLER LINES	
1	PAOZZ	11862	14028922	BOLT,MACHINE	2
2	PAOZZ	11862	15599246	BRACKET,ANGLE	1
3	PAOZZ	11862	14055585	SEAL RING,METAL UOC:194,208,209,230,231,252,254,256	4
4	PAOZZ	11862	14063337	HOSE ASSEMBLY,NONME UOC:194,208,209,230,231,252,254,256	1
5	PAOZZ	11862	14063336	HOSE ASSEMBLY,NONME UOC:194,208,209,230,231,252,254,256	1

END OF FIGURE

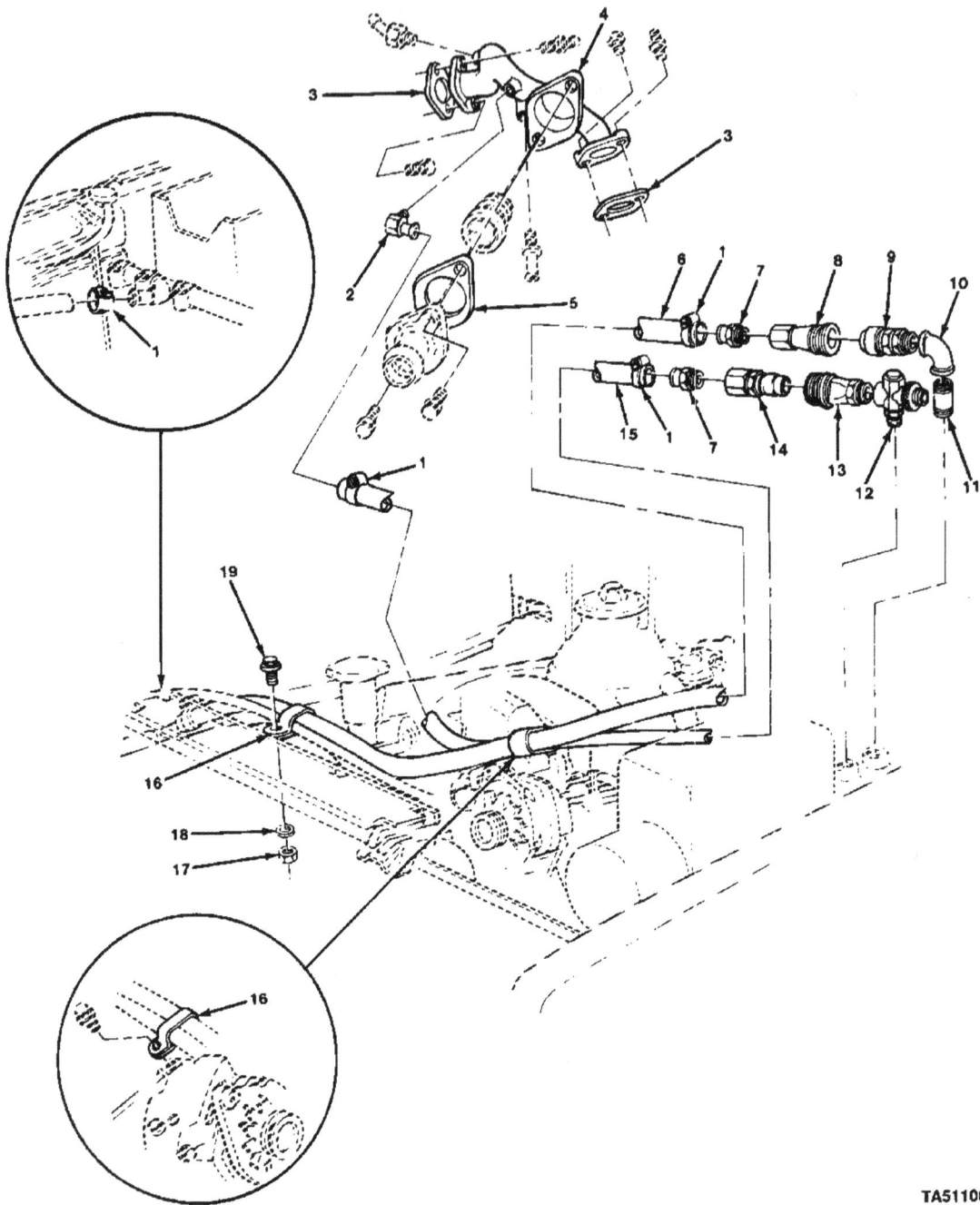

FIGURE 220. ENGINE COOLANT CROSSOVER HOUSING, HOSES, AND FITTINGS.

TA511068

(1) ITEM NO	(2) SMR CODE	(3) CAGEC	(4) PART NUMBER	(5) DESCRIPTION AND USABLE ON CODES (UOC)	(6) QTY
				GROUP 3303 WINTERIZATION KITS	
				FIG. 220 ENGINE COOLANT CROSSOVER HOUSING, HOSES, AND FITTINGS	
1	PAOZZ	96906	MS35842-11	CLAMP,HOSE	4
2	PAOZZ	11862	10005327	ELBOW,PIPE TO HOSE	1
3	PAOZZ	11862	23500846	GASKET	2
4	PAOZZ	11862	14063338	WATER OUTLET,ENGINE	1
5	PAOZZ	11862	14028916	GASKET	1
6	MOOZZ	11862	14063370	HOSE ENG CLT HTR OU (43.00" LG.) MAKE FOR HOSE, P/N MS521304B203R	1
7	PAOZZ	11862	354501	ADAPTER,STRAIGHT,PI	2
8	PAOZZ	73992	8200	COUPLING HALF,QUICK	1
9	PAOZZ	73992	B-84	COUPLING HALF,QUICK UOC:194,208,209,210,230,231,252	1
10	PAOZZ	96906	MS51845-4	ELBOW,PIPE	1
11	PAOZZ	96906	MS51846-64	NIPPLE,PIPE	1
12	PAOZZ	17769	4641	SENSOR ASSEMBLY,ENG	1
13	PAOZZ	73992	8100	COUPLING HALF,QUICK	1
14	PAOZZ	73992	B-85	COUPLING HALF,QUICK	1
15	MOOZZ	11862	14063373	HOSE ENG CLT HTR IN (23.00" LG.) MAKE FROM HOSE, P/N MS521304B203R	1
16	PO	11862	3825416	CLAMP,LOOP	2
17	PAOZZ	24617	456004	NUT,SELF-LOCKING,HE	1
18	PAOZZ	96906	MS27183-14	WASHER,FLAT UOC:194,208,209,210,230,231,252	1
19	PAOZZ	11862	9440034	BOLT,MACHINE	1

END OF FIGURE

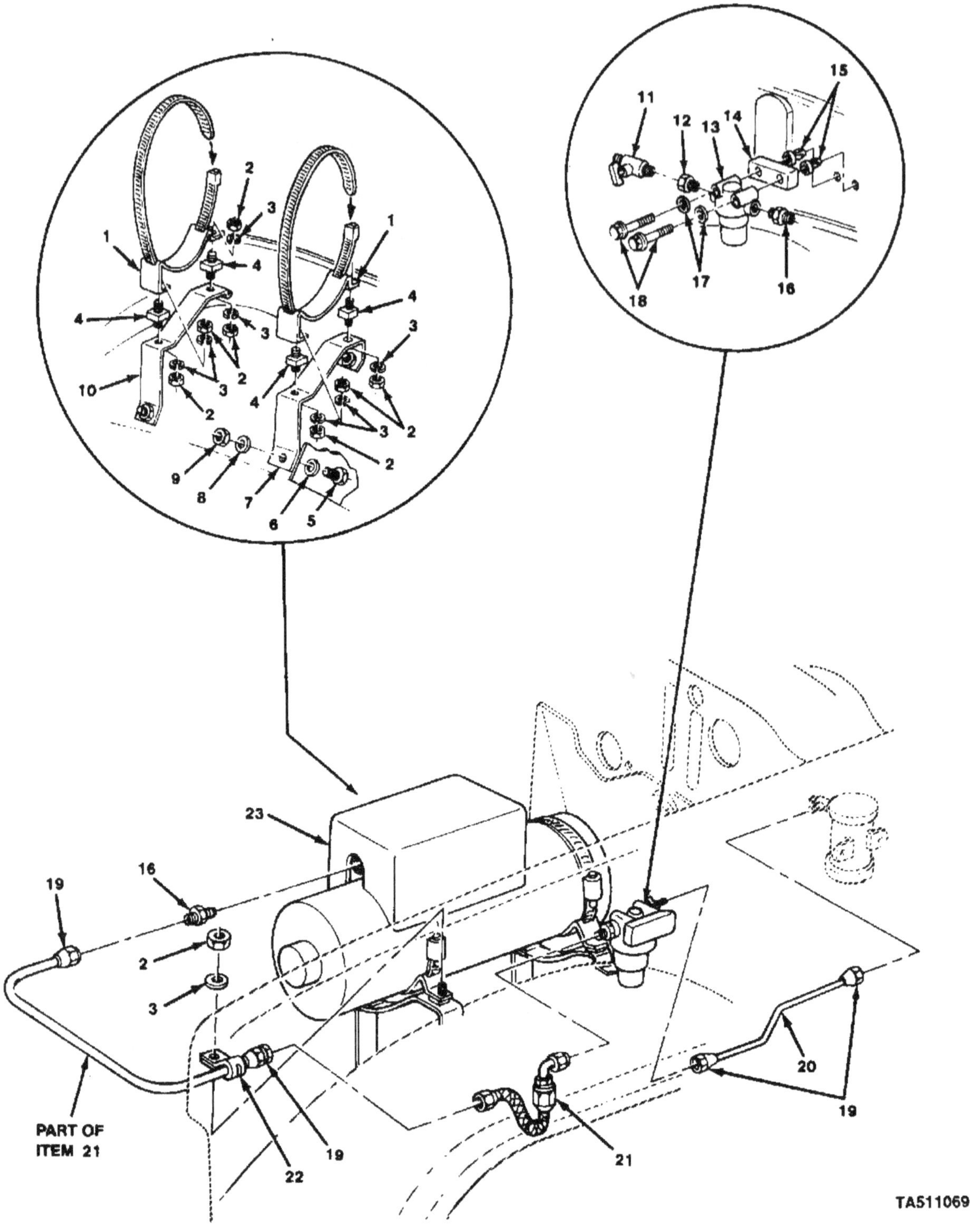

FIGURE 221. COOLANT HEATER, FUEL FILTER, FUEL LINE, AND MOUNTING BRACKETS.

TA511069

(1) ITEM NO	(2) SMR CODE	(3) CAGEC	(4) PART NUMBER	(5) DESCRIPTION AND USABLE ON CODES (UOC)	(6) QTY
				GROUP 3303 WINTERIZATION KITS	
				FIG. 221 COOLANT HEATER, FUEL FILTER, FUEL LINE, AND MOUNTING BRACKETS	
1	PAOZZ	11862	14074457	BRACKET	2
2	PAOZZ	96906	MS35691-406	NUT,PLAIN,HEXAGON	8
3	PAOZZ	96906	MS35338-44	WASHER,LOCK	8
4	PAOZZ	19207	10922334	MOUNT,RESILIENT	4
5	PAOZZ	96906	MS90728-32	BOLT,MACHINE	4
6	PAOZZ	24617	9418924	WASHER,FLAT	4
7	PAOZZ	11862	14074458	BRACKET,MOUNTING	1
8	PAOZZ	96906	MS35338-45	WASHER,LOCK	4
9	PAOZZ	96906	MS51967-6	NUT,PLAIN,HEXAGON	4
10	PAOZZ	11862	14074459	BRACKET,MOUNTING	1
11	XDOZZ	11862	9440173	VALVE FUEL SHUTOFF	1
12	PAOZZ	17769	443998	COUPLING,PIPE	1
13	PAOZZ	96906	MS51085-1	FILTER,FLUID	1
14	PAOZZ	11862	14072374	SPACER,HEATR FUEL	1
15	PAOZZ	00613	C-5139-2	RECEPTACLE,TURNLOCK	2
16	PAOZZ	81240	GM118749	ADAPTER,STRAIGHT,PI	2
17	PAOZZ	96906	MS27183-8	WASHER,FLAT	2
18	PAOZZ	24617	456748	SCREW,CAP,HEXAGON H	2
19	PAOZZ	81343	5 010111B	NUT,TUBE COUPLING	4
20	MFOZZ	11862	14072372	PIPE HTR FLTR INL (7.92" LG.) MAKE FROM TUBE, P/N 1324714	1
21	PAOZZ	11862	15599234	HOSE,ASSEMBLY,NONME	1
22	PAOZZ	96906	MS21333-110	CLAMP,LOOP	1
23	PAOFH	46522	D55395-G1	HEATER,COOLANT,ENGI	1

END OF FIGURE

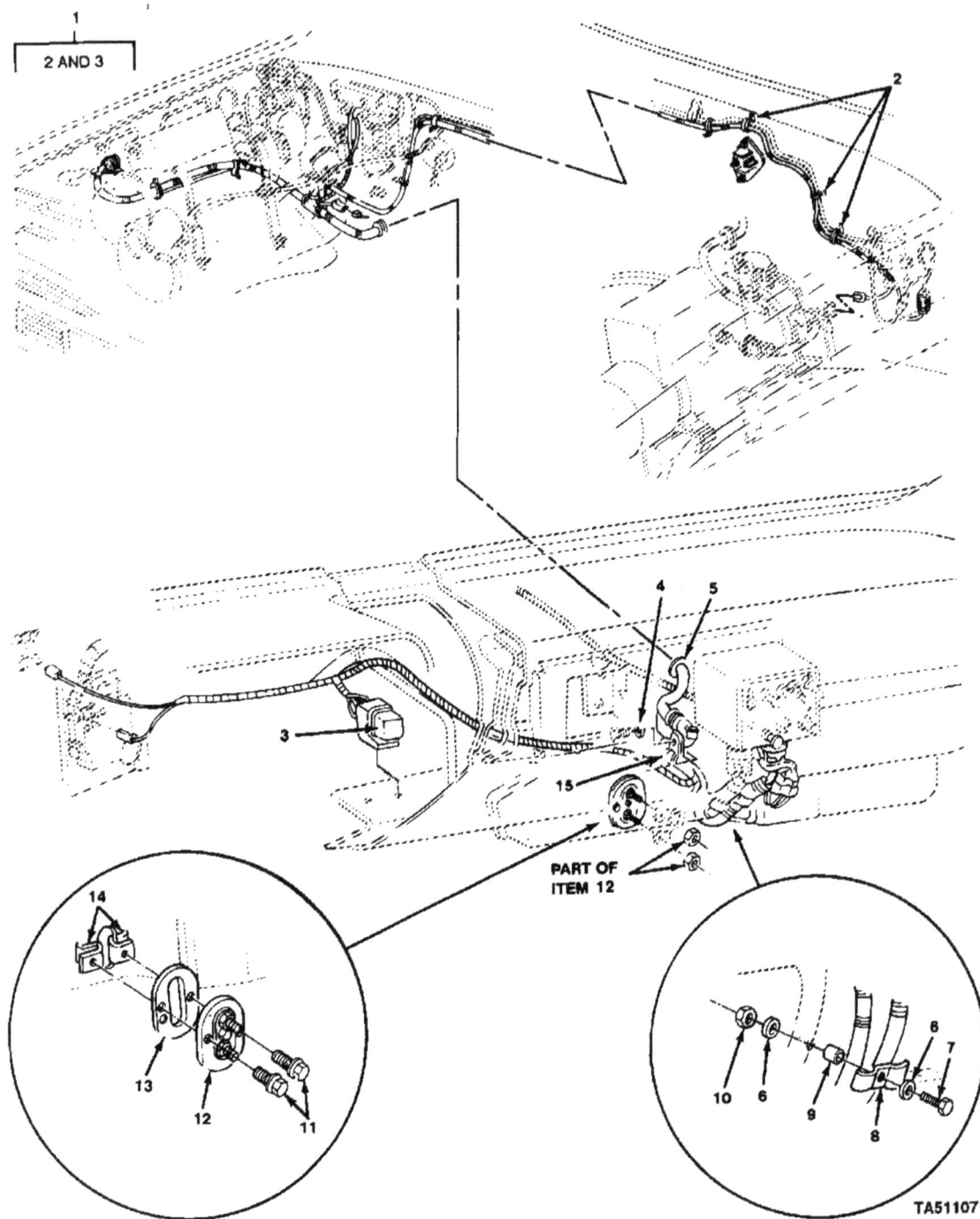

FIGURE 222. WARM AIR HEATER WIRING HARNESS .

TA511071

(1) ITEM NO	(2) SMR CODE	(3) CAGEC	(4) PART NUMBER	(5) DESCRIPTION AND USABLE ON CODES (UOC)	(6) QTY
				GROUP 3303 WINTERIZATION KITS	
				FIG. 222 WARM AIR HEATER WIRING HARNESS	
1	PAOZZ	11862	14076236	WIRING HARNESS,BRAN	1
2	PAOZZ	11862	3816659	.STRAP,LINE SUPPORTI	10
3	PAOZZ	11862	2098912	.RELAY	1
4	PAOZZ	96906	MS27183-10	WASHER,FLAT	1
5	PAOZZ	96906	MS35489-121	GROMMET,NONMETALLIC	1
6	PAOZZ	96906	MS9549-10	WASHER,FLAT	2
7	PAOZZ	96906	MS90728-3	SCREW,CAP,HEXAGON H	1
8	PAOZZ	11862	14061352	STRAP,RETAINING	1
9	PAOZZ	11862	15599920	SPACER,SLEEVE	1
10	PAOZZ	96906	MS35691-406	NUT,PLAIN,HEXAGON	1
11	PAOZZ	24617	9415163	SCREW,ASSEMBLED WAS	2
12	PAOZZ	78385	G704410-1	SWITCH,THERMOSTATIC	1
13	PAOZZ	11862	14076270	GASKET	1
14	PAOZZ	11862	9440178	NUT,PLAIN,DODECAGON	2
15	PAOZZ	96906	MS21333-62	CLAMP,LOOP	1

END OF FIGURE

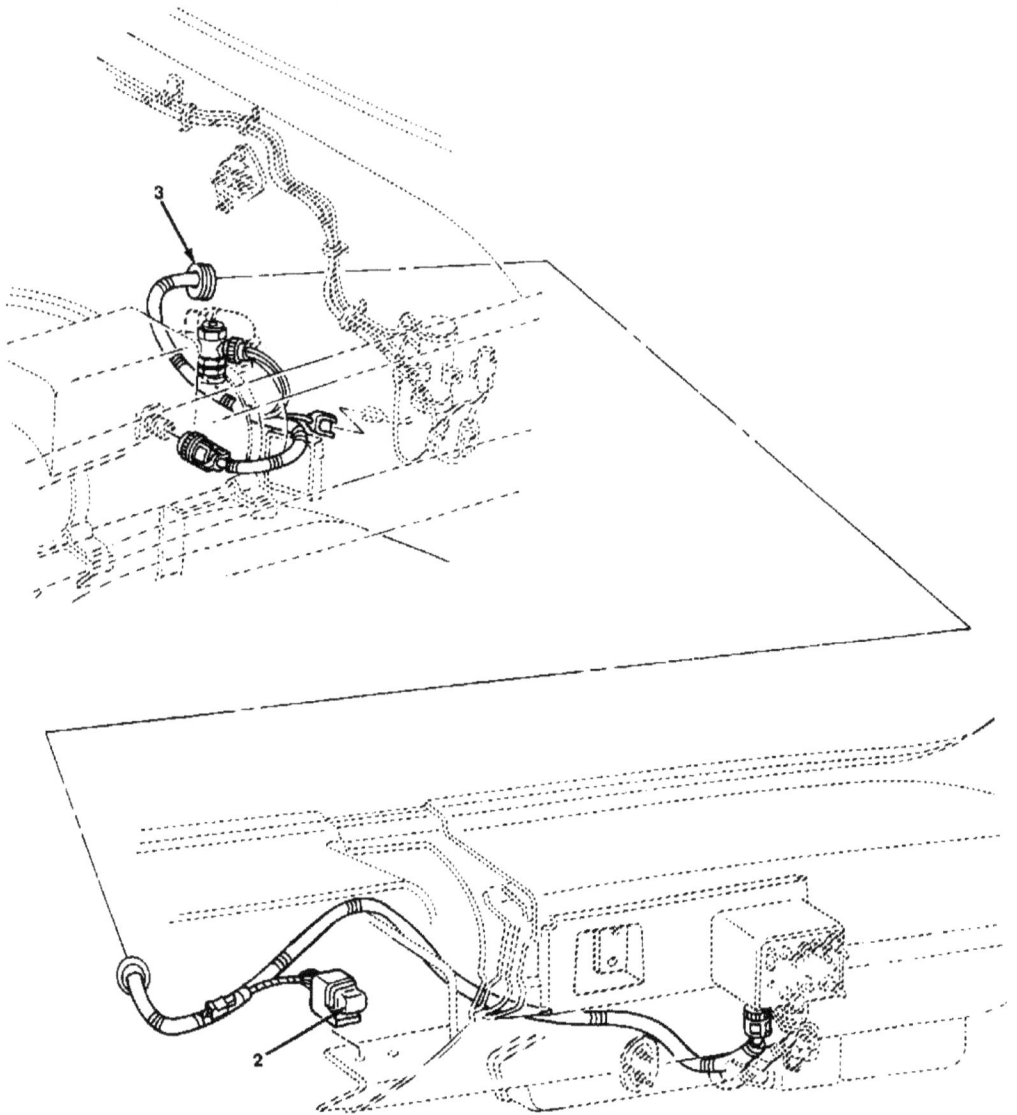

TA511072

FIGURE 223. COOLANT HEATER WIRING HARNESS

(1)	(2)	(3)	(4)	(5)	(6)
ITEM	SMR		PART		
NO	CODE	CAGEC	NUMBER	DESCRIPTION AND USABLE ON CODES (UOC)	QTY

GROUP 3303 WINTERIZATION KITS

FIG. 223 COOLANT HEATER WIRING
HARNESS

1	PAOOO	11862	14075888	WIRING HARNESS,BRAN	1
2	PAOZZ	11862	14074461PC6	.RELAY	1
3	PAOZZ	96906	MS35489-121	GROMMET,NONMETALLIC	1

END OF FIGURE

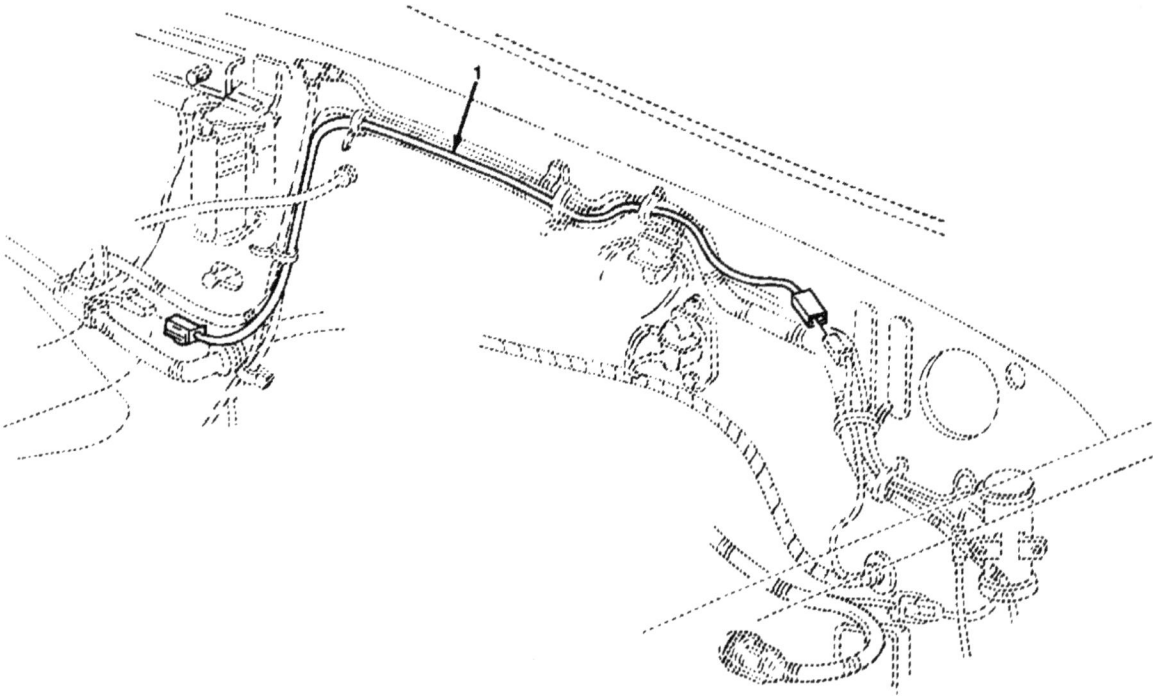

TA511073

FIGURE 224. WARM AIR FUEL PUMP EXTENSION HARNESS (M1010).

(1) ITEM NO	(2) SMR CODE	(3) CAGEC	(4) PART NUMBER	(5) DESCRIPTION AND USABLE ON CODES (UOC)	(6) QTY
				GROUP 3303 WINTERIZATION KITS	
				FIG. 224 WARM AIR FUEL PUMP EXTENSION HARNESS (M1010)	
1	PAOZZ	11862	15599968	LEAD,ELECTRICAL UOC:210	1
				END OF FIGURE	

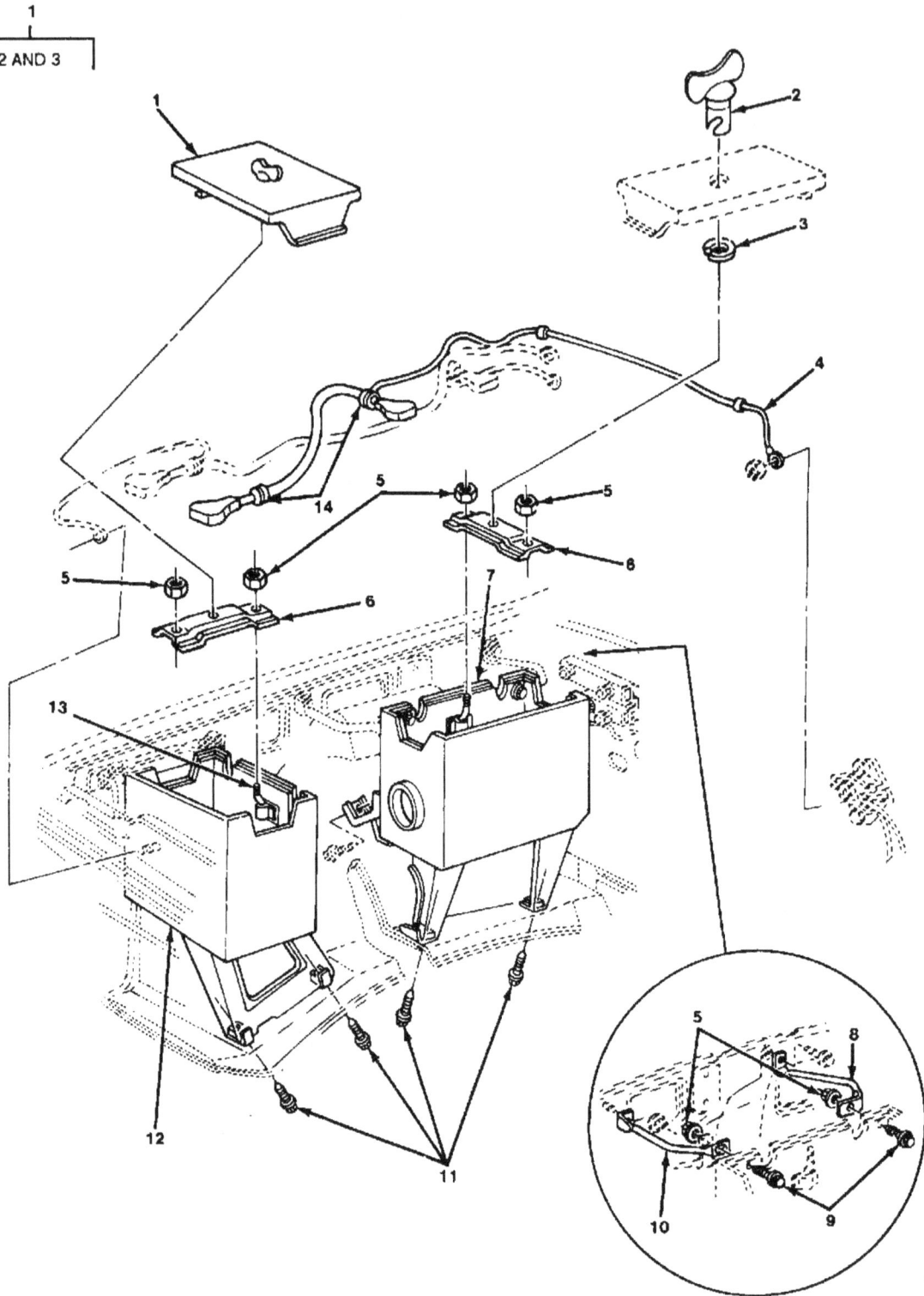

FIGURE 225. BATTERY BOXES AND CABLES.

TA511074

(1) ITEM NO	(2) SMR CODE	(3) CAGEC	(4) PART NUMBER	(5) DESCRIPTION AND USABLE ON CODES (UOC)	(6) QTY
				GROUP 3303 WINTERIZATION KITS	
				FIG. 225 BATTERY BOXES AND CABLES	
1	PAOZZ	11862	14076246	COVER,BATTERY BOX	2
2	PAOZZ	72794	AJW7-70	.STUD,TURNLOCK FASTE	2
3	PAOZZ	72794	X-840-SR7C	.RING,RETAINING	2
4	PAOZZ	11862	12039294	LEAD,STORAGE BATTER	1
5	PAOZZ	24617	11506003	NUT,PLAIN,ASSEMBLED	6
6	PAOZZ	11862	14076852	RETAINER,BATTERY	2
7	PAOZZ	11862	14076243	BATTERY BOX	1
8	PAOZZ	11862	14076250	SUPPORT,BATTERY BOX	1
9	PAOZZ	11862	9440334	BOLT,ASSEMBLED WASH	2
10	PFOZZ	11862	14076249	SUPPORT,BATTERY BOX	1
11	PAOZZ	11862	2014469	BOLT,ASSEMBLED WASH	4
12	PAOZZ	11862	14076241	BOX AND SUPPORT ASS	1
13	PAOZZ	11862	14076248	BOLT,HOOK	4
14	PAOZZ	96906	MS35489-11	GROMMET,NONMETALLIC	4

END OF FIGURE

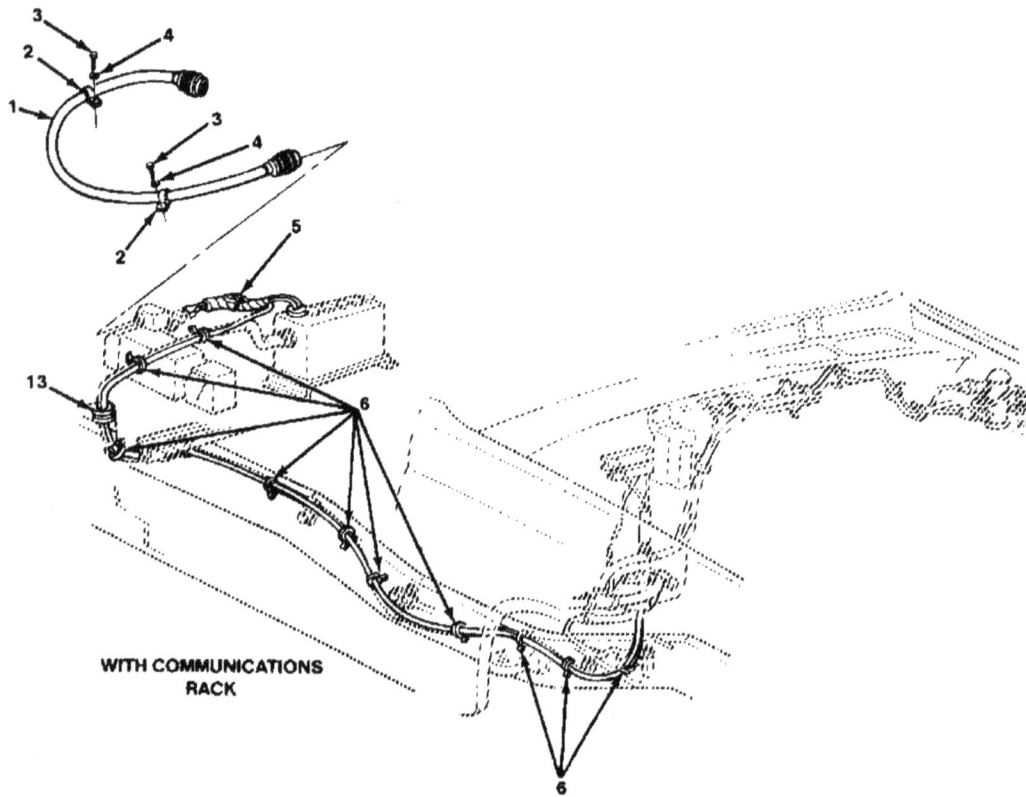

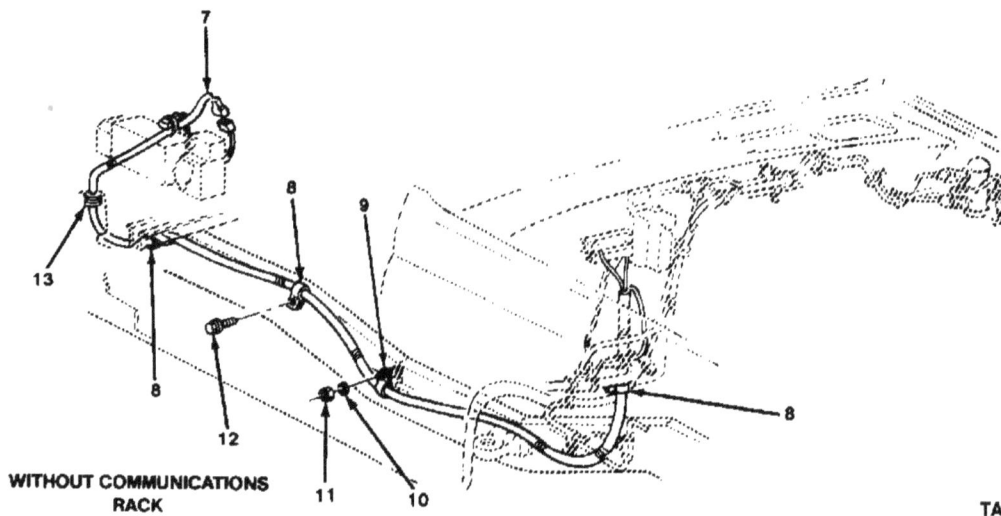

WITH COMMUNICATIONS
RACK

WITHOUT COMMUNICATIONS
RACK

TA511075

FIGURE 226. PERSONNEL HEATER WIRING HARNESS.

(1) ITEM NO	(2) SMR CODE	(3) CAGEC	(4) PART NUMBER	(5) DESCRIPTION AND USABLE ON CODES (UOC)	(6) QTY
				GROUP 3303 WINTERIZATION KITS	
				FIG. 226 PERSONNEL HEATER WIRING HARNESS	
1	PAOZZ	11862	14076269	LEAD,ELECTRICAL UOC:194,208	1
2	PAOZZ	96906	MS21333-112	CLAMP,LOOP UOC:194,208	2
3	PAOZZ	24617	9423768	SCREW,CAP,HEXAGON H UOC:194,208	2
4	PAOZZ	24617	9417714	WASHER,FLAT UOC:194,208	2
5	PAOZZ	11862	14076811	WIRING HARNESS,BRAN UOC:194,208	1
6	PAOZZ	11862	3816659	STRAP,LINE SUPPORTI UOC:194,208	11
7	PAOZZ	11862	14076240	WIRING HARNESS,BRAN UOC:194,208	1
8	PAOZZ	96906	MS21333-123	CLAMP,LOOP UOC:194,208	3
9	PAOZZ	96906	MS21333-114	CLAMP,LOOP UOC:194,208	1
10	PAOZZ	96906	MS35338-44	WASHER,LOCK UOC:194,208	1
11	PAOZZ	96906	MS35691-406	NUT,PLAIN,HEXAGON UOC:194,208	1
12	PAOZZ	11862	11504447	SCREW.TAPPING UOC:194,208	2
13	PAOZZ	11862	3886908	GROMMET,NONMETALLIC UOC:194,208	1

END OF FIGURE

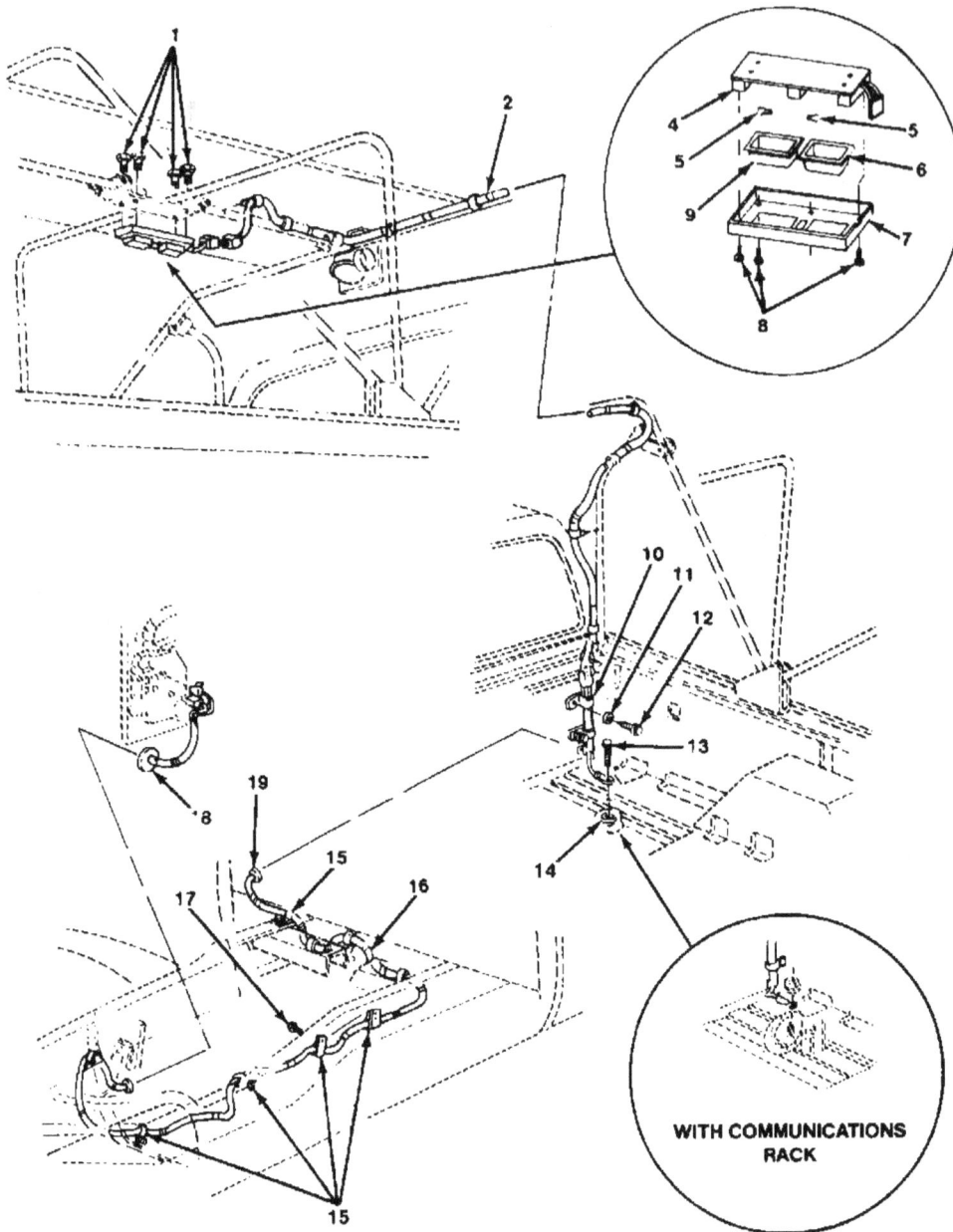

FIGURE 227. DOMELIGHT LAMP AND WIRING HARNESS (M1008 AND M1008A1).

TA511076

GROUP 3303 WINTERIZATION KITS

FIG. 227 DOMELIGHT LAMP AND WIRING
HARNESS (M1008)

ITEM NO	SMR CODE	CAGEC	PART NUMBER	DESCRIPTION AND USABLE ON CODES (UOC)	QTY
1	PAOZZ	96906	MS35206-245	SCREW,MACHINE UOC:194,208	4
2	PAOZZ	11862	14076238	LEAD,ELECTRICAL UOC:194,208	1
3	PAOOO	22973	922-900-00	LIGHT,DOME UOC:194,208	1
4	PAOZZ	22973	922-910-00	.MOUNTING BASE,LIGHT UOC:194,208	1
5	PAOZZ	08806	1003	.LAMP,INCANDESCENT UOC:194,208	2
6	PAOZZ	22973	922-901-02	.LENS,LIGHT WHITE UOC:194,208	1
7	PAOZZ	22973	922-904-02	.HOUSING,LIGHT UOC:194,208	1
8	PAOZZ	96906	MS35206-226	.SCREW,MACHINE UOC:194,208	6
9	PAOZZ	22973	922-901-01	.LENS,LIGHT BLUE UOC:194,208	1
10	PAOZZ	96906	MS21333-112	CLAMP,LOOP UOC:194,208	2
11	PAOZZ	24617	9417714	WASHER,FLAT UOC:194,208	2
12	PAOZZ	96906	MS51850-64	SCREW,CAP,HEXAGON H UOC:194,208	1
13	PAOZZ	96906	MS90728-6	SCREW,CAP,HEXAGON H UOC:194,208	1
14	PAOZZ	24617	271172	NUT,SELF-LOCKING,AS UOC:194,208	1
15	PAOZZ	96906	MS21333-123	CLAMP,LOOP UOC:194,208	5
16	PAOZZ	11862	14076239	WIRING HARNESS,BRAN UOC:194,208	1
17	PAOZZ	11862	11504447	SCREW,TAPPING UOC:194,208	5
18	PAOZZ	11862	3918889	GROMMET,NONMETALLIC UOC:194,208	1
19	PAOZZ	11862	15591130	GROMMET,NONMETALLIC UOC:194,208	1

END OF FIGURE

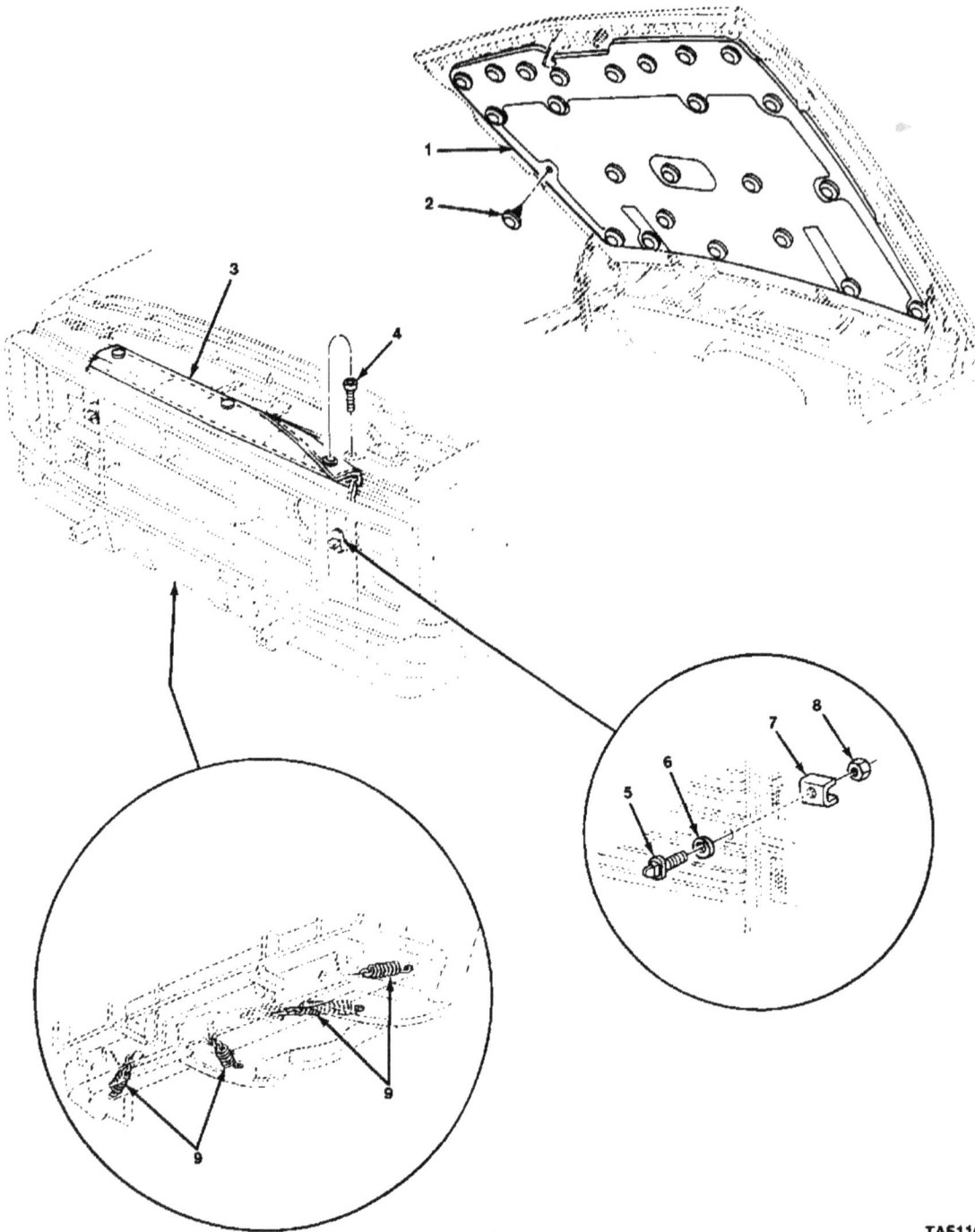

TA511077

FIGURE 228. HOOD AND RADIATOR INSULATORS.

(1)	(2)	(3)	(4)	(5)	(6)
ITEM	SMR		PART		
NO	CODE	CAGEC	NUMBER	DESCRIPTION AND USABLE ON CODES (UOC)	QTY

GROUP 3303 WINTERIZATION KITS

FIG. 228 HOOD AND RADIATOR
INSULATORS

1	MOOZZ	11862	15593599	INSULATOR HOOD MAKE FROM	1
				INSULATION,P/N 12306178	
2	PAOZZ	11862	3977775	FASTENER,SPRING TEN	24
				UOC:194,208,209,230,231,252,254,256	
3	PAOZZ	11862	14063365	INSULATOR,WINTERIZA	1
4	PAOZZ	11862	107413	STUD,SELF-LOCKING	3
5	PAOZZ	19207	12255564-2	STUD,TURNBUTTON FAS	2
6	PAOZZ	96906	MS27183-10	WASHER,FLAT	2
7	PFOZZ	11862	14063366	REINFORCEMENT,RADIA	2
8	PAOZZ	21450	131245	NUT,SELF-LOCKING,HE	2
9	PAOZZ	19207	7717066	SPRING,HELICAL,EXTE	4

END OF FIGURE

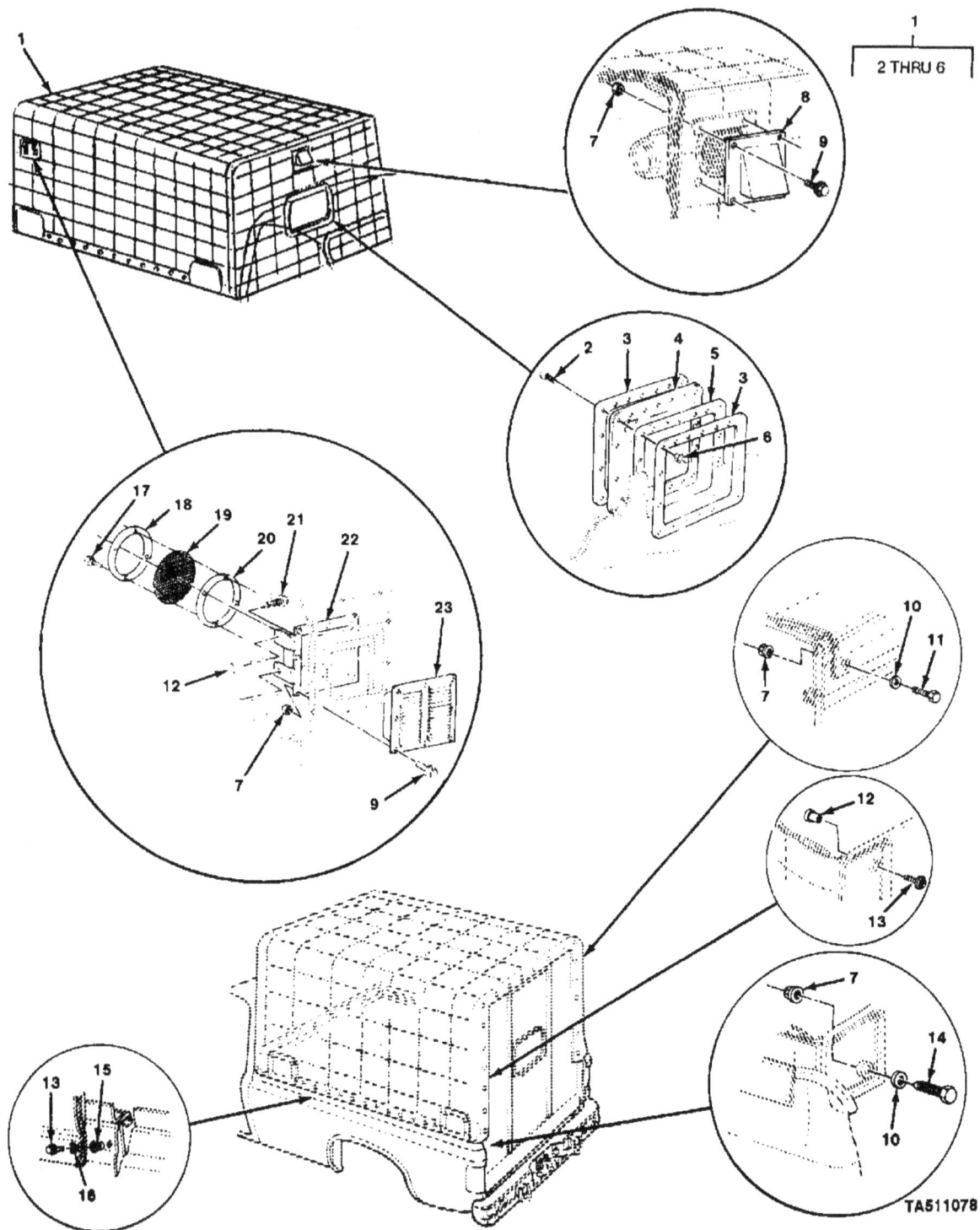

FIGURE 229. ROOF COVER, INTAKE DEFLECTOR, WINDOW, VENT, AND
RELATED PARTS (M1008 AND M1008A1).

TA511078

(1) ITEM NO	(2) SMR CODE	(3) CAGEC	(4) PART NUMBER	(5) DESCRIPTION AND USABLE ON CODES (UOC)	(6) QTY
				GROUP 3303 WINTERIZATION KITS	
				FIG. 229 ROOF COVER, INTAKE DEFLECTOR, WINDOW, VENT, AND RELATED PARTS (M1008 AND M1008A1)	
1	PAOFF	11862	14076228	COVER,FITTED,VEHICU UOC:194,208	1
2	PAOZZ	96906	MS51957-33	.SCREW,MACHINE UOC:194,208	18
3	PAOZZ	11862	14076216	.RETAINER,WINDOW UOC:194,208	2
4	PAOZZ	19207	7353960	.WINDOW,VEHICULAR UOC:194,208	1
5	PAOZZ	11862	14076215	.GASKET UOC:194,208	1
6	PAOZZ	11862	9414031	.NUT,SELF-LOCKING,RO UOC:194,208	18
7	PAOZZ	24617	9416918	NUT,PLAIN,EXTENDED UOC:194,208	20
8	PAOZZ	11862	14075845	VENTILATOR,AIR CIRC UOC:194,208	1
9	PAOZZ	11862	9440033	BOLT,MACHINE UOC:194,208	12
10	PAOZZ	81795	30489	WASHER,FLAT UOC:194,208	8
11	PAOZZ	96906	MS90728-14	SCREW,CAP,HEXAGON H UOC:194,208	6
12	PAOZZ	21450	587227	NUT,PLAIN,PLATE UOC:194,208	12
13	PAOZZ	96906	MS51957-84	SCREW,MACHINE UOC:194,208	44
14	PAOZZ	96906	MS90728-13	SCREW,CAP,HEXAGON H UOC:194,208	2
15	PAOZZ	11862	14005953	SHIELD,EXPANSION UOC:194,208	32
16	PAOZZ	24617	9419265	WASHER,FLAT UOC:194,208	44
17	PAOZZ	11862	20365263	SCREW,TAPPING UOC:194,208	4
18	PAOZZ	11862	14072367	DOOR,ACCESS UOC:194,208	1
19	PAOZZ	11862	14072366	STRAINER ELEMENT,SE UOC:194,208	1
20	PAOZZ	11862	14075857	GASKET UOC:194,208	1
21	PAOZZ	11862	9440334	BOLT,ASSEMBLED WASH UOC:194,208	2
22	PAOZZ	11862	14072365	COVER,ACCESS UOC:194,208	1
23	PAOZZ	11862	14072364	VENTILATOR,AIR CIRC UOC:194,208	1

END OF FIGURE

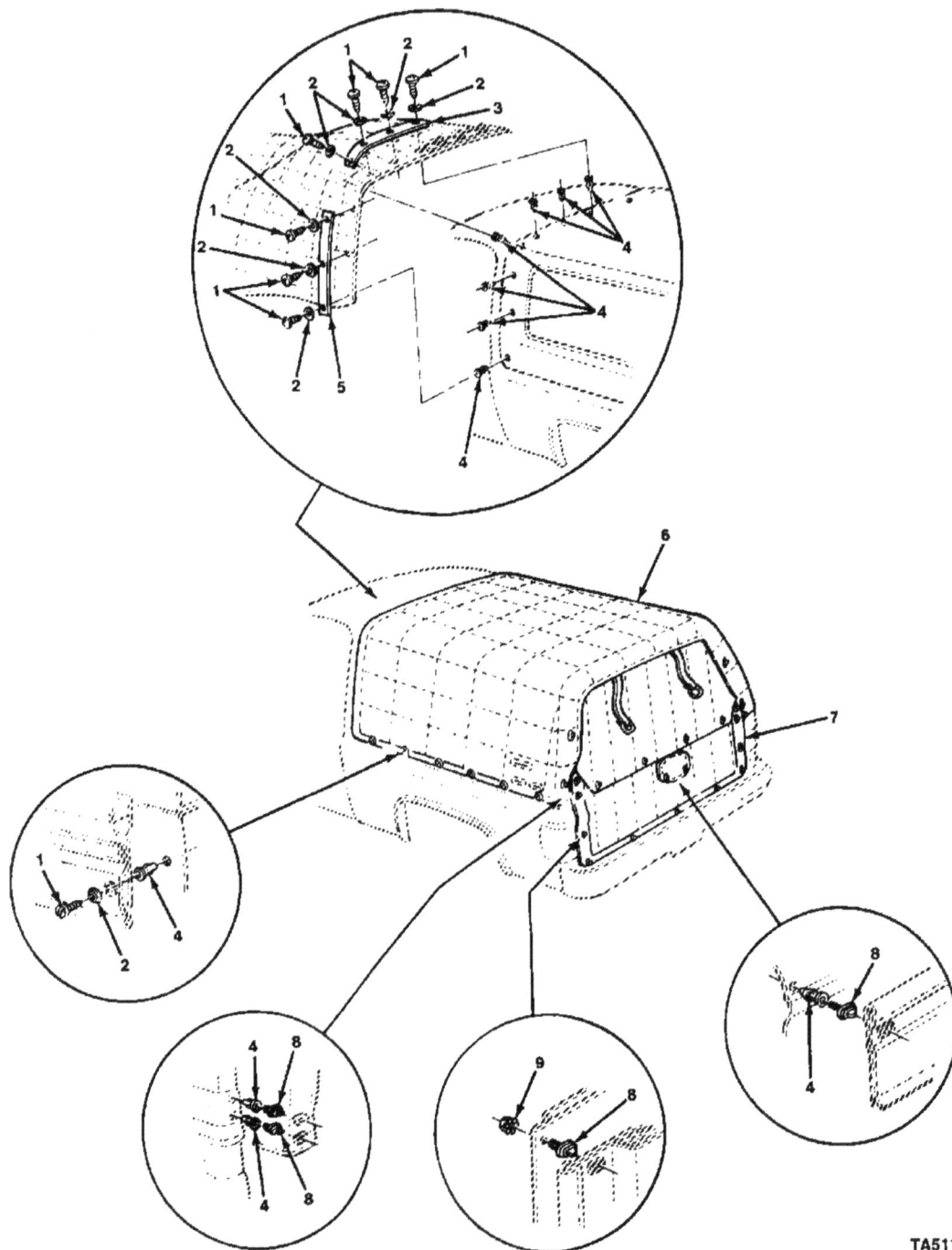

TA511079

FIGURE 230. ROOF AND ENDGATE COVERS AND MOUNTING PARTS (M1009).

(1) ITEM NO	(2) SMR CODE	(3) CAGEC	(4) PART NUMBER	(5) DESCRIPTION AND USABLE ON CODES (UOC)	(6) QTY
				GROUP 3303 WINTERIZATION KITS	
				FIG. 230 ROOF AND ENDGATE COVERS AND MOUNTING PARTS (M1009)	
1	PAOZZ	96906	MS51957-83	SCREW,MACHINE UOC:209	26
2	PAOZZ	24617	9419265	WASHER,FLAT UOC:209	26
3	MOOZZ	11862	14075884	RETAINER (1"X 29.6"X 0.54") MAKE FROM STRIP,P/N MS520390079 UOC:209	2
4	PAOZZ	11862	14005953	SHIELD,EXPANSION UOC:209	44
5	MOOZZ	11862	14075883	RETAINER (1"X 24.2"X 0.54")MAKE FROM STRIP,P/N MS520390079 UOC:209	2
6	PAOFF	11862	14075881	COVER,FITTED,VEHICU UOC:209	1
7	PAOZZ	11862	14075882	CURTAIN,VEHICULAR UOC:209	1
8	PAOZZ	19207	12255564-2	STUD,TURNBUUTON FAS UOC:209	20
9	PAOZZ	24617	271172	NUT,SELF-LOCKING,AS UOC:209	8

END OF FIGURE

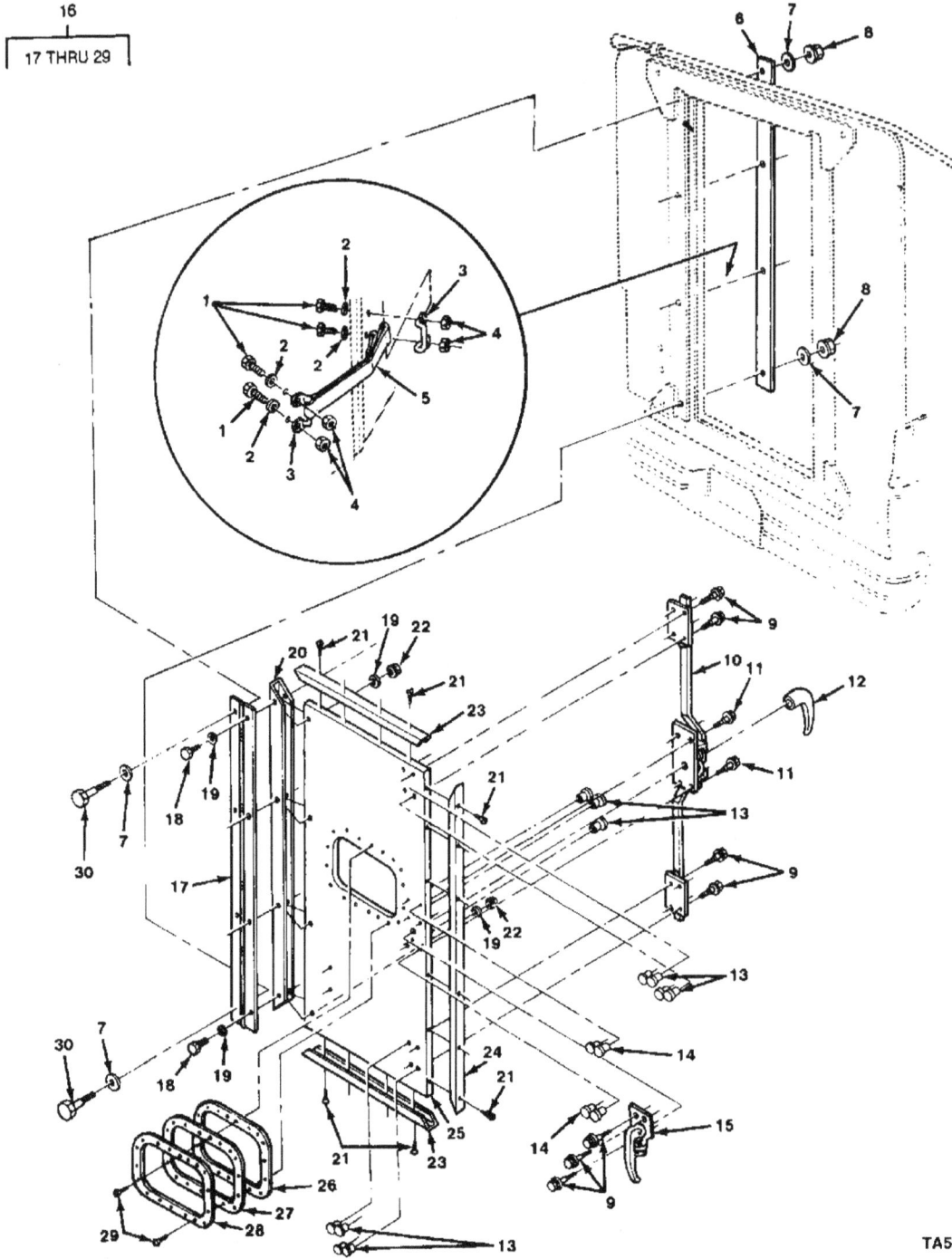

FIGURE 231. REAR DOOR ASSEMBLY (M1008).

TA511080

(1) ITEM NO	(2) SMR CODE	(3) CAGEC	(4) PART NUMBER	(5) DESCRIPTION AND USABLE ON CODES (UOC)	(6) QTY
				GROUP 3303 WINTERIZATION KITS	
				FIG. 231 REAR DOOR ASSEMBY (M1008)	
1	PAOZZ	96906	MS90728-13	SCREW,CAP,HEXAGON H UOC:194,208	4
2	PAOZZ	81795	30489	WASHER,FLAT UOC:194,208	4
3	PAOZZ	11862	3794767	HOLDER,DOOR UOC:194,208	2
4	PAOZZ	24617	9416918	NUT,PLAIN,EXTENDED UOC:194,208	4
5	PAOZZ	11862	370349	STRAP AND FITTING UOC:194,208	1
6	XAOZZ	11862	14076204	MOULDING,REAR DOOR UOC:194,208	1
7	PAOZZ	96906	MS27183-14	WASHER,FLAT UOC:194,208	8
8	PAOZZ	24647	9413534	NUT,SELF-LOCKING,HE UOC:194,208	4
9	PAOZZ	96906	MS51849-78	SCREW,MACHINE UOC:194,208	11
10	PAOZZ	11862	14076882	LATCH ASSEMBLY,DOOR UOC:194,208	1
11	PAOZZ	96906	MS90725-5	SCREW,CAP,HEXAGON H UOC:194,208	4
12	PAOZZ	11862	15599951	HANDLE,DOOR UOC:194,208	1
13	PAOZZ	11862	9411281	STUD,TURNLOCK FASTE UOC:194,208	11
14	PAOZZ	21450	587227	NUT,PLAIN,PLATE UOC:194,208	4
15	PAOZZ	11862	15599950	HANDLE ASSEMBLY,OUT UOC:194,208	1
16	PFOOO	11862	14076875	DOOR,VEHICULAR UOC:194,208	1
17	PAOZZ	11862	14076217	HINGE,BUTT UOC:194,208	1
18	PAOZZ	96906	MS90728-66	.SCREW,CAP,HEXAGON H UOC:194,208	4
19	PAOZZ	96906	MS27183-14	.WASHER,FLAT UOC:1094,208	8
20	XAOZZ	11862	14076210	.FRAME,DOOR UOC:194,208	1
21	PAOZZ	96906	MS35492-54	.SCREW,WOOD UOC:194,208	14
22	PAOZZ	24617	9413534	.NUT,SELF-LOCKING,HE UOC:194,208	4
23	XAOZZ	11862	14076211	.FRAME REAR DOOR UOC:194,208	2
24	XAOZZ	11862	14076884	.FRAME REAR DOOR UOC:194,208	1

(1) ITEM NO	(2) SMR CODE	(3) CAGEC	(4) PART NUMBER	(5) DESCRIPTION AND USABLE ON CODES (UOC)	(6) QTY
			TM9-2320-289-20P		
25	MOOZZ	11862	14076209	.DOOR,REAR (29.72"X 56.0")MAKE FROM PLYWOOD,P/N NN-P-53 UOC:194,208	1
26	PAOZZ	19207	7353960	.WINDOW,VEHICULAR UOC:194,208	1
27	PAOZZ	11862	14076215	.GASKET UOC:194,208	1
28	PAOZZ	11862	14076216	.RETAINER,WINDOW UOC:194,208	1
29	PAOZZ	96906	MS35493-37	.SCREW,WOOD UOC:194,208	18
30	PAOZZ	96906	MS90728-66	SCREW,CAP,HEXAGON H UOC:194,208	4

END OF FIGURE

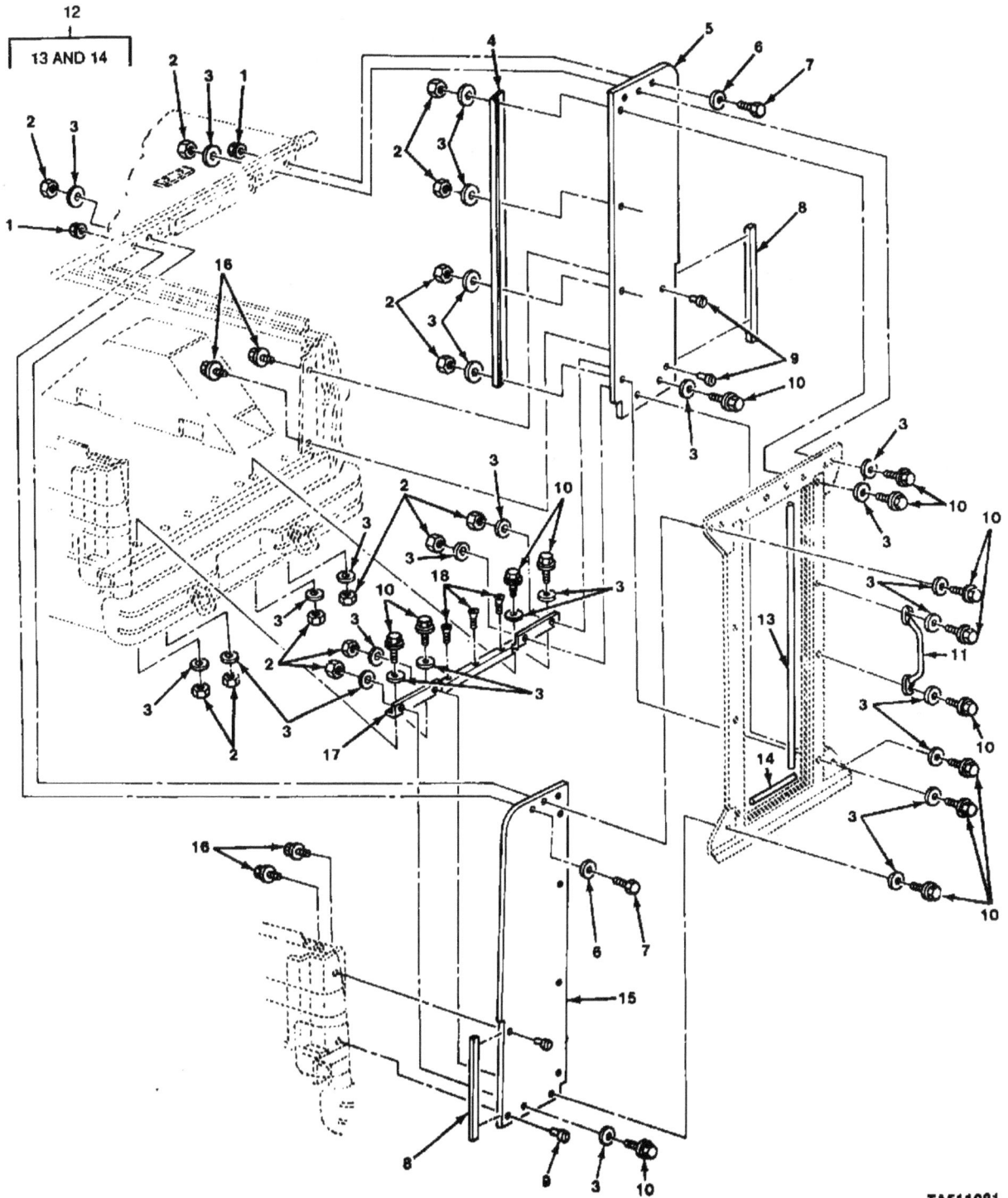

FIGURE 232. REAR PANEL COMPONENTS (M1008).

TA511081

(1) ITEM NO	(2) SMR CODE	(3) CAGEC	(4) PART NUMBER	(5) DESCRIPTION AND USABLE ON CODES (UOC)	(6) QTY
				GROUP 3303 WINTERIZATION KITS	
				FIG. 232 REAR PANEL COMPONENTS (M1008)	
1	PAOZZ	24617	9416918	NUT,PLAIN,EXTENDED UOC:194,208	2
2	PAOZZ	24617	9413534	NUT,SELF-LOCKING,HE UOC:194,208	14
3	PAOZZ	96906	MS27183-14	WASHER,FLAT UOC:194,208	28
4	XAOZZ	11862	14076204	MOULDING,REAR DOOR UOC:194,208	1
5	MOOZZ	11862	14076872	PANEL ASM RR DR R H (19.32"X 59.09") MAKE FROM PLYWOOD,P/N NN-P- UOC:194,208	1
6	PAOZZ	81795	30489	WASHER,FLAT UOC:194,208	2
7	PAOZZ	96906	MS90728-13	SCREW,CAP,HEXAGON H UOC:194,208	2
8	PAOZZ	11862	14076862	RUBBER STRIP UOC:194,208	2
9	PAOZZ	21450	587227	NUT,PLAIN,PLATE UOC:194,208	4
10	PAOZZ	96906	MS90728-66	SCREW,CAP,HEXAGON H UOC:194,208	14
11	PAOZZ	11862	14076221	HANDLE,BOW UOC:194,208	1
12	PAOOO	11862	15599910	FRAME,DOOR,METAL UOC:194,208	1
13	XDOZZ	11862	14076212	.SEAL UOC:194,208	2
14	XDOZZ	11862	14076864	.SEAL UOC:194,208	2
15	MOOZZ	11862	14076871	PANEL ASM RR DR LH (19.32"X 59.09") MAKE FROM PLYWOOD, P/N NNP530 UOC:194,208	1
16	PAOZZ	11862	9440334	BOLT,ASSEMBLED WASH UOC:194,208	4
17	PAOZZ	11862	14076208	MOULDING,METAL UOC:194,208	1
18	PAOZZ	96906	MS35492-54	SCREW,WOOD UOC:194,208	3

END OF FIGURE

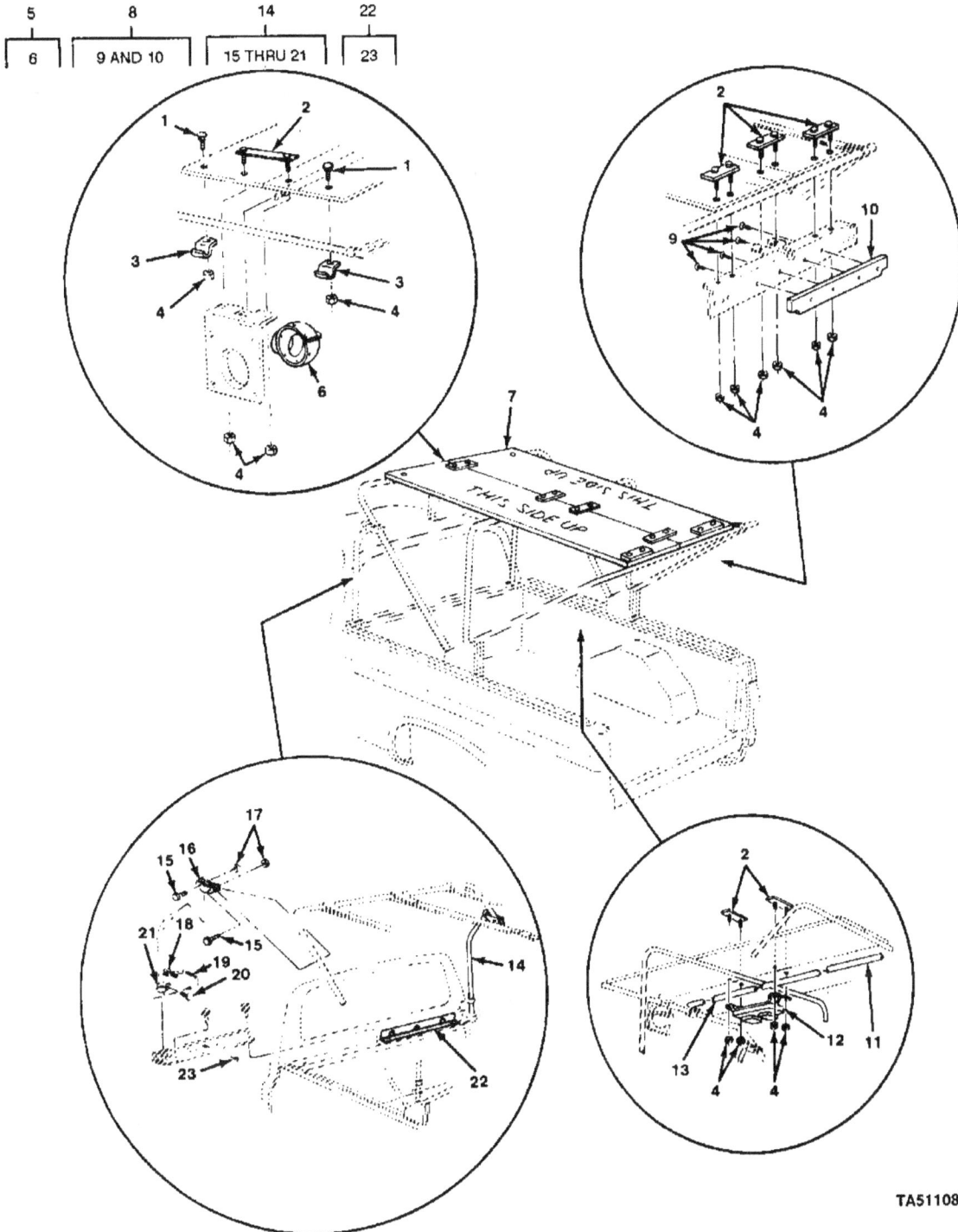

FIGURE 233. ROOF PANEL COMPONENTS (M1008).

TA511082

(1) ITEM NO	(2) SMR CODE	(3) CAGEC	(4) PART NUMBER	(5) DESCRIPTION AND USABLE ON CODES (UOC)	(6) QTY
				GROUP 3303 WINTERIZATION KITS	
				FIG. 233 ROOF PANEL COMPONENTS (M1008)	
1	PAOZZ	96906	MS35751-17	BOLT,SQUARE NECK UOC:194,208	2
2	PAOZZ	11862	14076233	BRACKET,SUPPORT,ROD UOC:194,208	6
3	PAOZZ	11862	14076230	STRAP,RETAINING UOC:194,208	2
4	PAOZZ	24617	9416918	NUT,PLAIN,EXTENDED UOC:194,208	14
5	PAOOO	11862	14075843	ADAPTER ASSEMBLY,AI UOC:194,208	1
6	PAOZZ	19207	7951738	.ADAPTER,AIR INLET UOC:194,208	1
7	MOOZZ	11862	14076222	PANEL ROOF (24.0"X 96.0") MAKE FROM PLYWOOD,P/N NNP530 UOC:194,208	2
8	PFOOO	17769	14076861	PANEL ASSEMBLY,REAR UOC:194,208	1
9	PAOZZ	96906	MS35493-76	.SCREW,WOOD UOC:194,208	2
10	MOOZZ	11862	14076201	.PANEL REAR DOOR (2.28"X 30.88") MAKE FOR PLYWOOD,P/N NNP530 UOC:194,208	1
11	MOOZZ	11862	15599916	SUPPORT (1.00"X 46.50") MAKE FROM TUBE,P/N MILT16343TYPE1 UOC:194,208	1
12	PAOZZ	11862	14076231	BRACKET,SUPPORT,ROO UOC:194,208	1
13	MOOZZ	11862	14076232	SUPPORT (46.50") MAKE FROM TUBE,P/ N MILT16343TYPE1 UOC:194,208	1
14	PAOOO	11862	15599917	SUPPORT,ROOF BOW LE UOC:194,208	1
14	PAOOO	11862	15599918	SUPPORT,ROOF BOW RT UOC:194,208	1
15	PAOZZ	96906	MS90728-13	.SCREW,CAP,HEXAGON H UOC:194-208	2
16	PAOZZ	11862	14076226	.STRAP,RETAINING UOC:194,208	1
17	PAOZZ	24617	9416918	.NUT,PLAIN,EXTENDED UOC:194,208	2
18	PAOZZ	24617	9423530	.NUT,PLAIN,ASSEMBLED UOC:194,208	1
19	PAOZZ	19207	11669126-1	.PIN,QUICK RELEASE UOC:194,208	1
20	PAOZZ	96906	MS51957-30	.SCREW,MACHINE UOC:194,208	1
21	PAOZZ	19207	12255561	.CLAMP,LOOP	1

(1) ITEM NO	(2) SMR CODE	(3) CAGEC	(4) PART NUMBER	(5) DESCRIPTION AND USABLE ON CODES (UOC)	(6) QTY
				UOC:194,208	
22	PAOOO	11862	14076299	RAIL,CARGO COVER,VE LEFT	1
				UOC:194,208	
22	PAOOO	11862	14076300	RAIL,CARGO COVER,VE RIGHT	1
				UOC:194,208	
23	PAOZZ	19207	12255564-1	.STUD,TURNBUTTON FAS	4
				UOC:194,208	

END OF FIGURE

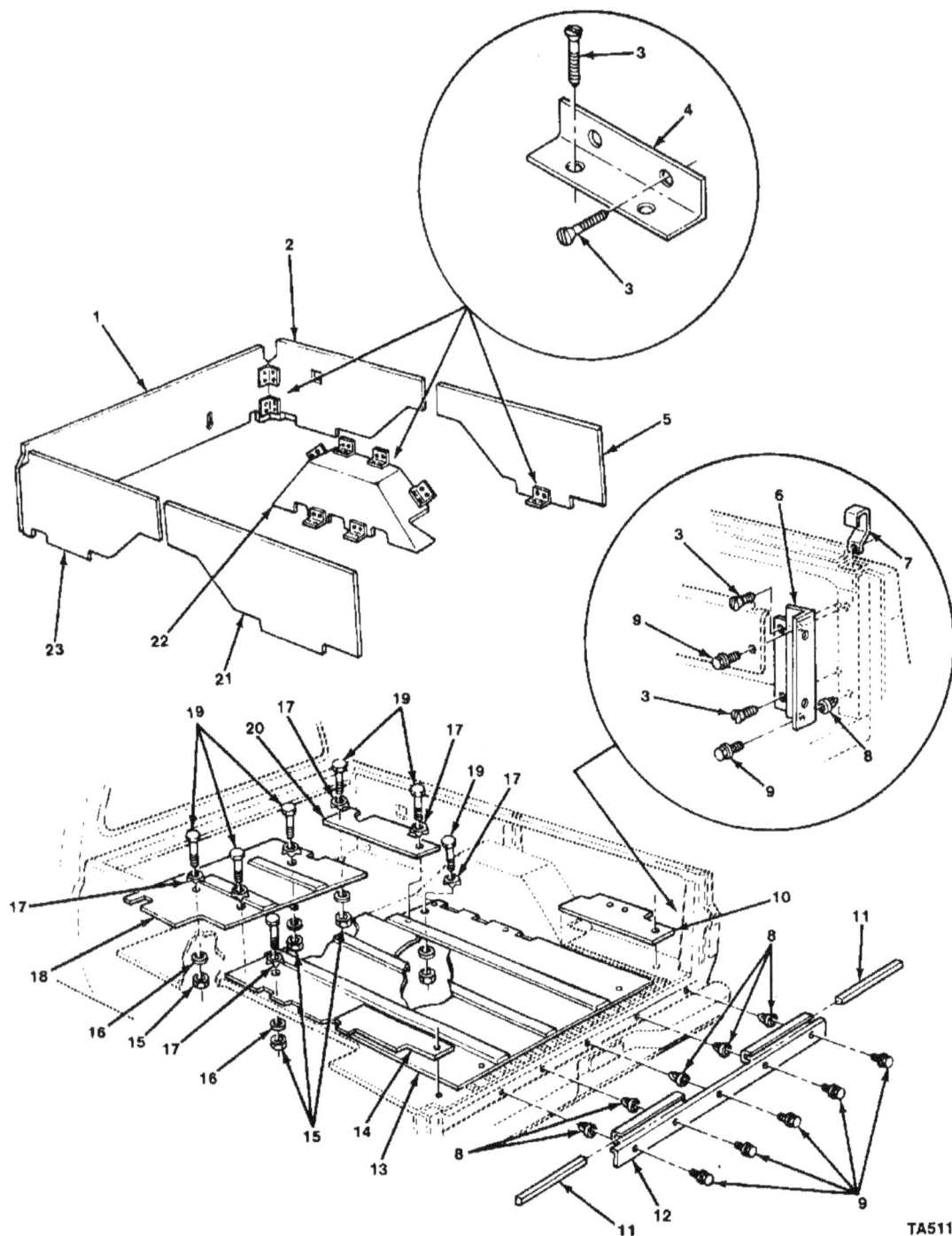

FIGURE 234. FLOOR AND SIDEWALL PANELS (MI 008).

TA511083

GROUP 3303 WINTERIZATION KITS

FIG. 234 FLOOR AND SIDEWALL PANELS
(M1008)

ITEM NO	SMR CODE	CAGEC	PART NUMBER	DESCRIPTION AND USABLE ON CODES (UOC)	QTY
1	MOOZZ	11862	14076281	INSULATOR (70.00"X 16.74") MAKE FROM PLYWOOD, P/N NNP530 UOC:194,208	1
2	MOOZZ	11862	14076278	INSULATOR (52.26"X 18.28") MAKE FROM PLYWOOD, P/N NNP530 UOC:194,208	1
3	PAOZZ	96906	MS35492-57	SCREW,WOOD UOC:194,208	76
4	PAOZZ	11862	14063349	BRACKET,ANGLE UOC:194,208	18
5	MOOZZ	11862	14076280	INSULATOR (38.12"X 16.80") MAKE FROM PLYWOOD, P/N NNP530 UOC:194,208	1
6	PAOZZ	11862	15599273	BRACKET,MOUNTING LEFT UOC:194,208	1
6	PAOZZ	11862	15599274	BRACKET,MOUNTING RIGHT UOC:194,208	1
7	PAOZZ	11862	14076889	HOOK,SUPPORT UOC:194,208	2
8	PAOZZ	11862	14005953	SHIELD,EXPANSION UOC:194,208	7
9	PAOZZ	11862	9440334	BOLT,ASSEMBLED WASH UOC:194,208	9
10	MOOZZ	11862	14076276	INSULATOR (17.84"X 10.75") MAKE FROM PLYWOOD, P/N NNP530 UOC:194,208	1
11	PAOZZ	11862	14076235	GASKET UOC:194,208	2
12	PFOFF	11862	14076206	MOULDING,PANEL,INSU UOC:194,208	1
13	MOOZZ	11862	14076272	INSULATOR (66.62"X 48.00") MAKE FROM PLYWOOD, P/N NNP530 UOC:194,208	1
14	MOOZZ	11862	14076275	INSULATOR (17.84"X 10.75") MAKE FROM PLYWOOD, P/N NNP530 UOC:194,208	1
15	PAOZZ	80205	NAS1408A6	NUT,SELF-LOCKING,HE UOC:194,208	7
16	PAOZZ	96906	MS27183-16	WASHER,FLAT UOC:194,208	7
17	PAOZZ	96906	MS27183-17	WASHER,FLAT UOC:194,208	7
18	MOOZZ	11862	14076271	INSULATOR (46.15"X 28.62") MAKE FROM PLYWOOD, P/N NNP530 UOC:194,208	1
19	PAOZZ	96906	MS35751-46	BOLT,SQUARE NECK UOC:194,208	7

(1)	(2)	(3)	(4)	(5)	(6)
ITEM NO	SMR CODE	CAGEC	PART NUMBER	DESCRIPTION AND USABLE ON CODES (UOC)	QTY
20	MOOZZ	11862	14076229	INSULATOR (28.62"X 10.09") MAKE FROM PLYWOOD, P/N NNP530 UOC:194,208	1
21	MOOZZ	11862	14076279	INSULATOR (38.12"X 16.80") MAKE FROM PLYWOOD,P/N NNP530 UOC:194,208	1
22	MOOZZ	11862	14076273	INSULATOR LEFT, MAKE FROM PLYWOOD P/N NNP530 UOC:194,208	1
22	MOOZZ	11862	14076274	INSULATOR RIGHT, MAKE FROM PLYWOOD, P/N NNP530 UOC:194,208	1
23	MOOZZ	11862	14076277	INSULATOR (52.26"X 18.28") MAKE FROM PLYWOOD,P/N NNP530 UOC:194,208	1

END OF FIGURE

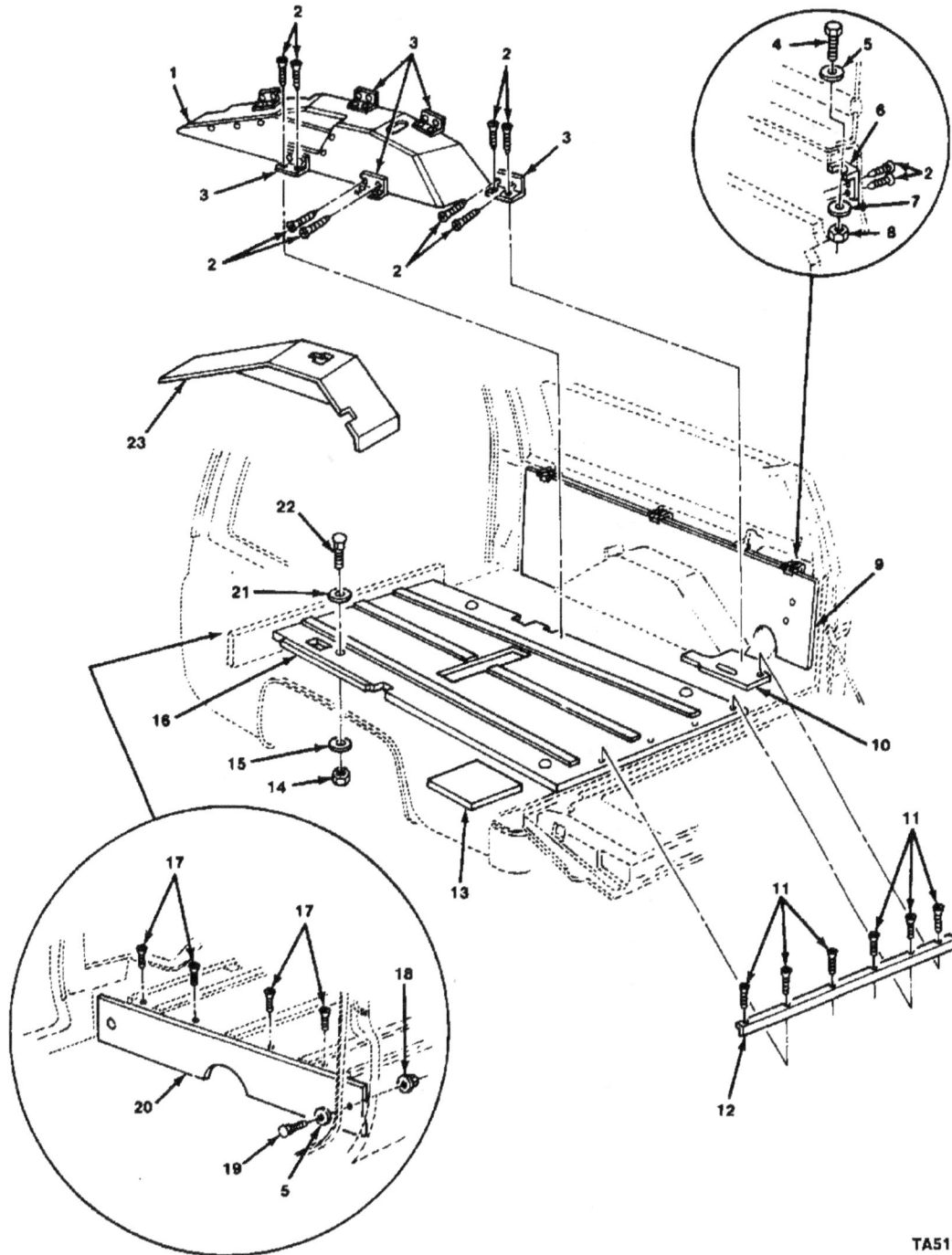

FIGURE 235. FLOOR AND SIDEWALL PANELS (M1009).

TA511084

(1) ITEM NO	(2) SMR CODE	(3) CAGEC	(4) PART NUMBER	(5) DESCRIPTION AND USABLE ON CODES (UOC)	(6) QTY
				GROUP 3303 WINTERIZATION KIT	
				FIG. 235 FLOOR AND SIDEWALL PANELS (M1009)	
1	MOOZZ	11862	14063348	INSULATION (RIGHT) MAKE FROM PLYWOOD, P/N NNP530 UOC:209	1
2	PAOZZ	96906	MS35492-54	SCREW,WOOD UOC:209	60
3	MOOZZ	11862	14063349	BRACKET,ANGLE MAKE FROM P/N QQS741 UOC:209	12
4	PAOZZ	96906	MS90728-37	BOLT,MACHINE UOC:209	6
5	PAOZZ	96906	MS27183-12	WASHER,FLAT UOC:209	8
6	MOOZZ	11862	14063342	BRACKET MAKE FROM ANGLE, P/N MILS20166 UOC:209	6
7	PAOZZ	11862	9417793	WASHER,FLAT UOC:209	6
8	PAOZZ	24617	9422295	NUT,SELF-LOCKING,CO UOC:209	6
9	MOOZZ	11862	14063343	INSULATION PANEL (LEFT) MAKE FROM PLYWOOD, P/N NNP530 UOC:209	1
9	MOOZZ	11862	14063344	INSULATION PANEL (RIGHT) MAKE FROM PLYWOOD, P/N NNP530 UOC:209	1
10	MOOZZ	11862	14063346	INSULATION FLOOR (RIGHT) MAKE FROM PLYWOOD, P/N NNP530 UOC:209	1
11	PAOZZ	96906	MS35494-83	SCREW,WOOD UOC:209	6
12	MOOZZ	11862	14063350	MOLDING (56.0" LG) MAKE FROM ANGLE P/N QQS741 UOC:209	1
13	MOOZZ	11862	14063345	INSL-FLR PNL L.R. O (LEFT) MAKE FROM PLYWOOD, P/N NNP530 UOC:209	1
14	PAOZZ	80205	NAS1408A6	NUT,SELF-LOCKING,HE UOC:209	4
15	PAOZZ	96906	MS27183-16	WASHER,FLAT UOC:209	4
16	MOOZZ	11862	14063341	INSULATION ASSEMBLY MAKE FROM PLYWOOD, P/N NNP530 UOC:209	1
17	PAOZZ	96906	MS35492-82	SCREW,WOOD UOC:209	4
18	PAOZZ	24617	11506003	NUT,PLAIN,ASSEMBLED UOC:209	2
19	PAOZZ	96906	MS35751-19	BOLT,SQUARE NECK	2

(1) ITEM NO	(2) SMR CODE	(3) CAGEC	(4) PART NUMBER	(5) DESCRIPTION AND USABLE ON CODES (UOC)	(6) QTY
				UOC:209	
20	MOOZZ	11862	14063351	INSULATION FLOOR MAKE FROM PLYWOOD P/N NNP530	1
				UOC:209	
21	PAOZZ	96906	MS27183-17	WASHER,FLAT	4
				UOC:209	
22	PAOZZ	96906	MS35751-73	BOLT,SQUARE NECK	4
				UOC:209	
23	MOOZZ	11862	14063347	INSULATION (LEFT) MAKE FROM PLYWOOD,P/N NNP530	1
				UOC:209	

END OF FIGURE

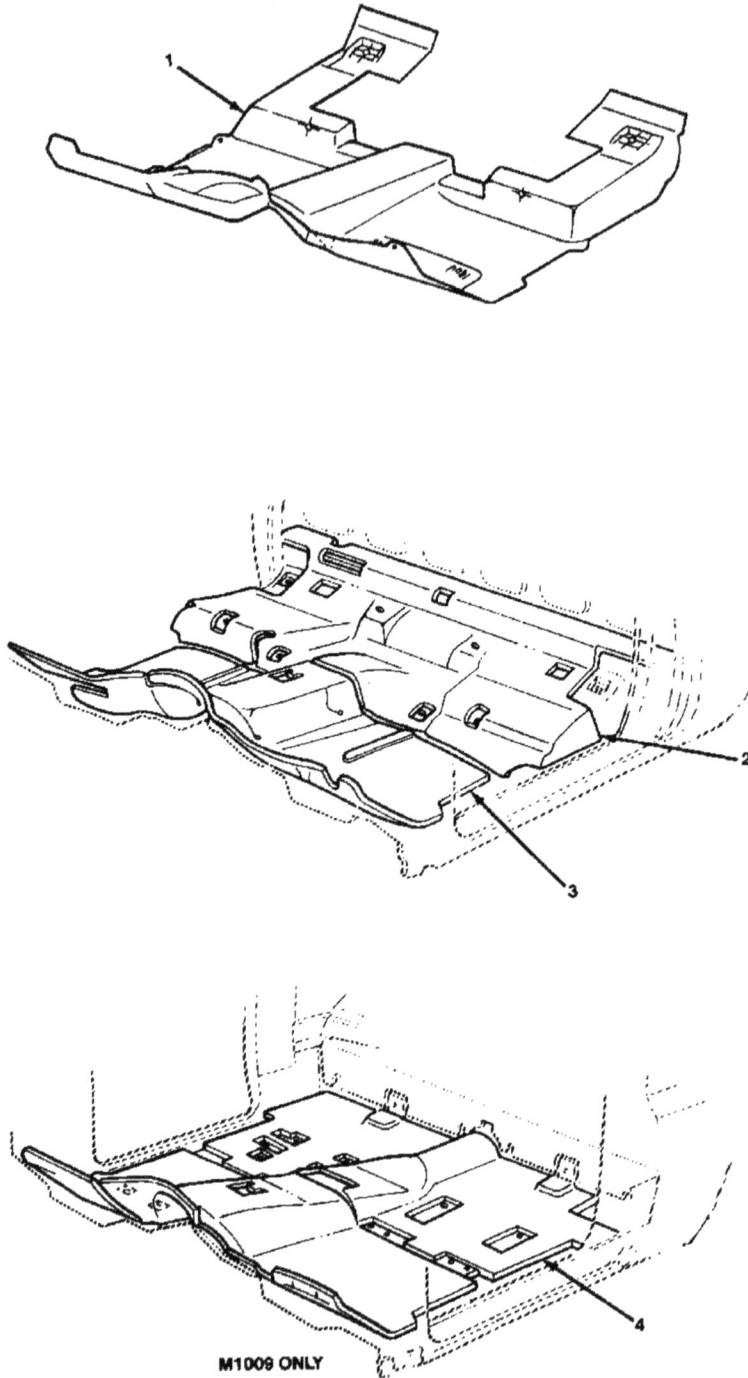

M1009 ONLY

TA511085

FIGURE 236. CAB FLOOR INSULATORS

(1) ITEM NO	(2) SMR CODE	(3) CAGEC	(4) PART NUMBER	(5) DESCRIPTION AND USABLE ON CODES (UOC)	(6) QTY
				GROUP 3303 WINTERIZATION KITS	
				FIG. 236 FLOOR INSULATORS	
1	PAOZZ	11862	15594983	MAT,FLOOR UOC:194,208,210,230,231,252,254,256	1
2	MOOZZ	11862	14075862	INSULATOR FL PNL RR (36.0"X 36.0")MAKE FROM INSULATOR,P/N 462233 UOC:194,208,230,231,252,254,256	1
2	MOOZZ	11862	14075864	INSULATOR,FLOOR,VEH (36.0" X 36.0") MAKE FROM INSULATION, P/N 462233 UOC:210	1
3	MOOZZ	11862	14076802	INSULATOIR FLR PNL (36.0" X 36.0") MAKE FROM INSULATOR, P/N 462233 UOC:194,208,209,230,231,252,254,256	1
3	MOOZZ	11862	14076803	INSULATION,FLOOR PA (36.0" X 36.0") MAKE FROM INSULATION, P/N 462233 UOC:210	1
4	MOOZZ	11862	14075863	INSUL-FLR PNL RR (36.0" X 36.0") MAKE FROM INSULATOR, P/N 462233 UOC:209	1

END OF FIGURE

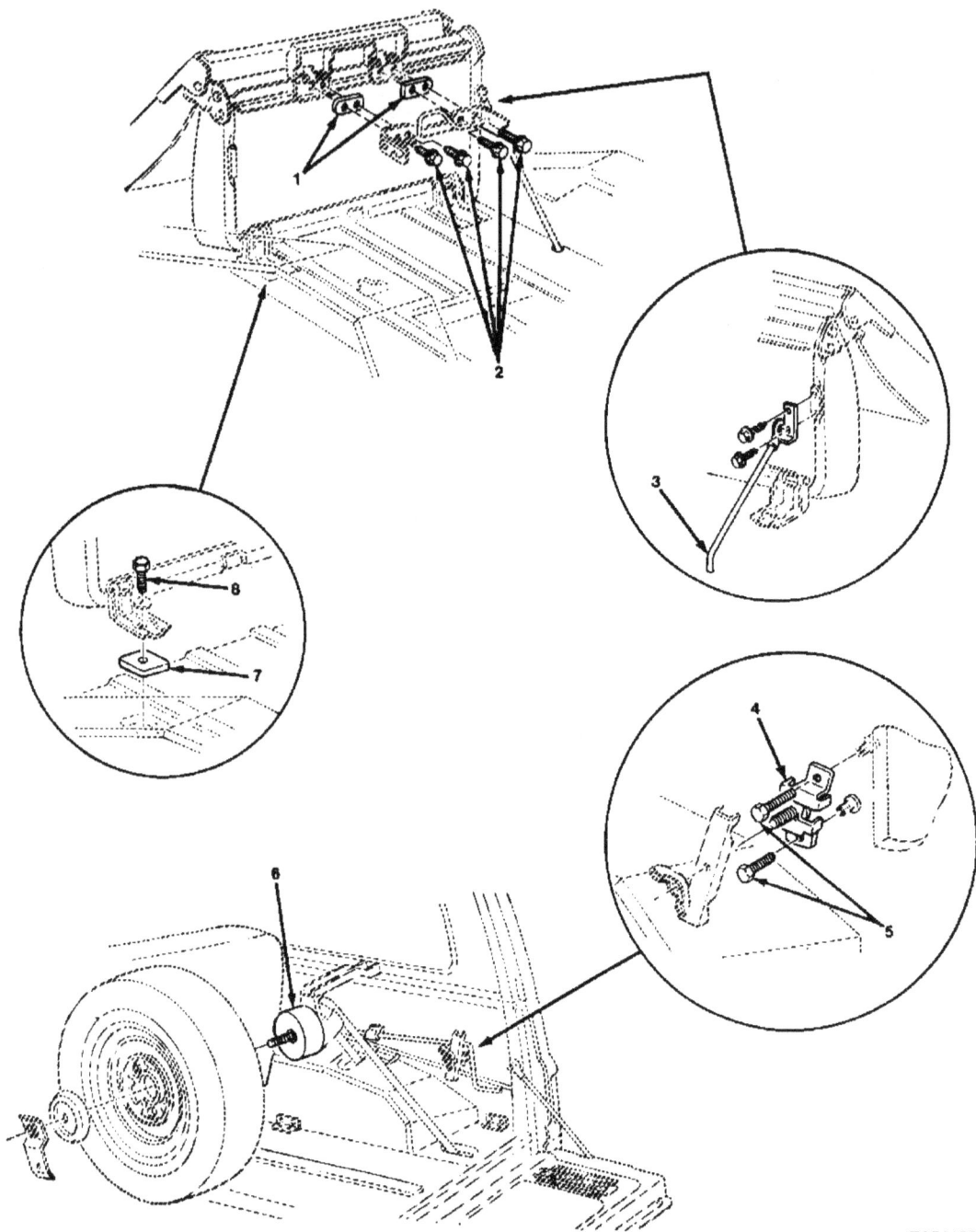

TA511086

FIGURE 237. SEAT AND SPARE TIRE SPACERS (M1009).

(1)	(2)	(3)	(4)	(5)	(6)
ITEM NO	SMR CODE	CAGEC	PART NUMBER	DESCRIPTION AND USABLE ON CODES (UOC)	QTY

GROUP 3303 WINTERIZATION KITS

FIG. 237 SEAT AND SPARE TIRE SPACERS (M1009)

1	PAOZZ	11862	14063353	PLATE,RESILIENT MOU UOC:209	2
2	XDOZZ	24617	9409103	BOLT,ASSEMBLED WASH UOC:209	4
3	PAOZZ	11862	14063359	LEVER,LOCK-RELEASE UOC:209	1
4	PFOZZ	11862	14074431	BRACKET,MOUNTING UOC:209	1
5	PAOZZ	96906	MS90728-6	SCREW,CAP,HEXAGON H UOC:209	2
6	PAOZZ	11862	14063358	RETAINER,SPARE TIRE UOC:209	1
7	XDOZZ	11862	14063352	SPACER UOC:209	2
8	PAOZZ	96906	MS90728-115	SCREW,CAP,HEXAGON H UOC:209	2

END OF FIGURE

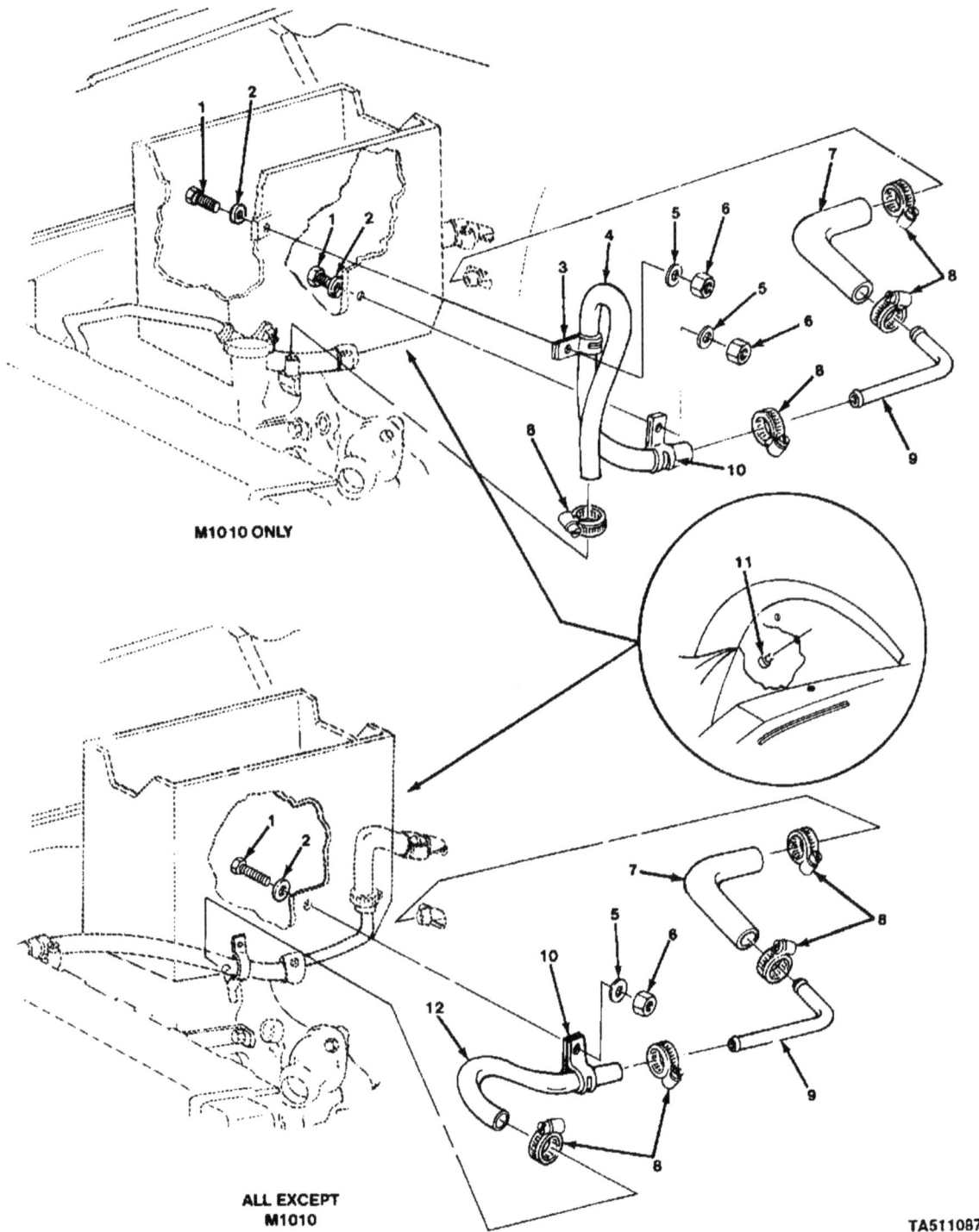

M1010 ONLY

**ALL EXCEPT
M1010**

TA511087

FIGURE 238. BASE HEATER INLET HOSE, PIPE, AND RELATED PARTS.

(1) ITEM NO	(2) SMR CODE	(3) CAGEC	(4) PART NUMBER	(5) DESCRIPTION AND USABLE ON CODES (UOC)	(6) QTY
				GROUP 3303 WINTERIZATION KITS	
				FIG. 238 BASE HEATER INLET HOSE, PIPE, AND RELATED PARTS	
1	PAOZZ	96906	MS90728-34	BOLT,MACHINE UOC:194,208,209,230,231,252,254,256	1
1	PAOZZ	96906	MS90728-34	BOLT,MACHINE UOC:210	2
2	PAOZZ	96906	MS35340-45	WASHER,LOCK UOC:194,208,209,230,231,252,254,256	1
2	PAOZZ	96906	MS35340-45	WASHER,LOCK UOC:210	2
3	PAOZZ	96906	MS21333-78	CLAMP,LOOP UOC:210	1
4	MOOZZ	11862	14074444	HOSE,NONMETALLIC (28.75" LG) MAKE FROM HOSE, P/N MS521304B203R UOC:210	1
5	PAOZZ	96906	MS27183-12	WASHER,FLAT UOC:194,208,209,230,231,252,254,256	1
5	PAOZZ	96906	MS27183-12	WASHER,FLAT UOC:210	2
6	PAOZZ	96906	MS51943-33	NUT,SELF-LOCKING,HE UOC:194,208,209,230,231,252,254,256	1
6	PAOZZ	96906	MS51943-33	NUT,SELF-LOCKING,HE UOC:210	2
7	MOOZZ	11862	14074446	HOSE,PREFORMED (3.20" LG) MAKE FROM HOSE, P/N MS521304B203R	1
8	PAOZZ	96906	MS35842-11	CLAMP,HOSE	4
9	PAOZZ	11862	14074445	TUBE,BENT,METALLIC	1
10	PAOZZ	96906	MS21333-128	CLAMP,LOOP UOC:194,208,209,230,231,252,254,256	1
11	PAOZZ	11862	3738198	CAP-PLUG,PROTECTIVE	1
12	MOOZZ	11862	14075856	HOSE HEATER INL FRT (24" LG) FROM HOSE, P/N MS521304B203R UOC:194,208,209,230,231,252,254,256	1

END OF FIGURE

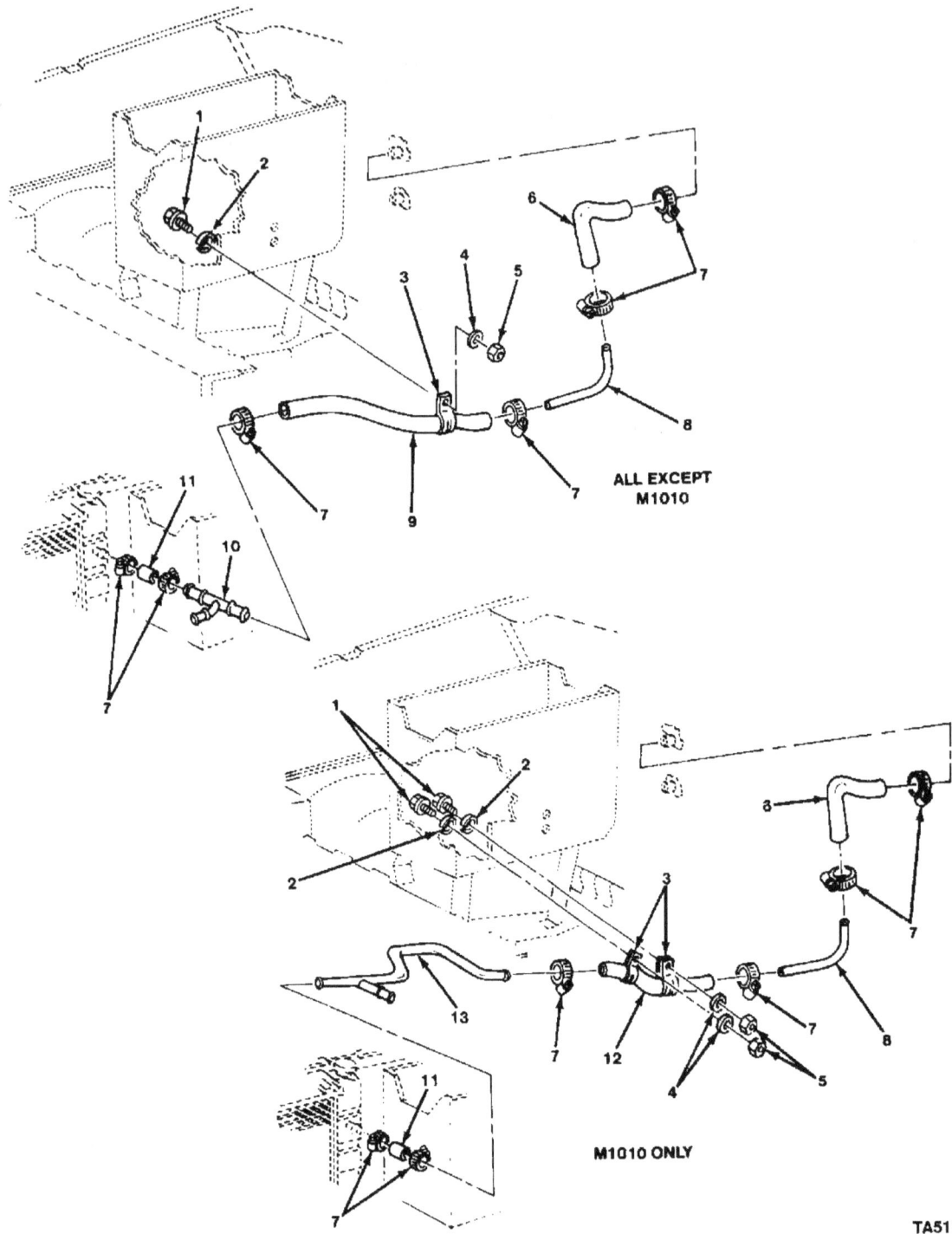

FIGURE 239. BASE HEATER OUTLET HOSE, PIPE, AND RELATED PARTS.

ALL EXCEPT
M1010

M1010 ONLY

TA511088

(1) ITEM NO	(2) SMR CODE	(3) CAGEC	(4) PART NUMBER	(5) DESCRIPTION AND USABLE ON CODES (UOC)	(6) QTY
				GROUP 3303 WINTERIZATION KITS	
				FIG. 239 BASE HEATER OUTLET HOSE, PIPE, AND RELATED PARTS	
1	PAOZZ	96906	MS90728-34	BOLT,MACHINE	1
1	PAOZZ	96906	MS90728-34	BOLT,MACHINE UOC:210	2
2	PAOZZ	96906	MS35340-45	WASHER,LOCK	1
2	PAOZZ	96906	MS35340-45	WASHER,LOCK UOC:210	2
3	PAOZZ	96906	MS21333-128	CLAMP,LOOP UOC:210	2
3	PAOZZ	96906	MS21333-128	CLAMP,LOOP	1
4	PAOZZ	96906	MS27183-12	WASHER,FLAT UOC:194,208,209,210,230,231,252,254	1
4	PAOZZ	96906	MS27183-12	WASHER,FLAT UOC:210	2
5	PAOZZ	96906	MS51943-33	NUT,SELF-LOCKING,HE	1
5	PAOZZ	96906	MS51943-33	NUT,SELF-LOCKING,HE UOC:210	2
6	PAOZZ	11862	14074451	HOSE,PREFORMED	1
7	PAOZZ	96906	MS35842-11	CLAMP,HOSE	6
8	PAOZZ	11862	14074450	TUBE,BENT,METALLIC	1
9	MOOZZ	11862	14074449	HOSE HTR OUT INTER (21.5" LG) MAKE FROM HOSE,P/N 482420 UOC:194,208,209,230,231,252,254,256	1
10	PAOZZ	11862	14074448	PIPE ASSEMBLY,HEATE UOC:194,208,209,230,231,252,254,256	1
11	MOOZZ	11862	14074447	HOSE HEATER INLET (2.50" LG) MAKE FROM HOSE,P/N 482420	1
12	MOOZZ	11862	14074453	HOSE HEATER INLET (11" LG) MAKE FROM HOSE,P/N 482420 UOC:210	1
13	PAOZZ	11862	14074452	TUBE,BENT,METALLIC UOC:210	1

END OF FIGURE

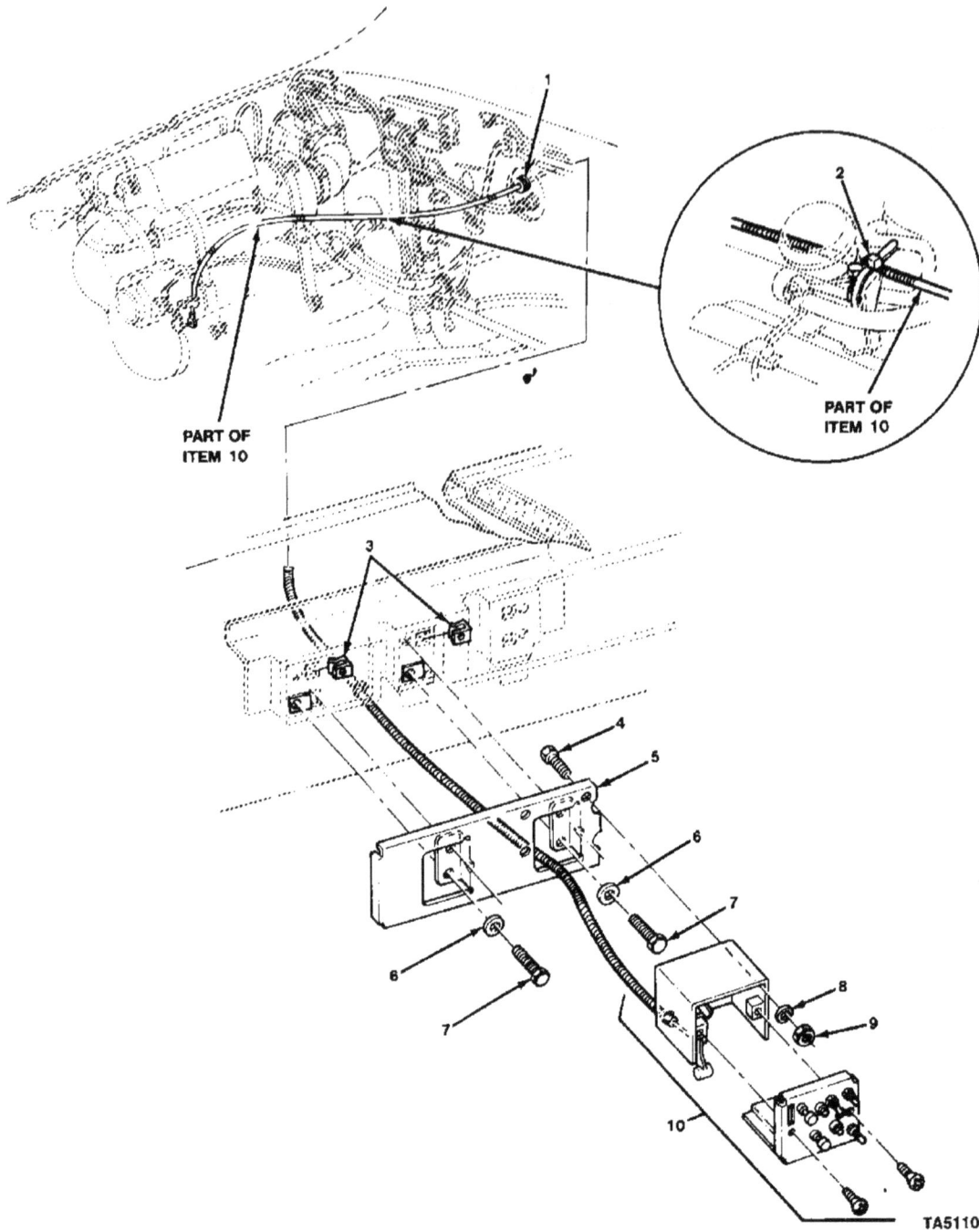

FIGURE 240. HEATER CONTROL MOUNTING AND CABLE.

PART OF ITEM 10

PART OF ITEM 10

TA511089

(1) ITEM NO	(2) SMR CODE	(3) CAGEC	(4) PART NUMBER	(5) DESCRIPTION AND USABLE ON CODES (UOC)	(6) QTY
				GROUP 3303 WINTERIZATION KITS	
				FIG. 240 HEATER CONTROL MOUNTING AND CABLE	
1	PAOZZ	96906	MS35489-5	GROMMET,NONMETALLIC	1
2	PAOZZ	11862	3816659	STRAP,LINE SUPPORTI	1
3	PAOZZ	11862	3982098	NUT,PLAIN,HEXAGON	4
4	PAOZZ	96906	MS90728-3	SCREW,CAP,HEXAGON H	3
5	PAOZZ	11862	14072415	BRACKET,MOUNTING	1
6	PAOZZ	96906	MS9549-10	WASHER,FLAT	2
7	PAOZZ	96906	MS90728-6	SCREW,CAP,HEXAGON H	4
8	PAOZZ	96906	MS35338-44	WASHER,LOCK	3
9	PAOZZ	96906	MS35691-406	NUT,PLAIN,HEXAGON	3
10	PAOOO	11862	14076284	CONTROL ASSEMBLY,HE	1

END OF FIGURE

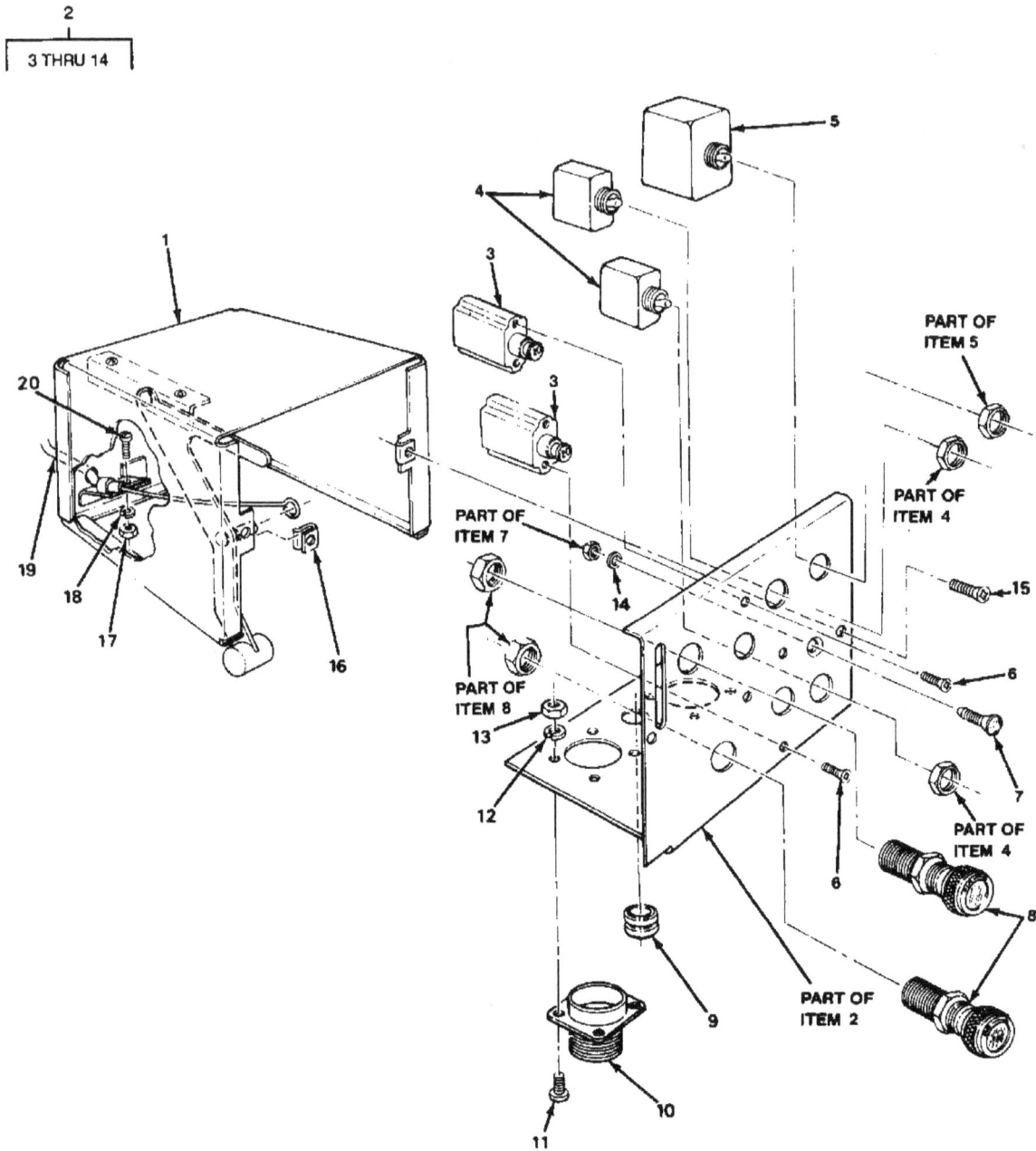

2
┌─────────────┐
│ 3 THRU 14   │
└─────────────┘

FIGURE 241. HEATER CONTROL ASSEMBLY COMPONENT PARTS.

TA511090

GROUP 3303 WINTERIZATION KITS

FIG. 241 HEATER CONTROL ASSEMBLY
COMPONENT PARTS

ITEM NO	SMR CODE	CAGEC	PART NUMBER	DESCRIPTION AND USABLE ON CODES (UOC)	QTY
1	PAOZZ	11862	14076285	HOUSING,HEATER CONT	1
2	PAOOO	11862	14076287	PANEL ASSEMBLY,HEAT	1
3	PAOZZ	96906	MS25244-P-20	.CIRCUIT BREAKER	2
4	PAOZZ	96906	MS35058-22	.SWITCH,TOGGLE	2
5	PAOZZ	96906	MS25307-312	.SWITCH,TOGGLE	1
6	PAOZZ	96906	MS51957-26	.SCREW,MACHINE	4
7	PAOZZ	81640	L30200R	.LIGHT,INDICATOR	1
8	PAOZZ	96906	MS25331-4-313S	.LIGHT,INDICATOR	2
9	PAOZZ	96906	MS35489-6	.GROMMET,NONMETALLIC	1
10	PAOZZ	96906	MS3452W18-11P	.CONNECTOR,RECEPTACL	2
11	PAOZZ	96906	MS51957-17	.SCREW,MACHINE	8
12	PAOZZ	96906	MS35333-70	.WASHER,LOCK	8
13	PAOZZ	96906	MS35649-244	.NUT,PLAIN,HEXAGON	8
14	PAOZZ	96906	MS27183-42	.WASHER,FLAT	1
15	PAOZZ	96906	MS51957-45	SCREW,MACHINE	2
16	PAOZZ	96906	MS90724-7	NUT,SHEET SPRING	2
17	PAOZZ	96906	MS35649-202	NUT,PLAIN,HEXAGON	1
18	PAOZZ	96906	MS35338-43	WASHER,LOCK	1
19	PFOZZ	11862	14076295	CABLE,HEATER CONTRO	1
20	PAOZZ	96906	MS35206-263	SCREW,MACHINE	1

END OF FIGURE

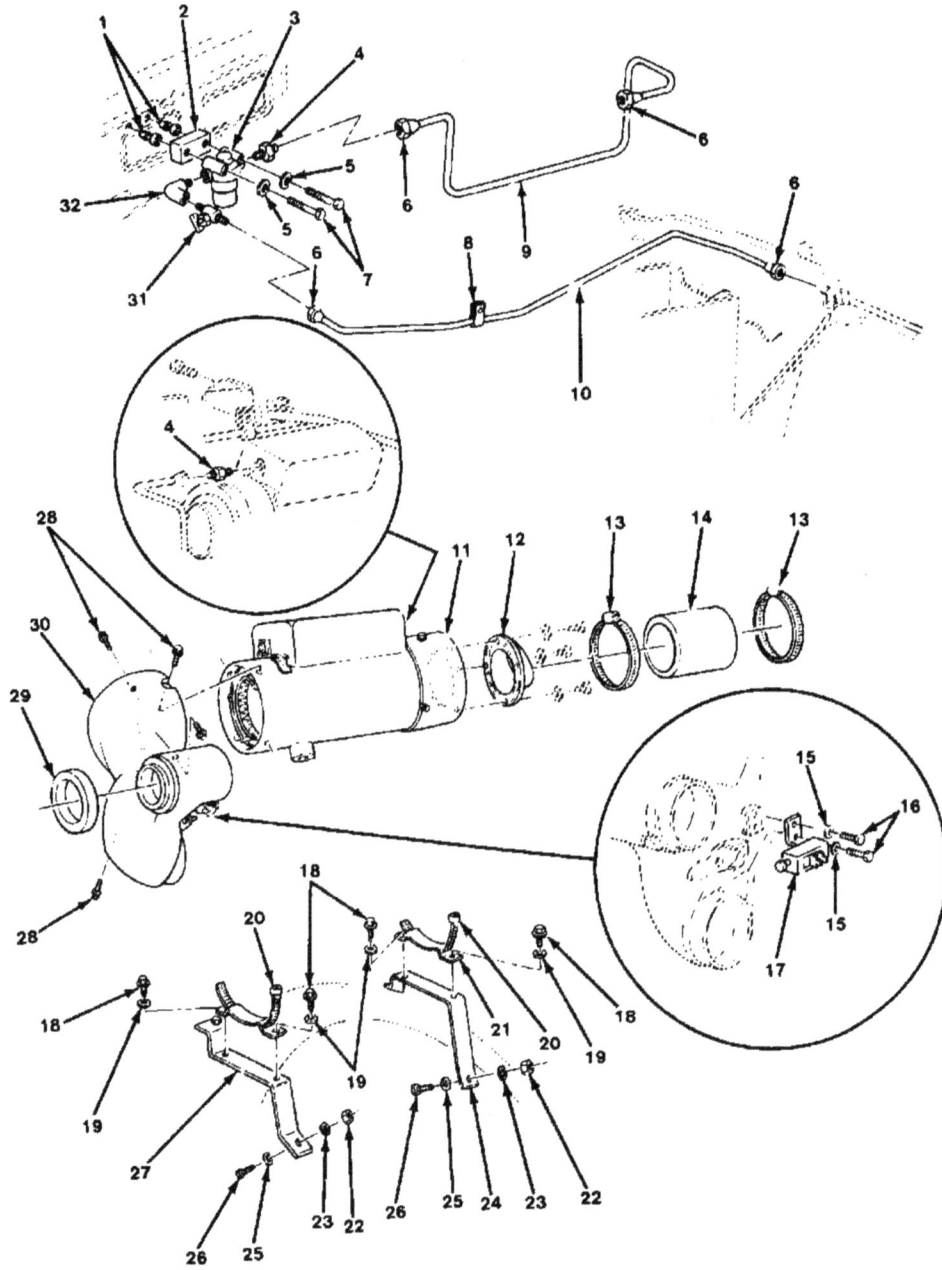

TA511091

FIGURE 242. HEATER AND MOUNTING PARTS.

(1) ITEM NO	(2) SMR CODE	(3) CAGEC	(4) PART NUMBER	(5) DESCRIPTION AND USABLE ON CODES (UOC)	(6) QTY
				GROUP 3303 WINTERIZATION KITS	
				FIG. 242 HEATER AND MOUNTING PARTS	
1	PAOZZ	00613	C-5139-2	RECEPTACLE,TURNLOCK	2
2	PAOZZ	11862	14072374	SPACER,HEATER FUEL	1
3	PAOZZ	96906	MS51085-1	FILTER,FLUID	1
4	PAOZZ	81240	GM118749	ADAPTER,STRAIGHT,PI	2
5	PAOZZ	96906	MS27183-8	WASHER,FLAT	2
6	PAOZZ	81343	5 010111B	NUT,TUBE COUPLING	4
7	PAOZZ	24617	456748	SCREW,CAP,HEXAGON H	2
8	PAOZZ	96906	MS21333-110	CLAMP,LOOP	1
9	MFOZZ	11862	14072378	PIPE F/F;TR OUTLT (29.99" LG) MAKE FROM TUBE, P/N 1324714	1
10	MFOZZ	11862	15599203	PIPE (43.79" LG) MAKE FROM TUBE, P/N 1324714	1
11	PAOFF	78385	10530B	HEATER,VEHICULAR,CO	1
12	PAOZZ	11862	14074466	ADAPTER,HEATER,VEHI	1
13	PAOZZ	96906	MS35842-14	CLAMP,HOSE	2
14	PAOZZ	16632	CHE2015-0001	HOSE,AIR DUCT	1
15	PAOZZ	96906	MS27183-10	WASHER,FLAT	2
16	PAOZZ	24617	9419663	SCREW,TAPPING	2
17	PAOZZ	11862	15599972	SWITCH,PUSH	1
18	PAOZZ	11862	9439771	BOLT,ASSEMBLED WASH	4
19	PAOZZ	19207	5287638	WASHER,FLAT	4
20	PAOZZ	96906	MS35842-16	CLAMP,HOSE	2
21	PAOZZ	11862	14074469	BRACKET,HEATER,VEHI	2
22	PAOZZ	96906	MS51967-6	NUT,PLAIN,HEXAGON	4
23	PAOZZ	96906	MS35338-45	WASHER,LOCK	4
24	PAOZZ	11862	14074471	BRACKET,MOUNTING	1
25	PAOZZ	24617	9418924	WASHER,FLAT	4
26	PAOZZ	96906	MS90728-32	BOLT,MACHINE	4
27	PAOZZ	11862	14074470	BRACKET,HEATER FRON	1
28	PAOZZ	24617	423532	SCREW,ASSEMBLED WAS	4
29	PAOZZ	16632	CHE2017	GASKET	1
30	PAOZZ	11862	14074473	VALVE ASSEMBLY,HEAT	1
31	XDOZZ	11862	9440173	VALVE FUEL SHUTOFF	1
32	PAOZZ	96906	MS51952-1	ELBOW,PIPE	1

END OF FIGURE

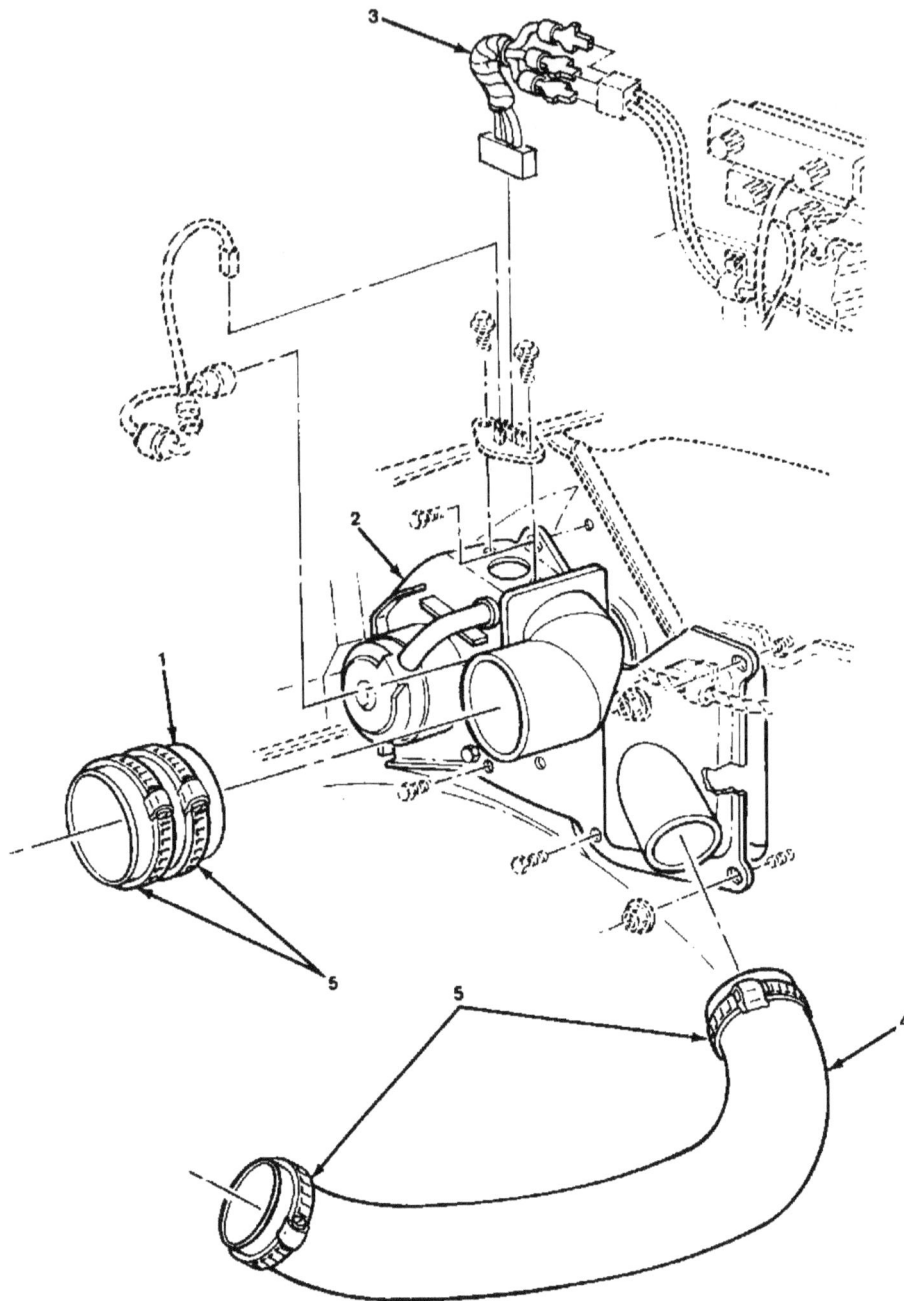

TA511092

FIGURE 243. HEATER BLOWER AND HOSES.

(1) ITEM NO	(2) SMR CODE	(3) CAGEC	(4) PART NUMBER	(5) DESCRIPTION AND USABLE ON CODES (UOC)	(6) QTY
				GROUP 3303 WINTERIZATION KITS	
				FIG. 243 HEATER BLOWER AND HOSES	
1	PAOZZ	16632	CHE2015-0001	HOSE,AIR DUCT	1
2	PAOOO	11862	14074465	BLOWER ASSEMBLY,HEA FOR COMPONENT PARTS SEE FIG 244	1
3	PAOZZ	11862	14076237	LEAD ASSEMBLY,ELECT UOC:194,208,209,210,230,231,252,254	1
4	PAOZZ	16632	CHE2015-0002	HOSE,AIR DUCT	1
5	PAOZZ	96906	MS35842-15	CLAMP,HOSE	4

END OF FIGURE

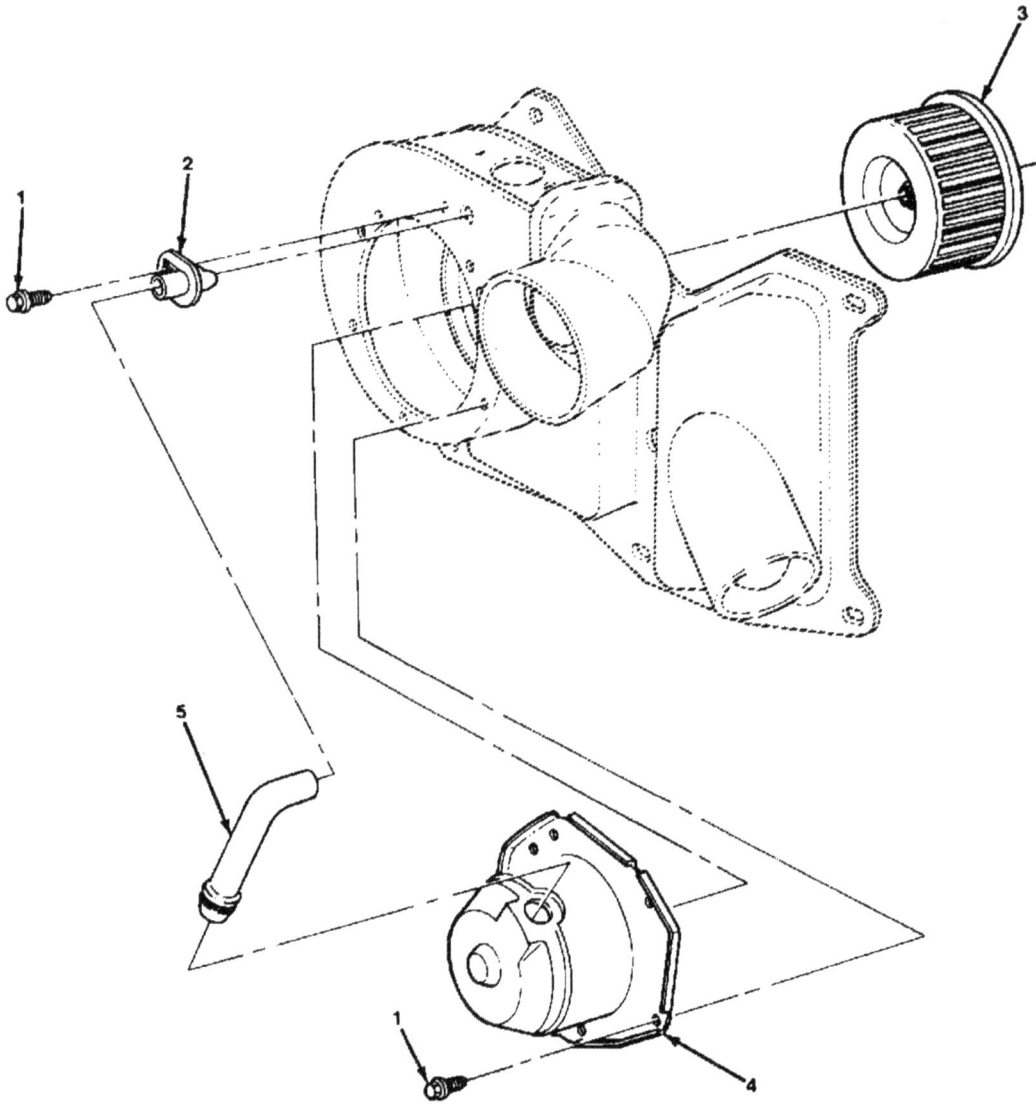

TA511093

FIGURE 244. BLOWER COMPONENT PARTS.

(1) ITEM NO	(2) SMR CODE	(3) CAGEC	(4) PART NUMBER	(5) DESCRIPTION AND USABLE ON CODES (UOC)	(6) QTY
				GROUP 3303 WINTERIZATION KITS	
				FIG. 244 BLOWER COMPONENT PARTS	
1	PAOZZ	24617	9419663	SCREW,TAPPING	6
2	PAOZZ	11862	3037476	PIPE,AIR CONDITIONI	1
3	PAOZZ	11862	3055734	MOTOR,HEATER FAN	1
4	PAOZZ	11862	22098841	MOTOR,DIRECT CURREN	1
5	PAOZZ	11862	3035192	PIPE,AIR CONDITIONI	1

END OF FIGURE

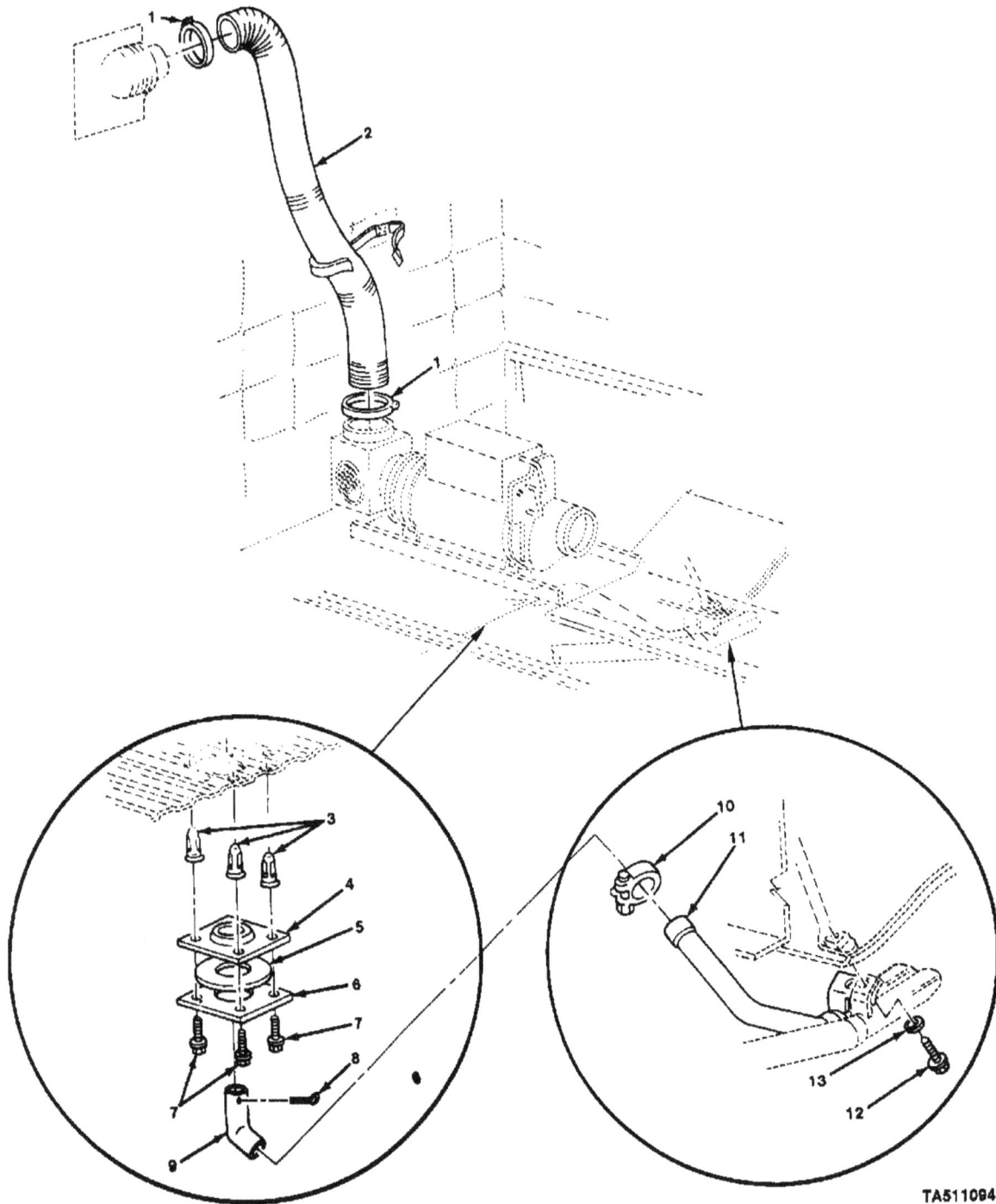

FIGURE 245. INLET HOSE AND EXHAUST PIPE.

TA511094

(1) ITEM NO	(2) SMR CODE	(3) CAGEC	(4) PART NUMBER	(5) DESCRIPTION AND USABLE ON CODES (UOC)	(6) QTY
				GROUP 3303 WINTERIZATION KITS	
				FIG. 245 INLET HOSE AND EXHAUST PIPE	
1	PAOZZ	96906	MS35842-15	CLAMP,HOSE UOC:194,208	2
2	PAOZZ	16632	CHE2013-0001	HOSE,AIR DUCT UOC:194,208	1
3	PAOZZ	11862	14005953	SHIELD,EXPANSION UOC:194,208	4
4	PAOZZ	16632	CHE2016-0002	GASKET UOC:194,208	1
5	PAOZZ	16632	CHE2023	GASKET UOC:194,208	1
6	PAOZZ	11862	15599942	CONNECTOR,EXHAUST P UOC:194,208	1
7	PAOZZ	11862	9440344	BOLT,ASSEMBLED WASH UOC:194,208	4
8	PAOZZ	96906	MS24665-516	PIN,COTTER UOC:194,208	1
9	PAOZZ	11862	15599940	ADAPTER,EXHAUST,HEA UOC:194,208	1
10	PAOZZ	63208	650-24	CLAMP,HOSE UOC:194,208	1
11	PAOZZ	11862	14076805	PIPE,EXHAUST UOC:194,208	1
12	PAOZZ	96906	MS90728-35	BOLT,MACHINE UOC:194,208	1
13	PAOZZ	96906	MS35340-45	WASHER,LOCK UOC:194,208	1

END OF FIGURE

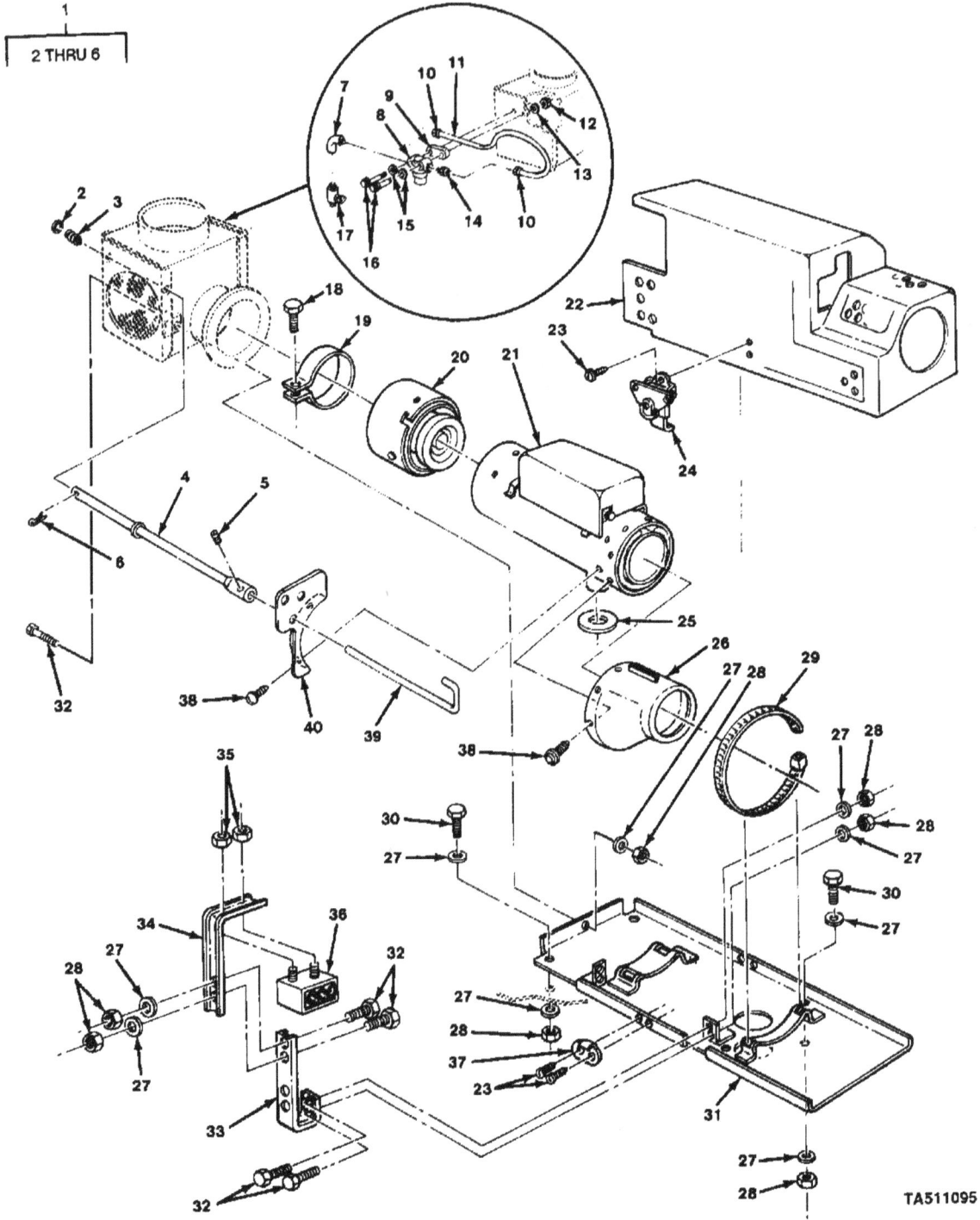

FIGURE 246. PERSONNEL/CARGO HEATER (M1008)

TA511095

(1) ITEM NO	(2) SMR CODE	(3) CAGEC	(4) PART NUMBER	(5) DESCRIPTION AND USABLE ON CODES (UOC)	(6) QTY
				GROUP 3303 WINTERIZATION KITS	
				FIG. 246 PERSONNEL/CARGO HEATER (M1008)	
1	PAOZZ	11862	14076252	VENTILATOR,AIR CIRC UOC:194,208	1
2	PAOZZ	96906	MS27183-10	.WASHER,FLAT UOC:194,208	1
3	PAOZZ	96906	MS24585-1276	.SPRING,HELICAL,COMP UOC:194,208	1
4	PAOZZ	11862	14076253	.ROD ASSEMBLY,AIR IN UOC:194,208	1
5	PAOZZ	96906	MS51023-49	.SETSCREW UOC:194,208	1
6	PAOZZ	96152	A82-1	.PIN,COTTER UOC:194,208	1
7	PAOZZ	96906	MS51952-1	ELBOW,PIPE UOC:194,208	1
8	PAOZZ	96906	MS51085-1	FILTER,FLUID UOC:194,208	1
9	PAOZZ	11862	14072374	SPACER,HEATER FUEL UOC:194,208	1
10	PAOZZ	81343	5 010111B	NUT,TUBE COUPLING UOC:194,208	2
11	MFOZZ	11862	14076255	PIPE HTR FUEL (18.44" LG) MAKE FROM TUBE, P/N 1324714 UOC:194,208	1
12	PAOZZ	88044	AN365-1024A	NUT,SELF-LOCKING,HE UOC:194,208	2
13	PAOZZ	24617	9417714	WASHER,FLAT UOC:194,208	2
14	PAOZZ	81240	GM118749	ADAPTER,STRAIGHT,PI UOC:194,208	1
15	PAOZZ	96906	MS27183-8	WASHER,FLAT UOC:194,208	2
16	PAOZZ	24617	456748	SCREW,CAP,HEXAGON H UOC:194,208	2
17	XDOZZ	11862	9440173	VALVE FUEL SHUTOFF UOC:194,208	1
18	PAOZZ	11862	9440334	BOLT,ASSEMBLED WASH UOC:194,208	1
19	PAOZZ	96906	MS35842-16	CLAMP,HOSE UOC:194,208	1
20	PAOZZ	11862	15599952	ADAPTER,AIR DUCT HO UOC:194,208	1
21	PAOFF	78385	10530B	HEATER,VEHICULAR,CO UOC:194,208	1
22	PAOZZ	11862	14076265	SHIELD,HEATER,AUXIL UOC:194,208	1
23	PAOZZ	96906	MS20600-B4W4	RIVET,BLIND UOC:194,208	8

(1) ITEM NO	(2) SMR CODE	(3) CAGEC	(4) PART NUMBER	(5) DESCRIPTION AND USABLE ON CODES (UOC)	(6) QTY
24	PAOZZ	82240	SPEC-3-10-L-L	CATCH,CLAMPING UOC:194,208	2
25	PAOZZ	16632	CHE2018	GASKET UOC:194,208	1
26	PAOZZ	19207	7524078	ADAPTER ASSEMBLY,CO UOC:194,208	1
27	PAOZZ	96906	MS27183-10	WASHER,FLAT UOC:194,208	13
28	PAOZZ	21450	131245	NUT,SELF-LOCKING,HE UOC:194,208	9
29	PAOZZ	96906	MS35842-16	CLAMP,HOSE UOC:194,208	2
30	PAOZZ	96906	MS90728-8	SCREW,CAP,HEXAGON H UOC:194,208	4
31	PAOZZ	11862	14076259	PLATE,MOUNTING,HEAT UOC:194,208	1
32	PAOZZ	96906	MS90728-5	SCREW,CAP,HEXAGON UOC:194,208	4
33	PFOZZ	11862	14076261	BRACKET,DOUBLE ANGL UOC:194,208	1
34	PAOZZ	11862	14076262	BRACKET,ANGLE UOC:194,208	1
35	PAOZZ	96906	MS51967-2	NUT,PLAIN,HEXAGON UOC:194,208	2
36	PAOZZ	11862	14076801	CONTROL BOX,ELECTRI UOC:194,208	1
37	PAOZZ	82240	B-1900-334	STRIKE,CATCH UOC:194,208	2
38	PAOZZ	24617	423532	SCREW,ASSEMBLED WAS UOC:194,208	6
39	PAOZZ	11862	14076258	LEVER,MANUAL CONTRO UOC:194,208	1
40	PAOZZ	11862	14076257	BRACKET,HEATER AIR UOC:194,208	1

END OF FIGURE

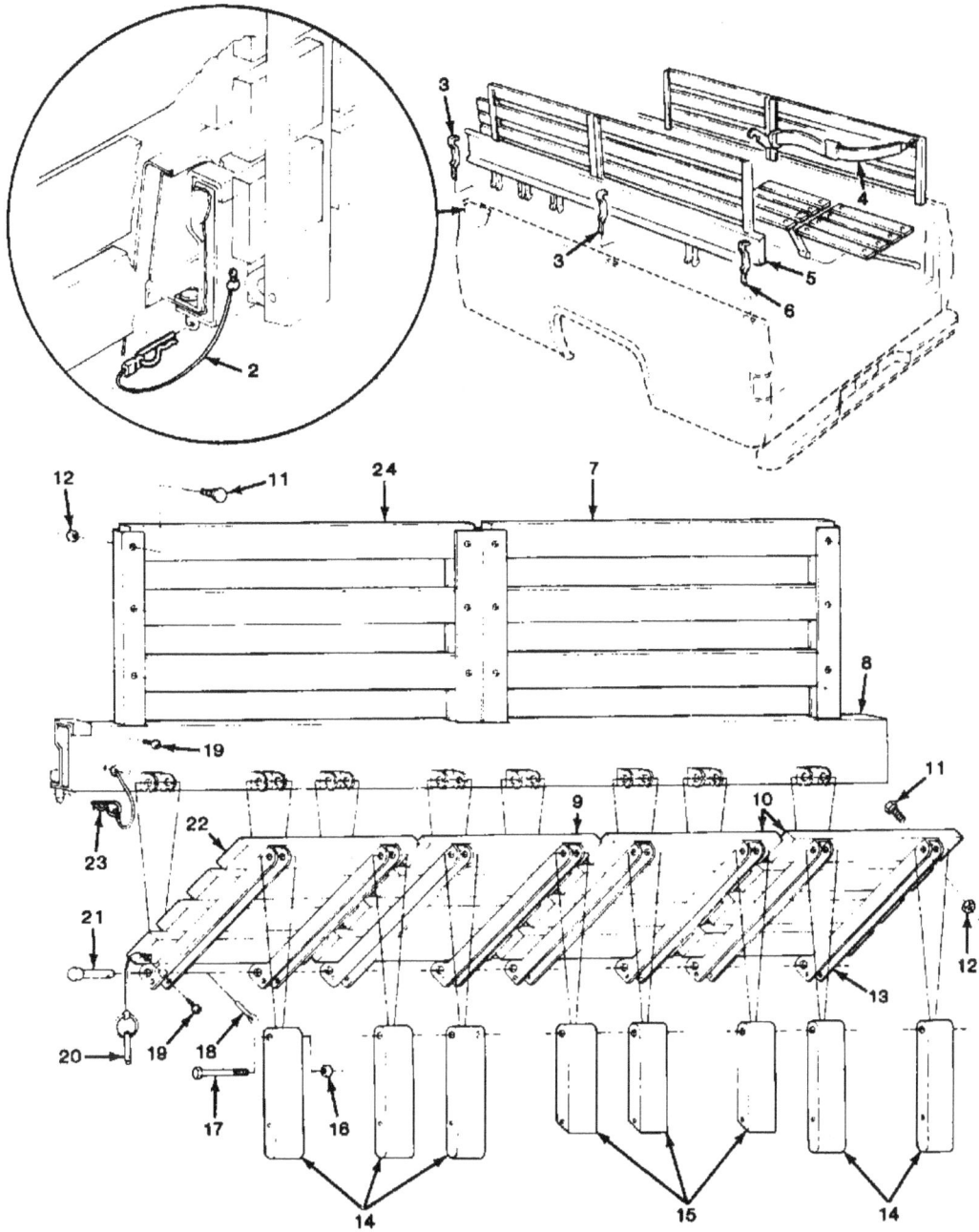

FIGURE 247. TROOP SEAT ASSEMBLY AND COMPONENT PARTS

TA511096

(1) ITEM NO	(2) SMR CODE	(3) CAGEC	(4) PART NUMBER	(5) DESCRIPTION AND USABLE ON CODES (UOC)	(6) QTY
				GROUP 3307 SPECIAL PURPOSE KITS FIG. 247 TROOP SEAT ASSEMBLY AND COMPONENT PARTS	
1	AOOOO	11862	14072308	SEAT ASM TROOP UOC:194,208	1
2	PAOZZ	11862	14072314	.LANYARD,SEAT UOC:194,208	6
3	PAOZZ	11862	14072325	.STRAP,RETAINING UOC:194,208	4
4	PAOZZ	19207	11682088-1	.STRAP,WEBBING UOC:194,208	1
5	PAOZZ	11862	14075811	.FRAME,SEAT,VEHICULA LEFT UOC:194,208	1
6	PAOZZ	11862	14072324	.CLAMP UOC:194,208	2
7	PAOZZ	19207	12343359-3	.SLAT,TROOP SEAT UOC:194,208	6
8	PAOZZ	11862	14075812	.SUPPORT ASSY,SEAT,R RIGHT UOC:194,208	1
9	PAOZZ	19207	12343359-5	.SLAT,TROOP SEAT FRA UOC:194,208	8
10	PAOZZ	19207	12343359-1	.BOARD,TROOP SEAT UOC:194,208	16
11	PAOZZ	21450	126373	.BOLT,SQUARE NECK UOC:194,208	88
12	PAOZZ	24617	271184	.NUT,PLAIN,ASSEMBLED UOC:194,208	88
13	PAOZZ	11862	14072319	.FRAME,SEAT,VEHICULA UOC:194,208	16
14	PAOZZ	11862	14072323	.LEG,SEAT UOC:194,208	10
15	PAOZZ	11862	14072322	.SEAT,TROOP,LEG UOC:194,208	6
16	PAOZZ	80205	NAS1408A6	.NUT,SELF-LOCKING,HE UOC:194,208	16
17	PAOZZ	96906	MS90728-68	.SCREW,CAP,HEXAGON H UOC:194,208	16
18	PAOZZ	96906	MS24665-283	.PIN,COTTER UOC:194,208	16
19	PAOZZ	96906	MS51850-44	.SCREW,TAPPING UOC:194,208	14
20	PAOZZ	19207	12255608	.PIN,QUICK RELEASE UOC:194,208	8
21	PAOZZ	19207	7370134	.PIN,STRAIGHT,HEADED UOC:194,208	16
22	PAOZZ	19207	12343359-4	.SLAT,TROOP SEAT FRA UOC:194,208	8
23	PAOZZ	11862	14072380	.CLIP UOC:194,208	6
24	PAOZZ	19207	12343359-2	.SLAT,TROOP SEAT UOC:194,208	6

END OF FIGURE

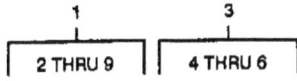

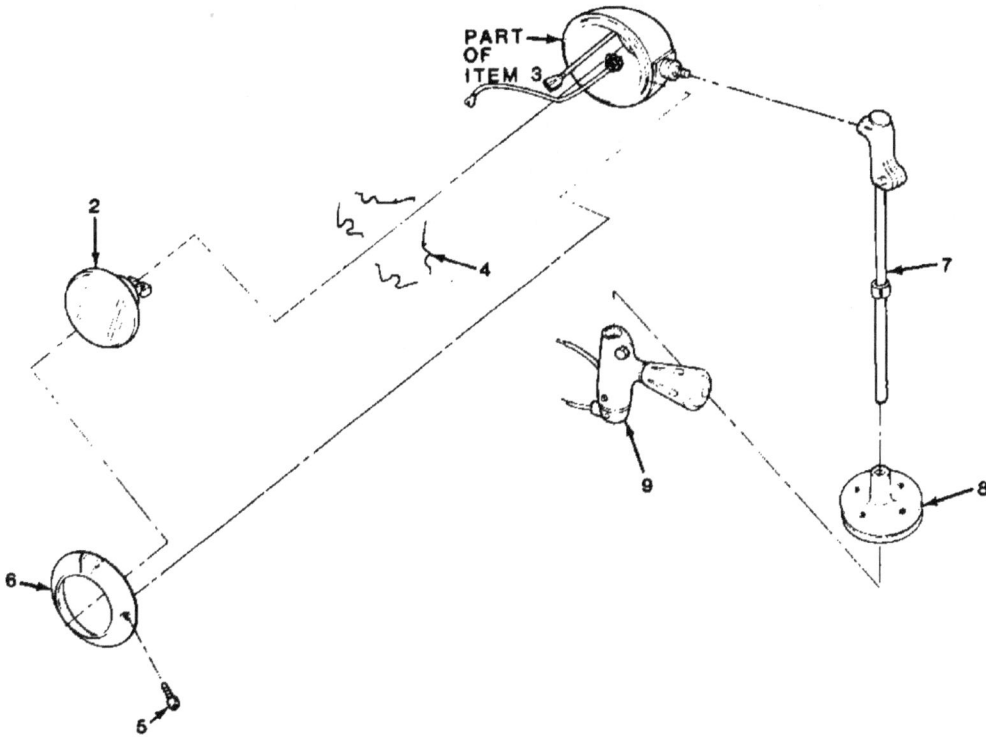

FIGURE 248. SPOTLIGHT ASSEMBLY AND COMPONENTS PARTS (M1010).

TA511097

(1) ITEM NO	(2) SMR CODE	(3) CAGEC	(4) PART NUMBER	(5) DESCRIPTION AND USABLE ON CODES (UOC)	(6) QTY
				GROUP 39 SEARCHLIGHT AND ELECTRICAL ILLUMINATING EQUIPMENT	
				GROUP 3901 SEARCHLIGHT CR ILLUMINATING LIGHT ASSEMBLY	
				FIG. 248 SPOTLIGHT ASSEMBLY AND COMPONENT PARTS (M1010)	
1	PAOOO	81349	M4510-1A4435	SPOTLIGHT UOC:210	1
2	PAOZZ	08806	4435	.LAMP,INCANDESCENT UOC:210	1
3	PAOOO	78977	650U-0016	.BRACKET UOC:210	1
4	PAOZZ	78977	6598	..CLIP,RETAINING UOC:210	4
5	PAOZZ	78977	6471	..SCREW,MACHINE UOC:210	1
6	PAOZZ	78977	6566-0004	..RETAINER,LENS UOC:210	1
7	PAOZZ	78977	6710-BU-2	.TUBE,SPOTLIGHT UOC:210	1
8	PAOZZ	78977	100-7-3	.PARTS KIT,MOUNTING UOC:210	1
9	PAOZZ	78977	6701-0025	.HANDLE,MANUAL CONTR UOC:210	1

END OF FIGURE

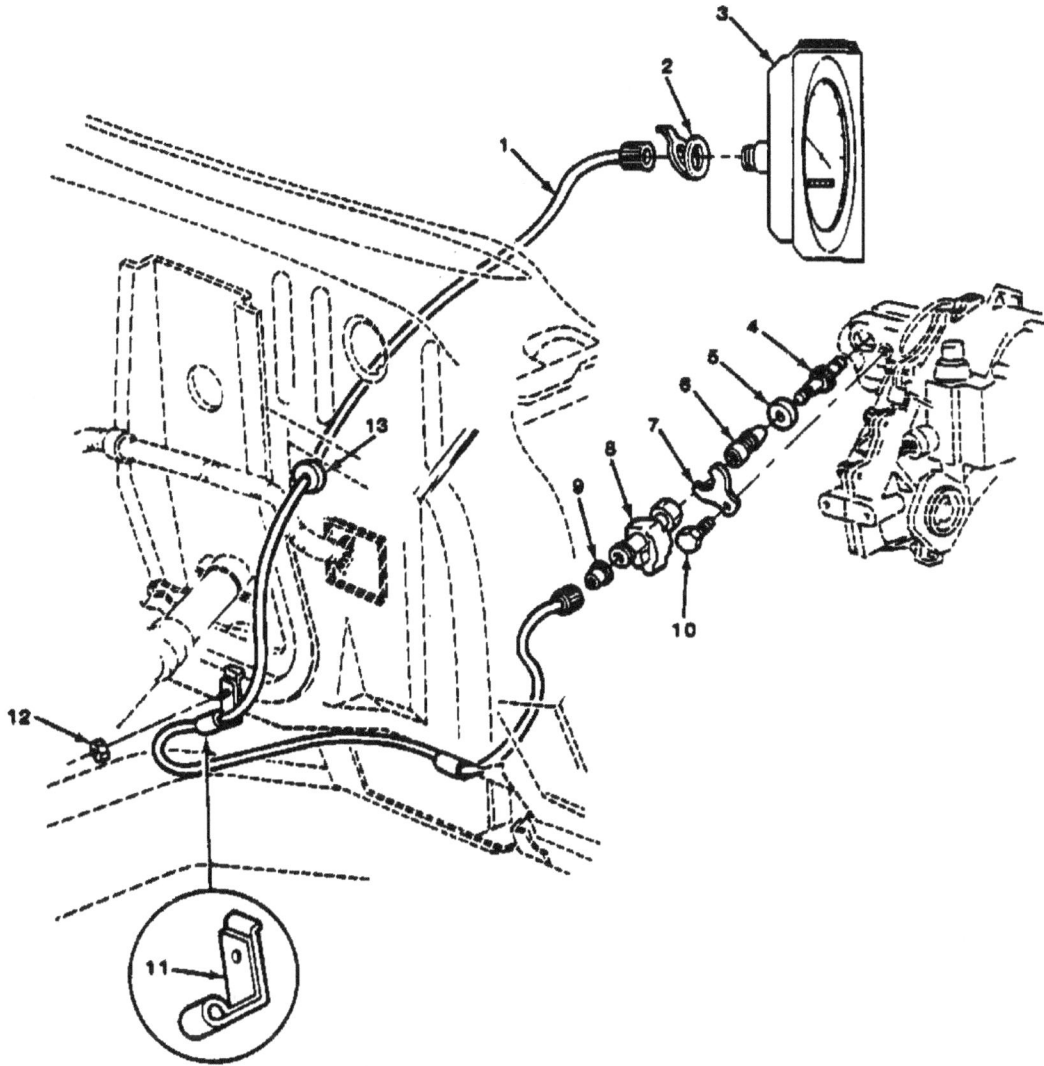

TA511098

FIGURE 249. SPEEDOMETER AND CABLE ASSEMBLY AND RELATED PARTS.

(1) ITEM NO	(2) SMR CODE	(3) CAGEC	(4) PART NUMBER	(5) DESCRIPTION AND USABLE ON CODES (UOC)	(6) QTY
				GROUP 47 GAGES, (NONELECTRICAL), WEIGHING AND MEASURING DEVICES	
				GROUP 4701 INSTRUMENTS	
				FIG. 249 SPEEDOMETER AND CABLE ASSEMBLY AND RELATED PARTS	
1	PAOZZ	11862	25033627	SHAFT ASSEMBLY,FLEX	1
2	PAOZZ	11862	25020687	CLIP,SPRING TENSION	1
3	PAOZZ	11862	25052373	SPEEDOMETER	1
4	PAOZZ	11862	1362195	GEAR,SPEEDOMETER UOC:209	1
4	PAOZZ	11862	9780470	GEAR SHAFT,HELICAL UOC:194,208,210,230	1
4	XDOZZ	11862	3866918	GEAR,SPUR UOC:231,252,254,256	1
5	PAOZZ	11862	15562374	SEAL	1
6	PAOZZ	11862	326561	SLEEVE UOC:231,252,254,256	1
6	PAOZZ	11862	1362293	SLEEVE AND SEAL ASS UOC:194,208,209,210,230	1
7	PAOZZ	11862	1254856	RETAINER,SPEEDOMETE	1
8	PAOZZ	11862	368026	ADAPTER,SPEEDOMETER UOC:209	1
9	PAOZZ	11862	14018671	RUBBER ROUND SECTIO	1
10	PAOZZ	11862	8639743	SCREW,CAP,HEXAGON H UOC:194,208,209,210,230,231,252,254	1
11	PAOZZ	11862	378362	CLIP,CABLE,SPEEDOME	1
12	PAOZZ	11862	11506101	NUT	1
13	PAOZZ	11862	474579	GROMMET,NONMETALLIC	1

END OF FIGURE

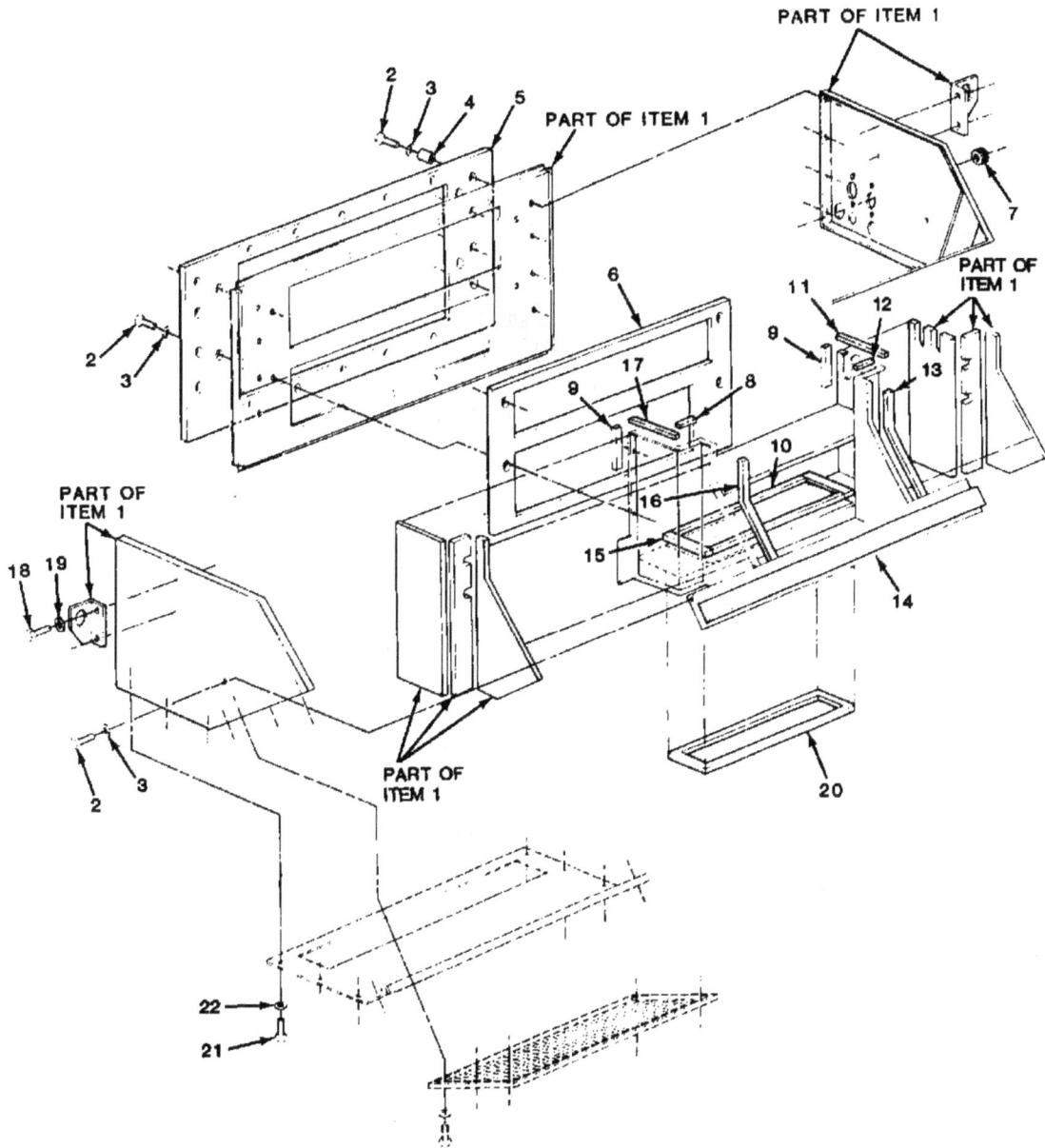

FIGURE 250. MAIN CASE ASSEMBLY AND COMPONENT PARTS (M1010).

TA511101

(1) ITEM NO	(2) SMR CODE	(3) CAGEC	(4) PART NUMBER	(5) DESCRIPTION AND USABLE ON CODES (UOC)	(6) QTY
				GROUP 52 REFRIGERATION, AIR CONDITIONER/HEATER, AND AIR CONDITIONING COMPONENTS GROUP 5200 AIR CONDITIONER/HEATER ASSEMBLY AND GAS COMPRESSOR ASSEMBLY FIG. 250 MAIN CASE ASSEMBLY AND COMPONENT PARTS (M1010)	
1	PAOOO	99688	85927	MAIN CASE,AIR CONDI UOC:210	1
2	PAOZZ	96906	MS51869-26	.SCREW,TAPPING UOC:210	23
3	PAOZZ	96906	MS35338-44	.WASHER,LOCK UOC:210	23
4	PAOZZ	99688	58606	.SPACER,SLEEVE UOC:210	16
5	PAOZZ	99688	58608	.GASKET UOC:210	1
6	PAOZZ	99688	58618	.GASKET UOC:210	1
7	PAOZZ	96906	MS35489-135	.GROMMET,NONMETALLIC UOC:210	3
8	PAOZZ	99688	58610	.INSULATION BLANKET UOC:210	1
9	PAOZZ	99688	58607	.SEAL,NONMETALLIC ST UOC:210	2
10	PAOZZ	99688	58617	.GASKET UOC:210	1
11	PAOZZ	99688	58615	.INSULATION BLANKET UOC:210	1
12	PAOZZ	99688	58614	.INSULATION BLANKET UOC:210	1
13	PAOZZ	99688	58613	.INSULATION BLANKET UOC:210	1
14	PAOZZ	99688	58612	.INSULATION BLANKET UOC:210	1
15	PAOZZ	99688	58616	.SEAL,RUBBER STRIP UOC:210	1
16	PAOZZ	99688	58611	.INSULATION BLANKET UOC:210	1
17	PAOZZ	99688	58609	.INSULATION BLANKET UOC:210	1
18	PAOZZ	96906	MS51871-14	.SCREW,TAPPING UOC:210	4
19	PAOZZ	96906	MS35338-46	.WASHER,LOCK UOC:210	4
20	PAOZZ	99688	58586	GASKET UOC:210	1
21	PAOZZ	96906	MS51869-26	SCREW,TAPPING UOC:210	39
22	PAOZZ	96906	MS35338-44	WASHER,LOCK UOC:210	45

END OF FIGURE

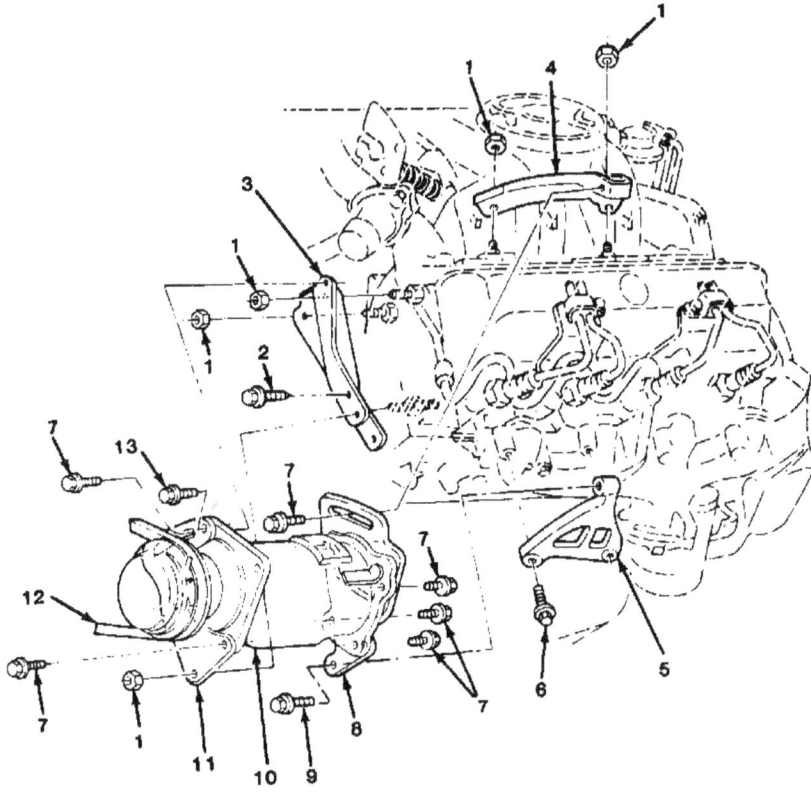

TA511102

FIGURE 251. GAS COMPRESSOR ASSEMBLY AND MOUNTING BRACKETS (M1010).

(1) ITEM NO	(2) SMR CODE	(3) CAGEC	(4) PART NUMBER	(5) DESCRIPTION AND USABLE ON CODES (UOC)	(6) QTY
				GROUP 5200 AIR CONDITIONER/HEATER ASSEMBLY AND GAS COMPRESSOR ASSEMBLY	
				FIG. 251 GAS COMPRESSOR ASSEMBLY AND MOUNTING BRACKETS (M1010)	
1	PAOZZ	11862	11506101	NUT UOC:210,230	5
7	PAOZZ	11862	1635490	BOLT,SELF-LOCKING UOC:210	6
9	PAOZZ	11862	1635490	BOLT,SELF-LOCKING UOC:210	1
12	PAOZZ	20796	42-4877	BELT,V UOC:210,230	1

END OF FIGURE

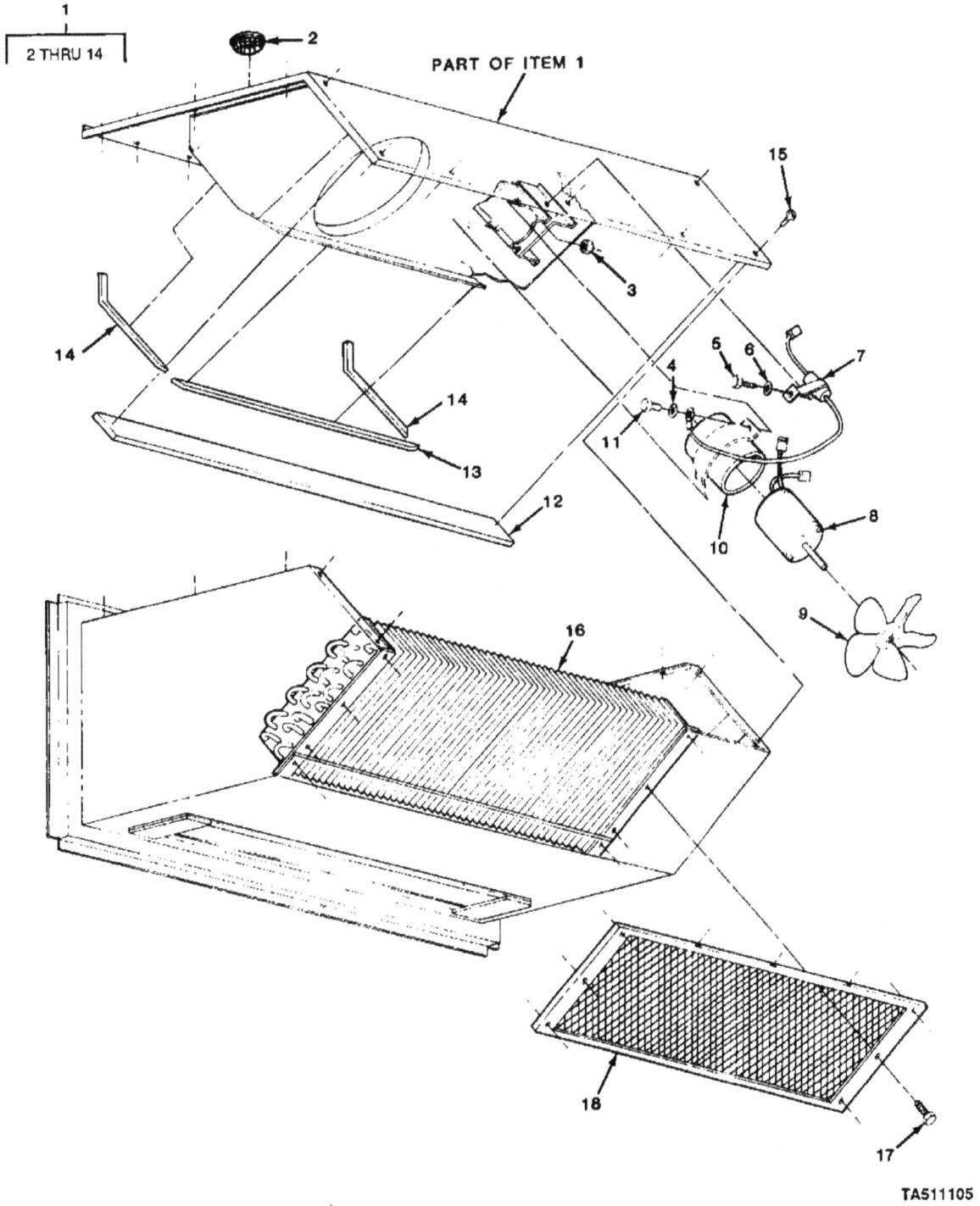

FIGURE 252. CONDENSER, COVER ASSEMBLY, AND COMPONENT PARTS (M1010).

TA511105

(1) ITEM NO	(2) SMR CODE	(3) CAGEC	(4) PART NUMBER	(5) DESCRIPTION AND USABLE ON CODES (UOC)	(6) QTY
				GROUP 5230 CONDENSER	
				FIG. 252 CONDENSER, COVER ASSEMBLY, AND COMPONENT PARTS (M1010)	
1	PAOZZ	99688	85923	FAN,CIRCULATING UOC:210	1
2	PAOZZ	03743	S150	.BUTTON,PLUG UOC:210	1
3	PAOZZ	99688	62218	.NUT UOC:210	2
4	PAOZZ	96906	MS35335-33	.WASHER,LOCK UOC:210	2
5	PAOZZ	24617	9421073	.SCREW,TAPPING UOC:210	2
6	PAOZZ	96906	MS35335-32	.WASHER,LOCK UOC:210	2
7	PAOZZ	99688	65134	.CAPACITOR,FIXED,ELE UOC:210	2
8	PAOZZ	99688	20566	.MOTOR,DIRECT CURREN UOC:210	2
9	PAOZZ	99688	58595	.IMPELLER,FAN,AXIAL UOC:210	2
10	PAOZZ	99688	58701	.RUBBER,ROUND SECTIO UOC:210	2
11	PAOZZ	96906	MS90728-10	.SCREW,CAP,HEXAGON H UOC:210	2
12	PAOZZ	99688	58598	.GASKET UOC:210	1
13	PAOZZ	99688	58597	.RUBBER STRIP UOC:210	1
14	PAOZZ	99688	58596	.SEAL,PLAIN UOC:210	2
15	PAOZZ	24617	9440025	SCREW,TAPPING UOC:210	20
17	PAOZZ	96906	MS90728-3	SCREW,CAP,HEXAGON H UOC:210	6
18	XDOZZ	99688	85928	GRILLE,METAL UOC:210	1

END OF FIGURE

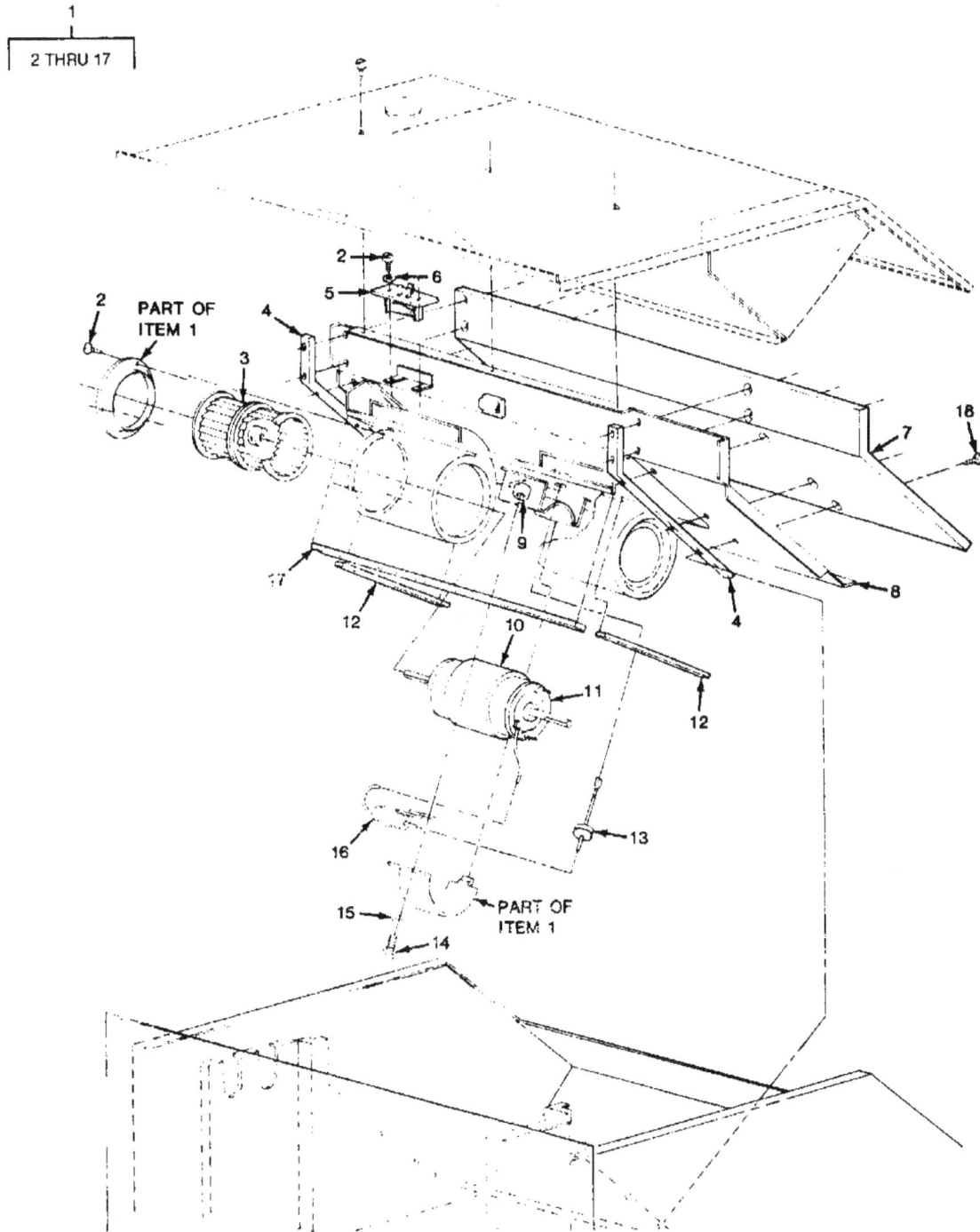

TA511107

FIGURE 253. BLOWER ASSEMBLY COMPONENT PARTS (M1010).

(1) ITEM NO	(2) SMR CODE	(3) CAGEC	(4) PART NUMBER	(5) DESCRIPTION AND USABLE ON CODES (UOC)	(6) QTY
				GROUP 5243 BLOWER ASSEMBLY	
				FIG. 253 BLOWER ASSEMBLY COMPONENT PARTS (M1010)	
1	PAOOO	99688	85922	FAN,CENTRIFUGAL UOC:210	1
2	PAOZZ	24617	9421073	.SCREW,TAPPING UOC:210	9
3	PAOZZ	99688	58590	.IMPELLER,FAN,CENTRI RIGHT UOC:210	1
3	PAOZZ	99688	58589	.IMPELLER,FAN,CENTRI LEFT UOC:210	1
4	PAOZZ	99688	58592	.SEAL,NONMETALLIC ST UOC:210	2
5	PAOZZ	99688	65158	.RESISTOR ASSEMBLY UOC:210	1
6	PAOZZ	96906	MS35335-32	.WASHER,LOCK UOC:210	2
7	PAOZZ	99688	58594	.INSULATION BLANKET UOC:210	1
8	PAOZZ	99688	85931	.COVER,ACCESS UOC:210	1
9	PAOZZ	99688	62218	.NUT UOC:210	1
10	PAOZZ	99688	58701	.RUBBER ROUND SECTIO UOC:210	1
11	PAOZZ	99688	20565	.MOTOR,DIRECT CURREN UOC:210	1
12	PAOZZ	99688	58591	.RUBBER STRIP UOC:210	2
13	PAOZZ	59875	TD97203	.GROMMET,NONMETALLIC UOC:210	1
14	PAOZZ	96906	MS90728-10	.SCREW,CAP,HEXAGON H UOC:210	1
15	PAOZZ	96906	MS35338-52	.WASHER,LOCK UOC:210	1
16	PAOZZ	99688	65134	.CAPACITOR,FIXED,ELE UOC:210	1
17	PAOZZ	99688	58593	.RUBBER STRIP UOC:210	1
18	PAOZZ	24617	9421073	SCREW,TAPPING UOC:210	13

END OF FIGURE

(1) ITEM NO	(2) SMR CODE	(3) CAGEC	(4) PART NUMBER	(5) DESCRIPTION AND USABLE ON CODES (UOC)	(6) QTY
				GROUP 94 REPAIR KITS	
				GROUP 9401 REPAIR KITS	
				FIG. KITS	
	PAOZZ	27647	11967	PARTS KIT,HUB BODY UOC:209 RING,RETAINING (2) 97-5 RING,RETAINING (1) 97-7 SCREW (6) 97-3	2
	PAOZZ	27647	15528	PARTS KIT,FOUR WHEE UOC:194,208,210,230,231,252,254,256 RING,RETAINING (1) 96-7 RING,RETAINING (1) 96-9 SCREW (6) 96-5 SEAL "O" RING (1) 96-8	1
	PAOZZ	11862	6258545	LINK UNIT,STABILIZE UOC:254,256 BOLT,STAB,LINK (2) 124-10 GROMMET STABIL LINK(4) 124-3 NUT,SPECIAL (2) 124-1 RETAINER,WASHER SPE(4) 124-2 SPACER,STAB,LINK (2) 124-11	2
				END OF FIGURE	

GROUP 95 GENERAL USE STANDARDIZED
PARTS

GROUP 9501 BULK MATERIAL

FIG. BULK

ITEM NO	SMR CODE	CAGEC	PART NUMBER	DESCRIPTION AND USABLE ON CODES (UOC)	QTY
1	PAOZZ	81348	QQS741	ANGLE,STRUCTURAL	V
2	PAOZZ	81349	MILS20166	ANGLE,STRUCTURAL	V
3	XDOZZ	74410	RRC271BTY2CLDIAO 72	CHAIN	V
4	PAOZZ	11862	8919355	CONDUIT,NONMETALLIC	1
5	PAOZZ	11862	8919356	CONDUIT,NONMETALLIC	1
6	PAOZZ	96906	MS18029-13S-8	COVER,TERMINAL BOAR	1
7	PAOZZ	96906	MS18029-4S-8	COVER,TERMINAL BOAR	1
8	PAOZZ	11862	6263877	FELT,MECHANICAL,PRE	1
9	PAOZZ	11862	370389	FILLER,BODY,GLASS C	1
10	PBOZZ	11862	6293923	FUSE LINK,ELECTRICA	1
11	PAOZZ	24234	319029	HOSE,AIR DUCT UOC:210	1
12	PAOZZ	11862	482420	HOSE,NONMETALLIC	V
13	PAOZZ	11862	7828506	HOSE,NONMETALLIC	1
14	PAOZZ	11862	9439104	HOSE,NONMETALLIC	1
15	PAOZZ	11862	9438383	HOSE,NONMETALLIC	1
16	PAOZZ	11862	9438257	HOSE,NONMETALLIC	1
17	PAOZZ	11862	9439162	HOSE,NONMETALLIC	1
18	PAOZZ	11862	9439046	HOSE,NONMETALLIC	1
19	PAOZZ	11862	9438381	HOSE,NONMETALLIC	1
20	PAOZZ	11862	1359744	HOSE,NONMETALLIC	1
21	PAOZZ	96906	MS521304B203R	HOSE,NONMETALLIC	1
22	PAOZZ	11862	9438373	HOSE,NONMETALLIC	1
23	PAOZZ	11862	9439402	HOSE,NONMETALLIC	1
24	PAOZZ	11862	9438315	HOSE,NONMETALLIC	1
25	XDOZZ	11862	9439274	HOSE,NONMETALLIC	1
26	PAOZZ	24617	9438124	HOSE,NONMETALLIC	1
27	PAOZZ	11862	3987364	HOSE,WIPER	1
28	PAOZZ	11862	12306178	INSULATION BLANKET	1
29	PAOZZ	11862	462233	INSULATOR,FLOOR,VEH	V
30	PAOZZ	81348	NNP530	PLYWOOD,CONSTRUCTIO	V
31	PAOZZ	11862	370390	RUBBER STRIP	1
32	PAOZZ	11862	363139	SEAL,FRONT DOOR	1
33	PAOZZ	96906	MS52039C079	STRIP,METAL	1
34	PAOZZ	96906	MS27212-4-8	TERMINAL BOARD	1
35	XDOZZ	81349	MILT16343TYPE1	TUBE,METALLIC	1

END OF FIGURE

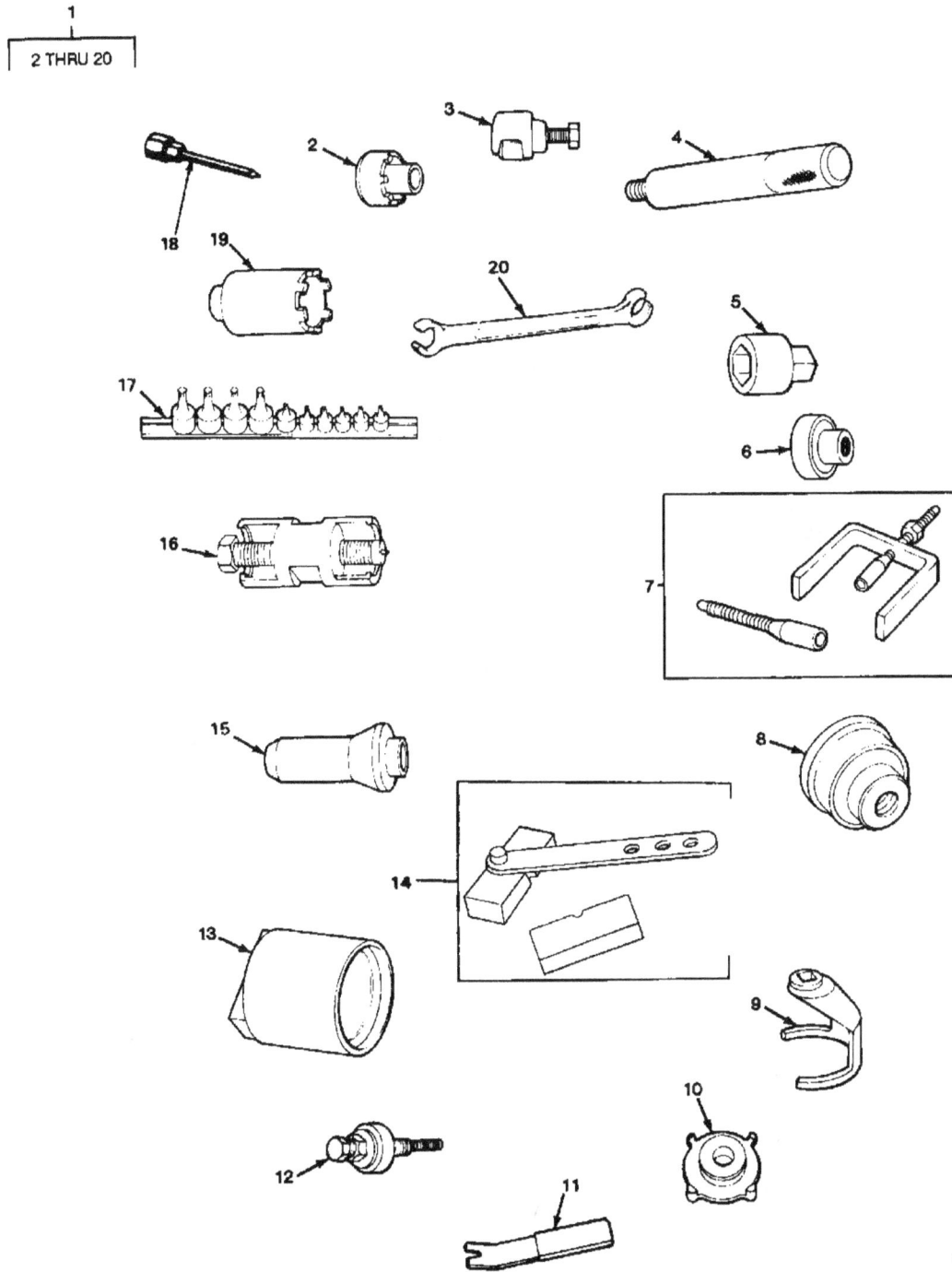

FIGURE 254. SPECIAL TOOLS.

(1) ITEM NO	(2) SMR CODE	(3) CAGEC	(4) PART NUMBER	(5) DESCRIPTION AND USABLE ON CODES (UOC)	(6) QTY
				GROUP 26 TOOLS AND TEST EQUIPMENT	
				GROUP 2604 SPECIAL TOOLS	
				FIG. 254 SPECIAL TOOLS	
1	ADOOO	19207	12314542	TOOL KIT,GENERAL ME	
2	PEOZZ	25341	J-2222-C	.WRENCH,WHEEL BEARIN UOC:194,208,210,231,252,254,256	
3	PEOZZ	25341	J-6632-01	.PULLER,MECHANICAL	
4	PEOZZ	33287	J-8092	.HANDLE,DRIVE	
5	PEOZZ	25341	J-21757-03	.SOCKET,OIL SWITCH	
6	PEOZZ	25341	J-23445-A	.INSERTER,BEARING AN UOC:194,208,210,230,231,252,254,256	
7	PEOZZ	25341	J-23653-C	.LOCK PLATE,COMPRESS	
				.INSERTER,BEARING AN UOC:209	
9	PEOZZ	25341	J-24187	.REMOVER,INSTALLER,F	
10	PEOZZ	25341	J-24426	.REMOVER,BEARING AND UOC:194,208,210,230,231,252,254,256	
11	PEOZZ	25341	J-24595-C	.REMOVER,CLIP,RETAIN	
12	PEOZZ	30282	553	.INSTALLER,POWER STE	
13	PEOZZ	25341	J-26878-A	.WRENCH NUT UOC:194,208,210,230,231,252,254,256	
14	PEOZZ	25341	J-33043	.BLOCK,VALVE GAGE	
15	PEOZZ	25341	J-29713	.DRIVE TOOL,SEAL UOC:209	
16	PEOZZ	25341	J-25034-B	.REMOVER,PULLEY,WATE	
17	PEOZZ	33287	J-29843	.SOCKET WRENCH ATTAC	
18	PEOZZ	33627	J25512-2	.COUPLING,GREASE GUN UOC:194,208,209,210,230,231,252,254	1
19	PEOZZ	25341	J-34616	.WRENCH,SPANNER WRENCH WHEELBEARING	
19	PEOZZ	25341	J-6893-D	.WRENCH,HUB UOC:194,209	
20	PEOZZ	25341	J-33124	.WRENCH,OPEN END	

END OF FIGURE

CROSS-REFERENCE INDEXES

NATIONAL STOCK NUMBER INDEX

STOCK NUMBER	FIG	ITEM	STOCK NUMBER	FIG	ITEM
5310-00-010-3028	100	18	5305-00-052-7472	194	6
4730-00-011-8538	214	4	4730-00-053-0266	242	32
	221	19		246	7
	242	6	5305-00-054-5651	241	11
	246	10	5305-00-054-6650	241	6
5310-00-013-1245	32	6	5305-00-054-6654	196	16
	68	12		233	20
	215	6	5305-00-054-6657	229	2
	215	6	5305-00-054-6670	241	15
	216	4	5340-00-057-3034	75	9
	218	2		212	2
	218	2		214	21
	228	8		221	22
	246	28		242	8
5315-00-013-7238	101	5	5340-00-057-3037	16	2
5315-00-013-7258	113	4		17	5
	114	26		17	6
	115	32	5340-00-057-3043	75	2
4730-00-013-7398	62	1		80	7
4730-00-014-2432	90	7		81	3
4730-00-014-2433	16	4		226	2
	17	7		227	10
5310-00-014-5850	210	29	5340-00-057-3052	23	10
	241	14		226	9
5305-00-014-9926	233	9	5315-00-057-5541	188	22
2910-00-025-3493	210	30	5305-00-057-9608	193	12
	221	13	4730-00-058-7558	215	10
	242	3		217	1
	246	8		218	1
5306-00-027-0722	235	19		245	10
5310-00-044-3342	100	20	5320-00-061-9648	185	2
4730-00-044-4587	66	4		186	6
4730-00-044-4789	26	1		189	3
	83	4	5320-00-061-9662	180	2
	84	1		181	14
5310-00-045-3296	179	10	5305-00-068-0501	17	19
	241	18		231	11
5310-00-045-5001	122	2	5305-00-068-0502	172	3
4730-00-050-4203	69	1	5305-00-068-0508	5	14
	70	10		37	3
	71	11		49	6
	72	10		51	10
	73	10		68	25
	100	13		148	4
	101	4		172	13
	102	5		227	13
	114	3		237	5
	115	12		240	7
5305-00-050-9237	179	16	5305-00-068-0509	5	20
5310-00-052-6454	87	2		185	12

CROSS-REFERENCE INDEXES

NATIONAL STOCK NUMBER INDEX

STOCK NUMBER	FIG	ITEM	STOCK NUMBER	FIG	ITEM
5305-00-068-0509	252	11	5305-00-071-2510	229	14
	253	14		231	1
5305-00-068-0510	41	20		232	7
	45	3		233	15
	111	22	5305-00-071-2511	229	11
	115	29	5930-00-073-0390	46	4
	118	2	2540-00-078-6633	114	1
	119	2		114	12
	176	3		115	10
	177	3		115	19
	180	12	5310-00-080-6004	63	8
	181	4		64	11
5305-00-068-0511	63	7		69	13
	64	13		115	28
	118	5		118	1
5310-00-068-5285	100	21		119	1
5305-00-068-7837	246	32		197	1
5305-00-071-1318	230	1		220	18
5305-00-071-1784	59	9		231	7
5305-00-071-1787	70	13		231	19
	71	13		232	3
	72	13	5310-00-081-4219	14	32
	73	13		17	35
5305-00-071-1788	107	2		68	14
	109	6		196	5
	115	37		215	1
5305-00-071-2055	123	5		218	7
5305-00-071-2058	115	33		218	7
5305-00-071-2066	30	7		235	5
5305-00-071-2067	107	4		238	5
	108	9		238	5
	110	2		239	4
	115	8		239	4
5305-00-071-2069	114	17	5310-00-082-1404	38	2
5305-00-071-2070	153	5	2940-00-082-6034	4	13
	182	10	5310-00-087-7493	180	11
5305-00-071-2071	237	8		181	5
5305-00-071-2073	115	39		188	26
5305-00-071-2075	107	8	4030-00-088-1881	113	6
	108	7	3110-00-100-0251	85	16
	114	23	5330-00-107-3925	4	18
	115	9		213	8
	120	5	5360-00-113-9490	87	17
5305-00-071-2077	120	3		88	19
5305-00-071-2081	153	6	5305-00-115-9526	18	17
5305-00-071-2087	229	13		22	4
5305-00-071-2506	188	13	5305-00-115-9934	39	7
	222	7	5360-00-123-0137	87	15
	240	4		88	17
	252	17	2530-00-125-2769	87	14

CROSS-REFERENCE INDEXES

NATIONAL STOCK NUMBER INDEX

STOCK NUMBER	FIG	ITEM	STOCK NUMBER	FIG	ITEM
2530-00-125-2769	88	16	5305-00-225-3843	215	8
4730-00-132-4625	16	6		215	8
	17	9		216	2
4730-00-142-2177	214	12		218	4
	221	16		218	4
	242	4		246	30
	246	14	5306-00-226-4822	178	16
3110-00-142-4387	85	15	5306-00-226-4824	91	5
6240-00-144-4693	34	21		212	7
	35	1		214	20
	35	5	5306-00-226-4825	17	36
	43	8		106	1
	44	5		221	5
5310-00-144-8453	241	16		242	26
5305-00-146-2524	14	24	5306-00-226-4826	14	30
	51	1		17	38
	57	9		86	4
	208	2	5306-00-226-4827	22	14
5310-00-167-0680	121	9		182	19
	122	8		202	6
5310-00-167-0721	40	6		203	8
4820-00-174-0315	5	6		238	1
5325-00-174-5314	240	1		238	1
5306-00-177-5707	235	22		239	1
5305-00-182-9584	95	6		239	1
4730-00-187-4210	77	16	5306-00-226-4828	245	12
4730-00-196-1991	220	11	5306-00-226-4829	179	18
5365-00-200-7377	168	22	5306-00-226-4830	21	4
2910-00-203-3322	210	32		22	2
5310-00-208-1918	193	6		235	4
	246	12	5306-00-226-4832	196	1
5310-00-209-0786	37	4	5306-00-226-4833	90	14
	39	10		176	9
	44	2		177	9
	45	2	5305-00-227-1543	36	10
	51	2		38	1
	52	3	3110-00-227-4667	85	9
	54	22	2530-00-228-6992	87	25
	172	12	5360-00-229-5312	87	24
	252	4	4720-00-230-6523	BULK	20
5310-00-209-0965	188	12	5930-00-234-1390	222	12
5310-00-209-2811	102	1	5340-00-237-7779	247	23
5305-00-217-9183	248	5	5305-00-240-6668	231	9
5306-00-225-2864	70	14	5315-00-243-1169	114	15
	71	14		115	22
5305-00-225-3843	5	3	5315-00-243-1170	245	8
	182	2	5310-00-245-3424	17	32
	182	15		86	13
	194	8	5305-00-245-4144	235	11
	197	3	4730-00-249-3885	220	10

CROSS-REFERENCE INDEXES

NATIONAL STOCK NUMBER INDEX

STOCK NUMBER	FIG	ITEM	STOCK NUMBER	FIG	ITEM
6240-00-252-7138	248	2	5310-00-407-9566	21	3
5310-00-252-8748	36	3		22	8
	38	8		55	8
5305-00-253-5626	114	16		70	15
	115	23		71	15
5325-00-263-6632	241	9		100	3
5325-00-263-6648	250	7		176	10
5325-00-263-6651	253	13		177	10
5310-00-264-1930	97	24		203	7
5330-00-265-1089	210	31		221	8
4730-00-266-0535	211	6		242	23
4730-00-266-0536	211	15	5340-00-411-4508	248	4
	214	18	4730-00-415-3172	221	12
5305-00-269-3233	49	25	5310-00-429-3135	31	2
5305-00-272-3533	246	5	5305-00-432-4163	210	5
4730-00-277-8269	5	5	5305-00-432-4171	214	7
4730-00-278-8886	90	12	5305-00-432-4201	142	7
5325-00-279-1248	214	26	5305-00-432-7953	43	3
5340-00-282-7509	222	15	5305-00-432-8220	145	16
5340-00-282-7539	214	23	6250-00-433-5946	34	19
5340-00-285-8868	134	18	6210-00-438-4745	241	7
4730-00-288-9390	5	4	5305-00-446-9901	227	12
	90	11	5315-00-450-9163	99	73
	91	12	5340-00-455-5899	173	2
4730-00-288-9440	5	8	5310-00-472-3214	229	10
5325-00-291-9366	225	14		231	2
5315-00-298-1481	100	10		232	6
5360-00-310-4493	88	25	2590-00-476-5459	136	8
5310-00-316-6513	21	15		136	17
	22	25	5305-00-483-0554	42	13
	63	9		158	5
	64	12	5340-00-486-1765	75	4
	111	4	5310-00-490-4639	134	3
	111	9	2910-00-493-2138	9	12
	234	15	2530-00-494-8165	87	14
	235	14		88	16
	247	16	5310-00-514-6674	22	15
4730-00-317-4231	220	8		36	4
5340-00-329-4420	252	2		38	7
5325-00-337-6636	225	2		49	9
5310-00-350-2655	42	7		53	3
3030-00-357-5506	30	11		198	3
5330-00-360-7881	147	3	5310-00-516-2701	31	1
5310-00-380-1514	90	8	9515-00-516-5756	BULK	33
4210-00-383-7127	203	3	5310-00-528-7638	242	19
5360-00-392-3453	87	22	5305-00-533-5542	231	21
	88	24		232	18
5940-00-405-8976	BULK	7		235	2
5310-00-407-9566	14	26	4030-00-542-3183	114	25
	17	21		115	31

CROSS-REFERENCE INDEXES

NATIONAL STOCK NUMBER INDEX

STOCK NUMBER	FIG	ITEM	STOCK NUMBER	FIG	ITEM
5305-00-543-2866	247	17	5310-00-637-9541	22	5
5930-00-548-5640	179	5		41	21
5940-00-549-6581	49	39		42	8
5940-00-549-6583	49	39		49	26
5310-00-550-3503	49	12		100	6
	54	21		111	21
5310-00-550-3715	241	12		115	27
2640-00-555-2829	96	29		118	4
2640-00-555-2840	97	1		119	4
3110-00-580-3708	85	6		121	6
3110-00-580-3709	85	7		122	4
4730-00-580-6738	19	1		124	5
5320-00-582-3521	176	2		180	14
	177	1		181	3
	178	8		188	23
	180	18		250	19
	181	26	5930-00-655-1514	241	4
5310-00-582-5965	5	13	5310-00-655-9370	109	5
	17	18	5320-00-660-0821	180	9
	37	9		181	9
	40	4	5120-00-677-2259	254	4
	148	6	5365-00-682-1762	87	13
	221	3		88	15
	226	10	5340-00-685-5899	246	37
	240	8	5306-00-685-7790	234	19
	250	3	5305-00-688-2111	91	15
	250	22		112	24
5310-00-584-5272	100	19		119	5
5310-00-596-6897	197	16	6210-00-688-5088	241	8
	220	17	3110-00-690-8923	97	22
5310-00-596-7691	252	6	5310-00-696-5172	54	4
	253	6	5340-00-700-1423	86	11
3110-00-606-9576	85	10		97	18
5320-00-616-4346	176	13	5340-00-702-2848	238	10
	177	15		239	3
	178	1		239	3
	180	31	5305-00-709-8517	188	7
	181	31	2910-00-710-6054	211	11
	183	3		214	10
	184	3	5305-00-719-5184	87	4
	185	16	5305-00-719-5240	114	11
	186	10		115	25
	192	4	5365-00-720-8064	144	10
	210	38	5365-00-721-6876	97	5
6240-00-617-0991	42	4		97	9
5530-00-618-6955	BULK	30	2520-00-722-7074	70	2
4730-00-619-9362	211	7		71	2
	214	6		72	2
5930-00-636-1584	179	6		73	2
5310-00-637-9541	18	18	5305-00-725-2317	9	7

CROSS-REFERENCE INDEXES

NATIONAL STOCK NUMBER INDEX

STOCK NUMBER	FIG	ITEM	STOCK NUMBER	FIG	ITEM
5310-00-732-0558	22	6	5310-00-792-3617	102	8
	41	22	5365-00-803-7317	96	7
	42	9	5325-00-807-0580	222	5
	45	5		223	3
	111	19	5340-00-809-1490	15	17
	115	26		16	11
	118	3		91	21
	119	3	5310-00-809-3078	86	20
	121	5		182	18
	122	3	5310-00-809-3079	107	12
	124	4		114	22
	214	29		145	20
5310-00-732-0559	188	24	5310-00-809-4058	32	7
5315-00-737-0134	247	21		49	17
2540-00-752-4078	246	26		51	11
5306-00-753-6996	247	11		222	4
5330-00-753-8036	BULK	31		228	6
5310-00-754-2005	253	15		242	15
5310-00-761-6882	37	8		246	2
	44	1		246	27
	45	1	5310-00-809-4061	13	6
	52	2		14	38
	246	35		115	36
5310-00-763-8894	87	1		188	10
5310-00-763-8905	122	1	5310-00-809-4085	21	16
5310-00-763-8913	121	8		22	26
	122	7		28	7
5340-00-764-7052	37	10		29	7
5310-00-768-0318	107	6		111	3
	108	3		118	6
	109	8		145	18
	114	27		234	16
	115	2		235	15
	116	1	5310-00-809-5997	182	9
	118	7		234	17
	119	6		235	21
	120	1	5310-00-809-5998	107	5
	121	4		108	5
	140	4		109	10
	147	10		114	18
	152	7		115	38
	182	5		117	8
4730-00-768-8880	220	13		121	2
5360-00-771-7066	228	9		140	3
5935-00-773-1428	51	9	5310-00-809-8546	221	17
5310-00-775-5139	31	6		242	5
5305-00-782-9489	231	18		246	15
	231	30	5310-00-814-0673	196	7
	232	10		215	2
5310-00-785-1762	100	5		218	8

CROSS-REFERENCE INDEXES

NATIONAL STOCK NUMBER INDEX

STOCK NUMBER	FIG	ITEM	STOCK NUMBER	FIG	ITEM
5310-00-814-0673	218	11	5320-00-845-9501	178	14
	238	6		180	3
	238	6		181	15
	239	5		185	17
	239	5		192	9
5315-00-814-3530	189	8		246	23
5315-00-814-3531	188	29	5315-00-846-0126	114	7
5315-00-816-1794	68	17		115	16
	69	12	5310-00-849-6882	114	6
	100	16		115	15
5305-00-821-3869	91	16	6240-00-850-4280	33	17
	124	8		191	3
5320-00-822-6257	183	9		227	5
	184	2	5310-00-851-2674	182	4
5310-00-823-8804	49	5		182	12
	182	3		185	9
	182	14	5310-00-880-7744	176	11
5305-00-823-9139	247	19		177	11
4730-00-826-4268	15	9	5310-00-880-7746	40	1
	16	9	5340-00-881-5303	8	11
	17	1		17	16
	18	21		90	2
5320-00-828-1284	183	13		91	21
	184	15		91	24
5330-00-830-1745	9	11	6240-00-889-1799	45	11
5310-00-834-7606	87	3		178	4
	108	4	5310-00-889-2528	172	15
	109	9	5306-00-889-2943	233	1
	114	28	5940-00-890-2831	36	1
	115	3		38	10
	118	8	5310-00-891-1709	182	17
	119	7		203	10
	120	2	5310-00-896-0903	13	5
	147	9		14	37
	153	4		109	4
	168	17		115	4
	182	6	5315-00-899-4119	210	35
5310-00-835-2036	68	18	5365-00-900-0982	144	8
	69	9	4730-00-900-3296	210	12
	188	11	5305-00-901-3110	234	3
6240-00-836-2079	176	5	5305-00-901-3144	235	17
	177	5	5310-00-903-5966	172	5
5315-00-839-2325	246	6	5310-00-905-4600	100	4
5315-00-839-5820	188	4	4730-00-908-3194	6	2
5310-00-842-1490	100	17		14	40
5315-00-842-3044	68	13		15	27
	247	18		25	17
5310-00-842-7783	100	9		209	1
4730-00-844-5721	62	7		220	1
4820-00-844-6744	23	16		238	8

CROSS-REFERENCE INDEXES

NATIONAL STOCK NUMBER INDEX

STOCK NUMBER	FIG	ITEM	STOCK NUMBER	FIG	ITEM
4730-00-908-3194	239	7	5310-00-934-9747	36	7
4730-00-908-3195	18	23		38	5
	23	8	5310-00-934-9748	241	13
	67	2	5310-00-934-9758	179	9
	75	6		241	17
	80	5	5310-00-934-9764	40	2
	81	5	5305-00-935-7506	231	29
4730-00-908-6292	14	10	5330-00-935-9136	4	8
	242	13		213	2
4730-00-908-6293	210	16	5310-00-938-8387	68	26
	215	7		222	6
	215	7		240	6
	216	3	6240-00-944-1264	34	18
	218	3		34	20
	218	3		42	17
	243	5		53	1
	245	1		56	1
4730-00-908-6294	210	10	5940-00-950-7783	BULK	34
	242	20	5340-00-958-8457	238	3
	246	19	5310-00-959-4675	45	4
	246	29		112	22
4730-00-909-8627	14	39	5310-00-959-4679	86	5
	15	22		91	6
	25	1		106	12
5340-00-914-1000	221	4		202	5
4030-00-916-2141	114	14		238	2
	115	21		238	2
5340-00-916-6539	197	9		239	2
	197	14		239	2
	197	19		245	13
6240-00-924-7526	43	7	6220-00-961-0783	248	1
	45	10	3030-00-967-4898	30	4
5940-00-926-8034	BULK	6	5310-00-975-2075	79	8
4720-00-930-2231	BULK	21		79	25
5310-00-931-8167	14	25	5930-00-978-8805	241	5
	17	20	5320-00-982-3815	180	24
	21	2		181	19
	22	9		190	6
	27	5		193	7
	70	16	5945-00-983-4374	41	29
	71	16	5305-00-984-4983	227	8
	86	19	5305-00-984-6191	178	18
	91	10	5305-00-984-6193	56	9
	106	11		227	1
	141	4	5305-00-984-6195	210	14
	221	9	5305-00-984-6210	241	20
	242	22	5305-00-984-6214	37	12
5310-00-933-4310	247	12	5340-00-989-1771	226	8
5310-00-933-8121	172	2		227	15
5310-00-933-8123	121	3	5945-00-992-5415	41	31

CROSS-REFERENCE INDEXES

NATIONAL STOCK NUMBER INDEX

STOCK NUMBER	FIG	ITEM	STOCK NUMBER	FIG	ITEM
5320-00-994-7076	48	9	5340-01-044-8389	196	15
5930-00-998-9211	41	18		233	21
2510-00-999-9856	229	4	5970-01-044-8391	49	27
	231	26	2990-01-046-1170	21	9
5310-01-012-8962	215	12	5325-01-050-6192	197	10
	217	2		197	12
	229	7		197	18
	231	4		228	5
	232	1		230	8
	233	4	5340-01-059-0114	49	23
	233	17	5935-01-059-0117	49	22
5930-01-014-0187	41	15	5330-01-059-4286	49	28
5305-01-019-1884	96	19	4710-01-062-3719	179	7
5330-01-020-9319	83	10	5925-01-067-2926	241	3
5310-01-021-9027	96	1	5310-01-069-5243	39	5
5935-01-022-2377	185	18		42	21
2520-01-024-0279	70	5		43	10
	71	6		45	14
	72	5		56	11
	73	7	4730-01-069-6408	211	3
	74	3		214	3
	74	3	4730-01-075-7310	16	5
2540-01-025-0433	189	9		17	8
5315-01-025-0930	179	11	5330-01-076-3009	96	27
5820-01-026-0983	172	4	5330-01-076-6172	42	3
5975-01-027-0253	172	6	5310-01-076-6196	42	6
3110-01-027-4475	96	17	5310-01-077-6817	154	3
2540-01-028-0574	181	17		155	2
5930-01-028-1949	192	10	5330-01-080-3253	61	7
5340-01-028-9063	183	6	5330-01-084-2410	84	6
	184	6	5310-01-084-4491	134	5
	185	7	5920-01-085-0825	41	28
	186	3		41	35
	189	5	5330-01-085-0918	96	20
	190	4	2930-01-085-0926	23	11
3110-01-030-8475	96	15	5355-01-085-0995	99	71
6140-01-031-6882	48	11	5306-01-085-1953	93	1
4730-01-034-8228	76	15	9320-01-085-2889	252	10
6130-01-035-6412	178	22		253	10
5340-01-036-7665	196	11	2590-01-085-6956	47	1
5330-01-037-0663	42	5	5330-01-086-3503	77	5
5340-01-038-3428	196	10	5330-01-086-3504	77	3
2520-01-038-7283	82	1	5330-01-086-3506	97	16
6220-01-039-9809	178	19	2540-01-086-5433	200	1
2520-01-040-2160	82	2	5305-01-087-1917	210	28
2540-01-041-4912	247	10	3110-01-087-2653	97	19
5340-01-043-5214	196	18	5330-01-087-4714	249	5
	233	19	6240-01-089-6149	178	20
3030-01-043-6749	251	12	5310-01-093-2907	78	1
5935-01-044-8382	49	24	5340-01-094-9025	247	20

CROSS-REFERENCE INDEXES

NATIONAL STOCK NUMBER INDEX

STOCK NUMBER	FIG	ITEM	STOCK NUMBER	FIG	ITEM
2530-01-096-6752	87	27	5305-01-140-9118	142	2
2510-01-096-6758	43	4		214	24
2530-01-096-6764	94	4	5310-01-143-0512	104	4
5330-01-096-7698	BULK	32	5310-01-143-0542	20	2
4720-01-096-7718	BULK	27	5310-01-143-1719	31	3
2530-01-096-7731	96	23	5305-01-143-7411	31	8
5330-01-096-9649	76	5	5305-01-143-7412	31	5
2540-01-096-9664	132	11	5970-01-144-1291	31	4
2530-01-096-9670	96	16	2920-01-145-0993	31	7
5310-01-097-8222	231	8	5940-01-145-7817	54	7
	231	22	4140-01-145-8099	27	4
	232	2	6220-01-146-4455	43	1
5310-01-097-9414	112	3	6220-01-146-4469	43	4
	123	3	6620-01-146-8006	25	13
4730-01-098-5229	78	5	5340-01-147-2268	104	5
9330-01-098-6554	185	3	2590-01-147-2269	116	8
	186	5	2990-01-147-3953	22	13
	189	2	2990-01-147-3954	112	6
5310-01-099-7945	78	2	2520-01-147-4005	74	1
5330-01-106-7938	96	14	2930-01-147-4198	25	7
	96	14	5330-01-147-4208	60	8
1430-01-106-8451	231	15	2530-01-147-4209	97	21
6220-01-107-2613	42	2	5330-01-147-4212	21	13
5310-01-107-4051	96	1		22	23
2530-01-110-5304	94	4	2530-01-147-4214	86	15
5330-01-112-1533	9	9	2910-01-147-4218	14	15
5340-01-114-7712	247	4	2910-01-147-4219	13	12
5310-01-119-3668	14	31	2930-01-147-4221	24	4
	17	37	2930-01-147-4222	23	5
	68	8	2920-01-147-4272	28	1
	90	23	2815-01-147-4275	4	21
	235	8	2920-01-147-4278	29	2
2940-01-121-6350	61	10	2590-01-147-4285	4	2
2930-01-123-4941	23	3	2990-01-147-4289	22	22
5920-01-123-5211	41	27	2990-01-147-4290	22	1
5920-01-123-5212	41	26	6680-01-147-4629	4	4
5325-01-123-6798	61	9	6680-01-147-5497	23	7
2530-01-124-3422	90	21	2540-01-147-5537	57	5
2920-01-131-4932	30	2	2590-01-147-5538	117	9
5305-01-132-2166	42	28	2520-01-147-5539	96	25
	198	16	2530-01-147-5541	123	9
5310-01-132-8275	221	6	3030-01-147-6410	29	4
	242	25	2530-01-147-6421	99	70
5310-01-133-7215	196	13	2530-01-147-6423	92	2
5330-01-138-2106	18	10	2530-01-147-6424	92	10
2530-01-140-6144	87	10	4730-01-147-6425	81	6
5305-01-140-9118	13	1	6680-01-147-6583	60	10
	14	36	3020-01-147-7935	30	3
	111	11	2530-01-147-8556	104	6
	130	5	2920-01-147-8559	29	8

CROSS-REFERENCE INDEXES

NATIONAL STOCK NUMBER INDEX

STOCK NUMBER	FIG	ITEM	STOCK NUMBER	FIG	ITEM
2920-01-147-8562	30	9	4720-01-148-5981	BULK	13
5310-01-147-8743	12	2	3040-01-148-5982	72	15
	107	3		73	15
	115	5	2940-01-148-5992	12	5
5310-01-147-8748	123	2	5306-01-148-6765	84	4
2990-01-147-9284	6	14	4720-01-148-6946	90	18
2530-01-147-9329	93	7	4720-01-148-6947	90	18
2930-01-147-9330	27	6	3020-01-148-6983	2	11
3020-01-147-9359	2	11	4720-01-148-6984	14	41
5310-01-147-9792	30	8	4720-01-148-7398	90	18
2930-01-147-9916	25	11	5306-01-148-7457	117	6
2510-01-147-9917	195	1	5305-01-148-7460	1	6
2530-01-148-1463	86	17		2	12
2610-01-148-1634	98	1		28	3
2610-01-148-1635	98	1		104	8
4710-01-148-2659	8	9	5310-01-148-7474	4	6
5310-01-148-2676	96	24	5330-01-148-7492	60	4
5310-01-148-2682	68	16	5330-01-148-7497	25	14
5340-01-148-2730	83	9		220	5
4730-01-148-2755	25	10	5330-01-148-7499	89	28
4730-01-148-2758	25	15	5340-01-148-7529	11	12
	26	2	5305-01-148-8208	92	15
	220	7	4730-01-148-8242	25	10
4720-01-148-2761	106	10	5340-01-148-8351	86	10
4720-01-148-2762	106	5	5340-01-148-8352	86	8
4720-01-148-2763	90	18	4710-01-148-8354	5	2
4720-01-148-2768	BULK	24	2815-01-148-9560	7	11
3030-01-148-2792	104	1	5330-01-149-0874	25	9
5340-01-148-2818	22	18		220	3
2910-01-148-2910	14	13	5365-01-149-0880	4	19
2530-01-148-2914	96	22		213	7
2520-01-148-2919	74	1	2530-01-149-1886	94	3
2990-01-148-2928	20	1	4710-01-149-1899	5	25
2990-01-148-2929	86	9	5305-01-149-1936	100	1
5995-01-148-2930	86	18	5360-01-149-1959	21	14
2510-01-148-2942	120	4		22	24
2540-01-148-2943	121	1	2530-01-149-3375	92	17
3020-01-148-2948	104	13	5340-01-149-3376	92	17
3020-01-148-2949	27	2	2520-01-149-3461	60	6
3020-01-148-2950	27	2	2910-01-149-3786	20	7
4710-01-148-2969	67	1	2530-01-149-3827	77	1
4720-01-148-2970	25	4		77	1
5306-01-148-3667	8	10	5306-01-149-4398	55	7
	104	11	5310-01-149-4407	108	2
5305-01-148-3685	7	10		110	4
5305-01-148-3687	116	9		114	20
5310-01-148-3693	12	3	5340-01-149-4434	23	9
4710-01-148-4989	60	9		49	8
4720-01-148-5000	5	21		90	5
5310-01-148-5922	214	28		129	3

CROSS-REFERNCE INDEXES

NATIONAL STOCK NUMBER INDEX

STOCK NUMBER	FIG	ITEM	STOCK NUMBER	FIG	ITEM
5340-01-149-4434	198	8	5340-01-150-4105	29	1
	222	2		36	11
	226	6		38	12
	240	2		39	8
4720-01-149-4659	91	25		42	11
2990-01-149-4966	3	6		48	10
5306-01-149-6278	7	8		49	7
	219	1		49	11
5306-01-149-6279	27	3		49	33
5306-01-149-6280	3	7		54	15
	25	8		54	20
	28	2		174	4
	28	4		197	2
	29	3		200	14
	59	1		211	10
	104	7		214	9
	251	7		229	15
	251	9		230	4
5325-01-149-6293	12	6		234	8
	86	14		245	3
5360-01-149-6309	42	36	5340-01-150-4106	11	10
5920-01-149-6952	41	33	5340-01-150-4991	25	2
	187	12	5340-01-150-4992	49	20
5920-01-149-6953	41	30	5305-01-150-5785	42	32
	187	14	5340-01-150-5785	1	5
5305-01-149-7356	41	24	5307-01-150-5992	4	20
2920-01-149-8606	28	8	5340-01-150-6026	11	7
5930-01-149-9305	65	51	5340-01-150-6249	5	17
5930-01-149-9306	41	25	5340-01-150-6275	11	11
5365-01-149-9710	65	17	4720-01-150-7575	5	10
5340-01-149-9729	74	5	5330-01-150-7744	4	15
5340-01-150-0197	5	24		213	3
4710-01-150-0842	4	5	5307-01-150-7764	30	12
4730-01-150-0879	4	12	5340-01-150-7774	11	19
2930-01-150-0895	25	19	5306-01-150-9493	29	5
5306-01-150-1197	97	20	5306-01-150-9497	61	11
5307-01-150-1228	27	1	5305-01-150-9500	79	9
5325-01-150-1229	68	15		79	13
5340-01-150-1377	5	19	2530-01-150-9757	103	1
	222	8	5305-01-150-9781	4	17
5305-01-150-1521	11	9		249	10
5355-01-150-1541	41	7	5360-01-151-1120	20	9
5340-01-150-1545	32	5	5360-01-151-1121	20	3
2920-01-150-1610	41	1	2920-01-151-3627	19	3
2815-01-150-2181	7	6	5315-01-151-4180	9	10
2910-01-150-3675	20	5	5306-01-151-4925	9	13
2910-01-150-3676	20	11	2530-01-151-5967	89	1
5310-01-150-4003	95	4	5365-01-151-6111	100	2
	112	2	5325-01-151-6117	4	3
	123	4	5340-01-151-7409	14	21

CROSS-REFERNCE INDEXES

NATIONAL STOCK NUMBER INDEX

STOCK NUMBER	FIG	ITEM	STOCK NUMBER	FIG	ITEM
4730-01-151-7972	90	19	2530-01-152-9312	102	4
2520-01-151-8043	74	4	2530-01-152-9313	102	9
2990-01-151-8115	86	9	2530-01-152-9314	102	7
5305-01-151-8288	42	14	3120-01-153-0281	76	2
5310-01-151-8347	87	19	5315-01-153-0317	96	28
	88	21	5315-01-153-0318	68	20
5310-01-151-8353	95	13	5307-01-153-0873	12	7
5307-01-151-8374	7	9	5306-01-153-1368	82	3
5305-01-151-9285	23	2	5310-01-153-1381	77	4
5340-01-151-9956	8	3	2530-01-153-1492	88	29
5340-01-151-9957	8	8	5340-01-153-1631	123	7
2530-01-152-0180	87	29	2530-01-153-1813	89	25
	88	31	2530-01-153-1814	121	7
2990-01-152-0251	86	12		122	5
5310-01-152-0598	39	6	4820-01-153-1851	4	10
	49	3	6615-01-153-1852	4	9
	54	5	4730-01-153-2718	75	8
	144	12	2520-01-153-8430	72	12
	172	10		73	12
	197	7	2520-01-153-8431	70	9
	197	13		72	9
	197	21	5310-01-153-9301	102	6
	227	14	5310-01-153-9302	97	14
	230	9	2530-01-153-9449	88	30
2920-01-152-2414	35	10	2530-01-153-9450	88	30
5306-01-152-2582	91	14	2540-01-153-9470	95	11
6680-01-152-2845	105	18	2510-01-153-9473	118	15
5306-01-152-4693	20	10		119	14
2910-01-152-5516	14	34	2510-01-153-9584	120	4
4710-01-152-5798	61	8	3020-01-153-9586	104	13
2530-01-152-7115	87	5	4710-01-154-1230	15	29
5340-01-152-7155	92	14	2510-01-154-1261	118	11
5365-01-152-7439	70	3		119	10
	71	3	2530-01-154-1262	100	12
	72	3	2530-01-154-1263	94	5
	73	3	2540-01-154-1293	95	10
3040-01-152-7786	88	18	2530-01-154-1294	89	1
2530-01-152-7787	88	18	2990-01-154-1323	22	16
2990-01-152-7788	22	17	2990-01-154-1324	21	10
2990-01-152-7828	22	20	4730-01-154-1366	90	3
5305-01-152-8193	72	14	6150-01-154-1381	49	13
	73	14	5310-01-154-2273	34	1
	74	6		42	16
5305-01-152-8945	174	2		43	6
2520-01-152-9171	84	5		44	8
2530-01-152-9258	88	29		125	3
2530-01-152-9305	97	17		131	3
2530-01-152-9306	93	11		132	9
2530-01-152-9307	93	11		134	1
2530-01-152-9308	88	5		136	21

CROSS-REFERENCE INDEXES

NATIONAL STOCK NUMBER INDEX

STOCK NUMBER	FIG	ITEM	STOCK NUMBER	FIG	ITEM
5310-01-154-2273	159	2	2910-01-155-5138	15	20
5905-01-154-2354	253	5		17	30
5945-01-154-3143	20	14	2910-01-155-5139	14	8
2990-01-154-3743	21	1	2590-01-155-5140	14	22
5310-01-154-3990	97	12	2910-01-155-5147	14	9
5310-01-154-3993	90	20	2910-01-155-5148	14	9
5310-01-154-4341	87	9	2990-01-155-5149	21	12
	88	8	2990-01-155-5150	21	11
5365-01-154-4365	29	9	2990-01-155-5151	21	8
5310-01-154-5263	89	27	2590-01-155-5177	14	12
5340-01-154-5269	91	7	4720-01-155-5194	14	11
5935-01-154-6264	241	10	2510-01-155-5432	156	4
2510-01-154-6906	130	1	2510-01-155-5433	156	2
2530-01-154-6952	96	3	2510-01-155-5434	156	1
5340-01-154-7163	104	9	2510-01-155-5435	156	7
2530-01-154-8146	97	23	2540-01-155-5824	171	8
5365-01-154-8514	95	9	2510-01-155-5825	151	3
5365-01-154-8577	88	28		152	9
4140-01-154-9615	253	3	2910-01-155-5845	17	34
3040-01-155-0194	170	8	2510-01-155-5846	141	3
3040-01-155-0195	170	15	2510-01-155-5848	13	9
3040-01-155-0371	137	1	2510-01-155-5849	142	20
3040-01-155-0372	137	9	2510-01-155-5850	142	19
3040-01-155-0373	137	9	2510-01-155-5851	142	13
2540-01-155-0376	200	7	2510-01-155-5853	142	10
5310-01-155-1897	97	13	2510-01-155-5854	142	3
5310-01-155-1898	88	3	2510-01-155-5857	142	8
5365-01-155-1941	70	6	3040-01-155-5864	161	18
	71	9	5306-01-155-6108	123	1
	72	6	5305-01-155-6113	121	10
	73	8		122	9
	74	2	6220-01-155-6515	42	31
5310-01-155-2503	6	4	6220-01-155-6521	42	27
5340-01-155-2614	90	1	6150-01-155-6522	37	15
	90	15	6140-01-155-6530	49	40
5340-01-155-2616	106	13	6140-01-155-6531	49	15
2940-01-155-3190	12	4	6250-01-155-6547	45	15
5340-01-155-3668	91	19	2540-01-155-6823	161	13
5330-01-155-4388	70	8	2540-01-155-6824	161	13
	72	8	2540-01-155-6825	161	12
5330-01-155-4393	65	50	3040-01-155-6912	161	22
5325-01-155-4482	86	3	2520-01-155-6936	74	4
2910-01-155-5063	14	2	6140-01-155-6997	48	15
	15	25	6140-01-155-6998	48	12
2540-01-155-5110	171	5	5975-01-155-7084	172	1
2540-01-155-5111	171	3	2540-01-155-7278	230	7
2510-01-155-5112	152	6	2540-01-155-7298	137	6
4730-01-155-5135	106	7	2540-01-155-7299	205	7
2910-01-155-5136	14	29	2510-01-155-7425	125	1
2910-01-155-5137	14	27	2530-01-155-7457	100	8

CROSS-REFERENCE INDEXES

NATIONAL STOCK NUMBER INDEX

STOCK NUMBER	FIG	ITEM	STOCK NUMBER	FIG	ITEM
2540-01-155-7496	122	6	4720-01-156-0085	17	2
2540-01-155-7502	135	3	2540-01-156-0088	158	7
2540-01-155-7503	135	3		236	1
2540-01-155-7535	109	12	4720-01-156-0547	BULK	14
2540-01-155-7542	229	1	4720-01-156-0548	BULK	17
2540-01-155-7543	230	6	4720-01-156-0549	BULK	18
5306-01-155-7659	203	1	4720-01-156-0550	BULK	19
5330-01-155-7700	101	3	2540-01-156-0564	132	10
	101	8	2540-01-156-0565	137	3
	102	3	2590-01-156-0583	86	12
2590-01-155-7711	13	7	2540-01-156-0584	198	4
	BULK	8	6620-01-156-0712	35	6
5340-01-155-7744	104	10	6220-01-156-4475	42	24
4720-01-155-7784	BULK	16	6220-01-156-4476	43	11
2510-01-155-7877	142	20		45	12
2910-01-155-7878	13	8	2540-01-156-4855	200	6
2990-01-155-7879	13	14	2540-01-156-4869	137	3
2910-01-155-7880	15	7	2540-01-156-4870	133	2
2910-01-155-7881	15	2		133	11
2590-01-155-7882	13	10	2510-01-156-4871	136	24
2510-01-155-7942	113	1	2510-01-156-4872	134	11
2530-01-155-7943	87	27	2510-01-156-4873	134	11
2910-01-155-7965	15	26	2540-01-156-4874	205	8
2590-01-155-7966	51	7	2530-01-156-4875	87	21
4720-01-155-8062	14	11	2540-01-156-4885	134	19
2530-01-155-8460	88	23	2530-01-156-4900	87	30
5306-01-155-8528	205	1	2530-01-156-4901	87	30
5365-01-155-8576	136	26	2540-01-156-4903	134	13
2510-01-155-8785	142	6	2540-01-156-4904	134	13
2540-01-155-8786	161	12	2540-01-156-4907	136	20
2510-01-155-8787	125	5	2540-01-156-4908	136	20
2510-01-155-8799	133	6	5305-01-156-5006	88	27
2510-01-155-8800	133	5	5340-01-156-5061	180	15
5340-01-155-9861	22	19		181	2
2910-01-156-0045	18	1	5330-01-156-5141	106	8
4730-01-156-0055	80	6	5330-01-156-5147	3	5
2510-01-156-0062	151	6	6140-01-156-5326	48	5
2540-01-156-0068	199	28	5306-01-156-5435	83	8
2540-01-156-0069	199	7	5305-01-156-5438	15	15
2540-01-156-0070	205	10		16	7
2540-01-156-0071	205	11		17	11
2540-01-156-0072	205	4		37	5
2540-01-156-0073	205	13		49	19
2590-01-156-0074	174	1		53	2
2590-01-156-0076	173	1		75	1
2590-01-156-0077	173	4		80	4
2590-01-156-0078	173	4		81	2
2590-01-156-0080	173	6		90	10
5315-01-156-0081	87	7		91	22
4720-01-156-0085	16	16		141	11

CROSS-REFERENCE INDEXES

NATIONAL STOCK NUMBER INDEX

STOCK NUMBER	FIG	ITEM	STOCK NUMBER	FIG	ITEM
5305-01-156-5438	212	1	5306-01-157-3279	163	4
	226	12		169	4
	227	17	5306-01-157-3330	107	11
2540-01-156-5882	198	10		108	8
2530-01-156-5883	87	16		109	11
2540-01-156-6107	135	2		114	30
2540-01-156-6108	135	2	4140-01-157-3501	253	3
2530-01-156-6190	93	2	5360-01-157-3662	87	20
6150-01-156-6326	54	19	2920-01-157-3765	32	8
	55	9	5930-01-157-4060	46	2
5315-01-156-6562	95	14	5310-01-157-4855	199	8
2530-01-156-7016	89	30	2530-01-157-5164	88	20
3040-01-156-7182	87	8	5305-01-157-5625	132	16
2540-01-156-7233	99	75	5310-01-157-5670	111	10
2540-01-156-7238	133	9		161	7
2510-01-156-8092	132	29	5310-01-157-5672	133	16
6220-01-156-8247	45	7		145	2
3040-01-156-8307	87	18	5330-01-157-5684	133	14
2530-01-156-8308	87	18	5365-01-157-5752	91	17
2540-01-156-8315	137	6	5340-01-157-6092	133	7
2530-01-156-8317	90	21	2540-01-157-6414	200	5
2910-01-156-8361	18	2	5340-01-157-6428	23	18
5340-01-156-8395	87	16	5340-01-157-6429	23	17
6220-01-156-8420	45	7	5340-01-157-6697	201	2
5305-01-156-8692	111	2		202	3
2540-01-156-9675	142	15	5306-01-157-6796	133	19
3040-01-156-9729	137	4		145	22
5360-01-156-9730	88	22		147	4
2540-01-156-9740	200	2		242	18
3040-01-156-9994	86	6	5306-01-157-6797	39	2
6240-01-157-0635	42	26		134	4
6240-01-157-0636	43	5		135	4
2510-01-157-1382	156	8		136	19
5325-01-157-1698	42	20		136	25
	125	4		137	7
	159	8	5330-01-157-6827	134	9
5355-01-157-1865	208	6	5330-01-157-6828	134	9
5355-01-157-1866	161	19	5305-01-157-7388	142	9
	170	9	5330-01-157-7458	133	8
5330-01-157-1916	89	35	5330-01-157-7459	133	4
5330-01-157-1952	204	1	5340-01-157-7471	133	25
5340-01-157-1955	89	33	5365-01-157-7476	161	6
5305-01-157-1987	136	23	5310-01-157-7560	116	4
	159	3	5310-01-157-7582	79	11
5340-01-157-2101	88	12	5330-01-157-7604	15	3
2540-01-157-2966	170	5	5340-01-157-7607	170	6
5315-01-157-3004	92	16	5340-01-157-7608	170	17
2540-01-157-3032	198	1	2540-01-157-7907	171	2
5306-01-157-3279	160	5	2530-01-157-7933	100	11
	162	5	3040-01-157-7970	87	8

CROSS-REFERENCE INDEXES

NATIONAL STOCK NUMBER INDEX

STOCK NUMBER	FIG	ITEM	STOCK NUMBER	FIG	ITEM
3040-01-157-7997	133	13	5365-01-158-5381	145	3
3040-01-157-7998	67	4	5305-01-158-6235	131	6
	75	3	5310-01-158-6257	49	21
	80	2	5310-01-158-6260	38	15
	81	1		42	22
2540-01-157-8008	115	35		43	9
2540-01-157-8009	145	25		48	4
3040-01-157-8021	144	14		54	2
6220-01-157-9046	43	1		206	1
5305-01-157-9720	15	1		225	5
	146	4		235	18
	168	14	5307-01-158-6312	7	7
5306-01-157-9817	116	2	4010-01-158-6331	145	5
5340-01-157-9825	15	21	5340-01-158-6354	161	21
5306-01-157-9936	133	17	6210-01-158-6575	34	13
5340-01-158-0297	86	16	5306-01-158-6682	96	13
5340-01-158-0303	80	3	5330-01-158-6683	134	8
5340-01-158-0314	15	16	5330-01-158-6725	76	3
	16	1	5310-01-158-6780	200	16
	17	4	5340-01-158-6816	205	5
5340-01-158-0321	89	37	4820-01-158-6836	10	10
5305-01-158-0335	137	2	5340-01-158-6892	168	19
	146	12	2540-01-158-6893	168	15
6210-01-158-0396	35	2	2540-01-158-6894	168	30
5340-01-158-0503	133	20	5340-01-158-6895	168	11
2540-01-158-0602	180	28	2540-01-158-6896	168	2
2540-01-158-1569	198	11	2510-01-158-6904	141	5
2540-01-158-1721	134	22	2540-01-158-6906	206	5
5365-01-158-2004	151	4	6350-01-158-7035	56	14
	152	8	2540-01-158-7551	168	13
5305-01-158-2032	14	3	2510-01-158-7575	127	1
	14	6	2540-01-158-7583	168	21
	15	4	5305-01-158-7820	14	7
	142	5		15	24
	157	5		125	2
3120-01-158-2096	95	8		128	5
5365-01-158-2191	87	26		159	7
5365-01-158-2193	97	10	2540-01-158-8548	114	19
2540-01-158-3576	133	1	5340-01-158-8549	154	7
6210-01-158-3857	34	11		155	1
5930-01-158-4428	35	11	2590-01-158-8551	208	4
5340-01-158-4583	146	3	2540-01-158-8553	115	1
2540-01-158-4599	115	40	2540-01-158-8554	143	2
2540-01-158-4600	145	12	2540-01-158-8555	148	8
2540-01-158-4601	147	8	2540-01-158-8556	148	2
2540-01-158-4602	144	2	2540-01-158-8557	146	9
2540-01-158-4603	164	12	2540-01-158-8558	164	8
	165	12	2540-01-158-8559	166	9
6210-01-158-4668	34	12	2540-01-158-8560	167	11
5930-01-158-4808	41	37	2540-01-158-8561	165	5

CROSS-REFERENCE INDEXES

NATIONAL STOCK NUMBER INDEX

STOCK NUMBER	FIG	ITEM	STOCK NUMBER	FIG	ITEM
2540-01-158-8611	198	15	5360-01-159-1449	87	23
2540-01-158-8612	198	6	5340-01-159-1460	172	9
5340-01-158-8624	1	2	3040-01-159-1775	146	5
2540-01-158-8626	34	3	2510-01-159-1790	234	12
3040-01-158-8703	148	5	2510-01-159-1791	232	12
4730-01-158-8717	198	17	2510-01-159-1792	229	3
2590-01-158-8784	129	5		231	28
2540-01-158-8812	166	1	2540-01-159-1793	183	2
2540-01-158-8813	143	5		184	7
5306-01-158-9018	23	12	6210-01-159-1794	191	1
	48	14	2510-01-159-1795	192	7
	127	2	5340-01-159-1796	179	17
	130	3		192	11
	141	8	2510-01-159-1797	192	1
	142	18	2510-01-159-1798	183	14
	145	7		184	16
	161	16	2540-01-159-1800	241	19
	168	3	2990-01-159-1801	215	5
	170	13	2930-01-159-1802	220	4
	171	6	5970-01-159-1803	228	3
	225	11	5895-01-159-1804	187	17
5310-01-158-9205	126	3	4720-01-159-1839	25	18
	134	16	6105-01-159-2223	253	11
5999-01-158-9249	34	4	6105-01-159-2666	252	8
5970-01-158-9337	158	11	5306-01-159-2772	145	21
	BULK	29	5305-01-159-2779	159	6
5307-01-158-9932	48	7	5305-01-159-2780	131	5
5905-01-159-0771	206	2	5305-01-159-2781	205	9
2910-01-159-0867	9	8	5305-01-159-2783	148	9
2510-01-159-0868	131	4	5306-01-159-2784	14	35
2540-01-159-0874	168	9	5330-01-159-2807	200	4
5930-01-159-0925	41	17	5330-01-159-2816	149	3
3040-01-159-0930	249	4	5325-01-159-2843	49	34
3040-01-159-0996	148	11	5340-01-159-2901	23	6
5306-01-159-1130	160	4	2930-01-159-2902	23	13
	162	2	2540-01-159-2928	114	32
	163	1	2510-01-159-2929	127	11
	169	3	2540-01-159-2992	108	10
5330-01-159-1152	149	1	5340-01-159-2996	153	2
5330-01-159-1153	134	8	2590-01-159-3505	51	8
5340-01-159-1185	17	24	2530-01-159-3604	99	64
5330-01-159-1298	13	4	5340-01-159-4517	202	13
	14	19	5340-01-159-4518	172	7
3120-01-159-1311	145	15	5340-01-159-4519	202	12
	168	12	5330-01-159-4777	147	6
5340-01-159-1321	37	6	5365-01-159-4833	88	10
	38	13	5999-01-159-5603	34	17
	49	4	5306-01-159-5710	94	1
5340-01-159-1324	209	4	5340-01-159-5762	42	23
	220	16	5340-01-159-5765	43	13

CROSS-REFERENCE INDEXES

NATIONAL STOCK NUMBER INDEX

STOCK NUMBER	FIG	ITEM	STOCK NUMBER	FIG	ITEM
4720-01-159-5796	BULK	22	2510-01-159-8761	128	3
5360-01-159-5952	41	8	2510-01-159-8762	126	2
2530-01-159-5958	100	14	2590-01-159-8763	208	5
5340-01-159-6174	151	2	2530-01-159-8764	249	6
2540-01-159-6198	233	6	2510-01-159-8765	42	33
5305-01-159-6567	168	1	2590-01-159-8766	41	23
5306-01-159-6574	154	1	2530-01-159-8802	86	2
	155	5	2590-01-159-8857	208	1
5310-01-159-6586	49	18	2590-01-159-8861	126	5
5310-01-159-6587	99	60	5360-01-159-8862	144	13
5355-01-159-6622	68	29	2540-01-159-8874	159	1
5307-01-159-6632	30	6	2540-01-159-8875	159	1
6150-01-159-6901	36	6	2540-01-159-8878	86	1
	38	6	2540-01-159-8880	136	5
5340-01-159-6905	142	14	2540-01-159-8881	107	10
5640-01-159-6935	5	12	3120-01-159-9386	77	2
2510-01-159-7120	145	24	5305-01-160-0331	161	14
2540-01-159-7740	113	2	5340-01-160-0367	14	23
2540-01-159-7741	114	31	3120-01-160-0570	166	11
2540-01-159-7744	165	9		167	15
3010-01-159-7750	144	9	5315-01-160-0575	133	22
2530-01-159-7754	92	18		133	28
2530-01-159-7755	92	18		145	14
2520-01-159-7757	60	5	5306-01-160-0769	164	7
	83	11		165	7
	84	7	4730-01-160-0814	206	11
3040-01-159-7950	137	4	2590-01-160-1047	198	19
2540-01-159-7954	198	14	2590-01-160-1496	50	9
2540-01-159-7963	160	2	4730-01-160-1505	46	3
5310-01-159-8264	252	3	2540-01-160-1591	128	2
	253	9	2930-01-160-1597	23	4
5330-01-159-8504	148	10	5306-01-160-1952	145	4
5310-01-159-8559	5	11	5306-01-160-1968	200	12
	17	17		211	12
	51	12		214	11
	148	7	5305-01-160-1974	206	10
	221	2	5305-01-160-1975	23	1
	222	10		24	3
	226	11		25	3
	240	9		130	13
5315-01-159-8660	168	20	5340-01-160-2155	89	29
2540-01-159-8705	205	12	5340-01-160-2171	113	3
2590-01-159-8716	111	12	5340-01-160-2172	147	7
2540-01-159-8721	159	5	5325-01-160-2237	134	20
2540-01-159-8722	205	6	5325-01-160-2238	86	7
2530-01-159-8725	100	15	5340-01-160-2239	18	16
2510-01-159-8726	153	7	5340-01-160-2346	128	7
2540-01-159-8727	168	23	5340-01-160-2367	145	6
2540-01-159-8759	142	1	5360-01-160-2411	161	20
2540-01-159-8760	200	9		161	23

CROSS-REFERENCE INDEXES

NATIONAL STOCK NUMBER INDEX

STOCK NUMBER	FIG	ITEM	STOCK NUMBER	FIG	ITEM
5360-01-160-2411	170	10	6220-01-160-5187	227	3
	170	16	6140-01-160-5196	225	4
5360-01-160-2415	95	7	6680-01-160-5276	249	8
5340-01-160-2445	21	5	5310-01-160-5708	200	10
	22	7	4720-01-160-5781	15	23
5340-01-160-2470	146	10	2510-01-160-5837	141	5
5365-01-160-2483	134	23	2540-01-160-5840	167	7
5340-01-160-2488	142	11	2590-01-160-5841	41	23
	146	7	2990-01-160-5873	141	12
2510-01-160-3634	146	6	3040-01-160-5913	148	12
2540-01-160-3651	163	2	2540-01-160-5918	143	3
2540-01-160-3652	168	25	5340-01-160-5922	137	8
2540-01-160-3653	168	28		146	8
2540-01-160-3654	168	27	5306-01-160-7553	198	20
4720-01-160-3664	206	12	4140-01-160-7664	253	1
6220-01-160-3686	178	17	4130-01-160-7695	250	1
6220-01-160-3687	178	3	2910-01-160-8107	13	13
6220-01-160-3705	178	5	5975-01-160-8458	BULK	4
6680-01-160-3870	34	7	4140-01-160-8503	252	1
5305-01-160-3937	133	24	5310-01-160-9529	23	19
	161	15		157	4
	164	1		212	6
	165	8		214	22
	170	11	5365-01-160-9530	99	69
	171	1	2540-01-161-1356	167	1
5305-01-160-3938	50	8	6680-01-161-1439	13	2
	217	5		14	18
5305-01-160-3945	41	10	5340-01-161-1440	249	11
5305-01-160-3955	166	13	2590-01-161-2119	86	18
	167	17	6210-01-161-2138	34	14
5320-01-160-3999	41	14	5310-01-161-2374	222	14
	173	3	5310-01-161-2531	229	6
5325-01-160-4028	134	6	5305-01-161-2581	138	1
5340-01-160-4130	168	16		161	11
6220-01-160-4247	42	18	5330-01-161-2608	198	21
6220-01-160-4254	42	30	5340-01-161-2749	164	5
5340-01-160-4397	3	8		165	3
5305-01-160-4494	168	24	5340-01-161-2789	159	4
5305-01-160-4528	161	10	6680-01-161-3656	249	7
5310-01-160-4536	23	21	5305-01-161-3995	49	35
	152	10	5305-01-161-3997	42	19
5340-01-160-4592	56	7	5340-01-161-4025	91	18
5340-01-160-4597	56	8	5365-01-161-4055	96	21
5325-01-160-4618	11	8	6220-01-161-5016	42	30
5315-01-160-4639	113	5	5306-01-161-5489	20	13
	114	24	5340-01-161-5522	134	2
	115	30	5306-01-161-6178	36	12
2510-01-160-4970	126	1		38	11
6220-01-160-5094	176	4		39	11
	177	4		47	5

CROSS-REFERENCE INDEXES

NATIONAL STOCK NUMBER INDEX

STOCK NUMBER	FIG	ITEM	STOCK NUMBER	FIG	ITEM
5306-01-161-6178	54	14	2540-01-162-4411	165	1
4710-01-161-6406	239	8	2540-01-162-4412	229	23
6220-01-161-6439	42	18	2990-01-162-4416	218	12
4730-01-161-6618	229	19	2590-01-162-4417	226	5
5310-01-161-7308	210	4	2590-01-162-4418	226	7
5360-01-161-7561	133	3	9390-01-162-4500	136	27
	133	10	5340-01-162-4774	49	30
5340-01-161-9188	132	7	5340-01-162-4775	115	7
5305-01-162-0015	200	11	5340-01-162-4820	203	2
3120-01-162-0060	161	8	5340-01-162-4852	129	1
4730-01-162-0095	220	2	4720-01-162-5113	211	16
4720-01-162-0119	5	10		214	16
	219	5	2510-01-162-5172	130	4
4720-01-162-0120	5	21	2510-01-162-5173	130	4
	219	4	2540-01-162-5174	241	1
4720-01-162-0121	214	27	2540-01-162-5175	241	2
3040-01-162-0255	133	13	2540-01-162-5176	246	4
4720-01-162-0283	239	6	2540-01-162-5177	246	40
5945-01-162-0516	223	2	2540-01-162-5178	246	31
5945-01-162-0517	222	3	2540-01-162-5189	246	39
5930-01-162-0803	41	36	5340-01-162-5619	180	23
5360-01-162-2849	161	17		181	21
	164	10		190	8
	165	6	5305-01-162-5707	150	10
	170	7	9340-01-162-5947	193	2
2510-01-162-3623	130	7	9340-01-162-5948	180	13
2530-01-162-3626	131	7		181	6
5340-01-162-3627	35	3	5305-01-162-5995	42	29
5340-01-162-3628	35	3	5305-01-162-5996	166	6
5930-01-162-3669	41	9		167	6
2510-01-162-3679	131	8	5340-01-162-6061	42	12
5330-01-162-3744	43	2	5340-01-162-6062	202	7
5340-01-162-3747	111	13	5340-01-162-6077	45	13
5340-01-162-3748	111	7	2540-01-162-6418	246	22
5340-01-162-3749	111	7	2540-01-162-6493	246	36
5340-01-162-3850	181	28	4710-01-162-7080	239	13
5340-01-162-3853	176	1	4720-01-162-7097	243	4
	177	2	4720-01-162-7098	242	14
	178	9		243	1
	180	19	2540-01-162-7110	231	10
	181	25	2510-01-162-7111	233	22
5340-01-162-3854	178	13	2510-01-162-7112	147	1
	179	1	2540-01-162-7113	218	5
5305-01-162-3961	134	14	2540-01-162-7114	216	1
	166	5	2540-01-162-7116	193	10
	167	12	2540-01-162-7117	182	7
2590-01-162-4352	226	1	2510-01-162-7119	133	21
2590-01-162-4353	227	2	2510-01-162-7120	133	21
2510-01-162-4407	233	2	2590-01-162-7130	227	16
2510-01-162-4408	233	12	2590-01-162-7139	183	17

CROSS-REFERENCE INDEXES

NATIONAL STOCK NUMBER INDEX

STOCK NUMBER	FIG	ITEM	STOCK NUMBER	FIG	ITEM
2590-01-162-7139	184	9	5340-01-163-0919	18	25
2510-01-162-7224	BULK	28	6140-01-163-1081	49	1
2590-01-162-7367	132	12	4720-01-163-1089	212	3
5305-01-162-7885	130	6		214	30
5305-01-162-7890	117	7	2510-01-163-1139	130	12
	162	3	2540-01-163-1140	243	2
	163	3	2540-01-163-1141	211	8
	168	26		214	8
5310-01-162-7912	166	14	5365-01-163-1142	221	14
	167	16		242	2
6625-01-162-8124	35	7		246	9
5305-01-162-8512	210	8	2540-01-163-1143	242	21
	252	5	2510-01-163-1146	109	1
	253	2	5365-01-163-1147	182	8
	253	18	2540-01-163-1175	246	1
5305-01-162-8514	158	8	2990-01-163-1179	217	6
5306-01-162-8525	42	25	2990-01-163-1180	218	5
	43	12	2990-01-163-1182	245	11
5330-01-162-8595	149	2	5995-01-163-1183	223	1
5340-01-162-8759	114	33	2590-01-163-1184	222	1
5340-01-162-8760	114	21	2590-01-163-1238	126	4
5365-01-162-8876	145	9	6150-01-163-1384	49	37
2540-01-162-8983	233	5	6150-01-163-1385	49	36
2530-01-162-8986	87	28	5340-01-163-1388	22	3
5306-01-162-9678	145	11	5340-01-163-1389	111	6
5305-01-162-9689	129	4	5340-01-163-1390	111	15
	207	5	5340-01-163-1401	92	7
5305-01-162-9695	45	8		93	6
	142	17		94	2
	145	23	5930-01-163-1439	35	13
5340-01-162-9777	14	33	5340-01-163-1973	58	4
5340-01-162-9781	14	28	5330-01-163-1992	34	10
5340-01-162-9782	43	13	9390-01-163-2028	136	27
5340-01-162-9844	133	18	5330-01-163-2055	232	8
5360-01-162-9935	88	26	5305-01-163-2423	250	18
4710-01-163-0594	238	9	5305-01-163-2438	152	12
2540-01-163-0765	240	10		201	4
2540-01-163-0766	233	22		202	4
2990-01-163-0771	215	9	5305-01-163-2439	168	18
2540-01-163-0772	188	19	5930-01-163-2583	179	4
3040-01-163-0797	96	4	2510-01-163-2681	141	7
2530-01-163-0798	96	6	2510-01-163-2709	136	9
2530-01-163-0799	96	10	2540-01-163-2719	136	14
2530-01-163-0800	KITS		5930-01-163-2779	184	14
2540-01-163-0801	247	15		192	3
2540-01-163-0834	193	9	5330-01-163-3150	242	29
5360-01-163-0885	130	9	5330-01-163-3151	246	25
5360-01-163-0886	99	61	5340-01-163-3294	231	17
2540-01-163-0894	194	5	2520-01-163-3494	213	6
5340-01-163-0917	130	10	2590-01-163-3529	243	3

CROSS-REFERENCE INDEXES

NATIONAL STOCK NUMBER INDEX

STOCK NUMBER	FIG	ITEM	STOCK NUMBER	FIG	ITEM
2530-01-163-3557	118	10	3040-01-163-7315	68	6
2990-01-163-3575	213	5	2520-01-163-7316	68	2
2540-01-163-3585	193	13	3040-01-163-7347	97	8
5340-01-163-4337	132	13	5340-01-163-7501	249	2
5355-01-163-4940	41	16	2590-01-163-7626	176	16
5360-01-163-5578	188	17		177	16
5360-01-163-5579	188	18	2590-01-163-7669	183	11
5360-01-163-5580	188	20		184	17
5330-01-163-5706	193	3	4720-01-163-7833	BULK	23
5305-01-163-5761	250	2	2540-01-163-7874	180	20
	250	21		181	24
5330-01-163-5850	234	11	2530-01-163-7878	93	5
5340-01-163-5902	17	31		93	8
5340-01-163-5908	130	8	2510-01-163-7879	180	16
5325-01-163-5973	201	1		181	7
5365-01-163-6195	115	34	2510-01-163-8014	181	10
5680-01-163-6347	138	3	2540-01-163-8017	169	2
5305-01-163-6466	43	14	4720-01-163-8039	18	20
	44	7	5340-01-163-8520	145	1
2510-01-163-7016	130	12	2540-01-163-8595	115	6
2540-01-163-7017	247	8	2590-01-163-8596	189	1
3040-01-163-7018	68	23	2540-01-163-8598	188	2
4730-01-163-7163	62	2	2540-01-163-8599	188	16
4730-01-163-7194	8	6	2540-01-163-8600	188	15
	15	10	2540-01-163-8623	176	12
	16	12		177	23
	17	13	2540-01-163-8624	177	14
	18	19	2540-01-163-8638	188	1
	106	2	5930-01-163-8851	184	12
2540-01-163-7225	245	9		192	6
2530-01-163-7227	88	6	5930-01-163-8924	184	13
2510-01-163-7228	109	3		192	5
2510-01-163-7229	141	7	5340-01-163-9400	17	22
2510-01-163-7231	145	8	2540-01-164-0032	225	12
5360-01-163-7234	90	17	2530-01-164-0039	87	28
	91	3	2540-01-164-0046	180	8
2540-01-163-7281	34	16		181	13
5930-01-163-7282	41	11	2540-01-164-0122	225	7
2520-01-163-7283	68	21	2590-01-164-0134	126	4
2520-01-163-7284	68	19	2590-01-164-0135	225	1
3040-01-163-7285	97	4	5340-01-164-0746	177	21
3040-01-163-7286	KITS		5340-01-164-0747	179	12
2590-01-163-7287	178	15	5340-01-164-0748	248	3
2540-01-163-7288	183	15	5340-01-164-0958	183	12
	184	10		184	18
2590-01-163-7290	185	4	5340-01-164-0974	179	2
	186	7	5340-01-164-1048	203	6
2540-01-163-7305	136	10	5340-01-164-1075	203	9
2510-01-163-7306	136	1	5340-01-164-1076	190	3
2520-01-163-7314	99	72	5340-01-164-1077	190	5

CROSS-REFERENCE INDEXES

NATIONAL STOCK NUMBER INDEX

STOCK NUMBER	FIG	ITEM	STOCK NUMBER	FIG	ITEM
5340-01-164-1078	185	13	5340-01-164-6473	214	14
	186	11	5340-01-164-6474	211	13
5340-01-164-1100	177	22		214	13
2510-01-164-1532	180	5	5340-01-164-6524	240	5
2540-01-164-1562	188	8	5340-01-164-6526	221	7
5305-01-164-1604	206	14	5340-01-164-6527	221	10
5330-01-164-1653	34	5	5340-01-164-6528	221	1
5340-01-164-1743	59	8	6105-01-164-6546	206	13
2540-01-164-1842	115	6	5340-01-164-6589	233	16
2540-01-164-1843	164	2	5340-01-164-6591	233	3
2540-01-164-1844	164	4	5340-01-164-6595	237	3
2540-01-164-1886	229	8	5340-01-164-7021	63	10
2540-01-164-1891	133	26	2590-01-164-7024	176	6
5360-01-164-1949	165	2		177	6
6220-01-164-2271	42	35	4730-01-164-7028	6	12
5305-01-164-2313	35	12	2510-01-164-7116	108	1
	132	17	2510-01-164-7117	108	6
	208	9	2510-01-164-7118	107	7
	211	9	2510-01-164-7119	107	1
	222	11	2510-01-164-7120	107	13
5310-01-164-2336	206	6	2540-01-164-7121	239	10
5310-01-164-2338	49	32	2540-01-164-7123	242	12
5325-01-164-2377	52	5	2540-01-164-7124	242	30
	227	19	2530-01-164-7126	88	6
5340-01-164-2397	232	11	2510-01-164-7127	109	7
5360-01-164-2404	145	19	2510-01-164-7128	109	2
5360-01-164-2405	145	19	2510-01-164-7152	136	18
6250-01-164-3266	183	8	2590-01-164-7177	17	33
	184	1	2990-01-164-7178	112	6
5340-01-164-3269	23	20	2540-01-164-7260	200	15
5365-01-164-4525	88	9	5330-01-164-7506	68	27
5680-01-164-4964	136	6	5330-01-164-7509	245	4
6220-01-164-5227	34	9	5325-01-164-7550	228	2
6220-01-164-5228	34	6	2590-01-164-7825	99	62
5315-01-164-5334	188	30	2520-01-164-7851	68	2
5315-01-164-5336	188	5	2590-01-164-7898	178	23
5310-01-164-5600	153	3	5340-01-164-8137	180	25
5330-01-164-5603	229	20		181	20
2520-01-164-6228	68	4		190	7
2540-01-164-6251	182	11	5340-01-164-8171	36	9
5305-01-164-6319	47	2	5330-01-164-8385	134	7
5305-01-164-6321	179	3	5325-01-164-8655	214	25
	187	16		226	13
	192	2	5340-01-164-8757	139	6
5340-01-164-6410	202	8		141	6
5340-01-164-6411	202	9	5340-01-164-8761	132	8
5340-01-164-6412	202	10	2520-01-164-9229	68	24
5325-01-164-6431	37	7	2540-01-164-9278	247	14
5340-01-164-6435	229	22	6680-01-164-9433	14	20
5340-01-164-6473	211	14	6150-01-165-0168	49	16

CROSS-REFERENCE INDEXES

NATIONAL STOCK NUMBER INDEX

STOCK NUMBER	FIG	ITEM	STOCK NUMBER	FIG	ITEM
5310-01-165-0464	42	15	5306-01-165-5583	165	11
2540-01-165-0466	242	27	5305-01-165-5591	213	4
9905-01-165-0541	176	17	5340-01-165-5617	246	34
	177	18	2520-01-165-5974	97	2
9905-01-165-0542	176	18	2540-01-165-5996	207	6
	177	17	2530-01-165-6005	101	9
9905-01-165-0544	178	7	2540-01-165-6145	200	15
5340-01-165-0564	142	4	5895-01-165-6792	35	9
5340-01-165-0602	189	7	2540-01-165-6793	189	11
5340-01-165-0657	143	7	7230-01-165-6795	193	8
5930-01-165-0732	208	7	5340-01-165-6797	237	4
2540-01-165-0813	247	5	9905-01-165-6901	180	17
2540-01-165-0895	166	10		181	27
5310-01-165-1327	68	9	5325-01-165-6975	233	23
5330-01-165-1358	89	31	2520-01-165-7885	68	11
5340-01-165-1494	247	6	2540-01-165-7931	188	6
2510-01-165-1495	107	9	2510-01-165-8101	68	28
5360-01-165-1574	68	3	2540-01-165-8177	179	8
5305-01-165-2260	96	5	5305-01-165-8612	198	2
	97	3	5340-01-165-8986	129	2
5340-01-165-2526	50	7	2530-01-165-9653	101	6
5325-01-165-2551	158	1	2530-01-165-9654	101	1
5310-01-165-3331	4	7	5340-01-166-0568	246	33
	5	18	2815-01-166-0621	4	11
	6	6	2510-01-166-1146	132	15
	8	4	2540-01-166-1370	170	1
	11	13	5340-01-166-1470	58	2
	58	1	5305-01-166-1471	178	21
5340-01-165-3417	45	6	5305-01-166-1473	187	13
5325-01-165-3475	249	13	5320-01-166-1477	193	14
5315-01-165-3536	68	5	5340-01-166-1534	8	1
5340-01-165-3717	205	3	5305-01-166-1610	180	27
5306-01-165-4286	140	1	5306-01-166-1665	193	4
5340-01-165-4351	147	2	2540-01-166-2009	225	10
5340-01-165-4353	115	7	2540-01-166-2010	225	8
5325-01-165-4372	231	13	5340-01-166-2011	176	14
5340-01-165-4379	229	18		177	20
5340-01-165-4429	247	3	5945-01-166-2012	187	8
5340-01-165-4543	242	24	2510-01-166-2015	179	14
5340-01-165-4544	155	4	4520-01-166-2133	244	2
6105-01-165-4561	206	8	4520-01-166-2134	244	5
6160-01-165-4637	48	6	5340-01-166-2152	215	3
6160-01-165-4638	48	2		217	3
5340-01-165-4705	14	1		218	9
	15	6	2530-01-166-3033	88	14
5340-01-165-4791	136	2	3040-01-166-4497	95	12
5340-01-165-4792	136	11	5340-01-166-5652	145	8
2510-01-165-4932	147	5	5340-01-166-5654	183	10
5306-01-165-5583	32	4		184	4
	164	11	5340-01-166-5861	162	4

TM9-2320-289-20P

CROSS-REFERENCE INDEXES

NATIONAL STOCK NUMBER INDEX

STOCK NUMBER	FIG	ITEM	STOCK NUMBER	FIG	ITEM
5340-01-166-5861	163	5	5120-01-170-0628	254	13
	169	5	5120-01-170-3279	254	8
2540-01-166-5913	189	4	5120-01-170-5473	254	20
3120-01-166-6724	133	23	5340-01-170-5530	134	2
	133	29	5330-01-170-6303	130	2
3020-01-166-6802	249	4	5120-01-170-6664	254	19
5306-01-166-8556	140	2	5310-01-170-8765	229	16
5340-01-167-0136	133	26		230	2
5325-01-167-0510	200	8	5310-01-170-9100	24	1
5680-01-167-1068	136	15		49	29
7230-01-167-2075	180	4		128	4
	181	16		240	3
2540-01-167-2985	169	1	5940-01-171-3195	187	7
5305-01-167-5498	68	7	5306-01-171-8076	60	7
5330-01-167-6335	229	5	5360-01-171-8248	165	4
	231	27	5935-01-171-8273	37	14
2930-01-167-7250	228	7	6220-01-171-9557	176	8
6695-01-167-8108	34	8		177	8
5330-01-167-8123	147	3	4710-01-172-0471	91	2
5305-01-167-8334	68	22	5310-01-172-1591	96	18
	229	17	5340-01-172-1942	193	15
5310-01-167-8344	154	2	5340-01-172-2087	14	4
	155	6		15	5
5325-01-167-8372	199	12	2510-01-172-3022	131	2
4720-01-167-9137	245	2	6220-01-172-5300	176	7
5340-01-167-9694	62	3		177	7
5340-01-168-0939	246	24	4730-01-172-6683	5	15
4030-01-168-1282	178	12	2530-01-173-1248	88	20
5340-01-168-1501	41	19	2540-01-173-1249	188	27
5330-01-168-1535	249	9	4820-01-173-1250	188	3
5306-01-168-4481	24	2	2520-01-173-1362	70	7
	42	10		72	7
	48	3	5945-01-173-7760	187	2
	49	31	5365-01-174-8657	76	4
	172	11	6680-01-175-0565	13	3
	225	9	5120-01-178-6342	254	17
	229	21	5330-01-178-7351	136	3
	232	16	2510-01-178-8867	146	11
	234	9	5120-01-179-1034	254	10
	245	7	5120-01-179-1318	254	3
	246	18	4910-01-179-2516	254	15
5325-01-168-5677	227	18	4910-01-179-2517	254	12
2530-01-168-6369	89	32	4910-01-179-2518	254	11
5340-01-168-6372	118	9	4820-01-179-4869	254	14
	119	8	4910-01-179-6340	254	9
5310-01-169-2849	153	1	4910-01-179-6341	254	5
2510-01-169-3785	180	7	5120-01-180-0558	254	2
	181	11	2990-01-180-2988	22	21
5120-01-169-4878	254	6	4910-01-180-6155	254	7
3120-01-169-6440	68	10	6240-01-180-9022	42	34

CROSS-REFERENCE INDEXES

NATIONAL STOCK NUMBER INDEX

STOCK NUMBER	FIG	ITEM	STOCK NUMBER	FIG	ITEM
4910-01-181-1959	254	16	2590-01-191-4357	210	36
5330-01-181-2454	136	12	5340-01-191-4827	253	8
5360-01-181-2482	14	5	2540-01-191-6510	57	8
	15	8	2590-01-191-6511	173	8
2990-01-181-6725	112	32	2540-01-191-6512	198	12
4720-01-182-3457	BULK	15	2540-01-191-6536	182	13
5330-01-182-4121	144	11	2540-01-191-6538	194	7
2590-01-182-4455	116	3	2540-01-191-6539	188	9
2530-01-183-8860	87	6	2540-01-191-6541	210	34
4720-01-184-0432	8	14	2920-01-191-6635	28	11
5310-01-184-5418	117	3	2510-01-191-6638	186	9
5310-01-184-5866	136	7	2540-01-191-8439	117	1
	136	16	2540-01-191-8440	167	8
5930-01-184-6370	242	17	2540-01-191-8441	167	9
5360-01-185-0341	148	1	2920-01-191-8442	30	5
5330-01-185-4676	88	11	2540-01-191-8443	197	5
5306-01-185-7048	25	6	2540-01-191-8444	197	6
5306-01-185-7049	104	12	2540-01-191-8445	197	11
5306-01-185-7050	28	9	2540-01-191-8446	197	17
4140-01-186-9753	252	9	2510-01-191-8447	158	6
5360-01-187-0301	99	65	2540-01-191-8462	182	16
5310-01-187-7610	112	23	4720-01-191-8463	210	43
5340-01-187-8673	134	17	2540-01-191-8467	247	13
8040-01-188-2953	33	1	2540-01-191-8549	195	2
5920-01-188-6294	41	32	2540-01-191-8668	162	1
	41	34	2590-01-191-9276	210	39
	187	11	2520-01-191-9518	71	1
4140-01-188-6977	210	42	2540-01-191-9564	196	9
6105-01-188-7154	210	40	5975-01-191-9851	BULK	5
2520-01-189-0596	70	1	2520-01-192-1257	205	5
	71	1	4720-01-192-1631	BULK	11
5910-01-189-3011	252	7	6130-01-192-1643	33	4
	253	16		54	10
6250-01-189-4981	51	3		55	3
5910-01-189-5109	56	2	2520-01-192-1793	71	10
5910-01-189-5110	54	3		73	9
5910-01-189-5152	36	5	2540-01-192-1823	20	4
5910-01-189-5153	54	16	2520-01-192-1919	90	21
6250-01-189-6926	51	5	2920-01-192-3020	32	1
5925-01-190-1211	187	5	4720-01-192-3510	210	13
6140-01-190-2516	48	16	2540-01-192-3572	116	7
6140-01-190-2517	48	8	2540-01-192-3573	197	24
5910-01-190-4600	47	4	2540-01-192-3574	197	23
6230-01-191-3856	191	4	2540-01-192-3575	197	22
2510-01-191-4259	210	9	2540-01-192-3576	196	8
2540-01-191-4327	210	19	2520-01-192-4314	71	5
2540-01-191-4331	210	41		73	5
2510-01-191-4334	186	8	5995-01-192-4374	187	4
2510-01-191-4335	185	15	2920-01-192-4375	39	1
2510-01-191-4336	185	14	2920-01-192-4376	39	9

CROSS-REFERENCE INDEXES

NATIONAL STOCK NUMBER INDEX

STOCK NUMBER	FIG	ITEM	STOCK NUMBER	FIG	ITEM
4730-01-192-4434	210	22	3120-01-194-0754	196	2
2540-01-192-4479	196	12	5315-01-194-0819	144	7
2990-01-192-4576	210	25	4730-01-194-2002	25	5
2990-01-192-4597	210	21	5340-01-194-3188	137	5
6685-01-192-4834	46	1	2540-01-194-3323	210	11
2590-01-192-5911	210	37		242	11
2815-01-192-5962	6	5		246	21
4520-01-192-6005	210	23	5330-01-194-4751	250	5
4520-01-192-6073	210	15	5330-01-194-4752	250	10
4710-01-192-7967	6	8	5330-01-194-4753	250	20
2520-01-192-7979	69	11	5330-01-194-4754	210	24
5945-01-192-7985	32	3	5306-01-194-4977	151	1
2520-01-192-8282	64	10		152	1
4720-01-192-8533	18	22	5365-01-194-5074	140	5
5945-01-192-8653	40	5	5340-01-194-5805	180	10
5330-01-192-8904	210	33		181	8
5330-01-192-8905	210	27	4710-01-194-6590	248	7
5330-01-192-8906	210	7	6220-01-194-6591	248	8
5330-01-192-9335	210	2	4710-01-194-6775	67	5
2520-01-192-9729	69	16	2540-01-194-6875	39	3
2990-01-192-9730	6	13	5310-01-194-7081	69	14
2510-01-192-9752	193	1	5640-01-194-7193	253	7
	193	5	5310-01-194-9208	211	1
2540-01-192-9754	144	1		214	1
2530-01-192-9778	89	34	5310-01-194-9217	115	41
4720-01-192-9823	14	41	5310-01-194-9220	69	4
5330-01-193-0226	253	4	5310-01-194-9233	69	3
5330-01-193-0227	250	9	5310-01-194-9234	144	4
5365-01-193-0458	32	11	5330-01-195-1564	250	15
5330-01-193-1840	134	7	5640-01-195-4633	250	17
2590-01-193-3443	116	5	5640-01-195-4634	250	8
2540-01-193-3623	180	22	5640-01-195-4635	250	16
	181	22	5640-01-195-4636	250	14
5680-01-193-5078	180	26	5330-01-195-4880	206	9
	181	18	5365-01-195-4948	140	5
5310-01-193-6927	211	2	5310-01-195-5088	69	5
	214	2	5320-01-195-5106	35	4
5360-01-193-7130	57	6	5305-01-195-5807	49	10
5905-01-193-7212	39	4	5365-01-195-5934	250	4
2520-01-193-7870	69	7	4720-01-195-7603	6	7
2540-01-193-7884	158	2	5306-01-195-7915	112	5
2540-01-193-7895	160	3	5640-01-195-9786	250	11
2540-01-193-7896	160	1	2540-01-196-1622	41	13
5340-01-193-9565	188	31	5310-01-196-5587	12	1
4730-01-194-0126	10	6	5340-01-196-6463	179	13
2510-01-194-0206	128	1	5315-01-196-6464	193	11
2540-01-194-0261	133	12	5640-01-196-7002	250	13
2520-01-194-0278	69	10	5640-01-196-7003	250	12
4720-01-194-0336	6	3	6220-01-197-0486	191	2
5305-01-194-0614	100	7	5360-01-197-0870	164	6

CROSS-REFERENCE INDEXES

NATIONAL STOCK NUMBER INDEX

STOCK NUMBER	FIG	ITEM	STOCK NUMBER	FIG	ITEM
5330-01-197-0897	250	6	5325-01-199-3461	47	3
5340-01-197-1199	18	8		221	15
5340-01-197-1259	28	5		242	1
5320-01-197-1394	116	6	5340-01-199-4993	210	3
5305-01-197-1475	117	4	2510-01-200-1021	158	6
5315-01-197-1482	188	28	2540-01-200-3167	114	29
5315-01-197-1483	188	21	5320-01-200-4017	176	15
5306-01-197-1492	54	1		177	19
5355-01-197-1501	168	10		179	15
5340-01-197-1550	188	25		180	21
5340-01-197-1585	248	9		181	23
5365-01-197-2286	161	9		183	7
5305-01-197-2320	207	4		184	5
	252	15		185	6
5305-01-197-2536	40	3		186	2
5306-01-197-3089	44	3		189	10
	52	4		190	2
	173	5		192	8
	229	9		197	8
5305-01-197-3112	20	8		197	15
5355-01-197-3172	69	8		197	20
5340-01-197-3244	140	6		210	18
5305-01-197-3287	32	2	2910-01-200-4338	10	9
	208	8	5340-01-200-5843	247	2
	242	16	5305-01-200-7735	180	6
	244	1		181	12
5305-01-197-3290	152	4	5340-01-200-8473	209	3
5340-01-197-3433	6	10	2520-01-201-2501	82	1
5340-01-197-3434	5	16	6250-01-201-3300	50	6
5325-01-197-3540	69	15	5305-01-201-3334	183	16
6220-01-197-3938	248	6		184	11
5340-01-197-4600	117	2	5305-01-201-3788	187	10
5310-01-197-5499	48	13	2520-01-201-4096	96	2
	157	1	5340-01-201-7954	172	8
5305-01-197-6351	196	14	5320-01-201-9453	189	6
5305-01-197-6576	197	4	5330-01-201-9681	253	12
5310-01-197-6621	196	17	5330-01-201-9682	252	13
	233	18	5340-01-202-2517	71	4
5365-01-197-8165	97	7		73	4
4710-01-198-2701	6	9	5340-01-202-2622	18	9
5340-01-198-3434	202	11	5310-01-202-2695	151	5
5305-01-198-4154	69	6	5930-01-202-3573	66	2
5365-01-198-5516	144	5	4730-01-202-8523	69	2
5325-01-198-8040	124	3	5305-01-203-2289	30	1
5325-01-198-8239	167	10	2990-01-203-2426	22	12
5340-01-198-8591	110	1	5360-01-203-6365	210	6
	110	3	5306-01-203-9082	200	13
5340-01-199-2312	21	6	5340-01-204-4268	21	7
	22	10		22	11
5325-01-199-3461	37	11	5330-01-204-4312	253	17

CROSS-REFERENCE INDEXES

NATIONAL STOCK NUMBER INDEX

STOCK NUMBER	FIG	ITEM	STOCK NUMBER	FIG	ITEM
2540-01-205-2509	247	7	6220-01-216-5288	227	9
2540-01-205-2510	247	24	6220-01-216-5289	227	6
2540-01-205-2511	247	22	6140-01-216-7923	225	6
2540-01-205-2512	247	9	5340-01-217-2168	231	3
5310-01-205-2536	96	11	5340-01-217-2278	231	5
5310-01-205-2537	96	11	5310-01-217-5205	226	4
5325-01-205-2545	134	10		227	11
6685-01-205-3676	19	2		246	13
5330-01-205-5056	252	12	2940-01-217-8089	4	1
5360-01-205-8888	130	11	5330-01-218-0862	5	1
5340-01-206-2995	133	27		219	3
5340-01-206-2996	133	27	5360-01-218-1610	164	3
5360-01-206-6616	249	6	5306-01-218-3119	220	19
5330-01-207-9421	146	2	5305-01-218-3139	226	3
5930-01-208-6292	18	15	5340-01-218-5823	234	7
4820-01-209-0473	18	14	4730-01-218-6690	220	14
5365-01-209-6943	96	12	4730-01-218-6691	220	9
5315-01-209-7063	188	14	2540-01-218-6833	144	6
2910-01-210-1322	18	4	2540-01-218-8099	237	6
2910-01-210-1323	18	7	5305-01-219-5399	242	28
2520-01-210-1382	74	1		246	38
6140-01-210-1964	48	11	5120-01-219-6753	254	19
5340-01-210-8824	158	10	5340-01-219-7272	217	4
5305-01-210-9425	134	12	5340-01-219-7275	234	4
5310-01-211-1648	206	7	5365-01-219-7285	222	9
5305-01-211-3031	18	12	2590-01-219-7808	117	5
5305-01-211-3032	18	11	5330-01-220-3117	245	5
5340-01-211-3086	18	6	5330-01-220-6153	222	13
5310-01-211-3811	235	7	5340-01-221-0264	238	11
2540-01-211-4621	144	3	6620-01-221-1942	220	12
2520-01-211-6755	73	1	2510-01-221-2094	BULK	9
5305-01-211-7464	10	11	5365-01-221-9717	96	9
3120-01-211-7528	123	6	5340-01-221-9972	219	2
2920-01-212-4771	18	13	2530-01-222-8068	91	9
2510-01-212-5819	128	6	6140-01-223-9144	49	14
5340-01-212-6716	234	6	5935-01-223-9420	37	13
5340-01-212-6717	234	6	2510-01-224-8839	143	6
2590-01-212-7639	51	6	2510-01-225-0997	119	9
2520-01-213-1680	60	6	2510-01-225-0998	145	17
5340-01-213-6934	62	4	2510-01-225-0999	145	13
5330-01-213-9811	252	14	2510-01-225-1004	111	41
5330-01-213-9966	18	3	2510-01-225-1006	142	12
2540-01-214-2634	233	14	2540-01-225-1023	142	16
2540-01-214-2635	233	14	2530-01-225-1024	91	8
5365-01-214-4927	123	8	2990-01-225-1028	21	11
4730-01-216-0021	246	20	2990-01-225-1029	21	1
2510-01-216-0039	183	1	2520-01-225-1033	99	72
	184	8	2990-01-225-1052	21	9
2540-01-216-3188	231	12	2910-01-225-1068	20	6
2530-01-216-4554	96	16	2530-01-225-2236	91	4

CROSS-REFERENCE INDEXES

NATIONAL STOCK NUMBER INDEX

STOCK NUMBER	FIG	ITEM	STOCK NUMBER	FIG	ITEM
5995-01-225-2534	38	18	5330-01-244-2277	199	10
6680-01-225-4432	33	5	5340-01-244-7925	13	11
6680-01-225-4475	249	3	5360-01-245-0405	246	3
2510-01-225-5865	111	5	2510-01-246-4236	233	8
5430-01-225-8971	5	9	2510-01-246-4237	231	16
5365-01-226-2342	225	3	5305-01-246-5770	198	7
5306-01-227-1454	225	13	5306-01-246-7459	56	10
4730-01-227-1929	5	23		143	1
5306-01-227-9085	32	9		148	3
5310-01-228-1405	101	2	2590-01-247-3286	158	10
	101	7	4720-01-247-4680	221	21
5340-01-228-1659	38	3	2540-01-248-2477	167	13
5320-01-229-8183	38	16	6220-01-248-6269	42	1
5325-01-230-1844	202	2	5310-01-249-4210	114	9
5306-01-230-3354	4	16		115	18
	38	14	2530-01-249-5401	77	1
6680-01-230-5684	249	1	2510-01-249-6434	138	2
5305-01-230-9846	136	28	3120-01-250-0583	124	6
5340-01-231-0925	74	5	5310-01-250-3301	32	10
5305-01-231-1297	136	22	2530-01-250-6472	89	36
5305-01-231-1298	54	6	5310-01-250-7679	29	6
	134	15		30	10
2990-01-231-2938	22	22		104	2
5320-01-231-3889	38	17		249	12
5305-01-231-7384	158	9		251	1
3120-01-232-6781	99	74	2990-01-250-8612	245	6
5340-01-232-8179	95	5	5355-01-251-0633	57	7
4710-01-232-8478	214	19	5315-01-251-1701	102	2
5340-01-234-1465	5	7	2540-01-251-1714	166	7
6150-01-234-3253	224	1	2540-01-251-1715	166	8
2590-01-234-6468	152	2	2510-01-251-5487	138	2
5355-01-235-6616	99	71	5340-01-253-2102	173	7
5330-01-236-1724	18	5	5306-01-253-7073	6	1
5330-01-237-7512	146	1	6105-01-254-9496	244	4
5340-01-238-5923	152	11	4730-01-255-2976	91	11
5340-01-238-5924	152	5	2990-01-257-1569	48	1
2520-01-239-3800	72	1	3030-01-258-5125	28	10
5305-01-239-9265	175	7	2510-01-259-5587	158	4
2540-01-241-4238	152	3	5307-01-259-7656	228	4
2590-01-242-1050	152	3	2930-01-264-3480	23	15
5305-01-242-1148	221	18	5310-01-264-5903	229	12
	242	7		231	14
	246	16		232	9
6220-01-242-7557	45	9	5306-01-266-2419	215	4
2590-01-242-8068	232	17		218	6
5310-01-242-8561	201	3		218	10
	202	1	5305-01-266-9194	158	3
5945-01-243-1702	47	6	2540-01-267-1360	114	10
2540-01-243-4934	199	9		115	24
5310-01-244-2259	97	11	4720-01-267-2052	BULK	26

CROSS-REFERENCE INDEXES

NATIONAL STOCK NUMBER INDEX

STOCK NUMBER	FIG	ITEM	STOCK NUMBER	FIG	ITEM
5310-01-267-3043	131	1	2640-01-323-2632	96	29
3040-01-267-4283	114	2	5306-01-323-5544	74	6
	115	11	5330-01-323-5567	111	24
5310-01-267-6293	114	5	2590-01-323-5857	124	7
	115	14	2540-01-323-6049	200	7
5340-01-267-6296	114	4	2540-01-323-6050	200	7
	115	13	5340-01-323-9727	86	10
2540-01-268-7202	244	3	2520-01-324-4895	74	1
6220-01-268-8795	227	4	2590-01-324-5042	74	5
5310-01-268-8948	208	3	5340-01-324-6756	111	23
5340-01-268-9064	17	10	5340-01-324-9553	111	23
	90	4	2510-01-325-9069	124	9
	214	17	2530-01-325-9112	96	3
6220-01-269-0465	227	7	2510-01-326-0762	KITS	
5340-01-269-1361	20	12	2530-01-326-1462	96	23
5305-01-269-4329	34	2	5365-01-326-4346	96	26
	206	3	6220-01-327-1025	44	6
5307-01-269-4336	1	3	6220-01-327-3252	44	4
	25	12	2520-01-328-4898	74	1
5365-01-269-8614	178	6	2520-01-330-3249	83	9
5365-01-270-1977	99	66	5330-01-331-7230	97	6
5305-01-270-3030	99	68	5340-01-335-9359	86	8
5340-01-270-7423	10	2	5340-01-335-9360	91	19
5310-01-271-1793	187	6	3120-01-338-6380	143	2
6210-01-271-6871	34	15			
5305-01-273-4486	6	11			
	132	14			
6220-01-276-0635	175	8			
5355-01-280-2975	137	10			
2990-01-287-2158	221	23			
2530-01-287-3980	99	67			
5340-01-293-1200	237	1			
2640-01-302-1388	96	29			
6220-01-306-4265	44	6			
5340-01-307-2247	178	10			
5340-01-307-2248	178	11			
5340-01-307-2249	176	22			
	177	25			
5340-01-307-2250	176	21			
	177	24			
5340-01-307-2251	176	20			
	177	13			
5340-01-307-2252	176	19			
	177	12			
5340-01-307-2253	180	29			
	181	29			
5340-01-307-2254	180	30			
	181	30			
6350-01-321-7005	56	13			
4930-01-323-0998	254	18			

CROSS-REFERENCE INDEXES

PART NUMBER INDEX

CAGEC	PART NUMBER	STOCK NUMBER	FIG	ITEM
79846	ABA64LBA	5320-01-231-3889	38	17
72794	AJW7-70	5325-00-337-6636	225	2
88044	AN365-1024A	5310-00-208-1918	193	6
			246	12
70040	A644C	2940-01-155-3190	12	4
96152	A82-1	5315-00-839-2325	246	6
82240	B-1900-334	5340-00-685-5899	246	37
73992	B-84	4730-01-218-6691	220	9
73992	B-85	4730-01-218-6690	220	14
00613	C-5139-2	5325-01-199-3461	37	11
			47	3
			221	15
			242	1
16632	CHE2013-0001	4720-01-167-9137	245	2
16632	CHE2015-0001	4720-01-162-7098	242	14
			243	1
16632	CHE2015-0002	4720-01-162-7097	243	4
16632	CHE2016-0002	5330-01-164-7509	245	4
16632	CHE2017	5330-01-163-3150	242	29
16632	CHE2018	5330-01-163-3151	246	25
16632	CHE2023	5330-01-220-3117	245	5
5A910	DC8211	5330-01-037-0663	42	5
5A910	DC8218	6220-01-107-2613	42	2
34904	DC8226	5330-01-076-6172	42	3
5A910	DC8228	5310-01-076-6196	42	6
80063	DL-SC-B-691368	5820-01-026-0983	172	4
72210	D23980-J	2530-01-165-9654	101	1
46522	D55395-G1	2990-01-287-2158	221	23
70040	FC106	2940-01-217-8089	4	1
11862	FLW-12		49	2
08805	F48T12/CW/WM	6240-01-089-6149	178	20
81240	GM118749	4730-00-142-2177	214	12
			221	16
			242	4
			246	14
81348	GP2A/LT235/85R16 /E/LTAW	2610-01-148-1635	98	1
78385	G704410-1	5930-00-234-1390	222	12
60038	HM807010	3110-00-227-4667	85	9
60038	HM807040	3110-00-606-9576	85	10
60038	HM88542	3110-00-580-3708	85	6
08806	H6054	6240-01-180-9022	42	34
89749	IF316	5315-00-816-1794	68	17
			69	12
			100	16
25341	J-21757-03	4910-01-179-6341	254	5
25341	J-2222-C	5120-01-180-0558	254	2
25341	J-23445-A	5120-01-169-4878	254	6
25341	J-23653-C	4910-01-180-6155	254	7
25341	J-23690	5120-01-170-3279	254	8
25341	J-24187	4910-01-179-6340	254	9

CROSS-REFERENCE INDEXES

PART NUMBER INDEX

CAGEC	PART NUMBER	STOCK NUMBER	FIG	ITEM
25341	J-24426	5120-01-179-1034	254	10
25341	J-24595-C	4910-01-179-2518	254	11
25341	J-25034-B	4910-01-181-1959	254	16
25341	J-26878-A	5120-01-170-0628	254	13
25341	J-29713	4910-01-179-2516	254	15
33287	J-29843	5120-01-178-6342	254	17
25341	J-33043	4820-01-179-4869	254	14
25341	J-33124	5120-01-170-5473	254	20
25341	J-34616	5120-01-170-6664	254	19
25341	J-6632-01	5120-01-179-1318	254	3
25341	J-6893-D	5120-01-219-6753	254	19
33287	J-8092	5120-00-677-2259	254	4
33627	J25512-2	4930-01-323-0998	254	18
43334	LM104949LM104911	3110-01-027-4475	96	17
43334	LM501349-LM501310	3110-00-690-8923	97	22
81640	L30200R	6210-00-438-4745	241	7
81349	MILS20166		BULK	2
81349	MILT16343TYPE1		BULK	35
96906	MS15001-1	4730-00-050-4203	114	3
			115	12
96906	MS16562-147	5315-00-057-5541	188	22
96906	MS16562-35	5315-00-814-3530	189	8
96906	MS16562-50	5315-00-814-3531	188	29
96906	MS16624-1024	5365-00-720-8064	144	10
96906	MS16624-1125	5365-00-721-6876	97	5
			97	9
96906	MS16624-1131	5365-00-803-7317	96	7
96906	MS16633-1015	5365-00-200-7377	168	22
96906	MS16633-1021	5365-00-900-0982	144	8
96906	MS16633-1031	5365-00-682-1762	87	13
			88	15
96906	MS17829-5C	5310-00-245-3424	17	32
			86	13
96906	MS18029-13L-5		36	2
			38	9
96906	MS18029-13S-3		36	15
96906	MS18029-13S-8	5940-00-926-8034	BULK	6
96906	MS18029-24	5940-00-890-2831	36	1
			38	10
96906	MS18029-4S-8	5940-00-405-8976	BULK	7
96906	MS18154-58	5305-00-115-9526	18	17
			22	4
96906	MS18154-96	5305-00-182-9584	95	6
96906	MS20600-B4W3	5320-00-582-3521	176	2
			177	1
			178	8
			180	18
			181	26
96906	MS20600-B4W4	5320-00-845-9501	178	14
			180	3

CROSS-REFERENCE INDEXES

PART NUMBER INDEX

CAGEC	PART NUMBER	STOCK NUMBER	FIG	ITEM
96906	MS20600-B4W4	5320-00-845-9501	181	15
			185	17
			192	9
			246	23
96906	MS20600-B6W10	5320-00-822-6257	183	9
			184	2
96906	MS20600-B6W5	5320-00-061-9662	180	2
			181	14
96906	MS20600B6W4	5320-00-616-4346	176	13
			177	15
			178	1
			180	31
			181	31
			183	3
			184	3
			185	16
			186	10
			192	4
			210	38
96906	MS20600MP6W10	5320-00-660-0821	180	9
			181	9
96906	MS20601-B6W6	5320-00-061-9648	185	2
			186	6
			189	3
96906	MS20613-4P4	5320-00-994-7076	48	9
96906	MS21141-U0604	5320-01-200-4017	176	15
			177	19
			179	15
			180	21
			181	23
			183	7
			184	5
			185	6
			186	2
			189	10
			190	2
			192	8
			197	8
			197	15
			197	20
			210	18
96906	MS21141-U0607	5320-01-201-9453	189	6
96906	MS21207-10-10	5305-00-057-9608	193	12
96906	MS21318-47	5305-00-253-5626	114	16
			115	23
96906	MS21333-110	5340-00-057-3034	75	9
			212	2
			214	21
			221	22
			242	8
96906	MS21333-111	5340-00-057-3037	16	2

CROSS-REFERENCE INDEXES

PART NUMBER INDEX

CAGEC	PART NUMBER	STOCK NUMBER	FIG	ITEM
96906	MS21333-111	5340-00-057-3037	17	5
			17	6
96906	MS21333-112	5340-00-057-3043	75	2
			80	7
			81	3
			226	2
			227	10
96906	MS21333-114	5340-00-057-3052	23	10
			226	9
96906	MS21333-116	5340-00-764-7052	37	10
96906	MS21333-123	5340-00-989-1771	226	8
			227	15
96906	MS21333-128	5340-00-702-2848	238	10
			239	3
			239	3
96906	MS21333-45	5340-00-881-5303	8	11
			17	16
			91	21
96906	MS21333-46	5340-00-282-7539	214	23
96906	MS21333-48	5340-00-486-1765	75	4
96906	MS21333-62	5340-00-282-7509	222	15
96906	MS21333-78	5340-00-958-8457	238	3
96906	MS21333-98	5340-00-809-1490	15	17
			16	11
			91	21
96906	MS24585-1276	5360-01-245-0405	246	3
96906	MS24627-67	5305-00-052-7472	194	6
96906	MS24662-153	5320-00-982-3815	180	24
			181	19
			190	6
			193	7
96906	MS24662-155	5320-00-828-1284	183	13
			184	15
96906	MS24665-134	5315-00-839-5820	188	4
96906	MS24665-283	5315-00-842-3044	68	13
			247	18
96906	MS24665-357	5315-00-298-1481	100	10
96906	MS24665-425	5315-00-013-7238	101	5
96906	MS24665-446	5315-00-899-4119	210	35
96906	MS24665-497	5315-00-013-7258	113	4
			114	26
			115	32
96906	MS24665-516	5315-00-243-1170	245	8
96906	MS24665-628	5315-00-846-0126	114	7
			115	16
96906	MS25043-32DA	5935-01-223-9420	37	13
96906	MS25244-P-20	5925-01-067-2926	241	3
96906	MS25307-312	5930-00-978-8805	241	5
96906	MS25331-4-313S	6210-00-688-5088	241	8
96906	MS27183-10	5310-00-809-4058	32	7
			49	17

CROSS-REFERENCE INDEXES

PART NUMBER INDEX

CAGEC	PART NUMBER	STOCK NUMBER	FIG	ITEM
96906	MS27183-10	5310-00-809-4058	51	11
			222	4
			228	6
			242	15
			246	2
			246	27
96906	MS27183-11	5310-00-809-3078	86	20
			182	18
96906	MS27183-12	5310-00-081-4219	14	32
			17	35
			68	14
			196	5
			215	1
			218	7
			218	7
			235	5
			238	5
			238	5
			239	4
			239	4
96906	MS27183-13	5310-00-087-7493	180	11
			181	5
			188	26
96906	MS27183-14	5310-00-080-6004	63	8
			64	11
			69	13
			115	28
			118	1
			119	1
			197	1
			220	18
			231	7
			231	19
			232	3
96906	MS27183-15	5310-00-809-4061	13	6
			14	38
			115	36
			188	10
96906	MS27183-16	5310-00-809-4085	21	16
			22	26
			28	7
			29	7
			111	3
			118	6
			145	18
			234	16
			235	15
96906	MS27183-17	5310-00-809-5997	182	9
			234	17
			235	21
96906	MS27183-18	5310-00-809-5998	107	5

PART NUMBER INDEX

CAGEC	PART NUMBER	STOCK NUMBER	FIG	ITEM
96906	MS27183-18	5310-00-809-5998	108	5
			109	10
			114	18
			115	38
			117	8
			121	2
			140	3
96906	MS27183-19	5310-00-809-3079	107	12
			114	22
			145	20
96906	MS27183-20	5310-00-068-5285	100	21
96906	MS27183-42	5310-00-014-5850	210	29
			241	14
96906	MS27183-6	5310-00-082-1404	38	2
96906	MS27183-8	5310-00-809-8546	221	17
			242	5
			246	15
96906	MS27183-9	5310-00-823-8804	49	5
			182	3
			182	14
96906	MS27212-4-3		36	13
96906	MS27212-4-5		36	8
			38	4
96906	MS27212-4-8	5940-00-950-7783	BULK	34
96906	MS29513-125	5330-00-265-1089	210	31
96906	MS3452W18-11P	5935-01-154-6264	241	10
96906	MS35058-22	5930-00-655-1514	241	4
96906	MS35206-226	5305-00-984-4983	227	8
96906	MS35206-243	5305-00-984-6191	178	18
96906	MS35206-245	5305-00-984-6193	56	9
			227	1
96906	MS35206-247	5305-00-984-6195	210	14
96906	MS35206-263	5305-00-984-6210	241	20
96906	MS35206-267	5305-00-984-6214	37	12
96906	MS35333-41	5310-00-167-0721	40	6
96906	MS35333-70	5310-00-550-3715	241	12
96906	MS35335-32	5310-00-596-7691	252	6
			253	6
96906	MS35335-33	5310-00-209-0786	37	4
			39	10
			44	2
			45	2
			51	2
			52	3
			54	22
			172	12
			252	4
96906	MS35335-34	5310-00-514-6674	22	15
			36	4
			38	7
			49	9

CROSS-REFERENCE INDEXES

PART NUMBER INDEX

CAGEC	PART NUMBER	STOCK NUMBER	FIG	ITEM
96906	MS35335-34	5310-00-514-6674	53	3
			198	3
96906	MS35335-36	5310-00-550-3503	49	12
			54	21
96906	MS35338-139	5310-00-933-8121	172	2
96906	MS35338-43	5310-00-045-3296	179	10
			241	18
96906	MS35338-44	5310-00-582-5965	5	13
			17	18
			37	9
			40	4
			148	6
			221	3
			226	10
			240	8
			250	3
			250	22
96906	MS35338-45	5310-00-407-9566	14	26
			17	21
			21	3
			22	8
			55	8
			70	15
			71	15
			100	3
			176	10
			177	10
			203	7
			221	8
			242	23
96906	MS35338-46	5310-00-637-9541	18	18
			22	5
			41	21
			42	8
			49	26
			100	6
			111	21
			115	27
			118	4
			119	4
			121	6
			122	4
			124	5
			180	14
			181	3
			188	23
			250	19
96906	MS35338-47	5310-00-209-0965	188	12
96906	MS35338-48	5310-00-584-5272	100	19
96906	MS35338-49	5310-00-167-0680	121	9
			122	8

CROSS-REFERENCE INDEXES

PART NUMBER INDEX

CAGEC	PART NUMBER	STOCK NUMBER	FIG	ITEM
96906	MS35338-52	5310-00-754-2005	253	15
96906	MS35340-45	5310-00-959-4679	86	5
			91	6
			106	12
			202	5
			238	2
			238	2
			239	2
			239	2
			245	13
96906	MS35340-46	5310-00-959-4675	45	4
			112	22
96906	MS35340-47	5310-00-655-9370	109	5
96906	MS35340-48	5310-00-834-7606	87	3
			108	4
			109	9
			114	28
			115	3
			118	8
			119	7
			120	2
			147	9
			153	4
			168	17
			182	6
96906	MS35340-49	5310-00-933-8123	121	3
96906	MS35340-50	5310-00-045-5001	122	2
96906	MS35340-51	5310-00-052-6454	87	2
96906	MS35425-72	5310-01-077-6817	154	3
			155	2
96906	MS35478-1073	6240-00-617-0991	42	4
96906	MS35489-103	5325-00-279-1248	214	26
96906	MS35489-11	5325-00-291-9366	225	14
96906	MS35489-121	5325-00-807-0580	222	5
			223	3
96906	MS35489-135	5325-00-263-6648	250	7
96906	MS35489-5	5325-00-174-5314	240	1
96906	MS35489-6	5325-00-263-6632	241	9
96906	MS35492-54	5305-00-533-5542	231	21
			232	18
			235	2
96906	MS35492-57	5305-00-901-3110	234	3
96906	MS35492-82	5305-00-901-3144	235	17
96906	MS35493-37	5305-00-935-7506	231	29
96906	MS35493-76	5305-00-014-9926	233	9
96906	MS35494-83	5305-00-245-4144	235	11
96906	MS35649-202	5310-00-934-9758	179	9
			241	17
96906	MS35649-205	5310-00-934-9764	40	2
96906	MS35649-244	5310-00-934-9748	241	13
96906	MS35649-262	5310-00-934-9747	36	7

CROSS-REFERENCE INDEXES

CAGEC	PART NUMBER	PART NUMBER INDEX STOCK NUMBER	FIG	ITEM
96906	MS35649-262	5310-00-934-9747	38	5
96906	MS35650-3314	5310-00-252-8748	36	3
			38	8
96906	MS35690-824	5310-00-010-3028	100	18
96906	MS35691-1	5310-00-851-2674	182	4
			182	12
			185	9
96906	MS35691-21	5310-00-975-2075	79	8
			79	25
96906	MS35691-29	5310-00-835-2036	68	18
			69	9
			188	11
96906	MS35691-406	5310-01-159-8559	5	11
			17	17
			51	12
			148	7
			221	2
			222	10
			226	11
			240	9
96906	MS35691-9	5310-00-891-1709	182	17
			203	10
96906	MS35692-37	5310-00-842-1490	100	17
96906	MS35692-53	5310-00-842-7783	100	9
96906	MS35692-94	5310-00-849-6882	114	6
			115	15
96906	MS35751-17	5306-00-889-2943	233	1
96906	MS35751-19	5306-00-027-0722	235	19
96906	MS35751-46	5306-00-685-7790	234	19
96906	MS35751-73	5306-00-177-5707	235	22
96906	MS35842-10	4730-00-908-3195	18	23
			23	8
			67	2
			75	6
			80	5
			81	5
96906	MS35842-11	4730-00-908-3194	6	2
			14	40
			15	27
			25	17
			209	1
			220	1
			238	8
			239	7
96906	MS35842-13	4730-00-909-8627	14	39
			15	22
			25	1
96906	MS35842-14	4730-00-908-6292	14	10
			242	13
96906	MS35842-15	4730-00-908-6293	210	16
			215	7

CROSS-REFERENCE INDEXES

PART NUMBER INDEX

CAGEC	PART NUMBER	STOCK NUMBER	FIG	ITEM
96906	MS35842-15	4730-00-908-6293	215	7
			216	3
			218	3
			218	3
			243	5
			245	1
96906	MS35842-16	4730-00-908-6294	210	10
			242	20
			246	19
			246	29
96906	MS45904-68	5310-00-889-2528	172	15
96906	MS51023-49	5305-00-272-3533	246	5
96906	MS51085-1	2910-00-025-3493	210	30
			221	13
			242	3
			246	8
96906	MS51321-1	2910-00-710-6054	211	11
			214	10
96906	MS51335-1	2540-00-078-6633	114	1
			114	12
			115	10
			115	19
96906	MS51845-4	4730-00-249-3885	220	10
96906	MS51846-64	4730-00-196-1991	220	11
96906	MS51849-33	5305-00-227-1543	36	10
			38	1
96906	MS51849-55	5305-00-115-9934	39	7
96906	MS51849-70	5305-01-087-1917	210	28
96906	MS51849-78	5305-00-240-6668	231	9
96906	MS51850-44	5305-00-823-9139	247	19
96906	MS51850-64	5305-00-446-9901	227	12
96906	MS51850-86	5305-00-146-2524	14	24
			51	1
			57	9
			208	2
96906	MS51861-24	5305-00-432-4163	210	5
96906	MS51861-38	5305-00-432-7953	43	3
96906	MS51861-45	5305-00-432-4201	142	7
96906	MS51862-26	5305-00-483-0554	42	13
			158	5
96906	MS51862-35	5305-00-432-8220	145	16
96906	MS51869-24	5305-01-158-2032	14	3
			14	6
			15	4
			142	5
			157	5
96906	MS51869-26	5305-01-163-5761	250	2
			250	21
96906	MS51869-28	5305-01-211-7464	10	11
96906	MS51871-14	5305-01-163-2423	250	18
96906	MS51871-4	5305-01-132-2166	42	28

TM9-2320-289-20P

CROSS-REFERENCE INDEXES

PART NUMBER INDEX

CAGEC	PART NUMBER	STOCK NUMBER	FIG	ITEM
96906	MS51871-4	5305-01-132-2166	198	16
96906	MS51877-4	4730-00-278-8886	90	12
96906	MS51884-9	4730-00-187-4210	77	16
96906	MS51939-2	5340-00-916-6539	197	9
			197	14
			197	19
96906	MS51943-33	5310-00-814-0673	196	7
			215	2
			218	8
			218	11
			238	6
			238	6
			239	5
			239	5
96906	MS51952-1	4730-00-053-0266	242	32
			246	7
96906	MS51957-17	5305-00-054-5651	241	11
96906	MS51957-26	5305-00-054-6650	241	6
96906	MS51957-30	5305-00-054-6654	196	16
			233	20
96906	MS51957-33	5305-00-054-6657	229	2
96906	MS51957-45	5305-00-054-6670	241	15
96906	MS51957-71	5305-00-050-9237	179	16
96906	MS51957-83	5305-00-071-1318	230	1
96906	MS51957-84	5305-00-071-2087	229	13
96906	MS51967-12	5310-00-896-0903	13	5
			14	37
			109	4
			115	4
96906	MS51967-14	5310-00-768-0318	107	6
			108	3
			109	8
			114	27
			115	2
			116	1
			118	7
			119	6
			120	1
			121	4
			140	4
			147	10
			152	7
			182	5
96906	MS51967-17	5310-00-763-8913	121	8
			122	7
96906	MS51967-2	5310-00-761-6882	37	8
			44	1
			45	1
			52	2
			246	35
96906	MS51967-5	5310-00-880-7744	176	11

CROSS-REFERENCE INDEXES

PART NUMBER INDEX

CAGEC	PART NUMBER	STOCK NUMBER	FIG	ITEM
96906	MS51967-5	5310-00-880-7744	177	11
96906	MS51967-6	5310-00-931-8167	14	25
			17	20
			21	2
			22	9
			27	5
			70	16
			71	16
			86	19
			91	10
			106	11
			141	4
			221	9
			242	22
96906	MS51967-8	5310-00-732-0558	22	6
			41	22
			42	9
			45	5
			111	19
			115	26
			118	3
			119	3
			121	5
			122	3
			124	4
			214	29
96906	MS51968-20	5310-00-763-8905	122	1
96906	MS51968-24	5310-00-763-8894	87	1
96906	MS51968-5	5310-00-880-7746	40	1
96906	MS51968-6	5310-00-905-4600	100	4
96906	MS51968-8	5310-00-732-0559	188	24
96906	MS51968-9	5310-00-785-1762	100	5
96906	MS51971-1	5310-00-903-5966	172	5
96906	MS52039C079	9515-00-516-5756	BULK	33
96906	MS521304B203R	4720-00-930-2231	BULK	21
96906	MS52149-1	6140-01-210-1964	48	11
96906	MS52150-30HE	5340-01-204-4268	21	7
			22	11
96906	MS52150-31HE	5340-01-199-2312	21	6
			22	10
96906	MS75004-1	5940-00-549-6581	49	39
96906	MS75004-2	5940-00-549-6583	49	39
96906	MS87006-53	4030-00-916-2141	114	14
			115	21
96906	MS90724-34	5310-01-154-2273	34	1
			42	16
			43	6
			44	8
			125	3
			131	3
			132	9

CROSS-REFERENCE INDEXES

CAGEC	PART NUMBER	PART NUMBER INDEX STOCK NUMBER	FIG	ITEM
96906	MS90724-34	5310-01-154-2273	134	1
			136	21
			159	2
96906	MS90724-40	5310-00-490-4639	134	3
96906	MS90724-7	5310-00-144-8453	241	16
96906	MS90725-5	5305-00-068-0501	17	19
			231	11
96906	MS90725-6	5305-00-068-0502	172	3
96906	MS90727-109	5305-00-719-5184	87	4
96906	MS90727-117	5305-00-719-5240	114	11
			115	25
96906	MS90727-145	5305-01-194-0614	100	7
96906	MS90727-57	5305-00-269-3233	49	25
96906	MS90727-85	5305-00-709-8517	188	7
96906	MS90728-10	5305-00-068-0509	5	20
			185	12
			252	11
			253	14
96906	MS90728-109	5305-00-071-2066	30	7
96906	MS90728-111	5305-00-071-2067	107	4
			108	9
			110	2
			115	8
96906	MS90728-113	5305-00-071-2069	114	17
96906	MS90728-114	5305-00-071-2070	153	5
			182	10
96906	MS90728-115	5305-00-071-2071	237	8
96906	MS90728-117	5305-00-071-2073	115	39
96906	MS90728-119	5305-00-071-2075	107	8
			108	7
			114	23
			115	9
			120	5
96906	MS90728-121	5305-00-071-2077	120	3
96906	MS90728-125	5305-00-071-2081	153	6
96906	MS90728-13	5305-00-071-2510	229	14
			231	1
			232	7
			233	15
96906	MS90728-14	5305-00-071-2511	229	11
96906	MS90728-29	5306-00-226-4822	178	16
96906	MS90728-3	5305-00-071-2506	188	13
			222	7
			240	4
			252	17
96906	MS90728-31	5306-00-226-4824	91	5
			212	7
			214	20
96906	MS90728-32	5306-00-226-4825	17	36
			106	1
			221	5

CROSS-REFERENCE INDEXES

PART NUMBER INDEX

CAGEC	PART NUMBER	STOCK NUMBER	FIG	ITEM
96906	MS90728-32	5306-00-226-4825	242	26
96906	MS90728-33	5306-00-226-4826	14	30
			17	38
			86	4
96906	MS90728-34	5306-00-226-4827	22	14
			182	19
			202	6
			203	8
			238	1
			238	1
			239	1
			239	1
96906	MS90728-35	5306-00-226-4828	245	12
96906	MS90728-36	5306-00-226-4829	179	18
96906	MS90728-37	5306-00-226-4830	21	4
			22	2
			235	4
96906	MS90728-39	5306-00-226-4832	196	1
96906	MS90728-40	5306-00-226-4833	90	14
			176	9
			177	9
96906	MS90728-5	5305-00-068-7837	246	32
96906	MS90728-59	5305-01-140-9118	13	1
			14	36
			111	11
			130	5
			142	2
			214	24
96906	MS90728-6	5305-00-068-0508	5	14
			37	3
			49	6
			51	10
			68	25
			148	4
			172	13
			227	13
			237	5
			240	7
96906	MS90728-60	5305-00-068-0510	41	20
			45	3
			111	22
			115	29
			118	2
			119	2
			176	3
			177	3
			180	12
			181	4
96906	MS90728-62	5305-00-068-0511	63	7
			64	13
			118	5

CROSS-REFERENCE INDEXES

PART NUMBER INDEX

CAGEC	PART NUMBER	STOCK NUMBER	FIG	ITEM
96906	MS90728-63	5305-00-688-2111	91	15
			112	24
			119	5
96906	MS90728-64	5305-00-725-2317	9	7
96906	MS90728-65	5305-00-821-3869	124	8
96906	MS90728-66	5305-00-782-9489	231	18
			231	30
			232	10
96906	MS90728-68	5305-00-543-2866	247	17
96906	MS90728-8	5305-00-225-3843	5	3
			182	2
			182	15
			194	8
			197	3
			215	8
			215	8
			216	2
			218	4
			218	4
			246	30
96906	MS90728-83	5305-00-071-1784	59	9
96906	MS90728-86	5305-00-071-1787	70	13
			71	13
			72	13
			73	13
96906	MS90728-87	5305-00-071-1788	107	2
			109	6
			115	37
96906	MS90728-89	5305-00-071-2055	123	5
96906	MS90728-92	5305-00-071-2058	115	33
96906	MS9549-10	5310-00-938-8387	68	26
			222	6
			240	6
11862	M127		10	8
11862	M140		10	5
27647	M257	2520-01-165-5974	97	2
81349	M4510-1A4435	6220-00-961-0783	248	1
11862	M495		10	7
11862	M51		10	4
80205	NAS1408A6	5310-00-316-6513	21	15
			22	25
			63	9
			64	12
			111	4
			111	9
			234	15
			235	14
			247	16
81348	NNP530	5530-00-618-6955	BULK	30
70040	PF-35	2940-00-082-6034	4	13
0A7R8	PV23135R	6105-01-188-7154	210	40

CROSS-REFERENCE INDEXES

PART NUMBER INDEX

CAGEC	PART NUMBER	STOCK NUMBER	FIG	ITEM
81348	QQS741		BULK	1
74410	RRC271BTY2CLDIA0 72		BULK	3
81343	SAEJ513	4730-00-266-0535	211	6
80063	SC-B-75180-IV		172	14
80063	SC-B-75180-IV		37	1
80063	SC-C-691545	5340-01-159-4518	172	7
80063	SC-D-691375	5975-01-027-0253	172	6
80063	SC-D-691391		37	2
80063	SC-D-866091	5975-01-155-7084	172	1
82240	SPEC-3-10-L-L	5340-01-168-0939	246	24
70411	SP2489-FM	5430-01-225-8971	5	9
09386	SR104396	2530-01-096-9670	96	16
03743	S150	5340-00-329-4420	252	2
97271	S19587-T	5330-01-155-7700	101	8
72210	S23981-H	2530-01-165-6005	101	9
59875	TD97203	5325-00-263-6651	253	13
74410	TH-0681	5365-01-163-1147	182	8
11862	TX001487		112	21
11862	TX001488		112	4
17875	T14R	2640-00-555-2840	97	1
81348	WC596/9-1	5935-01-022-2377	185	18
72794	X-840-SR7C	5365-01-226-2342	225	3
74410	XA-T-61-SF	2540-01-267-1360	114	10
			115	24
74410	XA-T-61-SR	3040-01-267-4283	114	2
			115	11
74410	XA-T-88	5310-01-267-6293	114	5
			115	14
74410	XB-T-45-1	5310-01-249-4210	114	9
			115	18
74410	XB-766		114	8
			115	17
74410	XB-767-10	5340-01-267-6296	114	4
			115	13
74410	XX123		114	13
			115	20
25022	06-0075	4710-01-062-3719	179	7
25022	07-01-01	5310-01-271-1793	187	6
25022	07-1016	5305-01-239-9265	175	7
25022	08-0475	2540-01-163-3585	193	13
25022	09-0056	2540-01-163-0772	188	19
25022	09-0093	5340-01-166-2011	176	14
			177	20
25022	09-0951	2540-01-163-0834	193	9
25022	09-0952	2540-01-162-7116	193	10
25022	09-0954	5340-01-162-3853	176	1
			177	2
			178	9
			180	19
			181	25

CROSS-REFERENCE INDEXES

PART NUMBER INDEX

CAGEC	PART NUMBER	STOCK NUMBER	FIG	ITEM
25022	09-0955	2540-01-162-7117	182	7
25022	09-0959	5340-01-162-3854	178	13
			179	1
25022	09-0963	5340-01-196-6463	179	13
25022	09-0965	2540-01-163-7288	183	15
			184	10
6N299	0917425	4730-00-132-4625	16	6
78977	100-7-3	6220-01-194-6591	248	8
11862	10005327	4730-01-162-0095	220	2
11862	10008936	5306-01-148-6765	84	4
11862	10012288-45		209	5
08806	1003	6240-00-850-4280	33	17
			191	3
			227	5
70040	10045847	6685-01-205-3676	19	2
14569	1007-2	4730-00-844-5721	62	7
09386	102007	5306-01-158-6682	96	13
89346	103868	4730-00-044-4587	66	4
09386	104192	2530-01-216-4554	96	16
78385	10530B	2540-01-194-3323	210	11
			242	11
			246	21
11862	107413	5307-01-259-7656	228	4
19207	10922334	5340-00-914-1000	221	4
16764	110200	4730-00-266-0536	211	15
			214	18
11862	1105500	2920-01-149-8606	28	8
16764	1113591	2920-01-157-3765	32	8
11862	11500046	5310-01-148-5922	214	28
11862	11500668	5305-01-266-9194	158	3
11862	11500742	5305-01-160-1974	206	10
24617	11500997	5305-01-164-1604	206	14
24617	11500999	5305-01-159-2781	205	9
73342	11501033	5310-01-143-0512	104	4
11862	11501047	5310-01-267-3043	131	1
11862	11501095	5306-01-161-5489	20	13
11862	11501149	5305-01-157-1987	136	23
			159	3
24617	11501151	5305-01-158-6235	131	6
24617	11501153	5305-01-159-2780	131	5
11862	11501812	5305-01-164-6319	47	2
11862	11501937	5310-01-268-8948	208	3
24617	11502488	5310-01-155-2503	6	4
11862	11502634	5305-01-162-8514	158	8
11862	11502656	5306-01-149-4398	55	7
11862	11502812	5310-01-154-5263	89	27
24617	11503395	5305-01-158-7820	125	2
			159	7
24617	11503396	5305-01-162-9689	129	4
			207	5
11862	11503537	5305-01-162-3961	134	14

CROSS-REFERENCE INDEXES

PART NUMBER INDEX

CAGEC	PART NUMBER	STOCK NUMBER	FIG	ITEM
11862	11503537	5305-01-162-3961	166	5
			167	12
24617	11503606	5305-01-231-7384	158	9
11862	11503617	5305-01-150-1521	11	9
11862	11503643		28	6
			104	3
11862	11503739	5310-01-158-6257	49	21
24617	11503778	5306-01-162-8525	42	25
			43	12
11862	11504108	5310-01-159-6586	49	18
11862	11504115	5305-01-151-9285	23	2
11862	11504447	5305-01-156-5438	15	15
			16	7
			17	11
			37	5
			49	19
			53	2
			75	1
			80	4
			81	2
			90	10
			91	22
			141	11
			212	1
			226	12
			227	17
11862	11504512	5306-01-148-3667	8	10
			104	11
11862	11504595	5305-01-148-7460	1	6
			2	12
			28	3
			104	8
11862	11504655	5305-01-163-6466	43	14
			44	7
11862	11504656	5305-01-162-5995	42	29
11862	11504736	5305-01-162-9695	45	8
24617	11504986	5306-01-152-4693	20	10
11862	11505299	5306-01-185-7049	104	12
24617	11506003	5310-01-158-6260	38	15
			42	22
			43	9
			48	4
			54	2
			206	1
			225	5
			235	18
11862	11506101	5310-01-250-7679	29	6
			30	10
			104	2
			249	12
			251	1

CROSS-REFERENCE INDEXES

PART NUMBER INDEX

CAGEC	PART NUMBER	STOCK NUMBER	FIG	ITEM
24617	11507029	5305-01-150-9781	4	17
11862	11508164	5305-01-162-7885	130	6
11862	11508353	5306-01-253-7073	6	1
11862	11508446	5310-01-164-2338	49	32
11862	11508534	5306-01-230-3354	4	16
			38	14
11862	11508566	5305-01-160-1975	23	1
			24	3
			25	3
			130	13
24617	11508687	5306-01-197-1492	54	1
11862	11508858	5305-01-161-3995	49	35
11862	11509135	5305-01-273-4486	6	11
			132	14
11862	11509371	5305-01-195-5807	49	10
11862	11509669	5306-01-151-4925	9	13
11862	11513606	5306-01-185-7048	25	6
11862	11513932	5305-01-269-4329	34	2
			206	3
11862	11514337	5315-01-251-1701	102	2
11862	1155445	2530-01-166-3033	88	14
08806	1156	6240-00-924-7526	43	7
			45	10
08806	1157	6240-00-889-1799	45	11
			178	4
19207	11608950-4	4730-00-826-4268	15	9
			18	21
11862	11663000		8	2
19207	11669126-1	5340-01-043-5214	196	18
			233	19
19207	11674728	5935-01-059-0117	49	22
19207	11674729	5330-01-059-4286	49	28
19207	11674730	5970-01-044-8391	49	27
19207	11675004	5340-01-059-0114	49	23
19207	11682088-1	5340-01-114-7712	247	4
19207	11682345	5935-01-044-8382	49	24
72582	118754	4730-00-288-9440	5	8
27647	11967	3040-01-163-7286	KITS	
11862	12001184	2590-01-160-1496	50	9
11862	12004005	5920-01-123-5212	41	26
11862	12004007	5920-01-123-5211	41	27
11862	12004008	5920-01-149-6952	41	33
			187	12
11862	12004009	5920-01-085-0825	41	28
			41	35
11862	12004010	5920-01-149-6953	41	30
			187	14
11862	12004011	5920-01-188-6294	41	32
			41	34
			187	11
11862	12006377	6130-01-192-1643	33	4

CROSS-REFERENCE INDEXES

PART NUMBER INDEX

CAGEC	PART NUMBER	STOCK NUMBER	FIG	ITEM
11862	12006377	6130-01-192-1643	54	10
			55	3
11862	12013813	6250-01-201-3300	50	6
11862	12039205	2590-01-155-7966	51	7
11862	12039208	2590-01-159-3505	51	8
11862	12039253	6150-01-156-6326	54	19
			55	9
11862	12039254	6150-01-155-6522	37	15
11862	12039257	6150-01-163-1385	49	36
11862	12039267	6150-01-163-1384	49	37
11862	12039271	6150-01-154-1381	49	13
11862	12039272	6150-01-165-0168	49	16
11862	12039293	6140-01-163-1081	49	1
11862	12039294	6140-01-160-5196	225	4
77060	12039297	2920-01-192-4375	39	1
77060	12039298	2920-01-192-4376	39	9
11862	12044586	5995-01-225-2534	38	18
11862	120877	5340-01-166-2152	215	3
			217	3
			218	9
19207	12255559	5340-01-038-3428	196	10
19207	12255561	5340-01-044-8389	196	15
			233	21
19207	12255564-1	5325-01-165-6975	233	23
19207	12255564-2	5325-01-050-6192	197	10
			197	12
			197	18
			228	5
			230	8
19207	12255567	5340-01-036-7665	196	11
19207	12255608	5340-01-094-9025	247	20
11862	1226174	2590-01-159-8763	208	5
11862	12300197	2510-01-164-7152	136	18
11862	12306178	2510-01-162-7224	BULK	28
19207	12314542		254	1
11862	12321435		88	13
11862	12337820	5340-01-200-8473	209	3
19207	12343359-1	2540-01-041-4912	247	10
19207	12343359-2	2540-01-205-2510	247	24
19207	12343359-3	2540-01-205-2509	247	7
19207	12343359-4	2540-01-205-2511	247	22
19207	12343359-5	2540-01-205-2512	247	9
11862	1234418	5325-01-150-1229	68	15
11862	1239146	5306-01-152-2582	91	14
11862	1242101	5930-01-163-7282	41	11
11862	1244067	5306-01-246-7459	56	10
			143	1
			148	3
11862	1244707	5315-01-156-6562	95	14
11862	1252415	2520-01-152-9171	84	5
11862	1253637	6350-01-158-7035	56	14

CROSS-REFERENCE INDEXES

PART NUMBER INDEX

CAGEC	PART NUMBER	STOCK NUMBER	FIG	ITEM
24617	125384	5310-01-228-1405	101	2
			101	7
11862	1254856	6680-01-161-3656	249	7
11862	1257087	2520-01-192-1919	90	21
11862	1257203	2530-01-124-3422	90	21
11862	1259475	5330-01-147-4208	60	8
11862	1260895	5310-01-157-5672	133	16
			145	2
11862	1261219	5930-00-998-9211	41	18
21450	126281	5306-01-166-1665	193	4
21450	126373	5306-00-753-6996	247	11
14892	129494		89	12
25022	13-1104	2510-01-163-8014	181	10
25022	13-1105	2510-01-164-1532	180	5
27647	13109	2530-01-163-0799	96	10
27647	13113	3040-01-163-7347	97	8
11862	1312281	5360-00-392-3453	87	22
			88	24
21450	131245	5310-00-013-1245	32	6
			68	12
			215	6
			215	6
			216	4
			218	2
			218	2
			228	8
			246	28
27647	13446	5330-01-331-7230	97	6
11862	1355003	5310-01-084-4491	134	5
72712	1358938	5306-00-225-2864	70	14
			71	14
11862	1359744	4720-00-230-6523	BULK	20
11862	1359887	5310-01-197-5499	48	13
			157	1
11862	1361699	5340-01-168-1501	41	19
11862	1362195	3020-01-166-6802	249	4
11862	1362293	2530-01-159-8764	249	6
11862	1365065		124	1
11862	137396	4730-00-288-9390	5	4
24617	137397	4730-00-014-2432	90	7
72582	137398	4730-00-013-7398	62	1
11862	14000091	2510-01-162-7119	133	21
11862	14000092	2510-01-162-7120	133	21
11862	14000093	2540-01-164-1891	133	26
11862	14000094	5340-01-167-0136	133	26
11862	14000172	5310-01-154-3993	90	20
11862	14000217	2930-01-150-0895	25	19
11862	14000395	2590-01-159-8766	41	23
11862	14001067	5340-01-324-9553	111	23
11862	14001068	5340-01-324-6756	111	23
11862	14001197	5310-01-148-3693	12	3

CROSS-REFERENCE INDEXES

PART NUMBER INDEX

CAGEC	PART NUMBER	STOCK NUMBER	FIG	ITEM
11862	14002543	2530-01-147-6423	92	2
11862	14004512	5340-01-164-6473	211	14
			214	14
11862	14004810	5330-01-148-7499	89	28
11862	14005953	5340-01-150-4105	29	1
			36	11
			38	12
			39	8
			42	11
			48	10
			49	7
			49	11
			49	33
			54	15
			54	20
			174	4
			197	2
			200	14
			211	10
			214	9
			229	15
			230	4
			234	8
			245	3
11862	14007142	2990-01-181-6725	112	32
11862	14007429	2540-01-157-6414	200	5
11862	14007430	2540-01-156-4855	200	6
11862	14007435	5325-01-167-0510	200	8
11862	14007449	5340-01-160-2488	142	11
			146	7
11862	14007511	5306-01-160-1968	200	12
			211	12
			214	11
11862	14007539	5310-01-158-6780	200	16
11862	14007541	2540-01-165-6145	200	15
11862	14007542	2540-01-164-7260	200	15
11862	14007545	2590-01-219-7808	117	5
11862	14007644	2530-01-154-1262	100	12
11862	14008191	5330-01-159-2807	200	4
11862	14009313	4730-01-202-8523	69	2
11862	14009626	3120-01-153-0281	76	2
11862	14009982	2530-01-152-9308	88	5
11862	14010707	5340-01-165-4705	14	1
			15	6
11862	14010954	5340-01-187-8673	134	17
11862	14011345	2930-01-085-0926	23	11
11862	14013122	2540-01-165-5996	207	6
11862	14013724	5305-01-159-6567	168	1
11862	14013753	2540-01-159-8874	159	1
11862	14013754	2540-01-159-8875	159	1
11862	14013789	5365-01-155-8576	136	26

CROSS-REFERENCE INDEXES

PART NUMBER INDEX

CAGEC	PART NUMBER	STOCK NUMBER	FIG	ITEM
11862	14014293	2540-01-159-0874	168	9
11862	14014799	2510-01-164-7116	108	1
11862	14014800	2510-01-164-7117	108	6
11862	14015724	5365-01-214-4927	123	8
11862	14015726	5340-01-153-1631	123	7
11862	14016511	2510-01-249-6434	138	2
11862	14016512	2510-01-251-5487	138	2
11862	14018523	5330-01-170-6303	130	2
11862	14018526	5340-01-163-0917	130	10
11862	14018529	5360-01-205-8888	130	11
11862	14018531	5340-01-163-5908	130	8
11862	14018532	5360-01-163-0885	130	9
11862	14018630	5340-01-157-9825	15	21
11862	14018647		15	18
11862	14018658		15	14
11862	14018671	5330-01-168-1535	249	9
11862	14018700	5305-01-152-8193	72	14
			73	14
			74	6
11862	14020403	2520-01-210-1382	74	1
11862	14020478	2990-01-147-3954	112	6
11862	14020491	2910-01-155-7878	13	8
11862	14020492	2990-01-155-7879	13	14
11862	14020698	5306-01-149-6279	27	3
11862	14021209	2540-01-155-6823	161	13
11862	14021210	2540-01-155-6824	161	13
11862	14021211	5305-01-160-4528	161	10
11862	14021213	5305-01-160-0331	161	14
11862	14021243	2510-01-158-7575	127	1
11862	14021253	2510-01-163-7016	130	12
11862	14021254	2510-01-163-1139	130	12
11862	14021275	2540-01-156-9675	142	15
11862	14021292	5365-01-158-5381	145	3
11862	14021315	5360-01-164-2404	145	19
11862	14021316	5360-01-164-2405	145	19
11862	14021317	5306-01-159-2772	145	21
11862	14021357	2510-01-164-7128	109	2
11862	14021358	2510-01-163-7228	109	3
11862	14021385	2510-01-155-7877	142	20
11862	14021386	2510-01-155-5849	142	20
11862	14021389	2510-01-155-5853	142	10
11862	14022537	5340-01-163-1390	111	15
11862	14022538	5340-01-163-1389	111	6
11862	14022649	5330-01-156-5147	3	5
11862	14022650	5340-01-160-4397	3	8
11862	14022654	5307-01-151-8374	7	9
11862	14022657	2815-01-150-2181	7	6
11862	14022683	5330-01-150-7744	4	15
			213	3
11862	14022700	4730-01-150-0879	4	12
11862	14022777	3040-01-155-5864	161	18

PART NUMBER INDEX

CAGEC	PART NUMBER	STOCK NUMBER	FIG	ITEM
11862	14022778	3040-01-155-6912	161	22
11862	14022786	5340-01-158-6354	161	21
75829	14022841	2510-01-155-5435	156	7
75829	14022842	2510-01-155-5434	156	1
11862	14022885	5305-01-161-2581	138	1
11862	14023008	2530-01-162-3626	131	7
11862	14023039	2510-01-172-3022	131	2
11862	14023174	3020-01-153-9586	104	13
11862	14023429	2530-01-152-9306	93	11
11862	14023430	2530-01-152-9307	93	11
11862	14023439	5315-01-157-3004	92	16
11862	14023889	3040-01-155-0194	170	8
11862	14023890	3040-01-155-0195	170	15
11862	14024561	5340-01-155-9861	22	19
11862	14024997	5360-01-151-1120	20	9
11862	14025568	2815-01-148-9560	7	11
11862	14025673	5340-01-157-7607	170	6
11862	14025674	5340-01-157-7608	170	17
11862	14025679	2540-01-157-2966	170	5
11862	14026247	5305-01-158-7820	14	7
			15	24
			128	5
11862	14026383	5330-01-157-6827	134	9
11862	14026384	5330-01-157-6828	134	9
11862	14026409	2540-01-156-4903	134	13
11862	14026410	2540-01-156-4904	134	13
11862	14026765	2530-01-147-4209	97	21
11862	14026802	2530-01-152-9313	102	9
11862	14026803	2530-01-152-9312	102	4
11862	14026804	2530-01-152-9314	102	7
11862	14026805	5310-01-153-9301	102	6
11862	14027345	2540-01-155-5824	171	8
11862	14027346	2540-01-157-7907	171	2
11862	14027347	2540-01-155-5110	171	5
11862	14027348	2540-01-155-5111	171	3
11862	14027431	2540-01-155-7502	135	3
11862	14027432	2540-01-155-7503	135	3
11862	14027451	2510-01-160-5837	141	5
11862	14027454	2510-01-158-6904	141	5
11862	14027542		143	4
11862	14027555	5340-01-160-2346	128	7
11862	14027775	5330-01-164-8385	134	7
11862	14027776	5330-01-193-1840	134	7
11862	14027777	9390-01-162-4500	136	27
11862	14027778	9390-01-163-2028	136	27
11862	14027799	5340-01-160-4130	168	16
11862	14027926	5340-01-197-4600	117	2
11862	14028916	5330-01-148-7497	25	14
			220	5
11862	14028917	2930-01-147-9916	25	11
11862	14028918	2930-01-147-4198	25	7

CROSS-REFERENCE INDEXES

PART NUMBER INDEX

CAGEC	PART NUMBER	STOCK NUMBER	FIG	ITEM
11862	14028922	5306-01-149-6278	7	8
			219	1
11862	14028923	5305-01-148-3685	7	10
11862	14028924	5307-01-158-6312	7	7
11862	14028931	5340-01-150-1545	32	5
11862	14028942	5325-01-151-6117	4	3
11862	14029107	2520-01-164-6228	68	4
11862	14029108	5360-01-165-1574	68	3
11862	14029111	5315-01-165-3536	68	5
11862	14029116	2520-01-164-9229	68	24
11862	14029117	2520-01-163-7283	68	21
11862	14029122	5315-01-153-0318	68	20
11862	14029158	2520-01-192-8282	64	10
11862	14029200	5340-01-168-6372	118	9
			119	8
11862	14029235		75	10
11862	14029852	2520-01-151-8043	74	4
11862	14029956	2990-01-154-1324	21	10
11862	14030586	2540-01-156-4885	134	19
11862	14031893	5340-01-161-2789	159	4
11862	14032395	2930-01-147-9330	27	6
11862	14032787	5340-01-165-0564	142	4
11862	14032789	2520-01-193-7870	69	7
11862	14032812	5340-01-165-4544	155	4
11862	14032814	5306-01-159-6574	154	1
			155	5
11862	14032995	4710-01-148-2969	67	1
11862	14032996	4710-01-194-6775	67	5
11862	14033823		25	16
11862	14033879	5340-01-147-2268	104	5
11862	14033880	5340-01-154-7163	104	9
11862	14033881	5340-01-155-7744	104	10
11862	14033893	5340-01-151-9956	8	3
11862	14033895	5340-01-151-9957	8	8
11862	14033921	5340-01-150-4106	11	10
11862	14033922	5340-01-150-6275	11	11
11862	1403394-6		1	1
11862	14033945	5340-01-158-8624	1	2
11862	14033947	5340-01-150-5986	1	5
11862	14033948	5307-01-153-0873	12	7
11862	14033953	5340-01-150-7774	11	19
11862	14033955	5340-01-150-6026	11	7
11862	14034410	5310-01-155-1897	97	13
11862	14034413	5310-01-244-2259	97	11
11862	14034501	5340-01-162-3747	111	13
11862	14034503	5340-01-162-3748	111	7
11862	14034504	5340-01-162-3749	111	7
11862	14034513	2990-01-1645-7178	112	6
11862	14034543	5340-01-159-1185	17	24
11862	14034546	2910-01-155-5845	17	34
11862	14034547	5340-01-148-2818	22	18

CROSS-REFERENCE INDEXES

PART NUMBER INDEX

CAGEC	PART NUMBER	STOCK NUMBER	FIG	ITEM
11862	14034571		90	16
11862	14034572		90	22
11862	14034586		90	13
11862	14034599		91	23
11862	14034728	2520-01-163-7314	99	72
11862	14035374	2530-01-154-6952	96	3
11862	14036369	5310-01-148-7474	4	6
11862	14036705		91	20
11862	14036706		91	13
11862	14036711		91	20
11862	14036712		91	13
11862	14036723	4720-01-148-7398	90	18
11862	14036736	4720-01-148-2763	90	18
11862	14036744	4720-01-148-2970	25	4
11862	14036751	4720-01-148-6984	14	41
11862	14036773	5340-01-154-5269	91	7
11862	14036775	4730-01-255-2976	91	11
11862	14036779	5340-01-150-4991	25	2
11862	14036784	5340-01-150-0197	5	24
11862	14036792	4710-01-172-0471	91	2
11862	14036797		91	1
11862	14037059	2540-01-155-6825	161	12
11862	14037060	2540-01-155-8786	161	12
11862	14037808	5340-01-163-1388	22	3
11862	14037812	2990-01-147-3953	22	13
11862	14037836	2990-01-203-2426	22	12
11862	14037856	2990-01-154-3743	21	1
11862	14037889	3040-01-163-7315	68	6
11862	14037893	3040-01-163-7018	68	23
11862	14037986	5930-01-149-9305	65	51
11862	14037987	5365-01-149-9710	65	17
11862	14038051	5365-01-209-6943	96	12
11862	14038644	2990-01-148-2928	20	1
11862	14038647	2910-01-150-3676	20	11
11862	14039710	2510-01-160-3634	146	6
11862	14039712	3040-01-160-5913	148	12
11862	14039716	3040-01-159-1775	146	5
11862	14039763	2540-01-156-0565	137	3
11862	14039764	2540-01-156-4869	137	3
11862	14039765	3040-01-159-7950	137	4
11862	14039766	3040-01-156-9729	137	4
11862	14039767	3040-01-155-0372	137	9
11862	14039768	3040-01-155-0373	137	9
11862	14039924	5306-01-165-4286	140	1
11862	14039948	2930-01-160-1597	23	4
11862	14039949	5340-01-164-3269	23	20
11862	14039950	5340-01-159-2901	23	6
11862	14039963	2590-01-158-8784	129	5
11862	14040525	2590-01-160-5841	41	21
11862	14040735		106	4
11862	14040775		80	1

CROSS-REFERENCE INDEXES

PART NUMBER INDEX

CAGEC	PART NUMBER	STOCK NUMBER	FIG	ITEM
11862	14040813	5340-01-150-4992	49	20
11862	14040817	4730-01-160-1505	46	3
11862	14041258		15	28
11862	1403724	5340-01-160-2239	18	16
11862	14043823	2510-01-162-5172	130	4
11862	14043824	2510-01-162-5173	130	4
11862	14043873	6220-01-160-4254	42	30
11862	14043874	6220-01-161-5016	42	30
11862	14043880	2510-01-159-2929	127	11
11862	14044340	5305-01-159-2779	159	6
11862	1404471	2540-01-156-0564	132	10
11862	14044931		198	5
11862	14044995	2990-01-152-7828	22	20
11862	14044996	2990-01-154-1323	22	16
11862	14045233		10	1
11862	14045268	4710-01-150-0842	4	5
11862	14045504	5305-01-167-5498	68	7
11862	14045515	2510-01-164-7118	107	7
11862	14045516	2510-01-164-7119	107	1
11862	14045521	2990-01-155-5149	21	12
11862	14045525	2990-01-155-5150	21	11
11862	14045605		17	23
11862	14045626		62	5
11862	14045628		62	6
11862	14045642	4710-01-148-4989	60	9
11862	14045654	2530-01-163-3557	118	10
11862	14045658	2520-01-163-7316	68	2
11862	14045697	2510-01-165-8101	68	28
11862	14045698	5340-01-160-2155	89	29
11862	14046907	2590-01-324-5042	74	5
11862	14047899	5340-01-197-3434	5	16
11862	14049351	5355-01-085-0995	99	71
11862	14049494	4720-01-160-5781	15	23
11862	14049556	5325-01-197-3540	69	15
11862	14049810	5340-01-164-8757	139	6
			141	6
11862	14050425	5315-01-151-4180	9	10
11862	14050440	5340-01-163-8520	145	1
11862	14050441	5340-01-197-3433	6	10
11862	14050442	4710-01-192-7967	6	8
11862	14050443	4710-01-198-2701	6	9
11862	14050444	4730-01-164-7028	6	12
11862	14050445	4720-01-195-7603	6	7
11862	14050446	2990-01-192-9730	6	13
11862	14050523	6680-01-147-4629	4	4
11862	14050679	5310-01-205-2536	96	11
11862	14050685	2910-01-160-8107	13	13
11862	14052026	5340-01-172-2087	14	4
			15	5
11862	14052221	2930-01-159-2902	23	13
11862	14053591	3040-01-156-9994	86	6

CROSS-REFERENCE INDEXES

PART NUMBER INDEX

CAGEC	PART NUMBER	STOCK NUMBER	FIG	ITEM
11862	14053593	2590-01-161-2119	86	18
11862	14054120	5340-01-323-9727	86	10
11862	14054122	5340-01-148-8352	86	8
11862	14054173	2990-01-152-0251	86	12
11862	14054174	2990-01-151-8115	86	9
11862	14054220	2520-01-192-9729	69	16
11862	14054257		90	16
11862	14054269	4720-01-148-6947	90	18
11862	14054270	4720-01-148-6946	90	18
11862	14055315	2530-01-157-5164	88	20
11862	14055531	2520-01-194-0278	69	10
11862	14055556	5365-01-157-5752	91	17
11862	14055585	5330-01-218-0862	5	1
			219	3
11862	14055586	4730-01-172-6683	5	15
11862	14055591	5995-01-148-2930	86	18
11862	14056133	5310-01-157-7582	79	11
11862	14056297	4730-01-156-0055	80	6
11862	14056299	4730-01-153-2718	75	8
11862	14056723	5305-01-160-3955	166	13
			167	17
11862	14057219	4820-01-158-6836	10	10
11862	14059238	3120-01-160-0570	166	11
			167	15
11862	14060613	5306-01-165-5583	32	4
			164	11
			165	11
11862	14061223		17	29
11862	14061227		17	25
11862	14061344	4710-01-148-8354	5	2
11862	14061345	4710-01-149-1899	5	25
11862	14061348	5340-01-150-6249	5	17
11862	14061350	5640-01-159-6935	5	12
11862	14061352	5340-01-150-1377	5	19
			222	8
11862	14061396	2530-01-222-8068	91	9
11862	14061569	4710-01-148-2659	8	9
11862	14061649	2815-01-147-4275	4	21
11862	14061661	5307-01-150-1228	27	1
11862	14063301	4720-01-192-8533	18	22
11862	14063302	4720-01-163-8039	18	20
11862	14063307	2530-01-154-8146	97	23
11862	14063314		17	15
11862	14063315		16	8
11862	14063317		15	19
11862	14063319	2910-01-155-5138	15	20
			17	30
11862	14063323	4710-01-232-8478	214	19
11862	14063324	4720-01-163-1089	212	3
			214	30
11862	14063325	2910-01-155-7965	15	26

CROSS-REFERENCE INDEXES

PART NUMBER INDEX

CAGEC	PART NUMBER	STOCK NUMBER	FIG	ITEM
11862	14063326	2910-01-155-5063	14	2
			15	25
11862	14063327	2910-01-155-5148	14	9
11862	14063328	4720-01-155-8062	14	11
11862	14063329	2910-01-155-7880	15	7
11862	14063331		68	1
11862	14063332	2520-01-164-7851	68	2
11862	14063333	2910-01-155-5147	14	9
11862	14063334	4720-01-155-5194	14	11
11862	14063335	4720-01-192-9823	14	41
11862	14063336	4720-01-162-0119	5	10
			219	5
11862	14063337	4720-01-162-0120	5	21
			219	4
11862	14063338	2930-01-159-1802	220	4
11862	14063341		235	16
11862	14063342		235	6
11862	14063343		235	9
11862	14063344		235	9
11862	14063345		235	13
11862	14063346		235	10
11862	14063347		235	23
11862	14063348		235	1
11862	14063349	5340-01-219-7275	234	4
			235	3
11862	14063350		235	12
11862	14063351		235	20
11862	14063352		237	7
11862	14063353	5340-01-293-1200	237	1
11862	14063358	2540-01-218-8099	237	6
11862	14063359	5340-01-164-6595	237	3
11862	14063363	2910-01-155-5139	14	8
11862	14063365	5970-01-159-1803	228	3
11862	14063366	2930-01-167-7250	228	7
11862	14063370		220	6
11862	14063373		220	15
11862	14063391	4720-01-156-0085	16	16
			17	2
11862	14063795	2990-01-046-1170	21	9
24617	140642	4730-00-619-9362	211	7
			214	6
11862	14064660	2530-01-155-7457	100	8
11862	14064663	2590-01-156-0583	86	12
11862	14064664	2990-01-148-2929	86	9
11862	14066195	3120-01-162-0060	161	8
11862	14066196	5365-01-197-2286	161	9
11862	14066255	5945-01-154-3143	20	14
11862	14066301	5340-01-166-1534	8	1
11862	14066305	4720-01-184-0432	8	14
11862	14066306		8	5
11862	14066307	5307-01-150-5992	4	20

CROSS-REFERENCE INDEXES

PART NUMBER INDEX

CAGEC	PART NUMBER	STOCK NUMBER	FIG	ITEM
11862	14066310	2815-01-166-0621	4	11
11862	14066657	2920-01-192-3020	32	1
11862	14066662	6210-01-158-0396	35	2
11862	14067429	2990-01-180-2988	22	21
11862	14067430	2990-01-152-7788	22	17
11862	14067701	3020-01-148-2948	104	13
11862	14067702	3020-01-148-6983	2	11
11862	14067703	3020-01-147-9359	2	11
11862	14067704	3020-01-148-2949	27	2
11862	14067705	3020-01-148-2950	27	2
11862	14067714	2920-01-147-8559	29	8
11862	14067715	2920-01-191-8442	30	5
11862	14067717	5306-01-150-9493	29	5
11862	14067718	5307-01-159-6632	30	6
11862	14067721	2920-01-147-8562	30	9
11862	14067724	2920-01-147-4278	29	2
11862	14067725	5365-01-154-4365	29	9
11862	14067727	4730-01-148-2755	25	10
11862	14067732	4720-01-194-0336	6	3
11862	14067733	2815-01-192-5962	6	5
11862	14067737	4730-01-148-8242	25	10
11862	14067759	2990-01-147-4289	22	22
11862	14067762	2520-01-147-4005	74	1
11862	14067763	4720-01-159-1839	25	18
11862	14067764	5340-01-164-7021	63	10
11862	14067770	2540-01-158-8553	115	1
11862	14067771	5340-01-165-4353	115	7
11862	14067772	5340-01-162-4775	115	7
11862	14067773	2540-01-163-8595	115	6
11862	14067774	2540-01-164-1842	115	6
11862	14067775	2540-01-158-4599	115	40
11862	14067776	2540-01-157-8008	115	35
11862	14067779	5340-01-162-8759	114	33
11862	14067780	5340-01-162-8760	114	21
11862	14067783	2510-01-163-1146	109	1
11862	14067784	2510-01-164-7127	109	7
11862	14067785	2540-01-159-2928	114	32
11862	14067786	2540-01-158-8548	114	19
11862	14067787	2540-01-159-7741	114	31
11862	14067789	5365-01-163-6195	115	34
11862	14067790	2510-01-155-7942	113	1
11862	14067791	2510-01-165-1495	107	9
11862	14067792	2510-01-164-7120	107	13
11862	14067793	4030-00-542-3183	114	25
			115	31
11862	14067794	5315-01-160-4639	113	5
			114	24
			115	30
11862	14067795	2540-01-159-7740	113	2
11862	14067796	5340-01-160-2171	113	3
11862	14068905	2530-01-156-4900	87	30

CROSS-REFERENCE INDEXES

CAGEC	PART NUMBER	PART NUMBER INDEX STOCK NUMBER	FIG	ITEM
11862	14068906	2530-01-156-4901	87	30
11862	14069636	5305-01-160-4494	168	24
11862	14070348	5365-01-197-8165	97	7
11862	14070352	2530-01-152-9305	97	17
11862	14070396	5365-01-221-9717	96	9
11862	14070703	2510-01-162-3623	130	7
11862	14071047	5930-01-157-4060	46	2
11862	14071059	2590-01-147-4285	4	2
11862	14071884	2520-01-330-3249	83	9
11862	14071950		68	1
11862	14071952	2520-01-165-7885	68	11
11862	14071954	5330-01-164-7506	68	27
11862	14071955	2520-01-192-7979	69	11
11862	14071980	2520-01-328-4898	74	1
11862	14071983	4730-01-194-2002	25	5
11862	14071984	2910-01-148-2910	14	13
11862	14072305	5340-01-159-2996	153	2
11862	14072306	2510-01-159-8726	153	7
11862	14072307	5310-01-169-2849	153	1
11862	14072308		247	1
11862	14072314	5340-01-200-5843	247	2
11862	14072319	2540-01-191-8467	247	13
11862	14072322	2540-01-163-0801	247	15
11862	14072323	2540-01-164-9278	247	14
11862	14072324	5340-01-165-1494	247	6
11862	14072325	5340-01-165-4429	247	3
11862	14072333	6220-01-248-6269	42	1
11862	14072336	6150-01-159-6901	36	6
			38	6
11862	14072337		36	14
11862	14072338	5930-01-158-4428	35	11
11862	14072339	5930-01-158-4808	41	37
11862	14072340	5340-01-160-4592	56	7
11862	14072347	2540-01-163-1141	211	8
			214	8
11862	14072358	5930-01-162-0803	41	36
11862	14072364	2540-01-162-4412	229	23
11862	14072365	5340-01-164-6435	229	22
11862	14072366	4730-01-161-6618	229	19
11862	14072367	5340-01-165-4379	229	18
11862	14072368	4720-01-162-5113	211	16
			214	16
11862	14072369		211	17
			214	15
11862	14072371		211	5
			214	5
11862	14072372		221	20
11862	14072374	5365-01-163-1142	221	14
			242	2
			246	9
11862	14072378		242	9

CROSS-REFERENCE INDEXES

PART NUMBER INDEX

CAGEC	PART NUMBER	STOCK NUMBER	FIG	ITEM
11862	14072380	5340-00-237-7779	247	23
11862	14072405	2510-01-159-0868	131	4
11862	14072406	5340-01-162-3627	35	3
11862	14072409	5340-01-162-3628	35	3
11862	14072410	5895-01-165-6792	35	9
11862	14072412	5930-01-163-1439	35	13
11862	14072413	5930-01-159-0925	41	17
11862	14072415	5340-01-164-6524	240	5
11862	14072421	5340-01-159-5762	42	23
11862	14072422	2540-01-159-8881	107	10
11862	14072425	5306-01-157-3330	107	11
			108	8
			109	11
			114	30
11862	14072426	5340-01-157-6428	23	18
11862	14072427	5340-01-157-6429	23	17
11862	14072430		23	14
11862	14072431	5340-01-162-6061	42	12
11862	14072432	5340-01-162-4774	49	30
11862	14072433	5340-01-159-5765	43	13
11862	14072434	5340-01-162-9782	43	13
11862	14072435	2540-01-159-2992	108	10
11862	14072436	2540-01-155-7535	109	12
11862	14072439	5340-01-164-6412	202	10
11862	14072440	5340-01-164-6411	202	9
11862	14072441	5340-01-164-6410	202	8
11862	14072442	5340-01-159-4517	202	13
11862	14072445	5340-01-157-6697	201	2
			202	3
11862	14072448	2920-01-152-2414	35	10
11862	14072452	5340-01-159-6174	151	2
11862	14072454	5365-01-158-2004	151	4
			152	8
11862	14072455	2510-01-155-5112	152	6
11862	14072458	5305-01-197-3290	152	4
11862	14072459	2510-01-156-0062	151	6
11862	14072460	2510-01-155-5825	151	3
			152	9
11862	14072461	2540-01-191-8443	197	5
11862	14072462	2540-01-191-8444	197	6
11862	14072463	2540-01-192-3573	197	24
11862	14072464	2540-01-191-8445	197	11
11862	14072465	2540-01-192-3574	197	23
11862	14072466	2540-01-191-8446	197	17
11862	14072467	2540-01-192-3575	197	22
11862	14072468	2540-01-192-3576	196	8
11862	14072469	2540-01-192-4479	196	12
11862	14072470	2540-01-191-9564	196	9
11862	14072471		196	3
11862	14072472		196	4
11862	14072473		196	6

CROSS-REFERENCE INDEXES

PART NUMBER INDEX

CAGEC	PART NUMBER	STOCK NUMBER	FIG	ITEM
11862	14072475	2540-01-191-8549	195	2
11862	14072479	2510-01-147-9917	195	1
11862	14072481	5340-01-162-6077	45	13
11862	14072485		200	3
11862	14072486		200	3
11862	14072487	2540-01-155-0376	200	7
11862	14072488	2510-01-155-8787	125	5
11862	14072489	2540-01-159-8760	200	9
11862	14072493	2540-01-156-7238	133	9
11862	14072494	2540-01-158-3576	133	1
11862	14072497	2540-01-158-4602	144	2
11862	14072499	2540-01-211-4621	144	3
11862	145072666	5306-01-159-2784	14	35
11862	14072686	5330-01-147-4212	21	13
			22	23
11862	14072692	2530-01-147-4214	86	15
11862	14072697	5340-01-148-8351	86	10
11862	14072850	2510-01-159-8762	126	2
11862	14072919	2530-01-149-3827	77	1
11862	14072921	5365-01-158-2193	97	10
11862	14072927		97	15
11862	14072930	4730-01-147-6425	81	6
11862	14074431	5340-01-165-6797	237	4
11862	14074435	2590-01-156-0076	173	1
11862	14074437	5340-00-455-5899	173	2
11862	14074438	2590-01-156-0080	173	6
11862	14074439	2590-01-156-0074	174	1
11862	14074441	2590-01-156-0077	173	4
11862	14074442	2590-01-156-0078	173	4
11862	14074444		238	4
11862	14074445	4710-01-163-0594	238	9
11862	14074446		238	7
11862	14074447		239	11
11862	14074448	2540-01-164-7121	239	10
11862	14074449		239	9
11862	14074450	4710-01-161-6406	239	8
11862	14074451	4720-01-162-0283	239	6
11862	14074452	4710-01-162-7080	239	13
11862	14074453		239	12
11862	14074457	5340-01-164-6528	221	1
11862	14074458	5340-01-164-6526	221	7
11862	14074459	5340-01-164-6527	221	10
11862	14074461PC6	5945-01-162-0516	223	2
11862	14074465	2540-01-163-1140	243	2
11862	14074466	2540-01-164-7123	242	12
11862	14074469	2540-01-163-1143	242	21
11862	14074470	2540-01-165-0466	242	27
11862	14074471	5340-01-165-4543	242	24
11862	14074473	2540-01-164-7124	242	30
11862	14074479	2540-01-159-8727	168	23
11862	14074480	5340-01-160-4597	56	8

CROSS-REFERENCE INDEXES

PART NUMBER INDEX

CAGEC	PART NUMBER	STOCK NUMBER	FIG	ITEM
11862	14074499	2540-01-162-7113	218	5
11862	14075347	2910-01-156-8361	18	2
11862	14075374	2540-01-160-3654	168	27
11862	14075375	2540-01-160-3652	168	25
11862	14075376	2540-01-160-3653	168	28
11862	14075379	2540-01-163-8017	169	2
11862	14075388	6140-01-155-6997	48	15
11862	14075389	6140-01-155-6998	48	12
11862	14075801	2990-01-159-1801	215	5
11862	14075811	2540-01-165-0813	247	5
11862	14075812	2540-01-163-7017	247	8
11862	14075815	2540-01-166-1370	170	1
11862	14075818	2540-01-165-0895	166	10
11862	14075819	2540-01-161-1356	167	1
11862	14075820	2540-01-158-8812	166	1
11862	14075821	2540-01-158-8558	164	8
11862	14075822	2540-01-159-7744	165	9
11862	14075823	2540-01-164-1843	164	2
11862	14075824	2540-01-164-1844	164	4
11862	14075843	2540-01-162-8983	233	5
11862	14075845	2540-01-164-1886	229	8
11862	14075846	5340-01-162-4820	203	2
11862	14075856		238	12
11862	14075857	5330-01-164-5603	229	20
11862	14075858	6620-01-156-0712	35	6
11862	14075862		236	2
11862	14075863		236	4
11862	14075864		236	2
11862	14075881	2540-01-155-7543	230	6
11862	14075882	2540-01-155-7278	230	7
11862	14075883		230	5
11862	14075884		230	3
11862	14075888	5995-01-163-1183	223	1
11862	14075894	5307-01-158-9932	48	7
11862	14075896	6140-01-156-5326	48	5
11862	14075900	5340-01-164-8171	36	9
11862	14076201		233	10
11862	14076204		231	6
			232	4
11862	14076206	2510-01-159-1790	234	12
11862	14076208	2590-01-242-8068	232	17
11862	14076209		231	25
11862	14076210		231	20
11862	14076211		231	23
11862	14076212		232	13
11862	14076215	5330-01-167-6335	229	5
			231	27
11862	14076216	2510-01-159-1792	229	3
			231	28
11862	14076217	5340-01-163-3294	231	17
11862	14076221	5340-01-164-2397	232	11

CROSS-REFERENCE INDEXES

PART NUMBER INDEX

CAGEC	PART NUMBER	STOCK NUMBER	FIG	ITEM
11862	14076222		233	7
11862	14076226	5340-01-164-6589	233	16
11862	14076228	2540-01-155-7542	229	1
11862	14076229		234	20
11862	14076230	5340-01-164-6591	233	3
11862	14076231	2510-01-162-4408	233	12
11862	14076232		233	13
11862	14076233	2510-01-162-4407	233	2
11862	14076235	5330-01-163-5850	234	11
11862	14076236	2590-01-163-1184	222	1
11862	14076237	2590-01-163-3529	243	3
11862	14076238	2590-01-162-4353	227	2
11862	14076239	2590-01-162-7130	227	16
11862	14076240	2590-01-162-4418	226	7
11862	14076241	2540-01-164-0032	225	12
11862	14076243	2540-01-164-0122	225	7
11862	14076246	2590-01-164-0135	225	1
11862	14076248	5306-01-227-1454	225	13
11862	14076249	2540-01-166-2009	225	10
11862	14076250	2540-01-166-2010	225	8
11862	14076252	2540-01-163-1175	246	1
11862	14076253	2540-01-162-5176	246	4
11862	14076255		246	11
11862	14076257	2540-01-162-5177	246	40
11862	14076258	2540-01-162-5189	246	39
11862	14076259	2540-01-162-5178	246	31
11862	14076261	5340-01-166-0568	246	33
11862	14076262	5340-01-165-5617	246	34
11862	14076265	2540-01-162-6418	246	22
11862	14076269	2590-01-162-4352	226	1
11862	14076270	5330-01-220-6153	222	13
11862	14076271		234	18
11862	14076272		234	13
11862	14076273		234	22
11862	14076274		234	22
11862	14076275		234	14
11862	14076276		234	10
11862	14076277		234	23
11862	14076278		234	2
11862	14076279		234	21
11862	14076280		234	5
11862	14076281		234	1
11862	14076284	2540-01-163-0765	240	10
11862	14076285	2540-01-162-5174	241	1
11862	14076287	2540-01-162-5175	241	2
11862	14076295	2540-01-159-1800	241	19
11862	14076298	5325-01-163-5973	201	1
11862	14076299	2510-01-162-7111	233	22
11862	14076300	2540-01-163-0766	233	22
11862	14076390	4720-01-162-0121	214	27
11862	14076801	2540-01-162-6493	246	36

CROSS-REFERENCE INDEXES

PART NUMBER INDEX

CAGEC	PART NUMBER	STOCK NUMBER	FIG	ITEM
11862	14076802		236	3
11862	14076803		236	3
11862	14076805	2990-01-163-1182	245	11
11862	14076811	2590-01-162-4417	226	5
11862	14076838	2540-01-158-8612	198	6
11862	14076847	5905-01-193-7212	39	4
11862	14076848	2540-01-194-6875	39	3
11862	14076852	6140-01-216-7923	225	6
11862	14076856	6160-01-165-4638	48	2
11862	14076857	6160-01-165-4637	48	6
17769	14076861	2510-01-246-4236	233	8
11862	14076862	5330-01-163-2055	232	8
11862	14076864		232	14
11862	14076871		232	15
11862	14076872		232	5
11862	14076875	2510-01-246-4237	231	16
11862	14076882	2540-01-162-7110	231	10
11862	14076884		231	24
11862	14076887	5340-01-197-3244	140	6
11862	14076889	5340-01-218-5823	234	7
11862	14076894	5365-01-195-4948	140	5
75829	14076899	2510-01-157-1382	156	8
11862	14077122	6620-01-146-8006	25	13
11862	14077147	2920-01-191-6635	28	11
11862	14077149	2920-01-147-4272	28	1
11862	14077151	5340-01-197-1259	28	5
11862	14077928	4140-01-145-8099	27	4
11862	14078806	2540-01-200-3167	114	29
11862	14079056	2540-01-159-7963	160	2
11862	14079057	2540-01-193-7895	160	3
11862	14079058	2540-01-193-7896	160	1
11862	14079550	5330-00-107-3925	4	18
			213	8
11862	14081915	2520-01-225-1033	99	72
11862	14089132	2990-01-225-1052	21	9
11862	14094948	4730-01-151-7972	90	19
24617	142433	4730-00-014-2433	16	4
			17	7
96061	144F-5	4730-01-069-6408	211	3
			214	3
08806	1445		35	8
11862	1456507	5365-01-155-1941	70	6
			71	9
			72	6
			73	8
			74	2
11862	1488565		106	6
24617	1494253	5310-01-160-9529	23	19
			157	4
			212	6
			214	22

PART NUMBER INDEX

CAGEC	PART NUMBER	STOCK NUMBER	FIG	ITEM
27647	15147	3040-01-163-7285	97	4
27647	15149	2530-01-163-0798	96	6
84760	15349	5330-01-138-2106	18	10
11862	15517986	5340-01-213-6934	62	4
11862	15521977	5306-01-156-5435	83	8
11862	15522022	5340-01-164-1743	59	8
11862	1522077	2530-01-096-6752	87	27
11862	15522078	2530-01-155-7943	87	27
11862	15522079	2530-01-162-8986	87	28
11862	15522080	2530-01-164-0039	87	28
11862	15522081	2530-00-228-6992	87	25
11862	15522095	2540-01-154-1293	95	10
11862	15522381	2510-01-225-0997	119	9
11862	15522392	2590-01-164-7177	17	33
11862	15522444		90	13
11862	15522697	2930-01-147-4221	24	4
11862	15522707	2510-01-225-0998	145	17
11862	15522708	2510-01-225-0999	145	13
11862	15522764	5680-01-163-6347	138	3
27647	15528	2530-01-163-0800	KITS	
11862	15530620	5325-01-149-6293	12	6
			86	14
11862	15531547	5305-01-231-1297	136	22
11862	15538215	2530-01-225-1024	91	8
11862	15544950	5306-01-227-9085	32	9
11862	15545178	5340-01-160-5922	137	8
			146	8
11862	15548901	4720-01-150-7575	5	10
11862	15548902	4720-01-148-5000	5	21
11862	15549248	2530-01-225-2236	91	4
11862	15554576	5305-01-162-0015	200	11
11862	15554915	2510-01-155-7425	125	1
11862	15557723	5340-01-335-9359	86	8
11862	15559312	6220-01-156-4476	43	11
			45	12
11862	15559316	6220-01-156-4475	42	24
11862	15562374	5330-01-087-4714	249	5
11862	15567924	5340-01-269-1361	20	12
11862	15569009	5340-01-158-6895	168	11
11862	15569010	2540-01-158-6896	168	2
11862	15569071	5330-01-158-6683	134	8
11862	15569072	5330-01-159-1153	134	8
11862	15571643	2510-01-155-8799	133	6
11862	15577694	2540-01-167-2985	169	1
11862	15582233	5310-01-205-2537	96	11
11862	15588503	5355-01-159-6622	68	29
11862	15588504	5355-01-197-3172	69	8
11862	15590123	2910-01-225-1068	20	6
11862	15590401	2540-01-156-6107	135	2
11862	15590402	2540-01-156-6108	135	2
11862	15590415		134	21

CROSS-REFERENCE INDEXES

PART NUMBER INDEX

CAGEC	PART NUMBER	STOCK NUMBER	FIG	ITEM
11862	15590422	2540-01-158-1721	134	22
11862	15590443	5305-01-230-9846	136	28
11862	15591130	5325-01-164-2377	52	5
			227	19
11862	15591138	6680-01-225-4432	33	5
11862	15591247	2540-01-191-8668	162	1
11862	15591248	2540-01-160-3651	163	2
11862	15591702	2540-01-193-7884	158	2
11862	15591703	2540-01-157-3032	198	1
11862	15591704	2540-01-156-0584	198	4
11862	15591705	2590-01-234-6468	152	2
23862	15591706	2540-01-241-4238	152	3
11862	15591707	5340-01-238-5923	152	11
11862	15591709	2590-01-242-1050	152	3
1T998	15591710	5340-01-238-5924	152	5
11862	15591718	5945-01-192-7985	32	3
11862	15593230	2510-01-155-8800	133	5
11862	15593570	5330-01-237-7512	146	1
11862	15593571	5330-01-207-9421	146	2
11862	15593599		228	1
11862	15593849	5340-01-232-8179	95	5
11862	15593866	5360-01-185-0341	148	1
11862	15594176	5930-01-202-3573	66	2
11862	15594177	2530-01-164-7126	88	6
11862	15594178	2530-01-163-7227	88	6
11862	15594643	2540-01-225-1023	142	16
11862	15594644	2510-01-225-1006	142	12
11862	15594895	5340-01-210-8824	158	10
11862	15594896	2590-01-247-3286	158	10
11862	15594983	2540-01-156-0088	158	7
			236	1
11862	15595211	2590-01-159-8716	111	12
11862	15595216	2990-01-147-4290	22	1
11862	15595224	2990-01-225-1029	21	1
11862	15595271	2990-01-225-1028	21	11
61928	15596614	5930-01-208-6292	18	15
11862	15596686	2520-01-153-8431	70	9
			72	9
11862	15596975	2510-01-155-5850	142	19
11862	15596976	2510-01-155-5851	142	13
11862	15597653	2540-01-155-7298	137	6
11862	15597654	2540-01-156-8315	137	6
11862	15597667	2510-01-156-4872	134	11
11862	15597668	2510-01-156-4873	134	11
11862	15598706	2510-01-156-8092	132	29
11862	15598708	2510-01-159-8761	128	3
11862	15598709	2510-01-212-5819	128	6
11862	15598769	2540-01-160-1591	128	2
11862	15598770	2510-01-194-0206	128	1
11862	15599200	2990-01-163-3575	213	5
11862	15599201	2520-01-163-3494	213	6

CROSS-REFERENCE INDEXES

PART NUMBER INDEX

CAGEC	PART NUMBER	STOCK NUMBER	FIG	ITEM
11862	15599203		242	10
11862	15599204	3020-01-147-7935	30	3
11862	15599209		16	3
			17	3
11862	15599211	2990-01-163-0771	215	9
11862	15599212	2990-01-162-4416	218	12
11862	15599215	2990-01-163-1180	218	5
11862	15599216		22	1
11862	15599219	5340-01-198-8591	110	1
11862	15599220	5340-01-198-8591	110	3
11862	15599221	5340-01-162-9777	14	33
11862	15599222	5940-01-189-5153	54	16
11862	15599223	5910-01-189-5109	56	2
11862	15599224	5910-01-190-4600	47	4
11862	15599225	5910-01-189-5152	36	5
11862	15599234	4720-01-247-4680	221	21
11862	15599235		58	3
11862	15599243	2990-01-163-1179	217	6
11862	15599245	5340-01-219-7272	217	4
11862	15599246	5340-01-221-9972	219	2
11862	15599250	5365-01-194-5074	140	5
11862	15599259		90	9
11862	15599260		90	6
11862	15599261		90	9
11862	15599262		90	6
11862	15599269	2990-01-231-2938	22	22
11862	15599271	2590-01-191-6511	173	8
11862	15599273	5340-01-212-6716	234	6
11862	15599274	5340-01-212-6717	234	6
11862	15599283	2590-01-163-1238	126	4
11862	15599284	2590-01-164-0134	126	4
11862	15599285	2510-01-160-4970	126	1
11862	15599286	2590-01-159-8861	126	5
11862	15599287		215	11
11862	15599290	2540-01-162-7114	216	1
11862	15599432	5306-01-148-7457	117	6
11862	15599677	2540-01-194-0261	133	12
11862	15599678	2540-01-192-9754	144	1
11862	15599687	2520-01-201-2501	82	1
11862	15599900	2990-01-257-1569	48	1
11862	15599901	6140-01-190-2516	48	16
11862	15599902	6140-01-190-2517	48	8
11862	15599910	2510-01-159-1791	232	12
11862	15599915	2590-01-182-4455	116	3
11862	15599916		233	11
11862	15599917	2540-01-214-2634	233	14
11862	15599918	2540-01-214-2635	233	14
11862	15599919	3120-01-194-0754	196	2
11862	15599920	5365-01-219-7285	222	9
11862	15599929	5306-01-194-4977	151	1
			152	1

CROSS-REFERENCE INDEXES

PART NUMBER INDEX

CAGEC	PART NUMBER	STOCK NUMBER	FIG	ITEM
11862	15599940	2540-01-163-7225	245	9
11862	15599942	2990-01-250-8612	245	6
11862	15599950	1430-01-106-8451	231	15
11862	15599951	2540-01-216-3188	231	12
11862	15599952	4730-01-216-0021	246	20
11862	15599958	5340-01-159-1460	172	9
11862	15599959	5340-01-201-7954	172	8
11862	15599962	5340-01-162-6062	202	7
11862	15599963	5340-01-159-4519	202	12
11862	15599964	5340-01-198-3434	202	11
11862	15599965	5340-01-253-2102	173	7
11862	15599968	6150-01-234-3253	224	1
11862	15599971	5306-01-166-8556	140	2
11862	15599972	5930-01-184-6370	242	17
11862	15599973	5340-00-881-5303	90	2
			91	24
11862	15599975	2540-01-162-4411	165	1
11862	15599976	2540-01-158-8561	165	5
11862	15599986		5	22
11862	15599987	4730-01-227-1929	5	23
11862	15599988	5340-01-234-1465	5	7
11862	15599989	5340-01-228-1659	38	3
11862	15599990	5325-01-230-1844	202	2
11862	15599994	5310-01-242-8561	201	3
			202	1
11862	15599997	2510-01-225-1004	111	41
11862	15599998	2510-01-225-5865	111	5
11862	15599999		17	39
11862	15605040	5305-01-161-3997	42	19
11862	15607227	5310-00-380-1514	90	8
11862	15614462	2510-01-224-8839	143	6
11862	15617126	2510-01-163-2709	136	9
11862	15627452	2540-01-158-8560	167	11
11862	15628608	2510-01-155-5857	142	8
11862	15629509	2510-01-154-6906	130	1
11862	15634658		96	13
11862	15634659	2540-01-323-6049	200	7
11862	15634660	2540-01-323-6050	200	7
11862	15634661	5365-01-326-4346	96	26
11862	15634663	2530-01-326-1462	96	23
11862	15635684	2540-01-163-7305	136	10
11862	15635685	2510-01-163-7306	136	1
11862	15641780	2540-01-158-8554	143	2
11862	15646949	2540-01-159-8721	159	5
11862	15668598	2530-01-325-9112	96	3
24617	157456	5305-01-197-6351	196	14
16758	16015256	5930-01-165-0732	208	7
11862	16034561	2590-01-158-8551	208	4
11862	1604854	3120-01-232-6781	99	74
30076	160635	5310-00-792-3617	102	8
11862	1610819	5306-01-185-7050	28	9

CROSS-REFERENCE INDEXES

PART NUMBER INDEX

CAGEC	PART NUMBER	STOCK NUMBER	FIG	ITEM
11862	1623159	5307-01-150-7764	30	12
11862	1635490	5306-01-149-6280	3	7
			25	8
			28	2
			28	4
			29	3
			59	1
			104	7
			251	7
			251	9
11862	1638274	5340-01-158-0314	15	16
			16	1
			17	4
24617	163881	5320-01-166-1477	193	14
24617	1640810	5305-01-231-1298	54	6
			134	15
11862	1640902	5305-01-160-3945	41	10
11862	16500591	6220-01-155-6515	42	31
11862	16501759	2510-01-159-8765	42	33
24617	165079	5305-01-166-1610	180	27
11862	16604537	2540-01-158-8559	166	9
08806	168	6240-00-144-4693	34	21
			35	1
			35	5
			43	8
			44	5
79410	17-01-014-001	5310-01-154-3990	97	12
25022	17-0177	5340-01-164-8137	180	25
			181	20
			190	7
25022	17-0178	5340-01-162-5619	180	23
			181	21
			190	8
25022	17-0195	2540-01-163-0894	194	5
25022	17-0201	5680-01-193-5078	181	18
25022	17-0202	5680-01-193-5078	180	26
25022	17-0209	2540-01-193-3623	180	22
			181	22
24617	171108	5305-01-201-3334	183	16
			184	11
11862	1727059	5310-01-162-7912	166	14
			167	16
11862	1731168	5340-01-166-5861	162	4
			163	5
			169	5
72582	178917	4730-01-075-7310	16	5
			17	8
11862	17981073	4720-01-149-4659	91	25
11862	17983936	2530-01-287-3980	99	67
11862	17987489	2530-01-147-6421	99	70
76462	18001032	5365-01-159-4833	88	10

CROSS-REFERENCE INDEXES

PART NUMBER INDEX

CAGEC	PART NUMBER	STOCK NUMBER	FIG	ITEM
11862	18002428	5310-01-151-8347	87	19
			88	21
11862	18003151	2530-01-149-1886	94	3
11862	18004057	5365-01-164-4525	88	9
11862	18004794	2530-01-096-6764	94	4
11862	18004890	2530-01-110-5304	94	4
11862	18007952	2530-01-147-9329	93	7
11862	18013395	2530-01-163-7878	93	5
			93	8
11862	18015381	2530-01-156-6190	93	2
11862	1892163	2590-01-085-6956	47	1
24617	189448	5320-01-197-1394	116	6
25022	19-0445		178	2
25022	19-0816	6210-01-159-1794	191	1
25022	19-0817	6220-01-160-5094	176	4
			177	4
25022	19-0818	6220-01-160-3686	178	17
25022	19-0820	2590-01-164-7898	178	23
25022	19-0849	5340-01-166-5654	183	10
			184	4
25022	19-0861	6220-01-160-3705	178	5
25022	19-0875	5945-01-173-7760	187	2
25022	19-0876	5945-01-166-2012	187	8
25022	19-0877	5940-01-171-3195	187	7
25022	19-0882	6220-01-172-5300	176	7
			177	7
25022	19-0884	2590-01-164-7024	176	6
			177	6
25022	19-0885	6220-01-171-9557	176	8
			177	8
25022	19-0893	6220-01-160-3687	178	3
25022	19-0909	5925-01-190-1211	187	5
25022	19-0910	5995-01-192-4374	187	4
25022	19-0940	6220-01-197-0486	191	2
25022	19-0941	6230-01-191-3856	191	4
25022	190-0941-1		191	5
25022	19-0942	6250-01-164-3266	183	8
			184	1
25022	19-0969	5365-01-269-8614	178	6
08806	194	6240-00-944-1264	34	18
			34	20
			42	17
			53	1
			56	1
11862	1988380	5910-01-189-5110	54	3
11862	1995217	5930-01-014-0187	41	15
11862	20025648	5305-01-162-5996	166	6
			167	6
11862	20030401	5325-01-165-2551	158	1
11862	20056525	5360-01-162-2849	161	17
			164	10

CROSS-REFERENCE INDEXES

PART NUMBER INDEX

CAGEC	PART NUMBER	STOCK NUMBER	FIG	ITEM
11862	20056525	5360-01-162-2849	165	6
			170	7
11862	2014469	5306-01-158-9018	23	12
			48	14
			127	2
			130	3
			141	8
			142	18
			145	7
			161	16
			168	3
			170	13
			171	6
			225	11
11862	20171141	2540-01-160-5918	143	3
11862	20243999	2540-01-158-4603	164	12
			165	12
11862	20264728	5340-01-165-4792	136	11
11862	20264729	5340-01-165-4791	136	2
11862	20264730	5330-01-181-2454	136	12
11862	20264731	5330-01-178-7351	136	3
11862	20264736	2540-01-163-2719	136	14
11862	20264737	2540-01-159-8880	136	5
11862	20264743	2510-01-155-5432	156	4
11862	20264744	2510-01-155-5433	156	2
11862	20289493	2540-01-251-1715	166	8
11862	20293842	2540-01-160-5840	167	7
11862	20293843	2540-01-251-1714	166	7
11862	20351007	5360-01-197-0870	164	6
11862	20354945	5680-01-167-1068	136	15
11862	20354946	5680-01-164-4964	136	6
11862	20365263	5305-01-167-8334	68	22
			229	17
11862	20369919	2540-01-191-8440	167	8
11862	20369920	2540-01-191-8441	167	9
11862	20410901	2540-01-248-2477	167	12
11862	2043150	5340-01-163-1973	58	4
11862	2043151	5340-01-159-1321	37	6
			38	13
			49	4
11862	2044779	5340-01-166-1470	58	2
11862	20489125	5330-01-161-2608	198	21
99688	20565	6105-01-159-2223	253	11
99688	20566	6105-01-159-2666	252	8
08806	2057	6240-01-157-0636	43	5
08806	2057NA	6240-01-157-0635	42	26
11862	20573776	5325-01-198-8239	167	10
11862	20696927	5325-01-160-4028	134	6
11862	2098912	5945-01-162-0517	222	3
22337	212-776	2610-01-148-1634	98	1
25022	22-0832	2510-01-216-0039	183	1

CROSS-REFERENCE INDEXES

PART NUMBER INDEX

CAGEC	PART NUMBER	STOCK NUMBER	FIG	ITEM
25022	22-0832	2510-01-216-0039	184	8
25022	22-0860	2540-01-166-5913	189	4
25022	22-0861	2590-01-163-7669	183	11
			184	17
25022	22-0864	2510-01-192-9752	193	5
25022	22-0865	2590-01-163-8596	189	1
25022	22-0867		185	5
25022	22-0871		210	1
25022	22-0873	7230-01-165-6795	193	8
25022	22-0875	2590-01-163-7287	178	15
25022	22-0876	5340-01-164-1076	190	3
25022	22-0877	5340-01-164-0958	183	12
			184	18
25022	22-0878	5340-01-164-1077	190	5
25022	22-0880	2590-01-1693-7290	185	4
			186	7
25022	22-0881	5340-01-164-0746	177	21
25022	22-0884	2540-01-159-1793	183	2
			184	7
11862	22020945	6105-01-164-6546	206	13
11862	22021655		198	9
11862	22021679	5325-01-167-8372	199	12
11862	22029629	2540-01-156-5882	198	10
11862	22029630	2540-01-191-6512	198	12
11862	22038927	2540-01-243-4934	199	9
11862	22038928	2540-01-156-0068	199	28
72560	22048352	2540-01-159-7954	198	14
11862	22049531	2540-01-156-0069	199	7
11862	22054153	5310-01-157-4855	199	8
11862	22054156	5330-01-244-2277	199	10
11862	22098841	6105-01-254-9496	244	4
14892	2227168	5330-01-157-1916	89	35
14892	2229044	5330-01-165-1358	89	32
14892	2229046	5340-01-157-1955	89	33
14892	2229448	5340-01-158-0321	89	37
14892	2232072	2530-01-192-9778	89	34
14892	2232073	2530-01-156-7016	89	30
14892	2232076	2530-01-168-6369	89	32
14892	2232077	2530-01-250-6472	89	36
14892	2238739		92	1
14892	2238740		92	8
14892	2238742	2530-01-147-6424	92	10
94988	224-12V	5945-00-992-5415	41	31
72582	224425	4732-00-277-8269	5	5
11862	22506637	2910-01-200-4338	10	9
11862	22507977	5355-01-150-1541	41	7
11862	22510143	2540-01-156-7233	99	75
11862	22514738	4730-01-155-5135	106	7
11862	22514861	2920-01-150-1610	41	1
11862	22515965	5330-01-159-1298	13	4
			14	19

CROSS-REFERENCE INDEXES

PART NUMBER INDEX

CAGEC	PART NUMBER	STOCK NUMBER	FIG	ITEM
11862	22516548	6680-01-161-1439	13	2
			14	18
11862	22521054	5310-01-250-3301	32	10
11862	22521550	5310-01-165-3331	4	7
			5	18
			6	6
			8	4
			11	13
			58	1
11862	22527167	5360-01-163-7234	90	17
			91	3
11862	22529441	6350-01-321-7005	56	13
11862	22535073	5307-01-269-4336	1	3
			25	12
84760	22591	5330-01-213-9966	18	3
25022	23-0193	9905-01-165-0542	176	18
			177	17
25022	23-0196	9905-01-165-0541	176	17
			177	18
25022	23-0198	9905-01-165-0544	178	7
25022	23-0200	9905-01-165-6901	180	17
			181	27
11862	23500396	5365-01-193-0458	32	11
11862	23500846	5330-01-149-0874	25	9
			220	3
84760	23796	4820-01-209-0473	18	14
72210	24004-J	2530-01-165-9653	101	6
11862	2423517	5310-01-195-5088	69	5
84760	24265	5340-01-197-1199	18	8
84760	24267	5340-01-211-3086	18	6
84760	24281	5340-01-202-2622	18	9
84760	24285	2910-01-210-1322	18	4
84760	24322	5305-01-211-3031	18	12
35510	2434	5310-00-775-5139	31	6
84760	24437	5305-01-211-3032	18	11
11862	2477054	5320-01-160-3999	41	14
			173	3
72983	248X4	4730-00-900-3296	210	12
11862	25004137	6680-01-164-9433	14	20
11862	25004140	6680-01-175-0565	13	3
11862	25011206	4820-01-153-1851	4	10
11862	25011208	6615-01-153-1852	4	9
11862	25015099	5330-01-164-1653	34	5
11862	25017376	6695-01-167-8108	34	8
11862	25020687	5340-01-163-7501	249	2
11862	25022883	6220-01-164-5228	34	6
11862	25022884	6210-01-158-4668	34	12
70040	25023641	5355-01-251-0633	57	7
11862	25033627	6680-01-230-5684	249	1
11862	25037177	6685-01-192-4834	46	1
11862	25041910	2940-01-148-5992	12	5

CROSS-REFERENCE INDEXES

PART NUMBER INDEX

CAGEC	PART NUMBER	STOCK NUMBER	FIG	ITEM
11862	25042462	2990-01-147-9284	6	14
11862	25052373	6680-01-225-4475	249	3
11862	25052807	2540-01-158-8626	34	3
11862	25053500	6210-01-161-2138	34	14
11862	25053501	6210-01-158-6575	34	13
11862	25053622	2540-01-163-7281	34	16
11862	25053623	5999-01-158-9249	34	4
11862	25076586	6210-01-271-6871	34	15
11862	25078571	2540-01-147-5537	57	5
11862	25078578	2540-01-191-6510	57	8
27647	25113	3040-01-163-0797	96	4
11862	25515635	2530-01-156-8317	90	21
11862	25516531	5340-01-158-0297	86	16
11862	25518880	4730-01-163-7194	8	6
			15	10
			16	12
			17	13
			18	19
			106	2
11862	25523703	5945-01-243-1702	47	6
11862	25527423	5340-01-268-9064	17	10
			90	4
			214	17
11862	26013911	2520-01-211-6755	73	1
11862	26013913	2520-01-191-9518	71	1
11862	26016662	5330-01-084-2410	84	6
11862	2622667	2530-01-154-1263	94	5
90005	26422-B	2910-00-203-3322	210	32
72582	271163	5310-01-069-5243	39	5
			42	21
			43	10
			45	14
			56	11
24617	271166	5310-00-696-5172	54	4
24617	271172	5310-01-152-0598	39	6
			49	3
			54	5
			144	12
			172	10
			197	7
			197	13
			197	21
			227	14
			230	9
24617	271184	5310-00-933-4310	247	12
84760	27284	2920-01-212-4771	18	13
84760	27290	2910-01-156-0045	18	1
11862	273487	2640-00-555-2829	96	29
24617	274244	5330-00-935-9136	4	8
			213	2
80201	27467	5330-01-106-7938	96	14

CROSS-REFERENCE INDEXES

PART NUMBER INDEX

CAGEC	PART NUMBER	STOCK NUMBER	FIG	ITEM
80201	27467	5330-01-106-7938	96	14
14892	2770209	2530-01-151-5967	89	1
14892	2770317	2530-01-154-1294	89	1
14892	2770614		89	11
84760	27820	5330-01-236-1724	18	5
84760	29090	2910-01-210-1323	18	7
77060	2973932	6250-00-433-5946	34	19
97271	29907X	2530-01-149-3827	77	1
6V625	30-600	2640-01-302-1388	96	29
22593	30103	5330-00-360-7881	147	3
11862	3013475	4730-01-160-0814	206	11
11862	3015545	5310-01-211-1648	206	7
11862	3024673	5340-01-165-3717	205	3
11862	3024867	2540-01-155-7299	205	7
11862	3025501	5340-01-158-6816	205	2
11862	3027247	2540-01-156-0072	205	4
11862	3027308	2540-01-159-8705	205	12
11862	3029730	2540-01-158-6906	206	5
11862	3030072	2540-01-156-0071	205	11
11862	3030075	2540-01-156-4874	205	8
11862	3035192	4520-01-166-2134	244	5
11862	3036927	4720-01-160-3664	206	12
11862	3037476	4520-01-166-2133	244	2
11862	3037550	6105-01-165-4561	206	8
11862	3039873	5330-01-195-4880	206	9
11862	3042351	5310-01-164-2336	206	6
11862	3048067	2540-01-156-0073	205	13
11862	3048083	2520-01-192-1257	205	5
81795	30489	5310-00-472-3214	229	10
			231	2
			232	6
11862	3054308		204	2
11862	3054315	2540-01-159-8722	205	6
27462	3054316	2540-01-156-0070	205	10
11862	3055734	2540-01-268-7202	244	3
11862	3058097		206	4
61928	3058966	2930-01-264-3480	23	15
25022	31-0030	2540-01-163-8623	176	12
			177	23
81343	31-620	6140-01-031-6882	48	11
35510	31256	5310-01-143-1719	31	3
11862	3187843	2510-01-153-9584	120	4
11862	3187844	2540-01-155-7496	122	6
11862	3187845	2540-01-148-2943	121	1
11862	3187846	2510-01-148-2942	120	4
24234	319029	4720-01-192-1631	BULK	11
14894	3203465	5340-01-149-3376	92	17
14892	3203466	2530-01-149-3375	92	17
11862	326560		58	5
11862	326561	5360-01-206-6616	249	6
11862	326934	5330-01-159-1152	149	1

CROSS-REFERENCE INDEXES

PART NUMBER INDEX

CAGEC	PART NUMBER	STOCK NUMBER	FIG	ITEM
11862	327005	5330-01-159-2816	149	3
11862	327006	5330-01-162-8595	149	2
11862	327015	5330-01-182-4121	144	11
11862	327062	2540-01-156-4870	133	2
			133	11
11862	327065	5360-01-161-7561	133	3
			133	10
11862	327067	3040-01-155-0371	137	1
24617	327739	5330-01-076-3009	96	27
11862	327959	5340-01-206-2995	133	27
11862	327960	5340-01-206-2996	133	27
11862	328107	2510-01-325-9069	124	9
11862	328108		124	11
11862	328111		124	10
11862	328128	3120-01-211-7528	123	6
11862	328130	5306-01-155-6108	123	1
11862	328131	5310-01-147-8748	123	2
11862	328132	2530-01-147-5541	123	9
11862	329198		198	18
11862	329457	5360-01-160-2411	161	20
			161	23
			170	10
			170	16
11862	330046	2540-01-191-8439	117	1
11862	330438	2510-01-155-5846	141	3
11862	330485	5325-01-205-2545	134	10
11862	330492	6220-01-327-3252	44	4
11862	331416	5340-01-155-3668	91	19
11862	331478	5305-01-148-8208	92	15
11862	331638	2540-01-158-8556	148	2
11862	334101	2510-01-162-7112	147	1
11862	334102	2510-01-165-4932	147	5
11862	334104	5330-01-167-8123	147	3
11862	334132	2510-01-159-7120	145	24
11862	334195	5306-01-160-0769	167	7
			165	7
11862	334307	3040-01-156-7182	87	8
11862	334308	3040-01-157-7970	87	8
23862	334387	5310-01-107-4051	96	1
11862	334521	2590-01-155-5140	14	22
11862	334522	5340-01-160-0367	14	23
11862	334523	2590-01-155-5177	14	12
11862	334532	6680-01-147-6583	60	10
11862	334540	2530-01-159-8802	86	2
11862	334541	5325-01-160-2238	86	7
11862	334675	5340-01-244-7925	13	11
11862	335452	3040-01-158-8703	148	5
11862	335524	3120-01-159-1311	145	15
			168	12
11862	336406	5355-01-157-1865	208	6
14892	3368689	2530-01-183-8860	87	6

CROSS-REFERENCE INDEXES

PART NUMBER INDEX

CAGEC	PART NUMBER	STOCK NUMBER	FIG	ITEM
11862	336926	3040-01-166-4497	95	12
11862	336989	5360-01-151-1121	20	3
11862	337185	5365-01-149-0880	4	19
			213	7
97271	33734	5310-01-172-1591	96	18
11862	337714		198	22
11862	337715	2540-01-156-4907	136	20
11862	337716	2540-01-156-4908	136	20
11862	337788	5340-01-160-2367	145	6
11862	337899	5340-01-160-2172	147	7
11862	337957	5330-01-323-5567	111	24
11862	338696	5340-01-155-2616	106	13
11862	339885	6220-01-306-4265	44	6
11862	339887	6220-01-327-1025	44	6
11862	340053	2540-01-158-8813	143	5
11862	341160	5340-01-160-2445	21	5
			22	7
11862	341287	2910-01-155-5137	14	27
11862	341509	5310-01-148-2676	96	24
11862	341510	5315-01-153-0317	96	28
11862	341511	2520-01-147-5539	96	25
11862	341990	5325-01-155-4482	86	3
11862	342221	5306-01-159-1130	160	4
			162	2
			163	1
			169	3
11862	342405	2910-01-149-3786	20	7
11862	342677	5340-01-155-2614	90	15
11862	343124	5325-01-164-6431	37	7
11862	343178	5305-01-149-1936	100	1
11862	343179	5365-01-151-6111	100	2
11862	343350	5340-01-270-7423	10	2
11862	343438	5340-01-155-2614	90	1
11862	343444	5340-01-164-6474	211	13
			214	13
11862	343915	2510-01-166-1146	132	15
11862	343951	2590-01-147-5538	117	9
11862	343978	5365-01-157-7476	161	6
11862	344714	5340-01-162-9781	14	28
11862	345683	2530-01-153-1813	89	25
11862	345943	2530-01-152-9258	88	29
11862	345944	2530-01-153-1492	88	29
11862	346381	3120-01-158-2096	95	8
11862	347347	5325-01-157-1698	42	20
			125	4
			159	8
11862	350036	2590-01-147-2269	116	8
11862	350037	2590-01-193-3443	116	5
11862	350371		106	3
11862	354501	4730-01-148-2758	25	15
			26	2

CROSS-REFERENCE INDEXES

PART NUMBER INDEX

CAGEC	PART NUMBER	STOCK NUMBER	FIG	ITEM
11862	354501	4730-01-148-2758	220	7
11862	355561	2540-01-153-9470	95	11
11862	357845	2530-01-156-5883	87	16
11862	357846	5340-01-156-8395	87	16
11862	357889	2530-01-152-7787	88	18
11862	357890	3040-01-152-7786	88	18
11862	358375	6680-01-147-5497	23	7
11862	358501	5310-00-264-1930	97	24
11862	359816	5340-01-161-4025	91	18
11862	359847	5340-01-151-7409	14	21
11862	359877	2510-01-153-9473	118	15
			119	14
11862	359878	2510-01-154-1261	118	11
			119	10
25022	36-0039	2540-01-163-8638	188	1
25022	36-0043	2540-01-173-1249	188	27
25022	36-0044	4820-01-173-1250	188	3
25022	36-0045	2540-01-163-8598	188	2
25022	36-0046	2540-01-163-8599	188	16
25022	36-0047	2540-01-163-8600	188	15
25022	36-0048	5360-01-163-5578	188	17
25022	36-0049	5360-01-163-5579	188	18
25022	36-0050	5360-01-163-5580	188	20
25022	36-0051	5315-01-164-5334	188	30
25022	36-0054	2540-01-164-1562	188	8
25022	36-0055	2540-01-165-7931	188	6
25022	36-0056	5315-01-164-5336	188	5
25022	36-0066	2540-01-025-0433	189	9
25022	36-0070	2540-01-191-6539	188	9
25022	36-0071	5315-01-209-7063	188	14
25022	36-0072	5340-01-193-9565	188	31
25022	36-0073	5315-01-197-1482	188	28
25022	36-0074	5340-01-197-1550	188	25
25022	36-0075	5315-01-197-1483	188	21
11862	362297	2530-01-159-5958	100	14
11862	362298	2530-01-159-8725	100	15
11862	362379	5310-01-165-0464	42	15
11862	362433	5340-01-170-5530	134	2
11862	362434	5340-01-161-5522	134	2
11862	363137	5325-01-160-2237	134	20
11862	363139	5330-01-096-7698	BULK	32
80020	36344N24	5315-00-243-1169	114	15
			115	22
11862	364372	5365-01-160-2483	134	23
72447	36472	4730-01-034-8228	76	15
11862	365443	5310-01-184-5866	136	7
			136	16
11862	365953		135	1
11862	365953-1		136	4
			136	13
11862	368026	6680-01-160-5276	249	8

CROSS-REFERENCE INDEXES

PART NUMBER INDEX

CAGEC	PART NUMBER	STOCK NUMBER	FIG	ITEM
11862	368752	2910-01-147-4219	13	12
11862	368786	2530-01-148-1463	86	17
97271	36880	5310-01-093-2907	78	1
11862	3694822	5360-00-310-4493	88	25
25022	37-0019	5930-01-163-2779	184	14
			192	3
25022	37-0020	5930-01-163-8851	184	12
			192	6
25022	37-0051	5340-01-165-0602	189	7
11862	3702807	5310-01-151-8353	95	13
11862	370349	5340-01-217-2278	231	5
11862	370389	2510-01-221-2094	BULK	9
11862	370390	5330-00-753-8036	BULK	31
11862	3705044	5330-00-830-1745	9	11
11862	370867	6220-01-156-8420	45	7
11862	370868	6220-01-156-8247	45	7
11862	370873	5340-01-165-3417	45	6
11862	370874	6250-01-155-6547	45	15
11862	3711876	5305-01-150-9500	79	9
			79	13
11862	371603	5305-01-148-3687	116	9
11862	3719599	2910-00-493-2138	9	12
11862	3721887	5365-01-152-7439	70	3
			71	3
			72	3
			73	3
11862	372249	2530-01-152-0180	87	29
			88	31
11862	372379	2530-01-140-6144	87	10
11862	3725668	5310-01-184-5418	117	3
97271	37312	5365-01-174-8657	76	4
11862	3738198	5340-01-221-0264	238	11
11862	375180	5340-01-194-3188	137	5
11862	3760300	5310-01-155-1898	88	3
11862	3762400	2590-00-476-5459	136	8
			136	17
11862	3764438	2530-01-153-1814	121	7
			122	5
11862	3765243	5340-01-161-9188	132	7
11862	3767138	5360-01-159-1449	87	23
11862	376851	5330-01-086-3503	77	5
11862	376852	5310-01-153-1381	77	4
11862	376855	5330-01-086-3504	77	3
11862	376869	5306-01-153-1368	82	3
11862	3773687		106	9
11862	3782730		198	13
11862	3782732		198	23
11862	378362	5340-01-161-1440	249	11
11862	3787240	2520-01-159-7757	60	5
			83	11
			84	7

CROSS-REFERENCE INDEXES

PART NUMBER INDEX

CAGEC	PART NUMBER	STOCK NUMBER	FIG	ITEM
11862	3790768	5310-01-147-8743	12	2
			107	3
			115	5
11862	3792287	5310-01-160-4536	23	21
			152	10
11862	3793014	5315-00-450-9163	99	73
11862	3794767	5340-01-217-2168	231	3
11862	3798372	2590-01-160-1047	198	19
97271	38000	2530-01-159-7755	92	18
97271	38001	2530-01-159-7754	92	18
97271	38081-1	5310-01-099-7945	78	2
11862	3815936	5930-00-073-0390	46	4
11862	3816659	5340-01-149-4434	23	9
			49	8
			90	5
			129	3
			198	8
			222	2
			226	6
			240	2
11862	3820163	5360-01-156-9730	88	22
11862	382105	5310-01-148-2682	68	16
11862	3824124	5306-01-160-7553	198	20
11862	3825416	5340-01-159-1324	209	4
			220	16
11862	3827499	5310-01-196-5587	12	1
11862	3838153	5310-01-194-9220	69	4
11862	3850084	5360-01-160-2415	95	7
11862	3856834	5315-01-156-0081	87	7
11862	3856843	5360-01-157-3662	87	20
11862	3856849	5365-01-158-2191	87	26
11862	3856850	5360-00-229-5312	87	24
11862	3856855	2530-00-494-8165	87	14
			88	16
11862	3856856	2530-00-125-2769	87	14
			88	16
11862	3856857	3040-01-156-8307	87	18
11862	3856858	2530-01-156-8308	87	18
11862	386451	2520-00-722-7074	70	2
			71	2
			72	2
			73	2
11862	3866187	5340-01-158-0303	80	3
11862	3866918		249	4
60038	387AS-382A	3110-01-030-8475	96	15
11862	3882979	3040-01-148-5982	72	15
			73	15
11862	3886908	5325-01-164-8655	214	25
			226	13
11862	3887347	5360-01-162-9935	88	26
11862	3889864	5340-01-159-6905	142	14

CROSS-REFERENCE INDEXES

PART NUMBER INDEX

CAGEC	PART NUMBER	STOCK NUMBER	FIG	ITEM
11862	3893181	2540-01-159-8878	86	1
11862	3898059	2530-01-156-4875	87	21
11862	3900684	5340-01-158-0503	133	20
11862	3905674	5340-01-160-2470	146	10
73342	3909063	5310-01-143-0542	20	2
11862	3914674	5310-01-157-5670	111	10
			161	7
11862	3918889	5325-01-168-5677	227	18
11862	3920486	5340-01-149-9729	74	5
11862	3929059	5315-01-025-0930	179	11
11862	3944769	5340-01-157-7471	133	25
11862	3953987	5310-01-194-7081	69	14
11862	3954730	5305-01-162-7890	117	7
			162	3
			163	3
			168	26
11862	3954735	5310-01-147-9792	30	8
11862	3957093	2590-01-162-7367	132	12
11862	3965121	3120-01-159-9386	77	2
11862	3970076		10	3
11862	3977383	2520-01-040-2160	82	2
11862	3977384	2520-01-038-7283	82	1
11862	3977386	5340-01-148-2730	83	9
11862	3977387	5330-01-020-9319	83	10
11862	3977397	2530-01-096-7731	96	23
11862	3977775	5325-01-164-7550	228	2
11862	3978901	5310-01-021-9027	96	1
11862	3979756	5325-01-159-2843	49	34
11862	3982098	5310-01-170-9100	24	1
			49	29
			128	4
			240	3
11862	3986821	4730-01-158-8717	198	17
11862	3987364	4720-01-096-7718	BULK	27
11862	3988538	5305-01-019-1884	96	19
24617	3990160	5310-01-097-9414	112	3
			123	3
11862	3990892	2540-01-158-8611	198	15
11862	3991022	5306-01-157-9817	116	2
11862	3992925	3120-01-169-6440	68	10
11862	3993087	2910-01-150-3675	20	5
11862	3993729		124	2
11862	3996270	5940-01-145-7817	54	7
11862	3997718	5340-01-167-9694	62	3
11862	3999572	8040-01-188-2953	33	1
11862	404062	3120-01-250-0583	124	6
11862	404234	5360-01-163-0886	99	61
76445	40424	5310-01-153-9302	97	14
11862	406887	2590-01-323-5857	124	7
11862	409190		99	63
14892	4150514	5340-01-152-7155	92	14

CROSS-REFERENCE INDEXES

PART NUMBER INDEX

CAGEC	PART NUMBER	STOCK NUMBER	FIG	ITEM
14892	4150515	2530-01-152-7115	87	5
11862	4158246	3120-01-338-6380	143	2
11862	4168122	5340-00-285-8868	134	18
11862	419454	5365-01-160-9530	99	69
20796	42-4877	3030-01-043-6749	251	12
20796	42-5023	3030-01-148-2792	104	1
20796	42-6919	3030-00-967-4898	30	4
20796	42-6921	3030-00-357-5506	30	11
20796	42-6923	3030-01-147-6410	29	4
24617	423532	5305-01-219-5399	242	28
			246	38
20796	43-3226	3030-01-258-5125	28	10
11862	4303911	5360-01-159-8862	144	13
35510	4340	5310-00-429-3135	31	2
11862	4410574	5340-01-157-6092	133	7
08806	4411	6240-00-836-2079	176	5
			177	5
08806	4435	6240-00-252-7138	248	2
24617	443945	5305-01-197-1475	117	4
17769	443998	4730-00-415-3172	221	12
24617	444034	4730-00-580-6738	19	1
24617	444620	4730-00-132-4625	17	9
30379	444789	4730-00-044-4789	26	1
			83	4
			84	1
24617	447143	5305-01-200-7735	180	6
			181	12
11862	4495180	2540-01-158-8555	148	8
11862	4497001	5310-01-194-9233	69	3
60038	453X	3110-00-142-4387	85	15
24617	456004	5310-00-596-6897	197	16
			220	17
24617	456697	5306-01-159-5710	94	1
24617	456748	5305-01-242-1148	221	18
			242	7
			246	16
11862	458025	2510-01-155-5854	142	3
11862	458026	2510-01-155-8785	142	6
79260	45823	2990-01-155-5151	21	8
11862	458300	5306-01-323-5544	74	6
11862	458418	2520-01-173-1362	70	7
			72	7
11862	4587931	5330-01-157-5684	133	14
11862	458985	5305-01-162-5707	150	10
11862	459461	5360-01-149-6309	42	36
99688	459461	2540-01-191-4331	210	41
99688	46023	4520-01-192-6005	210	23
11862	461610	2510-01-156-4871	136	24
11862	462233	5970-01-158-9337	158	11
			BULK	29
11862	462811	5330-01-096-9649	76	5

CROSS-REFERENCE INDEXES

PART NUMBER INDEX

CAGEC	PART NUMBER	STOCK NUMBER	FIG	ITEM
35510	4629JA	2920-01-131-4932	30	2
11862	464039	2530-01-249-5401	77	1
17769	4641	6620-01-221-1942	220	12
11862	465536	5355-01-157-1866	161	19
			170	9
11862	466578	5310-01-165-1327	68	9
11862	467117	5310-00-209-2811	102	1
11862	467247	2510-01-191-8447	158	6
11862	467248	2510-01-200-1021	158	6
11862	467299	5340-01-158-8549	154	7
			155	1
11862	467509	5340-01-163-5902	17	31
11862	467524	5340-01-163-9400	17	22
11862	467525	2910-01-155-5136	14	29
11862	467911	2510-01-163-2681	141	7
11862	467912	2510-01-163-7229	141	7
11862	468234	2540-01-192-1823	20	4
11862	468484	4710-01-154-1230	15	29
11862	468661	2530-01-155-8460	88	23
11862	468673	2530-01-153-9449	88	30
11862	468674	2530-01-153-9450	88	30
11862	468675	5305-01-156-5006	88	27
60038	469	3110-00-100-0251	85	16
11862	469302	5355-01-163-4940	41	16
11862	469339	5340-01-165-2526	50	7
11862	469694	5330-01-085-0918	96	20
11862	470205	5355-01-235-6616	99	71
11862	470949	2540-01-157-8009	145	25
11862	470974	5315-01-159-8660	168	20
11862	470984	2540-01-158-7551	168	13
11862	470993	5330-01-159-8504	148	10
11862	471010	2540-01-158-7583	168	21
11862	471018	5340-01-158-6892	168	19
11862	471079	2540-01-158-6894	168	30
11862	471083	5306-01-157-3279	160	5
			162	5
			163	4
			169	4
11862	471089	2990-01-160-5873	141	12
11862	472450	5340-01-162-4852	129	1
11862	472536	2520-01-201-4096	96	2
11862	473187	5355-01-197-1501	168	10
11862	473197	2540-01-158-6893	168	15
11862	473894	2540-01-158-4601	147	8
11862	473917	2540-01-158-8557	146	9
11862	473995	2510-01-178-8867	146	11
11862	474022	2510-01-259-5587	158	4
11862	474102	2590-01-164-7825	99	62
11862	474309	5365-01-161-4055	96	21
11862	474579	5325-01-165-3475	249	13
11862	474935		80	8

CROSS-REFERENCE INDEXES

PART NUMBER INDEX

CAGEC	PART NUMBER	STOCK NUMBER	FIG	ITEM
11862	474935		81	4
11862	474955	2910-01-152-5516	14	34
11862	474957		16	14
11862	475922	6220-01-242-7557	45	9
11862	476916	2910-01-155-7881	15	2
11862	476927	5330-01-157-7604	15	3
11862	477361	5930-01-149-9306	41	25
11862	477402	4730-00-826-4268	16	9
			17	1
11862	480534	2510-01-155-5848	13	9
11862	480567	5310-01-194-9217	115	41
11862	4813235	5360-01-181-2482	14	5
			15	8
11862	482420		BULK	12
11862	482995		209	2
11862	487425		209	2
11862	4918562	2540-01-158-1569	198	11
11862	4993563	2530-01-157-7933	100	11
81343	5 010111B	4730-00-011-8538	214	4
			221	19
			242	6
			246	10
11862	500890	5905-01-159-0771	206	2
25022	51-0979	5340-01-028-9063	183	6
			184	6
			185	7
			186	3
			189	5
			190	4
25022	51-0985	2540-01-165-6793	189	11
25022	51-0988	2540-01-158-0602	180	28
25022	51-0989	2540-01-028-0574	181	17
25022	51-0991	5340-01-164-1078	185	13
			186	11
25022	51-0998	5340-01-156-5061	180	15
			181	2
25022	51-0999	2540-01-164-0046	180	8
			181	13
25022	51-1304	5340-01-159-1796	179	17
			192	11
25022	51-1305	2510-01-166-2015	179	14
25022	51-1603	9340-01-162-5948	180	13
			181	6
25022	51-1604	9340-01-162-5947	193	2
25022	51-1721	2510-01-163-7879	180	16
			181	7
25022	51-1724	5330-01-163-5706	193	3
25022	51-1901	5930-00-636-1584	179	6
25022	51-1902	5930-00-548-5640	179	5
25022	51-1926	5930-01-028-1949	192	10
25022	51-1942	6220-01-039-9809	178	19

CROSS-REFERENCE INDEXES

PART NUMBER INDEX

CAGEC	PART NUMBER	STOCK NUMBER	FIG	ITEM
25022	51-1959	5930-01-163-8924	184	13
			192	5
25022	51-1991	6130-01-035-6412	178	22
25022	51-2204	2510-01-169-3785	180	7
			181	11
25022	51-2294	7230-01-167-2075	180	4
			181	16
25022	51-2297	9330-01-098-6554	185	3
			186	5
			189	2
25022	52-0914	2540-01-163-7874	180	20
			181	24
11862	52351724	5310-01-160-5708	200	10
19207	5287638	5310-00-528-7638	242	19
19207	5294507	5310-00-350-2655	42	7
35510	5413	5310-00-516-2701	31	1
11862	5454797	5310-01-154-4341	87	9
			88	8
11862	5461145	5360-00-123-0137	87	15
			88	17
11862	5461156	2530-01-173-1248	88	20
11862	5461984	5360-00-113-9490	87	17
			88	19
11862	5462496	5365-01-154-8577	88	28
11862	5468226	5306-01-085-1953	93	1
11862	5469497	5340-01-157-2101	88	12
11862	5469581	5340-01-163-1401	92	7
			93	6
			94	2
11862	5470497	5330-01-185-4676	88	11
94988	552-12V	5945-00-983-4374	41	29
30282	553	4910-01-179-2517	254	12
11862	556742	5930-01-162-3669	41	9
11862	556743	5360-01-159-5952	41	8
11862	560613	5340-01-148-7529	11	12
11862	560614	5325-01-160-4618	11	8
11862	560625	4730-01-194-0126	10	6
11862	5613939	2920-01-151-3627	19	3
11862	5713268	3040-01-157-8021	144	14
11862	5713274	5310-01-194-9234	144	4
11862	5713276	5365-01-198-5516	144	5
11862	5717887	5315-01-194-0819	144	7
99688	58586	5330-01-194-4753	250	20
99688	58589	4140-01-157-3501	253	3
99688	58590	4140-01-154-9615	253	3
99688	58591	5330-01-201-9681	253	12
99688	58592	5330-01-193-0226	253	4
99688	58593	5330-01-204-4312	253	17
99688	58594	5640-01-194-7193	253	7
99688	58595	4140-01-186-9753	252	9
99688	58596	5330-01-213-9811	252	14

CROSS-REFERENCE INDEXES

PART NUMBER INDEX

CAGEC	PART NUMBER	STOCK NUMBER	FIG	ITEM
99688	58597	5330-01-201-9682	252	13
99688	58598	5330-01-205-5056	252	12
99688	58606	5365-01-195-5934	250	4
99688	58607	5330-01-193-0227	250	9
99688	58608	5330-01-194-4751	250	5
99688	58609	5640-01-195-4633	250	17
99688	58610	5640-01-195-4634	250	8
99688	58611	5640-01-195-4635	250	16
99688	58612	5640-01-195-4636	250	14
99688	58613	5640-01-196-7002	250	13
99688	58614	5640-01-196-7003	250	12
99688	58615	5640-01-195-9786	250	11
99688	58616	5330-01-195-1564	250	15
99688	58617	5330-01-194-4752	250	10
99688	58618	5330-01-197-0897	250	6
99688	58620	4730-01-192-4434	210	22
99688	58623	4520-01-192-6073	210	15
99688	58624	5330-01-192-8904	210	33
99688	58625	4720-01-192-3510	210	13
99688	58627	5360-01-203-6365	210	6
99688	58628		210	17
99688	58629		210	26
99688	58632	5330-01-192-8905	210	27
99688	58634	4140-01-188-6977	210	42
99688	58635	5330-01-194-4754	210	24
99688	58636	5330-01-192-9335	210	2
99688	58637	5330-01-192-8906	210	7
99688	58649	2990-01-192-4597	210	21
99688	58651	2990-01-192-4576	210	25
99688	58659	5340-01-199-4993	210	3
99688	58701	9320-01-085-2889	252	10
			253	10
21450	587227	5310-01-264-5903	229	12
			231	14
			232	9
11862	587575	5360-01-149-1959	21	14
			22	24
11862	5965748	5330-01-162-3744	43	2
11862	5965771	6220-01-146-4469	43	4
11862	5965772	2510-01-096-6758	43	4
11862	5965775	6220-01-146-4455	43	1
11862	5965776	6220-01-157-9046	43	1
11862	5966249	5305-01-150-5785	42	32
11862	5968095	6220-01-164-2271	42	35
97271	620062-B	5330-01-158-6725	76	3
99688	62218	5310-01-159-8264	252	3
			253	9
99688	62229	5310-01-161-7308	210	4
58499	6258	6140-01-155-6531	49	15
11862	6258213	2540-01-196-1622	41	13
11862	6258364	2590-01-159-8857	208	1

CROSS-REFERENCE INDEXES

CAGEC	PART NUMBER	PART NUMBER INDEX STOCK NUMBER	FIG	ITEM
11862	6258545	2510-01-326-0762	KITS	
11862	6258561	5330-01-157-7458	133	8
11862	6258562	5330-01-157-7459	133	4
11862	6259071	5340-01-335-9360	91	19
11862	6259074	5330-01-155-7700	101	3
			102	3
11862	6259423	2940-01-121-6350	61	10
11862	6260421	2540-01-096-9664	132	11
11862	6260631	2590-01-155-7882	13	10
11862	6260830	2530-01-148-2914	96	22
58499	6262	6140-01-155-6530	49	40
11862	6262029	2540-01-159-8759	142	1
11862	6262054	5340-01-165-8986	129	2
19207	6262328	5340-00-700-1423	97	18
11862	6262755	2910-01-147-4218	14	15
11862	6263870		14	14
11862	6263871		14	17
11862	6263877	2590-01-155-7711	13	7
			BULK	8
11862	6264100	2930-01-147-4222	23	5
11862	6264131	5340-01-163-4337	132	13
11862	6264951	5365-01-154-8514	95	9
11862	6270704	5325-01-198-8040	124	3
11862	6271989	5315-01-160-0575	133	22
			133	28
			145	14
11862	6272627		133	15
11862	6273325	5330-01-157-1952	204	1
11862	6273948	5330-01-086-3506	97	16
11862	6274031	5310-01-157-7560	116	4
11862	6274036	2540-01-192-3572	116	7
11862	6274550	5340-01-164-8761	132	8
11862	6274836	2540-01-158-4600	145	12
11862	6274847	5340-01-166-5652	145	8
11862	6274848	2510-01-163-7231	145	8
11862	6274849	5365-01-162-8876	145	9
11862	6274850	4010-01-158-6331	145	5
11862	6274853	5330-01-159-4777	147	6
11862	6274854	5340-01-165-4351	147	2
11862	6274890	5340-01-158-4583	146	3
11862	6274970	2510-01-162-3679	131	8
11862	6287160	6140-01-223-9144	49	14
11862	6293923		BULK	10
11862	6298886	6250-01-189-4981	51	3
11862	6410785	2930-01-123-4941	23	3
70040	6433429	6680-01-160-3870	34	7
11862	6437746	5325-01-123-6798	61	9
78977	6471	5305-00-217-9183	248	5
11862	6471831	2910-01-159-0867	9	8
70040	6474942A	6625-01-162-8124	35	7
11862	6497475	6210-01-158-3857	34	11

CROSS-REFERENCE INDEXES

PART NUMBER INDEX

CAGEC	PART NUMBER	STOCK NUMBER	FIG	ITEM
11862	6497476	6220-01-164-5227	34	9
11862	6497483	5330-01-163-1992	34	10
63208	650-24	4730-00-058-7558	215	10
			217	1
			218	1
			245	10
78977	650U-0016	5340-01-164-0748	248	3
99688	65134	5910-01-189-3011	252	7
			253	16
99688	65148	2590-01-191-4357	210	36
99688	65149	2590-01-191-9276	210	39
99688	65158	5905-01-154-2354	253	5
78977	6566-0004	6220-01-197-3938	248	6
78977	6598	5340-00-411-4508	248	4
78977	6701-0025	5340-01-197-1585	248	9
78977	6710-BU-2	4710-01-194-6590	248	7
73342	6771005	5330-01-080-3253	61	7
79470	6820	4820-00-174-0315	5	6
97271	700013L		76	1
19207	7001423	5340-00-700-1423	86	11
11862	7040173	3040-01-162-0255	133	13
11862	7040174	3040-01-157-7997	133	13
11862	718368	2520-01-163-7284	68	19
19207	7353960	2510-00-999-9856	229	4
			231	26
19207	7357009	4210-00-383-7127	203	3
19207	7358030	4030-00-088-1881	113	6
19207	7370134	5315-00-737-0134	247	21
11862	7455617	3110-01-087-2653	97	19
19207	7524078	2540-00-752-4078	246	26
11862	7591126	5355-01-280-2975	137	10
19207	7717066	5360-00-771-7066	228	9
19207	7731428	5935-00-773-1428	51	9
11862	7740374	5306-01-160-1952	145	4
11862	7806140	2520-01-024-0279	70	5
			71	6
			72	5
			73	7
			74	3
			74	3
11862	7815849	2520-01-153-8430	72	12
			73	12
11862	7827942	5330-01-155-4388	70	8
			72	8
11862	7828506	4720-01-148-5981	BULK	13
11862	7829923	5330-01-156-5141	106	8
11862	7830927	2520-01-239-3800	72	1
11862	7834183	6680-01-152-2845	105	18
11862	7838665	2520-01-155-6936	74	4
52788	7838936	2530-01-147-8556	104	6
11862	7838941	4720-01-148-2762	106	5

CROSS-REFERENCE INDEXES

PART NUMBER INDEX

CAGEC	PART NUMBER	STOCK NUMBER	FIG	ITEM
11862	7838942	4720-01-148-2761	106	10
11862	7840235	5340-01-202-2517	71	4
			73	4
99688	784030	2540-01-191-4327	210	19
99688	78404	2540-01-163-8624	177	14
99688	78405		210	20
99688	78406	4720-01-191-8463	210	43
11862	7844074	2520-01-148-2919	74	1
11862	7845102	2520-01-189-0596	70	1
			71	1
11862	7845119	2520-01-192-1793	71	10
			73	9
11862	7845127	2520-01-192-4314	71	5
			73	5
11862	7846740	5340-01-231-0925	74	5
11862	7846959	2530-01-150-9757	103	1
11862	7846970	5310-01-159-6587	99	60
11862	7849302	2990-01-149-4966	3	6
19207	7951738	2540-01-159-6198	233	6
35510	7983	5970-01-144-1291	31	4
73992	8100	4730-00-768-8880	220	13
73992	8200	4730-00-317-4231	220	8
99688	85922	4140-01-160-7664	253	1
99688	85923	4140-01-160-8503	252	1
99688	85927	4130-01-160-7695	250	1
99688	85928		252	18
99688	85931	5340-01-191-4827	253	8
99688	85941	2510-01-191-4259	210	9
99688	85942	2540-01-191-6541	210	34
99688	859430	2590-01-192-5911	210	37
11862	8629526	4710-01-152-5798	61	8
11862	8633203	2520-01-149-3461	60	6
11862	8633208	5306-01-150-9497	61	11
11862	8637742	4730-01-163-7163	62	2
11862	8639743	5305-01-150-9781	249	10
11862	8640496	3040-01-157-7998	67	4
			75	3
			80	2
			81	1
11862	8655020	2520-01-213-1680	60	6
11862	8655625	5330-01-148-7492	60	4
19207	8701347	5935-01-171-8273	37	14
11862	8742340	3040-01-159-0996	148	12
11862	8782501	5305-01-159-2783	148	9
11862	8785295	5340-01-165-0657	143	7
60038	88510	3110-00-580-3709	85	7
11862	8906150	2590-01-212-7639	51	6
11862	8909518	6250-01-189-6926	51	5
11862	8914822		51	4
11862	8919163		49	38
11862	8919355	5975-01-160-8458	BULK	4

CROSS-REFERENCE INDEXES

PART NUMBER INDEX

CAGEC	PART NUMBER	STOCK NUMBER	FIG	ITEM
11862	8919356	5975-01-191-9851	BULK	5
11862	8985418	5360-01-193-7130	57	6
11862	8986000	5999-01-159-5603	34	17
97271	911105-5130	2520-01-324-4895	74	1
11862	915449	6220-01-160-4247	42	18
11862	915450	6220-01-161-6439	42	18
11862	915908	6220-01-155-6521	42	27
11862	918656	2540-01-156-9740	200	2
22973	922-900-00	6220-01-160-5187	227	3
22973	922-901-01	6220-01-216-5288	227	9
22973	922-901-02	6220-01-216-5289	227	6
22973	922-904-02	6220-01-269-0465	227	7
22973	922-910-00	6220-01-268-8795	227	4
11862	94009398	5310-01-164-5600	153	3
24617	9409103		237	2
24617	9409613	5310-01-167-8344	154	2
			155	6
11862	9409754	5310-01-193-6927	211	2
			214	2
24617	9409761	5310-01-194-9208	211	1
			214	1
24617	9411031	4730-01-098-5229	78	5
11862	9411281	5325-01-165-4372	231	13
24617	9413534	5310-01-097-8222	231	8
			231	22
			232	2
11862	9414031	5310-01-161-2531	229	6
24617	9414238	5305-01-166-1471	178	21
24617	9414411		14	16
24617	9414712	5305-01-162-9695	142	17
			145	23
24617	9414713	5305-00-432-4171	214	7
24617	9414714	5305-01-164-6321	179	3
			187	16
			192	2
24617	9414724	5305-01-210-9425	134	12
24617	9415153	5305-01-197-6576	197	4
24617	9415163	5305-01-164-2313	35	12
			132	17
			208	9
			211	9
			222	11
24617	9416187	5305-01-160-3938	50	8
			217	5
24617	9416918	5310-01-012-8962	215	12
			217	2
			229	7
			231	4
			232	1
			233	4
			233	17

CROSS-REFERENCE INDEXES

PART NUMBER INDEX

CAGEC	PART NUMBER	STOCK NUMBER	FIG	ITEM
24617	9417325	5305-01-161-2581	161	11
24617	9417350	5306-01-266-2419	215	4
			218	6
			218	10
24617	9417714	5310-01-217-5205	226	4
			227	11
			246	13
11862	9417793	5310-01-211-3811	235	7
11862	9417901	4730-00-050-4203	69	1
			70	10
			71	11
			72	10
			73	10
			100	13
			101	4
			102	5
24617	9418719	5305-01-166-1473	187	13
24617	9418924	5310-01-132-8275	221	6
			242	25
11862	9418931	5310-01-187-7610	112	23
11862	9418944	5305-01-149-7356	41	24
11862	9419138	5305-01-155-6113	121	10
			122	9
24617	9419163	5305-01-246-5770	198	7
24617	9419265	5310-01-170-8765	229	16
			230	2
24617	9419327	5305-01-157-9720	15	1
			146	4
			168	14
72582	9419454	5310-01-133-7215	196	13
24617	9419663	5305-01-197-3287	32	2
			208	8
			242	16
			244	1
24617	9419699	5306-01-155-8528	205	1
24617	9420408	5305-01-157-5625	132	16
24617	9420621	5310-01-158-9205	126	3
			134	16
24617	9421073	5305-01-162-8512	210	8
			252	5
			253	2
			253	18
24617	9421432	5305-01-152-8945	174	2
24617	9421985	5305-01-165-8612	198	2
24617	9422295	5310-01-119-3668	14	31
			17	37
			68	8
			90	23
			235	8
11862	9422299	5310-01-150-4003	95	4
			112	2

PART NUMBER INDEX

CAGEC	PART NUMBER	STOCK NUMBER	FIG	ITEM
11862	9422299	5310-01-150-4003	123	4
24617	9422301	5310-01-149-4407	108	2
			110	4
			114	20
11862	9422303	5310-00-044-3342	100	20
24617	9422956	5305-01-197-3112	20	8
24617	9423530	5310-01-197-6621	196	17
			233	18
24617	9423768	5305-01-218-3139	226	3
11862	9424320	5305-01-156-8692	111	2
11862	9424955	4730-01-154-1366	90	3
24617	9425117	5306-01-155-7659	203	1
24617	9426277	5306-01-203-9082	200	13
24617	9426623	5305-01-201-3788	187	10
11862	9431663	5305-01-157-7388	142	9
24617	9431995	5305-01-198-4154	69	6
24617	9432075	4730-00-288-9390	90	11
			91	12
24617	9432194	5305-01-163-2439	168	18
11862	9436175	5320-01-229-8183	38	16
11862	9437207	4820-00-844-6744	23	16
11862	9437242	5306-01-162-9678	145	11
11862	9437702	5306-01-161-6178	36	12
			38	11
			39	11
			47	5
			54	14
11862	9438039		145	10
24617	9438124	4720-01-267-2052	BULK	26
11862	9438150	5305-01-151-8288	42	14
11862	9438227		16	15
			17	40
11862	9438257	4720-01-155-7784	BULK	16
11862	9438315	4720-01-148-2768	BULK	24
11862	9438373	4720-01-159-5796	BULK	22
11862	9438381	4720-01-156-0550	BULK	19
11862	9438383	4720-01-182-3457	BULK	15
11862	9438916	5305-01-160-3937	133	24
			161	15
			164	1
			165	8
			170	11
			171	1
11862	9439001		16	13
11862	9439004		17	26
11862	9439010		15	13
			17	14
11862	9439046	4720-01-156-0549	BULK	18
11862	9439048		67	3
11862	9439059		17	27
11862	9439068		15	11

CROSS-REFERENCE INDEXES

PART NUMBER INDEX

CAGEC	PART NUMBER	STOCK NUMBER	FIG	ITEM
11862	9439088		75	5
11862	9439091		75	7
11862	9439092		18	24
11862	9439104	4720-01-156-0547	BULK	14
11862	9439117		16	10
			17	12
11862	9439120		17	28
11862	9439128		15	12
11862	9439162	4720-01-156-0548	BULK	17
11862	9439274		BULK	25
11862	9439363		8	7
11862	9439402	4720-01-163-7833	BULK	23
11862	9439637	5305-00-821-3869	91	16
11862	9439757	5310-01-202-2695	151	5
11862	9439770	5306-01-157-6797	39	2
			134	4
			135	4
			136	19
			136	25
			137	7
11862	9439771	5306-01-157-6796	133	19
			145	22
			147	4
			242	18
11862	9439772	5305-01-158-0335	137	2
			146	12
11862	9439930	5305-01-165-5591	213	4
24617	9440025	5305-01-197-2320	207	4
			252	15
11862	9440033	5306-01-197-3089	44	3
			52	4
			173	5
			229	9
11862	9440034	5306-01-218-3119	220	19
11862	9440166	5305-01-197-2536	40	3
11862	9440173		221	11
			242	31
			246	17
11862	9440178	5310-01-161-2374	222	14
11862	9440224	5306-01-171-8076	60	7
11862	9440280	5305-01-203-2289	30	1
11862	9440300	5305-01-163-2438	152	12
			201	4
			202	4
11862	9440334	5306-01-168-4481	24	2
			42	10
			48	3
			49	31
			172	11
			225	9
			229	21

CROSS-REFERENCE INDEXES

PART NUMBER INDEX

CAGEC	PART NUMBER	STOCK NUMBER	FIG	ITEM
11862	9440334	5306-01-168-4481	232	16
			234	9
			245	7
			246	18
11862	9440344	5306-01-195-7915	112	5
11862	9441669	5320-01-195-5106	35	4
27647	9477	5305-01-165-2260	96	5
			97	3
35510	95300	2920-01-145-0993	31	7
11862	9591270	2640-01-323-2632	96	29
11862	9601750	5306-01-157-9936	133	17
11862	9645073	5360-01-164-1949	165	2
09386	96735	5306-01-150-1197	97	20
11862	9702916	3010-01-159-7750	144	9
11862	9703344	2540-01-218-6833	144	6
11862	9711038	5360-01-218-1610	164	3
11862	9721917	3120-01-166-6724	133	23
			133	29
11862	9728247	5340-01-162-9844	133	18
24617	9749363	5360-01-187-0301	99	65
11862	9754764	5365-01-270-1977	99	66
11862	9762199	2530-01-159-3604	99	64
11862	9767270	5305-01-270-3030	99	68
11862	9776705	5330-01-112-1533	9	9
11862	9780470	3040-01-159-0930	249	4
11862	9785074	5340-01-163-0919	18	25
72055	98226	5945-01-192-8653	40	5
11862	9826897	5360-01-171-8248	165	4
11862	9831062	2540-01-086-5433	200	1
11862	9834636	5340-01-161-2749	164	5
			165	3
25022	99-1088-0	4030-01-168-1282	178	12
25022	99-1265-01		180	1
25022	99-1265-02		181	1
25022	99-4256-0	5930-01-163-2583	179	4
25022	99-4256-2	2540-01-165-8177	179	8
25022	99-4257-1	5340-01-172-1942	193	15
25022	99-4282-1	2510-01-159-1797	192	1
25022	99-4308-1	2590-01-163-7626	176	16
			177	16
25022	99-4315-1	5340-01-164-0747	179	12
25022	99-4324-0	2510-01-192-9752	193	1
25022	99-4340-0	2540-01-164-6251	182	11
25022	99-4341-1	5340-01-164-1075	203	9
25022	99-4356-1	5340-01-164-0974	179	2
25022	99-4360-1	5895-01-159-1804	187	17
25022	99-4408-1	2510-01-159-1795	192	7
25022	99-4420-1	2590-01-162-7139	183	17
			184	9
25022	99-4420-2	2510-01-159-1798	183	14
			184	16

CROSS-REFERENCE INDEXES

PART NUMBER INDEX

CAGEC	PART NUMBER	STOCK NUMBER	FIG	ITEM
25022	99-4447-0		185	1
25022	99-4456-0	2540-01-191-8462	182	16
25022	99-4469-0	2540-01-191-6536	182	13
25022	99-4577-1	5340-01-307-2247	178	10
25022	99-4578-1	5340-01-307-2248	178	11
25022	99-4579-1	5340-01-307-2249	176	22
			177	25
25022	99-4580-1	5340-01-307-2250	176	21
			177	24
25022	99-4581-1	5340-01-307-2251	176	20
			177	13
25022	99-4582-1	5340-01-307-2252	176	19
			177	12
25022	99-4583-1	5340-01-307-2253	180	29
			181	29
25022	99-4584-1	5340-01-307-2254	180	30
			181	30
25022	99-4602-1	5340-01-164-1048	203	6
25022	99-4675-1	5340-01-194-5805	180	10
			181	8
25022	99-4680-1	5340-01-162-3850	181	28
25022	99-4683-1	5315-01-196-6464	193	11
25022	99-4888-0	5340-01-164-1100	177	22
25022	99-4892-0	2540-01-191-6538	194	7
25022	99-4893-01	2510-01-191-4334	186	8
25022	99-4893-02	2510-01-191-6638	186	9
25022	99-4894-01	2510-01-191-4335	185	15
25022	99-4894-02	2510-01-191-4336	185	14
13548	99012R	6220-01-276-0635	175	8
35510	99459	5305-01-143-7411	31	8
27647	9952		96	8
35510	99525	5305-01-143-7412	31	5
76760	99780	5330-01-155-4393	65	50

CROSS-REFERENCE INDEXES

FIGURE AND ITEM NUMBER INDEX

FIG	ITEM	STOCK NUMBER	CAGEC	PART NUMBER
BULK	1		81348	QQS741
BULK	2		81349	MILS20166
BULK	3		74410	RRC271BTY2CLDIA0 72
BULK	4	5975-01-160-8458	11862	8919355
BULK	5	5975-01-191-9851	11862	8919356
BULK	6	5940-00-926-8034	96906	MS18029-13S-8
BULK	7	5940-00-405-8976	96906	MS18029-4S-8
BULK	8	2590-01-155-7711	11862	6263877
BULK	9	2510-01-221-2094	11862	370389
BULK	10		11862	6293923
BULK	11	4720-01-192-1631	24234	319029
BULK	12		11862	482420
BULK	13	4720-01-148-5981	11862	7828506
BULK	14	4720-01-156-0547	11862	9439104
BULK	15	4720-01-182-3457	11862	9438383
BULK	16	4720-01-155-7784	11862	9438257
BULK	17	4720-01-156-0548	11862	9439162
BULK	18	4720-01-156-0549	11862	9439046
BULK	19	4720-01-156-0550	11862	9438381
BULK	20	4720-00-230-6523	11862	1359744
BULK	21	4720-00-930-2231	96906	MS521304B203R
BULK	22	4720-01-159-5796	11862	9438373
BULK	23	4720-01-163-7833	11862	9439402
BULK	24	4720-01-148-2768	11862	9438315
BULK	25		11862	9439274
BULK	26	4720-01-267-2052	24617	9438124
BULK	27	4720-01-096-7718	11862	3987364
BULK	28	2510-01-162-7224	11862	12306178
BULK	29	5970-01-158-9337	11862	462233
BULK	30	5530-00-618-6955	81348	NNP530
BULK	31	5330-00-753-8036	11862	370390
BULK	32	5330-01-096-7698	11862	363139
BULK	33	9515-00-516-5756	96906	MS52039C079
BULK	34	5940-00-950-7783	96906	MS27212-4-8
BULK	35		81349	MILT16343TYPE1
KITS		2510-01-326-0762	11862	6258545
KITS		2530-01-163-0800	27647	15528
KITS		3040-01-163-7286	27647	11967
1	1		11862	1403394-6
1	2	5340-01-158-8624	11862	14033945
1	3	5307-01-269-4336	11862	22535073
1	5	5340-01-150-5986	11862	14033947
1	6	5305-01-148-7460	11862	11504595
2	11	3020-01-147-9359	11862	14067703
2	11	3020-01-148-6983	11862	14067702
2	12	5305-01-148-7460	11862	11504595
3	5	5330-01-156-5147	11862	14022649
3	6	2990-01-149-4966	11862	7849302
3	7	5306-01-149-6280	11862	1635490
3	8	5340-01-160-4397	11862	14022650

CROSS-REFERENCE INDEXES

FIGURE AND ITEM NUMBER INDEX

FIG	ITEM	STOCK NUMBER	CAGEC	PART NUMBER
4	1	2940-01-217-8089	70040	FC106
4	2	2590-01-147-4285	11862	14071059
4	3	5325-01-151-6117	11862	14028942
4	4	6680-01-147-4629	11862	14050523
4	5	4710-01-150-0842	11862	14045268
4	6	5310-01-148-7474	11862	14036369
4	7	5310-01-165-3331	11862	22521550
4	8	5330-00-935-9136	24617	274244
4	9	6615-01-153-1852	11862	25011208
4	10	4820-01-153-1851	11862	25011206
4	11	2815-01-166-0621	11862	14066310
4	12	4730-01-150-0879	11862	14022700
4	13	2940-00-082-6034	70040	PF-35
4	15	5330-01-150-7744	11862	14022683
4	16	5306-01-230-3354	11862	11508534
4	17	5305-01-150-9781	24617	11507029
4	18	5330-00-107-3925	11862	14079550
4	19	5365-01-149-0880	11862	337185
4	20	5307-01-150-5992	11862	14066307
4	21	2815-01-147-4275	11862	14061649
5	1	5330-01-218-0862	11862	14055585
5	2	4710-01-148-8354	11862	14061344
5	3	5305-00-225-3843	96906	MS90728-8
5	4	4730-00-288-9390	11862	137396
5	5	4730-00-277-8269	72582	224425
5	6	4820-00-174-0315	79470	6820
5	7	5340-01-234-1465	11862	15599988
5	8	4730-00-288-9440	72582	118754
5	9	5430-01-225-8971	70411	SP2489-FM
5	10	4720-01-150-7575	11862	15548901
5	10	4720-01-162-0119	11892	14063336
5	11	5310-01-159-8559	96906	MS35691-406
5	12	5640-01-159-6935	11862	14061350
5	13	5310-00-582-5965	96906	MS35338-44
5	14	5305-00-068-0508	96906	MS90728-6
5	15	4730-01-172-6683	11862	14055586
5	16	5340-01-197-3434	11862	14047899
5	17	5340-01-150-6249	11862	14061348
5	18	5310-01-165-3331	11862	22521550
5	19	5340-01-150-1377	11862	14061352
5	20	5305-00-068-0509	96906	MS90728-10
5	21	4720-01-148-5000	11862	15548902
5	21	4720-01-162-0120	11862	14063337
5	22		11862	15599986
5	23	4730-01-227-1929	11862	15599987
5	24	5340-01-150-0197	11862	14036784
5	25	4710-01-149-1899	11862	14061345
6	1	5306-01-253-7073	11862	11508353
6	2	4730-00-908-3194	96906	MS35842-11
6	3	4720-01-194-0336	11862	14067732
6	4	5310-01-155-2503	24617	11502488

CROSS-REFERENCE INDEXES

FIGURE AND ITEM NUMBER INDEX

FIG	ITEM	STOCK NUMBER	CAGEC	PART NUMBER
6	5	2815-01-192-5962	11862	14067733
6	6	5310-01-165-3331	11862	22521550
6	7	4720-01-195-7603	11862	14050445
6	8	4710-01-192-7967	11862	14050442
6	9	4710-01-198-2701	11862	14050443
6	10	5340-01-197-3433	11862	14050441
6	11	5305-01-273-4486	11862	11509135
6	12	4730-01-164-7028	11862	14050444
6	13	2990-01-192-9730	11862	14050446
6	14	2990-01-147-9284	11862	25042462
7	6	2815-01-150-2181	11862	14022657
7	7	5307-01-158-6312	11862	14028924
7	8	5306-01-149-6278	11862	14028922
7	9	5307-01-151-8374	11862	14022654
7	10	5305-01-148-3685	11862	14028923
7	11	2815-01-148-9560	11862	14025568
8	1	5340-01-166-1534	11862	14066301
8	2		11862	11663000
8	3	5340-01-151-9956	11862	14033893
8	4	5310-01-165-3331	11862	22521550
8	5		11862	14066306
8	6	4730-01-163-7194	11862	25518880
8	7		11862	9439363
8	8	5340-01-151-9957	11862	14033895
8	9	4710-01-148-2659	11862	14061569
8	10	5306-01-148-3667	11862	11504512
8	11	5340-00-881-5303	96906	MS21333-45
8	14	4720-01-184-0432	11862	14066305
9	7	5305-00-725-2317	96906	MS90728-64
9	8	2910-01-159-0867	11862	6471831
9	9	5330-01-112-1533	11862	9776705
9	10	5315-01-151-4180	11862	14050425
9	11	5330-00-830-1745	11862	3705044
9	12	2910-00-493-2138	11862	3719599
9	13	5306-01-151-4925	11862	11509669
10	1		11862	14045233
10	2	5340-01-270-7423	11862	343350
10	3		11862	3970076
10	4		11862	M51
10	5		11862	M140
10	6	4730-01-194-0126	11862	560625
10	7		11862	M495
10	8		11862	M127
10	9	2910-01-200-4338	11862	22506637
10	10	4820-01-158-6836	11862	14057219
10	11	5305-01-211-7464	96906	MS51869-28
11	7	5340-01-150-6026	11862	14033955
11	8	5325-01-160-4618	11862	560614
11	9	5305-01-150-1521	11862	11503617
11	10	5340-01-150-4106	11862	14033921
11	11	5340-01-150-6275	11862	14033922

CROSS-REFERENCE INDEXES

FIGURE AND ITEM NUMBER INDEX

FIG	ITEM	STOCK NUMBER	CAGEC	PART NUMBER
11	12	5340-01-148-7529	11862	560613
11	13	5310-01-165-3331	11862	22521550
11	19	5340-01-150-7774	11862	14033953
12	1	5310-01-196-5587	11862	3827499
12	2	5310-01-147-8743	11862	3790768
12	3	5310-01-148-3693	11862	14001197
12	4	2940-01-155-3190	7004C	A644C
12	5	2940-01-148-5992	11862	25041910
12	6	5325-01-149-6293	11862	15530620
12	7	5307-01-153-0873	11862	14033948
13	1	5305-01-140-9118	96906	MS90728-59
13	2	6680-01-161-1439	11862	22516548
13	3	6680-01-175-0565	11862	25004140
13	4	5330-01-159-1298	11862	22515965
13	5	5310-00-896-0903	96906	MS51967-12
13	6	5310-00-809-4061	96906	MS27183-15
13	7	2590-01-155-7711	11862	6263877
13	8	2910-01-155-7878	11862	14020491
13	9	2510-01-155-5848	11862	480534
13	10	2590-01-155-7882	11862	6260631
13	11	5340-01-244-7925	11862	334675
13	12	2910-01-147-4219	11862	368752
13	13	2910-01-160-8107	11862	14050685
13	14	2990-01-155-7879	11862	14020492
14	1	5340-01-165-4705	11862	14010707
14	2	2910-01-155-5063	11862	14063326
14	3	5305-01-158-2032	96906	MS51869-24
14	4	5340-01-172-2087	11862	14052026
14	5	5360-01-181-2482	11862	4813235
14	6	5305-01-158-2032	96906	MS51869-24
14	7	5305-01-158-7820	11862	14026247
14	8	2910-01-155-5139	11862	14063363
14	9	2910-01-155-5147	11862	14063333
14	9	2910-01-155-5148	11862	14063327
14	10	4730-00-908-6292	96906	MS35842-14
14	11	4720-01-155-5194	11862	14063334
14	11	4720-01-155-8062	11862	14063328
14	12	2590-01-155-5177	11862	334523
14	13	2910-01-148-2910	11862	14071984
14	14		11862	6263870
14	15	2910-01-147-4218	11862	6262755
14	16		24617	9414411
14	17		11862	6263871
14	18	6680-01-161-1439	11862	22516548
14	19	5330-01-159-1298	11862	22515965
14	20	6680-01-164-9433	11862	25004137
14	21	5340-01-151-7409	11862	359847
14	22	2590-01-155-5140	11862	334521
14	23	5340-01-160-0367	11862	334522
14	24	5305-00-146-2524	96906	MS51850-86
14	25	5310-00-931-8167	96906	MS51967-6

CROSS-REFERENCE INDEXES

FIGURE AND ITEM NUMBER INDEX

FIG	ITEM	STOCK NUMBER	CAGEC	PART NUMBER
14	26	5310-00-407-9566	96906	MS35338-45
14	27	2910-01-155-5137	11862	341287
14	28	5340-01-162-9781	11862	344714
14	29	2910-01-155-5136	11862	467525
14	30	5306-00-226-4826	96906	MS90728-33
14	31	5310-01-119-3668	24617	9422295
14	32	5310-00-081-4219	96906	MS27183-12
14	33	5340-01-162-9777	11862	15599221
14	34	2910-01-152-5516	11862	474955
14	35	5306-01-159-2784	11862	14072666
14	36	5305-01-140-9118	96906	MS90728-59
14	37	5310-00-896-0903	96906	MS51967-12
14	38	5310-00-809-4061	96906	MS27183-15
14	39	4730-00-909-8627	96906	MS35842-13
14	40	4730-00-908-3194	96906	MS35842-11
14	41	4720-01-148-6984	11862	14036751
14	41	4720-01-192-9823	11862	14063335
15	1	5305-01-157-9720	24617	9419327
15	2	2910-01-155-7881	11862	476916
15	3	5330-01-157-7604	11862	476927
15	4	5305-01-158-2032	96906	MS51869-24
15	5	5340-01-172-2087	11862	14052026
15	6	5340-01-165-4705	11862	14010707
15	7	2910-01-155-7880	11862	14063329
15	8	5360-01-181-2482	11862	4813235
15	9	4730-00-826-4268	19207	11608950-4
15	10	4730-01-163-7194	11862	25518880
15	11		11862	9439068
15	12		11862	9439128
15	13		11862	9439010
15	14		11862	14018658
15	15	5305-01-156-5438	11862	11504447
15	16	5340-01-158-0314	11862	1638274
15	17	5340-00-809-1490	96906	MS21333-98
15	18		11862	14018647
15	19		11862	14063317
15	20	2910-01-155-5138	11862	14063319
15	21	5340-01-157-9825	11862	14018630
15	22	4730-00-909-8627	96906	MS35842-13
15	23	4720-01-160-5781	11862	14049494
15	24	5305-01-158-7820	11862	14026247
15	25	2910-01-155-5063	11862	14063326
15	26	2910-01-155-7965	11862	14063325
15	27	4730-00-908-3194	96906	MS35842-11
15	28		11862	14041258
15	29	4710-01-154-1230	11862	468484
16	1	5340-01-158-0314	11862	1638274
16	2	5340-00-057-3037	96906	MS21333-111
16	3		11862	15599209
16	4	4730-00-014-2433	24617	142433
16	5	4730-01-075-7310	72582	178917

CROSS-REFERENCE INDEXES

FIGURE AND ITEM NUMBER INDEX

FIG	ITEM	STOCK NUMBER	CAGEC	PART NUMBER
16	6	4730-00-132-4625	6N299	0917425
16	7	5305-01-156-5438	11862	11504447
16	8		11862	14063315
16	9	4730-00-826-4268	11862	477402
16	10		11862	9439117
16	11	5340-00-809-1490	96906	MS21333-98
16	12	4730-01-163-7194	11862	25518880
16	13		11862	9439001
16	14		11862	474957
16	15		11862	9438227
16	16	4720-01-156-0085	11862	14063391
17	1	4730-00-826-4268	11862	477402
17	2	4720-01-156-0085	11862	14063391
17	3		11862	15599209
17	4	5340-01-158-0314	11862	1638274
17	5	5340-00-057-3037	96906	MS21333-111
17	6	5340-00-057-3037	96906	MS21333-111
17	7	4730-00-014-2433	24617	142433
17	8	4730-01-075-7310	72582	178917
17	9	4730-00-132-4625	24617	444620
17	10	5340-01-268-9064	11862	25527423
17	11	5305-01-156-5438	11862	11504447
17	12		11862	9439117
17	13	4730-01-163-7194	11862	25518880
17	14		11862	9439010
17	15		11862	14063314
17	16	5340-00-881-5303	96906	MS21333-45
17	17	5310-01-159-8559	96906	MS35691-406
17	18	5310-00-582-5965	96906	MS35338-44
17	19	5305-00-068-0501	96906	MS90725-5
17	20	5310-00-931-8167	96906	MS51967-6
17	21	5310-00-407-9566	96906	MS35338-45
17	22	5340-01-163-9400	11862	467524
17	23		11862	14045605
17	24	5340-01-159-1185	11862	14034543
17	25		11862	14061227
17	26		11862	9439004
17	27		11862	9439059
17	28		11862	9439120
17	29		11862	14061223
17	30	2910-01-155-5138	11862	14063319
17	31	5340-01-163-5902	11862	467509
17	32	5310-00-245-3424	96906	MS17829-5C
17	33	2590-01-164-7177	11862	15522392
17	34	2910-01-155-5845	11862	14034546
17	35	5310-00-081-4219	96906	MS27183-12
17	36	5306-00-226-4825	96906	MS90728-32
17	37	5310-01-119-3668	24617	9422295
17	38	5306-00-226-4826	96906	MS90728-33
17	39		11862	15599999
17	40		11862	9438227

CROSS-REFERENCE INDEXES

FIGURE AND ITEM NUMBER INDEX

FIG	ITEM	STOCK NUMBER	CAGEC	PART NUMBER
18	1	2910-01-156-0045	84760	27290
18	2	2910-01-156-8361	11862	14075347
18	3	5330-01-213-9966	84760	22591
18	4	2910-01-210-1322	84760	24285
18	5	5330-01-236-1724	84760	27820
18	6	5340-01-211-3086	84760	24267
18	7	2910-01-210-1323	84760	29090
18	8	5340-01-197-1199	84760	24265
18	9	5340-01-202-2622	84760	24281
18	10	5330-01-138-2106	84760	15349
18	11	5305-01-211-3032	84760	24437
18	12	5305-01-211-3031	84760	24322
18	13	2920-01-212-4771	84760	27284
18	14	4820-01-209-0473	84760	23796
18	15	5930-01-208-6292	61928	15596614
18	16	5340-01-160-2239	11862	14043724
18	17	5305-00-115-9526	96906	MS18154-58
18	18	5310-00-637-9541	96906	MS35338-46
18	19	4730-01-163-7194	11862	25518880
18	20	4720-01-163-8039	11862	14063302
18	21	4730-00-826-4268	19207	11608950-4
18	22	4720-01-192-8533	11862	14063301
18	23	4730-00-908-3195	96906	MS35842-10
18	24		11862	9439092
18	25	5340-01-163-0919	11862	9785074
19	1	4730-00-580-6738	24617	444034
19	2	6685-01-205-3676	70040	10045847
19	3	2920-01-151-3627	11862	5613939
20	1	2990-01-148-2928	11862	14038644
20	2	5310-01-143-0542	73342	3909063
20	3	5360-01-151-1121	11862	336989
20	4	2540-01-192-1823	11862	468234
20	5	2910-01-150-3675	11862	3993087
20	6	2910-01-225-1068	11862	15590123
20	7	2910-01-149-3786	11862	342405
20	8	5305-01-197-3112	24617	9422956
20	9	5360-01-151-1120	11862	14024997
20	10	5306-01-152-4693	24617	11504986
20	11	2910-01-150-3676	11862	14038647
20	12	5340-01-269-1361	11862	15567924
20	13	5306-01-161-5489	11862	11501095
20	14	5945-01-154-3143	11862	14066255
21	1	2990-01-154-3743	11862	14037856
21	1	2990-01-225-1029	11862	15595224
21	2	5310-00-931-8167	96906	MS51967-6
21	3	5310-00-407-9566	96906	MS35338-45
21	4	5306-00-226-4830	96906	MS90728-37
21	5	5340-01-160-2445	11862	341160
21	6	5340-01-199-2312	96906	MS52150-31HE
21	7	5340-01-204-4268	96906	MS52150-30HE
21	8	2990-01-155-5151	79260	45823

CROSS-REFERENCE INDEXES

FIGURE AND ITEM NUMBER INDEX

FIG	ITEM	STOCK NUMBER	CAGEC	PART NUMBER
21	9	2990-01-046-1170	11862	14063795
21	9	2990-01-225-1052	11862	14089132
21	10	2990-01-154-1324	11862	14029956
21	11	2990-01-155-5150	11862	14045525
21	11	2990-01-225-1028	11862	15595271
21	12	2990-01-155-5149	11862	14045521
21	13	5330-01-147-4212	11862	14072686
21	14	5360-01-149-1959	11862	587575
21	15	5310-00-316-6513	80205	NAS1408A6
21	16	5310-00-809-4085	96906	MS27183-16
22	1		11862	15599216
22	1	2990-01-147-4290	11862	15595216
22	2	5306-00-226-4830	96906	MS90728-37
22	3	5340-01-163-1388	11862	14037808
22	4	5305-00-115-9526	96906	MS18154-58
22	5	5310-00-637-9541	96906	MS35338-46
22	6	5310-00-732-0558	96906	MS51967-8
22	7	5340-01-160-2445	11862	341160
22	8	5310-00-407-9566	96906	MS35338-45
22	9	5310-00-931-8167	96906	MS51967-6
22	10	5340-01-199-2312	96906	MS52150-31HE
22	11	5340-01-204-4268	96906	MS52150-30HE
22	12	2990-01-203-2426	11862	14037836
22	13	2990-01-147-3953	11862	14037812
22	14	5306-00-226-4827	96906	MS90728-34
22	15	5310-00-514-6674	96906	MS35335-34
22	16	2990-01-154-1323	11862	14044996
22	17	2990-01-152-7788	11862	14067430
22	18	5340-01-148-2818	11862	14034547
22	19	5340-01-155-9861	11862	14024561
22	20	2990-01-152-7828	11862	14044995
22	21	2990-01-180-2988	11862	14067429
22	22	2990-01-147-4289	11862	14067759
22	22	2990-01-231-2938	11862	15599269
22	23	5330-01-147-4212	11862	14072686
22	24	5360-01-149-1959	11862	587575
22	25	5310-00-316-6513	80205	NAS1408A6
22	26	5310-00-809-4085	96906	MS27183-16
23	1	5305-01-160-1975	11862	11508566
23	2	5305-01-151-9285	11862	11504115
23	3	2930-01-123-4941	11862	6410785
23	4	2930-01-160-1597	11862	14039948
23	5	2930-01-147-4222	11862	6264100
23	6	5340-01-159-2901	11862	14039950
23	7	6680-01-147-5497	11862	358375
23	8	4730-00-908-3195	96906	MS35842-10
23	9	5340-01-149-4434	11862	3816659
23	10	5340-00-057-3052	96906	MS21333-114
23	11	2930-01-085-0926	11862	14011345
23	12	5306-01-158-9018	11862	2014469
23	13	2930-01-159-2902	11862	14052221

CROSS-REFERENCE INDEXES

FIGURE AND ITEM NUMBER INDEX

FIG	ITEM	STOCK NUMBER	CAGEC	PART NUMBER
23	14		11862	14072430
23	15	2930-01-264-3480	61928	3058966
23	16	4820-00-844-6744	11862	9437207
23	17	5340-01-157-6429	11862	14072427
23	18	5340-01-157-6428	11862	14072426
23	19	5310-01-160-9529	24617	1494253
23	20	5340-01-164-3269	11862	14039949
23	21	5310-01-160-4536	11862	3792287
24	1	5310-01-170-9100	11862	3982098
24	2	5306-01-168-4481	11862	9440334
24	3	5305-01-160-1975	11862	11508566
24	4	2930-01-147-4221	11862	15522697
25	1	4730-00-909-8627	96906	MS35842-13
25	2	5340-01-150-4991	11862	14036779
25	3	5305-01-160-1975	11862	11508566
25	4	4720-01-148-2970	11862	14036744
25	5	4730-01-194-2002	11862	14071983
25	6	5306-01-185-7048	11862	11513606
25	7	2930-01-147-4198	11862	14028918
25	8	5306-01-149-6280	11862	1635490
25	9	5330-01-149-0874	11862	23500846
25	10	4730-01-148-2755	11862	14067727
25	10	4730-01-148-8242	11862	14067737
25	11	2930-01-147-9916	11862	14028917
25	12	5307-01-269-4336	11862	22535073
25	13	6620-01-146-8006	11862	14077122
25	14	5330-01-148-7497	11862	14028916
25	15	4730-01-148-2758	11862	354501
25	16		11862	14033823
25	17	4730-00-908-3194	96906	MS35842-11
25	18	4720-01-159-1839	11862	14067763
25	19	2930-01-150-0895	11862	14000217
26	1	4730-00-044-4789	30379	444789
26	2	4730-01-148-2758	11862	354501
27	1	5307-01-150-1228	11862	14061661
27	2	3020-01-148-2949	11862	14067704
27	2	3020-01-148-2950	11862	14067705
27	3	5306-01-149-6279	11862	14020698
27	4	4140-01-145-8099	11862	14077928
27	5	5310-00-931-8167	96906	MS51967-6
27	6	2930-01-147-9330	11862	14032395
28	1	2920-01-147-4272	11862	14077149
28	2	5306-01-149-6280	11862	1635490
28	3	5305-01-148-7460	11862	11504595
28	4	5306-01-149-6280	11862	1635490
28	5	5340-01-197-1259	11862	14077151
28	6		11862	11503643
28	7	5310-00-809-4085	96906	MS27183-16
28	8	2920-01-149-8606	11862	1105500
28	9	5306-01-185-7050	11862	1610819
28	10	3030-01-258-5125	20796	43-3226

CROSS-REFERENCE INDEXES

FIGURE AND ITEM NUMBER INDEX

FIG	ITEM	STOCK NUMBER	CAGEC	PART NUMBER
28	11	2920-01-191-6635	11862	14077147
29	1	5340-01-150-4105	11862	14005953
29	2	2920-01-147-4278	11862	14067724
29	3	5306-01-149-6280	11862	1635490
29	4	3030-01-147-6410	20796	42-6923
29	5	5306-01-150-9493	11862	14067717
29	6	5310-01-250-7679	11862	11506101
29	7	5310-00-809-4085	96906	MS27183-16
29	8	2920-01-147-8559	11862	14067714
29	9	5365-01-154-4365	11862	14067725
30	1	5305-01-203-2289	11862	9440280
30	2	2920-01-131-4932	35510	4629JA
30	3	3020-01-147-7935	11862	15599204
30	4	3030-00-967-4898	20796	42-6919
30	5	2920-01-191-8442	11862	14067715
30	6	5307-01-159-6632	11862	14067718
30	7	5305-00-071-2066	96906	MS90728-109
30	8	5310-01-147-9792	11862	3954735
30	9	2920-01-147-8562	11862	14067721
30	10	5310-01-250-7679	11862	11506101
30	11	3030-00-357-5506	20796	42-6921
30	12	5307-01-150-7764	11862	1623159
31	1	5310-00-516-2701	35510	5413
31	2	5310-00-429-3135	35510	4340
31	3	5310-01-143-1719	35510	31256
31	4	5970-01-144-1291	35510	7983
31	5	5305-01-143-7412	35510	99525
31	6	5310-00-775-5139	35510	2434
31	7	2920-01-145-0993	35510	95300
31	8	5305-01-143-7411	35510	99459
32	1	2920-01-192-3020	11862	14066657
32	2	5305-01-197-3287	24617	9419663
32	3	5945-01-192-7985	11862	15591718
32	4	5306-01-165-5583	11862	14060613
32	5	5340-01-150-1545	11862	14028931
32	6	5310-00-013-1245	21450	131245
32	7	5310-00-809-4058	96906	MS27183-10
32	8	2920-01-157-3765	16764	1113591
32	9	5306-01-227-9085	11862	15544950
32	10	5310-01-250-3301	11862	22521054
32	11	5365-01-193-0458	11862	23500396
33	1	8040-01-188-2953	11862	3999572
33	4	6130-01-192-1643	11862	12006377
33	5	6680-01-225-4432	11862	15591138
33	17	6240-00-850-4280	08806	1003
34	1	5310-01-154-2273	96906	MS90724-34
34	2	5305-01-269-4329	11862	11513932
34	3	2540-01-158-8626	11862	25052807
34	4	5999-01-158-9249	11862	25053623
34	5	5330-01-164-1653	11862	25015099
34	6	6220-01-164-5228	11862	25022883

CROSS-REFERENCE INDEXES

FIGURE AND ITEM NUMBER INDEX

FIG	ITEM	STOCK NUMBER	CAGEC	PART NUMBER
34	7	6680-01-160-3870	70040	6433429
34	8	6695-01-167-8108	11862	25017376
34	9	6220-01-164-5227	11862	6497476
34	10	5330-01-163-1992	11862	6497483
34	11	6210-01-158-3857	11862	6497475
34	12	6210-01-158-4668	11862	25022884
34	13	6210-01-158-6575	11862	25053501
34	14	6210-01-161-2138	11862	25053500
34	15	6210-01-271-6871	11862	25076586
34	16	2540-01-163-7281	11862	25053622
34	17	5999-01-159-5603	11862	8986000
34	18	6240-00-944-1264	08806	194
34	19	6250-00-433-5946	77060	2973932
34	20	6240-00-944-1264	08806	194
34	21	6240-00-144-4693	08806	168
35	1	6240-00-144-4693	08806	168
35	2	6210-01-158-0396	11862	14066662
35	3	5340-01-162-3627	11862	14072406
35	3	5340-01-162-3628	11862	14072409
35	4	5320-01-195-5106	11862	9441669
35	5	6240-00-144-4693	08806	168
35	6	6620-01-156-0712	11862	14075858
35	7	6625-01-162-8124	70040	6474942A
35	8		08806	1445
35	9	5895-01-165-6792	11862	14072410
35	10	2920-01-152-2414	11862	14072448
35	11	5930-01-158-4428	11862	14072338
35	12	5305-01-164-2313	24617	9415163
35	13	5930-01-163-1439	11862	14072412
36	1	5940-00-890-2831	96906	MS18029-24
36	2		96906	MS18029-13L-5
36	3	5310-00-252-8748	96906	MS35650-3314
36	4	5310-00-514-6674	96906	MS35335-34
36	5	5910-01-189-5152	11862	15599225
36	6	6150-01-159-6901	11862	14072336
36	7	5310-00-934-9747	96906	MS35649-262
36	8		96906	MS27212-4-5
36	9	5340-01-164-8171	11862	14075900
36	10	5305-00-227-1543	96906	MS51849-33
36	11	5340-01-150-4105	11862	14005953
36	12	5306-01-161-6178	11862	9437702
36	13		96906	MS27212-4-3
36	14		11862	14072337
36	15		96906	MS18029-13S-3
37	1		80063	SC-B-75180-1V
37	2		80063	SC-D-691391
37	3	5305-00-068-0508	96906	MS90728-6
37	4	5310-00-209-0786	96906	MS35335-33
37	5	5305-01-156-5438	11862	11504447
37	6	5340-01-159-1321	11862	2043151
37	7	5325-01-164-6431	11862	343124

CROSS-REFERENCE INDEXES

FIGURE AND ITEM NUMBER INDEX

FIG	ITEM	STOCK NUMBER	CAGEC	PART NUMBER
37	8	5310-00-761-6882	96906	MS51967-2
37	9	5310-00-582-5965	96906	MS35338-44
37	10	5340-00-764-7052	96906	MS21333-116
37	11	5325-01-199-3461	00613	C-5139-2
37	12	5305-00-984-6214	96906	MS35206-267
37	13	5935-01-223-9420	96906	MS25043-32CA
37	14	5935-01-171-8273	19207	8701347
37	15	6150-01-155-6522	11862	12039254
38	1	5305-00-227-1543	96906	MS51849-33
38	2	5310-00-082-1404	96906	MS27183-6
38	3	5340-01-228-1659	11862	15599989
38	4		96906	MS27212-4-5
38	5	5310-00-934-9747	96906	MS35649-262
38	6	6150-01-159-6901	11862	14072336
38	7	5310-00-514-6674	96906	MS35335-34
38	8	5310-00-252-8748	96906	MS35650-3314
38	9		96906	MS18029-13L-5
38	10	5940-00-809-2831	96906	MS18029-24
38	11	5306-01-161-6178	11862	9437702
38	12	5340-01-150-4105	11862	14005953
38	13	5340-01-159-1321	11862	2043151
38	14	5306-01-230-3354	11862	11508534
38	15	5310-01-158-6260	24617	11506003
38	16	5320-01-229-8183	11862	9436175
38	17	5320-01-231-3889	79846	ABA64LBA
38	18	5995-01-225-2534	11862	12044586
39	1	2920-01-192-4375	77060	12039297
39	2	5306-01-157-6797	11862	9439770
39	3	2540-01-194-6875	11862	14076848
39	4	5905-01-193-7212	11862	14076847
39	5	5310-01-069-5243	72582	271163
39	6	5310-01-152-0598	24617	271172
39	7	5305-00-115-9934	96906	MS51849-55
39	8	5340-01-150-4105	11862	14005953
39	9	2920-01-192-4376	77060	12039298
39	10	5310-00-209-0786	96906	MS35335-33
39	11	5306-01-161-6178	11862	9437702
40	1	5310-00-880-7746	96906	MS51968-5
40	2	5310-00-934-9764	96906	MS35649-205
40	3	5305-01-197-2536	11862	9440166
40	4	5310-00-582-5965	96906	MS35338-44
40	5	5945-01-192-8653	72055	98226
40	6	5310-00-167-0721	96906	MS35333-41
41	1	2920-01-150-1610	11862	22514861
41	7	5355-01-150-1541	11862	22507977
41	8	5360-01-159-5952	11862	556743
41	9	5930-01-162-3669	11862	556742
41	10	5305-01-160-3945	11862	1640902
41	11	5930-01-163-7282	11862	1242101
41	13	2540-01-196-1622	11862	6258213
41	14	5320-01-160-3999	11862	2477054

CROSS-REFERENCE INDEXES

FIGURE AND ITEM NUMBER INDEX

FIG	ITEM	STOCK NUMBER	CAGEC	PART NUMBER
41	15	5930-01-014-0187	11862	1995217
41	16	5355-01-163-4940	11862	469302
41	17	5930-01-159-0925	11862	14072413
41	18	5930-00-998-9211	11862	1261219
41	19	5340-01-168-1501	11862	1361699
41	20	5305-00-068-0510	96906	MS90728-60
41	21	5310-00-637-9541	96906	MS35338-46
41	22	5310-00-732-0558	96906	MS51967-8
41	23	2590-01-159-8766	11862	14000395
41	23	2590-01-160-5841	11862	14040525
41	24	5305-01-149-7356	11862	9418944
41	25	5930-01-149-9306	11862	477361
41	26	5920-01-123-5212	11862	12004005
41	27	5920-01-123-5211	11862	12004007
41	28	5920-01-085-0825	11862	12004009
41	29	5945-00-983-4374	94988	552-12V
41	30	5920-01-149-6953	11862	12004010
41	31	5945-00-992-5415	94988	224-12V
41	32	5920-01-188-6294	11862	12004011
41	33	5920-01-149-6952	11862	12004008
41	34	5920-01-188-6294	11862	12004011
41	35	5920-01-085-0825	11862	12004009
41	36	5930-01-162-0803	11862	14072358
41	37	5930-01-158-4808	11862	14072339
42	1	6220-01-248-6269	11862	14072333
42	2	6220-01-107-2613	5A910	DC8218
42	3	5330-01-076-6172	34904	DC8226
42	4	6240-00-617-0991	96906	MS35478-1073
42	5	5330-01-037-0663	5A910	DC8211
42	6	5310-01-076-6196	5A910	DC8228
42	7	5310-00-350-2655	19207	5294507
42	8	5310-00-637-9541	96906	MS35338-46
42	9	5310-00-732-0558	96906	MS51967-8
42	10	5306-01-168-4481	11862	9440334
42	11	5340-01-150-4105	11862	14005953
42	12	5340-01-162-6061	11862	14072431
42	13	5305-00-483-0554	96906	MS51862-26
42	14	5305-01-151-8288	11862	9438150
42	15	5310-01-165-0464	11862	362379
42	16	5310-01-154-2273	96906	MS90724-34
42	17	6240-00-944-1264	08806	194
42	18	6220-01-160-4247	11862	915449
42	18	6220-01-161-6439	11862	915450
42	19	5305-01-161-3997	11862	15605040
42	20	5325-01-157-1698	11862	347347
42	21	5310-01-069-5243	72582	271163
42	22	5310-01-158-6260	24617	11506003
42	23	5340-01-159-5762	11862	14072421
42	24	6220-01-156-4475	11862	15559316
42	25	5306-01-162-8525	24617	11503778
42	26	6240-01-157-0635	08806	2057NA

CROSS-REFERENCE INDEXES

FIGURE AND ITEM NUMBER INDEX

FIG	ITEM	STOCK NUMBER	CAGEC	PART NUMBER
42	27	6220-01-155-6521	11862	915908
42	28	5305-01-132-2166	96906	MS51871-4
42	29	5305-01-162-5995	11862	11504656
42	30	6220-01-160-4254	11862	14043873
42	30	6220-01-161-5016	11862	14043874
42	31	6220-01-155-6515	11862	16500591
42	32	5305-01-150-5785	11862	5966249
42	33	2510-01-159-8765	11862	16501759
42	34	6240-01-180-9022	08806	H6054
42	35	6220-01-164-2271	11862	5968095
42	36	5360-01-149-6309	11862	459461
43	1	6220-01-146-4455	11862	5965775
43	1	6220-01-157-9046	11862	5965776
43	2	5330-01-162-3744	11862	5965748
43	3	5305-00-432-7953	96906	MS51861-38
43	4	2510-01-096-6758	11862	5965772
43	4	6220-01-146-4469	11862	5965771
43	5	6240-01-157-0636	08806	2057
43	6	5310-01-154-2273	96906	MS90724-34
43	7	6240-00-924-7526	08806	1156
43	8	6240-00-144-4693	08806	168
43	9	5310-01-158-6260	24617	11506003
43	10	5310-01-069-5243	72582	271163
43	11	6220-01-156-4476	11862	15559312
43	12	5306-01-162-8525	24617	11503778
43	13	5340-01-159-5765	11862	14072433
43	13	5340-01-162-9782	11862	14072434
43	14	5305-01-163-6466	11862	11504655
44	1	5310-00-761-6882	96906	MS51967-2
44	2	5310-00-209-0786	96906	MS35335-33
44	3	5306-01-197-3089	11862	9440033
44	4	6220-01-327-3252	11862	330492
44	5	6240-00-144-4693	08806	168
44	6	6220-01-306-4265	11862	339885
44	6	6220-01-327-1025	11862	339887
44	7	5305-01-163-6466	11862	11504655
44	8	5310-01-154-2273	96906	MS90724-34
45	1	5310-00-761-6882	96906	MS51967-2
45	2	5310-00-209-0786	96906	MS35335-33
45	3	5305-00-068-0510	96906	MS90728-60
45	4	5310-00-959-4675	96906	MS35340-46
45	5	5310-00-732-0558	96906	MS51967-8
45	6	5340-01-165-3417	11862	370873
45	7	6220-01-156-8247	11862	370868
45	7	6220-01-156-8420	11862	370867
45	8	5305-01-162-9695	11862	11504736
45	9	6220-01-242-7557	11862	475922
45	10	6240-00-924-7526	08806	1156
45	11	6240-00-889-1799	08806	1157
45	12	6220-01-156-4476	11862	15559312
45	13	5340-01-162-6077	11862	14072481

CROSS-REFERENCE INDEXES

FIGURE AND ITEM NUMBER INDEX

FIG	ITEM	STOCK NUMBER	CAGEC	PART NUMBER
45	14	5310-01-069-5243	72582	271163
45	15	6250-01-155-6547	11862	370874
46	1	6685-01-192-4834	11862	25037177
46	2	5930-01-157-4060	11862	14071047
46	3	4730-01-160-1505	11862	14040817
46	4	5930-00-073-0390	11862	3815936
47	1	2590-01-085-6956	11862	1892163
47	2	5305-01-164-6319	11862	11501812
47	3	5325-01-199-3461	00613	C-5139-2
47	4	5910-01-190-4600	11862	15599224
47	5	5306-01-161-6178	11862	9437702
47	6	5945-01-243-1702	11862	25523703
48	1	2990-01-257-1569	11862	15599900
48	2	6160-01-165-4638	11862	14076856
48	3	5306-01-168-4481	11862	9440334
48	4	5310-01-158-6260	24617	11506003
48	5	6140-01-156-5326	11862	14075896
48	6	6160-01-165-4637	11862	14076857
48	7	5307-01-158-9932	11862	14075894
48	8	6140-01-190-2517	11862	15599902
48	9	5320-00-994-7076	96906	MS20613-4P4
48	10	5340-01-150-4105	11862	14005953
48	11	6140-01-031-6882	81343	31-620
48	11	6140-01-210-1964	96906	MS52149-1
48	12	6140-01-155-6998	11862	14075389
48	13	5310-01-197-5499	11862	1359887
48	14	5306-01-158-9018	11862	2014469
48	15	6140-01-155-6997	11862	14075388
48	16	6140-01-190-2516	11862	15599901
49	1	6140-01-163-1081	11862	12039293
49	2		11862	FLW-12
49	3	5310-01-152-0598	24617	271172
49	4	5340-01-159-1321	11862	2043151
49	5	5310-00-823-8804	96906	MS27183-9
49	6	5305-00-068-0508	96906	MS90728-6
49	7	5340-01-150-4105	11862	14005953
49	8	5340-01-149-4434	11862	3816659
49	9	5310-00-514-6674	96906	MS35335-34
49	10	5305-01-195-5807	11862	11509371
49	11	5340-01-150-4105	11862	14005953
49	12	5310-00-550-3503	96906	MS35335-36
49	13	6150-01-154-1381	11862	12039271
49	14	6140-01-223-9144	11862	6287160
49	15	6140-01-155-6531	58499	6258
49	16	6150-01-165-0168	11862	12039272
49	17	5310-00-809-4058	96906	MS27183-10
49	18	5310-01-159-6586	11862	11504108
49	19	5305-01-156-5438	11862	11504447
49	20	5340-01-150-4992	11862	14040813
49	21	5310-01-158-6257	11862	11503739
49	22	5935-01-059-0117	19207	11674728

CROSS-REFERENCE INDEXES

FIGURE AND ITEM NUMBER INDEX

FIG	ITEM	STOCK NUMBER	CAGEC	PART NUMBER
49	23	5340-01-059-0114	19207	11675004
49	24	5935-01-044-8382	19207	11682345
49	25	5305-00-269-3233	96906	MS90727-57
49	26	5310-00-637-9541	96906	MS35338-46
49	27	5970-01-044-8391	19207	11674730
49	28	5330-01-059-4286	19207	11674729
49	29	5310-01-170-9100	11862	3982098
49	30	5340-01-162-4774	11862	14072432
49	31	5306-01-168-4481	11862	9440334
49	32	5310-01-164-2338	11862	11508446
49	33	5340-01-150-4105	11862	14005953
49	34	5325-01-159-2843	11862	3979756
49	35	5305-01-161-3995	11862	11508858
49	36	6150-01-163-1385	11862	12039257
49	37	6150-01-163-1384	11862	12039267
49	38		11862	8919163
49	39	5940-00-549-6581	96906	MS75004-1
49	39	5940-00-549-6583	96906	MS75004-2
49	40	6140-01-155-6530	58499	6262
50	6	6250-01-201-3300	11862	12013813
50	7	5340-01-165-2526	11862	469339
50	8	5305-01-160-3938	24617	9416187
50	9	2590-01-160-1496	11862	12001184
51	1	5305-00-146-2524	96906	MS51850-86
51	2	5310-00-209-0786	96906	MS35335-33
51	3	6250-01-189-4981	11862	6298886
51	4		11862	8914822
51	5	6250-01-189-6926	11862	8909518
51	6	2590-01-212-7639	11862	8906150
51	7	2590-01-155-7966	11862	12039205
51	8	2590-01-159-3505	11862	12039208
51	9	5935-00-773-1428	19207	7731428
51	10	5305-00-068-0508	96906	MS90728-6
51	11	5310-00-809-4058	96906	MS27183-10
51	12	5310-01-159-8559	96906	MS35691-406
52	2	5310-00-761-6882	96906	MS51967-2
52	3	5310-00-209-0786	96906	MS35335-33
52	4	5306-01-197-3089	11862	9440033
52	5	5325-01-164-2377	11862	15591130
53	1	6240-00-944-1264	08806	194
53	2	5305-01-156-5438	11862	11504447
53	3	5310-00-514-6674	96906	MS35335-34
54	1	5306-01-197-1492	24617	11508687
54	2	5310-01-158-6260	24617	11506003
54	3	5910-01-189-5110	11862	1988380
54	4	5310-00-696-5172	24617	271166
54	5	5310-01-152-0598	24617	271172
54	6	5305-01-231-1298	24617	1640810
54	7	5940-01-145-7817	11862	3996270
54	10	6130-01-192-1643	11862	12006377
54	14	5306-01-161-6178	11862	9437702

CROSS-REFERENCE INDEXES

FIGURE AND ITEM NUMBER INDEX

FIG	ITEM	STOCK NUMBER	CAGEC	PART NUMBER
54	15	5340-01-150-4105	11862	14005953
54	16	5910-01-189-5153	11862	15599222
54	19	6150-01-156-6326	11862	12039253
54	20	5340-01-150-4105	11862	14005953
54	21	5310-00-550-3503	96906	MS35335-36
54	22	5310-00-209-0786	96906	MS35335-33
55	3	6130-01-192-1643	11862	12006377
55	7	5306-01-149-4398	11862	11502656
55	8	5310-00-407-9566	96906	MS35338-45
55	9	6150-01-156-6326	11862	12039253
56	1	6240-00-944-1264	08806	194
56	2	5910-01-189-5109	11862	15599223
56	7	5340-01-160-4592	11862	14072340
56	8	5340-01-160-4597	11862	14074480
56	9	5305-00-984-6193	96906	MS35206-245
56	10	5306-01-246-7459	11862	1244067
56	11	5310-01-069-5243	72582	271163
56	13	6350-01-321-7005	11862	22529441
56	14	6350-01-158-7035	11862	1253637
57	5	2540-01-147-5537	11862	25078571
57	6	5360-01-193-7130	11862	8985418
57	7	5355-01-251-0633	70040	25023641
57	8	2540-01-191-6510	11862	25078578
57	9	5305-00-146-2524	96906	MS51850-86
58	1	5310-01-165-3331	11862	22521550
58	2	5340-01-166-1470	11862	2044779
58	3		11862	15599235
58	4	5340-01-163-1973	11862	2043150
58	5		11862	326560
59	1	5306-01-149-6280	11862	1635490
59	8	5340-01-164-1743	11862	15522022
59	9	5305-00-071-1784	96906	MS90728-83
60	4	5330-01-148-7492	11862	8655625
60	5	2520-01-159-7757	11862	3787240
60	6	2520-01-149-3461	11862	8633203
60	6	2520-01-213-1680	11862	8655020
60	7	5306-01-171-8076	11862	9440224
60	8	5330-01-147-4208	11862	1259475
60	9	4710-01-148-4989	11862	14045642
60	10	6680-01-147-6583	11862	334532
61	7	5330-01-080-3253	73342	6771005
61	8	4710-01-152-5798	11862	8629526
61	9	5325-01-123-6798	11862	6437746
61	10	2940-01-121-6350	11862	6259423
61	11	5306-01-150-9497	11862	8633208
62	1	4730-00-013-7398	72582	137398
62	2	4730-01-163-7163	11862	8637742
62	3	5340-01-167-9694	11862	3997718
62	4	5340-01-213-6934	11862	15517986
62	5		11862	14045626
62	6		11862	14045628

CROSS-REFERENCE INDEXES

FIGURE AND ITEM NUMBER INDEX

FIG	ITEM	STOCK NUMBER	CAGEC	PART NUMBER
62	7	4730-00-844-5721	14569	1007-2
63	7	5305-00-068-0511	96906	MS90728-62
63	8	5310-00-080-6004	96906	MS27183-14
63	9	5310-00-316-6513	80205	NAS1408A6
63	10	5340-01-164-7021	11862	14067764
64	10	2520-01-192-8282	11862	14029158
64	11	5310-00-080-6004	96906	MS27183-14
64	12	5310-00-316-6513	80205	NAS1408A6
64	13	5305-00-068-0511	96906	MS90728-62
65	17	5365-01-149-9710	11862	14037987
65	50	5330-01-155-4393	76760	99780
65	51	5930-01-149-9305	11862	14037986
66	2	5930-01-202-3573	11862	15594176
66	4	4730-00-044-4587	89346	103868
67	1	4710-01-148-2969	11862	14032995
67	2	4730-00-908-3195	96906	MS35842-10
67	3		11862	9439048
67	4	3040-01-157-7998	11862	8640496
67	5	4710-01-194-6775	11862	14032996
68	1		11862	14063331
68	1		11862	14071950
68	2	2520-01-163-7316	11862	14045658
68	2	2520-01-164-7851	11862	14063332
68	3	5360-01-165-1574	11862	14029108
68	4	2520-01-164-6228	11862	14029107
68	5	5315-01-165-3536	11862	14029111
68	6	3040-01-163-7315	11862	14037889
68	7	5305-01-167-5498	11862	14045504
68	8	5310-01-119-3668	24617	9422295
68	9	5310-01-165-1327	11862	466578
68	10	3120-01-169-6440	11862	3992925
68	11	2520-01-165-7885	11862	14071952
68	12	5310-00-013-1245	21450	131245
68	13	5315-00-842-3044	96906	MS24665-283
68	14	5310-00-081-4219	96906	MS27183-12
68	15	5325-01-150-1229	11862	1234418
68	16	5310-01-148-2682	11862	382105
68	17	5315-00-816-1794	89749	IF316
68	18	5310-00-835-2036	96906	MS35691-29
68	19	2520-01-163-7284	11862	718368
68	20	5315-01-153-0318	11862	14029122
68	21	2520-01-163-7283	11862	14029117
68	22	5305-01-167-8334	11862	20365263
68	23	3040-01-163-7018	11862	14037893
68	24	2520-01-164-9229	11862	14029116
68	25	5305-00-068-0508	96906	MS90728-6
68	26	5310-00-938-8387	96906	MS9549-10
68	27	5330-01-164-7506	11862	14071954
68	28	2510-01-165-8101	11862	14045697
68	29	5355-01-159-6622	11862	15588503
69	1	4730-00-050-4203	11862	9417901

CROSS-REFERENCE INDEXES

FIGURE AND ITEM NUMBER INDEX

FIG	ITEM	STOCK NUMBER	CAGEC	PART NUMBER
69	2	4730-01-202-8523	11862	14009313
69	3	5310-01-194-9233	11862	4497001
69	4	5310-01-194-9220	11862	3838153
69	5	5310-01-195-5088	11862	2423517
69	6	5305-01-198-4154	24617	9431995
69	7	2520-01-193-7870	11862	14032789
69	8	5355-01-197-3172	11862	15588504
69	9	5310-00-835-2036	96906	MS35691-29
69	10	2520-01-194-0278	11862	14055531
69	11	2520-01-192-7979	11862	14071955
69	12	5315-00-816-1794	89749	IF316
69	13	5310-00-080-6004	96906	MS27183-14
69	14	5310-01-194-7081	11862	3953987
69	15	5325-01-197-3540	11862	14049556
69	16	2520-01-192-9729	11862	14054220
70	1	2520-01-189-0596	11862	7845102
70	2	2520-00-722-7074	11862	386451
70	3	5365-01-152-7439	11862	3721887
70	5	2520-01-024-0279	11862	7806140
70	6	5365-01-155-1941	11862	1456507
70	7	2520-01-173-1362	11862	458418
70	8	5330-01-155-4388	11862	7827942
70	9	2520-01-153-8431	11862	15596686
70	10	4730-00-050-4203	11862	9417901
70	13	5305-00-071-1787	96906	MS90728-86
70	14	5306-00-225-2864	72712	1358938
70	15	5310-00-407-9566	96906	MS35338-45
70	16	5310-00-931-8167	96906	MS51967-6
71	1	2520-01-189-0596	11862	7845102
71	1	2520-01-191-9518	11862	26013913
71	2	2520-00-722-7074	11862	386451
71	3	5365-01-152-7439	11862	3721887
71	4	5340-01-202-2517	11862	7840235
71	5	2520-01-192-4314	11862	7845127
71	6	2520-01-024-0279	11862	7806140
71	9	5365-01-155-1941	11862	1456507
71	10	2520-01-192-1793	11862	7845119
71	11	4730-00-050-4203	11862	9417901
71	13	5305-00-071-1787	96906	MS90728-86
71	14	5306-00-225-2864	11862	1358938
71	15	5310-00-407-9566	96906	MS35338-45
71	16	5310-00-931-8167	96906	MS51967-6
72	1	2520-01-239-3800	11862	7830927
72	2	2520-00-722-7074	11862	386451
72	3	5365-01-152-7439	11862	3721887
72	5	2520-01-024-0279	11862	7806140
72	6	5365-01-155-1941	11862	1456507
72	7	2520-01-173-1362	11862	458418
72	8	5330-01-155-4388	11862	7827942
72	9	2520-01-153-8431	11862	15596686
72	10	4730-00-050-4203	11862	9417901

CROSS-REFERENCE INDEXES

FIGURE AND ITEM NUMBER INDEX

FIG	ITEM	STOCK NUMBER	CAGEC	PART NUMBER
72	12	2520-01-153-8430	11862	7815849
72	13	5305-00-071-1787	96906	MS90728-86
72	14	5305-01-152-8193	11862	14018700
72	15	3040-01-148-5982	11862	3882979
73	1	2520-01-211-6755	11862	26013911
73	2	2520-00-722-7074	11862	386451
73	3	5365-01-152-7439	11862	3721887
73	4	5340-01-202-2517	11862	7840235
73	5	2520-01-192-4314	11862	7845127
73	7	2520-01-024-0279	11862	7806140
73	8	5365-01-155-1941	11862	1456507
73	9	2520-01-192-1793	11862	7845119
73	10	4730-00-050-4203	11862	9417901
73	12	2520-01-153-8430	11862	7815849
73	13	5305-00-071-1787	96906	MS90728-86
73	14	5305-01-152-8193	11862	14018700
73	15	3040-01-148-5982	11862	3882979
74	1	2520-01-147-4005	11862	14067762
74	1	2520-01-148-2919	11862	7844074
74	1	2520-01-210-1382	11862	14020403
74	1	2520-01-324-4895	97271	911105-5130
74	1	2520-01-328-4898	11862	14071980
74	2	5365-01-155-1941	11862	1456507
74	3	2520-01-024-0279	11862	7806140
74	3	2520-01-024-0279	11862	7806140
74	4	2520-01-151-8043	11862	14029852
74	4	2520-01-155-6936	11862	7838665
74	5	2590-01-324-5042	11862	14046907
74	5	5340-01-149-9729	11862	3920486
74	5	5340-01-231-0925	11862	7846740
74	6	5305-01-152-8193	11862	14018700
74	6	5306-01-323-5544	11862	458300
75	1	5305-01-156-5438	11862	11504447
75	2	5340-00-057-3043	96906	MS21333-112
75	3	3040-01-157-7998	11862	8640496
75	4	5340-00-486-1765	96906	MS21333-48
75	5		11862	9439088
75	6	4730-00-908-3195	96906	MS35842-10
75	7		11862	9439091
75	8	4730-01-153-2718	11862	14056299
75	9	5340-00-057-3034	96906	MS21333-110
75	10		11862	14029235
76	1		97271	700013L
76	2	3120-01-153-0281	11862	14009626
76	3	5330-01-158-6725	97271	620062-B
76	4	5365-01-174-8657	97271	37312
76	5	5330-01-096-9649	11862	462811
76	15	4730-01-034-8228	72447	36472
77	1	2530-01-149-3827	11862	14072919
77	1	2530-01-149-3827	97271	29907X
77	1	2530-01-249-5401	11862	464039

CROSS-REFERENCE INDEXES

FIGURE AND ITEM NUMBER INDEX

FIG	ITEM	STOCK NUMBER	CAGEC	PART NUMBER
77	2	3120-01-159-9386	11862	3965121
77	3	5330-01-086-3504	11862	376855
77	4	5310-01-153-1381	11862	376852
77	5	5330-01-086-3503	11862	376851
77	16	4730-00-187-4210	96906	MS51884-9
78	1	5310-01-093-2907	97271	36880
78	2	5310-01-099-7945	97271	38081-1
78	5	4730-01-098-5229	24617	9411031
79	8	5310-00-975-2075	96906	MS35691-21
79	9	5305-01-150-9500	11862	3711876
79	11	5310-01-157-7582	11862	14056133
79	13	5305-01-150-9500	11862	3711876
79	25	5310-00-975-2075	96906	MS35691-21
80	1		11862	14040775
80	2	3040-01-157-7998	11862	8640496
80	3	5340-01-158-0303	11862	3866187
80	4	5305-01-156-5438	11862	11504447
80	5	4730-00-908-3195	96906	MS35842-10
80	6	4730-01-156-0055	11862	14056297
80	7	5340-00-057-3043	96906	MS21333-112
80	8		11862	474935
81	1	3040-01-157-7998	11862	8640496
81	2	5305-01-156-5438	11862	11504447
81	3	5340-00-057-3043	96906	MS21333-112
81	4		11862	474935
81	5	4730-00-908-3195	96906	MS35842-10
81	6	4730-01-147-6425	11862	14072930
82	1	2520-01-038-7283	11862	3977384
82	1	2520-01-201-2501	11862	15599687
82	2	2520-01-040-2160	11862	3977383
82	3	5306-01-153-1368	11862	376869
83	4	4730-00-044-4789	30379	444789
83	8	5306-01-156-5435	11862	15521977
83	9	2520-01-330-3249	11862	14071884
83	9	5340-01-148-2730	11862	3977386
83	10	5330-01-020-9319	11862	3977387
83	11	2520-01-159-7757	11862	3787240
84	1	4730-00-044-4789	30379	444789
84	4	5306-01-148-6765	11862	10008936
84	5	2520-01-152-9171	11862	1252415
84	6	5330-01-084-2410	11862	26016662
84	7	2520-01-159-7757	11862	3787240
85	6	3110-00-580-3708	60038	HM88542
85	7	3110-00-580-3709	60038	88510
85	9	3110-00-227-4667	60038	HM807010
85	10	3110-00-606-9576	60038	HM807040
85	15	3110-00-142-4387	60038	453X
85	16	3110-00-100-0251	60038	469
86	1	2540-01-159-8878	11862	3893181
86	2	2530-01-159-8802	11862	334540
86	3	5325-01-155-4482	11862	341990

CROSS-REFERENCE INDEXES

FIGURE AND ITEM NUMBER INDEX

FIG	ITEM	STOCK NUMBER	CAGEC	PART NUMBER
86	4	5306-00-226-4826	96906	MS90728-33
86	5	5310-00-959-4679	96906	MS35340-45
86	6	3040-01-156-9994	11862	14053591
86	7	5325-01-160-2238	11862	334541
86	8	5340-01-148-8352	11862	14054122
86	8	5340-01-335-9359	11862	15557723
86	9	2990-01-148-2929	11862	14064664
86	9	2990-01-151-8115	11862	14054174
86	10	5340-01-148-8351	11862	14072697
86	10	5340-01-323-9727	11862	14054120
86	11	5340-00-700-1423	19207	7001423
86	12	2590-01-156-0583	11862	14064663
86	12	2990-01-152-0251	11862	14054173
86	13	5310-00-245-3424	96906	MS17829-5C
86	14	5325-01-149-6293	11862	15530620
86	15	2530-01-147-4214	11862	14072692
86	16	5340-01-158-0297	11862	25516531
86	17	2530-01-148-1463	11862	368786
86	18	2590-01-161-2119	11862	14053593
86	18	5995-01-148-2930	11862	14055591
86	19	5310-00-931-8167	96906	MS51967-6
86	20	5310-00-809-3078	96906	MS27183-11
87	1	5310-00-763-8894	96906	MS51968-24
87	2	5310-00-052-6454	96906	MS35340-51
87	3	5310-00-834-7606	96906	MS35340-48
87	4	5305-00-719-5184	96906	MS90727-109
87	5	2530-01-152-7115	14892	4150515
87	6	2530-01-183-8860	14892	3368689
87	7	5315-01-156-0081	11862	3856834
87	8	3040-01-156-7182	11862	334307
87	8	3040-01-157-7970	11862	334308
87	9	5310-01-154-4341	11862	5454797
87	10	2530-01-140-6144	11862	372379
87	13	5365-00-682-1762	96906	MS16633-1031
87	14	2530-00-125-2769	11862	3856856
87	14	2530-00-494-8165	11862	3856855
87	15	5360-00-123-0137	11862	5461145
87	16	2530-01-156-5883	11862	357845
87	16	5340-01-156-8395	11862	357846
87	17	5360-00-113-9490	11862	5461984
87	18	2530-01-156-8308	11862	3856858
87	18	3040-01-156-8307	11862	3856857
87	19	5310-01-151-8347	11862	18002428
87	20	5360-01-157-3662	11862	3856843
87	21	2530-01-156-4875	11862	3898059
87	22	5360-00-392-3453	11862	1312281
87	23	5360-01-159-1449	11862	3767138
87	24	5360-00-229-5312	11862	3856850
87	25	2530-00-228-6992	11862	15522081
87	26	5365-01-158-2191	11862	3856849
87	27	2530-01-096-6752	11862	15522077

CROSS-REFERENCE INDEXES

FIGURE AND ITEM NUMBER INDEX

FIG	ITEM	STOCK NUMBER	CAGEC	PART NUMBER
87	27	2530-01-155-7943	11862	15522078
87	28	2530-01-162-8986	11862	15522079
87	29	2530-01-164-0039	11862	15522080
87	29	2530-01-152-0180	11862	372249
87	30	2530-01-156-4900	11862	14068905
87	30	2530-01-156-4901	11862	14068906
88	3	5310-01-155-1898	11862	3760300
88	5	2530-01-152-9308	11862	14009982
88	6	2530-01-163-7227	11862	15594178
88	6	2530-01-164-7126	11862	15594177
88	8	5310-01-154-4341	11862	5454797
88	9	5365-01-164-4525	11862	18004057
88	10	5365-01-159-4833	76462	18001032
88	11	5330-01-185-4676	11862	5470497
88	12	5340-01-157-2101	11862	5469497
88	13		11862	12321435
88	14	2530-01-166-3033	11862	1155445
88	15	5365-00-682-1762	96906	MS16633-1031
88	16	2530-00-125-2769	11862	3856856
88	16	2530-00-494-8165	11862	3856855
88	17	5360-00-123-0137	11862	5461145
88	18	2530-01-152-7787	11862	357889
88	18	3040-01-152-7786	11862	357890
88	19	5360-00-113-9490	11862	5461984
88	20	2530-01-157-5164	11862	14055315
88	20	2530-01-173-1248	11862	5461156
88	21	5310-01-151-8347	11862	18002428
88	22	5360-01-156-9730	11862	3820163
88	23	2530-01-155-8460	11862	468661
88	24	5360-00-392-3453	11862	1312281
88	25	5360-00-310-4493	11862	3694822
88	26	5360-01-162-9935	11862	3887347
88	27	5305-01-156-5006	11862	468675
88	28	5365-01-154-8577	11862	5462496
88	29	2530-01-152-9258	11862	345943
88	29	2530-01-153-1492	11862	345944
88	30	2530-01-153-9449	11862	468673
88	30	2530-01-153-9450	11862	468674
88	31	2530-01-152-0180	11862	372249
89	1	2530-01-151-5967	14892	2770209
89	1	2530-01-154-1294	14892	2770317
89	11		14892	2770614
89	12		14892	129494
89	25	2530-01-153-1813	11862	345683
89	27	5310-01-154-5263	11862	11502812
89	28	5330-01-148-7499	11862	14004810
89	29	5340-01-160-2155	11862	14045698
89	30	2530-01-156-7016	14892	2232073
89	31	5330-01-165-1358	14892	2229044
89	32	2530-01-168-6369	14892	2232076
89	33	5340-01-157-1955	14892	2229046

CROSS-REFERENCE INDEXES

FIGURE AND ITEM NUMBER INDEX

FIG	ITEM	STOCK NUMBER	CAGEC	PART NUMBER
89	34	2530-01-192-9778	14892	2232072
89	35	5330-01-157-1916	14892	2227168
89	36	2530-01-250-6472	14892	2232077
89	37	5340-01-158-0321	14892	2229448
90	1	5340-01-155-2614	18862	343438
90	2	5340-00-881-5303	11862	15599973
90	3	4730-01-154-1366	11862	9424955
90	4	5340-01-268-9064	11862	25527423
90	5	5340-01-149-4434	11862	3816659
90	6		11862	15599260
90	6		11862	15599262
90	7	4730-00-014-2432	24617	137397
90	8	5310-00-380-1514	11862	15607227
90	9		11862	15599259
90	9		11862	15599261
90	10	5305-01-156-5438	11862	11504447
90	11	4730-00-288-9390	24617	9432075
90	12	4730-00-278-8886	96906	MS51877-4
90	13		11862	14034586
90	13		11862	15522444
90	14	5306-00-226-4833	96906	MS90728-40
90	15	5340-01-155-2614	11862	342677
90	16		11862	14034571
90	16		11862	14054257
90	17	5360-01-163-7234	11862	22527167
90	18	4720-01-148-2763	11862	14036736
90	18	4720-01-148-6946	11862	14054270
90	18	4720-01-148-6947	11862	14054269
90	18	4720-01-148-7398	11862	14036723
90	19	4730-01-151-7972	11862	14094948
90	20	5310-01-154-3993	11862	14000172
90	21	2520-01-192-1919	11862	1257087
90	21	2530-01-124-3422	11862	1257203
90	21	2530-01-156-8317	11862	25515635
90	22		11862	14034572
90	23	5310-01-119-3668	24617	9422295
91	1		11862	14036797
91	2	4710-01-172-0471	11862	14036792
91	3	5360-01-163-7234	11862	22527167
91	4	2530-01-225-2236	11862	15549248
91	5	5306-00-226-4824	96906	MS90728-31
91	6	5310-00-959-4679	96906	MS35340-45
91	7	5340-01-154-5269	11862	14036736
91	8	2530-01-225-1024	11862	15538215
91	9	2530-01-222-8068	11862	14061396
91	10	5310-00-931-8167	96906	MS51967-6
91	11	4730-01-255-2976	11862	14036775
91	12	4730-00-288-9390	24617	9432075
91	13		11862	14036706
91	13		11862	14036712
91	14	5306-01-152-2582	11862	1239146

CROSS-REFERENCE INDEXES

FIGURE AND ITEM NUMBER INDEX

FIG	ITEM	STOCK NUMBER	CAGEC	PART NUMBER
91	15	5305-00-688-2111	96906	MS90728-63
91	16	5305-00-821-3869	11862	9439637
91	17	5365-01-157-5752	11862	14055556
91	18	5340-01-161-4025	11862	359816
91	19	5340-01-155-3668	11862	331416
91	19	5340-01-335-9360	11862	6259071
91	20		11862	14036705
91	20		11862	14036711
91	21	5340-00-809-1490	96906	MS21333-98
91	21	5340-00-881-5303	96906	MS21333-45
91	22	5305-01-156-5438	11862	11504447
91	23		11862	14034599
91	24	5340-00-881-5303	11862	15599973
91	25	4720-01-149-4659	11862	17981073
92	1		14892	2238739
92	2	2530-01-147-6423	11862	14002543
92	7	5340-01-163-1401	11862	5469581
92	8		14892	2238740
92	10	2530-01-147-6424	14892	2238742
92	14	5340-01-152-7155	14892	4150514
92	15	5305-01-148-8208	11862	331478
92	16	5315-01-157-3004	11862	14023439
92	17	2530-01-149-3375	14892	3203466
92	17	5340-01-149-3376	14894	3203465
92	18	2530-01-159-7754	97271	38001
92	18	2530-01-159-7755	97271	38000
93	1	5306-01-085-1953	11862	5468226
93	2	2530-01-156-6190	11862	18015381
93	5	2530-01-163-7878	11862	18013395
93	6	5340-01-163-1401	11862	5469581
93	7	2530-01-147-9329	11862	18007952
93	8	2530-01-163-7878	11862	18013395
93	11	2530-01-152-9306	11862	14023429
93	11	2530-01-152-9307	11862	14023430
94	1	5306-01-159-5710	24617	456697
94	2	5340-01-163-1401	11862	5469581
94	3	2530-01-149-1886	11862	18003151
94	4	2530-01-096-6764	11862	18004794
94	4	2530-01-110-5304	11862	18004890
94	5	2530-01-154-1263	11862	2622667
95	4	5310-01-150-4003	11862	9422299
95	5	5340-01-232-8179	11862	15593849
95	6	5305-00-182-9584	96906	MS18154-96
95	7	5360-01-160-2415	11862	3850084
95	8	3120-01-158-2096	11862	346381
95	9	5365-01-154-8514	11862	6264951
95	10	2540-01-154-1293	11862	15522095
95	11	2540-01-153-9470	11862	355561
95	12	3040-01-166-4497	11862	336926
95	13	5310-01-151-8353	11862	3702807
95	14	5315-01-156-6562	11862	1244707

CROSS-REFERENCE INDEXES

FIGURE AND ITEM NUMBER INDEX

FIG	ITEM	STOCK NUMBER	CAGEC	PART NUMBER
96	1	5310-01-021-9027	11862	3978901
96	1	5310-01-107-4051	23862	334387
96	2	2520-01-201-4096	11862	472536
96	3	2530-01-154-6952	11862	14035374
96	3	2530-01-325-9112	11862	15668598
96	4	3040-01-163-0797	27647	25113
96	5	5305-01-165-2260	27647	9477
96	6	2530-01-163-0798	27647	15149
96	7	5365-00-803-7317	96906	MS16624-1131
96	8		27647	9952
96	9	5365-01-221-9717	11862	14070396
96	10	2530-01-163-0799	27647	13109
96	11	5310-01-205-2536	11862	14050679
96	11	5310-01-205-2537	11862	15582233
96	12	5365-01-209-6943	11862	14038051
96	13		11862	15634658
96	13	5306-01-158-6682	09386	102007
96	14	5330-01-106-7938	80201	27467
96	14	5330-01-106-7938	80201	27467
96	15	3110-01-030-8475	60038	387AS-382A
96	16	2530-01-096-9670	09386	SR104396
96	16	2530-01-216-4554	09386	104192
96	17	3110-01-027-4475	43334	LM104949LM104911
96	18	5310-01-172-1591	97271	33734
96	19	5305-01-019-1884	11862	3988538
96	20	5330-01-085-0918	11862	469694
96	21	5365-01-161-4055	11862	474309
96	22	2530-01-148-2914	11862	6260830
96	23	2530-01-096-7731	11862	3977397
96	23	2530-01-326-1462	11862	15634663
96	24	5310-01-148-2676	11862	341509
96	25	2520-01-147-5539	11862	341511
96	26	5365-01-326-4346	11862	15634661
96	27	5330-01-076-3009	24617	327739
96	28	5315-01-153-0317	11862	341510
96	29	2640-00-555-2829	11862	273487
96	29	2640-01-302-1388	6V625	30-600
96	29	2640-01-323-2632	11862	9591270
97	1	2640-00-555-2840	17875	T14R
97	2	2520-01-165-5974	27647	M257
97	3	5305-01-165-2260	27647	9477
97	4	3040-01-163-7285	27647	15147
97	5	5365-00-721-6876	96906	MS16624-1125
97	6	5330-01-331-7230	27647	13446
97	7	5365-01-197-8165	11862	14070348
97	8	3040-01-163-7347	27647	13113
97	9	5365-00-721-6876	96906	MS16624-1125
97	10	5365-01-158-2193	11862	14072921
97	11	5310-01-244-2259	11862	14034413
97	12	5310-01-154-3990	79410	17-01-014-001
97	13	5310-01-155-1897	11862	14034410

CROSS-REFERENCE INDEXES

FIGURE AND ITEM NUMBER INDEX

FIG	ITEM	STOCK NUMBER	CAGEC	PART NUMBER
97	14	5310-01-153-9302	76445	40424
97	15		11862	14072927
97	16	5330-01-086-3506	11862	6273948
97	17	2530-01-152-9305	11862	14070352
97	18	5340-00-700-1423	19207	6262328
97	19	3110-01-087-2653	11862	7455617
97	20	5306-01-150-1197	09386	96735
97	21	2530-01-147-4209	11862	14026765
97	22	3110-00-690-8923	43334	LM501349-LM501310
97	23	2530-01-154-8146	11862	14063307
97	24	5310-00-264-1930	11862	358501
98	1	2610-01-148-1634	22337	212-776
98	1	2610-01-148-1635	81348	GP2A/LT235/85R16/E/LTAW
99	60	5310-01-159-6587	11862	7846970
99	61	5360-01-163-0886	11862	404234
99	62	2590-01-164-7825	11862	474102
99	63		11862	409190
99	64	2530-01-159-3604	11862	9762199
99	65	5360-01-187-0301	24617	9749363
99	66	5365-01-270-1977	11862	9754764
99	67	2530-01-287-3980	11862	17983936
99	68	5305-01-270-3030	11862	9767270
99	69	5365-01-160-9530	11862	419454
99	70	2530-01-147-6421	11862	17987489
99	71	5355-01-085-0995	11862	14049351
99	71	5355-01-235-6616	11862	470205
99	72	2520-01-163-7314	11862	14034728
99	72	2520-01-225-1033	11862	14081915
99	73	5315-00-450-9163	11862	3793014
99	74	3120-01-232-6781	11862	1604854
99	75	2540-01-156-7233	11862	22510143
100	1	5305-01-149-1936	11862	343178
100	2	5365-01-151-6111	11862	343179
100	3	5310-00-407-9566	96906	MS35338-45
100	4	5310-00-905-4600	96906	MS51968-6
100	5	5310-00-785-1762	96906	MS51968-9
100	6	5310-00-637-9541	96906	MS35338-46
100	7	5305-01-194-0614	96906	MS90727-145
100	8	2530-01-155-7457	11862	14064660
100	9	5310-00-842-7783	96906	MS35692-53
100	10	5315-00-298-1481	96906	MS24665-357
100	11	2530-01-157-7933	11862	4993563
100	12	2530-01-154-1262	11862	14007644
100	13	4730-00-050-4203	11862	9417901
100	14	2530-01-159-5958	11862	362297
100	15	2530-01-159-8725	11862	362298
100	16	5315-00-816-1794	89749	IF316
100	17	5310-00-842-1490	96906	MS35692-37
100	18	5310-00-010-3028	96906	MS35690-824

CROSS-REFERENCE INDEXES

FIGURE AND ITEM NUMBER INDEX

FIG	ITEM	STOCK NUMBER	CAGEC	PART NUMBER
100	19	5310-00-584-5272	96906	MS35338-48
100	20	5310-00-044-3342	11862	9422303
100	21	5310-00-068-5285	96906	MS27183-20
101	1	2530-01-165-9654	72210	O23980-J
101	2	5310-01-228-1405	24617	125384
101	3	5330-01-155-7700	11862	6259074
101	4	4730-00-050-4203	11862	9417901
101	5	5315-00-013-7238	96906	MS24665-425
101	6	2530-01-165-9653	72210	24004-J
101	7	5310-01-228-1405	24617	125384
101	8	5330-01-155-7700	97271	S19587-T
101	9	2530-01-165-6005	72210	S23981-H
102	1	5310-00-209-2811	11862	467117
102	2	5315-01-251-1701	11862	11514337
102	3	5330-01-155-7700	11862	6259074
102	4	2530-01-152-9312	11862	14026803
102	5	4730-00-050-4203	11862	9417901
102	6	5310-01-153-9301	11862	14026805
102	7	2530-01-152-9314	11862	14026804
102	8	5310-00-792-3617	30076	160635
102	9	2530-01-152-9313	11862	14026802
103	1	2530-01-150-9757	11862	7846959
104	1	3030-01-148-2792	20796	42-5023
104	2	5310-01-250-7679	11862	11506101
104	3		11862	11503643
104	4	5310-01-143-0512	73342	11501033
104	5	5340-01-147-2268	11862	14033879
104	6	2530-01-147-8556	52788	7838936
104	7	5306-01-149-6280	11862	1635490
104	8	5305-01-148-7460	11862	11504595
104	9	5340-01-154-7163	11862	14033880
104	10	5340-01-155-7744	11862	14033881
104	11	5306-01-148-3667	11862	11504512
104	12	5306-01-185-7049	11862	11505299
104	13	3020-01-148-2948	11862	14067701
104	13	3020-01-153-9586	11862	14023174
105	18	6680-01-152-2845	11862	7834183
106	1	5306-00-226-4825	96906	MS90728-32
106	2	4730-01-163-7194	11862	25518880
106	3		11862	350371
106	4		11862	14040735
106	5	4720-01-148-2762	11862	7838941
106	6		11862	1488565
106	7	4730-01-155-5135	11862	22514738
106	8	5330-01-156-5141	11862	7829923
106	9		11862	3773687
106	10	4720-01-148-2761	11862	7838942
106	11	5310-00-931-8167	96906	MS51967-6
106	12	5310-00-959-4679	96906	MS35340-45
106	13	5340-01-155-2616	11862	338696
107	1	2510-01-164-7119	11862	14045516

CROSS-REFERENCE INDEXES

FIGURE AND ITEM NUMBER INDEX

FIG	ITEM	STOCK NUMBER	CAGEC	PART NUMBER
107	2	5305-00-071-1788	96906	MS90728-87
107	3	5310-01-147-8743	11862	3790768
107	4	5305-00-071-2067	96906	MS90728-111
107	5	5310-00-809-5998	96906	MS27183-18
107	6	5310-00-768-0318	96906	MS51967-14
107	7	2510-01-164-7118	11862	14045515
107	8	5305-00-071-2075	96906	MS90728-119
107	9	2510-01-165-1495	11862	14067791
107	10	2540-01-159-8881	11862	14072422
107	11	5306-01-157-3330	11862	14072425
107	12	5310-00-809-3079	96906	MS27183-19
107	13	2510-01-164-7120	11862	14067792
108	1	2510-01-164-7116	11862	14014799
108	2	5310-01-149-4407	24617	9422301
108	3	5310-00-768-0318	96906	MS51967-14
108	4	5310-00-834-7606	96906	MS35340-48
108	5	5310-00-809-5998	96906	MS27183-18
108	6	2510-01-164-7117	11862	14014800
108	7	5305-00-071-2075	96906	MS90728-119
108	8	5306-01-157-3330	11862	14072425
108	9	5305-00-071-2067	96906	MS90728-111
108	10	2540-01-159-2992	11862	14072435
109	1	2510-01-163-1146	11862	14067783
109	2	2510-01-164-7128	11862	14021357
109	3	2510-01-163-7228	11862	14021358
109	4	5310-00-896-0903	96906	MS51967-12
109	5	5310-00-655-9370	96906	MS35340-47
109	6	5305-00-071-1788	96906	MS90728-87
109	7	2510-01-164-7127	11862	14067784
109	8	5310-00-768-0318	96906	MS51967-14
109	9	5310-00-834-7606	96906	MS35340-48
109	10	5310-00-809-5998	96906	MS27183-18
109	11	5306-01-157-3330	11862	14072425
109	12	2540-01-155-7535	11862	14072436
110	1	5340-01-198-8591	11862	15599219
110	2	5305-00-071-2067	96906	MS90728-111
110	3	5340-01-198-8591	11862	15599220
110	4	5310-01-149-4407	24617	9422301
111	2	5305-01-156-8692	11862	9424320
111	3	5310-00-809-4085	96906	MS27183-16
111	4	5310-00-316-6513	80205	NAS1408A6
111	5	2510-01-225-5865	11862	15599998
111	6	5340-01-163-1389	11862	14022538
111	7	5340-01-162-3748	11862	14034503
111	7	5340-01-162-3749	11862	14034504
111	9	5310-00-316-6513	80205	NAS1408A6
111	10	5310-01-157-5670	11862	3914674
111	11	5305-01-140-9118	96906	MS90728-59
111	12	2590-01-159-8716	11862	15595211
111	13	5340-01-162-3747	11862	14034501
111	15	5340-01-163-1390	11862	14022537

CROSS-REFERENCE INDEXES

FIGURE AND PART NUMBER INDEX

FIG	ITEM	STOCK NUMBER	CAGEC	PART NUMBER
111	19	5310-00-732-0558	96906	MS51967-8
111	21	5310-00-637-9541	96906	MS35338-46
111	22	5305-00-068-0510	96906	MS90728-60
111	23	5340-01-324-6756	11862	14001068
111	23	5340-01-324-9553	11862	14001067
111	24	5330-01-323-5567	11862	337957
111	41	2510-01-225-1004	11862	15599997
112	2	5310-01-150-4003	11862	9422299
112	3	5310-01-097-9414	24617	3990160
112	4		11862	TX001488
112	5	5306-01-195-7915	11862	9440344
112	6	2990-01-147-3954	11862	14020478
112	6	2990-01-164-7178	11862	14034513
112	21		11862	TX001487
112	22	5310-00-959-4675	96906	MS35340-46
112	23	5310-01-187-7610	11862	9418931
112	24	5305-00-688-2111	96906	MS90728-63
112	32	2990-01-181-6725	11862	14007142
113	1	2510-01-155-7942	11862	14067790
113	2	2540-01-159-7740	11862	14067795
113	3	5340-01-160-2171	11862	14067796
113	4	5315-00-013-7258	96906	MS24665-497
113	5	5315-01-160-4639	11862	14067794
113	6	4030-00-088-1881	19207	7358030
114	1	2540-00-078-6633	96906	MS51335-1
114	2	3040-01-267-4283	74410	XA-T-61-SR
114	3	4730-00-050-4203	96906	MS15001-1
114	4	5340-01-267-6296	74410	XB-767-10
114	5	5310-01-267-6293	74410	XA-T-88
114	6	5310-00-849-6882	96906	MS35692-94
114	7	5315-00-846-0126	96906	MS24665-628
114	8		74410	XB-766
114	9	5310-01-249-4210	74410	XB-T-45-1
114	10	2540-01-267-1360	74410	XA-T-61-SF
114	11	5305-00-719-5240	96906	MS90727-117
114	12	2540-00-078-6633	96906	MS51335-1
114	13		74410	XX123
114	14	4030-00-916-2141	96906	MS87006-53
114	15	5315-00-243-1169	80020	36344N24
114	16	5305-00-253-5626	96906	MS21318-47
114	17	5305-00-071-2069	96906	MS90728-113
114	18	5310-00-809-5998	96906	MS27183-18
114	19	2540-01-158-8548	11862	14067786
114	20	5310-01-149-4407	24617	9422301
114	21	5340-01-162-8760	11862	14067780
114	22	5310-00-809-3079	96906	MS27183-19
114	23	5305-00-071-2075	96906	MS90728-119
114	24	5315-01-160-4639	11862	14067794
114	25	4030-00-542-3183	11862	14067793
114	26	5315-00-013-7258	96906	MS24665-497
114	27	5310-00-768-0318	96906	MS51967-14

CROSS-REFERENCE INDEXES

FIGURE AND ITEM NUMBER INDEX

FIG	ITEM	STOCK NUMBER	CAGEC	PART NUMBER
114	28	5310-00-834-7606	96906	MS35340-48
114	29	2540-01-200-3167	11862	14078806
114	30	5306-01-157-3330	11862	14072425
114	31	2540-01-159-7741	11862	14067787
114	32	2540-01-159-2928	11862	14067785
114	33	5340-01-162-8759	11862	14067779
115	1	2540-01-158-8553	11862	14067770
115	2	5310-00-768-0318	96906	MS51967-14
115	3	5310-00-834-7606	96906	MS35340-48
115	4	5310-00-896-0903	96906	MS51967-12
115	5	5310-01-147-8743	11862	3790768
115	6	2540-01-163-8595	11862	14067773
115	6	2540-01-164-1842	11862	14067774
115	7	5340-01-162-4775	11862	14067772
115	7	5340-01-165-4353	11862	14067771
115	8	5305-00-071-2067	96906	MS90728-111
115	9	5305-00-071-2075	96906	MS90728-119
115	10	2540-00-078-6633	96906	MS51335-1
115	11	3040-01-267-4283	74410	XA-T-61-SR
115	12	4730-00-050-4203	96906	MS15001-1
115	13	5340-01-267-6296	74410	XB-767-10
115	14	5310-01-267-6293	74410	XA-T-88
115	15	5310-00-849-6882	96906	MS35692-94
115	16	5315-00-846-0126	96906	MS24665-628
115	17		74410	XB-766
115	18	5310-01-249-4210	74410	XB-T-45-1
115	19	2540-00-078-6633	96906	MS51335-1
115	20		74410	XX123
115	21	4030-00-916-2141	96906	MS87006-53
115	22	5315-00-243-1169	80020	36344N24
115	23	5305-00-253-5626	96906	MS21318-47
115	24	2540-01-267-1360	74410	XA-T-61-SF
115	25	5305-00-719-5240	96906	MS90727-117
115	26	5310-00-732-0558	96906	MS51967-8
115	27	5310-00-637-9541	96906	MS35338-46
115	28	5310-00-080-6004	96906	MS27183-14
115	29	5305-00-068-0510	96906	MS90728-60
115	30	5315-01-160-4639	11862	14067794
115	31	4030-00-542-3183	11862	14067793
115	32	5315-00-013-7258	96906	MS24665-497
115	33	5305-00-071-2058	96906	MS90728-92
115	34	5365-01-163-6195	11862	14067789
115	35	2540-01-157-8008	11862	14067776
115	36	5310-00-809-4061	96906	MS27183-15
115	37	5305-00-071-1788	96906	MS90728-87
115	38	5310-00-809-5998	96906	MS27183-18
115	39	5305-00-071-2073	96906	MS90728-117
115	40	2540-01-158-4599	11862	14067775
115	41	5310-01-194-9217	11862	480567
116	1	5310-00-768-0318	96906	MS51967-14
116	2	5306-01-157-9817	11862	3991022

CROSS-REFERENCE INDEXES

FIGURE AND ITEM NUMBER INDEX

FIG	ITEM	STOCK NUMBER	CAGEC	PART NUMBER
116	3	2590-01-182-4455	11862	15599915
116	4	5310-01-157-7560	11862	6274031
116	5	2590-01-193-3443	11862	350037
116	6	5320-01-197-1394	24617	189448
116	7	2540-01-192-3572	11862	6274036
116	8	2590-01-147-2269	11862	350036
116	9	5305-01-148-3687	11862	371603
117	1	2540-01-191-8439	11862	330046
117	2	5340-01-197-4600	11862	14027926
117	3	5310-01-184-5418	11862	3725668
117	4	5305-01-197-1475	24617	443945
117	5	2590-01-219-7808	11862	14007545
117	6	5306-01-148-7457	11862	15599432
117	7	5305-01-162-7890	11862	3954730
117	8	5310-00-809-5998	96906	MS27183-18
117	9	2590-01-147-5538	11862	343951
118	1	5310-00-080-6004	96906	MS27183-14
118	2	5305-00-068-0510	96906	MS90728-60
118	3	5310-00-732-0558	96906	MS51967-8
118	4	5310-00-637-9541	96906	MS35338-46
118	5	5305-00-068-0511	96906	MS90728-62
118	6	5310-00-809-4085	96906	MS27183-16
118	7	5310-00-768-0318	96906	MS51967-14
118	8	5310-00-834-7606	96906	MS35340-48
118	9	5340-01-168-6372	11862	14029200
118	10	2530-01-163-3557	11862	14045654
118	11	2510-01-154-1261	11862	359878
118	15	2510-01-153-9473	11862	359877
119	1	5310-00-080-6004	96906	MS27183-14
119	2	5305-00-068-0510	96906	MS90728-60
119	3	5310-00-732-0558	96906	MS51967-8
119	4	5310-00-637-9541	96906	MS35338-46
119	5	5305-00-688-2111	96906	MS90728-63
119	6	5310-00-768-0318	96906	MS51967-14
119	7	5310-00-834-7606	96906	MS35340-48
119	8	5340-01-168-6372	11862	14029200
119	9	2510-01-225-0997	11862	15522381
119	10	2510-01-154-1261	11862	359878
119	14	2510-01-153-9473	11862	359877
120	1	5310-00-768-0318	96906	MS51967-14
120	2	5310-00-834-7606	96906	MS35340-48
120	3	5305-00-071-2077	96906	MS90728-121
120	4	2510-01-148-2942	11862	3187846
120	4	2510-01-153-9584	11862	3187843
120	5	5305-00-071-2075	96906	MS90728-119
121	1	2540-01-148-2943	11862	3187845
121	2	5310-00-809-5998	96906	MS27183-18
121	3	5310-00-933-8123	96906	MS35340-49
121	4	5310-00-768-0318	96906	MS51967-14
121	5	5310-00-732-0558	96906	MS51967-8
121	6	5310-00-637-9541	96906	MS35338-46

CROSS-REFERENCE INDEXES

FIGURE AND ITEM NUMBER INDEX

FIG	ITEM	STOCK NUMBER	CAGEC	PART NUMBER
121	7	2530-01-153-1814	11862	3764438
121	8	5310-00-763-8913	96906	MS51967-17
121	9	5310-00-167-0680	96906	MS35338-49
121	10	5305-01-155-6113	11862	9419138
122	1	5310-00-763-8905	96906	MS51968-20
122	2	5310-00-045-5001	96906	MS35340-50
122	3	5310-00-732-0558	96906	MS51967-8
122	4	5310-00-637-9541	96906	MS35338-46
122	5	2530-01-153-1814	11862	3764438
122	6	2540-01-155-7496	11862	3187844
122	7	5310-00-763-8913	96906	MS51967-17
122	8	5310-00-167-0680	96906	MS35338-49
122	9	5305-01-155-6113	11862	9419138
123	1	5306-01-155-6108	11862	328130
123	2	5310-01-147-8748	11862	328131
123	3	5310-01-097-9414	24617	3990160
123	4	5310-01-150-4003	11862	9422299
123	5	5305-00-071-2055	96906	MS90728-89
123	6	3120-01-211-7528	11862	328128
123	7	5340-01-153-1631	11862	14015726
123	8	5365-01-214-4927	11862	14015724
123	9	2530-01-147-5541	11862	328132
124	1		11862	1365065
124	2		11862	3993729
124	3	5325-01-198-8040	11862	6270704
124	4	5310-00-732-0558	96906	MS51967-8
124	5	5310-00-637-9541	96906	MS35338-46
124	6	3120-01-250-0583	11862	404062
124	7	2590-01-323-5857	11862	4(6887
124	8	5305-00-821-3869	96906	MS90728-65
124	9	2510-01-325-9069	11862	328107
124	10		11862	328111
124	11		11862	328108
125	1	2510-01-155-7425	11862	15554915
125	2	5305-01-158-7820	24617	11503395
125	3	5310-01-154-2273	96906	MS90724-34
125	4	5325-01-157-1698	11862	347347
125	5	2510-01-155-8787	11862	14072488
126	1	2510-01-160-4970	11862	15599285
126	2	2510-01-159-8762	11862	14072850
126	3	5310-01-158-9205	24617	9420621
126	4	2590-01-163-1238	11862	15599283
126	4	2590-01-164-0134	11862	15599284
126	5	2590-01-159-8861	11862	15599286
127	1	2510-01-158-7575	11862	14021243
127	2	5306-01-158-9018	11862	2014469
127	11	2510-01-159-2929	11862	14043880
128	1	2510-01-194-0206	11862	15598770
128	2	2540-01-160-1591	11862	15598769
128	3	2510-01-159-8761	11862	15598708
128	4	5310-01-170-9100	11862	3982098

CROSS-REFERENCE INDEXES

FIGURE AND ITEM NUMBER INDEX

FIG	ITEM	STOCK NUMBER	CAGEC	PART NUMBER
128	5	5305-01-158-7820	11862	14026247
128	6	2510-01-212-5819	11862	15598709
128	7	5340-01-160-2346	11862	14027555
129	1	5340-01-162-4852	11862	472450
129	2	5340-01-165-8986	11862	6262054
129	3	5340-01-149-4434	11862	3816659
129	4	5305-01-162-9689	24617	11503396
129	5	2590-01-158-8784	11862	14039963
130	1	2510-01-154-6906	11862	15629509
130	2	5330-01-170-6303	11862	14018523
130	3	5306-01-158-9018	11862	2014469
130	4	2510-01-162-5172	11862	14043823
130	4	2510-01-162-5173	11862	14043824
130	5	5305-01-140-9118	96906	MS90728-59
130	6	5305-01-162-7885	11862	11508164
130	7	2510-01-162-3623	11862	14070703
130	8	5340-01-163-5908	11862	14018531
130	9	5360-01-163-0885	11862	14018532
130	10	5340-01-163-0917	11862	14018526
130	11	5360-01-205-8888	11862	14018529
130	12	2510-01-163-1139	11862	14021254
130	12	2510-01-163-7016	11862	14021253
130	13	5305-01-160-1975	11862	11508566
131	1	5310-01-267-3043	11862	11501047
131	2	2510-01-172-3022	11862	14023039
131	3	5310-01-154-2273	96906	MS90724-34
131	4	2510-01-159-0868	11862	14072405
131	5	5305-01-159-2780	24617	11501153
131	6	5305-01-158-6235	24617	11501151
131	7	2530-01-162-3626	11862	14023008
131	8	2510-01-162-3679	11862	6274970
132	7	5340-01-161-9188	11862	3765243
132	8	5340-01-164-8761	11862	6274550
132	9	5310-01-154-2273	96906	MS90724-34
132	10	2540-01-156-0564	11862	14044471
132	11	2540-01-096-9664	11862	6260421
132	12	2590-01-162-7367	11862	3957093
132	13	5340-01-163-4337	11862	6264131
132	14	5305-01-273-4486	11862	11509135
132	15	2510-01-166-1146	11862	343915
132	16	5305-01-157-5625	24617	9420408
132	17	5305-01-164-2313	24617	9415163
132	29	2510-01-156-8092	11862	15598706
133	1	2540-01-158-3576	11862	14072494
133	2	2540-01-156-4870	11862	327062
133	3	5360-01-161-7561	11862	327065
133	4	5330-01-157-7459	11862	6258562
133	5	2510-01-155-8800	11862	15593230
133	6	2510-01-155-8799	11862	15571643
133	7	5340-01-157-6092	11862	4410574
133	8	5330-01-157-7458	11862	6258561

CROSS-REFERENCE INDEXES

FIGURE AND ITEM NUMBER INDEX

FIG	ITEM	STOCK NUMBER	CAGEC	PART NUMBER
133	9	2540-01-156-7238	11862	14072493
133	10	5360-01-161-7561	11862	327065
133	11	2540-01-156-4870	11862	327062
133	12	2540-01-194-0261	11862	15599677
133	13	3040-01-157-7997	11862	7040174
133	13	3040-01-162-0255	11862	7040173
133	14	5330-01-157-5684	11862	4587931
133	15		11862	6272627
133	16	5310-01-157-5672	11862	1260895
133	17	5306-01-157-9936	11862	9601750
133	18	5340-01-162-9844	11862	9728247
133	19	5306-01-157-6796	11862	9439771
133	20	5340-01-158-0503	11862	3900684
133	21	2510-01-162-7119	11862	14000091
133	21	2510-01-162-7120	11862	14000092
133	22	5315-01-160-0575	11862	6271989
133	23	3120-01-166-6724	11862	9721917
133	24	5305-01-160-3937	11862	9438916
133	25	5340-01-157-7471	11862	3944769
133	26	2540-01-164-1891	11862	14000093
133	26	5340-01-167-0136	11862	14000094
133	27	5340-01-206-2995	11862	327959
133	27	5340-01-206-2996	11862	327960
133	28	5315-01-160-0575	11862	6271989
133	29	3120-01-166-6724	11862	9721917
134	1	5310-01-154-2273	96906	MS90724-34
134	2	5340-01-161-5522	11862	362434
134	2	5340-01-170-5530	11862	362433
134	3	5310-00-490-4639	96906	MS90724-40
134	4	5306-01-157-6797	11862	9439770
134	5	5310-01-084-4491	11862	1355003
134	6	5325-01-160-4028	11862	20696927
134	7	5330-01-164-8385	11862	14027775
134	7	5330-01-193-1840	11862	14027776
134	8	5330-01-158-6683	11862	15569071
134	8	5330-01-159-1153	11862	15569072
134	9	5330-01-157-6827	11862	14026383
134	9	5330-01-157-6828	11862	14026384
134	10	5325-01-205-2545	11862	330485
134	11	2510-01-156-4872	11862	15597667
134	11	2510-01-156-4873	11862	15597668
134	12	5305-01-210-9425	24617	9414724
134	13	2540-01-156-4903	11862	14026409
134	13	2540-01-156-4904	11862	14026410
134	14	5305-01-162-3961	11862	11503537
134	15	5305-01-231-1298	24617	1640810
134	16	5310-01-158-9205	24617	9420621
134	17	5340-01-187-8673	11862	14010954
134	18	5340-00-285-8868	11862	4168122
134	19	2540-01-156-4885	11862	14030586
134	20	5325-01-160-2237	11862	363137

CROSS-REFERENCE INDEXES

FIGURE AND ITEM NUMBER INDEX

FIG	ITEM	STOCK NUMBER	CAGEC	PART NUMBER
134	21		11862	15590415
134	22	2540-01-158-1721	11862	15590422
134	23	5365-01-160-2483	11862	364372
135	1		11862	365953
135	2	2540-01-156-6107	11862	15590401
135	2	2540-01-156-6108	11862	15590402
135	3	2540-01-155-7502	11862	14027431
135	3	2540-01-155-7503	11862	14027432
135	4	5306-01-157-6797	11862	9439770
136	1	2510-01-163-7306	11862	15635685
136	2	5340-01-165-4791	11862	20264729
136	3	5330-01-178-7351	11862	20264731
136	4		11862	365953-1
136	5	2540-01-159-8880	11862	20264737
136	6	5680-01-164-4964	11862	20354946
136	7	5310-01-184-5866	11862	365443
136	8	2590-00-476-5459	11862	3762400
136	9	2510-01-163-2709	11862	15617126
136	10	2540-01-163-7305	11862	15635684
136	11	5340-01-165-4792	11862	20264728
136	12	5330-01-181-2454	11862	20264730
136	13		11862	365953-1
136	14	2540-01-163-2719	11862	20264736
136	15	5680-01-167-1068	11862	20354945
136	16	5310-01-184-5866	11862	365443
136	17	2590-00-476-5459	11862	3762400
136	18	2510-01-164-7152	11862	12300197
136	19	5306-01-157-6797	11862	9439770
136	20	2540-01-156-4907	11862	337715
136	20	2540-01-156-4908	11862	337716
136	21	5310-01-154-2273	96906	MS90724-34
136	22	5305-01-231-1297	11862	15531547
136	23	5305-01-157-1987	11862	11501149
136	24	2510-01-156-4871	11862	461610
136	25	5306-01-157-6797	11862	9439770
136	26	5365-01-155-8576	11862	14013789
136	27	9390-01-162-4500	11862	14027777
136	27	9390-01-163-2028	11862	14027778
136	28	5305-01-230-9846	11862	15590443
137	1	3040-01-155-0371	11862	327067
137	2	5305-01-158-0335	11862	9439772
137	3	2540-01-156-0565	11862	14039763
137	3	2540-01-156-4869	11862	14039764
137	4	3040-01-156-9729	11862	14039766
137	4	3040-01-159-7950	11862	14039765
137	5	5340-01-194-3188	11862	375180
137	6	2540-01-155-7298	11862	15597653
137	6	2540-01-156-8315	11862	15597654
137	7	5306-01-157-6797	11862	9439770
137	8	5340-01-160-5922	11862	15545178
137	9	3040-01-155-0372	11862	14039767

CROSS-REFERENCE INDEXES

FIGURE AND ITEM NUMBER INDEX

FIG	ITEM	STOCK NUMBER	CAGEC	PART NUMBER
137	9	3040-01-155-0373	11862	14039768
137	10	5355-01-280-2975	11862	7591126
138	1	5305-01-161-2581	11862	14022885
138	2	2510-01-249-6434	11862	14016511
138	2	2510-01-251-5487	11862	14016512
138	3	5680-01-163-6347	11862	15522764
139	6	5340-01-164-8757	11862	14049810
140	1	5306-01-165-4286	11862	14039924
140	2	5306-01-166-8556	11862	15599971
140	3	5310-00-809-5998	96906	MS27183-18
140	4	5310-00-768-0318	96906	MS51967-14
140	5	5365-01-194-5074	11862	15599250
140	5	5365-01-195-4948	11862	14076894
140	6	5340-01-197-3244	11862	14076887
141	3	2510-01-155-5846	11862	330438
141	4	5310-00-931-8167	96906	MS51967-6
141	5	2510-01-158-6904	11862	14027454
141	5	2510-01-160-5837	11862	14027451
141	6	5340-01-164-8757	11862	14049810
141	7	2510-01-163-2681	11862	467911
141	7	2510-01-163-7229	11862	467912
141	8	5306-01-158-9018	11862	2014469
141	11	5305-01-156-5438	11862	11504447
141	12	2990-01-160-5873	11862	471089
142	1	2540-01-159-8759	11862	6262029
142	2	5305-01-140-9118	96906	MS90728-59
142	3	2510-01-155-5854	11862	458025
142	4	5340-01-165-0564	11862	14032787
142	5	5305-01-158-2032	96906	MS51869-24
142	6	2510-01-155-8785	11862	458026
142	7	5305-00-432-4201	96906	MS51861-45
142	8	2510-01-155-5857	11862	15628608
142	9	5305-01-157-7388	11862	9431663
142	10	2510-01-155-5853	11862	14021389
142	11	5340-01-160-2488	11862	14007449
142	12	2510-01-225-1006	11862	15594644
142	13	2510-01-155-5851	11862	15596976
142	14	5340-01-159-6905	11862	3889864
142	15	2540-01-156-9675	11862	14021275
142	16	2540-01-225-1023	11862	15594643
142	17	5305-01-162-9695	24617	9414712
142	18	5306-01-158-9018	11862	2014469
142	19	2510-01-155-5850	11862	15596975
142	20	2510-01-155-5849	11862	14021386
142	20	2510-01-155-7877	11862	14021385
143	1	5306-01-246-7459	11862	1244067
143	2	2540-01-158-8554	11862	15641780
143	2	3120-01-338-6380	11862	4158246
143	3	2540-01-160-5918	11862	20171141
143	4		11862	14027542
143	5	2540-01-158-8813	11862	340053

CROSS-REFERENCE INDEXES

FIGURE AND ITEM NUMBER INDEX

FIG	ITEM	STOCK NUMBER	CAGEC	PART NUMBER
143	6	2510-01-224-8839	11862	15614462
143	7	5340-01-165-0657	11862	8785295
144	1	2540-01-192-9754	11862	15599678
144	2	2540-01-158-4602	11862	14072497
144	3	2540-01-211-4621	11862	14072499
144	4	5310-01-194-9234	11862	5713274
144	5	5365-01-198-5516	11862	5713276
144	6	2540-01-218-6833	11862	9703344
144	7	5315-01-194-0819	11862	5717887
144	8	5365-00-900-0982	96906	MS16633-1021
144	9	3010-01-159-7750	11862	9702916
144	10	5365-00-720-8064	96906	MS16624-1C24
144	11	5330-01-182-4121	11862	327015
144	12	5310-01-152-0598	24617	271172
144	13	5360-01-159-8862	11862	4303911
144	14	3040-01-157-8021	11862	5713268
145	1	5340-01-163-8520	11862	14050440
145	2	5310-01-157-5672	11862	1260895
145	3	5365-01-158-5381	11862	14021292
145	4	5306-01-160-1952	11862	7740374
145	5	4010-01-158-6331	11862	6274850
145	6	5340-01-160-2367	11862	337788
145	7	5306-01-158-9018	11862	2014469
145	8	2510-01-163-7231	11862	6274848
145	8	5340-01-166-5652	11862	6274847
145	9	5365-01-162-8876	11862	6274849
145	10		11862	9438039
145	11	5306-01-162-9678	11862	9437242
145	12	2540-01-158-4600	11862	6274836
145	13	2510-01-225-0999	11862	15522708
145	14	5315-01-160-0575	11862	6271989
145	15	3120-01-159-1311	11862	335524
145	16	5305-00-432-8220	96906	MS51862-35
145	17	2510-01-225-0998	11862	15522707
145	18	5310-00-809-4085	96906	MS27183-16
145	19	5360-01-164-2404	11862	14021315
145	19	5360-01-164-2405	11862	14021316
145	20	5310-00-809-3079	96906	MS27183-19
145	21	5306-01-159-2772	11862	14021317
145	22	5306-01-157-6796	11862	9439771
145	23	5305-01-162-9695	24617	9414712
145	24	2510-01-159-7120	11862	334132
145	25	2540-01-157-8009	11862	470949
146	1	5330-01-237-7512	11862	15593570
146	2	5330-01-207-9421	11862	15593571
146	3	5340-01-158-4583	11862	6274890
146	4	5305-01-157-9720	24617	9419327
146	5	3040-01-159-1775	11862	14039716
146	6	2510-01-160-3634	11862	14039710
146	7	5340-01-160-2488	11862	14007449
146	8	5340-01-160-5922	11862	15545178

CROSS-REFERENCE INDEXES

FIGURE AND ITEM NUMBER INDEX

FIG	ITEM	STOCK NUMBER	CAGEC	PART NUMBER
146	9	2540-01-158-8557	11862	473917
146	10	5340-01-160-2470	11862	3905674
146	11	2510-01-178-8867	11862	473995
146	12	5305-01-158-0335	11862	9439772
147	1	2510-01-162-7112	11862	334101
147	2	5340-01-165-4351	11862	6274854
147	3	5330-00-360-7881	22593	30103
147	3	5330-01-167-8123	11862	334104
147	4	5306-01-157-6796	11862	9439771
147	5	2510-01-165-4932	11862	334102
147	6	5330-01-159-4777	11862	6274853
147	7	5340-01-160-2172	11862	337899
147	8	2540-01-158-4601	11862	473894
147	9	5310-00-834-7606	96906	MS35340-48
147	10	5310-00-768-0318	96906	MS51967-14
148	1	5360-01-185-0341	11862	15593866
148	2	2540-01-158-8556	11862	331638
148	3	5306-01-246-7459	11862	1244067
148	4	5305-00-068-0508	96906	MS90728-6
148	5	3040-01-158-8703	11862	335452
148	6	5310-00-582-5965	96906	MS35338-44
148	7	5310-01-159-8559	96906	MS35691-406
148	8	2540-01-158-8555	11862	4495180
148	9	5305-01-159-2783	11862	8782501
148	10	5330-01-159-8504	11862	470993
148	11	3040-01-159-0996	11862	8742340
148	12	3040-01-160-5913	11862	14039712
149	1	5330-01-159-1152	11862	326934
149	2	5330-01-162-8595	11862	327006
149	3	5330-01-159-2816	11862	327005
150	10	5305-01-162-5707	11862	458985
151	1	5306-01-194-4977	11862	15599929
151	2	5340-01-159-6174	11862	14072452
151	3	2510-01-155-5825	11862	14072460
151	4	5365-01-158-2004	11862	14072454
151	5	5310-01-202-2695	11862	9439757
151	6	2510-01-156-0062	11862	14072459
152	1	5306-01-194-4977	11862	15599929
152	2	2590-01-234-6468	11862	15591705
152	3	2540-01-241-4238	23862	15591706
152	3	2590-01-242-1050	11862	15591709
152	4	5305-01-197-3290	11862	14072458
152	5	5340-01-238-5924	1T998	15591710
152	6	2510-01-155-5112	11862	14072455
152	7	5310-00-768-0318	96906	MS51967-14
152	8	5365-01-158-2004	11862	14072454
152	9	2510-01-155-5825	11862	14072460
152	10	5310-01-160-4536	11862	3792287
152	11	5340-01-238-5923	11862	15591707
152	12	5305-01-163-2438	11862	9440300
153	1	5310-01-169-2849	11862	14072307

CROSS-REFERENCE INDEXES

FIGURE AND ITEM NUMBER INDEX

FIG	ITEM	STOCK NUMBER	CAGEC	PART NUMBER
153	2	5340-01-159-2996	11862	14072305
153	3	5310-01-164-5600	11862	94009398
153	4	5310-00-834-7606	96906	MS35340-48
153	5	5305-00-071-2070	96906	MS90728-114
153	6	5305-00-071-2081	96906	MS90728-125
153	7	2510-01-159-8726	11862	14072306
154	1	5306-01-159-6574	11862	14032814
154	2	5310-01-167-8344	24617	9409613
154	3	5310-01-077-6817	96906	MS35425-72
154	7	5340-01-158-8549	11862	467299
155	1	5340-01-158-8549	11862	467299
155	2	5310-01-077-6817	96906	MS35425-72
155	4	5340-01-165-4544	11862	14032812
155	5	5306-01-159-6574	11862	14032814
155	6	5310-01-167-8344	24617	9409613
156	1	2510-01-155-5434	75829	14022842
156	2	2510-01-155-5433	11862	20264744
156	4	2510-01-155-5432	11862	20264743
156	7	2510-01-155-5435	75829	14022841
156	8	2510-01-157-1382	75829	14076899
157	1	5310-01-197-5499	11862	1359887
157	4	5310-01-160-9529	24617	1494253
157	5	5305-01-158-2032	96906	MS51869-24
158	1	5325-01-165-2551	11862	20030401
158	2	2540-01-193-7884	11862	15591702
158	3	5305-01-266-9194	11862	11500668
158	4	2510-01-259-5587	11862	474022
158	5	5305-00-483-0554	96906	MS51862-26
158	6	2510-01-191-8447	11862	467247
158	6	2510-01-200-1021	11862	467248
158	7	2540-01-156-0088	11862	15594983
158	8	5305-01-162-8514	11862	11502634
158	9	5305-01-231-7384	24617	11503606
158	10	2590-01-247-3286	11862	15594896
158	10	5340-01-210-8824	11862	15594895
158	11	5970-01-158-9337	11862	462233
159	1	2540-01-159-8874	11862	14013753
159	1	2540-01-159-8875	11862	14013754
159	2	5310-01-154-2273	96906	MS90724-34
159	3	5305-01-157-1987	11862	11501149
159	4	5340-01-161-2789	11862	14031893
159	5	2540-01-159-8721	11862	15646949
159	6	5305-01-159-2779	11862	14044340
159	7	5305-01-158-7820	24617	11503395
159	8	5325-01-157-1698	11862	347347
160	1	2540-01-193-7896	11862	14079058
160	2	2540-01-159-7963	11862	14079056
160	3	2540-01-193-7895	11862	14079057
160	4	5306-01-159-1130	11862	342221
160	5	5306-01-157-3279	11862	471083
161	6	5365-01-157-7476	11862	343978

CROSS-REFERENCE INDEXES

FIGURE AND ITEM NUMBER INDEX

FIG	ITEM	STOCK NUMBER	CAGEC	PART NUMBER
161	7	5310-01-157-5670	11862	3914674
161	8	3120-01-162-0060	11862	14066195
161	9	5365-01-197-2286	11862	14066196
161	10	5305-01-160-4528	11862	14021211
161	11	5305-01-161-2581	24617	9417325
161	12	2540-01-155-6825	11862	14037059
161	12	2540-01-155-8786	11862	14037060
161	13	2540-01-155-6823	11862	14021209
161	13	2540-01-155-6824	11862	14021210
161	14	5305-01-160-0331	11862	14021213
161	15	5305-01-160-3937	11862	9438916
161	16	5306-01-158-9018	11862	2014469
161	17	5360-01-162-2849	11862	20056525
161	18	3040-01-155-5864	11862	14022777
161	19	5355-01-157-1866	11862	465536
161	20	5360-01-160-2411	11862	329457
161	21	5340-01-158-6354	11862	14022786
161	22	3040-01-155-6912	11862	14022778
161	23	5360-01-160-2411	11862	329457
162	1	2540-01-191-8668	11862	15591247
162	2	5306-01-159-1130	11862	342221
162	3	5305-01-162-7890	11862	3954730
162	4	5340-01-166-5861	11862	1731168
162	5	5306-01-157-3279	11862	471083
163	1	5306-01-159-1130	11862	342221
163	2	2540-01-160-3651	11862	15591248
163	3	5305-01-162-7890	11862	3954730
163	4	5306-01-157-3279	11862	471083
163	5	5340-01-166-5861	11862	1731168
164	1	5305-01-160-3937	11862	9438916
164	2	2540-01-164-1843	11862	14075823
164	3	5360-01-218-1610	11862	9711038
164	4	2540-01-164-1844	11862	14075824
164	5	5340-01-161-2749	11862	9834636
164	6	5360-01-197-0870	11862	20351007
164	7	5306-01-160-0769	11862	334195
164	8	2540-01-158-8558	11862	14075821
164	10	5360-01-162-2849	11862	20056525
164	11	5306-01-165-5583	11862	14060613
164	12	2540-01-158-4603	11862	20243999
165	1	2540-01-162-4411	11862	15599975
165	2	5360-01-164-1949	11862	9645073
165	3	5340-01-161-2749	11862	9834636
165	4	5360-01-171-8248	11862	9826897
165	5	2540-01-158-8561	11862	15599976
165	6	5360-01-162-2849	11862	20056525
165	7	5306-01-160-0769	11862	334195
165	8	5305-01-160-3937	11862	9438916
165	9	2540-01-159-7744	11862	14075822
165	11	5306-01-165-5583	11862	14060613
165	12	2540-01-158-4603	11862	20243999

CROSS-REFERENCE INDEXES

FIGURE AND ITEM NUMBER INDEX

FIG	ITEM	STOCK NUMBER	CAGEC	PART NUMBER
166	1	2540-01-158-8812	11862	14075820
166	5	5305-01-162-3961	11862	11503537
166	6	5305-01-162-5996	11862	20025648
166	7	2540-01-251-1714	11862	20293843
166	8	2540-01-251-1715	11862	20289493
166	9	2540-01-158-8559	11862	16604537
166	10	2540-01-165-0895	11862	14075818
166	11	3120-01-160-0570	11862	14059238
166	13	5305-01-160-3955	11862	14056723
166	14	5310-01-162-7912	11862	1727059
167	1	2540-01-161-1356	11862	14075819
167	6	5305-01-162-5996	11862	20025648
167	7	2540-01-160-5840	11862	20293842
167	8	2540-01-191-8440	11862	20369919
167	9	2540-01-191-8441	11862	20369920
167	10	5325-01-198-8239	11862	20573776
167	11	2540-01-158-8560	11862	15627452
167	12	5305-01-162-3961	11862	11503537
167	13	2540-01-248-2477	11862	20410901
167	15	3120-01-160-0570	11862	14059238
167	16	5310-01-162-7912	11862	1727059
167	17	5305-01-160-3955	11862	14056723
168	1	5305-01-159-6567	11862	14013724
168	2	2540-01-158-6896	11862	15569010
168	3	5306-01-158-9018	11862	2014469
168	9	2540-01-159-0874	11862	14014293
168	10	5355-01-197-1501	11862	473187
168	11	5340-01-158-6895	11862	15569009
168	12	3120-01-159-1311	11862	335524
168	13	2540-01-158-7551	11862	470984
168	14	5305-01-157-9720	24617	9419327
168	15	2540-01-158-6893	11862	473197
168	16	5340-01-160-4130	11862	14027799
168	17	5310-00-834-7606	96906	MS35340-48
168	18	5305-01-163-2439	24617	9432194
168	19	5340-01-158-6892	11862	471018
168	20	5315-01-159-8660	11862	470974
168	21	2540-01-158-7583	11862	471010
168	22	5365-00-200-7377	96906	MS16633-1015
168	23	2540-01-159-8727	11862	14074479
168	24	5305-01-160-4494	11862	14069636
168	25	2540-01-160-3652	11862	14075375
168	26	5305-01-162-7890	11862	3954730
168	27	2540-01-160-3654	11862	14075374
168	28	2540-01-160-3653	11862	14075376
168	30	2540-01-158-6894	11862	471079
169	1	2540-01-167-2985	11862	15577694
169	2	2540-01-163-8017	11862	14075379
169	3	5306-01-159-1130	11862	342221
169	4	5306-01-157-3279	11862	471083
169	5	5340-01-166-5861	11862	1731168

CROSS-REFERENCE INDEXES

FIGURE AND ITEM NUMBER INDEX

FIG	ITEM	STOCK NUMBER	CAGEC	PART NUMBER
170	1	2540-01-166-1370	11862	14075815
170	5	2540-01-157-2966	11862	14025679
170	6	5340-01-157-7607	11862	14025673
170	7	5360-01-162-2849	11862	20056525
170	8	3040-01-155-0194	11862	14023889
170	9	5355-01-157-1866	11862	465536
170	10	5360-01-160-2411	11862	329457
170	11	5305-01-160-3937	11862	9438916
170	13	5306-01-158-9018	11862	2014469
170	15	3040-01-155-0195	11862	14023890
170	16	5360-01-160-2411	11862	329457
170	17	5340-01-157-7608	11862	14025674
171	1	5305-01-160-3937	11862	9438916
171	2	2540-01-157-7907	11862	14027346
171	3	2540-01-155-5111	11862	14027348
171	5	2540-01-155-5110	11862	14027347
171	6	5306-01-158-9018	11862	2014469
171	8	2540-01-155-5824	11862	14027345
172	1	5975-01-155-7084	80063	SC-D-866091
172	2	5310-00-933-8121	96906	MS35338-139
172	3	5305-00-068-0502	96906	MS90725-6
172	4	5820-01-026-0983	80063	DL-SC-B-691368
172	5	5310-00-903-5966	96906	MS51971-1
172	6	5975-01-027-0253	80063	SC-D-691375
172	7	5340-01-159-4518	80063	SC-C-691545
172	8	5340-01-201-7954	11862	15599959
172	9	5340-01-159-1460	11862	15599958
172	10	5310-01-152-0598	24617	271172
172	11	5306-01-168-4481	11862	9440334
172	12	5310-00-209-0786	96906	MS35335-33
172	13	5305-00-068-0508	96906	MS90728-6
172	14		80063	SC-B-75180-IV
172	15	5310-00-889-2528	96906	MS45904-68
173	1	2590-01-156-0076	11862	14074435
173	2	5340-00-455-5899	11862	14074437
173	3	5320-01-160-3999	11862	2477054
173	4	2590-01-156-0077	11862	14074441
173	4	2590-01-156-0078	11862	14074442
173	5	5306-01-197-3089	11862	9440033
173	6	2590-01-156-0080	11862	14074438
173	7	5340-01-253-2102	11862	15599965
173	8	2590-01-191-6511	11862	15599271
174	1	2590-01-156-0074	11862	14074439
174	2	5305-01-152-8945	24617	9421432
174	4	5340-01-150-4105	11862	14005953
175	7	5305-01-239-9265	25022	07-1016
175	8	6220-01-276-0635	13548	99012R
176	1	5340-01-162-3853	25022	09-0954
176	2	5320-00-582-3521	96906	MS20600-B4W3
176	3	5305-00-068-0510	96906	MS90728-60
176	4	6220-01-160-5094	25022	19-0817

CROSS-REFERENCE INDEXES

FIGURE AND ITEM NUMBER INDEX

FIG	ITEM	STOCK NUMBER	CAGEC	PART NUMBER
176	5	6240-00-836-2079	08806	4411
176	6	2590-01-164-7024	25022	19-0884
176	7	6220-01-172-5300	25022	19-0882
176	8	6220-01-171-9557	25022	19-0885
176	9	5306-00-226-4833	96906	MS90728-40
176	10	5310-00-407-9566	96906	MS35338-45
176	11	5310-00-880-7744	96906	MS51967-5
176	12	2540-01-163-8623	25022	31-0030
176	13	5320-00-616-4346	96906	MS20600B6W4
176	14	5340-01-166-2011	25022	09-0093
176	15	5320-01-200-4017	96906	MS21141-U0604
176	16	2590-01-163-7626	25022	99-4308-1
176	17	9905-01-165-0541	25022	23-0196
176	18	9905-01-165-0542	25022	23-0193
176	19	5340-01-307-2252	25022	99-4582-1
176	20	5340-01-307-2251	25022	99-4581-1
176	21	5340-01-307-2250	25022	99-4580-1
176	22	5340-01-307-2249	25022	99-4579-1
177	1	5320-00-582-3521	96906	MS20600-B4W3
177	2	5340-01-162-3853	25022	09-0954
177	3	5305-00-068-0510	96906	MS90728-60
177	4	6220-01-160-5094	25022	19-0817
177	5	6240-00-836-2079	08806	4411
177	6	2590-01-164-7024	25022	19-0884
177	7	6220-01-172-5300	25022	19-0882
177	8	6220-01-171-9557	25022	19-0885
177	9	5306-00-226-483	96906	MS90728-40
177	10	5310-00-407-9566	96906	MS35338-45
177	11	5310-00-880-7744	96906	MS51967-5
177	12	5340-01-307-2252	25022	99-4582-1
177	13	5340-01-307-2251	25022	99-4581-1
177	14	2540-01-163-8624	99688	78404
177	15	5320-00-616-4346	96906	MS20600B6W4
177	16	2590-01-163-7626	25022	99-4308-1
177	17	9905-01-165-0542	25022	23-0193
177	18	9905-01-165-0541	25022	23-0196
177	19	5320-01-200-4017	96906	MS21141-U0604
177	20	5340-01-166-2011	25022	09-0093
177	21	5340-01-164-0746	25022	22-0881
177	22	5340-01-164-1100	25022	99-4888-0
177	23	2540-01-163-8623	25022	31-0030
177	24	5340-01-307-2250	25022	99-4580-1
177	25	5340-01-307-2249	25022	99-4579-1
178	1	5320-00-616-4346	96906	MS20600B6W4
178	2		25022	19-0445
178	3	6220-01-160-3687	25022	19-0893
178	4	6240-00-889-1799	08806	1157
178	5	6220-01-160-3705	25022	19-0861
178	6	5365-01-269-8614	25022	19-0969
178	7	9905-01-165-0544	25022	23-0198
178	8	5320-00-582-3521	96906	MS20600-B4W3

CROSS-REFERENCE INDEXES

FIGURE AND ITEM NUMBER INDEX

FIG	ITEM	STOCK NUMBER	CAGEC	PART NUMBER
178	9	5340-01-162-3853	25022	09-0954
178	10	5340-01-307-2247	25022	99-4577-1
178	11	5340-01-307-2248	25022	99-4578-1
178	12	4030-01-168-1282	25022	99-1088-0
178	13	5340-01-162-3854	25022	09-0959
178	14	5320-00-845-9501	96906	MS20600-B4W4
178	15	2590-01-163-7287	25022	22-0875
178	16	5306-00-226-4822	96906	MS90728-29
178	17	6220-01-160-3686	25022	19-0818
178	18	5305-00-984-6191	96906	MS35206-243
178	19	6220-01-039-9809	25022	51-1942
178	20	6240-01-089-6149	08805	F48T12/CW/WM
178	21	5305-01-166-1471	24617	9414238
178	22	6130-01-035-6412	25022	51-1991
178	23	2590-01-164-7898	25022	19-0820
179	1	5340-01-162-3854	25022	09-0959
179	2	5340-01-164-0974	25022	99-4356-1
179	3	5305-01-164-6321	24617	9414714
179	4	5930-01-163-2583	25022	99-4256-0
179	5	5930-00-548-5640	25022	51-1902
179	6	5930-00-636-1584	25022	51-1901
179	7	4710-01-062-3719	25022	06-0075
179	8	2540-01-165-8177	25022	99-4256-2
179	9	5310-00-934-9758	96906	MS35649-202
179	10	5310-00-045-3296	96906	MS35338-43
179	11	5315-01-025-0930	11862	3929059
179	12	5340-01-164-0747	25022	99-4315-1
179	13	5340-01-196-6463	25022	09-0963
179	14	2510-01-166-2015	25022	51-1305
179	15	5320-01-200-4017	96906	MS21141-U0604
177	16	5305-00-050-9237	96906	MS51957-71
179	17	5340-01-159-1796	25022	51-1304
179	18	5306-00-226-4829	96906	MS90728-36
180	1		25022	99-1265-01
180	2	5320-00-061-9662	96906	MS20600-B6W5
180	3	5320-00-845-9501	96906	MS20600-B4W4
180	4	7230-01-167-2075	25022	51-2294
180	5	2510-01-164-1532	25022	13-1105
180	6	5305-01-200-7735	24617	447143
180	7	2510-01-169-3785	25022	51-2204
180	8	2540-01-164-0046	25022	51-0999
180	9	5320-00-660-0821	96906	MS20600MP6W10
180	10	5340-01-194-5805	25022	99-4675-1
180	11	5310-00-087-7493	96906	MS27183-13
180	12	5305-00-068-0510	96906	MS90728-60
180	13	9340-01-162-5948	25022	51-1603
180	14	5310-00-637-9541	96906	MS35338-46
180	15	5340-01-156-5061	25022	51-0998
180	16	2510-01-163-7879	25022	51-1721
180	17	9905-01-165-6901	25022	23-0200
180	18	5320-00-582-3521	96906	MS20600-B4W3

CROSS-REFERENCE INDEXES

FIGURE AND ITEM NUMBER INDEX

FIG	ITEM	STOCK NUMBER	CAGEC	PART NUMBER
180	19	5340-01-162-3853	25022	09-0954
180	20	2540-01-163-7874	25022	52-0914
180	21	5320-01-200-4017	96906	MS21141-U0604
180	22	2540-01-193-3623	25022	17-0209
180	23	5340-01-162-5619	25022	17-0178
180	24	5320-00-982-3815	96906	MS24662-153
180	25	5340-01-164-8137	25022	17-0177
180	26	5680-01-193-5078	25022	17-0202
180	27	5305-01-166-1610	24617	165079
180	28	2540-01-158-0602	25022	51-0988
180	29	5340-01-307-2253	25022	99-4583-1
180	30	5340-01-307-2254	25022	99-4584-1
180	31	5320-00-616-4346	96906	MS20600B6W4
181	1		25022	99-1265-02
181	2	5340-01-156-5061	25022	51-0998
181	3	5310-00-637-9541	96906	MS35338-46
181	4	5305-00-068-0510	96906	MS90728-60
181	5	5310-00-087-7493	96906	MS27183-13
181	6	9340-01-162-5948	25022	51-1603
181	7	2510-01-163-7879	25022	51-1721
181	8	5340-01-194-5805	25022	99-4675-1
181	9	5320-00-660-0821	96906	MS20600MP6W10
181	10	2510-01-163-8014	25022	13-1104
181	11	2510-01-169-3785	25022	51-2204
181	12	5305-01-200-7735	24617	447143
181	13	2540-01-164-0046	25022	51-0999
181	14	5320-00-061-9662	96906	MS20600-B6W5
181	15	5320-00-845-9501	96906	MS20600-B4W4
181	16	7230-01-167-2075	25022	51-2294
181	17	2540-01-028-0574	25022	51-0989
181	18	5680-01-193-5078	25022	17-0201
181	19	5320-00-982-3815	96906	MS24662-153
181	20	5340-01-164-8137	25022	17-0177
181	21	5340-01-162-5619	25022	17-0178
181	22	2540-01-193-3623	25022	17-0209
181	23	5320-01-200-4017	96906	MS21141-U0604
181	24	2540-01-163-7874	25022	52-0914
181	25	5340-01-162-3853	25022	09-0954
181	26	5320-00-582-3521	96906	MS20600-B4W3
181	27	9905-01-165-6901	25022	23-0200
181	28	5340-01-162-3850	25022	99-4680-1
181	29	5340-01-307-2253	25022	99-4583-1
181	30	5340-01-307-2254	25022	99-4584-1
181	31	5320-00-616-4346	96906	MS20600B6W4
182	2	5305-00-225-3843	96906	MS90728-8
182	3	5310-00-823-8804	96906	MS27183-9
182	4	5310-00-851-2674	96906	MS35691-1
182	5	5310-00-768-0318	96906	MS51967-14
182	6	5310-00-834-7606	96906	MS35340-48
182	7	2540-01-162-7117	25022	09-0955
182	8	5365-01-163-1147	74410	TF-0681

CROSS-REFERENCE INDEXES

FIGURE AND ITEM NUMBER INDEX

FIG	ITEM	STOCK NUMBER	CAGEC	PART NUMBER
182	9	5310-00-809-5997	96906	MS27183-17
182	10	5305-00-071-2070	96906	MS90728-114
182	11	2540-01-164-6251	25022	99-4340-0
182	12	5310-00-851-2674	96906	MS35691-1
182	13	2540-01-191-6536	25022	99-4469-0
182	14	5310-00-823-8804	96906	MS27183-9
182	15	5305-00-225-3843	96906	MS90728-8
182	16	2540-01-191-8462	25022	99-4456-0
182	17	5310-00-891-1709	96906	MS35691-9
182	18	5310-00-809-3078	96906	MS27183-11
182	19	5306-00-226-4827	96906	MS90728-34
183	1	2510-01-216-0039	25022	22-0832
183	2	2540-01-159-1793	25022	22-0884
183	3	5320-00-616-4346	96906	MS20600B6W4
183	6	5340-01-028-9063	25022	51-0979
183	7	5320-01-200-4017	96906	MS21141-U0604
183	8	6250-01-164-3266	25022	19-0942
183	9	5320-00-822-6257	96906	MS20600-B6W10
183	10	5340-01-166-5654	25022	19-0849
183	11	2590-01-163-7669	25022	22-0861
183	12	5340-01-164-0958	25022	22-0877
183	13	5320-00-828-1284	96906	MS24662-155
183	14	2510-01-159-1798	25022	99-4420-2
183	15	2540-01-163-7288	25022	09-0965
183	16	5305-01-201-3334	24617	171108
183	17	2590-01-162-7139	25022	99-4420-1
184	1	6250-01-164-3266	25022	19-0942
184	2	5320-00-822-6257	96906	MS20600-B6W10
184	3	5320-00-616-4346	96906	MS20600B6W4
184	4	5340-01-166-5654	25022	19-0849
184	5	5320-01-200-4017	96906	MS21141-U0604
184	6	5340-01-028-9063	25022	51-0979
184	7	2540-01-159-1793	25022	22-0884
184	8	2510-01-216-0039	25022	22-0832
184	9	2590-01-162-7139	25022	99-4420-1
184	10	2540-01-163-7288	25022	09-0965
184	11	5305-01-201-3334	24617	171108
184	12	5930-01-163-8851	25022	37-0020
184	13	5930-01-163-8924	25022	51-1959
184	14	5930-01-163-2779	25022	37-0019
184	15	5320-00-828-1284	96906	MS24662-155
184	16	2510-01-159-1798	25022	99-4420-2
184	17	2590-01-163-7669	25022	22-0861
184	18	5340-01-164-0958	25022	22-0877
185	1		25022	99-4447-0
185	2	5320-00-061-9648	96906	MS20601-B6W6
185	3	9330-01-098-6554	25022	51-2297
185	4	2590-01-163-7290	25022	22-0880
185	5		25022	22-0867
185	6	5320-01-200-4017	96906	MS21141-U0604
185	7	5340-01-028-9063	25022	51-0979

CROSS-REFERENCE INDEXES

FIGURE AND ITEM NUMBER INDEX

FIG	ITEM	STOCK NUMBER	CAGEC	PART NUMBER
185	9	5310-00-851-2674	96906	MS35691-1
185	12	5305-00-068-0509	96906	MS90728-10
185	13	5340-01-164-1078	25022	51-0991
185	14	2510-01-191-4336	25022	99-4894-02
185	15	2510-01-191-4335	25022	99-4894-01
185	16	5320-00-616-4346	96906	MS20600B6W4
185	17	5320-00-845-9501	96906	MS20600-B4W4
185	18	5935-01-022-2377	81348	WC596/9-1
186	2	5320-01-200-4017	96906	MS21141-U0604
186	3	5340-01-028-9063	25022	51-0979
186	5	9330-01-098-6554	25022	51-2297
186	6	5320-00-061-9648	96906	MS20601-B6W6
186	7	2590-01-163-7290	25022	22-0880
186	8	2510-01-191-4334	25022	99-4893-01
186	9	2510-01-191-6638	25022	99-4893-02
186	10	5320-00-616-4346	96906	MS20600B6W4
186	11	5340-01-164-1078	25022	51-0991
187	2	5945-01-173-7760	25022	19-0875
187	4	5995-01-192-4374	25022	19-0910
187	5	5925-01-190-1211	25022	19-0909
187	6	5310-01-271-1793	25022	07-01-01
187	7	5940-01-171-3195	25022	19-0877
187	8	5945-01-166-2012	25022	19-0876
187	10	5305-01-201-3788	24617	9426623
187	11	5920-01-188-6294	11862	12004011
187	12	5920-01-149-6952	11862	12004008
187	13	5305-01-166-1473	24617	9418719
187	14	5920-01-149-6953	11862	12004010
187	16	5305-01-164-6321	24617	9414714
187	17	5895-01-159-1804	25022	99-4360-1
188	1	2540-01-163-8638	25022	36-0039
188	2	2540-01-163-8598	25022	36-0045
188	3	4820-01-173-1250	25022	36-0044
188	4	5315-00-839-5820	96906	MS24665-134
188	5	5315-01-164-5336	25022	36-0056
188	6	2540-01-165-7931	25022	36-0055
188	7	5305-00-709-8517	96906	MS90727-85
188	8	2540-01-164-1562	25022	36-0054
188	9	2540-01-191-6539	25022	36-0070
188	10	5310-00-809-4061	96906	MS27183-15
188	11	5310-00-835-2036	96906	MS35691-29
188	12	5310-00-209-0965	96906	MS35338-47
188	13	5305-00-071-2506	96906	MS90728-3
188	14	5315-01-209-7063	25022	36-0071
188	15	2540-01-163-8600	25022	36-0047
188	16	2540-01-163-8599	25022	36-0046
188	17	5360-01-163-5578	25022	36-0048
188	18	5360-01-163-5579	25022	36-0049
188	19	2540-01-163-0772	25022	09-0056
188	20	5360-01-163-5580	25022	36-0050
188	21	5315-01-197-1483	25022	36-0075

CROSS-REFERENCE INDEXES

FIGURE AND ITEM NUMBER INDEX

FIG	ITEM	STOCK NUMBER	CAGEC	PART NUMBER
188	22	5315-00-057-5541	96906	MS16562-147
188	23	5310-00-637-9541	96906	MS35338-46
188	24	5310-00-732-0559	96906	MS51968-8
188	25	5340-01-197-1550	25022	36-0074
188	26	5310-00-087-7493	96906	MS27183-13
188	27	2540-01-173-1249	25022	36-0043
188	28	5315-01-197-1482	25022	36-0073
188	29	5315-00-814-3531	96906	MS16562-50
188	30	5315-01-164-5334	25022	36-0051
188	31	5340-01-193-9565	25022	36-0072
189	1	2590-01-163-8596	25022	22-0865
189	2	9330-01-098-6554	25022	51-2297
189	3	5320-00-061-9648	96906	MS20601-B6W6
189	4	2540-01-166-5913	25022	22-0860
189	5	5340-01-028-9063	25022	51-0979
189	6	5320-01-201-9453	96906	MS21141-U0607
189	7	5340-01-165-0602	25022	37-0051
189	8	5315-00-814-3530	96906	MS16562-35
189	9	2540-01-025-0433	25022	36-0066
189	10	5320-01-200-4017	96906	MS21141-U0604
189	11	2540-01-165-6793	25022	51-0985
190	2	5320-01-200-4017	96906	MS21141-U0604
190	3	5340-01-164-1076	25022	22-0876
190	4	5340-01-028-9063	25022	51-0979
190	5	5340-01-164-1077	25022	22-0878
190	6	5320-00-982-3815	96906	MS24662-153
190	7	5340-01-164-8137	25022	17-0177
190	8	5340-01-162-5619	25022	17-0178
191	1	6210-01-159-1794	25022	19-0816
191	2	6220-01-197-0486	25022	19-0940
191	3	6240-00-850-4280	08806	1003
191	4	6230-01-191-3856	25022	19-0941
191	5		25022	19-0941-1
192	1	2510-01-159-1797	25022	99-4282-1
192	2	5305-01-164-6321	24617	9414714
192	3	5930-01-163-2779	25022	37-0019
192	4	5320-00-616-4346	96906	MS20600B6W4
192	5	5930-01-163-8924	25022	51-1959
192	6	5930-01-163-8851	25022	37-0020
192	7	2510-01-159-1795	25022	99-4408-1
192	8	5320-01-200-4017	96906	MS21141-U0604
192	9	5320-00-845-9501	96906	MS20600-B4W4
192	10	5930-01-028-1949	25022	51-1926
192	11	5340-01-159-1796	25022	51-1304
193	1	2510-01-192-9752	25022	99-4324-0
193	2	9340-01-162-5947	25022	51-1604
193	3	5330-01-163-5706	25022	51-1724
193	4	5306-01-166-1665	21450	126281
193	5	2510-01-192-9752	25022	22-0864
193	6	5310-00-208-1918	88044	AN365-1024A
193	7	5320-00-982-3815	96906	MS24662-153

CROSS-REFERENCE INDEXES

FIGURE AND ITEM NUMBER INDEX

FIG	ITEM	STOCK NUMBER	CAGEC	PART NUMBER
193	8	7230-01-165-6795	25022	22-0873
193	9	2540-01-163-0834	25022	09-0951
193	10	2540-01-162-7116	25022	09-0952
193	11	5315-01-196-6464	25022	99-4683-1
193	12	5305-00-057-9608	96906	MS21207-10-10
193	13	2540-01-163-3585	25022	08-0475
193	14	5320-01-166-1477	24617	163881
193	15	5340-01-172-1942	25022	99-4257-1
194	5	2540-01-163-0894	25022	17-0195
194	6	5305-00-052-7472	96906	MS24627-67
194	7	2540-01-191-6538	25022	99-4892-0
194	8	5305-00-225-3843	96906	MS90728-8
195	1	2510-01-147-9917	11862	14072479
195	2	2540-01-191-8549	11862	14072475
196	1	5306-00-226-4832	96906	MS90728-39
196	2	3120-01-194-0754	11862	15599919
196	3		11862	14072471
196	4		11862	14072472
196	5	5310-00-081-4219	96906	MS27183-12
196	6		11862	14072473
196	7	5310-00-814-0673	96906	MS51943-33
196	8	2540-01-192-3576	11862	14072468
196	9	2540-01-191-9564	11862	14072470
196	10	5340-01-038-3428	19207	12255559
196	11	5340-01-036-7665	19207	12255567
196	12	2540-01-192-4479	11862	14072469
196	13	5310-01-133-7215	72582	9419454
196	14	5305-01-197-6351	24617	157456
196	15	5340-01-044-8389	19207	12255561
196	16	5305-00-054-6654	96906	MS51957-30
196	17	5310-01-197-6621	24617	9423530
196	18	5340-01-043-5214	19207	11669126-1
197	1	5310-00-080-6004	96906	MS27183-14
197	2	5340-01-150-4105	11862	14005953
197	3	5305-00-225-3843	96906	MS90728-8
197	4	5305-01-197-6576	24617	9415153
197	5	2540-01-191-8443	11862	14072461
197	6	2540-01-191-8444	11862	14072462
197	7	5310-01-152-0598	24617	271172
197	8	5320-01-200-4017	96906	MS21141-U0604
197	9	5340-00-916-6539	96906	MS51939-2
197	10	5325-01-050-6192	19207	12255564-2
197	11	2540-01-191-8445	11862	14072464
197	12	5325-01-050-6192	19207	12255564-2
197	13	5310-01-152-0598	24617	271172
197	14	5340-00-916-6539	96906	MS51939-2
197	15	5320-01-200-4017	96906	MS21141-U0604
197	16	5310-00-596-6897	24617	456004
197	17	2540-01-191-8446	11862	14072466
197	18	5325-01-050-6192	19207	12255564-2
197	19	5340-00-916-6539	96906	MS51939-2

CROSS-REFERENCE INDEXES

FIGURE AND ITEM NUMBER INDEX

FIG	ITEM	STOCK NUMBER	CAGEC	PART NUMBER
197	20	5320-01-200-4017	96906	MS21141-U0604
197	21	5310-01-152-0598	24617	271172
197	22	2540-01-192-3575	11862	14072467
197	23	2540-01-192-3574	11862	14072465
197	24	2540-01-192-3573	11862	14072463
198	1	2540-01-157-3032	11862	15591703
198	2	5305-01-165-8612	24617	9421985
198	3	5310-00-514-6674	96906	MS35335-34
198	4	2540-01-156-0584	11862	15591704
198	5		11862	14044931
198	6	2540-01-158-8612	11862	14076838
198	7	5305-01-246-5770	24617	9419163
198	8	5340-01-149-4434	11862	3816659
198	9		11862	22021655
198	10	2540-01-156-5882	11862	22029629
198	11	2540-01-158-1569	11862	4918562
198	12	2540-01-191-6512	11862	22029630
198	13		11862	3782730
198	14	2540-01-159-7954	72560	22048352
198	15	2540-01-158-8611	11862	3990892
198	16	5305-01-132-2166	96906	MS51871-4
198	17	4730-01-158-8717	11862	3986821
198	18		11862	329198
198	19	2590-01-160-1047	11862	3798372
198	20	5306-01-160-7553	11862	3824124
198	21	5330-01-161-2608	11862	20489125
198	22		11862	337714
198	23		11862	3782732
199	7	2540-01-156-0069	11862	22049531
199	8	5310-01-157-4855	11862	22054153
199	9	2540-01-243-4934	11862	22038927
199	10	5330-01-244-2277	11862	22054156
199	12	5325-01-167-8372	11862	22021679
199	28	2540-01-156-0068	11862	22038928
200	1	2540-01-086-5433	11862	9831062
200	2	2540-01-156-9740	11862	918656
200	3		11862	14072485
200	3		11862	14072486
200	4	5330-01-159-2807	11862	14008191
200	5	2540-01-157-6414	11862	14007429
200	6	2540-01-156-4855	11862	14007430
200	7	2540-01-155-0376	11862	14072487
200	7	2540-01-323-6049	11862	15634659
200	7	2540-01-323-6050	11862	15634660
200	8	5325-01-167-0510	11862	14007435
200	9	2540-01-159-8760	11862	14072489
200	10	5310-01-160-5708	11862	52351724
200	11	5305-01-162-0015	11862	15554576
200	12	5306-01-160-1968	11862	14007511
200	13	5306-01-203-9082	24617	9426277
200	14	5340-01-150-4105	11862	14005953

CROSS-REFERENCE INDEXES

FIGURE AND ITEM NUMBER INDEX

FIG	ITEM	STOCK NUMBER	CAGEC	PART NUMBER
200	15	2540-01-164-7260	11862	14007542
200	15	2540-01-165-6145	11862	14007541
200	16	5310-01-158-6780	11862	14007539
201	1	5325-01-163-5973	11862	14076298
201	2	5340-01-157-6697	11862	14072445
201	3	5310-01-242-8561	11862	15599994
201	4	5305-01-163-2438	11862	9440300
202	1	5310-01-242-8561	11862	15599994
202	2	5325-01-230-1844	11862	15599990
202	3	5340-01-157-6697	11862	14072445
202	4	5305-01-163-2438	11862	9440300
202	5	5310-00-959-4679	96906	MS35340-45
202	6	5306-00-226-4827	96906	MS90728-34
202	7	5340-01-162-6062	11862	15599962
202	8	5340-01-164-6410	11862	14072441
202	9	5340-01-164-6411	11862	14072440
202	10	5340-01-164-6412	11862	14072439
202	11	5340-01-198-3434	11862	15599964
202	12	5340-01-159-4519	11862	15599963
202	13	5340-01-159-4517	11862	14072442
203	1	5306-01-155-7659	24617	9425117
203	2	5340-01-162-4820	11862	14075846
203	3	4210-00-383-7127	19207	7357009
203	6	5340-01-164-1048	25022	99-4602-1
203	7	5310-00-407-9566	96906	MS35338-45
203	8	5306-00-226-4827	96906	MS90728-34
203	9	5340-01-164-1075	25022	99-4341-1
203	10	5310-00-891-1709	96906	MS35691-9
204	1	5330-01-157-1952	11862	6273325
204	2		11862	3054308
205	1	5306-01-155-8528	24617	9419699
205	2	5340-01-158-6816	11862	3025501
205	3	5340-01-165-3717	11862	3024673
205	4	2540-01-156-0072	11862	3027247
205	5	2520-01-192-1257	11862	3048083
205	6	2540-01-159-8722	11862	3054315
205	7	2540-01-155-7299	11862	3024867
205	8	2540-01-156-4874	11862	3030075
205	9	5305-01-159-2781	24617	11500999
205	10	2540-01-156-0070	27462	3054316
205	11	2540-01-156-0071	11862	3030072
205	12	2540-01-159-8705	11862	3027308
205	13	2540-01-156-0073	11862	3048067
206	1	5310-01-158-6260	24617	11506003
206	2	5905-01-159-0771	11862	500890
206	3	5305-01-269-4329	11862	11513932
206	4		11862	3058097
206	5	2540-01-158-6906	11862	3029730
206	6	5310-01-164-2336	11862	3042351
206	7	5310-01-211-1648	11862	3015545
206	8	6105-01-165-4561	11862	3037550

CROSS-REFERENCE INDEXES

FIGURE AND ITEM NUMBER INDEX

FIG	ITEM	STOCK NUMBER	CAGEC	PART NUMBER
206	9	5330-01-195-4880	11862	3039873
206	10	5305-01-160-1974	11862	11500742
206	11	4730-01-160-0814	11862	3013475
206	12	4720-01-160-3664	11862	3036927
206	13	6105-01-164-6546	11862	22020945
206	14	5305-01-164-1604	24617	11500997
207	4	5305-01-197-2320	24617	9440025
207	5	5305-01-162-9689	24617	11503396
207	6	2540-01-165-5996	11862	14013122
208	1	2590-01-159-8857	11862	6258364
208	2	5305-00-146-2524	96906	MS51850-86
208	3	5310-01-268-8948	11862	11501937
208	4	2590-01-158-8551	11862	16034561
208	5	2590-01-159-8763	11862	1226174
208	6	5355-01-157-1865	11862	336406
208	7	5930-01-165-0732	16758	16015256
208	8	5305-01-197-3287	24617	9419663
208	9	5305-01-164-2313	24617	9415163
209	1	4730-00-908-3194	96906	MS35842-11
209	2		11862	482995
209	2		11862	487425
209	3	5340-01-200-8473	11862	12337820
209	4	5340-01-159-1324	11862	3825416
209	5		11862	10012288-45
210	1		25022	22-0871
210	2	5330-01-192-9335	99688	58636
210	3	5340-01-199-4993	99688	58659
210	4	5310-01-161-7308	99688	62229
210	5	5305-00-432-4163	96906	MS51861-24
210	6	5360-01-203-6365	99688	58627
210	7	5330-01-192-8906	99688	58637
210	8	5305-01-162-8512	24617	9421073
210	9	2510-01-191-4259	99688	85941
210	10	4730-00-908-6294	96906	MS35842-16
210	11	2540-01-194-3323	78385	10530B
210	12	4730-00-900-3296	72983	248X4
210	13	4720-01-192-3510	99688	58625
210	14	5305-00-984-6195	96906	MS35206-247
210	15	4520-01-192-6073	99688	58623
210	16	4730-00-908-6293	96906	MS35842-15
210	17		99688	58628
210	18	5320-01-200-4017	96906	MS21141-U0604
210	19	2540-01-191-4327	99688	784030
210	20		99688	78405
210	21	2990-01-192-4597	99688	58649
210	22	4730-01-192-4434	99688	58620
210	23	4520-01-192-6005	99688	46090
210	24	5330-01-194-4754	99688	58635
210	25	2990-01-192-4576	99688	58651
210	26		99688	58629
210	27	5330-01-192-8905	99688	58632

CROSS-REFERENCE INDEXES

FIGURE AND ITEM NUMBER INDEX

FIG	ITEM	STOCK NUMBER	CAGEC	PART NUMBER
210	28	5305-01-087-1917	96906	MS51849-70
210	29	5310-00-014-5850	96906	MS27183-42
210	30	2910-00-025-3493	96906	MS51085-1
210	31	5330-00-265-1089	96906	MS29513-125
210	32	2910-00-203-3322	90005	26422-B
210	33	5330-01-192-8904	99688	58624
210	34	2540-01-191-6541	99688	85942
210	35	5315-00-899-4119	96906	MS24665-446
210	36	2590-01-191-4357	99688	65148
210	37	2590-01-192-5911	99688	859430
210	38	5320-00-616-4346	96906	MS20600B6W4
210	39	2590-01-191-9276	99688	65149
210	40	6105-01-188-7154	0A7R8	PV23135R
210	41	2540-01-191-4331	99688	46023
210	42	4140-01-188-6977	99688	58634
210	43	4720-01-191-8463	99688	78406
211	1	5310-01-194-9208	24617	9409761
211	2	5310-01-193-6927	11862	9409754
211	3	4730-01-069-6408	93061	144F-5
211	5		11862	14072371
211	6	4730-00-266-0535	81343	SAEJ513
211	7	4730-00-619-9362	24617	140642
211	8	2540-01-163-1141	11862	14072347
211	9	5305-01-164-2313	24617	9415163
211	10	5340-01-150-4105	11862	14005953
211	11	2910-00-710-6054	96906	MS51321-1
211	12	5306-01-160-1968	11862	14007511
211	13	5340-01-164-6474	11862	343444
211	14	5340-01-164-6473	11862	14004512
211	15	4730-00-266-0536	16764	110200
211	16	4720-01-162-5113	11862	14072368
211	17		11862	14072369
212	1	5305-01-156-5438	11862	11504447
212	2	5340-00-057-3034	96906	MS21333-110
212	3	4720-01-163-1089	11862	14063324
212	6	5310-01-160-9529	24617	1494253
212	7	5306-00-226-4824	96906	MS90728-31
213	2	5330-00-935-9136	24617	274244
213	3	5330-01-150-7744	11862	14022683
213	4	5305-01-165-5591	11862	9439930
213	5	2990-01-163-3575	11862	15599200
213	6	2520-01-163-3494	11862	15599201
213	7	5365-01-149-0880	11862	337185
213	8	5330-00-107-3925	11862	14079550
214	1	5310-01-194-9208	24617	9409761
214	2	5310-01-193-6927	11862	9409754
214	3	4730-01-069-6408	93061	144P-5
214	4	4730-00-011-8538	81343	5 010111B
214	5		11862	14072371
214	6	4730-00-619-9362	24617	140642
214	7	5305-00-432-4171	24617	9414713

CROSS-REFERENCE INDEXES

FIGURE AND ITEM NUMBER INDEX

FIG	ITEM	STOCK NUMBER	CAGEC	PART NUMBER
214	8	2540-01-163-1141	11862	14072347
214	9	5340-01-150-4105	11862	14005953
214	10	2910-00-710-6054	96906	MS51321-1
214	11	5306-01-160-1968	11862	14007511
214	12	4730-00-142-2177	81240	GM118749
214	13	5340-01-164-6474	11862	343444
214	14	5340-01-164-6473	11862	14004512
214	15		11862	14072369
214	16	4720-01-162-5113	11862	14072368
214	17	5340-01-268-9064	11862	25527423
214	18	4730-00-266-0536	16764	110200
214	19	4710-01-232-8478	11862	14063323
214	20	5306-00-226-4824	96906	MS90728-31
214	21	5340-00-057-3034	96906	MS21333-110
214	22	5310-01-160-9529	24617	1494253
214	23	5340-00-282-7539	96906	MS21333-46
214	24	5305-01-140-9118	96906	MS90728-59
214	25	5325-01-164-8655	11862	3886908
214	26	5325-00-279-1248	96906	MS35489-103
214	27	4720-01-162-0121	11862	14076390
214	28	5310-01-148-5922	11862	11500046
214	29	5310-00-732-0558	96906	MS51967-8
214	30	4720-01-163-1089	11862	14063324
215	1	5310-00-081-4219	96906	MS27183-12
215	2	5310-00-814-0673	96906	MS51943-33
215	3	5340-01-166-2152	11862	120877
215	4	5306-01-266-2419	24617	9417350
215	5	2990-01-159-1801	11862	14075801
215	6	5310-00-013-1245	21450	131245
215	6	5310-00-013-1245	21450	131245
215	7	4730-00-908-6293	96906	MS35842-15
215	7	4730-00-908-6293	96906	MS35842-15
215	8	5305-00-225-3843	96906	MS90728-8
215	8	5305-00-225-3843	96906	MS90728-8
215	9	2990-01-163-0771	11862	15599211
215	10	4730-00-058-7558	63208	650-24
215	11		11862	15599287
215	12	5310-01-012-8962	24617	9416918
216	1	2540-01-162-7114	11862	15599290
216	2	5305-00-225-3843	96906	MS90728-8
216	3	4730-00-908-6293	96906	MS35842-15
216	4	5310-00-013-1245	21450	131245
217	1	4730-00-058-7558	63208	650-24
217	2	5310-01-012-8962	24617	9416918
217	3	5340-01-166-2152	11862	120877
217	4	5340-01-219-7272	11862	15599245
217	5	5305-01-160-3938	24617	9416187
217	6	2990-01-163-1179	11862	15599243
218	1	4730-00-058-7558	63208	650-24
218	2	5310-00-013-1245	21450	131245
218	2	5310-00-013-1245	21450	131245

CROSS-REFERENCE INDEXES

FIGURE AND ITEM NUMBER INDEX

FIG	ITEM	STOCK NUMBER	CAGEC	PART NUMBER
218	3	4730-00-908-6293	96906	MS35842-15
218	3	4730-00-908-6293	96906	MS35842-15
218	4	5305-00-225-3843	96906	MS90728-8
218	4	5305-00-225-3843	96906	MS90728-8
218	5	2540-01-162-7113	11862	14074499
218	5	2990-01-163-1180	11862	15599215
218	6	5306-01-266-2419	24617	9417350
218	7	5310-00-081-4219	96906	MS27183-12
218	7	5310-00-081-4219	96906	MS27183-12
218	8	5310-00-814-0673	96906	MS51943-33
218	9	5340-01-166-2152	11862	120877
218	10	5306-01-266-2419	24617	9417350
218	11	5310-00-814-0673	96906	MS51943-33
218	12	2990-01-162-4416	11862	15599212
219	1	5306-01-149-6278	11862	14028922
219	2	5340-01-221-9972	11862	15599246
219	3	5330-01-218-0862	11862	14055585
219	4	4720-01-162-0120	11862	14063337
219	5	4720-01-162-0119	11862	14063336
220	1	4730-00-908-3194	96906	MS35842-11
220	2	4730-01-162-0095	11862	10005327
220	3	5330-01-149-0874	11862	23500846
220	4	2930-01-159-1802	11862	14063338
220	5	5330-01-148-7497	11862	14028916
220	6		11862	14063370
220	7	4730-01-148-2758	11862	354501
220	8	4730-00-317-4231	73992	8200
220	9	4730-01-218-6691	73992	B-84
220	10	4730-00-249-3885	96906	MS51845-4
220	11	4730-00-196-1991	96906	MS51846-64
220	12	6620-01-221-1942	17769	4641
220	13	4730-00-768-8880	73992	8100
220	14	4730-01-218-6690	73992	B-85
220	15		11862	14063373
220	16	5340-01-159-1324	11862	3825416
220	17	5310-00-596-6897	24617	456004
220	18	5310-00-080-6004	96906	MS27183-14
220	19	5306-01-218-3119	11862	9440034
221	1	5340-01-164-6528	11862	14074457
221	2	5310-01-159-8559	96906	MS35691-406
221	3	5310-00-582-5965	96906	MS35338-44
221	4	5340-00-914-1000	19207	10922334
221	5	5306-00-226-4825	96906	MS90728-32
221	6	5310-01-132-8275	24617	9418924
221	7	5340-01-164-6526	11862	14074458
221	8	5310-00-407-9566	96906	MS35338-45
221	9	5310-00-931-8167	96906	MS51967-6
221	10	5340-01-164-6527	11862	14074459
221	11		11862	9440173
221	12	4730-00-415-3172	17769	443998
221	13	2910-00-025-3493	96906	MS51085-1

CROSS-REFERENCE INDEXES

FIGURE AND ITEM NUMBER INDEX

FIG	ITEM	STOCK NUMBER	CAGEC	PART NUMBER
221	14	5365-01-163-1142	11862	14072374
221	15	5325-01-199-3461	00613	C-5139-2
221	16	4730-00-142-2177	81240	GM118749
221	17	5310-00-809-8546	96906	MS27183-8
221	18	5305-01-242-1148	24617	456748
221	19	4730-00-011-8538	81343	5 010111B
221	20		11862	14072372
221	21	4720-01-247-4680	11862	15599234
221	22	5340-00-057-3034	96906	MS21333-110
221	23	2990-01-287-2158	46522	D55395-G1
222	1	2590-01-163-1184	11862	14076236
222	2	5340-01-149-4434	11862	3816659
222	3	5945-01-162-0517	11862	2098912
222	4	5310-00-809-4058	96906	MS27183-10
222	5	5325-00-807-0580	96906	MS35489-121
222	6	5310-00-938-8387	96906	MS9549-10
222	7	5305-00-071-2506	96906	MS90728-3
222	8	5340-01-150-1377	11862	14061352
222	9	5365-01-219-7285	11862	15599920
222	10	5310-01-159-8559	96906	MS35691-406
222	11	5305-01-164-2313	24617	9415163
222	12	5930-00-234-1390	78385	G704410-1
222	13	5330-01-220-6153	11862	14076270
222	14	5310-01-161-2374	11862	9440178
222	15	5340-00-282-7509	96906	MS21333-62
223	1	5995-01-163-1183	11862	14075888
223	2	5945-01-162-0516	11862	14074461PC6
223	3	5325-00-807-0580	96906	MS35489-121
224	1	6150-01-234-3253	11862	15599968
225	1	2590-01-164-0135	11862	14076246
225	2	5325-00-337-6636	72794	AJW7-70
225	3	5365-01-226-2342	72794	X-840-SR7C
225	4	6140-01-160-5196	11862	12039294
225	5	5310-01-158-6260	24617	11506003
225	6	6140-01-216-7923	11862	14076852
225	7	2540-01-164-0122	11862	14076243
225	8	2540-01-166-2010	11862	14076250
225	9	5306-01-168-4481	11862	9440334
225	10	2540-01-166-2009	11862	14076249
225	11	5306-01-158-9018	11862	2014469
225	12	2540-01-164-0032	11862	14076241
225	13	5306-01-227-1454	11862	14076248
225	14	5325-00-291-9366	96906	MS35489-11
226	1	2590-01-162-4352	11862	14076269
226	2	5340-00-057-3043	96906	MS21333-112
226	3	5305-01-218-3139	24617	9423768
226	4	5310-01-217-5205	24617	9417714
226	5	2590-01-162-4417	11862	14076811
226	6	5340-01-149-4434	11862	3816659
226	7	2590-01-162-4418	11862	14076240
226	8	5340-00-989-1771	96906	MS21333-123

CROSS-REFERENCE INDEXES

FIGURE AND ITEM NUMBER INDEX

FIG	ITEM	STOCK NUMBER	CAGEC	PART NUMBER
226	9	5340-00-057-3052	96906	MS21333-114
226	10	5310-00-582-5965	96906	MS35338-44
226	11	5310-01-159-8559	96906	MS35691-406
226	12	5305-01-156-5438	11862	11504447
226	13	5325-01-164-8655	11862	3886908
227	1	5305-00-984-6193	96906	MS35206-245
227	2	2590-01-162-4353	11862	14076238
227	3	6220-01-160-5187	22973	922-900-00
227	4	6220-01-268-8795	22973	922-910-00
227	5	6240-00-850-4280	08806	1003
227	6	6220-01-216-5289	22973	922-901-02
227	7	6220-01-269-0465	22973	922-904-02
227	8	5305-00-984-4983	96906	MS35206-226
227	9	6220-01-216-5288	22973	922-901-01
227	10	5340-00-057-3043	96906	MS21333-112
227	11	5310-01-217-5205	24617	9417714
227	12	5305-00-446-9901	96906	MS51850-64
227	13	5305-00-068-0508	96906	MS90728-6
227	14	5310-01-152-0598	24617	271172
227	15	5340-00-989-1771	96906	MS21333-123
227	16	2590-01-162-7130	11862	14076239
227	17	5305-01-156-5438	11862	11504447
227	18	5325-01-168-5677	11862	3918889
227	19	5325-01-164-2377	11862	15591130
228	1		11862	15593599
228	2	5325-01-164-7550	11862	3977775
228	3	5970-01-159-1803	11862	14063365
228	4	5307-01-259-7656	11862	107413
228	5	5325-01-050-6192	19207	12255564-2
228	6	5310-00-809-4058	96906	MS27183-10
228	7	2930-01-167-7250	11862	14063366
228	8	5310-00-013-1245	21450	131245
228	9	5360-00-771-7066	19207	7717066
229	1	2540-01-155-7542	11862	14076228
229	2	5305-00-054-6657	96906	MS51957-33
229	3	2510-01-159-1792	11862	14076216
229	4	2510-00-999-9856	19207	7353960
229	5	5330-01-167-6335	11862	14076215
229	6	5310-01-161-2531	11862	9414031
229	7	5310-01-012-8962	24617	9416918
229	8	2540-01-164-1886	11862	14075845
229	9	5306-01-197-3089	11862	9440033
229	10	5310-00-472-3214	81795	30489
229	11	5305-00-071-2511	96906	MS90728-14
229	12	5310-01-264-5903	21450	587227
229	13	5305-00-071-2087	96906	MS51957-84
229	14	5305-00-071-2510	96906	MS90728-13
229	15	5340-01-150-4105	11862	14005953
229	16	5310-01-170-8765	24617	9419265
229	17	5305-01-167-8334	11862	20365263
229	18	5340-01-165-4379	11862	14072367

CROSS-REFERENCE INDEXES

FIGURE AND ITEM NUMBER INDEX

FIG	ITEM	STOCK NUMBER	CAGEC	PART NUMBER
229	19	4730-01-161-6618	11862	14072366
229	20	5330-01-164-5603	11862	14075857
229	21	5306-01-168-4481	11862	9440334
229	22	5340-01-164-6435	11862	14072365
229	23	2540-01-162-4412	11862	14072364
230	1	5305-00-071-1318	96906	MS51957-83
230	2	5310-01-170-8765	24617	9419265
230	3		11862	14075884
230	4	5340-01-150-4105	11862	14005953
230	5		11862	14075883
230	6	2540-01-155-7543	11862	14075881
230	7	2540-01-155-7278	11862	14075882
230	8	5325-01-050-6192	19207	12255564-2
230	9	5310-01-152-0598	24617	271172
231	1	5305-00-071-2510	96906	MS90728-13
231	2	5310-00-472-3214	81795	30489
231	3	5340-01-217-2168	11862	3794767
231	4	5310-01-012-8962	24617	9416918
231	5	5340-01-217-2278	11862	370349
231	6		11862	14076204
231	7	5310-00-080-6004	96906	MS27183-14
231	8	5310-01-097-8222	24617	9413534
231	9	5305-00-240-6668	96906	MS51849-78
231	10	2540-01-162-7110	11862	14076882
231	11	5305-00-068-0501	96906	MS90725-5
231	12	2540-01-216-3188	11862	15599951
231	13	5325-01-165-4372	11862	9411281
231	14	5310-01-264-5903	21450	587227
231	15	1430-01-106-8451	11862	15599950
231	16	2510-01-246-4237	11862	14076875
231	17	5340-01-163-3294	11862	14076217
231	18	5305-00-782-9489	96906	MS90728-66
231	19	5310-00-080-6004	96906	MS27183-14
231	20		11862	14076210
231	21	5305-00-533-5542	96906	MS35492-54
231	22	5310-01-097-8222	24617	9413534
231	23		11862	14076211
231	24		11862	14076884
231	25		11862	14076209
231	26	2510-00-999-9856	19207	7353960
231	27	5330-01-167-6335	11862	14076215
231	28	2510-01-159-1792	11862	14076216
231	29	5305-00-935-7506	96906	MS35493-37
231	30	5305-00-782-9489	96906	MS90728-66
232	1	5310-01-012-8962	24617	9416918
232	2	5310-01-097-8222	24617	9413534
232	3	5310-00-080-6004	96906	MS27183-14
232	4		11862	14076204
232	5		11862	14076872
232	6	5310-00-472-3214	81795	30489
232	7	5305-00-071-2510	96906	MS90728-13

CROSS-REFERENCE INDEXES

FIGURE AND ITEM NUMBER INDEX

FIG	ITEM	STOCK NUMBER	CAGEC	PART NUMBER
232	8	5330-01-163-2055	11862	14076862
232	9	5310-01-264-5903	21450	587227
232	10	5305-00-782-9489	96906	MS90728-66
232	11	5340-01-164-2397	11862	14076221
232	12	2510-01-159-1791	11862	15599910
232	13		11862	14076212
232	14		11862	14076864
232	15		11862	14076871
232	16	5306-01-168-4481	11862	9440334
232	17	2590-01-242-8068	11862	14076208
232	18	5305-00-533-5542	96906	MS35492-54
233	1	5306-00-889-2943	96906	MS35751-17
233	2	2510-01-162-4407	11862	14076233
233	3	5340-01-164-6591	11862	14076230
233	4	5310-01-012-8962	24617	9416918
233	5	2540-01-162-8983	11862	14075843
233	6	2540-01-159-6198	19207	7951738
233	7		11862	14076222
233	8	2510-01-246-4236	17769	14076861
233	9	5305-00-014-9926	96906	MS35493-76
233	10		11862	14076201
233	11		11862	15599916
233	12	2510-01-162-4408	11862	14076231
233	13		11862	14076232
233	14	2540-01-214-2634	11862	15599917
233	14	2540-01-214-2635	11862	15599918
233	15	5305-00-071-2510	96906	MS90728-13
233	16	5340-01-164-6589	11862	14076226
233	17	5310-01-012-8962	24617	9416918
233	18	5310-01-197-6621	24617	9423530
233	19	5340-01-043-5214	19207	11669126-1
233	20	5305-00-054-6654	96906	MS51957-30
233	21	5340-01-044-8389	19207	12255561
233	22	2510-01-162-7111	11862	14076299
233	22	2540-01-163-0766	11862	14076300
233	23	5325-01-165-6975	19207	12255564-1
234	1		11862	14076281
234	2		11862	14076278
234	3	5305-00-901-3110	96906	MS35492-57
234	4	5340-01-219-7275	11862	14063349
234	5		11862	14076280
234	6	5340-01-212-6716	11862	15599273
234	6	5340-01-212-6717	11862	15599274
234	7	5340-01-218-5823	11862	14076889
234	8	5340-01-150-4105	11862	14005953
234	9	5306-01-168-4481	11862	9440334
234	10		11862	14076276
234	11	5330-01-163-5850	11862	14076235
234	12	2510-01-159-1790	11862	14076206
234	13		11862	14076272
234	14		11862	14076275

CROSS-REFERENCE INDEXES

FIGURE AND ITEM NUMBER INDEX

FIG	ITEM	STOCK NUMBER	CAGEC	PART NUMBER
234	15	5310-00-316-6513	80205	NAS1408A6
234	16	5310-00-809-4085	96906	MS27183-16
234	17	5310-00-809-5997	96906	MS27183-17
234	18		11862	14076271
234	19	5306-00-685-7790	96906	MS35751-46
234	20		11862	14076229
234	21		11862	14076279
234	22		11862	14076273
234	22		11862	14076274
234	23		11862	14076277
235	1		11862	14063348
235	2	5305-00-533-5542	96906	MS35492-54
235	3		11862	14063349
235	4	5306-00-226-4830	96906	MS90728-37
235	5	5310-00-081-4219	96906	MS27183-12
235	6		11862	14063342
235	7	5310-01-211-3811	11862	9417793
235	8	5310-01-119-3668	24617	9422295
235	9		11862	14063343
235	9		11862	14063344
235	10		11862	14063346
235	11	5305-00-245-4144	96906	MS35494-83
235	12		11862	14063350
235	13		11862	14063345
235	14	5310-00-316-6513	80205	NAS1408A6
235	15	5310-00-809-4085	96906	MS27183-16
235	16		11862	14063341
235	17	5305-00-901-3144	96906	MS35492-82
235	18	5310-01-158-6260	24617	11506003
235	19	5306-00-027-0722	96906	MS35751-19
235	20		11862	14063351
235	21	5310-00-809-5997	96906	MS27183-17
235	22	5306-00-177-5707	96906	MS35751-73
235	23		11862	14063347
236	1	2540-01-156-0088	11862	15594983
236	2		11862	14075862
236	2		11862	14075864
236	3		11862	14076802
236	3		11862	14076803
236	4		11862	14075863
237	1	5340-01-293-1200	11862	14063353
237	2		24617	9409103
237	3	5340-01-164-6595	11862	14063359
237	4	5340-01-165-6797	11862	14074431
237	5	5305-00-068-0508	96906	MS90728-6
237	6	2540-01-218-8099	11862	14063358
237	7		11862	14063352
237	8	5305-00-071-2071	96906	MS90728-115
238	1	5306-00-226-4827	96906	MS90728-34
238	1	5306-00-226-4827	96906	MS90728-34
238	2	5310-00-959-4679	96906	MS35340-45

CROSS-REFERENCE INDEXES

FIGURE AND ITEM NUMBER INDEX

FIG	ITEM	STOCK NUMBER	CAGEC	PART NUMBER
238	2	5310-00-959-4679	96906	MS35340-45
238	3	5340-00-958-8457	96906	MS21333-78
238	4		11862	14074444
238	5	5310-00-081-4219	96906	MS27183-12
238	5	5310-00-081-4219	96906	MS27183-12
238	6	5310-00-814-0673	96906	MS51943-33
238	6	5310-00-814-0673	96906	MS51943-33
238	7		11862	14074446
238	8	4730-00-908-3194	96906	MS35842-11
238	9	4710-01-163-0594	11862	14074445
238	10	5340-00-702-2848	96906	MS21333-128
238	11	5340-01-221-0264	11862	3738198
238	12		11862	14075856
239	1	5306-00-226-4827	96906	MS90728-34
239	1	5306-00-226-4827	96906	MS90728-34
239	2	5310-00-959-4679	96906	MS35340-45
239	2	5310-00-959-4679	96906	MS35340-45
239	3	5340-00-702-2848	96906	MS21333-128
239	3	5340-00-702-2848	96906	MS21333-128
239	4	5310-00-081-4219	96906	MS27183-12
239	4	5310-00-081-4219	96906	MS27183-12
239	5	5310-00-814-0673	96906	MS51943-33
239	5	5310-00-814-0673	96906	MS51943-33
239	6	4720-01-162-0283	11862	14074451
239	7	4730-00-908-3194	96906	MS35842-11
239	8	4710-01-161-6406	11862	14074450
239	9		11862	14074449
239	10	2540-01-164-7121	11862	14074448
239	11		11862	14074447
239	12		11862	14074453
239	13	4710-01-162-7080	11862	14074452
240	1	5325-00-174-5314	96906	MS35489-5
240	2	5340-01-149-4434	11862	3816659
240	3	5310-01-170-9100	11862	3982098
240	4	5305-00-071-2506	96906	MS90728-3
240	5	5340-01-164-6524	11862	14072415
240	6	5310-00-938-8387	96906	MS9549-10
240	7	5305-00-068-0508	96906	MS90728-6
240	8	5310-00-582-5965	96906	MS35338-44
240	9	5310-01-159-8559	96906	MS35691-406
240	10	2540-01-163-0765	11862	14076284
241	1	2540-01-162-5174	11862	14076285
241	2	2540-01-162-5175	11862	14076287
241	3	5925-01-067-2926	96906	MS25244-P-20
241	4	5930-00-655-1514	96906	MS35058-22
241	5	5930-00-978-8805	96906	MS25307-312
241	6	5305-00-054-6650	96906	MS51957-26
241	7	6210-00-438-4745	81640	L30200R
241	8	6210-00-688-5088	96906	MS25331-4-313S
241	9	5325-00-263-6632	96906	MS35489-6
241	10	5935-01-154-6264	96906	MS3452W18-11P

CROSS-REFERENCE INDEXES

FIGURE AND ITEM NUMBER INDEX

FIG	ITEM	STOCK NUMBER	CAGEC	PART NUMBER
241	11	5305-00-054-5651	96906	MS51957-17
241	12	5310-00-550-3715	96906	MS35333-70
241	13	5310-00-934-9748	96906	MS35649-244
241	14	5310-00-014-5850	96906	MS27183-42
241	15	5305-00-054-6670	96906	MS51957-45
241	16	5310-00-144-8453	96906	MS90724-7
241	17	5310-00-934-9758	96906	MS35649-202
241	18	5310-00-045-3296	96906	MS35338-43
241	19	2540-01-159-1800	11862	14076295
241	20	5305-00-984-6210	96906	MS35206-263
242	1	5325-01-199-3461	00613	C-5139-2
242	2	5365-01-163-1142	11862	14072374
242	3	2910-00-025-3493	96906	MS51085-1
242	4	4730-00-142-2177	81240	GM118749
242	5	5310-00-809-8546	96906	MS27183-8
242	6	4730-00-011-8538	81343	5 010111B
242	7	5305-01-242-1148	24617	456748
242	8	5340-00-057-3034	96906	MS21333-110
242	9		11862	14072378
242	10		11862	15599203
242	11	2540-01-194-3323	78385	10530B
242	12	2540-01-164-7123	11862	14074466
242	13	4730-00-908-6292	96906	MS35842-14
242	14	4720-01-162-7098	16632	CHE2015-0001
242	15	5310-00-809-4058	96906	MS27183-10
242	16	5305-01-197-3287	24617	9419663
242	17	5930-01-184-6370	11862	15599972
242	18	5306-01-157-6796	11862	9439771
242	19	5310-00-528-7638	19207	5287638
242	20	4730-00-908-6294	96906	MS35842-16
242	21	2540-01-163-1143	11862	14074469
242	22	5310-00-931-8167	96906	MS51967-6
242	23	5310-00-407-9566	96906	MS35338-45
242	24	5340-01-165-4543	11862	14074471
242	25	5310-01-132-8275	24617	9418924
242	26	5306-00-226-4825	96906	MS90728-32
242	27	2540-01-165-0466	11862	14074470
242	28	5305-01-219-5399	24617	423532
242	29	5330-01-163-3150	16632	CHE2017
242	30	2540-01-164-7124	11862	14074473
242	31		11862	9440173
242	32	4730-00-053-0266	96906	MS51952-1
243	1	4720-01-162-7098	16632	CHE2015-0001
243	2	2540-01-163-1140	11862	14074465
243	3	2590-01-163-3529	11862	14076237
243	4	4720-01-162-7097	16632	CHE2015-0002
243	5	4730-00-908-6293	96906	MS35842-15
244	1	5305-01-197-3287	24617	9419663
244	2	4520-01-166-2133	11862	3037476
244	3	2540-01-268-7202	11862	3055734
244	4	6105-01-254-9496	11862	22098841

CROSS-REFERENCE INDEXES

FIGURE AND ITEM NUMBER INDEX

FIG	ITEM	STOCK NUMBER	CAGEC	PART NUMBER
244	5	4520-01-166-2134	11862	3035192
245	1	4730-00-908-6293	96906	MS35842-15
245	2	4720-01-167-9137	16632	CHE2013-0001
245	3	5340-01-150-4105	11862	14005953
245	4	5330-01-164-7509	16632	CHE2016-0002
245	5	5330-01-220-3117	16632	CHE2023
245	6	2990-01-250-8612	11862	15599942
245	7	5306-01-168-4481	11862	9440334
245	8	5315-00-243-1170	96906	MS24665-516
245	9	2540-01-163-7225	11862	15599940
245	10	4730-00-058-7558	63208	650-24
245	11	2990-01-163-1182	11862	14076805
245	12	5306-00-226-4828	96906	MS90728-35
245	13	5310-00-959-4679	96906	MS35340-45
246	1	2540-01-163-1175	11862	14076252
246	2	5310-00-809-4058	96906	MS27183-10
246	3	5360-01-245-0405	96906	MS24585-1276
246	4	2540-01-162-5176	11862	14076253
246	5	5305-00-272-3533	96906	MS51023-49
246	6	5315-00-839-2325	96152	A82-1
246	7	4730-00-053-0266	96906	MS51952-1
246	8	2910-00-025-3493	96906	MS51085-1
246	9	5365-01-163-1142	11862	14072374
246	10	4730-00-011-8538	81343	5 010111B
246	11		11862	14076255
246	12	5310-00-208-1918	88044	AN365-1024A
246	13	5310-01-217-5205	24617	9417714
246	14	4730-00-142-2177	81240	GM118749
246	15	5310-00-809-8546	96906	MS27183-8
246	16	5305-01-242-1148	24617	456748
246	17		11862	9440173
246	18	5306-01-168-4481	11862	9440334
246	19	4730-00-908-6294	96906	MS35842-16
246	20	4730-01-216-0021	11862	15599952
246	21	2540-01-194-3323	78385	10530B
246	22	2540-01-162-6418	11862	14076265
246	23	5320-00-845-9501	96906	MS20600-B4W4
246	24	5340-01-168-0939	82240	SPEC-3-10-L-L
246	25	5330-01-163-3151	16632	CHE2018
246	26	2540-00-752-4078	19207	7524078
246	27	5310-00-809-4058	96906	MS27183-10
246	28	5310-00-013-1245	21450	131245
246	29	4730-00-908-6294	96906	MS35842-16
246	30	5305-00-225-3843	96906	MS90728-8
246	31	2540-01-162-5178	11862	14076259
246	32	5305-00-068-7837	96906	MS90728-5
246	33	5340-01-166-0568	11862	14076261
246	34	5340-01-165-5617	11862	14076262
246	35	5310-00-761-6882	96906	MS51967-2
246	36	2540-01-162-6493	11862	14076801
246	37	5340-00-685-5899	82240	B-1900-334

CROSS-REFERENCE INDEXES

FIGURE AND ITEM NUMBER INDEX

FIG	ITEM	STOCK NUMBER	CAGEC	PART NUMBER
246	38	5305-01-219-5399	24617	423532
246	39	2540-01-162-5189	11862	14076258
246	40	2540-01-162-5177	11862	14076257
247	1		11862	14072308
247	2	5340-01-200-5843	11862	14072314
247	3	5340-01-165-4429	11862	14072325
247	4	5340-01-114-7712	19207	11682088-1
247	5	2540-01-165-0813	11862	14075811
247	6	5340-01-165-1494	11862	14072324
247	7	2540-01-205-2509	19207	12343359-3
247	8	2540-01-163-7017	11862	14075812
247	9	2540-01-205-2512	19207	12343359-5
247	10	2540-01-041-4912	19207	12343359-1
247	11	5306-00-753-6996	21450	126373
247	12	5310-00-933-4310	24617	271184
247	13	2540-01-191-8467	11862	14072319
247	14	2540-01-164-9278	11862	14072323
247	15	2540-01-163-0801	11862	14072322
247	16	5310-00-316-6513	80205	NAS1408A6
247	17	5305-00-543-2866	96906	MS90728-68
247	18	5315-00-842-3044	96906	MS24665-283
247	19	5305-00-823-9139	96906	MS51850-44
247	20	5340-01-094-9025	19207	12255608
247	21	5315-00-737-0134	19207	7370134
247	22	2540-01-205-2511	19207	12343359-4
247	23	5340-00-237-7779	11862	14072380
247	24	2540-01-205-2510	19207	12343359-2
248	1	6220-00-961-0783	81349	M4510-1A4435
248	2	6240-00-252-7138	08806	4435
248	3	5340-01-164-0748	78977	6500-0016
248	4	5340-00-411-4508	78977	6598
248	5	5305-00-217-9183	78977	6471
248	6	6220-01-197-3938	78977	6566-0004
248	7	4710-01-194-6590	78977	6710-BU-2
248	8	6220-01-194-6591	78977	100-7-3
248	9	5340-01-197-1585	78977	6701-0025
249	1	6680-01-230-5684	11862	25033627
249	2	5340-01-163-7501	11862	25020687
249	3	6680-01-225-4475	11862	25052373
249	4		11862	3866918
249	4	3020-01-166-6802	11862	1362195
249	4	3040-01-159-0930	11862	9780470
249	5	5330-01-087-4714	11862	15562374
249	6	2530-01-159-8764	11862	1362293
249	6	5360-01-206-6616	11862	326561
249	7	6680-01-161-3656	11862	1254856
249	8	6680-01-160-5276	11862	368026
249	9	5330-01-168-1535	11862	14018671
249	10	5305-01-150-9781	11862	8639743
249	11	5340-01-161-1440	11862	378362
249	12	5310-01-250-7679	11862	11506101

CROSS-REFERENCE INDEXES

FIGURE AND ITEM NUMBER INDEX

FIG	ITEM	STOCK NUMBER	CAGEC	PART NUMBER
249	13	5325-01-165-3475	11862	474579
250	1	4130-01-160-7695	99688	85927
250	2	5305-01-163-5761	96906	MS51869-26
250	3	5310-00-582-5965	96906	MS35338-44
250	4	5365-01-195-5934	99688	58606
250	5	5330-01-194-4751	99688	58608
250	6	5330-01-197-0897	99688	58618
250	7	5325-00-263-6648	96906	MS35489-135
250	8	5640-01-195-4634	99688	58610
250	9	5330-01-193-0227	99688	58607
250	10	5330-01-194-4752	99688	58617
250	11	5640-01-195-9786	99688	58615
250	12	5640-01-196-7003	99688	58614
250	13	5640-01-196-7002	99688	58613
250	14	5640-01-195-4636	99688	58612
250	15	5330-01-195-1564	99688	58616
250	16	5640-01-195-4635	99688	58611
250	17	5640-01-195-4633	99688	58609
250	18	5305-01-163-2423	96906	MS51871-14
250	19	5310-00-637-9541	96906	MS35338-46
250	20	5330-01-194-4753	99688	58586
250	21	5305-01-163-5761	96906	MS51869-26
250	22	5310-00-582-5965	96906	MS35338-44
251	1	5310-01-250-7679	11862	11506101
251	7	5306-01-149-6280	11862	1635490
251	9	5306-01-149-6280	11862	1635490
251	12	3030-01-043-6749	20796	42-4877
252	1	4140-01-160-8503	99688	85923
252	2	5340-00-329-4420	03743	S150
252	3	5310-01-159-8264	99688	62218
252	4	5310-00-209-0786	96906	MS35335-33
252	5	5305-01-162-8512	24617	9421073
252	6	5310-00-596-7691	96906	MS35335-32
252	7	5910-01-189-3011	99688	65134
252	8	6105-01-159-2666	99688	20566
252	9	4140-01-186-9753	99688	58595
252	10	9320-01-085-2889	99688	58701
252	11	5305-00-068-0509	96906	MS90728-10
252	12	5330-01-205-5056	99688	58598
252	13	5330-01-201-9682	99688	58597
252	14	5330-01-213-9811	99688	58596
252	15	5305-01-197-2320	24617	9440025
252	17	5305-00-071-2506	96906	MS90728-3
252	18		99688	85928
253	1	4140-01-160-7664	99688	85922
253	2	5305-01-162-8512	24617	9421073
253	3	4140-01-154-9615	99688	58590
253	3	4140-01-157-3501	99688	58589
253	4	5330-01-193-0226	99688	58592
253	5	5905-01-154-2354	99688	65158
253	6	5310-00-596-7691	96906	MS35335-32

CROSS-REFERENCE INDEXES

FIGURE AND ITEM NUMBER INDEX

FIG	ITEM	STOCK NUMBER	CAGEC	PART NUMBER
253	7	5640-01-194-7193	99688	58594
253	8	5340-01-191-4827	99688	85931
253	9	5310-01-159-8264	99688	62218
253	10	9320-01-085-2889	99688	58701
253	11	6105-01-159-2223	99688	20565
253	12	5330-01-201-9681	99688	58591
253	13	5325-00-263-6651	59875	TD97203
253	14	5305-00-068-0509	96906	MS90728-10
253	15	5310-00-754-2005	96906	MS35338-52
253	16	5910-01-189-3011	99688	65134
253	17	5330-01-204-4312	99688	58593
253	18	5305-01-162-8512	24617	9421073
254	1		19207	12314542
254	2	5120-01-180-0558	25341	J-2222-C
254	3	5120-01-179-1318	25341	J-6632-01
254	4	5120-00-677-2259	33287	J-8092
254	5	4910-01-179-6341	25341	J-21757-03
254	6	5120-01-169-4878	25341	J-23445-A
254	7	4910-01-180-6155	25341	J-23653-C
254	8	5120-01-170-3279	25341	J-23690
254	9	4910-01-179-6340	25341	J-24187
254	10	5120-01-179-1034	25341	J-24426
254	11	4910-01-179-2518	25341	J-24595-C
254	12	4910-01-179-2517	30282	553
254	13	5120-01-170-0628	25341	J-26878-A
254	14	4820-01-179-4869	25341	J-33043
254	15	4910-01-179-2516	25341	J-29713
254	16	4910-01-181-1959	25341	J-25034-B
254	17	5120-01-178-6342	33287	J-29843
254	18	4930-01-323-0998	33627	J25512-2
254	19	5120-01-170-6664	25341	J-34616
254	19	5120-01-219-6753	25341	J-6893-D
254	20	5120-01-170-5473	25341	J-33124

www.ingramcontent.com/pod-product-compliance
Lightning Source LLC
Chambersburg PA
CBHW080413030426
42335CB00020B/2438